T0350758

Alternative Investments

Alternative Investments

An Allocator's Approach

Fourth Edition

DONALD R. CHAMBERS
HOSSEIN B. KAZEMI
KEITH H. BLACK

WILEY

Published by John Wiley & Sons, Inc., Hoboken, New Jersey.
Published simultaneously in Canada.

Library of Congress Cataloging-in-Publication Data

Names: Kazemi, Hossein, 1954- author. | Black, Keith H., author. |
   Chambers, Donald R., author.
Title: Alternative investments : CAIA level II / Hossein B. Kazemi, Keith
   H. Black, Donald R. Chambers.
Description: Fourth edition. | Hoboken, New Jersey : John Wiley & Sons,
   Inc., [2020] | Includes index.
Identifiers: LCCN 2020028777 (print) | LCCN 2020028778 (ebook) | ISBN
   9781119651680 (hardback) | ISBN 9781119651697 (adobe pdf) | ISBN
   9781119651703 (epub)
Subjects: LCSH: Investments. | Securities. | Portfolio management.
Classification: LCC HG4521 .K295 2020 (print) | LCC HG4521 (ebook) | DDC
   174/.93326—dc23
LC record available at https://lccn.loc.gov/2020028777
LC ebook record available at https://lccn.loc.gov/2020028778

Cover Design: Zoe Design Works
Cover Image: © Getty Images

Contents

PART 2

Models

CHAPTER 6

Modeling Overview and Interest Rate Models **93**

CHAPTER 7

Credit Risk Models **105**

CHAPTER 8
Multi-Factor Equity Pricing Models

PART 3

Institutional Asset Owners and Investment Policies

CHAPTER 11

Types of Asset Owners and the Investment Policy Statement   **197**

CHAPTER 14
Sovereign Wealth Funds   269

PART 5

Methods for Alternative Investing

CHAPTER 21

Valuation and Hedging Using Binomial Trees   **439**

CHAPTER 22

Directional Strategies and Methods

PART 6

Accessing Alternative Investments

CHAPTER 26

Hedge Fund Replication   **543**

CHAPTER 39

Insurance-Linked Products and Hybrid Securities   **845**

Preface

Alternative Investments: An Allocator's View is designed to provide information on the top-down process used by institutional investors when adding alternative investments to a traditional portfolio of stock and bond investments. The material reflects up-to-date practices in the area of alternative investments generated by CAIA Association members and staff including leading industry professionals and academics. While some of these CAIA members and staff members helped directly by writing some of the chapters of this book, others provided valuable inputs as reviewers and members of our advisory board. Without their immense talent and dedication, this would not have been completed.

Since its inception in 2002, the CAIA Association has striven to be the leader in alternative investment education worldwide, and to be the catalyst for the best education in the field wherever it lies. The CAIA program was established with the help of a core group of faculty and industry experts who were associated with the Center for International Securities and Derivatives Markets (CISDM) at Isenberg School of Management and the Alternative Investment Management Association (AIMA). From the beginning, the CAIA Association recognized that a meaningful portion of its curriculum must be devoted to codes of conduct and ethical behavior in the investment profession. To this end, with the permission and cooperation of the CFA Institute, we have incorporated its Code of Ethics and its Standards of Practice Handbook into our curriculum in Level 1 and the Asset Manager Code in Level 2. We have leveraged the experience and contributions of our members and other alternative investment professionals who serve on our board and committees to create and update the CAIA Association program's curriculum and its associated readings.

The quality, rigor, and relevance of our curriculum readings derive from the ideals upon which the CAIA Association was based. The CAIA program offered its first Level I examination in February 2003. Our first class consisted of 43 dedicated investment professionals who passed the Levels I and II exams, and met the other requirements of membership. Many of these founding members were instrumental in establishing the CAIA designation as the global mark of excellence in alternative investment education. Through their support and with the help of the founding cosponsors—the AIMA and the CISDM—the CAIA Association is now firmly established as the most comprehensive and credible designation in the rapidly growing sphere of alternative investments.

The CAIA Association has experienced rapid growth in its membership since 2003. It is now a truly global professional organization, with over 11,000 members in over 95 countries. We strive to stay nimble in our process so that curriculum remains relevant and keeps pace with the constant changes in this dynamic industry.

Although the CAIA Association's origins are largely based in the efforts of professionals in the hedge fund and managed futures space, these founders correctly identified a void in the wider understanding of alternative investments as a whole. From the beginning, the CAIA curriculum has also covered private equity, commodities, and real assets, always with an eye toward shifts in the industry. Today, several hundred CAIA members identify their main area of expertise as real estate or private credit, and several hundred more are from family offices, pension funds, endowments, and sovereign wealth funds, which allocate across multiple classes within the alternative investment industry. To ensure benefit to the widest spectrum of members, we have developed curriculum subcommittees that represent each area of coverage within the curriculum.

Alternative investment areas and products share some distinct features, such as the relative freedom on the part of investment managers to act in the best interests of their investors, alignment of interests between asset owners and asset managers, and relative illiquidity of the investment positions of some investment products. These characteristics necessitate conceptual and actual modifications to the standard investment performance analysis and decision-making paradigms.

This series is designed with two goals in mind. First, to provide readers with the tools needed to solve problems they encounter in performing their professional duties. Second, to provide them with a conceptual framework that is essential for investment professionals who strive to keep up with new developments in the alternative investment industry.

Readers will find the publications in our series to be beneficial, whether from the standpoint of allocating to new asset classes and strategies in order to gain broader diversification or from the standpoint of a specialist needing to better understand the competing options available to sophisticated investors globally. In both cases, readers will be better equipped to serve their clients' needs.

Candidates are encouraged to visit https://caia.org/content/curriculum-study-tools for the most up-to-date information regarding the required readings for the CAIA level II exam. We will continue to update the CAIA Level II Study Guide every six months (each exam cycle). The study guide outlines all of the readings and corresponding learning objectives (LOs) that candidates are responsible for meeting. The guide also contains important information for candidates regarding the use of LOs, testing policies, topic weightings, where to find and report errata, and much more. The entire exam process is outlined in the CAIA Candidate Handbook. Candidates can also access a workbook that solves the problems presented at the end of each chapter and other important study aids.

We believe you will find this series to be the most comprehensive, rigorous, and globally relevant source of educational material available within the field of alternative investments.

Hossein Kazemi, PhD
Senior Adviser to the CAIA Association

Acknowlegements

We would like to thank the many individuals who played important roles in producing this book. In particular, we owe great thanks to William Kelly, Chief Executive Officer of the CAIA Association, and our committee members:

CAIA Allocator Advisory Board and CAIA Job Task Analysis Committee

Sean Anthonisz, CAIA, Mine Super & The University of Sydney Business School

Frank Barbarino, CAIA, Templum, Inc

James Bennett, CAIA, Maine Public Employees Retirement System

Robert Bennett-Lovesey, CAIA, Global ARC & CAIA Singapore

Jim Bethea, CAIA, University of Iowa Foundation

Ryan Bisch, CAIA, Ontario Power Generation

Cameron Black, CAIA, Blue Cross Blue Shield of Arizona

Dominic Blais, CAIA, Canadian Medical Protective Association

Joseph Borda, CAIA

Alex Bradford, CAIA, Starwood Capital

Elizabeth Burton, CAIA, Hawaii Employees Retirement System

Nathan Butler, CAIA, Voya Financial

Jenny Chan, CAIA, Children's Hospital of Philadelphia

Gang Chen, CAIA, PIMCO

Anthony (Tony) Cowell, KPMG

Edward (Ned) Creedon, University of Illinois Foundation

Pamela Fennelly Campbell, CAIA, Washington University

Darren Foreman, CAIA, Public School Employees Retirement System of Penn

Marcus Frampton, CAIA Alaska Permanent Fund

Chase Frei, CAIA, Ashland Partners & Company LLP

John Freihammer, CAIA, Chicago Teachers Pension Fund

Craig Grenier, CAIA, Northeastern University Endowment

Weiyu Guo, CAIA, Huajin Capital (International) Ltd

Bobby Hagedorn, CAIA, Missouri Patrol Employees' Retirement System

Sajal Heda, CAIA, DAMAC Investment Company (Dubai)

Jeremy Heer, CAIA, The University of Chicago

Katy Huang, CAIA, Deutsche Bank (Suisse) SA

Drew Lerardi, CAIA, Exelon Corporation

Jason Josephiac, CAIA, United Technologies Corporation

Panayiotis Lambropoulos, CAIA, Employees Retirement Sysyem of Texas

Julia H. Lee, CAIA, Michigan State University

Grant Leslie, CAIA Tennessee Consolidated Retirement System

Yasir Mallick, CAIA, University of Toronto Asset Management

Tom Masthay, CAIA Texas Municipal Retirement System

Jason Morrow, CAIA, Utah Retirement Systems

Courtney Ann, CAIA, InvestorSpeak

Chad Myhre, CAIA, Public School & Education Employee Retirement Systems of Missouri

Michael Nicks, CAIA, Pepperdine University Endowment

Mansco Perry, CAIA Minnesota State Board of Investment

Steven Price, CAIA, Ohio School Employees Retirement System

Lin Qu, CAIA, Independent

Brian Quinn, CAIA, Newton Investment Management

Sarah Samuels, CAIA, NEPC

Andrew Sawyer, CAIA, Maine Public Employees Retirement System

Wolfdieter Schnee, CAIA, VP Fund Solutions (Liechtenstein) AG

Jamey Sharpe, CAIA, Blue Cross Blue Shield Association

Joseph Simonian, Quantitative Research, Natixis Investment Managers

Gaurav Singh, CAIA, Kuwait International Bank

Benjamin Skrodzki, CAIA, Teachers' Retirement System of the State of Illinois

Ken Stemme, CAIA, UAW Retiree Medical Benefits Trust

Graham Tedesco, CAIA, Storage Deluxe

Ryan Tidwell, CAIA, Oklahoma State University Foundation

Hilary Wiek, CAIA, Formerly the Saint Paul & Minnesota Community Foundations

Shane Willoughby, CAIA, State Universities Retirement System of Illinois

Michael Weinberg, CIO, MOV37

Thomas Woodbury, CAIA, University of Pennsylvania Investment Office

Gerald Yahoudy, CAIA, New York State Teachers

Ernest Yeung, CAIA, Changsheng Fund Management Ltd

Jasmine Yu, CAIA, BNY Mellon

Contributing Authors

Mark Anson

Richard Bliss

Jim Campasano

Michal E. Crowder

Satyabrota Das, CAIA

Malay K. Dey

Jaeson Dubrovay, CAIA

Urbi Garay

Kathryn Kaminski , CAIA

Jim Kyung-Soo Liew

Natalie Maniaci Roberts

George Martin

Pierre-Yves Mathonet

Thomas Meyer

Bob Murphy, CAIA

Putri Pascualy

Mark Potter

Jason Scharfman, CAIA

Lois Suruki

Ed Szado

Reviewers and Members of Curriculum Committee

James Bachman, CAIA

Gordon Barnes

Ann Blamire

David Blitz

Douglas Cumming

James Curley

Eric Dorflinger

Samuel Gallo, CAIA

Antolin Garza

James T Gillies, CAIA

Daniel Golyanov, CAIA

Mark Hutchinson

Georg Inderest

Tom Johnson, CAIA

Kathryn Kaminski, CAIA

Steve Karsh

Tom Kehoe, CAIA

Malinda Khauv

Eric Klein

Mike Kurz, CAIA

Jeff H Li

Greg Lyle

David McCarthy

Matthew Miracola, CAIA

Bob Murphy, CAIA

Ryan Murphy

Sanjay Nawalkha

Ludovic Phalippou

Ty Powers

Neena Prakash

Thomas Reigert

Mark Rzepczynski

Danny Santiago, CAIA

Christopher Schelling, CAIA

Shelly Talaye, CAIA

Richard Spurgin

Justin Toumey, CAIA

Laura Valdez, CAIA

Evgeny Vostretsov, CAIA

Mark Wiltshire, CAIA

Andrew Zimmerman

Special credit goes to CAIA staff for their valuable contributions in painstakingly bringing the fourth edition to completion.

CAIA Staff

Aaron Filbeck, CAIA, Associate Director, Content Development

Yaseen Gholizadeh, Curriculum Intern

Nelson Lacey, Director of Exams

Kristaps Licis, Senior Associate Director of Exams

Jack Neureuter, Curriculum Intern

Nancy E. Perry, Curriculum and Exams Associate

About the Authors

The CAIA Association is an independent, not-for-profit global organization committed to education and professionalism in the field of alternative investments. The Association was established in 2002 by industry leaders under the guidance of the Alternative Investment Management Association (AIMA) and the Center for International Securities and Derivatives Markets (CISDM) with the belief that a strong foundation of knowledge is essential for all professionals. The curriculum includes two exams (Level I and Level II) administered to professional analysts in this growing field so that, upon successful completion, the individuals are designated "Chartered Alternative Investment Analysts" (CAIA). The CAIA designation has a great deal of prestige in the global community. Members come from over 90 countries on six continents.

Dr. Donald R. Chambers, CAIA, is Associate Director of Programs at the CAIA Association; Chief Investment Officer of Biltmore Capital Advisors and Emeritus Professor at Lafayette College in Easton, Pennsylvania. Dr. Chambers previously served as Director of Alternative Investments at Karpus Investment Management. He is a member of the editorial board of the *Journal of Alternative Investments*.

Dr. Keith H. Black, CAIA, FDP, is Managing Director of Content Strategy at the CAIA Association. He was previously an Associate at Ennis Knupp and, before that, an Assistant Professor at Illinois Institute of Technology. He is a member of the editorial board of the *Journal of Alternative Investments*.

Dr. Hossein Kazemi is a senior adviser to the CAIA Association. He is the Michael and Cheryl Philipp Professor of Finance at the University of Massachusetts, Amherst; Director of the Center for International Securities and Derivatives Markets; a cofounder of the CAIA Association; and Editor-in-Chief of the *Journal of Alternative Investments*—the official publication of the CAIA Association and a member of the editorial board of the *Journal of Financial Data Science*.

Alternative Investments

Ethics Regulations and ESG

Investors in both traditional and alternative investments need to consider ethics, regulations, as well as environmental, social, and governance (ESG) issues when allocating assets. Part 1 begins with two chapters (Chapters 1 and 2) that lists the standards of the Asset Manager Code from the CFA Institute as well as recommendations and guidance. Chapter 3 details the global regulatory landscape, detailing regulations in the US, Europe, and in Asia. Chapters 4 and 5 detail ESG considerations, both generally and in the context of specific applications to alternative investments.

CHAPTER 1

Asset Manager Code

The CFA Institute Asset Manager Code outlines the ethical and professional responsibilities of firms ("Managers") that manage assets on behalf of clients.[1] By adopting and enforcing a code of conduct for their organizations, Managers demonstrate their commitment to ethical behavior and the protection of investors' interests.

1.1   GENERAL PRINCIPLES OF CONDUCT

Managers have the following responsibilities to their clients.
  Managers must:

1. Act in a professional and ethical manner at all times.
2. Act for the benefit of clients.
3. Act with independence and objectivity.
4. Act with skill, competence, and diligence.
5. Communicate with clients in a timely and accurate manner.
6. Uphold the applicable rules governing capital markets.

1.2   ASSET MANAGER CODE

(A) **Loyalty to Clients**
    Managers must:
    1. Place client interests before their own.
    2. Preserve the confidentiality of information communicated by clients within the scope of the Manager–client relationship.
    3. Refuse to participate in any business relationship or accept any gift that could reasonably be expected to affect their independence, objectivity, or loyalty to clients.
(B) **Investment Process and Actions**
    Managers must:
    1. Use reasonable care and prudent judgment when managing client assets.
    2. Not engage in practices designed to distort prices or artificially inflate trading volume with the intent to mislead market participants.
    3. Deal fairly and objectively with all clients when providing investment information, making investment recommendations, or taking investment action.

4. Have a reasonable and adequate basis for investment decisions.
5. When managing a portfolio or pooled fund according to a specific mandate, strategy, or style:
   a. Take only investment actions that are consistent with the stated objectives and constraints of that portfolio or fund.
   b. Provide adequate disclosures and information so investors can consider whether any proposed changes in the investment style or strategy meet their investment needs.
6. When managing separate accounts and before providing investment advice or taking investment action on behalf of the client:
   a. Evaluate and understand the client's investment objectives, tolerance for risk, time horizon, liquidity needs, financial constraints, any unique circumstances (including tax considerations, legal or regulatory constraints, etc.), and any other relevant information that would affect investment policy.
   b. Determine that an investment is suitable to a client's financial situation.

(C) **Trading**
Managers must:
1. Not act or cause others to act on material nonpublic information that could affect the value of a publicly traded investment.
2. Give priority to investments made on behalf of the client over those that benefit the Managers' own interests.
3. Use commissions generated from client trades to pay for only investment-related products or services that directly assist the Manager in its investment decision-making process, and not in the management of the firm.
4. Maximize client portfolio value by seeking best execution for all client transactions.
5. Establish policies to ensure fair and equitable trade allocation among client accounts.

(D) **Risk Management, Compliance, and Support**
Managers must:
1. Develop and maintain policies and procedures to ensure that their activities comply with the provisions of this Code and all applicable legal and regulatory requirements.
2. Appoint a compliance officer responsible for administering the policies and procedures and for investigating complaints regarding the conduct of the Manager or its personnel.
3. Ensure that portfolio information provided to clients by the Manager is accurate and complete and arrange for independent third-party confirmation or review of such information.
4. Maintain records for an appropriate period of time in an easily accessible format.
5. Employ qualified staff and sufficient human and technological resources to thoroughly investigate, analyze, implement, and monitor investment decisions and actions.
6. Establish a business-continuity plan to address disaster recovery or periodic disruptions of the financial markets.

7. Establish a firmwide risk management process that identifies, measures, and manages the risk position of the Manager and its investments, including the sources, nature, and degree of risk exposure.

(E) Performance and Valuation

Managers must:

1. Present performance information that is fair, accurate, relevant, timely, and complete. Managers must not misrepresent the performance of individual portfolios or of their firm.
2. Use fair-market prices to value client holdings and apply, in good faith, methods to determine the fair value of any securities for which no independent, third-party market quotation is readily available.

(F) Disclosures

Managers must:

1. Communicate with clients on an ongoing and timely basis.
2. Ensure that disclosures are truthful, accurate, complete, and understandable and are presented in a format that communicates the information effectively.
3. Include any material facts when making disclosures or providing information to clients regarding themselves, their personnel, investments, or the investment process.
4. Disclose the following:
   a. Conflicts of interests generated by any relationships with brokers or other entities, other client accounts, fee structures, or other matters.
   b. Regulatory or disciplinary action taken against the Manager or its personnel related to professional conduct.
   c. The investment process, including information regarding lock-up periods, strategies, risk factors, and use of derivatives and leverage.
   d. Management fees and other investment costs charged to investors, including what costs are included in the fees and the methodologies for determining fees and costs.
   e. The amount of any soft or bundled commissions, the goods and/or services received in return, and how those goods and/or services benefit the client.
   f. The performance of clients' investments on a regular and timely basis.
   g. Valuation methods used to make investment decisions and value client holdings.
   h. Shareholder voting policies.
   i. Trade allocation policies.
   j. Results of the review or audit of the fund or account.
   k. Significant personnel or organizational changes that have occurred at the Manager.
   l. Risk management processes.

1.3 NOTIFICATION OF COMPLIANCE

Managers must notify the CFA Institute of their claim of compliance through the Asset Manager Code claim of compliance form at www.cfainstitute.org/assetcode. This form is for communication and information-gathering purposes only and does not represent that CFA Institute engages in enforcement or quality control of an organization's claim of compliance. CFA Institute does not verify either the Manager's claim of compliance or actual compliance with the Code.

For additional information on complying, please visit www.cfainstitute.org/assetcode.

1.4   ADDITIONAL GUIDANCE FOR THE ASSET MANAGER CODE

The following interpretations of the Asset Manager Code are responses to inquiries received from firms seeking to comply with the Code. These interpretations serve as additional guidance to the Asset Manager Code from CFA Institute and should be considered official and authoritative explanations of the requirements of the relevant Code provisions.

1.4.1   Defining a Firm

How does the Asset Manager Code apply to large investment advisers that are the parent of a group of smaller managers? Does compliance by the parent company signify that all of the related firms are in compliance? Can the smaller firms claim compliance separately?

In the case of a common parent of several individual asset managers, each individual manager may claim compliance or the parent firm may claim compliance for all individual members. However, if the parent claims compliance for the group, then each individual member firm of that group must comply with the provisions of the Code. Additionally, both the parent and the underlying firms may claim compliance with the Code and appear on the CFA Institute list of compliant firms.

1.4.2   Claiming Compliance

If a firm claims compliance with the Asset Manager Code, is it required to include a statement of compliance on its marketing materials or in GIPS-compliant presentations?

The Code does not require firms to include a claim of compliance on marketing materials. If the firm claims compliance with the GIPS standards and the Code, the firm is not required to include a claim of Code compliance on GIPS-compliant performance. If the firm chooses to include a claim of compliance with the Code on its marketing materials, it must include the following statement: "[Firm] claims compliance with the CFA Institute Asset Manager Code. This claim has not been verified by CFA Institute."

1.4.3   Suitability

Is a Code-compliant asset manager required to meet the suitability provision (Provision B.6) for large, sophisticated asset owners or for asset owners working through a third-party consultant?

Provision B.6 applies to firms managing client assets with a variety of strategies and mandates. For instances when an institutional investor, either directly or through a third-party consultant, hires an investment manager to manage a specific portion of the institutional assets to a particular mandate, strategy, or style, Provision B.5 would be the applicable suitability provision. Provision B.5 requires the manager to take investment actions that are consistent with the mandate but does not require a suitability assessment of the mandate itself in relation to the client's other assets. Meeting either of these provisions can be documented through the investment policy statement or through the manager contract.

1.4.4 Protecting Client Interests

Provision C.2 states that clients must be given "priority" over investments that benefit the manager's own interests. If a manager's trade allocation policies treat all accounts "equitably" but do not necessarily give "priority" to an account or fund that is not invested in by the manager, does that comply with Code?

Trade allocation policies that (1) treat all accounts or funds equitably without consideration of a manager's participation; and (2) do not disadvantage clients for the manager's benefit are not incompatible with this provision. Provision C.2 highlights the duty to act in the best interest of clients. Giving client accounts priority in the context of this provision prohibits manager accounts from being favored over client accounts. The guidance to Provision C.2 makes clear that investment activities of the manager for his or her own investments must not adversely affect or disadvantage the manager's clients.

1.4.5 Best Execution

Provision C.4 states that compliant managers are to seek best execution for all client transactions. If a client directs the manager to trade with a specific broker that may not offer best execution but does provide some other service to the client, can the manager still claim compliance with the Code?

Directed brokerage arrangements that do not allow the firm to obtain best execution do not violate this provision. Best execution in this case can only be done within the confines of the client mandate.

Provision C.4 highlights the duty to maximize client portfolio value by trading though the appropriate channels for the particular circumstances for the trade. When a client directs the manager to trade through a specific broker, this may prevent the manager from using a broker that could provide more favorable execution terms for the client. Best practice dictates that the manager alert the client of the potential impact of his or her directed brokerage on execution prices.

1.4.6 Third-Party Confirmation of Client Information

Does the routine reconciliation process provided for by the custodial bank meet the "independent third-party confirmation" requirement of Provision D.3 of the Code? Does a manager need some separate, formal confirmation to a client?

Provision D.3 considers the routine reconciliation process of custodians to constitute "independent third-party confirmation" as required by the Code. No additional confirmation statement is required.

1.4.7   Risk Management

Regarding Provision D.7, can you describe what sort of risk management process you are seeing in managers adopting the Code?

CFA Institute does not require firms to disclose their risk management processes to the organization prior to or as part of their claim of compliance. We are not privy to the processes adopted by managers. It is up to each manager to adopt adequate risk management processes to meet this provision that are appropriate and relevant to the firm. The guidance to Provision D.7 outlines generally what constitutes an effective risk management process.

1.4.8   Valuation of Assets

Provision E.2 states that compliant managers are to use fair-market prices for traded securities. When a manager feels that the market quotation for a specific security or type of security no longer reflects the current value of the security, would the manager be prohibited from using alternative methods for calculating the holding value?

When the manager feels that the market quotation price no longer reflects the current value of a security because of an unforeseen market event (e.g., a sudden and protracted decline in trading liquidity), then the manager may treat that security like other investment assets without market quotation for valuation purposes. The manager may use widely accepted valuations methods common for the industry or turn to an independent third party for the security valuations.

1.4.9   Disclosures

Regarding providing the required disclosures in Section F, does the Code allow for some accounts to receive full disclosure documents (such as Form ADV or a fund prospectus) but others that do not?

The guidance to Provision F.1 states that "managers must determine how best to establish lines of communication that fit their circumstances and enable clients to evaluate their financial status." It is up to managers to determine how best to communicate with their clients. Provision F.4 lists the information that the Code requires to be made available (disclosed) to clients. Each manager has discretion regarding how disclosures are accomplished so long as the required information is available to the clients.

Managers need not disclose the full details of all required information with every communication. For example, for Provision F.4.b, a manager may state at the outset of the relationship that "information on regulatory or disciplinary action taken against this firm or our employees is available on request."

1.4.10   Soft Dollars

Does the requirement under Provision F.4.e that managers disclose to clients "the amount of any soft or bundled commissions" require the unbundling of commissions for each trade or each client? Does a description of the manager's execution process, which includes soft dollar and research practices, meet this requirement?

Disclosure under Provision F.4.e allows investors to make informed decisions about whether their commissions are used to purchase goods and services (including research) beyond execution and whether they are receiving a benefit from these goods and services. Disclosure enables investors to determine whether to use advisers who enter into soft dollar arrangements. However, Provision F.4.e does not require firms to unbundle each trade for each client. Firms should disclose to clients what amount (i.e., dollars) or portion (i.e., percentage) of their total commissions was paid under a soft dollar arrangement, along with the services received from the soft dollars and the benefit of those services to the clients. Boilerplate or general statements regarding use of soft dollars are not sufficient. In situations in which investors buy into a particular investment fund and the trading of the fund generates soft dollars, the firm is not required to break down the soft dollar commissions for each individual investor in the fund. Similarly, in programs in which holdings for many individual accounts are aggregated with other clients for trading or recordkeeping, disclosure of soft dollar information in aggregate is sufficient. Individual investors are then free to request information about soft dollars for their individual accounts. With disclosure in hand, the investor can make an informed decision about engaging the manager.

1.4.11 Investment Process

Does the requirement under Provision F.4.g require the manager to publicly disclose the full operations of the security selection process? For instance, is the manager required to disclose all elements of a proprietary quantitative model?

Provision F.4.g, in conjunction Provision F.4.c, highlights the need for a manager to provide clients and prospective clients with sufficient information to make an informed decision about the investment methodology used in managing the portfolio. The provisions do not require the firm to publish a proprietary investment model or analytical process. However, the communications with clients and prospective clients should be sufficiently detailed to give them sufficient information to understand the nature and the risks of the investment process. The timing and frequency of such disclosures by the manager may be determined based on the relationship that exists with the individual clients.

1.4.12 Additional Q&As

What are the registration options for a diverse organization with many operating subsidiaries?

Any legal operating entity providing investment management services is permitted to claim compliance with the Asset Manager Code. This permits the parent-level organization to claim compliance, as well as the individual subsidiaries. It is up to the firm to determine the most appropriate entities to submit claims of compliance to accurately reflect the information to clients.

If the organization registers compliance for the parent-level organization, then all operating subsidiaries would be covered by that registration. Thus, the registration of the subsidiaries, is not needed, but is permitted to add clarity.

When registration is completed at the subsidiary-level, only the specific organization and any subsidiaries under it are deemed as complying with the Code. The registration of a subsidiary does not create an obligation of the parent to comply with the Code.

A firm has only one legal structure but operates in different divisions for providing services to clients. Is the firm permitted to register compliance for only one specific operating division?

A firm may not register compliance for a division that is not operated as a separate legal entity. Any legal operating entity providing investment management services is permitted to claim compliance with the Asset Manager Code. The CFA Institute website then displays the names of the firms claiming compliance. Users of the website would not be able to tell if only a portion of the listed firm complied with the requirements of the Code.

Additional questions? Contact the helpdesk at industrystandards@cfainstitute .org.

NOTE

1. Copyright CFA Institute. Used by permission.

CHAPTER 2

Recommendations and Guidance

doption of the Asset Manager Code of the CFA Institute is insufficient by itself for a Manager to meet its ethical and regulatory responsibilities. Managers must adopt detailed policies and procedures to effectively implement the Code.[1] This section provides guidance explaining the Code and includes recommendations and illustrative examples to assist Managers that are seeking to implement the Code. These examples are not meant to be exhaustive, and the policies and procedures needed to support the Code will depend on the particular circumstances of each organization and the legal and regulatory environment in which the Manager operates. The following guidance highlights particular issues that Managers should consider when developing their internal policies and procedures that accompany the Code. The guidance is not intended to cover all issues or aspects of a Manager's operations that would have to be included in such policies and procedures to fully implement and support the Code.

(A) **Loyalty to Clients**
   Managers must:
   1. **Place client interests before their own.**
       Client interests are paramount. Managers should institute policies and procedures to ensure that client interests supersede Manager interests in all aspects of the Manager–client relationship, including (but not limited to) investment selection, transactions, monitoring, and custody. Managers should take reasonable steps to avoid situations in which the Manager's interests and client interests conflict and should institute operational safeguards to protect client interests. Managers should implement compensation arrangements that align the financial interests of clients and managers and avoid incentives that could result in Managers taking action in conflict with client interests.
   2. **Preserve the confidentiality of information communicated by clients within the scope of the Manager–client relationship.**
       As part of their ethical duties, Managers must hold information communicated to them by clients or other sources within the context of the Manager–client relationship strictly confidential and must take all reasonable measures to preserve that confidentiality. This duty applies when Managers obtain information on the basis of their confidential relationship with the client or their special ability to conduct a portion of the client's business or personal affairs. Managers should create a privacy policy that addresses how confidential client information will be collected, stored, protected, and used.

The duty to maintain confidentiality does not supersede a duty (and in some cases the legal requirement) to report suspected illegal activities involving client accounts to the appropriate authorities. Where appropriate, Managers should consider creating and implementing a written anti-money-laundering policy to prevent their organizations from being used for money laundering or the financing of any illegal activities.

3. **Refuse to participate in any business relationship or accept any gift that could reasonably be expected to affect their independence, objectivity, or loyalty to clients.**

    As part of holding clients' interests paramount, Managers must establish policies for accepting gifts or entertainment in a variety of contexts. To avoid the appearance of a conflict, Managers must refuse to accept gifts or entertainment from service providers, potential investment targets, or other business partners of more than a minimal value. Managers should define what the minimum value is and should confer with local regulations, which may also establish limits.

    Managers should establish a written policy limiting the acceptance of gifts and entertainment to items of minimal value. Managers should consider creating specific limits for accepting gifts (e.g., amount per time period per vendor) and prohibit the acceptance of any cash gifts. Employees should be required to document and disclose to the Manager, through their supervisor, the firm's compliance office, or senior management, the acceptance of any gift or entertainment.

    This provision is not meant to preclude Managers from maintaining multiple business relationships with a client as long as potential conflicts of interest are managed and disclosed.

(B) **Investment Process and Actions**

  Managers must:

  1. **Use reasonable care and prudent judgment when managing client assets.**

      Managers must exhibit the care and prudence necessary to meet their obligations to clients. Prudence requires caution and discretion. The exercise of prudence requires acting with the care, skill, and diligence that a person acting in a like capacity and familiar with such matters would use under the same circumstances. In the context of managing a client's portfolio, prudence requires following the investment parameters set forth by the client and balancing risk and return. Acting with care requires Managers to act in a prudent and judicious manner in avoiding harm to clients.

  2. **Not engage in practices designed to distort prices or artificially inflate trading volume with the intent to mislead market participants.**

      Market manipulation is illegal in most jurisdictions and damages the interests of all investors by disrupting the efficient functioning of financial markets and causing deterioration in investor confidence.

      Market manipulation includes practices that distort security prices or values or artificially inflate trading volumes with the intent to deceive persons or entities that rely on information in the market. Such practices may involve, for example, transactions that deceive market participants by distorting the price-setting mechanism of financial instruments and the dissemination of false or misleading information. Transaction-based manipulation includes, but is not limited to, transactions that artificially distort prices or volume to give the impression of activity or price movement in a financial instrument (e.g., trading in illiquid stocks at the end of a measurement period to drive up the price and improve Manager performance) and securing a large position with the intent to exploit and manipulate the price of an asset and/or a related derivative. Information-based manipulation includes, but is not limited to, spreading knowingly false rumors to induce trading by others and pressuring sell-side analysts to rate or recommend a security in such a way that benefits the manager or the Manager's clients.

3. **Deal fairly and objectively with all clients when providing investment information, making investment recommendations, or taking investment action.**

    To maintain the trust that clients place in them, Managers must deal with all clients in a fair and objective manner. Managers must not give preferential treatment to favored clients to the detriment of other clients. In some cases, clients may pay for a higher level of service or certain services and certain products may only be made available to certain qualifying clients (e.g., certain funds may be open only to clients with assets above a certain level). These practices are permitted as long as they are disclosed and made available to all clients.

    This provision is not intended to prevent Managers from engaging in secondary investment opportunities—referred to in some jurisdictions as "side-letter," "sidecar," or "tag-along" arrangements—with certain clients as long as such opportunities are fairly allocated among similarly situated clients for whom the opportunity is suitable.

4. **Have a reasonable and adequate basis for investment decisions.**

    Managers must act with prudence and make sure their decisions have a reasonable and adequate basis. Prior to taking action on behalf of their clients, Managers must analyze the investment opportunities in question and should act only after undertaking due diligence to ensure there is sufficient knowledge about specific investments or strategies. Such analysis will depend on the style and strategy being used. For example, a Manager implementing a passive strategy will have a very different basis for investment actions from that of a Manager that uses an active strategy.

    Managers can rely on external third-party research as long as Managers have made reasonable and diligent efforts to determine that such research has a reasonable basis. When evaluating investment research, Managers should consider the assumptions used, the thoroughness of the analysis performed, the timeliness of the information, and the objectivity and independence of the source.

    Managers should have a thorough understanding of the securities in which they invest and the strategies they use on behalf of clients. Managers should understand the structure and function of the securities, how they are traded, their liquidity, and any other risks (including counterparty risk).

    Managers who implement complex and sophisticated investment strategies should understand the structure and potential vulnerabilities of such strategies and communicate these in an understandable manner to their clients. For example, when implementing complex derivative strategies, Managers should understand the various risks and conduct statistical analysis (i.e., stress testing) to determine how the strategy will perform under different conditions. By undertaking adequate due diligence, Managers can better judge the suitability of investments for their clients.

5. **When managing a portfolio or pooled fund according to a specific mandate, strategy, or style:**

   a. **Take only investment actions that are consistent with the stated objectives and constraints of that portfolio or fund.**

   When Managers are given a specific mandate by clients or offer a product, such as a pooled fund for which the Managers do not know the specific financial situation of each client, the Managers must manage the funds or portfolios within the stated mandates or strategies. Clients need to be able to evaluate the suitability of the investment funds or strategies for themselves. Subsequently, they must be able to trust that Managers will not diverge from the stated or agreed-on mandates or strategies. When market events or opportunities change to such a degree that Managers wish to have flexibility to take advantage of those occurrences, such flexibility is not improper but should be expressly understood and agreed to by Managers and clients. Best practice is for Managers to disclose such events to clients when they occur or, at the very least, in the course of normal client reporting.

   b. **Provide adequate disclosures and information so investors can consider whether any proposed changes in the investment style or strategy meet their investment needs.**

   To give clients an opportunity to evaluate the suitability of investments, Managers need to provide adequate information to them about any proposed material changes to their investment strategies or styles. They must provide this information well in advance of such changes. Clients should be given enough time to consider the proposed changes and take any actions that may be necessary. If the Manager decides to make a material change in the investment strategy or style, clients should be permitted to redeem their investment, if desired, without incurring any undue penalties.

6. **When managing separate accounts and before providing investment advice or taking investment action on behalf of the client:**

   a. **Evaluate and understand the client's investment objectives, tolerance for risk, time horizon, liquidity needs, financial constraints, any unique circumstances (including tax considerations, legal or regulatory constraints, etc.), and any other relevant information that would affect investment policy.**

   Prior to taking any investment actions for clients, Managers must take the necessary steps to understand and evaluate the client's financial situation, constraints, and other relevant factors. Without understanding the client's situation, the Manager cannot select and implement an appropriate investment strategy. Ideally, each client will have an investment policy statement (IPS) that includes a discussion of risk tolerances (both the ability and willingness of the client to bear risk), return objectives, time horizon, liquidity requirements, liabilities, tax considerations, and any legal, regulatory, or other unique circumstances.

The purpose of the IPS is to provide Managers with written strategic plans to direct investment decisions for each client. The Manager should take an opportunity to review the IPS for each client, offer any suggestions on clarifying the IPS, and discuss with the client the various techniques and strategies to be used to meet the client's investment goals. Managers should review each client's IPS with the client at least annually and whenever circumstances suggest changes may be needed.

The information contained in an IPS allows Managers to assess whether a particular strategy or security is suitable for a client (in the context of the rest of the client's portfolio), and the IPS serves as the basis for establishing the client's strategic asset allocation. (Note: in some cases, the client will determine the strategic asset allocation; in other cases, that duty will be delegated to the Manager.) The IPS should also specify the Manager's role and responsibilities in managing the client's assets and establish schedules for review and evaluation. The Manager should reach agreement with the client as to an appropriate benchmark or benchmarks by which the Manager's performance will be measured and any other details of the performance evaluation process (e.g., when performance measurement should begin).

b. **Determine that an investment is suitable to a client's financial situation.**

Managers must evaluate investment actions and strategies in light of each client's circumstances. Not all investments are suitable for every client, and Managers have a responsibility to ensure that only appropriate investments and investment strategies are included in a client's portfolio. Ideally, individual investments should be evaluated in the context of clients' total assets and liabilities, which may include assets held outside of the Manager's account, to the extent that such information is made available to the Manager and is explicitly included in the context of the client's IPS.

(C) **Trading**

Managers must:

1. **Not act or cause others to act on material nonpublic information that could affect the value of a publicly traded investment.**

Trading on material nonpublic information, which is illegal in most jurisdictions, erodes confidence in capital markets, institutions, and investment professionals and promotes the perception that those with inside and special access can take unfair advantage of the general investing public. Although trading on such information may lead to short-term profitability, over time, individuals and the profession as a whole suffer if investors avoid capital markets because they perceive them to be unfair by favoring the knowledgeable insider.

Different jurisdictions and regulatory regimes may define materiality differently, but in general, information is "material" if it is likely that a reasonable investor would consider it important and if it would be viewed as significantly altering the total mix of information available. Information is "nonpublic" until it has been widely disseminated to the marketplace (as opposed to a select group of investors).

Managers must adopt compliance procedures, such as establishing information barriers (e.g., fire walls), to prevent the disclosure and misuse of material nonpublic information. In many cases, pending trades or client or fund holdings may be considered material nonpublic information, and Managers must be sure to keep such information confidential. In addition, merger and acquisition information, prior to its public disclosure, is generally considered material nonpublic information. Managers should evaluate company-specific information that they may receive and determine whether it meets the definition of material nonpublic information.

This provision is not meant to prevent Managers from using the mosaic theory to draw conclusions—that is, combine pieces of material public information with pieces of nonmaterial nonpublic information to draw conclusions that are actionable.

2. **Give priority to investments made on behalf of the client over those that benefit the Managers' own interests.**

Managers must not execute their own trades in a security prior to client transactions in the same security. Investment activities that benefit the Manager must not adversely affect client interests. Managers must not engage in trading activities that work to the disadvantage of clients (e.g., front-running client trades).

In some investment arrangements, such as limited partnerships or pooled funds, Managers put their own capital at risk alongside that of their clients to align their interests with the interests of their clients. These arrangements are permissible only if clients are not disadvantaged.

Managers should develop policies and procedures to monitor and, where appropriate, limit the personal trading of their employees. In particular, Managers should require employees to receive approval prior to any personal investments in initial public offerings or private placements. Managers should develop policies and processes designed to ensure that client transactions take precedence over employee or firm transactions. One method is to create a restricted list and/or watch list of securities that are owned in client accounts or may be bought or sold on behalf of clients in the near future; prior to trading securities on such a list, employees would be required to seek approval. In addition, Managers could require employees to provide the compliance officer with copies of trade confirmations each quarter and annual statements of personal holdings.

3. **Use commissions generated from client trades to pay for only investment related products or services that directly assist the Manager in its investment decision-making process, and not in the management of the firm.**

Managers must recognize that commissions paid (and any benefits received in return for commissions paid) are the property of the client. Consequently, any benefits offered in return for commissions must benefit the Manager's clients.

To determine whether a benefit generated from client commissions is appropriate, Managers must determine whether it will directly assist in the Manager's investment decision-making process. The investment decision-making process can be considered the qualitative and quantitative process and the related tools used by the Manager in rendering investment advice to clients. The process includes financial analysis, trading and risk analysis, securities selection, broker selection, asset allocation, and suitability analysis.

Some Managers have chosen to eliminate the use of soft commissions (also known as soft dollars) to avoid any conflicts of interest that may exist. Managers should disclose their policy on how benefits are evaluated and used for the client's benefit. If Managers choose to use a soft commission or bundled brokerage arrangement, they should disclose this use to their clients. Managers should consider complying with industry best practices regarding the use and reporting of such an arrangement, which can be found in the CFA Institute Soft Dollar Standards.

4. **Maximize client portfolio value by seeking best execution for all client transactions.**

When placing client trades, Managers have a duty to seek terms that secure best execution for and maximize the value of each client's portfolio (i.e., ensure the best possible result overall). Managers must seek the most favorable terms for client trades within each trades' particular circumstances (such as transaction size, market characteristics, liquidity of security, and security type). Managers also must decide which brokers or venues provide best execution while considering, among other things, commission rates, timeliness of trade executions, and the ability to maintain anonymity, minimize incomplete trades, and minimize market impact.

When a client directs the Manager to place trades through a specific broker or through a particular type of broker, Managers should alert the client that by limiting the Manager's ability to select the broker, the client may not be receiving best execution. The Manager should seek written acknowledgment from the client of receiving this information.

5. **Establish policies to ensure fair and equitable trade allocation among client accounts.**

When placing trades for client accounts, Managers must allocate trades fairly so that some client accounts are not routinely traded first or receive preferential treatment. Where possible, Managers should use block trades and allocate shares on a pro-rata basis by using an average price or some other method that ensures fair and equitable allocations. When allocating shares of an initial or secondary offering, Managers should strive to ensure that all clients for whom the security is suitable are given opportunities to participate. When Managers do not receive a large enough allocation to allow all eligible clients to participate fully in a particular offering, they must ensure that certain clients are not given preferential treatment and should establish a system to ensure that new issues are allocated fairly (e.g., pro rata). Manager's trade allocation policies should specifically address how initial public offerings and private placements are to be handled.

(D) **Risk Management, Compliance, and Support**
Managers must:
1. **Develop and maintain policies and procedures to ensure that their activities comply with the provisions of this Code and all applicable legal and regulatory requirements.**

Detailed and firmwide compliance policies and procedures are critical tools to ensure that Managers meet their legal requirements when managing client assets. In addition, the fundamental, principle-based, ethical concepts embodied in the Code should be put into operation by the implementation of specific policies and procedures.

Documented compliance procedures assist Managers in fulfilling the responsibilities enumerated in the Code and ensure that the standards expressed in the Code are adhered to in the day-to-day operation of the firms. The appropriate compliance programs, internal controls, and self-assessment tools for each Manager will depend on such factors as the size of the firm and the nature of its investment management business.

2. **Appoint a compliance officer responsible for administering the policies and procedures and for investigating complaints regarding the conduct of the Manager or its personnel.**

Effective compliance programs require Managers to appoint a compliance officer who is competent, knowledgeable, and credible and is empowered to carry out his or her duties. Depending on the size and complexity of the Manager's operations, Managers may designate an existing employee to also serve as the compliance officer, may hire a separate individual for that role, or may establish an entire compliance department. Where possible, the compliance officer should be independent from the investment and operations personnel and should report directly to the CEO or board of directors. The compliance officer and senior management should regularly make clear to all employees that adherence to compliance policies and procedures is crucial and that anyone who violates them will be held liable. Managers should consider requiring all employees to acknowledge that they have received a copy of the Code (as well as any subsequent material amendments), that they understand and agree to comply with it, and that they will report any suspected violations of the Code to the designated compliance officer. Compliance officers should take steps to implement appropriate employee training and conduct continuing self-evaluation of the Manager's compliance practices to assess the effectiveness of the practices. Among other things, the compliance officer should be charged with reviewing firm and employee transactions to ensure the priority of client interests. Because personnel, regulations, business practices, and products constantly change, the role of the compliance officer (particularly the role of keeping the firm up to date on such matters) is particularly important. The compliance officer should document and act expeditiously to address any compliance breaches and work with management to take appropriate disciplinary action.

3. **Ensure that portfolio information provided to clients by the Manager is accurate and complete and arrange for independent third-party confirmation or review of such information.**

Managers have a responsibility to ensure that the information they provide to clients is accurate and complete. By receiving an independent third-party confirmation or review of that information, clients have an additional level of confidence that the information is correct, which may enhance the Manager's credibility. Such verification is also good business practice because it may serve as a risk management tool to help the Manager identify potential problems. The confirmation of portfolio information may take the form of an audit or review, as is the case with most pooled vehicles, or may take the form of copies of account statements and trade confirmations from the custodian bank where the client assets are held.

4. **Maintain records for an appropriate period of time in an easily accessible format.**

    Managers must retain records that substantiate their investment activities, the scope of their research, the basis for their conclusions, and the reasons for actions taken on behalf of their clients. Managers should also retain copies of other compliance related records that support and substantiate the implementation of the Code and related policies and procedures, as well as records of any violations and resulting actions taken. Records can be maintained either in hard copy or electronic form.

    Regulators often impose requirements related to record retention. In the absence of such regulation, Managers must determine the appropriate minimum time frame for keeping the organization's records. Unless otherwise required by local law or regulation, Managers should keep records for at least seven years.

5. **Employ qualified staff and sufficient human and technological resources to thoroughly investigate, analyze, implement, and monitor investment decisions and actions.**

    To safeguard the Manager–client relationship, Managers need to allocate all the resources necessary to ensure that client interests are not compromised. Clients pay significant sums to Managers for professional asset management services, and client assets should be handled with the greatest possible care.

    Managers of all sizes and investment styles struggle with issues of cost and efficiency and tend to be cautious about adding staff in important operational areas. Nevertheless, adequate protection of client assets requires appropriate administrative, back-office, and compliance support. Managers should ensure that adequate internal controls are in place to prevent fraudulent behavior. A critical consideration is employing only *qualified* staff. Managers must ensure that client assets are invested, administered, and protected by qualified and experienced staff. Employing qualified staff reflects a client-first attitude and helps ensure that Managers are applying the care and prudence necessary to meet their obligations to clients. This provision is not meant to prohibit the outsourcing of certain functions, but the Manager retains the liability and responsibility for any outsourced work.

    Managers have a responsibility to clients to deliver the actual services they claim to offer. Managers must use adequate resources to carry out the necessary research and analysis to implement their investment strategies with due diligence and care. Also, Managers must have adequate resources to monitor the portfolio holdings and investment strategies. As investment strategies and instruments become increasingly sophisticated, the need for sufficient resources to analyze and monitor them becomes ever more important.

6. **Establish a business-continuity plan to address disaster recovery or periodic disruptions of the financial markets.**

    Part of safeguarding client interests is establishing procedures for handling client accounts and inquiries in situations of national, regional, or local emergency or market disruption. Commonly referred to as business-continuity or disaster-recovery planning, such preparation is increasingly important in an industry and world highly susceptible to a wide variety of disasters and disruptions. The level and complexity of business-continuity planning depends on the size, nature, and complexity of the organization. At a minimum, Managers should consider having the following:

- adequate backup, preferably off-site, for all account information;
- alternative plans for monitoring, analyzing, and trading investments if primary systems become unavailable;
- plans for communicating with critical vendors and suppliers;
- plans for employee communication and coverage of critical business functions in the event of a facility or communication disruption; and
- plans for contacting and communicating with clients during a period of extended disruption.

Numerous other factors may need to be considered when creating the plan. According to the needs of the organization, these factors may include establishing backup office and operational space in the event of an extended disruption and dealing with key employee deaths or departures.

As with any important business planning, Managers should ensure that employees and staff are knowledgeable about the plan and are specifically trained in areas of responsibility. Plans should be tested on a firmwide basis at intervals to promote employee understanding and identify any needed adjustments.

7. **Establish a firmwide risk management process that identifies, measures, and manages the risk position of the Manager and its investments, including the sources, nature, and degree of risk exposure.**

Many investors, including those investing in hedge funds and alternative investments or leveraged strategies, invest specifically to increase their risk-adjusted returns. Assuming some risk is a necessary part of that process. The key to sound risk management by Managers is seeking to ensure that the risk profile desired by clients matches the risk profile of their investments. Risk management should complement rather than compete with the investment management process. Investment Managers must implement risk management techniques that are consistent with their investment style and philosophy.

The types of risks faced by Managers include, but are not limited to, market risk, credit risk, liquidity risk, counterparty risk, concentration risk, and various types of operational risk. Such types of risks should be analyzed by Managers as part of a comprehensive risk management process for portfolios, investment strategies, and the firm. These examples are illustrative only and may not be applicable to all investment organizations.

Although portfolio Managers consider risk issues as part of formulating an investment strategy, the firm's risk management process must be objective, independent, and insulated from influence of portfolio managers. Managers may wish to describe to clients how the risk management framework complements the portfolio management process while remaining separate from that process. Managers should consider outsourcing risk management activities if a separate risk management function is not appropriate or feasible because of the size of the organization.

An effective risk management process will identify risk factors for individual portfolios as well as for the Manager's activities as whole. It will often be appropriate for Managers to perform stress tests, scenario tests, and backtests as part of developing risk models that comprehensively capture the full range of their actual and contingent risk exposures. The goal of such models is to determine how various changes in market and investment conditions could affect investments. The risk models should be continuously evaluated and challenged, and Managers should be prepared to describe the models to clients. Despite the importance of risk models, however, effective risk management ultimately depends on the experience, judgment, and ability of the managers in analyzing their risk metrics.

(E) **Performance and Valuation**

   Managers must:

   1. **Present performance information that is fair, accurate, relevant, timely, and complete. Managers must not misrepresent the performance of individual portfolios or of their firm.**

      Although past performance is not necessarily indicative of future performance, historical performance records are often used by prospective clients as part of the evaluation process when hiring asset Managers. Managers have a duty to present performance information that is a fair representation of their record and includes all relevant factors. In particular, Managers should be certain not to misrepresent their track records by taking credit for performance that is not their own (i.e., when they were not managing a particular portfolio or product) or by selectively presenting certain time periods or investments (i.e., cherry picking). Any hypothetical or backtested performance must be clearly identified as such. Managers should provide as much additional portfolio transparency as feasibly possible. Any forward-looking information provided to clients must also be fair, accurate, and complete.

      A model for fair, accurate, and complete performance reporting is embodied in the Global Investment Performance Standards (GIPS®), which are based on the principles of fair representation and full disclosure and are designed to meet the needs of a broad range of global markets. By adhering to these standards for reporting investment performance, Managers help assure investors that the performance information being provided is both complete and fairly presented. When Managers comply with the GIPS standards, both prospective and existing clients benefit because they can have a high degree of confidence in the reliability of the performance numbers the Managers are presenting. This confidence may, in turn, enhance clients' sense of trust in their Managers.

   2. **Use fair-market prices to value client holdings and apply, in good faith, methods to determine the fair value of any securities for which no independent, third-party market quotation is readily available.**

      In general, fund Managers' fees are calculated as a percentage of assets under management. In some cases, an additional fee is calculated as a percentage of the annual returns earned on the assets. Consequently, a conflict of interest may arise where the portfolio Manager has the additional responsibility of determining end-of-period valuations and returns on the assets.

      These conflicts may be overcome by transferring responsibility for the valuation of assets (including foreign currencies) to an independent third party. For pooled funds that have boards of directors comprising independent members, the independent members should have the responsibility of approving the asset valuation policies and procedures and reviewing the valuations. For pooled funds without independent directors, we recommend that this function be undertaken by independent third parties who are expert in providing such valuations.

Managers should use widely accepted valuation methods and techniques to appraise portfolio holdings of securities and other investments and should apply these methods on a consistent basis.

(F) Disclosures

Managers must:

1. **Communicate with clients on an ongoing and timely basis.**

    Developing and maintaining clear, frequent, and thorough communication practices is critical to providing high-quality financial services to clients. Understanding the information communicated to them allows clients to know how Managers are acting on their behalf and gives clients the opportunity to make well informed decisions regarding their investments. Managers must determine how best to establish lines of communication that fit their circumstances and that enable clients to evaluate their financial status.

2. **Ensure that disclosures are truthful, accurate, complete, and understandable and are presented in a format that communicates the information effectively.**

    Managers must not misrepresent any aspect of their services or activities, including (but not limited to) their qualifications or credentials, the services they provide, their performance records, and characteristics of the investments or strategies they use. A misrepresentation is any untrue statement or omission of fact or any statement that is otherwise false or misleading. Managers must ensure that misrepresentation does not occur in oral representations, marketing (whether through mass media or printed brochures), electronic communications, or written materials (whether publicly disseminated or not). To be effective, disclosures must be made in plain language and in a manner designed to effectively communicate the information to clients and prospective clients. Managers must determine how often, in what manner, and under what particular circumstances disclosures must be made.

3. **Include any material facts when making disclosures or providing information to clients regarding themselves, their personnel, investments, or the investment process.**

    Clients must have full and complete information to judge the abilities of managers and their actions in investing client assets. "Material" information is information that reasonable investors would want to know relative to whether or not they would choose to use or continue to use the Manager.

4. **Disclose the following:**

    a. **Conflicts of interests generated by any relationships with brokers or other entities, other client accounts, fee structures, or other matters.**

        Conflicts of interests often arise in the investment management profession and can take many forms. Best practice is to avoid such conflicts if possible. When Managers cannot reasonably avoid conflicts, they must carefully manage them and disclose them to clients. Disclosure of conflicts of interests protects investors by providing them with the information they need to evaluate the objectivity of their Managers' investment advice and actions taken on behalf of clients and by giving them the information to judge the circumstances, motives, and possible Manager bias for themselves. Examples of some of the types of activities that can constitute actual or potential conflicts of interest are the use of soft dollars or bundled commissions, referral and placement fees, trailing commissions, sales incentives, directed brokerage arrangements, allocation of investment opportunities among similar portfolios, Manager or employee holdings in the same securities as clients, whether the Manager co-invests alongside clients, and use of affiliated brokers.

b. **Regulatory or disciplinary action taken against the Manager or its personnel related to professional conduct.**

Past professional conduct records are an important factor in an investor's selection of a Manager. Such records include actions taken against a Manager by any regulator or other organization. Managers must fully disclose any significant instances in which the Manager or an employee was found to have violated standards of conduct or other standards in such a way that reflects badly on the integrity, ethics, or competence of the organization or the individual.

c. **The investment process, including information regarding lock-up periods, strategies, risk factors, and use of derivatives and leverage.**

Managers must disclose to clients and prospects the manner in which investment decisions are made and implemented. Such disclosures should address the overall investment strategy and should include a discussion of the specific risk factors inherent in such a strategy.

Understanding the basic characteristics of an investment is an important factor in judging the suitability of each investment on a standalone basis, but it is especially important in determining the effect each investment will have on the characteristics of the client's portfolio. Only by thoroughly understanding the nature of the investment product or service can a client determine whether changes to that product or service could materially affect his or her investment objectives.

d. **Management fees and other investment costs charged to investors, including what costs are included in the fees and the methodologies for determining fees and costs.**

Investors are entitled to full and fair disclosures of costs associated with the investment management services provided. Material that should be disclosed includes information relating to any fees to be paid to the Managers on an ongoing basis and periodic costs that are known to the Managers and that will affect investors' overall investment expenses. At a minimum, Managers should provide clients with gross- and net-of-fees returns and disclose any unusual expenses.

A general statement that certain fees and other costs will be assessed to investors may not adequately communicate the total amount of expenses that investors may incur as a result of investing. Therefore, Managers must not only use plain language in presenting this information but must clearly explain the methods for determining all fixed and contingent fees and costs that will be borne by investors and also must explain the transactions that will trigger the imposition of these expenses.

Managers should also retrospectively disclose to each client the actual fees and other costs charged to the clients, together with itemizations of such charges when requested by clients. This disclosure should include the specific management fee, any incentive fee, and the amount of commissions Managers paid on behalf of clients during the period. In addition, Managers must disclose to prospective clients the average or expected expenses or fees clients are likely to incur.

e. **The amount of any soft or bundled commissions, the goods and/or services received in return, and how those goods and/or services benefit the client.**

Commissions belong to the client and should be used in their best interests. Any soft or bundled commissions should be used only to benefit the client. Clients deserve to know how their commissions are spent, what is received in return for them, and how those goods and/or services benefit them.

f. **The performance of clients' investments on a regular and timely basis.**

Clients may reasonably expect to receive regular performance reporting about their accounts. Without such performance information, even for investment vehicles with lock-up periods, clients cannot evaluate their overall asset allocations (i.e., including assets not held or managed by the Managers) and determine whether rebalancing is necessary. Accordingly, unless otherwise specified by the client, Managers must provide regular, ongoing performance reporting. Managers should report to clients at least quarterly, and when possible, such reporting should be provided within 30 days after the end of the quarter.

g. **Valuation methods used to make investment decisions and value client holdings.**

Clients deserve to know whether the assets in their portfolios are valued on the basis of closing market values, third-party valuations, internal valuation models, or other methods. This type of disclosure allows clients to compare performance results and determine whether different valuation sources and methods may explain differences in performance results. This disclosure should be made by asset class and must be meaningful (i.e., not general or boilerplate) so that clients can understand how the securities are valued.

h. **Shareholder voting policies.**

As part of their fiduciary duties, Managers that exercise voting authority over client shares must vote them in an informed and responsible manner. This obligation includes the paramount duty to vote shares in the best interests of clients.

To fulfill their duties, Managers must adopt policies and procedures for the voting of shares and disclose those policies and procedures to clients. These disclosures should specify, among other things, guidelines for instituting regular reviews for new or controversial issues, mechanisms for reviewing unusual proposals, guidance in deciding whether additional actions are warranted when votes are against corporate management, and systems to monitor any delegation of share-voting responsibilities to others. Managers also must disclose to clients how to obtain information on the manner in which their shares were voted.

i. **Trade allocation policies.**

By disclosing their trade allocation policies, Managers give clients a clear understanding of how trades are allocated and provide realistic expectations of what priority they will receive in the investment allocation process. Managers must disclose to clients any changes in the trade allocation policies. By establishing and disclosing trade allocation policies that treat clients fairly, Managers foster an atmosphere of openness and trust with their clients.

j. **Results of the review or audit of the fund or account.**

If a Manager submits its funds or accounts (generally pooled or mutual funds) for an annual review or audit, it must disclose the results to clients. Such disclosure enables clients to hold Managers accountable and alerts them to any potential problems.

k. **Significant personnel or organizational changes that have occurred at the Manager.**

Clients should be made aware of significant changes at the Manager in a timely manner. "Significant" changes would include personnel turnover, merger and acquisition activities of the Manager, and similar actions.

l. **Risk management processes.**

Managers must disclose their risk management processes to clients. Material changes to the risk management process also must be disclosed. Managers should further consider regularly disclosing specific risk information and specific information regarding investment strategies related to each client. Managers must provide clients information detailing what relevant risk metrics they can expect to receive at the individual product/portfolio level.

NOTES

1. Copyright CFA Institute. Used by permission.

CHAPTER 3

Global Regulation

This chapter begins with an overview of regulation including a discussion of the importance of regulation in understanding some skill-based trading strategies. The remainder of the chapter provides a summary of key securities regulations in the US, Europe, and Asia. Throughout this chapter, the focus is on alternative investments.

This chapter is designed to provide basic information. While reading this chapter, the following should be understood: (1) some material may become dated subsequent to publication because the regulatory environment is constantly changing; and (2) this chapter is a brief overview of key aspects of major regulations and therefore should be viewed as an introduction to regulation and not as a comprehensive resource for due diligence.

3.1 OVERVIEW OF FINANCIAL MARKET REGULATION

Investors and financial industry professionals occupy a world of regulation and compliance. Understanding regulations therefore is a key responsibility and opportunity for financial industry professionals.

3.1.1 Theories of Regulation

Various theories of economic regulation are increasingly valued by the extent to which they are based on consistently applied assumptions regarding the primary motives for regulating economic activity. The **public interest theory of regulation** proposes that people act through government for the benefit of the society and seek to prevent and control problems associated with free markets such as imperfect competition, environmental damage, and other market failures with potential dangers to the public. **Private interest theories of regulation** view regulation as primarily emanating from self-interested motivations of various parties including legislators and other government employees as well as business competitors and industry groups.

3.1.2 Principles of Securities Economic Regulation

Capital markets are built on trust. Financial market regulations are based on principles of: (1) transparency; (2) market integrity or fundamental fairness; and (3) government protection of its economic and social systems through the rule of law. Although regulations will change from country to country, these guiding principles are intended to provide the investor or industry professional with a foundation for analysis. Regulations are typically a compromise between and among governments and business interests. Regulatory oversight and enforcement are the way governments and political entities ensure adherence to these compromises and policies.

3.1.3 Importance of Regulation to Some Trading Strategies

Changes in regulations can create and destroy investment opportunities. Accordingly, quality investment management requires analysis of threats and opportunities due to new information regarding regulations.

Increased regulation can inhibit the activities of those encumbered by the regulations and simultaneously generate opportunities for expansion of activities that use less-regulated pathways to meet the demand for goods and services. For example, in the wake of the global financial crisis, increased US regulations of commercial bank lending (e.g., the Dodd–Frank Act) led to the emergence and expansion of the shadow banking system. The shadow banking system consists of less-regulated nontraditional financial institutions and methods that act to provide lending more efficiently than traditional and highly regulated banks.

Decreased regulation and taxation can also open up potentially valuable opportunities. For example, in 2017 the US government authorized potentially valuable reductions in income taxes for real estate investment in so-called opportunity zones. **Qualified opportunity zones** are geographical areas in the US designated for special income tax breaks for investors funding private equity projects and real estate developments in those zones. The legislation led to a rush to create private real estate vehicles and suitable projects.

In summary, regulatory and taxation changes and uncertainty can be an important source of value-creating opportunities for investors and alternative asset managers.

3.2 REGULATION OF ALTERNATIVE INVESTMENTS WITHIN THE UNITED STATES

The primary regulators for entities and individuals engaged in the securities and investment-related activities in the US are the Securities and Exchange Commission (SEC), Financial Industry Regulatory Authority (FINRA), state securities agencies, the US Commodity Futures Trading Commission (CFTC), and the National Futures Association (NFA).

3.2.1 Overview of Regulatory Bodies in the US

SECURITIES AND EXCHANGE COMMISSION (SEC): Established in 1934, the SEC is an independent agency of the US federal government. The SEC oversees the key participants in the US securities markets, including securities exchanges, securities brokers and dealers, investment advisers, and mutual funds. As the primary overseer and regulator of the US securities markets, the **SEC's responsibilities** include: protecting investors; maintaining fair, orderly, and efficient markets; and facilitating capital formation.

The SEC disclosure regime includes **principles-based disclosure requirements,** which are intended to provide investors with the material information they need about companies and their securities offerings to make informed investment decisions.

FINANCIAL INDUSTRY REGULATORY AUTHORITY **(FINRA):** Overseen by the SEC, FINRA is a nongovernmental, self-regulatory organization (SRO) that supervises and regulates the broker-dealer industry to ensure that it operates fairly and honestly, including writing and enforcing rules governing the activities of all registered broker-dealer firms and registered brokers in the US.

Each state also has a securities commission that supervises the securities and investment activities within the state.

US COMMODITY FUTURES TRADING COMMISSION **(CFTC):** The derivatives market is overseen by the CFTC. The CFTC oversees individuals and organizations, including commodity pool operators and futures commission merchants, and seeks to protect market users and their funds, consumers, and the public from fraud, manipulation, and abusive practices related to derivatives.

NATIONAL FUTURES ASSOCIATION **(NFA):** The NFA was designated a registered futures association in 1981 and charged with the role of a self-regulatory organization (SRO). The NFA is responsible for the regulation of firms and individuals that engage in futures trading with and for investors.

States promulgate so-called blue sky laws. **Blue sky laws** in the US are a state's own set of securities laws designed to protect state interests and prevent fraudulent activities within its borders. Due to the nature of governance in the US, the SEC shares oversight authority and enforcement with each of the 50 state securities commissions.

3.2.2 Regulatory Framework

Many US laws and regulations govern securities and investment-related activities, products, and services. The primary federal statutes are:

- **The Securities Act of 1933 (Securities Act):** requires registration of securities with the SEC, unless an exemption is available, to ensure that investors receive financial and other significant information concerning the securities being offered and prohibits deceit, misrepresentations, and other fraud in the sale of securities. A private fund falls within the definition of a "security" and unless an exemption is available, the Securities Act requires the issuer to register the security.
- **The Securities Exchange Act of 1934 (Exchange Act):** provides governance of securities transactions on the secondary market (i.e., after the initial public offering) and regulates the exchanges and broker-dealers in order to protect the investing public.
- **The Investment Advisers Act of 1940 (Advisers Act):** provides for the registration and regulation of persons and entities who are engaged in providing advice to others regarding securities investments by the SEC and defines the role and responsibilities of an investment adviser. In the US, an **investment adviser** is any

person or firm that, for compensation, is engaged in the business of providing advice to others or issuing reports or analyses regarding securities.
- **The Investment Company Act of 1940 (40 Act)**: regulates the organization of companies, including mutual funds, that engage primarily in investing, reinvesting, and trading in securities, and whose own securities are offered to the investing public.

Another important US federal legislation relevant to the US securities industry is the Dodd–Frank Wall Street Reform and Consumer Protection Act of 2010 (Dodd–Frank Act) that was enacted after the global financial crisis. The **Dodd–Frank Act** was enacted to promote the financial stability of the US by improving accountability and transparency in the financial system, to end "too big to fail," to protect the American taxpayer by ending bailouts, to protect consumers from abusive financial services practices, and for other purposes. The Dodd–Frank Act is widely regarded as the most sweeping reform of asset management regulation in the US since the 1940s.

The US regulatory framework is complex and only the primary laws applicable to the investment industry are discussed above. Depending on the type of client and the nature of the investments, other laws and rules may apply, such as the Commodity Exchange Act (CEA), which must be considered when derivatives are included in the investment universe. If a fund has certain types of retirement plan investors, the Employee Retirement Income Security Act of 1974 (ERISA) is relevant. Finally, FINRA registration as a broker may be required if any person is engaged in the business of effecting transactions in securities for the account of others.

Taken together, these interlocking laws and statutes constitute the general regulatory framework that governs the US securities industry. Due to the plethora of US regulations applicable to investment advisory activities and private funds, managers should consider the advisory activities to be performed, types of investments, and fund distribution plans to determine the applicable laws.

3.2.3   Regulation of Private Funds: Registration as an Investment Adviser

The US regulatory scheme applicable to investment advisers is essentially a joint venture between the SEC and the states' securities commissions. This section outlines the choices and rules governing investment adviser registration. As each state security commission has its own rules and regulations, there may be wide variances between and among the states. Thus, care should be taken in understanding and complying with each applicable jurisdiction's regulations.

A fund manager who meets the basic investment adviser definition and is unable (or chooses not) to rely on a registration exemption must register as an investment adviser with either a state commission agency or the SEC. The determination of whether the adviser must register with the SEC or one or more states is generally determined by the adviser's assets under management (AUM).

If registration is required, the fund manager may not provide investment advisory services until the applicable SEC or state registration is obtained. Exhibit 3.1 provides guidelines to determine whether and with which government agency to register. Private fund managers with AUM between $25 million and $100 million are considered midsize advisers and are given a $10 million buffer so that they do not

EXHIBIT 3.1   Guidelines on Fund Manager Registration Requirements

Assets under Management	Registration Required?	Regulator
Under $25 million	Generally, no, unless the state securities commission requires	None, unless state securities commission requires
▪ Manages hedge funds whose AUM is between $25 million and $100 million; and ▪ Maintains a principal office and place of business in a state that requires the registration of investment advisers	Yes	State securities commission where the adviser is doing business, unless each of the states does not require registration
▪ Manages hedge funds whose AUM is between $25 million and $100 million; and ▪ Maintains a principal office and place of business in a state that does not require the registration of investment advisers	Yes State notice filing may be required	SEC
▪ Manages hedge funds whose AUM is between $25 million and $100 million; and ▪ Maintains a principal office and place of business in a state where the investment adviser would not be subject to examination by the state securities commissioner	Yes State notice filing may be required	SEC
Manages only hedge funds whose AUM is greater than $100 million and maintains managed accounts	Yes State notice filing may be required	SEC
Manages hedge funds whose AUM is greater than $150 million and does not maintain managed accounts	Yes State notice filing may be required	SEC

have to continually switch back and forth between state and SEC registration as their AUM fluctuates.

In addition to AUM triggering registration requirements, registration with the SEC as an investment adviser is also required if : (1) the fund manager manages a registered investment company or a business development company; or (2) it is a non-US-based hedge fund with more than 15 US clients and investors with assets under management of more than $25 million. On the other hand, two exemptions from registration that many fund managers may rely upon are: (1) the exemption for any adviser solely to one or more venture capital funds (venture capital fund adviser exemption); and (2) the exemption for any adviser solely to private funds with less than $150 million in assets under management (private fund adviser exemption).

Thus, **SEC registration requirements for non-US hedge funds** is triggered for funds with more than 15 US clients and investors with assets under management of more than $25 million unless exempted for an adviser solely advising private funds with less than $150 million in assets under management (i.e., the private fund adviser exemption).

Advisers relying on the above exemptions are not subject to reporting or record-keeping provisions under the Advisers Act or examination by the SEC. They are, however, required to file with the SEC a subset of the information requested by Form ADV. Registration with the state or the SEC imposes substantial disclosure and regulatory requirements on a hedge fund manager. Furthermore, if investments in derivatives are involved, registration under the CEA as a Commodity Trading Adviser (CTA) may be required.

In addition, SEC registered investment advisers will have to comply with certain state security laws, including state anti-fraud prohibitions. **Anti-fraud prohibitions** include that it is unlawful to employ any device, scheme, or artifice to obtain money or property by using material misstatements or omission, or to engage in any transaction, practice, or course of business which operates or would operate as a fraud or deceit upon the purchaser.

3.2.4 Regulation of Private Funds: Investment Adviser Obligations

Investment advisers are subject to many substantive legal obligations as fiduciaries, including an affirmative duty of care, loyalty, honesty, and good faith to act in the client's best interest. As fiduciaries, investment advisers have a fundamental obligation to: act in the best interests of their clients (including the funds they manage) and provide investment advice in their client's best interests.

Consistent with the fiduciary obligations, individuals in the securities industry must avoid insider trading. **Illegal insider trading** refers generally to buying or selling a security, in breach of a fiduciary duty or other relationship of trust and confidence, on the basis of material, nonpublic information about the security, and may also include "tipping" such information, securities trading by the person "tipped," and securities trading by those who misappropriate such information.

Additionally, fund managers required to register with the SEC are subject to many substantive requirements of the Advisers Act and other regulations. The Advisers Act imposes broad anti-fraud prohibitions that extend to dealings with fund investors and prospective investors in a fund that is advised by the adviser. Furthermore, the Advisers Act identifies investment advisers' liability. Among other matters, **twelve matters regulated under the Advisers Act** are: (1) advisory agreement terms; (2) performance fees; (3) client solicitation; (4) political contributions; (5) trading practices; (6) advertising; (7) record-keeping; (8) personal securities reporting; (9) custody; (10) proxy voting; (11) compliance program; and (12) gifts and entertainment.

Consistent with the principles-based disclosure regulatory regime, SEC registered advisers are obligated to complete and file Form ADV with the SEC. Form ADV is a uniform form used by investment advisers to register with both the SEC and the state securities authorities. In addition to filing the Form ADV with the SEC, Form ADV is used by advisers to satisfy the legal requirement to provide certain written disclosures to prospective and existing clients. Form ADV consists of three parts. Part 1 provides information about the hedge fund, its manager, and all associated persons, and is primarily designed for use by regulators for administrative purposes. Part 2 (broken into Part 2A and Part 2B) acts as a disclosure document for prospective and existing clients of the business and includes extensive information, including, but not limited to: types of advisory services offered, fees charged, conflicts of interest, and disciplinary information. An **adviser's legal obligation includes** delivering Form ADV Part 2 to its clients initially, annually, and when certain disclosure items are updated. However, where an adviser manages hedge funds or similar private fund clients, the fund itself, and not the fund investors, is considered the client and thus an adviser can meet its delivery obligation by providing the Form ADV Part 2 to the fund's general partner or managing member. However, as a best practice, many hedge funds typically deliver Form ADV Part 2 to fund investors to ensure that the investors have complete information about the adviser and its activities. Form CRS is to be provided to investors before committing to a fund investment. This form explains how the fund interacts with investors, such as fees, costs, conflicts of interest, and the firm's legal or disciplinary history.

An area requiring the increasing attention and focus of investment advisers is cybersecurity. **Cybersecurity** concerns include a broad range of risks such as threats through cyber intrusion, denial of service attacks, manipulation, misuse by insiders, and other cyber misconduct. An adviser is required to safeguard client information; thus, advisers are expected to properly consider and address cybersecurity related risks. Advisers are required to adopt comprehensive policies and procedures relating to cybersecurity risks and incidents. The SEC and state regulators have enacted rules, regulations, and provided guidance on cybersecurity as the impact of a successful cyberattack may have far reaching consequences that affect not only the adviser, but also its clients.

3.2.5 Hedge Fund Registration in the United States

Alternative investments fall under the SEC's regulatory authority. SEC regulation of alternative investment products has been premised on the assumption that these products are designed for wealthy individuals who are sophisticated investors or who, at minimum, have sufficient resources to protect themselves. When combined with the premise that government should play a limited role in overseeing private affairs—with the exception being issues of fraud or insider trading—regulation of alternative investment products within the US is based more on monitoring and controlling systemic risks to the US economy than on the protection of individual investors. A similar theme is found in hedge fund regulation as well as in private equity investment products.

To determine whether registration of an alternative investment product is required, analysis should be performed under two statutes: the Securities Act and the 1940 Act.

3.2.6 Public Securities, Private Securities, and Securities Act Registration

The Securities Act was passed to protect investors after the market crash of 1929 and the ensuing Great Depression. Through its rules and regulations, the SEC attempts to balance the protection of investors against not overly restricting access to capital. As such, the Securities Act requires securities offered for purchase and sale (e.g., interests in private funds) to be registered unless an exemption is available. The goal of requiring registration of the fund interests is to provide investors with full and fair disclosure of material information to enable investors to make their own investment decisions.

Registering securities is expensive and a slow process. Therefore, private funds typically structure their offers and sales of interests as private placements in reliance on an exemption available under the Securities Act. While an IPO sells shares of a company for the first time, **initial coin offerings (ICOs)**, which sell ownership of an asset as tracked through a coin or a digital token, may be securities offerings and thus the securities laws would apply, such as registration of the securities with the SEC (unless an exemption is available).

The designation of a category of accredited investors is "intended to encompass those persons whose financial sophistication and ability to sustain the risk of loss of investment or ability to fend for themselves render the protections of the Securities Act's registration process unnecessary." More precisely, the definition of an **accredited investor** includes a natural person who either has a net worth (along with his or her spouse) that exceeds $1 million, excluding the value of the person's primary residence; or income in excess of $200,000 (or joint income in excess of $300,000 with spouse) in each of the prior 2 years with a reasonable expectation of reaching the same income level in the current year. The definition also provides for various entities such as trusts. Unregistered interests (i.e., private placement) in a fund may be offered through general solicitations or general advertising if: (1) all purchasers are accredited investors; (2) the issuer takes reasonable steps to verify the purchasers' accredited investor status; and (3) certain other conditions set out in Rule 506(c) of the Securities Act are satisfied.

Private placements are generally made in accordance with Rule 506 of the Securities Act. This rule permits sales of fund interests to an unlimited number of accredited investors. A fund could also sell to a maximum of 35 nonaccredited investors as long as the fund is not offered through general solicitations or general advertising. The nonaccredited investors must have sufficient knowledge and experience in financial and business matters to make them capable of evaluating the merits and risks of the investment.

3.2.7 Investment Company Act Registration

In addition to finding an exemption from registration under the Securities Act, funds also rely on exemptions from the registration requirements under the 1940 Act. Although most hedge funds meet the definition of an "investment company" under the 1940 Act due to their securities investment and trading activities, most private funds commonly utilize one of the following exemptions: private investment fund exemption (Section 3(c)(1) of the 1940 Act), and qualified purchaser fund exemption (Section 3(c)(7) of the 1940 Act).

The fund must meet **two tests for the private investment fund exemption:** (1) it must have no more than 100 beneficial owners; and (2) it must not make or propose to make any public offering. The funds must only be offered to qualified purchasers to receive the qualified purchaser fund exemption. A **qualified purchaser** is either (1) a natural person with at least $5 million in investments; (2) an institutional investor with at least $25 million in investments; or (3) an entity of which each beneficial owner is a qualified purchaser.

A fund that relies on one of these two exemptions is not classified as an investment company and is not subject to virtually all of the 1940 Act provisions. Depending on whether or not the fund invests in derivatives, registration under the CEA as a Commodity Pool Operator (CPO) may be required.

3.2.8 Compliance Culture and the Role of the Chief Compliance Officer

Under the Advisers Act, regulators will evaluate an adviser's culture of compliance. A fund's culture is collective. Thus, senior corporate leadership and the Chief Compliance Officer (CCO) lead the effort to instill a culture of compliance. The **Chief Compliance Officer (CCO)** has the role of being primarily responsible for overseeing and managing regulatory compliance issues. However, it is the obligation of each team member to act with honesty and integrity. Culture is not just what is said by management or written in policies and procedures, but what actions are taken daily throughout the firm.

Under the Advisers Act, a registered adviser must: (1) designate a CCO who is responsible for administering the policies and procedures; and (2) adopt and implement written policies and procedures that are reasonably designed to prevent, detect, and correct violations of the Advisers Act. A CCO may be an employee with other duties, but it is essential that this employee be knowledgeable about the statutes and laws applicable to the adviser and the fund and have the authority to implement compliance procedures.

In addition to setting the general tone for the organization in conjunction with senior management about the importance of compliance, the CCO is responsible for administering the compliance program, including: (1) compliance (or forensic testing and reporting) which includes testing the effectiveness of the policies and procedures; and (2) reporting to senior management.

An investment adviser is prohibited from engaging in fraudulent, deceptive, or manipulative activities. Therefore, the CCO must review documents that communicate information to investors and prospects to make sure the materials conform to regulatory guidelines.

Registered investment advisers have extensive obligations with regard to record-keeping rules, and the CCO is responsible for making sure that all supervisory persons understand their obligations regarding the proper maintenance of certain books and records. The CCO is required to conduct a review of the policies and procedures to determine their effectiveness on at least an annual basis.

A **code of ethics** sets forth standards of conduct and requires compliance with federal securities laws and is required to be established in writing, maintained, and enforced in the US for any fund manager registered under the Advisers Act, and must include requiring access persons to: (1) report personal securities transactions and holdings periodically; and (2) obtain the adviser's preapproval before investing in reportable securities, including but not limited to IPOs or limited offerings (such as interests in hedge funds). **Access persons** include the adviser's directors, officers, partners, and supervised persons who have access to nonpublic information regarding securities transactions.

3.2.9 Review of Marketing Materials

With respect to marketing materials (advertisements), private fund managers are not allowed to use testimonials or endorsements from investors. Furthermore, performance must represent long periods of time and not highlight specific time frames or only successful trades (e.g., no cherry-picked stock selections).

Fostering a culture of compliance is important, as some of the most common violations that lead to SEC investigations include misrepresentation or omission of important information about securities. An **advertisement** includes any written communication addressed to more than one person, or any notice or other announcement in any publication or by radio or television, that offers any analysis, report, or publication regarding securities; any graph, chart, formula, or other device for making securities decisions; or any other investment advisory services regarding securities. Examples include marketing presentations, fact sheets, and electronic advertisements.

3.2.10 SEC Exams

Examinations of SEC registered advisers are administered by the SEC's Office of Compliance, Inspections, and Examinations (OCIE). While SEC exams may be conducted on an announced or unannounced basis, exams usually are announced. SEC exams are designed to "improve compliance, prevent fraud, monitor risk and inform regulatory policy."

There are **three types of SEC exams:** (1) regular periodic inspections; (2) cause inspections; and (3) sweep inspections. Regular periodic inspections are generally based on an adviser's promotional materials, including what is written in Form ADV, and are looking to ensure that there are no misleading or fraudulent statements. **Cause exams** are triggered by tips, complaints, and referrals. **Sweep exams** (or theme inspections) are used to review a compliance issue that the SEC considers a risk across multiple firms.

Once violations have been found, the SEC can bring charges in both administrative and civil suits; the end result can be large fines and/or loss of licenses or registrations for managers and their funds.

3.2.11 Reporting Requirements

Private fund advisers are subject to a number of regulatory reporting requirements and other compliance obligations, many of which must be completed annually. Examples of the reporting obligations include, but are not limited to, those described in Exhibit 3.2. The list in Exhibit 3.2 is not comprehensive and is only intended

EXHIBIT 3.2   Reporting Requirements for US Investment Advisers

Reporting Obligation	Summary Description
Significant Acquisition and Ownership Positions (**Section 13(d) of the Exchange Act**)	An adviser who beneficially owns, in aggregate, more than 5% of a class of publicly traded voting equity securities may be required to file disclosure reports identifying, among other things, the source and amount of funds used for the acquisition and the purpose of the acquisition.
Discretion over $100 Million in Public Equity (**Section 13(f) of the Exchange Act**)	An investment adviser managing discretionary accounts, that, in aggregate, hold publicly traded equity securities with an aggregate fair market value of $100 million or more may be required to file reports disclosing those holdings and the type of investment and voting authority exercised by the manager.
Form PF	A registered investment adviser with regulatory assets under management attributable to private funds exceeding $150 million is required to file Form PF with the SEC. The form requires information on fund size, leverage, investor types and concentration, liquidity, and fund performance. Hedge fund managers must also include information regarding their investment strategy, counterparty credit risk, and use of trading and clearing mechanisms.
Form CPO-PQR	Advisers registered with the CFTC as a commodity pool operator (CPO) or commodity trading adviser (CTA) due to their investments in derivatives may also have to file Form CPO-PQR with the CFTC.
Regulation D and Blue Sky Renewal Filings	A private fund that engages in private offerings that last more than 1 year may be subject to annual renewal filing requirements.
Pay-to-Play and Lobbyist Registration laws	A private fund adviser that solicits US state or local government entities may be subject to registration and reporting obligations under applicable state or municipal statutes.
Short Selling Reporting	Many countries, such as in the EU and Hong Kong, require reporting by investors who hold net short positions in certain financial instruments.

to give a sense of the extensive reporting obligations to which investment advisers are subject.

With respect to investor reporting, private funds are not required to furnish investors with any particular type of information aside from the disclosures necessary to prevent misleading investors. Institutional investors, however, generally demand fund transparency because they owe fiduciary duties to their own investors. The transparency allows for these institutional investors to conduct the necessary due diligence and monitoring of the fund's activities to ensure that the fund adheres to its investment strategies and risk parameters. In order to meet the demands of these investors, hedge funds typically provide the following types of information to their investors: inspection of fund books and records; quarterly or periodic letters; and annual audited financial statements.

3.3   ALTERNATIVE INVESTMENT REGULATION IN EUROPE

Each of the European countries has its own scheme for regulation and compliance. Accordingly, each has its own system of enforcement and associated penalties for noncompliance. Thus, an alternative investment manager doing business in Europe must comply with the regulatory scheme of each country it is doing business in and subject itself to the rules, regulations, social and market concerns, and judicial authority of that country.

An exception to this general rule is when a manager seeks to conduct business within the European Union (the EU) and its associated member states. The EU has designed and implemented a program whereby managers who are domiciled in one of its member states can provide services and market such services to other member states under a single regulatory scheme.

3.3.1   An Overview of the Supervisory Framework

The European System of Financial Supervisors (ESFS) is the supervisory architecture for the EU financial system. ESFS consists of three authorities: (1) a network of national competent authorities where a **competent authority** is any regulator or other authority that possesses the authorized power to regulate or otherwise exert control; (2) a joint committee of the European supervisory authorities; and (3) the following:

EUROPEAN SECURITIES AND MARKETS AUTHORITY (ESMA). **ESMA** is responsible for safeguarding the stability of the EU's financial system by enhancing investor protection and promoting orderly markets and financial stability, and has the power to write technical standards and bring about systems of mutual recognition. ESMA's role in the AIFMD is one of legislation.

EUROPEAN BANKING AUTHORITY (EBA). The **EBA** has as its main objective to safeguard the integrity, efficiency, and orderly functioning of the banking sector.

EUROPEAN INSURANCE AND OCCUPATIONAL PENSIONS AUTHORITY (EIOPA): **EIOPA** is responsible for occupational pensions and insurance.

EUROPEAN SYSTEMIC RISK BOARD (ESRB): The **ESRB** is an independent body within the EU responsible for macro-prudential oversight of the financial system within the EU.

ESMA, the EBA, and EIOPA were established to oversee the financial system at a micro-prudential level, and to achieve convergence between EU member countries on technical rules and coordination between national supervisors. The legislative process adopted by the EU for development of legislation for the financial services industry (the Lamfalussy Framework) involves the four levels detailed in Exhibit 3.3.

EXHIBIT 3.3   The Legislative Process of the EU for the Financial Industry

Level 1: Legislative Act	The framework legislation is proposed and adopted under the ordinary legislative procedure
Level 2: Implementing Measures	Implementing measures are drafted and adopted by the EU Commission, following advice from the specialist committees such as ESMA. The Commission can take the advice or implement on its own
Level 3: Supervisory Convergence	Consideration and guidance by the European Supervisory Authorities to ensure consistent application across the EU
Level 4: Supervision and Enforcement	Principally by the regulators in each member state

3.3.2   The European Regulatory Framework

The European regulatory framework is complex for many reasons including that not all European nations are members of the EU and not all EU members have the same status within the EU. Furthermore, certain countries, such as Switzerland, are not a member of the EU and thus have their own regulations applicable to alternative asset managers and their products. European regulation of alternative investments can be especially complex, and this section therefore reviews only the key regulations applicable to alternative asset managers in the EU. **National private placement rules** impose rules for selling non-EU funds in the EU at an EU level, but also each EU member country may impose their own requirements on any sale of fund interests within their own border.

Undertakings for Collective Investments in Transferable Securities (UCITS), is the main European framework covering collective investment schemes. UCITS funds must be open-ended and liquid and typically invest in securities listed on public stock exchanges and regulated markets.

The **Alternative Investment Fund Managers Directive (AIFMD)** regulates alternative investment managers—meaning any whose regular business is managing one or more alternative investment funds (AIFs). The AIFMD does not regulate AIFs directly. The AIFMD applies to non-UCITS investments such as private equity, venture capital, hedge funds, and real estate funds. **Collective investment schemes (CIS)** are either a UCITS or an AIF. Exhibit 3.4 provides an overview of the different laws that apply to UCITS and AIFs.

The AIFMD plays an important role in helping to create a market in the EU for AIFs and a harmonized regulatory and supervisory framework for AIFMs. **AIFMD key features** include, among others: (1) AIFMs managing AIFs must be authorized, unless an exemption is available; (2) restrictions are placed on the levels of remuneration for senior management and risk-takers; (3) AIFMs are required to set a maximum level of leverage for each AIF; and (4) AIFMs are required to manage and monitor liquidity risks and conduct regular stress tests.

Compliance with the AIFMD is intended to provide investors comfort as to the market integrity of financial products purchased from such firms, and to provide investment managers with common regulations across EU member countries, as well as a "passport" to market and deliver their services across EU borders (detailed in

EXHIBIT 3.4   Overview of Principal Differences Between UCITS and AIFs

UCITS	AIFs
Generally for retail investors with small investment amounts	For investors with higher investments
Investments are restricted to "safe" and liquid assets	Fewer investment restrictions. All investment types are possible including private equity and real estate
Limits leverage	Allows AIFM to set reasonable leverage limit

a subsequent section). In so doing, the model implicit in the AIFMD significantly reduces the administrative and operating costs of investment managers conducting business in multiple EU jurisdictions. Within this model, the member state where the manager is domiciled has initial authority over registration, compliance, and enforcement matters.

3.3.3   Registration and Exemptions in European Regulation

As noted above, AIFMs managing AIFs must be authorized by the competent authority of its home member state. The **home member state** is the EU country where the AIFM is authorized. Once an authority is delegated to perform a certain act, only the competent authority is entitled to take accounts therefrom and no one else. The AIFMD has a wide scope with few exceptions. The AIFMD applies to: (1) AIFMs that manage or market AIFs (wherever those funds are established) in the EU; (2) AIFMs established outside the EU that manage AIFs established in the EU; and (3) non-EU AIFMs that market one or more AIFs (wherever established) within the EU.

The AIFMD does include a number of exemptions for managers and funds which would otherwise fall within the broad definitions contained in the AIFMD:

EXEMPT ENTITIES: Holding companies, family offices (provided they do not raise external capital), entities which manage pension schemes, employee savings schemes, employee participation schemes, securitization special purpose entities, national central banks, national, regional, and local governments and bodies, other institutions which manage social security and pension funds, and supranational institutions and similar international organizations that manage AIFs where those AIFs act in the public interest.

PARENT/SUBSIDIARY RELATIONSHIP: An AIFM is exempt from AIFMD to the extent it manages one or more AIFs whose only investors are the AIFM or the parent or the subsidiaries of the AIFM or other subsidiaries of the parent, provided that none of those investors is itself an AIF.

MINIMUM AUM THRESHOLDS: AIFMs whose AUM are below certain thresholds do not have to obtain full AIFMD authorization. The minimum thresholds are: (1) less than €100 million; or (2) less than €500 million unleveraged and which do not grant investors redemption rights for 5 years.

The smaller AIFMs relying on the minimum AUM threshold exception above are not completely exempt from AIFMD. They are required to register with their local authority among other obligations. The disadvantage to funds not having a full AIFMD registration is that they will not be entitled to the marketing passport (discussed below) and are thus subject to direct oversight by each member state where they are doing business.

AIFMD REQUIREMENTS: In order to obtain and maintain authorization from the competent authority, an EU AIFM must, among other requirements: (1) satisfy specific initial and ongoing capital requirements; (2) put in place remuneration policies applicable to senior managers and staff whose professional activities have a material impact on the risk profile of the AIFM or any AIF that it manages; (3) separate risk management functions from other operating units, including the portfolio management functions; (4) disclose certain information to investors in an AIF that is marketed into the EU, both initial and ongoing disclosure; (5) comply with regulatory reporting requirements of the competent authority of the home member country; and (6) make available an annual report for the AIF.

3.3.4 Disclosures and Marketing

The disclosure requirements for marketing are quite extensive and are in many ways similar to those of the US Securities and Exchange Commission. Generally, the disclosure is made in the fund's offering memorandum. The required disclosure includes, among other things: description of investment strategy and objective; valuation methodology; liquidity; fees; preferential treatment received by an investor; and the identity of fund service providers.

Marketing a fund with the EU triggers AIFMD compliance obligations for an AIFM (whether EU or non-EU). There are two methods that allow marketing of AIFMs in the EU. **Marketing of AIFs by AIFMs** is allowed by: (1) using a marketing passport available under the AIFMD that provides that once a fund is approved in one EU member country, the AIF can be marketed to professional investors located in other EU countries; and (2) marketing in a specific EU member country in accordance with that country's private placement regime, subject to certain conditions being met.

Provisions in AIFMD allow AIFMs to use a marketing passport. A **marketing passport** permits marketing across the EU as a single marketplace for the marketing of AIFs to professional investors. Upcoming legislation will permit pre-marketing in EU member states.

3.3.5 Formal Risk Management

The AIFMD includes stringent risk management requirements that are intended to ensure that AIFs are appropriately managed in order to protect investors. The risk management function must operate based on formal written procedures, with the risk management procedures (RMP) as the core document detailing the structure and operations.

The risk management activity must be functionally and hierarchically segregated from the portfolio management function and must operate independently and with sufficient expertise, authority, and resources to ensure all risk in the AIFM and AIFs are appropriately measured, monitored, and managed on an ongoing basis.

The rules regarding risk management include assessment of risks based on the amount of leverage used. Rather than provide specific guidelines for the amount of leverage to be used, the AIFMD requires "reasonable" limits. Risk monitoring is expected to be ongoing and includes periodic stress tests, back tests, and random scenario analysis for potential variances in market conditions for each AIF and AIFM. Furthermore, the risk policy must take into account the measurements and analysis of risk relative to market risk, liquidity, counterparty risk, and other risks, including operational risk. Operational risk includes such items as network security, monitoring of depositaries, prime brokers, and other risks that are not directly financial, including cybersecurity.

3.3.6 Required Reporting in European Regulation

AIFMs must comply with a comprehensive set of reporting requirements under the AIFMD. Reporting under the AIFMD consists of annual reports to investors and regulators, periodic reports based on the size of the AIF/AIFM, and reports that must be filed when there is a material change within the AIF. Examples of the reporting obligations include, but are not limited to those summarized in Exhibit 3.5.

Private equity funds or any fund that invests directly in private companies are also required to report certain actions regarding their ownership, including reporting whenever one or more of their AIFs acquire more than 50%, or control, of a nonlisted company. In addition to reporting controlling ownership, the manager must also report how the acquisition was made, if leverage was used, where the leverage came from, the intentions for the future of the company, effects on employment, and employment conditions.

AIFs that acquire nonlisted companies are subject to asset stripping rules. **Asset stripping rules** prevent an AIF from making a controlling private equity investment,

EXHIBIT 3.5 Key Reporting Obligations of AIFMs

Reporting Obligation	Summary Description
Annual Report	Must include a balance sheet and an income statement, as well as any material changes for the past year and details regarding remuneration
Reporting to Regulator	Periodic reporting includes, but is not limited to, information pertaining to:
	▪ principal markets and instruments in which the AIFM trades on behalf of the AIFs it manages
	▪ main instruments traded
	▪ principal exposures and most important concentrations of each AIF managed
	▪ current risk profile of the AIF and risk management systems employed by the AIFM to manage market risk, liquidity risk, counterparty risk, operational and other risks
	▪ stress test results

having the nonlisted company take a loan, and then distributing the loan proceeds to themselves, and thereby creating leverage that may or may not create unnecessary risk. Asset stripping rules apply for a period of 2 years after acquiring control of a nonlisted company, during which time the AIF and/or AIFM is not permitted to influence or set distributions, make reductions in capital, or share redemptions.

3.3.7 Legal Structures

An AIF can be domiciled anywhere and take many different forms. However, Luxembourg and Ireland are well developed alternative fund jurisdictions and, as such, many asset managers set up new AIF products in these countries to avail themselves of the passport. There are a number of legal structures available in the EU, including but not limited to those summarized in Exhibit 3.6. Note that not all of the legal structures in the table are available in every EU country.

3.3.8 Enforcement of European Regulation

The enforcement of EU rules is left to the member states; however, should member states not enforce the AIFMD, ESMA may bring them before the EU to enforce the EU's intent of equalizing the playing field regarding alternative investment regulations. All member states have a national regulator who sits on ESMA's board. To the extent that two member states disagree on violations or enforcement procedures, the model provides for ESMA to mediate and, if necessary, take steps to bring action before the European Parliament for resolution.

Recall that the EU home member state is the EU country where the AIFM is authorized. On the other hand, **host state** refers to the EU country (other than the home country) where the AIF is being marketed. Host competent authorities can inspect AIFs without notice. The competent authorities can also issue cease and desist orders, freeze assets of an AIF or AIFM, request the prohibition of professional activity, suspend issues of units or shares, withdraw the authorization of an AIFM, and refer matters for criminal prosecution. In this instance, a competent authority refers to a regulator with oversight of the AIF in the particular EU country. However, if an AIF violates regulations or commits a crime, such as fraud, in a host state where it markets or manages a fund, the AIFMD does provide the structure for investigation and sanction.

In cases in which the host state and home state disagree on issues, either party can bring the issue to the ESMA. The ESMA will facilitate negotiations between the parties and does have the power to impose binding mediation. When a host state believes a violation has occurred and the violation is not within the host state's jurisdiction, the host state may refer this information to the authorities in the home state of the AIFM.

An important exception to the enforcement powers of the ESMA is the sovereignty exception. The **AIFMD sovereignty exception** provides that member states may refuse to cooperate if "cooperating adversely affects the sovereignty, security, or public order of the member state addressed."

EXHIBIT 3.6 Legal Structures Available in the EU

Type	Description
Investment Company/Variable Capital Company	Shareholders enjoy limited liability. The main aim of funds set up as investment companies is the collective investment of its funds and property with the aim of spreading investment risk. Used by both UCITS and AIFs
Irish Collective Asset-Management Vehicle (ICAV)	Designed specifically for Irish investment funds. The purpose of the vehicle is to minimize the administrative complexity and cost of establishing and maintaining collective investment schemes in Ireland. Can be used by both UCITS and AIFs
Unit Trust	Unit Trust is a contractual fund structure constituted by a trust deed between a trustee and a management company (manager). A Unit Trust is not a separate legal entity and, therefore, the trustee acts as legal owner of the fund's assets on behalf of the investors. A separate management company is always required and managerial responsibility rests with the board of directors of the management company
Common Contractual Fund (CCF)	A contractual arrangement established under a deed, which provides that investors participate as co-owners of the assets of the fund. The CCF is an unincorporated body, not a separate legal entity, and is transparent for Irish legal and tax purposes. As a result, investors are treated as if they directly own a proportionate share of the underlying investments rather than shares or units in an entity which itself owns the underlying investments. Can be established as a UCITS or an AIF
Reserved Alternative Investment Fund (RAIF)	Luxembourg vehicle used by many AIFs. RAIF combines the characteristics and structuring flexibilities of Luxembourg-regulated SIFs and SICARs qualifying as AIFs managed by an authorized AIFM. RAIFs are not subject to approval by the Luxembourg regulator, CSSF, before they are launched. SICARS are investment companies in risk capital (Société d'Investissement en Capital à Risqué)
Société d'Investissement à Capital Variable (SICAV)	Formed in Luxembourg as a public limited company (e.g., PLC or SA) with variable share capital
Specialised Investment Funds (SIF)	Formed in Luxembourg and limited to "qualified investors"

3.3.9 Non-EU Managers in Europe

The primary consideration for non-EU fund managers is marketing, since AIFMD requirements apply where an AIF is being marketed. Fund managers who actively market their funds must find out what the requirements are in each EU member country in which it plans to market or manage funds.

3.4 HEDGE FUND REGULATION IN ASIA

Each country in Asia has its own regulatory scheme for alternative investment funds. As such, regulations and licensing requirements vary widely resulting in a challenging process for fund managers to access Asian markets. For example, Hong Kong and Singapore generally require hedge funds to register with the appropriate government regulatory body. By contrast, Shanghai is largely off-limits to investors outside mainland China.

Cross-border offerings across Asian countries are being facilitated by the ASEAN CIS Framework and the Asia Region Funds Passport (ARFP). As both of these efforts continue to expand and obtain the necessary local regulatory approvals, the cross-border offerings of collective investment vehicles should become challenging.

This section discusses four key Asian countries with a focus on authorization requirements and marketing.

3.4.1 Hong Kong

Many factors induce fund managers to set up in Hong Kong, such as:

1. developed and sophisticated securities and banking infrastructure;
2. serves as the Asian hub for many of the world's leading prime brokers, custodians, and administrators; and
3. leading financial market for the greater China region.

The **Securities and Futures Ordinance (SFO)** is the primary legislation for the regulation of asset management activity in Hong Kong. The **Securities and Futures Commission (SFC)** is the regulator responsible for overseeing the SFO in Hong Kong.

Authorizations Required: Under the SFO, a fund manager may operate in Hong Kong once it registers with the SFC, provided the manager meets other licensing requirements. Additionally, the public offer and sale of interests in a fund to Hong Kong investors would generally require the fund to be authorized by the SFC. To avoid the cost of the registration process, alternative fund managers generally offer their funds on a private placement basis as there no requirement to obtain authorization from the SFC. However, use of the private placement alternative is limited to only certain types of funds and can only be offered by certain persons.

Generally, funds offered on a private placement basis or unsolicited basis do not need to be authorized by the SFC in the case in which all four of the following conditions are met:

1. offers are made to no more than 50 persons;
2. offers where the minimum subscription amount is HKD 500,000;
3. offers where the maximum offering of shares is valued at HKD 5 million; and
4. an offer made to a professional investor.

"Professional investor" under HK regulation includes most financial institutions and intermediaries, but not individual investors or a holding company owned by an individual.

MARKETING: The sale of shares of a fund on an unsolicited basis (or solicited outside of Hong Kong) to a resident of Hong Kong on a private placement basis does not trigger licensing or fund registration under Hong Kong law. To avoid running afoul of the SFO rules, fund managers should ensure that the offer and marketing of the fund is not regarded as being made to the public, as funds offered to the public are required to be authorized by the SFC.

3.4.2 Singapore

Many factors induce fund managers to set up in Singapore, such as licensing requirements that are not very stringent; a large number of high net worth individuals; a highly skilled workforce; a stable political environment; and world-class infrastructure. The primary investors in offshore funds include institutional, professional, and wealthy individuals.

The **Securities and Futures Act (SFA)** is the primary legislation for the regulation of asset management activity in Singapore. The **Monetary Authority of Singapore (MAS)** is the regulator responsible for administering the SFA. The MAS regulates all financial institutions in Singapore including fund managers. A **collective investment scheme (CIS)** is the statutory term used in Singapore to describe an investment fund.

AUTHORIZATIONS REQUIRED: Hedge fund managers in Singapore are subject to licensing requirements. The regulatory framework is set out in the SFA. Any person that carries on business in fund management in Singapore is required to hold a capital markets services (CMS) license or be registered with the MAS as a registered fund management company (RFMC).

Hedge fund managers frequently utilize an exemption from the CMS licensing requirement. Generally, a fund manager would not be required to obtain a CMS license if:

1. it carries on fund management in Singapore on behalf of not more than 30 qualified investors, (of which not more than 15 may be funds or limited partnerships);
2. the total value of the assets managed does not exceed a specific amount set out in the regulations (e.g., S$250 million); and
3. it is registered with the MAS as a RFMC.

Venture capital managers can utilize the venture capital fund manager (VCFM) regime. Under the VCFM regime, venture capital managers are still required to hold a CMS license. However, the application process is shortened and simplified, and regulatory requirements such as business conduct, base capital, risk-based capital, and competence of key individuals' requirements are removed.

Generally, offers of interests in a fund to residents of Singapore may be made only: (1) if the fund has been authorized or recognized by the MAS; and (2) the offer is accompanied by a prospectus prepared in accordance with the SFA that have been registered with the MAS. Authorization is the process by which MAS registers a fund that is established locally while recognition is the process under which MAS registers a fund that is established oversees. Offers of interests in an investment fund cannot be made unless:

1. the fund is authorized or recognized under the rules of the SFA; and
2. offers of interests are accompanied by a prospectus prepared in accordance with the requirements prescribed in the MAS.

However, there are several exemptions that fund managers may take advantage of pursuant to which the authorization process and prospectus requirement can be avoided if certain criteria are satisfied.

> MARKETING: The offering/marketing of interests of a fund in Singapore is considered a regulated activity and viewed separately from the authorization/recognition and prospectus requirements for the fund itself. To offer interests of a foreign CIS in Singapore, a license is required or the offer would need to be made through a local licensed intermediary (i.e., placement agent).

3.4.3 South Korea

The **Financial Investment Services and Capital Markets Act (FSCMA)** and its regulations are the primary legislation for the regulation of asset management activity in South Korea. The **Financial Services Commission (FSC)** is the primary regulator in South Korea and directs the **Financial Supervisory Service (FSS)**. The **FSS** is responsible for inspection of financial institutions as well as enforcement of relevant regulations as directed by the FSC.

> AUTHORIZATIONS REQUIRED: Pursuant to FSCMA, all offshore funds that are offered or sold to Korean investors are required to be registered with the FSC. The funds offered to only "qualified professional investors" are subject to lower eligibility requirements than funds sold publicly. "Qualified professional investors" include the Korean government, the Bank of Korea, certain financial institutions, certain pension funds, certain corporate investors such as listed companies, and certain high net worth individuals.

> MARKETING: Under the FSCMA, marketing activities, even when directed towards qualified professional investors only, are required to be carried out through a local Korean distributor, which includes Korean securities companies, banks, and insurance companies that are licensed to distribute funds. A sale on an unsolicited basis should not trigger fund registration.

3.4.4 Japan

The **Financial Instruments and Exchange Act (FIEA)** and **The Act on Investment Trust and Investment Corporation (ITIC)** are the primary legislation for the regulation of asset management activity in Japan. **The Kanto Local Finance Bureau of Ministry of Finance Japan (KLFB)** is the regulator for the purposes of disclosure in Japan under the FIEA.

AUTHORIZATIONS REQUIRED: Registration as an investment manager is required for any entity that engages in the discretionary investment management of assets of a Japanese client, including certain types of collective investment schemes, as well as providing continuing reports to the regulator on the actual business condition of the fund. Offshore fund general partners that have representatives in Japan may be able to utilize a registration exemption under Article 63 of FIEA. However, this exemption is limited, and fund operators taking advantage of the exemption still have to comply with a heavy regulatory burden.

MARKETING: The marketing of fund interests in Japan is heavily regulated. Generally, any entity wanting to market funds to investors in Japan is required to be registered with Financial Services Agency of Japan. Registration is not required for offshore funds not directly marketed to Japanese investor. Additionally, Japanese regulators may, from time to time, ban the acquisition of certain types of investments.

CHAPTER 4

ESG and Alternative Investments

ESG stands for environmental, social, and governance, and refers to the use of these three issues as key factors when making decisions including investment and business decisions. It is a generic term used in capital markets and commonly used by investors to evaluate the behavior and intention of companies, as well as estimating their future financial performance, alongside environmental and social performance.

This chapter provides an advocational perspective of ESG-related issues through its description of a broad and deep ESG role in investment practices. It is important for investment professionals to understand the potentially increasing role of these perspectives in society, as ESG issues can affect both the risk and return of investments.

4.1 BACKGROUND ON ESG AND ALTERNATIVE INVESTING

In a growing alternative investment industry, incorporating ESG factors into investment decisions has become increasingly important. This trend is expected to continue and is primarily being driven by the interests of institutional investors like pension funds, sovereign wealth funds, and endowments. As these developments unfold, all stakeholders face challenges as they endeavor to objectively measure ESG factors and understand their impact on risk and return.

4.1.1 Growth in Alternatives Assets

From 2016 to 2018, ESG assets under management (AUM) in alternative investments vehicles almost tripled, increasing from $206 billion to $588 billion.[1] Recent estimates are that alternatives AUM will increase by nearly 60% from 2017 to 2023.[2] Private equity and hedge funds account for over two-thirds of that 2023 asset base, but double-digit growth is forecast for every alternative asset class.[3]

4.1.2 ESG and Institutional Investors

In a recent survey of global institutional investors, 76% said they incorporate ESG criteria into their investment decisions.[4] Of those that did, 57% believed it increased risk-adjusted returns and 70% said reputational risk management was a consideration.[5] Over two-thirds (69%) said their stakeholders were concerned about ESG issues,[6] and both investors and fund managers believe ESG will increase in importance over the next 5 years.[7]

Let's examine these goals for incorporating ESG issues into institutional portfolios.

INCREASING RISK-ADJUSTED RETURNS: Evidence shows that publicly listed companies with better ESG scores have lower idiosyncratic risk.[8] In many ways, ESG is a risk management exercise, where companies seek to reduce the risk of their operations damaging the environment or controlling the potential negative outcomes from failures in corporate governance. Evidence regarding the ability of companies with strong ESG ratings to earn higher total returns is mixed.

REDUCING REPUTATIONAL RISK: Companies that focus on good management of ESG issues are likely to reduce the volatility of their stock price as well as the risk of being involved in scandals. Investors who wish to not be linked to scandals at companies held in their portfolio can benefit from this reduced risk.

ADDRESSING STAKEHOLDER CONCERNS: In many cases, endowments and foundations have the ultimate investment flexibility as they are generally untaxed and much less regulated than pension funds. However, university endowments are increasingly being urged by their students to divest investments from companies with exposure to potentially negative ESG issues. Most recently, these conversations surrounded climate change issues at companies that extract and distribute fossil fuels.

DOING THE RIGHT THING OR IMPROVING THE PLANET: Many endowments and foundations are founded or funded to explicitly benefit a specific cause, often education, healthcare, or religion. Many of these endowments were the first to divest, or never invest in, certain companies due to their strong convictions, such as a hospital system choosing not to invest in the tobacco or cannabis industries.

At the same time, a large majority (65%) of institutional investors said that most of the investment managers they considered did not incorporate ESG into their investment decision process.[9] This mismatch between demand for ESG-driven investment decisions and the number of managers currently incorporating ESG factors suggests an opportunity for asset managers.

Which ESG factors carry the most weight for a specific investor can vary based on asset class and geography. A US-based real estate development fund might be most concerned about the environment, focusing on energy efficiency, carbon footprint, and greenhouse gas emissions. By contrast, an infrastructure investor in an emerging market would put more emphasis on governance and social issues, paying particular attention to bribery concerns and workers' rights. Each institutional investor and asset manager needs to determine where to direct their ESG efforts based on their own and their stakeholders' objectives.

4.1.3 ESG Challenges

As the alternatives industry grows and ESG considerations become more important to both institutional investors and asset managers, there are challenges that need to be recognized and eventually overcome: ESG adoption, lack of standards, and cost.

ESG ADOPTION: The previously discussed data portray an investment landscape where asset managers are not yet fulfilling institutional investor demand for ESG investing strategies. In an industry where returns have long been the main measure of success, this hesitancy to change is not surprising. However, as more data emerge that effective ESG policies can produce better risk-adjusted returns and reduce reputational risk, undecided asset managers will come to realize that not having an ESG strategy puts them at a competitive disadvantage.

LACK OF STANDARDS: There is a dearth of clear guidance when it comes to establishing and implementing ESG policy. Almost two-thirds of institutional investors said that "clarity on techniques and strategies for ESG incorporation" would support further integration of ESG.[10] Even investors already employing ESG factors report a lack of consistent benchmarks which can lead to confusing and contradictory results.[11] Efforts to address this problem are ongoing and there has been significant consolidation in the ESG ratings industry.[12] However, emerging tools like the Sustainable Accounting Standards Board (SASB), and widely used ESG ratings from MSCI, Sustainalytics, Bloomberg, RepRisk, and Thomson Reuters are still in their infancy and largely geared to investments in large public companies which are already subject to considerable disclosure requirements. Unfortunately, much of the currently available data is not relevant to alternative assets like private equity and real estate.[13]

COST: The lack of consistent and easily accessible assessment data and industry-standard tools means that alternative asset managers need to develop their own ESG data sources and then collect and analyze that information. This requires establishing internal capabilities and operations to ensure consistent application of ESG principles in investment decision-making. All of this requires expertise and knowledge that most alternative asset managers do not currently possess. This is not an insurmountable hurdle, but will require a significant investment of both time and money in order to be done successfully.

4.2 ESG AND REAL ASSETS: NATURAL RESOURCES

Natural resource investments demand a high level of management oversight and skill. Whether done by direct ownership or through indirect investment vehicles, the environmental, social, and governance issues are similar.

4.2.1 Natural Resources and Environmental Issues

This section discusses eight environmental issues with respect to investment in natural resources.

CONSERVE WATER: Natural resource investments such as farming and mining can use large quantities of water and, in some cases, significantly degrade the quality of that water. Investors look for projects that use efficient means of water delivery and use while ensuring that polluted or hazardous effluent is either remediated, stored safely, or removed from the site.

ENCOURAGE BIODIVERSITY: Diversity of flora and fauna are important factors in environmental sustainability. The development and operation of natural resource investments includes adopting techniques that minimize the negative impact on biodiversity.

REDUCE SOIL EROSION: Farming, timbering, and mining can cause considerable disruption to and degradation of soil conditions. Investors should ensure that projects employ well-designed access roads, drainage infrastructure, and erosion control techniques to maintain both the quantity and quality of soil on the site.

MINIMIZE GREENHOUSE GAS EMISSIONS: The flaring or burning off of natural gas at oil wells and leakage of methane produce large quantities of greenhouse gases (GHGs). Both of these can be reduced significantly with current technology and careful oversight. In farm and forestry operations, efficient use of fossil fuel equipment can minimize GHG emissions.

PROTECT ENDANGERED SPECIES: Natural resource development can negatively impact threatened or endangered species. Studies are undertaken prior to any disruption and monitoring and mitigation plans put in place to ensure that any detrimental impact is minimized.

SAFE CHEMICAL USAGE: Avoid agrochemicals banned by international standards and pesticides that persist in the food chain. Ensure that in all projects, compliance with regulations and industry best practices around chemical storage, handling, and usage are documented thoroughly.

MAINTAIN PROPER PERMITS AND LICENSING: Where relevant ensure that, with respect to all natural resource assets, necessary environmental permits and licenses are obtained and maintained.

DECOMMISSIONING: All natural resource investments with a finite life should have a plan in place for site closure that returns the site as close to its original environmental state as possible and ensures a safe and sustainable future.

4.2.2   Natural Resources and Social Issues

COMPLIANCE WITH HEALTH AND SAFETY STANDARDS: Investors verify that all natural resource investments comply with regulations meant to protect workers, customers, and the surrounding community.

MEET ALL LABOR LAWS AND REGULATIONS: For example, all employees, whether direct or subcontracted, are paid on a timely basis according to prevailing minimum wage and overtime laws and that required breaks are granted on schedule.

PROVIDE SAFETY TRAINING/CERTIFICATIONS: All employees that operate machinery, handle chemicals, or are in other dangerous positions are given both initial and ongoing training to ensure they are properly prepared for their roles. Monitoring procedures are in place to ensure compliance with training and either retraining or reassignment for employees that do not observe best practices.

RESPECT WORKER'S RIGHTS: The rights of free association and collective bargaining must be allowed where provided by law or international standards. Zero tolerance should be applied for child labor, human trafficking, discrimination, and harassment. All employees should feel free to submit complaints without fear of reprisal or loss of their job.

RESPECT INDIGENOUS PEOPLE'S RIGHTS: Many natural resource assets are proximate to indigenous populations and cultural sites. All investments should implement procedures to identify, recognize, and accommodate these considerations for the life of the project.

ENGAGE RESPECTFULLY WITH THE COMMUNITY: In addition to providing quality employment opportunities, managers of natural resource assets understand the culture and practice of the surrounding community. Investors seek projects that actively engage local community members in initiatives that promote their education, health, and well-being. Mechanisms are in place to facilitate communication, resolve grievances, and provide fair compensation in the case of unavoidable loss or damage affecting the community.

4.2.3 Natural Resources and Governance Issues

Managers of natural resource assets should monitor and ensure compliance with all laws and regulations. This includes subcontractors and any other entities that work at the site.

COOPERATE WITH REGULATORS AND NGOs: Management assists outside organizations, e.g., the World Wildlife Fund, Rainforest Alliance, etc., via research and inspections.

ACHIEVE INDUSTRY BEST PRACTICES AND/OR SUSTAINABILITY CERTIFICATIONS: Investors prefer natural resources with certifications that support sustainable business practices. Examples include FSC certified timber harvesting or USDA certified organic farming.

MAINTAIN APPROPRIATE ANTI-CORRUPTION PROCEDURES: All natural resource investments comply with anti-money laundering laws and are party to the Foreign Corrupt Practices Act or other relevant anti-bribery laws. All employees receive training around identifying and reporting corrupt practices.

MAINTAIN TRANSPARENCY ON ASSET HOLDINGS AND ESG CRITERIA: Investors receive regular and audited reports on asset holdings, their ESG risks, and compliance/mitigation strategies.

4.3 ESG AND REAL ASSETS: COMMODITIES

Commodities are real assets that are further defined as being homogeneous goods that are widely available and readily tradeable. Their production can have a substantial impact on people and the environment.

4.3.1 Commodity Derivatives and Speculation

Exposure to returns of commodities can be accessed in two ways: via derivative contracts (e.g., futures) or by direct investment in the physical commodity. Futures contracts are used by both commercial investors (producers and users of the under-lying commodity) and noncommercial investors (hedge funds, mutual funds, and retail investors). For most agricultural commodities, the percentage of contracts held by commercial and noncommercial investors are approximately equal. For other commodities, e.g., oil and gold, noncommercial investors hold 70–90% of the out-standing contracts.

4.3.2   Commodity Speculation and Volatility

The presence of noncommercial speculative investors can lead to increased price volatility. This has implications across all commodities, but can be especially prob-lematic for food-related products. The world's poorest economies rely heavily on agriculture and volatile food prices can make it costly for them to import food and reduce the ability of local farmers to make a steady living.

Because of these factors, ESG investors in commodity futures should consider the following: (1) never take delivery of the physical commodity as it may disrupt supply/demand dynamics and distort prices; (2) only trade the most liquid contracts where the potential for increasing price volatility is low; (3) demand that hedge funds disclose their strategies and holdings of commodity futures; (4) avoid funds whose trading is likely to contribute to price volatility; and (5) limit investment in agri-cultural contracts—especially smaller and less liquid markets—due to the potential impact of price volatility on poorer countries/populations. Following these guide-lines, however, may reduce pricing efficiency in the commodity markets and reduce profits from ESG-oriented investors in commodity markets.

4.3.3   Physical Commodities and ESG

Direct investment in physical commodities brings additional ESG factors into play.

SOURCING: Long positions in a physical commodity may expose the investor to ESG issues regarding how the commodity is produced and delivered. The diamond and gold industries are notorious for examples of working con-ditions rife with human rights violations. These industries are comprised of global firms with multiple distribution channels. The commodities are high-value, fungible, and in some cases indistinguishable, which can make tracing their origin and provenance impossible. This makes consistent appli-cation of ESG criteria difficult.

HOARDING: From an ESG perspective, there may be issues with investing in pro-ductive commodities that have a limited supply solely for financial gain. Buying a physical commodity impacts demand and will therefore have a more direct effect on price (and possibly volatility). In extreme cases, it could produce shortages that have negative effects on countries, industries, com-panies, and workers.

MONEY LAUNDERING: Diamonds, precious metals, and oil can be bought and sold outside of the regulated banking industry. A significant proportion of the global production of these commodities comes from developing countries with higher levels of corruption. This makes them attractive for money laun-dering and creates an additional ESG challenge for investors.

All of these factors may make direct investment in most physical commodities unattractive to committed ESG investors. A strategy might be direct investment in the natural resources at their origin (i.e., a mine or well) where management oversight and control can ensure that sustainable business practices are implemented. Alternatively, investing in mining companies or commodity producers and actively engaging with management about their ESG practices may yield better results than directly purchasing the physical commodities.

4.4 ESG AND REAL ASSETS: REAL ESTATE

Real estate development takes place at the intersection of many important ESG issues, including inequality, food, water, energy, and climate change. Buildings and construction activity account for 36% of global final energy use and are responsible for 39% of global CO_2 emissions.[14] Because of this, the ESG emphasis in real estate is on environmental factors, but there are also important social and governance factors. The ESG discussion below follows the life cycle of real estate from land acquisition to development, to use, and finally, to recovery.[15]

4.4.1 Real Estate Development and ESG

The initial acquisition and development of real estate is where many important decisions are made that will impact the life of the investment. Poor planning at this stage may be costly and difficulty to correct later. Because of this, the integration of ESG considerations at this first stage is especially important.

LAND ACQUISITION AND GOVERNANCE: Land is by its nature part of the local community and any development should recognize and respect ESG issues. Prior to finalizing an acquisition of real estate, a developer should prepare a complete ESG impact assessment of the project including: (1) assessment and consultation with all stakeholders at critical stages of project approval; (2) recognition and respect of the rights of indigenous peoples; and (3) a fair and equitable process for resolving disputes involving workers and the community.

Acquisition of land should include market value compensation. Involuntary resettlement of people should be avoided whenever possible and, where unavoidable, those displaced should be included in the planning and implementation of their relocation. The goal of relocation should be the restoration of prior standards of living and economic standing. Investors should ensure all government and legal requirements are followed in the acquisition process in order to guarantee clear and secure title and avoid future disputes.

TRANSPARENCY: Bribery, corruption, bid-rigging, etc. may create value for investors in the short term, but can create long-term problems. Such practices can result in the use of substandard construction materials and techniques, leading to property damage and loss of life and significantly increase project costs. Policies should be put in place to ensure all contracts, payments, and documents are available and transparent and that all transactions are done at "arm's length." These policies can include using sealed bids and anonymous applications. All interactions with governing or regulatory agencies should be conducted in public or available to anyone. Employees and workers should be encouraged to report issues without fear of recrimination.

WORKERS' RIGHTS: Construction is too often characterized by large numbers of low-skilled workers performing dangerous work, often for long hours and low pay. Because of this, large development projects have an important role in the promotion of workers' rights. These include freedom of association, collective bargaining, and protection from discrimination, harassment, and forced or child labor. Companies should establish a safe and healthy work environment and ensure workers are properly trained and have necessary safety equipment. All subcontractors and suppliers should be audited to ensure compliance with labor laws. Where possible, local small businesses and underrepresented populations should be employed.

ENVIRONMENTAL STEWARDSHIP: Real estate development consumes significant resources and can impact ecosystems and biodiversity, both directly and indirectly. Investors should seek companies that incorporate the following best practices into their developments: (1) project design should include buildings and infrastructure that make efficient use of the land area; (2) walkability, proximity to public transportation, and green spaces can all enhance the environmental sustainability of a development; (3) environmental impact assessment including energy consumption and GHG emissions, impact on biodiversity, water management, and climate change mitigation; (4) selection of sustainably sourced building materials; (5) adopting site development and construction techniques that minimize soil erosion and materials waste; and (6) encouraging recycling of materials when possible.

QUALITY OF DESIGN, PLANNING, AND CONSTRUCTION: Building safety is the primary concern and involves design, materials selection, and construction techniques. To ensure that buildings provide occupants with a safe, productive, and sustainable environment, companies should: (1) design and construct buildings to accommodate the impact of reasonably predictable future weather, seismic, and climate change events; (2) adhere to international building codes and construction standards (e.g., ISO 9001 and 14001); (3) conduct a sustainability analysis of the planned building to assess the optimal design solution when balancing economic, social, and environmental costs and benefits; (4) plan for alternative future uses of the building by incorporating adaptable design principles and material choices; and (5) enhance the productivity and health of building occupants by ensuring adequate levels of natural light, indoor air quality, and common spaces.

4.4.2   Real Estate Use and ESG

The use phase in real estate commences when buildings are occupied and lasts for the life of the asset. Stakeholders during this phase include investors, tenants, facility managers, and service providers. Commercial real estate, e.g., factories, warehouses, office buildings, hospitals, etc., may involve additional ESG considerations based on the specific use.

TRANSPARENCY AND DISCLOSURE: The operation of real estate assets is susceptible to numerous practices that can encourage corruption and lead to environmental problems. By implementing comprehensive and transparent practices, managers of real estate assets can avoid problems and maintain the confidence of all stakeholders. These practices include the following: (1) robust internal and external compliance programs, including employee training and supplier reporting, to ensure proper oversight of all transactions and identify possible corrupt practices, e.g., money laundering; (2) creating a transparent framework for the collection, use, and secure storage of data on tenants and building operations: in all cases, privacy policies should be clearly stated and communicated; (3) establish clear criteria for evaluating building performance against appropriate economic, environmental, and social benchmarks; and (4) develop communication protocols for all stakeholders to ensure regular reporting of building performance, management effectiveness, and investment results.

ENVIRONMENTAL STEWARDSHIP: Buildings use large amounts of energy and water in their day-to-day operations. It was noted earlier that buildings and construction activity account for 36% of global final energy use and are responsible for 39% of global CO_2 emissions.[16] They may also create significant amounts of waste. Because of this, effective oversight and management of the environmental impact of all real estate assets during their use is critical to an ESG policy.

ENERGY CONSUMPTION: residential and commercial buildings consume large amounts of energy—mainly in the form of fossil fuels and electricity—and this is a major contributor to global carbon emissions. The energy is used primarily for climate control (heating and air conditioning), indoor and outdoor lighting, heating water, and appliances. To ensure efficient energy use and minimize environmental impact, companies should: (1) make energy efficiency and tracking an integral aspect of facilities management by adopting recognized global standards like LEED or ISO 50001; (2) employ energy efficient lighting and motion controls to conserve electricity; (3) explore the feasibility of becoming energy self-sufficient through the deployment of solar panels, wind turbines, and other forms of renewable energy; (4) utilize "smart" building control systems to track energy usage data and minimize inefficient heating and cooling practices; (5) incorporate environmental clauses in leases that encourage tenants to adopt energy efficient practices and sharing with them the financial benefits of such practices; (6) use public spaces to display data on the building's energy utilization and carbon footprint to encourage all employees and tenants to embrace efficiency and conservation.

WATER: Most buildings utilize water, many in large quantities. The water is used for heating and cooling, landscaping, and day-to-day activity in restrooms, kitchens, labs, etc. Many industrial processes employ large volumes of water as well. Recent research predicts that climate change and population growth will lead to widespread water shortages in the US within 50 years.[17] In addition, the delivery of water to buildings and subsequent treatment of wastewater are energy-intensive activities. For these reasons, the following best practices are recommended: (1) use low-flow plumbing fixtures when permitted by code; (2) employ metering and submetering equipment to track water usage and for early leak detection; (3) explore alternative onsite water sources e.g., capturing rainwater and storm runoff for irrigation or reusing "graywater"; (4) utilize native plants and low-irrigation landscape plans; and (5) educate all building users and tenants on water conservation best practices.

WASTE MANAGEMENT: From 1980 to 2015, per capita municipal solid waste (MSW) in the US increased 22% to 4.5 pounds per person each day. Total MSW in 2015 was 262 million tons, and 53% of that total wound up in land-fills.[18] MSW has a significant environmental impact, as its collection, transportation, and disposal or recycling requires substantial resources. Most MSW originates in buildings. To mitigate the negative impact companies may: (1) collect accurate data on the volume and categories of MSW generated by a facility and report this information to all tenants on a regular basis; (2) provide onsite diversion programs for recyclables, organic waste for composting; and specialty items like batteries, light bulbs, electronics, etc.; (3) educate tenants on opportunities for recycling, composting, etc.; (4) adopt practices that avoid material generation, e.g. replacing paper towels with high-efficiency hand dryers, ordering supplies in bulk to reduce packaging materials, providing reusable dishware, cutlery, and water bottles and ensuring those disposable products are recyclable; and (5) minimize waste from tenant turnover by encouraging new tenants to reuse improvements and fixtures left by prior occupants.

4.4.3   ESG Issues in the Treatment of Tenants, Community, and Workers

Most municipalities have laws in place to protect tenant's rights. However, specific laws can vary by location and many tenants continue to suffer unfair treatment at the hands of their landlords.

Discrimination on many grounds persists in the sale and rental of real estate. Tenants can also face harassment, onerous contractual terms, unsafe and unhealthy living conditions, and unfair evictions.

The owners and managers of buildings should work to enhance relationships between themselves, their tenants, and members of the local community. To achieve these goals, companies are encouraged to consider the following:

ADOPTION OF COMPREHENSIVE NONDISCRIMINATION POLICIES: Such policies should govern all rental and sale of real estate and should: (1) extend to any buildings that provide public access; (2) use transparent and fair contracting documents and procedures; (3) provide a clear and regular process for collecting tenant feedback and handling grievances; and (4) develop activities and programs to engage local community members, particularly ethnic and racial minorities, women, children, the elderly, disabled, and other underrepresented groups.

PROCUREMENT POLICIES: Should require local sourcing for labor and materials whenever possible.

HEALTH, SAFETY, AND WELL-BEING OF OCCUPANTS: Health and safety of indoor environments is critical to tenants and workers in both commercial and residential buildings since many people spend much of their time indoors. For example, a recent study indicates that Americans spend an approximate average of 90% of their time indoors.[19] Some issues can be addressed during the design and development phases of real estate. The following practices can help ensure the safety and well-being of occupants during the operating life of the building: (1) all parts of buildings should be accessible to and usable by people with mobility challenges, as well as those who are visually or hearing impaired; (2) companies should have clear policies and procedures in place around fire safety, active shooter training, weather-related evacuation/shelter, etc.; (3) these policies should be clearly communicated and visible to all building occupants; (4) where appropriate, relevant training should be provided; (5) adherence to all health/safety laws and regulations by both tenants and staff should be monitored and reported on regularly; (6) any potential public health risks created by the building or its occupants should be clearly disclosed; (7) access to water and convenient and private sanitation facilities should be guaranteed to all building occupants; (8) building managers should ensure adequate indoor air quality by using nontoxic and zero-VOC products in building materials and cleaning supplies.

WORKER'S RIGHTS ACROSS THE SUPPLY CHAIN: Once real estate assets are put into use, policies to ensure that workers' rights are protected should be put into place. These policies should: (1) cover both direct employees of the owner/manager as well as subcontracted workers responsible for the maintenance and repair of the building and companies; (2) include a diversity and inclusion policy that ensures diversity and gender equality; (3) ensure strict adherence to all child labor laws; (4) provide the proper equipment and training to ensure the safety of all workers and occupants; (5) pay wages that comply with all local wage laws, including against gender pay discrimination and require their subcontractors to do the same; (6) clearly communicate and monitor compliance with relevant occupational health and safety issues; and (7) implement a regular policy of inspection and routine maintenance around all aspects of building health and safety.

4.4.4 ESG Issues in Recovery and Disposal

Real estate assets have long lives. The median age of owner-occupied homes in 2016 was 37 years[20] and at the end of 2017, the average US commercial building was 50 years old.[21] Even with these long lives, real estate is regularly rebuilt, repurposed, or in some cases, decommissioned. Each of these options involves numerous stakeholders and the potential for significant impact on the environment and people.

STRATEGIC SITE-USE EVALUATION: The first stage of the process is determining the optimal strategy for a real estate asset at the end of its useful life. Options include renovation/refurbishment, redevelopment, or decommissioning, and the decision is often driven by investor preferences and economic factors.

As part of a thorough and transparent decision-making process, companies are encouraged to:

REVIEW MARKET CONDITIONS AND THE LONG-TERM DEMAND FOR THE EXISTING BUILDING/SITE: Conduct a comprehensive cost/benefit analysis of potential options. This analysis should include both direct and indirect costs and should also incorporate any intangible benefits that might come with sustainable redevelopment.

CONSIDER THE SOCIAL AND COMMUNITY IMPACT OF CHANGING THE USE OF THE BUILDING: For example, consider the potential impact of reduced affordability due to gentrification. Respect local historical, cultural, and archeological standards and incorporate them into the renovation or redevelopment assessment.

Use standard sustainability assessment tools and methodologies to evaluate the economic, social, and environmental impact of each option.

4.4.5   ESG Issues in Refurbishment and Retro-fitting

All buildings will eventually require updating due to age, condition, market demand, investor preferences, or changing technologies. For buildings originally designed carefully and constructed well, renovations should not be extensive and will have minimal economic and environmental impact. Other buildings may require extensive refurbishment or even complete reconstruction and these projects will face many of the same issues encountered in the development phase, the quality of planning, design and construction, including environmental stewardship and workers' rights.

Whatever the extent of the project, companies should adopt the following practices: (1) evaluate existing buildings in the context of strategic and long-term requirements to determine the optimal level of renovation, e.g., a low level renovation geared to energy efficiency might include installation of LED lighting and insulating curtains while a more extensive renovation with the same goals could include solar panels, wind turbines, or triple-glazed windows; (2) assess potential levels of refurbishment to determine the optimal combination of cost-effectiveness, energy efficiency, and environmental impact; and (3) consider the effect on the building and site of changing environmental conditions and the increased risk related to the current and projected impact of climate change.

4.4.6   Waste Management, Resource Conservation, and Recycling During Demolition

Most refurbishment activity involves some level of demolition, which is responsible for significant waste generation in the construction industry. This can include common construction materials like wood and concrete, but may also involve hazardous materials like asbestos, lead, etc. Even materials that are safe in use, e.g., drywall, can become hazardous when dumped in landfills where they may release toxic off-gases. Landfill disposal may carry significant social and environmental costs. All of this creates significant benefits from reuse and recycle practices for demolition waste.

Companies are encouraged to: (1) conduct a pre-demolition audit with the goal of minimizing the amount of waste going into a landfill and ensuring the safe handling of hazardous materials; (2) minimize the impact of demolition/disposal activities on surrounding communities; (3) prepare a risk assessment of all demolition activities and then develop site-specific procedures to manage those risks; (4) ensure adequate insurance and emergency procedures are in place to address demolition accidents; (5) comply with all laws for the handling and disposal of waste materials and obtain necessary permits and certifications; (6) provide for the safe handling of site waste water and ensure the safety of groundwater supplies; and (7) process demolition materials for reuse and/or recycling. Ideally, these activities are done onsite.

4.4.7 Land Recovery and Rehabilitation

Although rare, some real estate assets are abandoned at the end of their useful life. In these cases, land recovery and site rehabilitation activities should be undertaken to ensure land is restored to a safe and environmentally sustainable condition. To achieve this goal, companies should: (1) review legal and regulatory requirements for preparing environmental impact assessments; (2) identify specific considerations to be included in an environmental impact assessment, examples include: wildlife surveys, flora, agricultural, ecological, hydrologic, geomorphological, geological, historical/cultural, and archeological; (3) recruit appropriate specialists and commission a comprehensive environmental impact report; (4) survey site conditions to determine specific rehabilitation methods and technologies required to return the site to desired environmental standards; (5) develop an integrated plan of action that incorporates the following issues where relevant: interaction with local communities, promotion of native species, protection of animal migration routes, management of forestry and water resources, and reuse of construction materials.

4.5   ESG AND HEDGE FUNDS

ESG investing has begun to attract significant attention from both hedge fund investors as well as hedge fund managers. According to a recent report, 65% of hedge fund investors believe that ESG will become more important in the next 5 years. However, only 37% of hedge fund managers are in agreement regarding the importance of ESG in the near future.[22] While hedge fund manager beliefs are migrating towards ESG-linked strategies, there is still a sizable potential gap between hedge fund investor and manager objectives. Other recent data report that over 10% of hedge funds' assets under management are from the application of environmental, social, and governance principles to investment strategies.[23] Additionally, a recent report measuring the assets invested with hedge fund managers rated "poor" using ESG standards stood at 4% in 2018, compared with 32% from 2013.[24] Finally, key drivers behind the shift towards hedge funds' migration towards ESG include regulation, risk management, client demand, and search for new sources of alpha.

4.5.1   Hedge Fund Investment Strategies and ESG

There are many hedge fund strategies, instruments, and techniques. Hedge funds have more flexibility than long-only investment strategies. This can present unique challenges particularly in the governance, transparency, and credit-granting arenas.

4.5.2 Hedge Fund Governance and ESG

The governance of hedge funds has come under increased scrutiny for several ESG-related reasons including a lack of appropriate governance. The financial industry in general has been linked to scandals, frauds, and the financial crisis. These challenges have resulted in magnification of recent regulatory scrutiny related to hedge funds, including hedge funds moving offshore for the primary purpose of avoiding such scrutiny and potential future regulation. ESG concerns may increase as the hedge fund customer base includes more universities, pension plans, insurance companies, and retail investors.[25]

Most often, governance spans two main themes: the backgrounds, role, and independence of directors; and the transparency of the fund's leadership team, holdings, restrictions, and risks.

> DIRECTORS: The role of directors in the hedge fund universe is similar to that in other alternative investment areas, except that the idiosyncratic nature of hedge funds can lead to a variety of director structures due to jurisdiction and practice, the legal structure of the fund, and the particulars of the investor base. That said, the preferred practice of selecting and maintaining a strong governance base revolves around the independence of the directors; the skill level, background, and integrity of the directors; and the operational processes of hedge fund governance bodies. This is in order to ensure adherence to objectives and controls, clarity of purpose, and modifications to policies over time as regulations, conditions, and the investor base changes. The preferred model baseline starts with a fund governing body that consists of, if possible: (1) a majority of independent directors; (2) directors who are qualified and experienced; (3) directors who are representative of a potentially diverse and broadening set of investors; and (4) independent directors, as they may be called upon to represent the investors in situations where there are potential conflicts of interest between management and investors.

Examples of potential conflicts of interest between management and investors include changes in fee structures, legal structure, or the fund's investment objective. In the event that there are legitimate reasons that independent directors are not serving in the governance structure of the fund, the hedge fund should disclose this to investors as well as provide information about any governance guidelines, proxy voting procedures, and how directors are selected. Also, hedge funds should consider the extent of, and circumstances within which directors may, serve on many other funds' boards as this can raise questions around true independence, practical availability, and ability to serve each fund's investors appropriately.[26]

Two blossoming areas related to governance of hedge funds revolve around succession planning for the hedge fund, and how commingled accounts can be employed to provide lower cost processes to implement ESG screening, especially as data become more available to overlay quantitative screening techniques.

4.5.3 Hedge Fund Transparency and ESG

By their nature and by construction, hedge funds tend to be opaque. At the same time, hedge funds have strategic mandates. When coupled with unique transactions fees, risk metrics, operations, and other characteristics, these vehicles are not generally organized to be transparent. Investors—particularly institutional investors—need to understand risk characteristics in order to map to existing portfolios, and in order to explain their understanding of the hedge fund to their own customers.

More transparency on the part of the hedge fund allows for greater alignment of strategy with their investors. An effort to bridge investors' needs for risk and portfolio metrics against hedge funds needs to maintain some level of privacy around detailed data is the effort referred to as Open Protocol Hedge Fund Reporting.[27] In short, this process involves standardizing risk monitoring, managing, and reporting at the portfolio level in order to provide important information to investors while protecting specific asset allocation data for hedge fund investments. More specifically, **Open Protocol**[28] provides a standard and consistent framework around: (1) data and inputs; (2) calculations and methods; (3) timely and regular reporting; and (4) protocols and standards, where appropriate.

In addition to needing to manage the gap between investor needs and traditional hedge fund transparency revolving around investments and asset allocation, hedge funds should be encouraged to provide transparency around liquidity levels, risk management and monitoring processes, valuation steps and process (not the valuations themselves), investment gates, lock-ups, and fee structure. Also, migrating from individual investors with segregated accounts (which will notably incorporate more customized objectives for investors) towards share classes will improve cost control and efficiencies for the hedge fund but may result in less transparency for investors. Finally, transparency may relate to geography of the fund as regulators in the EU are looking for fund managers and institutions to disclose how they account for sustainability risks in the capital allocation process.[29]

Advocates for more transparency on the part of hedge funds will push for additional information on the underlying investments, including data about specific investment types, asset allocation, geographic mix, governance guidelines, and proxy voting particulars, as well as specifics around how ESG issues are considered by investment processes and guidelines.

4.5.4 Hedge Fund Investment Techniques and Instruments and ESG

Hedge funds employ a number of advanced techniques and instruments that are consistent with a specific fund strategy to optimize their risk–return profile. These techniques and instruments include derivatives, short-selling, leverage, and high-frequency trading. By their nature, each of these is designed to either modify the return payoff distribution or take advantage of disequilibrium in securities markets, or both. They all have the potential to radically alter or amplify the risk structure as well, and consequently are not a good fit for some investors. Ultimately, whether or not the hedge fund employs these tactics should be transparent to investors.

> SHORT-SELLING: Because, in a sense, short-sellers are hoping for price declines, some believe this tactic is potentially harmful to market sentiment, and can potentially increase market volatility. Others counterargue that short-selling performs a vital function in the marketplace as it allows for a vehicle to dampen the potential for overpriced securities or to prevent or punish corporate

fraud and mismanagement. Most of the research on short-selling supports the notion that it is effective for promoting markets that are well-functioning and efficient, but not all investors may agree, and there may also be restrictions on short-selling by some institutional investors. Finally, there are some hedge funds that are taking an active role in governance by purposefully shorting the stocks of firms that have low ESG scores, especially those with potential fraud and serious concerns around governance.

LEVERAGE: Some hedge funds borrow or alter the balance sheet of the fund in order to amplify potential future returns. This has a corresponding impact on the fund's risk structure as well. If mismanaged or left unchecked, leverage can have a significant negative impact on the fund. If there is increased systematic leverage in the economy, there can be greater consequences should market conditions deteriorate, liquidity dry up, or prices become more volatile. The fund should consider disclosing: (1) the conditions under which leverage may be used; (2) restrictions and sources of the leverage; (3) additional risks as a consequence of leverage (counterparty credit risk, for example); (4) details about how leverage is defined and measured by the fund; and (5) the match or mismatch of the maturity of the leverage relative to the maturity of the assets.

DERIVATIVES: Hedge funds can use options, swaps, forwards, and futures contracts to create custom risk–return payoff structures, many of which are asymmetric in nature. Because of their complexity, it can be difficult for investors to completely understand how the use of these instruments could potentially influence future risk and return patterns. Derivatives can promote efficiency and allow for a wider array of directional bets from the hedge fund managers, while entailing a greater set of both financial and operating risks, such as counterparty credit risk and margin calls. Hedge funds should consider disclosing: (1) whether or not derivatives are used by the fund; (2) if the use of derivatives is a central and key tactic used by the fund, as opposed to the use of derivatives as an occasional support feature, for example; and (3) the existence of regulatory and operating risk factors investors will be exposed to if they invest in the hedge fund.

HIGH-FREQUENCY TRADING: Some hedge funds focus on active and short-term trading to generate returns. At times, algorithmic or quantitative trading techniques are used to take advantage of even small mispricing in securities markets. This technique can be perceived as running counter to a focus on ESG strategies, which can be designed to promote longer-term investments in companies that are dedicated to environmental or sustainability objectives. Some argue that high-frequency trading can promote destabilization of markets where others counter that taking advantage of mispricing helps to bring markets back into equilibrium. In any event, hedge funds that focus on this primarily on this technique may not be a good fit for ESG strategies, unless and until data inputs for quantitative trading using ESG factors are sufficiently high quality to be usable for day-to-day trading strategies.

HEDGE FUND STRATEGIES: There are potential benefits and drawbacks of hedge funds employing ESG into their investment processes and choices. On the one hand, ESG can be a source of strategic choice and differentiation, leading to new investment client groups and understanding trends in the marketplace. In addition, migrating to an ESG-related strategy can attract new and different employees. Finally, when skillfully utilized, ESG can be a potential source of returns and a tool for improving return attribution and risk analytics. However, on the other hand, some customers and employees and other stakeholders may be skeptical of this approach, unsure about the level and magnitude of opportunities and risks when considering ESG-related factors. ESG performance and risk measurements are still being refined and developed, and there remains a notable lack of transparency here.

FORMS OF INTERSECTION BETWEEN HEDGE FUND STRATEGY AND ESG: Major hedge fund strategies include fundamental, equity or credit long/short, relative value, arbitrage, volatility, event-driven, distressed/restructuring, global macro, FX, fixed income, mortgage/asset-backed, and commodity. As an asset allocator drills down into specific hedge fund strategies to determine the most direct intersections between their portfolio strategy and ESG-related issues, the asset allocator should use a client viewpoint. That is, how might clients view ESG activities contingent upon a specific hedge fund strategy?

Aspects of ESG processes and investments fall into several categories: (1) underlying investments—to what degree does the hedge fund strategically allocate resources to specific investments or asset classes that are consistent with ESG objectives?; (2) activism—to what degree does the hedge fund strategically employ their role as asset owners to engage in ESG objectives, via voting rights, pressure, marketing, publicity, or policy changes?; (3) avoidance—does the hedge fund strategically avoid processes and/or investments that are potentially inconsistent with ESG objectives? Each of these three categories is discussed in detail in the next three sections.

4.5.5 Hedge Fund Strategies and Underlying Investments

There are a number of hedge fund strategies where the specific underlying investment is analyzed for potential inclusion in a portfolio. For hedge fund strategies that involve fundamental analysis, in either equity or credit markets, ESG characteristics of the underlying investment can be considered more directly than for other hedge fund strategies. Said differently, if there is a fundamental hedge fund that involves analyzing equities and/or credit, ESG characteristics of the equity or credit can be used as one of the factors the hedge fund manager can use to determine whether the underlying investment should be held as a long or short position in the portfolio. Relative value, and long/short equity hedge funds, may screen for ESG data for inclusion in their portfolios, and as the data improve in terms of quality and acceptance, quantitative-oriented strategies will focus more and more heavily on ESG factors in their analysis, if they so choose. In sum, fundamental equity and credit long/short hedge funds, as well as hedge funds with quantitative strategies, can be most closely associated with using ESG factors when analyzing their underlying investments.

4.5.6 Hedge Fund Strategies and Activism

Some hedge funds have begun to take a more participatory role with their positions, which dovetails nicely when coupled with ESG-related decisions. For example, event-driven and activist hedge fund strategies can also focus on screening for firms that have a higher "ESG IQ" which they would then, presumably, support actively. Moreover, this hedge fund strategy can urge or pressure management to take a more positive position when working with stakeholders such as employees, communities, customers, and suppliers. To the extent that event-driven hedge fund strategies make this tactic transparent to their own customers, they may be more attractive. In fact, hedge funds are uniquely positioned to leverage their activeness to ESG-oriented investors compared against traditional mutual funds.

4.5.7   Hedge Fund Strategies and Avoidance

There are several hedge fund strategies that are not directly consistent with ESG analysis of underlying investments or could easily promote an activist owner environment for their customers. For example, hedge funds that focus on government fixed income securities may not be able to employ ESG factors for the underlying instruments in their portfolios, but could analyze country social considerations and avoid sovereign debt of oppressive governments as well as those countries that have a spotty human rights record. Collectively, the industry could exert pressure on government leaders to improve their record related to ESG strategies. Hedge fund strategies that focus on mortgage- and asset-backed securities similar could avoid areas that have been called out for exploitive practices, issues with broad accessibility or loan servicing, or aggressive collections policies. FX and commodity related hedge funds, particularly for larger firms, may want to analyze whether their positions help to stabilize or destabilize markets.

4.6   ESG AND PRIVATE EQUITY

ESG strategies, practices, processes, and tactics have grown markedly in the private equity space in recent years. In a 2018 assessment of nearly 300 private equity managers, the percentage of those rated either excellent or good in terms of ESG has improved from 27% in 2014 to 58% in 2018, and those rated poor has declined from 43% to 17%.[30] This is true across managers in Europe, Asia, and the United States, although European managers appear to be leading the effort. As interest in ESG investing continues to grow, two notable characteristics in particular are relevant to private equity firms and processes related to ESG. The first is the general partner (GP)–limited partner (LP) relationship, and the second is the private equity investment process.

4.6.1   ESG within a Partnership Organization and the GP–LP Relationship

For private equity firms interested in engaging in ESG activities, it is crucial for the organizational structure to create and support an ESG culture. This starts at the top, with the GP or team leading the PE firm. This should include the following three elements:[31] (1) establishing a formal commitment to ESG integration; (2) setting ESG related objectives and metrics; and (3) engaging and communicating with all stakeholders. These three elements are discussed further in the following three paragraphs.

ESTABLISHING A FORMAL COMMITMENT TO ESG INTEGRATION: In order to maintain an organization that is committed to sustained ESG integration, a number of practices should be initiated and maintained: (1) there needs to be a formal commitment from the organization's leadership who should make resource commitments and guarantees transparent; (2) there should be a person or persons put in charge of this effort, and such individual(s) should have some experience or expertise in ESG integration; (3) employees should be educated on why the firm is engaging in ESG integration, how it can help the firm, investors, and other stakeholders, and also what they are likely to see as a result in an ESG-related and engaged strategy, processes, and tactics; and (4) finally, achieving ESG objectives needs to be linked to employee and firm performance objectives and results.

SETTING ESG-RELATED OBJECTIVES AND METRICS: In addition to leadership's formalized commitment to ESG integration into the private equity organization, the firm needs to set specific, tangible, and achievable goals and objectives. These objectives need to be set and clearly communicated to employees. Moreover, a back office operations group (including development and human resources) should be involved in articulating the goals so that they comport with and are in alignment with to-be-established employee performance benchmarks. Linking these objectives back to trainings held is an important part of this process.

ENGAGING AND COMMUNICATING WITH ALL STAKEHOLDERS: In addition to communicating and involving employees, other stakeholders need to be engaged. Most importantly, limited partners need to be involved early on so that they can better understand what is likely to occur, so that they can better understand whether this aligns with their own goals and objectives, and to provide them with time to make decisions as a result. The early stage is an opportunity for the PE firm to gauge the interest of the LPs to determine any specific interest and intent. This is also an opportunity for the firm to collaborate with the broader private equity and investment and wider communities.

4.6.2 ESG and the Private Equity Investment Process

As with previous asset classes, the allocation and rebalancing of significant resources is an important construct from which to employ an ESG-related strategy. Capital allocation is likely to remain the most critical "vote" for PE firms to engage with new and existing investments. The investment process can be divided into three areas to evaluate relative to ESG: (1) due diligence; (2) the investment decision and agreement; and (3) ownership. These three areas are discussed further in the following three paragraphs.

DUE DILIGENCE: The due diligence process for PE firms could be adapted to incorporate ESG-related screening mechanisms, including a high-level checklist for ESG factors, as well as exclusionary criteria. Target firms that make it through the initial screening process can then be examined more fully. Rather than create a new ESG process, there are a number of industry-specific ESG standards and toolkits that already exist, and these will likely improve and expand in the future. One decision the PE firm needs to make is whether to hire or use an in-house individual or team to assist in this filtering and targeting process, or whether to employ an external consultant. One key benefit of an in-house employee is that this individual is likely to understand the purpose and alignment of ESG with their PE firm. One benefit of an external consultant is that they are likely to be more objective and not subconsciously tilt their views on particular firms when it comes to ESG factors and analysis. A consultant can also help save on due diligence-related legal costs and risks.

According to a recent report,[32] the top ten ESG metrics sought by private equity fund investors are: (1) Does the firm have an ESG Policy? (2) Is there an individual or team that is specifically assigned to administer ESG policy? (3) Is there a Corporate Code of Ethics? (4) Presence of litigation. (5) People diversity. (6) Net employee composition (e.g., percentage of full-time to part-time workers, etc.). (7) Environmental policy. (8) Estimation of CO_2 footprint. (9) Data and cybersecurity incidents. (10) Health and safety events. Additionally, investors are concerned with materiality, the degree to which ESG factors are expected to have a substantial effect on the financial risk or returns of a specific investment.

THE INVESTMENT DECISION AND INVESTMENT AGREEMENT: Generally speaking, the investment decision approach combined with ESG considerations does not differ markedly from other alternative investment ESG approaches, namely whether or not to incorporate ESG factors as a standard practice in investment committee discussions and decisions, and incorporating information from the due diligence process in any investment summarization or decision. What differs for private equity firms is the commitment that the PE firm might make to or ask from their portfolio companies. This "investment agreement" should consist of standard and shared ESG objectives and policies and practices, templates from industry toolkits to embed ESG clauses into the agreements, deal documents, and near-term immediate objectives upon consummation of a deal. Of course, collaborating with and getting buy-in from portfolio companies as well as their committed leadership is paramount. Finally, longer horizon ESG goals and objectives should be part of clear process and objectives-based benchmarks.

OWNERSHIP: Engagement of the portfolio companies on ESG tactics and practices can involve the following: (1) the private equity firm can engage with the portfolio company on understanding of ESG related risks and opportunities; (2) the portfolio company should have ESG policies and processes in place that are at least as strong at the private equity firm; (3) the portfolio company can share any best practices throughout the private equity firm and other portfolio companies; and (4) all governance boards should be accountable for ESG related initiatives.

4.6.3 ESG and the Monitoring Process

Monitoring the portfolio companies should be consistent, transparent, and incorporate ESG metrics. Investors should: (1) ensure that ESG issues and risks (as well as opportunities) remain on the board's agenda; (2) provide tools for measuring ESG practices as well as prepare structured and consistent reporting practices across portfolio companies; and (3) ensure that ESG performance is a part of quarterly/annual reviews.

NOTES

1. https://www.ussif.org/sribasics (accessed July 3, 2019).
2. See Preqin Ltd. (2018). Data included Hedge Funds, Private Equity, Real Estate, Natural Resources, Infrastructure and Private Debt.
3. Ibid.
4. See Mercer and LGT Capital Partners (2015).
5. Ibid.
6. Ibid.
7. See Preqin Ltd. (2018).
8. Andersson et al. (2016); Sassen et al. (2016).
9. See Mercer and LGT Capital Partners (2015).
10. Ibid.
11. A survey conducted in 2018 by State Street Global Advisors found that over half of those institutional investors already implementing some form of ESG strategy in their portfolios were struggling with clarity around standards and terminology. https://blogs.cfainstitute.org/investor/2018/07/18/four-challenges-in-the-esg-market-whats-next/ (accessed July 3, 2019).
12. See Escrig-Olmedo et al. (2019).
13. Some efforts are underway to develop criteria applicable to private companies. See page 15 of "ESG Report 2018," LGT Capital Partners (2018). https://www.lgtcp.com/shared/.content/publikationen/cp/esg_download/LGT-CP-ESG-Report-2018_en.pdf (accessed July 2, 2019).
14. See International Energy Agency (2017, p. 14).
15. This section parallels and is adapted from *Advancing Responsible Business Practices in Land, Construction and Real Estate Use and Investment,* Royal Institution of Chartered Surveyors (2015).
16. See International Energy Agency (2017, p. 14).
17. See Brown et al. (2019).
18. http://css.umich.edu/factsheets/municipal-solid-waste-factsheet (accessed June 11, 2019).
19. https://www.epa.gov/report-environment/indoor-air-quality (accessed June 22, 2019).
20. https://www.housingwire.com/articles/46427-housing-stock-age-shows-desperate-need-for-new-construction (accessed June 21, 2019).
21. http://www.commbuildings.com/ResearchComm.html (accessed June 28, 2019).
22. See McElhaney (2019).
23. See Financial Times (2019).
24. See LGT Capital Partners (2018).
25. This section in particular has been guided by "Responsible Investment and Hedge Funds: A Discussion Paper," UNPRI (2012).
26. See Standards Board for Alternative Investments (2017).
27. See Fioravante (2012).
28. The Open Protocol description, information, and toolkit can be found at www.sbai.org/toolbox/open-protocol-op-risk-reporting/.
29. See Ward (2019).
30. See LGT Capital Partners (2018).

31. Many of the ideas from this specific section stem from the report "Integrating ESG in Private Equity: A Guide for General Partners," UN Principles for Responsible Investment, 2014.
32. "The Top 10 ESG Metrics Private Equity Funds Should Collect," by Sarah Broderick, IHS Markit.

REFERENCES

Andersson, M., P. Bolton, and F. Samama. 2016. "Hedging Climate Risk." *Financial Analysts Journal* 72 (3): 13–32. 10.2469/faj.v72.n3.4.

Brown, T. C., V. Mahat, and J. A. Ramirez. 2019. "Adaptation to Future Water Shortages in the United States Caused by Population Growth and Climate Change." *Earth's Future* 7 (3): 219–34. doi.org/10.1029/2018EF001091

Escrig-Olmedo, E., M. A. Fernandez-Izquierdo, I. Ferrero-Ferrero, et al. 2019. "Rating the Raters: Evaluating how ESG Rating Agencies Integrate Sustainability Principles." *Sustainability* 11 (3): 915. DOI: 10.3390/su11030915.

Financial Times. 2019. "ESG strategies lengthen hedge fund holding periods." 16 May.

Fioravante, J. 2012. "Open Protocol Hedge Fund Reporting a Boost for Pensions." *Institutional Investor*, 16 July.

International Energy Agency. 2017. *Global Status Report 2017*. International Energy Agency for the Global Alliance for Buildings and Construction, © United Nations Environment Programme, p. 14. https://www.worldgbc.org/sites/default/files/UNEP%20188_GABC_en%20%28web%29.pdf.

LGT Capital Partners. 2018. "ESG Report 2018." https://www.lgtcp.com/shared/.content/publikationen/cp/esg_download/LGT-CP-ESG-Report-2018_en.pdf.

McElhaney, A. 2019. "Hedge Funds Drag Their Feet When It Comes to ESG." *Institutional Investor*, 8 May.

Mercer and LGT Capital Partners. 2015. "Global Insights on ESG in Alternative Investing." https://www.mercer.com/content/dam/mercer/attachments/global/investments/responsible-investment/Global-Insights-ESG-in-Alternative-Investing-2015-Mercer-LGT.pdf. March.

Preqin Ltd. 2018, "The Future of Alternatives." https://www.preqin.com/insights/special-reports-and-factsheets/the-future-of-alternatives/23610.

Royal Institution of Chartered Surveyors (RICS). 2015. "Advancing Responsible Business Practices in Land, Construction and Real Estate Use and Investment." https://www.unglobalcompact.org/library/1361.

Sassen, R., A. Hinze, and I. Hardeck. 2016. Impact of ESG factors on firm risk in Europe. *Journal of Business Economy* 86: 867–904. doi.org/10.1007/s11573-016-0819-3.

Standards Board for Alternative Investments. July 2017. "The Alternative Investment Standards." https://www.sbai.org/wp-content/uploads/2016/04/SBAI-Standards-2017.pdf.

UNPRI. 2012. "Responsible Investment and Hedge Funds: A Discussion Paper," UN Principles for Responsible Investment, March 12. unpri.org/download?ac=4155.

Ward, C. 2019 "Implementing Responsible Investment at Discretionary Hedge Funds." *Man GLG Report*, February. https://www.man.com/maninstitute/implementing-ri-at-discretionary-hfs.

CHAPTER 5

ESG Analysis and Application

Chapter 4 delineated the myriad potential issues to be considered regarding ESG concerns within the alternative investment industry. This chapter discusses potential ways to analyze and operationalize ESG issues in portfolio construction and management.

5.1 BACKGROUND ON ESG

ESG as a popular determinant of investment decisions is a relatively recent development, so it should be expected that its theory and practices are more primitive and in more flux than traditional determinants of investment decisions. This section provides background on ESG as an investment criterion.

5.1.1 History of ESG

According to Forbes[1] the term ESG dates back to at least 2005. ESG has its roots in the socially responsible investing (SRI) movement which dates back to at least the 1980s and corporate social responsibility (CSR) which dates back to the late 1960s. Newsweek[2] cites two "landmark accords" that "marked a turning point for [responsible investing]: the signing by world leaders of the UN Sustainable Development Goals (SDGs) in September 2015, followed by the Paris Climate Agreement later that year."

5.1.2 The Global Reporting Initiative (GRI) Standards

A key issue in ESG is the decision of what an entity should report regarding ESG and how to report it. The Global Reporting Initiative (GRI) is an independent not-for-profit organization that describes itself as helping "businesses and governments worldwide understand and communicate their impact on critical sustainability issues such as climate change, human rights, governance and social well-being."[3] In 2016, GRI launched the Global Reporting Initiative (GRI) Standards, developed by the Global Sustainability Standards Board (GSSB). The GRI standards (formerly known as the G4 Sustainability reporting Guidelines) are designed to "enable all organizations to report publicly on their economic, environmental and social impacts – and show how they contribute towards sustainable development"[4] and to serve as a "reference for policy makers and regulators."[5] The KPMG Survey of Corporate Responsibility Reporting 2017[6] notes that the vast majority of the world's largest firms are using "some sort of [corporate responsibility] reporting" and that "The GRI framework is the most commonly used."

5.1.3   Social Responsibility, ESG, and Evidence Regarding Stakeholder Wealth

There are numerous studies that associate metrics of ESG and social investing with various accounting ratios, such as return on equity. However, such methods are not considered best practices within the field of finance with which to evaluate performance from the perspective of shareholders. Best practices in financial research of equity performance focus on market equity returns with attempts to adjust for risk differentials. While shareholders clearly prefer to focus on metrics of total return, one of the goals of ESG advocates may be not to maximize shareholder returns, but to more equitably distribute returns across all stakeholders. That is, some ESG advocates may prefer lower corporate profits and lower stock returns if it means paying higher compensation to employees or greater corporate spending to improve the community or slow the effects of climate change.

There are numerous empirical studies on the relationship between social investing (e.g., ESG) and shareholder returns in public markets. For example, using a data set on global ESG investing at the industry level, Auer and Schuhmacher[7] find that "Selection of high- or low-rated stocks does not provide superior performance; in the Asia-Pacific region and the US, ESG investors perform similar to the market; in Europe, investors tend to pay a price for socially responsible investing." Belghitar, Clark, and Deshmukh[8] conclude: "We find strong evidence that ethical investors pay a price for investing ethically."

Giese and Lee[9] examined extensive research on ESG and equity returns. They conclude: "the bulk of academic and industry studies fail to achieve consensus on whether ESG characteristics have affected performance" and "the finding supported with the highest statistical confidence level is the result that ESG characteristics had a positive effect on risk, in particular in mitigating tail risks."

Hvidkjær[10] performs a literature review of ESG investing and concludes: (1) "some authors do appear to wish to make the business case for ESG investing rather than applying a more dispassionate scientific approach"; (2) "no simple answer exists to the question of the profitability of ESG investing"; (3) "the most consistent finding in the current review is that sin stocks exhibit outperformance"; (4) "There is evidence that stocks with high ESG ratings exhibit high future returns. The evidence is strongest in 1991–2004, while the returns of stocks with high ESG ratings do not appear to differ from benchmarks in 2005–2012. Some evidence suggests that returns again have been high since 2012"; (5) "Event studies indicate that the stock market does not respond positively to ESG/CSR initiatives taken by firms"; and (6) "Finally, there is evidence that active ownership by ESG investors can create value, both for shareholders and other stakeholders. Specifically, successful ESG engagements by a large institutional investor into U.S. firms were followed by abnormal returns in the subsequent year."

Rabener[11] performs a robust analysis of equity returns based on factor analysis. Factor analysis is on the leading edge of equity return analysis and is discussed in detail in Chapter 8. Rabener writes:

> *The notion that companies that care about the environment, look after their employees, and exhibit good governance outperform is likely too good to be true. The drivers of performance since 2009 were common equity factors. While factor exposure might change over time, ESG investors currently run the risk of missing out if small and cheap stocks start outperforming low-risk and high-quality stocks. Historically, speculating on small and cheap stocks hasn't been a bad bet. That may be true again.*

Rabener's results are based on US equity returns only. Those returns provide evidence that incorporating a variety of return factors into an empirical analysis of equity returns can generate results that contrast with more primitive methods. It should be noted that the overwhelming majority of empirical studies of equity performance with regard to ESG issues are based on single-factor risk adjustment, no risk-adjustment, or all too often on accounting metrics such as ROE (return on equity). In all cases, empirical studies should be careful to avoid sample biases from using performance data on firms that pre-date the assignment of an ESG rating or other measure of ESG compliance.

5.2 ESG RATINGS AND SCORES

ESG ratings and scores attempt to measure and convey the extent to which an entity is operating with conformity to the best practices advocated from an ESG perspective. ESG ratings are compiled by major financial rating firms (e.g., Moody's and Fitch), major index providers (e.g., FTSE Russell and MSCI), and companies specializing in ESG-related issues (e.g., Sustainalytics and ISS). The explosive growth and substantial popularity of such ratings indicate the extent to which inclusion of ESG-related issues has become important to fund managers and institutional investors.

One issue of importance in ESG ratings is whether the ratings are relative to a particular industry or not. For example, a particular oil and gas firm may be viewed as deserving of a negative ESG rating based on environmental concerns due to its line of business, but may be viewed as deserving a positive rating if it is a leader in ESG-related concerns within its industry.

There has been criticism of the heterogeneity of ESG-related ratings for the same firms across ratings agencies. Barnett, CEO of a corporation with a vision of "a world in which all capital allocation is driven by environmental, social and financial returns,"[12] asserts that "ESG ratings don't actually rate anything (if by which we mean assigning a comparable estimation on the likelihood of a future event),"[13] and reports that "The big three credit rating agencies (Moody's, S&P, Fitch) have a [credit] ratings correlation of 0.9. Three of the largest ESG ratings organizations (MSCI, Sustainalytics, Reprisk) have an ESG ratings correlation of 0.32."[14]

In other words, while there is a high average correlation between credit ratings of the same firms across different rating agencies, there is a low correlation for ESG ratings between the same firms across different rating agencies.

5.3   ESG MATERIALITY AND DISCLOSURE

> **ESG materiality** is the property of being likely to be considered important (i.e., potentially having a substantial impact) from the reasonable perspective of stakeholders in the context of ESG principles. The concept of materiality has been used throughout legal, business, and regulatory analyses to denote subsets of issues requiring serious consideration. This section discusses materiality and its assessment in the context of ESG.

There have been numerous methods proposed to assist corporate managers in reducing the myriad ESG issues potentially useful in implementing ESG into a more manageable framework. The issue of ESG materiality includes which matters have sufficient importance to both: (1) warrant consideration in a firm's operational and investment decisions; and (2) warrant disclosure to a firm's investors and others. This section reviews several methods of utilizing or implementing materiality with ESG.

5.3.1   ESG Materiality, ESG Disclosure, and the Global Reporting Initiative

The Global Reporting Initiative (GRI) is a nongovernmental organization (NGO) that promotes improved reporting principles and disclosure of ESG-related issues through the development of the GRI Standards. The GRI Standards is an ESG-related reporting standard developed in 2016. The term, GRI Standards, can be used to refer to those organizations that create and use the standard. The fourth set of GRI Standards is known as the G4.

The G4 includes enhanced coverage of ESG materiality including a "Materiality Principle." The **G4 Materiality Principle** asserts that: "[An ESG-related] report should cover aspects that: reflect the organization's significant economic, environmental, and social impacts; or substantively influence the assessments and decisions of stakeholders."[15] The Materiality Principle asserts that relevant topics within reports should include those topics that "may reasonably be considered important for reflecting the organization's economic, environmental, and social impacts, or influencing the decisions of stakeholders, and, therefore, potentially merit inclusion in the report."[16] The G4 describes materiality as the second of four steps in defining the boundaries of a report and as the process of "prioritization." The G4 notes that "This 'materiality' focus will make reports more relevant, more credible, and more user-friendly. This will, in turn, enable organizations to better inform markets and society on sustainability matters."[17]

Two other groups that have created guidance used by fiduciaries and others in respect of ESG investing are: the Sustainability Accounting Standards Board (SASB) and the Task Force on Climate-Related Financial Disclosures (TCFD). SASB has created industry-specific sustainability reporting standards intended to allow ESG comparisons of businesses within the same industry. SASB emphasizes financial materiality as the appropriate threshold for issuer reporting on ESG topics. The mission of the TCFD is to "develop voluntary, consistent, climate-related financial risk disclosures for use by companies in providing information to investors, lenders, insurers, and other stakeholders."[18]

5.3.2 A Framework for ESG Materiality Assessment

KPMG[19] proposes a six-step process for materiality assessments: (1) identify and analyze; (2) assess and plan; (3) implement and integrate; (4) monitor and measure; (5) assure and report; and (6) evaluate and revise. The assessment is designed for use in developing strategy, reporting regarding ESG, communicating importance, and spotting future trends.

Antea Group proposes a seven-step process centered on surveying internal and external stakeholders who have been identified:[20]

> *To get the best results, materiality assessments should be formal, structured engagements with stakeholders—not informal Q&A's or workshops. We suggest using a traditional survey format to make it easy for stakeholders to complete and easy for you to analyze results. In the survey, ask stakeholders to rate the importance and impact of each indicator you've identified on a numerical scale, such as 1-5 or 1-10. This will give you quantitative data that can be analyzed and explained visually. Leave additional space for written insights and comments to enhance...*[21]

5.3.3 ESG Materiality Maps

The SASB is a not-for-profit organization with a mission "to establish industry-specific disclosure standards across environmental, social, and governance topics that facilitate communication between companies and investors about financially material, decision-useful information."[22]

The **SASB Materiality Map**[23] analyzes ESG-related issues along two major dimensions: ESG category (e.g., environment) and industry (e.g., consumer goods). There are five ESG categories (environment; social capital; human capital; business model and innovation; and leadership and governance). These five ESG categories (such as environment), are further broken down into a total of 25+ subcategories. For example, environment can be broken into air quality, energy management, and four other concerns.

The other major dimension is industry. There are ten industry categories (e.g., consumer goods, financials, and infrastructure) that are further broken down into subcategories. For example, the consumer goods industry is broken down into seven subcategories (e.g., e-commerce and appliance manufacturing). Thus, the map has had a dimension of roughly 25 ESG subcategories by 75 industry subcategories for a total of almost 2,000 locations on the map.

Each location on the map (i.e., each possible combination of subcategories) is rated as falling into one of three categories: (1) likely to be material for more than 50% of the firms; (2) likely to be material for fewer than 50% of the firms; or (3) not likely at all. For example, within e-commerce, energy management is indicated as being likely to be "material for more than 50% of industries in sector". However, the other environmental issues (e.g., GHG emissions and air quality) were rated as being unlikely to be material.

In summary, the SASB's Materiality Map offers firms and investors an easy-to-use indication of the various ESG-related issues that may or may not be material for various industries. This facilitates the analysis of evaluating the impact of ESG issues for an investment or a firm in a particular industry subgroup.

5.3.4 ESG Materiality Measurement

ESG materiality can be viewed as the product of the likelihood of a material ESG issue multiplied by its expected financial loss.[24] A valuable goal of analysis is the improved ability to assess the materiality of each ESG issue for each industry based on its likelihood of having an impact and the degree of that impact. Cornerstone Capital Group suggests plotting the likelihood of an adverse ESG event against its potential impact in the form of an ESG Materiality Matrix.[25] Their publication suggests that the matrix evolves through time and that the likelihood and potential impacts can be viewed as "ESG life cycles". ESG lifecycles evolve as "awareness of the issue grows and social norms emerge."

Cornerstone describes **three phases of the impact of adverse ESG events:**

1. In the emerging, or "pre-financial" phase of an ESG life cycle, a shift (subtle or overt) commences that ultimately has environmental, social, and/or governance consequences for a sector.
2. In the "transitional" phase, the ESG shift becomes increasingly visible, but neither its timing nor its ultimate financial impact are particularly clear.
3. In the ultimate phase of the life cycle—the "financial" phase—the full financial impacts of the ESG event are felt.[26]

Cornerstone's approach includes a method of associating ESG risks with metrics. Particular risks, associated with particular sectors, can be associated with their drivers. For example, in the telecom sector a social risk is driven by data privacy and data security. A metric of that ESG exposure may be the number of confirmed data breaches.[27] Their suggested approach provides observable metrics on which to perform empirical analysis and, potentially, form informed opinions with regard to future impact. An example of a broad overview of the ESG exposures in the health care sector summarizes the analysis of ESG materiality:

> In Health Care—where governance (product safety and quality) and social (product affordability and access) factors are estimated to have almost equal importance—ESG risks have likely increased in recent years.
>
> With regard to product safety and quality issues, the number of fatalities associated with pharmaceutical products reported by the U.S. Food and Drug Administration doubled in the most recent five-year period. Separately, Interpol estimates that, in some areas of Asia, Africa and Latin America, counterfeit medical goods can form up to 30% of the market. As for product affordability and access, in many developed economies the rate of increase in the price of prescription drugs has exceeded the general inflation level, thereby increasing the risk of price regulation.[28]

5.4 THE UNITED NATIONS ROLE IN ESG ISSUES

The United Nations is taking a leading role in improving the sustainability of our world, including goals for investors, citizens, and corporate entities.

5.4.1 The Six Principles for Responsible Investment (PRI)

The **Principles for Responsible Investment (PRI)**, formerly known as the UN PRI or United Nations Principles for Responsible Investment, is a nonexhaustive set of six proposals designed to "provide a global standard for responsible investing as it relates to environmental, social, and corporate governance (ESG) factors."[29] The six voluntary and aspirational principles are:[30]

> *Principle 1: We will incorporate ESG issues into investment analysis and decision-making processes.*
> *Principle 2: We will be active owners and incorporate ESG issues into our ownership policies and practices.*
> *Principle 3: We will seek appropriate disclosure on ESG issues by the entities in which we invest.*
> *Principle 4: We will promote acceptance and implementation of the Principles within the investment industry.*
> *Principle 5: We will work together to enhance our effectiveness in implementing the Principles.*
> *Principle 6: We will each report on our activities and progress towards implementing the Principles.*

5.4.2 The Sustainable Development Goals (SDGs)

In 2015, the United Nations published a list of 17 goals to improve the plight of the human race, seeking to improve incomes, living conditions, and reduce poverty and inequality worldwide while stalling or reversing the impact of climate change. These goals are meant to drastically improve global conditions by the year 2030.

EXHIBIT 5.1 The United Nations Sustainable Development Goals
Source: United Nations www.un.org.

5.5   ESG FIDUCIARY RESPONSIBILITIES AND REGULATION

Regulations regarding fiduciary responsibilities in the context of ESG issues are in a state of change throughout the world. This section is an interpretation of these regulations as of mid-2019.

5.5.1   ESG and Fiduciary Responsibilities in the US

There is no doubt that, if from no other perspective than that of potential fines and litigation, ESG matters should be included in all investment decisions in which ESG issues can affect future potential expected cash flows and their risks. The nontrivial question is whether, from a fiduciary perspective, financial managers should consider ESG issues beyond their direct financial effect on an investment. Simply put, is it appropriate for a financial manager to base investment decisions on a desire to improve the world without the express direction of the investor?

Under the Investment Advisers Act of 1940, fiduciary duties cannot conflict with the clients' best interests. Schanzenbach and Sitkoff[31] show that:

> *ESG investing is permissible under trust fiduciary law only if two conditions are satisfied: (1) the fiduciary believes in good faith that ESG investing will benefit the beneficiary directly by improving risk-adjusted return, and (2) the fiduciary's exclusive motive for ESG investing is to obtain this direct benefit. We reject the claim that the law imposes any specific investment strategy on fiduciary investors, ESG or otherwise.*

Schanzenbach and Sitkoff note that:

> *In the context of a private trust, a trustee must conduct the trust's investment program in the sole interest of the beneficiary as defined by the terms and purpose of the trust. To be sure, in some cases the terms and purpose of the trust might point to an objective for the investment program other than portfolio efficiency.*

Thus, Schanzenbach and Sitkoff recognize the legitimacy of issues such as ESG if a trust directs purposes considered other than financial considerations.

Schanzenbach and Sitkoff conclude by noting:

> *Fiduciaries who reasonably conclude that ESG factors will improve portfolio performance, and are solely motivated by this possibility, should have no hesitation in using them.*

Unless explicitly directed by the investor, fiduciaries in the US are directed to only invest with a goal of maximizing returns relative to the financial risk constraints of the client. In 2015 and 2016, the US Department of Labor confirmed that fiduciaries may consider ESG issues while investing, but only if those issues are directly relevant to the return, risk, and economic outlook of each investment. The rules appear to specifically prohibit an investment that has, say, a social goal of improving employment in a specific industry or region, if that investment would create jobs while reducing the risk-adjusted financial return to plan beneficiaries. That is, investments should be made in the interest of plan beneficiaries with secondary goals of ESG being allowable if those goals do not negatively impact the risk and return outlook for the investment.

As noted above, ESG regulation in the US is still in development, however, the Securities and Exchange Commission and federal securities laws require public companies to disclose material ESG topics in offering materials, 10-Ks, and other reports. As there are currently few formal regulations enacted around ESG investing in the US, regulators are concerned with "greenwashing." **Greenwashing** occurs when investment promoters mislead prospective investors with overstated claims regarding the likely social impact of an investment opportunity.

5.5.2 ESG and Fiduciary Responsibilities in Europe

The European Commission (EC) as of 2019 set forth proposals to require disclosure of and transparency with regard to sustainable finance (i.e., ESG-related issues) "to clarify asset managers' and institutional investors' duties regarding sustainability," and to strengthen "the transparency of companies on their environmental, social, and governance (ESG) policies."[32]

European regulation is increasingly supporting mandatory disclosure and consideration of ESG-related issues. However, the exact implication of increased consideration of ESG issues is uncertain. To be clear, there should be no doubt that at least indirect consideration of ESG issues by investment fiduciaries and other professionals is part of best practices to the extent that such issues can alter expected return and risk. In other words, ESG issues can affect risk and return of investments if for no other reason than through potential fines and litigation.

The key issue is whether investment professionals are being allowed—or even forced—to sacrifice risk-adjusted returns to pursue perceived societal goals of ESG. While requirements for sacrificing returns on private investments for ESG goals are not clear and explicit, the existing proposals and discussions make clear that a major goal of the legislation supporting sustainable finance is to reduce pressures on the environment, reduce emissions, and minimize waste in the use of natural resources.[33]

As of this writing, the ultimate outcome of legislative proposals in Europe is unclear with regard to the key issue: are fiduciaries and/or other investors being required to tilt portfolios through incorporation of ESG issues in a way that can be expected to result in less financially attractive combinations of risk and return?

5.5.3 ESG and Fiduciary Responsibilities in Asia

In referring to regulations in China, Hong Kong, India, Malaysia, Singapore, and South Korea, the 60-page "Investor obligations and duties in six Asian markets" comments:[34]

> *despite growing awareness of responsible investment, many investors have yet to fully integrate ESG factors into their investment decision-making processes. Public policy and regulation are a key influence. Currently, these markets have few formal requirements to integrate ESG factors, but investor obligations and duties are dynamic concepts that continuously evolve as society changes.*

Hong Kong appears to be slightly ahead of other Asian countries with respect to considering ESG investing. The Hong Kong Strategic Framework for Green Finance was announced by the Securities and Futures Commission in September 2018 to promote Hong Kong as an international green finance center. The goal of the framework is to facilitate the development of a wide range of green-related investments (including listed green products, as well as unlisted, exchange-traded, and OTC green products) with disclosure guidance, harmonized criteria, and frameworks to facilitate disclosure and reporting.

5.5.4   ESG Compliance and Risk Management for Asset Managers

Since the regulations in ESG investing continue to evolve, creating ESG compliance and risk management processes and procedures can be challenging. The extent of controls needed depends on the extent of the firm's ESG investing and its commitments to ESG. Generally, the Chief Compliance Officer is in the best position to test and document the firm's adherence to ESG commitments. Examples of areas that a firm's compliance and risk management framework should address include, but are not limited to:

- Reviewing any marketing materials to confirm that greenwashing is not occurring.
- Creating ESG policies and procedures that are tailored to the firm's ESG fund offerings.
- Implementing controls around the portfolio management process to ensure appropriate adherence to: (1) ESG-related commitment/directives in client management agreements and fund offering documents; and (2) ESG-related investment objectives, strategies, and policies.
- With respect to private fund management companies, consideration as to whether or not they align with ESG principles of the fund and/or its adviser.
- Developing methods to analyze and act on ESG-related investment risks.
- Testing investment decisions over time to measure contributions to or exceptions from ESG policies and/or strategies.

5.6   METHODS OF ESG INVESTING

There are four broad methods of approaching ESG investments: negative or exclusionary screening; positive or inclusionary screening; engagement and proxy voting; and impact investing.

5.6.1   Negative versus Positive Screening

Some of the earliest investors focused on socially responsible investing (SRI), often due to their strong religious or moral beliefs. These investors focused on **negative or exclusionary screening,** which chose not to invest in entire industries of publicly-traded companies due to the firm's involvement in activities deemed objectionable, often based on the morals or religion of the investor. This style of investing specifically excluded investments in **sin stocks,** such as firms profiting from gambling, tobacco, or alcohol sales. Investors found the underlying activity drivers of these sin stocks so objectionable that an investment in such firms was avoided regardless of the potential return that could be earned on these investments.

A subsequent version of screening was **positive screening,** where an investor's portfolio was designed to focus on publicly-traded firms that were judged to have operations that performed in an exemplary manner on one or more ESG issue. This could be investing in a company that embraces renewable energy sources to power its operations, a company that has equitable pay regardless of gender, or significant diversity in board and executive roles. Investors who employ a positive screening methodology may do so with the belief that funds invested in the most sustainable companies may offer lower downside risk than the broader market.[35]

5.6.2 Engagement and Proxy Voting

Some investors may prefer to not build portfolios using either positive or negative screening, as their view is that every share of stock is owned by an investor and that the company's operations are not penalized by someone who sells the stock or helped by someone who buys the stock. The simple fact of one investor buying or selling a stock will not influence the company to change or improve their ESG standing. Investors with this view may choose to take a more active role, either through impact investing in private ventures or directly engaging with publicly-traded companies.

In an **engagement strategy,** an investor with a long position in the stock starts a dialogue with the company with a specific agenda on how to improve the ESG standing of the company. Investors may have a variety of agendas. For companies involved in energy or manufacturing, the agenda is often to improve the environmental footprint of a company. Other investors may engage with a company around board issues, such as diversity or executive compensation. For some, the agenda is simply to improve disclosure, prompting the company to be more transparent about how the firm ranks on behaviors and disclosures of ESG issues.

In some cases, this conversation may be collaborative and private, where the company and the investor work behind the scenes to improve one or more concerns regarding the company's operations. In other cases, the conversation may be public and combative, where the investor believes that the company will not cooperate without the negative publicity that an investor can create. In extreme cases, an investor will create an opportunity for proxy voting by sponsoring an initiative for all shareholders to vote on how the company should change their operations. This differs from standard or passive **proxy voting,** where shareholders vote on issues put up for election by management, typically focused on routine elections of board members and service providers.

5.6.3 Impact Investing

Closely related to materiality is impact investing. Materiality, in the context of ESG, examines the extent to which particular ESG issues can have an impact and it is an important attribute in the processes of evaluation and analysis. **Impact investing** is the inclusion of ESG and related issues in the asset allocation and security decisions of the investor with the goal of generating positive environmental and social influence alongside financial returns. Impact investing focuses on the process of asset allocation and the prioritization of investments by the perceived degree of influence or materiality that the investment offers regarding nonfinancial issues addressed by ESG concerns. Successful impact investing is often discussed as optimizing the combination of (risk-adjusted) financial return and ESG-related impact. Advocates view impact investing as the continuum between (the nexus of) philanthropy and financially-driven investing.

Many believe that impact investing is most effective in venture capital and private equity, where an investment is specifically targeted to a new project that would not otherwise receive funding, such as entrepreneurs or water quality in emerging markets.

The Global Impact Investing Network (GIIN) notes that impact investments can be made across asset classes and proposes elements of impact investing, three of which are summarized as follows:[36]

INTENTIONALITY: "Impact investments intentionally contribute to social and environmental solutions. This differentiates them from other strategies such as ESG investing, Responsible Investing, and screening strategies."[37]

FINANCIAL RETURNS: "Impact investments seek a financial return on capital that can range from below market rate to risk-adjusted market rate. This distinguishes them from philanthropy."[38]

IMPACT MEASUREMENT: "A hallmark of impact investing is the commitment of the investor to measure and report the social and environmental performance of underlying investments."[39]

5.6.3.1 Two Categories Of Impact Investments

There are two categories important to impact investing in the US based on tax considerations:

MISSION-RELATED INVESTMENTS (MRIs): **Mission-related investments (MRI)** are investments viewed as offering a combination of ESG impact as well as financial return. MRIs are often further defined as offering competitive risk-adjusted returns along with ESG impact.

PROGRAM-RELATED INVESTMENTS (PRIs): **Program-related investments (PRI)** are investments offering ESG impact and no financial return or offering a combination of ESG impact as well as a subcompetitive risk adjusted financial return.

The importance of the distinction is primarily based on US tax rules for not-for-profit organizations. The US Internal Revenue Service specifies **three characteristics of a program-related investment:**[40]

1. *The primary purpose is to accomplish one or more of the foundation's exempt purposes,*
2. *Production of income or appreciation of property is not a significant purpose, and*
3. *Influencing legislation or taking part in political campaigns on behalf of candidates is not a purpose.*

Investments in PRIs qualify for tax advantages to charitable organizations in the US. For example, PRIs can be treated as a qualifying distribution for a foundation similar to direct charitable grants.

Finally, the distinction between philanthropy, MRIs, and PRIs is related to enviropreneurship. **Enviropreneurship** is an emerging branch of entrepreneurship that deals with a mixed motive of profit-seeking and concern regarding ESG-related issues, specifically using entrepreneurship to address environmental issues.[41] Enviropreneurship tends to emanate from opportunities created by entrepreneurs rather than directed by investors or governments.

5.6.3.2 The Five Steps of Implementing Impact Investing

There are many approaches to implementing impact investing. This section provides an overview of common steps. The first part of the process of implementation of impact investing involves mission and themes:[42]

ARTICULATING MISSION AND VALUES: Articulating the missions and values relevant to a program of impact investing emanates from the investor's core motives, values, and mission. The goal of this step is to clarify and build consensus regarding the mission and values of the program of impact investing, expressed in part as the identification of target areas.

CREATING IMPACT THEMES OR THESES: Selecting the themes or theses of an impact investment program begins at the broadest levels, such as environmental, social, governance, and other issues, and drills down towards more specific themes. The themes may be from one or several of the broad categories of ESG-related issues and may share substantial commonalities, or may be highly diverse depending on the investor's mission and values. The inclusion of materiality in this step can be used to identify priorities between missions. The resulting themes or theses form the social target of the impact investment program.

Common next steps in the process of implementing an impact investing program are incorporating the targets of the social program into an investment framework or set of policies. Saltuk and El Idrissi describe the use of target graphs to reflect the balance among three targets: return, risk, and impact.[43]

DEVELOPING IMPACT INVESTMENT POLICY: The investment policy specifies the method by which the ESG-related targets of the impact investing program will be included into the portfolio construction and management processes. For example, Saltuk and El Idrissi[44] describe target portfolio graphs. Exhibit 5.2 illustrates a sample target portfolio graph with three axes: return, risk, and (social) impact. The closer any point on the graph is to each of the three labels, the more that label represents a high priority. The shaded areas of Exhibit 5.2 depict targeted combinations of return, risk, and impact for an investor with a high priority for low risk, a high priority for impact, and a relatively low priority for return.

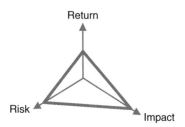

EXHIBIT 5.2 Target Portfolio
Graphs for Return, Impact, and
Risk[45]

GENERATE AND EVALUATE DEAL FLOW: Target graphs, discussed in the previous section
in the context of a portfolio, can be used to depict the evaluation of individual assets. Data such as ESG ratings and materiality analysis can be used to
assess the likely impact of various investments.

PORTFOLIO CONSTRUCTION AND MANAGEMENT: The top-down asset allocation decision should reflect the tendency of different asset classes to offer markedly
different opportunities for various ESG-related issues (as well as differences
in risk and return). For example, timber would tend to be low risk, low
expected return, and would have an impact factor that depends on the
nature of the opportunities—such as timber with sustainable practices.
The portfolio construction begins with an optimization of a top-down
tradeoff between the three goals of high expected return, low risk, and high
impact and the opportunities afforded by different asset classes. Finally,
the selection and weighting of individual investment opportunities—the
bottom-up process—involves the tradeoffs between the expected returns,
risks, and impacts of the individual investments.

5.6.3.3 Evidence from Research on Impact Investing in Illiquid Investments

Barber, Morse, and Yasuda[45] examined whether investors have sacrificed expected
returns for social impact in the case of private equity (PE) funds. They examined
the performance of 159 impact private equity funds (venture capital and growth
equity) that intentionally and explicitly asserted a dual purpose of financial return
and ESG-related goals over the period 1995–2014 relative to a total sample of over
5,000 funds. It should be noted that the possibility exists that some funds are green-
washed.

LOWER IRRs FOR IMPACT FUNDS: Barber, Morse and Yasuda document that "the
annualized internal rate of return (IRR) on impact funds is 4.7 percentage points
lower than traditional VC funds, after controlling for industry, vintage year, fund
sequence, and geography."[46]

LOWER IRRs ACCEPTED BY SOME INVESTORS: The authors then form an estimate of
ESG impact as one of many potential variables in modeling the investment decision of investors. Other variables included to explain investor fund choices included

"a rich array of fund (e.g., manager quality) and investor characteristics as controls."[47] Their empirical analysis finds that "Using estimates from logit models, the average investor exhibits a willingness to pay 3.4 percentage points in expected excess IRR for impact funds."[48] This willingness to pay is the lower expected return apparently accepted by investors exhibiting a preference for investment opportunities in private equity with an expressed objective of social impact.

LOWER IRRs ACCEPTED BY PARTICULAR TYPES OF INVESTORS: Their research further identifies the following organization types as having higher willingness to pay: developmental organizations, banks, insurance companies, public pension funds, UN PRI signatories, and investors in Europe, Latin America, and Africa. Further they find that program-focused investors and investors facing political or regulatory pressures exhibit higher willingness to pay for social impact in the form of lower expected returns. Investors that are required to maximize risk-adjusted financial returns (i.e., required to be shareholder wealth maximizers) were not found to be willing to accept lower IRRs for social impact.

Do investors knowingly bear lower risk-adjusted expected returns in private equity to generate higher social impact benefits or does the high demand for social impact investments result in too many dollars chasing too few attractive opportunities? In cases of high investor demand for social impact and in the case of private equity, perhaps investors with a social mission end up with inferior managers (who need to promote themselves as being attractive from an ESG perspective) or with managers who are forced to select portfolio companies with inferior financial prospects due to their mandate.

Several notes of caution regarding the empirics cited in this section include: (1) aggregated IRRs of PE funds may be poor indicators of performance; (2) the research paper has been widely presented to and commented on by leading academic scholars and the paper won the Moskowitz Prize for the "best paper on socially responsible investing" (which is a global award recognizing outstanding quantitative research in sustainable and responsible investing), but the paper was not published in a refereed journal as of July 2019; and (3) the methods used in the paper to infer willingness to pay may not be highly reliable in ascertaining the mindset of investors regarding relative preferences for financial return and social objectives.

5.7 MARKET-BASED METHODS OF ADDRESSING ESG ISSUES

This section discusses theories of economic behavior in free markets and regulated markets as well as some potential market-based methods of dealing with ESG-related issues. Nobel laureate Friedrich Hayek noted the inability of subsets of individuals to possess the knowledge to make and impose efficient economic decisions for an entire economy or society. Hayek asserts the importance of decentralized decision making in which individuals make decisions regarding and involving the information sets that only they possess. As Shawn Regan puts it:

> *the problem facing human societies is not how any one authority or group of experts can direct economic activity as it relates to the use or conservation of resources. Instead, the challenge is for the knowledge that is dispersed*

throughout society to be conveyed in a way so that individual market actors can adjust their behavior in response to changes of which they could not be fully aware. Hayek referred to this challenge as one of "rapid adaptation to changes in the particular circumstances of time and place," and viewed the price system as the mechanism for humans to adapt to changing market circumstance.[49]

5.7.1 Background on Externalities and Markets

In financial economics, ESG-related issues are often approached in the context of theories of law and regulation, negative externalities, and the tragedy of the commons. **Negative externalities** are adverse consequences on third-party entities caused by contracts or transactions controlled by two or more primary parties and can include pollution, noise, congestion, and other potentially deleterious consequences to parties that did not have control of the contract or transaction. The problem of negative externalities is related to the tragedy of the commons. In economics, the **tragedy of the commons** is the problem that individuals or entities will tend to overconsume or undervalue natural resources and other assets that are available for common use (i.e., shared or nonexcludable) since the costs are borne by all. When an individual or entity consumes assets that belong to them only, the cost is borne solely by the asset's owner and so the level of consumption will be optimal.

The tragedy of the commons is useful in understanding a variety of ESG concerns. In particular, environmental concerns clearly deal with the problem of one or more entities causing widespread environmental damage (perhaps to billions of people) that taken as a whole may cause substantial harm. However, the people with direct control over each entity's operations (e.g., management and shareholders) likely bear only a miniscule quantity of the total environmental damage.

5.7.2 The Coase Theorem

The **Coase theorem** asserts that, in competitive and frictionless markets, economically efficient production and distribution will occur regardless of how governments divide property rights. In other words and in the context of the ESG discussion, Coase asserts that whether the law sides with shareholders who claim a right to generate negative externalities or with the victims of negative externalities will not interfere with the ability of the parties to negotiate the most efficient resolution to the dispute so that they can share in the net benefits (or least costs).

For example, consider a noisy manufacturer situated next to a hotel that is generating noise that is harming the hotel's ability to attract and please guests. The cost to soundproof the hotel is $2 million, the cost to soundproof the manufacturer's building is $3 million, and the loss in revenues and guest satisfaction to the hotel from the noise is estimated to have a present value cost of $1 million. The hotel sues the manufacturer in court. The Coase theorem asserts that in the absence of transactions costs, the optimal solution will ensue regardless of the legal decision. Regardless of the ruling, the total wealth-maximizing solution is for the hotel not to install soundproofing because the cost of the soundproofing exceeds its value.

5.7.3   Cap and Trade Programs

Cap and trade is a government program regarding pollution or other externalities that specifies caps (allowances) on the activity for each entity but allows each entity to trade its rights (e.g., its allotment of pollution). Thus, each entity can be viewed as having a private property right to, for example, pollute up to its assigned cap. Importantly, cap and trade programs allow each entity to exchange these rights. Economic reasoning finds that these exchange rights serve as a mechanism through which pollution reductions or other goals will be generated by those entities who can accomplish the reductions at the least financial cost (i.e., least economic burdens to society based on market prices).

For example, Anderson and Leal[50] describe a US cap and trade program to reduce sulfur dioxide emissions in the 1990s. The program's success was remarkable—quickly exceeding its stated goals of emission reductions. Eventually, the market value of the rights to emit sulfur dioxide plummeted causing large losses to those entities that had purchased them. The losses may have been caused by a combination of the program's success or by government-imposed changes to the rules. Regardless, the program illustrated the potential advantages to an approach to reducing negative externalities (or, potentially, increasing positive externalities) that harnesses results-based incentives and comparative advantages rather than an approach of strict and uniform regulations.

5.8   ESG AND SPECIAL INVESTMENT CONSIDERATION

This section addresses the key issue of the extent, if any, to which ESG issues should receive special consideration in the valuation of investments and the management of investment portfolios.

5.8.1   Special Consideration, Cash Flows, Returns, and Risk

Traditional financial principles base asset valuation on cash flows adjusted for time and risk. ESG considerations obviously affect future cash flows and therefore ESG issues should, at a minimum, be considered (similar to any other effects) to the extent that they are determinants of future cash flows and their likelihoods. The key issue is whether investments viewed as attractive for their ESG profiles deserve "favorable" consideration above and beyond their possible effects on future cash flows. In other words, should analysts assign higher value to those investments with attractive ESG profiles through the use of lower discount rates? In this sense, special consideration of ESG issues would suggest that expected future cash flows of investments with attractive ESG profiles should receive higher values than otherwise identical cash flows from investments with less attractive ESG profiles.

5.8.2   The Case for Special Consideration of ESG Issues

Three primary justifications for special consideration of ESG issues (i.e., considerations above and beyond an investment's direct effects on anticipated cash flows and risk) may be hypothesized as follows:

1. The historic total returns from portfolios of listed securities based on ESG concerns and adjusted for risk based on single-market-factor methods appear to be equally attractive, and perhaps in some cases or jurisdictions more attractive, than portfolios that ignore or eschew ESG concerns.[51]
2. Investment managers have a duty to protect shareholders from the deleterious effects of ESG-related risks such as litigation, penalties, and adverse public images of those firms that do not aggressively incorporate ESG issues in their corporate policies and decisions.
3. Investment managers who favor ESG-compatible investments with higher allocations contribute to a better world which in turn confers noncash benefits on its investors along with all other living beings.

5.8.3 The Case Against Special Consideration of ESG Issues

Three primary justifications against special consideration of ESG issues (i.e., not adding value above and beyond their direct effects on anticipated cash flows to estimated valuations of investments with favorable ESG profiles) may be hypothesized as follows:

1. The historic total returns from portfolios based on ESG concerns and adjusted for risk based on multi-factor methods appear to be only equally attractive to portfolios with similar factor exposures that ignore or eschew ESG concerns.[51]
2. Investment managers, in the absence of directions to the contrary from their clients, have a legal fiduciary duty in the US and possibly elsewhere to invest solely to benefit the client from a financial perspective.
3. Investment managers who favor ESG-compatible investments with higher allocations for nonfinancial reasons or by applying lower risk-adjusted discount rates are redirecting the wealth of their clients to their personally-favored causes.

NOTES

1. See Kell, 2018
2. See Hummels et al. (2018).
3. See https://www.globalreporting.org/Information/about-gri/Pages/default.aspx. (accessed July 2019).
4. Ibid.
5. Ibid.
6. See KPMG (2017).
7. See Auer and Schuhmacher (2016).
8. See Belghitar, et al. (2014).
9. See Giese and Lee (2019).
10. See Hvidkjær (2017).
11. See Rabener (2019).
12. Util.co, "About us." https://www.util.co/about-us (accessed July 2019).
13. See Barnett (2018).
14. Ibid.
15. "G4 Sustainability Reporting Guidelines, the Global Reporting Initiative," accessed July 2019 at https://www2.globalreporting.org/standards/g4/Pages/default.aspx.

16. Ibid., p. 17.
17. Ibid., p. 3.
18. "Our Mission." https://www.fsb-tcfd.org/ (accessed July 2019).
19. See KPMG/NZ (2017).
20. See Anteagroup (2019).
21. Ibid.
22. https://www.sasb.org/governance/ (accessed July 2019).
23. (https://materiality.sasb.org/) (accessed July 2019).
24. Adapted from Cornerstone Capital Group's *Global Markets Strategy*, "A Shifting ESG Materiality Matrix: What Has Mattered, What May Matter." 21 October 2015. https://cornerstonecapinc.com/wp-content/uploads/2015/10/Materiality-Matrix-2-October-21.pdf
25. Ibid.
26. Ibid.
27. Ibid.
28. Ibid.
29. See Chen, James, "UN Principles for Responsible Investment," (PRI), https://www.investopedia.com/terms/u/un-principles-responsible-investment-pri.asp.
30. "What are the Principles for Responsible Investment?" https://www.unpri.org/pri/what-are-the-principles-for-responsible-investment.
31. See Schanzenbach and Sitkoff (2018).
32. See "Sustainable Finance." https://ec.europa.eu/info/business-economy-euro/banking-and-finance/sustainable-finance_en.
33. Ibid.
34. UNPRI in collaboration with UNEP FI and Generation Foundation. 2016. "Investor obligations and duties in six Asian markets." https://www.unpri.org/fiduciary-duty/investor-obligations-and-duties-in-six-asian-markets/266.article.
35. Morgan Stanley "Sustainable Reality: Analyzing Risk and Returns of Sustainable Funds." https://www.morganstanley.com/pub/content/dam/msdotcom/ideas/sustainable-investing-offers-financial-performance-lowered-risk/Sustainable_Reality_Analyzing_Risk_and_Returns_of_Sustainable_Funds.pdf.
36. The Global Impact Investing Network (GIIN), "Core Characteristics of Impact Investing." https://thegiin.org/assets/Core%20Characteristics_webfile.pdf.
37. Ibid.
38. Ibid.
39. Ibid.
40. "Program-Related Investments." https://www.irs.gov/charities-non-profits/private-foundations/program-related-investments.
41. Lofthouse, J. "The Power of Entrepreneurs to Solve Environmental Problems." Strata.org, 2019. https://www.strata.org/wp-content/uploads/2019/06/power-of-entrepreneurs.pdf.
42. See Godeke and Pomares (2009).
43. See Saltuk and El Idrissi (2012).
44. Ibid.
45. Ibid.
46. See Barber et al. (2019).
47. Ibid.
48. Ibid.
49. Ibid.
50. See Anderson and Leal (2001, p. 23).
51. See Rabener (2019).

REFERENCES

Anderson T. L. and D. R. Leal. 2001. *Free Market Environmentalism*. New York, NY: Palgrave. 10.1057/9780312299736.

Anteagroup. 2019. "7 Basic Steps for Conducting a Successful Materiality Assessment." https://us.anteagroup.com/en-us/blog/7-basic-steps-conducting-successful-materiality-assessment.

Auer, B. R. and F. Schuhmacher. 2016. "Do Socially (Ir)responsible Investments Pay? New evidence from International ESG Data." 59 (February): 51–62. 10.1016/j.qref.2015.07.002.

Barber, B. M., A. Morse, and A. Yasuda. 2019. "Impact Investing." https://ssrn.com/abstract=2705556 or http://dx.doi.org/10.2139/ssrn.2705556.

Barnett, S. 2018. "The Curious Case of ESG Ratings." https://medium.com/@stephenjbarnett/the-curious-case-of-esg-ratings-5ad2d6947bf2.

Belghitar, Y., E. Clark, and N. Deshmukh. 2014. "Does It Pay to be Ethical? Evidence from the FTSE4Good." *Journal of Banking & Finance* 47: 54–62.

Giese, G. and L.-E. Lee. 2019."Weighing the Evidence: ESG and Equity Returns," MCSI ESG Research LLC, April. https://www.eticanews.it/wp-content/uploads/2019/06/Research_Insight_Weighing_the_Evidence_ESG-and-Equity-Returns.pdf.

Godeke, S. and R. Pomares. 2009. *Solutions for Impact Investors: From Strategy to Implementation*. New York, NY: The Rockefeller Philanthropy Advisors, https://thegiin.org/assets/binary-data/RESOURCE/download_file/000/000/53-1.pdf, accessed July 2019.

Hummels, H., R. Bauer, and J. Mertens. 2018. "Going Mainstream- The Future of ESG Investing," *Newsweek Vantage*, September 16. https://d.newsweek.com/en/file/459599/newsweek-vantage-future-esg.pdf

Hvidkjær, S. 2017. "ESG Investing: A Literature Review." Dansif. https://dansif.dk/wp-content/uploads/2019/01/Litterature-review-UK-Sep-2017.pdf.

Kell, G. 2018. "The Remarkable Rise of ESG." *Forbes*, July 11. https://www.forbes.com/sites/georgkell/2018/07/11/the-remarkable-rise-of-esg/#257770731695.

KPMG. 2017. "The Road Ahead: The KPMG Survey of Corporate responsibility Reporting 2017." https://assets.kpmg/content/dam/kpmg/xx/pdf/2017/10/kpmg-survey-of-corporate-responsibility-reporting-2017.pdf.

KPMG/NZ, 2017. "Environmental, Social and Governance (ESG) Materiality, Assessment." https://assets.kpmg/content/dam/kpmg/nz/pdf/September/esg-materiality-assessment-2017-kpmg-nz.pdf.

Rabener, N. 2019. "ESG Investing: Too Good to Be True?" https://blogs.cfainstitute.org/investor/2019/01/14/esg-factor-investing-too-good-to-be-true/.

Saltuk, Y. and A. El Idrissi. 2012. "A Portfolio Approach to Impact Investment." JPMorgan, https://www.jpmorganchase.com/corporate/socialfinance/document/121001_A_Portfolio_Approach_to_Impact_Investment.pdf.

Schanzenbach, M. M. and R. H. Sitkoff. 2018. "The Law and Economics of Environmental, Social, and Governance Investing by a Fiduciary," Draft of September 5, 2018, Discussion Paper No. 971, 09/2018, Harvard Law School, Cambridge, MA. https://corpgov.law.harvard.edu/2018/09/20/the-law-and-economics-of-environmental-social-and-governance-investing-by-a-fiduciary/.

Models

The complex task of managing an institutional-quality portfolio of traditional and alternative investments requires careful analysis and sound reasoning. Financial models are essential tools of modern portfolio management. Part 2 begins with an overview of types of models and then reviews foundational financial models from interest rate models, to credit models, and finally to multi-factor equity models.

CHAPTER 6

Modeling Overview and Interest Rate Models

Financial models are abstractions or simplifications of reality designed to provide insights into the essential relations that underlie the complex world of financial instruments and financial markets. Models express the foundational concepts underlying investment strategies and approaches to risk management.

Models contain exogenous and endogenous values. An **exogenous variable** is a value that is determined outside a model and is therefore taken as a given. An **endogenous variable** is determined inside a model and therefore takes on whatever value the model prescribes.

For example, a cash management model for an endowment may take as exogenous the amount of cash being received from donations and generated as income from investments. Endogenous variables may include decision variables such as the amount of money to be invested in new deals.

This chapter provides an overview of different types of models, such as theoretical versus empirical, and provides details regarding financial models beginning with the simplest interest rate models.

6.1 TYPES OF MODELS UNDERLYING INVESTMENT STRATEGIES

Numerous ways of distinguishing between financial models exist. For example, one of the primary distinctions between models of importance in alternative investments is the one between single-factor and multiple-factor models. The CAIA Level I curriculum focuses on single-factor models, while this level emphasizes multi-factor models. Additionally, there are other distinctions.

A better understanding of the differences between models can prove helpful. For example, investment strategies may be viewed as differing by their underlying models. Understanding the types of models may assist an asset allocator in forming portfolios that are better diversified across model types. This section begins by briefly touching on four common methodological distinctions.

6.1.1 Normative Strategies versus Positive Strategies

Evaluating the potential effectiveness of an investment strategy is a key aspect of alternative investing. Understanding whether a strategy is based on normative reasoning, positive reasoning, or both is essential.

In financial economics, a **normative model** attempts to describe how people and prices *ought* to behave. A **positive model** attempts to describe how people and prices *actually* behave. For example, when a hedge fund manager implements a trade in an attempt to benefit from a forecasted change in prices, did the manager base that forecast on how prices should behave or by observing how prices have behaved in the past? This essential issue is at the heart of analyzing many trading strategies and is perhaps the most fundamental aspect of a trading strategy that should be understood.

Normative economic models tend to be most useful in helping explain underlying forces that might drive rational financial decisions under idealized circumstances and, to a lesser extent, under more realistic conditions. Normative approaches can be used to identify the potential mispricing of securities by identifying how securities should be priced. Trading strategies based on normative reasoning anticipate that actual prices will converge toward normatively derived values if the models are well designed. Arbitrage-free pricing models are normative models. Arbitrage-free models describe relationships that should hold given that the actions of arbitrageurs will eliminate arbitrage opportunities. For example, strategies based on put–call parity are normative strategies.

Often, people do not behave in adherence to the rational prescriptions of economic theory. Positive economic models try to explain past behavior and then predict future behavior. Positive economic models are often used to try to identify mispricing of securities by recognizing patterns in actual price movement. Technical trading strategies are based on positive economic modeling. For example, a strategy based on point-and-figure charts is a positive strategy.

Alternative investment analysis uses both normative and positive modeling. The effectiveness of models should not be judged solely on the reality of their assumptions or on their ability to explain the past. Primary attention should be given to their ability to predict the future. Both normative and positive models can be useful in understanding and predicting future behavior.

6.1.2 Theoretical versus Empirical Approaches

An issue closely related to normative and positive modeling is theoretical and empirical modeling. **Theoretical models** describe behavior using deduction and assumptions that reflect well-established underlying behavior. For example, the price of simple options can be deduced through a number of underlying assumptions, including that financial markets are perfect, that stock prices follow a particular process, and that arbitrage opportunities do not exist. Empirical models are primarily based on observed behavior. For example, the relationship between the observed prices of option trades and particular underlying variables might be analyzed through time and fitted with an approximation function. Whether the theoretical approach or the empirical approach is more effective in explaining and predicting behavior depends on the complexity of the relationships and the reliability of the data.

Theoretical models tend to explain behavior accurately in more simplified situations, in which the relationships among variables can be somewhat clearly understood through logic. Arbitrage-free models are developed by theory.

Empirical models tend to explain complex behavior relatively well when there are many data points available and when the relative behavior of the variables is fixed or is changing in predictable ways. For example, an empirical model might be better than a theoretical model in the case of a frequently traded but extremely complex security with many overlapping option features. In such a complex case, the most accurate models might simply fit curves to the relationships based on observations of past data. The numerous and complex attributes of the security may make theoretical modeling impractical.

Alternative investing tends to lend itself more to empirical models than to theoretical models. The reason is that alternative investments tend to be characterized by illiquidity, changing risks, dynamic strategies, or other complexities that can foil theoretical modeling. Empirical modeling in the midst of such complexities, however, may also be inadequate, especially when data are limited.

6.1.3 Applied versus Abstract Approaches

The distinction between applied and abstract approaches is perhaps the easiest in understanding research methods. **Applied models** are designed to address immediate real-world challenges and opportunities. For example, Markowitz's model, which is an applied model, provides useful insights for accomplishing diversification efficiently. Many Markowitz-style models are used throughout traditional and alternative investing to manage portfolios. Most asset pricing models are applied models.

Abstract models, also called basic models, tend to have applicability only in solving real-world challenges of the future. Abstract models tend to be theoretical models that explain hypothetical behavior in less realistic scenarios. For example, a model might be constructed that describes how two people with specific utility functions might bargain with regard to prices in a world with only two people and two risk factors. Eventually, abstract models can lead to innovative applications. Models in alternative investing, especially those described in this book, are applied models. They are intended and used for solving immediate real-world problems, such as managing risk and evaluating potentially profitable investment opportunities.

6.1.4 Cross-Sectional versus Time-Series Approaches

Both cross-sectional and time-series models are used throughout economic modeling in alternative investments. **Cross-sectional models** analyze relationships across characteristics or variables observed at a single point in time such as when investment returns are used to explain the differences in risk premiums. **Time-series models** analyze behavior of a single subject or set of subjects through time. When a data set includes multiple subjects and multiple time periods, it is often called a panel data set, and it is analyzed with a panel model. **Panel data sets** combine the two approaches by tracking multiple subjects through time and can also be referred to as longitudinal data sets and cross-sectional time-series data sets.

For example, consider a researcher analyzing returns on REITs (real estate investment trusts) using a particular REIT index where the index is simply an arithmetic average of the returns of each of the REITs. At first, the researcher builds a model that explains the index returns of the REITs through time using such variables as changes in Treasury rates, mortgage rates, and equity prices. This time-series model might tell the researcher how the average REIT returns are explained in terms of various market factors. The researcher might then use a cross-sectional model to attempt to explain why the long-term average returns of various REITs differed. The researcher might regress the long-term returns of the individual REITs against such variables as geographic region, property type, and leverage. If the researcher put all of the short-term returns for each time period and for each REIT into a single data set and econometric model, it would be a panel study.

A large and growing body of time-series analysis focuses on the way an asset's unexplained price risk, measured as its volatility, might change through time. Examples of this approach include autoregressive conditional heteroskedasticity (ARCH) and generalized autoregressive conditional heteroskedasticity (GARCH) analyses, which focus on time-series behavior such as potential patterns through time in the variance of unexplained return.

6.1.5 Importance of Methodology

The primary purpose of this section has been to describe how to identify the nature of a model using four distinctions: normative versus positive, theoretical versus empirical, applied versus abstract, and cross-sectional versus time-series models. It is important to be able to understand investment analysis from a methodological perspective in order to better organize and compare investment strategies. For example, one manager may have identified a profitable trading opportunity by specifying the proper equilibrium price of an asset and recommending trades when the actual price deviated from the ideal price. Another manager may have detected a statistical pattern to actual trading on the last day of each month and used that as a signal for trades. The first manager used a theoretical and normative model, whereas the other manager used an empirical and positive model. Both models were applied. By evaluating these managers in the context of their methods of modeling, an analyst may be able to better evaluate the prospects for investment success.

6.2 EQUILIBRIUM FIXED-INCOME MODELS

Since the time value of money underlies the determination of all asset prices, this first chapter begins with models of default-free fixed-income securities. While theories have been proposed to explain the shape of yield curves (the market expectations hypothesis, liquidity preference hypothesis, market segmentation hypothesis, and preferred habitat hypothesis discussed in Level 1 of the CAIA curriculum), the focus here is on introducing the models that have been developed to explain the evolution of bond values. These models are then used to value fixed-income derivatives.

Equilibrium models of the term structure (also referred to as first-generation models) make assumptions about the structure of fixed-income markets and then use economic reasoning to model bond prices and the term structure of interest rates. The first set of models introduced in this area took the process followed by the short-term interest rate as given. These models assumed that the unbiased expectation hypothesis holds for bond prices, meaning that the expected short-term rates of return on all bonds that are free from credit risk are assumed to be the same. This assumption, along with the exogenously specified process, was then used to model the entire term structure of interest rates. Here, we will introduce two of these models: Vasicek (1977) and Cox, Ingersoll, and Ross (1985).

6.2.1 Vasicek's Short-Term Interest Rate Process

Vasicek's model is a single-factor model of the term structure that assumes constant volatility and that the short-term interest rate drifts toward a prespecified long-term mean level. The model specifies the following mean-reverting process for the short-term rate of interest:

$$\tilde{r}_{t+1} = r_t + k(\mu - r_t) + \sigma\tilde{\varepsilon}_{t+1} \tag{6.1}$$

This model states that next period's short-term rate, $\tilde{r}_{t+1}$, is equal to the current short-term rate, r_t, plus two adjustments. In the first adjustment term, k and μ are constants and positive. According to the first adjustment term, $k(\mu - r_t)$, the next period rate will be higher than the current rate if $\mu > r_t$. Therefore, one can think of μ as the long-term average value of the short-term rate. This means that the short-term rate is likely to increase if it is currently below its long-term value and decrease if it is above the long-term value. This process is said to be mean-reverting, as the short-term rate tends to revert to its long-term mean. The speed of adjustment to the long-term rate is determined by the parameter k. The higher its value k, the faster the short-term rate will approach its long-term mean. The second adjustment factor, $\sigma\tilde{\varepsilon}_{t+1}$, introduces some noise into this adjustment process. The volatility of changes in interest rates is represented by σ and the noise is represented by $\tilde{\varepsilon}_{t+1}$, which is assumed to be a normally distributed random variable with a mean of zero and a standard deviation of 1.

6.2.2   Vasicek's Model and Expected Interest Rates

In terms of expected rates, Equation 6.1 can be used as illustrated in Equation 6.2:

$$E[r_{t+1}] = r_t + \kappa(\mu - r_t) \tag{6.2}$$

In this model, the expected change in the short-term rate $E[r_{t+1} - r_t]$, is given by $\kappa(\mu - r_t)$. For example, if the current short-term rate is 5% and the long-term expected rate is 10%, the next period's short-term rate would be 5.5% for a κ *value of 0.10 and 6% for a κ value of 0.2*. Note that the unexpected change in the short-term rate is given by $\sigma \times \tilde{\varepsilon}$ and that the standard deviation of changes in the short-term rate is σ.

APPLICATION 6.2.2

Suppose the parameters of the Vasicek model are $\mu = 5\%$ *(i.e., the long-term mean level of the short-term interest rate), and the following speed of adjustment parameter is given as $\kappa = 0.8$ and $\sigma = 1\%$*. If the current short-term rate is 4%, what would be the expected short-term rate for the next period? Inserting the given values into Equation 6.2 produces

$$E[r_{t+1}] = 0.04 + 0.8(0.05 - 0.04) = 4.8\%$$

If the current short-term rate is 6%, next year's short-term rate is expected to be 5.2%. Of course, Equation 6.2 has four variables, any one of which could be calculated given the other three.

In Vasicek's model, the volatility of changes in interest rates is constant and does not change as the level of interest rates change. In the previous example, the volatility of interest rate changes will be 1% regardless of the level of interest rates. This is one of the criticisms directed at Vasicek's model.

6.2.3   Vasicek's Model and the Term Structure of Interest Rates

In Vasicek's model, all bond prices are driven by one factor: the short-term interest rate. That is, the only source of uncertainty in the bond market is the random change in the short-term rate of interest. At this point, one may use several approaches to develop a mathematical formula for bond prices. For example, one could assume that the unbiased expectations hypothesis about the term structure holds. Under one form of this hypothesis, all bonds that are free from credit risk (regardless of their maturity) are expected to earn the same rate of return in the short run. Under this assumption, one can then obtain a mathematical formula for the yield to maturity of a zero-coupon bond and the yield curve, or the term structure of interest rates, in Vasicek's model.

6.2.4   Robustness of Vasicek's Model of the Term Structure of Interest Rates

The values of the parameters in Vasicek's model can generate a downward-sloping, an upward-sloping, or a humped term structure. The term structure generated by Vasicek's model can be illustrated using the following example. Suppose that the current short-term interest rate is 5%, the long-term mean (μ) is 7%, the standard deviation is 1%, and the speed of adjustment (κ) is 0.1. Using this set of values generates an upward-sloping term structure of interest rates, as illustrated in the middle structure in Exhibit 6.1.

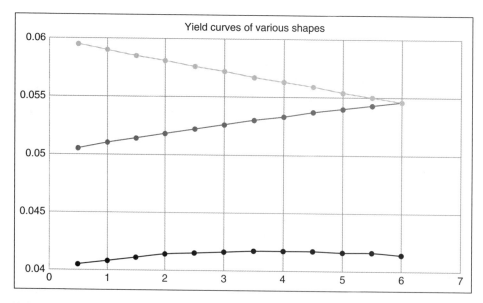

EXHIBIT 6.1   Illustration of Vasicek's Model

Exhibit 6.1 also illustrates the case of a downward-sloping yield curve generated by Vasicek's model (the top structure) and the case of a humped yield curve (the bottom structure). The general slope is driven by the relation between the short rate and the long-term average rate. The hump reflects risk aversion.

6.2.5   The Cox, Ingersoll, and Ross Model of Interest Rates

Vasicek's model has been criticized because it allows the short-term interest rate to be negative. The **Cox, Ingersoll, and Ross model** (CIR model) is a single-factor model that alters the Vasicek model to make the variance of the short-term interest rate proportional to the rate itself, thereby disallowing negative interest rates. In other words, negative rates are prevented because as rates approach zero, their volatility approaches zero. The following equation represents the short-term interest rate process proposed by the CIR model:

$$r_{t+1} = r_t + \kappa(\mu - r_t) + \sqrt{r_t}\sigma\tilde{\varepsilon}_{t+1} \tag{6.3}$$

where the three (constant) parameters κ, μ, and σ have the same meanings as before. The major difference between this model and Vasicek's is that the variance of the change in the short-term rate, $\sigma^2 r_t$, is proportional to the short-term rate. This makes sense, as we observe higher volatility for interest rate changes when the short-term rate is relatively high. The CIR model can generate yield curves with different shapes.

6.3   ARBITRAGE-FREE MODELS OF THE TERM STRUCTURE

Arbitrage-free models of the term structure (also referred to as second-generation models) use a different approach to model bond prices and the yield curve that is parametrized based on observed current interest rates.

6.3.1   Overview of Arbitrage-Free Interest Rate Models

First, a mathematical formula describing bond prices is obtained by arguing that the bond prices should not allow for arbitrage opportunities. In particular, we know that under risk-neutral modeling, the rates of returns on all investments—including bonds—should be equal to the short-term rate. Another distinguishing feature of arbitrage-free models is that the currently observed term structure is used to determine the parameters of the model. As a result, the theoretically derived term-structure model is consistent with the observed term structure. Therefore, any fixed-income derivative security that is priced using this theoretical model will be consistent with the current term structure and will also preclude arbitrage opportunities involving those derivatives and available bonds.

6.3.2   A Single-Factor Arbitrage-Free Model of Interest Rates

Ho and Lee (1986) proposed the first arbitrage-free model of interest rates. The **Ho and Lee model** is a single-factor model that assumes that the short-term interest rate follows a normally distributed process, with a drift parameter that is chosen so that the modeled term structure of interest rates fits the observed term structure of interest rates. Ho and Lee's model of the short-term rate is shown in Equation 6.4:

$$r_{t+1} = r_t + \theta_t + \sigma \tilde{\varepsilon}_{t+1} \tag{6.4}$$

where θ_t is a time-dependent mean change in the short-term rate (chosen to ensure that the model fits the initial term structure of interest rates), σ is the (constant) standard deviation of changes in the short rate, and $\tilde{\varepsilon}_{t+1}$ is a binomial random variable assuming values of $+1$ or -1. Notice that, unlike Vasicek's model, one of the parameters of Ho and Lee's model, θ_t, is not constant and is determined by the current term structure of interest rates.

6.3.3   The Ho and Lee Model in a Binomial Framework

Ho and Lee used the simple model introduced in the previous section as the basis of a binomial model for bond prices. The current zero-coupon bond prices are taken as given and are used to value the parameters of the model based on the currently observed term structure of interest rates. Thereafter, the term structure is assumed to be affected by random changes in interest rates.

   Bond prices evolve in response to random changes in interest rates. Ho and Lee use the well known result that under risk-neutral probabilities the bond price in every state is equal to the expected value of the same bond in the next period discounted at the riskless rate. Using this result and the assumption about the source of uncertainty in the market, Ho and Lee are able to obtain analytical solutions for all bond prices in each future state.

6.3.4   Evaluation of the Ho and Lee Model of Interest Rates

Since the Ho–Lee model is calibrated to fit the currently observed term structure of interest rates, the resulting prices for callable bonds, bond options, swaptions, and other interest rate derivatives will be consistent with the current term structure. In other words, the actions of arbitrageurs will be able to ensure that derivative prices are tied to observable bond prices, so that arbitrage profits are not possible—hence the title of section: "Arbitrage-Free Models of the Term Structure." Binomial interest rate trees will be used to value callable bonds in a subsequent chapter. The main disadvantages of the Ho and Lee model are that interest rates can be negative and that it assumes a very simple binomial process for bond prices. In the years since this model was devised, more sophisticated models that prevent negative interest rates and allow for richer processes for bond prices have been developed.

6.4   THE BLACK–DERMAN–TOY MODEL

The **Black–Derman–Toy Model (BDT model)** (Black and Toy 1990) is a popular interest rate model useful for valuing fixed income derivatives consistent with both the observed term structure of interest rates and the implied volatilities of interest rate caplets.

The BDT model can be used to directly model spot rates, forward rates, and/or discount factors. Further, the model can be used with any compounding assumption. The model centers on two relations: one focused on average forward rates and one on interest rate volatilities. These two key relations are discussed in the second and third subsections.

6.4.1 Evolution of a Binomial BDT Tree

Consider a two-period (2-year) binomial tree with a current short-term (1-year) spot rate, r_0, of 5%. Assume that there are two paths forward from the current 5% spot rate to the next 1-year spot rate: an up path to r_u and a down path to r_d. In other words, there are two possible values next year to the short-term (1-year) interest rate: r_u and r_d. For simplicity, the following analysis will assume that each rate (path) will occur with a probability of 50%. The diagram in Exhibit 6.2 illustrates the current 1-year rate (5%) either rising to or falling to one of two values as next year's short-term (1-year) spot rate.

The two possible rates in Exhibit 6.2 (r_u and r_d) were calibrated based on two key constraints: (1) the average two-period return of the two paths must be equal to the return of the 2-year discount bond; and (2) the spread between the up and down rates must be consistent with the implied rate volatility of the short-term rate from a 1-year caplet on the short-term rate. These two constraints and the math involved in finding r_u and r_d based on those constraints (i.e., calibration of the model) are detailed in the next two sections.

6.4.2 Calibrating the Level of Rates Based on Average Returns

Calibration refers to the adjustment of potential outcomes within a model being formulated so as to prevent arbitrage opportunities given observed market rates and prices. In this case, the above values for r_u and r_d (6.50% and 4.70%) are found (calibrated) as the only no-arbitrage values that are consistent with the 2-year zero-coupon bond yield being 5.30% and the lognormal rate volatility of the short-rate in 1 year being 16.21%. Calibration of rates is based on the yield of a 2-year discount bond.

The rates in a BDT tree are calibrated so that the averaged future value of the paths based on rolling over N single-period bonds equals the observed total return on an N-year zero-coupon bond. To illustrate, consider the case of the two-period tree in Exhibit 6.2. Note that the yield on the 2-year bond is given as 5.30% which

EXHIBIT 6.2   A Two-Period Black–Derman–Toy (BDT) Binomial Tree

$$r_u = 6.50\%$$

$$r_0 = 5.00\% <$$

$$r_u = 4.70\%$$

Note:
(1) The yield on a 2-year zero coupon bond is 5.30%.
(2) The lognormal rate volatility of the short-rate in 1 year is 16.21%.
(3) The rates are all based on annual compounding.

generates a total 2-year return of 10.88%. Next, consider the averaged return of the two paths of investing in the short-rate for 2 years:

$$\text{Averaged short-rate total return} = 0.5[(1 + r_0)(1 + r_u) + (1 + r_0)(1 + r_d)] - 1 \quad (6.5)$$

The numbers in Exhibit 6.2 were calibrated so that the value from Equation 6.5 would equal the 2-year return on zero coupon bond:

$$\text{Averaged short-rate total return} = 0.5[(1.05)(1.065) + (1.05)(1.047) - 1 = 10.88\%$$

$$\text{2-year return on zero coupon bond} = (1.053\char`^2) - 1 = 10.88\%.$$

The issue of *how* these particular rates were selected is discussed in the final subsection.

APPLICATION 6.4.2

An analyst is calibrating a Black–Derman–Toy binomial tree model and obtains the following values for the current short rate ($r_0 = 0.06$) and its two potential realizations after one period ($r_d = 0.05$ and $r_u = 0.08$). What is the total 2-year return obtained from investing in the current two-period short rate? Use annual compounding. Inserting the given values into Equation 6.5 to find the averaged of the two-period short-rate returns:

$$\text{Averaged short-rate return} = 0.5[(1 + r_0)(1 + r_u) + (1 + r_0)(1 + r_d)] - 1$$

$$\text{Averaged short-rate return} = 0.5[(1.06)(1.05) + (1.06)(1.08)] - 1 = 12.89\%$$

Given any two of the three rates (r_0, r_d, and r_u) the missing rate can be found. Note that the total 2-year return of 12.89% corresponds to an annualized return of 6.25%: $[(1 + 0.1289)\char`^0.5] - 1$.

6.4.3 Calibrating the Spread of Rates Based on Volatilities

The second constraint is that the spread between the possible values of the short-rate in 1 year (r_d and r_u) must be consistent with the observed volatility of the short-term rate on a caplet with an expiration date of 1 year. The implied volatility of the short-rate is expressed in a form such that the relation between r_d and r_u is:

$$r_u = r_d \, e^{2\sigma} \quad (6.6)$$

Suppose, for instance, that the implied volatility (expressed as a continuous rate) of the 1-year caplet on the short-term rate is 16.21%. In the simple example in Exhibit 6.2, the unique values satisfying the average return condition and exhibiting the observed spread (16.21%) are 4.70% and 6.50%. The relation can be verified by inserting the values for r_u, r_d, and σ into Equation 6.6: $0.065 = 0.047 \, e^{2*0.1621}$.

APPLICATION 6.4.3

An analyst is calibrating a Black–Derman–Toy binomial tree model and observes the following values: r_d, the next period short-rate in the down state, is 0.04, and the implied continuous volatility of the short-rate next period, σ, is 0.25. What is the value for the next period short-rate in the up state, r_u?

Inserting the given values into Equation 6.6 to find next period short-rate in the up state:

$$r_u = r_d \ e^{2\sigma}$$

$$r_u = .04 * e^{2 \times 0.25} = 0.06595$$

Given any two of the three values the missing value can be found. Note that the continuous implied volatility requires the use of the exponential function.

6.4.4 Summary of BDT Calibration

The previous two sections examined the two conditions that identify the rates in the second period of a two-period BDT binomial tree. Understanding the intuition of imposing these two conditions helps in understanding the essence of the BDT model. The spot rates in the currently observed term structure drive the overall *levels* of the rates that are projected throughout the binomial tree. The implied volatilities of options trading on short-term rates (i.e., interest rate caplets) drives the *spreads* between the "up rates" and the "down rates" corresponding to the expiration dates of the caplets. Together the two conditions identify the entire tree.

Even in the case of a two-period tree, the rates that solve these two conditions must be found using a somewhat complex approach such as a quadratic equation or a solver function. In practice, the tree typically has 30 or more time steps and requires considerable programming. While the solution may be cumbersome, the concepts illustrated in the previous sections do not change. The concepts are actually intuitive and straightforward: the BDT model allows construction of no-arbitrage interest rate trees using the observed term structures of interest rates and rate volatilities. The tree can then be used to find no-arbitrage values for financial derivatives on fixed income securities.

6.5 P-MEASURES AND Q-MEASURES

One of the most important concepts in the modeling of financial derivative values is the use of P-Measures and Q-Measures. A **P-Measure** indicates a probability or other value that reflects an actual statistical probability meaning that the probability is an unbiased indication of the chance occurring.

A **Q-Measure** is based on a quasi probability in the sense that it functions as if based on an actual statistical probability but it is generally a biased indication of the chance occurring. A Q-Measure in finance is typically based on an assumption of risk neutrality. In some frameworks, Q-Measures can be used to generate unbiased valuations even when risk premiums are not zero. Much more will be discussed regarding this topic in Chapter 21.

The probability and values used in the BDT model of Section 6.4 were based on Q-Measures. In other words, market participants were assumed to be risk neutral so that interest rates could be projected without having to assume or specify a risk premium for bearing interest rate risk. This simplification, when valid, allows financial analysts to determine no-arbitrage values based on observations of riskless interest rates that are unbiased estimates of values in a "real world" of risk aversion.

REFERENCES

Black, F., E. Derman, and W. Toy. 1990. "A One Factor Model of Interest Rates and Its Applications to Treasury Bond Options." *Financial Analysts Journal* 46 (1): 33–39.

Cox, J. C., J. E. Ingersoll, and S. A. Ross. 1985. "A Theory of the Term Structure of Interest Rates." *Econometrica* 53: 385–407.

Thomas, S. Y. Ho, and Sang-Bin Lee. 1986. "Term Structure Movements and Pricing Interest Rate Contingent Claims." *Journal of Finance* 41 (5): 1011–29.

Vasicek, O. 1977. "An Equilibrium Characterization of the Term Structure." *Journal of Financial Economics* 5 (2): 177–88.

CHAPTER 7

Credit Risk Models

This chapter discusses the modeling of credit risk. The issuers of these instruments can be either corporate or sovereign borrowers, and the instruments typically bear lower than investment-grade ratings. The lower rating implies that there is a significant default risk associated with these instruments, which partially explains the higher yield and the premium that investors can expect for investing in them.

This chapter discusses the nature of credit risk and presents three approaches to credit risk modeling. While these models can be very complex, our goal is to provide readers with a basic understanding of these models and highlight the strengths and weaknesses of each approach.

7.1 THE ECONOMICS OF CREDIT RISK

Credit risk is the risk of loss resulting from some type of credit event with a counterparty. **Credit** is money or funds granted by a creditor or lender to a debtor or borrower. The types of credit issued could be bank loans, corporate bonds, or government (sovereign) bonds. For a variety of reasons, the debtor may not be able or willing to meet all the obligations that the credit contract stipulates. For example, if the debtor does not have the funds to make the regular interest payments on a loan, the debtor will be in default. However, credit risk could arise from a set of credit events, of which nonpayment of obligations is just one example. **Credit events** that give rise to credit risk include bankruptcy, downgrading, failure to make timely payments, certain corporate events, and government actions:

- Bankruptcy: This arises if an entity is dissolved or becomes insolvent and therefore is unable to meet its obligations.
- Downgrading of credit rating: This arises when the external credit rating agencies lower the credit rating of an entity due to changes in the financial condition of the entity or changes in overall economic conditions.
- Failure to make timely payments: A borrower may fail to make timely interest or principal payments even if the entity is not dissolved and does not face economic hardships.
- Corporate events: Certain corporate events, such as mergers or spin-offs, could weaken the financial condition of a firm, making it more difficult for the entity to meet its financial obligations.
- Government actions: Capital controls and other government restrictions could prevent a borrower from meeting its financial obligations.

The extent and the consequence of credit risk depend on a number of factors, of which credit exposure or exposure at default (EAD) is the most important. EAD measures the *potential* loss to the creditor in the case of a credit event. Closely related to EAD is loss given default (LGD), which takes into account any potential recovery should default take place. In other words, if 100% of EAD is lost in a case of default, then LGD = EAD. However, in most cases the creditor is likely to recover some of the losses; therefore, LGD is typically less than EAD.

7.1.1 Adverse Selection and Credit Risk

Adverse selection refers to an economic process in which negative or undesirable outcomes take place when the parties to a transaction have asymmetric information (i.e., they have access to different information).[1] It is often the case that borrowers have more information than lenders about the borrowers' ability and willingness to meet their obligations. In this case, there is asymmetric information between borrowers and lenders, with borrowers having more information about their circumstances than lenders. This asymmetric information leads to adverse selection. Since the lender is at a disadvantage, it may decide to raise the rate of interest it would charge potential borrowers. However, this will have some unintended consequences. As the cost of borrowing increases, a disproportionate fraction of borrowers willing to pay the high cost of borrowing will be privately aware of their own poor credit quality and will therefore find borrowing at such a high cost still attractive. If the lender were to raise the cost of borrowing any further in order to compensate for this adverse selection, the proportion of poor credit quality would continue to increase. At the extreme, the very high interest rate will drive all borrowers away, and the lender will be left with unused capital. Akerlof (1970) describes a market with asymmetric quality information as a "market for lemons." Lemon is a slang term for a poor-quality used car. Akerlof describes the implications of asymmetric information between the seller and potential buyers. Akerlof reasons that poor quality cars will drive good quality cars from the market (since sellers will refuse to sell good quality cars at low prices to buyers who fear the car is of poor quality and who refuse to offer high prices). Accordingly, economists cite markets for lemons as an example of potential market failure.

Financial institutions have developed a variety of tools and processes to reduce the impact of adverse selection and the potential problem of market failure. In addition to taking into account a borrower's credit history and reputation, lenders may ask for collateral, since it is often easier to verify the economic value of collateral. Also, lenders may limit the size of their loans to an individual or a group of borrowers in order to diversify their risk and reduce the impact of adverse selection.

7.1.2 Moral Hazard and Credit Risk

Whereas adverse selection is a potential problem before a financial transaction is completed, moral hazard can come into play after the transaction is completed, such as when one party to an economic transaction takes actions or takes on more risks while the counterparty bears the consequences. For example, after a loan transaction has been completed, the corporate borrower may decide to use the loan's proceeds to pay large dividends to its shareholders or invest in projects with unexpectedly high risk. This action may weaken the financial condition of the borrower and therefore increase the risk of default faced by the lender. Another important example is the case of financial lending institutions that can raise money at a very low rate of interest because their deposits are insured by a government agency. Moral hazard is exacerbated when these financial institutions are allowed to use the funds they have raised at low interest rates to make risky loans and earn a large spread. If the borrowers default on their loans, governments and their citizenry will bear the cost of those defaults. To reduce moral hazard, lenders monitor the behavior of borrowers, impose restrictions on how the loans' proceeds may be used, and limit the size of their loans to risky borrowers.

7.1.3 Probability of Default

As previously noted, EAD and LGD are two important factors determining the extent and the consequence of credit risk. Another important factor that affects credit risk is the probability of default (PD), which refers to the probability that the borrower will be unable to meet its financial obligations. The task of assigning a default probability to each borrower in a lender's credit portfolio is a difficult task, as it is affected by a number of firm-specific as well as macroeconomic conditions. Adverse selection and moral hazard impact the probability of default; thus, any actions taken to mitigate their impacts are done with the aim of reducing the probability of default.

Lenders use their own experience as well as market data and credit ratings to improve the accuracy of their estimates of PD. As discussed in the next section, certain credit risk models use market data such as credit spreads to improve estimates of the PD. Credit spreads refer to the higher yields that instruments exposed to credit risk must offer lenders in order to meet the credit needs of borrowers. A credit model that relates credit spreads to the PD can be used to infer the PD from the observed credit spreads. Alternatively, lenders can use credit ratings assigned by external credit rating agencies to improve their estimates of PD. Using historical data available from these agencies, one can obtain empirical estimates of defaults for each credit rating. For example, we may observe that 0.15% of firms rated Baa1 have historically defaulted on their loans. Assuming that these historical relations are relatively stable, one can use the current rating of a Baa1 bond to estimate that its PD is 0.15%.

7.1.4 Expected Credit Loss

EAD and LGD are related to each other through the recovery rate (RR), which gives the percentage of EAD that can be recovered through legal and economic processes. Typically, the recovery does not take place at the time of default; indeed, it may take years to gain control of the recovered amount. In such cases, the present value of the recovered amount may be used to calculate the recovery rate. Note that the recovery rate can be expressed as:

Present Value of Sum to Be Recovered/EAD

The EAD can be expressed as the sum of the principal and interest due.

APPLICATION 7.1.4A

Example: Suppose the EAD of a loan due at the end of this year is $100 million. Should there be a default, the lender expects to recover 40% of the principal after 5 years. If the appropriate annual rate of interest for discounting the cash flows of the same riskiness as the recovered amount is 6%, the actual recovery rate is:

Sum to be recovered $= 0.4 \times 100 = \$40$ million

Present Value of Sum to be Recovered $= \dfrac{\$40 \text{ million}}{(1 + 0.06)^5} = \$29.9$ million

Recovery rate $= \dfrac{29.9}{100} = 29.9\%$

Given the definitions of EAD, LGD, RR, and PD, we can obtain an estimate of loss and expected loss from credit risk. In particular,

$$LGD = EAD \times (1 - RR) \qquad (7.1)$$

$$E[Loss] = LGD \times PD = EAD \times (1 - RR) \times PD \qquad (7.2)$$

APPLICATION 7.1.4B

Suppose a loan has $100 million of principal and $10 million of interest due at the end of the year. If there is a default, the lender expects to recover $25 million 3 years after the default. The PD for the borrower is estimated to be 1%. Find the exposure at default, the present value (PV) of the sum to be recovered, the recovery rate, the loss given default, and the expected loss using an interest rate of 8%. These values are given as follows:

EAD $= \$100$ million principal $+ \$10$ million interest $= \$110$ million

PV of sum to be recovered $= \dfrac{\$25 \text{ million}}{1.08^3} = \$19.8458$ million

RR $=$ PV of sum to be recovered/EAD $= \$19.8458$ million/$110 million

$\quad = 0.1804164$

LGD $=$ EAD$(1 - RR) = \$110$ million$(1.0 - 0.1804164) = \$90.1542$ million

Expected Loss $=$ LGD $\times$ PD $= \$90.1542$ million $\times 1\% = \$0.901542$ million

Note that LGD can also be found as EAD $-$ Present Value of Sum to be Recovered.

7.2 OVERVIEW OF CREDIT RISK MODELING

In constructing a fixed-income portfolio, an investor faces the decision of how much, if any, interest rate risk or credit risk should be taken. Owners of government bonds, such as US Treasuries or German bunds, predominantly face interest rate risk, as the risk that the US or German government would default on its obligations is considered to be extremely low.

However, owners of bonds issued by levered entities (i.e., borrowers with significant amounts of leverage on their balance sheets) face the risk that the credit quality of the borrower will deteriorate, resulting in a credit event taking place. As discussed earlier, default is one extreme example of a credit event, one in which the firm is failing to operating as a going concern. In practice, default is not a terminal end—that is, a company does not cease to exist at the point of default. In fact, the process of workout or restructuring is one in which the underlying business practices, management, and liabilities of the borrower are changed in order to enable the business to emerge as a going concern or otherwise face liquidation. Nonetheless, the focus on many credit risk models assumes default as an end point.

To invest in instruments that are exposed to credit risk and to take advantage of investment opportunities offered by such instruments, investors must have a thorough understanding of the credit risk and credit exposures of these instruments. For instance, in a relative value strategy, an investor may decide to compare returns on two instruments with different levels of exposure to credit risk to determine if both offer the appropriate credit spreads given their levels of credit risk. A credit risk model can be used to evaluate both instruments in order to determine whether the instruments are correctly priced relative to each other.

There are **three types of credit risk modeling approaches:** the structural approach, the reduced-form approach, and the empirical approach. In the structural approach, the framework is set around an explicit relationship between capital structure and default. The value of a firm's assets is set equal to the value of its equity plus the value of its debt. Equity of the firm is viewed as a call option on the firm's assets, with the strike price being the face value of the debt due at the time of exercise. In contrast, bondholders are viewed as having a risk-free bond and a short position in a put option on the firm's assets. If the value of assets is less than the face value of the debt, the put option will be exercised on the bondholders, resulting in their giving up the risk-free bond and receiving the firm's assets.

In the reduced-form approach, default is modeled as an exogenous event that is driven by a random signal. The behavior of this random signal is the deciding factor of default rather than the value or the dynamics of the firm's assets. Reduced form models are built on the assumption that default is a random event that can be described using statistical and economic models.

The **empirical approach to credit risk modeling** is based on the assumption that it is too difficult to model the company and its environment accurately. Instead, an investor examines historical evidence regarding companies that have defaulted and evaluates their financial data to understand the credit risk of the firm. This approach produces a credit score that is used to rank firms in terms of their credit worthiness.

7.3   THE MERTON MODEL

The best known of the structural modeling approaches is Merton's structuring model (see Merton 1974), which was introduced in the CAIA Level I curriculum.

7.3.1   Capital Structure in the Merton Model

The approach starts with a simple capital structure of Assets = Liabilities (Debt) + Equity.

$$A_t = D_t + E_t \tag{7.3}$$

It assumes that default happens at the maturity of the debt if the asset value falls below the face value of the debt. Other assumptions of this model are that there is no cost to bankruptcy, that debt and equity can be traded without friction, and that the debt is a zero-coupon bond with the face value of K and a maturity date of T. Equity value at time T is:

$$E_T = \max(A_T - K, 0) \tag{7.4}$$

Note that this payoff is the payoff of a European call option on underlying assets A_T, strike K, and maturity T. The payoff to bondholders at time T is:

$$D_T = K - \max(K - A_T, 0) \tag{7.5}$$

Equation 7.5 indicates that bondholders will receive the face value unless the face value is less than the value of the assets. In that case, bondholders will receive the assets. In other words, the equity holders first pay creditors the face value of the debt. Then they exercise the put option given to them by creditors, receiving back the face value in exchange for the firm's assets.

7.3.2   The Merton Model and the Black–Scholes Option Pricing Model

Since the Merton model views capital structure with options, the model can be applied using option pricing models, such as the Black–Scholes option pricing model (Black and Scholes 1973), to value a firm's equity as a call option on the assets of the underlying company. This use of a well known option model is intuitive and one of the most appealing aspects of the Merton model. Using the Black–Scholes formula for valuing a European call option results in:

$$E_t = A_t \times N(d) - K \times e^{-r \times t} \times N(d - \sigma_A \sqrt{\tau}) \tag{7.6}$$

Here, r is the annualized continually compounded short-term rate of interest on risk-free debt, $\tau = T - t$ is the time left to maturity of the debt, σ_A is the annualized volatility of the rate of return on the firm's assets, and

$$d = \frac{\ln(A_t/K) + (r + 0.5\sigma_A^2) \times \tau}{\sigma_A \sqrt{\tau}} \tag{7.7}$$

The symbol $N(\cdot)$ refers to the cumulative probability distribution function for a standard normal distribution. That is, $N(d) = \text{Probability } (Z \leq d)$, where Z is a standard normal random variable. In this scenario, debt holders face a potential loss of the shortfall between the asset value A_T and the face value of the debt K (note that the equity holders cannot lose more than their equity stake). Hypothetically, if debt holders were to buy a put option with a strike K that pays off if asset value A_T falls below K, the debt holders would be hedged against the loss in the event of default. Thus, at any given time t, the debt combined with the put option guarantee a payoff of K at maturity time T.

As previously discussed, the value of a risky debt issue at any time is equal to the price of a portfolio that consists of a long position in risk-free debt with the same maturity as the original debt, and a short position in a put option with a strike price equal to the face value of the bond and the same maturity date as the bond. That is,

$$D_t = K \times e^{-r \times \tau} - (Put\ Price)_t \tag{7.8}$$

Using the Black–Scholes formula for a European put option, the put value is given by:

$$P_t = K \times e^{-r \times \tau} \times N(-d + \sigma_A \sqrt{\tau}) - A_t \times N(-d) \tag{7.9}$$

7.3.3   The Role of the Credit Spread in the Structural Model

This section describes a model of pricing of the risky debt in terms of the credit spread. The common practice in valuing risky debt is to account for the credit risk in terms of a spread above the risk-free rate. In the current context, the value of the zero-coupon debt can be expressed as:

$$D_t = K \times e^{-(r + s_t) \times \tau} \tag{7.10}$$

where s_t is the annual spread due to credit risk expressed as a continuously compounded rate. Equations 7.8, 7.9, and 7.10 can be combined to obtain an expression for the credit spread as it relates to the parameters of the Merton model.[2]

Example: The ABC Corporation has the following balance sheet: Its assets are worth €100 million, and it has 4-year maturity zero-coupon debt with a face value of €70 million. The volatility of its assets is 20% per year, and the risk-free rate is 5% per year. To value ABC's debt and equity, use Equation 7.7 to calculate d:

$$d = \frac{\ln\left(\frac{100}{70}\right) + (0.05 + 0.5 \times 0.2^2) \times 4}{0.2 \times \sqrt{4}} = 1.592$$

$$d - 0.2 \times \sqrt{4} \qquad\qquad\qquad\qquad\qquad = 1.192$$

Then, calculate the area under the standard normal distribution for the value of 1.592 and 1.192. That is, $N(1.592) = 0.944$ and $N(1.192) = 0.883$. Next, apply Equation 7.6:

$$E_t = 100 \times 0.944 - 70 \times e^{-0.05 \times 4} \times 0.883 = 43.79$$

This means that the current value of the debt must be: $D_t = 100 - 43.79 = 56.21$.

Next, calculate the value of the put option given to equity holders. As previously stated, the value of the put option given to equity holders is equal to the difference between current value of the risk-free debt and the risky debt:

$$Put\ Option = Risk - Free\ Debt - Risky\ Debt$$

$$= (70 \times e^{-0.05 \times 4}) - 56.21 = 1.1$$

Therefore, the value of the put option given to equity holders is €1.1 million. Finally, note that the credit spread is:

$$s = -\frac{1}{4} \times \ln\left[0.883 + \frac{100}{10} \times e^{0.05 \times 4} \times (1 - 0.944)\right] = 0.49\%$$

Note that the spread correctly prices the risky debt. That is, 56.21 is the present value of 70 discounted back at 5.49% for 4 years.

7.3.4 Evaluation of the Merton Model

In its simplest form, the Merton model is just the starting point of credit risk modeling. Because its underlying assumptions are highly restrictive, it cannot be applied to real-world situations in which firms have different types of coupon bonds and interest rates are random through time. Still, the Merton model has many intuitive properties and is a useful point of departure for more complex models. For example, it can be shown that the risk-neutral probability of default (i.e., the Q-Measure) can be expressed as $\Pr[A_T \leq K] = 1 - N(d - \sigma_A \sqrt{\tau})$. It is important to note that this is not the true probability of default; rather, as a Q-Measure, it is a version of that probability implied by current prices if those prices were determined in markets where investors were risk neutral. It is equally important to realize that even if investors were risk neutral, they would still care about credit risk due to the effect of credit risk on potential loss of principal. However, risk-neutral investors do not demand an extra risk premium for systematic risk (i.e., the beta of the asset in the capital asset pricing model [CAPM]) of the investment that contains credit risk.

The shortcomings of the Merton model are discussed in CAIA Level I. It was pointed out that some of the parameters of the model are not readily observable—particularly the market value of assets and the return volatility. The KMV model, discussed in the next main section, attempts to overcome this difficulty. From an empirical point of view, the Merton model performs poorly in explaining the credit spread on short-term securities. In other words, if the parameters of the model are selected so that they correspond to available historical data, the result would predict a very low credit spread for short-term assets, results that are contradicted by available empirical evidence.

7.3.5 Four Important Properties of the Merton Model

This section takes a closer look at four important properties of the Merton model. As discussed so far, two key outputs from the Merton model are the credit spread and the probability of default. Let's examine how these two outputs are affected if there are changes in some of the inputs to the model. For example, what will happen to the credit spread if the maturity of the debt increases? The answer to this question is neither obvious nor simple. To facilitate our discussion, let's recall the two expressions that the Merton model provides for the two key outputs:

Credit Spread:

$$s_t = -\frac{1}{\tau} \times \ln \times \left[N(d - \sigma_A \sqrt{\tau}) + \frac{A_t}{K} e^{r \times \tau} \times N(-d) \right] \tag{7.11}$$

Probability of default:

$$\Pr[A_T \leq K] = 1 - N(d) \tag{7.12}$$

$$d = \frac{\ln(A_t/K) + (r + 0.5\sigma_A^2) \times \tau}{\sigma_A \sqrt{\tau}} \tag{7.13}$$

The following are four important properties of the Merton model:

1. SENSITIVITY TO MATURITY: The cumulative probability of default increases as the debt's time to maturity increases. This is an intuitive result, because as the time to maturity increases, the firm's assets have more chances to decline below the face value of the debt. Note, however, that the (noncumulative) probability of default may increase or decrease through each prospective point in time.

   The behavior of the default probability through time (for a particular degree of leverage, asset volatility, and riskless rate) forms the shape of the term structure of credit spreads. Accordingly, the sensitivity of credit spreads to maturity can be analyzed by examining the shape of the term structure of credit spreads for different levels of leverage, asset volatility, and riskless rates. This section focuses on the sensitivity of credit spreads to maturity over different levels of the firm's leverage.

   Exhibit 7.1 depicts the credit spreads over different maturities for three levels of leverage from a low leverage of 10% in Panel A to a moderately high level of leverage of 60% in Panel C. Note in Panel A that for low levels of leverage there is a low credit spread and therefore a low probability of default for bonds with short maturities. The reason is that over short intervals of time there is a low probability that the assets of a firm will decline below the debt's face value. However, as the time to the debt's maturity is increased, the probabilities of default (and credit spreads) increase. Therefore, for firms with low leverage the term structure of credit spreads tends to be upward sloping.

   Panel C depicts the credit spreads over different bond maturities for a relatively high degree of leverage (60%). Highly leveraged firms can quickly rise to high short-term probabilities of default. But at more distant prospective points in time the credit spreads can decline (i.e., the slope of the term structure of credit spreads can decline causing a humped shape). The explanation for the decline is that if a firm that started with high leverage is able to survive for several years

A. Debt/Assets = 0.10:

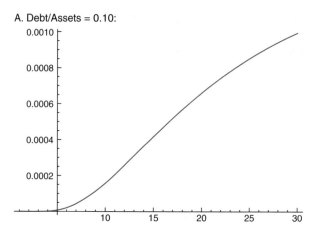

B. Debt/Assets = 0.30:

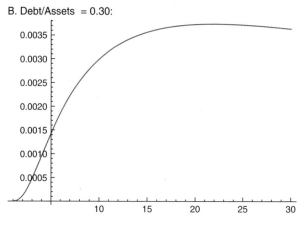

C. Debt/Assets = 0.60:

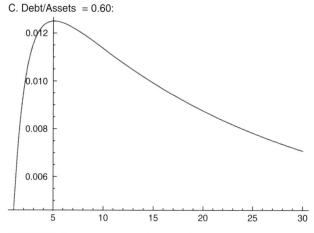

EXHIBIT 7.1   Credit Spreads for Differing Leverage
(r_f = 5%; Vol = 30%)

without default, the positive expected rates of return on the firm's assets will drive long-term probabilities of default lower.

Thus, the shape of the term structure of credit spreads can vary from uniformly upward sloping (for firms with very low leverage) to various humped shapes depending on leverage. For a more extensive discussion see Wang (2009).

For further intuition regarding these results, recall that risky debt is really a portfolio consisting of risk-free debt and a short position in a put option on the firm's assets. Because this put can be exercised only on the maturity date of the debt, it is a European option. While the value of an American put option will always increase as its maturity increases, the same cannot be said of a European put option. For example, if it is optimal to exercise a put option today, the value of the put option declines if the owner of the put option is forced to delay its exercise. The same phenomenon affects the value of the put option owned by shareholders. Especially as indicated in cases of high leverage, as the maturity date of the put option exceeds the optimal exercise date, the value of the put option begins to decline, reducing the credit spread that must be used to calculate the price of the risk debt (note that the risky debt is short the put option).

2. SENSITIVITY TO ASSET VOLATILITY: As expected, the probability of default increases as the volatility of the asset increases. Again, similar to an increase in maturity, the default probability increases at a decreasing rate. The credit spread will also increase as the volatility of the asset increases. However, the credit spread may increase by a smaller amount for longer-maturity bonds compared to short-term bonds. The reason for this is that as volatility increases, there is a greater chance for the value of assets to end up very far above or below the face value of the debt. However, there is a lower bound to the value of assets that cannot become negative. For this reason, at very high levels of asset volatility, the increase in credit spread will be smaller for long-term bonds. That is, the negative impact of the higher volatility is limited to the downside, while the positive impact of higher volatility is unlimited to the upside.

Exhibit 7.2 depicts the credit spreads over different maturities for three levels of asset volatility from a low volatility of 10% in Panel A to a high level of volatility of 60% in Panel C. All three panels assume moderate leverage (30%). Note in Panel A of Exhibit 7.2 that for low levels of volatility and moderate leverage, credit spreads tend to rise slowly to a distant peak. However, for high levels of volatility (in Panel C of Exhibit 7.2) the hump occurs much earlier.

3. SENSITIVITY TO LEVERAGE: As leverage increases, both the probability of default and the credit spread increase. While the probability of default increases by a larger amount for long-term bonds as leverage increases, the credit spread may increase by a relatively smaller amount for long-term bonds. The reason behind this reaction is the same as the one discussed in the context of the sensitivity to increases in asset volatility.

4. SENSITIVITY TO THE RISKLESS RATE: How default probability and credit spreads react to changes in the short-term riskless rate depends very much on how the rate of return on the asset is assumed to react as the riskless rate changes. The Merton model implicitly assumes that the expected rate of return on the firm's assets is equal to the riskless rate plus a constant risk premium. Under this assumption, as the riskless rate increases, the mean return on the firm's assets increases, reducing the probability of default and the credit spread. However, if this assumption is

A. Volatility = 0.10:

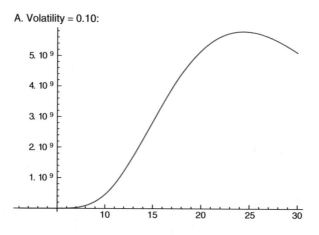

B. Volatility = 0.30:

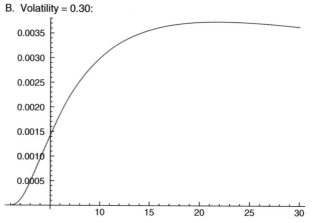

C. Volatility = 0.60:

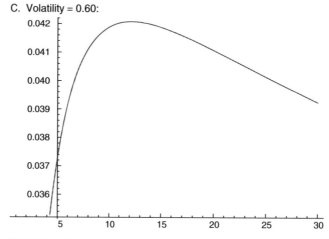

EXHIBIT 7.2 Credit Rates for Differing Volatility ($r_f = 5\%$; Debt/Assets = 30%)

EXHIBIT 7.3 Sensitivities of Credit Spread, and Probability of Default
in Merton Structural Model

	Maturity	Asset Volatility	Leverage	Riskless Rate
Credit Spread	Initially +	+	+	-
Prob. of Default	+	+	+	-

relaxed, then the reaction to an increase in the riskless rate will be difficult to
predict. Exhibit 7.3 summarizes the sensitivity of the credit spread and probability of default in the Merton structural model to the maturity of the debt, the
volatility of the assets, the firm's leverage, and the riskless interest rate.

The four properties discussed above illustrate a key argument for financial modeling. Merton's structural model was used to analyze credit spreads for various determinants. While Merton's model, like all models, does not describe the world with
perfect precision, the model's simplifications can permit enormous insight into the
key issues faced by investors regarding asset valuation and risk.

7.4 OTHER STRUCTURAL MODELS: KMV

Another variation of a structural model that is widely implemented in the industry is
the KMV model. KMV stands for Kealhover, McQuown, and Vasicek, who founded
the firm KMV in 2002 (Crosbie and Bohn 2003). The firm was sold to Moody's
Investors Service, and the model is now the basis of Moody's modeling approach.

7.4.1 Overview of the KMV Credit Risk Model

The **KMV model** is a structural credit risk model that uses Merton's model and estimates of the volatility and total value of the firm's underlying equity and assets to
estimate the credit risk of the debt. The KMV model turns the creditor's lending problem around and considers the loan repayment incentive problem from the viewpoint
of the borrowing firm's equity holders. As previously discussed, the value of assets,
A_t, and its volatility, σ_A, cannot be observed or estimated directly. The KMV model
attempts to solve this problem by estimating them simultaneously using the Merton
model and the economic relationship between equity values and firm values. To solve
for the two unknowns, the model uses: (1) the structural relationship between the
market value of a firm's equity and the market value of its assets (see Equation 7.6);
and (2) the relationship between the volatility of a firm's assets and the volatility of
a firm's equity. This relationship is expressed as:

$$\sigma_E = \frac{A_t}{E_t} \times \Delta \times \sigma_A \tag{7.14}$$

The term Δ is the delta of the equity with respect to changes in the value of the
assets and, under the Merton model, is equal to $N(d)$. Note that the market value
of equity is observable for publicly traded firms, and the value of the equity return

volatility can be estimated from historical equity returns or implied from options on the firm's equity. Once the values of E_t and σ_E are obtained, the two relations previously stated can be used to solve for the two unknowns, A_t and σ_A.

If the implied volatility of the firm's equity is used to estimate σ_ε rather than the historic volatility of the equity, then the resulting estimate of σ_A is a forward-looking and market-based estimate. This estimate of σ_A can then be used as an important input to the analysis of the credit risk of the firm's debt.

Two important outputs of the KMV model are the probability of default—or, using KMV's terms, the expected default frequency—and a credit score known as distance to default. The next section will briefly discuss how these two figures are calculated.

An important difference between the KMV model and the Merton model is the way default is modeled. The KMV model uses a default trigger to model default. The Merton model **default trigger** for the firm's total asset value is the face value of the zero-coupon bond, because it represents the asset value at which the firm would be on the brink of default. If the total value of the firm's assets falls below the face value of the debt, the firm is modeled as being in default. In practice, firms have short-term and long-term debt. KMV argues that short-term debt is more pressing, since the firm will have to service this debt, but it has some leeway on how to service longer-term debt. Thus, the default trigger is calculated when the value of the firm's assets falls below the full amount of the short-term debt and a partial amount of longer-term debt.[3]

7.4.2 Using the KMV Model to Estimate a Credit Score

One of the main outputs of the KMV model is a credit score, which is measured as distance to default for a borrower. The **distance to default (DD)** is the number of standard deviations away from default and is approximately measured as the percentage difference between a firm's assets and its default trigger relative to the volatility of its assets:

$$DD_t = \frac{A_t - K}{A_t \times \sigma_A} \qquad (7.15)$$

Here, K is the default trigger of the firm, which would be the face value of the debt in the Merton model and a function of the face values of short-term and long-term debt in the KMV model. For example, suppose that a firm's assets are valued at $100 million and the default trigger is $80 million, reducing the equation to $DD = 0.2/\sigma A$. The firm's assets must decline 20% in this example to trigger default. The annual standard deviation of the returns of the assets is σA. The resulting ratio (DD) is the number of standard deviations that the assets must lose in order to decline in value to reach the default trigger. Suppose that the standard deviation (σ_A) in this example is 0.1, so that $DD = 2$. The value of 2 indicates that this firm will enter the default region if the value of its assets drops by two standard deviations of its value—that is, by $20 million. Thus, if the DD of a firm is reported to be n, then the firm will enter the default region if the value of its assets drops by $n \times \sigma_A$. Alternatively, the firm can be viewed as being n standard deviations away from default due to asset value declines.

APPLICATION 7.4.2

Suppose the assets of KYZ Corporation are worth $200 million. Its default trigger is estimated to be $120 million, and the volatility of its assets is 40% per year. What is KYZ's distance to default?

The DD of KYZ is found using Equation 7.15 as: $DD = \dfrac{200 - 120}{200 \times 0.4} = 1$ standard deviation.

KYZ Corporation is one standard deviation of asset volatility away from default.

7.4.3 Using the KMV Model to Estimate an Expected Default Frequency

As mentioned in the last section, an important output from the KMV model is the calculation of the **expected default frequency (EDF)**, which will measure theoretically or empirically the probability that loans of certain characteristics could default. The value of DD can be used to ask the following question: What is the probability that the value of a firm's assets could drop by n standard deviations over the t periods? Here we discuss how the empirical EDF can be calculated. Suppose that we have a large historical database of firm defaults and loan repayments, and we calculate that the firm we are analyzing has a distance to default of $n(DD = n)$. We then ask the empirical question: What percentage of firms in the database actually defaulted within the 1-year time horizon when their asset values placed them a distance of n standard deviations away from default at the beginning of the year, and how does that compare to the total population of firms that were n standard deviations away from default at the beginning of the year? This produces an empirical EDF:

$$EDF = \frac{\text{Number of Firms That Defaulted within One Year with } DD = n}{\text{Total Number of firms in the Population with } DD = n} \quad (7.16)$$

APPLICATION 7.4.3

Suppose there were 500 firms with $DD = 2$ at the beginning of 2019 in a sample of European corporations. Of this total, 8 defaulted by the end of the year. Estimate EDF empirically. The estimate of the EDF is found using Equation 7.16:

$EDF = \dfrac{8}{500} = 1.6\%$ Based on historical observation, we might expect 1.6% of European firms with $DD = 2$ to default within 1 year. The estimated EDF can be used to obtain other valuable estimates, such as the credit spread that bonds issued by such firms should command.

7.5   REDUCED-FORM MODELS

In a reduced-form model, the framework does not consider the causes of default; that is, default is exogenous. Key drivers in a reduced-form model include time to default (or default time) and recovery in the event of default (conversely, loss given default). The difference between various reduced-form models typically involves the processes of modeling when default occurs and estimating the recovery if default happens.

7.5.1   Default Intensity in Reduced-Form Models

Under certain assumptions about the nature of the random process that leads to default, the probability of survival for a given number of years can be shown to have an exponential distribution. Assuming an exponential distribution and denoting $p(t)$ as the probability that a firm has survived for t years, this probability can be expressed as:

$$p(t) = \exp(-\lambda \times t) \tag{7.17}$$

where λ is called the default intensity of the model. The parameter λ determines both the expected time to default and the probability of survival. Specifically, given a default intensity of $\lambda = 0.2$, the expected time to default is $(1/\lambda)$, or 5.00. The higher the **default intensity,** the shorter the expected time to default. The probability of default at or before t is given by $1 - p(t)$. The default intensity that appears in Equation 7.17 may refer to the actual or physical default intensity or to the risk-neutral version of the same variable. If the actual default intensity is used, then the analyst obtains an estimate of the actual expected time of default. The risk-neutral version of the default intensity is used exclusively for valuation purposes and to estimate credit spreads on investments exposed to credit risk.

7.5.2   Default Intensity and the Probabilities of Default

Suppose default time is continuous, meaning that default can take place at any time, and not just at discrete points of time (e.g., at the end of each quarter). Then, given Equation 7.17, the probability of default in the time interval of $(t, t + \Delta t)$, assuming there has been no default up to time t, is given by $\lambda \times \Delta t$, where Δt is a relatively small length of time. This is the conditional probability of default. On the other hand, the unconditional probability of default in the time interval of $(t, t + \Delta t)$ is given by $\exp(-\lambda \times t)\lambda \times \Delta t$, which is equal to the probability of surviving up to time t multiplied by the conditional probability of defaulting between t and Δt. It is important to note that λ is not the probability of default within 1 year, as 1 year is a relatively long length of time. Finally, the probability that default could take place between s and t, assuming that no default has taken place up to time s, is given by:

$$p(s) - p(t) = \exp(-\lambda \times s) - \exp(-\lambda \times t) \tag{7.18}$$

For example, suppose a start-up company has an actual default intensity of 5%. At the time the firm is established (i.e., time 0), the probability that the firm will default within Year 3, assuming that it has already survived for 2 years, is:

$$\text{Probability of Default in Year 3} = \exp(-0.05 \times 2) - \exp(-0.05 \times 3)$$

$$= 0.905 - 0.861 = 4.4\%$$

That is, at time zero, there is a 4.4% chance that the firm will not survive beyond the third year, provided that it has already survived for 2 years. Also, the expected time to default is $(1/0.05) = 20$ years.

APPLICATION 7.5.2

Company A has an actual default intensity of 0.10, and Company B has a 17% probability of defaulting in the next three periods. Find: (1) the probability of default; (2) the probability of survival; and (3) the expected time to default for Company A over the next two periods and the default intensity (λ) for Company B.

 The expected time to default of any company is simply $(1/\lambda)$, which in the case of Company A is 10 periods. Both remaining problems for Company A are solved using Equation 7.17. For Company A, the probability of survival is $e^{-0.10 \times 2}$, which equals 0.819. The probability of default is simply 1.0 minus the probability of survival: $1.0 - 0.819$, or 0.181. Company B has a probability of survival of 83%, or 0.83 (since its default probability is 17%). Therefore, the default intensity can be found by inserting 0.83 into the left side of Equation 7.17 and taking the natural logarithm of both sides. This generates the value that is equal to $-\lambda t$, specifically, $\ln(0.83)$, or -0.18633. Dividing that quantity by -3 (i.e., $-t$) generates a default intensity (λ) of 6.21%.

A reduced-form model can be used to relate default intensities to various financial and economic variables. Credit analysts have built models in which the default intensity is related to financial conditions of a firm as well as to macroeconomic conditions. The model is typically calibrated by selecting its parameters so that it can explain historical default patterns as well as current conditions in credit markets (e.g., credit spreads for various credit ratings). The resulting model is then used to value new issues or credit instruments, which is crucial to the development of some credit investment strategies.

7.5.3 Valuing Risky Debt with Default Intensity

The default intensity model can be incorporated into the valuation model for risky debt. To see the intuition of this model, consider a zero-coupon bond with a face value of K and time to maturity of T. If the bond is risk-free, then its current price is given by $K \times e^{-r \times T}$. Suppose the bond is exposed to default risk with a default intensity of λ. The probability of survival up to time T is $e^{-\lambda \times T}$, which means the probability of default by time T is $(1 - e^{-\lambda \times T})$. Assume that in the case of default the bond will have zero recovery. Then the price is given by:

$$D_0 = e^{-r \times T}(\text{Prob}_{\text{No Default}} \times K + \text{Prob}_{\text{Default}} \times 0)$$
$$= e^{-r \times T}(e^{-\lambda \times T} \times K + (1 - e^{-\lambda \times T}) \times 0) = K\, e^{-(r+\lambda) \times T} \tag{7.19}$$

APPLICATION 7.5.3

Assume the riskless rate is 2%. What is the current price of a 1-year zero-coupon bond issued by a start-up firm with a default intensity of 5%? The face value of the bond is $50 million. The value ($46.62 million) can be found using Equation 7.19:

$$D_0 = e^{-(0.02+0.05)\times 1} \times 50 = \$46.62 \text{ million}$$

Note that Equation 7.19 can be solved for any of its variables given the others.

It is important to note that Equation 7.19 was obtained under the assumption that investors do not care about potential systematic risk of the bond, and the only risk that enters into their calculations is the default risk. In other words, the default intensity and the resulting probability of default are assumed to be under risk neutrality (i.e., are Q-Measures).

The calculation in Application 7.5.3 can be reversed and, using observed market prices, one can calculate the implied risk-neutral default intensity. For example, suppose the market price of the bond in the previous example is actually $45.24 million. The implied risk-neutral default intensity would be 8%. That is,

$$45.24 = e^{-(0.02+0.08)\times 1} \times 50$$

7.5.4 Relating the Credit Spread to Default Intensity and the Recovery Rate

Finally, let's consider the case where in the event of default there is some recovery of face value. This amount is represented by $K \times RR$, where RR is the recovery rate. For simplicity, assume that the recovered amount is paid at time T. In this case, the value of the bond is given by:

$$D_0 = e^{-r\times T}(RR \times K \times (1 - e^{-\lambda\times T}) + K \times e^{-\lambda\times T})$$
$$\approx e^{-(r+\lambda(1-RR))\times T} \times K \tag{7.20}$$

When there is some recovery in case of default, the default intensity is reduced by the factor related to the recovery rate. The higher the recovery rate, the lower the impact of a default. The term $\lambda(1 - RR)$ in the second line of Equation 7.20 could be interpreted as an approximation to the credit spread that is added to the risk-free rate to obtain the appropriate discount rate:

$$\lambda \times (1 - RR) \approx \text{Credit Spread} \tag{7.21}$$

The credit spread is smaller for bonds with higher recovery rates or lower default intensity.

APPLICATION 7.5.4

Suppose the credit spread on a 1-year zero-coupon bond is 2%, and the recovery rate is estimated to be 80%. Find the risk-neutral default intensity. Using Equation 7.21, the approximated implied risk-neutral default intensity is 0.10:

$$0.02 \approx \lambda \times (1 - 0.8)$$

$$\lambda \approx 10\%$$

Note that Equation 7.21 contains three variables, any one of which can be solved using the other two.

7.5.5   The Two Predominant Reduced-Form Credit Models

Two models are most commonly cited when referring to the reduced-form models: the Jarrow–Turnbull (1995) model and the Duffie–Singleton (2003) model. The Jarrow–Turnbull model assumes that regardless of timing of default, recovery is received at the maturity date. The Jarrow–Lando–Turnbull (1997) model extends the original model further by taking into account various credit ratings beyond just two simple states of default or survival. Here, the model takes into account that there is migration risk (i.e., that the bond will be downgraded rather than experiencing outright default). The probability of moving from one rating to the next can be obtained from rating transition tables, published by the credit rating agencies. The Duffie–Singleton model allows the recovery process to occur at any time and sets the recovery amount to be a fraction of the nondefaulting bond price at the time of default.

7.6   EMPIRICAL CREDIT MODELS

Structural and reduced-form models attempt to model the economic and statistical underpinnings of bankruptcy and default. This section discusses empirical models.

7.6.1   Two Features of Empirical Credit Models

The empirical credit models differ from reduced form and structural credit models in two important ways. First, empirical models are based on the belief that the default process is too complex to be modeled mathematically. Therefore, the focus is on using historical data on default to understand credit risk in a rather crude way. Second, empirical models do not attempt to generate an estimate of the probability of default or credit spread, at least not directly. The primary goal of empirical models is to create a credit score. A **credit score** is a measure that can be used to rank or assess the relative riskiness of firms or securities. The absolute values of these credit scores usually do not contain much useful information but rather are used on a relative basis to rank firms or securities in terms of their credit risk. For this reason, empirical models are sometimes referred to as credit scoring models.

7.6.2 The Purpose of Altman's Z-Score Model

In this section, we provide a brief overview of an important credit scoring model: Altman's Z-score (Altman 1968; Saunders and Allen 2010). First, we discuss certain characteristics of a business, to specify and quantify the variables that are effective indicators and predictors of corporate distress. Second, we discuss how a set of financial and economic ratios can be analyzed in a context of corporate distress prediction by creating a credit score for the business.

The **Z-score model** focuses on a set of financial ratios that are based on a firm's financial statements as well as the market value of the firm's equity to generate a Z-score which is a relative rank of the likelihood of default. The ratios focus on those characteristics of firms that have proven to be useful in predicting financial distress, taking into account liquidity, profitability, leverage, solvency, and activity of a firm. Altman, who created the Z-score in the 1960s, used a linear econometric model to determine how important each characteristic is in predicting financial distress. The following equation displays the econometric model estimated by Altman:

$$Z = (1.2 \times X_1) + (1.4 \times X_2) + (3.3 \times X_3) + (0.6 \times X_4) + (1.0 \times X_5) \qquad (7.22)$$

In this expression, Z is the resulting Z-score, or the credit score. The five X variables determine the credit score and are detailed in the next section.

7.6.3 The Five Determinants of Altman's Z-Scores

There are five variables that determine Altman's Z-scores as depicted in Equation 7.22:

1. X_1: Working Capital/Total Assets. This ratio, frequently found in studies of corporate problems, is a measure of the net liquid assets of the firm relative to its total capitalization. Working capital is defined as the difference between current assets and current liabilities. Liquidity and size characteristics are explicitly considered. Ordinarily, a firm experiencing consistent operating losses will have shrinking current assets in relation to total assets.

2. X_2: Retained Earnings/Total Assets. This ratio measures the relative size of the total amount of reinvested earnings and/or losses of a firm over its entire life. This is a measure of the cumulative profitability of the firm over time and is likely to be low for young firms. This ratio is indirectly related to leverage, since those firms with relatively high ratios are more likely to have financed their assets through retention of profits and not to have used as much debt.

3. X_3: Earnings before Interest and Taxes/Total Assets. This ratio is a measure of the true productivity of the firm's assets, independent of any tax or leverage factors. Since a firm's ultimate existence is based on the earning power of its assets, this ratio appears to be particularly appropriate for studies dealing with corporate failure. Furthermore, insolvency in a bankruptcy sense occurs when the total liabilities exceed a fair valuation of the firm's assets, with the value determined by the earning power of the assets.

4. X_4: Market Value of Equity/Book Value of Total Liabilities. With the knowledge that assets minus liabilities equals equity, this measure shows how much the

firm's assets can decline in value before the liabilities exceed the assets and the firm becomes insolvent. For example, the value of X_4 will be equal to 2 for a firm with a market value of its equity equal to $1,000 and debt of $500, and the firm could experience a two-thirds $[2/(2 + 1)]$ drop in asset value before insolvency. However, the same firm with $500 equity will be insolvent if assets drop by only one-half in value.

5. X_5: Sales/Total Assets. This ratio, which is known as the asset-turnover ratio, is a standard financial ratio illustrating the sales-generating ability of the firm's assets. It is one measure of management's capacity in dealing with competitive conditions.

Altman used these five variables and historical data on a sample of firms— of which some defaulted and some survived—to estimate the coefficients that appear in Equation 7.22. The goal was to find coefficients to explanatory variables that maximized the maximum predictability power of default for the firms in the sample.

7.6.4 Solving for the Z-Score in Altman's Credit Scoring Model

Consider the information for PQR Corporation in Exhibit 7.4.

Given the definitions of X1 through X5, their values can be calculated as shown:

$$X1 = 5,000,000/30,000,000 = 0.167$$

$$X2 = 3,000,000/30,000,000 = 0.1$$

$$X3 = 5,000,000/30,000,000 = 0.167$$

$$X4 = 18,000,000/(5,000,000 + 10,000,000) = 1.2$$

$$X5 = 60,000,000/30,000,000 = 2$$

Finally, the Z-score can be calculated as 3.61 using these five values and the coefficients in Equation 7.22.

7.6.5 Interpreting Z-Scores in Altman's Credit Scoring Model

The absolute values of Z-scores do not have intuitive interpretations; one can use them to rank firms in terms of their levels of credit risk or likelihood of default. Using

EXHIBIT 7.4 Financial Information of PQR Corporation

Assets	€	Liabilities and Equity	€
Current Assets	10,000,000	Current Liabilities	5,000,000
Fixed Assets	20,000,000	Long-Term Liabilities	10,000,000
		Retained Earnings	3,000,000
		Common Stocks	12,000,000
Total Assets	30,000,000	Total Liabilities and Equity	30,000,000
Sales	60,000,000	Market Value of Equity	18,000,000
Cost and Expenses	55,000,000		
Income before Taxes and Interest	5,000,000		

historical data on the performance of firms for which the Z-scores were calculated. Altman has developed the following rule for interpreting the absolute values of these scores:

- $Z < 1.81$: Default group
- $1.81 \leq Z \leq 2.99$: Gray zone
- $Z > 2.99$: Nondefault group

The 3.61 Z-score for the sample firm (PQR Corporation) indicates that this firm belongs to the nondefault group.

NOTES

1. For further discussion of adverse selection and moral hazard in financial markets, see Mishkin (2012).
2. For further discussion of credit risk models, see Duffie and Singleton (2003).
3. For further discussion of Merton, KMV, and reduced-form models, see Saunders and Allen (2010).

REFERENCES

Akerlof, George A. 1970. "The Market for 'Lemons': Quality Uncertainty and the Market Mechanism." *The Quarterly Journal of Economics* 84 (3): 488–500.

Altman, E. 1968. "Financial Ratios, Discriminant Analysis and Prediction of Corporate Bankruptcy." *Journal of Finance* 23 (4): 589–609.

Black, F. and M. Scholes. 1973. "The Pricing of Options and Corporate Liabilities." *Journal of Political Economy* 8 (3): 637–54.

Crosbie, P. and J. Bohn. 2003. "Modeling Default Risk." White Paper, Moody's KMV Company.

Duffie, D. and K. Singleton. 2003. *Credit Risk: Pricing, Measurement and Management.* Princeton, NJ: Princeton University Press.

Jarrow, R., D. Lando, and S. Turnbull. 1997. "A Markov Model for the Term Structure of Credit Spreads." *Review of Financial Studies* (Summer): 481–523.

Jarrow R. and S. M. Turnbull. 1995. "Pricing Derivatives on Financial Securities Subject to Credit Risk." *Journal of Finance* 50 (1): 53–85.

Merton, R. 1974. "On the Pricing of Corporate Debt: The Risk Structure of Interest Rates." *Journal of Finance* 29 (2): 449–70.

Mishkin, F. S. 2012. *The Economics of Money, Banking, and Financial Markets*, Harlow: Pearson Education.

Saunders, A. and L. Allen. 2010. *Credit Risk Management in and out of the Financial Crisis: New Approaches to Value at Risk and Other Paradigms.* Hoboken, NJ: John Wiley & Sons.

Wang, Yu. 2009. "Structural Credit Risk Modeling: Merton and Beyond." *Risk Management* 16: 30–33.

CHAPTER 8

Multi-Factor Equity Pricing Models

Chapters 6 and 7 discussed interest rate risk and credit risk. In some cases, the risks were explicitly linked to factors. This chapter focuses on factors in equity markets, but can be generalized to all assets.

Level I of the CAIA curriculum emphasized single-factor asset pricing models, namely the capital asset pricing model (CAPM) in which the single factor is the total market portfolio of risky assets. This chapter emphasizes multi-factor asset pricing models. While these models are described as asset pricing models, their purpose is to describe the return generating process of risky assets.

8.1 MULTI-FACTOR ASSET PRICING MODELS

This section discusses a multi-factor market model. A **factor** represents a unique source of return and a unique premium in financial markets such that the observed return cannot be fully explained by other factors. In other words, return factors are not supposed to be highly correlated with each other. In addition, factors should have a sound economic foundation with rigorous academic and industry research supporting their presence. Finally, factors must show that their factor premiums persist over long periods.

8.1.1 Multi-factor Asset Pricing

Multi-factor models of asset pricing express systematic risk using multiple factors and are extremely popular throughout traditional and alternative investing. The reason is simple: multi-factor models tend to explain systematic returns much better than do single-factor models. By doing so, multi-factor models are generally believed to produce better estimates of idiosyncratic returns. A multi-factor asset pricing model has factors either in addition to the market portfolio or in place of the market portfolio. An example of a factor could be the size of the firm or the spread between the returns of small stocks and large stocks. Equation 8.1 represents a general ex ante form of a multi-factor asset pricing model assuming that the factors can be traded:

$$E(R_i) - R_f = \sum_{j=1}^{J} \beta_{ij}[E(R_j) - R_f] \tag{8.1}$$

where β_{ij} represents the responsiveness, or beta, of asset i to factor j; $E(R_j)$ is the expected return of factor j; and J is the number of factors. Single-factor models represent the case of $J = 1$, whereas multi-factor models represent the case of $J > 1$. Equation 8.2 represents an ex post form:

$$R_{it} - R_f = \sum_{j=1}^{J} \beta_{ij}[R_{jt} - R_f] + \varepsilon_{it} \qquad (8.2)$$

As detailed in Level I of the CAIA curriculum, ex ante models describe expected returns while ex post models describe realized returns.

Multi-factor models are primarily used to estimate the variance–covariance matrix of asset returns in order to inform investors about the exposures of their portfolios. Researchers use cross-sectional models to identify the return attributable to various systematic factors and therefore identify the portion of return differences across securities that would be attributable to idiosyncratic risk. The most popular multi-factor asset pricing model for equity returns is the Fama–French (1992) model, which links the returns of equities to two factors in addition to the market factor: (1) a factor representing a growth versus value effect; and (2) a factor representing a size effect.

The following sections explore empirical models and the distinction between empirical and theoretical multi-factor asset pricing models. Then the next several sections review especially important empirical models: the Fama–French model, the Fama–French–Carhart (Cahart 1997) model and extensions to those models.

8.1.2 Asset Factors and the Role of Marginal Investor Utility in the CAPM

An important characteristic of a factor in a factor-based asset pricing model is whether the payoffs to the factor (i.e., the payoffs to assets with high exposures to that factor) are related to the marginal utility that investors derive from those payoffs. For example, the CAPM has as its single factor the return of the overall market. Clearly, investors derive higher marginal utility from payoffs when the market generates negative returns (i.e., "bad economic times") than from payoffs received when markets are strong. A stock with a high beta generates great returns when wealth levels are high and poor returns when wealth levels are low. Declining marginal utility of wealth drives such undesirable assets (high beta assets) to require relatively high-risk premiums.

8.1.3 Multiple Factors and "Bad Times"

Outside of a single-factor world, the relation between factor payoffs and good economic times or bad economic times still matters. Factors that pay well in bad times are desirable and command low or negative risk premiums.

However, in a CAPM world only one factor commands a risk premium (the market beta) and all investors are assumed to share the same definition of what differentiates good economic times from bad economic times. In a multi-factor world, investors differ with regard to the impact of good overall economies and bad overall economies on their utility as well as differing with regard to the attractiveness of various factors in the economic outcomes.

For example, investors with human capital tied to occupations that suffer financially during periods of high inflation may especially prefer factor exposures that cause their financial assets to do well during periods of high inflation.

The key takeaway is as follows. Differences among investors with regard to the attractiveness of various factor exposures can lead to valuation effects that cause asset prices to be driven by multiple factors rather than a single market factor.

8.1.4 Factors Based on Expected Utility or Anomalies

Factors, like financial markets, can be driven by influences that are linked to expected utility maximization or by anomalies. Expected utility maximization by market participants drives factors that contain systematic risks to offer risk premiums. Factor premiums that cannot be explained by expected utility maximization (and risk premiums) are entitled anomalies. For example, the tendency of stocks that generate substantially improved cash flows in good economic times to have positive returns supports the existence of the market return factor to offer a risk premium. Alternatively, the potential tendency of investors to consistently react to recent market performance in a way that generates predictable patterns in subsequent returns that can be used to earn superior returns would indicate an anomaly. In other words, when a return premium related to a factor cannot be explained by expected utility models (i.e., cannot be explained by risk aversion), then it is an anomaly.

8.1.5 Three Major Categories of Factors

There are three major categories of factors that drive asset returns. **Macroeconomic factors** drive asset returns throughout the entire economy and across asset classes, and include productivity, inflation, credit, economic growth, and liquidity. For example, a spike in anticipated inflation is generally expected to have effects throughout an economy and is expected to affect some firms (e.g., utilities) more than other firms (e.g., commodity producers).

Fundamental, style, investment, or dynamic factors tend to drive equity returns within asset classes and include well known style factors such as value, size, momentum, quality, and low volatility. These factors are linked to fundamental firm attributes that have been empirically identified as being important drivers of different investment returns across various firms, industries, and sectors. These factors are used in smart beta and alternative beta approaches.

Statistical factors drive asset returns within an entire economy, asset class, or sector and are distinguished by having been identified purely on empirical characteristics rather than style or economic characteristics. For example, principal component analysis of security returns through time may find that much of the return differences between assets can be explained by perhaps three to five components. The economic identity of these factors and economic cause of the relation between the factor and the asset returns is often not known. Statistical factors have been identified in bond returns, for example.

8.1.6 Theoretically versus Empirically Derived Multifactor Return Models

A crucial distinction between asset pricing models is whether the factors are derived theoretically or identified empirically. Simply put: were the factors deduced through reasoning, or were they determined statistically? In the former case, there is a potentially logical explanation for the relationship. In the latter case, it may simply be an observed phenomenon. In a theoretical model, the factors are derived from reasoning based on known facts and relations. An example of a multi-factor asset pricing model based on theory rather than empirics would be a model that recognizes that the returns of some alternative assets should depend on statistical parameters other than just mean and variance, such as skewness. The key is that the factors are identified based on an understanding of financial economics: there is a reason to believe that investors should be concerned with skewness and that the related factor should therefore be related to expected and realized returns. Another example would be a model linking the returns of a hybrid security containing equity and bond features to the market returns of equity markets and bond markets.

An empirical model is derived from observation. An example would be a model that recognizes that the returns of some traditional assets are correlated with their market-to-book ratios. The key would be that the factors were observed to be correlated using historical data rather than identified ahead of time based on arguments relying on well-established economic reasoning. Of course, the observed correlations should be identified using sound statistical techniques.

8.1.7 Fundamentals of Empirical Models

Empirical models of returns are derived from historical observations and are typically based on the following steps: (1) the risk-free rate is subtracted from the past returns of each security or fund to form the excess return for each asset, which is then used as the dependent variable, traditionally located on the left side of a regression equation; (2) the researcher selects a set of potential factors that serve as independent variables; and (3) statistical analysis is used to identify those factors that are significantly correlated with the returns.

The factors may represent tradable assets, such as indices (e.g., the return on bonds) or spreads between the returns of two indices (e.g., the return on a large-capitalization index minus the return on a small-capitalization index). As its name implies, a **tradable asset** is a position that can be readily established and liquidated in the financial market, such as a stock position, a bond position, or a portfolio of liquid positions. Alternatively, the factors may represent nontradable variables, such as inflation or economic productivity.

8.1.8 The Tradability of Factors and the Intercept

A key characteristic of using tradable assets in asset pricing models is that if all of the factors in the model are tradable, and if the model includes all potential systematic return factors, then the intercept of the model (i.e., the mean of the residual term) can be interpreted as indicating any superior or inferior risk-adjusted return. In an informationally efficient market, if Equation 8.2 contained all of the systematic return factors, and all of the factors were tradable, then the idiosyncratic error term would have a mean of zero. The reason is that with all the factors being tradable, an arbitrageur could use market positions to hedge out all of the systematic risk of any asset, leaving only the diversifiable (idiosyncratic) risk. The actions of arbitrageurs would drive the expected returns toward zero. In a statistical test, if an intercept term generated a value significantly different from zero, it would indicate that the asset was mispriced. This property does not necessarily hold for models with an incomplete set of factors or models with nontradable factors.

8.2 FAMA–FRENCH MODELS

The next three sections review seminal and still-popular empirical asset pricing models developed by Fama and French for equity returns.

8.2.1 The Original Fama–French Model

The Fama–French model and other models discussed in Section 8.2 are empirical asset pricing models that have shown substantial power in explaining the returns of traditional equities and equity-oriented alternative investments. The **Fama–French model** links the returns of assets to three factors: (1) the market portfolio; (2) a factor representing a value versus growth effect; and (3) a factor representing a small-cap versus large-cap effect.[1] The first factor is the same as the one found in the CAPM (the return of the market portfolio). The other two factors reflect the tendency of common stocks to fluctuate both in proportion to their book-to-market ratios (as a proxy for value versus growth) and in proportion to their capitalization size. Support for the model is empirically based: many years of data support the idea that realized returns, and arguably expected returns, are correlated with these factors. Equation 8.3 is the ex ante form of the Fama–French model:

$$E(R_i) - R_f = \beta_i[E(R_m) - R_f] + \beta_{1i}[E(R_s - R_b)] + \beta_{2i}[E(R_h - R_l)] \qquad (8.3)$$

where R_s is the return to a diversified portfolio consisting of small-capitalization stocks, R_b is the return to a diversified portfolio consisting of big-capitalization stocks, β_{1i} is the responsiveness of asset i to the spread $(R_s - R_b)$, R_h is the return to a diversified portfolio consisting of high book-to-market ratio (value) stocks, R_l is the return to a diversified portfolio consisting of low book-to-market ratio (growth) stocks, and β_{2i} is the responsiveness of asset i to the spread $(R_h - R_l)$.

The two additional factors are expressed as spreads between the returns of two indices. For example, the size factor is the spread between the returns earned on small stocks and the returns earned on large stocks. An investor can earn and trade the return of each factor by being long the index that is added and short the index that is subtracted in forming the return spread. As discussed in the previous section, because the factors are tradable, any intercept of the model and of the related regression can be interpreted as an indication of asset mispricing.

8.2.2 The Fama–French–Carhart Model

The **Fama–French–Carhart model**, shown in Equation 8.4, adds a fourth factor to the Fama–French model: momentum.[2] The idea is that whether a common stock has risen or fallen recently helps explain subsequent performance. This fourth factor, in theory, may be important, because many investors, including mutual funds, follow momentum strategies. Momentum demonstrates very strong explanatory power, especially relative to the size factor.

$$E(R_i) - R_f = \beta_i[E(R_m) - R_f] + \beta_{1i}[E(R_s - R_b)] + \beta_{2i}[E(R_h - R_l)] + \beta_{3i}[E(R_w - R_d)]$$

$$(8.4)$$

where R_w is the return to a diversified portfolio consisting of winning stocks, in the sense that they have better performance over a previous period; R_d is the return to a diversified portfolio consisting of declining stocks, in the sense that they have worse performance over a previous period; and β_{3i} is the responsiveness of asset i to the spread $(R_w - R_d)$.

Asset pricing models can be used to analyze cross-sectional return variations (the returns of many assets at a point in time) or time-series variations (the returns of one asset over many points in time). There is little doubt that both the Fama–French model and the Fama–French–Carhart model provide higher explanatory power of past equity returns than do single-factor models. Higher explanatory power can be useful in return attribution. The more return variation that is explained by a given number of common factors, the more likely it is that the remaining return variation can be more accurately attributed to idiosyncratic return and, presumably, abnormal performance. Thus, these models may better allow an analyst to separate manager skill from the returns earned by accepting exposure to systematic factors such as size, value, and momentum.

8.2.3   Models with Numerous Factors

The Fama–French model and the Fama–French–Carhart model were the dominant multi-factor return models in academic studies for the analysis of traditional equity markets. More recently, Fama and French have developed a five-factor model. **The Fama–French five-factor model** adds two factors to the Fama–French three-factor model: robust minus weak, and conservative minus aggressive.

Robust minus weak is "the average return on ... robust operating profitability portfolios minus the average return on ... weak operating profitability portfolios."[3] Conservative minus aggressive is "the average return on ... conservative investment portfolios minus the average return on ... aggressive investment portfolios."[4] The **robust minus weak factor** is designed to distinguish firms by a specific measure of their reported accounting profitability (with robust firms having exhibited higher accounting profits as a proportion of equity). The **conservative minus aggressive factor** is designed to distinguish firms by the rate of reported corporate asset investment (with conservative firms exhibiting a lower rate of investment in corporate assets).

There now exist a multitude of models developed and used by practitioners that include numerous factors to describe equity returns. The Fama–French five-factor model and models with five or six factors developed by other researchers have become the industry standards for analysis of equity market returns. As described by Christopherson, Carino, and Ferson, the factors included in a multi-factor model vary from model to model and can even include dozens of factors in a single model.[5] Factors can include measures of trading activity, historical growth, historical profitability, earnings-to-price ratios, variability of earnings, leverage, currency sensitivity, dividend yield, and sector exposures.

Alternative assets do not tend to have the same factor exposures as traditional assets. Therefore, the Fama–French models are of limited application to alternative asset returns that do not involve public equities. However, analogous multi-factor return models have been proposed and tested for various types of alternative assets and various management strategies. Although results vary between the types of alternative assets being analyzed, many multi-factor asset pricing models have performed quite well by displaying substantial levels of explanatory power in empirical tests.

For example, a hedge fund strategy like convertible bond arbitrage can be associated with the return factors of bonds, due to the bond part of the convertible bond, and with the return factors of equity options, including volatility, due to the conversion feature of the bond.[6] The idea is simply to identify those common sources of return (i.e., return factors) that appear to be related to the given type of investment return, either through economic reasoning or through empirical testing.

8.3   THREE CHALLENGES OF EMPIRICAL MULTI-FACTOR MODELS

Academics and practitioners have identified various multi-factor models that appear to offer the high explanatory power of past returns, especially in public equity markets. This section begins by raising two important issues that analysts should consider when using these models to perform return attribution or to forecast future expected returns.

8.3.1   False Identification of Factors

First, widespread searches for statistically significant factors run the risk of false identification of useful factors. In the absence of solid theory, research is often performed in which a multitude of potential variables are tested to locate those that are statistically significant. For example, a researcher might test for correlations between stock returns and their characteristics, such as: their accounting ratios; their past return behaviors; and descriptive variables relating to each firm's size, location, industry, number of employees, number of products, and so forth. The list could contain hundreds of potentially important variables. If the researcher requires a factor to be statistically significant in an empirical test with a confidence level of 99%, then a test of 200 to 300 variables typically generates two to three statistically significant factors, even if there is no true underlying relationship. Of course, such randomly identified factors would not have any value in predicting future behavior. Therefore, it is vital that factors be identified with solid theoretical reasoning, with rigorous statistical testing, or with both. The key is to understand how many variables have been tested as potential factors.

APPLICATION 8.3.1A

A researcher wishes to test for statistically significant and independent factors in explaining asset returns. Using a confidence level of 90%, how many statistically significant independent factors would the researcher expect to identify by testing 50 variables, independent from one another, that had no true relationship to the returns?

The answer is 5, which is found by multiplying the number of unrelated variables (50) by the probability of mistakenly concluding that the variables were true factors (10%). What if research were performed with a confidence level of 99.9% but with 100 researchers, each testing 50 different variables on different data sets? The answer is also 5, as there are 5,000 variables (50 times 100) multiplied by the probability of mistakenly concluding that the variables were true factors (0.1%).

8.3.2 Factor Return Correlation versus Causation

A second potential difficulty is in differentiating between factors that are correlated with returns and those that cause returns. For example, consider a market in which the Fama–French model describes equity returns well (i.e., the systematic component of all returns is substantially explained by three factors: the market, a value effect, and a size effect). Suppose that the firms in the equity market belong to 20 industries, and within each industry, the characteristics of the firms tend to be rather similar with regard to the three Fama–French factors. It is quite possible that an empirical model with 20 industry factors would perform better in terms of r-squared (i.e., explanatory power) than would the Fama–French model. But the 20 factors corresponding to the 20 industries do not cause investment returns in this example; they are simply *correlated* with investment returns. Why does causation matter? The analyst can benefit from understanding why a phenomenon exists in order to make better decisions. For example, if a firm is a mix of businesses related to two industries, it would be important to know whether its valuation is driven by the industry label assigned to the firm or by its Fama–French factors.

8.3.3 Why the CAPM May Not Be Sufficient

A key challenge in using an empirical multi-factor model lies in justifying why it should perform better than the CAPM in describing the tradeoff between risk and return. In other words, why are multiple factors necessary if the CAPM provides a single-factor explanation? In a CAPM-based view of risk and return, all investors fully diversify into the market portfolio so that their returns are subject to only one factor: the market portfolio. The justification for using a multi-factor approach implicitly assumes that various investors receive benefit from selecting different exposures to different factors. Why would investors choose high exposures to some factors and low exposures to others when the CAPM implies that all investors obtain their highest expected utility from allocating to market-weighted exposures?

One potential inability of the CAPM (as a single-factor model) to capture all relevant variation in asset pricing is the CAPM's reliance on mean and variance. The justifications for mean-variance analysis are either that utility investor functions are quadratic or that investment returns are normally distributed. Both justifications are violated in the real world, so multi-factor models may be needed.

Other justifications for multiple-factor asset pricing approaches include investor-specific differences, including heterogeneous expectations, positions in illiquid assets (e.g., human capital and private real estate), liabilities such as mortgages, different investment time horizons (e.g., different ages), and the existence of and heterogeneous exposure to transaction costs and taxes.

These issues are especially problematic when considering alternative investments. In the case of traditional investments, there is a strong case to be made for the idea that investors are increasingly able and willing to fully diversify into a market-weighted portfolio. But for many alternative investments, there is a strong case for expected returns to depend on multiple factors, because, unlike traditional investments, it is nearly impossible to invest in a market-weighted portfolio of alternative investments. For example, many alternative investments are privately held rather than publicly traded. Much of the wealth throughout the world is in private assets, such as real estate and intellectual property, which are not regularly offered for sale. Therefore, idiosyncratic risks of many alternative assets are not easily diversified. An important takeaway message to the conflict between using single-factor and multi-factor approaches is this: rather than using multi-factor models purely because of impressive empirical results, an analyst should investigate the economic reasoning behind why a single-factor market model is inappropriate. Alternative investments offer substantial reasons to believe that a single-factor market model may be inadequate.

8.4 FACTOR INVESTING

Factor investing is a recent development in the area of asset allocation, and some aspects of it are closely tied to the developments of certain hedge fund strategies. The basic ideas behind factor investing were developed by academic researchers over the past 30 years. However, only in recent years have these ideas been synthesized and presented in practical form by the investment industry. This section offers a brief introduction to this topic; detailed discussions of this approach can be found in Ang (2014).

8.4.1 The Emergence of Return Factor Analysis and Three Important Observations

One of the central concepts in finance is that returns above the risk-free rate are compensation for exposure to risks. Stocks have earned a premium above the risk-free asset because they expose their owners to their underlying factors. The CAPM can be thought of as the first theory of return factors. According to the CAPM, the expected excess return on a risky asset is equal to the beta of the asset times the risk premium on the market portfolio. Under assumptions including that asset returns are normally distributed, the CAPM correctly identifies the only return factor to be the return on the market portfolio, and the measure of exposure of each stock to this factor to be its market beta. Further, each investor has an optimal beta.

By relaxing the assumptions of the CAPM, academic and industry researchers have extended the model, leading them to develop a long list of return factors.[7] Even though there is no consensus about the number of return factors in financial markets, it is well established that the market portfolio is not the only factor in the market. The risk premiums earned by stocks and other traditional assets are indeed a combination of various risk premiums. In a multiple factor model, each investor has optimal exposures to each beta.

Our discussion of factor investing begins with three important observations detailed by Ang (2014):

1. Factors matter, not assets: The factors behind the assets matter, not the assets themselves. Asset allocators should view assets as nothing more than means for accessing factors.
2. Assets are bundles of factors: Most asset classes expose investors to a set of return factors; therefore, the risk premium offered by an asset class represents a package of risk premiums offered by factor exposures. Exposures of assets and

risk premiums to factors can be used to estimate the risk premium that an asset should provide.

3. Different investors should focus on different factors: Asset owners differ in terms of time horizons, risk tolerances, objectives, and liabilities that should be funded. These differences require careful examination of factor exposures of a portfolio in order to ensure that the asset owners do not have too much or too little exposure to some factors.

If we consider the risk premium earned by each asset class to be a function of exposures to several return factors, then several important questions arise:

- How are factors described?
- Do all factors offer the same risk premium?
- How do the risk premiums for these factors behave through various stages of a business cycle?
- Are all factors investable?
- How does one perform risk allocation based on factors?
- Do allocations based on factors outperform allocations based on asset classes?

These questions are addressed in the next six sections.

8.4.2 How Return Factors Are Described

Consider two well known equity factors: momentum and value. To create the momentum factor, researchers examine the performance of equity prices through time. Two portfolios are created at the start of each period (e.g., each month). One equally weighted portfolio will contain those stocks that performed well during a previous period (e.g., past 12 months), and the other equally weighted portfolio will contain those stocks that performed poorly during the same period. This procedure is repeated every period and results in two return series. If one were to go long the portfolio of winners and go short the portfolio of losers, the return to this active strategy would be the return to the momentum factor. We can ascertain that this is indeed a new factor if the return to this strategy cannot be explained by other factors, such as returns to the market portfolio.

The value factor is constructed the same way except that stocks are sorted based on the ratio of their book values to their market values. Stocks with high ratios of book value to market value are considered value stocks, and those with low ratios are considered growth stocks. Two equally weighted portfolios are created each period. One will consist of those stocks with above-average book-to-market ratios, and the other one will consist of those stocks with below-average book-to-market ratios. Again, a strategy will go long the first portfolio and short the second portfolio. The return to this active strategy will represent the return to the value factor. Exhibit 8.1 displays properties of these two factors.

It is important to note that the average returns reported in Exhibit 8.1 are for portfolios that, at least in theory, do not require any investment. This is because each factor consists of equal-size long and short positions. Therefore, the initial capital is available to be invested in the riskless assets, the market portfolio, or some combination of the two.

EXHIBIT 8.1 Properties of Value and Momentum Factors

1927–2018	Value	Momentum	50/50 Portfolio
Annualized Mean	4.46%	7.94%	6.20%
Annualized Standard Deviation	12.06%	16.25%	7.87%
Correlation with Market Return	0.24	−0.34	−0.16
Correlation of Two Factors	−0.41		

Source: K. French Data Library.

During the same period, the return on the market in excess of the riskless rate and the standard deviation of that return were 7.72% and 18.71%, respectively.

Several important observations can be made from Exhibit 8.1. First, both factors have generated significant positive returns over a long period. Second, both factors are volatile, which means they may not consistently generate positive returns, and there will be periods during which they could generate negative returns. Third, the two factors are negatively correlated (−0.41) with each other and are not highly correlated with market risk. The fact that the two factors have been negatively correlated in the past is one of the key benefits of factor investing in the sense that two sources of returns have been discovered that are negatively correlated. This means a portfolio of the two should be far less volatile, which is confirmed by the last column of the exhibit. From Exhibit 8.1 the potential benefits of factor investing can already be seen. By isolating factors and investing in them, one might be able to avoid those risks that are not rewarded by the marketplace and, as a result, create portfolios that display more attractive risk–return properties.

Academic and industry research has uncovered a number of risk premiums. The following is a partial list of the best-known fundamental or investment return factors:

- Value premium: Based on the return earned by stocks with high book values relative to their market values. The strategy is to take long positions in stocks with a relatively high ratio and short positions in stocks with a relatively low ratio.
- Size premium: Based on the rate of return earned by small-cap stocks. The strategy is to take long positions in small-cap stocks and short positions in large-cap stocks.
- Momentum premium: Based on past performance of stocks. The strategy is to take long positions in past winners and short positions in past losers.
- Liquidity premium: Based on the risk premium earned by illiquid assets. The strategy is to take long positions in illiquid assets and short positions in similar but otherwise liquid assets.
- Credit risk premium: Based on the credit risk of bonds. The strategy is to take long positions in bonds with low credit quality and short positions in bonds with high credit quality.
- Term premium: Based on the riskiness of long-term bonds. The strategy is to take long positions in long-term bonds and short positions in short-term bonds.
- Implied volatility premium: Based on the risk premium earned by the volatility factor. The strategy is to be short the implied volatility of options (e.g., create a market-neutral position using short positions in out-of-the-money puts and

short positions in stocks) and long the realized volatility of options through delta hedging of the underlying stock.

- Low volatility premium: Based on the return to low volatility stocks. The strategy is to take long positions in low volatility stocks and short positions in high volatility stocks. The same strategy can be implemented using betas.
- Carry trade: Based on the return to investments in high-interest-rate currencies. The strategy is to take long positions in bonds denominated in currencies with high interest rates and short positions in bonds denominated in currencies with low interest rates.
- Roll premium: Based on the return earned on commodities that are in backwardation. The strategy is to take long positions in commodities that are in backwardation and short positions in commodities that are in contango.

8.4.3   Risk Premiums Vary across Return Factors

Do all factors offer the same risk premium? Evidence regarding this question has already been provided by the two factors that were presented in Exhibit 8.1. Those two factors offered different risk–return profiles. Different factors offer different risk premiums, and the sizes of the risk premiums are not constant through time. Therefore, while a passive allocation to several factors could produce attractive results, a more sophisticated approach would consider the size of the premium attached to each factor and create an asset allocation that would take advantage of differences in risk premiums. In other words, it might be beneficial to apply tactical asset allocation to factors by assigning higher weights to factors that are believed to be offering more attractive risk premiums. In addition, academic research has shown that those factors that provide poor returns during bad times are the ones that provide attractive returns during normal times. Risk premiums associated with legitimate factors are there because these factors perform poorly during bad times. Investors should be willing to hold them only if they provide attractive returns during normal times. Actually, the first step in determining whether an observed source of return is a legitimate factor is to compare its returns during good and bad times. If the factor provides an attractive return during good and bad times, then it is not a factor—it is an arbitrage opportunity.

8.4.4   Factor Returns Vary across Market Conditions

How do these risk premiums behave through various stages of a business cycle? Exhibit 8.2 displays the rolling 24-month average returns on the two factors discussed in Exhibit 8.1.

Clearly, these two factors display significant time variations. As previously mentioned, we must expect factor premiums to display some volatility and to perform differently during various stages of the business cycle. If there were no risks, then there would be no premiums. For instance, the book-to-market factor (i.e., value factor) tends to produce attractive risk-adjusted returns during normal market conditions but have poor risk-adjusted returns during economic downturns.[8] The momentum factor tends to produce positive returns most of the time but has a tendency to display large negative returns over a short period of time when a

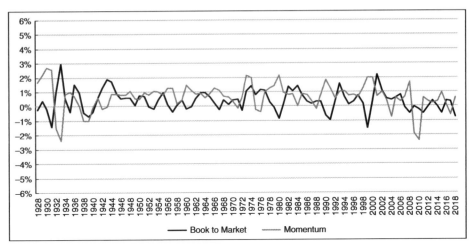

EXHIBIT 8.2 Rolling 24-Month Average Returns to Factors
Source: K. French Data Library.

market correction takes place. Momentum is notorious for performing poorly during momentum crashes. A **momentum crash** occurs when those assets with recent overperformance (i.e., those assets with momentum) experience extremely poor performance relative to other assets (Asness et al. 2010). In the same way that investors have learned to hold diversified portfolios in terms of asset classes, they should hold diversified portfolios in terms of factors.

8.4.5 Return Factors and Investability

Are all factors investable? While 25 years ago it might have been difficult and costly to create investment strategies that represented various factors, financial innovations of the past decades have substantially reduced the cost of such strategies. In recent years, exchange-traded funds (ETFs) have become available that track value, volatility, momentum, size, and roll factors. These strategies are often described as using smart beta. Another term for describing the investability of a factor is that it is tradable.

While many factors are tradable, they may not be fully implementable. For example, the value factor has been shown to be strongest for the very small-cap firms. However, there is limited capacity for investing in these firms, and the bid–ask spreads for their stocks are quite wide. Since creating the value factor would require frequent rebalancing of the portfolio, it may not be possible to fully implement factor investing in value stocks. Therefore, traded investment products designed to replicate the value factor tend to concentrate their allocations to large-cap stocks, which have shown to be poor representatives of the value factor.

Even when pure return factors may not be fully traded, their return properties are useful in measuring risk exposures of investment products (e.g., hedge funds) and in determining if they offer any alpha. If one were to regress the excess return of an investment product against the returns of several traded factors, the intercept would represent an estimate of the alpha of the investment product.

8.4.6 Risk Allocation Based on Return Factors

How does one perform risk allocation based on return factors? Factor or risk allocation is no different from asset allocation. After all, one has to use assets to isolate factors. Two issues related to factor investing should be considered. First, it is not possible to create a benchmark for a passive factor investing strategy. This is because factors involve long/short strategies, and therefore it is unclear what the passive weights of a diversified portfolio of factors should be. Should the factors be equally weighted, or should they be volatility weighted? There is no clear answer to this question.

Second, direct factor investing requires the investor to actively manage portfolios that are supposed to represent factors. Therefore, there is no such thing as passively managed factor portfolios. It should be pointed out that if there are enough investment products (e.g., funds and ETFs) replicating each factor, then the investor could follow a buy-and-hold strategy involving these investment products. However, unless one is willing to allow the weights of some factors to become very high or low, the investor will have to rebalance the portfolio on a regular basis. In addition, direct investments may not be a viable strategy for some institutional investors, as most factor strategies would require long and short positions in certain asset classes, and many institutional investors may not be prepared to take short positions.

Several hedge fund strategies earn their returns by exploiting these factors. For instance, the merger arbitrage strategy seeks a premium by exploiting a factor related to the uncertainty surrounding the completion of mergers. The convertible arbitrage strategy exploits a form of the implied volatility factor, and many equity long/short and equity market-neutral strategies have been shown to have significant exposures to factors of the equity markets (Zhang and Kazemi 2015). Finally, global macro strategies often rely heavily on the carry trade factor to generate returns.

8.4.7 Performance with Allocations Based on Return Factors

Do allocations based on factors outperform allocations based on asset classes? In theory, allocations based on factors should provide the same risk-adjusted return as allocations based on assets if the same information sets are used (Idzorek and Kowara 2013). It can be shown that in a perfect world, where all factors can be traded and all asset returns can be explained by factors, neither approach is inherently superior to the other. Research using real-world data has demonstrated that either approach may be superior over a given period of time (Idzorek and Kowara 2013). In particular, in some cases, the apparent superiority of factors is a simple result of the fact that factors can be conceptualized as being an alternative set of asset classes that can be identified when the long-only constraint is removed. For instance, a portion of the return earned by the value factor is due to the fact that it shorts growth stocks. Therefore, an asset allocation strategy that would permit the investor to short stocks should be able to match the performance of a portfolio that allocates to the value factor. If all return factors were traded and short sale constraints were removed, then it would be difficult to imagine that a portfolio constructed using risk allocation could outperform a portfolio constructed using asset allocation on a consistent basis.

Several practical issues associated with risk-factor-based asset allocation must be highlighted (Idzorek and Kowara 2013). First, portfolio construction using return factors is not likely to become globally adopted, because it implies allocation strategies that are not sustainable (i.e., not consistent on the macro level). That is, not everyone can be short growth stocks or commodities that are in contango. Therefore, the capacity is likely to be limited, and as more money is allocated to factor investing, the strategies will become expensive and the risk premium will shrink or disappear altogether. Second, risk allocation requires asset owners to take extreme positions in some asset classes. Many institutional investors are not allowed to make such allocations. For example, taking short positions in all growth stocks, including such names as Google, Amazon, and Facebook, is not something that most investors are prepared to do. Third, risk allocation is not a magic bullet that will automatically lead to asset allocations that will dominate those based on asset classes. Similar to other investment products, the cost of the strategy must be taken into account. Flows into some of these factors have already reduced the size of the premium (e.g., size and low volatility factors have not performed well in recent years). Finally, alternative investments are important vehicles for accessing some of these return factors, but they typically represent a bundle of factors; as such, a pure risk allocation approach cannot be applied to alternatives. However, measuring factor exposures of alternative assets can provide valuable information about their risk–return profiles, which should be taken into account when allocations to traditional asset classes are considered. For instance, factor exposure analysis of private equity will highlight the fact that it has significant exposures to size and credit factors. Therefore, the investor may choose to tilt the exposure of the portfolio's traditional assets to other factors.

8.5   THE ADAPTIVE MARKETS HYPOTHESIS

The Adaptive Markets Hypothesis is related to the importance of multiple factor return analysis. As first proposed by Lo (2004), the **Adaptive Markets Hypothesis (AMH)** is an approach to understanding how markets evolve, how opportunities occur, and how market players succeed or fail based on principles of evolutionary biology.

According to the AMH, concepts central to evolutionary biology govern market dynamics via the forces of competition, mutation, reproduction, and natural selection:

> *Prices reflect as much information as dictated by the combination of environmental conditions and the number and nature of "species" in the economy, or … ecology. Species are defined as distinct groups of market participants: e.g., pension funds, retail investors, hedge funds.* (Lo 2004)

According to the AMH, profit opportunities exist when more resources are present and competition is lower. Through the mechanism of natural selection, as competition increases, the players who have competitive advantage over others survive and adapt. Those who are not able to adapt disappear, reducing competition and starting the evolutionary cycle all over again. An excellent example of this phenomenon at work is the waxing and waning of hedge fund styles.

According to Lo (2012), the important practical implications of an adaptive view on markets include these four:

1. TIME-VARYING RISK PREMIUMS. The tradeoff between risk and return is not stable over time (risk premiums vary over time). In addition, changes in risk premiums could be predicted based on technical and fundamental variables.
2. MARKET EFFICIENCY IS A RELATIVE CONCEPT. Market efficiency should be measured and discussed in relative terms as opposed to absolute terms. Market efficiency is a continuum; it is not simply efficient or inefficient, and a market displays varying degrees of efficiency at different points in time and for different market participants.
3. ADAPTATION FOR SUCCESS AND SURVIVAL. It is necessary to use adaptable investment approaches to handle changes in the market environment. Opportunities are not always found in the same place; therefore, trading strategies must be altered as the economic environment evolves.
4. THE INEVITABLE DEGRADATION OF ALPHA. With time, what was once alpha becomes, due to innovation and competition, beta. Persistent alpha opportunities are not possible; however, fleeting alpha opportunities may be possible.

A key development in asset allocation has been recognition of the importance of time-varying volatility, and the related concepts of time-varying risk premiums and stochastic discount factors. Both of these issues relate to the importance of viewing the tradeoff between risk and return in the context of stochastic discount factors. Time-varying volatility and stochastic discount factors are discussed in the next sections.

8.6   TIME-VARYING VOLATILITY

Time-varying volatility is the characteristic of a return series in which the asset's returns experience varying levels of true (as opposed to realized) return variation.

8.6.1   Equity Market Volatility is Predictable

The fact that equity market volatility can be somewhat predictable can be consistent with informational efficiency. It is obvious that equity markets should be and are generally more volatile surrounding the revelation of fundamentally important information such as central bank announcements, major military conflicts, international trade negotiations, major legislative actions, and so forth. Equity market volatility is at least partially predictable with simple technical analysis: equity market volatility is persistent and therefore volatility immediately subsequent to a period of high observed volatility tends to be higher than volatility subsequent to a period of low observed volatility. Relatively sophisticated econometric models (e.g., ARCH and GARCH, discussed in Chapter 4 of the CAIA Level 1 curriculum) are popular tools for predicting future volatility on the basis of past volatility.

8.6.2   Volatility is Negatively Correlated with Average Returns

Equity market volatility is clearly correlated with the contemporaneous direction of the market. High volatility tends to occur during negative market returns and low volatility tends to occur during positive market returns. The negative correlation between equity market volatility and the change in the price level of the equity market is a key attribute of volatility that explains a negative volatility risk premium (i.e., a lower expected return from positive exposure to volatility tends to occur because the positive exposure to volatility has a negative beta and vice versa).

8.6.3 Time-Varying Volatility and Multiple Factors

Time-varying volatility simply means that the asset's volatility is not constant. There are two popular approaches to modeling time-varying volatility as a stochastic process: the Heston (1993) and Bates (1996) models.

The **Heston model** is much like the classic Brownian motion (Weiner process) used for equity returns in the Black–Scholes model except that the volatility coefficient is itself a mean-reverting stochastic process. The Heston model therefore allows the volatility of the asset to change randomly through time in a continuous process that reverts to a long-term average. Therefore, the key assumptions are that volatility is a continuous stochastic process and that volatility reverts towards a long-term mean.

The **Bates model** treats volatility as a stochastic process much like the Heston model except that it includes a jump process for the underlying asset's price that permits price jumps at random time intervals and with random magnitude. The modeling process comes down to a decision of whether random changes in equity prices through time are driven purely by a volatility process that is itself random or whether the price changes are also the result of random price shocks.

8.6.4 Time-Varying Volatility and Higher Moments

An important implication of time-varying volatility is that the distribution of an asset's returns will not generally be normally distributed over a finite length of time. Note that normally distributed returns over short periods of time combine to form lognormally distributed returns over longer periods of time as long as the volatilities of the returns are constant and the process is Markov (i.e., experience new returns that are independent of previous returns).

Hamdan, Pavlowsky, Roncalli, and Zheng (2016)[9] find evidence that skewness has associated risk premiums and that negative skewness to factor returns is an important driver of extreme risk. Skewness does not aggregate simply in the case of asset returns. While the volatility of a portfolio tends to diminish steadily as idiosyncratic risks are diversified through the inclusion of additional assets with modest correlation, skewness can increase. For example, hedging correlated alternative strategies will tend to reduce volatility but can increase negative skewness.

The implications of skewness for asset allocation are not straightforward. However, including skewness in the analysis of alternative investments may substantially increase an asset allocator's ability to manage multi-factor risk and return.

8.7 STOCHASTIC DISCOUNT FACTORS

Stochastic discount factors (pricing kernels) are used in asset valuation models to allow the present value of each cash flow (across each potential economic state) to be formed with potentially different discount rates rather than imposing that all potential cash flows be discounted with the same rate. For example, consider a one-period zero coupon bond with two potential cash flows: $100 in the no-default state and $50 in the default state. A stochastic discount factor approach would allow each potential cash flow to be discounted with its own factor based on the economic state in which it occurs, rather than imposing that the expected value of the bond's cash flow be discounted by a single factor.

8.7.1 Traditional Discount Factors

Traditional discount factors form present value based on expected cash flows as illustrated in Equations 8.5 and 8.6.

$$\text{Present Value} = \frac{E(x)}{(1+k)^t} \tag{8.5}$$

Where x is a stochastic value representing the cash flow of the next period.

$$\text{Discount Factor} = \frac{1}{(1+k)^t} \tag{8.6}$$

There is a single discount factor associated with each potential cash flow at time t. For example, a zero-coupon 1-year bond has a 60% chance of paying off $100 and a 40% chance of paying off $50. If the market price of the bond was $64 the discount factor would be $64/$80 = 0.80.

8.7.2 Stochastic Discount Factors Example

Stochastic discount factors allow different potential payoffs to be valued with different present value factors. For example, suppose the two potential cash flows of the 1-year bond in the previous example had a value of $50 for the $100 potential cash flow and $14 for the $60 potential cash flow:

Bond Price = ($100 × 60% × 0.833) + ($60 × 40% × 0.70)

Bond Price = $50 + $14 = $64

The traditional approach discounts the $80 expected value to $64 using a single factor (0.80). The stochastic discount factors approach uses two factors (0.833 and 0.70) which is equivalent to using different discount rates (20% and 42.4%) for two different cash flow outcomes ("states"): $100 and $50.

Details on the computation of stochastic discount factors based on the above example are provided in Chapter 21.

8.7.3 Stochastic Discount Factors Present Value Formula

The formula for the present value of a cash flow in one period based on stochastic discount factors (analogous to Equation 8.5 with $t = 1$) is shown in Equation 8.7.

$$\text{Present Value} = E(m \cdot x) \tag{8.7}$$

Where $E(\cdot)$ is the expectation operator, m is the stochastic discount factor, and x is the stochastic cash flow next period. Note that Equation 8.7 differs from Equation 8.5 because Equation 8.7 allows the discount factor to vary along with the cash flow. This difference embodies the key difference: stochastic discount factors value cash flows in different economic outcomes differently. Presumably, investors value $1 in "bad times" as providing greater utility than receiving $1 in "good times" due to diminishing marginal utility.

If m is constant across outcomes, then Equation 8.7 reverts to Equation 8.5 with $t = 1$ and $m = 1 + k$.

For example, in the previous section a bond with a price of $64 had an expected future cash flow of $80 $[(0.60 \times 100) + (0.40 \times 50)]$ generating a traditional discount factor of 0.80 and a discount rate of 25%. Now consider the same example in the context of Equation 8.7. Equation 8.7, as an expected value, can be expanded as follows for this case of two potential outcomes.

$$\text{Present Value} = \pi_u m_u x_u + \pi_d m_d x_d \qquad (8.8)$$

Where $\pi_u = 0.60$ and $\pi_d = 0.40$ represent the probabilities of the "up state" (when the higher potential cash flow, x_u equals 100) and "down state" (x_d equals 50), respectively.

The stochastic discount factors for the two states, m_u and x_d took on the values 0.833 and 0.700, respectively.

Finally, note that the example imposed the values of $50 and $14 to the two potential cash flows as well as the respective probabilities (60% and 40%). Other sets of probabilities and values to the cash flows could have been imposed. The values of the individual cash flows (i.e., $50 and $14) or other values could be specified using assumptions regarding the wealth and utility functions of investors.

8.7.4 The Importance of Stochastic Discount Factors

Stochastic discount factors are emblematic of the new generation of thinking with regard to asset allocation and alternative investments. In a traditional or CAPM-based world, a portfolio is viewed as having an expected return based on a single measure of risk (i.e., the asset mix or the portfolio beta). In a multi-factor world that includes alternative investments, different portfolio components offer potentially very distinct types of risk that require multi-factor methods, such as recognizing: (1) that cash flows in "good times" must be valued differently than cash flows in "bad times"; and (2) that different investors with different constraints, different time horizons, different liabilities, and different illiquid assets need to value potential cash flows with different risk premiums.

8.8 SUMMARY OF MULTIPLE-FACTOR ASSET ALLOCATION

The simplicity of the CAPM approach to asset allocation must be sacrificed for optimal asset allocation in a world with multiple factors, time-varying volatility, time-varying risk premiums, and unique circumstances to investors.

In a multi-factor world with both traditional and alternative investments, each investor seeks beta exposures to all factors that are optimal for his or her individual circumstances (i.e., time horizon, illiquid asset holdings).

The multi-factor asset pricing issues discussed in this chapter reflect the advances to asset allocation made available to allocators through advances dating back to Ross's seminal arbitrage pricing model of 1976. The material in this chapter is foundational material indicating both why alternative investments are important and how to allocate assets among both traditional and alternative opportunities.

NOTES

1. See Fama and French (1992).
2. See Carhart (1997).
3. See http://mba.tuck.dartmouth.edu/pages/faculty/ken.FRENCH/Data_Library/f-f_5 _factors_2x3.html [accessed October 2019].
4. Ibid.
5. See Christopherson et al. (2009).
6. See Black (2012).
7. A recent paper by Harvey, Liu, and Zhu (2016) documents the reported discovery of 316 factors. The authors demonstrate that most of these are not reliable sources of risk premium.
8. See Zhang (2005) and Santos and Veronesi (2005).
9. See Hamdan et al. (2016).

REFERENCES

Ang, A. 2014. *Asset Management: A Systematic Approach to Factor Investing.* New York: Oxford University Press.

Asness, C., T. Moskowitz, and L. H. Pedersen. 2010. "Value and Momentum Everywhere." AFA 2010 Atlanta Meetings Paper, March 6. http://ssrn.com/abstract=1363476.

Bates, D. 1996. "Jumps and stochastic volatility: Exchange rate processes implicit in Deutsche Mark options." *Review of Financial Studies* 9: 69–107.

Black, K. 2012. "The Role of Credit Default Swaps and other Alternative Betas in Hedge Fund Factor Analysis." *Journal of Derivatives and Hedge Funds* 18 (3): 201–22.

Carhart, M. 1997. "On Persistence in Mutual Fund Performance." *Journal of Finance* 52 (1): 57–82.

Christopherson, J., D. Carino, and W. Ferson. 2009. *Portfolio Performance Measurement and Benchmarking.* New York: McGraw-Hill.

Fama, E. and K. French, 1992. "The Cross-Section of Expected Stock Returns." *Journal of Finance* 47 (2): 427–65.

Harvey, C. R., Liu, Y., and Zhu, H. 2016. " . . . and the cross-section of expected returns." *Review of Financial Studies* 29 (1): 5–68, https://doi.org/10.1093/rfs/hhv059.

Hamdan, R., F. Pavlowsky, T. Roncalli, and B. Zheng. 2016. "A primer on alternative risk premia" *SSRN Electronic Journal.* https://ssrn.com/abstract=2766850 or http://dx.doi.org/10.2139/ssrn.2766850

Heston, S. 1993. "A closed-form solution for options with stochastic volatility with applications to bond and currency options." *Review of Financial Studies* 6: 327–43.

Idzorek, T. and M. Kowara. 2013. "Factor-Based Asset Allocation vs. Asset-Class-Based Asset Allocation." *Financial Analysts Journal* 69 (3): 1–11.

Lo, A. 2004. "The Adaptive Markets Hypothesis: Market Efficiency from an Evolutionary Perspective." *Journal of Portfolio Management* 30: 15–29.

Lo, Andrew W. 2012. "Adaptive Markets and the New World Order (corrected May 2012)." *Financial Analysts Journal* 68 (2): 18–29.

Santos, T. and P. Veronesi. 2005. "Cash-flow Risk, Discount Risk, and the Value Premium." NBER Working Paper.

Zhang, C., and H. Kazemi. 2015. "Hedge Funds Returns and Market Anomalies." CISDM Working Paper, University of Massachusetts.

Zhang, L. 2005. "The Value Premium." *Journal of Finance* 60: 67–103.

Asset Allocation Processes and the Mean-Variance Model

This is the first of two chapters discussing asset allocation, with a focus on the decision-making process of asset allocators who consider portfolios consisting of traditional as well as alternative asset classes. Chapter 9 explains the mean-variance approach, which is the best-known quantitative approach to allocation. Important limitations of the mean-variance approach and approaches to mitigating those limitations are discussed. Chapter 10 explores qualitative asset allocation approaches.

9.1 ASSET ALLOCATION PROCESSES AND THE MEAN-VARIANCE MODEL

In portfolio allocation, the top-level decision is a long-term target allocation decision, known as the strategic asset allocation decision. The **strategic asset allocation decision** is the long-term target asset allocation based on investor objectives and long-term expectations of returns and risk. For the passive investment manager or indexer, the strategic asset allocation decision is the only major decision.

For most investment managers, tactical decisions are also important decisions. **Tactical asset allocation** is the process of making portfolio decisions to alter the systematic risks of the portfolio through time in an attempt to earn superior risk-adjusted returns. Even though tactical decisions emphasize short-term management of a portfolio's beta, it may be argued that these tactical decisions are an attempt to earn alpha. In other words, systematic risk exposures are adjusted not for the purposes of earning appropriate risk premiums from bearing systematic risk, but to generate alpha by bearing those systematic risks that the allocator believes are being best rewarded at each point in time.

The models that follow in this chapter and Chapter 10 are primarily focused on an institution's strategic asset allocation decision.

9.1.1 Origin of Mean-Variance Optimization

The most appropriate investment process for a given manager depends on that manager's objectives and tolerance for risk. This means that tradeoffs are inevitable. Modern portfolio theory provides a useful starting point.

Modern portfolio theory (MPT) is based on Nobel Prize-winning economist Harry Markowitz's insight that because they have unique risk and return characteristics, less than perfectly correlated assets can be combined in a way that maximizes return for any given level of risk (Markowitz 1952). MPT relies on the fundamental principle of diversification and suggests that allocation choices are simple mean-variance efficient portfolios in perfect markets. Investors choose the appropriate combination of the risk-free asset and the market portfolio to create optimal portfolios that maximize expected return in line with their level of risk aversion (i.e., mean-variance efficient portfolios).

Despite its importance in finance in general, MPT's powerful mathematical apparatus is particularly difficult to apply in the context of alternative investments, where a sufficient quantity of data of a quality necessary for precise calculation simply does not exist. Risks, particularly those associated with investments in limited partnership funds, need to be modeled based on qualitative as well as available quantitative data. Realistically, portfolio management in alternative investments is about "satisficing"—a term coined by Herbert Simon, US Nobel laureate (1978)—which contrasts with optimum decision-making. Instead, we need to rely on heuristics for searching through available alternatives until an acceptable solution is found.

9.1.2 The Tradeoff Between Expected Return and Volatility

Throughout this chapter, the terms volatility, standard deviation, and variance refer to the volatility, standard deviation, and variance of the returns of an asset or portfolio unless otherwise stated.

Consider the following two investment choices available to an asset owner:

- Investment A will increase by 10% or decrease by 8% over the next year, with equal probabilities.
- Investment B will increase by 12% or decrease by 10% over the next year, with equal probabilities.
- The expected return on both investments is 1% (found as the probability weighted average of their potential returns); however, their volatilities will be different.
- Investment A: Standard Deviation
  $= \sqrt{0.5 \times (0.10 - 0.01)^2 + 0.5 \times (-0.08 - 0.01)^2} = 9\%$
- Investment: Standard Deviation
  $= \sqrt{0.5 \times (0.12 - 0.01)^2 + 0.5 \times (-0.10 - 0.01)^2} = 11\%$

If an asset owner expresses a preference for investment A over investment B, then we can claim that the asset owner is risk averse. Investment A dominates investment B because it offers lower risk with the same expected return.

A portfolio is said to **dominate** another portfolio if it offers a higher expected return with the same level of risk, a lower risk with the same expected return, or both higher expected return and lower risk.

Although it is rather obvious to see why a risk-averse asset owner would prefer A to B, it will not be easy to determine whether a risk-averse investor would prefer C to D from the following example:

- Investment C will increase by 10% or decrease by 8% over the next year, with equal probabilities.
- Investment D will increase by 12% or decrease by 9% over the next year, with equal probabilities.

In this case, compared to investment C, investment D has a higher expected return (1.5% to 1%) and a higher standard deviation (10.5% to 9%). Depending on their aversion to risk, some asset owners may prefer C to D, and others D to C. Academics explicitly use investor utility functions to describe decisions between added return and added risk. Investors use utility theory implicitly.

9.1.3 Evaluating Risk and Return with Utility

Different asset owners will have their own preferences regarding the level of risk to bear. Economists have developed a number of tools for expressing such preferences. Expected utility is the most common approach to specifying the preferences of an asset owner for risk and return. While a utility function is typically used to express preferences of individuals, there is nothing in the theory or application that would prevent us from applying utility to institutional investors as well. Therefore, in the context of investments, we define **utility** as a measurement of the satisfaction that an individual receives from investment wealth or return. **Expected utility** is the probability weighted average value of utility over all possible outcomes. Finally, in the context of investments, a **utility function** is the relationship that converts an investment's financial outcome into the investor's level of utility. Suppose the initial capital available for an investment is W and that the utility derived from W is $U(W)$. The expected utility for an investor with two potential outcomes to his or her wealth, W_1 and W_2, shown in Equation 9.1:

$$E[u(w)] = [\pi_1 \times u(w_1)] + [\pi_2 \times u(w_2)] \tag{9.1}$$

Where the probabilities of w_1 and w_2 are π_1 and π_2, respectively. Thus, the expected utilities associated with investments A and B can be expressed as follows:

$$E[U(W_A)] = 0.5 \times U(W \times 1.10) + 0.5 \times U(W \times 0.92)$$

$$E[U(W_B)] = 0.5 \times U(W \times 1.12) + 0.5 \times U(W \times 0.90)$$

The function $U(\cdot)$ is the utility function. The asset owner would prefer investment A to investment B if $E[U(W_A)] > E[U(W_B)]$.

Suppose the utility function can be represented by the log function, and assume that the initial investment is $100. Then:

$$E[U(W_A)] = 0.5 \times \ln(100 \times 1.10) + 0.5 \times \ln(100 \times 0.92) = 4.611$$

$$E[U(W_B)] = 0.5 \times \ln(100 \times 1.12) + 0.5 \times \ln(100 \times 0.90) = 4.609$$

In this case, the asset owner would prefer investment A to investment B because it has higher expected utility. Applying the same function to investments C and D, it can be seen that $E[U(W_C)] = 4.611$ and $E[U(W_D)] = 4.615$. In this case, the asset owner would prefer investment D to investment C.

APPLICATION 9.1.3

Suppose that an investor's utility is the following function of wealth (W):

$$U(W) = \sqrt{W}$$

Find the current and expected utility of the investor if the investor currently has $100 and is considering whether to speculate all the money in an investment with a 60% chance of earning 21% and a 40% chance of losing 19%. Should the investor take the speculation rather than hold the cash?

The current utility of holding the cash is 10, which can be found as $\sqrt{100}$. The expected utility of taking the speculation is found as:

$$E[U(W)] = \left(0.60 \times \sqrt{121}\right) + \left(0.40 \times \sqrt{81}\right) = 10.2$$

Because the investor's expected utility of holding the cash is only 10, the investor would prefer to take the speculation, which has an expected utility of 10.2.

9.1.4   Risk Aversion and the Shape of the Utility Function

Consider a more precise definition of risk aversion. An investor is said to be **risk averse** if his or her utility function is concave, which in turn means that the investor requires higher expected return to bear risk. Exhibit 9.1 displays the log function for various values of wealth. We can see that the level of utility increases but at a decreasing rate.

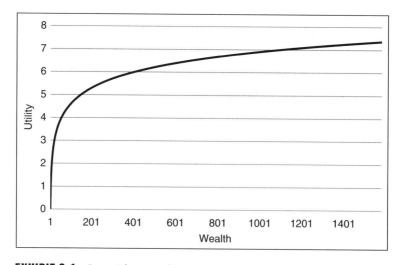

EXHIBIT 9.1   Logarithmic Utility Function

Alternatively, a risk-averse investor avoids taking risks with zero expected pay-offs. That is, for risk-averse investors, $E[U(W)] > E[U(W + \tilde{\epsilon})]$, where $\tilde{\epsilon}$ is a zero mean random error that is independent from W. A risk neutral investor's utility function is linear.

9.1.5 Expressing Utility Functions in Terms of Expected Return and Variance

The principle of selecting investment strategies and allocations to maximize expected utility provides a very flexible way of representing the asset owner's preferences regarding risk and return. The representation of expected utility can be made more operational by presenting it in terms of the parameters of the probability distribution functions of investment choices. The most common form among institutional investors is to present the expected utility of an investment in terms of the mean and variance of the investment returns. For example, consider a specific representation of utility based on expected return and variance shown in Equation 9.2.

$$E[U(W)] = \mu - \frac{\lambda}{2} \times \sigma^2 \qquad (9.2)$$

Here, μ is the expected rate of return on the investment, σ^2 is the variance of the rate of return, and λ is a constant that indicates the asset owner's degree of risk aversion. It can be seen that the higher the value of λ, the larger the negative effect of variance on the expected utility. For example, if λ is equal to zero, then the investor is said to be risk neutral and the investment is evaluated only on the basis of its expected return. A negative value of λ would indicate that the investor is a risk seeker and actually prefers more risk to less risk.

The **degree of risk aversion** indicates the tradeoff between risk and return for a particular investor and is often indicated by a particular parameter within a utility function, such as λ in Equation 9.2. The fact that the degree of risk aversion is divided by 2 will make its interpretation much easier. Specifically, a subsequent section demonstrates that if Equation 9.2 is used to select an optimal portfolio for an investor, then the ratio of the expected rate of return on the optimal portfolio in excess of the riskless rate divided by the portfolio's variance will be equal to the degree of risk aversion.

Example: Suppose $\lambda = 5$. Calculate the expected utility of investments C and D.

$$\mu_C - \frac{\lambda}{2} \times \sigma_C^2 = 1.0\% - \left(\frac{5}{2}\right) \times (9.0\%)^2 = -0.01025$$

$$\mu_D - \frac{\lambda}{2} \times \sigma_D^2 = 1.5\% - \left(\frac{5}{2}\right) \times (10.5\%)^2 = -0.01256$$

In this case, the expected utility of investment C is higher than that of investment D; therefore, it is the preferred choice. It can be verified that if $\lambda = 1$, then the expected utility of investments C and D will be 0.0059 and 0.00949, respectively, meaning that D will be preferred to C.

APPLICATION 9.1.5(Begins)

Suppose that an investor's expected utility, $E[U(W)]$, from an investment can be expressed as

$$E[U(W)] = \mu - \frac{\lambda}{2} \times \sigma^2$$

Where W is wealth, μ is the expected rate of return on the investment, σ^2 is the variance of the rate of return, and λ is a constant that represents the asset owner's degree of risk aversion.

Use the expected utility of an investor, $\lambda = 0.8$, to determine which of the following investments is more attractive:

Investment A: $\mu = 0.10$ and $\sigma^2 = 0.04$

Investment B: $\mu = 0.13$ and $\sigma^2 = 0.09$

The expected utility of A and B are found as:

Investment A: $E[U(W)] = 0.10 - \left(\dfrac{0.8}{2}\right) \times (.04)^2 = 0.084$

Investment B: $E[U(W)] = 0.13 - \left(\dfrac{0.8}{2}\right) \times (.09)^2 = 0.094$

Because the investor's expected utility of holding B is higher, investment B is more attractive.

9.1.6 Expressing Utility Functions with Higher Moments

The expected utility presented in Equation 9.2 assumes that risk can be measured using variance or standard deviation of returns. This assumption is reasonable if investment returns are approximately normally distributed. While the normal distribution might be a reasonable approximation to returns for equities, empirical evidence suggests that most alternative investments have return distributions that significantly depart from the normal distribution. In addition, return distributions from structured products tend to deviate from normality in significant ways. In these cases, Equation 9.2 will not be appropriate for evaluating investment choices that display significant skewness or excess kurtosis. It turns out that Equation 9.2 can be expanded to accommodate asset owners' preferences for higher moments (i.e., skewness and kurtosis) of return distributions. For example, one may present expected utility in the following form:

$$E[U(W)] = \mu - \frac{\lambda_1}{2} \times \sigma^2 + \lambda_2 \times S - \lambda_3 \times K \tag{9.3}$$

Here, S is the skewness of the portfolio value; K is the kurtosis of the portfolio; and λ_1, λ_2, and λ_3 represent preferences for variance, skewness, and kurtosis, respectively. The **assumed investor preferences** are that most investors dislike variance

EXHIBIT 9.2 Example: Properties of Two Hedge Fund Indices

Index (December 1990–December 2018)	Annualized Mean	Annualized Std. Dev.	Skewness
HFRI Fund Weighted Composite	9.31%	6.52%	−0.58
HFRI Fund of Funds Market Defensive	5.71%	5.24%	0.12

Source: HFR and authors' calculations.

($\lambda_1 > 0$), like positive skewness ($\lambda_2 > 0$), and dislike kurtosis ($\lambda_3 > 0$). Note that the signs of coefficients change.

Example: Consider the information about two hedge fund indices in Exhibit 9.2.

If we set $\lambda_1 = 10$ and ignore higher moments, the investor would select the Hedge Fund Research (HFRI) Fund Weighted Composite as the better investment, as it would have the higher expected utility (0.075 to 0.055). However, if we expand the objective function to include preference for positive skewness and set $\lambda_2 = 1$, then the investor would select the HFRI Fund of Fund Defensive as the better choice, because it would have a higher expected utility (0.29 to −0.54).

9.1.7 Expressing Utility Functions with Value at Risk

The preceding representation of preferences in terms of moments of the return distribution is the most common approach to modeling preferences involving uncertain choices. It is theoretically sound as well. However, the investment industry has developed a number of other measures of risk, most of which are not immediately comparable to the approach just presented. For instance, in the CAIA Level I book, we learned about value at risk (VaR) as a measure of downside risk. Is it possible to use this framework to model preferences in terms of VaR? It turns out that in a rather ad hoc way, one can use the preceding approach to model preferences on risk and return when risk is measured by VaR. That is, we can rank investment choices by calculating the following value:

$$E[U(W)] = \mu - \frac{\lambda}{2} \times VaR_\alpha \qquad (9.4)$$

Here, λ can be interpreted as the degree of risk aversion toward VaR, and VaR_α is the value at risk of the portfolio with a confidence level of α. We can further generalize Equation 9.4 and replace VaR with other measures of risk. For instance, one could use risk statistics, such as lower partial moments, beta with respect to a benchmark, or the expected maximum drawdown.

9.1.8 Finding Investor Risk Aversion from the Asset Allocation Decision

As mentioned previously, the value of the risk aversion has an intuitive interpretation. The expected excess rate of return on the optimal portfolio ($E[R_P] - R_f$) divided by its variance, σ_P^2, is equal to the degree of risk aversion, λ:

$$\lambda = \frac{E[R_P] - R_f}{\sigma_P^2} \qquad (9.5)$$

In other words, an investor (with access to the return on a riskless rate) who seeks to maximize expected utility as defined in Equation 9.2 will select a portfolio with expected return $E(R_P)$ and variance σ_p^2 such that Equation 9.5 will hold.

The value of the parameter of risk aversion, λ, is chosen in close consultation with the plan sponsor. There are qualitative methods that can help the portfolio manager select the appropriate value of the risk aversion. The portfolio manager may select a range of values for the parameters and present asset owners with resulting portfolios so that they can see how their level of risk aversion affects the risk–return characteristics of the portfolio under current market conditions.

Example: Consider the information for two well-diversified portfolios shown in Exhibit 9.3. The riskless rate is 2% per year.

Assuming that these are optimal portfolios for two asset owners, what are their degrees of risk aversion?

We know from Equation 9.5 that the expected excess return on the optimal portfolio for a particular investor divided by its variance will be equal to the degree of the risk aversion of that investor.

Aggressive investor:

$$(15\% - 2\%)/(16\%^2) = 5.1$$

Moderate investor:

$$(9\% - 2\%)/(8\%^2) = 10.9$$

As expected, the aggressive portfolio for the aggressive investor with a 5.1 degree of risk aversion represents the optimal portfolio for that more risk tolerant investor, while the moderate portfolio represents the optimal portfolio for the moderate investor with a 10.9 degree of risk aversion.

APPLICATION 9.1.8

Suppose that an investor's original portfolio has an expected return of 10%, which is 8% higher than the riskless rate. If the variance of the portfolio is 0.04, what is the investor's degree of risk aversion, λ?

Using Equation 9.5, λ can be found as:

$$\lambda = \frac{E[R_p] - R_f}{\sigma_P^2} = \frac{0.08}{0.04} = 2.0$$

The investor has a 2.0 degree of risk aversion and found that the portfolio with an expected return of 10% and a variance of 0.04 was optimal.

EXHIBIT 9.3   Optimal Portfolio for an Aggressive and Moderate Investor

Optimal Portfolio	Annualized Mean	Annualized Std. Dev.
Aggressive	15%	16%
Moderate	9%	8%

9.1.9 Managing Assets with Risk Aversion and Growing Liabilities

As mentioned earlier in the chapter, many institutional investors are concerned with funding future obligations using the income generated by the assets. Suppose the current value of these liabilities is L euros. Further, suppose the rate of growth in liabilities is given by G, which could be random. In this case, the objective function of Equation 9.6 can be restated as:

$$E[U(W)] = V \times E[R_p] - \frac{\lambda}{2} \times \text{Var}[V \times R_p - L \times G] \qquad (9.6)$$

In this case, the DB plan wishes to maximize the expected rate of return on the fund's assets, subject to its aversion toward deviations between the return on the fund and the growth in the fund's liabilities. In other words, the risk of the portfolio is measured relative to the growth in liabilities. Later in this chapter, this problem is solved.

One final comment about evaluating investment choices: although the framework outlined here is a flexible and relatively sound way of modeling preferences for risk and return, the presentation considered only one-period investments and decisions. Economists have developed methods for extending the framework to more than one period, where the investor has to withdraw some income from the portfolio. These problems are extremely complex and beyond the scope of this book. However, in many cases, the solutions that are based on the single-period approach provide a reasonable demonstration of the principles of approaches that are more complex.

9.2 IMPLEMENTATION OF MEAN-VARIANCE OPTIMIZATION

Section 9.1 discussed how the general expected utility approach could be used to represent preferences in terms of moments of a portfolio's return distribution. In particular, we noted that optimal portfolios could be constructed by selecting the weights such that the following function is maximized:

$$\mu - \frac{\lambda}{2} \times \sigma^2 \qquad (9.7)$$

where μ is the expected return on the portfolio, λ is a parameter that represents the degree of risk-aversion of the asset owner, and σ^2 is the variance of the portfolio's return. This section provides a description of a portfolio construction technique and examines the solution under some specific conditions. Later sections will discuss some of the problems associated with this portfolio optimization technique and offer some of the solutions that have been proposed by academic and industry researchers.

9.2.1 Mean-Variance Optimization

The portfolio construction problem discussed in this section is the simplest form of mean-variance optimization. The universe of risky investments available to the portfolio manager consists of N asset classes. The single-period total rate of return on the risky asset i is denoted by R_i, for $i = 1, \ldots, N$. Asset zero is riskless, and its rate of return is given by R_0. The weight of asset i in the portfolio is given by w_i. Therefore, the rate of return on a portfolio of the $N + 1$ risky and riskless asset can be expressed as:

$$R_p = w_0 R_0 + w_1 R_1 + \cdots + w_N R_N \tag{9.8}$$

$$w_0 + w_1 + \cdots + w_N = 1 \tag{9.9}$$

For now, no short-sale restriction is imposed, and therefore the weights could assume negative values.

Equation 9.9 can be written as $w_0 = 1 - \sum_{i=1}^{N} w_i$.

If this is substituted in Equation 9.8 and terms are collected, the rate of return on the portfolio can be expressed as:

$$R_p = w_1(R_1 - R_0) + \cdots + w_N(R_N - R_0) + R_0 \tag{9.10}$$

The advantage of writing the portfolio's rate of return in this form is that there is no longer need to impose a separate constraint that the weights appearing in Equation 9.10 will add up to one.

Next, we need to consider the risk of this portfolio. Suppose the covariance between asset i and asset j is given by σ_{ij}. Using this, the variance–covariance of the N risky assets is given by:

$$\Sigma = \begin{bmatrix} \sigma_{11} & \cdots & \sigma_{1N} \\ \vdots & \sigma_{ij} & \vdots \\ \sigma_{N1} & \cdots & \sigma_{NN} \end{bmatrix} \tag{9.11}$$

The portfolio problem can be written in this form, where the weights are selected to maximize the objective function:

$$\max_{w_1, \ldots w_N} E\left[\sum_{i=1}^{N} w_i(R_i - R_0) + R_0 \right] - \frac{\lambda}{2} \times \text{Var}\left[\sum_{i=1}^{N} w_i(R_i - R_0) + R_0 \right] \tag{9.12}$$

The objective function in Equation 9.12 turns out to have a simple and well known solution:

$$\begin{bmatrix} w_1 \\ \vdots \\ w_N \end{bmatrix} = \frac{1}{\lambda} \Sigma^{-1} \times \begin{bmatrix} E[R_1 - R_0] \\ \vdots \\ E[R_N - R_0] \end{bmatrix} \tag{9.13}$$

Note that in Equation 9.13 the term Σ^{-1} refers to the inverse of the variance-covariance matrix in Equation 9.11, not to a summation sign.

The solution requires one to obtain an estimate of the variance–covariance matrix of returns on risky assets. Then the inverse of this matrix will be multiplied into a vector of expected excess returns on the N risky assets. It is instructive to note the role of the degree of risk aversion. As the level of risk aversion λ increases, the portfolio weights of risky assets decline. Note also that regardless of the value of λ, those assets with large expected excess returns tend to have the largest weights in the portfolio.

9.2.2 Mean-Variance Optimization with a Risky and Riskless Asset

To gain a better understanding of the solution, consider the case of only one risky Asset, R, and a riskless asset, R_0. In this case, the optimal weight of the risky asset using Equation 9.13 is:

$$w = \frac{1}{\lambda} \frac{E[R - R_0]}{\sigma^2} \tag{9.14}$$

The optimal weight of the risky asset is proportional to its expected excess rate of return, $E[R - R_0]$, divided by its variance, σ^2. Again, the higher the degree of risk aversion, the lower the weight of the risky asset.

For example, with an excess return of 10%, a degree of risk aversion (λ) of 3, and a variance of 0.05, the optimal portfolio weight is 0.67. This is found as $(1/3) \times (0.10/0.05)$. Note that Equation 9.14 may be used to solve for any of the variables given the values of the remaining variables.

APPLICATION 9.2.2

Consider the case of mean-variance optimization with one risky asset and a riskless asset. Suppose the expected rate of return on the risky asset is 9% per year. The annual standard deviation of the index is estimated to be 13% per year. If the riskless rate is 1%, what is the optimal investment in the risky asset for an investor with a risk-aversion degree of 10?

The solution based on Equation 9.14 is:

$$w = \frac{1}{10} \times \frac{0.09 - 0.01}{0.13^2} = 47.3\%$$

$$w_0 = 1 - 47.3\% = 52.7\%$$

That is, this investor will invest 47.3% in the risky asset and 52.7% in the riskless asset. By varying the degree of risk aversion, we can obtain the full set of optimal portfolios for investors of any degree of risk aversion. Note that as the degree of risk aversion approaches zero, the allocation to the risky asset approaches infinity.

9.2.3 Mean-Variance Optimization with Growing Liabilities

Equation 9.6 displayed the formulation of the problem when the asset owner is concerned with the tracking error between the value of the assets and the value of the liabilities. Similar to Equation 9.13, a general solution for that problem can be obtained as well. A simple version of it is when there is only one risky asset. The covariance between the rate of growth in the liabilities and the growth in assets is denoted by δ, and L is the value of liabilities relative to the size of assets:

$$w = \frac{1}{\lambda} \frac{E[R - R_0]}{\sigma^2} + L \frac{\delta}{\sigma^2} \tag{9.15}$$

It can be seen that if the risky asset is positively correlated with the growth in liabilities (i.e., $\delta > 0$), then the fund will hold more of that risky asset. The reason is that the risky asset will help reduce the risk associated with growth in liabilities. For instance, if the liabilities behaved like bonds, then the fund would invest more in fixed-income instruments, as they would reduce the risk of the fund. Note that the rightmost term in Equation 9.15 $\left(\frac{\delta}{\sigma^2}\right)$ can be viewed as the beta of L with respect to the risky asset.

Example: Based on Equation 9.15 and the example given in Application 9.2.2, suppose the covariance between the risky asset and the growth rate in the fund's liabilities is 0.002, and the value of liabilities is 20% higher than the value of assets. What will be the optimal weight of the equity allocation? Based on Equation 9.15:

$$w = \frac{1}{10}\frac{0.09 - 0.01}{0.13^2} + 1.2\frac{0.002}{0.13^2} = 61.5\%$$

It can be seen that, compared to the previous example, the fund will hold about 14% more in the risky asset because it can hedge some of the liability risk.

APPLICATION 9.2.3

Consider the case of mean-variance optimization with one risky asset and a riskless asset. Assume that the riskless rate is 3%, the expected return of the risky asset is 7%, the standard deviation of the risky asset is 20%, and an investor has a risk-aversion degree (λ) of 8. Given that L = 0.02, find the optimal portfolio allocation, w, of the risky asset.

Substituting the given values into Equation 9.15:

$$w = \frac{1}{8}\frac{0.07 - 0.03}{20^2} + 0.8\frac{0.02}{0.20^2} = 52.5\%$$

Note that the rightmost term in Equation 9.15 does not contain λ. That term increases with both the size of the liability stream, L, and the size of the covariance of the growth rate of L with the return of the risky portfolio, R (assuming that the covariance is positive). This makes sense because the portfolio's liabilities and assets hedge each other when $\delta > 0$, permitting higher allocations to the risky asset.

9.2.4 Mean-Variance Optimization and λ

This section explores mean-variance outcomes for different values of the degree of risk-aversion, λ. Return to the case of $L = 0$, $R_0 = 1\%$, $R = 9\%$, and $\sigma = 13\%$ in Application 9.2.2. Note that the weight of the risky asset, w, in terms of the degree of risk aversion can be written as:

$$w = \frac{1}{\lambda}\left(\frac{0.09 - 0.01}{0.13^2}\right)$$

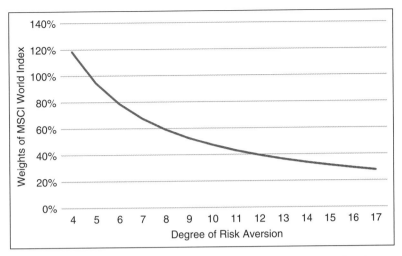

EXHIBIT 9.4   Optimal Weights of Risky Investment and Degree of Risk Aversion

The above equation demonstrates the simplicity of the relation between optimal total portfolio risk (i.e., the allocation to the risky asset and the degree of risk aversion (λ)).

Exhibit 9.4 plots the relation between w and λ for the above equation. As expected, higher degrees of risk aversion generate lower allocations to the risky asset (e.g., the MSCI World Index) and higher allocation to the riskless asset.

It can be seen that at low degrees of risk aversion (e.g., 4), the investor will be investing more than 100% in the MSCI World Index, which means a leveraged position will be used. Exhibit 9.5 plots the full set of expected returns and volatility that the optimal portfolios will assume, which is referred to as the efficient frontier. The points appearing in Exhibit 9.5 correspond to various degrees of risk aversion.

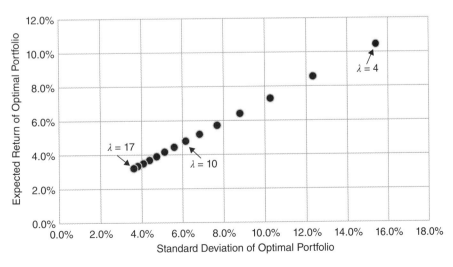

EXHIBIT 9.5   Expected Returns and Standard Deviations of Optimal Portfolios

For instance, the optimal risk–return tradeoff for an investor with a degree of risk aversion of 4 has an expected return of 10.5% and a volatility of about 15.4%, so its high return and high risk places the observation in Exhibit 9.5's upper right-hand corner.

9.3 MEAN-VARIANCE OPTIMIZATION WITH MULTIPLE RISKY ASSETS

It turns out that a graph similar to Exhibit 9.5 is obtained even if the number of asset classes is greater than one. In that case, the graph is referred to as the efficient frontier. The **efficient frontier** is the set of all feasible combinations of expected return and standard deviation that can serve as an optimal solution for one or more risk-averse investors. Put differently, no portfolio can be constructed with the same expected return as the portfolio on the frontier but with a lower standard deviation, or, conversely, no portfolio can be constructed with the same standard deviation as the portfolio on the frontier but with a higher expected return.

9.3.1 A Riskless Asset and the Linearity of Efficient Frontier

The possible optimal portfolios formed by combining a riskless and otherwise optimal risky portfolio in Section 9.2.4 culminated in Exhibit 9.5. Exhibit 9.5 illustrates that a portfolio comprised of a risky and riskless asset form a linear relation between expected return and standard deviation of returns. The optimal portfolio for a particular investor depends on his or her risk aversion (e.g., λ).

9.3.2 A Riskless Asset with Multiple Risky Assets

This section discusses mean-variance optimization with a riskless asset and multiple risky assets using an example. In this example, the set of risky asset classes is expanded to three. The necessary information is provided in Exhibit 9.6. The figures are estimated using monthly data in terms of USD. The annual riskless rate is assumed to be 1%. Note that these estimates are typically adjusted to reflect current market conditions. This example is meant to illustrate an application of the model. Using

EXHIBIT 9.6   Statistical Properties of Three Risky Asset Classes

Index (December 1990–December 2018)	Annual Mean	Annual Standard Deviation	Annual variance–covariance		
			MSCI World	Barclays Global Aggregate	HFRI Fund Weighted Composite
MSCI World	8%	14%	0.0204	0.0021	0.0072
Barclays Global Aggregate	5%	5%	0.0021	0.0028	0.0005
HFRI Fund Weighted Composite	9%	7%	0.0072	0.0005	0.0043

Source: Bloomberg and authors' calculations.

EXHIBIT 9.7 Optimal Weights and Statistics for Different Degrees of Risk Aversion

	Degree of Risk Aversion			
	10	15	20	40
MSCI World	−108%	−72%	−54%	−27%
Barclays Global Aggregate	165%	110%	82%	41%
HFRI Fund Weighted Composite	357%	238%	179%	89%
Treasury Bills	−314%	−176%	−107%	−3%
Optimal Portfolio Statistics				
Annual Mean	30%	21%	16%	8%
Annual Standard Deviation	17%	11%	9%	4%

Source: Authors' calculations

the optimal solution that was displayed in Equation 9.13, the optimal weights of a portfolio consisting of the three risky assets and one riskless asset can be calculated for different degrees of risk aversion. The results are displayed in Exhibit 9.7 for $\lambda = 10, 15, 20$ *and* 40.

A number of interesting observations can be drawn from these results. First, notice that the optimal weights are not very realistic. For example, for every degree of risk aversion, the optimal portfolio requires us to take a short position in the MSCI World Index. Second, the optimal investment in the HFRI index exceeds 100% for some degrees of risk aversion considered here. Third, unless the degree of risk aversion is increased beyond 40, the optimal portfolio requires some degree of leverage (i.e., a negative weight for the Treasury bills).

The bottom two rows of Exhibit 9.7 display annual mean and annual standard deviation of the optimal portfolios. These represent points on the efficient frontier. Note that the three risky assets in Exhibits 9.6 and 9.7 are held in the same proportions to each other over all values of λ. This is because inclusion of a riskless asset always generates a linear efficient frontier consisting of two assets: a riskless asset and the risky portfolio with the highest ratio of expected excess return to volatility.

9.3.3 Unconstrained Optimization and Unrealistic Weights

As we just saw, mean-variance optimization typically leads to unrealistic weights. A simple way to overcome this problem is to impose limits on the weights. For instance, in the example just provided, we can impose the constraint that the weights must be nonnegative. Unfortunately, when constraints are imposed on the weights, a closed-form solution of the type presented in Equation 9.13 can no longer be obtained, and we must use a numerical optimization package to solve the problem.[1]

If we repeat the example but impose the constraint that weights cannot be negative, the resulting optimal portfolios will reflect those displayed in Exhibit 9.8.

It can be seen that the weight of the MSCI World Index is constantly zero for all degrees of risk aversion. This means that portfolios that are on the efficient frontier in this case do not have any allocation to the MSCI World Index. Another important point to consider is that the optimal portfolios do not have the same attractive risk–return properties. By imposing a constraint, the resulting portfolios are not as optimal as they were when there were no constraints.

EXHIBIT 9.8 Optimal Weights without Short Sale Constraints

	Degree of Risk Aversion			
	10	15	20	40
MSCI World	0%	0%	0%	0%
Barclays Global Aggregate	120%	80%	60%	30%
HFRI Fund Weighted Composite	180%	120%	90%	45%
Treasury Bills	–200%	–100%	–50%	25%
Optimal Portfolio Statistics				
Annual Mean	21%	14%	11%	6%
Annual Standard Deviation	14%	9%	7%	4%

9.4 MEAN-VARIANCE OPTIMIZATION AND HURDLE RATES

The **hurdle rate** is the minimum expected rate of return that a new asset (i.e., an asset not already included in a portfolio) must offer in order to be a beneficial inclusion in an otherwise existing optimal portfolio. The hurdle rate in this context should not be confused with the term hurdle rate as used in the context of allocating fund incentive fees between managers and investors. This section describes the investment hurdle rate in the context of a mean-variance optimal portfolio.

An interesting implication of mean-variance portfolio optimization when there is a riskless asset is that the benefits of diversification can be shown to cause low-return assets to be desirable for inclusion in a portfolio. It is easy to show that the addition of a new asset to an already optimal portfolio will improve its risk–return properties (i.e., increases the expected utility) if the expected rate of return on this new asset exceeds a hurdle rate. The hurdle rate is an expected rate of return that a new asset must offer to be included in an already optimal portfolio. An asset being considered for addition to a portfolio should be included in the portfolio when the following expression is satisfied:

$$E[R_{New}] - R_f > (E[R_p] - R_f) \times \beta_{New} \tag{9.16}$$

Here, $E[R_{New}]$ is the expected rate of return or hurdle rate on the new asset, $E[R_p]$ is the expected rate of return on the optimal portfolio, R_f is the riskless rate, and β_{New} is the beta of the new asset with respect to the optimal portfolio.[2] In other words, β_{New} is the covariance of R_{New} and R_p divided by variance of R_p.

Equation 9.16 states that the addition of the new asset to an optimal portfolio will improve the risk–return properties of the portfolio if the expected excess rate of return on the new asset exceeds the expected excess rate of return on the optimal portfolio times the beta of the new asset. If the new asset satisfies Equation 9.16, then its addition to the optimal portfolio will move the efficient frontier in the northwest direction. For example, if the beta of the new asset is zero, then the new asset will improve the optimal portfolio as long as its expected rate of return exceeds the riskless rate. If the new asset has a negative beta, then it could improve the optimal portfolio even if its expected rate of return is negative. In other words, assets that can serve as hedging instruments could have negative expected returns and still improve the performance of a portfolio.

APPLICATION 9.4

Suppose that an investor is using mean-variance optimization, the expected annual rate of return of an optimal portfolio is 16%, and the riskless rate is 1% per year. What is the hurdle rate for a new asset that has a beta of 0.5 with respect to the optimal portfolio?

Given the formula of Equation 9.16, the hurdle rate, $E[R_{New}]$ would be:

$$E[R_{New}] - 1\% > (16\% - 1\%) \times 0.5$$

$$[R_{New}] > 8.5\%$$

What if the new asset has a beta of −0.3, which means that it can hedge some of the portfolio's risk?

$$E[R_{New}] - 1\% > (16\% - 1\%) \times (-0.3)$$

$$E[R_{New}] > -3.5\%$$

In this case, even if the new asset is expected to lose some money (i.e., lose less than losing 3.5%), its addition to the optimal portfolio would still improve its risk–return properties.

9.5 ISSUES IN USING OPTIMIZATION FOR PORTFOLIO SELECTION

Previous sections indicated that, even in the case of three risky asset classes and a riskless rate, reasonable estimates of the weights could not be obtained unless short sale restrictions were imposed, and even in that case, allocations to the assets are not always reasonable. In practice, implementing an optimization method (mean-variance optimization, in particular) for portfolio allocation decisions raises major challenges.

9.5.1 Optimizers as Error Maximizers

Portfolio optimizers are powerful tools for finding the best allocation of assets to achieve superior diversification, given accurate estimates of the parameters of the return distributions. When the mean-variance method is used, there is a need for accurate estimates of expected returns and the variance–covariance matrix of asset returns. However, portfolio optimizers that use historical estimates of the return distributions have been derogatorily called "error maximizers" due to their tendency to generate solutions with extreme portfolio weights.

For example, very large portfolio weights are often allocated to the assets with the highest mean returns and lowest volatility; and very small portfolio weights are allocated to the assets with the lowest mean returns and high volatility. Assets with the highest estimated means are likely to have the largest positive estimation errors, whereas assets with the lowest estimated means are likely to have the largest negative estimation errors. Hence, mean-variance optimization is likely to maximize errors. Therefore, if an analyst overstates mean returns for an asset, then the weights that the model recommends are likely to be much larger than an institutional investor would consider reasonable. Further, other assets are virtually omitted from the portfolio if the analyst supplies low estimates of mean returns.

In light of this well known challenge, a typical attempt to use a mean-variance optimization model for portfolio allocation is this: (1) the portfolio manager supplies estimates of the mean return, volatility, and covariance for all assets; (2) the optimizer generates a highly unrealistic solution that places very large portfolio weights on what are considered the most attractive assets (with high mean returns and low volatility), and zero or minuscule portfolio weights on what are considered the least attractive assets, with low mean return; and (3) the portfolio manager then, often subjectively, modifies the model by adding constraints or altering the estimated inputs—including mean, variance, and covariance—until the resulting portfolio solutions appear reasonable.

The problem with this process is when the portfolio weights become driven by the subjective judgments of the analyst rather than by the analyst's best forecasts of risk and return.

The difficulty in deriving estimates of expected return and risk for each asset class is that return and risk are nonstationary, meaning that the levels of risk and return vary substantially over time. Therefore, the true risk and return over one period may be substantially different from the risk and return of a different period. Thus, in addition to traditional estimation errors for a stationary process, estimates for security returns may include errors from shooting at a moving target.

9.5.2 Portfolio Optimization and Smoothing of Illiquid Returns

As noted, mean-variance optimizers can be error maximizers. Therefore, erroneous forecasts of the means, variances, and covariances can result in extreme portfolio weights, with a resulting portfolio concentration in a few assets with estimated high means, attractive estimated covariances, and estimated low volatilities. Most institutions view such concentrated positions as unacceptable speculation on the validity of the forecasted mean and volatility. This issue is discussed in detail in Section 9.8.

Although higher frequency of observed data can improve the accuracy of the estimated variance and covariance, for most alternative assets, high-frequency data are not available. More important, the assets whose prices cannot be observed with high frequency tend to be illiquid, and the reported quarterly returns are based on appraisals such as those used in real estate and private equity. These prices tend to be smoothed and therefore can substantially understate the variance and covariance of returns. Because volatility and covariance are key inputs in the optimization process, asset classes with underestimated correlation and volatility receive relatively large weights in the optimal portfolio according to the model.

Anson (2016) details problems of smoothed return data for private equity and venture capital, and empirically analyzes the effects of return unsmoothing on asset allocation. Anson, after unsmoothing the returns, reports volatility estimates that are twice those based on the smoothed returns as well as reporting substantially higher estimated correlations of private equity and venture capital returns with equities, credit, and government bonds. Unsmoothing is also found to be useful in better estimating higher moments (skew and excess kurtosis). Most importantly, Anson finds "very large differences" in optimal allocations determined with and without return smoothing. Specifically, optimal allocations based on unsmoothed returns were 20% lower for private equity and 30% lower for venture capital than allocations based on smoothed returns.

9.5.3 Data Issues for Large-Scale Optimization

A problem with covariance estimation includes the potentially large scale of the inputs required. This is typically not an issue when working at the asset class level, at which the investor may consider 10 asset classes for inclusion in the portfolio. However, optimizing an equity portfolio selected from a universe of 500 stocks has very large data requirements. A 500-asset optimization problem requires estimates of covariance between each pair of the 500 assets. Not only does this problem require $n(n - 1)/2$, or 124,750 covariance estimates, but it is also difficult to be confident in these estimates, especially when there are too many to analyze individually. Also, notice that to estimate 124,750 covariance terms, we need more than 124,750 observations, or more than 10,000 years of monthly data or more than 340 years of daily data.

The problem of needing to calculate thousands of covariance estimates can be reduced with factor models. Rather than estimating the relation between each pair of stocks in a 500-stock universe, an analyst can estimate the relations between each stock and a limited number of factors. The analyst also needs to estimate the covariances between the factors.

9.5.4 Mean-Variance Ignores Higher Moments

A problem that is especially acute with alternative investments is that the mean-variance optimization approach considers only the mean and variance of returns. This means that the optimization model does not explicitly account for skewness and kurtosis. Investors' expected utility can be expressed in terms of mean and variance alone if returns are normally distributed or if investor utility is quadratic. Usually, neither condition is usual. When making allocations to alternative investments and other investments with nonzero skewness and nonzero excess kurtosis, portfolio optimizers tend to suggest portfolios with desirable combinations of mean and variance but with highly undesirable skewness and kurtosis. In other words, mean-variance optimizers may be adding large and unfavorable levels of skewness and kurtosis to the portfolio. For example, two assets with returns that have the same variance may have very different skews. In a competitive market, the expected return of the asset with the large negative skew might be substantially higher than that of the asset with the positive skew to compensate investors willing to bear the higher downside risk. A mean-variance optimizer typically places a much higher portfolio weight on the negatively skewed asset because it offers a higher mean return with the same level of variance as the other asset. The mean-variance optimizer ignores the unattractiveness of an asset's large negative skew and, in so doing, maximizes the error.

9.5.5 Three Ways to Address Skewness and Kurtosis

There are three common ways to address this complication. First, it is possible to expand our optimization method to account for skewness and perhaps kurtosis of asset returns. Second, continue with mean-variance optimization but add the desired levels of the skewness and kurtosis as explicit constraints on the allowed solutions to the mean-variance optimizer, such as when the excess kurtosis of the portfolio returns is not allowed to exceed 3, or when the skewness must be greater than –0.5. A problem with incorporating higher moments in portfolio optimization is that these moments are extremely difficult to predict, as they are highly influenced by a few large negative or positive observations. In addition, in the second approach, a portfolio with a desired level of skewness or kurtosis may not be feasible at all. Third, the analyst may choose to explicitly constrain the weight of those investments that have undesirable skew or kurtosis. For example, the allocation to a hedge fund strategy that is known to have large tail risk (e.g., negative skew) might be restricted to some maximum weight.

9.6 ADJUSTMENT OF THE MEAN-VARIANCE APPROACH FOR ILLIQUIDITY

There are two types of illiquidity risks: market liquidity risk and funding liquidity risk (Hibbert et al. 2009). **Market liquidity risk** arises when an event forces an investor to sell an asset that is not actively traded and there are a limited number of active market participants. Under such a circumstance, the price of the asset may have to be reduced significantly in order to bring a bid from market participants. **Funding liquidity risk** arises when a borrower or investor is unable to immediately pay what is owed. A forced liquidation of assets may occur; for example, when an investor in futures markets is unable to meet a margin call and the clearing corporation closes out the affected positions.

9.6.1 The Liquidity Penalty Function

In this section, the focus is on market liquidity risk and its incorporation into the mean-variance framework. The following presentation is kept simple to highlight the impact of liquidity risk on optimal allocations. In particular, it presents a model that modifies the mean-variance optimization framework by incorporating a liquidity penalty function, the purpose of which is to allow for an explicit, easily communicated, natural specification of liquidity preferences that works in conjunction with the standard mean-variance approach.[3]

The **liquidity penalty function** reflects the cost of illiquidity and the preference for liquidity. By incorporating this penalty function into the traditional mean-variance optimization model, we can construct a framework for asset allocation involving illiquid assets.

To account for illiquidity, we begin by assigning each asset class i an illiquidity level, denoted by L_i, which takes values between 0 and 1. Perfectly liquid assets are assigned 0 and highly illiquid assets are assigned 1. The liquidity level of the portfolio is measured by $L_p = \sum_{i=1}^{N} w_i L_i$. The objective function of the mean-variance approach is now adjusted to reflect a penalty for the extent that each feasible portfolio displays illiquidity when the investor has a preference for liquidity:

$$\max \overline{R}_p - \frac{\lambda}{2}\sigma_p^2 - \phi L_p \quad \text{subject to } w_i \geq 0 \ \ i = 1, \ldots, N \qquad (9.17)$$

Here, ϕ is a positive number and it represents the investor's preference for liquidity (i.e., aversion to illiquidity). If all assets are highly liquid, then $L_p = 0$ and the liquidity preference will have no impact. However, when some assets are illiquid, $L_p > 0$, the investor's aversion to illiquidity will reduce the attractiveness of portfolios with illiquidity. The impact of the liquidity penalty will be to reduce the value of the objective function by subtracting the illiquidity penalty from the expected returns on illiquid assets. The most illiquid assets have a penalty, $L_i = 1$, which reduces the expected returns on such assets by ϕ. This insight can help the portfolio manager select a reasonable value for ϕ.

9.6.2 Examples of Adjusting for Illiquidity

For example, a portfolio manager has assigned a liquidity level of 0.5 to the private equity asset class. The expected annual mean return on this asset class is estimated to be 18%. The asset owner is an endowment and therefore does not have a strong preference for liquidity; this has led the portfolio manager to set $\phi = 0.10$. The adjustment to the mean return of the private equity asset class is:

$$\overline{R} - \phi L_i = 0.18 - 0.1 \times 0.5 = 13\%$$

The manager of a family office portfolio is considering the same asset class and assigns a liquidity level of 0.5 as well. However, liquidity is more important to this family office, and therefore the manager has set $\phi = 0.20$. The adjustment to the estimated expected return of the private equity asset class for the family office inside the model is:

$$\overline{R} - \phi L_i = 0.18 - 0.2 \times 0.5 = 8\%$$

Obviously, everything else being equal, the family office will make a smaller allocation to the private equity class.

9.6.3 Takeaway Points on Illiquidity Adjustments

The key takeaway points on adjusting for asset illiquidity in a mean-variance optimization framework using a penalty function are:

1. The penalty function, ϕ, is a positive number that reflects the investor's disutility for illiquidity.
2. Each asset is assigned an illiquidity level, L_i, that reflects the asset's market illiquidity from 0 (fully liquid) to 1 (maximum illiquidity).
3. The product of ϕL_i for each asset i serves to penalize (lower) the expected return of that asset within the mean-variance optimization. The optimal allocation to each asset will be inversely related to illiquidity (L_i) assuming that $\phi > 0$.

9.7 ADJUSTMENT OF THE MEAN-VARIANCE APPROACH FOR FACTOR EXPOSURE

In the process of asset allocation, whether strategic or tactical, the investor may wish to limit the exposure of the portfolio to certain sources of risk (and potentially some returns) other than or in addition to the risk of the overall market. For example, the investor may wish to cap the exposure of the portfolio to changes in the price of oil. As long as an observable factor representing the source of risk exists, the constraints on factor exposures can be incorporated into the mean-variance approach with little difficulty.

The first step is to estimate the factor exposures of the assets that are being considered for inclusion in the portfolio. To do this, a linear regression of the following form is run:

$$R_{it} = a_i + b_i F_t + \varepsilon_{it} \tag{9.18}$$

Here, R_{it} is the rate of return on asset i; a_i and b_i are the intercept and the slope of the regression, respectively; F_t is the risk factor that is of interest; and ε_{it} is the residual. For example, F_t might be the percentage change in the price of oil. In this regression, b_i measures the factor exposure of asset i. Since the factor exposure of the portfolio is a weighted average of the individual asset's exposures, the factor exposure of the portfolio can be expressed as $b_P = \sum_{i=1}^{N} w_i b_i$.

The following constraint can now be added to the mean-variance optimization of Equation 9.17:

$$b_P \leq \overline{b} \tag{9.19}$$

In this case, the constraint is that the total factor exposure of a potential portfolio must be less than or equal to the target, $\overline{b}$, in order for the portfolio to be a feasible solution. The impact of imposing this constraint is to reduce allocations to those asset classes that have large exposures to the source of risk being considered. It is important to note that since short sales are not allowed, it may not be feasible to create a portfolio with the desired level of factor exposure. For example, suppose an investor decides to have a negative exposure of the portfolio to the equity risk of the overall equity market. It may not be possible to create a negative equity beta portfolio when short positions are not permitted.

9.8 MITIGATING ESTIMATION ERROR RISK IN MEAN-VARIANCE OPTIMIZATION

The inputs to the portfolio allocation process (estimates of expected returns, variances, and covariances) are unknown and are therefore estimated with error. Estimation errors of those inputs can be large when, as is typically the case, the asset returns have fat-tailed distributions (i.e., have far more outliers than expected in a normal distribution), limited return histories, illiquidity, or shifting risks. As a result, the level of confidence in the estimated means, variances, and covariances of the assets is low (i.e., the risk of estimation error is high).

As discussed in Section 9.5.1, the use of portfolio optimization approaches. such as mean-variance optimization, are criticized as being potential "error maximizers" due to their tendency to place extreme weights on assets that have the most extreme values for inputs (means, variances, or covariances). Placing extreme weights based on extreme inputs (when there is reason to believe that there is substantial risk of estimation errors in their inputs) will generally result in suboptimal portfolio allocations.

This section reviews techniques developed to mitigate problems of mean-variance portfolio optimization with regard to the estimation errors and estimation error risk in the inputted values.

9.8.1 Estimation Error Risk Reduction through Objective Measures of Estimation Error Risk

Consider the process of overall asset allocation among asset classes where the number of asset classes is relatively small. In this case informal and *subjective* adjustments may be useful in reducing error estimation risk as briefly discussed in Section 9.5.1. However, *objective* measures of potential estimation error risk (other than market returns) that are based on the characteristics of prospective investments can also be used.

For example, assets or asset classes with shorter return histories and lower trading frequency are likely to have higher risks of estimation errors. Typically, asset allocators should consider reducing allocations to assets or asset classes that exhibited attractive historic combinations of risk and return but that had characteristics (e.g., short return histories or illiquidity) consistent with high risk of large estimation errors.

The following sections discuss methods including resampling and shrinkage to control for estimation error risk in the cases of large portfolios or for portfolios in which such objective measures of estimation error risk do not exist.

9.8.2 Resampling to Reduce the Effect of Estimation Error

A popular method within statistics and mean-variance portfolio optimization is resampling. There are numerous methods of resampling historic returns for portfolio optimization.

Consider a portfolio allocator with access to a sample of returns on currently held and potential new investments. In the context of mean-variance portfolio optimization (i.e., estimation of the efficient frontier), the method of **resampling returns** strives to reduce estimation error and typically is executed by: (1) repeated analysis of *hypothetical* returns simulated from the statistical parameters estimated from the original sample of returns; or (2) repeated analysis of new samples of returns generated from the original sample using draws with *replacement*.

To explore the two common applications of resampling discussed above, consider an analyst with a sample of returns for five asset classes over the previous 60 months. The analyst wishes to estimate the efficient frontier based on that data and begins by estimating the vector of eight mean returns and the historical 8×8 variance–covariance matrix of returns. However, financial research has shown that directly using these estimated statistical parameters in a mean-variance optimization tends to generate extreme portfolio weights, suboptimal portfolio selection, and suboptimal prediction of future risk and return. The analyst considers the two resampling approaches: one based on hypothetical returns and the other on hypothetical samples. These two approaches are discussed in the next two paragraphs.

In the hypothetical return method, the analyst estimates the statistical parameters (e.g., the means and the variance–covariance matrix) based on the actual historical return data of the eight asset classes. The analyst then applies Monte Carlo simulation by generating a large number of hypothetical returns for the eight asset classes based on their estimated statistical parameters (the means and variance–covariance matrix derived from the original sample) and based on an assumed distribution of the returns (e.g., the normal distribution or a *t*-distribution). The analyst uses numerous samples of these hypothetical (simulated) returns to derive an efficient frontier of optimized portfolios. Research indicates that the efficient portfolios derived from analysis of the simulated returns provide better diversification and better prediction than the original optimized portfolio based on the original sample of actual returns.

To apply the other approach to resampling returns (hypothetical samples of actual returns), the analyst uses returns from the original data set but creates new return samples by drawing randomly from the historical data (with replacement). In other words, rather than analyzing the actual 60 months of eight returns corresponding to the eight asset classes, the analyst randomly draws 60 sets of eight monthly returns from different periods (months) in the original sample of returns. The analysts "replaces" each set of eight returns. For example, if the time periods in the original data set are sequential from time 1 to time 60 with each time period appearing once in the sample, each resampling done by the analysts may contains several time periods (i.e., sets of eight returns) that are included multiple times and several time periods that do not get drawn even once.

Note that due to the use of replacement in resampling, if the historical data set included a month with very extreme returns (e.g., October 2008), the resampling will vary with some samples having no draws of October 2008, many having one draw of October 2008, and some having two or more such draws. In doing so, the resampling mimics the idea that future five-year returns for the assets are likely to vary with respect to the number of months with returns as extreme as those encountered in October 2008. Of course the original sample only has one month with October 2008 returns.

Research indicates that the efficient portfolios derived from randomly selected hypothetical sets of returns (with replacement) from actual data provide better portfolio solutions and better estimates of future statistical parameters than the original optimal portfolio based on the actual return histories.

9.8.3 Shrinkage to Reduce the Effect of Estimation Error

A popular method of tempering extreme portfolio allocations, providing improved risk-adjusted performance and better predictive capabilities, is shrinkage. Shrinkage is a popular approach within the field of statistics for narrowing confidence intervals and reducing estimation errors relative to basing predictions directly from unadjusted statistical parameters derived from historical data.

In the context of mean-variance portfolio optimization, **shrinkage** is the process of implementing a statistical method designed to generate estimated statistical parameters (means, variances, and/or covariances of returns) that differ from those obtained from an unconstrained analysis of historical returns and that provide improved solutions with narrower confidence intervals. In other words, rather than directly using the statistical parameters of historical return data, the analyst applies shrinkage to the statistical parameters to improve prediction. Improvements through shrinkage emanate from the imposition of structure or a target model—to be discussed below.

Consider a mean-variance optimization problem involving a large number of securities. A few securities are observed to have experienced extremely high volatility (i.e., standard deviation of returns) and a few securities experienced extremely low volatility. In many cases of observing historic returns, it might be reasonable to believe that using these extreme historic volatilities as unbiased predictors of future volatility would be likely to cause suboptimal estimation error. Shrinkage involves applying statistical methods that provide better predictions than a naïve approach that assumes that statistical parameters generated from historic data are unbiased predictors of future statistical parameters.

For example, consider the simple task of forecasting the statistical parameters of a set of assets. The forecasted mean, volatility, and covariances of each asset's returns are intended to be used in a mean-variance optimization model. Without shrinkage, an asset allocator might estimate the variance–covariance matrix of returns using the simple formulas for variance and covariance applied directly to the historical returns. But this simple estimate of the variance–covariance matrix is likely subject to substantial estimation error. A pair of assets with an outlier historic correlation coefficient of −0.20 might be viewed as possessing substantial estimation error if used (without adjustment) as an input to the portfolio optimization model. An analyst may *shrink* that observed statistical parameter (−0.20) towards a better estimate produced by imposing *structure* to the variance–covariance matrix, such as imposing that the correlation coefficients between all security pairs are equal. Shrinkage in this example may provide a better estimate of future volatility if the model being imposed on the data (equal return correlations) provides a beneficial structure.

Shrinkage methods consistent with shrinkage theory from statistics do not directly "shrink" portfolio weights. Shrinkage methods are used to reduce confidence intervals. Note that reducing the portfolio weight of one long position causes the portfolio weights of one or more other positions to be increased. The goal is better forecasts of the statistical parameters that are used as inputs to the optimization model.

Ledoit and Wolf (2004) describe linearly adjusting those statistical parameters estimated based entirely on historical analysis (i.e., the unadjusted historical means and variance–covariance matrix of asset returns) towards the statistical parameters consistent with one or more "structured" models, such as a model that forces all off-diagonal elements of the variance–covariance matrix to be the same value. The degree of shrinkage can be set by the asset allocator and determines the extent to which the means and variance–covariance matrix used in the portfolio optimization are driven by: (1) an unconstrained computation based entirely on historical returns; versus (2) a constrained estimation such as a matrix driven in part by imposition of the structures through a target model.

The key issue in shrinkage methods is the method by which the statistical parameters of a sample of historical data should be adjusted. In other words, on what basis should estimates based on historical data be modified based on a view that full reliance on sampled historical returns injects substantial estimation error? Ledoit and Wolf (2004) describe multi-factor return models as the "industry standard." In that case, the multi-factor return model is used as the basis for parameterizing the return data for input into the portfolio optimization model. The potential multi-factor models that can provide structure to improve the optimization include not only the most popular approaches detailed in Chapter 8 (the factor approach referred to synonymously as fundamental, style, investment, or dynamic factors), but also *statistical* factor models (briefly discussed in Chapter 8) that can be estimated using approaches such as principal component analysis, detailed in Chapter 23.

9.8.4 Mean-Variance Optimization and the Black–Litterman Approach

Perhaps the most popular modification to account for managerial views on outliers and obtain reasonable estimates of weights is described by Black and Litterman (1991). The first problem addressed by the Black–Litterman approach is the tendency of the user's estimates of mean and variance to generate extreme portfolio weights in a mean-variance optimizer. Note that, in a competitive market, if a security truly and clearly offered a large expected return, low risk, and high diversification potential, then demand for the security would drive its price upward and its expected return downward until the demand for the security equaled the quantity available. The Black–Litterman approach imposes that a security offers an equilibrium expected return if the portfolio manager has no views about the future performance of a particular asset class and that a market-cap-weighted portfolio is optimal. However, note that market-cap weights are not well defined for some asset classes, and so the Black–Litterman approach will need to be adjusted for application to alternative assets.

The primary innovation of the Black–Litterman approach is that it allows the investor to blend asset-specific views of each asset's expected return with views that would be consistent with market weights in a market equilibrium model. A major difference between the Black–Litterman approach and shrinkage methods is that the Black–Litterman approach allows adjustments directly to portfolio weights (the outputs of the optimization model), while shrinkage methods tend to impose adjustments on the statistical parameters used as inputs to the optimization model. The use of constraints is discussed in the next section.

9.8.5 Mean-Variance Optimization and the Use Of Constraints

Whereas some asset allocators employ advanced techniques such as the Black–Litterman approach to reduce the sensitivity of the weights to the expected risks and returns, a much larger number of asset allocators choose to add additional constraints to the optimization model to circumvent the difficulties and sensitivities of mean-variance optimization (including estimation errors). Common additional constraints include the following:

- Limiting weights to be nonnegative (i.e., no short sales).
- Limits on the maximum allocation to one or more assets.
- Limits on estimated correlations.
- Limits on divergences of portfolio weights from benchmark weights or market weights.

The first constraint, disallowing negative portfolio weights, is the most popular. Jagannathan and Ma (2003) discuss the efficacy of weight constraints on asset allocation generated by mean-variance portfolio optimizers. They report that constraining weights to be nonnegative has similar effects to the use of shrinkage to reduce large portfolio weights. In effect, weight constraints can perform some of the goals sought by methods such as shrinkage and resampling.

Note that the existence of optimal solutions that involve nontrivial short sales in applications of mean-variance optimizers for asset allocation is surprising because negative weights per se increase portfolio variance and require offsetting increases in positive weights to keep the weights summed to one. Intuitively, negative weights substantially increase portfolio variance and should only be used when the assets being shorted are extremely unattractive and/or when there are long positions so attractive that they should be increased through short sales of other assets. Such extreme views on the relative attractiveness of assets in a competitive market would seem quite speculative for overall asset allocation. Much more likely in the case of asset allocation among asset classes would be that negative portfolio weights and extremely large portfolio weights prescribed by an optimization model are caused by estimation errors of their statistical parameters. Hence, restrictions of short sales may serve as a method of controlling estimation error risk.

In practice, however, many investors use so many constraints that the constraints have more influence on the final asset allocation than does the mean-variance optimization process. While each of the added constraints may help the asset allocator avoid extreme weights, the approach may ultimately lead to having the constraints define the allocation rather than the objective function.

NOTES

1. The problem is still a rather standard optimization program and can be solved using Solver from Excel or similar packages.
2. From linear regression and the CAPM we know that $\beta_{\text{New}} = \text{Cov}[R_P, R_{\text{New}}]/\text{Var}[R_p]$.
3. The following model is based on Lo, Petrov, and Wierzbicki (2003) and Hayes, Primbs, and Chiquoine (2015).

REFERENCES

Anson, M. 2016. "Asset Allocation with Private Equity." *The Journal of Investment Consulting* 17 (1): 31–36.

Black, F. and R. Litterman. 1991. "Asset Allocation: Combining Investors' Views with Market Equilibrium." *Journal of Fixed Income* (September): 7–18.

Hayes, M., J. Primbs, and B. Chiquoine. 2015. "A Penalty Cost Approach to Strategic Asset Allocation with Illiquid Asset Classes." *Journal of Portfolio Management* 41 (2 Winter): 33–41.

Hibbert, J., A. Kirchner, G. Kretzschmar, R. Li, and A. McNeil. 2009. "Liquidity Premium: Literature Review of Theoretical and Empirical Evidence." *Barrie & Hibbert Research Report version* 1.1.

Jagannathan, R. and Ma, T. 2003, "Risk Reduction in Large Portfolios: Why Imposing the Wrong Constraints Helps." *Journal of Finance* 58: 1651–83.

Ledoit, O. and M. Wolf. 2004. "Honey, I Shrunk the Sample Covariance Matrix." *Journal of Portfolio Management* 30 (4): 110–24.

Lo, A., C. Petrov, and M.Wierzbicki. 2003. "It's 11pm—Do You Know Where Your Liquidity Is?" *Journal of Investment Management* 1 (1): 55–93.

Markowitz, H. 1952. "Portfolio Selection." *Journal of Finance* 7 (1): 77–91.

Other Asset Allocation Approaches

Moment-optimization approaches discussed in Chapter 9 offer precise quantitative frameworks within which to model ideal asset allocations. However, due to its potential to maximize the impact of estimation errors, numerous other approaches are applied in practice along with or in the place of moment-based models.

Chapter 10 begins with two nonquantitative distinctions regarding asset allocation approaches that are useful to consider as part of a multi-model approach. Chapter 10 then continues with two somewhat elegant and instructive asset allocation models: risk budgeting and risk parity.

Regardless of the asset allocation approach or approaches taken, there are many constraints that should be taken into account. This chapter discusses liquidity, but other topics affecting asset allocation decisions include smoothing, minimum investment requirements, due diligence costs, subscription and redemption limits, gates, and so forth. These topics are discussed in subsequent chapters.

10.1 THE CORE–SATELLITE APPROACH

Broadly speaking, the **Core–Satellite approach** seeks to merge passive investing with active management in an attempt to outperform a benchmark. Typically, the **core portfolio** consists of passive and often low-cost investments that track the overall performance of an asset class. Positions in the **satellite portfolio** are added in the form of actively managed and higher-cost investments. The core is related to an investor's strategic asset allocation, while the satellite component is an effort to add alpha through tactical asset allocation.

This means that the portfolio is structured in various subportfolios, which can then be designed using one of the construction techniques (bottom-up, top-down, or mixed), and the portfolios can be constructed as layered pyramids (see Exhibit 10.1). For example, a well-diversified core, or bottom layer, may provide downside protection for the portfolio (risk aversion), while a less diversified satellite, or top layer, may look to generate upside gains (risk seeking).[1] This approach aims to increase risk control, reduce costs, and add value. This may be an effective strategy for institutions that want to diversify their portfolios without giving up the potential for higher returns generated by selected active management strategies. Another advantage is the flexibility to customize a portfolio to meet specific investment objectives and preferences. The Core–Satellite approach also provides the framework for targeting and controlling those areas in which investors believe they are better able to

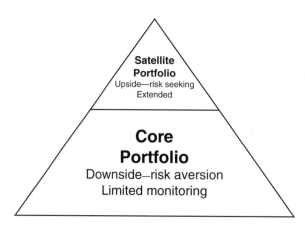

EXHIBIT 10.1   Core–Satellite Pyramid

control risks or are simply willing to take more risks. What constitutes core versus satellite depends on the investor's focus and expertise. Some see venture capital as satellite, while others view a core portfolio as being balanced between buyout and VC funds. Another benefit to this approach is that it facilitates concentrating more effort on the satellite portfolio, which is expected to generate excess performance by incurring additional risk, and less time on the more straightforward, benchmarked, lower-risk core portfolio.

10.2   TOP-DOWN AND BOTTOM-UP ASSET ALLOCATION APPROACHES

Portfolios can be constructed either from the bottom up or from the top down, or by using a combination of the two approaches.

10.2.1   Overview of Bottom-Up and Top-Down Approaches

Approaches to constructing portfolios are usually described as either bottom-up or top-down. The **bottom-up approach** is based on fund manager or security specific research, in which the emphasis is on screening all investment opportunities and picking the perceived best. A **top-down approach** analyzes the macroeconomic environment and then determines the weights and the combination of industry sectors, countries, and so on that best meet the program objectives under the likely scenarios.

While appearing to be in opposition, the bottom-up and top-down approaches can be complementary and are typically used in tandem. This method, called the **mixed approach**, either starts with a bottom-up strategy, to which increasing top-down optimization is added, or starts as an iterative short process cycle, in which bottom-up screenings are followed by top-down analysis and then by bottom-up screenings.

10.2.2   Bottom-Up Approach

The starting point of a bottom-up approach, also called the screening technique, is the identification of suitable investments, or those perceived to be the best. This is followed by intensive analysis and due diligence in order to rank the opportunities by their attractiveness and identify which are the likely top performers.

The bottom-up approach has several compelling features. As it depends solely on ranking, this approach is simple, easy to understand, and robust. It enhances the expected performance by concentrating the portfolio in the highest-alpha opportunities, with the highest expected performance adjusted for correlation with the market.

However, the bottom-up approach is not without problems. As it is very opportunistic, it can lead to an unbalanced portfolio (e.g., a portfolio excessively concentrated) carrying considerably more risk than intended or can miss some important macroeconomic changes or opportunities.

10.2.3 Top-Down Approach

The top-down approach takes the big picture as its starting point as opposed to individual fund selection. Investors who follow a top-down approach place more emphasis on the management of the strategy, asset allocation, portfolio diversification, and macroeconomic considerations. The top-down approach is a process that analyzes the macroeconomic conditions surrounding the targeted markets and attempts to determine the strategic asset allocation (i.e., the combination of industry sectors, geographies, and fund styles that are expected to be the most likely to meet the program objectives under the likely scenarios). The main criteria used in the evaluation process are political, economic, and currency risks. Other criteria examined include, for example, the extent to which each particular market has accepted private equity as a form of financing and investment, and the degree to which the environment is conducive to entrepreneurial activity. In this context, the investor takes into account various factors influencing the ability to invest, such as due diligence standards, accounting and tax issues, and the enforceability of legal rights (this last issue is particularly relevant in the case of many emerging markets). Finally, the availability of both attractive investment opportunities and exit opportunities for investments is considered.

The major shortcoming of a top-down approach is that, in reality, strict allocations are not possible. In practice, it may be difficult to find and have access to a sufficient number of superior managers to fill each predetermined subclass allocation. Therefore, in order to adopt a top-down approach, investors cannot just wait for investment opportunities to arise but must proactively search for them so as to have a sufficiently large number of funds available to fill their desired allocations.

10.2.4 Mixed Approach

As both pure bottom-up and pure top-down approaches are not problem-free, most investors follow a combined, or mixed, approach. Even a strong believer in the top-down approach would rarely invest in opportunities that are known to be of inferior quality just to fulfill a target allocation. Likewise, it may not be prudent for fund pickers to commit all of their money to a single sector based solely on the opportunity to invest in outstanding teams. Investors are conscious of the importance of diversification, but instead of diversifying on the basis of the correlations among the different asset classes, they define their target allocations on the basis of the investment strategies of the funds in which they invest.

Shearburn and Griffiths (2002) describe a modus operandi that can be considered representative of that followed by many private equity (PE) funds of funds. They invest exclusively in established PE markets, such as the United States, the United Kingdom, and selected European economies; target the premier league of PE funds in Europe and the United States; and diversify by stage, focus, geography, and vintage year. The goal is to create a portfolio that is diversified according to specified investment strategies or dimensions. In this portfolio, all the strategies or dimensions have equal weight. More specifically, these authors describe an approach that "consists in creating a portfolio of unique PE strategies that are diversified from one another over multiple dimensions. These dimensions might include industry focus, investment size, geographic focus, and PE subasset class (such as leveraged buyouts, venture capital, growth capital and distressed investments)." They then assemble a portfolio of superior managers capable of generating extraordinary returns, with each manager's strategy being as distinct (i.e., uncorrelated) as possible from all the other strategies in the portfolio. Investors using this approach weight each strategy equally in the portfolio to minimize the concentration of funds. This means, for example, investing the same amount in a London-based large buyout PE manager as in a Silicon Valley-based early-stage venture capitalist. This manager-driven, equally weighted approach to portfolio construction also drives the weighting of PE subsectors, despite situations in which an investor may have a strong point of view.

Finally, there is an evolution in the adoption of the different approaches. For the early stages of an investment program, one of the main objectives is to quickly put capital to work with the best available funds in order to minimize performance drag resulting from idle liquidity. Young programs often cannot count on an established relationship, so the available universe of investment opportunities is likely restricted to a limited number of accessible wish-list funds. This makes a top-down approach difficult to implement, as allocation targets would make little sense. Once a sizable portfolio has been built, however, a top-down approach becomes a more appropriate means of identifying concentration (e.g., in sectors or in teams).

10.3 RISK BUDGETING

Risk budgeting refers to a broad spectrum of approaches to portfolio construction and maintenance that emphasize the selection of targeted amounts of risk and the allocation of the portfolio's aggregate risk to those various categories of risk.

10.3.1 Overview of Risk Budgeting

Risk budgeting is only part of an asset allocation process because *by itself* risk budgeting limits the range of possible allocations (via constraints) but does not identify a unique portfolio through optimization. Risk budgeting must be combined with other methods or goals in order to identify a unique, optimal portfolio.

Risk budgeting is often described as the setting of *target risk levels* (risk budgets) in which the asset allocator *spends* risk across risky investments (i.e., bears various risks judiciously for the sake of receiving benefits, such as higher expected return). The asset allocator can set a risk budget for the total portfolio and also can parse the acceptable amount of risk (the risk budget) into risk allocations for or within asset classes.

A risk budget is therefore analogous to an ordinary household budget for expenses in which an aggregate level is determined and is spent among various categories. Similarly, a risk budgeting process might decide that an appropriate level of risk is 15% and then might allocate that acceptable level of risk among the various asset classes—each of which might also have a budgeted risk level.

10.3.2 Specifications in Risk Budgeting

Risk budgeting requires a specification of how risk is measured, but the risk budgeting approach can be used with virtually any quantitative approach. Common examples of risk measurements to use in a risk budgeting process include standard deviation of returns (volatility), standard deviation of tracking error against a benchmark, value at risk, and beta. Risk budgeting requires a clear specification of the relation between the measured risk of the total portfolio and the measured risks of the portfolio's constituent assets. The quantitative link between the risk of the portfolio and the risks of its constituent assets permits risk to be budgeted among the available assets.

Risk budgeting by itself does not require or even consider expected returns, although it typically is used in asset allocation frameworks that explicitly or implicitly utilize expected returns. For example, consider an asset allocator managing the total risk of a portfolio using the portfolio's annual volatility (i.e., standard deviation of returns). The allocator may set a target aggregate risk exposure of, say, 12% for the portfolio. Furthermore, the allocator may specify the portion of that risk that each asset subclass is allowed to exhibit (e.g., 3% from bonds and 9% from stocks). In this example, the risk budgeting approach constrains the allocation decision to those portfolios such that the risk of the total portfolio is 12%. The allocator might construct a portfolio that keeps total risk (and perhaps the risks of various asset classes) at their target level while identifying the optimal portfolio through an objective function.

In more advanced applications, allocations to each asset subgroup are formed to equate each group's *marginal contribution* to that risk. The goals of risk budgeting are typically twofold: (1) to organize and quantify the process of allocating portfolio risk exposures; and (2) to identify portfolio allocations that bear risks as efficiently as possible relative to other goals determined by the asset allocator.

10.3.3 Defining Risk in Risk Budgeting and Risk Buckets

Risk bucketing describes the gathering of each type of risk into a value of that risk for the entire portfolio. A **risk bucket** indicates the amount of a particular type of risk that can be tolerated. The risk-bucketing approach typically uses multiple risk buckets. Risk budgeting typically *forces* the portfolio to contain the budgeted or targeted levels of each type of risk—no more and no less.

A key aspect that differentiates risk budgeting approaches is the specification of the risk being budgeted. That specification may be linked to a set of factors such as an equity risk bucket, an interest rate risk bucket, an illiquidity risk bucket, and a credit risk bucket. Other common choices include buckets for total risk (volatility), systematic risk, multiple beta risks (e.g., factor risks), value-at-risk (VaR), and active risks.

Having already determined the optimal or target exposure of the portfolio to each type of risk, the allocator then "fills" each bucket with an appropriate level of risk by selecting assets—noting that each asset likely has an impact on multiple risk buckets (via correlations) and perhaps considering other important characteristics such as taxes or liquidity.

10.3.4 Defining an Objective to Obtain a Unique Solution

Some objective must identify the preferred solution from the myriad of possible solutions that meet the constraints imposed by various risk buckets. To identify an optimal portfolio, a model must have an implicit or explicit *objective function*. Risk budgeting approaches are usually paired with some type of portfolio optimization (wherein the objective function is maximized). The most familiar kind of portfolio optimization to be paired with risk budgeting is mean-variance optimization. Other approaches include forcing the marginal contribution of each asset class to total portfolio risk to be equal, or to maximize diversification (e.g., minimize the sum of the squared portfolio weights).

10.3.5 Including Correlations and Viewing Marginal Risks

In relatively sophisticated applications of risk budgeting, the amount of risk for various potential portfolios is estimated by accounting for the covariances or correlation coefficients between assets or asset classes to adjust for the effects of diversification on total portfolio risk. In these more quantitative applications, the return correlations among asset classes or subclasses are estimated and inserted into computer programs that generate the total risk and the *marginal* contribution of each eligible investment to the risk of the portfolio. The use of marginal risks typically involves setting the marginal contribution of each asset to the risk of the portfolio equal to each other or equal to the budgeted values for each asset.

10.3.6 Including Expected Returns with Risk Budgeting

Although risk budgeting often does not explicitly attempt to *optimize* expected returns, the expected returns of some or all of the investments may enter into the process either explicitly or through variables as alpha. For example, the asset allocator may include target levels of alpha or target allocations to alpha generators within the risk budgeting approach. Furthermore, once allocations to each asset class have been determined, the process may allow allocations within each asset class to be optimized with respect to expected return while constraining the marginal risk of each asset class to remain within its budgeted amount.

The risk budgeting approach can be combined with mean-variance optimization quite simply by including the constraints from risk budgeting as constraints on the optimization.

A popular application of risk budgeting allocates a portfolio between passive investments (e.g., indexation) and active investments (e.g., alternative investments) based in part on estimates of the extent to which the active investments can be expected to have higher expected returns than the passive investments. For example, a risk budgeting framework may be designed to guide the asset allocator into deciding how much risk out of a total risk budget of 15% to allow for actively managed investments such as hedge funds in the pursuit of earning potential alpha. Other risk budgeting approaches may use a mean-variance framework in which the expected return of every asset is specified and optimized as part of the risk–return tradeoff.

Another case where expected returns are used in risk budgeting is when the asset allocator is using the standard deviation of the tracking errors between the portfolio's return and a benchmark's return. The asset allocator has to decide which managers will be allowed to deviate from a benchmark due to active risk. One important factor influencing this decision is the potential alpha of the manager. For instance, an asset allocator may decide that a large-cap equity investor is not likely to generate substantial alpha; therefore, the portfolio manager will not be allocated any tracking error risk. In other words, an index fund will be used for this asset class. On the other hand, the asset allocator will be willing to spend a substantial portion of the portfolio's tracking error risk on a small cap equity long/short manager who is believed to have the potential to generate a significant amount of alpha.

10.4 A FACTOR-BASED EXAMPLE OF IMPLEMENTING A RISK BUDGETING APPROACH

Level 1 of the CAIA curriculum detailed the formula for the variance of a portfolio:

$$\sigma_p^2 = \text{Var}\left[\sum_{i=1}^{N} w_i R_i\right] = \sum_{j=1}^{N}\sum_{i=1}^{N} w_i w_j \sigma_{ij}$$

Here, w_i is the weight of asset i in the portfolio, and σ_{ij} is the covariance between asset i and asset j. Risk budgeting attempts to measure the contribution of each asset class to the total risk of the portfolio, typically measured by the standard deviation of returns σ_p. This example of risk budgeting uses the above equation as a foundation.

10.4.1 Attributing the Risk of a Portfolio to Three Attributes of Each Asset

The previous equation can be used to measure the risk contributions of asset classes as well as contributions of return factors. Having selected standard deviation to represent the total risk of a portfolio, measuring each asset class's contribution to the total risk is straightforward, as indicated in Equation 10.1.

$$\sigma_p = \frac{\partial \sigma_p}{\partial w_1} w_1 + \cdots + \frac{\partial \sigma_p}{\partial w_N} w_N \tag{10.1}$$

Equation 10.1 states that the total risk of a portfolio can be decomposed into N components, with each measuring the contribution of an asset class to the total risk. The contribution of each class is measured by the asset's weight in the portfolio multiplied by the sensitivity of the portfolio's standard deviation to small changes in the weight of the asset $(\partial \sigma_p / \partial w_i)$.

The total risk of a portfolio can be decomposed into the contribution of each asset class to the total risk. A simple analytical formula allows us to calculate the risk contribution of each asset class. Because the contribution of each asset class to the total risk was measured by $(\partial \sigma_p / \partial w_i) \times w_i$, we can use the formula for the standard deviation of the portfolio to evaluate this contribution: in particular, the total risk can be decomposed in the following form:

$$\frac{\partial \sigma_p}{\partial w_i} \times w_i = \frac{\sigma_{iP}}{\sigma_P} \times w_i = \rho_i \times \sigma_i \times w_i \tag{10.2}$$

where σ_{iP} is the covariance of asset i with the portfolio, and ρ_i is the correlation of asset i with respect to the portfolio. Each term on the right side of Equation 10.1 can be expressed as the middle or right side of Equation 10.2. It can be seen from the right side of Equation 10.2 that the contribution of the risk of asset i to the total risk of a portfolio (with risk being measured as volatility of returns) is positively related to: (1) the correlation of that asset's returns with the returns of the total portfolio; (2) the volatility of that asset; and (3) the weight of that asset in the portfolio.

10.4.2   Using Factor-Based Returns and Factor-Based Risk Buckets

The preceding discussion focused on risk budgets associated with individual assets or asset classes. The total risk of a portfolio was decomposed into the contribution of each asset to that total risk. It is possible to use the same approach to decompose the total risk of a portfolio by measuring the contribution of each *factor* to the total risk.

Here we discuss how the contribution of factor volatilities to total risk of a portfolio can be measured. The contribution of factor volatilities to the total risk of a portfolio can be measured. To see this, suppose there are two factors, F_1 and F_2, that are the major drivers of the portfolio's return. Their degree of importance can be measured by regressing the portfolio's rate of return on these two factors (e.g., one factor could be changes in the credit spread and the other could be changes in the price of oil).

$$R_{Pt} = a + b_1 F_{1t} + b_2 F_{2t} + \varepsilon_t \tag{10.3}$$

Here, R_{Pt} is the rate of return on the portfolio; a, b_1, and b_2 are the estimated parameters (factor loadings or factor betas) of the regression model; and ε_t is the residual part of the regression that represents the part of the return that cannot be explained by the two factors.

A number of macroeconomic and financial factors can affect the performance of a portfolio. An asset owner may already have significant exposures to some of these factors. For example, the manufacturer of a product that is sold in foreign markets may have significant exposures to currency risk. That may lead the asset owner to instruct the portfolio manager to measure and then limit the exposure of the portfolio to currency risk. On the other hand, the same asset owner may wish to measure and adjust the risk exposure of the portfolio to the interest rate factor because it needs the assets to fund a liability that is interest rate sensitive.

10.4.3 Calculating the Risk Contribution to Each Factor

This section uses the approach in Sections 10.4.1 and 10.4.2 to decompose the total risk of a portfolio by measuring the contribution of each *factor* to the total risk (rather than each *asset*). The total risk of the portfolio can now be decomposed into the contributions of each factor:

$$\sigma_P = \underset{\text{Contribution of Factor 1}}{(\rho_{F_1} \times \sigma_{F_1} \times b_1)} + \underset{\text{Contribution of Factor 2}}{(\rho_{F_2} \times \sigma_{F_2} \times b_2)} + \underset{\text{Contribution of Unknown Sources}}{(\rho_\varepsilon \times \sigma_\varepsilon)} \qquad (10.4)$$

Here, ρ_{F_1}, ρ_{F_2}, and ρ_ε are the correlations of the two factors and the residual risk with the portfolio's return, respectively. Each of the first two terms that appear on the right-hand side of Equation 10.4 represents the contribution of a factor to the total risk of the portfolio. The last term represents the contribution of unknown sources of risk.

For example, suppose the correlation between changes in the oil price and the return on a portfolio with a standard deviation of 8.21% is 0.31. The standard deviation of changes in the oil price is estimated to be 20%, and the factor loading of the portfolio on oil (i.e., the coefficient of a regression of the portfolio returns on oil) is 0.757. What is the risk contribution of oil to the total risk of the portfolio?

$$\text{Contribution of Oil} = 0.31 \times 0.20 \times 0.757 = 4.69\%$$

Therefore, 4.69% of the total risk of 8.11% of the portfolio can be contributed to the volatility in oil prices. It can be seen how the risk budget associated with return factors can be helpful in understanding the risk profile of a portfolio. In addition, limits on risk budgets associated with factors can be incorporated into the mean-variance optimization.

APPLICATION 10.4.3

Portfolio XYZ, with a volatility of 12%, has been identified as being driven by three factors, one of which is credit spreads. Analysis indicates that 30% of the portfolio's volatility (i.e., 3.6% of the 12%) is due to the credit spread factor, which has a factor loading (beta coefficient) estimated to be 0.40 and a volatility estimate of 25%. What is the implied correlation coefficient between the credit spread factor and the returns of portfolio XYZ?

$$30\% \times 12\% = \rho \times 0.25 \times 0.40 \quad \rho = 3.6\%/(0.25 \times 0.40) = 0.36$$

The correlation coefficient between the credit spread factor and portfolio returns is 0.36.

10.5 RISK PARITY

Risk parity is an asset allocation approach that identifies asset allocations based on balancing the *contribution* of each asset to portfolio risk without regard for expected return. The goal and result of risk parity is to ensure that each asset class contributes the same amount of risk to the portfolio—hence the name *risk parity*. In a sense, the portfolio may be viewed as diversifying among risks such that each risk is equally weighted. In risk parity, there is no consideration given to the expected returns of each asset class or asset. Specifically, and as is detailed later, the risk-parity approach recommends that the allocation to each asset class should be set so that each asset class has the same marginal contribution to the total risk of the portfolio.

10.5.1   Overview of Risk Parity

The risk-parity approach to asset allocation seeks a portfolio in which all asset classes (except cash) contribute the same amount to the total risk of the portfolio. That is, the weights are numerically adjusted to locate a portfolio in which each asset contributes the same amount to the total risk. It is important to note that there is no volatility target, and the total risk of the portfolio is endogenous to the process (i.e., the risk is determined within the model).

As in the case of risk budgeting, allocations in a risk-parity portfolio-allocation approach are driven primarily by risk, not by expected return. Also, as in the case of risk budgeting, risk may be defined using any metric the allocator selects, such as volatility or VaR.

In risk parity, each asset's contribution to portfolio risk is equal. For example, in a stocks-versus-bonds allocation, bonds would be overweighted relative to stocks until the risk generated by the bond allocation equaled that of the stocks. By equating the combined risk contributions of each asset class to the total risk of the portfolio, the approach could be viewed in the context of risk budgeting as generating an efficient way to budget the total risk among various asset classes.

10.5.2   Risk Parity with Two Risky Assets

Returning to the classic decision to invest in just two asset classes: equities and bonds. Bonds tend to contain less risk than equities, so the "first" dollar of bonds contributes less risk than the first dollar of equities. Thus, in a risk-parity approach, bonds are initially overweighted relative to equities based in part on the inverse of their risk relative to the inverse of the risk of equities.

Risk parity, however, does not simply mean weighting each asset in inverse proportion to its volatility (as in an *inverse volatility approach* which is discussed later in this chapter). This is because the risk that an asset contributes to a portfolio depends on more than just its volatility and its portfolio weight—it depends on correlation. This correlation needs to be incorporated into the weights to reflect the diversification effects that are driven by correlations among the portfolio's assets.

Although low-volatility assets tend to be overweighted in risk parity, their weights are tempered by the method's recognition that, as bonds and other low-risk assets begin to dominate a portfolio, their marginal risk contribution to the portfolio rises because of reduced diversification (i.e., concentrated positions in low-risk asset classes). Eventually, the high-risk asset classes, such as equities, gain attractiveness as diversifiers. The risk-parity approach balances these effects to achieve allocations such that each asset class contributes the same amount to the portfolio's total risk.

The risk-parity approach tends to discourage investing in riskier assets. Application of the risk-parity approach in this example of a fixed-income and equity portfolio would therefore tend to overweight fixed-income assets and underweight equities relative to traditional asset allocations. This contrasts with modern portfolio theory which suggests that optimal portfolio diversification occurs when risky assets are weighted in direct proportion to their size—with each portfolio weight equal to the weight that each asset represents in the total market portfolio.

A focus on equating the contributions of each asset class to the total risk of the portfolio through the risk-parity approach tends to drive the entire portfolio toward being low risk. Therefore, unlevered portfolios based on risk-parity approaches tend to perform relatively poorly during periods when high-risk assets, such as equities, perform well.

10.5.3   Risk Parity, Leverage, and Sharpe Ratios

The risk-parity approach tends to create relatively low-risk portfolios through high allocations to low-risk assets and low allocations to higher-risk assets such as equities. A common criticism of low-risk portfolios is that in periods of high returns on high-risk assets (e.g., equities) they exhibit relatively poor performance. This criticism, however, ignores the potential role of leverage. The low-risk portfolios generated by the risk parity approach can be leveraged to generate risk comparable to that of other portfolios. In other words, leverage (through margin or financial derivatives) allows the asset allocator to reach whatever level of total portfolio risk is desired.

If the low-risk portfolios suggested by risk parity offer a higher expected excess return-to-risk ratio (i.e., Sharpe ratio), then the leveraged low-risk portfolios should be preferred to unleveraged high-risk portfolios. So the standard by which risk-parity approaches should be evaluated relative to other asset allocation approaches is their risk/return tradeoffs, not just their expected return. This assumes, however, that the investor is willing and able to apply leverage and is able to withstand the risks and monitoring costs specific to leveraged portfolios.

APPLICATION 10.5.3

The returns of a risk-parity portfolio have been estimated as having a standard deviation of 12%. A traditional portfolio has been estimated as offering an expected return of 8% with a standard deviation of 18%. The riskless rate of return is 2%. What return must the risk-parity portfolio offer to be equally attractive as the traditional portfolio?

To be equally attractive, the risk-parity portfolio must have the same Sharpe ratio. The Sharpe ratio of the traditional portfolio is (8% − 2%)/18% = 0.333. To be equally attractive, the expected return of the risk-parity portfolio (X%) must satisfy: 0.333 = (X% − 2%)/12%. Therefore, the equally attractive expected return of the risk-parity portfolio would be 6%.

10.5.4 Three Steps in Implementing the Risk-Parity Approach

There are three steps in implementing the risk-parity approach.

First, similar to risk budgeting, risk parity requires a definition of the total risk of a portfolio. Risk parity does not impose a uniform measure of total risk. However, total risk is typically measured by the standard deviation of the rate of return on the portfolio (volatility). Alternatively, one could use value at risk (VaR) or some other measure of risk. The advantage of using VaR as a measure of total risk, especially for portfolios with alternative investments, is that one can incorporate skewness and kurtosis into the measure of total risk. However, to simplify this discussion, volatility is used as a measure of total risk.

Second, risk parity requires a method to measure the marginal risk contribution of each asset class to the total risk of the portfolio. The marginal risk contribution of an asset to the total risk of a portfolio indicates the rate at which an additional unit of that asset would cause the portfolio's total risk to rise. The marginal risk contribution of an asset depends on the composition of the portfolio. For example, adding a hedge fund to an otherwise diversified portfolio may contribute little or no risk, since the hedge fund may offer substantial diversification benefits. However, as the hedge fund's allocation to the portfolio is increased, the effect of additional allocations of hedge funds (i.e., the marginal contribution) also increases. Accordingly, at high levels of allocation to hedge funds, additional allocations may increase risk substantially, as the portfolio becomes concentrated in hedge funds rather than diversified. The measurement of risk contributions was discussed in the previous section.

Third and finally, portfolio weights are determined for all available assets. The weights are typically identified using a trial-and-error process until the marginal contributions from all assets to the total risk of the portfolio are equal. The previous section showed that the marginal contribution of an asset class to the total risk of a portfolio is given by Equation 10.5:

$$\text{Contribution of Asset } i = \frac{\partial(\text{Total Risk})}{\partial(\text{Weight of Asset } i)} \times (\text{Weight of Asset } i) \qquad (10.5)$$

10.5.5 An Example of Creating a Portfolio Using the Risk-Parity Approach

This section addresses the central point of the risk-parity approach: how to determine portfolio weights. Equations 10.1 and 10.5 demonstrate that, in all cases, the total risk of a portfolio may be expressed as the sum of the marginal contributions of the portfolio's constituent assets. The risk-parity approach is the simple prescription that the portfolio's weights should be selected such that the marginal contribution of each asset is equal. Thus, to create a portfolio of N assets using the risk-parity approach, the weights need to be adjusted until the marginal contribution to risk for each asset in the portfolio is equal to $(1/N)$ times the total risk of the portfolio.

The portfolio weights that equalize all the marginal contributions to risk can be easily found using a trial-and-error approach such as that performed by an optimization package such as Microsoft Excel's Solver. Even under simplifying assumptions, it is difficult to obtain closed-form solutions. Consider the information for the two asset classes in Exhibit 10.2 based on actual return data. A trial-and-error search was

EXHIBIT 10.2   Sample Solution to Risk Parity for Two Assets

Input Data	Stocks	Bonds
Volatility of Returns	4.50%	1.62%
Covariance Between the Two	0.021%	
Output Data	Stocks	Bonds
Risk-Parity Weights	26.45%	73.55%
Marginal Contribution to Risk	0.955%	0.955%
Total Portfolio Volatility	1.91%	

used to generate the risk-parity solutions depicted in Exhibit 10.2 based on volatility as the measure of risk. Note that bonds received over 73% of the portfolio's allocation in order to generate the same contribution to risk as the stocks generated with an allocation of less than 27%.

The intuition of the solution in Exhibit 10.2 is straightforward. Based on Equation 10.2, the marginal contribution to the risk of a portfolio from each asset, say asset i, can be expressed as the product of three values: ρ_i, σ_i, and w_i. Accordingly, the marginal contribution for each asset being introduced to a portfolio "starts" at zero when its allocation is set to zero (because $w_i = 0$). The allocation to each asset then increases in inverse proportion to its volatility and correlation with the portfolio so that each asset contributes equally at the margin to portfolio risk.

Examination of the two assets in Exhibit 10.1 indicates that the stocks have higher volatility than the bonds, which means that the allocation to bonds must increase at a faster rate than stocks (both from a starting point of zero) to generate the same increase in marginal contribution to risk as the stocks. In a two-asset case, the exercise is nearly trivial since the only correlation to consider is the correlation between the returns of the two assets.

Nevertheless, the example illustrates the most important points. Risk parity tends to overweight low-risk assets and underweight high-risk assets relative to an equal weighting. However, the standalone volatility of each asset is not the only determinant. The weights are also driven by the correlation of each asset with the portfolio (which in turn is driven by correlation with all the other assets).

10.5.6   The Primary Economic Rationale for the Risk-Parity Approach

It would seem that portfolios generated by the risk-parity approach would tend to perform well only when traditionally low-risk assets (e.g., bonds) performed better than traditionally high-risk assets (e.g., stocks). However, performance should be based on risk adjusted returns and diversification attributes (e.g., which asset generated a higher Sharpe ratio and which asset provided better diversification).

Note, however, that to the extent that the market portfolio is optimal, a risk-parity portfolio that overweights low-volatility assets will tend to be suboptimal. Under what conditions, then, would low-risk portfolios become optimal for some investors? One obvious answer is that if an investor has a very high degree of risk aversion, then a risk-parity portfolio could be optimal. However, a low-volatility portfolio can also be constructed using the mean-variance framework or by allocating substantially to the riskless asset.

The most compelling arguments that can be put forward in support of the risk-parity approach also support the use of low-risk portfolios, including the minimum-volatility approach (discussed later). The economic rationale for low-volatility portfolios is that because of market imperfections, many investors are unable or unwilling to use leverage. This is referred to as leverage aversion. The **leverage aversion theory** argues that large classes of investors cannot lever up low-volatility portfolios to generate attractive returns and that, as a result, low-volatility stocks and portfolios are underpriced. Those investors who are not averse to leverage can exploit the potential underpricing of low-volatility portfolios and lever the attractive Sharpe ratios into attractive combinations of risk and return.

10.5.7   The Volatility Anomaly and Risk Parity

The **volatility anomaly** is the idea that low-volatility stocks are underpriced and therefore offer higher expected risk-adjusted returns and may be justified by market imperfections and the leverage aversion theory. A key question is why the low-volatility portfolio should provide a higher Sharpe ratio in the first place. The leverage aversion argument is that because many investors are not allowed to use leverage, demand for low-risk stocks is low, and therefore they are undervalued. For example, if a mutual fund manager wants to overweight stocks he judges to be undervalued, but still track a broad equity benchmark with some degree of accuracy, the manager cannot afford to overweight low-volatility stocks. Although low-risk stocks may offer attractive risk-adjusted returns, the mutual fund manager will not be able to lever up their low raw returns to match the overall market return; as a result, the fund will underperform its benchmark in terms of raw returns.

According to this anomaly, portfolios consisting of low-volatility stocks have historically outperformed the overall market. However, the evidence seems to indicate that the anomaly has weakened since its discovery by academic researchers. Related to the volatility anomaly is the "**betting against *beta***" anomaly, which has been documented with the observation that portfolios consisting of low-beta stocks have outperformed the market in the past on a risk-adjusted basis. The explanation for the betting against beta anomaly is rather similar to the one set forth for the low-volatility anomaly. Many investors are unwilling or unable to use leverage to increase the betas of low-beta portfolios. During periods of rising market prices, investors want to be invested in high-beta stocks. As a result, high-beta stocks are bid up, which reduces their future returns. Therefore, those investors who are willing and able to use leverage should experience a higher risk-adjusted return through investing in low-beta stocks.

10.5.8   Criticisms of Three Popular Rationales for Risk Parity

Market participants have set forth other arguments in support of the risk parity approach: (1) that past attractive performance of risk-parity portfolios will persist; (2) that the ability to lever a risk-parity portfolio means that high Sharpe ratios are always preferred; and (3) that risk parity guides portfolios to the optimal allocation to alternative assets. These arguments should be viewed with caution.

First, historic returns are not a reasonable basis on which to speculate that low-risk fixed-income instruments of developed and most emerging economies will continue to perform well. Note that many bonds now have yields far below yields observed in previous decades. Therefore, risk-parity portfolios that overweight fixed income are not highly likely to repeat superior historical performance.

Second, it is important to note that risk parity may introduce funding risks that are absent in other strategies. The assertion that leveraged risk-parity portfolios are attractive relative to equally volatile unleveraged portfolios does not recognize potential funding risk. **Funding liquidity risk** introduces a risk associated with leverage that is not present in unlevered portfolios. For example, during periods of market stress, the investor may be required to reduce the portfolio's leverage and therefore liquidate the portfolio at the most inopportune time.

A third potentially unsupported rationale for risk parity is that it better exploits anomalies that exist in alternative asset markets through higher allocations to alternatives. However, there have been no studies to show that the low volatility or "betting against beta" anomalies work in the alternative investment area. That is, the low-risk strategies may or may not provide the highest risk-adjusted returns. While there is some evidence that levered low-risk portfolios of traditional asset classes may provide attractive risk-adjusted returns, there is no evidence that such a strategy could work in the alternative investment area.

It is important to note that because some alternative investments have low volatility and low correlations with other asset classes, the allocations to alternative investments using the risk-parity approach will be relatively high compared to market weights and typical institutional portfolios. While risk parity may be a viable approach to asset allocation, it does not represent a trading strategy that can be employed by active managers seeking to maximize risk-adjusted return, because risk parity does not require or use any estimate of expected return. The risk-parity approach may be suitable for institutional and high-net-worth investors who do not face substantial constraints on their asset allocation policies and who are able to use leverage to adjust the total risk to meet their target total risk.

10.6 OTHER QUANTITATIVE PORTFOLIO ALLOCATION STRATEGIES

This section briefly describes several other quantitative asset allocation strategies.

10.6.1 The Market-Weighted Strategy

A standard asset allocation strategy in traditional investments is to allocate to each asset in proportion to its total market capitalization relative to the market capitalization of the entire market. Modern portfolio theory establishes that, under idealized conditions, market weighting provides optimal diversification. Passive indexation based on market weighting has soared in retail and institutional usage. In alternative investing the application of market-weighted asset allocation is problematic. First, the illiquid and granular nature of real assets such as real estate and natural resources makes precise market weighting impossible. The total size and value of privately traded asset sectors is difficult to estimate. Further, calculating the total underlying value of publicly traded assets sectors is complicated by publicly traded investment pools such as exchange traded funds (ETFs), structured products, and financial derivatives. These pools serve as conduits of underlying exposures and complicate the issue through potential double and triple counting of asset values.

10.6.2 An Equally Weighted or 1/N Diversification Strategy

An equally weighted 1/N, or **naïve asset allocation strategy** refers to constructing a portfolio with an equally sized allocation assigned to each asset (or sector). There are three primary justifications for implementing an equally weighted asset allocation strategy:

1. A 1/N diversification is the strategy that minimizes portfolio risk when the opportunity set of available investments is made up of assets with equal volatilities (and equal alphas), and asset pairs with equal correlations.
2. When forecasts of asset volatilities and/or correlations are quite difficult to make, a 1/N diversification strategy can make sense.
3. When long-term mean reversion of asset returns is deemed likely based on the hypothesis that very large assets have smaller long-term growth opportunities than very small assets.

On the other hand, the theoretical justification for using *market weights,* especially in allocating among traditional listed assets such as public equities, is generally persuasive. Beyond the issue of ideal diversification, the optimal weighting of assets, asset classes, and asset subclasses for a particular investor can vary due to that investor's unique circumstances. In practice, investors can differ in terms of their risk preferences, tax rates, information sets, expectations, borrowing costs, transaction costs, opportunities, and access. For all of these reasons, the use of market weights as portfolio weights may not be optimal for each investor. Nevertheless, the theoretical optimum of using market weights as portfolio weights can serve as a valuable reference point from which to depart. Whether deciding between domestic and international equity allocations, between sovereign bonds and corporate bonds, between infrastructure funds and high-yield bonds, or any other such decision, institutions should have a thoughtful process for asset allocation, especially when deciding to allocate based on weights other than market weights.

10.6.3 Inverse Volatility-Weighted Portfolio Strategies

Risk parity is one approach to creating a low-volatility portfolio. In many markets, another approach to obtain a low-volatility portfolio is to use an equally weighted portfolio. An equally weighted portfolio is, by definition, rather well diversified and, in practice, is likely to have relatively high allocations to less risky assets. The reason is that in most applications, equity serves as both the largest asset class and the riskiest. Thus, equal weighting typically underweights equities relative to a market portfolio. Another approach, as seen previously, is to use mean-variance optimization to identify the minimum variance portfolio.

An inverse volatility-weighted portfolio is the direct approach to a low-risk portfolio obtained by weighting each asset (or asset class) inversely to its volatility.

The inverse volatility-weighting approach uses the inverse of the volatility of each asset ($1/\sigma_i$) and the weight of each asset or asset class as shown in Equation 10.6.

$$w_i = \frac{\sigma_i^{-1}}{\sum_{j=1}^{N} \sigma_j^{-1}} \qquad i = 1, \ldots, N \qquad (10.6)$$

Equation 10.6 indicates that the portfolio weight for each asset or asset class is formed with: (1) the inverse of its volatility in the numerator; and (2) the sum of the inverses of every portfolio asset in the denominator. Thus, each asset's weight is simply its inverse volatility relative to the sum of all the inverse volatilities among the portfolio's assets. This ensures that the weights will add up to one. The inverse volatility-weighed approach and the risk-parity approach are rather similar.

The difference between the two is that the risk-parity approach takes into account the diversification that each asset offers, whereas the volatility-weighted approach allocates the portfolio solely on the basis of each asset's standalone risk (i.e., each asset's volatility). The volatility-weighted approach is identical to the risk-parity approach under conditions discussed in a subsequent section.

10.6.4　Minimum Volatility Portfolio Allocation Strategies

A minimum volatility portfolio strategy simply minimizes the well-known formula for volatility (or variance) in a Markowitz framework.

$$\sigma_p^2 = \text{Var}\left[\sum_{i=1}^{N} w_i R_i\right] = \sum_{j=1}^{N}\sum_{i=1}^{N} w_i w_j \sigma_{ij} \qquad (10.7)$$

Graphically, the **minimum volatility portfolio** may be envisioned in a mean-variance framework as the leftmost point on a mean-variance efficient frontier where the frontier is tangent to a vertical line. The weights of each asset will tend to be higher for low-volatility assets and higher for assets that have low correlations with the rest of the portfolio. The next section provides some further insight under three special cases.

10.6.5　Equivalence Between Allocation Strategies

Three equivalency cases are instructive involving the following allocation strategies described in this chapter: risk parity, equally weighted, inverse volatility-weighted, and minimum volatility.

1. In the case of *equally* volatile assets with *equal* return correlations between each pair of assets, the following strategies generate the same allocations: risk parity, equally weighted, inverse volatility-weighted, and minimum volatility.
2. In the case of *equally* volatile assets with *unequal* return correlations between pairs of assets, the following strategies generate the same allocations: equally weighted and inverse volatility-weighted. Note that minimum-volatility strategies and risk-parity strategies take into account correlations and so their solutions (portfolio weights) will depend on the correlations (and may differ from each other in the given case of *equally* volatile assets with *unequal* return correlations).

3. Finally, in the case of *unequally* volatile assets with *equal* return correlations between pairs of assets, only the risk-parity and inverse-volatility strategies generate the same allocations.

The first case demonstrates the volatility-diminishing nature of all four strategies. Note that none of the strategies, per se, take into account expected returns. The second case highlights the point that the equally weighted and volatility-weighted strategies ignore correlations. The third case demonstrates the similarity between risk parity and inverse volatility when the assumption of uniform correlations removes the impact on risk parity of diverse correlations.

10.6.6 Risk Allocation Based on Return Factors

Chapter 8 details the importance of factor analysis within modern investment analysis and portfolio management. This section discusses the allocation strategies in the context of factor analysis. How does one perform risk allocation based on return factors or at least include return factors in the strategy?

First, factor-based portfolios are not entirely passively managed. Unless one is willing to allow the weights of factors to become very high or low, the investor will have to rebalance the portfolio on a regular basis. In addition, direct investments designed to maintain specific factor exposures may not be a viable strategy for some institutional investors, as most factor strategies would require long and short positions in certain asset classes, and many institutional investors may not be prepared to take short positions.

However, investment pools such as hedge funds implement strategies designed to earn their returns by actively managing factors. For instance, the merger arbitrage strategy earns a premium by exploiting a factor related to the uncertainty surrounding the completion of mergers. The convertible arbitrage strategy exploits a form of the implied volatility factor, and many equity long/short and equity market-neutral strategies have been shown to have significant exposures to factors of the equity markets (Zhang and Kazemi 2015). Finally, global macro strategies often rely heavily on the carry trade factor to generate returns.

Do allocations based on factors outperform allocations based on asset classes? It can be shown that in a perfect world, where all factors can be traded and all asset returns can be explained by factors, a factor-based approach is not inherently superior to other strategies. In other words, if all factors were traded and short sale constraints were removed, then it would be difficult to imagine that a portfolio constructed using factor-based risk allocation could outperform on a consistent and long-term basis a portfolio constructed using other asset allocation approaches. Nevertheless, research using real-world data has demonstrated that factor approaches may offer superior returns over a given period of time (Idzorek and Kowara 2013).

10.6.7 Four Practical Issues with Allocating Based on Return Factors

Four practical issues associated with risk-factor-based asset allocation are important (Idzorek and Kowara 2013).

First, portfolio construction using return factors is not likely to become globally adopted, because it implies allocation strategies that are not sustainable (i.e., not consistent on the macro level). That is, not everyone can be short growth stocks or commodities that are in contango. Therefore, the capacity is likely to be limited, and as more money is allocated to factor investing, the strategies will become expensive and the risk premium will shrink or disappear altogether.

Second, factor-based risk allocation requires asset owners to take extreme positions in some assets or asset classes. Many institutional investors are not allowed to make such allocations. For example, taking short positions in all growth stocks—including such names as Google, Amazon, and Facebook—is not something that most investors are prepared to do.

Third, factor-based risk allocation is not a magic bullet that will automatically lead to asset allocations that will dominate those based on asset classes. Similar to other investment products, the cost of the strategy must be taken into account. Flows into some of these factors appear to have already reduced the size of the premium (e.g., size and low volatility factors have not performed well in recent years).

Finally, alternative investments are important vehicles for accessing some of these return factors, but they typically represent a bundle of factors and cannot be isolated in practice. For instance, factor exposure analysis indicates that private equity has significant exposures to both the size and credit factors. Therefore, an investor preferring one of the factor exposures but not the other may have difficulty in controlling the factor exposures of the entire portfolio.

10.7 THE NEW INVESTMENT MODEL

In the **new investment model,** investments are allocated with flexibility and in the explicit context of alpha and beta management.

Beta is sought through investment products that cost-effectively offer returns driven by beta so that the portfolio obtains efficient economic exposure to market risk and can earn the expected risk premiums associated with bearing systematic risks. Beta risk is managed with the purpose of implementing the strategic asset allocation strategy established by the investor.

Alpha is sought independently of beta. The professional investment staff can seek alpha from those investment products that are perceived to offer the best opportunities, even if those products fall outside the benchmark and traditional asset classes. Alternative assets can be highly useful with this flexible model. Alpha should be pursued in products related to less efficient markets, including hedge funds, real assets, commodities, private equity, and structured products. The management of systematic risk should be accomplished with those products that offer beta exposure efficiently. Key concepts in the new investment model are the ideas of the separation of alpha and beta and of portable alpha.

NOTE

1. See Statman (2002): "The desire to avoid poverty gives way to the desire for riches. Some investors fill the uppermost layers with the few stocks of an undiversified portfolio like

private individuals buy lottery tickets. Neither lottery buying nor undiversified portfolios are consistent with mean-variance portfolio theory but both are consistent with behavioral portfolio theory."

REFERENCES

Idzorek, T. and M. Kowara. 2013. "Factor-Based Asset Allocation vs. Asset-Class-Based Asset Allocation." *Financial Analysts Journal* 69 (3): 1–11.

Shearburn, J. and B. Griffiths. 2002. "Private Equity Building Blocks." *Pension Week* in association with Goldman Sachs, April.

Statman, M. 2002. "How Much Diversification Is Enough?" Leavey School of Business, Santa Clara University, September.

Zhang, C. and H. Kazemi. 2015. "Hedge Funds Returns and Market Anomalies." CISDM Working Paper, University of Massachusetts.

Institutional Asset Owners and Investment Policies

A systematic asset allocation process depends on the asset owners. Chapter 11 overviews four major types of asset owners and the components of an investment policy statement. Chapters 12-15 discuss the four major types of institutional asset owners in detail.

Types of Asset Owners and the Investment Policy Statement

The first part of this chapter briefly describes major classes of asset owners. Although the list of asset owners is not exhaustive, it should be sufficient to highlight the differences that exist among major types of asset owners and how their characteristics influence their asset allocation policies. The following four sections discuss four categories of asset owners:

1. Endowments and foundations
2. Pension funds
3. Sovereign wealth funds
4. Family offices.

This chapter concludes with a discussion of investment policies and investment policy statements.

11.1 ENDOWMENTS AND FOUNDATIONS

Endowments and foundations serve different purposes but, from an investment policy point of view, share many characteristics. Endowments are funds established by not-for-profit organizations to raise funds through charitable contributions of supporters and use the resources to support activities of the sponsoring organization. For example, a university endowment receives charitable contributions from its supporters (e.g., alumni) and uses the income generated by the fund to support the normal operations of the university. Endowments could be small or large, but since they have long investment horizons and are lightly regulated, the full menu of assets is available to them. In fact, among institutional investors, endowments are pioneers in allocating to alternative assets.

Foundations are similar to endowments in the sense that funds are raised through charitable contributions of supporters. These funds are then used to fund grants and support other charitable work that falls within the foundation's mandate. Most foundations are long-term investors and are lightly regulated in terms of their investment activities. However, in order to enjoy certain tax treatments, they are required to distribute a minimum percentage of their assets each year. Foundations are able to invest in the full menu of assets, including alternative asset classes.

11.2   PENSION FUNDS

Pension funds are set up to provide retirement benefits to a group of beneficiaries who typically belong to an organization, such as for-profit or not-for-profit businesses and government entities. The organization that sets up the pension fund is called the plan sponsor. There are four types of pension funds (Ang 2014):

1. NATIONAL PENSION FUNDS: **National pension funds** are run by national governments and are meant to provide basic retirement income to the citizens of a country. The US Social Security program, South Korea's National Pension Service, and the Central Provident Fund of Singapore are examples of such funds. These types of funds may not operate that differently from sovereign wealth funds, which are described later in this chapter and in Chapter 5 of this book. The investment allocation decisions of these large funds are controlled by national governments, which makes their management different from private pension funds. Given the size and long-term horizons of these funds, the menu of assets that are available for potential investments is large and includes various alternative assets.

2. PRIVATE DEFINED BENEFIT FUNDS: Private defined benefit (DB) funds are set up to provide prespecified pension benefits to employees of a private business. The plan sponsor promises the employees of the private entity a predefined retirement income, which is based on a set of predetermined factors. Typically, these factors include the number of years an employee has worked for the firm, as well as his or her age and salary. The plan may include provisions for changes in retirement income, such as a cost-of-living adjustment or a portion of the retirement income to be paid to the employee's surviving spouse or young children. The plan sponsor directs the management of the fund's assets. While these funds may not match the size or the length of time horizon of national funds, they are still large long-term investors, and therefore the full menu of asset classes, including alternative assets, are available to them.

3. PRIVATE DEFINED CONTRIBUTION FUNDS: Private defined contribution (DC) funds are set up to receive contributions made by the plan sponsor into the fund. The pension plan specifies the contributions that the plan sponsor is expected to make while the firm employs the beneficiary. The contributions are deposited into accounts that are tied to each beneficiary and, upon retirement, the employee receives the accumulated value of the account. The employee and the plan sponsor jointly manage the fund's assets, in that the sponsor decides on the menu of asset classes and fund products available, and the employee decides the asset allocation. The menu of asset classes available to these funds is smaller than both national funds and defined benefit funds. Lumpiness of alternative investments, lack of liquidity, and government regulations typically prevent these funds from investing in a full range of alternative asset classes, as most participants fall below the net worth requirements allowing them to invest in alternative funds. Historically, real estate is one alternative asset class that has been available to these funds. In recent years, liquid alternatives have slowly become available as well.

4. INDIVIDUALLY MANAGED ACCOUNTS: **Individually managed accounts** are no different from private savings plans, in which the asset allocation is directed entirely by the employee. Since the funds enjoy tax advantages, they are not free from regulations, and therefore the list of asset classes available to the beneficiary will be limited. In particular, privately placed alternative investments are not normally available to these funds.

11.3 SOVEREIGN WEALTH FUNDS

Sovereign wealth funds (SWFs) are funds set by national governments as a way to save and build on a portion of the country's current income for use by future generations of its citizens. SWFs are similar to national pension funds in the sense that they are owned and managed by national governments, but the goal is not to provide retirement income to the citizens of the country.

SWFs have become major players in global financial markets because of their sheer size and their long-term investment horizons. Most SWFs invest a portion of their assets in foreign assets. SWFs are relatively new, and their growth, especially in emerging economies, has been tied to the rise in prices of natural resources such as oil, copper, and gold. In some cases, SWFs are funded through the foreign currency reserves earned by countries that enjoy a significant trade surplus, such as China. SWFs are large and have very long horizons; therefore, the full menu of assets should be available to them. However, because national governments manage them, they may not invest in all available asset classes.

11.4 FAMILY OFFICES

Family offices refer to organizations dedicated to the management of a pool of capital owned by a wealthy individual or group of individuals. In effect, it is a private wealth advisory firm established by an ultra-high-net-worth individual or family.

The source of income for a family office can be as varied as the underlying family that it serves. In some cases, the capital is spun off from an operating company; while in other cases, it might be funded with what is known as legacy wealth, which refers to a second or third generation of family members that have inherited their wealth from a prior source of capital generation. The financial resources of a family office can be used for a variety of purposes, from maintaining the family's current standard of living, to providing benefits for many future generations, to distributing all or a portion of it through philanthropic activities in the current generation. Family offices tend to have relatively long time horizons and are typically large enough to invest in a full menu of assets, including alternative asset classes.

11.5 STRATEGIC ASSET ALLOCATION: RISK AND RETURN

The main decisions to address in the institutional investment process include strategic asset allocation, fund selection, method of diversification, and liquidity management. The strategic asset allocation (SAA) creates a portfolio allocation that will provide the asset owner with the optimal balance between risk and return over a long-term investment horizon, serves as the basis for creating a benchmark that will be used to measure the actual performance of the portfolio, and serves as the starting point of the tactical asset allocation process.

11.5.1 Basing Strategic Asset Allocations on Observation and Reasoning

SAA is based on long-term risk–return relationships that have been observed in the past and that, based on economic and financial reasoning, are expected to persist under normal economic conditions into the future. While historical risk–return relationships are used as the starting point of generating the inputs needed to create the optimal long-run allocation, these historical relationships should be adjusted to reflect fundamental and potentially long-lasting economic changes that are currently taking place. For example, although long-term historical returns to investment-grade corporate bonds were once high, the prevailing yields on those instruments would indicate that the long-run return from this asset class should be adjusted down. In developing long-term risk–return relationships for major asset classes, it is important to begin with fundamental factors affecting the economy. Macroeconomic performance of the global economy is the driving force behind the performance of various asset classes. The expected return on all asset classes can be expressed as the sum of three components:

$$\text{Asset Class Return} = \text{Short-Term Real Riskless Rate}$$

$$+ \text{Expected Inflation} + \text{Risk Premium} \qquad (11.1)$$

The real short-term riskless rate of interest is believed to be relatively stable and lower than the real growth rate in the economy. Typically, there is a lower bound of zero for this rate. Therefore, if the global economy is expected to grow at 3% per year going forward, the short-term real riskless rate is expected to be somewhere between 0 and 1%. In turn, population growth and increases in productivity are known to be the major drivers of economic growth. Long-term expected inflation is far less stable, as it depends on central banks' policies as well as long-term economic growth. Historically, it was believed that long-term expected inflation would depend on the growth rate in the supply of money relative to the real growth rate in the economy. For instance, it was believed that long-term inflation would be around 5% if the money supply were to increase at 8% in an economy that is growing at 3%. However, this long-term relationship has been challenged by empirical observations following the 2008–9 financial crisis. Once long-term estimates of the short-term real riskless rate and expected inflation have been obtained, the next step involves the estimation of the long-term risk premium of each asset class. At this stage, one may assume that historical risk premiums would prevail going forward. This would be particularly appropriate if we believe that historical estimates of volatilities, correlations, and risk exposures of various asset classes are likely to persist into the future. For instance, if the long-term historical risk premium on small-cap equities has been 5%, then, assuming 2% expected inflation and a 1% short-term real riskless rate, one could assume an 8% expected long-term return from this asset class.

11.5.2   Reasons That Alternative Assets Raise Return Estimation Challenges

For several reasons, long-term returns from alternative asset classes could be more difficult to estimate. First, while alternative assets such as real estate and commodities have a long history, some of the more modern alternative asset classes (e.g., hedge funds or private equity) do not have a long enough history to obtain accurate estimates of their risk exposures and risk premiums. Second, to the degree that alpha was a major source of return for alternative asset classes in the past, the same level of alpha may not be available going forward if there is increased allocation to this asset class by investors. That is, the supply of alpha is limited, and increased competition is bound to reduce it. Third, the alternative investment industry has been shown to be quite innovative and adaptive in response to changing economic conditions. Therefore, we should expect to see new classes of alternative assets going forward, with their potential place in investors' strategic asset allocations unknowable at this point.

A large body of economic research suggests that asset allocation is the main driver of the investment performance of well-diversified portfolios and that the added value provided by the selection of a particular asset within the class is minimal. The fundamental justification supporting the relative importance of strategic asset allocation is the notion that individual asset classes perform differently in various market and economic conditions, and, as a consequence, this type of diversification is viewed as the only "free lunch" available in financial markets.

In some cases, it is almost impossible to use standard risk–return optimization models to determine the appropriate allocation, because it is difficult to estimate the correct risk premiums and correlations between asset classes. An analysis of the correlations between asset classes may not be possible without making severe assumptions. In addition, some asset classes are lumpy, and desirable investments may not be available at the precise moment that an asset allocator decides to construct an optimal portfolio. Given the lack of information, most investors have to compromise and use naïve approaches, or a combination of quantitative optimization and naïve approaches, to construct portfolios.

11.5.3   Reasons for Placing Caps and Floors on Asset Allocations

While some institutions approach this by capping their various asset class exposures at around 5% to 10%, for some larger and more experienced institutions the allocation to some asset classes may exceed 30%. This naïve allocation can be estimated based on the analysis of three basic dimensions:

1. If the allocation is not large enough, the returns will not allow for the establishment of a dedicated team, which is a required condition if one expects to achieve above-average performance. Conversely, if the allocation is too large, it may not be possible to find sufficient investment opportunities, or it may drive performance down if lower-quality opportunities need to be selected.
2. If the allocation is not large enough relative to the overall portfolio, it will have an insignificant impact on the overall portfolio performance (i.e., fail to "move the needle"). If the allocation is too large compared to the overall portfolio, the investor risks being underdiversified and overexposed to risks specific to the asset class.
3. The institution's liquidity needs should also be considered as a component of the analysis. This constraint essentially depends on the institution's regular liquidity needs to support its ongoing business, an important consideration for endowments and foundations. The lower the ongoing liquidity needs and the higher the excess capital, the more funds the investor can allocate to private equity, which is the case for the largest endowment investors. An investor with high regular liquidity needs and no excess capital is in no position to launch a PE program.

In general, the more mature a PE program, the more liquidity it is likely to be generating, increasing the funds available for allocation to an illiquid asset class such as private equity.

11.6 ASSET ALLOCATION OBJECTIVES

An **objective** is a preference that distinguishes an optimal solution from a suboptimal solution.

Asset owners' objectives must be expressed in terms of consistent risk-adjusted performance values. Also, if the asset owner states that her objective is to earn 25% per year with no reference to the level of risk that she is willing to assume, then it could lead the portfolio manager to create a risky portfolio that is entirely inconsistent with her risk tolerance. Therefore, asset owners and portfolio managers need to communicate in a clear language regarding return objectives and risk levels that are acceptable to the asset owner and are consistent with current market conditions.

In other words, it is safe to assume that asset owners would prefer to earn a high rate of return on their assets. However, higher rates of return are associated with higher levels of risk. Therefore, asset owners should present their objectives in terms of combinations of risks and returns that are consistent with market conditions and their level of risk tolerance. For instance, the objective of earning 30% per year on a portfolio that has 8% annual volatility is not consistent with market conditions. Such a high return expectation would require a much higher level of volatility.

11.7 INVESTMENT POLICY CONSTRAINTS

A **constraint** is a condition that any solution must meet. This section discusses the typical set of constraints that must be taken into account when trying to select the investment strategy that maximizes the expected utility of the asset owner.

11.7.1 Internal and External Constraints

Internal constraints refer to those constraints that are imposed by the asset owner as a result of its specific needs and circumstances and may be a function of the owner's time horizon, liquidity needs, and desire to avoid certain sectors. **External constraints** refer to constraints that are driven by factors that are not directly under the control of the investor. External constraints result from market conditions and regulations. For instance, an asset owner may be prohibited from investing in certain asset classes, or fees and due diligence costs may prevent the owner from considering all available asset classes.

11.7.2 Three Types of Internal Constraints

Some of these internal constraints can be incorporated into the objective function previously discussed. For example, we noted how the constraint that allocations with positive skewness are preferred could be incorporated into the model. However, there are other types of constraints that may be expressed separately. Some examples of these internal constraints are:

LIQUIDITY: The asset owner may have certain liquidity needs that must be explicitly recognized. For example, a foundation may be anticipating a large outlay in the next few months and therefore would want to have enough liquid assets to cover those outflows. This will require the portfolio manager to impose a minimum investment requirement for cash and other liquid assets. Even if there are no anticipated liquidity events where cash outlays will be needed, the asset owner may require maintaining a certain level of liquidity by imposing minimum investment requirements for cash and cash-equivalent investments, and maximum investment levels for such illiquid assets as private equity and infrastructure.

TIME HORIZON: The asset owner's investment horizon can affect liquidity needs. In addition, it is often argued that investors with a short time horizon should take less risk in their asset allocation decisions, as there is not enough time to recover from a large drawdown. This impact of time horizon can be taken care of by changing the degree of risk aversion or by imposing a maximum limit on allocations to risky assets. Time horizon may impact asset allocation in other ways as well. For instance, certain asset classes are known to display mean reversion in the long run (e.g., commodities). As a result, an investor with a short time horizon may impose a maximum limit on the allocation to commodities, as there will not be enough time to enjoy the benefits of potential mean reversion.

SECTOR AND COUNTRY LIMITS: For a variety of reasons, an asset owner may wish to impose constraints on allocations to certain countries or sectors of the global economy. For instance, national pension plans may be prohibited from investing in certain countries, or a university endowment may have been instructed by its trustees to avoid investments in certain industries. Asset owners may have unique needs and constraints that have to be accommodated by the portfolio manager. However, it is instructive to present asset owners with alternative allocations in which those constraints are relaxed. This will help asset owners understand the potential costs associated with those constraints.

11.7.3 Two Types of External Constraints

External constraints are mostly driven by regulations and the tax status of the asset owner.

TAX STATUS: Most institutional investors are tax exempt, and therefore allocation to tax-exempt instruments are not warranted. Because these investments offer low returns, the optimization technique selected to execute the investment strategy should automatically exclude those assets. In contrast, family offices and high-net-worth investors are not tax exempt, and therefore the impact of taxes must be taken into account. For example, constraints can be imposed to sell asset classes that have suffered losses to offset realized gains from those that have increased in value.

REGULATIONS: Some institutional investors, such as public and private pension funds, are subject to rules and regulations regarding their investment strategies. In the US, the Employee Retirement Income Security Act (ERISA) represents a set of regulations that affect the management of private pension funds. In the UK, the rules and regulations set forth by the Financial Services Authority impact pension funds. In these and many other countries, regulations impose limits on the concentration of allocations in certain asset classes.

11.8 INVESTMENT POLICY STATEMENTS FOR INSTITUTIONAL ASSET OWNERS

A sound investment policy statement is an important component of many investment programs and serves as a roadmap for the asset owners, as well as their advisers and investment managers. At its core, the **investment policy statement (IPS)** is a document that describes the primary goals for an investment program and lays out a framework to achieve those goals. This section walks through the key components of a successful investment policy statement from the perspective of the four main categories of asset owners: endowments and foundations, pension funds, sovereign wealth funds, and family offices. Each of these asset owners were previously introduced in this chapter and are described in detail in Chapters 12 through 15.

11.8.1 Six Benefits to a Thoughtfully Developed IPS

While the underlying sections and implementation of an IPS may vary across investor type, a thoughtfully developed investment policy statement supports the ongoing oversight of investments by helping the asset owner in six areas:

1. Articulates the investor's long-term investment objectives and outline policies and procedures to help meet those objectives.
2. Provides guidance around the risk tolerance and investment beliefs of the investor and governing bodies.
3. Monitors the investment program and measures outcomes against objectives.
4. Helps new staff, board, and investment/finance committee members get up to speed on the investments.
5. Allows the investor to maintain focus on important strategic issues and take a holistic view of how the investment program ties back to goals and activities.
6. Serves as a road map for the fiduciaries and provides guidance through all phases of a market cycle.

There is no one-size-fits-all approach to investment policy statements. They commonly range from 2 to 50 or more pages. The specific structure and content of an IPS will be influenced by many factors, including the investor's governance structure, depth of internal resources and expertise, investment philosophy, and complexity of the portfolio. This discussion focuses on the key components most commonly observed across investment policy statements of institutional asset owners.

11.8.2   Introduction, Scope, and Purpose

The first section of the IPS establishes the context for the investment program. It should include a description of the asset owner, scope of the IPS, reference to appropriate fiduciary standards, and the purpose of the IPS.

DESCRIPTION OF THE ASSET OWNER AND MISSION: Include a brief overview of the investor and describe its mission. The objectives of the portfolio should link back to supporting the investing entity and its broader mission.

PURPOSE AND SCOPE OF THE IPS: Purpose and intent go hand in hand in setting the overarching role of the IPS and the tone for the guidelines that follow. Clearly state which asset pool(s) is/are subject to the IPS. This is particularly important when an organization has multiple asset pools.

INVESTMENT PHILOSOPHY: Acknowledge fiduciary standards that drive the principles and guidelines in the IPS. Make reference to appropriate law. For example, institutional investors in the US may refer to the Uniform Prudent Management of Institutional Funds Act (UPMIFA) for charitable organizations, or ERISA for applicable retirement plans. This includes referencing the fiduciary standard of "reasonable care, skill and caution of a prudent investor" and the concept that investment decisions should not be evaluated in isolation but rather in the context of the entire portfolio and overall investment strategy.

ONGOING REVIEW: As markets and investment needs evolve, how the IPS is implemented may also evolve accordingly. As such, it's important to highlight the need for IPS flexibility and periodic review.

Example of introduction, scope, and purpose: Foundation The Elemenopea Foundation (the "Foundation"), a New State nonprofit corporation, is committed to expanding educational opportunities for low-income residents of New City and surrounding regions. Elemenopea is governed by a Board of Trustees. The Board has determined that the Foundation should be viewed as a perpetual institution managed to benefit both present and future charitable programs and purposes that it serves.

The investment of assets must be made in accordance with the standards put forth in the Uniform Prudent Management of Institutional Funds Act (UPMIFA) as adopted by New State. UPMIFA requires fiduciaries to apply the standard of prudence with reasonable care and skill "to any investment as part of the total portfolio and overall investment strategy, rather than to individual investments." All investment actions and decisions must be based solely on the overarching long-term interests of the Foundation's mission.

This Investment Policy Statement (IPS) applies to all investable assets of the Foundation. All assets available for investment will be invested through an investment portfolio (the "Portfolio"). The purpose of this IPS is to define the investment objectives, policies, and procedures established by the Board to support the Foundation's mission. This IPS will serve as a framework for the management and review of the Portfolio, with sufficient flexibility to be practical, and is intended to:

- identify roles and responsibilities;
- establish investment objectives;

- define the annual spending policy;
- establish long-term asset allocation targets; and
- establish guidelines to monitor the performance in comparison to stated objectives.

The Board also recognizes that from time to time, short-term market fluctuations and dynamics make it impossible to precisely reflect all aspects of this policy at all times. This IPS is established to accommodate these short-term fluctuations, which should not necessitate IPS adjustments. It is expected that this IPS be reviewed periodically to ensure alignment with forward-looking market expectations and industry best thinking and best practices. This IPS may be modified or terminated, in whole or in part, by the Board at any time as the Board deems appropriate.

Example of introduction, scope, and purpose: Corporate Pension The Board of Trustees of Aebeecee Corporation is authorized and responsible to administer a Defined Benefit Plan (the "Plan") for its employees. Funding for benefits under the plan is provided by employer contributions and earnings on the investment of contributions.

This Investment Policy Statement ("Policy") defines the investment objectives, policies, and procedures that have been established by the Board of Trustees (the "Board"). The objectives, policies, and procedures outlined in this document were created as a framework for the management of the Plan and the statements contained in this document are intended to allow for sufficient flexibility in the investment process to capture opportunities, yet ensure prudence and care are maintained in the execution of the investment program. This Policy is intended to:

- Provide a mechanism to establish and review the Plan's investment objectives.
- Set forth an investment "structure" for managing assets. This structure includes various asset classes and investment styles that, in aggregate, are expected to produce a prudent level of diversification and investment return over time.
- Provide a single document identifying the roles of those responsible for selecting, monitoring, and reviewing the Plan's investments.
- Identify the criteria that may be used for selecting the investment funds (a collective reference as to investment managers, pooled investment funds, and investment fund organizations).
- Establish measurement standards and monitoring procedures to be used in evaluating the performance of investment funds.
- Establish procedures for evaluating investment funds.

The Board has arrived at this Policy through careful study of the returns and risks associated with the investment strategies in relation to the current and projected liabilities. This Policy has been chosen as the most appropriate policy for achieving the financial objectives of the Plan. The Plan's assets shall be invested in a manner consistent with the fiduciary standards of the Employee Retirement Income Security Act of 1974, as amended ("ERISA"), namely that the assets shall be invested (a) with the care, skill, prudence, and diligence under the circumstances prevailing from time-to-time that a prudent person acting in a like capacity and familiar with such matters would use in the investment of a fund, with like aims and with due consideration; (b) by diversifying the investments so as to minimize the risk of large losses unless, under the circumstances, it is clearly imprudent to do so; and (c) for the exclusive purposes of providing benefits to the Plan participants and beneficiaries and defraying reasonable expenses of administering the plan.

It is expected that this IPS be reviewed periodically to ensure alignment with forward-looking market expectations and industry best thinking and best practices. This IPS may be modified or terminated, in whole or in part, by the Board at any time as the Board deems appropriate.

11.8.3   Roles and Responsibilities

The IPS should clearly articulate the role and responsibilities of key parties involved in overseeing the investments. While a separate governance policy may be in place, including a description of key roles and responsibilities will confirm the applicable decision-making process for the investments and ensure that responsibilities are in-line with the policies and processes described in the IPS. The most common decision-making parties included in investment policy statements are:

BOARD: In most cases, the highest governing body (e.g., board of trustees) is primarily responsible for approving the investment policy statement and target asset allocation strategy. The board also reviews the investment program periodically to confirm whether the portfolio is meeting the objectives laid out in the IPS. The IPS should clearly describe specific areas where the board wishes to retain decision-making authority.

INVESTMENT COMMITTEE: A board typically delegates the role of making recommendations or final decisions to a finance or investment committee.

INTERNAL STAFF: Day-to-day activities and oversight of the investments are the responsibility of internal staff. Some asset owners may have dedicated internal investment staff (e.g., chief investment officer and investment staff) who may have higher levels of responsibility, such as discretion to implement tactical allocation decisions within IPS guidelines. Other asset owners may have limited or no internal staff and may delegate certain responsibilities to the chief financial officer and finance department.

INVESTMENT ADVISER(S) AND/OR OUTSOURCED CHIEF INVESTMENT OFFICER (OCIO): Listing the role of the adviser and scope of responsibilities is important to manage expectations on both sides. This may include frequency of communications, key deliverables, and acknowledgment of fiduciary responsibilities. In the case of an OCIO, the level of discretion (and fiduciary responsibility) is much greater and could include functions such as hiring and firing managers and shifting asset allocations.

TRUSTEE/CUSTODIAN: (or other external providers). The duties, expectations, and fiduciary responsibilities of important external providers such as the custodian should also be acknowledged.

Governance structure is unique to each asset owner and can vary based on the nature of the assets, size of the entity, or depth of internal resources. For example, a family office may follow a different decision-making process compared to a corporate pension sponsor. But for any asset owner, it is critical to identify who is responsible for key components of the investment oversight process, spanning from broad oversight (e.g., IPS approval) to implementation and review (e.g., manager selection and termination).

Example of IPS Roles and Responsibilities: University Endowment The following section outlines the roles and responsibilities of each of the parties involved with implementing this IPS.

The Board of Trustees (the "Board") has ultimate fiduciary responsibility for the ABC University Endowment. The Board is responsible for approving this Investment Policy Statement and must ensure that appropriate policies governing the management of the investable assets are in place and being effectively implemented. The Board is also responsible for establishing and approving changes to the Portfolio asset allocation targets and ranges. The Board has delegated to the Investment Committee the responsibility to oversee the investment activities of the Endowment on behalf of the Board.

The Investment Committee (the "Committee") has the responsibility to ensure that all investments are managed in a manner that is consistent with the policies and objectives for the Endowment. The Committee's responsibilities include but are not limited to:

- Periodically reviewing the IPS and recommending changes to the Board as needed.
- Periodically reviewing and evaluating investment results.
- Selecting, monitoring, and terminating investment managers.
- Selecting, monitoring, and terminating the Custodian, Adviser, and other service providers involved with servicing all or parts of the Portfolio.

The Committee may, at its discretion, delegate the execution of above responsibilities, in full or in part, to staff or external parties with appropriate expertise to assist the Committee in discharging its obligations. Other specialists may be employed by the Committee from time to time, on an as-needed basis, to ensure its responsibilities in providing oversight of Portfolio assets are prudently executed.

The Investment Staff ("Staff") responsibilities include but are not limited to:

- Acting as the liaison between the Committee and Adviser.
- Managing day-to-day investment activities of the Portfolio to ensure sufficient cash flow to meet the Endowment's distribution needs.
- Working with the Adviser to compile information on the investment return and performance for the Committee review.
- Interfacing with the Committee to ensure necessary action items are brought to the Committee and that Committee decisions are implemented.

The Adviser's responsibilities include but are not limited to:

- Assisting the Committee with manager selection, retention, and termination.
- Assisting the Committee with rebalancing and implementation of this IPS, as approved.

- Assisting the Committee with the development of investment policies, guidelines, and objectives.
- Proactively recommending investment strategies as warranted.
- Preparing and presenting performance measurement analysis and quarterly reports.
- Attending Committee meetings.
- Providing research/education on related issues and investment opportunities.
- Working with Staff to ensure sufficient cash flow availability to meet the Endowment's spending needs.

The Custodian's responsibilities include:

- Providing security safekeeping, collection of income, settlement of trades, collections of proceeds of maturing securities, and daily investment of cash.
- Providing monthly reports detailing investment holdings and transactions to Staff and Adviser.

11.8.4 Investment Objectives

Investment objectives should be realistic, attainable, and consistent with the organization's mission. Investors with multiple asset pools should identify separate investment objectives for each pool. Clearly stated investment objectives will lay the groundwork for establishing suitable asset-allocation guidelines and other policies and are important to understand when reviewing the investment results. Investment objectives are often stated as return targets in absolute terms, but investors should tie any specific return targets to the organization's goals that need to be met. For example, instead of requiring a fixed "7% long-term annual return," the objective could instead be framed as a "real return of 5% relative to CPI to support the organization's long-term spending needs" or "2% return over plan liabilities." Objectives do not always need to reference specific return targets if the appropriate context is provided.

Most endowments and foundations are long-term investors, so investment objectives should address the need for corpus growth to exceed inflation to maintain purchasing power and support the organization's spending needs over time. A foundation created for a very targeted and/or shorter-term purpose would state an investment objective that is focused less on maintaining purchasing power and more on preserving capital to support the specific goals. **A common investment objective of endowments** is a return target X% above inflation, specifically connected to long-term spending needs.

Investment objectives for pension funds are tied to the responsibilities the sponsor has to the plan beneficiaries. Objectives will differ based on the type of pension fund (e.g., defined benefit versus defined contribution plans), as well as the type of establishing entity (e.g., government versus private). Defined benefit plan investments are usually directed by the sponsoring entity, so the objective should focus on managing the investments to meet the retirement distributions to participants. **A common investment objective of pension funds** is a return target X% above the liability discount rate. In the case of defined contribution plans, the plan sponsor manages the selection of investment options available, while the beneficiaries choose from those options. Objectives are typically to offer a range of investment choices so participants are able to build diversified portfolios.

Sovereign wealth funds (SWFs) are state-owned investment funds held for the benefit of future generations and/or to stabilize the state currency. SWFs are typically long-term investors, but the investment objective will vary depending on the type of fund (stabilization funds, reserve funds, savings funds, and development funds).

A family office manages pools of capital owned by a wealthy individual or group of individuals. The investment objective for a family office can vary significantly depending on the family's goals or needs, which could range from preserving wealth for the next generation to a focus on philanthropy. In many cases, objectives can be framed similarly to an endowment (e.g., long-term real growth to support current and future spending needs).

Examples of investment objectives

> ENDOWMENT: The primary objective of Quearesstee Endowment is to ensure the Portfolio generates a real rate of return, above an appropriate inflation rate (i.e., the Consumer Price Index or CPI) over time, that is sufficient to support, in perpetuity, the mission of the Endowment and its spending needs.

> DEFINED BENEFIT PLAN: The primary investment objective of the Quearesstee Plan is to generate investment returns that, in combination with funding contributions from Quearesstee, provide adequate assets to meet all current and future obligations of the Plan.

> DEFINED CONTRIBUTION PLAN: Considering the varied attitudes, goals, expectations, investment time horizons, and risk tolerance levels of the participants, the primary objective of the ABC 401(k) Plan is to offer a broad array of investment options that allow participants to build portfolios consistent with their needs and objectives.

> SOVEREIGN WEALTH INVESTMENT FUND: The primary objective of the Fund is to invest revenue from Quearesstee country's commodity resources to generate a real rate of return of X% above an appropriate inflation rate over time, so that this wealth benefits both current and future generations in perpetuity.

11.8.5 Time Horizon

Time horizon is an example of an internal constraint. Defining the applicable time horizon is important to set the right perspective when evaluating outcomes. Longer horizons indicate a higher propensity to weather volatility and illiquidity. Liquidity needs are closely tied to time horizon and will directly impact an organization's capacity to invest in alternative investments.

The time horizon can be integrated with the investment objectives or defined in a separate section. As previously mentioned, many endowments and foundations are long-term investors seeking to maintain funds in perpetuity, in which case a time horizon in excess of 10 years would be appropriate. Sovereign wealth funds and family offices are also commonly long-term investors but may require shorter time horizons depending on the purpose of the portfolio and near-term spending needs. Time horizon for pensions (specifically defined benefit plans) will be influenced by funded status, the duration of liabilities, and whether the plan is open, closed, or frozen.

Examples of time horizon

ASSET OWNER WITH TIME HORIZON IN PERPETUITY (E.G. ENDOWMENT OR SOVEREIGN WEALTH SAVINGS FUND). The Board acknowledges that fluctuating rates of return characterize the securities markets, particularly during short-term time periods. Accordingly, the Board views interim fluctuations with an appropriate perspective, given the long-term perpetual objectives. Investment objectives are to be evaluated over a minimum long-term horizon, defined as rolling 10-year periods.

DEFINED BENEFIT PLAN. Given that the Plan is closed but not frozen, the longer duration of liabilities, and current funded status, the Board has adopted a long-term investment horizon and will evaluate Plan and manager performance over an appropriate period—generally across full market cycles, or at least on a rolling 5-year basis.

11.8.6 Risk Tolerance

Higher expected returns are usually accompanied by higher levels of volatility. Thinking through the appropriate risk language and parameters for an investment program, particularly the willingness to accept downside risk in the near term, can help the asset owner when assessing portfolio choices. Identify key variables to be considered when implementing the investment strategy to minimize risk, such as asset-class diversification.

Risk language must be reasonable given the objectives, time horizon, and asset-allocation strategy. For example, a low risk tolerance does not align with a portfolio that has a lengthy time horizon, high return objectives, and aggressive asset-allocation strategy.

While risk is often defined at the total portfolio level and in terms of volatility, additional measures of risk may also be used and should be clearly defined in the policy. Asset owners with a more complex investment program may have a comprehensive risk management policy in place that further defines policies related to specific areas of risk such as foreign currency exposure, overlay strategies, liquidity risk, and operational risk. Rather than restating these policies in the body of the IPS, reference should be made to the broader policy and included as an appendix.

Example of risk tolerance language: Defined Benefit Plan At the broadest level, the greatest risk is any portfolio value impairment that leads to a permanent loss of capital that reduces the Plan's ability to provide secure retirement benefits. As institutional investors with significant liability duration, Quearesstee Corporation takes a long-term perspective and will review Plan investment results in the context of risk-adjusted returns. Quearesstee's goal is to achieve its investment objective while assuming acceptable risk levels within a reasonable range around the targeted volatility of the adopted asset allocation policy. The general policy will be to diversify investments based on their role in the Portfolio to enhance total return while avoiding undue risk concentration in any single asset class or investment strategy.

To mitigate the probability of permanent capital loss and reduce risk to the downside, the variables to be considered by the Committee in all aspects of portfolio construction include:

- probability of missing objective;
- impact of inflation;
- asset class diversification;
- time horizon of investments versus funding needs;
- historical and prospective information regarding capital markets;
- broad economic factors; and
- current regulatory environment.

11.8.7 Spending Policy

Asset pools are often relied on to support both current and future spending needs of the asset owner, in which case a spending policy sets the right expectations for cash flow needs from the portfolio. Clearly defining ongoing spending needs helps the asset owner develop appropriate investment objectives and asset allocation policy. Spending policy is also relevant when evaluating the income characteristics or liquidity profile of portfolio investments and provides guidance to staff who are responsible for managing portfolio distributions.

Spending policies are often stated in terms of a fixed spending rate of $x\%$ of the portfolio's moving average market value over a trailing period of y quarters. Some asset owners may have more flexibility and establish a spending range from 0% to a maximum of $x\%$.

Spending policies are common for foundations and endowments (especially foundations with mandated distribution requirements). In the case of family offices, spending policies can serve as a level of protection for future generations by placing prudent controls on distributions to the current generation. Note that a formal spending policy is not applicable to all asset owners. For example, defined benefit plan distributions are driven by plan liabilities. Sovereign wealth reserve funds may invest funds for the long term with no near-term spending plans, but with the ability to be drawn on when required. Even when a spending policy is not specified, asset owners and related parties should have a clear understanding of both near-term and future distribution needs, as well as the governance process that drives spending decisions.

Example of spending policy: Foundation The Committee recognizes the dual funding role of the Portfolio assets in supporting both current and future funding needs (i.e., provide a stable and predictable stream of funds versus maintain purchasing power of the portfolio over time). It is the responsibility of the Committee to maintain this intergenerational equity and balance the needs between current and future beneficiaries. Unless otherwise prohibited by donor restrictions or law, dividends and interest income, capital gains, and principal may be used for spending purposes to the extent that such payments do not exceed the annual amount determined by the spending rate and formula below. The spending policy will be reviewed at least annually and adjusted as appropriate based on evolving trends with respect to the investment return of the Portfolio, capital market expectations, funding needs, and other resources available to the organization.

Unless otherwise directed and/or approved by the Board, the annual target spending rate should not exceed 5% of the Portfolio's trailing 3-year average market value as of the end of the most recent fiscal year.

11.8.8   Asset Allocation Guidelines

Asset allocation is the most important determinant of long-term success for the asset owner's investment program and establishing a strategic asset allocation policy is a critical component of the IPS. Institutional investors should consider establishing targets and ranges by broad asset category or asset role, rather than the more rigid approach of detailing targets by asset classes. This encourages an objective-oriented allocation policy and supports more dynamic management of the underlying portfolios. Additional detail for each asset category or role (as well as policy benchmarks) should be included to facilitate implementation and monitoring.

Note that asset allocation guidelines for defined benefit plans can be further customized to reflect the objective of reducing funded status volatility as the funded status improves, linking the management of plan assets to the liabilities. The Committee develops an initial asset allocation policy based on the Plan's funded status and other characteristics, then establishes a de-risking policy to reallocate the portfolio as the funded status improves (recognizing that the return requirements and risk tolerance will change over time). A hedge ratio policy (the goal of which is to reduce interest rate risk as funded status improves) is also an important component that goes hand in hand with the target allocation for defined benefit plans and should be incorporated into the IPS if applicable.

It is not uncommon for a portfolio to deviate from the stated targets. Rebalancing guidelines help guide the actions of staff (and/or advisers with discretionary oversight) without requiring additional committee approval. This is particularly important when managing cash flows in or out of the asset pool or addressing situations where an allocation may temporarily fall outside of the prescribed range.

Example of Asset Allocation and Rebalancing Guidelines: General The most important component of an investment strategy is the asset mix, or the resource allocation among the various classes of securities available to the Portfolio for investment purposes. The Board shall approve a target allocation framework based on long-term capital market assumptions (expected returns, risk, and correlations), which over time should provide an expected return equal to or greater than the primary objective of the Fund. To achieve these goals, the asset allocation will be set with the target percentages and within the ranges provided in Appendix A. Asset allocation studies should be conducted periodically to ensure the target asset allocation remains appropriate relative to the investment objectives, risk preference, and market outlook.

The basic guidelines for the allocation of assets based on asset categories is as follows:

Asset Category	Min	Target	Max
Equity	55%	60%	65%
Liquid Alternatives	0%	5%	10%
Real Assets	5%	10%	15%
Return-Seeking Fixed Income	10%	15%	20%
Opportunity	0%	0%	10%
Risk-Reducing	5%	10%	15%

Within each asset category, the CIO shall adopt and implement portfolio strategies to meet the overall objective of each asset class.

The Portfolio should be monitored by Staff at least quarterly to ensure compliance within the approved ranges. Staff has discretion to manage the Portfolio and rebalance within the ranges stated above or seek Board approval to remain outside of the ranges. Execution of the rebalancing may be implemented through any combination of actions: 1) purchase and sale of funds/securities; or 2) allocation of normal cash flows (e.g., contributions or distributions to cover spending needs).

The Board recognizes that rapid unanticipated market shifts or changes in economic conditions may lead to wide deviations from the target allocation and approved ranges. Generally, these divergences should be of a short-term or tactical nature in response to fluctuating market environments. Further, the Board also recognizes that private market assets, such as real estate, private equity, and infrastructure, may not be able to be managed within the stated ranges at all times, but should be prudently managed to the targets over time through distributions and strategic new investments.

11.8.9   Selection and Retention Criteria for Investment Managers or Funds

An IPS should include general criteria regarding the selection and retention of investment managers. Quantitatively focused standards and watch lists are generally discouraged as a means of monitoring managers, as this could put the asset owner in a position of being forced to prematurely terminate a manager. The decision to select and retain managers should be driven by a variety of considerations, including long-term performance versus both benchmarks and peers, consistency of investment style, and stability of the team and firm.

Example of investment manager selection and monitoring The Committee seeks to identify investment managers it believes will provide competitive risk and return performance relative to their asset classes and support the Fund in meeting its investment goals. The Committee recognizes that decisions regarding managers are always prospective. As such, a variety of factors may be considered when making changes to the investment manager structure, including (but not limited to) the following:

- Investment results compared to appropriate benchmarks and peer groups over multiple shorter- and longer-term periods (with a focus on longer-term), including trailing, rolling, and annual results.
- Consistency of the investment style given the asset class and stated investment philosophy.
- Stability of the investment's portfolio management team and/or changes in the compensation and incentives of key investment professionals.
- Changes in ownership or management of the investment organization.

Other areas of consideration may include (but are not limited to) the following:

- Suitability of the strategy and diversification benefit to the overall Portfolio.
- Adherence to any specified investment guidelines.
- Meaningful changes to the level of assets under management.
- Client service level.
- Investment fees.

11.8.10   Strategic Investment Guidelines

Including a section that outlines strategic investment guidelines for the investments and their primary purpose in the portfolio serves as an important framework for evaluating allocation choices across asset classes and investment strategies to achieve the portfolio's objectives. This also provides guidance for both staff and fiduciaries while conducting manager due diligence and implementing decisions around rebalancing and tactical asset allocation.

While certain investments may demonstrate risk and return characteristics at different time periods that could fulfill more than one portfolio role, it is the strategic nature of those investments that should dictate the primary purpose they serve in the portfolio. The purpose of an investment will also vary by the type of asset owner and their objectives. For example, endowments and foundations are more likely to invest in fixed income for diversification benefits and return premiums, while many pension plans would also allocate to fixed income specifically to hedge liabilities. A family office with concentrated holdings related to the family business might invest in strategies specifically aimed at hedging their concentrated exposure. A sovereign wealth development fund may choose to focus their private equity and infrastructure investments on local industries or sectors aimed at growing productivity and increasing the future wealth of the country.

Strategic investment guidelines are particularly useful for alternative investments given the wide spectrum of strategies within each category. For example, one investor may invest in more conservative, lower-volatility hedge fund strategies to reduce risk, while another investor might allocate to more aggressive and opportunistic hedge fund strategies with a focus on market return premium. In the case of real assets, certain investments may be selected primarily for stable income generation as opposed to capital appreciation or inflation hedging.

Note that the examples below reflect broader guidelines that allow more flexibility around portfolio construction and implementation. Some investors prefer to be more prescriptive with their strategic investment guidelines, such as stating specific percentages within asset categories (e.g., private equity should have X% in venture capital, Y% in buyouts, etc.) or a maximum allocation to specific managers or funds. This approach is also acceptable as long as the IPS is regularly reviewed to ensure that stricter guidelines do not become stale or no longer make sense in a given market environment.

Examples of Strategic Investment Guidelines

LONG-TERM INVESTOR DEFINING ROLE OF HEDGE FUND AS PART OF RISK REDUCTION CATEGORY: The primary role of hedge fund investments in the Portfolio is downside protection, diversification, and low correlation to other investments. The hedge fund portfolio should be diversified with allocations across many strategy types and should have low beta and limited directionality to the overall public equity market. The targeted net return should exceed cash/short-term instruments.

DEFINED BENEFIT PLAN DEFINING REAL ESTATE: The objective of global real estate investments is to diversify the equity beta in the return-seeking portfolio and to provide a return above that of the liability-hedging assets. The global real estate investments may consist of REITs, core real estate funds, value-added real estate funds, opportunistic real estate funds, or other real estate holdings.

ENDOWMENT DEFINING BROADER CATEGORY/ROLE OF "OPPORTUNITY ASSETS": Opportunity Assets have the potential to significantly enhance the portfolio's return and/or diversify risk based on market dislocations that create time-sensitive investment opportunities. Return is primarily driven either by alpha or the skill identified in the manager/strategy or by the idiosyncratic nature of the investment's risk/return profile. Return can also be derived from cyclical alternative beta opportunities that are less correlated to other investments in the portfolio. Investments can span the spectrum of liquidity profiles and may include, but would not be limited to, stressed/distressed assets, nonequity hedge funds, opportunistic credit, and multi-asset strategies.

11.8.11   Performance Measurement and Evaluation

A regular review of performance allows the asset owner to monitor the portfolio's progress toward the investment objectives and assess the appropriateness of the strategies. Identifying benchmarks to evaluate the portfolio's performance provides metrics to guide this process. Total portfolio performance should be evaluated based on a weighted benchmark consisting of broad market indices aligned with the strategic allocation targets, while performance of the underlying managers should be compared using an appropriate market index specific to each strategy or through the use of peer groups.

Example of performance measurement and evaluation The principal goal of the Portfolio is to maximize the likelihood of achieving and/or exceeding the investment objectives stated in this IPS over the long term. Performance evaluation is designed to monitor the asset allocation and manager selection decisions. The Committee should review performance at a minimum on a quarterly basis. It is expected that reporting for private equity, private infrastructure, private real estate, and other private market investments will lag public markets reporting by one or more quarters.

The primary benchmark for evaluating performance of the total Portfolio will be a weighted benchmark consisting of broad market indices for each main asset category as described in Appendix X. Total Portfolio performance will be evaluated on a net-of-fee basis relative to the representative weighted benchmark over various trailing time periods.

Performance for the underlying strategies will be compared with the risk and return of an appropriate market index and peer group (as described in Appendix X), on a net-of-fee basis over various trailing time periods.

11.8.12 Additional Considerations

Any other considerations that are important to the asset owner should be included in this section. The most common topics are described below:

RESPONSIBLE INVESTING: Responsible investing has become an important topic for many institutional asset owners. It covers a wide range of strategies, from divestment of particular investments to active engagement in others; implementing an impact-investing program; thoughtful consideration of environmental, social, and governance (ESG) issues; and identifying investments that more closely align with the asset owner's mission. Chapters 3 and 4 address ESG in detail. If an asset owner wants to incorporate any of these considerations in the investment program, the IPS should include a section articulating the organization's philosophy and approach. Many asset owners develop a more comprehensive responsible investing policy, which may be referenced and included as an appendix to the IPS.

PROXY VOTING: Typically, investment managers are responsible for voting proxies for the securities within their respective portfolios, while the organization (or discretionary adviser) is responsible for voting proxies related to fund-level issues for mutual funds or other commingled vehicles. Asset owners may want to include language to help the direct voting of proxies where relevant and appropriate to the assets to ensure that their investments are aligned to support the organization's mission and beliefs. Proxy voting may also be integrated as part of a responsible investing policy.

BROKERAGE AND OTHER INVESTMENT-RELATED EXPENSES: It is common for asset owners to include a statement regarding brokerage and other investment-related expenses, acknowledging that investment managers have discretion to select brokers and negotiate commissions, but requiring them to seek "best execution" services.

LIQUIDITY POLICY: As previously discussed, asset owners will require differing levels of liquidity depending on factors such as long-term spending needs, short-term cash needs, regulatory requirements, and risk tolerance. Defining a liquidity policy helps ensure that the portfolio maintains adequate liquidity and allows the asset owner to meet its cash needs when markets come under pressure.

Examples of additional considerations

RESPONSIBLE INVESTING: Quearesstee Inc. strives to incorporate responsible investing considerations into investment decision-making where possible and seeks to avoid investments that directly conflict with Quearesstee's mission and values. Please refer to Quearesstee's Responsible Investing policy, included as Appendix X to this IPS.

PROXY VOTING: The Committee delegates the responsibility for voting all proxies to the investment managers, with consideration of select issues described in the proxy voting section of Quearesstee's Responsible Investing policy, included as Appendix X. In evaluating current and prospective investment managers, the Committee will consider whether the investment manager's proxy voting policy is consistent with the responsible investing policy.

In the event that there are mutual funds or other commingled vehicles used in the management of the Fund's assets, the Committee delegates the responsibilities for voting proxies related to fund-level issues (e.g., changes to prospectus, board of directors, etc.) to Staff.

Managers should provide a copy of proxy voting policies and summaries of voting history to Staff on an annual basis.

BROKERAGE AND OTHER INVESTMENT-RELATED EXPENSES: Brokerage commissions, incurred in the normal course of trading securities, are expenses of Quearesstee Inc. Brokerage commissions must be managed in the best interest of the organization. The Portfolio's investment managers will have discretion to select brokers and negotiate commissions. In executing this responsibility, investment managers should seek "best execution" services.

LIQUIDITY POLICY: The investment program must have a minimum level of liquidity to meet the annual spending needs as outlined in the spending policy, and liquidity needs remain regardless of the performance of the Portfolio. As such, the Board has adopted the following liquidity guidelines for the Portfolio:

Category	Liquidity Characteristic	Min Allocation (%)	Max Allocation (%)	Min Balance ($)
Liquid	Daily	30%	100%	$150 million
Quasi-Liquid	Between daily and 1 year	0%	40%	–
Illiquid	Greater than 1 year	0%	30%	–

11.8.13 Conclusion

A clearly articulated investment policy statement is an important component of many investment programs and should be viewed as a living document to guide oversight of the investments. As discussed in this chapter, an effective IPS clearly lays out investment goals and objectives, roles and responsibilities, and asset allocation policy, as well as other considerations important to the asset owner. The IPS should also reflect sound governance practices and reference other policies that help ensure portfolio outcomes are aligned with objectives. Asset owners should periodically review their IPS taking an iterative approach to encourage constructive evaluation of the investment program, which is critical given the ever-changing market environment, particularly in alternative investments.

REFERENCE

Ang, A. 2014. *Asset Management: A Systematic Approach to Factor Investing*. Oxford: Oxford University Press.

CHAPTER 12

Foundations and the Endowment Model

Investors allocating assets to alternative investments need a framework on which to build their portfolios. What should the size of the allocation to traditional investments be, relative to alternative investments? Within alternative investments, how should the portfolio be diversified across asset classes, styles, and managers? For many, the answers come from a study of the investment practices of the managers of the largest endowment and foundation portfolios.

12.1 DEFINING ENDOWMENTS AND FOUNDATIONS

Endowments refer to the permanent pools of capital owned by institutions such as colleges, universities, hospitals, museums, and religious organizations. When well funded and well managed, an endowment can provide a permanent annual income to the organization, while maintaining the real value of its originally contributed assets in perpetuity. The idea of perpetuity is not a theoretical concept. Two of the largest US university endowments are owned by Harvard University and Yale University, which were founded in 1636 and 1701, respectively. Universities that are more than 310 years old with assets of over $30 billion can operate under the assumption that their assets will exist in perpetuity.

Most endowments are run by a single organization but may be funded by thousands of donors. In the United States, each organization is typically organized as a tax-free charity, in which individuals receive a tax deduction for making charitable donations. The investment income of the organization may also be tax exempt. Donations to the organization can be made in many forms, including cash, real estate, or equity securities, as well as art and other collectibles. Noncash donations are frequently sold and the proceeds reinvested according to the strategic asset allocation of the endowment manager. The endowment fund of a single university may be composed of thousands of smaller gifts, many of which are segregated to fund specific scholarships, professorships, or the maintenance of specific buildings or academic programs. An endowment fund may have specific restrictions on the capital, **restricted gifts,** that may require that the university maintain the **corpus,** the nominal value of the initial gift, while spending the income generated by the gift to benefit the stated purpose.

Exhibit 12.1 shows the significant asset size of the US and Canadian college and university endowment community. As of June 2018, the National Association of

EXHIBIT 12.1 Assets of the Largest North American University Endowments ($ Billions)

	Assets as of June 2008	Assets as of June 2018	Year Founded
Harvard University	$36.6	$38.3	1636
University of Texas System	$16.1	$30.9	1883–1895
Yale University	$22.9	$29.4	1701
Stanford University	$17.2	$26.5	1891
Princeton University	$16.3	$25.9	1746
Massachusetts Institute of Technology	$10.1	$16.5	1861
Total assets of the six largest endowments	$119.2	$167.5	
Total assets of U.S and Canadian endowments	$412.8	$623.6	
Number of endowments > $1 billion AUM	77	106	

Source: 2018 NACUBO-Commonfund Study of Endowments.

College and University Business Officers (NACUBO 2018) reported that endowment assets totaled nearly $624 billion, with over $167 billion held by the six universities with the largest endowment funds. The total value of endowments likely exceeded $624 billion, as this figure includes only those assets of the 809 endowments that responded to the survey.

The wealth of college and university endowments is highly concentrated at a small number of institutions. As of June 2018, 106 of the 809 colleges and universities reporting to the NACUBO survey had assets exceeding $1 billion. These largest endowments controlled 77% of the total endowment and foundation assets under management (AUM) held by US and Canadian colleges and universities.

Foundations are similar to endowments but tend to differ in a number of ways: (1) foundations are grant-making institutions, whereas endowments tend to be funds established by educational, healthcare, or religious organizations; (2) foundations tend to be finite lived, whereas endowments tend to be perpetual; (3) foundations are more subject to minimum spending requirements; and (4) foundations are less likely to be funded from ongoing donations.

Foundations located in the United States have even greater assets than college and university endowments. At the end of 2015, the latest period available in 2019, the Foundation Center estimated that US foundations controlled $860 billion in assets, the vast majority of which were held by independent, individual, and family foundations (see Exhibit 12.2). The Foundation Center estimates that 22% of the grants made by the top 1,000 foundations in 2012 were awarded to educational charities, 38% to health and human services, 10% to arts and cultural programs, 7% to the environment and animals, and the remaining 23% to charities with various other purposes. With an increase in health-related giving by the Gates foundation, grants to healthcare are now the majority of grants to all causes.

There are a number of different structures for foundations (see Exhibit 12.3). Some are similar to endowments, whereas others differ notably. **Operating foundations** have the greatest similarity to endowments, as the income generated by an

EXHIBIT 12.2   Assets of the Largest US Foundations ($ Billions)

	Assets 2015
Bill & Melinda Gates Foundation	$ 40.4
Ford Foundation	$ 12.2
J. Paul Getty Trust	$ 12.0
Lilly Endowment, Inc.	$ 11.8
The Robert Wood Johnson Foundation	$ 10.4
The William and Flora Hewlett Foundation	$ 9.0
Total assets of the six largest foundations	$ 95.8
Total assets of U.S foundations	$ 860.0
Number of foundations > $2.5 billion AUM	29

Source: The Foundation Center, 2018.

EXHIBIT 12.3   Assets, Gifts, and Giving at US Foundations ($ billions)

2015 ($ Billion)	2015 Total Assets	2015 Total Gifts Paid	2015 Total Gifts Received
Independent foundations	$704.0	$44.1	$32.0
Corporate foundations	$27.8	$5.5	$5.0
Community foundations	$84.3	$7.0	$8.6
Operating foundations	$43.9	$6.2	$7.5
All foundations	$860.0	$62.8	$53.1

Source: The Foundation Center, 2018.

endowment is used to fund the operations of the charitable organization. Some of the largest operating foundations are sponsored by global pharmaceutical companies with the goal of distributing medicine to patients who cannot afford to purchase these lifesaving remedies.

Community foundations are based in a specific geographical area, concentrating the charitable giving of the region's residents. The gifts and investment returns received by the community foundation are distributed in the form of grants to other charities in the community. In contrast to endowments and operating foundations, community foundations do not operate their own programs. A single community foundation may partially fund the operations of dozens of charities within a specific region, typically making grants to organizations with a variety of purposes.

Corporate foundations are sponsored by corporations, with gifts provided by the corporation and its employees. Like community foundations, corporate foundations frequently concentrate their financial donations to charities located in the communities where the firm has the greatest number of employees or customers.

Unlike endowments, many foundations find it difficult to survive in perpetuity. In fact, some foundations are designed to last for only a designated period of time.

The ability of endowments, operating foundations, and community foundations to solicit gifts greatly increases the probability of the organization's assets lasting into perpetuity.

Most **independent foundations** are funded by an individual or a family. These foundations may be founded by a single gift, often by the senior executive of a large corporation who donates wealth in the form of stock. Donating stock to any charity may provide significant tax benefits. The charitable donation may be tax deductible at the current market value, while capital gains on the appreciated stock position are eliminated for tax purposes by the donation. When tax law allows for this structure, the donors reduce their tax burden in two ways: (1) from the forgiven capital gains taxes on the stock's appreciation; and (2) from the tax deduction on the current market value of the charitable donation. Independent foundations may present an exceptional challenge for a portfolio manager. First, the wealth of the foundation is often concentrated in a single stock, which increases the idiosyncratic risk of the portfolio. Maintaining this undiversified portfolio can lead to spectacular wealth or gut-wrenching drawdowns, so foundations may wish to reduce the size of the single stock position either rapidly or on a specific schedule. Second, independent foundations do not typically receive gifts from external donors. Once the foundation has been established by the individual or the family donation, many independent foundations do not receive subsequent gifts.

12.2 INTERGENERATIONAL EQUITY, INFLATION, AND SPENDING CHALLENGES

James Tobin stated that the key task in managing an endowment is to preserve equity among generations. The investment goal of an endowment manager should be to maintain **intergenerational equity**, balancing the need for spending on the current generation of beneficiaries with the goal of maintaining a perpetual pool of assets that can fund the operations of the organization to benefit future generations. Stated quantitatively, intergenerational equity may be expressed by a 50% probability of maintaining the real, or inflation-adjusted, value of the endowment in perpetuity. When the probability of the endowment surviving perpetually is low, such as 25%, the current generation has an advantage due to the high spending rate of the endowment. Conversely, a high probability of perpetuity, such as 75%, gives an advantage to future generations, as the endowment would likely survive indefinitely even if the current rate of spending were increased.

Intergenerational equity may take on varying philosophical approaches to the investment objectives based on the levels of importance the original generations placed on longevity. If longevity is of mild importance, the current generation may place a greater emphasis on higher spending rates which will maximize the shorter term impacts from the capital. If maintaining the endowment in perpetuity is of moderate importance, they may place more emphasis on maintaining the real, or inflation-adjusted, value of the endowment while balancing a tempered level of distributions. Conversely, if the current generation desires the highest probability of the endowment lasting in perpetuity, the emphasis may be heavily focused on a barbell approach of long-term riskier assets and short-term conservative investments with only a portion of the portfolio yield being utilized for distributions.

The challenge of the endowment manager is to maintain the long-term, inflation-adjusted value of the endowment's corpus, or principal value. The value of the endowment is constantly changing: growing with gifts, falling with spending to fund the organization's mission, and changing with the net returns to the investment portfolio. External forces can also impact the assets and spending of an institution, as gifts, research grants, and governmental funding may change substantially from one year to the next:

Change in endowment or foundation value = Income from gifts − Spending

$$+ \text{ Net investment returns} \quad (12.1)$$

In fiscal year 2018, NACUBO estimated that the average endowment spent 4.4% of assets. In contrast to endowments, which typically have flexibility in their **spending rate** (which is the fraction of asset value spend each year), US law requires that foundations spend a minimum of 5% per year on operating expenses and charitable activities. Should charitable contributions received by endowments and foundations decline during times of weak investment returns or rising inflation, the real value of an endowment can fall substantially in a short period of time. Given that foundations have a minimum spending requirement of 5%, while endowments have flexibility in their spending rate, it is easier for endowments to operate in perpetuity than it is for foundations to do so. This is because endowments can reduce their spending rate below 5% of the endowment value during times of crisis.

For an endowment or a foundation to last in perpetuity and provide grants of growing value to its beneficiaries, the returns to its portfolio must exceed the rate of inflation by a wide margin. Exhibit 12.4 shows that the Consumer Price Index (CPI) measure of inflation rose by an annual average of 1.8% in the 10 years ending June 2018. (As of December 2018, the CPI was weighted 42.2% on Housing, 16.3% on Transportation, 15.3% on Medical Care and Education, and 26.2% on Other Goods and Services.)

During the same 10-year period, the Higher Education Price Index (HEPI), a measure of price inflation most relevant to US colleges and universities, rose by an

EXHIBIT 12.4 Return of North American University Endowments

	Ending June 2018			
Index	1 Year	3 Years	5 Years	10 Years
60% MSCI World Equity Index, 40% Barclays Global Aggregate Bond Index	7.1%	5.6%	6.6%	5.5%
60% Russell 3000 Equity Index, 40% Barclays U.S. Aggregate Bond Index	8.4%	6.9%	8.7%	8.1%
40% Russell 3000 Index, 20% MSCI World Equity Index, 40% Barclays	8.4%	6.8%	7.8%	6.9%
Global Aggregate Bond Index				
MSCI World Index Free U.S. Currency	10.9%	7.7%	10.0%	7.4%
Russell 3000 Index	14.2%	10.7%	13.0%	11.0%
Barclays Capital Global Aggregate	1.4%	2.5%	1.6%	2.7%
Barclays Capital U.S. Aggregate	−0.4%	1.3%	2.3%	3.7%
Endowments over $1 Billion	9.7%	6.8%	7.9%	5.9%
Total Endowment	8.0%	6.1%	7.2%	5.7%
Consumer Price Index	1.9%	2.0%	1.5%	1.8%
Higher Education Price Index	2.8%	2.6%	2.6%	2.2%

Source: Bloomberg, 2018 NACUBO-Commonfund Study of Endowments.

annual average of 2.2%. Salaries of faculty and administrators make up the largest percentage of HEPI at 46%; clerical and service employee salaries make up 26%; fringe benefits make up 13%; while miscellaneous services, supplies, and utilities make up 15%.

In order to maintain the real value of assets into perpetuity, as well as to fund the required spending rate, a foundation needs to achieve a return target. A **return target** is a level of performance deemed necessary to satisfy the goals of the owners or beneficiaries of the associated assets. A foundation that has a spending rate of 5%, does not have any regular gift income, and wishes to preserve the real value of its assets has a more aggressive return target: the rate of inflation plus 5%, or even higher when the foundation's spending rate exceeds 5%. When measured relative to CPI inflation over the prior 10 years, this return target is 6.8%, a rate higher than the returns to a blended global stock and bond portfolio over the same period. Return targets may face greater pressure with higher inflation rates, such as HEPI; however, this pressure can be offset by a substantial level of sustained donation income. For institutions without substantial gifts, endowment values likely declined in real terms over the previous decade due to investment returns that fell short of the targeted return of inflation plus 5%.

David Swensen, the chief investment officer of Yale University and author of *Pioneering Portfolio Management* (2009), challenges endowment managers to resist the temptation to increase spending rates after periods of extremely high returns. He argues that limiting spending will allow an endowment to better survive cyclical drawdowns and better compound wealth in perpetuity.

12.3 THE ENDOWMENT MODEL

Aggressive return targets, as well as the perpetual life of many endowments and foundations, have led to an equally aggressive asset allocation. The asset allocation of major endowments and foundations, which typically includes substantial allocations to alternative investments and limited investments to listed stocks and bonds, has been called the **endowment model**.

12.3.1 Asset Allocation in the Endowment Model

Universities with large endowments have been early adopters of alternative investments, well known as sophisticated investors across all areas of alternative investments. The financial success of these investors has been much discussed, even spawning a subset of investors who seek to earn higher returns by following similar investment strategies. Many credit the endowment model, or at least the most articulate description of the endowment model, to David Swensen. Most of the US colleges and universities with endowment assets in excess of $1 billion tend to invest large portions of their endowment portfolios in alternative investments, following the example of Yale University.

Notice from Exhibit 12.5 that the university endowments with over $1 billion in assets under management had an average exposure to alternative investments of 58%. Smaller endowments tend to hold much lower weights on alternative

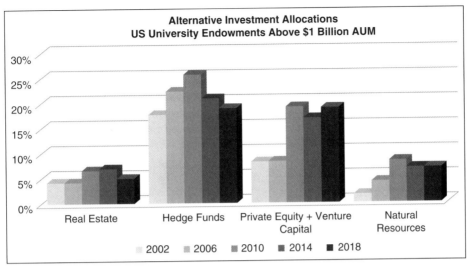

EXHIBIT 12.5 Exposure to Alternative Investments Within Large Endowment Funds
Source: NACUBO, 2018. Chart made from NACUBO data.

assets, with endowments between $101 million and $250 million holding 27% and the smallest endowments, those under $25 million, holding just 11%. The largest endowments hold just 10% in fixed income and cash, while smaller endowments typically hold between 15% and 30% in fixed income and cash. Notice the large weights held on real estate and natural resources, with the largest endowments holding one-eighth of their portfolio in these inflation-hedging assets.

12.3.2   The Endowment Model's Case Against Bonds

Swensen believes strongly in an equity orientation, seeking to participate in the ownership of both public and private equity securities and real assets. The role of fixed income is to provide liquidity and a tail hedge that serves to reduce potential losses in the portfolio. Yale University chooses not to invest in either investment grade or high-yield bonds due to the inherent principal–agent conflict. As Swensen explains the conflict, corporate management explicitly works for stockholders and may choose to make decisions that benefit stockholders, even when those decisions are to the detriment of bondholders. Given this conflict and the fact that the total returns to investment-grade corporate bonds are less than 1% above government bonds on a long-term, net-of-defaults basis, the incremental return to corporate bonds may not warrant inclusion in the endowment portfolio. While sovereign bonds provide liquidity and a tail hedge in a time of crisis, corporate bonds can experience a reduction in liquidity and a disastrous loss of value during extreme market events, producing the opposite effect to what fixed income should have on a portfolio. Similarly, foreign bonds are not held in the Yale University portfolio because, while the return may be similar to that of domestic sovereign bonds, the addition of currency risk and unknown performance during times of financial crisis is not consistent with Swensen's goals for the fixed-income portfolio.

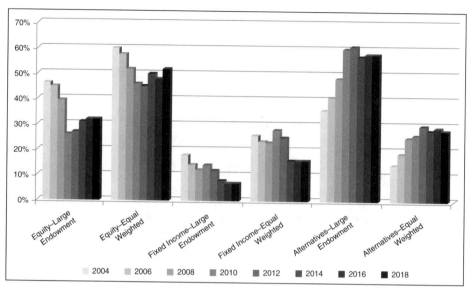

EXHIBIT 12.6   Asset Allocation of Large versus Average College and University
Endowments
Source: NACUBO, 2018. Chart made from NACUBO data.

12.3.3   Alternative Investments in the Endowment Models

Not all endowments have a similar affinity toward alternative investments.
Exhibit 12.6 shows the asset allocation of the equally weighted endowment, which
averages asset allocation across all 890 endowments surveyed by NACUBO, ranging
from those with assets below $25 million to those over $1 billion. While the average
endowment has a smaller allocation to alternatives than the largest endowments,
the equal-weighted average allocation to alternative investments more than doubled
(from 11.8% to 28%) between 2002 and 2018. In fact, the allocation to alternative
investments at college and university endowments increases monotonically with
asset size: endowments between $25 million and $50 million have a larger allocation
than those below $25 million, while those with $100 million to $500 million in
assets have larger allocations than endowments with assets between $50 million and
$100 million. Returns over the past 5 and 10 years reflect the same patterns: The
largest endowments have both the highest returns as well as the largest allocations
to alternative assets.

12.4   WHY MIGHT LARGE ENDOWMENTS OUTPERFORM?

Investors worldwide, from pensions, endowments, and foundations to individual
investors, have become attracted to the endowment model, seeking to emulate
the returns earned by the largest endowments over the past 25 years. However,
evidence shows that not all aggressive allocations toward alternative investments
necessarily earn similar returns. This may be due to key advantages particular to
large endowments.

12.4.1 Six Attributes of the Endowment Model

The literature discusses at least six attributes of the endowment model which may provide advantages that explain the past excellent returns earned by large endowments in recent years:

1. An aggressive asset allocation.
2. Effective investment manager research.
3. First-mover advantage.
4. Access to a network of talented alumni.
5. Acceptance of liquidity risk.
6. Sophisticated investment staff and board oversight.

The next six sections detail those six attributes.

12.4.2 An Aggressive Asset Allocation

In the world of traditional investments, a number of studies—including those by Ibbotson and Kaplan (2000); Brinson, Hood, and Beebower (1986); and Brinson, Singer, and Beebower (1991)—show that the strategic asset allocation of pension plans accounts for between 91.5% and 93.6% of the variance in fund returns. The remaining portion of the variance in fund returns, just 6.4% to 8.5%, can be explained by security selection and market timing. (Note that it was the variance in returns that was measured rather than the amount of returns.) Equation 12.2 attributes portfolio returns to three components:

$$\text{Return attribution} = \text{Contributions from strategic asset allocation}$$
$$+ \text{Security selection} + \text{Market timing or tactical allocation} \quad (12.2)$$

The returns from strategic asset allocation, the first component in Equation 12.2, are measured by multiplying the targeted long-term asset allocation weights by the benchmark returns to each asset class. **Security selection,** the second component, is defined as the return within asset classes relative to a benchmark such as the return to the domestic fixed-income portfolio when compared to the domestic fixed-income benchmark. Finally, **market timing or tactical asset allocation** is measured as the return earned from the variation of asset class weights versus the policy or target asset class weights. Value is added from market timing when the returns to over-weighted asset classes outperform the returns to underweighted asset classes. For example, when the actual equity allocation is 42% and the target equity allocation is 40%, the return to market timing is positive when the equity index outperforms the returns of the other asset classes in the portfolio. Swensen (2009) explains the role of tactical asset allocation and rebalancing. Investors are encouraged to be contrarian and consider valuation when making allocations.

Rather than considering what his peers were doing, Swensen entered alternative asset classes earlier and more aggressively than did other institutional investors. In contrast to the common practice of increasing allocations to asset classes after a period of outperformance, Swensen sought to aggressively **rebalance** (i.e., transact so as to cause portfolio weights to return to prespecified values) to strategic asset allocation weights by selling outperforming asset classes and buying underperforming ones. This can be psychologically difficult, as it requires buying equities during a crash and selling certain assets when other investors are clamoring to increase their allocations to those assets. Market timing between risky and less risky asset classes, such as equities versus cash, can be dangerous due to the large difference in expected returns. While generally eschewing market timing, Swensen suggests tilting the portfolio toward undervalued assets and away from overvalued assets between asset classes with similar long-term return expectations. Brown, Garlappi, and Tiu (2010) analyze the returns to endowment funds over the period 1984 to 2005 and find a much different story than that seen in prior literature regarding return attribution in pension plans. Their study shows that just 74.2% of the returns can be explained by the endowment's strategic asset allocation. With market timing explaining 14.6% of returns, and security selection explaining 8.4%, endowment funds show a much larger contribution to returns from dynamic asset allocation and manager selection.

While it can be easy to replicate the asset allocation of endowment funds, investors seeking to emulate the success of the endowment model will find it much more difficult to profit from market timing and security selection. One reason may be that while pension plans are seen to focus largely on passive allocations within each asset class, endowment funds place a much greater emphasis on manager selection. Brown, Garlappi, and Tiu also find that the return from policy allocation is quite similar across endowments. The contribution from asset allocation explains just 15.3% of the return differences across endowments, while selection explains 72.8% and timing contributes just 2.5%. The endowment model, then, may not seem to be an asset allocation story as much as a story of superior manager selection.

12.4.3 Effective Investment Manager Research

From a risk perspective, many endowment managers prefer to take the majority of their active risk in alternatives. On average, these large investors allocate to 8 managers within traditional asset classes and more than 11 managers in alternative asset classes. Endowments have exploited both their networks of successful alumni and their first-mover advantage in allocating to the best-performing managers, many of whom have now closed their funds to new investors. While common wisdom assumes that the sole secret to endowment success is the large allocation to alternative investments, the top endowments enhance performance further by allocating to managers who outperform. In fact, the largest endowments have historically outperformed in nearly every asset class, both traditional and alternative. Those investors seeking to replicate the success of endowments should be cautioned that although this outperformance within asset classes can add up to 2% per year to performance, it is unlikely to be replicated by an alternatives-heavy allocation if investors lack the talented staff and valuable network of invested managers that many endowments have cultivated. That is, investing in the median manager or exchange-listed alternative investments are unlikely to replicate the returns earned by the top university endowments.

Swensen (2009) demonstrates the importance of manager selection within the alternative investment universe. In liquid, efficient markets, the dispersion of returns across asset managers is relatively small. While fixed income markets may exhibit a mere 0.5% difference in returns between managers at the first and third quartiles of returns, equity markets often have return dispersion across managers of between 2% and 4.8%.

In contrast, the value added by active managers in alternative investments can be quite substantial. In inefficient markets, managers have a greater opportunity to profit from skill, information, and access to deal flow. Dispersion in alternative investments is much higher, with 5% in hedge funds, over 10% in private equity buyouts, and over 25% in venture capital. In many cases, especially in private equity, investments are not attractive when investing in the median manager. In order for a private equity investment to outperform public equity on a risk-adjusted basis and adequately compensate for the liquidity risk in these investments, investors need to allocate to managers who deliver returns far above the median manager in each asset class.

12.4.4 First-Mover Advantage

It appears that the largest endowments have significant skill in selecting the top performing managers within each asset class. Lerner, Schoar, and Wang (2008) explain that this ability to select top managers may be related to the **first-mover advantage** (i.e., benefits emanating from being an initial participant in a competitive environment): large endowments invested in many alternative asset classes years earlier than pension funds and smaller endowments did, and may therefore have an advantage. For example, Takahashi and Alexander (2002) explain that Yale University made its first investments in natural resources in 1950, leveraged buyouts in 1973, venture capital in 1976, and real estate in 1978. In contrast, Lerner, Schoar, and Wang explain that corporate pensions began investing in venture capital only in the 1980s, while public pension plans did not make their first venture capital investments until the 1990s.

Many of the funds offered by managers who have earned top-quartile performance in these asset classes have been closed to new investors for many years. Newer investors seeking access to top managers in alternative investment asset classes, especially in venture capital, are destined to underperform when the top managers allow commitments only from those investors who participated in their earlier funds.

Lerner, Schoar, and Wongsunwai (2007) show that endowments earn higher average returns in private equity, likely due to the greater sophistication of their fund selection process. Endowment funds may have higher returns than do other investors when making allocations to first-time private equity fund managers. Once an endowment fund has become a limited partner in a private equity fund, it seems to be more efficient at processing the information provided by each general partner. The follow-on funds that endowments select for future investment outperform funds to which endowments decline to make future commitments.

Mladina and Coyle (2010) identify Yale University's investments in private equity as the driving factor in the endowment's exceptional performance. It can be difficult to emulate Yale's outperformance in private equity and venture capital investments, as its venture capital portfolio has earned average annual returns of 31.4% since its inception through fiscal year 2007. In fact, this study suggests that without the private equity and venture capital investments, the returns to the Yale endowment would be close to that of the proxy portfolio.

12.4.5 Access to a Network of Talented Alumni

Perhaps the first-mover advantage and the manager-selection skill of top endowments can be attributed to the superior network effect. An institution has a positive **network effect** when it has built relationships with successful people and businesses that may be difficult for others to emulate. Alumni of the universities in Exhibit 12.1 are noted for being among the most successful US college graduates, in terms of both academics and business. Graduates of these schools tend to have the highest initial and midcareer salaries. A study by Li, Zhang, and Zhao (2011) correlated manager-specific characteristics to the returns of the hedge funds they managed. In contrast to the median SAT college entrance exam score of all college-bound students of 1,000, Li, Zhang, and Zhao found that the middle 50% of hedge fund managers attended colleges and universities with average SAT scores between 1,199 and 1,421 (the 79th and 97th percentiles, respectively), demonstrating that the majority of hedge fund managers attended the most competitive colleges and universities. Within the group of studied hedge fund managers, the research showed that those who attended undergraduate colleges with higher average SAT scores have higher returns and lower risk. For example, a 200-point difference in SAT scores, such as that between 1,280 and 1,480, was correlated with higher annual returns of 0.73%. Not only did managers who attended top universities have higher returns, but they did so at lower risk and earned greater inflows during their tenures as fund managers. The authors suggest that talented managers are attracted to hedge funds due to the incentive fee structure, which rewards performance over asset gathering. In contrast to their studies on hedge fund managers, Li, Zhang, and Zhao found that SAT scores did not seem to affect the asset gathering or excess returns earned by mutual fund managers, as these managers are compensated for gathering assets, not for earning excess returns.

Many alumni of top universities wish to continue an association with their alma mater, the university from which they received their undergraduate degree. The ability of top endowment funds to outperform can be perpetuated by this important network of relationships, to the extent that these talented professionals either choose to work for the university's endowment fund or guarantee the endowment investment access to the funds they manage.

Barber and Wang (2013) show that the strong returns earned by endowments are directly traced to the size of their alternative investment exposure. Alphas earned by Ivy League schools exceed 3%, while 30 other schools with top SAT scores earned an alpha exceeding 1.7%. There is a reliably positive alpha and return spread between schools with top SAT scores and schools with average scores.

12.4.6 Acceptance of Liquidity Risk

Endowments have a perpetual holding period. With low spending rates and limited liabilities, endowments have a much greater tolerance for risk, including liquidity risk. When viewed in light of the age of leading universities, which for Harvard and Yale now surpasses 300 years, the 10-year lockup period of private equity vehicles appears relatively short term. As the longest-term investors, charged with protecting the real value of endowment principal for future generations of students, universities are seeking to earn **illiquidity premiums,** which are higher returns earned by investing in less liquid assets that require long lockup periods. The idea is that the perpetual nature of endowments allows them to easily handle this liquidity risk. Anson (2010) estimates the liquidity premium for private equity at 2% and for direct real estate at 2.7%, while other studies estimate liquidity premiums as high as 10%.

Swensen (2009) explains that less liquid investments tend to have greater degrees of inefficient pricing. On average, investors overvalue liquid assets, leaving undervalued and less liquid assets for investors with long-term investment horizons. Investors making commitments to long-term assets, such as private equity and private real estate, know that these investments are typically held for 10 years or longer and so require a significant due diligence process before making such a long-term commitment. Investors in more liquid asset classes may not take their investments as seriously, knowing that the investment may be exited after a short-term holding period. Investments that appear to be liquid in normal markets may have constrained liquidity during times of crisis, which is when liquidity is most valued.

12.4.7 Sophisticated Investment Staff and Board Oversight

All investors need a process by which asset allocations are set and managers are selected. Traditionally, an institutional investor would have an internal staff that would make recommendations to an investment committee, which would then vote on recommendations at quarterly meetings. The quality of the votes and recommendations depends on the experience and composition of the members of the endowment's staff and investment committee.

Investors with smaller assets under management (e.g., less than $100 million) tend to have smaller staffs meaning that a single staff member, such as the chief financial officer or treasurer, is responsible for the endowment (along with a wide variety of other budget and financial issues). In contrast, the endowments with over $1 billion in assets tend to have large and sophisticated internal teams, averaging over 10 investment professionals. These teams tend to be well experienced and highly compensated, allowing them to manage some of the assets in-house as well as recommend investment managers.

In addition to internal staff and an investment committee, many endowments employ external consultants. A **nondiscretionary investment consultant** makes recommendations to the endowment on asset allocation, manager selection, and a wide variety of other issues, but leaves the ultimate decision to a vote of the investment committee. There is growing use of the **outsourced CIO (OCIO) model,** in which the endowment gives discretionary authority to an external consultant who may make and implement prespecified decisions, such as manager selection and asset allocation decisions, without taking those decisions to a vote. Endowments with smaller internal teams appear to find the outsourced CIO model attractive.

12.4.8 Outsourced CIO Model

The Commonfund Institute (2013) notes a number of benefits to hiring an OCIO, especially for endowments that are devoting ever-larger allocations to alternative investments. An OCIO firm will have a large staff and significant infrastructure resources that are shared across all its clients. This institutional-quality firm has resources that could not be afforded by smaller investors. There are economies of scale in manager research, as hedge fund and other alternative managers can visit the consultant or OCIO firm rather than visiting the dozens of underlying investors. An OCIO firm can be cost-effective when compared to attracting, training, and retaining investment professionals, who may be difficult to find and retain in a market where there is a growing demand for those who have experience managing foundation and endowment assets. For investors who do have staff, the OCIO may help train and educate their internal staff and shorten the overall learning curve or improve internal practices. While investment decisions often take more than three months when an investment committee retains discretion, the OCIO model can make investment and rebalancing decisions faster and more efficient by allowing the investment committee to take more of an oversight position rather than being involved in the day-to-day management of the fund. Lord (2014) studied the common factors shared by the largest and most successful endowments. Ideally, the investment committee would be staffed by investment professionals and others who have experience serving as corporate executives or board members. If those investors have experience in alternative investments and a wider variety of investment strategies, the resulting portfolio tends to be more diversified and experience higher risk-adjusted returns. Investment committees with significant representation from donors or employees of the universities tend to have lower allocations to alternative investments. Decision-making is improved when committee members have multiple perspectives and an ability and willingness to openly debate issues. When adding new members to the investment committee, endowments should seek members with knowledge and experience that differ from those of current committee members. Finally, prior to allocations being made, top-performing endowments make it a practice to educate their staff and committee members on new investment themes, trends, and asset classes.

12.5 RISKS OF THE ENDOWMENT MODEL

When applied by the largest investors, the endowment model has created impressive returns over the past 20 years. However, this style of portfolio management comes with a special set of risks. First, portfolio managers need to be concerned about the interactions among spending rates, inflation, and the long-term asset value of the endowment. Second, a portfolio with as much as 60% invested in alternative assets raises concerns of liquidity risk and the ability to rebalance the portfolio when necessary. Finally, portfolios with high allocations to assets with equity-like characteristics and low allocations to fixed income require the portfolio manager to consider how to protect the portfolio from tail risk, which is a large drawdown in portfolio value during times of increased systemic risk.

12.5.1 Spending Rates and Spending Rules

There is an important tension between the spending rate of the endowment, the risk of the endowment portfolio, and the goal of allowing the endowment to serve as a permanent source of capital for the university. When the endowment fund generates high returns with a low spending rate, the size of the endowment fund increases. This may lead to concerns about intergenerational equity, as the spending on current beneficiaries could likely be increased without compromising the probability of the endowment continuing into perpetuity. Conversely, a conservative asset allocation with a high spending rate may favor the current generation yet imperil the real value of the endowment in the long run. Once an asset allocation is determined, a spending rule must also be established. The earliest endowments spent income only, which tilted the portfolio toward income-producing securities. Later, endowments moved toward spending at a fixed percentage of the current value of the endowment, such as 4%. Between the 1950s and 1970s, endowment managers came to embrace the concept of spending rates as depending on total return. A **total return investor** who considers both income and capital appreciation as components of return may realize that a 5% current yield is not needed in order for the endowment to have a spending rate of 5%. Moving from a portfolio dominated by fixed income to one with a healthy mix of equity investments may reduce the yield to 3% while increasing total return to 7.5%. With a total return of 7.5%, including income and capital appreciation, the endowment can afford a spending rate of 5% while maintaining the real value of the portfolio, as the 2.5% return in excess of the spending rate can be used to offset the impact of inflation. In order to generate 5% spending, the entire income of 3% is spent, and 2% of the portfolio is sold each year to meet the spending rate. A fixed spending rate, however, created volatility in the amount of income available to the university. In a year when the return and gifts received by the endowment generated a 20% increase in endowment value, the income to be spent also increased by 20%. Conversely, during a 20% drawdown, the spending rate of the university was slashed by a significant amount. A sticky spending rate, such as $3 million per year, provides certainty of income to the university but can create concerns of intergenerational equity after a large gain or loss in the value of the endowment.

Recognizing that volatility in the income provided to university operations was unwelcome, more flexible spending rules were developed. Spending 4% of the average value of the endowment over the trailing 3 to 5 years creates a smoothing process that dampens the impact of the volatility of portfolio returns on the income provided to the university.

David Swensen developed a spending rule for Yale University: each year, the endowment could spend at a rate equal to 80% of the prior year's dollar spending plus 20% of the endowment's long-term spending rate (4.5%). This formula incorporates the prior 10 years of endowment value into the spending rate calculation, providing a stronger smoothing effect than a simple moving average rule.

Swensen (2009) expresses concern about the impact of inflation, market volatility, and high spending rates. Some 70% of endowments use spending rates of between 4% and 6%, with 5% being a popular choice. Yale has set its long-term spending rate at 4.5%, as simulations show that, based on a 5-year average of endowment values, a 5% spending rule has a 50% probability of losing half of the endowment's real value at some point over the course of a generation. Using a longer averaging period and a lower spending rate reduces the probability of this disastrous decline in the real value of the endowment portfolio.

12.5.2 Spending Rates and Inflation

Inflation has a particularly strong impact on the long-term real value of university endowments. Ideally, endowments should seek to maintain the real value of the corpus rather than the legal requirement of the notional value. When maintaining the real value of the corpus, long-term spending rates can keep up with inflation;

when maintaining the nominal value of the corpus, long-term spending has an ever-declining value in real terms.

The focus on inflation risk has led many endowments to increase allocations to real assets in recent years. Real asset investments include inflation-linked bonds; public and private real estate investments; commodity futures programs; and both direct and private equity fund investments in mining, oil and gas, timber, farmland, and infrastructure. Ideally, the real assets portfolio would earn long-term returns similar to those of equity markets, with yields similar to those of fixed income, while experiencing low volatility and low correlation to the fixed income and publicly traded equity assets in the portfolio, as well as higher returns during times of rising inflation.

A report from Alliance Bernstein (2010) calculated the inflation betas of several asset classes. An **inflation beta** is analogous to a market beta except that an index of price changes is used in place of the market index, creating a measure of the sensitivity of an asset's returns to changes in inflation. Only a few assets demonstrated a positive inflation beta, where the assets act as an effective inflation hedge. The majority of assets have a risk to rising inflation; that is, they have a negative inflation beta. According to Alliance Bernstein, commodity futures offered the greatest inflation beta at 6.5, whereas farmland had a beta of 1.7. In the fixed-income sector, 10-year Treasury Inflation-Protected Securities (TIPS) had a beta of 0.8, whereas 3-month Treasury bills had a beta of 0.3. Equities and long-term nominal bonds had a strong negative reaction to inflation, with the Standard & Poor's (S&P) 500 Index exhibiting an inflation beta of –2.4 and 20-year US Treasury bonds suffering returns at –3.1 times the rate of inflation. Of course, the default portfolio of 60% equities and 40% fixed income maintains this large negative exposure to inflation risk. Within equities, small-capitalization stocks had an even greater risk to rising inflation. Companies with lower capital expenditures and fewer physical assets also had a stronger negative response to rising inflation.

12.5.3 Spending Rates and Liquidity Issues

In the aftermath of the 2007–8 global financial crisis, many pension funds and endowments reevaluated their asset allocation policies and started paying increased attention to their risk and liquidity management practices. Liquidity in this context represents the ability of an entity to fund future investment opportunities and to meet obligations as they come due without incurring unacceptable losses. These obligations include the annual spending rate as well as the capital calls from private equity and real estate limited partnerships. If there are mismatches between the maturity of an entity's assets and its liabilities, the entity is exposed to liquidity risk.

While liquidity is certainly a risk for endowments, these funds have long lives and can afford to take a fair amount of liquidity risk. Investors should demand premiums to bear liquidity risk, as holding less liquid assets may cause investors to forfeit the lucrative opportunity to buy assets at distressed prices during a crisis. For 10-year lockups, this premium may be 6%, while 2-year lockups require a 2% premium. The size of this premium varies through time, with studies suggesting that illiquidity premiums declined in the years leading to the financial crisis. A portfolio manager has to consider carefully the tradeoff between the liquidity risk and the illiquidity premium in determining the size of the illiquid assets in the overall portfolio.

A long lockup period is a vital tool employed by fund managers to reduce the cost of liquidity risk. During the global financial crisis, funds with long lockup periods were not under pressure to sell their assets at distressed prices. It is important to note that if the underlying assets of a fund are less liquid than the liquidity provisions it offers to its investors, the cost of liquidity risk will increase for all investors, even if only a small fraction of the fund's investors decide to redeem their shares during periods of financial distress. Pension funds and endowments cannot afford to ignore such an important source of return if they are to meet the needs of their beneficiaries.

Due to lack of effective liquidity risk management, many funds experienced severe liquidity squeezes during the global financial crisis. This forced some to sell a portion of their illiquid assets at deep discounts in secondary markets, to delay the funding of important projects, and, in certain cases, to borrow funds in the debt market during a period of extreme market stress. These discouraged some pension funds and endowments from allocating a meaningful portion of their portfolios to alternative assets.

12.5.4 Spending Rates and Liquidity-Driven Investors

In *The Global Economic System*, Chacko et al. (2011) explain that liquidity risk rises during a crisis, as declining liquidity and rising volatility increase bid–ask spreads and reduce trading volumes. The book notes that alternative investments have a very high liquidity risk, with private equity, venture capital, real estate, hedge funds, and infrastructure exhibiting liquidity betas in excess of 1.0. While these investments tend to have higher returns over long periods of time, the underperformance during times of crisis can be substantial due to the large exposure to liquidity risk. Chacko et al. discuss **liquidity-driven investing**, an investment approach emphasizing the role of the liquidity of investments and the time horizon of the investor in the asset allocation decisions. Tier 1 assets are invested in short-term fixed income; tier 2 assets are invested in risky, liquid assets, such as stocks; and tier 3 assets are both risky and illiquid, such as investments in private equity and hedge funds. The endowment should estimate the spending and capital calls for the next 10 years and invest those assets exclusively in tier 1 and tier 2 assets, which can be liquidated quickly at relatively low cost. Tier 3 assets are designed as long-term investments; as such, the size of this allocation should be designed to prevent the need to liquidate these assets in the secondary market before maturity.

One measure of illiquidity is the sum of the endowment's allocation to private equity and real estate partnerships combined with the potential capital calls from commitments to funds of more recent vintage. Takahashi and Alexander (2002) from the Yale University endowment office discuss the importance of understanding the capital call and distribution schedule of private equity and real estate investments. In these private investment vehicles, investors commit capital to a new fund, and that capital is contributed to the fund on an unknown schedule. A typical private equity or real estate fund will call committed capital over a 3-year period, focus on investments for the next few years, and then distribute the proceeds from exited investments in years 7 to 12 of the partnership's life. Once an alternative investment program has matured, it may be possible for distributions from prior investments to fully fund capital commitments from new partnerships.

12.5.5 Avoiding Liquidity Losses from a Financial Crisis

During the global financial crisis, it became very difficult for managers to exit investments, as private equity funds could not float initial public offerings, and real estate funds could not sell properties. As a result, distributions were much slower than expected. When distributions slowed and capital calls continued, some endowments and foundations found it challenging to meet their commitments, as they had previously assumed that the pace of distributions would be sufficient to fund future capital calls. The price of a missed capital call can be steep (up to as much as a forfeiture of the prior contributed capital) and can result in being banned from participating in future funds offered by the general partner.

One feature of the endowment model is the minimal holdings of fixed income and cash. For example, going into 2008, Yale's target for fixed income was 4%, with leverage creating an effective cash position of –4%. Princeton had a combined weight of 4%, and Harvard held approximately 8%. Although income from dividends, bond interest, and distributions from private funds added to the available cash, in many cases the income, fixed income, and cash holdings were not sufficient to meet the current year's need for cash. With a 5% spending rate, it became necessary for these endowment funds to either borrow cash or sell assets at fire-sale prices in order to guarantee the university sufficient income to fund its operations. To the extent that the endowment also had capital calls for private equity and real estate funds, the need for immediate cash was even greater. In some cases, the universities cut spending, halting building programs and even eliminating some faculty and staff positions, while raising tuition at higher rates than in prior years.

Sheikh and Sun (2012) find that the cash and fixed-income holdings of an endowment should be at least 6% to 14% of assets to avoid liquidity crises in 95% of market conditions. To completely eliminate liquidity risk, cash and fixed-income holdings may need to be as high as 35%, far above the allocations that most endowments are comfortable making, given their high expected return targets. To avoid liquidity crises, Siegel (2008) suggests laddering allocations to private equity and real estate funds, ideally at a schedule in which distributions from maturing funds are sufficient to fund capital calls of partnerships of more recent vintages.

12.5.6 Leverage Risk and the Endowment Model

The use of leverage can also create liquidity issues for a portfolio manager. Short-term leverage, such as that provided by prime brokers to hedge funds, may not be sustainable or affordable during times of crisis. When credit lines are reduced or not renewed, investors may have to repay loans on short notice, which can require the sale of investments at very low prices. Many fixed-income arbitrage and convertible bond arbitrage funds suffered significant losses during the financial crisis, as a reduction in leverage from eight times to four times required the immediate sale of half of the portfolio. When the market knows that these sales are coming, and a number of hedge funds are simultaneously forced to sell due to credit line reductions as well as investor redemptions, liquidity risk is extreme as buyers of these fixed-income assets wait to purchase until the prices of the convertible and mortgage-backed bonds have fallen precipitously. Endowments and foundations that invest in leveraged hedge funds must be prepared for the potentially large drawdowns in these strategies, as well as the potential for the erection of gates that prevent investors from redeeming their assets from hedge funds during times of a financial crisis. Keating (2011) believes that after some tweaks in liquidity, conviction in the endowment model has strengthened. He notes that the Harvard University endowment has changed its cash target from −5% to +2%, while reducing its uncalled capital commitments to real estate and private equity partnerships by more than $4 billion in just 2 years. Similarly, Yale University increased its cash holdings to 4%, while putting external lines of credit into place. Keating (2010) states that the liquidity crisis was not caused by an overallocation to alternative investments, but by an underallocation to fixed-income and cash investments.

There are important lessons to be learned from the experiences of pension funds and endowments during the great financial crisis. Plan sponsors, portfolio managers, and asset allocators should establish sound processes for identifying, measuring, monitoring, and controlling liquidity risk. This process should include estimates of future cash flows arising from both assets and liabilities. A sound and robust risk management process should allow pension funds and endowments to take full advantage of the available investment opportunities, including earning premiums for bearing liquidity risk at levels their institutions can tolerate.

12.6   LIQUIDITY REBALANCING AND TACTICAL ASSET ALLOCATION

A reason to maintain liquidity in an endowment or a foundation portfolio is to facilitate rebalancing activity. Swensen (2009) believes strongly in keeping portfolio weights close to the long-term strategic weights, a practice that requires regular rebalancing. Without rebalancing, the asset allocation of the portfolio will drift, with the asset classes earning the highest returns rising in weight relative to the rest of the portfolio. If the highest-performing asset class becomes highly overvalued, the risk of the portfolio rises significantly when rebalancing activity is delayed. It is relatively easy to rebalance publicly-traded securities. However, it can take courage to buy an underweighted asset class when prices have fallen or to choose when to sell assets that have performed well.

Within alternatives, hedge funds may have quarterly redemption windows and lockup periods of 1 to 3 years. Private equity and real estate funds must typically be held until assets are fully distributed, a process that can take 10 to 12 years. Funding capital calls to private equity and real estate funds can change the asset mix, as traditional investments are typically sold to fund the increasing allocation to the less liquid alternative investments. To the extent that alternative investments have net asset values that are smoothed or reported with a time lag, publicly traded investments will decline in allocation rapidly during times of crisis. It is important to understand the role of pricing in these less liquid asset classes, as the net asset value adjusts slowly to changes in public market valuation. Investors may react by rebalancing only within the liquid alternatives and traditional assets, while slowly changing allocations to less liquid alternative investments by modifying the size of future commitments.

There are a number of approaches to rebalancing, such as those discussed by Kochard and Rittereiser (2008). Some investors will rebalance on a calendar basis;

for example, after discussions at a quarterly meeting of the investment committee. Other investors will tie the rebalancing activity to the actual asset allocation when compared to the long-term policy asset allocation. While some investors have exact targets for the domestic equity allocation, such as 30%, others might have ranges of 25% to 30%. Those with an exact target may establish a rebalancing deviation, such as a decision to rebalance when the equity allocation has strayed 2% from its target weight. Investors with asset allocation ranges may wait to rebalance until the allocation has moved outside the range. When range-based investors rebalance, they must also decide whether to rebalance to the closest edge of the range or to the center of the range. Rebalancing is an advantage when markets are mean reverting, but can reduce returns when markets are trending. Some portfolio managers will postpone rebalancing when markets are trending or rebalance halfway back to the target. The successful implementation of rebalancing rules can both improve returns and reduce risks.

Some endowments may employ internal tactical asset allocation (TAA) models or external asset managers offering TAA strategies. As opposed to strategic asset allocation, which regularly rebalances back to the long-term target weights, tactical asset allocation intentionally deviates from target weights in an attempt to earn excess returns or reduce portfolio risk. TAA models take a shorter-term view on asset classes, overweighting undervalued assets and underweighting overvalued assets. While the risk and return estimates underlying the strategic asset allocation are typically calculated for a 10- to 20-year period, the risk and return estimates used by tactical asset allocation are typically much shorter, often 1 quarter and 1 year. TAA models can employ valuation data, fundamental and macroeconomic data, price momentum data, or any combination of the three.

A number of alternative investment styles employ TAA analysis. Managed futures funds focus on price momentum, while global macro funds more commonly analyze governmental actions to predict moves in fixed-income and currency markets. TAA funds may employ both methods but are different from managed futures and macro funds. First, managed futures and macro funds take both long and short positions and often employ leverage; TAA funds are typically long-only, unlevered funds. Second, TAA funds may reallocate assets across a small number of macro markets, whereas managed futures and global macro funds may have a much larger universe of potential investments.

Because TAA strategies can be difficult to employ successfully, many investors will place limits on the size of tactical positions. For example, when stocks are perceived to be overvalued, the equity allocation may be 10% below the long-term target weight. If the fund were allowed to swing between 100% equity and 100% fixed-income allocations, substantial underperformance could occur. Due to the similarity in long-term return estimates, it is less risky to tactically allocate between assets of similar risk and return (e.g., commodities versus stocks) than between assets of different risk and return (equities versus cash).

12.7 TAIL RISK

In the foreword to Swensen (2009), Charles Ellis comments that Yale was good at playing defense, because the endowment was built to withstand the inevitable storms that face capital markets. This resiliency was put to a severe test, as the Yale endowment lost 25% of its value in the 12 months ending June 2009. This has been termed a *tail event,* in that the returns were at the extreme left tail of the endowment's return distribution. In times of market stress, correlations between many types of assets tend to rise. This increases portfolio volatility above that assumed in the mean-variance optimization that may have been used to determine the initial asset allocation. Tail events are discussed in detail in Chapter 16.

Bhansali (2008, 2010, 2011) has repeatedly encouraged investors to manage the risk of catastrophic loss of portfolio value, termed *tail risk.* When portfolios preserve value during bear markets, the long-term value of the endowment fund can be increased. The key to minimizing drawdowns is to build some protection into the portfolio by making an allocation to assets that will maintain value or even rise in value during times of crisis.

The most straightforward hedge is an increased weight on cash and risk-free debt in the portfolio. A rising allocation to cash, however, will reduce the expected return of the portfolio and potentially lead to lower long-term wealth. The most aggressive endowment and foundation investors have clearly not used cash and fixed income as a tail hedge, as the allocation to this defensive asset class is typically quite low.

A second method to reduce tail risk is to employ options hedges on the equity-linked portion of the portfolio. **Equity options hedges** are positions established in equity options for the primary purpose of reducing the equity risk of a portfolio, such as the purchase of a put option. Equity put options provide the purest hedge against tail risk, offering the potential to provide a greater than 500% return during times of large equity market declines. For example, an investor who spends 5% of portfolio value each year on equity put options may expect those options to be worth 25% of the portfolio value at the bottom of the bear market. However, the simple purchase of equity put options can be quite expensive. Further, this approach may simply be smoothing returns: transferring the losses on options in good years to profits on options in years of declining equity markets.

The cost of equity options hedges can be reduced through the use of collars or put spreads. In a collar, a call option is sold above the market. While this limits the potential return from the equity-linked portion of the portfolio, the premium earned from the sale of the call option can offset the cost of the put options or a put spread. In a put spread, the investor purchases one put option at perhaps 10% out-of-the-money, while selling a second put option at perhaps 25% out-of-the-money. This strategy can insure losses on the equity portfolio of up to 15%, but after the market has fallen 25%, the investor participates fully in market declines. The cost of a put spread may be 30% to 70% less than the cost of a long put option, depending on the implied volatility, strike price, and maturity of each option.

Within each asset class, investors can structure allocations to reduce exposure to extreme market events. Just as Swensen does at Yale, the fixed-income portfolio can focus on high-quality bonds, which will grow in value during a crisis, while avoiding corporate bonds, whose yield spreads widen quickly during a market stress event. With hedge funds, it may be wise to reduce allocations to arbitrage strategies, such as convertible arbitrage or mortgage-backed securities arbitrage, which rely on tightening spreads, the availability of leverage, and liquid markets to earn their returns.

Some hedge fund strategies have historically risen in value during times of market crisis. Macro, managed futures, and some volatility arbitrage funds are designed to have their largest returns during times of extreme market moves, so some investors specifically allocate assets to these strategies to reduce the tail risk of their portfolios. While these hedge fund strategies are not as certain to perform as a put options strategy during times of market stress, the expected cost of these strategies is lower, as their long-term return far exceeds the negative expected return of programs that regularly purchase equity put options.

12.8 CONCLUSION

It is important for investors and analysts to understand the endowment model, which seeks a high allocation to alternative investments in order to meet aggressive targets requiring long-term returns that exceed the rate of inflation by at least the rate of required spending. Portfolio managers and asset allocators seeking to emulate the returns of the most successful endowments must realize that simply mimicking the asset allocations of top endowments will not guarantee similar returns, as endowments have historically added significant value through manager selection and market timing. Those wishing to replicate the results of the most successful endowment and foundation investors need to consider the risks to inflation, liquidity, and extreme market events. A focus on alternative investments also requires a greater degree of investment manager due diligence, evaluating both investment and operational risks.

REFERENCES

Alliance Bernstein. 2010. "Deflating Inflation: Redefining the Inflation-Resistant Portfolio." https://www.alliancebernstein.com/CmsObjectABD/PDF/Research_WhitePaper/RWP_ DeflationInflationBlackbook.pdf. April.

Anson, M. J. P. 2010. "Measuring a Premium for Liquidity Risk." *Journal of Private Equity* 13 (2): 6–16.

Barber, B. M. and G. Wang. 2013. "Do (Some) University Endowments Earn Alpha?" *Financial Analysts Journal* 69 (5): 26–44.

Bhansali, V. 2008. "Tail Risk Management." *Journal of Portfolio Management* 34: 68–75.

———. 2010. "Vineer Bhansali Discusses PIMCO's Approach to Tail Risk Hedging." PIMCO. http://europe.pimco.com/EN/Insights/Pages/Bhansali%20QA% 20Tail%20Risk%20-% 20Feb%202010.aspx.

———. 2011. "Cash vs. Tail Risk Hedging: Which Is Better?" PIMCO. http://europe.pimco .com/EN/Insights/Pages/Cash-vs-Tail-Risk-Hedging-Which-Is-Better.aspx.

Brinson, G. P., L. R. Hood, and G. L. Beebower. 1986. "Determinants of Portfolio Performance." *Financial Analysts Journal* 42 (4): 39–44.

Brinson, G. P., B. D. Singer, and G. L. Beebower. 1991. "Determinants of Portfolio Performance II: An Update." *Financial Analysts Journal* 47 (3): 40–48.

Brown, K., L. Garlappi, and C. Tiu. 2010. "Asset Allocation and Portfolio Performance: Evidence from University Endowment Funds." *Journal of Financial Markets* 13 (2): 268–64.

Chacko, G., C. L. Evans, H. Gunawan, and A. L. Sjoman. 2011. *The Global Economic System: How Liquidity Shocks Affect Financial Institutions and Lead to Economic Crises.* Upper Saddle River, NJ: FT Press.

Commonfund Institute. 2013. "Outsourced Investment Management: An Overview for Institutional Decision Makers." November.

Ford Foundation. 1969. *Managing Educational Endowments: Report to the Ford Foundation.* New York: Ford Foundation.

Ibbotson, R. G. and P. D. Kaplan. 2000. "Does Asset Allocation Policy Explain 40, 90, or 100 Percent of Performance?" *Financial Analysts Journal* 56 (1): 26–33.

Keating, T. 2010. "The Yale Endowment Model of Investing Is Not Dead." RIABiz, April 20.

———. 2011. "How the Harvard and Yale Endowment Models Changed to Avoid a Repeat of 2009." RIABiz, February 15.

Kochard, L. E. and C. M. Rittereiser. 2008. *Foundation and Endowment Investing: Philosophies and Strategies of Top Investors and Institutions.* Hoboken, NJ: John Wiley & Sons.

Lerner, J., A. Schoar, and J. Wang. 2008. "Secrets of the Academy: The Drivers of University Endowment Success." *Journal of Economic Perspectives* 22: 207–22.

Lerner, J., A. Schoar, and W. Wongsunwai. 2007. "Smart Institutions, Foolish Choices? The Limited Partner Performance Puzzle." *Journal of Finance* 62 (2): 731–64.

Li, H., X. Zhang, and R. Zhao. 2011. "Investing in Talents: Manager Characteristics and Hedge Fund Performances." *Journal of Financial and Quantitative Analysis* 46 (2): 59–82.

Lord, M. 2014. "University Endowment Committees: How a Learning Orientation and Knowledge Factors Contribute to Portfolio Diversification and Performance." *European Journal of Finance.* doi:10.1080/1351847X.2013.879536.

Mladina, P. and J. Coyle. 2010. "Yale's Endowment Returns: Manager Skill or Risk Exposure?" *Journal of Wealth Management* 13 (2): 43–50.

National Association of College and University Business Officers. 2018. "NACUBO–TIAA Study of Endowments (NTSE)." http://nacubo.org/Research/2020/NACUBO-TIAA-Study-of-Endowments.

Sheikh, A. and J. Sun. 2012. "Defending the 'Endowment Model': Quantifying Liquidity Risk in a Post–Credit Crisis World." *Journal of Alternative Investments* 14 (4 Spring): 9–24.

Siegel, L. 2008. "Alternatives and Liquidity: Will Spending and Capital Calls Eat Your 'Modern' Portfolio?" *Journal of Portfolio Management* 35 (2): 103–14.

Swensen, D. 2009. *Pioneering Portfolio Management: An Unconventional Approach to Institutional Investment.* New York: Simon & Schuster.

Takahashi, D. and A. Alexander. 2002. "Illiquid Alternative Asset Fund Modeling." *Journal of Portfolio Management* 28 (2): 90–100.

The Foundation Center. 2018. http://data.foundationcenter.org/.

CHAPTER 13

Pension Fund Portfolio Management

Pension plans (also known as pension schemes or superannuation plans) manage assets that are used to provide employees with a flow of income during their retirement years. This chapter provides an overview of pension funds as they relate to alternative investing.

13.1 DEVELOPMENT, MOTIVATIONS, AND TYPES OF PENSION PLANS

Because pension schemes may control the largest pool of capital in the world, asset managers need to be aware of the goals and challenges of managing these plans.

13.1.1 Development of Pension Plans

World Bank data shows that 90% of the workforce in the high-income OECD countries is covered by some form of pension or government retirement plan. The world's top 15 pension plans controlled over $6.715 trillion in assets at the end of 2017 (see Exhibit 13.1). Employees need to save during their careers to maintain an adequate standard of living during retirement. It can be difficult for an individual worker to adequately plan for retirement, as investment returns and one's life expectancy are unknown. Depending on their chosen career and income, employees may lack either the ability to save or the investment knowledge to appropriately invest their assets.

13.1.2 Motivations for Using Pension Plans

There are a number of reasons why pension plans can be attractive, both for employers and for employees. Companies offering pension plans may be able to attract and retain higher-quality employees while employees may seek out companies offering strong pension benefits. Employees value the income promised by a pension plan, which may be used as a substitute for their personal savings. In many countries, retirement plan assets grow on a tax-deferred basis. Employees' and employers' contributions to retirement plans are not taxed in the year that the contributions are made. The gains on the investment portfolio are not taxed in the year they are earned, but taxes are paid by employees when the assets are withdrawn during retirement. Ideally, the employee will pay a lower tax rate during retirement than during their working years, which further increases the tax benefit of pension plans for employees. Pension funds have several advantages over individual savings for retirement

EXHIBIT 13.1 The World's Largest Pension Plan Sponsors

Fund	Country	Assets ($ million)
Government Pension Investment	Japan	$1,443,554
Government Pension Fund	Norway	$1,063,546
National Pension	South Korea	$582,938
Federal Retirement Thrift	U.S	$531,489
ABP	Netherlands	$494,796
National Social Security	China	$456,853
California Public Employees	U.S	$336,684
Canada Pension*	Canada	$283,545
Central Provident Fund	Singapore	$269,133
PFZW*	Netherlands	$235,995
California State Teachers	U.S	$216,193
Local Government Officials	Japan	$209,880
New York State Common	U.S	$201,263
Employees Provident Fund	Malaysia	$200,265
New York City Retirement	U.S	$189,794

* As of March 31, 2018
Source: Thinking Ahead Institute (2018).

in self-directed plans. First, the pension fund can hire internal staff and external managers who are highly trained in finance to watch the investment portfolio on a daily basis. There are economies of scale with large pension plans, with larger plans better able to meet substantial investment minimums required of many alternative investments. These economies of scale may allow pensions to negotiate preferential terms, which may allow the investment manager to potentially reduce investment fees with the fee savings allowing the pension to maintain a larger staff. The pooling of mortality risk also allows the pension plan to allocate a larger portion of assets to illiquid assets to earn an illiquidity premium.

Pension plans can also make long-term investments with a time horizon that may be as long as the lifetime of the youngest employee, thus the asset allocation decisions are made with the average employee's age in mind. When individual investors make retirement investments, asset allocation becomes inherently more conservative over time; as the employee nears retirement and a need to rely upon their assets, their ability to withstand and recover from investment losses is decreased. This provides a further advantage to pension plans with regards to mortality risk, which is the risk that someone will die earlier than expected, and is highly uncertain for an individual investor, but can be quite predictable when averaged over a large number of employees and retirees covered by a pension plan.

For an individual investor, spending rates may be conservative, again because the life span is uncertain and a longer lifetime will require a longer reliance on retirement assets. However, for a large pension plan with known benefits, the asset allocation and benefit levels are not significantly impacted by the death of a single beneficiary. Longevity risk, the risk that individuals will live longer than anticipated and outlive their resources, affects different investors in different ways. For individuals and pension plans, the risk is that lifetimes will be longer than anticipated, as retirement spending or retirement benefits will last for a longer period, requiring a larger number of monthly benefit payments or months of retirement spending. In contrast, for life insurance companies, the risk is that beneficiaries die at a younger age than predicted, as the life insurance benefit will be paid at an earlier date and a higher present value. Life insurance companies have an interest in selling hedges for longevity risk, as this is a natural fit for offsetting the longevity risk in their general account.

13.1.3 Three Basic Types of Pension Plans

There are three basic types of pension plans: defined benefit (DB), governmental social security plans, and defined contribution (DC). Each plan varies in the asset management risks and rewards, and whether the employer, the employee, or taxpayers have the ultimate risk for the performance of the investment portfolio.

There are also hybrid types of schemes, such as cash balance plans that share features with both defined benefit and defined contribution plans. A **cash balance plan** is basically a defined benefit plan, where the pension benefits are maintained in individual record-keeping accounts that show the participant the current value of his or her accrued benefit and facilitate portability to a new plan.

13.2 RISK TOLERANCE AND ASSET ALLOCATION

The first step in the asset allocation process is to identify the asset owner's objectives and constraints. This information is then used in the second step of crafting an investment policy statement which will guide the portfolio manager in the implementation of asset allocation strategies that are consistent with the asset owner's needs.

13.2.1 Three Approaches to Managing the Assets of Defined Benefit Plans

In managing a DB plan, the primary objective is to fund the plan's liabilities. In creating optimal portfolios, one needs to develop an appropriate measure of risk for the fund and account for factors that affect the plan sponsor's level of risk tolerance.

The risk of a DB plan can be measured from three difference perspectives: assets, assets and liabilities, and integrated. Different risk metrics such as volatility, value at risk, conditional value at risk, and risk budgeting can be employed for measuring or managing risk. Here, volatility is used as the risk metric.

ASSET-FOCUSED RISK MANAGEMENT: The portfolio manager could consider the volatility of the rate of return on the plan's assets as a measure of its riskiness when the risk of a DB plan is measured using assets only. In this context, cash and cash equivalents are considered riskless. Subject to the plan sponsor's degree of risk tolerance and other constraints (e.g., liquidity needs), optimal allocations are created so that the portfolio can earn the maximum expected return.

ASSET–LIABILITY RISK MANAGEMENT PERSPECTIVE: The risk of the DB plan is measured in terms of the volatility of its surplus from an asset–liability perspective. For example, suppose the plan's assets and liabilities at time t are given by A_t and L_t, respectively. Then the risk from an asset–liability framework can be measured using the standard deviation of $(A_t - L_t)$. Everything else being the same, the standard deviation is lower as the correlation between assets and liabilities increases. Therefore, in this context, cash or cash equivalents are not risk-minimizing assets. An asset that is volatile but positively correlated with changes in liabilities is considered to have a lower risk.

INTEGRATED ASSET–LIABILITY RISK MANAGEMENT: The plan's funding status is considered with the plan sponsor's operations in an integrated approach to risk management. In this case, it is recognized that future short-falls in the plan's funding status are likely to require larger contributions by the plan sponsor. Therefore, everything else being the same, it will be desirable if there is a negative correlation between $(A_t - L_t)$ and profitability of the plan sponsor. If a negative correlation is achieved, as a result, whenever there is a decline in $(A_t - L_t)$, there is likely to be an increase in the firm's profitability, making it easier for the firm to contribute to the plan. In this context, an asset that is positively correlated with liabilities may be con-sidered rather risky if it is positively correlated with the firm's operational strength as well.

There are other ways of measuring the riskiness of a pension fund in an integrated approach. For example, the plan sponsor may wish to reduce the volatility of the firm's equity. Equity is given by:

$$E_t = OA_t - OL_t + (A_t - L_t) \tag{13.1}$$

where E_t is the market value of the firm's equity, and OA_t and OL_t are the firm's operating assets and liabilities, respectively. In this context, the volatility of equity will depend on the correlations between the changes in surplus, operating assets, and operating liabilities. In particular, everything else being the same, assets that have low correlations with operating assets and high correlations with operating liabilities are considered less risky.

13.2.2 Four Factors Driving the Impact of Liabilities on a Plan's Risk

The primary liabilities of a pension plan are the benefits due to participants. Unless the fund measures risk from an assets-only perspective, changes in the plan's liabilities affect the plan's measure of riskiness. Four factors impact the value of liabilities the most: interest rates, inflation, retirement cycle, and mortality.

CHANGES IN INTEREST RATES are the most important factor, as they affect the discount rate used to calculate the present value of future obligations. A decline in interest rates will increase the present value of future liabilities.

INFLATION affects the future value of liabilities to the degree that benefits are directly or indirectly affected by inflation. For instance, pension bene-fits are typically tied to salary, and salaries tend to increase with inflation. In some cases, benefits might be tied to inflation directly through cost of living adjustments.

THE RETIREMENT CYCLE is the third factor, which tends to require modelling necessary data to include the age profile of employees, the firm's retirement policy, and the number of employees who are likely to retire in future years. However, some determinants may be difficult to predict, such as changes in the economic environment, the number of future employees and their tenure at the firm, if the firm reduces staff in a recession, or if employees leave during times of economic growth to seek other employment.

MORTALITY RATE is the final factor affecting liabilities. While longevity risk (i.e., a declining mortality rate) can pose a serious threat to the long-term financial viability of a DB plan, the risk is somewhat predictable and may have a small influence on the value of the liabilities in the short run.

13.2.3 Five Major Factors Affecting the Risk Tolerance of the Plan Sponsor

Having discussed various ways of measuring the riskiness of a fund, the next step is to examine factors that affect the risk tolerance of the plan sponsor. Five factors have the most impact on a plan sponsor's risk tolerance: the funding status of the plan, the size of the plan, the expected size of future contributions relative to the employer's cash flow, the employer's financial position, and the employees' characteristics.

THE DB PLAN CAN BE OVERFUNDED, UNDERFUNDED, OR FULLY FUNDED. In general, the larger the deficit, the less tolerance for risk the plan sponsor is likely to have. It is important to note that this does not mean that an underfunded plan will always be less risky. The amount of risk assumed by the plan is determined by the interaction of the sponsor's tolerance for risk and its objective. For instance, consider a slightly underfunded plan, where the plan sponsor has a low tolerance for risk. To improve the plan's funded status, the sponsor will have to assume some risk if the objective is to earn a higher rate of return than the growth rate of liabilities.

THE SIZE OF THE PLAN influences the sponsor's risk tolerance. The risk tolerance of the plan sponsor rises with the size of the plan's liabilities relative to the size of the sponsor's assets.

THE EXPECTED SIZE OF FUTURE CONTRIBUTIONS RELATIVE TO PROJECTED FREE CASH FLOWS is the third factor that influences the sponsor's risk tolerance. If the sponsor is expected to generate significant free cash flows in the future, then its capacity to take risk increases. The sponsor should evaluate the projected annual contributions that will be needed to cover current and future obligations. These potential contributions must then be compared to the firm's future free cash flows. If the future free cash flows are relatively small, then the firm's tolerance for risk is reduced.

THE SPONSOR'S FINANCIAL POSITION, including the potential free cash flows expected to be generated by the firm, is the fourth factor. Plan sponsors with a high debt-to-equity ratio will have a lower tolerance for risk. Not only are these organizations already exposed to business fluctuations, but they will not be able to issue debt to contribute to the fund. Employers that have little debt on their balance sheets may find it advantageous to issue debt to contribute to the fund.

THE DEMOGRAPHICS OF THE EMPLOYEES is the final factor affecting the sponsor's risk tolerance. In general, sponsors that have younger employees tend to have more tolerance for risk. The primary reason for this is that that there is more time to reduce any potential shortfall in the fund's assets. On the other hand, an employer with an aging workforce will have a smaller capacity for risk tolerance. Also, an aging workforce increases the sponsor's needs to have enough liquidity in the fund, which reduces the tolerance for liquidity risk.

13.2.4   Strategic Asset Allocation of a Pension Plan Using Two Buckets

As discussed in Chapter 11, the next step after evaluating the asset owner's objectives is to develop an investment policy statement. In an ASSET–LIABILITY framework, the focus will be on the relation between assets and liabilities. A simple approach to creating a strategic asset allocation for a DB plan is to consider the entire portfolio as consisting of two separate buckets: a hedging bucket and a growth bucket.[1]

The hedging portfolio bucket is created to mimic the growth of the liabilities. The goal is to reduce the volatility of the fund's surplus. This hedging portfolio is likely to consist of allocations to asset classes with returns that are negatively correlated with changes in interest rates, positively correlated with the inflation rate, and positively correlated with increased longevity in the population. For instance, a combination of long-term bonds, inflation-indexed bonds, healthcare stocks, or longevity-related derivatives could be used to create the hedging bucket. In addition, the investment policy statement may consider the correlation between the hedging portfolio and the sponsor's operating revenues. In this case, the hedging portfolio's return should not be highly correlated with changes in the sponsor's future free cash flows.

Three approaches may be used to create the hedging bucket in the ASSET–LIABILITY framework: duration matching, cash flow matching, and overlay. In the **duration matching approach,** the duration of the hedging bucket is matched to the duration of the liabilities. The approach is simple to implement but requires careful monitoring as changes in the yield curve and credit spreads will impact the duration of assets and therefore the portfolio will have to be rebalanced.

In the **cash flow matching approach,** the hedging portfolio is constructed such that its estimated future cash inflows match the expected outflows associated with liabilities at each prospective point in time. Compared to duration matching, this approach is harder to implement because appropriate instruments to match cash-flows at each perspective point in time may not be available. For example, very long-term zero-coupon bonds may not be available and may be costly to create using strips, which are principal-only securities created when the interest and principal of a bond are separated or stripped.

In the **overlay approach,** the plan sponsor employs finance derivatives to create a hedging bucket. It is important to note that this could lead to leveraged positions which will increase the overall risk of the portfolio. A potential advantage of this approach is that the sponsor might be able to create the hedging bucket without the need to sell portions of the growth bucket. For instance, the fund can enter into an interest rate swap to receive the fixed rate and pay the variable rate. If interest rates decline, the portfolio will benefit from the swap position as the value of liabilities increases. If the sponsor can maintain its allocation to the growth bucket, it may be able to benefit from outperformance by the growth portfolio.

The growth bucket is constructed with the expectation that it will outperform the liabilities and therefore reduce the sponsor's future contributions to the fund. The size of the allocation to the growth bucket depends on the capacity of the sponsor to assume some surplus risk. As the sponsor's tolerance for risk increases, two courses of action may be deemed appropriate. First, a larger portion of the overall assets can be allocated to the growth bucket. In this case, the riskiness of the growth bucket is held constant, but a larger portion of the portfolio is allocated to it. Second, the sponsor can decide to keep the relative sizes of hedging and growth buckets unchanged, but increase the growth bucket's allocations to less liquid and riskier asset classes in order to earn a higher rate of return. For instance, the sponsor may decide to increase allocations to private equity, timber, private real estate, and hedge funds with long lockups.

13.3 DEFINED BENEFIT PLANS

DB plans provide a guaranteed income to retirees, but the investment risk can increase the liabilities of employers. In a **defined benefit plan,** the employer takes all of the investment risk while offering a guaranteed, formulaic benefit to retirees.

For example, consider an employer that offers a retirement benefit of 1.5% of salary for each year the employee worked before retirement. Typically the salary used to calculate the benefit is based on a simple formula such as the average annual salary over the final 3 years of employment. If the salary to which the benefits apply is $50,000, and the employee has worked for 40 years, the retiree will be paid retirement benefits in the amount of $30,000 per year (15% × 40 years × $50,000) for the rest of the retiree's life. This provides the worker with a **retirement income-replacement ratio** of 60%, which is the pension benefit as a portion of final salary.

13.3.1 Pension Plan Portability and Job Mobility

DB plans are not portable. A plan is **portable** if benefits earned at one employer can continue to be accrued at another employer. In many cases, workers who die before retirement age receive no benefits from a DB plan and their heirs receive no lump sum or recurring benefit payments.

DB plans reward employees who spend their entire career with a single employer and punish workers who exercise job mobility. Contrast an employee who worked for 40 years at one firm to another employee who worked 20 years at each of two employers. Each employer provides a benefit of 1.5% of the average of the final 5 years of salary multiplied by the number of years of service. The worker started with an income of $15,787 in 1975 and retired in 2015 with an income of $50,000 after receiving annual salary increases of 3% over 40 years. If the worker served her entire career with one employer, the annual benefit would be $28,302 (1.5% × 40 years × the final 5-year salary average of $47,171). The benefits would be quite different had she worked for two employers. The retiree worked at the first employer from 1975 to 1995, with an average annual salary in the final 5 years of $26,117.

The annual benefits of $7,835 ($1.5\% \times 20$ years $\times \$26,117$) are determined in 1995, but not paid until retirement in 2015. The second employer pays annual benefits in the amount of $14,151 ($1.5\% \times 20$ years $\times \$47,171$).

Compared to the annual benefit of $28,302 after working the entire career for a single employer, the employee splitting careers between two firms earns an annual pension of only $21,986 ($7,835 plus $14,151), which is $6,316 per year less than if she had worked for a single firm.

A lack of portability may be an even greater issue for an employee who works a large number of jobs in a career, as many companies have vesting periods of 5 to 10 years. An employee must work for the entire vesting period to earn any retirement benefits. In a worst-case scenario, consider an employee who worked for 45 years, serving 9 years at each of five employers. If each employer required a minimum of 10 years of service to qualify for a DB pension, the employee would have earned no retirement benefits, even after working for 45 years at firms offering DB plans.

13.3.2 Defining Liabilities: Accumulated Benefit Obligation and Projected Benefit Obligation

It can be challenging to model the liability of an employer's DB plan. Estimating the value of the liability is important to plan for future benefit payments. A number of assumptions need to be made to calculate the amount owed in retiree benefits. These assumptions include:

- The amount of employee turnover and the years of service at the date of separation.
- Average wages at retirement, which requires the current wage, estimated retirement age, and annual wage inflation from today until retirement.
- The assumed age of employee death, as the number of years of benefits to be paid is the difference between the age at retirement and the age at death.
- The number of current employees, future employees, and their ages.

The **accumulated benefit obligation (ABO)** is the present value of the amount of benefits currently accumulated by workers and retirees. This number may be very small for a young firm with young workers, such as a 4-year-old technology startup filled with young college graduates. In this scenario, current workers have had only 4 years to accrue benefits and the firm may not anticipate retirements for another 40 years. The ABO is relatively easy to calculate, as the number of workers, their tenure, and average salary are all known. Of course, future wage growth and the average employee life span need to be estimated.

The **projected benefit obligation (PBO)** is the present value of the amount of benefits assumed to be paid to all future retirees of the firm. This number is much more challenging to calculate, as the number of workers at the firm in the future, employee turnover levels, future wage levels, and years of service are unknowns. As long as the company has current employees, the PBO is always greater than or equal to the ABO. When the firm and its employees are young, the ABO may be much smaller than the PBO. For example, the PBO may assume 40 years of service whereas employees at the young firm have accrued only 4 years of service. In a mature firm with a large number of retirees and an older workforce, the ABO will be of a similar magnitude to the PBO. The difference between the ABO and the PBO is also based on the current versus future salaries and years of service of current employees.

13.3.3 Funded Status and Surplus Risk

The **funded status** of a pension plan is a measure of the plan's current assets compared to its projected benefit obligation (PBO) or accumulated benefit obligation (ABO). The funded status may be expressed in terms of currency, such as €2 billion under-funded, or in percentage terms, such as 70% funded (or 30% underfunded) if a plan's assets are 70% of the PBO. Plans that are 100% funded are said to be fully funded. Overfunded plans, such as those with assets of 120% of PBO, may attract attention from employees who would like to receive larger benefits, or from corporate merger partners who may wish to disband the pension and keep the surplus value. Under-funded plans, such as those where assets are 70% of the PBO, may require larger employer contributions and may attract regulatory scrutiny.

The funded status of pension plans can vary sharply over time, as shown in Exhibit 13.2. The assets of the plan grow with employer contributions, decline with retiree benefit payments, and, most importantly, change daily with returns to the investment portfolio. The PBO also changes over time, as the present value factor is based on corporate bond yields. As corporate bond yields rise, the PBO declines. Conversely, declines in corporate bond yields lead to an increasing PBO. The effects of changing discount rates on PBOs can be dramatic. Consider the FTSE Pension Liability Index which tracks corporate bond yields that can be used to discount future values of the PBO. At December 31, 2009, the discount rate was 5.98%, by year end 2018, the discount rate had fallen to 4.22%. The pension plan's PBO can be compared to a short position in corporate bonds, which will change in value by the approximate amount of:

$$\%\text{Change in Liabilities} = -\text{Modified Duration} \times \text{Change in Yield} \qquad (13.2)$$

The duration of the PBO was estimated to be 16.2 years. Over the time period 2009–18, the 1.76% decline in corporate bond yields led to an increase of 28.5% in the PBO, assuming that duration and future benefits assumptions remain unchanged.

$$28.5\% = -16.2 \times (-1.76)$$

Note that Exhibit 13.2 funding ratios have improved due to very healthy global equity market returns over the last decade. The UK estimate of full pension buy-outs is the assets in the pension plan compared to the cost of fully purchasing the promised annuity pension benefits from an insurance company.

The **pension surplus** is the amount of assets in excess of a pension plan's projected pension benefit (PBO). The **surplus risk** of a pension plan is the economic exposure to the spread between the assets and liabilities of a pension plan and can be measured as the volatility and tracking error of the difference between the value of the assets relative to the present value of the liabilities. Consider the example in Exhibit 13.3, where assets are assumed invested 60% in the S&P 500 and 40% in the Barclays Aggregate Bond Index. The liabilities are assumed to have a duration of 16.2 years and a discount rate tracked by the FTSE Pension Liability Index. From 1997 to 2018,

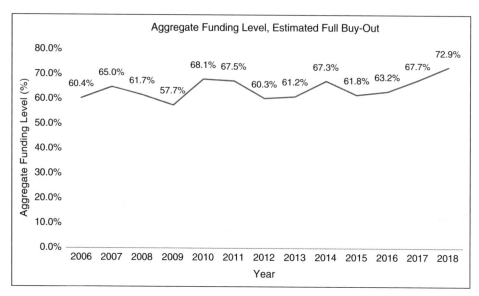

EXHIBIT 13.2   Aggregate Funding Level of UK Pensions
Source: The Purple Book (Pension Protection Fund, 2018).

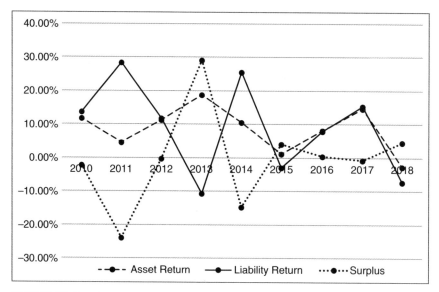

EXHIBIT 13.3   The Volatility of Pension Assets and Liabilities Creates Surplus Risk
Source: Authors' calculations based on returns to the S&P 500, Barclays Aggregate
Bond Index, and the FTSE Pension Liability Index.

the volatility of the asset portfolio was 7.2%, while the volatility of liabilities based only on the change in corporate bond yields was 11.1%. Because assets and liabilities had a correlation of −0.09 over this period, the surplus risk was even higher, as the volatility of the annual difference between asset and liability returns was 13.7%.

APPLICATION 13.3.3

Consider a DB plan that on January 1 has plan assets of $1 billion and is $0.2 billion underfunded. The plan's liabilities have a modified duration of 15 years. Assume that on January 2 of the same year the discount rate used to value the pension plan's projected benefit obligation fell by 2% and the portfolio's asset portfolio suffered a 10% loss. Based only on these assumptions, what would be the plan's funding status after the market events?

The liability originally at $1.2 billion ($1.0 billion + $0.2 billion) rises to: $1.2 billion − (−0.02 × $1.2 billion × 15.0) = $1.56 billion. The plan's assets fall by 10% to $0.9 billion. The plan would be $0.66 billion underfunded after the events.

Low investment returns and rising regulatory pressure may have motivated many employers to no longer offer DB plans. Employers that continue to provide DB plans are willing to experience surplus risk on their balance sheets and the variability of contributions to employee retirement plans. These employers will see pension costs rise during times of low investment returns; however, they will also earn the upside during times of high investment returns.

13.3.4 Why Defined Benefit Plans Are Withering

Each pension plan has a forward-looking return assumption that is used to calculate the employer's annual contribution. As shown in Exhibit 13.4, all of the 129 US public pension plans surveyed by the National Association of State Retirement Administrators (NASRA) and the National Council on Teacher Retirement (NCTR) used return assumptions of 8% or less in 2019, with only 4.65% using an estimate of 8%. Note that return estimates have been falling in recent years, as 44% of pensions used an 8% return assumption in 2010. Should actual long-term investment returns fall below this assumed return, either the plan will become underfunded or additional employer contributions will be required. The required (or projected) return is also a key driver of asset allocation, as investment policy is set in an attempt to earn the required return. That is, plans with higher return assumptions may pursue a more aggressive asset allocation to earn the investment profits needed to justify the current levels of benefits promised and the employer contributions.

Plan sponsors, whether in the public or private sector, are increasingly becoming concerned about the affordability of DB plans. While corporate plan sponsors use a corporate bond yield as the discount rate, public plans use the required projected return assumption as the discount rate. The calculations underlying Exhibit 13.3 show an average annual return on assets of 7.2% from 1997 to 2018 during a time period in which liabilities were increasing. When the public plan sponsor is making

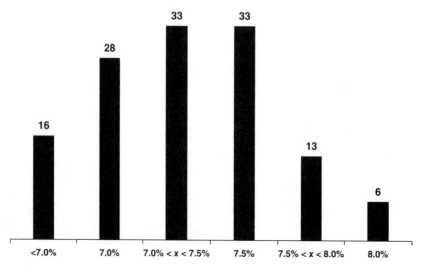

EXHIBIT 13.4　Distribution of Investment Return Assumptions
Source: NASRA, 2019 (updated February 2020).

contributions based on an 8% required return and actual returns are substantially lower, funded ratios will decrease over time.

Regulatory changes, at least in the US, are also making corporate DB plans less attractive. The Pension Protection Act of 2006 requires that corporate employers disclose the plan's funded status to plan participants. The Act also requires employer contributions to be commensurate with the funding status, with underfunded plans requiring greater contributions and overfunded plans requiring lower contributions. Underfunded plans must increase required contributions by an amount that projects the plan to be fully funded within 7 years. Investors are also concerned about the risk of investing in the equity securities of companies with underfunded pensions. The funded status of US pension plans is now required to be disclosed on corporate balance sheets. Employees are also concerned about DB plans. The declining number of DB plans offered by companies and their lack of portability make such plans less relevant today. Employees are working at a greater number of firms during their careers than did previous generations. It is therefore difficult for the majority of younger workers to accrue meaningful retirement income under a DB system. As a result, DB plans are declining as a share of assets among US pension plans.

Should a plan sponsor no longer wish to offer a DB plan to its employees, it has the option to freeze or terminate the plan. As a less drastic measure, the employer may move to a two-tier structure, offering newly hired employees a less generous pension benefit than previously hired employees. A **frozen pension plan** is one where employees scheduled to receive defined benefit pension benefits will no longer continue to accrue additional years of service in the plan. An employee with 20 years of service when the plan is frozen might retire 5 years later with 25 years of service, but the benefits would be tied to only 20 years of service. A **terminated pension plan** is no longer operated by the employer. Once a plan has been terminated, all assets leave the control of the employer and are either paid out in lump sums to employees or used to purchase annuities that will pay future benefits to retirees.

13.3.5 Asset Allocation and Liability-Driven Investing

Pension plan sponsors have conflicting goals when designing the asset allocation of the plan. The first goal is to earn a high return on pension assets, which will be used to reduce the employer's long-term contributions required to fund employee benefits. The second goal is to minimize the risk of underfunding (i.e., the amount of surplus risk incurred in the plan). As can be seen in Exhibit 13.5, Preqin surveyed a large number of institutional investors, noting the size of their allocation to alternative investments. Endowments and foundations (averaged here from Preqin data) and sovereign wealth funds are the leaders in allocating to alternative investments. While endowments and foundations and sovereign wealth funds may have reached the maximum practical allocation to alternative investments, it appears that pension plans are continuing to grow their allocations to alternative investments.

While investing in equity and alternative investments may earn higher long-term returns, these risky assets are subject to substantial short-term volatility, whether measured against a benchmark of zero, the plan's required return, or the change in the present value of the plan's liabilities. Companies wishing to reduce surplus risk may choose a very large fixed-income allocation. While this reduces surplus risk, the large fixed-income allocation reduces the likely return on assets, which increases the plan sponsor's long-term contributions, assuming the plan is less than fully funded.

13.3.6 Liability-Driven Pension Investing

Liability-driven investing (LDI) seeks to reduce surplus volatility by building a portfolio of assets that produces returns that are highly correlated with the change in the plan's liabilities. The simplest way to immunize pension liabilities is to invest in a corporate bond portfolio with a duration matching that of the liabilities. Other ways to reduce surplus risk include derivatives overlays, such as a swap receiving long-duration bond returns or a swaption that increases in value as interest rates decline.

Meder and Staub (2007) discuss the asset allocation necessary to hedge the ABO and PBO exposures. The ABO does not count future benefit accruals; it simply has exposure to declining nominal bond rates, which increases the present value of benefit payments. The PBO is more complicated, as future wage inflation may be correlated to both equities and inflation rates. Employers with younger workers may prefer have a higher allocation to equities. Some plans offer retirees a **cost of living adjustment**

EXHIBIT 13.5 Average Assets Allocated to Alternative Investments by Institutional Investors

	Private Pensions	Public Pensions	Sovereign Wealth Funds	Endowments and Foundations
Private Equity	4.71%	6.52%	14.57%	10.09%
Hedge Funds	10.81%	7.99%	8.98%	18.55%
Real Estate	8.39%	9.96%	8.74%	6.48%
Infrastructure	2.65%	3.30%	12.34%	3.31%
Total	26.55%	27.77%	44.62%	38.43%

Source: Preqin (2019).

(COLA), which increases the benefits paid to employees along with the rate of inflation. For example, consider a retiree earning a COLA pension of $2,000 per month.
After 5 years of 4% inflation rates and a 75% COLA (75% of 4%), the retiree's
pension will have risen by 3% per year to $2,318 per month. Plans offering benefits
with large percentage COLA adjustments would need to have large allocations to
inflation-protected assets, in order to reduce surplus risk.

Investors, then, may wish to protect their portfolios against inflation without
earning the low real returns offered by inflation-protected assets. A growing
number of investors are turning to real assets to gain inflation protection while
attempting to earn higher returns than offered by inflation-protected bonds, such
as Treasury Inflation-Protected Securities (TIPS). **Inflation-protected bonds** earn a
nominal coupon while the principal value rises with the rate of inflation. Their total
return tends to be low. Martin (2010) demonstrates that a number of real assets
can serve as long-horizon inflation hedges, including commodities, timber, and
farmland. Equities have not served in the past as a good hedge against long-horizon
inflation. It is uncertain whether infrastructure, real estate, or intellectual property
investments will be good hedges against inflation in the future. Specific investment
characteristics, such as revenues tied to inflation and fixed financing costs, improve
the potential of infrastructure or real estate to serve as an inflation hedge. Assets
with fixed-rate lease revenue and variable-rate debt expenses may actually be hurt
by inflation, even if they are real assets, such as real estate or infrastructure.

13.4 GOVERNMENTAL SOCIAL SECURITY PLANS

Government social security plans may provide retirement income to all previously
employed citizens of a given country, regardless of whether the worker was employed
in the public sector or in the private sector. The main requirements for earning benefits from these systems are that retirees must have worked for a minimum amount
of time, such as 10 years over the course of a career, and paid contributions into the
system.

Social security benefits are typically portable, meaning that employees continue
to accrue service credits whenever they are paying contributions into the system,
regardless of the number of employers in a career. Some employees, especially of
governmental entities, do not receive these benefits, as neither employees nor their
employers paid the required contribution.

DB plans often have benefits explicitly tied to employee income, without a cap on
the amount of benefits that may be earned. Social security plans are quite different, in
that there are caps on earnings, which means that retirees with lower career-average
incomes may earn a higher retirement income-replacement ratio than higher-income
retirees. This is a **progressive system,** where lower paid workers get relatively higher
benefits than those earned by higher paid workers when measured by a percentage
of salary. US workers retiring in 2019 at the age of 66 were eligible for a maximum
monthly retirement benefit of $2,861. This maximum benefit is paid to higher-income
workers, such as those with incomes over $132,900 in 2019. According to a 2015
study by the US Congressional Budget Office (CBO), workers born in the 1960s
are estimated to have a retirement income-replacement ratio of 82% for the lowest quintile of US workers, which declines to just 23% for the highest quintile of

workers based on their five highest years of earnings. Social security systems may also provide income security to the dependents of workers, paying benefits to the spouse or children of employees who die or become disabled during their working years.

13.5   CONTRASTING DEFINED BENEFIT AND CONTRIBUTION PLANS

Willis Towers Watson () estimates that global pension assets in 2016 were 49% DB plans and 48.4% DC plans. The mix between DB and DC plans varies widely by country, with 87% of Australian assets invested in DC plans, whereas 96% of Japanese assets are in DB plans. Using Investment Company Institute (ICI) (2019) estimates, assets in US DB and other plan assets of $8,600 billion are now smaller than the combined $16,200 billion in DC and individual retirement account assets.

13.5.1   Defined Contribution Plans

A **defined contribution plan** is offered by employers, where the employer and/or employee make a specified contribution on behalf of each covered employee on a regular basis, such as a percentage of the employee's salary. In a DC plan, there is no surplus risk for the employer, as assets always match liabilities. A common structure for a DC plan is one in which an employer offers each employee an annual amount of perhaps 3% of salary, with perhaps a matching contribution of, say, 50% of the amount contributed by the employee. A **matching contribution** is a voluntary contribution made by an employee that is augmented by additional contributions by the employer. For example, an employee will contribute 6% of salary to the DC plan while the employer will contribute 3% plus a matching contribution of 3% (50% of 6%). This employee would place 6% of salary into a retirement account, which, combined with the firm's contribution of 6%, totals a 12% contribution.

13.5.2   Plan Differences in Portability, Longevity Risk, and Investment Options

In contrast to DB plans, DC plans are portable, meaning that the employer contributions become the asset of the employee once the vesting period is completed. This portability is better for employees who work multiple jobs in a career, and for employees who work for firms that may not have the financial strength to pay long-term pension benefits in the amount promised. When leaving an employer, the employee is able to roll over the balance in the DC plan into the plan offered by the next employer or into an individual retirement account. Given that DC plans are personal accounts, the employee contribution, investment gains, and vested portion of employer contributions can be bequeathed to the employee's heirs should the employee die before retirement.

In a DB plan, the longevity risk is incurred by the employer. The employee is guaranteed the monthly benefit for life, whether that life is longer or shorter than anticipated. This means that employees cannot outlive their pension. In a DC plan, however, there is no guarantee as to the amount of assets accumulated or the amount of monthly income in retirement, meaning that longevity risks are borne by the employee. Employees with low contributions, low investment returns, or long lives may have a significant probability of outliving their assets, meaning that their assets may be exhausted or their spending rate curtailed in their final years of life.

The employer makes the asset allocation decisions in a DB plan, but asset allocation decisions in DC plans are made by the employees, typically using the fund choices provided by the employer. The employer may offer a range of investment choices, such as up to 20 mutual funds. Fees inside DC plans vary widely based on the funds offered by the employer and the funds selected by the employee.

13.5.3 Asset Allocation in Defined Contribution Plans

It is the employee's decision as to how to allocate the assets across the allowed investment choices. Leaving the decision-making to employees, most of whom are not trained in making investment decisions, can lead to a wide variety of employee outcomes. Some employees may retire without any retirement assets, either because they did not choose to participate in the plan or because they were allowed to invest all of their assets in their employer's stock, which ended up worthless at the end of a bankruptcy proceeding. Some employers may offer the option of a brokerage window, which allows employees to invest in a broader variety of mutual funds, or even individual stocks. While employees with a high degree of financial sophistication can benefit from a brokerage window, the sheer number of options or the ability to concentrate risk in more narrow investments can cause excessive risk for some plan participants.

On the other hand, a diligent saver with good investment returns can potentially earn a larger retirement benefit in a DC plan than in a DB plan. In the earlier example, the employee started with a salary of $15,787 and worked for 40 years, before retiring at a final salary of $50,000 with a single-employer DB pension plan income of $28,302. Assume that the same employee, when covered by a DC plan, invested 6% of her salary and received employer contributions of the same amount. Assuming salary raises of 3% per year, investment returns of 8% per year, and combined annual contributions in the amount of 12% of salary, the employee would have accumulated more than $699,000 at retirement. This amount includes employee and employer contributions of approximately $71,400 each over the course of the career and over $550,000 in investment earnings. With a spending rate of just 4.05%, the employee would earn the same amount as the DB pension plan income of $28,302. If the DC account earned annual returns of at least 4.05% during retirement, the nominal value of the retirement account would either be stable or rising for the rest of the employee's life. The principal balance, at the date of death, would be passed on to the retiree's heirs.

In contrast, most DB plans do not offer value to the family of the retiree, unless there is a promise to pay some portion of the pension income for the rest of the spouse's life. For a diligent saver who was blessed with high investment returns over the course of a career, the DC plan is often superior to a DB plan, in terms of both portability and the ability to pass significant assets along to heirs. Unfortunately, many DC plan participants either save too little or invest too conservatively and end up faced with the prospect of earning far fewer benefits from the DC plan than if the employee had worked for a single employer offering a DB plan. When plan participants have the ability to withdraw from or borrow against the assets in the DC plan before retirement, it may be even more difficult to accumulate the assets necessary to ensure a strong income during retirement.

Given that employees are making their own investment decisions, many employers offer simple fund choices for DC plan participants. In some cases, employees are allowed only the choice to allocate assets across domestic stocks, domestic bonds, cash, and global stocks. Other plans will allow participants to invest in equity securities of the employer, as well as more than 20 funds in a variety of geographies or asset classes.

Employees do not generally allocate DC plan assets in the same careful way that professional managers allocate DB plan assets. Employees sometimes invest in just a single fund, resulting in a 100% equity or 100% cash allocation, or they diversify contributions equally across many or all investment choices. Employees also do not frequently rebalance or change allocations when their investment needs become more conservative as retirement approaches. This lack of rebalancing results in a **drifting asset allocation,** where the allocations to asset classes change based on returns of each asset class with the highest-returning asset classes growing as a share of the portfolio. For example, an employee may have decided at age 30 to direct 70% of contributions to an equity fund and 30% to a fixed-income fund, given his investment preferences at the time. If stock returns were substantially higher than bond returns over the next 20 years, the now 50-year-old employee may find himself with a portfolio with 85% equity and 15% fixed-income allocations at a time when a 60% equity, 40% bond mix may be more appropriate for his circumstances.

13.5.4 Target-Date Funds and Alternative Investments within Pension Plans

Given that most DC plan participants are not accredited investors, few DC plans offer private placement alternative vehicles such as private equity. The limited number of fund choices in DC plans reduces diversification potential and the ability to switch to funds with better performance. Due to a lack of investor sophistication as well as regulatory restrictions, most DC plan participants do not have the ability to invest directly in alternative investments. When alternative investment choices are offered in DC plans, they typically focus on commodities or real estate. It is quite rare for individual employees to be able to invest in private equity or hedge funds through DC plans.

In the United States, after the Pension Protection Act of 2006, many employers made changes to their DC plans' designs in order to alleviate a number of problems with DC plan investments. In the past, employers may not have mandated DC plan participation, and when they did, all employee contributions were placed in cash, unless otherwise directed by the employee. Recently, employers have been automatically enrolling new employees in DC plans, setting the employee contribution at 1% to 3% of salary, and automatically increasing annual contributions by one-third of the employee's salary increase. For example, an employee contributing 2% of salary would have a contribution rate of 4% after earning 3% salary increases for 2 years. Finally, the default investment option may now be a target-date fund, rather than cash.

A **target-date fund** has risks that are managed relative to a specified horizon date, which allows employees to choose a single investment option without needing to rebalance or change investments as the horizon date approaches. A young employee hired in 2020 might invest in a target-date fund, anticipating retirement in the year 2060, while an employee approaching retirement may be invested in a fund targeting a retirement date of 2025. The 2060 target-date fund assumes that a young employee with an average risk tolerance may be invested 85% in equity and 15% in fixed income. This asset allocation would be regularly rebalanced by the fund manager, following a **glide path** where the allocation becomes more conservative over time. Ultimately, the 2060 fund (in 2055) would resemble the 2025 fund (today), with a more conservative asset allocation of matching the investment needs of an individual approaching retirement. Target-date funds are often managed as a fund of funds structure, with a mutual fund company allocating assets to between 3 and 20 mutual funds managed by the mutual fund firm. In this structure, funds with private equity, hedge funds, commodity, or real estate investments may be included in the target-date products at allocations between 5% and 20%.

While most DC plans do not offer alternatives as investment options, Kupperman and Kilgallen (2015) suggest that target-date funds investing in liquid alternative investments are likely to grow the ability for DC investors to allocate to alternatives. However, alternative investments are more likely to be held as an allocation within the professionally managed target-date funds than to be made available to plan participants as standalone investment options.

13.6   ANNUITIES FOR RETIREMENT INCOME

This section discusses annuities, which have two related major definitions. An annuity is often defined as any fixed stream of cash flows. Annuities also refer to specific insurance products that contain features that enable payouts in the form of a stream of cash flows.

13.6.1   Financial Phases Relative to Retirement

When individuals are working, they are in the **accumulation phase** of their lives where they are saving a portion of their income and growing their assets to provide for a comfortable retirement. After retirement, the ability to earn income declines substantially, and the investor enters the **decumulation phase,** where assets are drawn down to support spending during retirement. In the accumulation phase, income should exceed spending, so that during retirement the employee can have spending greater than income. Many retirees will not outlive their assets and will be able to bequeath assets to their heirs or charitable causes. However, some retirees will deplete their assets. These investors face longevity risk, in that a longer than expected lifetime will be highly likely to deplete their assets when spending at the desired rate.

13.6.2   Three Important Risks to Retirees

Starting with a lump sum of assets at retirement, retirees face at least three important risks. First is longevity risk, where the longer the life of the retiree, the more likely he is to deplete his assets. Second, there is the market risk of the investments, where a substantial investment loss will deplete the retiree's assets faster than the desired rate. Third, there is the risk of inflation, where a fixed amount of spending each year buys fewer goods and services in a rising inflation rate environment.

Actuaries calculate **mortality tables,** which show the distribution of the expected age of death or probability of death for various current ages across a specified population. Mortality tables can be quite accurate for large populations of people, but can err substantially as the sample size gets smaller or the health or occupation of the measured lives changes. The maximum error in mortality tables is likely to be on the life of a single person, which can be much longer or shorter than expected, even if it is in the range of the population distribution of mortality.

All three of these risks are crucial when investors choose to manage their own assets in retirement. Consider an investor with $1,000,000 in assets at retirement and a need for $40,000 in annual income to support his expenses, which are likely to grow at the rate of inflation over time. Should he earn 6% annual returns on his investment portfolio while spending 4% of assets each year and experiencing a 2% inflation rate, he can meet his annual spending rate after inflation and still leave the real value of the $1,000,000 to his heirs. This same investor, however, would have a substantial problem if investment returns averaged zero over time, if inflation rose, and if he outlived his actuarially expected life. Should this investor (the US male previously described) spend an inflation-adjusted $40,000 each year, he will have exhausted his entire retirement savings at his life expectancy of 83 years old. Should he live longer than his expected lifetime, he will have experienced substantial longevity risk, living longer than his assets have actually lasted.

13.6.3   Estimating Exposure to Longevity Risk

A retiree could use the information provided by mortality tables along with some financial data about her retirement fund and the cost of living to obtain rough estimates of her exposure to longevity risk. The expected economic life of a retirement fund can be approximated by the following expression:

$$EL = \frac{1}{\ln(1 + R)} \times \ln\left(\frac{\text{Payment} - R \times \text{Assets}}{\text{Payment}}\right) \tag{13.3}$$

Here, EL is the expected economic life of the retirement fund measured in years, R is the annual net of fees real rate of return (i.e., after inflation) that the assets are expected to earn each year, payment is the first annual withdrawal, which is expected to increase at the annual rate of inflation, and Assets is the current value of the fund's assets. Note that Equation 13.3 is valid as long as $R \times Assets <$ Payment. If the annual cash generated by the investment is greater than the annual payment, (i.e., $R \times Assets >$ Payment), then the fund will last forever.

APPLICATION 13.6.3

Suppose that the market value of the retirement fund of an individual is €2,500,000. The annual net of fees real rate of return on the fund is estimated to be 3%, and the retiree wants to withdraw €200,000 in the first year, and an amount each year thereafter that will grow at the rate of inflation. What is the expected economic life of the fund? Using Equation 13.3:

$$EL = -\frac{1}{\ln(1 + 0.03)} \times \ln\left(\frac{200,000 - 0.03 \times 2,500,000}{200,000}\right) = 15.9 \text{ Years}$$

The fund is expected to last 15.9 years.

Retirees in good health with relatively small amounts of retirement savings may wish to purchase an annuity from an insurance company that can offer income for the owner's life. Sweeting (2014) reports that annuitization of retirement assets is compulsory in the UK, the Netherlands, Germany, and Italy. While voluntary annuitization may appeal to the most healthy retirees who hope to live longer than the mortality tables suggest, compulsory annuitization avoids this moral hazard and makes insurance company experience closer to the general population mortality tables.

13.6.4   Two Major Types of Annuities

In an **immediate annuity,** an investor pays a lump sum to an insurance company for cash flows starting in the first year of the contract and guaranteed for some period. Some retirees may purchase a lifetime income annuity, which pays a set amount of income for life. While the use of a lifetime income annuity reduces longevity risk by guaranteeing that the retiree will never run out of income, the entire cost of the annuity is paid to the insurance company with no residual value available to heirs. That is, whether the investor dies in 1 day or 30 years, no assets are left over after the investor has received income. This desire to leave assets for heirs has led to a low popularity of annuities in the US.

Ezra (2016) advocates the use of a deferred annuity, which he calls longevity insurance. In a **deferred annuity,** an investor pays a lump sum to an insurance company for cash flows that are scheduled to start at some date in the future. Because the cash flows from the insurance company start at some future date, perhaps in 11 years, the cost of the deferred annuity is lower than the cost of the immediate annuity. Investors choosing a deferred annuity can keep some portion of their assets in an investment portfolio designed to provide income for 11 years or longer, while using the deferred annuity to provide lifetime income at an advanced age when longevity risk is experienced and when they are more likely to deplete their resources.

13.6.5   Analysis of the Value of a Growth Annuity

Consider the present value of an ordinary annuity, where r is the discount rate, and n is the number of annual payments. Several present values of an ordinary (immediate)

EXHIBIT 13.6 Cost of Purchasing an Annuity to Provide $1,000 in Annual Income

	Immediate Fixed Annuity	11-Year Deferred Fixed Annuity	Immediate Annuity with Income Growing at 3% Inflation
20-Year Annuity, 5% Discount Rate	$12,462	$ 7,651	$15,965
20-Year Annuity, 2% Discount Rate	$16,351	$13,413	$21,546
30-Year Annuity, 5% Discount Rate	$15,372	$ 9,437	$21,920
30-Year Annuity, 2% Discount Rate	$22,396	$18,372	$34,002

annuity for various values of r and n are provided in the first column of Exhibit 13.1 based on Equation 13.4.

$$PV_{\text{Growing Annuity}} = \frac{\text{Payment}}{r} \times \left[1 - \frac{1}{(1+r)^n} \right] \tag{13.4}$$

$$PV_{\text{Growing Annuity}} = \frac{\text{Initial Payment}}{r-g} \times \left[1 - \left(\frac{1+g}{1+r} \right)^n \right] \tag{13.5}$$

APPLICATION 13.6.5

A pension plan offers a choice of a fixed $100,000 initial annual benefit or an $80,000 initial annual benefit that will grow by 3% per year. Using a market interest rate of 5%, calculate the present value of both alternatives based on life expectancy of 20 years (based on annual compounding).

Both alternatives can be valued using Equation 13.5 by using a zero growth rate for the fixed payment alternative and 3% for the growth alternative (as well as the different initial payments).

$$PV_{\text{Growing Annuity}} = \frac{\text{Initial Payment}}{r-g} \times \left[1 - \left(\frac{1+g}{1+r} \right)^n \right]$$

PV of Fixed = $2,000,000^*(1 - 0.376889) = $1,246,222

PV of Growing = $4,000,000^*(1 - 0.680704) = $1,277,184

The growth annuity has a slightly higher value. Note that the present value annuity formulas are highly intuitive and easily memorized. An annuity may be viewed as a perpetuity that is received today and lost after n years. The first term on the right side of the PV growing and annuity formula (above) is the initial value of a perpetuity. The last term subtracts out the future value of the perpetuity. This interpretation can be seen in the solutions shown where the perpetuity values ($2 million and $4 million) are reduced for the payments not received after 20 years.

Comparing the cost of the immediate, deferred, and immediate growing annuities in Exhibit 13.6 for various discount rates and payment periods gives an important illustration of interest rate risk, inflation risk, and longevity risk for a retiree or a pension plan. It also illustrates the reduced cost of a deferred annuity relative to a growing annuity.

When designing a pension plan or a personal investment strategy, investors need to be aware of the cost of market risk, longevity risk, and inflation risk. Regarding interest rate risk or market risk, compare the cost of an immediate fixed-rate annuity with 20 annual payments using a 2% discount rate relative to a 5% discount rate. As interest rates decline from 5% to 2%, the cost of providing $1,000 in annual income rises from $12,462 to $16,351 per retiree. Longevity risk can also be illustrated, as the cost of providing $1,000 payments at a 5% discount rate for 20 years is $12,462 while the present value of 30 annual payments is $15,372. Finally, compare the cost of a growing annuity to a fixed annuity. For 20 annual payments with a 5% discount rate, adding 2% annual inflation benefits increases the cost from $12,462 to $15,965 per retiree.

The cost of a lifetime annuity would typically be based on the life expectancy and discount rate assumed by the insurance company, likely comparable to the 20-year example for a 65-year-old male shown earlier.

13.7   CONCLUSION

Retirement income can be sponsored by a government benefits plan, a corporate DB plan, and/or a DC plan. Investors and plan sponsors consider the market risk of investments, the interest rate risk of liabilities, inflation risk, and the expected lifetime of the retiree.

NOTES

1. See "Pension Risk Management." Cambridge Associates LLC, Boston, MA, 2011.

REFERENCES

Congressional Budget Office. 2015. "CBO's 2015 Long-Term Projections for Social Security: Additional Information." https://www.cbo.gov/publication/51047.

Ezra, D. 2016. "Most People Need Longevity Insurance Rather than an Immediate Annuity." *Financial Analysts Journal* 72 (2): 23–29.

Investment Company Institute. 2019. *2019 Investment Company Fact Book*. https://www.ici .org/pdf/2019_factbook.pdf.

Kupperman, D. and S. Kilgallen. 2015. "The Case for Liquid Alternatives in Defined Contribution Plans." *Journal of Alternative Investments* 18 (1): 59–66.

Martin, G. 2010. "The Long-Horizon Benefits of Traditional and New Real Assets in the Institutional Portfolio." *Journal of Alternative Investments* 13 (1): 6–29.

Meder, A. and R. Staub. 2007. "Linking Pension Liabilities to Assets." *Society of Actuaries*. https://www.soa.org/globalassets/assets/library/journals/actuarial-practice-forum/2007/ october/apf-2007-10-meder-staub.pdf.

NASRA. 2019. Pension Plan Investment Return Assumptions, February 2019 (updated February 2020). https://www.nasra.org/files/Issue%20Briefs/NASRAInvReturnAssumptBrief.pdf.

Pension Protection Fund. 2018. The Purple Book. https://www.ppf.co.uk/news/purple-book-2018.

Preqin. 2019. Investor Outlook: Alternative Assets. https://docs.preqin.com/reports/Preqin-Investor-Outlook-Alternative-Assets-H1-2019.pdf.

Sweeting, P. 2014. "*The Future of Pensions: A Plan for Defined Contribution.*" White Paper. JPMorgan.

Thinking Ahead Institute, Willis Towers Watson. 2018.Institute World 300, Year End 2017.

CHAPTER 14

Sovereign Wealth Funds

This chapter covers Sovereign Wealth Funds (SWFs), which are rapidly amassing assets to become one of the world's largest categories of investors in traditional as well as alternative assets. SWFs are state-owned investment funds held for the purpose of future generations and/or to stabilize the state currency. SWFs controlled nearly $8 trillion in 2018, which is similar to the combined assets under management (AUM) of the entire hedge fund and private equity industries. With over $1.6 trillion invested in alternative assets, it is important to understand the investment goals of SWF investors.

14.1 SOURCES OF SOVEREIGN WEALTH

The creation of a SWF generally results from a nation having an excess of savings, usually a result of substantial budget surpluses over the course of many years, whether from favorable macroeconomic conditions, planning, and/or restraint. More specifically, the source of such wealth is often associated with natural resources (usually oil and gas, and, to a lesser extent, copper, diamonds, and phosphates), strong and reliable trade surpluses, or the receipt of foreign aid money. In fact, two broad categories are responsible for nearly all SWF assets: oil and/or gas and noncommodity sources.

14.1.1 Accounting for Changes in the Reserve Account

The **reserve account** of a central bank consists of the central bank's holdings of foreign currencies and is operated by the central bank to conduct transactions involving foreign currencies. A country's balance of payments measures the inflows and outflows of currency that facilitate each country's foreign transactions. The **balance of payments** considers three accounts, which must offset each other in any given year as depicted in Equation 14.1:

$$\Delta\text{Reserve Account} = \Delta\text{Current Account} + \Delta\text{Capital Account} \qquad (14.1)$$

where ΔReserve Account is the change in the reserve account, and Current Account and Capital Account are positive numbers for surpluses and negative numbers for deficits. For example, a country with a €300,000 current account surplus and a €200,000 capital account deficit would experience a €100,000 increase in its reserve account.

APPLICATION 14.1.1

Country A experiences a €100,000 drop in its reserve account while having a €300,000 surplus in its capital account. What was the current account surplus or deficit of country A? Inserting the known values into Equation 14.1 and solving for the current account surplus generates a value of −€400,000.

The current account measures trade in goods and services along with investment income and gifts, such as foreign aid. A country is said to have a **current account deficit** when the value of its imports of goods and services exceeds the value of its exports, meaning that more currency is flowing out of the country to purchase these goods and services than is flowing in from selling goods and services. The capital account measures investment flows, where foreigners buy assets in a country or make loans. A **capital account surplus** occurs in a country when the amount of imported capital exceeds the amount of exported capital.

If a country regularly imports more goods and services than it exports, it runs a current account deficit and is dependent on capital account transactions continuing to flow into the country to finance those deficits. For example, the United States tends to run a current account deficit and a capital account surplus. Residents of the United States tend to buy a far greater amount of imported goods and services than the US economy exports. In order to finance this excess consumption, US residents need to sell assets or borrow money. China has the opposite profile, with a current account surplus and a capital account deficit, as they export goods and use the proceeds to increase their ownership of foreign assets.

If there is a situation of capital flight and that causes a capital account deficit while the country still has a current account deficit, the country's official reserve account may need to be quickly drawn down to maintain the balance of payments. When a country attempts to maintain a fixed exchange rate, the reserve account may be exhausted. This was the cause of the 1997 currency crisis that led to large declines in the currencies of Thailand, Malaysia, and Indonesia.

14.1.2   Changes in the Reserve Account and Five Drivers of Currency Exchange Rates

In the case of a free-floating currency, a capital account surplus tends to roughly offset a current account deficit in any given year keeping the reserve account stable. The currency price will adjust to make imports of goods or exports of capital equally attractive. For example, if a country's exports seem to be cheaply priced, the amount of exports is likely to increase, which creates demand for that country's currency that is likely to lead to the currency's appreciation. When the currency is freely floating, the change in the government's foreign currency reserves tends to be small, as the currency market tends to bring equilibration to the capital account and the current account.

Like any other asset, currency prices are typically set by supply and demand. Gwartney et al. (2003) explain that a country's currency is likely to appreciate when the country has:

1. A lower inflation rate than its trading partners.
2. Higher real interest rates than its trading partners.
3. Policies that attract an inflow of capital.
4. Slower income growth versus trading partners that reduces the demand for imports.
5. A competitive or comparative advantage in export-oriented industries.

These five values tend to drive changes in the value of the currency of a country with a free-floating currency. For example, a country's free-floating currency is likely to appreciate in value when foreigners buy the assets and exports of that country at a greater rate than that country's residents buy the assets and exports of other countries.

14.1.3 Fixed versus Floating Rule Policies

A central bank can attempt to manage the value of its currency or fix the value of its currency relative to another currency. For example, suppose that a central bank is able to lower the value of its currency by 10% relative to other currencies while the nominal prices of goods and services are constant. The prices of imports to that country will be roughly 10% higher in terms of the domestic currency to that country's citizens, while exports from that country will be roughly 10% cheaper to citizens of other countries when measured in their currencies. The intended effects are to expand the country's exports and cut the country's imports.

When currency prices are not allowed to adjust freely due to market forces, the official reserve account can grow or shrink, as the current account and the capital account will not naturally balance. For example, the value of the Chinese yuan was pegged at 8.28 to the US dollar from 1994 until 2005. Over much of this period, it appeared that Chinese labor costs were low and the yuan was undervalued. With low labor costs and an undervalued currency, China built a very large export economy, which created demand for the yuan. As foreign residents purchased these Chinese exports, they created a demand for the undervalued yuan. In order to support the currency at the pegged rate, the Chinese government was selling yuan at its undervalued price and buying foreign currency, predominately US dollars and euros. By keeping the yuan undervalued, Chinese exports were underpriced and imports overpriced, creating greater incentives for Chinese consumers and businesses to save. The Chinese government then channeled these savings into their SWFs.

SWFs of countries with persistent current account surpluses, such as China, Hong Kong, and Singapore, have grown markedly. One reason why countries may wish to amass foreign currency reserves is that flows in the capital account and the current account tend to move at different speeds. Foreign trade flows and foreign direct investment can move rather slowly, as the value of the currency takes time to impact trading and real asset investment decisions. However, portfolio investment flows can move much more quickly. This makes it dangerous for a country to run a current account deficit and a capital account surplus.

14.1.4 Commodity Exports and the Reserve Account

Current account flows can be differentiated into flows from manufactured goods, services, and commodities. While many countries, especially in Asia, export goods and services to earn foreign currency revenue, other countries, especially in the Middle East, earn foreign currency revenues through the export of commodities, such as oil, gas, and copper. Economies that export goods and services may feel comfortable at projecting similar or growing export revenues from year to year, as it can be relatively easy to project prices and quantities of manufactured goods. Commodity producers, however, have no such certainty. Crude oil prices have a higher volatility than that of most equity markets and many other commodities, which can make it difficult for a country to predict the value of their exports in any given year.

Government revenues in many countries are tightly linked to oil prices, either because the oil company is state owned or because the state earns taxes on the corporate sale of energy commodities. In some Middle Eastern countries, the vast majority of state revenues are linked to the energy sector.

Commodity exporting countries have three key concerns regarding these tax revenues. First, the volatility of oil prices can create a volatile income stream for a sovereign state, which is clearly unwelcome, as government spending is much more stable than commodity prices. Second, it is unclear how long these commodity revenues will continue, as the commodities in the ground will not last forever. Specifically, there is a concern regarding **depletion,** which is the rate of extraction of a commodity relative to the remaining in-ground stocks. Third, governments would like to have a diversified economy, ideally earning tax revenues from other industries, such as technology, finance, and tourism, rather than relying almost exclusively on commodity revenues.

14.2   FOUR TYPES OF SOVEREIGN WEALTH FUNDS

This section discusses four types of SWFs: stabilization funds, savings funds, reserve funds, and development funds.

14.2.1   Stabilization Funds

When an economy is building reserves, the initial store of wealth should be held in cash and liquid fixed income securities. In most countries, this wealth is held by the central bank and not segregated into a SWF. The central bank typically has three uses for official reserves: (1) implementing monetary policy through increasing and decreasing interest rates by trading fixed income securities; (2) intervening in the foreign exchange market, either to keep a currency at a fixed rate or to move a floating currency toward a desired level; and (3) injecting liquidity into the banking system to prevent crises. Most countries keep reserves in a central bank or other macroeconomic stabilization agency rather than separating these assets into a SWF charged with economic stabilization.

Countries with substantial commodity revenues have a much greater need for a stabilization fund, as commodity revenues are typically more volatile than the currency prices and interest rates typically of concern to central bankers. It may be problematic for the government to experience massive cuts in revenue during times of low commodity prices. It can be disruptive if economies substantially increase or decrease spending as commodity revenues change, so many governments seek to have relatively stable government spending. A sovereign wealth **stabilization fund** serves a countercyclical purpose through collecting excess commodity revenues during times of high commodity prices, and distributing saved wealth during times of low commodity prices.

Alsweilem et al. (2013) discuss rules on the size of commodity revenues transferred from the general government budget into the stabilization fund. The easiest rule to implement and communicate is a fixed percentage, where the stabilization fund receives perhaps 20% of commodity revenues. Note that this is procyclical, where the government budget still receives higher revenues during times of higher commodity prices and lower revenues during times of lower commodity prices. Another rule is a hurdle price rule, where the stabilization fund receives all commodity revenue above a certain price, such as $50 per barrel. This will save the windfall revenues during the good times, but does not explicitly release stabilization funds into the government budget during times of low commodity prices. A final rule could be the deviation from a moving average rule, where commodity prices higher than a moving average rule move proceeds into the stabilization fund, while prices below a moving average move proceeds from the stabilization fund into the government budget.

14.2.2 Savings Funds

A sovereign state may wish to avoid the opportunity costs of investing entirely in cash and fixed income. Once the reserve adequacy standard has been met, a sovereign wealth savings fund may be created with a total return objective. Sovereign wealth **savings funds** are designed to bring intergenerational equity to a commodity-producing country by investing today's commodity revenues into a total return fund designed to benefit future generations. Similar to the university endowment funds described in Chapter 12, a spending rate can be instituted that provides income to future generations of beneficiaries while maintaining or growing the corpus of the fund. This is especially important in commodity-producing countries, as the commodity supplies may be depleted in 20, 50, or 150 years. The country sets up a savings fund to benefit from commodity sales long after the in-ground supplies have been exhausted. Savings funds may be specifically invested in foreign currency assets designed to match the global distribution of where imported goods are purchased or the currency in which foreign debt is issued.

14.2.3 Reserve Funds

Many SWFs don't have clearly defined liabilities beyond a level spending rate. However, sovereign wealth **pension reserve funds** are designed to invest for high total returns in preparation for estimated future pension-like liabilities. In contrast to traditional pension funds that are funded with employer and/or employee contributions, pension reserve funds in the SWF category are funded with the proceeds of commodity or manufactured goods exports.

Sovereign wealth **reserve investment funds** are included in a country's reserve accounting as part of its reserves, but the funds invest in a total return portfolio in order to overcome the opportunity costs of the cash and fixed income dominated stabilization funds. Kunzel et al. (2010) note that there are very few pension reserve and reserve investment funds, but those funds that do exist are very prominent (Korea Investment Corporation, China Investment Corporation, and Government of Singapore Investment Corporation).

14.2.4   Development Funds

Castelli and Scacciavillani (2012) describe sovereign wealth **development funds** as investment holding companies that have socio-economic objectives such as economic diversification, the development of strategic industries, or poverty alleviation. Development funds may focus on the domestic economy or choose to invest regionally or globally. Compared to reserve and savings funds, development funds may focus more on growing employment or diversifying the economy than on maximizing total returns. Development funds may be exclusively dedicated or largely allocated to alternative investments such as private equity and infrastructure.

Consider an economy where the majority of government revenue is derived from commodity exports. This economy is subject to volatile revenue streams as commodity prices and export volumes can vary dramatically over time. In addition, commodities are subject to depletion, where there is no guarantee how long the commodity reserves will continue to produce revenue. It is important, then, to diversify the economy beyond natural resources, such as Dubai has done by growing robust tourism and financial services industries. If and when the wells run dry, investments made by development funds will have ideally grown the economy to the point where it can be well supported by these noncommodity industries.

While savings and reserve funds seek to increase financial wealth that may be distributed in the future, development funds invest in infrastructure, human capital, and local industry to grow productivity and increase the future wealth of the country. These funds will typically be more concentrated, and may take on the flavor of private equity or even venture capital incubators.

Development funds bring a special set of conflicts to SWFs. Therefore, it is important to segregate the development fund from political influence and other government agencies. For example, there can be a temptation for the governmental agency responsible for developing infrastructure to promote fewer projects as they are waiting for the SWF to develop projects that should be the responsibility of the infrastructure agency. Like any good private equity fund, projects or investments in a development fund should be evaluated on a financial basis, where the projects with the highest probability of success or the greatest profit potential should be financed. In some countries, there may be pressure to invest based on personal relationships that are more likely to enrich a corrupt friend of a politician than to create wealth or jobs for a country.

14.3   ESTABLISHMENT AND MANAGEMENT OF SOVEREIGN WEALTH FUNDS

This section discusses why SWFs are established and how they are managed.

14.3.1   Four Common Motivations to Establishing a Sovereign Wealth Fund

There are four common motivations which may lead to the establishment of a SWF:[1]

1. To protect a nation's economy (and fiscal budget) from a potential decline or volatility in revenues.
2. To help monetary authorities to counter unwanted liquidity.
3. To grow the level of savings for future generations, particularly if the condition that drove the surplus is at a reasonable risk for depletion or reversal.
4. To invest the money in infrastructure or economic growth projects today in order to strengthen a sector of the economy or grow a specific industry, especially to diversify away from commodity revenues.

14.3.2   Investment Management of Sovereign Wealth Funds

Exhibit 14.1 shows that the asset allocations of different types of SWFs vary dramatically. While stabilization funds invest nearly exclusively in cash and fixed income, savings and reserve funds have highly diversified investments resembling the asset allocations of pensions, endowments, or foundations. Exhibit 14.1 shows that savings funds, pension reserve funds, and reserve investment funds invest heavily in equities and other investments, which are largely alternative investments.

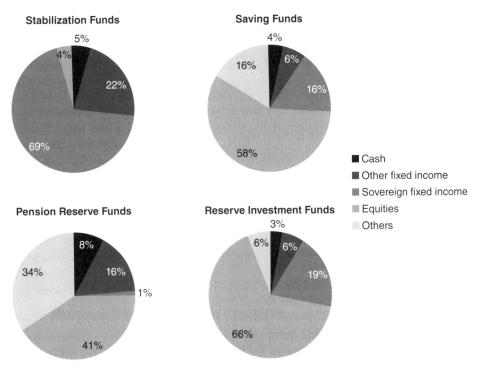

EXHIBIT 14.1   Asset Allocations at SWF, by Type of Fund
Source: IMF (2012), Al-Hassan et al. (2013).

Preqin data shows that over three-quarters of SWFs invest in alternative investments (Preqin 2016). The large size and long holding period of SWFs have led many investors to focus on direct investments rather than pooled investments, especially in infrastructure and real estate. Co-investments and joint ventures can reduce the fees of investing while the involvement of a general partner or joint venture partner can reduce the risk relative to a full direct investment program.

14.3.3   Dutch Disease and Sterilization Policies

A stabilization fund may be used to reduce the volatility in government revenues, or the value of the domestic currency. Consider a commodity-producing country during a time of high commodity prices. When the majority of the economy is focused on commodity exports and the size of the economy is small relative to the large currency inflows from commodity sales, it can be disruptive if all of the (typically US dollar) proceeds from commodity sales are converted into the local currency. There are two potential effects. First, inflation could result if the money supply increases faster than the availability of goods or investments in the local economy. Second, there is a fear of Dutch disease.

Dutch disease occurs when large currency inflows (such as from the sale of large quantities of commodities) damage the long-run health of a country's other sources of economic prosperity (such as the country's manufacturing sector). In particular, the discovery of a tradable natural resource or a substantial increase in the price of such a resource has two major impacts. First, it will increase local wages by shifting workers from other sectors of the economy to the commodity sector. It can also shift the focus of entrepreneurs and industry leaders to opportunities directly related to the export of the commodity. Second, the value of the local currency increases due to large inflows of cash. These results reduce the competitiveness of the country's manufacturing and export sectors, leading to its de-industrialization.

Many countries engage in sterilization. **Sterilization** is a macroeconomic policy in which a central bank or the government takes actions to counter the effects of an economic event (such as a commodity boom) and a balance of payments surplus on the country's economy. There are two types of sterilization.

First, a country that is running a trade surplus may decide to intervene in the foreign exchange markets to prevent its currency from appreciating. In this case, the central bank will sell local currency and buy foreign currency in order to satisfy the increased demand for local currency by foreign importers of its products.

Second, a country may accumulate a significant amount of reserves not because of intervention in the foreign currency markets, but rather because of the revenues generated through the sales of natural resources that are completely or partially controlled by the government. If the government were to spend the revenues in the local economy, it could cause major disruptions in the local economy, especially if the local economy is small compared to the size of the inflows. In this case, the government may choose to invest much of the commodity proceeds outside of the home economy. For example, Norway may choose to invest much of its sovereign assets in dollar or euro denominated securities of other countries in order to not disrupt the local economy and to prevent the appreciation of the krone.

14.3.4   Managing the Size of a Sovereign Wealth Fund

After an extended period of high commodity prices, the size of a stabilization fund may be relatively large compared to the immediate spending and stabilization needs of the country. As the size of the stabilization fund grows, a question arises as to how large the stabilization fund should be. Given that the stabilization fund is invested almost exclusively in cash and liquid fixed income securities, there is a large **conservative investment opportunity cost,** where the longer conservative assets are left in cash, the greater the lost returns relative to what could have been earned on a balanced portfolio that includes investments in risky assets.

Reserve adequacy is the estimated size for stabilization fund reserves that is considered necessary before starting to invest in risky assets and moving funds into a total return portfolio. The necessary size of stabilization reserves are measured relative to the size of the potential shocks that can come from crises, whether from changes in commodity prices, trade flows, investment flows, or losses in the banking sector.

14.4   GOVERNANCE AND POLITICAL RISKS OF SWFs

Many government funds have opaque investment policies and potentially substantial economic power from their large amounts of wealth. Uncertainty with regard to potential conflicts of interest can create costs that lower benefits to all parties. Transparency allows investors to better understand the impact that SWFs may have and may lessen the impacts of interest. Therefore, it may benefit SWFs to develop strong governance principles for enhanced transparency and improved ethics in their investments.

14.4.1   Governance of SWFs

Windfall commodity revenues in a country with tendencies toward corruption or underdeveloped financial systems must be used with caution. There can be temptations to steal the money, invest in unwise domestic projects, or simply invest without the skill that is more common in economies with more developed institutions.

SWFs should be independent of the government and the central bank, and managed in an external agency staffed with well-trained investment professionals. Bernstein et al. (2013) note that when politicians are involved in a SWF, there is a greater allocation toward domestic investments, which is seen as a sign of poor decision-making. Within the SWF, well-defined and transparent processes should be in place for investment management, risk management, and reporting of investment results. Efforts should be made to minimize the cost of an internally managed portfolio or to receive maximum value for the fees paid to external managers.

As will be seen later, Norway is the model of an independent, well-governed SWF with professional management, ultra-low investment costs, highly diversified portfolios, ethical investment policies, and well-developed transparency and governance policies. It is important to note that most of Norway's investments are made outside the country in minority stakes in publicly traded investments. This avoids the potential conflicts that can come with large domestic investments or with large stakes in foreign companies.

14.4.2   Impact of SWF Investments on Portfolio Companies

What are the impacts of SWF investments on their portfolio companies? Do the large investments of SWFs have a long-term impact on the stock price? Do SWF investors seek to control the actions of the portfolio companies in a way that would benefit the sponsoring government and their local economy? Avendaño and Santiso (2011) compare SWF holdings to those of private mutual funds and find that the investment decisions of SWF investors don't significantly differ from the decisions made by mutual fund managers. Furthermore, they did not find any evidence that SWF investment decisions are politically influenced, but rather that most SWFs go out of their way to not be perceived as controlling the interests of their portfolio companies.

Megginson and Fotak (2015) cite a variety of studies that show mixed evidence regarding the impact of SWF investors on asset prices. Stocks added to SWF portfolios tend to outperform around the date of the acquisition announcement, but underperform over the following year, especially when compared to stocks purchased by other acquirers or professional investors. When SWFs make investments in distressed firms, it appears that the credit risk and CDS spreads of the firms decline, perhaps due to the assumption that a sovereign bailout would likely prevent the bankruptcy of these firms should greater distress arise.

14.4.3   Ten Principles of the Linaburg–Maduell Transparency Index

A method of rating SWF transparency was developed at the Sovereign Wealth Fund Institute (SWFI) by Carl Linaburg and Michael Maduell. The **Linaburg–Maduell Transparency Index** consists of the following 10 principles, where one point is assigned to a given fund for having satisfied its requirement. The SWFI recommends an index score of no less than an 8 (out of a maximum of 10) for a SWF to claim its transparency is adequate.

- Fund provides history including reason for creation, origins of wealth, and government ownership structure.
- Fund provides up-to-date and independently audited annual reports.
- Fund provides ownership percentage of company holdings, and geographic locations of holdings.
- Fund provides total portfolio market value, returns, and management compensation.
- Fund provides guidelines in reference to ethical standards, investment policies, and enforcement of guidelines.
- Fund provides clear strategies and objectives.
- Fund clearly identifies subsidiaries and contact information, if applicable.
- Fund identifies external managers, if applicable.
- Fund manages its own website.
- Fund provides main office location address and contact information.

14.4.4   Santiago Principles

The International Working Group of SWFs (2008) set out the Santiago Principles, which define the generally accepted principles and practices (GAPP) of good governance of SWFs. Twenty-four governments have signed that they will seek to comply with the **Santiago Principles,** which are summarized in the following points:

- A clear investment policy.
- Diligence, prudence, and skill in investment practices.
- A robust risk management framework.
- Refraining from pursuit of any objectives other than maximization of risk-adjusted financial returns.
- Public disclosures of general approach to voting and board representation.
- Not seeking advances of privileged information.
- Description of the use of leverage or disclosure of other measures of financial risk exposure.
- Execution of ownership rights consistent with the SWF's investment policy.
- A transparent and sound operational control and risk management system.

14.5 ANALYSIS OF THREE SOVEREIGN WEALTH FUNDS

This section takes a closer look at three SWFs in order to analyze and illustrate the economics of their management.

14.5.1 Government Pension Fund Global (Norway)

Alsweilem et al. (2013) explain that Norway had a major advantage by being a wealthy, diversified, developed economy before oil was discovered in the North Sea in 1969. Given that Norway didn't need the revenues generated from oil production, those funds were treated as a windfall subject to a large savings rate. Today, as much as 80% of the country's revenues are outside of the energy sector, so the role of the SWF to stabilize the economy from volatile oil prices is less important than in other countries, where oil revenue can exceed 80% of state revenues. The Norwegian Government Pension Fund Global, can be categorized as a savings fund designed to allow future generations to benefit from this resource discovery.

All oil revenues are transferred to the SWF, while the fund transfers 4% of its value each year to the government budget. The government budget is designed to be able to balance its budget using the 4% income from the SWF. If the fund is able to earn a 4% real return, the real value of the fund can be maintained in perpetuity, even after the oil supplies have been exhausted.

After the discovery of oil in the North Sea in 1969, oil production rose steadily, peaking around the year 2000. While gas production has been increasing in recent years, oil production has declined, showing that oil supplies may be nearly exhausted in the next 20 years in the absence of new discoveries. After oil revenues cease to flow into the fund, the SWF should presumably be managed as a perpetual endowment, as the windfall experienced over the last 50 years is unlikely to be repeated, so future generations will rely on the savings of the SWF to benefit from this large oil discovery. Norway currently does not have large investments in inflation-hedging assets, as oil and gas reserves largely serve that purpose. However, as oil and gas reserves are depleted, it would be expected that investments in real assets would increase to serve the long-term inflation hedging role.

Chambers, Dimson, and Ilmanen (2012) contrast the Norway model to the endowment model or Yale model. In the **Norway model,** asset allocations are dominated by highly diversified liquid assets that are managed at extremely low costs, which seem to be the opposite of the Yale model, which maximizes exposure to illiquid assets invested with external managers. In 2019, Norway had invested over 65% in global equities, 30% in global fixed income, and a target to grow to 5% in unlisted real estate investments.

With a small staff of less than 500 employees and a large fund, the strategy is aimed at passive management, acknowledging that active management fees and the market impact of such a large fund can impair returns. Norway has a very large and diversified fund. The assets are largely internally managed at a very low cost.

Norway is seen as a leader in SWF transparency and governance as well as in its stance on social investing. The SWF publishes a 100-page annual report in addition to a separate report on responsible investment. In the annual report, detailed asset allocations are presented, including fund and benchmark returns for the entire fund as well as for subportfolios, such as European equities. Risk management policies are disclosed, as are specific breaches of risk management policies or operational risk events during each year. Compensation levels of top employees are disclosed, as is the structure of the performance-based pay program offered to nearly 200 employees. The rules for contributions to, and distributions from, the fund are clearly set and are stable over time. The Norwegian government maintains a list of prohibited investments,[23] that exclude a number of equity investments from the SWF portfolio. These exclusions ban investments in a number of industries, including the production or use of coal, certain types of weapon, and tobacco. Company-specific prohibited investments are listed for firms that are determined to have damaged the environment, violated human rights, or have issues with corruption, ethics, or conflict zones. The fund seeks investments in environmental technology firms and regularly votes at equity shareholder meetings.

14.5.2 China Investment Corporation

In 2019, China was reported to have held over $3 trillion in foreign exchange reserves, most of which was earned through the export of manufactured goods and a currency that was undervalued for an extended period of time (CNBC 2019). China and Hong Kong have four large funds, while the balance of the reserves are likely held by the central bank. China's State Administration of Foreign Exchange (SAFE) is located within the central bank and functions as a stabilization fund, with significant infusions into the state-owned banking system. Due to the size of SAFE, the fund has started to invest in risky assets in the pursuit of higher returns than earned with the previous focus on cash and fixed income investments. The Chinese funds operate quite differently than Norway, especially SAFE, which is not known for its transparency.

Alsweilem et al. (2013) explain that China Investment Corporation (CIC) was established in 2007 in order to increase independence of the investment arm from the central bank. CIC can be classified as a reserve investment fund, which seeks higher returns. While many SWFs focus investments outside of their home countries, CIC controls Central Huijin, a holding company originally started by SAFE's injections into the banking system, which owns between 35% and 66% of five state-owned Chinese banks. Other divisions of CIC are CIC International and CIC Capital.

While Norway is highly diversified and highly liquid, CIC has more concentrated investments, a large allocation to private equity, and significant exposure to external management, which is more similar to the Yale model.

Global leaders have expressed concern over the political influence of CIC, especially when investing in specific industries, such as oil and gas.[4] Alsweilem et al. (2013) report that CIC invested in distressed financial firms in 2008. Those firms were later hired by CIC to advise on $500 million in hedge funds and $800 million in real estate investments, respectively. With the size of these stakes, CIC is not a passive investor, but has taken seats on a number of corporate boards. CIC also invests heavily in real assets, especially those that are seen as providing inflation protection, or hedges against a falling US dollar, or those improving the resource security of the Chinese population. The allocation of CIC has been moving away from public equities and toward greater allocations in private equity and direct investments, especially in oil and gas, mining, utilities, and infrastructure. CIC includes these assets in the long-term investments category. CIC started CIC Capital in 2015, which has specific goals to oversee private investments in infrastructure and farmland.

14.5.3   Temasek Holdings (Singapore)

Like China, Singapore sponsors a number of funds, each with a different objective. Singapore's Government Investment Corporation (GIC) functions as a reserve investment fund, seeking to maximize returns on a global portfolio, with over 80% invested in a diversified portfolio of liquid equities and fixed income securities. Singapore's Temasek Holdings is an example of a development fund that has been funded with the proceeds of privatizations, which are the sale of government owned assets to private investors. While a primary goal of Temasek may be the growth of employment and economic development in Asia, a portion of the returns from Temasek's investments are paid as dividends to the government of Singapore.

As a development fund, Temasek makes large strategic investments to develop certain sectors. Singapore is a wealthy, but small, city state, which has developed its wealth through shipping, engineering, and financial services. Given its small size and high population density of 5.6 million people in just 719 square kilometers, Singapore focuses investments on areas driven more by intellectual capital than by natural resources or heavy manufacturing.

Temasek's portfolio is highly concentrated, with 26% of holdings in Singapore, and 40% in the rest of Asia. In 2019, nearly 80% of the portfolio was invested in financial services, transportation, industrials, consumer companies, real estate, as well as telecommunications, media, and technology (TMT). Temasek's portfolio focuses on public and private equity investments, with over 40% invested in unlisted assets, over 20% in listed large blocks above a 20% holding, and over one-third in liquid investments with less than a 20% stake in the underlying firms. While most SWFs take small stakes in firms, Temasek controls the majority of shares in firms such as Olam International, Singapore Airlines, and Singapore Telecommunications, while owning all of the equity of Singapore Technologies Telemedia, PSA International, Singapore Power, Mapletree Investments, and Pavilion Energy.

14.6 CONCLUSION

Since 2008, SWFs have increased their assets by over $4.4 trillion, including asset returns and the establishment of new funds from the proceeds of commodity and merchandise exports as well as privatizations. The initial allocation of a new SWF is often close to 100% in cash and fixed income, as the assets are used to stabilize the economy against volatility in export revenues, tax revenues, and foreign trade and capital flows. Once a central bank determines that the level of reserves is adequate for the purpose of economic stabilization, assets are moved into a vehicle seeking higher returns. As the AUM of a SWF rises and the sophistication of the investment team grows, allocations to alternative investments tend to increase. To date, these investments have been focused on private equity and real assets with lesser interest in hedge funds.

NOTES

1. See Rozanov (2005).
2. See Norwegian Government Pension Fund Global Annual Report (2018).
3. See www.nbim.no/en/responsibility/exclusion-of-companies/.
4. See Koch-Weser and Haacke (June 2013).

REFERENCES

Al-Hassan, A., M. Papaioannou, M. Skancke, and C. Chih Sung. 2013. "Sovereign Wealth Funds: Aspects of Governance Structures and Investment Management." Working Paper No. 13/231, International Monetary Fund, November 13. https://www.imf.org/external/pubs/cat/longres.aspx?sk=41046.0.

Alsweilem, K., A. Cummine, M. Rietveld, and K. Tweedie. 2013. "Sovereign Investor Models: Institutions and Policies for Managing Sovereign Wealth." Working Paper, Harvard Kennedy School.

Avendaño, R. and J. Santiso. 2011. "Are Sovereign Wealth Funds Politically Biased? A Comparison with Other Institutional Investors." In B. Narjess and C. Jean-Claude (eds), *Institutional Investors in Global Capital Markets* (pp. 313–53). Bradford, UK: Emerald Group Publishing Limited.

Bernstein, S., J. Lerner, and A. Schoar. 2013. "The Investment Strategies of Sovereign Wealth Funds." *Journal of Economic Perspectives* 27: 219–38.

Castelli, M. and F. Scacciavillani. 2012. *The New Economics of Sovereign Wealth Funds.* Chichester, UK: John Wiley & Sons.

Chambers, D., E. Dimson, and A. Ilmanen. 2012. "The Norway Model." *Journal of Portfolio Management* 38 (2): 67–81. Available at http://ssrn.com/abstract=1936806 or doi:10.2139/ssrn.1936806.

CNBC. 2019. "China is building up its 'shadow reserves' to counter its reliance on the US dollar". https://www.cnbc.com/2019/11/18/china-diversifying-fx-reserves-assets-to-counter-us-dollar-exposure.html.

Gwartney, J., R. Stroup, R. Sobel, and D. Macpherson. 2003. *Economics: Public and Private Choice.* 10th Edition. Mason, OH: South-Western College Publishing.

International Monetary Fund. 2012. "Global Financial Stability Report 2012."

International Working Group of Sovereign Wealth Funds. 2008. "Generally Accepted Principles and Practices (GAPP)—Santiago Principles," October. Available at www.iwgswf.org/pubs/eng/santiagoprinciples.pdf.

Koch-Weser, I. and O. Haacke. June 2013. China Investment Corporation: Recent Developments in Performance, Strategy, and Governance. US–China Economic and Security Review Commission. Available at https://www.uscc.gov/sites/default/files/Research/China%20Investment%20Corporation_Staff%20Report_0.pdf.

Kunzel, P., Y. Lu, I. Petrova, and J. Pihlman. 2010. "Investment Objectives of Sovereign Wealth Funds—A Shifting Paradigm." Working Paper, IMF.

Megginson, W. and V. Fotak. 2015. "Rise of the Fiduciary State: A Survey of Sovereign Wealth Fund Research." *Journal of Economic Surveys* 29 (4): 733–78.

Norwegian Government Pension Fund Global Annual Report. 2018. https://www.nbim.no/contentassets/02bfbbef416f4014b043e74b8405fa97/annual-report-2018-government-pension-fund-global.pdf.

Preqin. 2016. "2015 Preqin Sovereign Wealth Fund Review." Available at https://docs.preqin.com/reports/2015-Preqin-Sovereign-Wealth-Fund-Review-Exclusive-Extract-June-2015.pdf.

Rozanov, A. 2005. "Who Holds the Wealth of Nations?" State Street Global Advisors' Official Institutions Group, August. Available at http://piketty.pse.ens.fr/files/capital21c/xls/RawDataFiles/WealthReportsEtc/SovereignFunds/General/Rozanov2005.pdf.

CHAPTER 15

Family Offices and the Family Office Model

A family office refers to an organization dedicated to the management of a pool of capital owned by a wealthy individual or group of individuals. In effect it is a private wealth advisory firm established by an ultra high-net-worth individual (UHNWI). This chapter discusses the family office model, including the types of family offices, managing wealth and relationships across multiple generations of a family, taxes, lifestyle investments, and philanthropic activities.

15.1 IDENTIFYING FAMILY OFFICES

Information on the growth of family offices is limited because of the highly confidential and private nature of family offices and the wealthy individuals they serve. As of 2018, the number of family offices in the United States was approximately 3,000 to 5,000 while globally the number may be as high as 10,000. In total, these offices manage over $4 trillion.[1]

As a general rule of thumb, dedicated family offices are considered operational at $1 billion of assets under management (AUM). For amounts smaller than that size, it would make sense for the wealthy family to join a multi-family office to share expenses and achieve economies of scale. It is estimated that running a single-family office costs approximately 60 basis points of AUM per year.[2]

In some cases the family office is referred to a "single"-family office, and this means that the management of capital and financial affairs is dedicated to a single individual or a single family. Some offices are set up to serve multiple families—a multi-family office. This may be done to share operating expenses and back office administration, or to collectively pool investment ideas.

Note that a multi-family office typically starts as a single-family office and other families are later invited to join or several families may be involved at the inception. Typically, a multi-family office pools assets of a small number of **ultra high-net-worth** families, those with over $30 million in assets. While some investment advisers may call themselves multi-family offices, they are unlikely to truly function in this role if they have dozens or hundreds of clients who are not from ultra high-net-worth families.

The source of income for a family office can be as varied as the underlying family that it serves. In some cases, the capital is spun off from an operating company (e.g., Mark Zuckerberg of Facebook). In other cases, the family office might be funded with what is known as "legacy wealth." This refers to a second, third, or later generation of family members who have inherited their wealth from a prior source of capital generation. The family office can be funded with cash, real estate, natural resources, equity securities, or even art.

15.2   GOALS, BENEFITS, AND BUSINESS MODELS OF FAMILY OFFICES

Family offices are diverse with respect to their goals, benefits, and business models.

15.2.1   General Goals of the Family Office

The goals of the family office vary dramatically. One goal can be preserving wealth for the next generation. Another goal can be to give away all of the wealth. A third goal can be to place the family wealth into a foundation for long-term charitable goals. A more immediate goal might be to maintain a certain lifestyle. This can include funding purchases like homes, art, automobiles, private jets, and the like.

A survey of single-family offices found wealth management to be the most common goal for the family. Wealth management and accounting consolidation seem to be very important goals for every family office. More simply, a key benefit to a family office is to have a consolidated function for family office wealth management, accounting, and control.

The benchmark returns for the family offices are different. Some family offices are benchmarked to an absolute return hurdle: Treasury bills, LIBOR +X%, or an inflation target. Some families have benchmarks defined in terms of objectives instead of a certain percentage. For example, the benchmark for one family office is simple and clear on its face: Don't lose money. Not surprisingly, that family office has a very conservative asset.

15.2.2   Benefits of the Family Office

A family office provides several benefits over a private bank or traditional asset manager. A family office serves as the central source for financial management for a family or group of families. As a result, it is a key source of information and advice on all family financial affairs. Family offices also have the benefit of absolute privacy. Further, the family office is intimately aware of the personalities, risk tolerances, individual goals, and the spending needs of the family members. The staff of the family office is dedicated exclusively to the financial and philanthropic goals of the family and its members. Such dedicated advice and counsel are hard to duplicate outside of a family office.

Exhibit 15.1 shows what benefits or functions matter most to UHNWIs in setting up a family office.[3] Wealth management ranks highest. But also important is conflict-free advice—the benefit of a dedicated staff, confidentiality, and sophisticated investment advice. Further down the ranking are the softer benefits, such as education of family members, philanthropy, and concierge services. Yet these benefits were valued by over 50% of families.

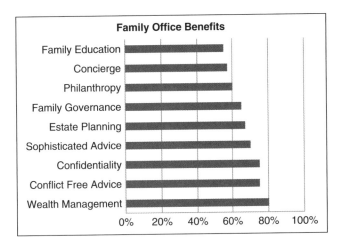

EXHIBIT 15.1 Benefits of a Family Office

Another key benefit is keeping the family money consolidated in one central core. This can become more difficult as more generations emerge with their individual goals and objectives. It is typically not an easy task to get family members to agree on matters related to money.

15.2.3 Models and Structure of the Family Office

Family offices manage capital for individuals whose goals are varied. Consequently, there is no "family office model" as a counterpart to the "endowment model" of universities. Each family office follows a unique game plan that reflects the individual members of that family, their specific goals, the source of their wealth, and their lifestyle needs.

Exhibit 15.2 presents the business models for several UHNW family offices.[4] First, note that in some cases the founding family is involved in the management of the family office. Sometimes, family members even make investments on behalf of the family. There is no right or wrong here; it really is the individual nature of the family office. The downside is that these family members may not have rigorous training or experience in asset allocation and portfolio management.

One dimension along which family offices differ is whether they manage outside capital for external clients. If a family office accepts money from a nonfamily member, it may be required to register with the US Securities and Exchange Commission (SEC) or another national financial regulatory agency. A family member is defined as any member of the direct bloodline of the founder of the family office plus spouses of family members. Anyone outside that family circle is considered an outside client and brings with it the full burden of SEC registration, regulatory adherence, and government agency scrutiny.

Family lines can become a bit murky regarding who, exactly, is a family member. Currently, the SEC allows family offices to advise up to 10 generations of family (and spouses) related to a common designated ancestor. However, in a recent well-publicized case, the SEC allowed the movie star Meryl Streep to keep her money with a family office even though she had divorced the family member from whom she gained access to the family office in the first place.[5]

EXHIBIT 15.2 Various Models of a Family Office

	Estimated AUM	Family Actively Engaged	Size of Team	Structure of Team	Benchmark	In/Out source Infrastructure	Hedge Funds	Direct Private Equity	External PE Firms	Real Assets	Internal Management	Asset Allocation	Accept Outside Clients
Family Office A	$14 B	Yes–in VC	25	7 in VC, 5 in PE, 5 in Public Markets, 4 in Credit, 4 for Risk & Asset Allocation, rest as analysts	Outperform the S&P 500.	In House– team size undisclosed	Only 10 to 15	Yes, $50 to $200 million	10 external Firms	Minimal– not their strength	Yes, direct VC investing	No formal Risk Budget or Allocation	Yes in their Capital Funds. Also willing to co-Invest.
Family Office B	$15+ B	No	25	By Asset Class	Would like to earn 10% across total portfolio	Full Back and Middle Office In house– Team of 50–full bookkeeping to performance attribution	None–they have their own L/S and macro trading in house	Yes, $50 million and up	8 to 10 PE Funds; US Mid Market, Distressed Debt, RE	Yes, but rely more on outside managers	Yes, Concentrated long only, L/S Equity, Bonds, Currency	Quarterly Risk and Asset Allocation meetings– can go to zero in any asset class	No, but will co-Invest in other direct deals
Family Office C	$7–8 B	No	20	2 to 4 persons per Asset Class team; 3 person Asset Allocation team, 3 person Operational Due Diligence team	Not disclosed: Tbills + a Premium	In house–12 people that handle everything on site–they like the immediate interaction	Yes, 90% of the capital is allocated externally to Hedge Funds	Very Limited	Only 2	Yes– allocated to external managers	Very active internal management across equities, bonds, credit, currency, commodities	Formerly meet with the Foundation 3 times a year	No, but willing to co-invest with other Family Offices
Family Office D	$5+ B	Yes	9	1 Direct Deal guy, 2 Structured Credit, 2 Traders, 2 for Public Equities, CIO for asset allocation, CEO makes ...	Tbills plus a premium	Outsource all back and middle office	Run their own internal Discretionary Macro portfolio plus external hedge funds to diversify	Yes, but very limited.	None yet	Don't invest in real assets: "not our expertise"	Left to the CIO but no formal meetings	No, but willing to co-invest with other family offices

Family Office E	$6+ B	Yes	10	Across traditional Asset Classes	T-Bills + 4 to 5%	Hybrid between Viteos system for accounting and in house for Capital Calls	Yes, portfolio is geared more towards Absolute Returns	No	very limited Yes		Focus on internal bond management: Investment Grade, Hi Yield, Short Term cash	Different allocations for different family members	Looking to accept 2 to 4 other families to spread costs and create economies of scale.
Multi Family Office F	$25 million to $250 million	No	22	Organized by Asset Class	Blended based on asset allocation	Outsource to custodian	Yes, significant source of their alpha	No	Only 3 firms	Commodities but limited RE	None	Formal Asset Allocation Committee once a year	Yes, 20 clients, and 8 client PMs to work on asset allocation
Family Office G	$3.3 Billion	No	8	4 Accountants, 4 Investors including the CIO	None. Goal is not to lose money.	Use their external bank for Performance, Custody, Risk Management	Yes, a significant commitment to hedge funds. No long only Public Equity.	No-consider their investments in the family OpCo to be similar to direct PE	Very small. They consider the Family Operating Companies to be their equivalent of PE	Some energy exposure through Riverstone PE fund-very small.	None. All outsourced primarily to HF and Stock and Bond Managers.	No Formal Asset Allocation Model. Meet quarterly.	No, they have several family members that keep them fully occupied.
Family Office H	$3+ Billion	Yes	7	4 Investment, 2 accountants, 1 support staff		Outsource Risk Management	A blend of HF managers but tilted towards those strategies with less market risk	None	Very limited	Oil and gas	None, all external managers	No formal asset allocation or committee	No, Regulatory burden is simply too high.

By accepting outside clients, the family office must develop an internal compliance department to ensure that all external clients are treated on an equal footing with the family members. In other words, the sponsoring family cannot be selective in choosing the best investment ideas just for their family; they must share all investments equally with their outside clients. This can be an especially prickly situation with family members who source the good investment ideas in the first place. They may not want to share their investment insights with outside clients who contribute nothing to the generation of investment ideas. In addition, the family office must develop a sophisticated reporting infrastructure to provide monthly and quarterly reports to the external clients. Last, there are ongoing reporting requirements to the SEC and other regulators that can require additional lawyers, accountants, and administrators.

The key point is that if a family office intends to accept outside clients, it must do so with the full knowledge that this is a very expensive proposition. One family office estimates that its operating costs more than doubled once it accepted outside clients. Other family offices—notably that of George Soros—immediately shut down their outside investment activities and returned capital to all of their external clients when the SEC began regulating family offices with nonfamily clients in 2010. Still other family offices—Rockefeller & Co., for example—continue to accept outside clients and have become fully registered with the SEC as investment advisers.

15.3 FAMILY OFFICE GOALS BY GENERATIONS

The number of generations has a substantial impact on asset allocation and risk taking.

15.3.1 First-Generation Wealth

The first generation of wealth creation (**new money**) is more likely to be concerned with wealth preservation—keeping the newly created wealth intact. It is successive generations (**old money**) that turn to generating wealth growth with an established pool of assets. However, family offices are more likely to be set up past the first generation. Exhibit 15.3 depicts the generational transfer of wealth and when it comes under the management of a family office.[6] This exhibit demonstrates that family offices are usually established after the first generation of wealth is created. This may not be as surprising as it looks. The first generation of family wealth is usually tied to an operating company. As a result, the first generation is typically focused on creating the wealth, not managing it. It is only after the wealth has been created and typically locked up in a transaction of some kind (e.g., the sale of an operating company) that the family begins to think about the ongoing maintenance of the wealth.

15.3.2 Risk Management of First-Generation Wealth

There are special concerns that arise from **concentrated wealth**, which occurs when the vast majority of the assets are poorly diversified, such as being held in a single company. Concentrated wealth positions typically arise because the newly wealthy often earn their fortune from a privately held family business or from serving as an

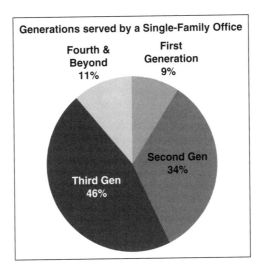

EXHIBIT 15.3 Generations Served by a
Family Office

entrepreneur or chief executive of a public company. While starting or managing a
public company can create substantial wealth, there are also regulations and shareholders to respect. Many executives of public companies are required to refrain from
trading their shares during times when they are in possession of material nonpublic
information, such as around announcements of corporate profits or merger transactions. Purchases or sales of company stock may also be required to be reported to
regulators and/or shareholders. Both the disclosure requirement and the restricted
holding periods serve to make the company stock less liquid for the executives at
the company than for other shareholders. Sales of stock may incur a substantial tax
liability, as they are often held at a large increase in value relative to the acquisition
or granting price.

Many chief executives regularly invest the vast majority of their wealth in the
stock of the company they lead. This may be a sign of confidence or solidarity with
shareholders or the result of receiving stock options or grants that may require some
price move or the passage of time before the sale is allowed. These executives may be
interested in regularly scheduled sales of stock, perhaps 1% of holdings sold immediately after the release of each quarterly earnings report, in order to diversify their
portfolios and grow assets outside of the company over time. The proceeds of these
sales may be invested in a completion portfolio. A **completion portfolio** is a collection of assets that is managed with the objective of diversifying the aggregated risks
of the concentrated portfolio. The assets purchased should have a low correlation
to the assets held in the company stock portfolio (the concentrated portfolio). For
example, an entrepreneur who owns a substantial stake in a US-based technology
company would not buy any technology stocks, but focus purchases on sovereign
debt, real assets, and foreign stocks, perhaps in the finance or healthcare sector, resulting in an increasingly diversified portfolio, even when including the concentrated
stock holding.

Some executives may partially hedge their concentrated holdings with long-term
stock options, such as through an options collar, which sells call options and buys

put options. This strategy delays realized gains for tax purposes, while limiting the potential gains and reducing the potential losses relative to the current market price. Shares can also be held as collateral for loans, which can provide liquidity, but can also multiply losses if the loan proceeds are invested in risky assets.

Generating wealth through a privately held business has even more extreme illiquidity than serving as the executive of a public company. Much of the wealth that is managed by family offices is generated by a **liquidity event** such as the sale of the family business in a merger transaction or in an initial public offering. These liquidity events may generate $10 million or more in proceeds in a single week, dramatically changing the wealth management strategies of the family. Before the liquidity event, nearly all of the family wealth is held in a private business that is highly illiquid and difficult to value. After the liquidity event, the family has a large amount of cash that can be easily invested in a diversified portfolio. Some advisers encourage sellers of private businesses to take some time to invest the proceeds of their life's work, perhaps a year or more, especially during times of overvaluation in the equity markets. This is the time for education on investment markets and reflection on family goals, including the distribution of the wealth and whether the goal is to preserve or multiply the wealth. The time can also be used to have discussions with attorneys and financial advisers as well as to consider whether to start a single-family office or join a multi-family office.

15.3.3 Benchmarking First-Generation Wealth

The T-bills/LIBOR + X% benchmarks reflect one style of family office management typically associated with first-generation wealth. Often the initial wealth is created, or continues to be created, by an operating company. The operating company, in many cases, produces a large concentration of wealth from a single source. There is considerable risk when a significant portion of wealth is concentrated in a single asset.

When this is the case, many family offices take more of an absolute return approach to their asset allocation. The family office portfolio is used to diversify the single company risk of the initial or ongoing wealth generation. Under this approach, more of the portfolio is geared toward hedge funds, credit, fixed income, relative value, and other assets that are exposed to market risk.

In fact, family offices that have an absolute return benchmark (like T-bills + X%) tend to have allocations to private equity that are limited. Again, this points toward taking less market risk in the family office to balance the risk contained in the family operating company.

15.3.4 Goals of the Second Generation and Beyond

Taxes play an important role in portfolio construction and asset allocation within family offices, particularly in relation to second- and third-generation wealth. At this stage of the family life cycle, the initial wealth has been created from an original underlying source—usually an operating company that has been sold. In this situation, the family office portfolio becomes the new source of wealth generation.

When constructing an optimal portfolio for a family office and building an efficient frontier, it is important to analyze after-tax returns. At this generation of the family life cycle, the family office portfolio is geared more toward growth

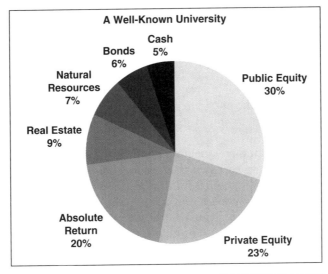

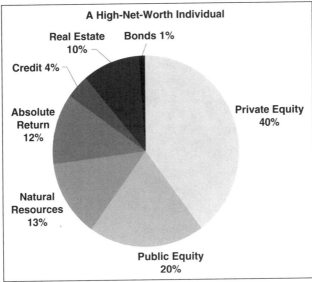

EXHIBIT 15.4 Sample Asset Allocations for an Endowment versus a Family Office

assets—those assets that generate long-term capital gains instead of assets that are more short-term oriented either in their income generation or capital gains.

Consider Exhibit 15.4, which shows the asset allocation of a well-known university endowment and that for an UHNWI. One observation is the much larger allocation to private equity for the individual versus the university. Endowment portfolios are usually considered to have an aggressive risk profile with a considerable portion of the endowment allocated to risky assets. However, family office portfolios may take this a step further.

Reviewing Exhibit 15.4, 87% of the family office portfolio is allocated to long-term risk-based assets that generate long-term capital gains: private equity, public equity, natural resources, credit, and real estate. By contrast, the university endowment has only 69% of its portfolio allocated to these long-term assets. Not surprisingly, the endowment has a much larger allocation to bonds, cash, and absolute return investments (31%) than the family office (13%).

The higher allocation to risky assets by the family office serves two goals: (1) tax efficiency; and (2) expected long-term wealth generation. Again, keep in mind that Exhibit 6.4 demonstrates the portfolio allocation for a family office that has already established its wealth from an initial source and now uses the family office portfolio as the driver of wealth growth.

Exhibit 15.4 raises another issue for a family office compared to an endowment. The higher allocation to private assets that generate long-term capital gains can result in a very illiquid portfolio. Exhibit 15.5 demonstrates this problem.

Next, compare the well-known university to the UHNWI along the dimensions of liquidity. Illiquid assets are defined as those assets that cannot be sold within 1 year without selling at a discount. Liquid assets are those assets that can be sold in less than 3 months without selling at a discount, and semiliquid assets fall into the 3-month to 1-year time frame. In reality, every asset can be sold within a year—a home, a private equity portfolio, a ranch. The problem is that chunky/illiquid assets generally must be sold at a discount if the UHNWI wants liquidity quickly.

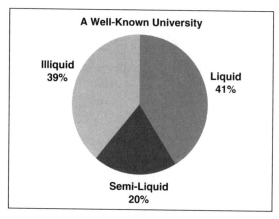

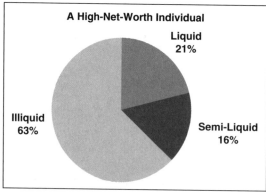

EXHIBIT 15.5 Liquidity Profiles for an Endowment versus a Family Office

Examining Exhibit 15.5 indicates how lopsided the UHNWI portfolio is with respect to illiquid assets compared to the university endowment. The university has achieved an almost perfect balance between its liquid and illiquid assets, with semiliquid assets filling the gap between the other two categories. However, for the UHNWI, illiquid assets represent 63% of the total portfolio. For this reason, many UHNWIs have a credit line or liquidity backstop negotiated with an external bank. Yet, this liquidity profile demonstrates an advantage of the family office over the endowment. Unlike an endowment, the family office does not have a university operating budget to support each year. To the extent that the family has a low spending rate, the family office can capture even more of the liquidity premium than sophisticated endowment offices can. If there is a desire for the family to sustain a high spending rate, the allocation to illiquid assets will be lower.

15.4 MACROECONOMIC EXPOSURES OF FAMILY OFFICES

Another difference between family offices and endowments is a concern for the overall macroeconomic variables that can affect an investment portfolio. Endowments, for example, are much more focused on beta drivers—the systematic risk premiums attached to asset classes. Beta drivers are effective tools for asset allocation, risk budgeting, and income generation. Exhibit 15.6 shows the beta drivers for both an endowment and a UHNWI.

However, there is a growing trend among wealthy families to better understand how their wealth is tied to global macroeconomic factors. The financial crisis of 2008 demonstrated to investors large and small that many asset classes became highly correlated with one another, resulting in significant declines in asset values. Macroeconomic factors are a way to look beyond asset classes and beta drivers to better understand the true economic forces that can impact a portfolio.

Exhibit 15.6 gives a simple diagram of how each asset class can be broken up into global economic factors. Each asset class can be shown to be a combination of four macroeconomic variables: (1) real return; (2) inflation (both realized and expected); (3) growth; and (4) risk premium. These are the global factors that impact the returns to all asset classes.

Not surprisingly, bonds tend to be affected mostly by the real return and inflation rate, whereas more risky assets like public equities are impacted more by growth and risk premium. Exhibit 15.7 shows how the US stock market maps out across these variables. Not surprisingly, public equities map out to mostly growth and risk premium; 78% of the return to the US equity markets can be explained by these two macroeconomic variables. Real rates and inflation also have an impact on the returns

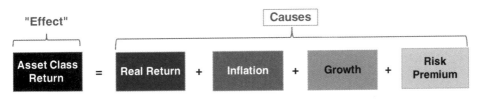

EXHIBIT 15.6 Macroeconomic Drivers of Asset Class Returns

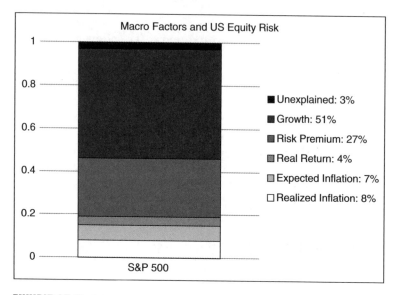

EXHIBIT 15.7   Macroeconomic Drivers of US Equity

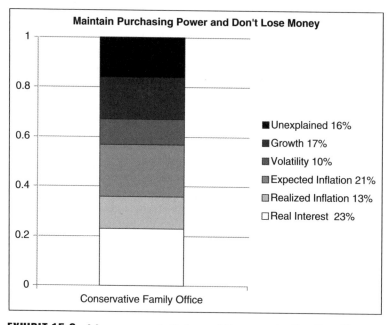

EXHIBIT 15.8   Macroeconomic Drivers of Conservative Family Office
Returns

to public equities, but their inputs are smaller. Overall, these economic variables explain 97% of the return variability of the US stock market.

Turn to a UHNWI, Exhibit 15.8. This portfolio is consistent with a family office whose benchmark is "Don't lose money." One would expect such a goal to have a more conservative portfolio—one tied less to growth assets or risk premiums.

Nearly 60% of this family office is dedicated to real interest rates and inflation factors. Clearly this is a portfolio that is tied much more to bonds than to stocks or other growth assets. The goal of this family office is to not lose money. It is not surprising that its portfolio would be most exposed to real interest rates and inflation—the key macroeconomic variables that affect bond portfolios.

There is a growing trend of family offices looking through their asset allocation and beta drivers to get a better understanding of what macro factors can impact their portfolio. The reason for this, compared to an endowment, is that family offices often have multiple goals: maintaining a lifestyle, growing wealth, and donating cash and other assets to charity. Given these sometimes competing goals, it is helpful for a family office to look at its beta portfolio to get a better understanding of how the portfolio will react to a spike in inflation, a global economic recession, a general hike in real returns, and so on. With this information, family offices can better adjust their beta drivers to ensure they have the right mix of macroeconomic factors to achieve their individual goals.

15.5   INCOME TAXES OF FAMILY OFFICES

Tax-exempt status is a luxury for endowments, foundations, and pension funds. They enjoy an income-tax-free environment where they do not have to worry about the taxable nature of the gains, losses, and cash yield that flows from an investment. To them, a cash dividend is equivalent in tax status to a capital distribution from a private equity investment.

Unfortunately for family offices, income taxes are a significant constraint. To a family office, there is a distinct difference between cash dividends and capital distributions from a private equity fund. In most jurisdictions, the former are considered ordinary income and taxed at a higher tax rate than distributions from a private equity fund.

15.5.1   Tax Efficiency and Wealth Management

Consider Exhibit 15.9. which shows the payoff profiles for three financial instruments: a swap, a privately negotiated forward contract, and an exchange-traded futures contract. Each of these instruments offers the 6-month return on the EURO STOXX Index. If the EURO STOXX Index increases in value over the next 6 months,

EXHIBIT 15.9   Payoff Diagrams for Swaps, Forwards, and Futures Contracts

each of these instruments will earn a positive return. Conversely, if the EURO STOXX declines in value, each of these instruments will have a negative return.

In the absence of transactions costs, the payoff profile should show the arrow passing through the zero intercept. However, each of these instruments intersects the y-axis slightly below zero. The reason is that there is a cost to each instrument. For example, the swap contract requires the EURO STOXX Index receiver to pay an interest rate, typically LIBOR + X%. Similarly, with respect to the forward contract, the negotiating broker will require the EURO STOXX Index receiver to make a deposit with the broker. Last, for the futures contract, the EURO STOXX Index receiver is required to post a cash amount called the initial margin with the futures broker to ensure that she will honor the contract at its completion.

The main point is that in a perfect market all of these contracts are economically equivalent. An investor should be indifferent between the swap, the forward, and the futures contract. This is roughly true for the endowment, foundation, or pension plan that does not have to worry about the tax consequences of its investments. However, for the family office, there is a very large difference. Taxable investors are concerned with **tax efficiency,** which is the efficacy with which wealth is managed so as to maximize after-tax risk-adjusted return. To pursue tax efficiency, investments should be structured in a way to incur the lowest possible tax liability for a given set of assets and the level of expected return.

15.5.2   Taxability of Short-Term and Long-Term Capital Gains

Gains from forward contracts or 6-month swap agreements are considered **short-term capital gains** in the United States, which are trading profits recognized on an investment held for less than 1 year. Short-term capital gains are typically taxed at ordinary income tax rates, the highest rate currently at 37% in the US (not including other potential state and local taxes). The tax rate on short-term capital gains is substantially higher than that of qualified dividends or long-term capital gains in the US.

Let's assume that the swap or forward contract increases in value by $100,000 over the 6-month investment period. Therefore, the net after-tax return to the high-net-worth investor in a 40% tax bracket is:

$$\$100,000 \times (1 - \text{Tax Rate}) = \$100,000 \times (1 - 40\%) = \$60,000$$

However, the treatment is different for the futures contract. For example, any gains from an exchange-traded futures contract are treated as having 60% long-term capital gains and 40% short-term capital gains, regardless of its holding period. This tax simplification creates an opportunity for sophisticated wealth managers to improve after-tax risk-adjusted returns in the US and is representative of opportunities that exist in other jurisdictions.

Securities that qualify for this special income tax treatment are known as Section 1256 contracts, and as such, trading in these securities in the US can be used as a major advantage for high-net-worth investors because 60% of the gains are favorably taxed at the long-term capital-gain tax rate, typically about 20% (i.e., just over half the ordinary income tax rate). In non-Section 1256 securities, the lower tax rate on

long-term capital gains is levied only on investment gains in which assets are held for longer than 1 year.

Denoting $T_{Ordinary}$ as the tax rate on short-term capital gains and T_{LTCG} as the tax rate on long-term capital gains, Equation 15.1 provides the blended tax rate on Section 1256 contract gains denoted as $T_{1256\ Contracts}$:

$$T_{1256\ Contracts} = (0.40\ T_{Ordinary}) + (0.60\ T_{LTCG}) \tag{15.1}$$

APPLICATION 15.5.2

Suppose that the portfolio of a family office generates $100,000 of profit from short-term trading and is in an ordinary income tax bracket of 40%. Assume that the long-term capital-gains tax rate is half the ordinary tax rate. Compare the after-tax profits if the gains were and were not from Section 1256 contracts. The after-tax profits for non-Section 1256 contracts were shown before to be $60,000. For Section 1256 contracts, the after-tax profit can be derived by first computing the tax rate using Equation 15.1:

$$T_{1256\ Contracts} = (0.40 \times 0.40) + (0.60 \times 0.40/2) = 0.28$$

The after-tax gain using the blended rate (0.28) raises the after-tax profits from $60,000 to $72,000:

$$\$100,000 \times (1 - 28\%) = \$72,000$$

Note that 60% of the income is taxed at an assumed long-term tax rate of 20% (half the assumed 40% ordinary rate) and 40% is taxed at the assumed ordinary rate of 40%. The net result is to lower the effective tax rate from 40% to 28%. Clearly, there is an advantage to trading futures contracts and other Section 1256 securities for the family office. This has significant implications with respect to the asset allocation, asset class strategy, and long-term funding goals of the family office. While tax structures vary worldwide, this example clearly shows that advisers, consultants, and family office staff need to understand the implications of different investment vehicles and how each investment affects the specific tax situations of each individual client.

15.5.3   Tax Efficiency and Hedge Fund Investment Strategies

Consider the potential role of hedge funds in improving the income tax efficiency of a family office. Many of these funds use short-term trading strategies, such as those associated with relative value and active macro managers who tend to use swaps and forward contracts more frequently than futures contracts. There are three major ways a family office can increase tax efficiency with hedge funds:

1. Focus more on strategies that have a long-term (12-month) horizon to them. This would be equity long/short and event driven.

2. Invest with hedge fund managers who trade more in Section 1256 securities, such as futures contracts.
3. Select tax-efficient managers by checking the trading and tax records of hedge fund managers to determine how much of their total return is short-term capital gain and how much is long-term gain.

In the US, hedge fund managers will provide investors with an annual reporting of the taxable gains and losses for the year. The US K-1 tax form lists the short-term capital gains, the long-term capital gains, return of capital, dividends, and ordinary income receipts from an investment fund over the course of the year. The K-1 form is not particularly relevant for tax-exempt investors such as endowments, foundations, or pension funds. However, for a family office, the K-1 form is an important source of information and a key part of the due diligence process for that hedge fund manager. Family offices routinely check the K-1 forms of prospective hedge fund managers to determine what portion of the hedge fund manager's gains are subject to ordinary income tax rates of 40% and long-term capital gains tax rates of 20%. Some taxable investors may choose not to invest in hedge funds that are likely to issue a K-1 form, as these forms can significantly complicate tax filings, especially when the K-1 forms are issued several months after the typical deadline for filing tax forms.

15.6   LIFESTYLE ASSETS OF FAMILY OFFICES

Another key difference between family offices and university endowments is the allocation to lifestyle assets. **Lifestyle assets or passion assets** include art, homes, wine, airplanes, cars, and boats, where the purchase and collection follows from the lifestyle preferences or the passions of one or more family members. Lifestyle assets can become a significant part of an UHNWI's overall wealth.

15.6.1   Art as a Lifestyle Asset

Art is the best example of a passion or lifestyle asset. There is significant debate about how these assets should be treated in an asset allocation model. Some family offices believe that art, for example, is an asset class that should be included in the asset allocation process. The reasoning is that art is a scarce commodity and typically increases in value over time. In fact, large money center banks, such as Citicorp and JPMorgan, even provide an outsourced curator function to look after a family's artwork.

More to the point, there are art indices that attempt to track the return to art. One index uses repeat sales of the same painting or sculpture. By using transaction pairs of the same artwork, the issue of heterogeneity or uniqueness is removed as a bias in the index calculation.[7] One problem with such a pairs index is that the time interval between the "paired trade" can be many years—even decades. Furthermore, museums are active purchasers of artwork, and these purchases may permanently remove the art from the trading market. Also, this type of index does not take into account the vast majority of single transactions in the art world. Last, this type of index ignores private transactions that account for up to 50% of all art transactions.[8]

Another type of index attempts to measure the premium paid for auctioned artworks above the estimated auction price quoted by dealers and auction houses. This index measures a rarity premium as the difference between the realized price at auction and the estimated value as established by the auction house. While this type of index attempts to be more empirical, ultimately, the rarity premium is based on the subjective estimate by a dealer or auction house of the estimated sales price for the artwork.[9]

Other family office managers take the view that art is not an asset class because there is no underlying systematic risk premium that can be used to risk budget art as an asset class. Without an underlying risk premium, it is hard to determine how art can be built into an efficient frontier of portfolio construction. Furthermore, unlike the homogeneous assets such as stocks and bonds, each artwork is unique and is defined by a set of physical and intangible characteristics.

Another argument against art as an asset class is that there is no cash flow associated with a piece of art. Therefore, a discounted cash flow model cannot be used to determine its present value. Similarly, it is very difficult to measure the underlying volatility of artwork—individual pieces trade infrequently such that there are very few data points upon which to build a distributional analysis of the returns to art. Last, art is an illiquid asset class; most family offices do not trade in and out of art. They purchase art for the personal enjoyment of the family without regard for trying to generate a capital gain.

15.6.2 Lifestyle Wealth Storage and Other Costs

Financial assets typically have little or no storage costs (custody costs) and in some cases net benefits from securities lending. Expense management can be an important component of lifestyle asset management. While lifestyle assets typically do not generate cash flow, there are ongoing costs of ownership. Expenses such as insurance, storage, curation, security, and general maintenance can increase rapidly as a collection of passion assets grows. And it is not just guarding against theft; for older and rarer collectibles like paintings or wine, the assets must be guarded against the elements like sunlight, dust, and water damage. The proper installation of the passion asset can also be expensive.

In order to reduce these costs and potentially generate cash flow, some art investors have chosen to lease their art, as described by Harris (2015). Demand for leasing can come from corporate art collections, which gives the advantage of tax deductible lease payments. Other lessees may include art investors who may wish to display art that they cannot afford to purchase or may wish to live with a piece of art before making a final purchase decision. Perhaps, leasing art could lead to greater appreciation, such as when a work is displayed in a museum that leads to a larger number of viewers, some of whom may potentially be interested in purchasing the piece. While leasing models vary, some lessors may intend to sell the art and may credit all or part of the lessee's payments toward the eventual purchase of the piece.

A significant trend is that artwork is often held in "free ports." **Free ports** are specialized, climate-controlled repositories for art and other valuable goods belonging to the very wealthy—similar to a custody bank for stock certificates. Not surprisingly, the best-known free ports are in Geneva and Zurich, Switzerland, home to many of the oldest and most private of wealth management firms. Additional free ports exist in Beijing, Singapore, and Luxembourg. More and more, UHNWIs may see art as a portable store of value where the physical display of the artwork is not necessary to achieve personal enjoyment or social status.

Some free ports, such as Singapore, offer complete confidentiality with regard to the nature of the art, its value, and the identity of the owner. However, other free ports, such as those in Zurich and Geneva, are governed by laws that require descriptions, values, and country of origin for the art stored.

Free ports have an important advantage for art collectors. With UHNWIs and museums, foundations, auction houses, and other private collectors, free ports have become an acceptable place of business for the purchase, sale, and transfer of art ownership. The key advantage is that free ports charge no sales taxes—taxes are charged by the country of destination when the art leaves the free port. Until then, while stored at the free port, the goods are considered "in transit" and typically not taxed. This makes free ports a convenient and often a permanent place of storage for art.[10]

15.6.3 Lifestyle Assets and Portfolio Management

Following this discussion, one way that lifestyle assets are used in portfolio construction for a family office is as a constraint on the asset allocation process. Exhibit 15.10 demonstrates this constraint. It shows three broad buckets of assets that are used to achieve three family member goals: (1) maintaining a lifestyle; (2) wealth growth; and (3) wealth transfer.

For this individual, two different portfolios are shown: a moderate portfolio and an aggressive portfolio. In each case, the lifestyle assets remain constant. It is the other two buckets of assets, wealth generation and wealth transfer, that must adjust to achieve the moderate and aggressive portfolio allocation.

Sometimes these two buckets are referred to as **balancing portfolios,** which are used as counterweights to a pool of assets that, for some reason, cannot be adjusted itself. In this case, the lifestyle assets are never expected to be sold or rebalanced. They exist for the personal enjoyment of the family member. Consequently, the wealth generation and wealth transfer buckets are used to balance the overall risk profile for the family member.

15.6.4 Concierge Services

Closely related to lifestyle assets is a growing part of family office management known as **concierge services,** where the family office will attend to mundane details that most people have to deal with in their daily lives such as personal shopping and travel arrangements. While concierge services may be offered by family offices, the UHNWIs can afford to pay a staff directly to manage these details for them rather than receiving them in conjunction with their wealth management services. A sample list of concierge services includes:

- personal shopping;
- art curation and purchase;
- travel arrangements;
- entertainment and sporting events;
- purchase and maintenance of transportation assets; and
- arranging medical services.

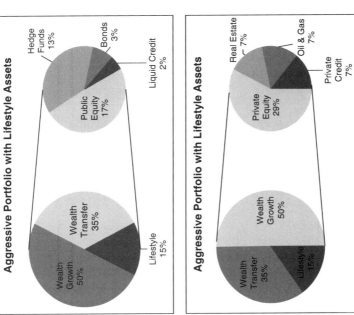

Moderate Portfolio with Lifestyle Assets

Wealth Growth 45%
Wealth Transfer 40%
Lifestyle 15%

Public Equity 20%
Hedge Funds 14%
Liquid Credit 3%
Bonds 3%

Aggressive Portfolio with Lifestyle Assets

Wealth Growth 50%
Wealth Transfer 35%
Lifestyle 15%

Public Equity 17%
Hedge Funds 13%
Bonds 3%
Liquid Credit 2%

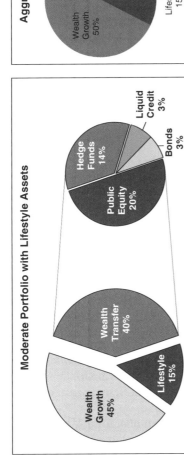

Moderate Portfolio: Allocation of Growth Assets

Wealth Growth 45%
Wealth Transfer 40%
Lifestyle 15%

Private Equity 27%
Real Estate 6%
Oil & Gas 6%
Private Credit 6%

Aggressive Portfolio with Lifestyle Assets

Wealth Growth 50%
Wealth Transfer 35%
Lifestyle 15%

Private Equity 29%
Real Estate 7%
Oil & Gas 7%
Private Credit 7%

EXHIBIT 15.10 Asset Allocation Including Lifestyle Assets

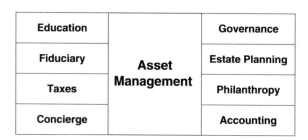

Education		Governance
Fiduciary	**Asset Management**	Estate Planning
Taxes		Philanthropy
Concierge		Accounting

EXHIBIT 15.11   Services Offered by a Family Office

Another part of concierge services is directly related to wealth management. These include tax preparation, administration of the assets, custody, estate planning, education, and philanthropy. Exhibit 15.11 shows the complete range of a full-service family office.

15.7   FAMILY OFFICE GOVERNANCE

Family offices operate very differently from one another. Again, there is no endowment model counterpart to family office management. In the endowment model, independent trustees form the bulk of the endowment board with, typically, only one university employee sitting on the board.

15.7.1   Governance Structures of Family Offices

Some family offices have a formal structure that includes a board of directors or trustees, much like an endowment or a foundation. However, in the family office case, almost all of the board members are family members. There may be one or two independent board members, but this is limited because of the confidentiality of the family wealth. In this case, there are formal board meetings, usually quarterly, where investment memos are proposed and vetted by the board of family members.

Other family offices have a less formal structure and are often controlled by a single person. This is especially true when the first generation that created the family wealth is still alive, has sold the family operating company, and now devotes his or her time to the family wealth. Usually, this is a patriarch or matriarch who forms the core of decision-making and governance for the family. In this case, the investment committee is typically the patriarch/matriarch and the chief investment officer.

Like everything else in life, there are pros and cons to formality in family office governance. The more formal style ensures a rigorous process with detailed investment memos to support every opportunity. Also, there is a forum for debate as well as ensuring that every family member's investments and interests are attended to fairly and completely.

On the other hand, the patriarch/matriarch model offers more flexibility. Investment committee meetings are whenever the patriarch/matriarch wants them or needs them. Decision-making is quick and decisive, and flexibility is an advantage.

There is no single model that is right for all situations. The more formal model is typically set up by the time the wealth is passed to the second generation, unless a member of the second generation is anointed to be the new patriarch/matriarch of the family. It really depends on the individual family's comfort zone with a patriarch/matriarch model versus a board of trustees model and the natural equilibrium for managing the family office depending upon the generation cycle of the family itself.

15.7.2 The Challenges of Family Wealth Sustainability

A common phrase in wealth management is "shirtsleeves to shirtsleeves in three generations," which acknowledges the fact that the vast majority of family fortunes never last beyond the third generation after the wealth was earned, as the first generation earns the wealth, the second preserves it, and the third spends it or distributes it across a large number of descendants. **Dynastic wealth** is an amount of wealth so large that is has substantial potential to be maintained for a large number of generations. The difficulty of maintaining dynastic wealth is evidenced by the fact that none of the 20 richest families in the United States in 1918, such as Ford, Rockefeller, or Carnegie, were among the 100 richest families in 2012 as measured by *Forbes*.[11]

There are four primary factors related to this loss of family wealth over time:

1. A growing number of descendants as the number of generations increases, which dilutes wealth among a larger number of people.
2. A lack of skill or interest in the family business by members of the younger generations.
3. A lack of education and planning with how to prepare younger generations to be productive and understand how to handle their share of the family wealth.
4. An intentional focus on philanthropy, where the assets are distributed to benefit broader society rather than being left for descendants.

These types of issues are described in detail in Daniell and McCullough (2013), who believe that it may be easier to become wealthy today than to stay wealthy over multiple generations.

15.7.3 Strategies to Maintain Family Wealth

In order to address the issue of diluting wealth across generations, it is recommended that wealth be held in a multi-generational trust controlled by the family office or the family business. Similar to an endowment, the assets are professionally managed with a focus on total return, while income to the descendants is limited to a sustainable spending rate that will allow the assets to maintain their value over multiple generations. Limiting overspending by family members and explaining a sustainable distribution rate are important factors in maintaining the wealth over time. The income or assets distributed per beneficiary inevitably decline over time, as there could be 60 **beneficiaries,** or descendants who receive a share of the family wealth, over the course of five generations or 120 years. With an annual spending rate of 2% to 4% and adequate investment returns, the family office may be able to operate in perpetuity, distributing income to many generations of descendants. The assets will be depleted quickly, perhaps within two generations, if the annual spending rate is 6% to 10%, which likely exceeds the real return to the portfolio.

Ideally, the trust would be protected from issues such as family disputes and divorces (dissolutions of marriage) that are well known to quickly reduce family wealth. A properly structured governance process would educate family members on the issues of wealth management and sponsor regular discussions designed to manage the financial conflicts within the family over time. If the family members agree on the vision, values, and goals of the family, the managers of the family office can structure operations in a way designed to meet these goals.

Managers of the family office may also be responsible for governance issues, planning family meetings, and educating family members on investments and wealth-management issues. Records within the family office can preserve and document the family vision, culture, and wishes over time. This institutional memory is very important when the family office changes financial advisers, accountants, and attorneys.

15.7.4 Family Office Inheritance and Succession Strategies

One of the key questions is determining a strategy for **inheritance**, which is the distribution of assets after the death of members of the older generation. Young family members should be educated regarding managing wealth on a continuous basis over time so that they will be prepared for when they receive a distribution of wealth. They receive education not only on wealth management, but also on ways of exercising diligence, discretion, and the avoidance of destructive behaviors. Realistic expectations on the size of the inheritance can serve to reduce anxiety and division within the family.

Daniell and McCullough (2013) explain that giving too much wealth too soon may reduce the work ethic of the beneficiary and create a sense of entitlement. To overcome these issues, it is recommended that wealth be distributed over time, ideally after the beneficiary reaches a series of milestones. Rather than giving $10 million to children once they turn 18 years old, perhaps $1 million is distributed at age 25 or 30 after they have graduated from college and worked for 3 to 10 years in a nonfamily business, proving that they can balance a budget on their own income. Further distributions, perhaps $10 million over the course of a lifetime, may take place as the beneficiaries continue to participate in society in a productive way, often at milestones such as when they are married, have children, buy a house, or need to fund their children's education. Some families choose to distribute assets to beneficiaries in a way that matches their income, as those with higher levels of income receive a larger share of the family wealth, as they have proven to be responsible and productive in their own affairs. It is important that all descendants understand their role in the stewardship of the family fortune.

Some believe that those who materially participate in the family business and in the governance of the family office should receive a substantially larger distribution than those who choose not to contribute in this way. This participation in the family business and family office would commence after the completion of their education as well as professional experience in the nonfamily business. Once the children have proven themselves both externally as well as in the management of the family business and family office, the **succession planning** process starts, which is the process of naming a new leader of the family business and potentially a new governance structure after the death or retirement of the founder or current leader of the business. Succession planning is important, as Daniell and McCullough (2013) state that 92% of family businesses do not last three generations and there is less than a 30% probability of maintaining family wealth across three generations. Training outside the family business is vital, as external experience can bring a greater diversity of views and experience into the family business once the family members complete their external training and move into the family business.

15.8 CHARITY, PHILANTHROPY, AND IMPACT INVESTING

When members of the oldest generation die, their assets are divided between tax liabilities, inheritances distributed to family members or other persons, and donations to benefit society beyond the family.

15.8.1 Charity and Philanthropy

Family estate planning is the process for planning the distribution of assets upon the death of preceding generations. The estate plan considers the goals of the family, the number and type of beneficiaries, the taxable nature of wealth upon death, as well as insurance and giving strategies. Distributing assets to family was discussed in the previous section, while tax and insurance strategies may vary widely across families and domiciles. **Estate taxes** are levied by governments in many jurisdictions on accumulated wealth after the death of its owner. While assets distributed to family members are often subject to these taxes, the estate tax law in many jurisdictions allows the distribution of assets outside of the family for charitable purposes on a pre-tax basis. This allows families to maximize their donations to institutions that seek to benefit society.

There are a variety of causes to which families contribute, but they tend to be focused on religion, healthcare, education, arts and museums, poverty and community development, as well as the environment and issues of social justice or inequality. Each family may have a different area of passion, and the family office team can assist the family in defining how and where this wealth can be distributed to best benefit the selected cause.

There are two terms for donating assets to benefit society: charity and philanthropy. Frumkin (2006) believes that these are very different concepts, even though they may be used interchangeably in conversation. **Charity** is the giving of money or time to social causes, typically to meet more immediate needs and without accountability on behalf of the recipient. For example, a donor may make a charitable gift to a homeless shelter that feeds and houses those with immediate need, without seeking to overcome the situation of poverty through counseling or job training. Without addressing the root causes of poverty, the poverty is sustained and the recipients of the charitable gifts may be in need for long periods of time. In contrast, Franklin describes **philanthropy** as the giving of money or time with the intent of making a lasting change. In the example of the homeless shelter, a philanthropic gift would seek longer term benefits to permanently improve the situation of the homeless by providing the counseling, education, and job training needed to reintegrate the homeless back into productive society.

Frumkin (2006) discusses philanthropy in the context of Andrew Carnegie, who stated that "the man who dies rich, dies disgraced." Carnegie believed that wealth should be distributed during the life of the donor, as the donor has no need for the assets after death. Carnegie is joined by twenty-first-century philanthropists Bill Gates, Warren Buffett, and Mark Zuckerberg, who are seeking to improve outcomes in global health and education during their lifetimes. Buffett has also encouraged other billionaires to leave nearly all of their wealth to philanthropic causes. Azim Premji, the chairman of Wipro Limited, donated a significant portion of his wealth to improve education in India. When signing Warren Buffett's giving pledge, he stated, "I strongly believe that those who are privileged to have wealth should contribute significantly to try to create a better world for the millions who are far less privileged."[12]

These individuals have amassed great wealth during their lifetime, but they have also developed global influence due to their business acumen. Rather than giving only money, many successful businesspeople seek to use their social and political influence and business skills to measure and improve the impact of their philanthropic ventures. Andrew Carnegie, along with John Rockefeller, had an interest in scientific philanthropy, which searched for the underlying causes of poverty and donated to organizations that were able to address these causes. If successful, the need for charity and social welfare would decrease. Ideally, philanthropy would allow recipients to become gainfully employed, ultimately becoming self-supporting and eventually accumulating their own wealth. Some philanthropists sponsor public policy research institutes that actively research ways in which to better the world. Through publication of the research and conversations with lawmakers, the institutes seek to influence legislations and regulations that would further their social agenda. For example, funding scientific research into climate change could influence government officials to create and enforce regulations that could reduce pollution and improve the environment. Just as venture capitalists may seek to invest in disruptive technologies to meet business goals, philanthropists are seeking to promote innovative thinking into solving global issues.

15.8.2 Impact Investing

The World Economic Forum (2014) defines **impact investing** as an investment approach that seeks to earn financial returns while generating measurable and positive social impact. While philanthropy and charity donate assets to worthy causes, impact investing seeks to earn a positive financial return and a return of capital while using the investment to drive social benefits. Impact investing is closely related to concepts such as socially responsible investing (SRI) and environmental, social, and governance (ESG) investing. The World Economic Forum estimates that 17% of family office assets are now allocated to impact investing, with interest greatest among women and younger family members who desire to use their wealth to make a difference in the world. In 2013, the *Financial Times* estimated that 68% of family offices have some involvement in impact investing.

Historically, many investors were introduced to this topic by using their social goals to tilt investments in their public equity portfolio. In **negative screening,** investors intentionally eliminate companies from their portfolio that are deemed to have a negative impact on the world, such as from pollution, harmful products, or unfair employment practices. A newer concept is **positive screening,** where companies are added to the portfolio when they are perceived to do good in the world, such as producing helpful products and having high wages and benefits and good working conditions for their workers and suppliers worldwide, even in areas of extreme poverty. The results of either version of screening have not been extremely beneficial, as the return and risk of screened portfolios may not provide stronger financial results than an indexed portfolio, and it is unclear how changes in portfolios of public companies impact the behavior of these very large and highly diversified firms.

As a result, many investors believe that the social impact can be magnified through focused investments in private equity and private debt structures. There is a wide variety of risk and return targets from private impact investments. Some investments are **impact first,** where investors have a greater focus on the social good of their investments and may accept projects with higher financial risk or lower financial returns. In an extreme case, investors may buy bonds with a zero yield and a simple expectation of the return of capital if the proceeds of the debt offering are used to meet their social goals, perhaps building affordable or environmentally efficient housing.

Finance first investors would like to earn an investment return competitive with market returns and commensurate with the risk of the investment and place relatively less priority on social impact. Once investments with competitive risk-adjusted returns are identified, finance first investors select the projects that most benefit the cause they have chosen to support. Some investors espouse impact alpha. **Impact alpha** is the theory that ventures choosing to do the right things from a social perspective will ultimately be rewarded in the marketplace with above-market financial returns, or that ventures that have socially objectionable operations have substantial risks of generating below-market financial returns. For example, a firm with operations that are negative for the environment may be faced with substantial future cleanup costs that are not currently factored into the stock price.

Impact investing has long had a reputation for earning below-market financial returns. If this is true, the assets allocated to these strategies by fiduciaries such as pension plans will be limited. However, if it can be proven that impact investments provide competitive risk-adjusted returns, then the amount of assets dedicated to impact investments may increase substantially. This increase in assets may start first with family offices and then move into endowments and foundations, many of which are already affiliated with organizations charged with benefiting the social good. Pension plans and others with the largest pools of capital will likely follow.

The Case Foundation (2015) notes that impact investments can be made across asset classes, many of which are clearly alternative. These include public and private equity, fixed income, real estate, and infrastructure. Investment structures can include funds, direct investments, or structured products such as community development bonds.

A key goal of impact investing is to be able to measure the outcomes of these investments. Measurement can be easier when the cause is well defined and the investment is relatively small and where the investor can have an influence on operations, if desired. Some examples of ways of measuring the impact of social investments are the number of jobs or housing units created, the decline in pollution or increase in the availability of clean water, or the number of children vaccinated against diseases. To the extent that investors become involved in the cause, their business acumen and political influence may further enhance the productivity, measurability, and long-term impact of these investments.

15.9   TEN COMPETITIVE ADVANTAGES OF FAMILY OFFICES

Almost every investor has some form of natural advantage that can be exploited as part of the portfolio management process. Pension funds, for example, have huge balance sheets that can bear a lot of liquidity risk over a long period of time. Endowments and foundations are tax-exempt so they can seek out hedge fund strategies without regard to whether short-term or long-term capital gains are generated.

Similarly, family offices have some natural advantages that can help manage the overall portfolio. For the purposes of this discussion we will refer to second- and later-generation family offices—after the initial wealth has been generate and the family operating company has been sold.

1. AGGRESSIVE ASSET ALLOCATION geared toward private equity, venture capital, hedge funds, and other alternative investments can enhance UHNWI expected returns. This flows from their ability to gain access to the best managers, as well as their larger risk appetite.
2. LIQUIDITY PREMIUM CAPTURE. Exhibit 15.5 showed that the liquidity profile for a UHNWI can be more aggressive than a well-known university endowment. This aggressiveness allows UHNWIs to capture the liquidity premium associated with illiquid asset classes. Family offices can commit even more of their wealth to long-dated assets compared to an endowment.
3. DEAL FLOW. UHNWIs are often approached by entrepreneurs and operating companies for direct infusions of capital. Most family offices prefer to make direct private investments in existing, operating companies with established cash flows rather than start-up ventures, but there is no hard-and-fast rule. Direct deals flow from the family's own network of contacts in the banking industry, other private family offices, and lawyers, accountants, and other service providers. Some family offices establish a reputation for direct deals that attracts even more operating companies seeking private capital.

   From an operating company's perspective, billionaire capital is an excellent source of funding. This capital tends to be long term and the family office is not looking to change the management of the company or the board of directors—unlike private equity managers, who often cause significant turnover and turmoil within an operating company. Also, the family office can often make introductions to other investors or customers for the company.

   From the family office perspective, with a direct deal, there are no "2 & 20" fees to be paid to a private equity manager. In addition, the family office gets complete transparency into the underlying investment, unlike allocating capital to a private equity fund where the family office has no control over the investments that will be made by the private equity manager. Last, the family office often contributes the private capital at a discount to the company's enterprise value, unlike private equity managers who typically have to pay a premium to acquire the company.
4. SPEED. Family offices can act quickly to jump on opportunities that a pension fund or an endowment would have to pass on because it cannot process the investment quickly enough. Pension fund and endowment governance requires committee approval to make investments. This can take several months to

schedule the investment opportunity on the investment committee agenda. By contrast, a family office can quickly convene family members to review an opportunity, typically in a matter of days rather than months.

5. GOVERNANCE AND MANAGEMENT OF ASSETS. Managing individual wealth can be complex because it needs to be transparent and devoid of conflicts of interest. An internal family office solves these problems by addressing the individual goals of the family members, providing tailored advice within a framework of complete confidentiality. In addition, the family office can blend the goals of the individual family members with the overall objectives of the family office: Cost savings, central control of the family wealth, and sophisticated asset management.

6. ALIGNMENT OF INTERESTS. When a wealthy family allocates capital to different financial advisers and managers, it will rarely lead to a perfect alignment of family interests. In fact, it often leads to competition among the outside money managers and behavior that can be counterproductive. A family office eliminates these potential conflicts by creating structures where the interests of the family members, the family office, and external money managers work together toward common goals. For example, by pooling the money of the total family, the family office can often negotiate fee breaks and other advantageous terms that a single family member may not be able to access. This has also led to family offices bringing more asset management in-house to avoid external conflicts of interest as well as harder negotiation of fees and promotes.

7. HIGHER RETURNS. The ability to manage the assets of the family in a centralized and professional office can generate the benefit of achieving higher returns. As previously mentioned, the family office can often negotiate fee breaks that a single family member cannot. Every basis point saved in fee negotiations goes straight to the bottom line of additional returns. Also, a central management structure for the family's wealth allows for economies of scale that generate a more efficient and cost-effective management of the family wealth. Last, internal professional management, devoid of any conflicts of interest, gives the family the best chance of achieving higher returns.

8. RISK MANAGEMENT. Centralization of asset management also has the benefit of centralization of risk management. All of the same benefits flow from this: cost-effective management, better alignment of interests, and ability to manage risks across asset classes and time horizons. Another key benefit is the centralization of risk reporting and performance attribution—a more cost-effective way for the family to ensure that their wealth is managed intelligently and prudently.

9. CENTRALIZATION OF SERVICES. The family office can also centralize all of the other services demanded by a UHNWI: estate planning, taxes, accounting, travel, art curation, philanthropy, and so on. The centralization provides two key benefits: cost savings and confidentiality.

10. LIFESTYLE ASSETS. Lifestyle assets flow from some passion of the family member. Art, wine, and other collectibles are prerogatives of the very wealthy. However, there is no consensus about how these assets should be accounted for as part of a well-diversified portfolio. One way to account for these assets is to use them as a constraint in the asset allocation process—a dedicated block of assets that provide a fixed allocation in the portfolio construction process.

NOTES

1. Kavanaugh (2018).
2. See Capgemini (2012).
3. See Amit et al. (2011).
4. This survey was conducted by the author as part of his own network of UHNW family offices.
5. See Collins (2015)
6. See Amit et al. (2011).
7. See the Mei Moses All World Art Index, Mei and Moses (2002).
8. See Geman and Velez (2015).
9. See Geman and Velez (2015).
10. See Geman and Velez (2015).
11. *Forbes* (2002); Kroll (2012).
12. *India Today*, February 23, 2013. http://indiatoday.intoday.in/story/azim-premji-wiprochairman-donates-millions/1/251436.html.

REFERENCES

Amit, R., H. Liechtenstein, M. J. Prats, T. Millay, and L. Pendleton. 2011. "Single Family Offices: Private Wealth Management in the Family Context." Wharton Global Family Alliance.

Capgemini. 2012. "The Global State of Family Offices." Internal White Paper. https://www.capgemini.com/wp-content/uploads/2017/07/The_Global_State_of_Family_Offices.pdf.

Case Foundation. 2015. "A Short Guide to Impact Investing." October. https://casefoundation.org/resource/short-guide-impact-investing/.

Collins, M. 2015. "Private Investment Firms Win the Right to Keep Money in the Family." *Bloomberg News*, February 10.

Daniell, M. H. and T. McCullough. 2013. *Family Wealth Management*. Hoboken, NJ: John Wiley & Sons.

Forbes. 2002. "The First Rich List." *Forbes*, September 27.

Frumkin, P. 2006. *Strategic Giving: The Art and Science of Philanthropy*. Chicago, IL: University of Chicago Press.

Geman, H., and T. Velez. 2015. "On Rarity Premium and Ownership Yield in Art." *Journal of Alternative Investments* (Summer): 8–21.

Harris, G. 2015. "Something Borrowed: The Growing Industry of Art Leasing." *Financial Times*, June 12.

Kavanaugh, J. 2018. "The Rise of Family Offices: 10-fold Growth in Less Than a Decade." *Real Assets Adviser*. March 1. https://irei.com/publications/article/rise-family-offices-10-fold-growth-less-decade/.

Kroll, L. 2012. "Forbes World's Billionaires 2012." *Forbes*, March 7.

Mei, J. and M. Moses. 2002. "Art as an Investment and the Underperformance of Masterpieces." *American Economic Review* 92 (5): 1656–68.

World Economic Forum. 2014. "Impact Investing: A Primer for Family Offices." http://www3.weforum.org/docs/WEFUSA_FamilyOfficePrimer_Report.pdf.

Risk and Risk Management

Risk and risk management are central to the analysis and management of portfolios containing traditional or alternative assets. Part 4 begins with a review of negative investment outcomes that serves to emphasize the importance of risk and the broad range of important risks. Chapters 16-20 discuss varied aspects of understanding and managing the challenges faced by asset allocators and risk managers in overseeing investment portfolios.

CHAPTER 16

Cases in Tail Risk

This chapter examines cases involving unusual events such as hedge fund collapses. The purposes of this review are to distill the events into underlying central causes and to develop insights to better prepare for future events.

16.1 PROBLEMS DRIVEN BY MARKET LOSSES

This section begins with three examples of the impact of market forces in generating tail events. Losses should be expected as a natural consequence of seeking profits with strategies involving risk. However, best practices require that prospective and current investors be provided with sufficient information to have a reasonable basis on which to understand the total potential risk.

This section is not about problems driven solely by market losses. When a fund collapses during a period of market stress, the collapse is often attributable to a combination of external pressures from markets and internal failures due to conditions that predate the market stress. For example, a poorly constructed building is most likely to fail during a stress such as a storm. In most cases, the true cause of the failure is the internal flaws in the structure, since storms are to be expected. Similarly, fund failures during market stress should be analyzed to see the internal mistakes that led to the weaknesses.

16.1.1 Amaranth Advisors, LLC

Amaranth Advisors, LLC, was a self-described multi-strategy hedge fund investing across asset classes and strategies. Multi-strategy hedge funds are generally designed to employ a variety of investment strategies. However, Amaranth's fall from glory came from an extremely concentrated bet in the energy markets. Although Amaranth was technically a multi-strategy hedge fund with positions across multiple asset classes, by 2006 it had devoted a large proportion of its risk capital to natural gas trading.

Amaranth was founded in 2000 by Nicholas Maounis and was headquartered in Greenwich, Connecticut. The founder's original expertise was in convertible bonds, but the fund later became involved in merger arbitrage, long/short equity, leveraged loans, and energy trading. As of June 30, 2006, energy trades accounted for about half of the fund's capital and generated about 75% of its profits.

Although Amaranth was based in Greenwich, its star trader, Brian Hunter, was based in Calgary, Alberta, Canada. The *Wall Street Journal* reported that Amaranth's head energy trader sometimes held "open positions to buy or sell tens of billions of dollars of commodities."[1] Due to the hedge fund fee structure, Amaranth had a big incentive to take big bets. This is also detailed in the *Wall Street Journal* article: "At Amaranth, star energy trader Brian Hunter won an estimated $75 million bonus after his team produced a $1.26 billion profit in 2005. Like many others at the fund, he had to keep about 30% of his pay in the fund. The fund's chief risk officer, Robert Jones, got a bonus of at least $5 million for 2005, say people familiar with the bonuses."

Amaranth engaged in a commodity futures strategy of establishing long positions in winter delivery contracts for natural gas and going short the nonwinter contracts. Understanding the nuances of natural gas trading requires some background. The key economic function for natural gas in the United States is to provide for heating demand during the winter in the northern United States, although natural gas is also a key energy source for generating electricity for air-conditioning demand during the summer. There is a long injection season, from spring through fall, in which natural gas is injected and stored in caverns for later use during the long winter season. By the end of February 2006, Amaranth held nearly 70% of the open interest in the November futures contracts on the New York Mercantile Exchange (NYMEX) and nearly 60% of the futures for January.

The size of those positions in natural gas contracts led to Amaranth's collapse. But Amaranth's fall did not happen overnight. After starting 2006 with $7.5 billion in investor assets, the fund soared to $9.2 billion, but then eventually tumbled to less than $3 billion. By the end of May 2006, at least some of Amaranth's traders and officers were aware of the firm's predicament, as it had lost approximately $1 billion in that month alone. Still, Amaranth continued to put more money into its natural gas bets. By the end of August, Amaranth was still pumping in more money to hold its positions, but the market continued to move against the fund. When natural gas prices fell in September 2006, Amaranth found itself losing a substantial amount of money on its very large positions. These losses led Amaranth to scramble to transfer its natural gas futures contracts to third-party financial institutions over the weekend of September 16.

Initially, Merrill Lynch agreed to take on 25% of Amaranth's positions for a payment of about $250 million. Amaranth lost another $800 million on Tuesday, September 19. The next day, on September 20, Amaranth succeeded in transferring its remaining energy positions to Citadel Investment Group and to its prime broker, JPMorgan Chase, at a $2.15 billion discount to their mark-to-market value, using the previous day's prices. In total, Amaranth lost $6.6 billion in a matter of months.

Prime brokers generally treat hedge funds as their most favored clients (MFCs). But when it comes to a quickly eroding hedge fund, MFC status can change quickly, and a hedge fund can find that prime brokers exacerbate the hedge fund's problems rather than alleviate them. This appears to be part of the story for Amaranth. On Monday, September 18, just when Amaranth thought it had a rescue plan negotiated with Goldman Sachs, its prime broker, JPMorgan, refused to release the collateral that Amaranth had deposited. This effectively killed any potential bailout of Amaranth.

What are the lessons to be learned here? A multi-strategy fund should clearly not have 50% of its capital dedicated to one specific market or trade, especially if that fund claims to be well diversified. Investors should watch for signs that a fund has concentrated positions, such as may be indicated by a volatility of monthly returns exceeding 10%. Fund management should closely supervise all traders, even those star traders who have previously earned billions of dollars in profits.

Risk managers at Amaranth may have allowed Hunter to take more risk than was justified simply because of the size of his prior trading gains. The geographic separation between Hunter and Amaranth may have also been a factor, as Hunter ran a small office in Alberta, far from Amaranth's Connecticut home. This separation could have made it difficult to discover any concealed dealings. Hunter apparently had a checkered past, which should have given some investors pause. It was said that in his prior career at Deutsche Bank, Hunter's trading privileges were revoked after a series of crippling losses on energy trades.

Hedge funds often operate in a lightly regulated environment. The lack of regulation over Amaranth was compounded by the fact that its trading schemes were conducted in the complex and uncoordinated world of natural gas markets. For example, the US regulatory umbrella covering energy trading has had a noteworthy gap in coverage. The exchange-traded futures markets are explicitly regulated by the Commodity Futures Trading Commission (CFTC), and the physical natural gas markets are explicitly regulated by the Federal Energy Regulatory Commission (FERC). However, over-the-counter energy derivatives trading has not been subject to the same regulatory scrutiny, and it was on such platforms that Amaranth carried out a substantial portion of its trading. Amaranth traded many of its natural gas positions on the Intercontinental Exchange (ICE) as opposed to the New York Mercantile Exchange (NYMEX). Both exchanges trade natural gas contracts; however, under what is known as the Enron loophole, electronic exchanges like the ICE are not as highly regulated as physical exchanges like the NYMEX.

The risk-management process at Amaranth may have understated the probability of long-term and large unidirectional price changes. When risk measures, such as value at risk, are estimated based on historical data that reflect an abnormally calm period of price changes, they understate reasonable anticipations of future risk. For example, estimations of risk based on historical data during periods of short-term price changes that are uncorrelated or mean-reverting typically understate the potential magnitude of longer-term price changes over periods of positively autocorrelated, or trending, markets.

Due to the larger position sizes, leverage magnifies the impact of underestimating underlying risks. Therefore, positions using leverage should be based on worst-case scenario losses rather than volatility estimates from a recently calm market. For example, if data over a longer time interval, such as a complete market cycle, show a maximum drawdown of 10%, then levering similar positions at rates of more than 10 times capital is likely to lead to a complete loss of investor capital during the next down cycle for that market. Also, Amaranth apparently had no formal stop-loss or concentration limits. High leverage, unanticipated large unidirectional moves, and insufficient processes to control risk can cause fund failure.

Amaranth illustrates another problem with large positions relative to the liquidity of the underlying markets. As a fund experiences financial stress, the fund's process of liquidating long positions in illiquid markets can drive prices down (and liquidating short positions in illiquid markets can drive prices up), fueling further losses and further liquidations. The problem is especially severe when, as is often the case, the events leading to a fund's trouble coincide with illiquidity in the market. Adding to the problem is the fact that during periods of market stress and the accompanying need for funds to receive credit to ride out the adverse price movements, financial institutions often experience similar stress and restrict credit.

16.1.2 Long-Term Capital Management

World financial markets faced a dramatic crisis in 1998 when a Greenwich, Connecticut, hedge fund named Long-Term Capital Management (LTCM) collapsed. At the time, LTCM was considered one of the largest and best-managed hedge funds in the world.

LTCM was founded in 1994 by several executives from Salomon Brothers Inc., and its board included two Nobel laureates in economics. Its troubles began in May 1998 with huge losses in its mortgage-backed arbitrage portfolio. LTCM's net worth shrank from a peak of $5 billion to about $2.3 billion in August 1998 and to just under $400 million by the end of September.[2] How did this huge fund with its stellar management team collapse so quickly when much of the world's economy was performing quite well?

LTCM focused on relative value strategies, such as fixed-income arbitrage. The premise for these trades was the expectation that the spread in prices or rates between two similar securities would converge over time. LTCM would buy the cheaper security and short the more expensive security and wait for the spread between the two similar securities to narrow before closing the trades.

LTCM used extensive leverage, based apparently on management's confidence that the fund's models could successfully identify mispriced securities and that large mispricings were virtually sure to be corrected on a timely basis. LTCM's massive degrees of leverage, including a leverage ratio of 25 to 1 in its cash positions, grew to over 50 to 1 in 1998. In addition, the fund had gross notional amounts of futures contracts that exceeded $500 billion, swap positions that exceeded $750 billion, and other derivative positions that exceeded $150 billion.[3] The leverage ratio implied by these positions approached 300 to 1.

LTCM's already weakened positions were pummeled in August 1998 when the Russian government defaulted on the payment of its outstanding bonds. As a result of the Russian bond default, there was a sudden and drastic liquidity crisis that caused spreads to widen across a broad range of markets rather than contract, as LTCM's models had predicted. The fund's positions quickly accumulated large losses that led to a margin call from its prime broker. LTCM was forced to liquidate some of its positions. But liquidating in the midst of illiquid market conditions caused spreads to widen further. LTCM's losses continued to grow, which in turn led to more margin calls as its finances spiraled downward.

The situation for LTCM was bleak, and large financial institutions feared that if it were forced to liquidate the majority of its portfolio, there would be a systemic impact in the financial markets. The US Federal Reserve Bank stepped in with three rate reductions within 6 months, but this action did not save LTCM. Finally, on September 23, at the neutral site of the Federal Reserve Bank of New York, 14 banks and brokerage firms met and agreed to provide capital infusions totaling $3.6 billion to LTCM. In return, the consortium of banks and brokerage firms received 90% ownership of the fund.

Although the cause of LTCM's demise was clear, the real question is: how was LTCM able to procure such a huge amount of credit that it could leverage its cash positions at a 25 to 1 ratio and its derivative positions at almost a 300 to 1 ratio? It was simple: LTCM never disclosed its full positions, because its counterparties did not demand information on the size of its total positions or its total credit exposure. As a result, LTCM was able to amass tremendous positions and credit.

It should be noted that LTCM's spread trades would have performed well if LTCM had had more time to work its way out of the liquidity crisis that gripped the markets. It was not that LTCM had poor trade ideas; on the contrary, its valuation models were robust. Instead, the problem was the inability to weather a major liquidity crisis due to the use of too much leverage. When the Russian bond default occurred, there was a flight to quality; LTCM's relative value positions diverged instead of converging and, with its very large amounts of leverage, LTCM collapsed.

16.1.3   Carlyle Capital Corporation

Another swift and stunning reversal of fortune was experienced by Carlyle Capital Corporation (CCC), which was created by the Carlyle Group in 2007. The Carlyle Group is one of the most successful alternative asset firms in the world, managing as of 2019 more than $220 billion in assets for some of the world's most sophisticated clients. The Carlyle Group created CCC as part of its efforts to diversify its business and to give public shareholders a way to get exposure to some of its funds.

Unlike most such funds, CCC was listed on Euronext Amsterdam. Therefore, it was available to the public starting with its listing in July 2007. Partners of the Carlyle Group retained a 15% ownership in CCC. Unfortunately, within weeks of its public listing, the Carlyle Group was forced to make its first bailout of the fund with additional injected capital. The fund's demise came just 8 months later and was a surprise to many. How could such a new and publicly traded fund with such a prestigious parent firm collapse so quickly?

CCC's strategy was not fraught with complex derivatives or secretive black box trading schemes. Its strategy was simple: it borrowed money at low short-term interest rates and invested this borrowed capital in long-term AAA-rated mortgage bonds issued by Freddie Mac and Fannie Mae. Fannie Mae, Freddie Mac, and Ginnie Mae are nicknames for three large US government-sponsored companies with the corresponding acronyms FNMA, FHLMC, and GNMA. These agencies bought mortgages and issued bonds backed by an explicit or implicit guarantee by the US government. Debate existed as to whether the full credit risk of the bonds issued by the agencies was unambiguously backed by the US government, but the bonds were considered safe enough by the rating agencies to receive AAA ratings.

CCC's investment strategy was to make money on the difference between the cost of funding the AAA-rated mortgage securities and the interest received on them. It used aggressive leverage; for every $1 in capital it raised from investors, CCC borrowed about $31 to invest in the US housing agency bonds. Its aim was to use this leverage to amplify the narrow spread between the return on its assets and the cost of its funding to generate an annual dividend of around 10%. It used only about $670 million in cash equity to finance its $21.7 billion portfolio of securities issued by Freddie Mac and Fannie Mae.

Although Freddie Mac and Fannie Mae securities were considered almost certain to be repaid, their value plummeted dramatically in February and March 2008, as investors worldwide shunned risk of any type and as the US housing market continued to suffer. CCC's financial health was vulnerable because of the highly leveraged nature of its investment strategy.

Dire funding problems first emerged on March 5, 2008, when CCC said it had been unable to meet margin calls from four banks on short-term repurchase agreements. Just 2 days earlier, the chief executive, John Stomber, had told investors on a conference call that the fund wasn't seeing increased margin pressure from its lenders. But within a week, the margin calls had reached more than $400 million, and lending banks had seized about three-quarters of CCC's assets. Efforts to put in place a standstill agreement with banks holding the remaining assets failed late in the week of March 10.

The substantial decline in value of Fannie Mae and Freddie Mac securities came to a head with margin calls from Deutsche Bank, JPMorgan Chase, and other lenders that reached more than $900 million. At that point, the lenders began to seize the fund's collateral and its chief assets, the AAA-rated mortgage-backed securities. The share price for CCC declined swiftly, from its public offering price of $20 in July 2007 to $0.31 in March 2008. During the week of March 10, 2008, CCC declared that it would wind up its operations and further stated that there would be no money left for shareholders.

CCC's collapse was a casualty of a liquidity crisis that led to more than $50 billion in losses at major investment banks. What was the lesson here? No security is safe from a liquidity crisis. The securities purchased by CCC were presumed to be US-government backed and immune from credit risk. But as the credit crisis took hold, even these safe investments declined substantially in value. Indeed, as history played out later in 2008, Fannie Mae and Freddie Mac were taken over by the US government, and the implicit guarantee of their bonds was finally made explicit. Even the Carlyle Group, with its clout and reputation, could not negotiate a grace period from its bankers to save CCC. Prime brokers and bankers have no patience or compassion when it comes to declining collateral values.

16.1.4 Declining Investment Opportunities and Leverage

Some funds choose to use aggressive levels of leverage from the start. Other funds drift into dangerous levels of leverage due to declining investment opportunities in a previously lucrative strategy or market. Declining profits can lead fund managers to take on increasing leverage and pursue riskier trades to maintain performance levels. This section reviews the mechanics of leverage and returns.

Return on equity (ROE) is profit after financing costs, expressed as a percentage of equity. **Return on assets (ROA)** is profit before financing costs (and taxes), expressed as a percentage of assets. ROE can be expressed as a function of ROA, leverage (L, which is defined here as the ratio of assets to equity), and interest costs on the financing (r):

$$ROE = (ROA \times L) - [r \times (L - 1)] \tag{16.1}$$

In Equation 16.1, the rightmost term in brackets is the total interest expense from leverage, expressed as a percentage of equity. Note that without leverage, such that $L = 1$, ROE will be equal to ROA. Equation 16.1 illustrates the sensitivity of ROE to ROA (i.e., asset performance) when L is large as well as the sensitivity of ROE to financing costs (r) when L is large.

APPLICATION 16.1.4

A firm with an ROE (return on equity) of 14% employs a leverage of 3 (which is defined here as the ratio of assets to equity). If the firm's interest cost on financing is 5%, what is its ROA (return on assets)?

Inserting the values into Equation 16.1:

$$14\% = (ROA \times 3) - (5\% \times 2)$$

ROA = 8%. Note that each variable in Equation 16.1 can be found given the other three.

16.1.5 Behavioral Biases and Risk Taking

Examining the use, measurement, and dangers of leverage is reasonably straightforward. However, the search for profitable trades in markets with increasing competition raises more challenging issues. Financial markets with substantially increased competition are often described as too much money chasing too few opportunities. The dynamics of these environments deserve careful consideration, since these environments are ripe for market-driven collapses and fraudulent schemes that attempt to mask losses.

Firms seeking to maintain trading profits in increasingly competitive markets may become overexposed to particular risks. First, when profitable trading opportunities are rare, fund managers may concentrate positions in particular bets that they perceive as having value. Second, managers may be more likely to invest in opportunities that they have misunderstood.

As competition increases and as truly valuable opportunities become rarer, it is increasingly likely that managers will expand their search for opportunities until they find a bet that appears unusually attractive. But even an overpriced opportunity can appear attractive to an analyst when that analyst errs by missing or misunderstanding the true risks. In a behavioral sense, an analyst may be biased toward concluding that an opportunity is truly attractive rather than interpreting the finding as the result of an error in evaluation. The result is that the fund may become overexposed to risks of which it is unaware.

Behavioral finance provides explanations of why these concerns are valid. **Behavioral finance** studies the potential impacts of cognitive, emotional, and social factors on financing decision-making. For example, confirmation bias is the tendency to disproportionately interpret results that confirm a previously held opinion as being true. The previous discussion provided an example. The analyst knows that profitability predictions are susceptible to error. But based on experience, the analyst believes that highly profitable trading opportunities can be identified.

The analyst then examines numerous trading opportunities. Since the evaluations of each opportunity are subject to error, the analyst may locate an investment opportunity based on a false prediction of high profitability. A confirmation bias would cause the analyst to be too likely to decide that the reason for the finding is that the opportunity will be highly profitable rather than to conclude that the prediction was made in error.

The analyst's belief that profitable trading opportunities exist in a particular market may be a result of anchoring. Anchoring may be viewed in this context as a tendency to rely too heavily on previous beliefs. An analyst observing past successful searches for profitable trades may disproportionately expect that new opportunities will be found, despite knowing that market conditions have changed.

Confirmation bias and anchoring are examples of behavioral biases. **Behavioral biases** are tendencies or patterns exhibited by humans that conflict with prescriptions based on rationality and empiricism. Behavioral biases are generally viewed as important explanations for some investment behavior and often conflict with rational long-term investment decision-making. There are numerous types of behavioral biases that have been described and observed.

In due diligence analysis, these biases should be presumed to affect both the fund managers being evaluated and the analysts charged with performing the analysis. For instance, analysts performing due diligence on a fund might desire to find that the fund represents a great investment opportunity and therefore be biased in favor of reaching a favorable conclusion. The primary methods of combating errors in decision-making due to behavioral biases are to rely on evidence, including academic research, and to use industry best practices that are based on careful analysis of empirical evidence and theory.

Analysts performing due diligence should be especially alert when analyzing funds using strategies that have become widely known as generating high returns. In these situations, increased use of leverage, increasing concentrations of positions, and reported returns out of line with competitors are valuable warning signals.

16.1.6 Volatility of Volatility Derivatives in February 2018

XIV was a volatility derivative structured as an exchange traded note (ETN). Long positions in XIV were structured to offer gains when anticipated S&P 500 volatility decreased (or held steady) but suffer declines when anticipated S&P 500 volatility increased. Volatility derivatives including XIV are detailed in Chapters 36 and 37.

From a speculator's or investor's point of view, establishing long positions in XIV was like selling insurance to portfolio managers against market turmoil (i.e., a long position in XIV was short volatility). As an exchange traded note, XIV represented a liability on the balance sheet of XIV's issuer (Credit Suisse). XIV maintained its target short volatility exposure by being short volatility futures contracts. The size of the futures hedge was continuously adjusted based on the value of XIV, the number of shares of XIV outstanding, and the contract prices of specified volatility futures contracts.

As a short volatility exposure, long positions in XIV were expected to offer a risk premium in normal economic environments to reward investors for bearing the highly undesirable risk of large losses during market crashes (i.e., volatility spikes). The profit potential is related to the shape of the CBOE Volatility Index (VIX) futures curve, with strong contango contributing to gains in short volatility positions. As expected, XIV generated consistent gains. XIV's truly remarkable history included its gain from early 2016 to January 2018 of over 600% as shown in Exhibit 16.1. Investors should realize, though, that any inverse product is expected to lose 100% of its value when the price of the underlying doubles.

As an ETN, the quantity and total value of the outstanding shares of XIV could grow with its market price as well as the issuance of additional shares. By late 2017, XIV and similar volatility products had total market values near $5 billion.

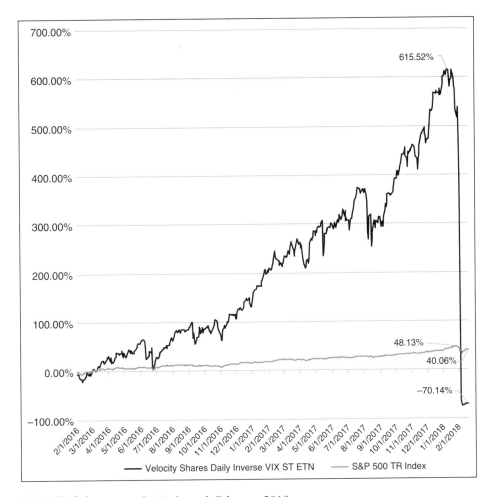

EXHIBIT 16.1 Prices of VIX through February 2018

XIV cranked out enormous gains. The gains were briefly interrupted by losses when volatility spiked, but holders of long positions in XIV were quickly rewarded when volatility returned to low levels and XIV set new highs.

All of that changed in a single day: February 5, 2018. On February 5, 2018, the market's anticipation of future volatility in the S&P 500 soared, causing the value of VIX to rise and XIV to fall. The decline in the value of XIV led to the unwinding of some of the massive short volatility futures positions in the XIV hedge (i.e., it caused huge orders for long positions in the volatility futures contracts). The buy orders for volatility futures from XIV's rebalancing as well as other similar products swamped the relatively small available liquidity in the volatility futures contracts—leading to further escalation in the futures contract's price. The soaring futures prices in turn caused more declines in the value of XIV and orders for more long positions in volatility futures to maintain the hedge.

XIV began the day trading at nearly $100 per share. XIV's historic fall on February 5, 2018 continued until the markets closed. The indicated value of XIV shares at the end of the day was only $4.22 per share.

Surely, most investors in XIV understood that XIV would decline in price if the market's perception of future S&P 500 volatility rose. However, it is likely that few investors understood that *the volatility products themselves could generate futures transactions that could swamp the liquidity of the futures market and cause their own destruction.*

An important and somewhat unique aspect of the demise of XIV is the difficult position faced by holders of XIV as its price plummeted. Great uncertainty existed in the marketplace as to what transactions were being taken inside XIV and what the impacts of those transactions were on the ETN's market value. While the reported hypothetical value of XIV was under $5 per share at the end of February 5 (down from almost $100), its closing market price was $16.39.

XIV was terminated shortly after its collapse, although similar products (SVXY) still exist. There are takeaways from the collapse of XIV. First, care should be taken to thoroughly understand complex products such as volatility products. Second, a trade with a history of fantastic profits becomes quite dangerous when the trade becomes highly crowded. Another lesson is that the returns from "insurance-writing" strategies come with negative skewness.

16.2 TRADING TECHNOLOGY AND FINANCIAL CRISES

Trading technology has increased dramatically in the last century, transforming relatively slow-paced financial markets based on verbal agreements and pencil-and-paper-based records into lightning-fast markets based on Internet-based communication and computerized algorithms. Although these technological gains have generated enormous reductions in trading costs, recent experiences suggest that technology may be increasing systemic risks. This section discusses three events.

16.2.1 Quant Crisis, August 2007

During the first half of 2007, events in the US subprime mortgage markets began affecting many parts of the US financial industry, setting the stage for eventual turmoil in financial markets. By the first week of August 2007, several quantitative long/short equity hedge funds had sustained tremendous losses. Researchers from MIT subsequently conducted simulations of long/short equity portfolios and found evidence that the unwinding of fund positions began in July 2007 and continued until the end of the year.[4] In 2011, Khandani and Lo analyzed what became known as the Quant Meltdown of August 2007 and proposed the unwind hypothesis to explain the events of the previous year. The **unwind hypothesis** suggests that hedge fund losses began with the forced liquidation of one or more large equity market-neutral portfolios, primarily to raise cash or reduce leverage. The subsequent price impact of this massive and sudden unwinding caused other similarly constructed portfolios to experience losses. These losses caused other funds to deleverage their portfolios, leading to a vicious spiral reminiscent of Long-Term Capital Management in 1998. Some of the most successful equity hedge funds in the history of the industry reported record losses, although equity markets were only moderately affected by these troubles. Many of the funds suffering large losses were equity market-neutral and statistical arbitrage hedge funds.

The unwind hypothesis and the events of 2007 underscore the potential commonality of strategies among many quantitative equity market-neutral hedge funds. When large investors hold substantial positions in the same asset or similar assets, it is known as a **crowded trade**. Crowded trades are viewed as risky positions due to the relatively large potential for massive sell orders or buy orders placed by investors at approximately the same time. The pursuit of similar strategies across a set of very large hedge funds combined with rapid trading techniques facilitated by new technologies broadens the concern regarding crowded trades into concerns regarding crowded strategies.

16.2.2 The Flash Crash of 2010

On the afternoon of May 6, 2010, the United States' Dow Jones Industrial Average (the Dow) was down about 3% on the day based on macroeconomic concerns, such as the debt crisis in Greece. Suddenly the Dow dropped another 600 points (about 6%) in a period of 5 minutes, bringing the Dow to a loss of 900 points by 2:47 p.m. Then the market turned abruptly and began a rapid rally. By 3:07 p.m., the Dow had bounced back by about 600 points and leveled off to end the day where it had stood prior to the flash crash. During the day of the flash crash, the Dow experienced its second largest point swing to that date.

What caused this wild swing in prices? While there were initial rumors of trading errors, high-frequency traders, and technical glitches, news emerged that an intentional but very large E-Mini S&P 500 sell order may have triggered the crash. A report by the SEC showed that "a large fundamental trader (a mutual fund complex) initiated a program to sell a total of 75,000 E-Mini S&P contracts (valued at approximately \$4.1 billion) as a hedge to an existing equity position."[5] In April 2015, the US Department of Justice attributed the large order to fraud and manipulation through spoofing and pursued criminal action against a British trader. **Spoofing** is the placing of large orders to influence market prices with no intention of honoring the orders if executed.

High-frequency trading firms and other traders jumped in and joined the selling of futures contracts. Arbitrageurs bought the depressed futures contracts and sold equities in the cash markets, driving down the cash equity market.

In the aftermath of the flash crash, circuit breakers were expanded. A **circuit breaker** is a decision rule and procedure wherein exchange authorities invoke trading restrictions (even exchange closures) in an attempt to mute market fluctuations and to give market participants time to digest information and formulate their trading responses. Despite their intended purposes, circuit breakers have also been argued to heighten risk due to concerns over illiquidity when exchanges suspend trading. These challenges and opportunities reflect the impact of advancing trading technologies on financial markets and their participants.

16.2.3 Knight Capital Group

Knight Capital Group was a global financial services firm engaged in market making, electronic execution, and institutional sales and trading. Knight was the largest trader in US equities, with a market share of about 17% of equity exchange volume according to information supplied by the firm on its website in late 2011. One of

Knight's major roles was receiving and executing order flow from large institutions, including investment companies, banks, and brokerage firms.

On Wednesday, August 1, 2012, Knight's trading caused a major disruption in the prices of about 150 companies listed on the NYSE. The problem was attributed to a technological breakdown, namely the installation of software that had caused Knight to enter millions of faulty trades in less than an hour. By the end of the day, Knight's losses from the error totaled $460 million.

Knight's technological issue appears to have stemmed from flaws in the oversight and management of a new technology deployed at Knight. According to an analysis by Nanex, a Knight algorithm appeared to have been repeatedly buying at the offer and selling at the bid, causing Knight to lose a small amount of money on each trade and resulting in the loss of huge sums due to the trades being repeated over and over again.

By Friday morning, Knight was in dire straits; as the *Wall Street Journal* explained, "In the span of two days, the company's market value had plunged to $253.4 million from $1.01 billion."[6] Major customers stopped doing business with Knight or were "dialing back" their trading through Knight. Ultimately, Knight reached an agreement with Getco LLC in December 2012 and was acquired for $1.4 billion in July 2013.

According to the *New York Times*, "The SEC blamed two 'technology missteps' for the trading fiasco on Aug. 1. It contends that Knight Capital failed to remove a defective function in one of its routers . . . [resulting] in a barrage of erroneous stock orders . . . The regulator also contends that an automated e-mail identifying the error ahead of the market opening on Aug. 1 was sent to a group of employees. While these messages were not intended to be alerts, they provided a chance for the firm to fix the problem."[7] Knight agreed to pay a $12 million fine imposed by the SEC to settle charges that it had violated trading rules.[8]

The fine against Knight marked the first time that the SEC used a market-access rule against a trading firm; the new rule had been adopted in 2010 and required brokers and dealers with direct access to American exchanges to institute controls to protect the markets from such trading errors.[9] Although regulatory efforts may mitigate some threats, risks from advanced trading technology remain and are relevant to all market participants. As in the case of Knight, rapid electronic trading can generate enormous benefits but can magnify even the smallest trading glitches. The problems at Knight disrupted markets and trade executions for several days. These events highlight the systemic risks posed by very large organizations, and indicate that the infrastructure supporting modern capital markets is highly technology dependent.

All three cases in this section emphasize not only the seriousness of technological failures but also the speed with which investors can lose money and the speed with which computer-driven trading systems need to be able to detect and correct errors.

16.3   FAILURES DRIVEN BY FRAUD

The next four cases are concerned with fraud (or alleged fraud) and have little or nothing to do with losses due to market stress. **Fraud** is intentional deception typically for the purpose of financial gain. Although fraud is often revealed during periods of market stress, market stress is inevitable. The true source of the problem is the fraud itself, and the fundamental underlying cause of investor losses to fraud is insufficient due diligence and controls.

16.3.1 Bayou Management

Bayou Management perpetrated one of the boldest of all hedge fund frauds. Bayou started out as a legitimate hedge fund but quickly degenerated into outright fraud. The two principals, founder Samuel Israel III and CFO Daniel Marino, were both eventually sentenced to more than 10 years in prison.

The story of Bayou began in 1996, when, within a few months after the Bayou fund opened and started trading, Bayou sustained trading losses and began lying to customers about the fund's profits and losses. Bayou concealed its true volatility and losses by fabricating results. In 1997, with profits falling short of the amount principals had projected, Bayou transferred back into the fund a portion of the trading commissions that the fund had paid to Bayou Securities during that year. Bayou Securities was a separate broker that Bayou Capital had set up to process the trades from the fund, meaning it was a captive brokerage firm and earned commissions on the Bayou fund's trades. It is typically a bad practice for hedge fund managers to earn brokerage fees on the trades of the funds they manage, as this gives the fund managers incentive to increase the number of trades. Further, there is an incentive for the managers to direct trades to their securities firm without demanding the best execution and lowest commission rates.

Bayou did not disclose to its clients that the fund's performance was being bolstered by these rebates of commissions. Consequently, Bayou's clients were left with a false impression that the fund had made a profit after commissions. Trading losses continued into 1998, when the fund sustained a net trading loss of millions of dollars. Over the course of the year, Israel and Marino concealed their losses by making material misstatements to clients about the Bayou fund's performance and the value of clients' investments. Israel, Marino, and a former Bayou principal concocted false investment returns to report to their clients and applied those false results to create inaccurate year-end financial statements.

By December 1998, the Bayou fund's mounting losses could not withstand an independent audit. So, Bayou dismissed the fund's independent auditing firm and created fictional auditor's reports, financial statements, and performance summaries. Marino, a certified public accountant, agreed to fabricate the annual audit of the Bayou fund to conceal the trading losses. He created a fictitious accounting firm, Richmond-Fairfield Associates, to pose as the independent auditor of the Bayou fund. But Marino was the sole principal of Richmond-Fairfield, and the firm had no other clients.

In 1999, the fund again suffered substantial losses. Bayou again concealed the loss by creating and distributing false performance summaries and financial statements that purportedly had been audited by Richmond-Fairfield Associates. The trading losses continued to mount, and fictional financial statements and summaries continued to be issued from 2000 to 2002 to create the appearance of modest, reliable, and believable growth. The performance summaries sent out by Bayou indicated that clients were earning 1% to 2% in net profits each month.

Throughout this time, Bayou actively solicited new investors and additional investments from current investors, raising tens of millions of dollars of additional capital. In January 2003, to attract more investors and capital, the managers liquidated the Bayou fund and created four successor funds: Accredited, Affiliates, No Leverage, and Superfund. While investor deposits peaked in 2003 at more than $125 million, the reorganization did not improve true performance. The new funds lost even more money from trading activities. In 2003, Bayou Superfund took in more than $90 million in capital but lost approximately $35 million through trading. However, according to its 2003 annual statement, Bayou Superfund had earned more than $25 million. Also, throughout this period, the managers of Bayou's funds continued to collect profit-sharing fees on the fraudulent gains, and Bayou Securities continued to earn millions of dollars in trading commissions. By 2004, Israel and Marino had stopped actual trading and transferred Bayou's depleted assets to Israel and other non-Bayou entities, effectively the managers' personal accounts. Nevertheless, the managers still sent periodic statements to investors describing profitable trades.

Things began to unravel for Bayou when, in May 2005, legal authorities from the state of Arizona seized $100 million. At the time, the Arizona authorities were investigating an unrelated financial fraud and became suspicious when they found that huge sums of money had been shifted between bank accounts in different countries in a rapid fashion. Unbeknownst to Arizona's authorities, they had stumbled onto what would become one of the most brazen hedge fund frauds of all time. The extent of the fraud was later confirmed in a several-page suicide note drafted by Marino. He did not commit suicide, but his note pieced together the extent and blatancy of the fraud. The $100 million recovered by Arizona's authorities, ultimately in a New Jersey bank account, was all that remained of the investors' money.

What are the lessons here? First, some fund managers are dishonest. A thorough due diligence process may uncover evidence of any dishonesty of the principals of a fund before money is invested. Israel's fund should have failed any standard due diligence checklist if prospective investors had looked carefully and in the right places. Israel's résumé overstated his position and his tenure at a previous firm. Although he claimed to have been a head trader at a large, respected hedge fund from 1992 to 1996, reference checks would have found that he had been an employee for only 17 months (in 1994 and 1995) and had no trading authority at the fund. Although Israel claimed that Bayou started in early 1997, it seems that the fund may have actually started in late 1996. The later start date allowed Israel to conceal substantial losses during the first several months of the fund's operations.

Second, audited information is only as reliable as the auditor. When a hedge fund uses a small outside auditing firm (in this case, one that was unknown outside of its Bayou purpose), red flags should go up. As noted in Part 7 on due diligence, contacting and interviewing outside auditors for a hedge fund is a critical step of any due diligence. The only employee of the Richmond-Fairfield accounting firm was Marino, and the only customer was Bayou.

Third, regulation and regulators are not a panacea and cannot be expected to prevent fraud or to discover fraud on a timely basis. Bayou's fraud was discovered 8 years after it began and only as part of an unrelated investigation into what regulators thought might be a money-laundering scheme. The conclusion here is that investors must perform thorough due diligence on their investments.

As a final and bizarre postscript to this whole mess, Samuel Israel went missing in 2008, the day before he was to begin serving his 20-year prison sentence. His abandoned car was found near a bridge in New York State. On the dust of his car's hood was written the message "suicide is painless." He was later captured at a trailer park, where he had been driven by his girlfriend after leaving his car at the bridge. Two years were added to his sentence as a result of this latest deception, leading to a 22-year jail sentence.

16.3.2 Bernie Madoff

The investment-related activities of Bernie Madoff have damaged lives and struck fear into the hearts of investors and investment professionals since December 2008. Early that month, Madoff allegedly confessed to running a giant Ponzi scheme. A **Ponzi scheme** is a fraudulent program that returns deposits to investors and identifies the returned capital as a distribution of profit in order to overstate the profitability of the enterprise and to attract additional and larger deposits.

The fictitious profits distributed to investors are actually the capital contributed by new investors to the scheme. A Ponzi scheme requires the continual recruiting of new investors to sustain the fraud. In the end, Madoff reportedly broke down and admitted to his family that his business was "all just one big lie" and basically a giant Ponzi scheme.[10] Along the way, Madoff managed to defraud high-net-worth investors, hedge fund managers, movie producers, movie stars, and university endowments. All told, the scheme was reputed to have grown to $50 billion before being unmasked.

What is amazing about this fraud is that questions, if not outright accusations, had been put forward about Madoff-related investments since 2000. That year, Harry Markopolos, a portfolio manager at Rampart Investment Management, and Neil Chelo, his top assistant, examined the performance numbers of Bernard L. Madoff Investment Securities. They suspected trickery because Madoff's performance rose with uncommonly stable, predictable returns year after year and market cycle after market cycle. The consistency of Madoff's performance seemed too good to be believed.

Markopolos and his assistant studied the strategy supposedly used by Madoff. Madoff called it a split strike conversion strategy, but most market participants call this strategy an option collar plus a position in the underlying. In an option collar, as introduced in the Level I CAIA curriculum, a manager (1) buys the underlying asset; (2) writes a call option at the higher of two strike prices; and (3) buys a put option at the lower of two strike prices. Both option positions have a neutral exposure inside the range of the two strike prices and hedge the underlier outside of the range. Accordingly, the options hedge the tail risks of the underlier and form a collar, limiting upside and downside, to the aggregated returns of the positions. In perfect markets, this strategy hedges most of the risk of the underlying equity position and should therefore be a risk-reducing and expected-return-reducing strategy relative to long positions without the options. The strategy as described had no realistic source of consistently high returns other than highly inefficient markets. Yet Madoff's positions apparently used somewhat common securities and strategies.

What made Markopolos especially suspicious of Madoff's investment claims was that he had managed a similar strategy but had not produced the consistent positive results that Madoff claimed to have earned. Markopolos went to the Securities and Exchange Commission (SEC) with his concerns. He approached the Boston office of the SEC first in 2000 and then again in 2001. Unfortunately, these initial visits did not lead to SEC action. Frank Casey, a coworker of Markopolos, tried to help by mentioning Madoff's amazing performance to a reporter from MarHedge, a publication that covers the hedge fund industry.

Both MarHedge and Barron's subsequently published stories calling into question the remarkable results produced by Bernie Madoff. But these stories did not generate effective regulatory scrutiny. In 2005, Markopolos contacted the SEC's New York office. He sent a 21-page report to the SEC's branch chief explaining why he had concluded that Madoff's business was "the world's largest Ponzi scheme."[11] He continued to send warnings to the SEC in 2006 and 2007, but no action followed. The SEC chairman at the time, Christopher Cox, later stated that he was "gravely concerned by the apparent multiple failures over at least a decade to thoroughly investigate these allegations."[12] Unfortunately, the grave concern came much too late.

Investors who performed careful due diligence at a firm like Madoff's should have been concerned about several issues. The most important is that the stated returns in terms of both positive mean and minimal volatility were clearly not consistent with the contemporaneous returns of similar strategies being observed in the market. Additionally, the quantity of assets under management and allegedly being deployed with the strategy would have required a trading volume too large relative to the trading activity in the underlying options markets. Another key red flag was that Madoff brokered, cleared, administered, and effectively audited his own fund, creating a lack of external accountability that allowed him to create fictitious accounting statements.

Madoff was arrested by federal agents on December 11, 2008, after being turned in to the authorities by his sons. Madoff is currently serving a 150-year prison sentence. Assets obtained by Madoff and those cooperating with the fraud have been obvious targets of repossession. In a Ponzi scheme or other types of fraud, investors who leave the scheme before it collapses are enriched at the expense of those who remain. Authorities in the Madoff scandal are seeking **restitution,** meaning restoration of lost funds, from both Madoff and his profitable investors. Courts can order investors who are enriched by a fraud to return the profits as restitution to those who suffered losses, even if the investors were unaware of the investment's fraudulent nature. In December 2010, Mark Madoff, the elder of Madoff's two sons (the younger of which died from cancer), committed suicide.

What can be learned from the Madoff experience? Most important, investors should ensure that performance numbers are audited by a reputable third-party auditor that provides an independent verification of the check on the stated returns. Returns that sound too good to be true are probably untrue. Also, investors should be especially alert to affinity fraud. **Affinity fraud** is the commission of fraud against people or entities with which the perpetrator of the fraud shares a common bond, such as race, ethnicity, or religious affiliation. Fraud is especially likely to be committed in the context of such affinities, since the perpetrators target their efforts toward people and groups who would be less likely to be suspicious. Madoff relied on affinities to market his fund, and he portrayed himself as a caring member of the community through public acts, such as philanthropy. Finally, investors should be aware that even if they enter a Ponzi scheme with no clear knowledge of its underlying fraud and exit the scheme before it collapses, the law generally requires return of profits to provide restitution to the eventual victims.

16.3.3 Lancer Group

At one time, Lancer Group was a highly successful hedge fund focused on trades in equity securities using a mix of private and public shares, typically of very small capitalization companies. The fund was run by Michael Lauer, who had a pedigree that other hedge fund managers dream about. He was a graduate of Columbia University and a six-time member of Institutional Investor's all-star equity analyst team. Over a 3-year period, Lauer is reported to have earned management and incentive fees totaling $44 million. The fund raised $613 million in investor capital, and at its peak, Lancer valued the assets at $1.2 billion. Then a collapse came that left the fund with only $70 million.

The story of Lancer raises several interesting issues and highlights important challenges for performing due diligence and avoiding harm as an investor. The key issue is the role of poor valuation procedures. That issue, combined with challenges of poor transparency, conflicts of interest, and loose oversight, allegedly led to huge investment losses and to the downfall of several professionals involved.

Beginning with the issue of transparency, Lancer did not offer transparency to its investors and refused to identify the stocks that were being held in the portfolio. Limited transparency can protect the investors when, as in this case, the fund has large positions in illiquid shares. The hesitancy to reveal the names of the holdings could have been related to legitimate concerns that the actions of other traders could inflict harm on the value of Lancer's stocks if they understood the magnitude of Lancer's positions in each stock. But transparency can also prevent investors from understanding the risks and threats.

The alleged fraud at Lancer also involved issues of valuation and conflicts of interest. Through the partnership agreements, Lauer's investors allowed him the personal discretion to value the restricted shares of these illiquid holdings. This violates one of the cardinal rules of operational risk management: never allow portfolio managers the ability to price their own positions, especially if their income depends on those valuations. Of course, most hedge fund managers earn large incentive fees on reported profits. The higher the valuation of the fund's securities, the higher the incentive fees earned by the fund. If portfolio managers are allowed to value their own holdings, the temptation to exaggerate performance to earn high incentive fees may overcome naturally honest personalities. A key issue is how Lancer calculated, and allegedly manipulated, the valuation of its portfolio.

Last, there is the issue of window dressing. **Window dressing** is a term used in the investment industry to denote a variety of legal and illegal strategies to improve the outward appearance of an investment vehicle. For example, some funds might liquidate their holdings of a stock before the end of a reporting period if the stock has generated very bad headlines so that the report does not embarrass the fund managers by having the stock appear in their list of holdings. Other window dressing is clearly illegal, such as manipulating the closing prices of stocks that represent large holdings of a fund so that the fund's total valuations, which are typically calculated at the end of each calendar month using closing prices, are higher. Lancer is alleged to have manipulated market prices to boost reported valuations of fund holdings.

Lancer purchased very large stakes in restricted shares of small companies. Restricted, or unregistered, shares are purchased directly from the issuing company and cannot be sold in public markets for prespecified lengths of time. Typically, unregistered shares are valued at a discount to the market price of the registered shares of the same firm. There is nothing inherently wrong with holding unregistered shares. The allegation against Lauer is that he manipulated the market price of the registered shares by placing trades at key points in time to print high prices in the stock's trading record and thereby justify placing high values on the fund's holdings. Placing transactions to record high or low prices on the transaction records of public markets is a fraudulent activity often termed **painting the tape,** in reference to the historical use of ticker tape to broadcast prices.

For example, Lauer is said to have purchased 1.7 million unregistered shares in a firm named SMX at 23 cents per share for a total cost of less than $0.5 million. Even though SMX had virtually no operations, Lancer soon valued the holding at nearly $200 million in market capitalization. How could such an enormous jump in value be justified? At the end of 1 month, Lauer is reported to have purchased 2,800 of the freely floating shares in the market at $19.50 per share, a large premium to the price trading just minutes earlier. Again, later in the year, he purchased 1,000 shares as the last trade of the month, this time at $27. These small trades in the registered, tradable shares were used to value or mark all the shares in the fund at a gain of 8,000% over the purchase price. Not only were the public shares not able to be sold at this price, but also the restricted shares were likely to trade at an even lower price than the registered shares.

Two primary potential safeguards to the problems discussed here are auditing and regulation. In both cases, the safeguards appear to have failed. For example, Lancer's auditor, a major accounting firm, eventually published an audit verifying the dubious valuations. The auditor apparently asked for full appraisals on ten companies yet received only four. Those four appraisals were written by parties alleged to have had a conflict of interest. Specifically, they may have had an ownership stake or a financial interest in the target companies. In the end, the audit stated that most of the fund value was based on unrealized gains, with prices based on the manager's valuation. The audit did not seem to have questioned the ultimate valuation of the target companies, leaving investors to decide from the auditor's language whether Lauer's valuations were warranted.

Another potential safeguard would have been revelation by regulators of potential irregularities. Lancer allegedly didn't file a Form 13D on 15 stocks in the portfolio for which it held more than 5% of the shares. (The SEC requires a 13D filing whenever an investor owns greater than a 5% stake in a firm.) Had Lancer filed these 13D reports as required, or had the SEC alerted the public to Lancer's failure to file timely reports, careful investors might have been able to realize the substantial illiquidity risk in the fund.

There is no reason to believe that excellent due diligence on the background of Michael Lauer would have raised any warning signals. But closer scrutiny of the auditing of the fund might have alerted careful analysts. One way to reduce the risk of this type of collapse is for investors to demand a private equity style of fee structure, in which incentive fees are paid only on realized gains. Another way is to separate the valuation and portfolio management processes so that the persons valuing the portfolio have no financial interest in the results of the valuation.

16.3.4 Venture Capital Startup: Theranos

Elizabeth Homes by all appearances was on the cusp of revolutionizing medical diagnosis and therapies in much the same manner as Steve Jobs revolutionized computing, music storage, and cell phones. Holmes dropped out of Stanford in 2003 at age 19 (much like Jobs dropped out of Reed College) with the goals of "changing the world" with a compact device that requires just a "tiny drop of blood" to quickly perform a multitude of blood tests. Holmes's original idea was for a skin patch that would harness nanotechnology to both test the user's blood and provide treatments (hence the name Theranos, derived from therapy and diagnosis).

Over a decade later Holmes was being featured in major magazines (e.g., *Fortune* June 14, 2015) and was celebrated in Silicon Valley and Washington DC. Eventually, Theranos reportedly raised $700 million with $100 million or more from each of the following: the DeVos family (Amway), the Walton family (Walmart), and Rupert Murdoch (media). Theranos retained over 500 employees and boasted a Board of Directors that included renowned politicians such as Henry Kissinger, George Shultz, Sam Nunn, and William Perry, and corporate leaders including Riley Bechtel (Bechtel) and Richard Kovacevich (Wells Fargo).

Holmes's claims of tremendous advances in blood testing were met with skepticism by some, especially a reporter for the *Wall Street Journal,* John Carreyrou. Carreyrou wrote a series of articles starting in October 2015 citing Theranos employees who claimed that the firm's technologies were being vastly overstated. Carreyrou's research indicated that after years of missed goals and delayed launches, most blood testing at Theranos was still being carried out using large commercial products made by other companies. Shockingly, some employees claimed that the few tests being performed on drops of blood from finger pricks (rather than large samples drawn directly from veins) were generating large errors on actual patient reports (as opposed to causing errors on blood tests being performed purely for research and product development purposes). Carreyrou's book on Theranos (*Bad Blood*) is a chilling account of a flawed corporate culture that reportedly led to fraudulent claims by senior management, evasion of regulation, and distribution of erroneous blood test results to doctors and patients.

By 2016, the company's practices were under investigation by the SEC and medical regulators. Eventually, Holmes (CEO) and Theranos's president were indicted for criminal fraud in June of 2018. A few months later, Theranos reportedly ceased operations. Most investors lost most or all of their investments in Theranos.

What went wrong? It is noteworthy that most if not all of Theranos's major investors and directors had relatively little experience in the main areas of Theranos's purported expertise: medical equipment development and blood testing. The lack of venture capital firms specializing in medical technologies that chose to make major investments in Theranos was telling—if anyone had been listening.

Perhaps the most surprising aspect of the Theranos saga is the reported extent to which Theranos's corporate partners, investors, and directors failed to require product demonstrations—especially when concerns were being expressed that the company's primary product was failing to deliver virtually all of the claimed capabilities. It appears that many Theranos employees, investors, directors, and commentators were enticed by Holmes, a passionate visionary, regarding the prospects of "changing the world" with medical advances.

In publicly traded firms there are two mechanisms that enhance fraud detection: short selling and regulatory oversight. As a private firm Theranos's stock could not be short sold and so there was little or no financial incentive to perform or publish research to expose fraud. The primary takeaway message is the seriousness of the tail risk of venture capital investment and the importance of rigorous due diligence performed by specialists with experience related to the technology they are evaluating.

16.4   FOUR MAJOR LESSONS FROM CASES IN TAIL EVENTS

What are the lessons to be learned from these failures?

First, a consistent theme across many of the cases is the danger of using large amounts of leverage.

Second, overconfidence can be a danger in trading. When convergence traders speculate that a pricing relationship appears out of line, they should prepare for a time when their discretion (or the traders' computer system) is in error, or when it may take a long time for prices to revert to a normal level. As convergence trades move against a trader, the trade appears to become even more attractive. But increasing the positions or leverage is especially risky and can lead to liquidation at the most unfavorable prices. Potentially related to this point, banks and prime brokers often act to magnify liquidity problems during periods of market stress by calling loans when the client most needs liquidity assistance.

Third, in highly quantitative financial systems, it is impossible to predict all of the risks that exist. It is important to keep abreast of technological changes and to develop good measures of detection, assessment, and mitigation.

Finally, the large fees and assets of the alternative investment world attract both geniuses and charlatans. Regulation has not been demonstrated to be a panacea against fraud. It is difficult, but not impossible, to detect fraud. Due diligence is the investor's best protection.

NOTES

1. See Davis et al. (2007).
2. See Jorion (2000).
3. Department of the Treasury, Board of Governors of the Federal Reserve System, Securities and Exchange Commission, and Commodity Futures Trading Commission, Hedge Funds, Leverage, and the Lessons of Long-Term Capital Management, Report of the President's Working Group on Financial Markets, Washington, DC, April 1999, 10–11. https://www.wsj.com/articles/SB1000087239639044386640457756477208396141 2.
4. This section is adapted from Khandani and Lo (2011).
5. "Findings Regarding the Market Events of May 6, 2010." Report of the Staffs of the CFTC and SEC to the Joint Advisory Committee on Emerging Regulatory Issues, September 30, 2010, www.sec.gov/news/studies/2010/marketevents-report.pdf.
6. See Strasburg and Bunge (2012).

7. See Stevenson, A. (2013). United States of America Before the Securities and Exchange Commission; Securities Exchange Act of 1934 Release No. 70694/October 16, 2013; Administrative Proceeding File No. 3-15570, "In the Matter of Knight Capital Americas LLC Respondent." www.sec.gov/litigation/admin/2013/34-70694.pdf.
8.
9. This section is adapted from Barbara J. Mack. 2015. "Fast Track to the Futures: Technological Innovation, Market Microstructure, Market Participants, and the Regulation of High Frequency Trading," in *The World Scientific Handbook of Futures Markets*, eds. Anastasios G. Malliaris and William T. Ziemba. Singapore: World Scientific.
10. See McCoy, K. (2009).
11. Ibid.
12. Ibid.

REFERENCES

Davis, A., G. Zuckerman, and H. Sender. 2007. "Hedge Fund Hardball." *Wall Street Journal*, January 30.

Jorion, P. 2000. "Risk Management Lessons from Long-Term Capital Management." *European Financial Management* 6 (September 2000): 277–300.

Khandani, A. E. and A. W. Lo, 2011. "What happened to the quants in August 2007? Evidence from factors and transactions data," *Journal of Financial Markets*, 14 (1): 1–46.

McCoy, K. 2009. "Pursuer of Madoff Blew a Whistle for Nine Years." *USA Today*, February 12.

Stevenson, A. 2013. "Knight Capital to Pay $12 Million Fine on Trading Violations." *New York Times*, October 16. http://dealbook.nytimes.com/2013/10/16/%knight-capital-to-pay-12-million-fine-on-trading-violations/.

Strasburg, J. and J. Bunge. 2012. "Loss Swamps Trading Firm: Knight Capital Searches for Partners as Tab for Computer Glitch Hits $440 Million." *Wall Street Journal*, August 3, A1. https://www.wsj.com/articles/SB10000872396390044386640457756477208396141

CHAPTER 17

Benchmarking and Performance Attribution

Benchmarking and performance attribution share many common attributes. Benchmarking tends to be a normative process of describing how asset returns ought to behave in terms of expected and realized returns. Performance attribution (return attribution) is a positive process of analyzing how past asset returns actually behaved relative to standards such as return factors or returns on similar assets.

Performance attribution is also known as return attribution. A performance analysis attempts to determine whether deviations of an investment's returns from its benchmark were the result of having different risk exposures than the benchmark or were attributable to nonrisk-related factors, such as superior management or luck.

17.1 BENCHMARKING AND PERFORMANCE ATTRIBUTION OVERVIEW

Benchmarking is often a simpler and more forward-looking process than performance attribution.

17.1.1 Active Return in Benchmarking

In benchmarking, the return of an asset is divided into two components: the benchmark return and the active return. The active return in the context of benchmarking is the deviation of an asset's return from its benchmark. The benchmark's return is subtracted from the asset's return for the same time period to form the active return. In effect, the benchmark return is attributed to the systematic performance of the asset, and the active return is attributed to the idiosyncratic performance of the asset.

Establishing a benchmark for fund managers of alternative investments or alternative strategies is one of the most challenging issues. One reason is the skill-based nature of many investment strategies. Manager skill cannot be adequately captured by a passive securities benchmark, such as the S&P 500 Index. Returns from skill, in fact, are often uncorrelated with returns from passive investing or may even be negatively correlated with the returns from passive investing for some skill-based strategies during stressed markets.

For instance, it can be argued that a long-only passive equity index is not an appropriate benchmark for an active equity long/short fund, particularly when the manager dynamically alters the fund's systematic risk exposure. In addition, fund managers often use derivative instruments, such as options, that have nonlinear payout functions, and most passive securities indices do not reflect nonlinear payouts. Another case against passive securities indices as an evaluation tool for hedge funds is that fund managers tend to maintain concentrated portfolios. The nature of this concentration makes the investment strategy of the fund manager distinct from that of a broad-based securities index.

Nonetheless, some measure to evaluate performance should be established for the fund manager. A **fund style index** is a performance index based on a collection of fund managers operating with a similar strategy to the fund manager in question that can be used as a benchmark. For example, a macro manager can be benchmarked against a macro index. Red flags should arise for an investor when the risk or return of the fund differs wildly from that of the style benchmark. It may be obvious that substantial underperformance and excessive volatility are warning signs, but even large gains and abnormally low volatility can be troubling, since outperformance relative to a benchmark can be evidence of large idiosyncratic risk exposures and/or weak risk management.

If the fund manager does not believe that any index is appropriate as a benchmark, then a hurdle rate should be established. Hurdle rates are most appropriate for absolute return fund managers whose rate of return should not depend on the general economic performance of a sector or a broad-based market index.

17.1.2   The Bailey Criteria for a Useful Benchmark

Bailey et al. (1990) define the so-called **Bailey criteria** as a grouping of seven characteristics or properties that an investment benchmark should possess in order to be a useful gauge: (1) unambiguous/knowable: the names and weights of entities that make up the benchmark should be clearly identifiable; (2) investable: there should be an option to forgo active management and simply hold all assets that make up the benchmark; (3) measurable: it is possible to frequently calculate the benchmark performance; (4) specified in advance: the benchmark is constructed and mutually agreed on before the manager's evaluation; (5) appropriate: the benchmark is consistent with the manager's investment style; (6) reflective of current investment opinion: this requires understanding a benchmark enough to have opinions about whether to deviate from it; and (7) owned: investment managers have to agree with their sponsor that they are being measured against this benchmark and are accountable for the results.

17.1.3   Selecting a Benchmark for Alternative Investments

Although it may be difficult to associate the risk and return profiles of some alternative investment products to specific benchmarks, in most cases the risk and return of an investment will have greater meaning if compared to the benchmark rather than analyzed in isolation. The selection of a benchmark is usually based on the investment's risk and perhaps other aspects, such as liquidity and the taxability of its returns. An **optimal benchmark** is a standard that best differentiates whether the investment manager has generated superior or inferior returns through skill and in so doing provides evidence to the asset owner regarding which assets to own.

A major theme throughout this chapter is the relation among risk, return, and diversification. Risk of and by itself is undesirable to an investor. Some risks can be reduced or eliminated by diversification. Understanding which risks can and cannot be diversified away is essential. Presumably, those risks that can be diversified away are not rewarded with higher expected returns, and those risks that cannot be fully diversified away are systematic and should be rewarded with higher expected returns. Rather than discussing the theme of risk and diversification in vague and qualitative terms, analysts can use asset pricing models as clear and concise representations of how assets should or do behave.

The next two sections examine benchmarking in detail. The next section performs a single-factor analysis while the section after that performs a multiple-factor analysis. Clearly a multi-factor analysis is more complex. However, the added complexity is worth the added benefits when the portfolio being analyzed is driven by more than one factor.

17.1.4 Benchmarking Liquid Alternative Investments

The entire universe of private funds, such as private equity and hedge funds, cannot be invested in or observed. However, that is not the case for liquid alternative investments due to their publicly traded nature and regulated transparency. Just because they have access characteristics similar to ETFs or mutual funds doesn't mean that all liquid alternative investments should be benchmarked to long-only stock or bond indices. Investors are bound to be disappointed by performance when compared to long-only stock indices during a bull market, which inhibits asset flows.

Hughen and Eckrich (2015) describe the challenges of benchmarking liquid alternatives. According to the Bailey criteria, Hughen and Eckrich explain that the key challenge to liquid alternatives benchmarking is appropriateness due to their lower correlations to typical long-only benchmarks. They encourage investors not to consider liquid alternatives as a single asset class, but look through to the strategy level and the typical risk exposures held by each liquid alternative fund. Their study segregates liquid alternatives into currency, long-short, market neutral, multi-alternative, and other alternative categories. Unfortunately, they found that long-only equity indices are the most frequent benchmark disclosed by liquid alternative managers, short-term interest rates are the second most frequent benchmark, and only 12% of fund managers suggest a liquid alternative peer group or strategy benchmark. Short-term interest rates may be a reasonable benchmark for market neutral funds that show little to no beta exposure to traditional asset classes, but may lead investors to infer that the liquid alternative fund is a low risk investment. Many liquid alternative funds use a long-only index as a primary benchmark and a strategy benchmark for secondary comparison. Chasing multiple benchmarks can be confusing to investors and may make it difficult for fund managers to understand or explain the return and risk goals of their funds.

While some investors may consider peer group benchmarks to be useful, there could also be issues with that approach. First, if there is heterogeneity within a category of funds it can be difficult to compare returns across those funds with differing strategies. Second, investability is difficult if the peer group experiences survivor bias or includes funds that are closed to new investors and do not offer index fund options. Regarding the seven characteristics suggested by Bailey, peer group benchmarks in alternative investments are likely to be measurable, but have issues with most of the other characteristics.

Beyond peer group benchmarks, investors should consider the correlation of returns between a fund and the benchmark as well as risk-adjusted return statistics such as the Sortino ratio or downside deviation.

17.2   SINGLE-FACTOR BENCHMARKING AND PERFORMANCE ATTRIBUTION

Single-factor benchmarking simply compares an investment's expected or realized performance with a single index. Performance attribution analyzes the components of the returns.

17.2.1   An Example of Single-Factor Benchmarking

Exhibit 17.1 lists the returns of 10 funds over 20.5 years of actual monthly data. The first eight rows of data summarize the returns of eight hedge funds chosen mostly at random. The next two rows contain the data for two well-known and diversified equity mutual funds (labeled Fund I and Fund J). The last row contains the returns of the MSCI World Index, a diversified equity index that includes stocks from 24 developed countries but excludes stocks from emerging markets. Exhibit 17.1 compares the average annualized return of each fund with the MSCI World Index as the benchmark, demonstrating that 9 of the 10 funds generated higher average performance, as shown in the final column. The calculations in the chart are rounded.

Focusing on the returns of Fund A, and assuming that the MSCI World Index is an appropriate benchmark for the fund, Exhibit 17.1 indicates that Fund A outperformed the MSCI World Index by 0.66% per year and did so with a standard deviation of returns (volatility) of 14.73%, a little less than the 15.46% volatility

EXHIBIT 17.1   Returns, Standard Deviations, and Excess Returns for 10 Funds

	Annualized Mean Return	Annualized Standard Deviation of Returns	Return in Excess of MSCI World Index
Fund A	6.80%	14.73%	0.66%
Fund B	13.45%	14.31%	7.32%
Fund C	11.50%	13.95%	5.36%
Fund D	17.44%	27.38%	11.30%
Fund E	15.28%	9.87%	9.14%
Fund F	4.60%	30.61%	−1.53%
Fund G	10.43%	13.64%	4.29%
Fund H	15.75%	16.84%	9.62%
Fund I	8.81%	17.16%	2.67%
Fund J	9.64%	19.71%	3.50%
MSCI World Index	6.14%	15.46%	

Source: Bloomberg and CISDM.

experienced by the MSCI World Index. Thus, Fund A outperformed the proposed benchmark on both a risk basis and a return basis based on this single-factor analysis (and using world equities as the index).

17.2.2 Three Considerations in Benchmarking

Three related questions arise regarding the previous analysis of the risk and return of Fund A relative to its assumed benchmark, the MSCI World Index: (1) Is the benchmark appropriate, meaning that the risk and return drivers of the fund are similar to the drivers of the benchmark? (2) Did the fund outperform the benchmark to an economically and statistically significant degree? (3) Why did the fund outperform its benchmark?

17.2.3 Single-Factor Market Model Performance Attribution

The purpose of this section is to discuss the use of a single-factor market model for performance attribution. Whether using a simple benchmark approach or a formal asset pricing model, virtually every investment professional who is evaluating performance must adjust for risk. Hence, every professional is explicitly or implicitly using an asset pricing model. This section is designed to: (1) equip analysts with more advanced and robust approaches than simple benchmarking; and (2) facilitate an explicit recognition of the assumed relations between risks and return that underlie a return attribution analysis.

The example uses a single-factor approach for simplicity, even though many alternative assets would likely benefit from a more robust multi-factor method. The single-factor market model approach is similar in many ways to the capital asset pricing model (CAPM); however, an important distinction should be kept in mind. The CAPM describes efficiently priced assets wherein the expected returns of all assets are directly and linearly related to their market betas (i.e., all assets have equal Treynor ratios). In practice, performance attribution is used to evaluate assets presumed to have potential price inefficiencies (i.e., different levels of risk-adjusted performance). The ex post form of the CAPM was given in Level I of the CAIA curriculum and is repeated here:

$$R_{it} - R_f = \beta_i(R_{mt} - R_f) + \varepsilon_{it}$$

In the CAPM, the error term on the far right-hand side of the equation is presumed to have a zero mean. The risk-free rate can serve as the intercept or, as is represented in the equation, can be subtracted from each asset's return to form an excess return. A single-factor market model allows an intercept that is not equal to the riskless rate and that can indicate abnormally high or low returns due to mispricing. Thus, a difference between a CAPM model and the single-factor market model is whether consistently abnormal returns are allowed to be captured in the intercept term or are disallowed due to a presumption of informational market efficiency.

The first component of asset i's realized return is from the effect of systematic risk: the effect of the realized return of the market portfolio. The error term is the effect of idiosyncratic risk. The equation can be used to perform a single-factor return attribution by inserting the known returns and estimating the unknown terms: the beta, the intercept, and the error terms.

APPLICATION 17.2.3

Find the systematic and idiosyncratic returns for the following: Assume that the risk-free rate is 2%, the realized return of asset I in year t was 16%, the realized return of the market portfolio was 14% (which was 12% more than the riskless rate), and the beta of asset i is 1.25.

The systematic portion of its realized return must be 15%, which is found using the first terms on the right-hand side of the equation 1.25(14% − 2%). Since the realized return of asset i in excess of the risk-free rate (the left-hand side of the equation) was 14% (found as the realized return of 16% minus the risk-free return of 2%), and since the systematic component of its realized return was 15% (found earlier), the idiosyncratic portion of asset i's return must be −1%, found by inserting −1% in the following equation:

$$16\% - 2\% = 1.25(14\% - 2\%) - 1\%.$$

The idiosyncratic return of asset i represents the portion of asset i's realized return that is not attributable to its market risk. In Application 17.2.3, the estimated idiosyncratic return of asset i in year t was −1%. Asset i's performance benefited from the higher-than-expected returns of the overall market and its high beta, but it suffered a small setback (−1%) from the combined impact of the idiosyncratic effects.

Asset i seemed at first to have performed well with its 16% realized return, but after risk adjustment, its realized return was found to be 1% lower than it should have been, given its level of risk. This example illustrates the return attribution process for a single security using a single factor. Return attribution can be similarly performed for the returns of portfolios of securities and for investment funds.

Performance attribution can be used to indicate whether the manager generated superior risk-adjusted returns or whether the returns can be attributed to other factors. As with any exercise involving randomness and unobserved components such as beta, the results of this return attribution analysis are estimates. For example, because the beta of the stock would typically be an estimated value with some level of error, the estimate of the attribution of returns into the portions due to systematic and idiosyncratic risks would similarly be subject to error. Further, another analyst may have measured the security's beta differently or may have used different returns to represent the risk-free and market portfolio returns.

Does estimated superior performance indicate skill on the part of the manager? First, there is the issue that the performance analysis may contain estimation errors due to flaws in the return attribution process, such as model misspecification. If systematic risks were ignored or misidentified, the returns will not be accurately attributed to risks. But even if this estimate could be considered accurate and reliable, an important issue remains: was the estimated superior return generated due to skill or to luck? Multiple observations of returns can be examined for persistence of positive or negative idiosyncratic returns.

17.2.4 Examining Time-Series Returns with a Single-Factor Market-Based Regression Model

The ex post form of the single-factor market model can be used in a time-series model to better understand and estimate the effects of systematic risk and idiosyncratic risks through time. This section focuses on using a single-factor model. Multi-factor models could be similarly used and should typically be used for alternative investments, but we are focusing on a single-factor model because of its relative simplicity. An *estimated* single-factor time-series model is typically written like this:

$$R_{it} - R_f = \alpha_i + B_i(R_{mt} - R_f) + e_{it} \qquad (17.1)$$

R_{it} is the return for the asset in period t, and R_{mt} is the return for the market. The equation's parameters (a and B) are usually estimated using a regression method, which is performed over a set of time periods for a particular asset (i).

The Greek letters α, β, and ε tend to be used to represent the true and unobservable variables, and the Latin letters a, B, and e are used to represent the estimates of those variables from a statistical procedure such as a regression. Thus, ε_{it} in the theoretical model represents the true portion of asset i's return attributable to the effects of idiosyncratic risks in time period t, whereas e_{it} in Equation 17.1 represents the researcher's estimate of ε_{it} using a statistical analysis, in this case a regression, and a particular model.

If the CAPM describes returns perfectly, then empirical tests of Equation 17.1 should indicate the following: (1) the intercept of the regression equation, a, should be statistically equal to zero; (2) the slope of the regression equation, B_i, should not be statistically unequal to the true beta of the asset; and (3) the residuals of the regressions, e_t, should reflect the effects of idiosyncratic, asset-specific risks. But many alternative assets may trade at prices that depart from perfectly efficient prices. Hence, analysts often use this time-series approach and interpret statistically nonzero intercepts as a signal of asset mispricing. Statistical testing using linear regression is an important and multi-faceted subject.

17.2.5 Application of Single-Factor Benchmarking

The application of single-factor performance attribution in Section 17.2.2 used the market portfolio as the factor. This section illustrates the use of the investment's benchmark as the single factor. We return to the example in the beginning of the chapter summarized in Exhibit 17.1. In the exhibit, the performance of Fund A was analyzed by directly comparing its return (as well as the return of the other funds) to the return of the MSCI World Index, assuming that the MSCI Index served as a reasonable benchmark and that the beta of each fund was one. This section examines the performance of the funds using the same benchmark but with a single-factor model framework, which allows each fund to have a different sensitivity or beta with respect to the benchmark/factor. In other words, the previous simplistic benchmarking example implicitly assumed that the beta of each fund with respect to the benchmark was 1. This section allows that beta to depart from 1 depending on the observed sensitivity of each fund's return to the return of the benchmark.

EXHIBIT 17.2   Analysis of Returns for Fund A
Using a Single-Factor Model

	Intercept	Beta
Fund A	1.30%	0.68

Source: Bloomberg and CISDM.

Equation 17.2 illustrates the concept of benchmarking with a single-factor linear regression model, in which the benchmark takes the place of the market factor:

$$R_t - R_f = \alpha + B(R_{benchmark,t} - R_f) + e_t \tag{17.2}$$

where R_t is the return of a fund in period t, R_f is the riskless rate, a is the intercept of the regression (usually viewed as an estimate of the average overperformance or underperformance of the fund through time), B is the sensitivity of the fund's return to the benchmark's return (which is typically expected to be near 1 for a benchmark with equivalent risk to the fund), $R_{benchmark,t}$ is the return of the fund's benchmark, and e_t is the fund's estimated idiosyncratic return above or below its risk-adjusted return.

Exhibit 17.2 shows results from this time-series analysis of the returns of Fund A as the variable on the left-hand side of Equation 17.2 (R_t) and the MSCI World Index as the benchmark return $(R_{benchmark,t})$ on the right-hand side. Fund A's return has an estimated beta of 0.68 based on actual historic returns not shown. This means that rather than containing the same level of systematic risk as the index, Fund A's return tended to move only 68% as far as the market each time the market moved. The analysis appears to magnify the favorable implications of Exhibit 17.1. The estimated annual performance of Fund A in Exhibit 17.2 was 1.3% higher than would be expected in a perfectly efficient market, as indicated by the intercept. Thus, a single-factor risk-adjusted analysis indicates that Fund A outperformed its benchmark by 1.3% per year while taking only 68% of the systematic risk of that benchmark.

17.3   MULTI-FACTOR BENCHMARKING

Exhibits 17.1 and 17.2 summarize return attribution of Fund A using a single benchmark. The first exhibit implicitly assumes that the beta of Fund A with respect to its benchmark is one, whereas the second exhibit allows the returns to be attributed to a different level of systematic risk than the benchmark. The analysis demonstrated the advantage of using a benchmarking approach that takes into account the beta (systematic risk) of the fund being analyzed. The next sections expand the benchmarking to a multi-factor approach.

17.3.1   An Example of Multi-factor Benchmarking

Now let's return to the example using a multi-factor model: the Fama–French–Carhart model detailed in Chapter 8. Using an ex post form of that model, the performance

EXHIBIT 17.3 Analysis of Return for Fund A Using the Fama–French–Carhart Model

	Intercept	Market Factor	Size Factor	Value Factor	Momentum Factor
Fund A	– 2.91%	0.66	0.16	0.10	0.15

Source: Bloomberg and CISDM.

of Fund A can be explained by three systematic risk factors, as indicated in Exhibit 17.3.

The estimated betas in Exhibit 17.3 indicate that Fund A's return included exposures to size, value, and momentum factors in addition to its exposure to the market index. Note that the annual idiosyncratic performance (the intercept) is now estimated as being 2.91% *lower* than would be obtained in a perfectly efficient market. What was previously estimated as a 1.3% positive alpha using a single-factor model is now estimated as a –2.9% alpha using multiple factors. Apparently, the intercept of Fund A using a single-factor model was erroneously identified as an indication of superior return rather than as compensation for the omitted risk exposures that the fund was incurring by investing in small-capitalization value stocks with a high degree of momentum. This indication that performance was inferior is in marked contrast to the estimated superior performance shown in Exhibits 17.1 and 17.2, using a simple benchmark and single-factor approach, respectively.

17.3.2 The Bias from Omitted Factors in Benchmarking

In an up market (i.e., a market in which major indices outperformed the riskless rate), the omission of systematic risk factors will result in an analysis that overestimates the risk-adjusted performance of assets positively exposed to the omitted risk factors and underestimates the performance of assets negatively exposed to the omitted risk factors. In a down market, the anticipated effect would be the opposite. Most long-term studies are more likely to be up markets, since risky assets on average tend to outperform the riskless asset.

17.3.3 Multi-factor versus Single-factor Methods

The analysis underscores the importance of the method being implemented. Benchmarking is only as accurate as the model that implicitly or explicitly serves as its foundation. Thus, the study of methods (methodology) and the careful selection of an appropriate method serve as key processes in the attribution of return performance.

The benchmarking examples of Exhibits 17.1, 17.2, and 17.3 illustrate the great differences between applying a single-factor model and applying a multi-factor model. There are solid reasons to believe that alternative investing is especially exposed to multiple systematic risk factors other than the market risk factor. Multi-factor models provide a more robust basis for understanding and estimating the sources of the realized and expected returns of alternative investments. Multi-factor models may allow analysts to better separate systematic risks from idiosyncratic risks and perhaps to separate sustainable superior performance based on skill from unsustainable superior performance based on luck.

17.4   DISTINCTIONS REGARDING ALTERNATIVE ASSET BENCHMARKING

The foundations of benchmarking discussed in the previous sections relate to the central issue of this book: the returns and multiple sources of risk in alternative assets. What level of risk and returns can investors expect to receive from alternative investments? Are higher returns attained only through bearing higher systematic risk? How can systematic and idiosyncratic risks be identified and separated?

These questions relate to a bigger picture. Many experts believe that the best traditional investment strategy is to allocate any capital available to be risked to a very broadly diversified portfolio with the lowest possible fees. An example would be to hold a highly diversified indexed mutual fund with fees of less than 10 basis points per year. Perhaps many investors in traditional assets would do well to heed this advice. But this low-cost indexation strategy is not generally feasible for alternative investments.

This section discusses reasons why multi-factor models may meet the needs of investors attempting to analyze the risks associated with alternative asset investing. The purpose is to provide a basis for understanding the potential sources of returns and risks, facilitating the establishment of benchmarks, and enabling return attribution.

17.4.1   Why Not Apply the CAPM to Alternative Assets?

In an ideal world without market imperfections, with normally distributed asset returns, and with a stationary distribution for the returns of the market portfolio, assets should tend to be priced well using the CAPM. The CAPM collapses all the potential complexities of investments into one simple assertion: all investors fully diversify into the same portfolio of risky assets, the market portfolio, which defines the one and only systematic risk factor. The CAPM separates systematic risk from idiosyncratic risk with a single factor, the return of the market portfolio, and specifies how expected and actual returns are determined. In a CAPM world, the only way that an investment manager can consistently earn higher returns is by taking more market risk, and any investor bearing idiosyncratic risk is acting irrationally. In a CAPM world, there is no distinction between traditional and alternative investment methods.

Are there solid theoretical reasons to believe that the CAPM does not hold for alternative assets? Can assets require higher returns for any risk other than the beta of an asset with the market portfolio? Does there need to be more than one risk factor in a performance attribution analysis? This section explores four primary reasons why the CAPM approach to investing may not work for alternative investing.

17.4.2   Reason 1: Multi-period Issues

The CAPM is a single-period model, in which it is assumed that all investors can make an optimal decision based only on analysis of the outcomes at the end of one period. Investors do so with assurance that by repeating the process of optimizing each single period's decision, the investor's lifetime decisions will be optimized. All investors are assumed to share the same one-period time horizon for their decision-making.

For the CAPM to hold in a world of multiple periods, it is usually assumed that, among other things, the market's return process behaves in similar patterns through time. If return distributions of securities or distributions of corporate earnings randomly change through time, Merton as well as Connor and Korajczyk demonstrate that additional systematic risk factors will emerge, and a single-factor approach will no longer hold.[1]

For example, assume that the expected return of the market portfolio varies through time in relation to the average credit spread risk in the marketplace. In that case, it is possible that credit spread risk can become an additional factor, and the single-factor CAPM approach must be expanded into a multi-factor model. Similar arguments for additional risk factors have been made if the variance or dispersion of the market changes through time in relation to an economic variable.

Multi-period issues could affect both traditional and alternative investment pricing. However, the relatively dynamic nature of alternative investments and their unusual return distributions (e.g., structured products) tend to make this issue more important for the analysis of alternative investments.

17.4.3 Reason 2: Nonnormality

The normal distribution can be specified with two parameters: mean and variance (or standard deviation). Traditional portfolio theory demonstrates that portfolios can be managed using these two parameters if returns are normally distributed or if investors have preferences that require analysis of only those two parameters (e.g., investors have quadratic utility functions). If returns are nonnormal, then investors may be concerned about additional parameters, such as skewness and kurtosis.

Alternative investment returns often tend to skew to one side or the other or to have excess kurtosis, with fatter tails on both sides. Nonnormality of returns tends to be greater for larger time intervals, and many alternative investments by their nature tend to be illiquid and are less likely to be managed with short-term portfolio adjustments. Another reason for the nonnormality of many alternative investment returns is the structuring of their cash flows into relatively risky and asymmetric patterns.

CAPM-style frameworks have been extended to include additional parameters that capture the nonnormality of returns. Rubinstein, Kraus and Litzenberger, and Harvey and Siddique developed models that incorporate skewness.[2] Homaifar and Graddy developed a model that incorporates kurtosis.[3] It should be noted that measures such as skewness and kurtosis can be difficult to estimate accurately and can change rapidly. Further, the higher moments of portfolios are often quite different than the higher moments of the portfolio's underlying assets. However, difficulty in forecasting quantitative measures of higher moments does not mean that higher moments are irrelevant.

17.4.4 Reason 3: Illiquidity of Returns and Other Barriers to Diversification

Illiquidity in this context refers to the risk of not being able to adjust portfolio holdings substantially and quickly at low costs. The idea within the CAPM that every investor should seek perfect diversification through holding the market portfolio is predicated on perfect liquidity. But in real life, there are substantial barriers to perfect diversification. First, transaction costs, taxes on the realized gains, and differential taxation on individual investments inhibit transactions and may offset the benefits of diversifying fully. Since many investors are unable to diversify well without substantial costs, they are exposed to risk factors other than simply the market factor, and therefore the CAPM may not adequately capture all the sources of risk that are priced.

Further, the illiquidity of a particular investment may be priced. Illiquidity of many alternative assets restricts an investor's ability to adjust a portfolio continuously, including the manager's ability to control risks and manage cash. The ultimate question of whether illiquidity is priced in is an empirical question explored in Part 6 on Access.

17.4.5   Reason 4: Investor-Specific Assets or Liabilities

Institutional investors, such as sovereign wealth funds and endowments, may possess substantial illiquid assets, such as real estate, that are not optimally hedged or diversified through investment solely in a market portfolio of liquid assets. Similarly, family offices and other individual investors with illiquid assets such as human capital, residences, and businesses will tend to find that investing liquid funds in the market portfolio provides suboptimal diversification of the substantial idiosyncratic risks that they face. A highly related issue involves investment uncertainty in generating cash for institutions such as pension funds and insurance companies to fund specific multi-period liabilities and uncertain liabilities. Many financial institutions manage their portfolios with the goal of funding a stream of future liabilities rather than simply trying to control risk and return one period into the future. Further, the liabilities themselves can be driven by risk exposures other than a single-market factor.

17.4.6   Summary of Why Multiple-Factor Models May be Preferable

The above reasons and issues relate to Chapter 8's discussion of return factors, "good times," and "bad times." In a CAPM world, all investors define good times and bad times identically (i.e., based on the return of the market portfolio) so all investors can invest optimally through the same asset (the market portfolio). For the reasons discussed above (e.g., heterogeneous time horizons, utility functions, other assets, liabilities) different investors define good times and bad times differently. Accordingly, their investment preferences differ and their optimal portfolios must be achieved through a multiple-factor approach.

17.5   BENCHMARKING OF COMMODITIES

Indexes are key tools; however, indexation of commodity returns raises four important issues: (1) specifying weights on value versus quantity; (2) weighting on market or other values; (3) specification of returns including returns on collateral (and collateral choice); and (4) roll method. The most important issue is the second issue: selecting a weighting scheme for sectors and their components.

17.5.1   Weighting All Positions on Value versus Quantity

Commodity indices can be value-based or quantity-based. A **value-based index** has fixed-component weights expressed as percentages of the value of the index. The number of futures contracts in the index changes dynamically to maintain constant value weights. A **quantity-based index** holds a fixed quantity of contracts for each commodity, so that the index weights change each day in terms of percentage of value as futures prices change. For example, the S&P 500 Index on US equities is quantity-based, since the number of shares of each company in the index changes only when the index constituents are changed, whereas the percentage of the index attributable to a particular constituent changes when the market price of that constituent changes. Conversely, an index that consists of 60% stocks and 40% bonds is value-based.

17.5.2   The Three Schemes Used to Weight Commodities Sectors and Components

The largest impact on index returns comes from the choice of an overall weighting method. For example, the S&P GSCI was targeted in 2019 for roughly 63% in energies, whereas the Bloomberg Commodity Index (BCOM) was targeted in 2019 for roughly 30% in energies.

There are a number of input variables an index provider can use to determine individual commodity or commodity-sector weights. The three primary criteria are as follows:

1. World production—for example, the S&P GSCI is a quantity-based, world production-weighted index.
2. Liquidity—for example, the BCOM uses a combination of liquidity and production measures to assign weights to individual commodities.
3. Open interest—the nominal value of the open futures contracts.

17.5.3   Total Return versus Excess Return

There are two major types of return indices available to commodity investors: total return and excess return. A **total return index** is a fully collateralized investment strategy, with the collateralization generally taking the form of Treasury bills. In a total return index, the overall calculation of the index return includes the cash return from the collateral (i.e., collateral yield). Generally, total return indices have returns and volatilities comparable to broad equity indices. An **excess return index** provides returns over cash and is linked to the price movements of a basket of commodity futures contracts.

17.5.4 Roll Method

The roll method can have a substantial impact on the returns of a commodity index. In its simplest form, roll methods involve two primary choices: (1) futures curve positioning; and (2) roll procedure.

> FUTURES CURVE POSITIONING: **Futures curve positioning** determines the time to expiration of a futures contract at the *initiation* of the position, and the length of time the contract will be held before rolling to a further-out contract. First-generation indices, such as the S&P GSCI (which has an average maturity of less than 2 months), generally position themselves at the near end of the futures curve and hold their contracts for a short period of time. Many of the newer indices position themselves further out on the forward curve and/or hold their positions for a longer time before rolling. Since forward curves of commodities are generally nonlinear, the impact of contango or backwardation on returns can vary significantly due to the choice of curve positioning strategy.
>
> ROLL PROCEDURE: The **roll procedure** refers to the method by which the timing of the closing of the old position and the opening of the new position is determined. A number of products have attempted to base roll procedures on the slope of the futures curve. However, they have the disadvantage of becoming close to an active strategy and therefore contradicting the initial goal of investing in a passive product. In response, passive products whose methods are curve-neutral have been developed. The actual roll procedure can have a significant impact on returns, particularly on the more popular indices, where the sheer trading volume of funds tied to the index can move markets due to insufficient liquidity. As a result, extremely large futures positions must typically be rolled over multiple days. In addition, the roll procedure is publicly available and thus entirely predictable, which can result in significant market impact—to the detriment of index returns but to the delight of alert traders who take advantage of the opportunity for profit. Many newer indices are designed to minimize the inefficiencies of their rolls. For example, an index may roll a small portion of its positions each day, resulting in a low-impact, almost continuous roll.

17.5.5 Three Generations of Commodity Indices

First-generation commodity indices tend to be heavily weighted in energy and hold long-only positions in front month contracts, rolling to the second month contracts at prespecified times regardless of the shape of the current term structure. **Second-generation commodity indices** attempt to enhance returns through forward curve positioning to spread the roll period across points along the forward curve or target different segments of the curve. **Third-generation commodity indices** add yet another enhancement to second-generation commodity indices by including active commodity selection, which may be predicated on objective rules (such as using algorithms to assign weights based on specific criteria related to momentum, inventory levels, term structure signals, and so on) or could be discretionary.

17.6 THREE APPROACHES TO BENCHMARKING MANAGED FUTURES FUNDS

There are three major approaches to benchmarking investment pools focused on futures contracts. This section focuses on commodity trading advisors (CTAs), a US-based subset of managed futures. Although benchmarking trend-following CTAs can be a reasonably straightforward exercise due to the high correlation among trend-following strategies, the same is not true of other managed futures trading styles, such as nontrend-following and relative value. There is considerable heterogeneity among managers in both of these styles. Finding or creating useful indices to benchmark nontrend-following CTA styles remains a significant challenge.

17.6.1 Benchmarking with Long-Only Futures Contracts

The simplest approach is to use an index of long-only futures contracts. Because CTAs are as likely to be short as to be long, this approach has not been found to be particularly useful. Schneeweis and Spurgin (1997) and Spurgin et al. (2001) note that there appears to be little connection between the absolute returns of major indices and the returns of CTA indices, suggesting that CTA-based indices (discussed next) provide a better benchmark for an actively managed futures portfolio than either passive or active long-only commodity-based performance indices.

17.6.2 Benchmarking CTAs with Peer Groups

The peer group approach uses the actual performance collected from investments considered to be of similar investment strategies. The peer group method is discussed in greater detail in the sections below on private equity benchmarking. There are a number of issues when using fund databases. Many funds report to only one provider and some of the best do not report to any database. Another problem is investability. For traditional asset classes, construction of investable indices is common; relatively inexpensive investable products, such as indexed mutual funds and exchange-traded funds (ETFs), are available to investors. In contrast, construction of truly investable indices in the CTA space is complex and may not result in a truly investable index that is an accurate representation of the industry.

17.6.3 Benchmarking CTAs with Algorithmic Indices

CTAs may be compared with passive indices of futures trading. These passive indices represent the performance of an individual algorithmic-based trading system, as opposed to the performance of the CTAs themselves. It is impossible to create accurate algorithmic passive indices for most discretionary CTAs because, as the name implies, these managers use a significant amount of discretion, which cannot be modeled through a systematic trading approach.

The oldest and most prominent of these algorithmic indices is the MLM Index. Since 1988, Mount Lucas Management has published the MLM Index, which represents the daily performance of a 252-day moving average trend-following system applied to a large set of futures markets. Such an algorithmic-based index can be quite useful because it provides the return that can be achieved from a simple trend-following trading model. This return can then be compared to the performance of active trend-following managers in order to examine the value added by more active (and expensive) strategies.

17.6.4   Five Conclusions from Evidence on CTA Benchmarking

Empirical studies of the performance of these systematic trend-following strategies and their comparisons to the performance of diversified portfolios of actual trend-following CTAs lead to the following five conclusions:

1. Passive trend-following indices, such as the MLM Index, can provide a reasonable benchmark for trend-following CTAs.
2. Less than half of the historical excess return earned by trend-following CTAs is due to their beta exposure to passive trend-following indices. More than half of the returns cannot be captured by such passive indices.
3. Trend-following CTAs display low exposures to traditional asset classes as well as long-only commodity indices. The same low exposure is provided by passive trend-following indices.
4. Discretionary CTAs display low exposures to traditional asset classes as well as long-only commodity and passive trend-following indices.
5. Peer groups appear to be the most suitable benchmark for discretionary CTAs.

17.7   BENCHMARKING PRIVATE EQUITY FUNDS

Swamy et al. (2011) see two broad approaches to the construction of benchmarks, resulting in asset-based and peer-group-based benchmarks. An asset-based benchmark is constructed using public or private securities as its constituents. A peer-group-based benchmark is constructed using portfolios of investment managers (e.g., funds) as its constituents.

17.7.1   Listed Asset-Based Benchmarks

A **listed PE index** refers to an index (such as the LPX 50) whose components are share prices of publicly traded PE firms. The primary listed private equity index opportunities in the US are indices of major global private equity firms or BDCs (business development companies) that are publicly listed. These firms include major PE firms such as KKR & Co. and Blackstone Group LP. Access to the major indices can be obtained using ETPs (exchange traded products including ETFs and ETNs) that track the indices, although the expense ratios of these major ETPs are generally relatively high.

However, these indices do not reflect the assets in which institutional investors typically invest: private limited partnerships. Rather, they reflect an entity receiving cash from GPs. For example, Blackstone Group LP is a partnership with revenues that include the fees earned by the GP but not the return LPs experience on the underlying investments. The statistical characteristics of listed PE indices, such as volatility and correlation to other assets, mainly depend on developments in the public markets (that is, short-term changes in supply and demand) rather than the intrinsic value of the underlying assets. Therefore, and due to its listed nature, listed private equity does not exhibit the same risk and return characteristics as nonlisted private equity.

17.7.2 Public Equity Indices and the Public Market Equivalent (PME) Method

A key approach to benchmarking private equity is the **Public Market Equivalent (PME) Method** which was introduced in Level I of the CAIA curriculum for investments involving only two cash flows: an initial cashflow into the investment and one liquidating cashflow out of the investment. This section details the challenges raised when there are multiple contributions to an investment (e.g., private equity capital calls) and multiple distributions from the investment (and perhaps a terminal NAV or value).

The seminal PME method was developed by Long and Nickels in a handbook by Kocis et al (2009). The Long–Nickels (or LN) PME method is described in this chapter. The **LN PME method** focuses on computing two IRRs, one based on the actual cash flows of private equity and another based on hypothetical use of a public market index, and comparing them. Due in part to difficulties with IRRs, other PME methods have emerged that use other performance metrics.

The PME method is a cash-weighted metric (like IRR) that considers multiple negative and/or multiple positive cash flows. The intuition of the PME method is that it indicates the attractiveness of a private investment by comparing the cash-weighted returns of two identical cash flow streams: one invested in a specified private project and the other a hypothetical investment of the same cash flows into and out of a public equity market index.

For example, consider a PE Fund investment requiring three cash contributions to the fund for the first three periods (from Period 0 to Period 2) and followed by three values: two cash distributions (in Period 6 and 7) followed by an NAV in Period 8. Further, assume that the public equity market experienced the returns in Exhibit 17.4 labeled "Market Return" (which is derived from the line labeled "Market Index").

> STEP 1: FINDING THE IRR OF THE PE FUND: The line "PE Fund Flows" contains the cash flows and NAV for a simplified PE fund investment. It is easy to calculate its interim IRR (using a financial calculator or a spreadsheet formula) as 12.75%. This value is found by inserting the cash flow stream (and the NAV) in software that finds the IRR using a trial and error search.

EXHIBIT 17.4 PMEs for a PE Fund with Multiple Cash Inflows and Outflows

Period	0	1	2	3	4	5	6	7	8
PE Fund Flows	−100	−50	−40	0	0	0	70	80	280 (NAV)
Market Index	100	60	75	90	99	110	132	165	198
Market Return	n.a.	−.40	.25	.20	.10	.1111	.20	.25	.20
Hyp Mkt Acc	100	110	177.5	213.0	234.3	260.3	242.4	223	−12.40
Hyp Cash Flows	−100	−50	−40	0	0	0	70	80	267.60 (NAV)

STEP 2: FINDING THE IRR OF THE PE'S CASH FLOW STREAM UNDER THE HYPOTHETICAL SCENARIO THAT THE CASH CONTRIBUTIONS WERE INVESTED INTO A PUBLIC EQUITY INDEX AND THE CASH DISTRIBUTIONS WERE WITHDRAWN FROM THAT SAME INDEX: Calculating this comparable return of investing in the public market is not easy when there are multiple cash "investments" and "withdrawals." The starting point is to gather annual total returns from a public (i.e., listed) equity index. The "Market Index" line of Exhibit 17.4 denotes the index values for the public equity market assuming dividend reinvestment of the public equity dividends. The "Market Return" line indicates the implied annual total returns for the market index.

The last two lines construct the hypothetical results of investing $100, $50, and $40 in the public market over the first 3 years rather than investing in the PE fund. The second to last line of Exhibit 17.4 (the hypothetical public market accumulation) denotes the hypothetical accumulation of investment of the PE fund's required cash contributions (capital calls) into a public equity index rather than the PE fund (and reflects cash distributions). The hypothetical PME cash flows are all the same as the PE fund cash flows except the final value (a quasi NAV). The difference between the fund's NAV (280) and the final hypothetical PME NAV (267.40) drives the difference between the IRR of the PE fund and the hypothetical IRR using the public market index.

In summary, the key computation is the final quasi-NAV (the last line of Period 8 in Exhibit 17.4). This $267.60 figure is the hypothetical accumulation within the public market generated by the cash contributions (capital calls) and distributions in Periods 0 to 7 and is driven by the returns of the public market index. It is the hypothetical $267.60 NAV in the final period (using the PME method in the last two lines of Exhibit 17.4) rather than the $280 (obtained from the PE fund's actual final distribution) that captures the difference between the IRR of the PE fund and the IRR of the PME Method applied to the same fund.

Step 3: Calculate the IRR for the hypothetical investment in the public index based on the contributions to the PE fund investment, the distributions from the fund prior to the final distribution, and the hypothetical NAV (or perhaps a final distribution) of the final period.

The key result in this example is that the PE fund's NAV of $280 would wipe out the hypothetical balance in the public equity index if distributed and create a deficit in the hypothetical market account of $12.40. Therefore, only $267.60 would be available to be distributed under the hypothetical (i.e., PME) approach. The IRR of the hypothetical investment in the public market is 12.30%, found using the bottom line cash flows and a spreadsheet or financial calculator. Recall that the IRR of the actual cash flows of the PE fund was 12.75%. The excess of the PE fund's 12.75% IRR above the PME IRR of 12.30% indicates that the PE fund outperformed the public equity index.

Thus the sign of the balance at the end of the last year (found in the second to last line of Exhibit 17.4) indicates whether the public market performed better (a positive balance) or worse (a negative balance) than the PE fund given the timing of the cash flows. Note that a change in the size and timing of the PE fund's cash flows (e.g., investing less in Period 0 and avoiding the catastrophic −40% return in the first year) could substantially change the results. This is the key point of the method: to examine the performance of the public market and private fund in the context of the same cash flows (the actual cash flows into and out of the private fund).

APPLICATION 17.7.2

A 5-year PE fund required a cash contribution (capital call) of $100 at the end of Year 0 and $100 and the end of Year 1. The PE fund has a NAV at the end of Year 5 of $350. In the meantime, the market index generated an annual return of −20% in the first year (Year 1) and 0% in the remaining four years (Year 2 to Year 5). Calculate and interpret the IRR of the PE fund and the IRR using the PME method.

   Inserting the cash flow stream of (−100, −100, 0, 0, 0, +350) generates an IRR of 13.19%. Investing the end-of-year 0 $100 contribution in the market index lowered its value to $80 at the end of Year 1 due to the −20% return in the public market index. That $80 combined with the $100 contributed at the end of Year 1 remained at $180 through the end of Year 5 due to the 0% public market returns in Years 2 to 5. Therefore, the final hypothetical accumulation in the public market is $180 at Year 5.

   Inserting the PME cash flow stream of (−100, −100, 0, 0, 0, +180) generates an IRR of −2.32%. The PE fund's IRR outperformed the public market index by 15.51%.

17.7.3 Key Computations in the Public Market Equivalent (PME) Method

The computations of the PME method in the previous section involve two challenges that are further explored in this section.

   First, recall that in the PME method the cash flows of a private investment (e.g., the contributions into and distributions out of a private equity fund) are compounded and accumulated from Period 0 to the final period as illustrated in Exhibit 17.4. That example used the return of the market index to form the hypothetical market accumulation. For example, between Periods 2 and 3 in Exhibit 17.4, the hypothetical market accumulation grew from 177.5 to 213.0 to simulate the hypothetical growth in value when the market index rose 20% [i.e., $213.0 = 177.5 \times (1 + 0.20)$]. The arithmetic could have been expressed equivalently using the ratio of the Period 3 index value to the Period 2 index value: (i.e., $213.0 = 177.5 \times 90 / 75$) rather than the percentage return.

   A common and equivalent (but more complex) approach to the same computation is to simulate the growth through "units" of the market index. According to this method the cash contributions are hypothetically used to "purchase" units in the index. So, the initial $100 cash contribution into the fund (in Period 0) would be simulated as having been used to purchase one unit of the index because the initial index value was 100.0. In Period 1, the $50 contribution would be simulated as having been used to purchase another 0.8333 index units (i.e., $50/$60) to bring the total accumulation to 1.833 units. The Period 1 hypothetical market accumulation could then be found as the number of units times the new index value: 1.833 × 60 = $110. The result is the same as that shown in the exhibit. The approach of accumulating units provides a helpful visualization.

The second key computation occurs in the final period. In Exhibit 17.4, the PE fund distributed $280 in Period 8. The hypothetical market accumulation (assuming the hypothetical cash flows included the $280 NAV) shows a value of −12.40 in the final period and a hypothetical cash flow or NAV of $267.60 (viewing the Period 8 value using public market returns and ignoring the $280 NAV). Different expositions of the PME method describe these two cash flows differently, but they are the key cash flows of the entire analysis. Accordingly, they are a major key to understanding the method.

When the actual PE fund's NAV (e.g., $280) happens to exactly match the hypothetical market accumulation *going into* the final period, then the PE fund and the PME method generate the same final distributions and the same IRRs. In other words, when the hypothetical market amount available to be distributed in the final period matches the NAV of the PE fund, then the performance (i.e., IRR) of the fund and the public method are equal. When the PE fund's actual NAV exceeds the amount available from the hypothetical public market accumulation (as it did in Exhibit 17.4 when there was only $267.60 available to distribute) then the PE fund outperformed the public index. The inferior performance of the market index is indicated by a negative ending balance in the hypothetical market accumulation (−$12.40) relative to the NAV of the fund.

There are three scenarios:

Scenario 1. The hypothetical market accumulation amount is negative going in the final period. In this case, the final hypothetical cash flow (the last line of Exhibit 17.4) that goes into the PME IRR computation will be negative and will be found as the previous hypothetical market accumulation amount minus the actual PE NAV (terminal distribution, in this case $280). The result would be a large negative number indicating that the PE fund performed much better than the public market.

Scenario 2. The hypothetical market accumulation amount is positive going into the final period but smaller than the PE fund's NAV. This is the case in Exhibit 17.4 where the hypothetical cash flow will be positive, but $12.40 smaller than the actual PE NAV (e.g., $280).

Scenario 3: The hypothetical market accumulation amount is positive going into the final period and equal to or larger than the PE fund's actual NAV. In this case, the hypothetical cash flow will be equal to or greater than the actual PE distribution (e.g., greater than or equal to $280).

In all scenarios, the goal is to determine the final hypothetical cash flow. The hypothetical cash flows are then used to compute the hypothetical IRR under the PME method.

17.7.4 Extensions to the PME Method and Other Related Performance Metrics

The IRR method, and by extension the LN PME method, have particularly troublesome shortcomings in terms of interpretation (i.e., as cash-weighted returns they are limited in their usefulness in comparison with time-weighted returns). Further, the performance levels generated by IRR and PME methods have substantial potential to be manipulated through manipulation of cash flow management (e.g., moving cash in and out of the underlying investment). Both of these issues are explored in more detail in Part 6 (Chapter 30) on Access. Metrics based on the PME method other than IRR can also be used to indicate performance such as PME ratios.

Also, it is important to bear in mind that there are substantial differences between private equity investments and public equity investments (e.g., illiquidity, governance, and taxation). Therefore, any direct comparison of a PE investment to public equity must be made with caution. Depending on how the PME is calculated, there will be a number of issues and problems that must be carefully examined. These are discussed in detail in Part 6 on Access.

17.8 GROUP PEER RETURNS AS BENCHMARKS

The most intuitive approach is to benchmark the performance of a PE fund (or many other types of funds for which asset-based benchmarks may be unavailable or unreliable) against the performance of a group of funds that have a similar risk profile (i.e., that have the same style or specialization)—that is, the fund's peer group.

In private equity, peer groups are formed based on characteristics such as vintage, geographic location, size, or development stage and often express performance in terms of the quartile within which it lies. A **peer-group cohort** refers to a group of private equity funds or investments that share some important characteristics. For example, one may consider European venture capital funds of a particular vintage to form a peer-group cohort. A top performer in a dismal vintage year may barely return the invested funds, whereas in some spectacular vintage years, even fourth-quartile funds have earned double-digit returns.

The mean return of a peer group is often viewed as a benchmark or as a risk-adjusted return in a performance analysis. Additionally, the distribution of the returns of each fund in a peer group can be used to indicate how superior or inferior a fund's return was. Performance relative to a peer group is often expressed in terms of quartiles. A top-quartile fund is typically defined as a fund that belongs to the 25% best-performing funds in its peer group at the time of benchmarking. This leads some people to conclude that only 25% of funds qualify as top quartile. The fact is that many more funds in the market are being labeled and marketed as top quartile. One reason for this is that except for the 25% ratio itself, nothing else in this definition is carved in stone. For example, different fund managers or consultants may use different peer groups to calculate the relative performance of different funds. In addition, different time periods may be used to compare the performance. Even if the same peer group and time period are used, different measures of performance (e.g., IRR, multiples, or PME) may be used to compare performance.

Sometimes there are too few observations within one peer-group cohort to benchmark. Extending the peer-group cohort by closely comparable funds can be a simple way out. For example, if the number of 2017 European early-stage funds is not sufficient, the universe of all 2017 European VC funds or the universe of all 2016–18 European early-stage funds could potentially be used as alternatives.

17.9 BENCHMARKING REAL ESTATE

Development of expected risk and return estimates for real estate properties can be based primarily on past returns and current metrics based on current valuations.

17.9.1 Benchmarking Core Real Estate with Cap Rates

Expected returns and benchmarks for core real estate are often assumed to be approximately equal to cap rates (discussed in Chapter 13 of the CAIA Level I curriculum). The cap rate of a real estate investment is the net operating income (NOI) of the investment divided by some measure of the real estate's total value, such as purchase price or appraised value: Cap Rate = NOI/Value.

The exact specifications of the NOI for the numerator of the cap rate (recent, current, forecasted) and the value (beginning of period versus end of period, transaction price versus appraised price) for the denominator of the cap rate vary between users and purposes. Note that NOI does not reflect financing costs, and therefore the NOI-based approach for estimating value is intended for analysis of unleveraged property values.

Cap rates are often viewed as direct estimates of expected returns. Thus, a property with a cap rate of 8% is expected to generate a return of 8% to the investor on an unleveraged basis. The view of a cap rate as an estimated expected return is at best a crude approximation in that it typically ignores anticipated capital gains or losses as well as anticipated growth or decline in income. Nevertheless, cap rates are a good starting point for an analysis of expected returns.

Cap rates are also viewed as required rates of return and are used to perform risk adjustment in valuation of properties. Thus, an investor may search for a core property that offers a cap rate of at least 6% while demanding a cap rate such as 8% on a value-added property that is perceived as having higher risk. Thus cap rates are often used to establish values for particular properties by rearranging the formula for the cap rate: Property Value = NOI/Cap Rate.

Cap rates are often expressed as a cap rate spread. The **cap rate spread** is the excess of the cap rate over the yield of a default-free 10-year bond (such as the 10-year Treasury rate in the United States). A typical cap rate spread for core real estate over the 10-year Treasury rate is 2% to 3%, or 200 to 300 basis points. Cap rates are a tool that is widely used in real estate but less so in other areas of finance.

17.9.2 Benchmarking Core Real Estate with a Risk Premium Formula

In the finance literature, expected investment returns are often modeled using a risk premium approach, which expresses a risky asset's expected return as the sum of a riskless return and a premium for bearing the risk of that asset. The risk premium approach is illustrated in Equation 17.3:

$$E(R_i) = R_f + Risk\ Premium_i \qquad (17.3)$$

where $E(R_i)$ is the expected return (or a required return) on asset i, R_f is the riskless interest rate, and $Risk\ Premium_i$ is the risk premium, or spread, of asset i relative to the riskless rate. Note that $Risk\ Premium_i$ is a premium peculiar to asset i; it is not a risk premium such as the premium on the market portfolio that is used to determine cross-sectional expected returns of other assets based on their correlation with the market.

The key contribution of the risk premium approach in Equation 17.3 is its potential to incorporate the current riskless interest rate in forming expectations of future returns for the same asset for different market conditions. Since riskless interest rates vary primarily due to inflation expectations, Equation 17.3 may be viewed as a method of adjusting return expectations for different anticipated inflation levels as well as different interest rate levels. For example, in the late 1970s, US inflation rates reached double-digit levels. It would be unreasonable to believe that investors expected single-digit nominal returns on competitively priced assets when there was double-digit inflation. Nominal after-tax interest rates must exceed expected inflation rates for real rates to be positive.

The maturity of the default-free interest rate used in the risk premium approach varies and is generally determined by the investment horizon of the application. Outside of real estate, analysts often use a very short-term rate, such as an overnight rate or a 3-month rate, to capture the rate earned in the absence of default risk and interest rate risk. In US real estate markets, the 10-year Treasury rate is typically used as the default-free interest rate against which to evaluate cap rates and risk premiums. Presumably, the 10-year bond is selected to more closely approximate the longevity of real estate holdings. The decision of which riskless interest-rate maturity to use is a matter of professional judgment.

APPLICATION 17.9.2

Solve for the average risk premiums of the NPI given a 7.8% NPI average annualized return and the 1-year and 10-year Treasury average returns of 3.3% and 4.9%.

Using Equation 17.5 generates 25-year average risk premiums of 4.5% and 2.9%, respectively.

17.9.3   Three Approaches to Benchmarking Noncore Real Estate

Development of an estimate of the expected returns of value-added and opportunistic real estate investing may take three primary approaches: (1) the use of observed cap rates for those styles of real estate investment; (2) the use of a risk premium approach (based on the estimation of their risks relative to the risks of core real estate investments); or (3) the use of absolute hurdle rates.

While data on core real estate returns are reasonably available and reliable, data on value-added and opportunistic risks and returns are more problematic. The direct use of observed cap rates in market transactions to estimate expected returns for value-added and especially opportunistic properties may be rather inaccurate because the estimates of net operating income for these styles are much less reliable than are the estimates of NOI for the core style. The use of absolute hurdle rates may be inappropriate due to their failure to consider different interest rates and expected inflation levels.

Accordingly, the expected risks and returns (and benchmarks) of value-added and opportunistic real estate investments are typically estimated and expressed relative to the risks and returns of core real estate investments. Risk-premium methods can serve as effective tools both in estimating the current expected returns of core properties and in developing expected returns for value-added and opportunistic properties.

17.9.4 Examples of Benchmark Return Estimates for Noncore Style Assets

At particular points in time, investors may develop benchmark or target rates of return for properties with value-added and opportunistic styles relative to core rates rather than relying on cap data from value-added and opportunistic styles. For example, Exhibit 17.5 illustrates the idea that expected returns for core real estate across the three real estate property markets (primary, secondary, and tertiary) are determined based on current metrics such as cap rates. Then, the rates for value-added and opportunistic are formed by adding in risk premiums associated with each style and market.

NCREIF and other organizations estimate cap rates for various commercial property types in the United States. The overall weighted average of cap rates for core commercial property in the United States has varied between roughly 5%

Gross Expected Returns Style Box

$E(R) = 7\%$	$E(R) = 7.5\%$	$E(R) = 10\%$	Primary
$E(R) = 7.5\%$	$E(R) = 8\%$	$E(R) = 11\%$	Secondary
$E(R) = 8\%$	$E(R) = 9.5\%$	$E(R) = 12\%$	Tertiary
Core	Value-Added	Opportunistic	

EXHIBIT 17.5 Suggestive Expected Real Estate Returns Style Boxes

and 10% since the mid-1980s. The higher end of the range was reached in the mid-1990s, whereas the lower end of the range was a result of the onset of the global financial crisis that began in 2007. Estimates of cap rates on US commercial property ranged below long-term averages (at between 4% and 6%) for core real estate properties in primary real estate markets leading into 2020.

NOTES

1. See Merton (1973); Connor and Korajczyk (1989).
2. See Rubinstein (1973); Harvey and Siddique (2000); Kraus and Litzenberger (1976).
3. See Homaifar and Graddy (1988).

REFERENCES

Bailey, J. V., T. M. Richards, and D. E. Tierney. 1990. "Benchmark Portfolios and the Manager/Plan Sponsor Relationship." 2025 In *Current Topics in Investment Management*, ed. F. J. Fabozzi and T. Dessa Fabozzi, New York: Harper & Row, pp. 71–85.

Connor, G. and R. A. Korajczyk. 1989. "An Intertemporal Equilibrium Beta Pricing Model." *Review of Financial Studies* 2 (3): 373–92.

Harvey, C. R. and A. Siddique. 2000. "Conditional Skewness in Asset Pricing Tests." *Journal of Finance LV* (3): 1263–95.

Homaifar, G. and D. Graddy. 1988. "Equity Yields in Models Considering Higher Moments of the Return Distribution." *Applied Economics* 20 (3): 325–34.

Hughen, J. and P. Eckrich. 2015. "Chasing Two Rabbits: Challenges in Benchmarking Liquid Alternatives." *Journal of Index Investing* 6 (2): 80–85.

Kocis, J., J. Bachman, A. Long, and C. Nickels. 2009. *Inside Private Equity: The Professional Investor's Handbook*. Chichester: John Wiley & Sons.

Kraus, A. and H. Litzenberger. 1976. "Skewness Preference and the Valuation of Risky Assets." *Journal of Finance* 31 (4): 1085–1100.

Merton, R. C. 1973. "An Intertemporal Capital Asset Pricing Model." *Econometrica* 41 (5): 867–87.

Rubinstein, M. 1973. "A Comparative Statics Analysis of Risk Premiums." *Journal of Business* 46 (4): 604–15.

Schneeweis, T. and R. Spurgin. 1997. "Comparison of Commodity and Managed Futures Benchmark Indices." *Journal of Derivatives* 4 (4): 33–50.

Spurgin, R., T. Schneeweis, and G. Georgiev. 2001. "Benchmarking Commodity Trading Advisor Performance with a Passive Futures-Based Index." CISDM Working Paper.

Swamy, G. M., I. Zeltser, H. Kazemi, and E. Szado. 2011. "Setting the Benchmark: Spotlight on Private Equity." *Alternative Investment Analyst Review*, CAIA. 1.

CHAPTER 18

Liquidity and Funding Risks

Funding and liquidity risks arise from the potential for an investor to be unable to meet commitments. This chapter begins with a discussion of liquidity and funding risks for levered portfolios with liquid assets (e.g., portfolios of futures contracts). The remainder of the chapter discusses funding risks for portfolios with illiquid assets (e.g., private equities).

18.1 MARGIN ACCOUNTS AND COLLATERAL MANAGEMENT

Commodity trading advisers (CTAs) use futures contracts and other leveraged products to manage exposures and risks. CTAs are faced with funding risks that provide an excellent example of the funding risks faced by all investors with highly leveraged exposures.

18.1.1 Three Specialized Terms for Futures Account Levels

Futures contracts do not have a single, clear measure of value. To cope with the specialized features of margin and collateral for futures portfolios, the CTA industry has adopted three specialized terms describing levels of value: (1) trading level; (2) funding level; and (3) notional funding.

Trading level is simply the base amount or denominator used in calculating returns of leveraged positions and is the amount of capital that is traded in the active risk account. It is also: (1) the account value that the CTA uses to calculate management and incentive fees; (2) the mutually agreed upon amount to be traded that determines the size of the actual positions that the CTA takes in futures markets, depending on the CTA's leverage goals; and (3) the account value that the CTA uses to translate profits and losses in futures contract trading into percentage returns.

The funding level is the total amount of cash or collateral that the investor posts or invests to support the trading level. The rock-bottom minimum funding level for any futures position or portfolio is the total value of margin collateral required by the various futures exchanges.

The notional funding is the added exposure to the trading level that the CTA allows above and beyond the trading level. Notional funding gives investors the ability to leverage their managed futures account to a higher trading level than would exist with cash funding. Notional funding in managed futures is favored by investors because it capitalizes on the ease of acquiring leverage through futures markets. In addition, implicit leverage may carry a relatively low cost because the notionally funded amount is not borrowed or deposited; the funding level is a good-faith deposit for the full value of the account.

For example, if an investor wants to invest with a CTA that requires a minimum investment of $600,000, the investor could either fully fund the account with $600,000 or, if notional funding was offered, partially fund the account (e.g., a funding level of $400,000) but still have it traded as if it were funded with $600,000. The account would therefore have a notional funding level of $200,000. In this case, the trading level—which is also the amount on which investor fees and returns are calculated—would be $600,000 with the account funded 67%. If the CTA returned 10% that year (on the trading level), the investor would have made $60,000 (a 10% gain on the trading level), but it would be a 16.7% gain on the funding level. Of course, if the CTA were to lose 10%, the loss would be magnified to 16.7%.

The relation is depicted in Equation 18.1:

$$\text{Trading Level} = \text{Funding Level} + \text{Notional Level} \qquad (18.1)$$

Exchange margins tend to be small relative to the face value or portfolio equivalent value of the underlying contracts. In a diversified portfolio of futures contracts, the actual day-to-day risk in the portfolio can be smaller still. As a result, funding levels can be much lower than trading levels.

APPLICATION 18.1.1

Consider an account with $100,000 cash invested but with a mandate that risk exposures, fees, and returns be based upon $200,000 through the use of leverage. Identify the trading level, funding level, and notional level.

Equation 18.1 provides the relation between the three levels. The $100,000 is the funding level, since it is the cash contributed. The $200,000 meets the definition of the trading level. Therefore, the $100,000 being used to lever the funding level to the trading level represents the notional level.

18.1.2 Collateral and Margin for Futures Portfolios

Futures markets require participants to post collateral to cover potential daily losses. The posting of collateral is typically called margin. Because futures contracts are exchange-traded instruments, CTAs need to satisfy the rules and restrictions put forth by these exchanges. One of these rules pertains to the amount of collateral or margin that a party to a futures contract must contribute or post. The amount of initial margin is the amount of cash or Treasury bills that must be in an account at a broker or futures commission merchant in order to initiate a trade in a specific futures contract. Minimum initial margins are set by the exchanges for each futures contract. This initial margin, which is generally only a small percentage of the notional value of the futures contract, is related to the volatility of the assets underlying the futures contract and can change over time.

More volatile contracts require larger margins. Futures exchanges have the ability to change margin requirements at any time. Margin requirements are often increased after a sharp rise in prices or price volatility. The maintenance margin, which is typically lower than the initial margin, is the amount of margin required to carry previously initiated positions. If a customer's margin account drops below the level required for the maintenance margin, then the customer has to add funds to restore the margin account to the level of the initial margin.

In certain circumstances, the initial margin may be less than the sum of the initial margins of the individual futures contracts. Futures exchanges take into account the fact that the manager is holding both long and short positions in related contracts. Since such spread positions may have less risk than outright directional positions, the exchanges apply a lower spread margin. For instance, a relative value trader might be long a nearby futures contract (e.g., long March corn) and short a distant contract (e.g., short September corn). In such cases, spread margins would apply.

The **margin-to-equity** ratio is expressed as the amount of assets held for meeting margin requirements as a percentage of the net asset value (NAV) of the investment account. For example, if the equity invested in a futures portfolio is valued at \$1,000,000 and the total margin required by various exchanges is \$61,000, then the margin-to-equity ratio would be 6.1%. It is often difficult to interpret margin-to-equity ratios. More conservative managers may build portfolios with margin-to-equity ratios between 5% and 10%, while more aggressive managers may have a margin-to-equity ratio above 20%. Margin-to-equity is closely correlated to fund volatility, as the implied leverage of higher margin-to-equity ratios leads to greater levels of fund volatility.

High levels could indicate highly levered trading; for instance, a margin-to-equity ratio of 100% means that the invested equity is just enough to cover the margins, indicating that the maximum amount of leverage provided by the contracts is being employed. However, high levels of the margin-to-equity ratio could equally result from a portfolio diversified across many futures markets where margin offsets are not available (e.g., partially offsetting positions at different exchanges). Still, the margin-to-equity ratio is a popular measure of CTA risk because it tells investors roughly how much of their investment could be used for margin purposes. This number will fluctuate from day to day for a given manager, but investors can obtain the average range. It should be noted that the exchange sets the margin to reflect the riskiness of the futures contract. The greater the exchange's estimate of the risk associated with a contract, the higher the level of the margin required by that exchange on the particular contract.

18.1.3 Margin Across Multiple Clearinghouses

The minimum margin for a globally diversified CTA portfolio would most likely be enough to meet the CTA's internal risk management objectives, since clearinghouse margin is only aggregated within each clearinghouse. Globally diversified CTAs trade across many clearinghouses and do not often get cross-margin benefits across exchanges. A **cross-margin benefit** is available when a CTA has multiple positions in contracts traded on the same exchange, which allows the total amount of margin that the CTA must post to be smaller than the sum of the margin amount of each contract.

In practice, each clearinghouse requires that margins be posted in the local currency, causing CTA portfolios to be exposed to currency risks. To alleviate this problem, many CTAs can use single-currency margining, in which the trading client can post the full margin in the form of dollars (or euros or any other allowed currency). Under this arrangement, the clearinghouse is responsible for converting the client's cash into collateral that is acceptable for various exchanges around the world.

For a well-diversified CTA portfolio, the passing of each trading day produces gains and losses in various currencies. In futures markets, it is standard practice to settle all gains and losses in cash every day. These daily cash settlements of gains and losses are known as **variation margin**. The practice of making daily cash settlements produces an ongoing stream of small transaction costs. Minimizing these costs is an important objective for CTAs and their investors.

The cash that flows into or out of an account also affects the ultimate return earned by the investor. Cash that flows in can be invested, whereas cash that flows out must be financed, either explicitly or out of pocket. Because all gains and losses are settled in cash daily, futures contracts have no net liquidating value beyond what they accumulate over the course of a single trading day. As a result, there is no natural denominator for estimating the return on a futures position. Interest earned on any cash or collateral invested in a fund or posted as collateral in a managed account is part of the total return.

18.1.4 Capital at Risk for Managed Futures

Managed futures traders normally employ stop-loss rules in their trading programs. These **stop losses** are specific prices at which the strategy will exit a futures position should the price move adversely. In the case of reversal systems, stops are effectively the price at which the system liquidates an existing directional position and establishes a new position in the opposite direction.

Capital at risk (**CaR**) represents the total loss that would be incurred should each position hit its stop-loss price level on that day. Exhibit 18.1 displays the CaR of a

EXHIBIT 18.1 Leverage and Capital at Risk (CaR) of a Sample Portfolio

Contract	Notional Contract Value	Loss at 1% Price Change
S&P 500 Index	$517,250.00	−$5,172.50
Corn	$19,060.00	−$190.60
Soybeans	$49,500.00	−$495.00
Eurodollars	$987,000.00	−$9,870.00
U.S. long bond	$155,000.00	−$1,550.00
Crude oil	$48,800.00	−$488.00
Gold	$108,000.00	−$1,080.00
Japanese yen	$154,800.00	−$1,548.00
Size of notional positions	$2,039,410.00	
Total CaR value		−$20,394.10
Assumed account value	$1,000,000.00	
Notional leverage	203.94%	
Capital at risk	−2.0394%	

sample portfolio of long futures positions. It assumes that each stop loss is set at 1% of the notional value of each contract (i.e., the position would be liquidated upon a 1% adverse price move).

The usefulness of CaR as a measure of maximum potential loss is dependent on the likelihood that the futures price could gap through the stop-loss level, resulting in a greater loss than that being reported by the CaR. This could occur while the market is closed or while the market is open in less liquid markets, such as futures on agricultural commodities. A **stop-loss order** becomes a market order when the loss level is reached. The market order may be partially or fully executed at a less favorable price if there are insufficient offsetting trade orders. A **stop-limit order** becomes a limit order when the loss level is reached, and may not be executed if the market price has moved quickly beyond the stated limit.

In another sense, though, CaR often overstates a portfolio's risk, since it does not account for the possibility that a portfolio might hold both long and short futures positions, which could offer some offset should significant price moves occur. That is, it is unlikely for all positions to hit their stop-loss levels simultaneously. Finally, a typical investor does not have the transparency to the CTA's positions that is needed to calculate CaR. The exception is when the investor uses a managed account platform to invest in a CTA program.

18.2 VALUE AT RISK FOR MANAGED FUTURES

Value at risk (VaR) is a method of measuring the potential loss in an investment portfolio given a particular holding period, with no changes to the portfolio during the holding period, and at a particular confidence level. The most common confidence levels used are 95% and 99%. A portfolio's 1-day VaR of $3,000,000 at a 95% confidence level means that there is a 95% probability that losses sustained by the portfolio over the next day will not exceed $3,000,000 and, thus, a 5% chance that losses will be greater than $3 million. In other words, during 100 trading days, losses exceeding $3,000,000 are expected in only 5 trading days. If the value of the portfolio is $100,000,000, then the VaR could be expressed as 3%.

18.2.1 Value at Risk for a Portfolio as a Quantile

For example, using the portfolio shown in Exhibit 18.1 (i.e., one long contract in each of the individual markets), a 1-day VaR can be inferred from daily data over a long period of time such as 100 trading days or more. At a 95% confidence level, the 1-day VaR might be estimated to be $10,000 or approximately 1% of the assumed account value of $1,000,000. That is, one would expect that 95% of the time, the daily loss on this portfolio would be less than $10,000.

A simple way of estimating VaR when sufficient data exist is to observe the returns on an actual portfolio (or construct hypothetical returns) over a long period of time such as 200 days. The daily profits and losses can then be ranked from largest profit to largest loss. A 1-day 95% VaR can then be approximated as the 190th ranked outcome and a 99% VaR can then be approximated as the 198th ranked outcome.

18.2.2   VaR Using a Parametric Approach with Variance Based on Equal Return Weighting

There are several methods for estimating the VaR of an investment. A simple and common method is the parametric approach. In the parametric approach, one assumes that return on the investment follows a known distribution (typically normal). In order to estimate the VaR of the investment, one has to estimate the parameters of the distribution (typically, mean and standard deviation). In fact, to obtain an accurate estimate of VaR, it is crucial to obtain an accurate estimate of return volatility. There are several methods for estimating return volatility, and, in general, the higher the frequency of available observations, the more accurate the estimated volatility.

The most common method for estimating volatility is to obtain daily returns on an investment, say a CTA, and then perform the following procedure on the data to obtain an estimate of daily volatility:

$$\mu = \frac{1}{T} \sum_{t=1}^{T} R_t \tag{18.2}$$

$$\sigma_T^2 = \frac{1}{T-1} \sum_{t=1}^{T} (\mu - R_t)^2 \tag{18.3}$$

Here, σ_T^2 is the estimate of the current daily variance, R_t is the daily rate of return, T is the number of observations, and μ is the estimated daily mean return. In this method, all observations have the same weight.

18.2.3   Parametric VaR Using a Variance based on Unequal Return Weighting

When an analyst believes that the more recent behavior of the asset better approximates the expected behavior of the asset in the near future, an alternative to the equally weighted method of estimating variance is to assign larger weights to the most recent observations and smaller weights to observations that occurred many periods ago. One simple and popular technique that uses this unequal weighting is the exponential weighting method. Under this approach, the estimated value of the variance is obtained using the following expression:

$$\mu_{T-1} = (1 - \lambda)\mu_{T-2} + \lambda(\mu_{T-2} - R_{T-1}) \tag{18.4}$$

$$\sigma_T^2 = (1 - \lambda) \times \sigma_{T-1}^2 + \lambda(\mu_{T-1} - R_T)^2 \tag{18.5}$$

Here, $0 < \lambda < 1$ is a parameter that is selected by the user. The larger the value of λ, the higher the weight assigned to the most recent observations in calculating both the mean and the variance. Note that the mean daily return is updated as new observations of returns are received. The updated mean is then used to calculate the daily variance. The estimated parameters (mean and variance) are then used to estimate VaR using the parametric VaR formulas as described in the next section.

18.2.4 Confidence Intervals with Parametric VaR

Once an estimate of the standard deviation is obtained, the user needs to specify the desired level of confidence. The higher the selected level of confidence, the higher the estimated value of VaR will be. After the desired confidence level is selected, the critical value of α is calculated as shown in Equation 18.6:

$$Pr\{Z \leq \alpha\} = 1 - \text{Confidence Level} \tag{18.6}$$

Here, Z is a standard normal random variable. This means α is the value for a standard normal random variable where the probability of observing a value less than α is equal to 1 minus the selected confidence level. To determine the value of α, one may use either a table of standard normal random variables or a spreadsheet program. Once this critical value is calculated, the VaR of the portfolio can be estimated using Equation 18.7.

$$\text{VaR}_\alpha = (\alpha \times \sigma_t) + \mu \tag{18.7}$$

The portion of the VaR in Equation 18.7 inside the parentheses is typically calculated as a negative number while μ is a positive number. It is customary to report the absolute value of the VaR value even as an indication of loss. In addition, since the daily mean, μ, is likely to be very small, it is common practice to ignore it (especially for short time intervals).

For example, assume that the daily returns for a CTA are used to obtain estimates of daily volatility, σ_t, and daily mean return, μ, of the CTA. These are reported to be 1.8% and 0.03%, respectively. What is the daily VaR of this CTA at the 95% confidence level? First, the critical value of α for the 95% confidence level is -1.6448. That is,

$$Pr\{Z \leq -1.6448\} = 1 - 0.95.$$

Thus, the daily VaR at the 95% confidence level is calculated as follows:

$$\text{VaR} = (-1.6448 \times 1.8\%) + 0.03\% = -2.93\%$$

Thus there is an estimated 5% probability that the daily loss experienced by this CTA will exceed 2.93%. One of the critical assumptions of using this approach to estimate VaR is that the probability distribution of the portfolio's daily return is approximately normal. If the probability distribution deviates substantially from normality, then alternative methods to estimate the VaR must be used. As a method of calculating risk, VaR is useful but should be used in conjunction with additional risk-measurement techniques. Its reliance on specific estimates of correlations and volatilities makes it prone to underestimating potential tail risk during periods of increased financial stress.

18.3 OTHER METHODS OF ESTIMATING LIQUIDITY NEEDS

VaR represents a versatile and straightforward method of estimating potential losses and the liquidity that may be necessary to meet those losses. This section discusses additional methods of estimating liquidity needs.

18.3.1   Simulation Analysis and Potential Managed Futures Losses

A portfolio **stress test** or **scenario analysis** is a simulation applied to a portfolio to determine how it will perform under different market scenarios. Commonly, these try to include extreme market events, both those historically encountered (e.g., the global financial crisis in 2008) and those based on simulated financial stress. This technique is often used in conjunction with VaR, since it examines scenarios in which volatility and correlations are assumed to change.

Exhibit 18.2 illustrates a stress test under simplified assumptions. It analyzes the demand on cash in an investment account should a set of futures positions have an eight-sigma (i.e., eight-standard-deviation) adverse price move and, at the same time, should futures exchanges double the required initial margin on these same positions. It should be noted that an eight-sigma move is incredibly unlikely for a normally distributed variable. However, the positive excess kurtosis of most return distributions makes very extreme events much more likely to happen than exists for a mesokurtic distribution.

Consider a portfolio that has a margin-to-equity ratio of 6.1%, a CaR of 1.66%, and a VaR of 1%. Under the conditions assumed in the stress test (see Exhibit 18.2), the portfolio could lose over 6.46% on a day with an eight-standard-deviation price move (6.46% = 64,640/1,000,000).

The stress test potential loss (based on an eight-sigma move) is substantially higher than indicated by the CaR or the VaR. In addition, the doubling of the initial

EXHIBIT 18.2   Portfolio Stress Test: Eight-Standard-Deviation Price Move; Doubling of Initial Margin

Contract	Notional Contract Value	1-Standard Deviation Price Move	8-Standard Deviation Price Move	Initial Margin Requirement
S&P 500 Index	$207,250	1.24%	−$20,559	$30,938
Corn	$17,913	1.68%	−$2,408	$2,025
Soybeans	$47,475	1.45%	−$5,507	$4,725
Eurodollars	$987,650	0.08%	−$6,321	$1,485
U.S. long bond	$126,640	0.63%	−$6,383	$4,320
Crude oil	$40,320	2.17%	−$7,000	$8,100
Gold	$90,166	1.26%	−$9,089	$5,399
Japanese yen	$139,636	0.66%	−$7,373	$4,860
Total loss from 8-standard-deviation price move			−$64,638	
Total required initial margin				$61,852

Potential Total Cash Demand

8-standard-deviation price move	$64,638
Initial margin at 2x level	$123,704
Total	$188,344
Assumed account value	$1,000,000
Potential total cash demand as % of account value	18.83%

margin creates a further demand on cash of 12.4% of the account value. The combined impact would be an 18.8% use of cash in the portfolio over 1 day. Although this may be an unlikely scenario, a major purpose of stress tests is to examine the potential impact of extreme events. It has been seen in the past that these low-probability events do occur (e.g., the failures of Long-Term Capital Management and Lehman Brothers).

18.3.2 Omega Ratio and Managed Futures

The omega ratio is a more general measure of risk that takes the entire return distribution of an investment (e.g., a CTA) into account. Traditional measures of risks and risk-adjusted returns such as the VaR, Sharpe ratio, Treynor ratio, and information ratio have been questioned by researchers because of their reliance on specific, and sometimes restrictive, assumptions about the distribution of returns.

Omega is an alternative to these and can provide a better assessment of downside risk and upside potential relative to a target return. The target level could be zero for an absolute return product such as a CTA or a hedge fund, while other rates, such as the inflation rate or a short-term nominal riskless rate, could be selected for a product that is supposed to protect the real value of an investor's portfolio.

The **omega ratio** is the ratio of the total realized returns in excess of a given target return relative to the total realized loss relative to the same target return. Exhibit 18.3 contains hypothetical monthly returns on a CTA. In this example, a 4% annual return (0.333% monthly return) is the stated target. For each realized monthly return, it is determined whether the realized return is greater or less than the target level. These differences in periods with positive deviations from the target are included in the upper partial moment and the others in the lower partial moment. For example, the January figure exceeds the target and is included in the upper partial moment column as follows:

$$18.22\% = \max(18.55\% - 0.333\%, 0)$$

EXHIBIT 18.3   Hypothetical Monthly Return (Target Rate = 4% per year)

	Realized Monthly Return	Above Target Return	Below Target Return	Upper Partial Moment	Lower Partial Moment
Jan	18.55%	1	0	18.22%	0.00%
Feb	−18.62%	0	1	0.00%	18.95%
Mar	8.58%	1	0	8.25%	0.00%
Apr	−4.68%	0	1	0.00%	5.01%
May	1.69%	1	0	1.36%	0.00%
June	−3.50%	0	1	0.00%	3.83%
July	−13.07%	0	1	0.00%	13.40%
Aug	−21.47%	0	1	0.00%	21.80%
Sept	−4.91%	0	1	0.00%	5.24%
Oct	8.13%	1	0	7.80%	0.00%
Nov	2.66%	1	0	2.33%	0.00%
Dec	−5.27%	0	1	0.00%	5.61%
Average				3.16%	6.15%
Omega					0.51
Target Annual Return					4.00%

and the February figure goes into the lower partial moment column because it was lower than the target:

$$18.95\% = \max(0.333\% - (-18.62\%),\ 0)$$

Exhibit 18.3 depicts the placement of the deviations from the target into two sets. The averages (based on the total number of observations) of these upper and lower partial moments are calculated to be 3.16% and 6.15%, respectively. The omega ratio is calculated to be 0.51, the ratio of these two figures (3.16/6.15). The same answer can be found by simply dividing the total of the upper partial moment column by the total of the lower partial moment column. Mathematically, omega is given by the expression in Equation 18.8:

$$\Omega = \frac{Upper\ Partial\ Moment}{Lower\ Partial\ Moment}$$

$$= \frac{\frac{1}{N}\sum_{i=1}^{N}\max(R_i - T, 0)}{\frac{1}{N}\sum_{i=1}^{N}\max(T - R_i, 0)} \tag{18.8}$$

where R_i is the rate of return on the investment in period i, N is the total number of observations, and T is the target rate. Note that the value of N (the total number of observations for all periods) is the same in the numerator and the denominator so the N can be canceled out. Thus the omega ratio compares the sum of the upside deviations with the sum of the downside deviations (relative to the target).

APPLICATION 18.3.2

Assume that the returns of an investment exceed the target rate in five periods by 1%, 3%, 4%, 5%, and 7%, while the returns fall short of the target in four periods by 4%, 6%, 8%, and 10%. What is the omega ratio?

The sums in the upper and lower partial moments are calculated to be 20% and 28%, respectively. Using Equation 18.8, and noting that the term 1/N cancels out, the omega ratio is simply 20%/28% = 0.71. Note that the return deviation explicitly provided in this example can be found as the absolute values of the quantity: total return − target return.

18.3.3   Interpreting the Omega Ratio

For a symmetrical distribution with a target return equal to the mean, the omega ratio should average one. When the omega ratio is less than one, it means the investment has failed to earn a summed return that exceeds the target level. Furthermore, it can be shown that higher volatility, lower skewness, and higher kurtosis will, in general, reduce the omega of a portfolio (Shadwick and Keating (2002) and Kazemi,

Schneeweis, and Gupta (2003)). In addition, increasing the target return will reduce the omega of the investment product. For instance, in the previous example, the omega will decline to 0.48 if the target return is raised to 8% per year (0.666% per month).

Using historical performance figures, studies have shown that for a target level of zero, the omega of a diversified portfolio of CTAs would be around four, and the omega measure of the MSCI World Equity Index would be around two.

18.4   SMOOTHED RETURNS ON ILLIQUID FUNDS

Chapter 25 discusses appraisal-based valuations and methods of forming indices of real estate. That chapter emphasizes the difficulties in obtaining accurate and timely reporting of values of illiquid assets. For example, Chapter 9 of the CAIA Level I Curriculum noted that the historic returns of farmland and timberland appear to falsely indicate extremely low levels of risk and therefore extremely high return-to-risk ratios (e.g., Sharpe and Treynor ratios). These performance distortions can be due to the use of appraisals in valuing the underlying prices of the return indices. This section contrasts appraised values versus market values for real estate indices and explores the risks and returns of liquid versus illiquid real estate funds. This chapter analyzes the problem and presents a quantitative solution.

18.4.1   Smoothed Asset Returns and Unsmoothing

Exhibit 18.4 provides a hypothetical numerical illustration of the concept of smoothed pricing. Overall equity market returns, shown in Column 2, are assumed to experience a 10% surge in prices in the midst of a larger time period of stable values. Three other return series with a true beta of 0.8 are illustrated in Columns 3, 4, and 5, each of which eventually responds with an 8% rise (ignoring compounding for simplicity). The unsmoothed return series experiences its entire price response (8%) to the market in the same time period as the equity market. The lightly smoothed return series reflects 75% of its 8% price response in the same period as the market, but reflects another 25% of its price response in the subsequent time period. The strongly smoothed return series experiences half of its price response in the same period as the market, and the other half in the subsequent period.

EXHIBIT 18.4   Illustration of Price Smoothing

(1) Time Period	(2) Market Returns	(3) Unsmoothed	(4) Lightly Smoothed	(5) Strongly Smoothed
1	0%	0%	0%	0%
2	10%	8%	6%	4%
3	0%	0%	2%	4%
4	0%	2%	0%	0%
Mean	2.5%	20%	2.0%	2.0%
Std. dev.	5.0%	4.0%	2.8%	2.3%
Corr. w/mkt	1.00	1.00	0.94	0.58
Beta	1.00	0.80	0.53	0.27

The remainder of this chapter focuses on one of the most crucial tasks in empirical analysis of returns of unlisted assets: data unsmoothing. **Return unsmoothing** is the process of removing the effects of smoothed changes from a return series by adjusting the data to eliminate, or at least reduce, the level of autocorrelation in a time series. When appraisal or other lagged methods are used to construct real estate price indices, the resulting indices are considered to be smoothed, as the index values will slowly adjust to changes in market conditions affecting real estate prices. Unsmoothing of an index is the process of adjusting the index values so that they reflect changes in economic conditions on a timely basis and with a level of volatility that reflects market realities rather than appraisals. The effects of smoothed data are not limited to values based on real estate appraisals. Smoothing can affect other alternative investments, such as other illiquid real assets (e.g., farmland and timberland) and private equity funds. The unsmoothing procedures discussed in this chapter are central to the analysis of alternative investments.

18.4.2 Price Smoothing and Arbitrage in a Perfect Market

In a perfect market (i.e., one without transaction costs or trading restrictions), arbitrageurs will attempt to exploit profit opportunities caused by the consistently delayed price responses contained in smoothed prices. Any asset with consistently delayed price responses will be purchased by arbitrageurs after general prices rise and will be short-sold after general prices decline. For example, in the context of Exhibit 18.4 an arbitrageur could buy a strongly price-smoothed asset at the end of time period 2 (immediately after the market rises) and expect, on average, to receive an alpha of 4% in time period 3, as the asset's price experiences a delayed response to the large market rise in time period 2. Note that the arbitrageur can hedge risk by taking offsetting positions in similar assets that are not smoothed.

Competition both to buy assets with smoothed prices before delayed price increases and to short-sell assets with smoothed prices before delayed price declines will drive away delayed prices in tradable assets by forcing prices to respond more quickly. Thus, in perfect markets, any smoothing of a market price (or a market return) will be unsmoothed by the actions of arbitrageurs whenever assets can be traded at the stated prices.

18.4.3 Persistence in Price Smoothing

There are two primary culprits that prevent smoothed return series from being unsmoothed by arbitrageurs. First, the return series may not indicate true trading opportunities. Appraisals of commercial properties performed for accounting purposes are indications of prices that do not represent either bids to buy or offers to sell.

Second, even if a smoothed return series indicates trading opportunities (i.e., prices at which transactions may be made), the underlying assets may have substantial transaction costs or other barriers to arbitrage. For example, in real estate, the time and transaction costs of buying and selling assets in order to exploit delayed pricing responses may be prohibitively expensive relative to the potential gains from moderate price smoothing. Real estate sales commissions, real estate transfer taxes, legal costs, financing costs, search costs, inspection costs, and so forth, provide substantial barriers to arbitrageurs seeking to exploit the lags in price changes caused by price smoothing.

In addition to transaction costs, there are other barriers to trading assets that exhibit smoothed pricing. For example, international open-end equity mutual funds were notorious for allowing stale prices to cause smoothing in their reported prices (net asset values). Arbitrageurs exploited the smoothed pricing by establishing long positions in international funds when domestic markets rose sharply (when foreign markets were already closed), and establishing neutral positions in international funds when domestic markets declined. Many mutual fund companies implemented more accurate pricing methods or erected powerful barriers against short-term trading of such funds, such as a 2% redemption fee on positions held for less than 90 days.

Due to the actions of arbitrageurs and other market participants, assets with tradable prices, low transaction costs, and minimal trading barriers do not typically require unsmoothing. The need to unsmooth prices tends to be greater for non-tradable prices and assets with high transaction costs or trading barriers.

18.4.4 Problems Resulting from Price Smoothing

The smoothing of the last two return series in Exhibit 18.4 generates lower standard deviations, lower correlations with the market, and much lower reported betas. For example, note that the true beta of 0.80 is indicated in the estimated beta of the unsmoothed return series, but the lightly smoothed return series has a reported beta one-third smaller than the unsmoothed return series, and the strongly smoothed return series has a reported beta two-thirds smaller. Similarly, the standard deviations of the smoothed series are substantially lower, as smoothing causes the largest outliers of the unsmoothed series to be muted. The primary problem resulting from price smoothing is that it causes substantial understatement of both volatility and correlation.

Risk understatement may cause inappropriately high allocations to assets with smoothed prices. Portfolio optimization models will tend to overweight assets with understated risk. Furthermore, underestimated price correlations due to price smoothing may distort the estimation of appropriate hedge ratios and interfere with optimal diversification and risk management.

Though risk can be understated through price smoothing, long-term historical mean returns are not substantially affected by the price-smoothing process. For example, in a 10-year analysis of asset returns, the only *values* that determine the average time-weighted return over the 10-year period are the first and last prices. If one of those prices is overstated or understated by 2% it would cause the average annual return of the series over 10 years to be misstated by only about 20 basis points. However, if many of the prices during the 10 years are smoothed by 2%, the reduction in measured risk could be very significant. Some investment managers may prefer investments with smoothed returns, low (and underestimated) risk statistics, and high Sharpe ratios.

18.5 MODELING PRICE AND RETURN SMOOTHING

In order to detect, correct, or even exploit smoothing, it is necessary to understand the form of the smoothing taking place, which can be achieved by modeling. A properly specified model can be used to determine a method for estimating unsmoothed prices or returns. This section discusses the primary approaches to modeling smoothing.

18.5.1 Reported Prices as Lags of True Prices

Define $P_{t,\text{reported}}$ as the reported or smoothed price of an asset at time t, and $P_{t,\text{true}}$ as the true price. An example of a reported price would be a price index based on appraisal values or a hedge fund's net asset value that is subject to smoothing by a fund manager. The true price of the asset is defined as the best indication of the market price at which the asset would trade with fully informed buyers and sellers.

A simple single-parameter model that specifies an exact relation between the reported price and true prices is shown in Equation 18.9:

$$P_{t,\text{reported}} = \alpha P_{t,\text{true}} + \alpha(1 - \alpha)P_{t-1,\,\text{true}} + \alpha(1 - \alpha)^2 P_{t-2,\,\text{true}} + \cdots \qquad (18.9)$$

where α is a decay parameter greater than zero and less than or equal to one that determines the speed of the decay function. A **decay function** in a valuation method is a numeric construct that puts less weight on older valuations and more weight on more recent valuations. Consider the case of $\alpha = 0.60$ in Equation 18.9. In this case, the current reported price depends 60% on the current true price, 24% on the true price of the previous observation date, 9.6% on the true price of the observation date from two periods before, and so on. The weights of the prices in Equation 18.9 sum to one. A value of $\alpha = 1.00$ indicates that true prices are immediately and fully reflected in reported prices. A value of α approaching zero indicates that the effect of a true price on reported prices occurs on a much more delayed basis. An intuitive interpretation of α is that it determines the extent to which the reported price (or return) in a particular time period is determined or driven by the value of the true price (or return) in the same time period. The higher the value of α, the more the current reported value is driven by current changes in the true value rather than by past changes.

Equation 18.9 can be factored to generate a simplified expression for true price as a function of the current reported price and the one-period-lagged value of the reported price, as shown in Equation 18.10:

$$P_{t,\text{true}} = P_{t-1,\text{reported}} + [(1/\alpha) \times (P_{t,\text{reported}} - P_{t-1,\text{reported}})] \qquad (18.10)$$

The importance of Equation 18.10 is that it expresses the most recent true but unobservable price as a simple equation involving the most recent smoothed index value (i.e., the reported value) and the previous smoothed index value, both of which are observable. Consider the case of a rising reported value, $P_{t,\text{reported}} > P_{t-1,\text{reported}}$, and note that in Equation 18.10, the expression $1/\alpha$ is greater than one (assuming that α is between zero and one). In this case, the true value of the asset is expressed as the previously reported value of the asset $(P_{t-1,\text{reported}})$ plus the reported price change increased by a factor of $1/\alpha$. For example, with $\alpha = 0.60$, a \$10 change in the reported price (muted by smoothing) implies a \$16.67 difference between the current true price and the previous reported price.

The primary importance of Equation 18.10 is that given an estimate of the parameter α, the equation can be used to generate the estimated true prices and their changes (i.e., the unsmoothed prices) from a series of smoothed prices. Fisher (2005) estimates a value of $\alpha = 0.40$ for private unleveraged annual real estate returns in the United States. Inserting $\alpha = 0.40$ into Equation 18.10 indicates that true prices should be estimated based on a price change that is 2.5 times larger than the most recent reported price change.

18.5.2 Modeling True Returns from Smoothed Returns

Section 18.5.1 focused on prices. Generally, there is only a small difference between the lagged structure specified by prices and the same structure on returns. As an approximation, Equation 18.11 can be formed in terms of returns and noting the use of ρ (autocorrelation) rather than α (decay parameter):

$$R_{t,\text{true}} \approx (R_{t,\text{reported}} - \rho R_{t-1,\text{reported}})/(1 - \rho) \tag{18.11}$$

where $R_{t,\text{true}}$ is the estimated true return in period t, $R_{t,\text{reported}}$ and $R_{t-1,\text{reported}}$ are the reported returns in periods t and $t - 1$, respectively, and ρ is the estimated first order autocorrelation coefficient of the reported return series.

Equation 18.11 provides the primary tool for converting a series of reported returns into a series of estimated true returns based on first-order autocorrelation of the reported return series.

Equation 18.11 indicates that true returns can be estimated from reported returns using the most two recent reported returns and the parameter ρ. Section 18.5.1 on prices used the parameter α. Equation 18.11 is formed in part by substituting $\alpha = 1 - \rho$. The use of ρ (the first-order autocorrelation coefficient) in place of α puts the emphasis on a statistical interpretation of the relations. The parameter ρ specifies the relative importance of the two explanatory variables, with higher values of ρ indicating greater smoothing (a larger impact from $R_{t-1,\text{reported}}$) and less reliance on the most recent reported return ($R_{t,\text{reported}}$).

18.5.3 Four Reasons for Smoothed Prices and Delayed Price Changes in an Index

There are four primary explanations for first-order autocorrelation in a price index such as an index of real estate prices.

One explanation for first-order autocorrelation is that a price index is being based on observed prices of the most recent transactions of each component of the index and that old or stale prices are being used for index components that have not recently traded. Let's examine a hypothetical case in which $\alpha = 0.60$ which means that $\rho = 40\%$ and a series of true underlying returns (price changes) in a particular asset class in the last five time periods is 0%, 0%, 10%, 0%, 0%.

A value of $\rho = 60\%$ would be consistent with the idea that 60% of the most recent underlying asset values were adjusted based on a transaction that occurred in the current time period (and reflected the true return of 10% in Period 3), while the impact of the 10% true return on the remaining 40% of the underlying asset values will be reflected through time as they transact in subsequent time periods. For example, approximately 24% (i.e., 60% of the remaining 40% of unadjusted prices) would become adjusted to the new market reality with a lag of one period, and approximately 9.6% would be adjusted with a lag of two periods and so forth.

Another explanation is that a professional appraiser may exhibit the behavioral phenomenon known as anchoring. Anchoring is the observed tendency of humans to give disproportionate weight or reliability to previous observations. In the previous example, an appraiser may be reluctant to believe that underlying assets have truly risen by 10%, and may move valuations 60% in the direction of 10% during the first period, and then continue to adjust valuations in the subsequent periods.

A third major reason for smoothed pricing is that even current transaction prices in an efficient market may be selected in a biased manner such that they provide lagged responses in prices. In a rapidly rising market with some real estate prices rising 15%, investors may be systematically biased toward transacting in those property types with characteristics that signaled higher or lower price growth. Simply put, more buyers are willing to buy property types with 5% higher prices than are willing to buy property types with 15% higher prices, even though prices overall rose 10%.

The final reason for smoothed prices is the potential delay between the setting of a price on a real estate transaction and the reporting of the transaction. A real estate price may be negotiated months before the transaction occurs, and the reported price of the transaction may become known to the appraiser or index on a delayed basis as well.

18.6   UNSMOOTHING A HYPOTHETICAL RETURN SERIES

The previous section discussed smoothing and provided simple examples of how smoothed prices and returns are formed through delayed responses to true price changes. But the objective in practice is to estimate true returns from smoothed returns. This section discusses **unsmoothing**: the process of estimating a true but unobservable price or return series from an observable but smoothed price or return series.

18.6.1   Unsmoothing Returns Based on First-Order Autocorrelation

Given an estimate of ρ, Equation 18.11 can be used to estimate smoothed returns from reported returns. Return to the example of the true return series used in the previous section (0%, 0%, 10%, 0%, and 0%) to generate the smoothed return series of 0%, 0%, 6%, 2.4%, and 0.96%. Equation 18.11 can be used along with $\rho = 0.40$ to back out the true return series from the reported series. Inserting the smoothed return series as the reported returns in Equation 18.11 and continuing to use $\rho = 0.40$, the implied true returns are as follows:

$$R_{3,\text{true}} = (R_{3,\text{reported}} - \rho R_{2,\text{reported}})/(1 - \rho) = [6\% - (0.40 \times 0\%)]/(1 - 0.40) = 10\%$$

$$R_{4,\text{true}} = (R_{4,\text{reported}} - \rho R_{3,\text{reported}})/(1 - \rho) = [2.4\% - (0.40 \times 6\%)]/(1 - 0.40) = 0\%$$

$$R_{5,\text{true}} = (R_{5,\text{reported}} - \rho R_{4,\text{reported}})/(1 - \rho) = [0.96\% - (0.40 \times 2.4\%)]/(1 - 0.40) = 0\%$$

Note that the smoothed return series can be used to find the underlying true return series if the process follows a first-order autocorrelation process and if ρ can be estimated accurately. Of course, in practice, the returns do not conform perfectly to the first-order autocorrelation model, and the coefficient ρ must be estimated and is subject to estimation error. Thus, the unsmoothed estimations contain errors.

APPLICATION 18.6.1

A smoothed return series has returns in two consecutive time periods of −2% and +10%. The estimated autocorrelation is 0.60. Find the estimated true return of the series in the second period. Inserting the two returns and the estimated autocorrelation coefficient into Equation 18.11 produces the following equation:

$$R_{2,true} = [10\% - (0.60 \times -2\%)]/(1 - 0.60)$$

$$R_{2,true} = (10\% + 1.2\%)/0.4 = 28\%$$

It would take a very high true return in the second period (i.e., 28%) to generate a smoothed return of 10% after a smoothed return of −2%. Note that the equation contains four variables. Given any three of the variables, the equation can be used to solve for the fourth variable.

More complex models may be appropriate when the smoothing takes place over more than one time period, such as a fourth-order autocorrelation model, when smoothing of quarterly returns takes place over a 1-year period. The following section summarizes the three-step process for unsmoothing a reported price or return series to estimate a true price or return series.

18.6.2 The Three Steps of Unsmoothing

Unsmoothing a return series containing autocorrelation involves three steps:

Step 1: Specifying the form of the autocorrelation.

Step 2: Estimating the parameter(s) of the assumed autocorrelation process.

Step 3: Inserting the estimated correlation coefficient in place of ρ in Equation 18.11 (or a model with a different autocorrelation specification) along with two reported returns.

18.6.3 An Example of Unsmoothing with the Three Steps

Return to the previous example of the reported (and smoothed) return series: 0%, 0%, 6%, 2.4%, and 0.96%.

Step 1: The first step is determining or specifying the form of the autocorrelation. As throughout this chapter, first-order autocorrelation is being assumed (and was assumed to derive Equation 18.11).

Step 2: The second step is estimating the parameter(s) of the assumed auto-correlation process. In our example of first-order autocorrelation, the only parameter is ρ, as indicated in Equation 18.11. The first-order autocorrelation coefficient of a series is found as the correlation coefficient between each observation and the observation from the same series in the previous time period, as depicted in Equation 18.12:

$$\rho = \text{corr}(R_{t,\text{reported}}, R_{t-1,\text{reported}}) \qquad (18.12)$$

The correlation coefficient between each observation (not including the earliest observation for which the previous value is unknown) and its value in the previous time period can be estimated using sample statistics. Using Equation 18.12, the estimated correlation coefficient between that series [0%, 0%, 6%, 2.4%, 0.96%] and the one-period lagged return series [0%, 0%, 0% 6%, 2.4%] is 0.037. Note that the estimated value of ρ (0.037) is far from its assumed and true value (0.40). The explanation for the difference is the small sample size and estimation error.

Step 3: The third step is inserting the estimated correlation coefficient in place of ρ in Equation 18.11 along with two reported returns and solving for $R_{t,\text{true}}$. Using Equation 18.11 and the estimated correlation coefficient (0.037) rather than the true correlation coefficient (0.40) generates the series 0%, 0%, 6.2%, 2.3%, and 0.9%:

$$R_{2,\text{true}} = [0\% - (0.037 \times 0\%)]/(1 - 0.037) = 0\%$$

$$R_{3,\text{true}} = [6\% - (0.037 \times 0\%)]/(1 - 0.037) = 6.2\%$$

$$R_{4,\text{true}} = [2.4\% - (0.037 \times 6\%)]/(1 - 0.037) = 2.3\%$$

$$R_{5,\text{true}} = [0.96\% - (0.037 \times 2.4\%)]/(1 - 0.037) = 0.9\%$$

The smoothed return series for time periods 2 through 5 (0%, 6%, 2.4%, and 0.96%) is unsmoothed as 0%, 6.2%, 2.3%, and 0.9%, slightly closer to the assumed true return series (0%, 10%, 0%, and 0%) from which the example was derived. The reason for the very limited success was the poor estimation of ρ (0.037 as an estimation of the assumed true correlation of 0.40). As was demonstrated earlier, the use of $\rho = 0.40$ to unsmooth the return series generates the exact true series. The success of the unsmoothing therefore depends on the proper specification of the autocorrelation scheme and especially the accurate estimation of the parameter(s). It would be expected that the estimation of ρ should improve as the sample size is increased and that the poor estimation of ρ in the example was attributable to the use of such a small sample.

18.7   UNSMOOTHING ACTUAL REAL ESTATE RETURN DATA

The purpose of this section is to provide a detailed example of the unsmoothing of an actual return series with autocorrelation. This section follows the three-step procedure discussed in Section 18.6 and assumes first-order autocorrelation.

18.7.1 The Smoothed Data and the Market Data

Exhibit 18.5 is based on 20 years of quarterly return data from two popular US real estate indices. The number of quarters actually shown in the exhibit is shortened to conserve space and to focus on the early years, the global financial crisis, and recent years. The returns labeled NAREIT are based on the all-equity REIT index of the FTSE National Association of Real Estate Investment Trusts (NAREIT) US Real Estate Index Series (henceforth NAREIT Index), which is based on closing market prices of publicly traded equity real estate investment trusts (REITs). The other returns are from the National Council of Real Estate Investment Fiduciaries (NCREIF) Property Index (henceforth NPI). The NPI is based on appraised prices of private real estate properties and is therefore likely to contain substantial price smoothing.

EXHIBIT 18.5   Returns of Appraised (NPI) and Market (NAREIT) Real Estate

Year	Quarter	Returns NAREIT	NPI	Lagged Returns NAREIT	Lagged Returns NPI	Unsmoothed Returns NAREIT	Unsmoothed Returns NPI
1999	1	−4.82%	2.59%				
1999	2	10.08%	2.62%	−4.82%	2.59%	12.13%	2.79%
1999	3	−8.04%	2.81%	10.08%	2.62%	−10.53%	3.89%
1999	4	−1.01%	2.89%	−8.04%	2.81%	−0.04%	3.35%
2000	1	2.39%	2.40%	−1.01%	2.89%	2.86%	−0.39%
2007	1	3.46%	3.62%	9.47%	4.51%	2.64%	−1.45%
2007	2	−9.04%	4.59%	3.46%	3.62%	−10.76%	10.12%
2007	3	2.59%	3.56%	−9.04%	4.59%	4.18%	−2.31%
2007	4	−12.67%	3.21%	2.59%	3.56%	−14.77%	1.22%
2008	1	1.40%	1.60%	−12.67%	3.21%	3.33%	−7.58%
2008	2	−4.93%	0.56%	1.40%	1.60%	−5.80%	−5.37%
2008	3	5.55%	−0.17%	−4.93%	0.56%	6.99%	−4.33%
2008	4	−38.80%	−8.29%	5.55%	−0.17%	−44.90%	−54.57%
2009	1	−31.87%	−7.33%	−38.80%	−8.29%	−30.92%	−1.86%
2009	2	28.85%	−5.20%	−31.87%	−7.33%	37.19%	6.94%
2009	3	33.28%	−3.32%	28.85%	−5.20%	33.88%	7.40%
2009	4	9.39%	−2.11%	33.28%	−3.32%	6.11%	4.79%
2017	1	2.55%	1.55%	−3.28%	1.73%	3.35%	0.52%
2017	2	2.27%	1.75%	2.55%	1.55%	2.24%	2.89%
2017	3	1.11%	1.70%	2.27%	1.75%	0.95%	1.42%
2017	4	2.48%	1.80%	1.11%	1.70%	2.67%	2.37%
2018	1	−6.66%	1.70%	2.48%	1.80%	−7.92%	1.13%
2018	2	8.50%	1.81%	−6.66%	1.70%	10.58%	2.44%
2018	3	0.87%	1.67%	8.50%	1.81%	−0.18%	0.87%
2018	4	−6.06%	1.37%	0.87%	1.67%	−7.02%	−0.34%
Arithmetic Mean		**2.95%**	**2.20%**				
StdDev		10.18%	2.27%			11.53%	8.05%
Autocorrelation of NAREIT			12.08%				
Autocorrelation of NPI			85.07%				

The NAREIT Index serves in the example as a proxy of a true return series and the NPI serves as a proxy of a smoothed return series. The effect of smoothing should be minimal on mean returns (as discussed in Section 18.4.4). However, the standard deviation of returns based on the NPI is substantially lower than that of the NAREIT Index, as shown near the bottom of Exhibit 18.5, and is consistent with the NPI being smoothed. Part of the volatility difference can be explained by the fact that the NPI reflects no leverage (i.e., reflects underlying real estate assets without leverage), whereas the NAREIT Index series reflects the returns of REITs that generally reflect levered real estate positions.

Note the very large negative returns of the NAREIT Index in the fourth quarter of 2008 and the first quarter of 2009. Note further that the appraised series (the NPI) shows only relatively modest negative returns in the same two quarters, apparently reflecting the tendency of appraised prices to move only in a partial response to true market price changes (although the muted reaction can also be explained at least in part by the lack of leverage in the NPI relative to the NAREIT Index). Note also that the NAREIT Index has very large gains in the next two quarters (the second and third quarters of 2009). However, the NPI continues to drift downward throughout 2009, possibly continuing to reflect the previous declines on a lagged basis.

Investors generally find it impossible to sell short private real estate at appraisal-based prices in order to take advantage of these smoothed returns, since private real estate funds are typically not available to short sell. During a time of extreme market turmoil, it is also difficult to sell funds of private real estate investments, as many open-end funds either cease redemptions or erect gates.

The subsequent sections continue to assume first-order autocorrelation between returns for simplicity, although there are many reasons to expect that autocorrelation of real estate appraisal prices extend to multiple quarters.

18.7.2   Estimating the First-Order Autocorrelation Coefficient

In Exhibit 18.5, the returns to the NCREIF and NAREIT indices for the first quarter of 2007 are 3.62% and 3.46%, respectively. The same returns, when lagged, are located in the row for the second quarter of 2007. The lagged time series, with 79 quarters of data, has one less observation than the unlagged time series, meaning that their estimated standard deviations will differ only slightly because they are based on mostly the same data. The lagged returns are shown to emphasize the computation of correlation coefficients. The correlation coefficients shown at the bottom of Exhibit 18.5 are estimated between the returns and lagged returns in data rows 2 to 80. Put differently, they are the correlations between the nonlagged returns in data rows 1 to 79 and the lagged returns in rows 2 to 80.

The estimated first-order autocorrelation of the appraisal-based NPI is 85.07%, whereas the market-price-based NAREIT Index has an estimated autocorrelation coefficient of only 12.08%. It should be noted that the sample period covers the highly unusual real estate market collapse that coincided with the global financial crisis that began in 2007. Accordingly, the observed correlations may not be representative of more normal economic conditions due to the presence of outliers and their potentially disproportionate influence, although with 20 years of data this effect should be somewhat modest.

18.7.3 Unsmoothing the Smoothed Return Series

Using the respective estimated correlation coefficients, Exhibit 18.5 unsmooths the original return data in the first and second data columns. The unsmoothed returns are computed using Equation 18.11. For example, the first unsmoothed return for the NPI is 2.79%, using Equation 18.11:

$$R_{t,\text{true}} = (R_{t,\text{reported}} - \rho R_{t-1,\text{reported}})/(1 - \rho)$$
$$2.79\% = [2.62\% - (0.8507 \times 2.59\%)]/(1 - 0.85070)$$

Note in the case of the NPI that relatively small changes in the returns between two adjacent time periods in the smoothed series often generate large changes in the unsmoothed returns. For example, the −8.29% smoothed return in the fourth quarter of 2008 generates a massive −54.57% decline in the unsmoothed return for the same quarter. However, the −7.33% smoothed return in the next quarter (the first quarter of 2009) generates only a −1.89% change in the unsmoothed return for the same quarter. The unsmoothing technique captures the likelihood that the second large negative return (−7.33% in the first quarter of 2009) was a lagged reaction to the events of the fourth quarter of 2008 due to smoothing.

18.7.4 The Relation between the Variances of True and Reported Returns

In addition to calculating (estimating) unsmoothed returns, the estimated autocorrelation can be used to calculate (estimate) the variance and volatility in this subsection. The next subsection discusses the beta of the unsmoothed return series. Bearing in mind that:

$$R_{t,\text{reported}} = \rho R_{t-1,\text{reported}} + (1 - \rho)R_{t,\text{true}}$$

Under the assumption that the variance of the true return series and the autocorrelation of the smoothed series are both constant through time, and by rearranging with some algebra, the variance of the unsmoothed (true) return series is shown in Equation 18.13:

$$\sigma^2_{\text{true}} = \sigma^2_{\text{reported}} \times (1 + \rho)/(1 - \rho) \tag{18.13}$$

Example: Suppose the annual variance of a smoothed (reported) return series is 0.03 per year (i.e., the volatility is 0.1732). The estimated autocorrelation is 22%. What is the variance and volatility of the true or unsmoothed return? Using Equation 18.13, the variance of the returns that have been unsmoothed is 0.047:

$$\sigma^2_{\text{true}} = 0.03 \times (1 + 0.22)/(1 - 0.22) = 0.047$$

The volatility is 0.202. As expected, the variance of the unsmoothed series is higher than the variance estimated using the smoothed series. Note that Equation 18.13 can be written as:

$$\text{True Volatility} = \text{Smoothed Volatility} \times \sqrt{\frac{1 + \rho}{1 - \rho}}$$

APPLICATION 18.7.4

The variance of a true return series is constant at 0.280. A smoothed series of those returns has an estimated autocorrelation coefficient of 0.75 that is assumed constant. What is the estimated variance of the reported (smoothed) return series? Using Equation 18.13, the solution can be found by inserting values and solving for σ^2(Reported):

$$0.280 = \sigma^2(\text{Reported})(1 + 0.75)/(1 - 0.75)$$

$$\sigma^2(\text{Reported}) = \frac{0.280}{\left(\frac{1.75}{0.25}\right)} = 0.280 * \left(\frac{0.25}{1.75}\right) = 0.04$$

Note that given any two of the three variables in Equation 18.13, it should be possible to estimate the value of the third variable. Also, it would be common for return dispersions to be discussed using standard deviation rather than variance.

18.7.5 The Relation between the Betas of True and Reported Returns

Using an approach similar to that from the previous subsection regarding variances, one is able to present the beta of the unsmoothed return series as a function of the beta of the smoothed series. For example, if the market beta of a smoothed series is estimated using the following one-factor regression, then one can obtain an estimate of the beta of the true return series using the value of autocorrelation:

$$R_{t,\text{reported}} = \alpha_{\text{reported}} + (\beta_{\text{reported}} \times R_{t,m}) + \varepsilon_t$$

The beta of the true return series is

$$\beta_{\text{true}} = \beta_{\text{reported}}/(1 - \rho) \tag{18.14}$$

According to Equation 18.14, if the autocorrelation is positive ($\rho > 0$), then the true beta will be greater than the estimated beta. Therefore, the systemic risk of a smoothed return series tends to be underestimated.

Example: The market risk of a smoothed return series is estimated to be 0.7. What is the estimate of the beta of the true return series if the autocorrelation is estimated to be 0.3?

Using Equation 18.15:

$$\beta_{\text{true}} = 0.7/(1 - 0.3) = 1.0 \tag{18.15}$$

The beta of the true return series is estimated to be 1.0.

APPLICATION 18.7.5

Assume that a reported (smoothed) return series has β equal to 0.20 and that the true but unobservable return series has β equal to 0.50. What would the estimated autocorrelation of the smoothed series be?

$$\beta_{\text{true series}} = \beta_{\text{smoothed series}}/(1-\rho)$$

so

$$(1-\rho) = \beta_{\text{smoothed series}}/\beta_{\text{true series}}$$

Inserting the two betas and solving for the correlation coefficient generates an estimated autocorrelation coefficient of 0.60.

$$(1-\rho) = .2/.5 = .4$$
$$\rho = .60$$

Exhibit 18.6 lists the estimated betas for the NPI and NAREIT return indices, both smoothed and unsmoothed, relative to the Russell 3000. A reduction in volatility (for example due to smoothing) will tend to reduce beta because lower volatility, everything else equal, causes beta to be closer to zero. Note that the beta of an asset with a market index can be written as the product of the correlation between the two returns and the ratio of the asset volatility to the market volatility. Unsmoothing the returns lowers the volatility of the returns, thereby reducing the ratio and, in turn, the beta.

EXHIBIT 18.6   Smoothed and Unsmoothed Return Statistics

	NPI	NAREIT
Volatilities—Smoothed	2.27%	10.18%
Betas—Smoothed	0.05	0.80
Volatilities—Unsmoothed	8.05%	11.53%
Betas—Unsmoothed	0.17	0.91
Correlation with Russell 3000:		
Smoothed REIT	0.648	
Smoothed NPI	0.180	
Unsmoothed REIT	0.654	
Unsmoothed NPI	0.382	
Correlations between NAREIT and NPI:		
Smoothed NAREIT and Smoothed NPI	0.25	
Unsmoothed NAREIT and Unsmoothed NPI	0.50	

APPLICATION 18.7.5

The smoothed returns of a return series with an autocorrelation of 0.40 have a true beta of 1.25 after adjusting for smoothing. What is the estimated reported beta (i.e., the beta of the smoothed returns)? Inserting the true beta and auto-correlation coefficient to Equation 18.14 generates the following equation:

$$1.25 = \beta_{\text{reported}}/(1 - 0.40)$$

$$\beta_{\text{reported}} = 1.25 \times 0.60 = 0.75$$

The smoothed series exhibits a much lower beta than the true return series. Note that given any two of the three variables in Equation 18.14, it should be possible to estimate the value of the third variable.

18.7.6 Interpreting the Results of Unsmoothing

Exhibit 18.6 summarizes the standard deviations (volatilities) of both the unsmoothed and the smoothed return series. Note that the standard deviation of the smoothed NPI returns (2.27%) increases to 8.05% when the returns are unsmoothed. To the extent that the return series has been properly and accurately unsmoothed to reflect true values, the true volatility of the asset is more than three times the volatility perceived based on smoothed values.

Note also that the NAREIT Index contains positive autocorrelation and that the estimated standard deviation of the unsmoothed NAREIT Index (11.53%) is slightly higher than the estimated standard deviation of the original NAREIT Index (10.18%).

It should be noted that statistics that rely on squared returns (e.g., the measures of dispersion in this chapter, but not the means) are quite sensitive to outlier returns. The returns during the incredible turmoil of the real estate market (and other securities markets) during the global financial crisis that began in 2007 exert a strong effect on many of the statistics.

The original (i.e., smoothed) NPI exhibited volatility about one-quarter that of the original NAREIT Index. The unsmoothed NPI exhibited volatility approximately two-thirds that of the unsmoothed NAREIT Index. These unsmoothed values appear somewhat in line with the higher risk of the securities in the NAREIT Index due to the use of leverage underlying the REITs. In other words, since the NPI is on unlevered real estate, it should be expected that the REITs—most of which use leverage—will have higher *true* (i.e., unsmoothed) return volatilities.

The dramatic increase in estimated risk for the NPI that results from unsmoothing the actual data highlights the importance of unsmoothing. Asset allocations based on volatilities of the smoothed data would dramatically overweight assets with smoothed returns in a mean-variance optimization framework. However, the effects of smoothing are probably underestimated in Exhibit 18.5 because the unsmoothing was performed based only on first-order autocorrelation.

More accurate unsmoothing of the return data in Exhibit 18.5 might be attained using autocorrelation techniques more general than the first-order autocorrelation model illustrated.

Smoothed returns generate dangerous perceptions of risk if the returns are not unsmoothed and if the short-term volatility of the returns is used without adjustment to estimate longer-term risk. The estimated quarterly standard deviation of the reported returns of the NPI in Exhibit 18.5 is approximately 2.3%. Without taking autocorrelation into account, the estimated annualized standard deviation of the same series would be about 4.5% (found by multiplying the quarterly standard deviation by the square root of the number of quarters in each year). Based on an annualized standard deviation of 4.5% and an expected annual return of perhaps 9%, a portfolio allocator might not expect a very large annual loss. However, the correlated string of quarterly losses from the fourth quarter of 2008 to the end of 2009 (totaling about 25%) shows the tremendous longer-term potential loss generated from positive autocorrelation even when short-term volatility appears modest.

Smoothed returns understate not only the volatility but also the correlation of the smoothed returns to the returns of other asset classes. Exhibit 18.6 shows the correlation between smoothed and unsmoothed return series. The smoothed, appraisal-based NPI returns had a correlation of 0.25 to the NAREIT Index and a 0.18 correlation to the Russell 3000 US stock index. After unsmoothing the NPI returns, the correlation between the NPI and the NAREIT Index rose to 0.50, while the correlation to the Russell 3000 rose to 0.38. Assets with true low volatility and low correlations to other asset classes are highly diversifying and earn large weights in a mean-variance optimization process. Using a simple first-order autocorrelation unsmoothing process finds that the unsmoothed NPI returns have twice the volatility and three times the beta of the stated, appraisal-based returns. Using unsmoothed returns rather than smoothed data in the mean-variance process leads to substantially lower weights for private real estate in the optimal portfolio.

Underestimating risk through examination of only smoothed returns results in inflated estimates of risk-adjusted returns, including the Sharpe ratio. In fact, overestimation of risk-adjusted performance due to smoothing of returns may explain the so-called real estate risk premium puzzle, which asks why private equity real estate investments seem to offer abnormally high risk-adjusted returns relative to other investments.

The lesson is clear. Autocorrelated returns can provide misleading indications of long-term risk relative to short-term risk. Smoothing of returns can dangerously mask true risk. Unsmoothing of returns is an important method of providing estimates that better indicate true risk and facilitate more appropriate decisions regarding asset allocation.

REFERENCES

Fisher, J. D. 2005. "U.S. Commercial Real Estate Indices: The NCREIF Property Index." BIS White Paper 21.

Kazemi, H., T. Schneeweis, and R. Gupta. 2003. "Omega as a Performance Measure." Working Paper, Isenberg School of Management, University of Massachusetts.

Shadwick, W. F. and C. Keating. 2002. "A Universal Performance Measure." *Journal of Performance Measurement* 6 (3): 59–84.

CHAPTER 19

Hedging, Rebalancing, and Monitoring

This chapter discusses three potential aspects of holding portfolios of risky investments: hedging, rebalancing, and monitoring.

19.1 MANAGING ALPHA AND SYSTEMATIC RISK

Whether as a long-term strategy of maintaining a target systematic risk exposure or as part of tactical asset allocation making a bet on systematic risk levels, hedging systematic risk can be an important part of an investment strategy. Similarly, the pursuit of alpha can be a key part of an investment strategy. This section discusses managing these two exposures independently.

19.1.1 Separating Alpha and Beta

Alpha can be sought independently of beta. The professional investment staff can seek alpha from those investment products that are perceived to offer the best opportunities, even if those products fall outside the benchmark and traditional asset classes. Alternative assets can be highly useful with this flexible model.

Beta is sought through investment products that cost-effectively offer returns driven by beta so that the investor obtains efficient economic exposure to market risk and can earn the expected risk premiums associated with bearing systematic risks.

The level of systematic risk in a portfolio can be separated from the level of systematic risk inherent in the investor's optimal portfolio from an alpha perspective. In other words, investors can seek a portfolio that is focused on maximizing alpha while controlling the systematic risk level through financial derivatives. Separating alpha and beta can be part of the portfolio management process that refers to attempts to independently manage a portfolio's alpha and its exposure to beta, each toward desired levels.

19.1.2 Hedging Systematic Risk

Derivative products can be used to substantially alter a portfolio's characteristics without having to redeem allocations to certain illiquid funds. For example, suppose the equity beta of a diversified portfolio of traditional and alternative asset classes is positive and is equal to β_{Port}. The portfolio manager can reduce the equity beta of this portfolio by selling equity futures contracts (i.e., establishing a short position). In particular, the new beta of the portfolio is equal to the weighted average of the betas of its assets and the futures positions, as shown in Equation 19.1.

$$\beta_{\text{New}} = \beta_{\text{Port}} + (F/P)\,\beta_{\text{Futures}} \tag{19.1}$$

Here, β_{New} is the new beta of the portfolio, which could serve as the target by the manager, (F/P) is the ratio of the notional amount of the positions in the futures contracts, F, to the size of the portfolio, P, and β_{Futures} is the beta of the futures contract with respect to the equity benchmark used to calculate the beta of the portfolio, β_{Port}. The beta of the futures contract is typically equal to one in the case of a futures contract on a broad equity index. An investor can engineer a new beta for the portfolio by adjusting the level of futures contracts, F.

APPLICATION 19.1.2

Suppose the beta of a diversified portfolio against the FTSE 100 Index is 0.9. The portfolio manager wants to increase the beta to 1.2 because of improving economic conditions. If the market value of the portfolio is $500 million, what notional position does the portfolio manager need to take, F, in the FTSE 100 futures market with a beta of 1 in order to achieve a beta of 1.2? What position would have lowered the beta to 0.4?

Inserting the known values into Equation 19.1:

$$1.2 = 0.9 + (F/\$500,000,000) \times 1$$

$$F = \$150 \text{ million}$$

That is, the manager has to take long positions in $150 million worth of FTSE 100 futures contracts. If the manager had decided to reduce the equity exposure to 0.4, the futures position would have been:

$$0.4 = 0.9 + (F/\$500,000,000) \times 1$$

$$F = -\$250 \text{ million}$$

In the second case, the manager has to establish a $250 million short position in S&P 500 futures contracts to lower the beta to 0.4 from 0.9.

Application 19.1.2 highlights how managers can use liquid futures (or other liquid derivative markets, such as swap markets) to effectively control the systematic risk of their portfolio.

19.1.3 Porting Alpha

Portable alpha is closely related to the concept of separation of alpha and beta. Portable alpha is the ability of a particular investment product or strategy with a perceived ability to generate alpha to be used in the separation of alpha and beta. Portable alpha is the ability to exploit alpha by investing in an alpha-producing strategy while simultaneously managing a target beta exposure. The manager can add the alpha of the strategy to the existing portfolio without substantially altering the final beta of the portfolio. Derivatives are the primary tool for controlling beta while porting alpha.

Consider an investment strategy involving small-cap US equities that is expected to generate alpha through active management. At times, the large-cap and small-cap segments of the US equity markets have diverged substantially in terms of returns. Therefore, an investor with a benchmark of the S&P 500 would be concerned about using the small-cap strategy due to its different systematic risk. Portable alpha would be the ability to invest in the small-cap strategy to receive its alpha while hedging the small-cap exposure from the strategy and replacing that risk with the risk of the S&P 500, typically using derivatives.

APPLICATION 19.1.3

The manager of a €400 million portfolio benchmarked to the equity index of Country A has decided to allocate €360 million to the equity index of Country A and €40 million to a hedge fund with an expected alpha of 150 basis points per year and a beta of 0.60 to the stocks of Country B. Futures contracts trade on the equity indices of Countries A and B. Country A's equity futures contract trades at 200 times the index, with a current index value of €125. Country B's equity futures contract trades at 500 times the index, with a current index value of €40.

Assume riskless interest rates are zero and dividend rates are zero, and ignore transaction costs. With respect to the €40 million allocation to the hedge fund, what position should be established in the futures contracts of the equity index of Country A, what position should be established in the futures contracts of the equity index of Country B, and how much alpha should the asset allocator expect expressed on the basis of the entire €400 million portfolio?

The position in Country A's equity index futures contracts should be a long position of €40 million/(200 × €125) = 1,600 contracts. Country B's equity index futures contracts should be a short position of (0.60 × €40 million)/(500 × €40) = 1,200 contracts. The expected alpha of the entire portfolio would be 15 basis points per year, found as the weighted average of the expected alphas of the positions comprising the portfolio: 90% with an expected alpha of 0, and 10% with an expected alpha of 150 basis points.

19.2 MANAGING THE RISK OF A PORTFOLIO WITH OPTIONS

This section discusses the management of risk pertaining to options.

19.2.1 Put–Call Parity as a Foundation for Risk Analysis

The Level I CAIA Curriculum discussed the concept of put–call parity, which can be expressed as follows:

$$+Stock + Put - Call = +Bond \qquad (19.2)$$

It is assumed in Equation 19.2 that the put and call are both European options with identical expiration dates and strike prices. Intuitively, the long position in a put (+Put) removes the downside risk exposure from being long the underlying asset (+Stock), whereas the short position in the call (−Call) gives up the profit potential from price increases in the underlying asset. The combination removes all risk, creating the equivalent of a long position in a riskless bond (+Bond). Therefore, the hedged position on the left side of Equation 19.2 is equal to owning a riskless bond. Specifically, the default-free bond has a maturity date equal to the expiration of the options, a face value equal to the strike price, no coupon, and a price equal to the strike price discounted at the riskless rate. This analysis (and the analyses that follow) ignores counterparty risk.

To the extent that markets are well functioning, the total value of the hedged position on the left side of Equation 19.2 evolves through time the same as that of the right-hand side: it grows at the riskless rate from being equal to the present value of the strike price to being equal to the strike price at the maturity or expiration of the options. The sensitivity of this hedged portfolio to the price and volatility of the underlying financial asset must be zero. This insight drives the relations discussed in the next section.

19.2.2 Option Sensitivities

Various sensitivities of option prices to underlying option parameters, including delta, gamma, and vega, were discussed in Level I of the CAIA curriculum. These sensitivities are often referred to as the Greeks, since most of them are denoted with letters of the Greek alphabet. Exhibit 19.1 summarizes the most important Greeks for the underlying stock, a put, a call, and a fully hedged position assuming identical strike prices and expiration dates. Specifically, both options are assumed to be European options on the stock (in the first column) and to have the same strike prices and expiration dates.

As discussed in the CAIA Level 1 Curriculum, sensitivities such as those shown in Exhibit 19.1 are partial derivatives that examine the effect of each underlying risk source in isolation. Portfolio managers with positions involving explicit or implicit options often use these option sensitivities in tandem to understand and analyze the total risks of a portfolio.

Note that a call and a put with identical strike prices and identical expiration dates have identical gammas and vegas. The reason that the gamma and vega values are the same is that a portfolio that is long the put and short the call must be gamma neutral and vega neutral. The logic is as follows: if the underlying asset (stock) is gamma and vega neutral, and if +Stock + Put − Call is gamma and vega neutral, then

EXHIBIT 19.1 Option Sensitivities and Put–Call Parity

	+Stock	+Put	+Call	+Stock + Put − Call
Delta	1	$\delta - 1$	δ	0
Gamma	0	γ	γ	0
Vega	0	v	v	0

δ = delta of a call option, γ = gamma of a call option, and v = vega of a call option the difference (Put − Call) must also be gamma and vega neutral. Note, however, that the delta risk of calls and puts are of opposite signs and always differ by 1.

Thus, from inspection of Exhibit 19.1, being long a call and short a put (+Call − Put), or being long a put and short a call (+Put − Call), is hedged with respect to gamma risk and vega risk but leaves delta risk at +1 or −1, respectively. The delta risk is laid off by either a long position in the underlying asset (which adds delta = +1) or a short position in the underlying asset (which adds delta = −1). Hedging involving options that differ by moneyness or by expiration date requires additional positions and hedge ratios based on the differences in delta, gamma, and vega.

19.2.3 Delta of a Simple Call Option and Put Option

Delta is the partial derivative of an asset to changes in an underlying asset. The delta of a call option within the Black–Scholes option pricing model is simply $N(d_1)$, with a cumulative probability that is bounded by 0 and 1. Note that put–call parity can be used to easily show that the delta of a put option is $N(d_1) - 1$. For example, if $N(d_1)$ is 0.4, then the delta of the call is 0.4 and the delta of the put is −0.6.

APPLICATION 19.2.3

An analyst has determined using the Black–Scholes option pricing model and specific parameters such as a strike price, tenor, volatility, and so forth that $N(d_1)$ equals 0.55. What is: (a) the delta of a call option; (b) the delta of a put option; (c) the delta of a portfolio that is long the call option and short the put option; and (d) the delta of a short straddle?

The delta of the call option is 0.55; the delta of the put option is $N(d_1)$ − 1 => −0.45; the delta of being long the call and short the put is 0.55 − (−0.45) => 1.0. Finally, the delta of the short straddle (short the call and short the put) is −0.55 − (−0.45) = −0.10.

19.2.4 Viewing Options as Volatility Bets

Option traders sometimes say that calls and puts are the same. This claim is in stark contrast to the view of many market participants less familiar with option hedging. Most market participants do not hedge risk with options and view calls and puts as complete opposites because long calls are bullish positions and long puts are bearish positions. But the claim that calls and puts are the same makes sense from the perspective of a trader who maintains delta-neutrality. From the trader's perspective, the difference in delta between a call and a put is trivialized by the trader's ease in managing delta by simply expanding or contracting a hedging position in the underlying asset (to maintain a target delta such as delta-neutrality). An option trader may view management of vega risk and gamma risk as more problematic due to trading costs such as bid–ask spreads. The trader can buy vega and gamma with either a long position in a call or a long position in a put. Similarly, the trader can short vega and gamma with short positions in either calls or puts.

In other words, the only difference between the call and put in Exhibit 19.1 is in the delta, and the delta of a single position to a trader who maintains delta-neutrality is easy to hedge using the underlying asset. Option traders often take bets with respect to volatility and view positions in the underlying asset as the slack variable that is used to control delta. A **slack variable** is the variable in an optimization problem that takes on whatever value is necessary to allow an optimum to be feasible but, while doing so, does not directly alter the value of the objective function. In this case, the position in the underlying asset keeps the portfolio from being affected by directional moves in the market (i.e., controls the delta) but is not a direct source of alpha and does not affect gamma or vega.

For those market participants who use options to place directional bets on the underlying assets, long positions in options provide leverage, positive skews, and limited downside risk, all of which can be especially attractive to aggressive investors with a view that an underlying asset is mispriced. One way of viewing these bets is that the traders are net long options when they view the implied volatilities of the options as being below expected volatility and are net short options when they view the implied volatilities of the options as being above expected volatility. Typically, these traders maintain delta-neutrality and therefore view the positions in mispriced options as pure bets on volatility that offer alpha. Chapters 36 and 37 discuss trading based on volatility in detail.

19.3 DELTA-HEDGING OF OPTION POSITIONS

One of the fundamental skills in financial engineering and risk management is delta-hedging of positions involving options and their underlying asset. This section begins with the description of the simplified scenario of hedging a single option with a position in its underlying asset. The goal of this material is to provide a foundation for a "top level" understanding of the goals and risk of strategies based on delta-hedging.

19.3.1 Construction of a Binomial Stock and Call Option Tree in a Risk-Neutral World

For simplicity, assume that a stock's price, S, is currently $50 and will move either upward or downward $5 per period with a 50%/50% probability of a move in either direction. To simplify further, assume that the riskless interest rate is zero and that the stock has a beta of zero (i.e., assume risk-neutrality).

A call option with a strike price of $55 expires at the end of two periods. Exhibit 19.2 projects the possible future values of S over the next two periods as well as the payoffs of the call option, c, at the option's expiration (the last column of values). The tree is recombining and each node is labeled in order to describe the sequence of moves in S (e.g., u, d, uu, ud, du, and dd).

The value of the option after one period can be determined as its expected payoff at the end of the second period given that all discount rates are zero (i.e., the riskless rate is zero and the beta is zero). To use backward induction: the call option is worth $5 in state uu and $0 in state ud which generates a value of $2.50 in state u. The call option is worthless in states du and dd which generates a value of $0 in state d.

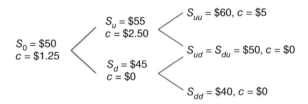

EXHIBIT 19.2 Risk-Neutral Two-Period Binomial Tree

The call option is worth $2.50 in state u and $0 in state d which generates a value of $1.25 at time 0. This makes sense because with all interest rates equal to 0% and a one-in-four chance of having value ($5), the option will be worth $1.25. The call values computed using backward induction are included in Exhibit 19.2. The six option values are derived within the model (endogenously) from the other variables rather than assumed externally (exogenously).

19.3.2 Performing Arbitrage on a Properly Priced Option

Consider a delta-neutral strategy of buying one call option from the previous section at time 0 for $1.25 and hedging the option's risk by short selling the underlying stock, S, based on the option's delta as it changes through time.

The delta of the call option at time 0 is found using the values of S and c at time 1 and the formula $\Delta c / \Delta S$; $\Delta c / \Delta S$ at node u is $0.25 = \$2.50 / \$10.00$ which means that it requires a short position of 0.25 shares to hedge one long call option at time 0. The purchase of the call option is a "set it and forget it" decision. However, the size of the short position needs to be changed as S changes.

APPLICATION 19.3.2

A delta-risk-neutral strategy between a put option and its underlying stock is being evaluated at a particular node. The stock's price in the next two equally possible nodes differs by $1.00. The option is a put option and its value is expected to differ by $0.40. What is the put's delta and how many shares of stock must be purchased or (short) sold in order to be hedge a position that is long 10 puts?

The answer is that 0.4 shares must be held long for each put option owned, for a total of 4.00 shares held long. The formula for hedging a put is analogous to that for a call: put delta $= \Delta p / \Delta S$. However, put deltas are negative, meaning that they move inversely to their underlying asset. Therefore, hedges are formed between a put option and its underlier with the same sign (i.e., long positions hedge each other and short positions hedge each other). In this case, put delta $= -\$0.40 / \$1.00 = -0.40$ with ten puts requiring four shares of the same sign.

EXHIBIT 19.3   Outcomes from Delta-Neutral Strategy with No-Arbitrage Option Price of $1.25

Final State	Shares Shorted $t = 0$	More Shares Shorted at $t = 1$	P/L on S	P/L on c	Total P/L
uu	0.25 @ $50	0.25 @ $55	−$3.75*	$3.75	$0
ud	0.25 @ $50	0.25 @ $55	$1.25**	−$1.25	$0
du or *dd*	0.25 @ $50	none	$1.25***	−$1.25	$0

* $[0.25 \times -\$10] + [0.25 \times -\$5]$
** $[0.25 \times -\$5]$
*** The position is liquidated at $t = 1$

Returning to Exhibit 19.2, the delta of the call option at time 1 depends on the node that occurs. For node *u* (after one upward shift in S) the option's delta is found using the possible values of S and c at time 2 and the formula $\Delta c / \Delta S$. $\Delta c / \Delta S$ at node *u* is $0.50 = \$5.00/\$10.00$ which means that it requires a short position of 0.50 shares to hedge one long call option. The delta of the call option at time 1 for node *d* is zero because the call is worthless in both nodes *du* and *dd*. At time 1 and node *d* all positions would be closed since the option's value is 0 and the strategy ends. In summary, the initial short sale of 0.25 shares of the underlier was followed either by the covering of that short position (in state *d*) or by the doubling of the position in state *u*. After two periods the option terminates and any position in the stock is closed.

Exhibit 19.3 explains the profits and losses of the components of the delta-neutral strategy of long one option and short the underlier. To understand Exhibit 19.3, follow the computation of the P&Ls (profits and losses) of the short stock positions and long option position through the tree. For example, at time 0 there were 0.25 shares shorted. If S shifts up to $55 the option's delta rises from 0.25 to 0.50 and the arbitrage requires that another 0.25 shares be shorted. If node *d* occurs all positions end. Because the option is priced at its no-arbitrage value, the delta-neutral strategy produces a profit of $0 in all states as shown in the right-most column.

19.3.3   Performing Arbitrage on a Mispriced Option

This section continues with the example in Exhibit 19.2 but supposes that the market price of the option in the above sections is only $1.00 (i.e., is underpriced). Given the zero interest rates and zero risk premium assumption, it is easy to see that a speculator could buy the option for $1 and have a one-in-four chance of winning net $4 and a three-in-four chance of losing $1 for a net expected, but risky, gain of $0.25 (i.e., the amount by which the option is assumed to be undervalued).

However, using delta-hedging an investor can lock in an arbitrage (i.e., guaranteed) profit of $0.25. The importance of this profit without risk is that permits leverage and potentially large-scale riskless profits. In this simplified example, the process of delta-hedging is quite simple.

Note that if state *u* occurs, the call option's $1.25 gain will be offset by the short stock's equal loss of $5 × 0.25 shares = $1.25 and if state *d* occurs the offset will

EXHIBIT 19.4   Outcomes from Delta-Neutral Strategy with Arbitrageable Option Price
of $1.00

Final State	Shares Shorted $t = 0$	More Shares Shorted at $t = 1$	P/L on S	P/L on c	Total P/L
uu	0.25 @ $50	0.25 @ $55	−$3.75*	$4.00	$0.25
ud	0.25 @ $50	0.25 @ $55	$1.25**	−$1.00	$0.25
du or *dd*	0.25 @ $50	none	$1.25***	−$1.00	$0.25

* $[0.25 \times -\$10] + [0.25 \times -\$5]$
** $[0.25 \times -\$5]$ The $t = 0$ option breaks even
*** $[0.25 \times -\$5]$ The position is liquidated at $t = 1$

occur with the signs simply reversed. In state d the option is worthless and the hedge
is liquidated. In state u the new hedge ratio is $\Delta c / \Delta S = \$5/\$10 = 0.50$. This requires
that a cumulative total of 0.50 shares of stock be held short from time period 1 to
time period 2. The P/L of the hedging strategy is shown in Exhibit 19.4.

Exhibit 19.4 shows that if the option were underpriced by $0.25 the arbitrageur
could delta-hedge a long position in the option and lock in a profit of $0.25 regard-
less of the path that the underlying stock takes over the life of the option. It is not
shown, but if the option were overvalued at $1.50 the speculator and investor would
write the call option and the investor would delta-hedge with a long position in the
underlying stock of 0.25 shares and would lock in a profit of $0.25.

APPLICATION 19.3.3

A delta-risk-neutral strategy between a call option and its underlying stock is
being evaluated at a particular node that occurs at time 0. The stock's price is
expected to rise or fall by $1 in its two equally likely states. The stock has a call
option with a delta of 0.20 that expires in one period (at Time 1). In a down
state, the call option will expire worthlessly. What is the option's current value
and what are the two possible values to the option when it expires, assuming
0% interest rates and 0% risk premiums? Please describe the risk-neutral hedge
involving a long call position and explain its outcomes.

The answer is that the call option will be worth $0.00 in state d. The call
option's value in state u must be $0.40 given that the stock price outcomes differ
by $2 ($1 up + $1 down) and that the call option's delta is 0.20. Therefore, the
call option must be worth $0.20. A risk-neutral strategy involves shorting 0.20
shares of stock. If state u occurs, the call gains $0.20 from $0.20 to $0.40 and
the short position of 0.20 shares of stock loses $0.20 found using a $1 increase
in the stock price.

Finally, note that given that the stock price is $50 and has two potential outcomes
($55 and $45) in Exhibit 19.2, the 50% probability of each outcome is consistent

with the stock's $50 value (and with the assumptions that interest rates are 0% and risk premiums are 0%). Note, however, that positive risk premiums could generate identical option values if the probabilities were allowed to shift to remain consistent with the stock's price being $50. Therefore, although this example assumes risk-neutrality, it generates the same values if certain other combinations of risk premiums and probabilities are assumed. This illustrates the incredible simplicity and value of the risk-neutral approach to option pricing. Also, the assumption that the interest rate is 0% is not necessary, but relaxing that assumption makes the arithmetic less clear.

19.3.4 Geometric Motion and Delta-Hedging

Exhibit 19.2 modeled an arithmetic motion in the underlying stock in which stock prices either added $5 to or subtracted $5 from the previous price. The exhibit was constructed this way to make the analysis easier to follow. In practice, most stock price models use geometric motion in which a stock price is either multiplied by $(1 + u)$ to represent an up movement or by $(1 + d)$ to represent a downward movement (with $u > 0$ and $d < 0$).

The results discussed in Sections 19.1–19.3 demonstrate the same principles whether the analysis is based on arithmetic or geometric motion. Nevertheless, this section briefly restates the key results using geometric motion of 10%.

The stock price tree starts with the same time 0 and time 1 values. However $Suu = \$60.50$ (rather than $60), $Sud = Sdu = \$49.50$ (rather than $50), and $Sdd = \$40.50$ (rather than $40). The call option with a strike price of $55 is still worthless in all states except uu in which case it has a payoff of $5.50. Therefore, the call price is $5.50/4 or $1.375 at node uu and, importantly, $2.75 at node u. The hedge ratio at node u remains at $\$5.50/\$11.00 = 0.50$. However, the hedge ratio at $t = 0$ is $\$2.75/\$10 = 0.275$ indicating that 0.275 shares need to be shorted at time 0. Also, the payoffs change as indicated in Exhibit 19.5.

Note in Exhibit 19.5 that all paths end with zero profit or loss, indicating that $1.375 is the no-arbitrage price of the option (continuing to assume interest rates and risk premiums are 0% for simplicity). Thus the economics of delta-neutral-hedging work whether the stock's underlying movement is arithmetic or geometric. However, the two processes generate different option values because the geometric process compounds the changes in value and therefore models a different path of volatility.

EXHIBIT 19.5   Outcomes from Delta-Neutral Strategy with Geometric Motion

Final State	Shares Shorted $t = 0$	More Shares Shorted at $t = 1$	P/L on S	P/L on c	Total P/L
uu	0.275 @ $50	0.225 @ $55	−$4.125*	$4.125	$0.00
ud	0.275 @ $50	0.225 @ $55	$1.375**	−$1.375	$0.00
du or dd	0.275 @ $50	none	$1.375***	−$1.375	−$0.00

* [0.275 × −$10.50] + [0.225 × −$5.50]
** [0.275 × −$0.50] + [0.225 × −$5.50]
*** [0.275 × −$5] The position is liquidated at $t = 1$

19.4 THREE KEY OBSERVATIONS ON DELTA-HEDGING

The financial economics of delta-hedging between an option and its underlying asset lead to three key observations:

DELTA-HEDGING IS NOT A DIRECTIONAL SPECULATION ON THE STOCK PRICE: Suppose that the market is dramatically underestimating (or overestimating) the value of the stock. For example, suppose that a speculator is convinced that there is a very high chance the stock will follow the *u* and *uu* paths in Exhibit 19.2 to $60. If the speculator delta-hedges a long position in the stock with a short position in its call option, the combined portfolio will tend to generate a profit of zero because the delta-hedging eliminates the risk of directional movements. If the stock is perceived as over- or under-valued the speculator should simply short sell or buy the stock, respectively. Delta-hedging is typically based on the belief that a derivative on an asset is mispriced relative to its underlying asset.

IF A STOCK IS EFFICIENTLY PRICED ALL TRADING STRATEGIES ON THAT STOCK HAVE A NET PRESENT VALUE (NPV) OF ZERO: If the stock's price is informationally efficient then there can be no sequence of stock trades that will generate an expected excess profit or loss (on a risk-adjusted basis if applicable). While this is obvious given the definition of informational market efficiency, the complexity of delta-hedging can mask this truth and lead some analysts to believe that the *expected* profits of a delta-hedging strategy are generated by the stock transactions even when the stock price is informationally efficient. Note that many commentaries on delta-hedging strategies such as convertible bond arbitrage are based on the belief that the stock transactions generate expected profits. In other words, some commentaries claim that the risk-adjusted excess return of the strategy is expected to be positive and that the profit is generated in part or in whole by the stock trades used to hedge the strategy. While realized returns on a stock in an efficient market may be positive or negative, it simply cannot be true that expected returns on the stock will be positive if the market for the stock is informationally efficient.

DELTA-HEDGING IS PART OF A SPECULATION ON VOLATILITY: A truly delta-neutral trader does not care about the direction or ultimate level of the stock (or other underlying asset) because the outcomes of the strategy are driven by volatility, not by directional movements. Suppose that a speculator believes that the market is dramatically misestimating the volatility of the stock. If true, this would mean that options are mispriced. In fact, that is the whole point of most delta-hedging: to remove the directional risk with a strategy that generates profits to a speculator that is able to identify when the implied volatility of an option is inconsistent with informational market efficiency. For example, suppose that the market anticipates stock price changes of $5 per period, but a trader is confident that the actual stock price changes will be $2.50 per period. In that scenario the option discussed relative to Exhibit 19.2 should be worth $0 because the stock will not exceed $55 in the two periods before the option expires. The relation between the true future volatility of the stock and its actual realized volatility drives the profitability of a delta-neutral strategy with the option.

19.5   THREE OBSERVATIONS ON REBALANCING DELTA-NEUTRAL OPTION PORTFOLIOS

The previous section detailed the role of delta-neutrality in managing directional risk. This section and the next two sections discuss rebalancing. In particular, this section discusses the role of gamma in describing the role of rebalancing a delta-neutral portfolio that includes options.

Generally, the primary driver of the returns to an option on an equity index is a directional move in the underlying equity index. A delta-neutral portfolio is a portfolio with a net delta of zero: the position-weighted-sum of the positive deltas equals the absolute value of the position-weighted-sum of the negative deltas. The portfolio is designed to be protected from exposure to changes in the *value* of the underlying index. However, the portfolio is typically designed to be a play on the *volatility* of the options' underlying asset. If the portfolio is long (short) options then it tends to be long (short) gamma and vega. A delta-neutral portfolio with positive gamma and vega benefits from high volatility, suffers from low volatility, and is neutral with respect to the direction of the underlying asset.

Chapters 36 and 37 discuss gamma exposure in detail. This section briefly discusses rebalancing a delta-neutral long gamma option portfolio. In particular, the *frequency* with which a delta-neutral long gamma portfolio is rehedged drives the portfolio's profitability differently depending on the *autocorrelation* of the underlying asset's realized returns (i.e., trending, mean-reverting, or Markov). For example, frequent rehedging performs well (relative to infrequent rehedging) if the underlying asset's returns experience negative autocorrelation (mean-reverts) and frequent rehedging performs poorly if the underlying asset's returns experience positive autocorrelation (trends).

INFREQUENT REHEDGING IS A BET ON POSITIVE AUTOCORRELATION: Without rebalancing, a delta-neutral, long gamma portfolio will benefit greatly from volatility that is directional but will have little or no benefit from volatility that is mean-reverting. For example, if the underlying stock price rises dramatically but then falls back to its original level (i.e., mean-reverts) before being rehedged, the short equity position will return to its value but the long option position will tend to decline in value due to its theta for a net loss (assuming no change in implied volatility). Conversely, if the stock trends up or down, the long gamma portfolio will earn a high return if the portfolio is not rebalanced because the call option's gamma will generate large option gains from an upward trend and small option losses from a downward trend. Thus, infrequent rebalancing is a bet that volatility will be directional (trending). A delta-neutral, long gamma portfolio with infrequent rebalancing will experience poor performance when the underlying asset mean-reverts even if the realized volatility in the short-term returns of the underlying asset is high.

FREQUENT REHEDGING IS A BET ON NEGATIVE AUTOCORRELATION (MEAN-REVERSION): A delta-neutral, long gamma portfolio that is frequently rebalanced to maintain delta-neutrality will benefit moderately from volatility that is mean-reverting (or at least random). However, the portfolio will tend to generate relatively high transaction costs. The virtue of frequent rehedging is that it can harvest returns from volatility even if the underlying asset price mean-reverts frequently (assuming that the rehedging interval matches the range within which the underlying asset's price tends to revert).

For example, if the asset underlying a delta-neutral portfolio with net long positions in options tends to mean-revert after a directional move of, say 1%, in the underlier, then a rebalancing strategy of rehedging whenever the underlier moves 1% will tend to be very profitable. A very frequent rebalancing strategy (say, every 0.10% movement in the underlier) or an infrequent rebalancing strategy (say, every 2.0% movement in the underlier) will tend to perform relatively poorly.

REHEDGING IS MORE EFFECTIVE WHEN OPTIONS ARE SHORT-DATED AND NEAR-THE-MONEY OPTIONS: The effect of rehedging long gamma, delta-neutral strategies depends on the *timing* of the volatility of the underlying asset with respect to the option's tenor and moneyness. For example, if the bulk of the underlying asset's volatility occurs when the option is deeply in-the-money or out-of-the-money (when the option's delta is near one or zero, respectively, and the option's gamma is near zero) the strategy will tend to underperform. Also, if most of the underlying asset's volatility occurs when the option has a very long time-to-expiration (another case when gamma will tend to be modest) the strategy will tend to underperform. A long gamma, delta-neutral strategy works best when most of the underlying asset's volatility occurs when the option(s) is (are) somewhat short-dated and somewhat near-the-money (when the gamma is large).

Generally, if the underlying stock returns are strongly upward trending, the stock trading will tend to lose money which will be offset by a high option payout. If the underlying stock returns are strongly downward trending, the stock trading will tend to make money which will be offset by a low option payout. If the stock returns are mean-reverting, then the stock trading will tend to make money (with higher volatility generating high profits) while the option will suffer time decay.

In summary, delta-neutral strategies between options and their underlying assets are driven by more complex issues other than simply whether or not the underlying asset's volatility is high or low. It depends on whether the volatility was directional or mean-reverting, on the frequency of rehedging, and on the moneyness and tenor of the option when the bulk of the volatility takes place.

19.6 REBALANCING PORTFOLIOS WITH DIRECTIONAL EXPOSURES

This section discusses the benefits and costs of rebalancing a directional exposure to a market such as an equity market or commodity market. Rebalancing simply refers to the extent to which the weights of the securities in the portfolio are being adjusted back to target values through time.

19.6.1 Rebalancing, Mean-Reversion, Trending, and Randomness

Simply put, the efficacy of rebalancing from an *expected value* perspective depends on whether the prices of the portfolio's underlying assets tend to trend, mean-revert, or move randomly over the time intervals for which the rebalancing is performed. The expected or average ending value of a portfolio with underlying assets that tend to *trend* is reduced by rebalancing, the expected or average ending value of a portfolio with underlying assets that tend to *mean-revert* is enhanced by rebalancing, while the expected or average ending value of a portfolio with underlying assets that follow a *random walk* is neither reduced nor enhanced.

19.6.2   Rebalancing When Assets Follow a Random Walk

Consider a portfolio of stocks each of which moves up or down 10% per period as indicated in the tree in Exhibit 19.6 from $t = 0$ to $t = 2$. For simplicity, it is helpful to assume that interest rates and risk premiums are all 0% and that the probabilities (p) of moves are all 50%.

With $p = 50\%$, the *uu* and *dd* states each have a probability of 25%, while the middle nodes of *ud* and *du* together have a 50% probability. Accordingly, the expected value of the stock in both $t = 1$ and $t = 2$ is $100, generating expected returns of 0% for both periods.

Consider a buy-and-hold investor of one share of stock with outcomes as shown in Exhibit 19.7. Note that the investor's expected profit or loss (P/L) after two periods is $0.

$$\text{Expected Profit/Loss} = \$0.00$$

Now consider an investor with an equally weighted stock portfolio that wishes to rebalance the portfolio to maintain a $100 exposure to each stock at the end of each period. Thus the investor keeps an exposure of exactly $100 to the stock in Exhibit 19.6. So in the *u* state the investor sells $10 of the stock (using partial

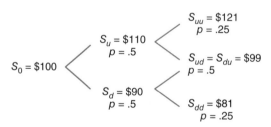

EXHIBIT 19.6   A Random Walk Two-Period Risk-Neutral Binomial Stock Price Tree

EXHIBIT 19.7   Two-Period Outcomes without Rebalancing

State	Value	P/L	Probability
uu	$121	+ $21	25%
ud	$ 99	– $1	25%
du	$ 99	– $1	25%
dd	$ 81	– $19	25%

EXHIBIT 19.8 Two-Period Outcomes with Rebalancing to $100 Exposure

State	Value	P/L	Probability
uu	$120	$20	+ 25%
ud	$100	$0	+ 25%
du	$100	$0	+ 25%
dd	$120	– $20	+ 25%

share amounts) and in the *d* state the investor buys $10 of the stock to maintain the $100 exposure. This rebalancing generates the outcomes shown in Exhibit 19.8:

$$\text{Expected Profit/Loss} = \$0.00$$

Given equal probabilities to each outcome, the rebalancing has a net return of $0 or 0%. Comparing Exhibits 19.7 and 19.8 indicates that both exhibits have the same expected P/L. But the risks differ. Without rebalancing (Exhibit 19.7) has a smaller possible drawdown (–$19) that is more favorable. But rebalancing (Exhibit 19.8) only has one outcome that is a loss.

TAKEAWAY POINT: **If stocks follow a random walk, then rebalancing does not change the expected value of a portfolio, it only alters the risk.** Whether rebalancing increases or decreases the risk depends on the target to which the portfolio is being rebalanced. From the perspective of an investor seeking equally weighted exposure, rebalancing makes sense (everything else equal). However, from the perspective of an investor seeking to keep a market-weighted exposure (which modern portfolio theory indicates is optimal), then rebalancing is counterproductive. Rebalancing keeps a growing asset's weight fixed and keeps a declining asset's weight fixed—both of which impede maintenance of a market-weighted exposure.

19.6.3 Rebalancing When Individual Assets Trend

Now return to the case in which at node 0 the stock has a 50%/50% chance of rising to node *u* or falling to node *d*. However, the stock price tends to trend. If the asset rises to node *u* it will have a 60% chance of rising again and if it falls to node *d* it will have a 60% chance of falling again. The price possibilities are the same, but the probabilities have now changed as indicated in Exhibit 19.9.

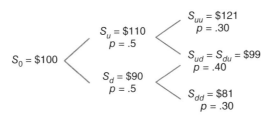

EXHIBIT 19.9 A Trending Two-Period Risk Neutral Binomial Stock Price Tree

EXHIBIT 19.10   Two-Period Outcomes of a Trending Asset
with and without Rebalancing

Not Rebalanced

State	Value	P/L	Probability
uu	$121	+ $21	30%
ud	$ 99	− $1	20%
du	$ 99	− $1	20%
dd	$ 81	− $19	30%

Expected Profit/Loss = $0.20

Rebalanced

State	Value	P/L	Probability
uu	$120	+ $20	30%
ud	$100	$0	20%
du	$100	$0	20%
dd	$80	− $20	30%

Expected Profit/Loss = $0.00

With $p = 60\%$ of trending and 40% of retracing, the *uu* and *dd* states each rise to a probability of 30% (compared to the 25% probabilities in a random walk), while the middle nodes of *ud* and *du* together each have a 20% probability. Although, the expected value of the stock in both $t = 1$ and $t = 2$ is $100, a decision to rebalance in a market that ends up trending will lower the expected value at $t = 2$. The relative performance is detailed in Exhibit 19.10. Note that trending allows a passive strategy (buy-and-hold generates $0.20) to outperform a rebalancing strategy.

> TAKEAWAY POINT: **If stock prices trend, then rebalancing lowers the expected value of a portfolio in addition to altering its risk.** Whether rebalancing increases or decreases the risk depends on the target to which the portfolio is being rebalanced as previously discussed.

19.6.4   Rebalancing When Individual Asset Prices Mean-Revert

Now consider again the case in which at node 0 the stock has a 50%/50% chance of rising to node *u* or falling to node *d*. However, Exhibit 19.11 models mean-reversion by assuming that if the asset rises to node *u* it will have only a 40% chance of rising again and if it falls to node *d* it will have only a 40% chance of falling again.

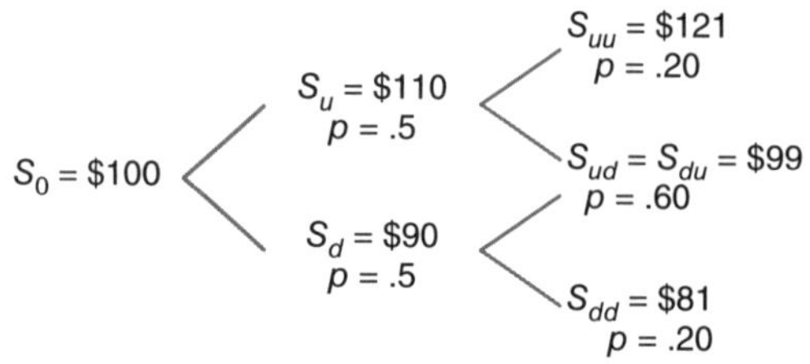

$S_0 = \$100$

$S_u = \$110$
$p = .5$

$S_d = \$90$
$p = .5$

$S_{uu} = \$121$
$p = .20$

$S_{ud} = S_{du} = \$99$
$p = .60$

$S_{dd} = \$81$
$p = .20$

EXHIBIT 19.11   A Trending Two-Period Risk
Neutral Binomial Stock Price Tree

EXHIBIT 19.12 Two-Period Outcomes of a Mean-Reverting Asset with and without Rebalancing

Not Rebalanced

State	Value	P/L	Probability
uu	$121	+$21	20%
ud	$ 99	−$1	30%
du	$ 99	−$1	30%
dd	$ 81	−$19	20%

Expected Profit/Loss = −$0.20

Rebalanced

State	Value	P/L	Probability
uu	$120	+$20	30%
ud	$100	$0	20%
du	$100	$0	20%
dd	$ 80	−$20	30%

Expected Profit/Loss = $0.00

With $p = 60\%$ that the asset(s) will mean-revert from nodes u and d the nodes uu and dd each have a probability of only 20%, while the middle nodes of ud and du together have a combined 60% probability. Although the expected value of the stock in both $t = 1$ and $t = 2$ is $100, a decision to rebalance in a market that ends up mean-reverting will increase the expected value at $t = 2$ as indicated in Exhibit 19.12 compared to a buy-and-hold strategy.

TAKEAWAY POINT: **If stock prices mean-revert then rebalancing increases the expected value of a portfolio relative to a buy-and-hold strategy and alters the risk.** Whether rebalancing increases or decreases the risk depends on the target to which the portfolio is being rebalanced as previously discussed.

19.6.5 Empirical Evidence on the Effect of Rebalancing on Return

The simulations in the last three sections were constructed to exhibit randomness, trending, or mean-reversion as indicated. Actual price data will typically depart from randomness and therefore the empirical results on the data will tend to be driven by the degree of trending or mean-reversion contained in the data. It should be noted that even data generated from a random simulation will exhibit random levels of trending or mean-reversion.

In a commodity futures portfolio context, Greer (2000) finds that rebalancing yield can provide a significant contribution to returns. **Rebalancing yield** is the additional observed or expected return produced by the periodic rebalancing of a portfolio to an initial set of weights. Returns can be enhanced by the tendency of commodity prices to be mean-reverting. The rebalancing yield of a fixed-weight portfolio is expected to provide a greater contribution to the returns of the portfolio when the portfolio constituents are volatile and have low correlations with each other. Erb and Harvey (2006) find that the average correlation across a set of 16 commodity futures from 1982 to 2004 was very low at about 9%, and the average volatility was relatively high at about 25%. Thus, one would expect that a commodity portfolio might achieve greater rebalancing benefits (from mean-reversion) than a stock or bond portfolio, which tends to have much higher average within-class correlations.

19.6.6   The Effects of Rebalancing When Prices Do Not Mean-Revert

To understand the rebalancing yield and the impact of diversification, it is important to note that in the absence of mean-reversion (or trending) in prices, Chambers and Zdanowicz (2014) show that rebalancing will have no impact on the expected future value of an investment in a portfolio of commodities. However, rebalancing changes volatility, which in turn will have an impact on the probabilities of future growth paths of the portfolio. Specifically, different portfolio volatilities from rebalancing will change the probability that the future value of the portfolio will exceed a particular value. In other words, certain statistical properties of the distribution of the future value of the portfolio (excluding its mean) will change as return volatility changes. These changes to the risk of a portfolio from rebalancing may be favorable or unfavorable depending on the investor's utility function.

The geometric mean return on an investment can be written as indicated in Equation 19.3:

$$R_C \approx \overline{R} - \frac{1}{2}\sigma^2 \tag{19.3}$$

Here, R_C is the per-period (e.g., annual) compounded rate of return, $\overline{R}$ is the per-period arithmetic mean return, and σ^2 is the per-period variance of the return. It can be seen that if the volatility of the return is reduced, the geometric mean return will increase. However, this will have no impact on the expected future value of the portfolio. Other statistical properties (e.g., median, mode, and skewness) of the distribution of the portfolio's future values are, of course, affected as the volatility of the per-period rate of return is changed.

To see this, consider two investments. Portfolio A can increase by 20% or decrease by 18% each year with equal probabilities, and Portfolio B can increase by 3% or decrease by 1% each year with equal probabilities. These values were chosen so that each portfolio has an arithmetic mean return of 1% per year. Clearly, the rate of return on Portfolio B is less volatile than the rate of return on Portfolio A. If the initial investment in both portfolios is $100, then their paths after two periods can be seen in Exhibit 19.13.

The expected values of the two portfolios after two periods are equal to each other and equal to $102.10, after an expected return of 1% each year, despite

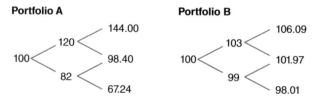

EXHIBIT 19.13   Paths of Two Portfolios

the difference in their volatilities. This illustrates a key point: the long-term future expected value of an investment depends directly on its arithmetic mean return, not its geometric mean return.

However, we can see that there is only a one in three chance that Portfolio A will make money after 2 years, while there is a two in three chance that portfolio B will make money after 2 years. In other words, the most likely outcome for Portfolio A is to lose money and for Portfolio B is to make money. In this sense, rebalancing the commodity portfolio in order to maintain a diversified portfolio and to reduce its return volatility can help to improve its standalone risk-adjusted performance through its reduced risk.

19.7 MEAN-REVERSION AND DIVERSIFICATION RETURN

Commodities have long been considered to exhibit mean-reversion in their prices. This section discusses the potential to generate diversification return in a market with mean-reverting prices.

19.7.1 Benefits of Mean-Reversion in Commodity Investing

Mean-reversion can be a great advantage in an asset allocation framework. To the extent that assets exhibit this property, they may provide enhanced return from rebalancing. While the degree of mean-reversion varies by commodity, the available evidence suggests that mean-reversion at different time horizons is a common feature of commodities. It is often said that the cure for high prices is high prices. This means that as commodity prices rise because of supply or demand shocks, marginal producers that could not compete at previously low prices begin to supply the market, eventually reducing the price. By the same token, marginal users will leave the market, reducing the demand and forcing the price lower. Similarly, a decline in prices will eventually force marginal producers out of business, reducing the supply and thus increasing the price.

19.7.2 Benefiting from Mean-Reversion through Portfolio Rebalancing

One approach to harvesting the benefits of mean-reversion is through rebalancing (an action that brings portfolio allocations back into line with target allocations). The enhanced average or expected geometric mean return from rebalancing (or other volatility reduction) is often termed **diversification return**. Diversification return is not unique to commodities. The term was first coined by Booth and Fama (1992), and has been studied for equities, bonds, emerging markets, and multi-asset-class portfolios. Commodities seem particularly well suited for obtaining this source of benefit for two reasons:

1. Diversification returns are highest when the individual assets in a portfolio are highly volatile and the correlation among those assets is low.
2. Most importantly, diversification returns are enhanced to the extent that the commodity prices tend to display mean-reversion.

Commodities have low correlations with one another and so can offer uncorrelated investment opportunities across various commodity markets. In particular, the energy sector does not have high positive correlation with other sectors, because higher energy prices, in particular, can weigh on economic growth and depress demand for other commodities. This correlation pattern can potentially generate diversification returns while lowering the risk of a diversified commodity portfolio.

19.7.3   Volatility Reduction Enhances Geometric Mean Returns, Not Expected Values

It is important to note that the increase in geometric mean return of the portfolio that results from lowering the portfolio's return volatility has no impact on the expected value of the portfolio. As discussed in Chapter 22, although reducing the volatility of a portfolio increases its average compounded rate of return,[1] it does not affect the expected future value of the portfolio.[2] This means that in the absence of mean-reversion, rebalancing will have no effect on the portfolio's future value.

However, even in the case when volatility is lowered, the most likely outcomes tend to be higher in value. On the other hand, when there is mean reversion in prices, rebalancing may increase the expected future value of the portfolio as well. Although rebalancing's only impact is to increase the likelihood that the portfolio will make money, the lower volatility means that the best outcomes will not be as rewarding as when the volatility is high.

Diversification return is related to the fact that rebalancing reduces the portfolio allocation to commodities whose weights have increased since the beginning of the period, while increasing the allocation to commodities that have declined in relative value. This return to contrarian trading benefits when prices exhibit mean-reversion (rather than momentum). Frequent rebalancing to initial allocations improves returns if asset values exhibit mean-reversion and detracts if there is significant price momentum.

19.7.4   Summary of Rebalancing

Rebalancing is the adjustment of portfolio weights towards a specified set of target weights, possibly to retain exposures determined to be desirable and possibly for the dubious justifications of improved diversification or enhanced return.

Rebalancing a portfolio on, say, a monthly basis will generally enhance expected portfolio values if monthly returns are mean-reverting (i.e., if monthly returns exhibit negative autocorrelation) and will reduce expected portfolio values if monthly returns are trending (i.e., if monthly returns exhibit positive autocorrelation).

The question of whether rebalancing enhances diversification depends on the definition of diversification. The textbook definition of optimal diversification is to market-weight a portfolio such that the weight of each asset in the portfolio is proportional to the weight of the asset in the market portfolio. Note that a market-weighted portfolio needs very little rebalancing since each asset in the portfolio will tend to maintain a constant market-weight without rebalancing (except for the effects of share repurchases by the company and secondary offerings).

Within this definition of optimal diversification (market-weighting), rebalancing a portfolio towards any other weighting scheme tends to make the portfolio less diversified. If optimal diversification is defined as equal weighting (i.e., $1/N$ or naïve diversification) then rebalancing a portfolio back towards equal weights would be, by definition, diversifying. However, it should be noted that there are extremely strong reasons (grounded in capital market theory) to view optimal diversification as using market-weights rather than equal weights.

Finally, note that a continuously rebalanced portfolio will approach a value of zero if any of its components approach a value of $0. The reason is that the portfolio will continuously allocate towards an asset that is vanishing. Also, long-term portfolio rebalancing to fixed weights means that the portfolio will retain modest exposures to the assets that have provided the greatest long-run returns (e.g., in the US equity markets long-term rebalancing to fixed weights would lead to a current portfolio with minimal gains from the massive growth of Apple, Microsoft, Amazon, Alphabet and Facebook).

19.8   INVESTMENT MONITORING

In the context of investments, monitoring is the ongoing process of gathering, reviewing, and analyzing financial and compliance-related information. Monitoring begins with the due diligence process and continues through the exit from the investment. The task of monitoring during the due diligence process is gathering information that will enable the investor to determine the scope of the information gathering and areas of analysis that are appropriate for each investment. Monitoring involves more goals than simply the issuance of warnings as needed. The monitoring process involves identifying problems and developing a plan to address them. Monitoring is different for different types of investments.

Monitoring of publicly traded assets is substantially easier than monitoring of private assets.

This section emphasizes the monitoring of a portfolio of private equity partnerships. Investing in and monitoring private investments involves more effort and higher costs relative to an otherwise equivalent publicly traded investment.

19.8.1   Portfolio and Individual Asset Monitoring

Monitoring is performed at the portfolio level and individual asset level.

At the portfolio level, monitoring includes analyzing concentration across all partnerships in the portfolio (e.g., in private equity by industry, investment style, stage, geography, vintage year, and cross-holdings between funds). In private equity, tracking overall commitment level, contributions and distributions, return on investment to date, and expected final return on investment is also important for liquidity management.

At the individual investment level, monitoring varies depending on the fund or asset. For publicly-traded indexed funds, monitoring can be as minimal as analyzing tracking error. However, for private partnerships proper monitoring can be extensive and involve due diligence on other limited partners.

19.8.2   Six Activities of Monitoring Private Partnerships

Monitoring of illiquid partnerships is based on regular meetings with all parties involved and should include the following six activities:

1. Tracking the planned strategy of the partnership versus the implemented strategy.
2. Reviewing the fund's financial investment, valuation, and divestment information.
3. Analyzing the impact of relevant market trends.
4. Assessing the risk of both individual investments and the overall portfolio.
5. Measuring performance against the benchmark.
6. Verifying each partnership's legal and tax compliance.

It is neither possible nor meaningful to anticipate at the signing of the partnership agreements all the challenges and potential conflicts of interest that will arise over a fund's lifetime of 10 or more years. Market conditions fluctuate, fund management teams evolve, co-investors change, investments do not materialize as planned, and new opportunities arise. In hindsight, limited partners (LPs) may conclude that certain provisions of the agreement were overly restrictive and worked against their interests, while other issues may not have been addressed in sufficient detail. The monitoring exercised by investors is intended to bridge this gap.

19.8.3   Monitoring Objectives

Monitoring is done to create benefits but monitoring has costs primarily from employee time (labor). The resources devoted to monitoring should be based on the potential benefits and results.

Monitoring is important for ensuring style discipline. Because LPs are investing in a blind pool, the investment is based mainly on the fund manager's declared investment strategy. LPs should be concerned with any change to a fund's strategy. That said, there are risks associated with adhering too closely to a declared investment strategy, especially when market conditions change significantly, creating new opportunities. Therefore, funds will not necessarily adhere to it, nor should they in certain instances. LPs nevertheless need to ensure that fund managers stay within the confines of their core expertise and style.

THREE CHARACTERISTICS OF AN INVESTMENT THAT INDICATE THAT THERE MAY BE SUBSTANTIAL BENEFITS FROM MONITORING: (1) greater options to liquidate the investment; (2) greater ability to exert control over the investment's management; and (3) larger implications for the portfolio's other assets. Monitoring an investment that cannot be liquidated or controlled and that has no implications for the management of the portfolio has little or no benefit beyond gaining confidence on whether to invest in the general partner's (GP's) next fund or to decide not to make that allocation.

19.8.4   Forms of Active Involvement in the Fund's Governance Process

The two forms of active involvement in the fund's governance process are:

1. RENEGOTIATION OF MANAGEMENT FEES: One of the more obvious and common monitoring actions is the increased use of renegotiation of management fees and fund

size toward the end of a fund's life. If it becomes clear that the original invest-ment strategy cannot be successfully implemented and no credible alternative is brought forward, investors can influence the fund manager to reduce manage-ment fees or even release LPs from portions of their commitments. More often than not, GPs give in to reducing fund size. This investor-friendly behavior can build up goodwill and ease the next fundraising exercise. However, GPs have the right to refuse such voluntary actions. However, this often results in pressure, activism, and even lawsuits from LPs who want some or all of their money back.

2. TERMINATION WITHOUT CAUSE: In the extreme, and if there is an agreement among LPs, the fund management team can be terminated without cause. Even without recourse to such extreme measures, the threat of action or the noise of complaints from investors can be highly damaging to the reputation of a fund manager. This in turn can have serious implications for future fundraising ambitions.

19.8.5 Forms of Active Involvement Outside the Fund's Governance Process

The three actions outside the fund's governance process are:

1. NOT TO COMMIT TO THE FOLLOW-ON FUND: In situations in which a fund manage-ment team has clearly demonstrated that it is not up to the job or that it is not cooperating with its LPs, the simplest and most obvious action of an LP is not to commit to the follow-on fund. This is also most feared by the fund manager, as often the loss of a reputable investor sends a clear negative signal to the market. Not only would the team need to go back to the capital market for fundraising, but it would also do so with a tarnished reputation.

2. INVESTOR DEFAULT: An investor who does not fulfill commitments when called (i.e., default) is a questionable action, as it constitutes a contractual breach. However, this refusal to pay capital calls when requested may be the instrument of last resort if the fund manager is clearly incompetent. There can be substantial penalties when an LP does not pay a requested drawdown. The LP would likely forfeit all prior investments in the fund. The investor might also find it difficult to continue investing in private equity, as other fund managers might refuse to accept new commitments from investors who did not fulfill their prior obligations.

3. DIVESTMENT INTO THE SECONDARY MARKET: Limited partnerships may be able to be divested on the secondary market.

19.8.6 Three Ways to Create Value through Monitoring

Three benefits from monitoring beyond potential benefits to the extant invest-ment are:

1. EVALUATE FOLLOW-ON INVESTMENT: Intensive contact with the fund managers is important when deciding whether to invest in a follow-on fund (i.e., re-ups). A study undertaken by Lerner, Schoar, and Wongsunwai (2007) found that endowment funds are less likely to reinvest in a partnership, but if they did invest in the follow-on fund, its subsequent performance was significantly better

than those of funds they let pass. This finding underscores the importance of monitoring for improved decision-making.

2. Enhanced Awareness of Other Investment Opportunities: Networking and liaising with other LPs is an important instrument for gathering intelligence on the overall market and gaining knowledge of other funds. Information gleaned from monitoring is important for screening interesting investment opportunities that may arise, and may help an investor gain access to deals that might otherwise not appear on the institution's radar screen.

3. Better Liquidity Management: Monitoring may provide information that helps an institutional investor optimize the management of commitments through more precise cash flow forecasting.

19.8.7 Two Limits to the Detail and Extent of Information Available from Monitoring

GPs are extremely reluctant to disclose all information to investors. On the one hand, there is an obligation to disclose information so that investors are able to understand the portfolio's progress. On the other hand, further information, especially at a level of detail that allows an independent risk assessment, may potentially lead to:

1. Loss of Limited Partners: Detailed information provided to an LP by the GP may increase the chance that LPs will start investing directly and not commit to follow-on funds.

2. Increased Competition: There is also the investment rationale for maintaining a high degree of confidentiality to prevent competition. A fund with a niche strategy that consistently yields above-average returns will attract competition.

NOTES

1. See Erb and Harvey (2006); Till and Eagleeye (2005); Willenbrock (2011).
2. See Chambers and Zdanowicz (2014).

REFERENCES

Booth, D. G. and E. F. Fama. 1992. "Diversification Returns and Asset Contributions." *Financial Analysts Journal* 48 (3): 26–32.

Chambers, D. and J. Zdanowicz. 2014. "The Limitations of Diversification Return." *Journal of Portfolio Management* 40 (4): 65–76.

Erb, C. B. and C. R. Harvey. 2006. "The Strategic and Tactical Value of Commodity Futures." *Financial Analysts Journal* 62 (2): 69–97.

Greer, R. J. 2000. "The Nature of Commodity Index Returns." *Journal of Alternative Investments* 3 (1): 45–52.

Lerner, J., A. Schoar, and W. Wongsunwai. 2007. "Smart Institutions, Foolish Choices? The Limited Partner Performance Puzzle." *Journal of Finance* 62 (2): 731–64.

Till, H. and J. Eagleeye. 2005. "Commodities: Active Strategies for Enhanced Returns." *Journal of Wealth Management* (Fall): 42–61. Also in *The Handbook of Inflation Hedging Investments*, ed. R. Greer, New York: McGraw-Hill, pp. 127–57.

Willenbrock, S. 2011. "Diversification Return, Portfolio Rebalancing, and the Commodity Return Puzzle." *Financial Analysts Journal* 67 (4): 42–49.

CHAPTER 20

Risk Measurement, Risk Management, and Risk Systems

Risk and return are arguably the most ubiquitous and important terms and concepts within investing. Generally, investors must bear risk in order to obtain the possibility of receiving returns in excess of the risk-free rate of return. This chapter discusses the concepts and practices of measuring, reporting, and managing the types and amounts of risk to which an investor is exposed. Risk measurement and risk management need to be reviewed as separate, consecutive, and intricately connected concepts and practices, and both need to be the foundation of any well-designed and functioning investment process.

Accordingly, this chapter discusses the concept of risk, including basic definitions and distinctions between risk-related terms. Next, risk aggregation and the use of systems to ensure consistency, repeatability, and mitigating associated data collection risks is detailed. From there, the chapter discusses cybersecurity and risk management structures. The chapter concludes with a discussion of the investment process as a risk process and a brief note on the evolution of risk reporting.

20.1 OVERVIEW OF RISK MEASUREMENT AND AGGREGATION

Risk management includes the decisions and actions associated with overseeing and controlling exposure to uncertainty. **Risk measurement** includes all the steps associated with gathering and reporting the information required to capture an investor's exposure to uncertainty. Risk measurement is effective only to the extent that the measurements associated with each investment are accurate. Therefore, risk management starts with risk measurement, and risk measurement starts with the performance reporting process. This section discusses capturing, measuring, aggregating, and reporting these exposures.

20.1.1 Risk and the Investment Mandate

Understanding the objectives of risk measurement and management starts with an understanding of information typically contained in a well-written investment policy statement ("IPS"). The IPS, detailed in Chapter 11, should sufficiently describe the investor's financial goals, objectives, circumstances, and constraints to understand appropriate types and levels of risk. Within the borders of the IPS, information underlying the construction of the portfolio will be described and the investment mandates for the portfolio should be detailed. The investment mandate, ideally communicated via an IPS, provides the context for risk measurement and management. Therefore, risk measurement and management start at the top and are subsequently developed across each level (asset class, strategy, geography, sector, position, etc.) from the top down.

The significance of the top-down nature of risk measurement and management is often ignored. The measurement, monitoring, reporting, and managing of the risk of each investment is informed by the top-down expectations associated with such investment and should: (1) be memorialized in each investment's respective mandate; and (2) form the foundation for risk management from the bottom up. The bottom foundation of risk measurement and management of each position is then aggregated up to each respective level of the portfolio. In summary, risk measurement should be incrementally aggregated across each investment level (position, sector, geography, strategy, asset class, etc.), ultimately providing information regarding the portfolio's risk exposures across all levels of investment positioning. From the bottom up, there are five component areas to address in order to measure the risk information as detailed in the next section.

20.1.2   The Five Components of Risk Measurement

This section discusses five components or aspects of risk measurement as relating to five popular interrogative terms: who, what, when, where, and how.

1. INVESTMENT/POSITION LEVEL (WHERE): The investment/position level requires designing an approach for data collection for each investment made by the allocator. This is the level from "where" the risk data will be collected.
2. FREQUENCY OF DATA COLLECTION (WHEN): The frequencies of various data collections are determined and ideally includes daily, weekly, monthly, quarterly, and annual data, based upon the type of investment and data to be reviewed. This is "when" (i.e., how often) the various types of risk data will be collected.
3. AGGREGATION AND SYSTEMS DEVELOPMENT (HOW): Aggregation and systems development involve creating a systematized, repeatable risk measurement and investment process that seeks to minimize the potential problems associated with effectuating the process. This is ultimately "how" the risk data will be collected.
4. DIMENSIONS OF RISK (WHAT): The dimensions of risk refer to the extent possible to all of the risks associated with each investment. This is "what" risk data, in addition to positioning and pricing data, will be collected.
5. RISK REPORTING (WHOM): Risk reporting forms the basis for risk managers to act upon the results of the risk measurement process. This will be used to inform for "whom" the risk data are collected.

The next five sections detail the above five components or aspects of risk measurement.

20.1.3   Risk Measurement at the Investment/Position Level

Risk measurement at the investment or position level includes designing an approach for data collection for each investment. Data collection includes position information such as amount invested, valuation, and whether the investment represents a long or short position. For fixed income and over-the-counter derivative positions, additional data will need to be obtained and retained, including terms such as rates, tenor, early redemption, optionality—if any, key covenants, exercise terms, and any extraordinary features.

While the initial amount invested will be known at the time of investment, interim or subsequent amounts invested in each position will simply be calculated based upon the number of shares, bonds, units, etc. owned multiplied by the price of each share, bond, unit, etc. on each valuation date. Valuation approaches differ. Greater confidence is placed on valuations associated with investments traded on highly liquid, frequently traded, publicly available capital market exchanges. The determination of value is critical to the measurement of risk, and risk exposure increases as position liquidity decreases. Confidence in valuations decreases with reduced price discovery due to infrequent transactions.

The construction of a formal *valuation policy* to ensure consistent valuation practices across different types of investments is a crucial risk mitigation step in the data collection phase of risk measurement. Such polices would typically be crafted by back office professionals with support from investment and trade execution professionals and external service providers (third-party custodians/administrators, accountants and pricing services, for example), and approved by both the allocator's operating and investment committees. Once in place, industry best practice is to contain all valuation activities within the back office and associated professionals to avoid any conflicts of interest that may arise should members of the investment team determine position valuations.

The valuation policy is then summarized into a pricing matrix or model. A **pricing matrix** describes valuation of assets typically with labels for the types of asset (e.g., the labels Level l, Level 2, and Level 3, as one dimension), with descriptions of the valuation model-type as the other dimension and total aggregated asset values as the data entries. As discussed in Chapter 33 on investment due diligence, Level 1 assets are highly liquid with prices accepted as valuations with a high degree of confidence, Level 2 assets can be valued using observable inputs, while Level 3 assets are illiquid with values based on models resulting in relatively low degrees of confidence. While not perfect, three methods for approximating short-term valuations for illiquid securities are capital balance statements, discounted cash flow models, and customized indices.

CAPITAL STATEMENT VALUATIONS: Capital statement valuations are normally provided on a quarterly basis by the entity or manager sponsoring a private investment and may be used as the basis from which to approximate expected variations in value from previously reported quarterly valuation estimates.

DISCOUNTED CASH FLOW MODEL-BASED CALCULATIONS: Discounted cash flow model-based calculations with defined parameters (such as growth and discount rates, compounding frequency, and expected salvage/exit value) may be employed to approximate valuations during interim periods.

CUSTOMIZED INDEX-BASED CALCULATIONS: A customized index may be created to proxy private investments versus comparable, publicly traded positions, utilizing key attributes and descriptive properties (industry, sector, geography, etc.) with a suitable discount ("haircut") for illiquidity (versus similar publicly traded investments) to approximate valuations on as frequent as a daily basis.

Over time, valuation practices and the valuation policy may evolve and improve, and the annual audit practice (discussed later) may serve as a source of useful value verification (i.e., a "sanity check") for an allocator's interim valuation practices.

20.1.4   Risk Measurement and Frequency of Data Collection

The frequency of particular data collection and risk measurement is a key issue that is so important in understanding a risk measurement and reporting system that it is the organizing principle underlying most of this chapter. In fact, Sections 20.4 to 20.8 detail issues from the perspective of five data collection frequencies: daily, weekly, monthly, quarterly, and annually. As detailed later, data collection refers to more than merely position and performance data. Data collection frequency is linked to the purposes of the data collection—especially risk and performance reporting. Also, illiquidity of private alternative investments is a key factor in determining appropriate practices.

Best practices in risk measurement and reporting optimize the level of detail of information and the frequency of reporting, including the role of the personnel being served. For example, detailed information on daily closing cash balances for various sub-accounts may be useful information for personnel designated to monitor liquidity on a short-term basis, but it may be distracting and time-wasting to report such information on a daily basis to senior personnel monitoring profitability and compliance.

Exception reporting can be used to optimize the efficiency of risk measurement and reporting. An **exception report** filters data to describe only those instances in which risk measures and other data are outside predetermined bands deemed to be appropriate for further analysis at a more senior level.

Specification of efficient risk measurement and reporting practices using different data collection frequencies is the foundation for an effective risk measurement, reporting, and management system. Exhibit 20.1 overviews risk identification, measurement, and management for the five data collection frequencies previously enumerated. All else being equal, using higher frequencies of data collection decreases the time period between successive position valuations, increases risk monitoring, and allows for more reliable risk measurement. Increased frequency of data collection is typically associated with increased transparency and position liquidity. However, as noted above, limiting the scope of information included in the reporting system is also important.

Increased frequency of data collection is very helpful in exception reporting, assessments of manager skill, and style drift and may result in the discovery of increasing risk exposures much earlier than delaying data collection to month or quarter ending dates. Subsequent sections discuss data collection for daily, weekly, monthly, quarterly, annual, and multi-year rolling time periods.

Note that the use of illiquid securities, such as private partnerships, typically means that much of the new information regarding estimates of value for those assets will tend to arrive perhaps quarterly rather than daily as in the case of listed securities. Similarly, the use of actively managed and dynamic strategies such as hedge funds means that new information beyond changes in positions will arrive with

EXHIBIT 20.1   Data Collection Frequency and Data Reporting

Frequency:	Data Collected:	Reporting Outcomes:
Daily:	Values, returns, position size, volume, index and benchmark data, and keyword alerts	Values, performance, risks, exceptions, events
	↓ ↓	↓ ↓
Weekly:	No additional data	Exposures, netted exposures and changes in exposures
	↓ ↓	↓ ↓
Monthly:	Position and manager changes Non-investment qualitative risks (business, legal, regulatory, and compliance risks)	Position and manager turnover, top positions, exposures, cash, cash flow, illiquid/miscellaneous positions and qualitative risks reports
	↓ ↓	↓ ↓
Quarterly:	Extensive manager calls and reports Quarterly valuations of illiquid positions	Summary of manager calls Illiquid position information
	↓ ↓	↓ ↓
Annually:	Annual site visits, annual audits of illiquid positions, and reference updates	Reports, summaries, and analyses of managers and illiquid positions

manager calls and visits, which occur perhaps quarterly or annually. Thus, the use of alternative investments (rather than entirely liquid listed securities) drives arrival of new value and risk exposure information further down the process depicted in Exhibit 20.1. Thus, allocators of portfolios with alternative assets face a more complex data collection and analysis process than in the case of a portfolio of only liquid (and perhaps primarily passive) investments.

20.1.5   Risk Aggregation and Systems Development

Risk aggregation is most often studied and reported with regard to banks or banking institutions, with an ultimate purpose of discovering and reporting one, or a few, summary statistic(s) to describe the expected total risk exposure of the institution. For these institutions, the focus is typically used to estimate tail loss risk metrics, such as value at risk ("VaR") and expected shortfall, over a defined period of time and within a defined level of probability. Such statistics are typically backward-looking and of limited value during actual loss events for individual banking institutions, such as during the onset of a financial crisis.

The principle of aggregating the components that comprise the risk factors—from risks of individual positions, to lines, and ultimately to firm-wide measures that are generally appropriate for banking institutions—are also appropriate for institutional investment portfolios. Institutional investment portfolios, especially those with alternative investments (such as long/short positions, diverse asset class exposures, private investments, and derivatives), may use numerous aggregation levels and are likely to include exposures from both sides of the balance sheet (and any off-balance sheet exposures).

AGGREGATION DEPENDS ON CORRELATION: While aggregating returns is an additive process from the bottom up, calculating and aggregating risk measurements ultimately to the top level of a portfolio is not simply the sum of the constituent risk measures. Due to the impacts of correlations between positions, strategies, sectors, and other exposures, aggregating risk measures up to the portfolio level is a nonlinear and more complex exercise.

STATIC AND DYNAMIC ELEMENTS: Risk reporting should include both static risk elements and dynamic elements. Static elements include measures such as those related to exception reporting (including, for example, prohibited investments and excess leverage). Dynamic elements include forward-looking elements, such as identifying potential risks, quantifying changes in risk exposures associated with proposed changes in allocations and risk budgets, and potentially including the impacts of hedges at the portfolio level to mitigate certain risk exposures.

NONLINEAR EXPOSURES AND SIMULATION MODELS: Given the nonlinear nature of many alternative investments and strategies, it is common to utilize various scenario and stress testing simulation models to measure potential risk exposures in the future and to inform any potential risk management activities, including portfolio level hedging activities. Also, the more complex and diverse the allocator's portfolio, the greater the probability that the portfolio is exposed to a greater number of risk factors. The use of multi-factor simulation models similarly increases the complexity of the model and the associated data needs. Therefore, developing proper systems of data collection, storage, and model validation frameworks are essential to proper risk measurement and to support risk management across the entire portfolio.

SPREADSHEET-BASED SYSTEMS: Risk measurement and reporting systems may be manual (i.e., spreadsheet-based) or automated, and developed and maintained internally, externally, or some combination of both. A common approach is to use locally developed, maintained, and stored spreadsheet-based methods of recording and measuring position and portfolio data, and calculating, aggregating, and reporting associated risk measures. While seemingly inexpensive to build and maintain, such a manual system potentially introduces data collection, calculation, and related accuracy, model, storage, cyber, reporting, conflict of interest, and fraud risks to the risk measurement process.

AUTOMATED SYSTEMS: More fully automated systems and software may connect pricing and valuation services directly to calculation and reporting systems, thereby decreasing transposition and transcription errors, increasing accuracy, and potentially mitigating, although not eliminating, other model and related risks. Automated systems may be proprietary, developed internally within the offices and utilizing the resources of the allocator, and may require substantial internal resources such as connecting a spectrum of various data sources to internally developed spreadsheets, purchased software and/or customized data storage, measurement, and reporting software.

EXTERNALLY PROVIDED SYSTEMS: A substantial amount of the systems work may be outsourced to external service providers, thereby allowing the allocator to focus more upon risk measurement and less upon software development. Many external service providers, including custodians, administrators, and pricing services have either developed risk measurement and reporting systems into their primary data systems, or formed joint ventures with software vendors to receive the position and related data and then to produce and provide risk measurement and other reporting services to the allocator. While this does not completely eliminate the need for internal systems development and/or maintenance professionals, it may provide a cost-effective alternative.

QUALITATIVE RISK SYSTEMS: The topics discussed in the preceding paragraphs clearly focus upon principles related to aggregating quantitative risks and briefly introduce the concepts of automated data and risk systems. However, risk measurement for alternative investments is incomplete if processes (systems) are not also in place to measure and record the *qualitative* risks associated with each alternative investment. Quantitative risk measures and associated diligence activities are related more closely to the revenue proposition associated with the investment. Qualitative risk measures and associated diligence activities are associated with managing the operations of the investment manager as an ongoing business concern.

20.1.6 Risk Measurement and Dimensions of Risk

The important concept for risk measurement is to use best efforts to know the risks to which one is exposed and from which one expects to obtain the possibility of receiving excess returns. The majority of risk measurement in practice focuses on: (1) deviations from expected results; and (2) capital market and related risks.

A well-structured investment process includes both quantitative and qualitative elements, effectuated by different professionals with different skill sets and gives equal weight to the results of both quantitative and qualitative due diligence processes such that a failing grade from either side normally disqualifies the potential investment from additional consideration or terminates an existing investment.

For alternative investments, qualitative risks are typically reviewed in the business operations, legal, regulatory, and compliance due diligence activities completed in conjunction with the initial investment process and updated at various times throughout the holding period of the investment. The need to follow a systematic and disciplined approach, including the recording of such activities, is critical to the risk measurement process and is indicative of an investment process that is better positioned to deliver more accurate information in the short term and repeatable results in the long term. The key to the efficacy of such a system is the ability and discipline to identify qualitative risk exposures.

In order to fully understand the risks associated with an alternative investment, it is helpful to create a report summarizing such risks and including investment, business operations, and any other nuanced, specific, or idiosyncratic risks associated with such investment. Third-party software is commercially available for tracking and storing such diligence and risk measurement activities over time.

This total risk summary report is herein referred to as the "Dimensions of Risk" associated with an alternative investment. The following is intended to present an overview of that which may be contained within the Dimensions of Risk report for an investment in a hedge fund. Clearly, the following is not specific to a particular investment, is not exhaustive, and the format may be altered to suit allocator needs. The main point is that the discovery of all the risks associated with an alternative investment gives a more complete review of risk-adjusted returns than merely relying upon a few quantitative measures calculated by multiplying or dividing a return measure by a risk measure.

20.1.7 An Example of Dimensions of Risk Reporting for an Alternative Investment

This section illustrates risk reporting for an alternative investment using an example of a hedge fund. The risk reporting is organized around twelve dimensions.

1. STRATEGY: Strategy risk reporting should include risks inherent to the particular alternative investment strategy:

   - A LONG/SHORT EQUITY EXAMPLE: Consider a long/short equity strategy utilizing both top-down macro analysis and fundamental bottom-up research to identify investment opportunities in mid- to large cap companies within the technology sector and predominately within the US. Inherent risks include macro analysis risk, sector-related risks, idiosyncratic security selection risk, dispersion risk, basis risk on derivative positions and portfolio hedges, if any, and, to a lesser extent, political/regulatory and currency risks.

   - AN EVENT DRIVEN MULTI-STRATEGY EXAMPLE: Consider an event driven multi-strategy–credit-oriented strategy with flexibility across the entire capital structure and a particular focus upon distressed and related events and special situations, primarily focused upon small and mid-cap North American domiciled companies, utilizing fundamental bottom-up security selection and event/catalyst identification for all positions. Inherent risks include mark-to-market risk, interest rate risk, credit risk, event risk, idiosyncratic security selection risk, dispersion risk, and basis risk on portfolio hedges, if any.

   - A LONG/SHORT FIXED INCOME/CREDIT STRATEGY: Consider a long/short fixed income/credit strategy focusing upon active trading of securitized assets, predominantly residential and commercial mortgages within the US by utilizing data intensive fundamental bottom-up security selection for all positions and employing active relative value trading. Inherent risks include mark-to-market risk, interest rate risk, prepayment risk, extension risk, credit risk, idiosyncratic security selection risk, dispersion risk, basis risk on position and portfolio hedges, if any, and regulatory risk.

   - A SYSTEMATIC MANAGED FUTURES STRATEGY: Consider a systematic managed futures strategy that utilizes pattern recognition, trend reversion models, and is diversified across time periods (short and intermediate terms) and markets (35 global markets). Inherent risks include model risk, trade execution (slippage and allocation) risk, lack of volatility within longer trends and trend reversal risks, and implicit leverage risk.

2. LIQUIDITY: Liquidity risk reporting should include the specifics for the strategy, generally:
   - Exchange traded, daily liquid investments imply lower liquidity risk.
   - Unlisted, private, and/or direct investments imply increased liquidity risk.
3. CONCENTRATION: Concentration risk generally decreases as diversification increases. This section may include information regarding the expected number of long, short, and total positions in the portfolio and the percentage of the portfolio expected to be represented by the top 5 or 10 long and short positions.
4. GEOGRAPHY: Geography-related risk reporting should include the potential for developed economies with strong "Rule of Law" regulatory systems in place to generally be regarded as less risky than emerging economies with less well-defined institutions established.
5. LEVERAGE: Leverage risk reporting should include the type(s) and extent to which leverage is expected to be utilized by the investment manager; generally:
   - The use of leverage may increase costs and investment returns are not normally commensurate with the amount of leverage employed.
   - Leverage may increase or add default risk and counterparty risk to the investment.
   - Borrowing activities may induce "forced selling" during times of market downturns or increased redemption activity.
6. TRANSPARENCY: If the risks are understood and appropriately managed, increasing transparency is typically associated with lower risk.
7. VALUATIONS: The determination of value is critical to the measurement of returns and risk. Valuation risk generally increases as position liquidity decreases.
8. KEY PERSON: Key person risk is the risk that valuable decision maker(s), managers, or other key talent may leave the investment manager or the firm in which one has invested. This risk may be mitigated:
   - If the investment manager's investment process and/or business is constructed so as to decrease the reliance on one individual for important intellectual capacity, knowledge, relationships, and decision-making.
   - Through the purchase of a key person insurance policy.
   - Using the presence of extraordinary redemption rights triggered by the departure of a key person.
   - With ongoing new idea generation and diligence processes to develop an active "bench" of alternative investment opportunities and adequately diversified portfolio construction.
9. BUSINESS OPERATIONS: Business operations risk includes any extraordinary or otherwise notable risks associated with the operations of the investment manager's business or operations. These risks should be reported, completely reviewed on an annual basis, proxied during interim time periods, and monitored through automated key word searches and news services.
10. LEGAL, REGULATORY, AND COMPLIANCE: Legal, regulatory, and compliance risks are similar to business operations risks in that any extraordinary or notable risks should be included in this report, monitored on a daily basis through exception reporting, automated key word searches, news and regulatory reporting services, and completely reviewed on an annual basis.

11. OTHER RISKS: Other risks include extraordinary, unique, or idiosyncratic risks that may be associated with the investment or investment manager, and may include growth through acquisitions, succession plans, capacity or other limitations, and disclosed conflicts of interest, among others.

12. EMERGING: Emerging risks may include any potential emerging risks to which the manager may become exposed, including risks associated with Environmental, Social, and Governance ("ESG") issues, and the impacts of big data and artificial intelligence, for example.

It is also possible to assign numeric ranks or weights to each category of risk listed above to arrive at a dimensions of risk score to allow for relative risk rankings across all investments within an allocator's portfolio.

20.2 CATEGORIES OF INFORMATION TO BE CONSIDERED

The purpose of this section is to discuss various quantitative and qualitative categories of information that allocators may find helpful to calculate or compile and review on at least a quarterly, and preferably on a monthly, basis. This information may be useful for both risk measurement of existing investments and potential identification of new opportunities through identification of emerging trends, dislocations, and other leading indicators. The information to be collected is nonexhaustive and subject to change and evolution as specific needs, markets, regulations, investments, technology, and other conditions emerge, evolve, or otherwise become impactful over time.

20.2.1 Quantitative Information Categories and Associated Statistics

This section describes seven categories of quantitative information.

1. HISTORICAL PERFORMANCE: Historical performance review includes analysis on an absolute basis and versus investment mandates, related indices, and appropriate benchmarks. These measures and statistics should be calculated over discrete time periods and compounded over various time frames. Charting and comparing each investment across daily, monthly, and other appropriate discrete and/or rolling measurement time periods, at each level, from the position level and aggregating up through each designated level to the total portfolio, yields a pictorial representation of each investment's contribution to performance over time. Overlaying appropriate comparison indices and benchmarks may also yield important insights into correlation, beta, and alpha that may otherwise be missed through a review based solely upon calculated summary statistics.

2. HISTORICAL RISK MEASUREMENT REVIEW: Historical risk measurement review starts by measuring the various statistics that are used to describe the distribution of returns for each position, related indices, and appropriate benchmarks. These descriptive statistics include minimum value, maximum value, range, standard deviation, downside deviation, skew, and (excess) kurtosis. Additional performance measures may include Sharpe, Sortino, Treynor, and Omega statistics. Based on related indices and benchmarks over similar time periods, additional information to calculate and review includes statistics that are intended to relate

each investment to its benchmarks, including estimates of correlation, beta, alpha, and up and down capture statistics.

3. ASSET ALLOCATIONS AND CAPITAL BALANCES: From performance information, asset allocations and capital balances are updated across all positions and aggregated through each level, sector, geography, asset class, and portfolio. Trend reports may be created for each level and are used to depict actual cash and valuation impacts of investment performance, potentially informing any upcoming rebalancing and exposure decisions.

4. GROSS CONTRIBUTION: As performance and risk measures are aggregated through each level of the portfolio, gross contribution (manager, sector, strategy, asset class and, if extraordinary, position level) and attribution information may be calculated and reviewed, potentially including assessments of manager skill.

5. VARIOUS ACTIVITY REPORTS: Information on activity includes investment mandate tracking, exception reports, exposure information, purchase, sale, and manager turnover, overlapping and offsetting positions, portfolio allocations, top positions and exposures, cash, cash flow (including transactions and trends), and illiquid and miscellaneous position reports.

6. FIXED INCOME REPORTS: For fixed income positions and exposures, it is also best practice to measure and/or maintain interest rate, various yield computations, duration (along with interest rates and spreads), convexity, credit, illiquidity, as well as gross and net exposure information.

7. CTA AND MANAGED FUTURES EXPOSURES: In the case of CTAs and managed futures exposures, it is important to measure and be aware of the level of diversification of the aggregate portfolio across geographies, markets, models, time frames, and margin-to-equity.

20.2.2 Due Diligence Tracking Matrices

In order to maintain a disciplined approach to obtaining such interim updates, best practice would include the development of a diligence monitoring system. One simple way to do this is to create a due diligence tracking matrix. A due diligence tracking matrix is a chart that tracks and summarizes diligence activities and highlights findings, risks, and actions associated with each activity. The matrix is helpful in guiding quarterly risk review discussions and focusing upon key potential action items. While such a matrix may be constructed and customized to include all investments, the matrix to be discussed here will focus on the use of external investment managers. Therefore, qualitative risk measurement for external investment managers may include the creation of a due diligence tracking matrix that may include the categories, topics, and summary information included in the next section.

20.2.3 Qualitative Information Categories

The intent of a monthly and/or quarterly qualitative risk measurement is to provide interim information related to the business operations, legal, regulatory, and compliance risks associated with each investment or investment manager. This section reviews five qualitative categories that may be included in the due diligence tracking matrix.

1. DESCRIPTIVE INFORMATION: Descriptive information for each manager may include the name of the manager, approval and funding status, and key dates, ranging from historic to recent (for example, initial approval date, initial investing date, most recent regulatory related dates, most recent onsite investment and business operations dates, and most recent third-party background and reference checks), and information related to the manager's investment strategy.

2. KEY INFORMATION: Key information for each manager may include the amount invested (current account value), performance concerns versus the associated investment mandate, liquidity concerns, key employee turnover, opening/closing of offices, changes in ownership, changes in regulatory registration status, and changes in the manager's assets under management, both with regard to absolute changes and versus previous representations from the firm with regard to the strategy or firm's capacity.

3. OTHER INFORMATION: Other information may include significant news and issues that may have come to light from ongoing monitoring activities, including investment mandate violations, regulatory audits, pending litigation, and areas which are monitored but occur infrequently.

4. WATCH OR FOCUS LIST SUMMARY: Managers are placed on a **watch list** when the investor wishes to monitor the manager more closely with a concern that investment performance or organizational changes may soon warrant redemption. A watch or focus list summary may be included to ensure that watch or focus list manager activities are consistently recorded and reviewed for further action, including removal from the list if concerns have been addressed, or termination if so warranted.

5. ACTIVITIES LOG: An activities log may be added as a separate page or addendum to the due diligence tracking matrix in which specifics related to investment and business operations discovered during the onsite diligence meetings may be recorded. Such information as dates, attendees, business purpose, reports filed, and summary comments for each meeting, among other things, may be recorded in the activities log.

While not specifically contained within the due diligence tracking matrix, beyond highlighting significant exceptions, another important area of the monthly and quarterly measurement of qualitative risk is to require and review an acceptable certification by the Chief Compliance Officer of each investment manager that addresses illiquid securities, soft dollar, regulatory oversight, and portfolio holdings reports for each investment manager hired by the allocator.

20.3   RISK MEASUREMENT WITH DAILY FREQUENCY OF DATA COLLECTION

Daily collection of data does not mean that the data must be reported daily. For example, daily volume data for a particular position might be collected daily but stored for later use to calculate minimum and maximum daily volume levels that are reported on a monthly basis. Also, daily collection of data used for a daily report does not mean that the specific data for that day will appear directly on a daily report.

For example, the daily volume for a position may be used to form a 5-day moving average volume that *is* reported on a daily basis.

Daily risk measurement is focused on position and performance measurement, and updating cumulative position, performance, and risk measures, as appropriate. By utilizing the appropriate valuation measure, summarized within the pricing matrix, performance for the just completed business day is discovered for each position and incrementally calculated for each fund, manager, sector, strategy and/or asset class, as appropriate. Basically, performance is discovered on a discrete, position by position basis, and measurement progresses through increasing levels of aggregation in order to arrive at specific sub-portfolio and total portfolio performance and asset valuations. Similarly, performance of appropriate and associated comparison indices and benchmarks are obtained for each portfolio position and level of aggregation.

From there, it is helpful to extend the information by calculating performance for each position and aggregation level, and associated indices and benchmarks, over various time periods from daily, to week to date, month to date, year to date, and appropriate rolling time frames of 1, 3, and 5 years to date, and from inception of the investment to date.

Performance information at each level is also used to calculate and update key information, such as exposures, allocations, leverage, and cash balances. All of these pieces of information can be combined to produce exception reports (versus investment mandates and/or expectations) on daily, position by position, and aggregated bases. The use of rolling time periods to capture such metrics as rolling daily returns, standard deviations, and drawdowns can be helpful in the early detection of risks.

Daily tracking of asset weightings versus strategic and tactical portfolio allocation ranges is a useful and comparatively easy daily update. Finally, key word alerts should be set, monitored, and maintained on various search engines and/or news services to include names and terms associated with portfolio investments and investment managers.

20.4 RISK MEASUREMENT WITH WEEKLY FREQUENCY OF DATA COLLECTION

Weekly risk measurement activities are normally focused upon calculating and reporting exposures, for all levels of the portfolio, from position information obtained from the daily performance data collected on the last day of each trading week. Weekly detailed exposure reporting is sufficient for most developed institutional investment portfolios as exposure shifts are not typically significant at the portfolio level on a daily basis.

Weekly information to be calculated and reported at each level of portfolio aggregation includes gross long, gross short, and net exposures (reflecting the amount and direction of leverage utilized within the portfolio) on accounting (cash), delta, and beta adjusted bases. For fixed income positions, exposures to credit and type of security should be included. Exposures for futures and forwards positions should capture notional exposures across time frames (short, intermediate, and long term) and margin-to-equity calculations. Exposure reporting should include comparisons, reflected in changes in exposures reports and charts depicting at least weekly changes over time.

20.5   RISK MEASUREMENT WITH MONTHLY FREQUENCY OF DATA COLLECTION

As should be apparent, each successive time period of data collection and risk measurement builds upon and utilizes the information developed during the shorter time periods. On a monthly basis, therefore, valuation and position information is used to develop various performance and risk statistics for each level of aggregation from the position level through the portfolio level. It is particularly helpful if such reports include comparisons based upon daily and monthly calculations. This is true because daily measurements may represent "noise," but they may also reflect manager skill, including risk management.

Additional information to be reviewed on a monthly basis includes exposure information, overlapping and offsetting position reports (aggregated across all appropriate levels, including position, sector, manager, strategy, asset class, and portfolio levels), and position and manager turnover reports. When using external managers, portfolio position turnover reports are helpful to obtain for each manager. It is particularly helpful to obtain both purchase and sales turnover reports for each manager as these reports may provide valuable insights into an external manager's trading activity, and prove useful for both mandate tracking and potential early indications of style drift or distress on the part of the manager. Portfolio allocations, top positions and exposures, cash, cash flow reports, and illiquid and miscellaneous position reports should also be included in monthly risk measurement activities.

During each monthly risk review, it is not unusual to discover investments exceeding expected risk exposures. This may occur generally because of changes in market conditions, including various political and regulatory changes, or changes in manager behavior, which may include unintended or undiscovered risks, or lack of manager skill. Regardless of the reason, risk measurement activities may result in the discovery of certain investments and/or managers that may require enhanced monitoring activities for the foreseeable future. Many allocators list such investments, class of investments and/or managers on a "watch" or "focus" list, and additional monitoring activities would ensue. Enhanced monitoring of investment managers may include monthly calls with the manager to review issues of concern and other related topics (potentially including all items listed as a part of a manager quarterly call program discussed in the next section). It is also not unusual to include such enhanced monitoring and communication activities in conjunction with the hiring of new investment managers for the initial 3 to 6 months of the investment.

While it is not the scope of this chapter to discuss specific risk measures and statistics in great detail, it is obvious that risk measurement deeply involves the calculation and interpretation of such measures. Accordingly, most adequately resourced institutional investors calculate and review many risk statistics across all levels of the portfolio as appropriate, on at least a quarterly basis, using either internal or external service provider resources. Industry best practices include the development of a fully integrated, automated (to the extent practicable), and systematic approach to calculate this information on at least a monthly basis.

Similarly, a well-developed investment and risk process includes ongoing measuring and monitoring of the risks associated with investments beyond merely those risks associated with the performance of the investment. Generally, these risks can be categorized as business operations, legal, regulatory, and compliance risks. Some may add ESG considerations within this category of diligence and risk measurement, and many may generalize this area by referring to it as merely operational due diligence, or ODD. For the purposes of this chapter, noninvestment performance risks are included as a subset within the qualitative risk measures. On a monthly basis, interim qualitative risk measurement and monitoring activities should be reported and highlighted, as available and appropriate, and a more complete report should be presented on quarterly and annual bases. Quantitative and qualitative risk measurement is discussed again in the following quarterly risk measurement section.

20.6   RISK MEASUREMENT WITH QUARTERLY FREQUENCY OF DATA COLLECTION

On a quarterly basis, significant time should be spent preparing, reviewing, discussing, and managing risks across all levels of the portfolio. Risk information from daily, weekly, and monthly measurement activities should be collected, combined, and augmented by additional risk measurement, monitoring, and diligence activities, culminating in complete investment monitoring each calendar quarter. A significant addition to risk measurement activities includes a quarterly investment manager call program. This type of deeper dive into each investment manager will most likely be effectuated over a 4- to 6-week period after the end of each calendar quarter. The timing is directly dependent upon the liquidity of the actual investments managed by each manager and the associated valuation method and related steps required to appropriately value such investments.

For qualitative risk measurement, the quarterly call program is designed to provide a disciplined approach to obtaining interim updates to initial and annual regulatory filings and site visits. Exhibit 20.2 provides details regarding potential best practices in the content of periodic (e.g., quarterly) manager calls. Compiling all the risks and opportunities listed by each manager during the entire quarterly call program can prove to be very insightful and helpful for future risk and portfolio management activities, as well as asset allocation and exposure decisions.

20.7   RISK MEASUREMENT WITH ANNUAL FREQUENCY OF DATA COLLECTION OR ROLLING TIME PERIODS

If well developed, the data, calculations, and related activities listed above should be followed for year-end as for the other quarter ending periods. Final valuations, performance, and related calculations may change following any adjustments made during annual audit activities. For longer and rolling time periods, calculations for quantitative performance and risk measurement will follow from that defined and as appropriate based upon, or relative to, the associated IPS and investment mandate for such allocator or specific investment.

From a risk measurement perspective, there are additional activities that would typically occur only on an annual basis, although not necessarily at year end. Such annual activities may be summarized in banking terms as "re-underwriting" each investment and pertain largely to investments made through external investment managers. Co-investment and direct investment activities will follow an annual audit

Asset allocators may find it helpful to include a reasonable number of investment professionals on each manager call, including risk analysts. Further, a potentially valuable practice is to assign each analyst participating in the call an area of focus and the task of noting all discussion related to that area of focus that occurs during the call.

Allocators should subscribe to, receive, and review information that is available regarding the manager through regulatory sources, public news, and search services. Therefore the focus of a periodic call should be on information not received through public sources and information that can change significantly in the short term. Each quarterly call should start with an update of the manager's business including: operations, legal, regulatory, and compliance topics. Questions regarding the business operations may also include any changes to the team and the office facilities, including the identification of significant hires and fires, and any planned opening or closing activities, respectively. These questions are typically followed by questions regarding any planned changes to the firm's organization or structure, such as additions of new partners or any potential merger or acquisition activity. Related to this, allocators should ask for updates and any changes to the firm's service providers and counterparties, and request appropriate follow up materials and/or meetings for further diligence if it appears to be warranted by the reply.

The next portion of the call may be handled by the manager's COO or CFO, and may start with questions regarding assets under management, the strategy in which the allocator is invested, any expected or known changes to come (such as subscription and redemption requests already received by the firm), updates to the capacity of the firm, and the strategy (normally answered by the portfolio manager).

Next, the manager's General Counsel or CCO may answer questions related to any litigation and regulation activity. Copies of updates to any regulatory filings, offering materials, marketing, and other documents should be requested as there may not exist any legal requirement to inform the allocator of such updates or changes. In addition, questions regarding the existence of any new side letters, or other unique agreements, entered into by the firm are worth asking along with the important open-end question: "Are there any other issues investors should know about?" Next, a quick review of issues related to cybersecurity, trading systems, valuations, interim and annual financial statements, capital balances, legal covenants, use of margin, ESG, and other related questions depending on the investment strategy.

As the call progresses, the focus moves to a deeper review of investment related topics potentially including:

- performance of the investments;
- comparison of investment performance versus any similar or related products offered by the manager (particularly relevant for separately managed accounts and co-investments);
- performance attribution information, cash, delta-, and beta-adjusted exposure information;
- duration, yield, and carry information, and other exposures, as appropriate;
- additional disclosures and comments on key performance drivers;
- identification and discussion regarding top contributors to and detractors from performance; and
- comments on outlier positions (with a focus on unusual positions).

Finally, the conversation should move towards completion with a shift towards forward-looking questions and attempts to shape the allocator's expectations for both the short and long terms. This may help with risk budgeting and asset allocation decisions and may lead to information to inform future monitoring activities and exception reporting. The allocator's internal follow-on to the call includes documenting the call along with the help of the other investment professionals that were on the call and took notes regarding their assigned areas of focus.

EXHIBIT 20.2   Conducting a Periodic Manager Call

process and may include an annual site visit to the location of the specific investment. For allocators utilizing external investment managers, the manager's firm should be the venue for the annual meeting, and it should follow much of the same diligence activities as those followed during the initial investment due diligence process.

As such, each allocator may schedule two separate onsite visits per year: one for an investment due diligence update meeting and another for a business operations due diligence update meeting. The expected participants for the external manager should be the same as during the initial investment process: the investment management team, including the Chief Investment Officer, Portfolio Manager, and other investment decision makers or support, as appropriate, and the Chief Operating Officer, Chief Financial Officer, General Counsel and/or Chief Compliance Officer, as appropriate, for the separate investment and business operations annual due diligence meetings, respectively. Follow-up reporting would be expected to reference and improve upon previous reports and action items should be highlighted.

On an annual basis, and taking into account all updated information, manager investment mandates and investment advisory agreements should be reviewed and renewed or updated/altered, if needed and as appropriate. Considerations for such actions may include peer group reviews, fee and expense analyses, and performance comparisons. This process may also include negotiations surrounding additional capacity with each manager, if desired.

Based upon investment performance, updated diligence activities, market conditions, including emerging risks and potential opportunities, regulatory and other leading indicators, it may make sense to review and revise portfolio construction, including the determination of strategic and tactical asset allocation ranges. In a typical year, this step may not be needed, particularly if the performance results and risk statistics for the past year are all contained, or reasonably expected to remain within the historic distribution of returns associated with each asset class, for time periods associated with the allocator's entire portfolio.

Codes of ethics, anti-money laundering documentation, and other regulatory and compliance certifications must be renewed annually. For allocators, it is recommended that they perform (renew) third-party background and reference checks on each external manager, every 3 years commencing 3 years from the date of original investment. Some allocators accomplish this by performing such reviews on one third of all external managers each year.

20.8 CYBERSECURITY FOR FUND MANAGERS

Mary Jo White, Chair of the SEC in 2016, cited cybersecurity as the biggest risk facing the financial system.[1] In most, if not all, investment organizations, the firm's most important assets are subject to threats from harmful activity executed through computer information systems and the Internet. As mentioned in Chapter 3, cybersecurity is required through regulation. This section focuses solely on cybersecurity and does not address the myriad of privacy laws enacted globally. However, privacy laws are an important issue with potentially serious repercussions. Privacy laws are a major reason that cybersecurity should be taken very seriously for firms with data that could compromise privacy.

20.8.1   Vulnerability of Investment Organizations to Cybersecurity Issues

Investment organizations have numerous potential exposures to shortcomings in cybersecurity. Firms can be subjected to ransomware attacks in which malware attacks the firm's information system and potentially shuts down its capabilities unless the firm meets the demands of the attacking party. Also, firms are exposed to loss of proprietary and other confidential information as briefly noted below.[2]

- Proprietary investment methods: Includes algorithms, models, analytics, and research.
- Confidential information on individuals and organizations: Includes personal information of employees, clients, and third parties.
- Confidential information on investments: Includes trade data, performance data, position data, and information on managers including due diligence files.
- Confidential information on sales and distribution: Includes identification of prospective clients, prospective clients' confidential information, and sales methods.
- Confidential information on business management: Includes business plans, information relative to litigation, the organization's accounting data and forecasts.

20.8.2   Achieving a State of Preparedness Regarding Cybersecurity

The SEC's National Exam Program Risk Alert seeks "to better understand how firms managed their cybersecurity preparedness by focusing on the following areas: (1) governance and risk assessment; (2) access rights and controls; (3) data loss prevention; (4) vendor management; (5) training; and (6) incident response."[3] The Program provides key insights regarding cybersecurity observed in SEC examinations. The next three subsections summarize key findings.

20.8.3   Evidence on Regularity with Which Cybersecurity Functions Were Observed

The SEC indicated the regularity of these four cybersecurity functions:

- Periodic risk assessments of critical systems: These assessments were conducted by the vast majority of advisers to "identify cybersecurity threats, vulnerabilities, and the potential business consequences of a cyber incident."
- Penetration tests and vulnerability scans: These tests and scans were conducted by almost half of the advisers.
- Had a process in place for ensuring regular system maintenance: These processes were in place for nearly all advisers "ensuring regular system maintenance, including the installation of software patches to address security vulnerabilities."
- Maintained cybersecurity organizational charts: A large majority of advisers "maintained cybersecurity organizational charts and/or identified and described cybersecurity roles and responsibilities for the firms' workforce."

20.8.4 Evidence on Areas Requiring Improved Policies

The SEC examinations of firm practices indicated issues that "the staff believes firms would benefit from considering in order to assess and improve their policies, procedures, and practices." Key examples of these issues include the following:

- Policies and procedures were not reasonably tailored: The policies and procedures were too general or were vague, as they did not articulate narrowly defined procedures for implementing the policies.
- Firm adherence was lax: "Firms did not appear to adhere to or enforce policies and procedures, or the policies and procedures did not reflect the firms' actual practices."
- Inadequate system maintenance: Examples included "Using outdated operating systems that were no longer supported by security patches" and "High-risk findings from penetration tests or vulnerability scans that did not appear to be fully remediated in a timely manner."

20.8.5 Evidence on Robust Policies and Procedures Worth Emulating

The SEC staff observed policies and procedures that they believed other firms may wish to consider, including the following key elements that are described here as policies and procedures that firms should implement:

- Maintenance of an inventory of data, information, and vendors: Policies and procedures should include a complete inventory of data and information, along with classifications of the risks, vulnerabilities, data, business consequences, and information regarding each service provider and vendor, if applicable.[4]
- Detailed cybersecurity-related instructions: Examples for which detailed instructions were encouraged include penetration tests, security monitoring and system auditing, access rights, and reporting.[5]
- Maintenance of prescriptive schedules and processes for testing data integrity and vulnerabilities: Examples cited for maintenance included vulnerability scans, patch management policies, an analysis of the problem the patch was designed to fix, the potential risk in applying the patch, and the method to use in applying the patch.[6]
- Established and enforced controls to access data and systems: For example, firms should: implement detailed "acceptable use" policies, require and enforce restrictions and controls for mobile devices that connected to the firms' systems, require third-party vendors to periodically provide logs of their activity on the firms' networks and require immediate termination of access for terminated employees and very prompt termination of access for employees that left voluntarily.[7]
- Mandatory employee training: Information security training should be mandatory for all employees at on-boarding and periodically thereafter to ensure that all employees completed the mandatory training.[8]
- Engaged senior management: Policies and procedures should be vetted and approved by senior management.[9]

20.8.6 Cybersecurity and EU Regulation

"The Directive on Security of Network and Information Systems (NIS)" was the first European Union-wide legislation on cybersecurity. The NIS came into force in August 2016 with countries having until May 2018 to implement the Directive. The objective of the NIS is to raise the overall level of security of network and information systems across the EU through:

- improved cybersecurity capabilities at the national level;
- increased EU-level cooperation;
- risk management and incident reporting obligations for operators of essential services and digital service providers.[10]

The Directive requires operators of essential services, including both banking and financial market infrastructures (e.g., trading venues, central counterparties), to take appropriate and proportionate technical and organizational measures to detect and manage the risks posed to networks and information systems. Also the Directive requires operators of essential services to notify, without undue delay, the competent authority of incidents that have a significant impact on continuity of the core services provided. Measures that entities should do to comply with the initiative include, but are not limited to:

- identifying critical systems and those containing confidential and sensitive data;
- performing penetration testing and cybersecurity risk assessments;
- training and awareness initiatives of all employees;
- establishing an incident response plan.

Even if entities are not within the scope of the NIS, many counterparties will expect compliance as best practice.

20.8.7 Cybersecurity and Asian Regulation

There is no overarching legal framework for cybersecurity in Asia, and therefore it is up to each country to enact legislation.

Hong Kong requires entities regulated by the Hong Kong Monetary Authority (HKMA) and Securities and Futures Commission (SFC) to comply with regulatory guidance (e.g., various guidelines and circulars) concerning cyber risk management. Japan has enacted the Basic Act of Cybersecurity, the Act on the Protection of Personal Information, and the Act on the Prohibition of Unauthorized Computer Access.

The Singapore government ranks cybersecurity threats high on its agenda and has established a Cyber Security Agency of Singapore (CSA). In 2018, Singapore adopted the Cybersecurity Act which focuses on ensuring that the country is prepared and can respond effectively and promptly when a cyberattack occurs.

20.9   RISK MANAGEMENT STRUCTURE AND PROCESS

A **risk manager** is a duly qualified professional with trading and investment enforcement authority to be able to review, analyze, and understand the information derived from the risk measurement process to take action, as appropriate, to ensure risk exposures within the portfolio are as intended and in compliance with the investment mandates associated with each investment and the portfolio as a whole. Historically, such a professional with this level of trading authority would be presented as a professional separate and apart from portfolio management and, therefore, dispassionate about portfolio positioning.

20.9.1 Three Models of Risk Management Structure

The structuring of the role of risk manager is a crucial decision. A risk manager without authority might only function as a measurer of risk. If the role of risk manager is assigned to a person of authority without the necessary time and interest, then the responsibilities of risk manager role will not be executed carefully and comprehensively.

Three models of such separate, dispassionate risk management structures have evolved: (1) the Chief Executive Officer or President of the firm as the Risk Manager; (2) the Chief Operating Officer or the Chief Financial Officer of the firm as the Risk Manager; and (3) the Chief Investment Officer of the firm as the Risk Manager.

The first two, the CEO/President and the COO/CFO serving as the risk manager are effectively similar and may merely reflect the size of the firm. Allocators with smaller levels of assets under management and fewer resources may empower the CEO/President to serve as risk manager. As assets under management increase and the firm's business or other activities grow, the COO/CFO may serve as risk manager as their levels of expertise and daily focus may be more appropriate to the role of risk manager.

The Chief Investment Officer as the Risk Manager is a more recent evolution of the risk management role. One drawback of the risk management function being completely separate from the investment professionals may be an incomplete understanding of the risks associated with an investment, such investment's role within the portfolio, and any nuances that may be associated with the proper interpretation of the various risk measures included in the risk reports. In addition, risk management decisions may not receive adequate prioritization when viewed in competition with activities associated with running the firm. Therefore, in some instances and if well resourced, the CIO has assumed the risk management role, and this has been particularly effective in those cases in which the CIO is not also serving as a portfolio manager. Clearly there is a danger to having a risk manager that also serves as CIO and portfolio manager. The risk manager may end up being the only person with authority that understands and monitors investing.

20.9.2 The Investment Process as Primarily a Risk Process

An institutional investment process may be simply described as a linear process starting with idea generation, flowing through various due diligence processes, internal investment committee approvals, formal presentation and board level approvals, if required, to portfolio construction, initial investment, and ongoing monitoring activities. The process is linear because each step along the flow of the process is looking for reasons to reject an investment, and subsequent steps do not ensue if an investment opportunity is rejected or otherwise fails an earlier step in the process. Therefore and arguably, the due diligence process is, with a particular focus on reasons to reject an investment, focused upon the various risks associated with the potential investment or manager.

Risk identification, measurement, and management permeates the entire investment process, at each level, and is aggregated from the bottom up. In fact, the focus of portfolio management is primarily on managing exposures to risks—risks for which the portfolio manager is expecting, and hoping to receive, excess returns. Therefore, if the investment process is not primarily a risk process, it is certainly a close second.

20.9.3 The Evolution of Risk Reporting

Since the early 1980s, the development of processes and systems have evolved rapidly and with increasing levels of sophistication. The ability to stay connected without connections (the use of wireless) continues to expand and increase speeds and flexibilities with regard to configurations and data transfer. There is every expectation that such advances will continue unabated for the foreseeable future. With all these changes, one thing that has not changed is that the key reason for the use of processes and systems is to provide information to support decision-makers as they endeavor to make the best decisions possible. Similarly, all data collected at each level and frequency of the risk measurement process is intended to support the decisions that need to be made by risk management professionals.

The final step in the risk management process is to present the acquired data and the derived position and risk information in a reporting format that is meaningful and helpful to the end user. Typically, all risk reports may initially be received by a risk analyst for review and escalation, if warranted. Risk reports should be designed to highlight key metrics and areas of concern automatically, and then direct further action, if warranted. The creation of daily dashboards greatly enhances risk monitoring and conditional formatting helps direct attention to measures requiring more immediate attention. The format of daily dashboards and monthly and quarterly reports are subject to individual preference, but should include the measures discussed herein or more, as appropriate to the measurement time period and the specifics of the investments within the portfolio.

NOTES

1. Reuters.com, 5/17/2016. See https://www.reuters.com/article/us-finance-summit-sec/sec-says-cyber-security-biggest-risk-to-financial-system-idUSKCN0Y82K4 (accessed July 2019).
2. Loosely based on https://www.accenture.com/_acnmedia/PDF-49/Accenture-InsideOps-Cybersecurity-Asset-Management.pdf (accessed July 2019).
3. See SEC's National Exam Program Risk Alert issued by the Office of Compliance Inspections and Examinations ("OCIE")1 Volume VI, Issue 5 August 7, 2017. See https://www.sec.gov/files/observations-from-cybersecurity-examinations.pdf (accessed July 2019).
4. Further information is available from the SEC: https://www.sec.gov/files/observations-from-cybersecurity-examinations.pdf (accessed July 2019).

5. Ibid.
6. Ibid.
7. Ibid.
8. Ibid.
9. Ibid.
10. Questions and Answers: Directive on Security of Network and Information systems, the first EU-wide legislation on cybersecurity; Europa.eu/rapid/press-release_MEMO-18-3651_en.pdf May 4, 2018.

Methods for
Alternative Investing

Part 5 details a number of alternative investment methods. Chapter 21 discusses the binomial tree method for valuation and hedging. Chapter 22 discusses directional investment strategies in which investors alter risk exposures in an attempt to time market movements based on the methods of technical analysis. Chapter 23 reviews multivariate empirical methods such as multiple regression. Chapter 24 discusses relative value strategies with a focus on the methods of fundamental analysis. Finally, Chapter 25 details the tax consequences of depreciation methods and transaction-based index construction methods for real assets such as real estate.

CHAPTER 21

Valuation and Hedging Using Binomial Trees

Chapter 5 of the Level 1 CAIA curriculum introduces recombining binomial stock price trees and its use in valuing options and Chapter 6 of this book discusses binomial trees of interest rates. This chapter begins with risk-neutral binomial trees and a discussion of P-measures and Q-measures.

21.1 A ONE-PERIOD BINOMIAL TREE AND RISK-NEUTRAL MODELING

A one-period binomial tree of short-term zero-coupon corporate bonds provides an excellent foundation through which to understand two key concepts in financial modeling: P-measures and Q-measures, and the role of risk-neutrality in valuation models.

21.1.1 A One-Period Model of Default Risk with Risk-Neutrality

Consider a one-period zero-coupon bond with a face value of $1 and with three major assumptions for simplicity: (1) interest rates are 0%; (2) investors are assumed to be risk-neutral so that all risk premiums are set to 0%; and (3) if default occurs there is zero recovery.

Given the above assumptions, there is a simple relation between the probability of default and the price of the bond. Specifically, the price of the bond equals the probability of nondefault. Exhibit 21.1 depicts the bond using a binomial tree. V_0 denotes the value of the bond at time zero and p denotes the probability of (total) default.

Exhibit 21.1 can be used to calculate the bond's value given a probability of default or infer the bond's probability of default from an observed bond price. For example, a bond price of $0.90 infers a probability of default of 10%. Thus, the up-path from Period 0 to Period 1 would be deemed to occur with a probability of 90%.

Alternatively, an assumption or conclusion that the actual probability of default is 15% would be consistent with the bond value being $0.85. Given the assumption that risk premiums are zero, Exhibit 21.1 is consistent with a world of risk-neutrality (a world in which risk-neutral investors drive relations between market prices).

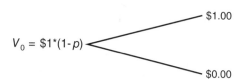

$V_0 = \$1^*(1-p)$

$\$1.00$

$\$0.00$

EXHIBIT 21.1 A One-Period Zero-Coupon Defaultable Bond with No Recovery

21.1.2 A One-Period Model With A Risk Premium For Default

This section returns to the example in Exhibit 21.1 but relaxes the assumption that the risk premium for bearing default risk has to be zero. In a world in which investors base their required returns on risk, the simple model of the previous section develops an interesting complexity: it is not possible to identify the extent to which the zero-coupon bond's discount is caused by a required risk premium or by its default probability.

This section delves into the above complexity—and in doing so addresses an extremely important issue in financial valuation. Consider a 1-year default-free bond with a yield of 5% and a 1-year defaultable bond with a yield of 7%. Note that the 2% credit spread has two potential sources: default likelihood and risk-aversion. In other words, one possibility is that the bond has a 2% probability of default and offers no risk premium (because the bond's risk is diversifiable). Another possibility is that the bond has a 1% probability of default and a 1% risk premium. It's even possible that the bond has a negative beta (and a negative risk premium) and that its probability of default is higher than 2%. This section introduces a foundation for understanding risk-neutral modeling in advance of their application later in the chapter to convertible and callable bonds.

For simplicity, this example assumes riskless interest rates are zero, but now explicitly models a continuous annual rate of default as δ (e.g., $\delta = 2\%$ indicates a 2% probability of default each year). Equation 21.1 provides a simplified valuation model for the one-period, zero-coupon, $1 face value defaultable bond of the previous section using continuous compounding.

$$V_0 = \$1e^{-(\delta+\pi)} \tag{21.1}$$

where: δ is the continuous annual rate of default and π is the continuously compounded risk premium. Taking the natural logarithm of both sides expresses a relation between δ and π for a particular bond that is depicted in Exhibit 21.2.

Exhibit 21.2 indicates that there are an infinite number of possible combinations of the probability of default and the associated risk premium (both of which are unobservable) that are consistent with an observed bond price (and its observable yield). As is discussed below, the ideal combination from the perspective of financial modeling is to use the intersection with the horizontal axis (i.e., risk-neutrality) in Exhibit 21.2.

The next section discusses these concepts using the terms P-measures and Q-measures.

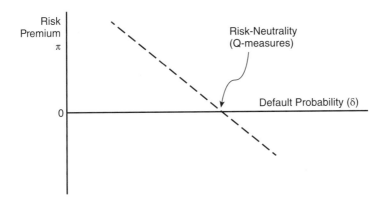

EXHIBIT 21.2 The Set of Risk Premiums and Probabilities

21.1.3 P-measures, Q-measures, and the Power of Risk-Neutral Modeling

Exhibit 21.2 illustrates the important point that risk premiums are generally not readily observable from market data because risk premiums depend (in the case of the defaultable bond) on the exact level of default risk (which is unobservable). Simply put, analysts cannot be sure whether a discounted price for a risky asset is due to its (unobservable) degree of risk, or the (unobservable) extent to which investors require a risk premium.

Exhibit 21.2 illustrates a key concept: there is one point on the dashed line (i.e., the line denoting the infinite combinations of risk-premiums and default probabilities) that is definitive: the point where the risk premium is zero due to risk neutrality. When an analyst assumes risk neutrality (knowing that it likely is unrealistic) and infers probabilities and other values from that assumption, the resulting values are known as Q-measures. Therefore, a Q-measure is a probability-like value or other related variable within a model derived for modeling purposes under the assumption that risk-neutrality holds when it is likely that the world is not risk-neutral.

On the other hand, in a world with risk premiums, the expected returns and values of asset will be determined in part by actual statistical probabilities, such as the probability of a bond defaulting and the probabilities of various recovery amounts given default. A P-measure is a statistical probability (or an estimate of that probability) that represents the likelihood of an outcome in the real world.

For example, consider the Black–Scholes Option Pricing model. The likelihood of the option being exercised can be derived from the model assuming risk-neutrality and that the expected return of the option and the stock equal the riskless rate. In that case, the result would be a quasi-probability or a Q-measure. If the stock's expected return is estimated based on the real world of risk aversion, the model can be used to infer an actual probability that the option will be exercised. In that case, the result would be a statistical probability or a P-measure.

21.1.4 Four Key Concepts of Risk-Neutral Modeling

1. There is often an infinite number of sets of values (P-measures such as probabilities, risk premiums, risk levels, recovery rates) that are consistent with a particular value for a financial derivative.

2. Expected risk premiums in a risk-averse world are generally unobservable. However, risk premiums are zero in a risk-neutral world. Therefore, there is one set of values (Q-measures) that has inputs that are readily observable and easy to apply.

3. In the case of many financial derivatives, the derivative's value obtained from Q-measures is identical to the no-arbitrage values that must exist in a risk-averse world using P-measures.

4. Since Q-measures are tractable, they are used in risk-neutral modeling under those conditions in which actual derivative prices must match risk-neutral model prices.

21.2   MULTI-PERIOD BINOMIAL TREES, VALUES, AND MEAN RATES

Binomial trees can be based on prices or rates. This section discusses a problem with using average rates of return in a tree model.

21.2.1   A Trinomial Tree Model Based on Prices

Consider the single-period trinomial model depicted in Exhibit 21.3. The model depicts three outcomes from a $1.00 asset with three associated probabilities. For simplicity, this section assumes that all interest rates are zero and that all risk premiums are zero.

The averaged dollar values of the three outcomes ($1.21, $0.99, and $0.81) weighted by the associated probabilities (25%, 50%, and 25%, respectively) is $1.00. This result is consistent with a net present value (NPV) of $0 because of the zero interest rate and zero risk premium assumptions. Note further that the total returns average 0% based on three return levels (+21%, −1%, and −19%) and the same three probabilities. It is clear from Exhibit 21.3 that the $1 current value of the asset is consistent with the model's assumptions (risk-neutrality and zero interest rates) based on the asset's expected value of $1.00 and return of 0%. The next section uses the same example but introduces multi-period compounding of rates.

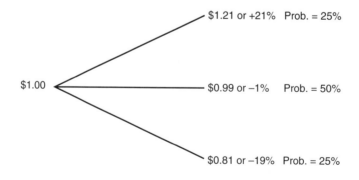

Expected Value = $1.00 and Expected Return = 0%

EXHIBIT 21.3   A One-Period Trinomial Model

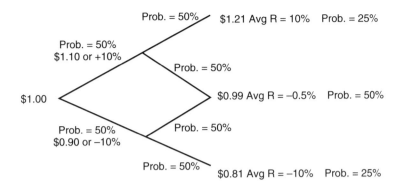

Expected Value = $1.00 and Average Return < 0%

EXHIBIT 21.4 A Two-Period Binomial Model

21.2.2 Two-Period Binomial Tree Model with Compounded Returns

Consider a two-period binomial tree that assumes a 50% probability from each node of either a 10% increase or a 10% decrease in the asset's value. Exhibit 21.4 depicts a two-period recombining binomial tree with the same ending values as Exhibit 21.3.

Note that Exhibits 21.3 and 21.4 generate the same ending values for the asset of $0.81, $0.99, and $1.21 with the same associated probabilities (25%, 50%, and 25%, respectively) and hence the same expected value of $1 and NPV = $0 when viewed using dollars.

However, using rates the two trees appear to be inconsistent. Exhibit 21.3 uses single period returns and reports three single period rates of −19%, −1%, and +21%. Exhibit 21.4 lists three mean or average rates (over two periods) of −10%, −0.5%, and +10%. Note, the average rate for the middle node is more precisely −.50126%, a fact that is of no consequence to this discussion.

In Exhibit 21.4, the outcomes of the three paths are expressed both in dollars and as average rates of return on the right side. When viewed as expected average rates of return, the asset appears to be overvalued (because the three rates, −10%, −0.5%, and +10%, average out to less than zero). But when viewed as dollars (the same as in Exhibit 21.3) the values average out to zero and therefore the asset is appropriately valued given that this example is in a risk-neutral world of zero interest rates.

How can Exhibit 21.4 show an expected negative return when the rates in Exhibit 21.3 (and the dollars in both exhibits) indicate an expected zero return and an expected zero profit? The answer is that average rates of compounded returns (e.g., realized geometric mean returns) can be deceiving.

The difficulty with expected compounded rates can be vividly illustrated by an asset offering a 50% probability of a +100% continuously compounded return and a 50% probability of a −100% continuously compounded return. Note that over a 1-year horizon a $100 initial investment would have a 50% probability of growing to $272 (the +100% continuously compounded return) and a 50% probability of declining to $37 (the −100% continuously compounded return) for an expected value of $154.31. The dollar values are computed with the formula $100e^r$.

The averaged dollar values indicate an increase of 54.31% over its current value and represent an accurate depiction of the attractiveness of the two potential outcomes. Yet its expected geometric mean return (based on continuous compounding) would be 0%. The point is that care must be used in analyzing expected average returns based on compounding.

21.2.3 Three Fallacies Generated by Averaging Compounded Rates of Return

This section uses tree models to illustrate three cases in which it is falsely claimed that strategies can be derived that have NPVs different from zero even when every asset underlying the strategy is efficiently priced (i.e., each underlying asset has NPV = 0). While trading costs and inefficiently priced assets (e.g., assets that exhibit mean-reversion of returns) can cause some strategies to have nonzero NPVs, in a well-functioning market an NPV>0 strategy cannot be formed from underlying assets that are all NPV = 0.

LEVERAGED EXCHANGE TRADED FUNDS (ETFs): It is sometimes contended that leveraged ETFs incur wealth-destroying performance when volatility occurs even in an efficient market. Consider Exhibit 21.5 which repeats the tree in Exhibit 21.4 except that u is raised from 1.1 to 1.2 and d is lowered from 0.9 to 0.8 (i.e., the single period rate of return is doubled from ±10% to ±20%). The result is that the average compounded returns become more negative due to the greater dispersion. However, the expected wealth remains constant at $1.00 (which is perfectly acceptable in the assumed risk-neutral world with 0% interest rates). In the real world, the leveraged ETF would offer twice the risk premium if it offered twice the leverage and volatility (using noncompounded values). The point is that the expected compounded rates of return falsely indicate that levered ETFs destroy wealth, as proved by the expected average return of −1% from possible returns of +20%, −2% and −20%, with probabilities of 25%, 50%, and 25%, respectively. However, the expected dollar values prove that no wealth has been destroyed by leverage—on average.

INVERSE ETFs: It is contended that inverse ETFs incur wealth-destroying performance through time. However, an inverse ETF rebalanced every period would be identical to a direct ETF as shown in Exhibit 21.4 except that the +10% and −10% returns would switch places. Exhibit 21.5 demonstrates the same idea with +20% and −20% rates. The trees are mirror images. For simplicity, view the interest rates and risk premiums as equaling zero.

DIVERSIFICATION RETURN: It is contended that rebalancing of a portfolio creates higher performance due to better diversification. However, rebalancing assets towards a lower expected volatility does not create wealth if the underlying assets are efficiently priced. Analyses that indicate otherwise are based on the use of expected compounded rates of return. Rebalancing of portfolios cannot generate positive NPVs when the underlying assets are, by assumption, efficiently priced and offer NPV = 0 for any sequence of trading. Diversification return is discussed further in Chapter 19.

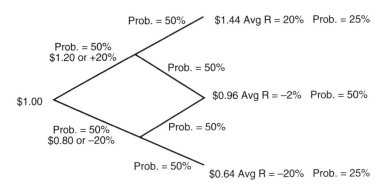

Prob. = 50% $1.44 Avg R = 20%   Prob. = 25%

Prob. = 50%
$1.20 or +20%

Prob. = 50%

$1.00

$0.96 Avg R = –2%   Prob. = 50%

Prob. = 50%
$0.80 or –20%

Prob. = 50%

Prob. = 50%
$0.64 Avg R = –20%   Prob. = 25%

EXHIBIT 21.5   Expected Value = $1.00 and Average Return <0%

Other examples of fallacies exist such as dollar-cost-averaging in which equal dollar purchases of a stock through time supposedly create positive NPVs. Dollar-cost-averaging will appear attractive in two scenarios: when the data or model contain mean-reversion or when the results are interpreted through the distorted lens of average compounded rates of return.

In summary, in a perfectly efficient market with no transaction frictions, it is not possible to devise a strategy comprised of market-traded assets that offers a nonzero net present value. If a strategy offered a nonzero NPV, arbitrageurs could establish a long position in the strategy (if its NPV>0) or a short position (if NPV<0) and hedge out any undesirable risks. Nevertheless, much is written about levered and inverse ETFs being negative NPV investments. Such claims may be valid if based on reasons such as inefficiencies in the pricing of the strategy's underlying assets, such as mean-reversion, or frictions, such as NPV<0 margin rates.

21.3   VALUATION OF CONVERTIBLE SECURITIES WITH A BINOMIAL TREE MODEL

Level I of the CAIA program detailed convertible bond valuation and convertible arbitrage trading strategies. At the heart of convertible bond arbitrage strategies is the method by which the arbitrageur decides which convertible bonds are overpriced and which are underpriced. This section describes a method of evaluating the prices of securities that contain options. It is in cases of options and other complexities where alternative investment strategies can be developed to identify arbitrage opportunities.

Investment managers use tree valuation models in practice to study complex options because tree models can deal with a wide range of contractual specifications while remaining relatively simple. This section demonstrates the flexibility of tree models in valuing convertible bonds.

21.3.1   Forming a Tree of Stock Prices

As detailed in Chapter 5 of the CAIA Level I curriculum, the evolution of equity prices through time are often modeled using a recombining binomial tree as shown in Exhibit 21.6. Binomial tree models of equity prices can be used to value derivatives

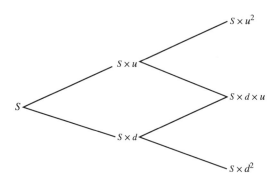

EXHIBIT 21.6 Possible Stock Price Movement (Two Periods)

on equities. Here, the procedure for calculating derivative values using the binomial tree approach is briefly discussed.

The potential prices of the underlying asset are projected with u and d as illustrated in Exhibit 21.6. That is, over the next period, the stock price can either go up by a multiplicative factor u or go down by a multiplicative factor d, where $u > d$. The parameters u and d are proportional to the volatility of the underlying asset and must be specified. As suggested by Cox, Ross, and Rubinstein (1979), commonly known as CRR, set u equal to the value in Equation 21.2:

$$u = e^{\sigma\sqrt{\Delta t}} \tag{21.2}$$

where Δt is the length of one period in the tree, σ is the volatility of the stock returns, and $d = 1/u$. This ensures that the resulting expected volatility of percentage changes in the stock price is σ.

APPLICATION 21.3.1A

Given that $\sigma = 0.20$ for $\Delta t = 1$ and r (i.e., one plus the riskless interest rate) is 1.10, compute the values of u and d based on a Cox, Ross, and Rubenstein (CRR) tree model.

The value of u is found using Equation 21.2.

$$u = e^{\sigma\sqrt{\Delta t}} = e^{0.20} = 1.2214$$

The value of d can be found as $1/u = 1/1.2214 = 0.81873$.

Note that r was extraneous to the computation of u and d.

Clearly, to prevent arbitrage, the rate of growth of the riskless asset must lie between the lower and upper movements of the risky asset (even though there is no risk premium): $d < r < u$.

Note that each value of S in a tree such as that in Exhibit 21.6 can be denoted with subscripts such that $S \times u = S_u, S \times u \times u = S_{uu}, S \times u \times u \times d = S_{uud}$, and so forth.

While the tree may be viewed as being projected from the left to the right based on u and d, insight can be gained by viewing each value of S as being equal to the following expression based on the two values of S in the next period, as shown in the following two equations:

$$S = [p \times S_u + (1-p) \times S_d]/r$$
$$S = [p \times S \times u + (1-p) \times S \times d]/r$$

where p is the risk-neutral probability of the up movement (u), and r is 1 plus the riskless rate.

The previous equation can be factored (starting with multiplication of each side by $1/S$) to obtain Equation 21.3:

$$p = \frac{r-d}{u-d} \tag{21.3}$$

Equation 21.3 can be used with u, d, and r to solve for the risk-neutral probability (Q-measure), p. For example, suppose $r = 1.05$, $u = 1.10$, and $d = 1/u$. The risk-neutral probability of an up movement is 0.738 and the probability of a down movement is 0.262 based on Equation 21.3.

APPLICATION 21.3.1B

Consider a CRR risk-neutral binomial tree. Suppose $r = 1.05$ and $u = 1.25$. Find d and p.

Because $d = 1/u$, $d = 1/1.25 = 0.80$. The risk-neutral probability of an up movement, p, is found using Equation 21.3 as:

$$p = \frac{r-d}{u-d}$$

which is $(1.05-0.80)/(1.25-0.80) = 0.556$. Therefore, the probability of a down movement is 0.444.

To summarize, a CRR tree can be viewed as being built around σ, which drives the spreads between the nodes of the tree, and r which drives the average level of the nodes. The sequence of computations is quite simple as summarized in Exhibit 21.7. The next section details the valuation process of a very simple one-period derivative. Later sections utilize the same five steps in a demonstration of valuing a convertible bond.

EXHIBIT 21.7   The Five Steps of Valuing a Derivative with a CRR Tree Model

(1)	The value for the volatility of the underlying equity's return, σ, can be used to specify u by the equation $u = e^{\sigma \sqrt{\Delta t}}$
(2)	d is then determined as $1/u$
(3)	The riskless rate, r, can be used (along with u and d) to find p (the up probability) as $(r - d)/(u - d)$
(4)	The prospective values of S at each node are used to find the payoffs of derivative contracts on S
(5)	The binomial tree of derivative payoffs (along with the values of r and p) is then used to recursively find the current value of the derivative backward from its expiration date to time 0

21.3.2   The Tree of Prices for a Call Option on an Equity

The first step in calculating an arbitrage-free current value for a derivative security (based on a tree of prices for the derivative's underlying asset) is to calculate the payoff of the derivative at each node corresponding to the expiration date or delivery date of the derivative based on the tree of prices for the underlying asset. Suppose there is a one-period call option on the stock (with current price S) that is depicted in Exhibit 21.6. As a result, the payoff from this call option will be $\max[(S \times u) - K, 0]$ in the top node (S_u) and $\max[(S \times d) - K, 0]$ in the bottom node (S_d), where K is the strike price of the call option.

The process of backward induction uses Equation 21.4 for each node prior to the derivative's expiration:

$$f = [p \times f_u + (1 - p) \times f_d]/r \tag{21.4}$$

where f is the value of the derivative at a node from which f_u is the value of f one period upward and f_d is the value of f one period downward. **Backward induction** is the recursive process of starting with the potential values of an asset in a final time period and working backwards through time finding the values in each previous period until the value at time 0 (i.e., the current value) is found.

Using $r = 1.05$, $u = 1.1$, and $d = 1/u$ the risk-neutral probability of an up movement, p, is 0.738 and a down movement to be 0.262. First confirm that the tree correctly values the stock:

$$S = [p \times S \times u + (1 - p) \times S \times d]/r$$

$$S = [(0.738*100*1.1) + (0.262*100*0.9091)]/1.05 = \$100$$

$$Su = \$110.00$$

$$Sd = \$90.91$$

Next, value the call option. If the initial stock price is $100 and the call option's strike price is $100, the up payoff is $10 and the down payoff is zero. Using the same approach as above (except inputting the option payoffs rather than the future values of the stock), the current value of the call option (c) is:

$$c = [(0.738*10) + (0.262*0)]/1.05 = \$7.0286.$$

APPLICATION 21.3.2

Consider a CRR risk-neutral binomial tree. Suppose $r = 1.05$ and $u = 1.25$. Find d and p. Then use the values to find the value of a one-period put option (with a strike price of $55) on a stock with a current price of $50.

Because $d = 1/u$, $d = 1/1.25 = 0.80$. The risk-neutral probability of an up movement, p, is found using Equation 21.3 as $p = \frac{r-d}{u-d}$ which is $(1.05 - 0.80)/(1.25 - 0.80) = 0.556$. Therefore, the probability of a down movement is 0.444. The up and down single-period stock values are:

$$S_u = S \times u = \$50 * 1.25 = \$62.50$$
$$S_d = S \times d = \$50 * 0.80 = \$40.00$$

Inputting the put option payoff ($15.00 in the down state), the current value of the put option (*put*) is:

$$put = [[0.556 * \$0 * 1.1] + [0.444 * \$15.00]]/1.05 = \$6.34.$$

21.3.3 The Tree of Prices for the Bond's Underlying Stock

Having discussed the basic approach to the valuation of derivative securities using the binomial approach, consider a multi-period convertible bond that can be exercised prior to its maturity.

Consider the convertible bond of XYZ corporation with a $1,000 principal or face value and 5 years to maturity that offers a coupon of 2% per year (paid annually) and is convertible into 8.00 shares of XYZ stock (i.e., has a conversion price of $125 per share). The underlying stock's volatility is estimated to be 30% per year and is currently trading at $100 per share. The bond is assumed to be able to be converted into common stock at the end of each of its 5 years to maturity. The riskless rate is assumed to be 4%, so $r = 1.04$.

To value the convertible bond, the number of time periods in the tree of underlying stock prices is set equal to the time-to-maturity of the convertible bond (5 years). For the sake of simplicity, the tree is made of $N = 5$ periods of $t = 1$ year, which reflects that the convertible bond pays its coupon annually.

The valuation process follows the five steps of Exhibit 21.7. A key input into the valuation of the convertible bond is the selection of the volatility of the returns of the underlying stock (σ). Based perhaps on historic volatility or, if options are traded on the stock, the implied volatility from the options, the stock's return volatility is assumed to be 0.30. Therefore, the size of the up move is $u = e^{(0.30)} = 1.3499$, which means that the down move is $d = 1/u = 0.7408$. The resulting stock price tree is given in Exhibit 21.8.

For example, the value of S_u in Exhibit 21.8 is found as 100.00×1.3499, with u and d used to generate the rest of the tree from the initial price of 100.00.

EXHIBIT 21.8   Binomial Tree for the Stock Price

$t = 0$	$t = 1Y$	$t = 2Y$	$t = 3Y$	$t = 4Y$	$t = 5Y$
					448.17
				332.01	
			245.96		245.96
		182.21		182.21	
	134.99		134.99		134.99
100.00		100.00		100.00	
	74.08		74.08		74.08
		54.88		54.88	
			40.66		40.66
				30.12	
					22.31

21.3.4   The Tree of Prices for the Convertible Bond's Underlying Stock

The next step is to determine the value of the stock into which the bond may be converted because that is a minimum price for the bond at each node (otherwise arbitrageurs would buy the bond and instantly convert it). The convertible bond's associated parity tree can be easily constructed, as shown in Exhibit 21.9 by multiplying each potential stock price (Exhibit 21.8) times the conversion ratio 8.00.

A minimum value of the convertible bond is given by the stock price times the conversion ratio at each node in Exhibit 21.9's tree. For example, the conversion value of the bond in the first node is $800 found as (8.00 × $100). In the final time period, when the option is expiring, the value of the bond will be the greater of its face value (plus coupon for a total of $1,020) or its parity value (conversion ratio times stock price).

For instance, in the uppermost node of the last period in Exhibit 21.9, the conversion value of the bond (8.00 × $448.17) is $3,585.36. Clearly, the bond's conversion value greatly exceeds its bond value ($1,020) in that state and therefore the bond would be converted rather than held for its principal and coupon.

EXHIBIT 21.9   Binomial Tree for Convertible Bond's Parity

$t = 0$	$t = 1Y$	$t = 2Y$	$t = 3Y$	$t = 4Y$	$t = 5Y$
					3585.36
				2656.08	
			1967.68		1967.68
		1457.68		1457.68	
	1079.92		1079.92		1079.92
800.00		800.00		800.00	
	592.64		592.64		592.64
		439.04		439.04	
			325.28		325.28
				240.96	
					178.48

Each node in the convertible bond's fifth and final time period can be valued as the greater of its promised payoff ($1,020) and its conversion value (which ranges from $178.48 to $3,585.36). For every final node with a conversion value of less than $1,020, the bond should be valued based on its principal and coupon. Here it is assumed that the bond will not default, although in practice an analyst may determine that the payoff (recovery) will be less than $1,020 in some of the nodes in which the stock prices are very low.

In summary, for the bottom three end nodes, no conversion should occur. Therefore, at time $t = 5$, there is a 100% probability of converting for the top three nodes, and a 0% probability of converting for the bottom three nodes. So the tree provides the payoff for the convertible bond at each node in the final time period. The next section discusses the key issue of valuing the convertible prior to the final time period.

21.3.5   Valuing the Convertible Bond One Period Prior to Its Maturity

The next step is to estimate the value of the convertible bond in the time period prior to its maturity (i.e., $t = 4$) using the values at maturity that were found in the previous section. This step requires the risk neutral probability of an up movement, p. That pseudo-probability (Q-measure) is found using Equation 21.3, displayed below:

$$p = \frac{r - d}{u - d}$$

Given $r = 1.04$, $u = 1.3499$, and $d = 1/u = 0.7408$, the value of p is 0.4912. The probability of the stock price going down (decreasing), is $(1 - p)$ or 0.5088. The risk-neutral probability for the problem at hand is 0.491 computed as follows:

$$p = (r - d)/(u - d) = (1.04 - 0.7408)/(1.3499 - 0.7408) = 0.491$$

The value of the derivative (i.e., the convertible bond) at each node for $t = 4$, is based on Equation 21.4, displayed again below, which is a simple function of its two potential next-period values (f_u and f_d), probability weighted by p and discounted by r:

$$f = [p \times f_u + (1{-}p) \times f_d]/r$$

Setting aside the issue of early conversion of the bond, the values f_u and f_d for $t = 4$ have three cases: (1) when both values (f_u and f_d) are the conversion-based values for the bond because the bond is worth more by being converted rather than being redeemed for the principal plus coupon ($1,020); (2) when both values are the redemption value of $1,020 rather than the conversion-based values for the bond because the bond is worth less from being converted because the stock price is low; and (3) when the f_u value is based on conversion and the f_d value is $1,020.

In the second case, $f = \$1,020/1.04 = \$980.77$. In the first case the value of f depends on the values on the right side of Exhibit 21.9, such as using $3,585 and $1,968 to find the value for f in the top node of $t = 4$. In the single instance of the third case (when the decision to convert or not convert is undecided), the value of f

depends both on the $1,080 value on the right side of Exhibit 21.9 and the $1,020 redemption value.

APPLICATION 21.3.5

Given that $p = .60$ and that the riskless interest rate is 0.10, compute the values of a derivative, f, given that the derivative's value in the next up state would be $6 and in the next down state would be $5.

The answer can be found using Equation 21.4:

$$f = [p \times f_u + [1 - p] \times f_d]/r$$

$$f = [(0.60 \times \$6) + (0.40 \times \$5)]/1.10 = \$5.091$$

21.3.6 Determining the Current Value of the Convertible Bond

The previous section detailed the process of finding the risk-neutral value for the convertible bond for all $t = 4$ nodes based on the $t = 5$ node values. The remainder of the recursive process involves finding f for each node in the tree from right ($t = 3$) to left ($t = 0$) and is done one period at a time using the process of backward induction demonstrated earlier in this chapter. The process continues to time 0 in which case f is the current value of the bond according to the model.

The process is mechanical and may initially appear to be unnecessary. But the process is easy to implement and allows tremendous flexibility in modeling various options. For example, in the case of a convertible bond, the decision of whether or not to exercise the conversion early can easily be modeled using a tree and can take into account whether or not the bond holder should exercise early or delay exercising in order to collect more coupons.

While the values of simple European options can often be quickly calculated with theoretical option pricing models, tree models are often necessary to model options with the potential for early exercise. Note that if a tree model is used for a simple European option, the resulting value will tend to converge towards the theoretical option value as the number of time steps is increased. So by simply modeling each period as a smaller and smaller length of time, the tree model's value for a derivative will approach the value based on theoretical models such as the Black–Scholes Option Pricing Model.

21.4 VALUING CALLABLE BONDS WITH A TREE MODEL

Callable bonds give the bond issuer the right to redeem the bond by returning a prespecified payment to the investor during the period designated in the terms of the bond. Usually, a callable bond will become callable at a premium. For example, a bond that matures in 2040 might become callable on or after 2030 at a price of

$102 per $100 of the principal amount. In the US, most municipal bonds contain call provisions and many corporate bonds are callable but almost all Treasury bonds and notes are noncallable. Callable bonds can also be found in Europe, Japan, Canada, Australia, Asia-Pacific, and Latin America.

While convertible bonds (discussed in the previous section) focus on an underlying tree of stock prices (into which the bond can be converted), this section discusses callable bonds with a focus on interest rate trees.

21.4.1 A Two-Period Binomial Tree

The call feature is a call option (held by the issuer who can call back the bond by buying it a prespecified price), so callable bonds can be valued using binomial interest rate trees, which depict a set of possible interest rate paths. For example, Exhibit 21.10 shows a two-period binomial interest rate tree.

In the tree, the interest rate for the first period is known today and is represented as $i(0, 0-1)$ in Node A. This is the rate that will prevail between today and the end of the first period. The "0" in $i(0,0-1)$ refers to the time period at which the rate is observed, while the "0-1" in $i(0,0-1)$ refers to the starting time period (before the dash) and the concluding time period (after the dash) over which the interest rate applies. For example, $i(0,1-3)$ would represent the forward rate observed today for the 2-year period between periods 1 and 3.

At the end of the first period the upward path to Node B indicates an upward movement in interest rates observed at time 1 and to be in effect between the first and the second period, or $i(1, U, 1-2)$. The U stands for "up." On the other hand, at the end of the first period the downward move to Node C implies a lower interest rate observed at time 1 to be in effect between the first and the second period. Therefore, the node's rate is $i(1, L, 1-2)$, where L stands for "low."

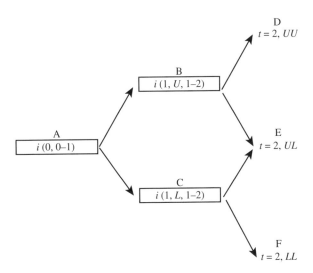

EXHIBIT 21.10 Two-Period Binomial Interest Rate Tree

21.4.2   Modeling the Spread Between Upward and Downward Shifting Rates

Changes in interest rates (for example, moving either from Node A to Node B, or from Node A to Node C) are assumed to be random events. The bond to be valued using the tree in Exhibit 21.10 matures at the end of the second period in either Nodes D, E, and F. The goal is to develop a tree that can provide an accurate value for a callable bond in time 0 using backward induction.

The construction of an interest rate tree requires important choices. The resulting tree should provide bond values that are arbitrage-free and that are consistent with a reasonable evolution of both the level and dispersion of actual interest rates. A well-regarded approach to modeling the interest rate process (the Black, Derman, and Toy (BDT) model detailed in Chapter 6) utilizes the interest rate volatility assumption in Equation 21.5 to capture the dispersion in possible future interest rates. Equation 21.5 depicts the relation between each up rate, $i(1, U, 1$–$2)$, and down rate, $i(1, L, 1$–$2)$, as depending on a single volatility parameter, σ:

$$i(1, U, 1 - 2) = i(1, L, 1 - 2) \times e^{2\sigma} \tag{21.5}$$

where σ is the assumed volatility of the one-period interest rate through time. Equation 21.5 is depicted for period one but is representative of the process at all nodes. As detailed in Chapter 6, the BDT model uses observed forward rates (i.e., the observed term structure) to identify the *levels* of the tree's rates in each time period, while Equation 21.5 dictates the spread between the upward and downward rates.

APPLICATION 21.4.2

Consider a binomial tree of interest rates consistent with the BDT model. Suppose that the 1-year interest rate 1 year from today after experiencing a downward shift (i.e., lower-rate shift) is projected to be 4.04% and that the volatility of the 1-year interest rate is constant at 20%. Calculate the 1-year interest rates between the first year and the second year from an upward shift.

The upward shift generates a 1-year interest rate 1 year from today of 6.03%. Using the 20% volatility of the 1-year interest rate, the upward shift rate as depicted in Equation 21.5 is 6.03%:

$$i(1, U, 1\text{–}2) = 4.04 \times e^{2(0.20)} = 6.03\%.$$

21.4.3   Calculating a Two-Period Straight Bond Price with a Binomial Tree

Suppose a 2-year bond pays an annual coupon of €5 and has a face value of €100. Exhibit 21.11 displays the binomial interest rate tree using the information from Application 21.4.2. Note that the bond values at the end of the second year (when the bond matures) are inserted into the tree for all of the period 2 nodes.

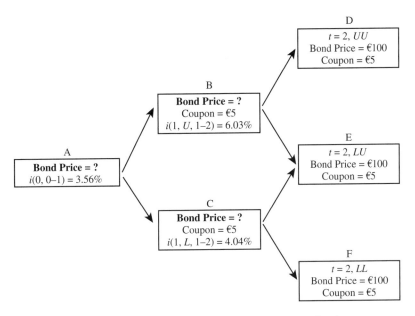

EXHIBIT 21.11   Two-Period Binomial Interest Tree (Example 1)

The next step is to find the value of the bond at Nodes B and C (at the end of the first year). The value of each bond at Nodes B and C is found as the discounted value of the two possible values (from D and E to value the bond at B, and from E and F to value the bond at C). The two values are calculated using different projected interest rates: 6.03% found in Node B to value the bond price at Node B, and 4.04% found in Node C to value the bond price at Node C. Thus, bond prices at Nodes B and C are as follows (note that these formulas assume that the probabilities of an up move and a down move are each 50%).

$$\text{Bond Price (Node B)} = \frac{1}{1+0.0603}[0.5 \times (100+5) + 0.5 \times (100+5)] = 99.029$$

$$\text{Bond Price (Node C)} = \frac{1}{1+0.0404}[0.5 \times (100+5) + 0.5 \times (100+5)] = 100.923$$

Finally, calculate the current value of the bond (at Node A) using the interest rate at Node A and the bond prices (calculated above for Nodes B and C):

$$\text{Bond Price (Node A)} = \frac{1}{1+0.0356}[0.5(99.029+5) + 0.5 \times (100.923+5)]$$

$$= 101.367$$

In a more advanced model, the probabilities would be determined with the assumption of risk-neutrality and the requirement that the 1-year rates all generate the same expected return as a 2-year investment in a 2-year zero coupon bond. The analysis here is being kept simple to focus on a callable bond's optionality as discussed in the next section.

21.4.4   Calculating a Two-Period Callable Bond Price with a Binomial Tree

Callability and other option features can be built into the valuation process of a binomial tree by recognizing the ability of an option owner to exercise the option at one or more nodes. For example, the option of a lender to call a bond issue for $102 can be included in a binomial option analysis by replacing any valuation over $102 with $102 if the bond is callable at that point in time and if it is assumed that the lender will call the bond if its value is in excess of $102.

Consider again the 2-year bond in Exhibit 21.11 that pays an annual coupon of €5 and has a face value of €100. The 1-year interest rate today is 3.56%, and 1-year interest rates between the first year and the second year will be either 6.03% or 4.04%. The volatility of the 1-year interest rate is still assumed to be 20%. Note that the rates between the first and second year are related, as depicted in Equation 21.5, because $i(1, U, 1-2) = 4.04 \times e^{2(0.20)} = 6.03\%$. As throughout these analyses of callable bonds, the upward and downward probabilities are set to 0.5 for simplicity.

Now assume that this bond can be called at €100 in one year. What should the current price be?

In this case, the bond would be called in Node C in year 1 because the market price of the bond at that node (€100.923 as indicated in the previous section for an otherwise identical straight bond) exceeds €100. The respective binomial interest rate tree, assuming the bond is called at $100 in Node C, is depicted in Exhibit 21.12.

Next, note that the ability to call the bond at Node C (replacing its previous value of €100.923 with €100.00) changes the current value of the bond (at Node A) as shown:

$$\text{Bond Price (Node A)} = \frac{1}{1 + 0.0356}[0.5 \times (99.029 + 5) + 0.5 \times (100 + 5)] = 100.921$$

As expected, the current value of the callable bond (€100.921) is now lower than the current value of the noncallable bond (€101.367). The reason is that the bond

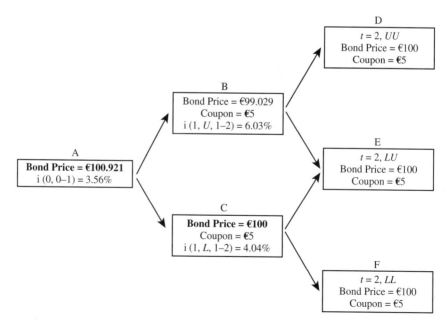

EXHIBIT 21.12   Two-Period Binomial Interest Rate Tree (Example 2)

would be called in 1 year if rates fall (Node C). The difference between the two bond values in the examples is the value of the implicit or embedded call option that the issuer owns to call the bond:

Value of Call Option = Value of Noncallable Bond − Value of Callable Bond

Value of Call Option = €101.367 − €100.921 = €0.446

Note that the reduction in value €0.446 is easy to calculate another way. The callable bond gets called for €100 when it is worth €100.923. This represents a €0.923 loss in value to the holder of the callable bond. The loss has a 50% probability of occurring ($d = 0.500$) and occurs in 1 year so it must be discounted at the 1-year rate of 3.56%:

$$€0.923*0.50/1.0356 = €0.446$$

This €0.446 decreased value of the callable bond relative to the noncallable bond matches the answer found by comparing the NodeA values of the callable and noncallable bonds.

APPLICATION 21.4.4

For simplicity, assume a binomial tree model in which the current price (at Node A) of a noncallable bond is $100. An otherwise identical (but callable) bond is callable in exactly 1 year at a price of $103. Only one of the two nodes at the end of the first period has a value in excess of $103 for the noncallable bond. That value is $107 and is Node C, which represents the effects of one downward shift in rates. Assume that the current 1-year rate is 4%, and that the upward and downward shift probabilities are 50%. What is the value of the callable bond?

The only differences in the tree for the noncallable and callable bonds are in Node C (where the $106 noncallable value drops to the call price of $102), and in Node A, the current value. The formula for Node A is:

$$\text{Bond Value} = (1/1.04)(.50)[(\text{node B Value} + \text{Coupon})$$

$$+ (\text{node C Value} + \text{Coupon})]$$

Note that the above formula factors out 0.5 from the bracketed expression and describes the node values and coupons rather than supplying numbers, because the only number on the right side that is changing is the Node C value from $106 to $102.

The $4 drop in the Node C value (due to a $106 bond being called for $102) has the following effect:

$$\text{Change in Bond Value} = (\$102 - \$106) * (0.5)/1.04 = -\$1.923.$$

The intuition is easy: the callable bond holder relative to the noncallable bond holder has a 50% chance of receiving $4 less in value. The discounted value of the expected $2 loss, discounted at 4% for 1 year, causes the callable bond to have a $1.923 lower value.

In the preceding sections, only the interest rate risk of the bond was considered. Corporate and municipal callable bonds are exposed to credit risk as well. Therefore, the model should account for both interest rate and credit risk. Credit risk of a callable bond may play a role in the issuer's decision to call a bond. More sophisticated tree models can use two factors, such as a stock price factor and an interest rate factor, in order to incorporate the two types of risk.

Note further that a defaultable callable bond might also be convertible. In this case, the firm could decide to call the bond in order to force conversion. If investors decide to convert rather than redeem the bonds, the firm's equity will increase and the default risk of the remaining liabilities will be reduced. The potential complexities make theoretical option pricing models intractable and makes tree models (or simulation models) attractive due to their flexibility and relative ease of use.

21.5 TREE MODELS, VISUALIZATION, AND TWO BENEFITS TO SPREADSHEETS

Large tree models are easily programmed using computer software such as Python and R. Small tree models can also be easily programmed using a spreadsheet program such as EXCEL. But very large models (i.e., involving many "steps" or time periods) might be much easier to program without a spreadsheet. However, there is a key advantage to the enhanced visualization offered by a spreadsheet. In the context of models, **visualization** refers to the ability to understand the relations between the components of a model and is often substantially enhanced by expressing the model via a spreadsheet.

There are two potentially important benefits to expressing a model using both a programming language and a spreadsheet: (1) the spreadsheet allows the programmer to verify the results obtained with a programming language; and (2) the spreadsheet allows the model to be communicated to senior managers who may be highly familiar with the securities and markets but who do not have the time or skills to ascertain the economics of the model through a programming language. A senior manager can literally see the interim results as well the assumptions on which the results are based.

The importance of using spreadsheets to communicate complex models extends well beyond tree models. Economy-wide crises, such as the collateralized debt obligation collapses of 1994 and 2008, occurred in part because market participants did not understand the complex "black-box" models that were used to value CDOs and to understand their risks. Individual firms also have failed due to a failure to understand complex valuation and risk assessment models. Many of these problems could have been lessened or avoided if senior managers understood the models better. Communication of the "nuts and bolts" (i.e., details) of financial models to managers and other colleagues using spreadsheets is a key way to lessen the dangers of black-box systems.

REFERENCE

Cox, J. C., S. A. Ross, and M. Rubinstein. 1979. "Options Pricing: A Simplified Approach." *Journal of Financial Economics* 7 (3): 229–63.

CHAPTER 22

Directional Strategies and Methods

Directional strategies have intentional exposures to a market's direction from either a net long or a net short exposure. While directional strategies can be implemented with traditional assets, such as exchange-traded funds (ETFs), when actively traded they often use listed derivatives (futures and options) and over-the-counter (OTC) derivatives. Directional strategies can be differentiated in several ways, including the market in which the positions are focused and the method used to select positions (such as technical analysis versus fundamental analysis).

22.1 EFFICIENTLY INEFFICIENT MARKETS

A buy-and-hold directional strategy can be justified entirely by expected risk premia associated with the systematic risks of the underlying market. This chapter focuses on active directional strategies in which risk exposures are intentionally altered in an effort to improve risk-adjusted returns. Active investment methods generally entail higher transactions costs and management fees. This section discusses efficiently inefficient markets as a potential justification for investing in active management strategies including directional strategies.

The degree of informational efficiency of prices in various markets is one of the central issues in asset allocation and the investment process. The thesis that security markets are perfectly efficient and that prices reflect all available information at all times leads to two paradoxes. The **two paradoxes of informational market efficiency** are: (1) if financial asset markets are perfectly efficient, no one will have an incentive to collect information and so there would be no mechanism to keep markets informationally efficient; and (2) if financial asset markets are perfectly efficient, then fees paid to active managers of financial assets imply that the markets for asset management are highly inefficient.

Efficiently inefficient markets occur when markets prices are, on average, just informationally inefficient enough to compensate managers and investors for the costs and risks of pursuing skill-based strategies, but not too inefficient to present a large number of money managers with easy-to-exploit arbitrage opportunities. Therefore, the flow of capital to actively managed strategies is limited in a world that is efficiently inefficient. In such a world, competition among active money managers will result in markets that are almost efficient; however, inefficiencies do exist that reward those who can identify and exploit them well.

The presence of active money managers and the need for active managers to exist in order for markets to reflect information provide support for the idea that markets are at least somewhat inefficient. However, markets cannot be highly inefficient, because if that were the case, then many more people would enter the active money management business to earn a portion of those fees and, in the process, help make markets more efficient. Therefore, it seems that there must be a fine balance between efficiency and inefficiency. Different markets with different levels of information availability, different sizes, and different levels of trading frictions should have different degrees of market inefficiency. Further, the degree of informational inefficiency should be expected to ebb and flow through time as the number of analysts change and as markets experience levels of relative calm or turmoil.

22.2 TECHNICAL DIRECTIONAL STRATEGIES OVERVIEW

Technical directional strategies purposefully take on exposure to one or more risk factors based on analysis of past trading information including past prices and volumes. At the heart of most technical directional strategies is the attempt to predict whether a particular asset or index is more likely to trend (exhibit momentum or positive return autocorrelation) or to mean-revert (exhibit negative return autocorrelation). Mean-reversion is not a random walk. **Mean-reversion** exists when an asset's future value changes (returns) are more likely to reverse from unusually high or low previous performance by exhibiting the opposite performance in the future (i.e., exhibiting negative autocorrelations of returns).

Level I of the CAIA curriculum discusses several metrics of technical analysis including various types of moving averages and the countertrend strategy of the relative strength index. This chapter discusses additional methods and metrics.

22.2.1 Metrics of Technical Analysis

Strategies based on technical analysis are designed to benefit from changes in prices (or rates). However, many methods or strategies focus on various metrics (e.g., simple metrics such as market breadth, market volume, open interest, and ratios such as advances-to-declines) to gauge market sentiment or otherwise generate trading signals. Several popular methods of analysis include various moving averages of prices and point-and-figure diagrams (detailed below).

The quantity and diversity of methods by which technical analysis is performed is astounding. Large books are written on even the subtopics of technical analysis. Charting is often used as a flexible and less quantitative method to interpret past data in an attempt to predict future data (e.g., prices or returns).

A popular form of charting is the use of point and figure charts. A **point and figure chart** is a diagram of X's and O's that denote upward and downward price movements through time (i.e., trends) in an attempt to discern tradeable patterns. Specifically, X's indicate that the price of the asset being studied has moved ("trended") upward by a threshold amount (e.g., $1.00), while O's indicate the asset has fallen by the same threshold amount. The X's and O's are placed on a grid with price level on the vertical axis and time along the horizontal axis as indicated in Exhibit 22.1:

EXHIBIT 22.1   Example of a Point and Figure Chart

```
  X                                          30
  X O      X                                 29
O X O      X O                               28
  O        X O X                             27
  O X    X O X O      X                       26
O X O X O X O X    X O X                      25
O X O X O    O X O X O X O                    24
O            O  O X O    O                    23
             O X        O                     22
             O          O                     21
                        O                     20
      Jan              Feb Mar
```

A point and figure chart does not move from left to right (i.e., forward in time) at an even rate, as illustrated in Exhibit 22.1 by the large gap on the horizontal axis between January and February, and the small gap between February and March. The X's and O's do not shift to the right until the underlying asset's price has reversed its direction by the threshold amount (e.g., $1).

For example, the second column of Exhibit 22.1 contains three X's indicating that the asset moved up steadily from $28 to over $30 (trended?) without a substantial reversal. Then, the asset returned to $29 or less causing the creation of a new column with a symbol change from X's to O's to denote the downward "trend." The period from February to March is quickly identified by the diagram as a relatively long period of time in which the asset trades within a somewhat narrow range.

Technical analysts use point and figure charts similarly to how price charts are used. Namely, they look for patterns such as increasing lows, decreasing lows, support levels, resistance levels, and various shapes such as V's. For example, a technical analyst may use Exhibit 22.1 to predict the continuation of a downtrend based on the lower highs and lower lows occurring from left to right. Lines are often sketched above and below the X's and O's in an attempt to indicate potential patterns.

22.2.2   Trend-Following or Momentum Models

A **momentum strategy** seeks to generate superior risk-adjusted performance by identifying assets more likely to continue the unusually high (or low) previous performance rather than to reverse a past trend.

There are two primary methods of implementing momentum strategies: cross-sectional (relative) and time series (absolute).

Cross-sectional momentum is defined and measured by the relative performance of a security within a group of securities, such as classifying a stock as having positive momentum if its recent performance is in the top 50% of all stocks. The cross-sectional approach is traditionally used to indicate momentum in factor return studies, including those of Fama and French.

Time-series momentum is defined and measured by the absolute performance of a security based on its own performance, such as classifying a stock as having positive momentum if its recent performance was positive. The time-series momentum approach is a form of trend following introduced by Moskowitz, Ooi and Pedersen 2012 in which momentum for a particular asset is measured based only on that asset's performance. For example, a simple time series momentum approach would be to go long each security that has risen in price over a given time period and to short each security that has declined over the same time period.

To implement a time-series momentum or trend-following strategy, an investor examines the relative performance of assets and establishes a long position in those assets whose values have appreciated in the recent past and establishes a short position in those assets whose values have declined in the recent past. Momentum strategies are flexible with regard to the time period (and potential risk adjustment) on which to examine past returns (or prices) as well as the exact criteria for entering a trade and exiting a trade.

A simple momentum strategy and its corresponding profits or losses are illustrated using the following:

$$\text{P\&L from Momentum Trade} = \begin{cases} S_{t+1} - S_t & \text{If } S_t > S_{t-1} \\ S_t - S_{t+1} & \text{If } S_t < S_{t-1} \end{cases}$$

where S_t is the value of asset S at time t. This means that if asset S increased in value during the previous period, one should establish a long position in S and thus the strategy would show a profit if the trend continues and $S_{t+1} > S_t$. In contrast, the long strategy would show a loss if the trend reverses and S declines in the next period—that is, $S_{t+1} < S_t$. Conversely, a negative price change in the previous period would trigger a short sale which would generate a profit if the price trended and a loss if the price mean-reverted.

Empirical academic and practitioner studies have shown instances of powerful momentum. Momentum has been found to exist across all asset classes and across various time periods. For example, in equity markets the cross-sectional momentum-based relation between past returns and subsequent returns has been so strong that a four-factor model for asset returns (Fama–French–Carhart model) is used as an extension of the Fama–French model in order to include a momentum factor. Evidence of momentum exists in other markets including evidence that, on average, currency momentum trades were historically profitable. For example, a study by Burnside, Eichenbaum, and Rebelo (2011) shows that a strategy that took long positions in a portfolio of previously-appreciating currencies and short positions in a portfolio of previously-depreciating currencies between 1976 and 2009 would have earned 4.5% per year. Finally, note that momentum is considered to be one of the core risk premia in various markets.

22.2.3 Market Divergence

In financial markets, **divergence** can be defined as the tendency or process of an asset, market index, or indicator to move in opposition to the movement or behavior anticipated by a particular model or expectation. For example, a stock's price may be described by a particular model as trading within a specific range. Divergence in this example would be said to have occurred if the price moved outside that range. Divergence strategies attempt to earn superior rates of return by trading in relation to occurrences of divergences as indicated by a particular view or model of prescribed behavior. If financial markets were perfectly efficient, divergence in market prices would not lead to the emergence of opportunities to use trading strategies with consistently high risk-adjusted returns.

22.2.4 Measuring Market Divergence of an Individual Asset

Similarly to how volatility can be measured by standard deviation, market divergence can be measured empirically. A popular measure of the level of divergence for a particular price series is the signal-to-noise ratio. The **signal-to-noise ratio** is the ratio of a measure of a potential trend to a measure of all price changes during the same period. Examining the formula that calculates the signal-to-noise ratio helps in understanding this concept. For any specific day, at time t, the signal-to-noise ratio (SNR_t) for a particular price series with look-back period (n) can be calculated mathematically using the following formula:

$$SNR_t(n) = \frac{|P_t - P_{t-n}|}{\sum_{i=0}^{n-1} |P_{t-i} - P_{t-i-1}|} \tag{22.1}$$

The signal-to-noise ratio can be viewed as the ratio of the *magnitude* of a trend (or overall price change) to the *volatility* of prices around that trend. The denominator of the formula (i.e., the "noise") for SNR_t in Equation 22.1 is the sum of the *absolute values* of the price changes observed over n periods. The numerator (i.e., the "signal of a trend") is the total change in price over the last n periods expressed as an absolute value. Thus, the numerator is the absolute value of the *netted* sum of the same price changes—the same price changes used in the denominator to indicate the total variation that occurred.

22.2.5 Interpreting Market Divergence

The SNR_t is designed to indicate the extent to which the price variation in an asset generated a trend (i.e., a total directional move). If, for instance, a small uptrend in the market is achieved through a large number of positive and negative changes in prices, then the signal-to-noise ratio is small. On the other hand, if a large uptrend is the summation of mostly positive changes in the price, then the signal-to-noise ratio is high.

The SNR_t varies between 0 (indicating all noise) to 1 (indicating all trend). For example, suppose an asset's price increased gradually over the past n days, with the price rising a little each day. In this case, the ratio will be equal to 1, indicating that there was no noise (i.e., all of the price variation contributed to the trend). Instead, if the price generally rises but in an uneven manner, increasing on some days and decreasing on other days, the ratio will be less than 1 and would indicate there was some noise but also perhaps a trend. If the variation created no net change, the ratio would be 0 indicating that all of the price action was noise.

Consider a stock observed over three days as having changed in price by $1 each day. It is instructive to calculate the signal to noise ratio (SNR) under the following four scenarios: (1) all three price changes were positive; (2) two price changes were positive; (3) one price change was positive; and (4) all price changes were negative. The SNR for the first and fourth scenarios are 1.0 because all price changes contributed to the trend. The SNR for the second and third scenarios are 0.33 because two of the price changes were "noise" that did not contribute to the trend. Note that the use of an absolute value in the numerator means that the SNR is always nonnegative whether the data formed an upward or downward trend.

APPLICATION 22.2.5

Consider a price series observed for 5 days. If the price series in chronological order is 50, 51, 52, 50, and 53, what is the SNR and how might it be interpreted? The SNR can be found using Equation 22.1 as |50 − 53| divided by the sum: |51 − 50 | + |52 − 51| + |50 − 52| + |53 − 50|. The ratio is 3/7 which is 0.43. This indicates that the trend is reasonably strong. If the final price were 51 instead of 53, the SNR would be 0.2, indicating a weaker trend.

Exhibit 22.2 depicts six hypothetical price series to illustrate SNRs. The upper left series depicts a uniform price trend with equal price changes, no noise, and an SNR=1. The upper right series depicts a price trend with no noise, two periods of trend, one period of no change, and an SNR=1. Note that all of the days in the upper right diagram have a positive or zero price change and that the days of a constant price are not viewed as having created noise.

The two middle series add short-term, moderately-sized noises to the series in the first row. The bottom two series add large noises to the series in the first row. The moderately noisy linear price series (the two middle diagrams) have a return volatility of 10%, and the very noisy linear price series (the two bottom diagrams) have a volatility of 40%. The expected size of all six of the trends is the same: a $10 increase in price.

Exhibit 22.2 lists the 100-day SNR for each price series. Note that as noise (or volatility) enters into price trends, SNR becomes lower, as the trend is difficult to distinguish from the noise. For example, the SNRs for the noisy and very noisy linear price trends (on the left side) are 0.1728 and 0.0314, respectively. The right side of Exhibit 22.2 plots a shorter trend, with the same increase in the price over a 100-day period. Note that the SNR for the noisy linear price trend is 0.1728 versus 0.1598 for the short-term price trend. The noisy linear price trend would be interesting for a trend-follower, but the very noisy linear price trend might be deemed too volatile.

Exhibit 22.2 illustrates the challenges faced by analysis of actual data and how volatility can make it difficult to ascertain a trend. The same noise series (randomness of the prices) is used in this example to make the SNRs comparable. When the annualized volatility is 40% (the very noisy series), both the steady and short-term price trends (bottom left and bottom right diagrams) generate near-zero SNRs that are relatively useless to a technical analyst.

The key to the analysis of SNRs is the extent to which the historical data is useful in predicting future trends (or lack of trends). Empirical results are somewhat mixed.

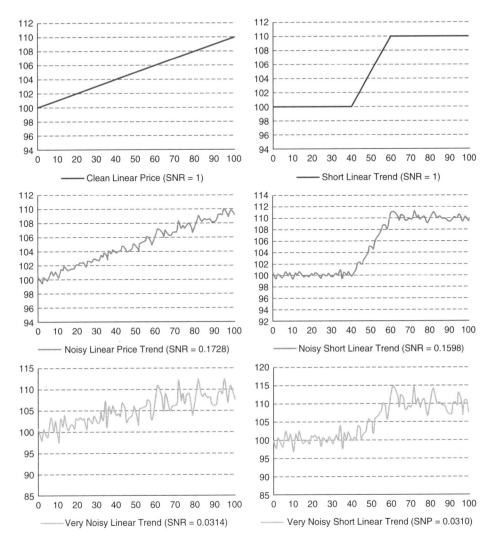

EXHIBIT 22.2 Examples of Price Trends with and without Noise

While numerous studies indicate trends, it is not always clear whether the trends are statistically significant since it is unknown how many markets, assets, time intervals, and time periods are being tested.

22.2.6 Measuring Market Divergence

The SNR can be calculated for various markets or asset groups. The SNRs for each individual market i, can be used to calculate the divergence of the total market, defined as the market divergence index. The **market divergence index (MDI)** is the average signal-to-noise ratio for a group of submarkets. The MDI is found for a collection of M markets as an arithmetic average of the individual SNRs as follows:

$$MDI_t(n) = \frac{1}{M} \sum_{i=1}^{M} SNR_t^i(n) \qquad (22.2)$$

where SNR^i_t is the signal-to-noise ratio for an individual market i, at time t and with signal observation window of length n. The MDI is a simple aggregate measure of divergence in prices, taking into account the level of volatility (or noise) in the M markets or asset groups. When the MDI is higher, this corresponds to a market environment with stronger trends across markets. For example, if a group of markets being analyzed is half comprised of markets with SNRs of 0.60 and half with SNRs of 0.40, the MDI would be $[(0.50*0.60)+(0.50*0.40)] = 0.50$. The MDI is interpreted much like the SRI except that it tends to be applicable to overall asset allocation decisions rather than individual asset decisions.

APPLICATION 22.2.6

Suppose the S&P 500 Index, Japanese government bonds (JGBs), corn, wheat, crude oil, and Treasury bonds have 100-day SNRs of 0.3, 0.2, 0.3, 0.1, 0.4, and 0.3, respectively. Crude oil has the largest SNR, which means that the trend signal is the highest for crude oil over the past 100 days relative to its volatility. Wheat prices have the smallest SNR, which means that the trend signal is the lowest. What is the MDI for the six markets?

Using Equation 22.2, the MDI for all included markets would be the average SNR. In this case, MDI = 0.267. This figure can be compared to SNRs and/or MDIs from previous periods to determine the extent to which these markets, viewed as a group, may be considered to have been trending.

22.2.7 Technical Strategies Based on Machine Learning

Technical strategies have evolved from early, simple linear models with which analysts search for performance correlations through time. Increasingly, analysts are programming computers to search with advanced nonlinear models and/or massive data sets in an attempt to identify profitable trading strategies. For example, **genetic algorithms** seek to identify patterns in data using an approach modeled after the natural selection process found in biological evolution with various "genes" representing trading rules that survive within the model or perish based on the their estimated value in generating trading profits. Artificial **neural network** software seeks to identify patterns in data using an approach modeled after the learning process of the human brain with various "nodes" and "layers" forming connections and associations that are modified within the model (are "learned") to form trading rules that are included or omitted based on the their estimated value in generating trading profits.

Artificial intelligence approaches can utilize the tremendous quantity of technical and fundamental data, not just in their most basic forms (e.g., prices) but also in a myriad of popular forms such as various moving averages of prices (simple, weighted, and exponential moving averages). Such approaches offer power beyond that capable of being generated solely by the human brain, but also offer increased danger of data dredging that explains the past well but fails to enhance predictions of the future.

EXHIBIT 22.3 The Characteristics of Trend Following and Their Implications during Period of Equity Market Crisis

Characteristics of Trend Following	Implications during Equity Market Crisis
Highly liquid, adaptable strategies based exclusively in futures, with minimal credit exposure	Less susceptible to the illiquidity and credit traps that most investors experience during equity market crises
Systematic trading strategies, lack of long equity bias	Less susceptible to behavioral biases and emotionally based decision-making triggered by experiencing losses
Active across a wide range of asset classes in futures	Poised to profit from trends across a wide range of asset classes

22.2.8 Risks of Directional Technical Strategies

Times of market crisis, for both behavioral and institutional reasons, represent times when market participants become synchronized in their actions, creating trends in markets. Note that the relation between the total value of assets being sold equals the total value of assets being purchased at all times (ignoring creation and destruction of available assets through, for example, new issuances of common stock and company repurchases of common stock). The synchronization in a financial crisis described above refers to herd behavior, such as willingness to transact at prices far below recent norms.

The potential for some strategies to generate superior return during periods of financial crisis can be termed **crisis alpha**. Perhaps only the most adaptable market players—a select few— can take advantage of these "crisis alpha" opportunities. When equity markets go down, the vast majority of investors may experience losses. At these times, investor decisions may be influenced by behavioral biases and emotionally based decision-making. When coupled with the widespread use of institutionalized leverage—along with risk limits triggered by losses, increased volatility, and increased correlation—these losses will drive large groups of investors into action. When large groups of investors are forced into action, liquidity disappears, credit issues come to the forefront, fundamental valuation becomes less relevant, and, arguably, persistent trends occur across various markets while many investors fervently attempt to exit positions. Opportunistic systematic strategies that are highly adaptive, liquid, and void of a long equity bias have identified and benefited from crisis alpha opportunities.

It is important to note that systematic strategies do not time the onset of an extreme event, like an equity market crisis, but may profit from opportunities in the aftermath of a crisis in currencies, bonds, short rates, equities, and commodities. Using systematic trend following as an example, its characteristics and their implications during an equity market crisis are summarized in Exhibit 22.3.

22.3 FUNDAMENTAL DIRECTIONAL STRATEGIES

This section discusses strategies of discretionary directional managers that use fundamental information in the search for alpha.

22.3.1   Overview of Fundamental Directional Strategies

Discretionary directional managers take fewer bets and larger position sizes because their approach is more labor intensive, and each investment opportunity needs to be analyzed carefully and separately. Therefore, information gathering and analysis aspects of the strategy make it difficult to build portfolios consisting of hundreds of positions. Quantitative approaches, in contrast, rely on computing power to apply their algorithms and models to large sets of investments rather quickly. Since each individual investment has not been the subject of hours of analysis by the manager, it is generally prudent to diversify the risk and make smaller allocations.

Discretionary managers rely heavily on information flow and their personal synthesis of such information incorporated into their own investment thesis. Many have argued that discretionary managers are thus much more skill-based than nondiscretionary or systematic managers, as the alpha that discretionary managers attempt to extract is less obvious and not well publicized.

22.3.2   The Bottom-Up Approach of Fundamental Analysis

The strategy of **bottom-up fundamental analysis** is to estimate the value of a company's stock based on firm-level forecasted sales, expenses, earnings, and other data linked economically to the eventual cash distributions of a firm in an attempt to enhance portfolio returns. The forecasts of these bottom-up fundamental analysts provide an estimated cash flow stream, which is discounted to arrive at the perceived value of the company. The equity value is found after subtracting the value of the company's debt. Given that forecasting the future is challenging at best, analysts may generate a set of valuations based on good, medium, and bad scenarios, and then use the weighted average of these valuations where the weights correspond to the probability of the scenarios occurring.

Bottom-up managers often have researchers on the ground ferreting out any useful information that is not included in public documents. They perform detailed due diligence on the companies they hold and in which they intend to invest. For example, managers may ask industry experts about their views on a company's products and processes, competitive advantages, patents, and political and regulatory risks. Typically, this strategy focuses on companies that have limited analyst coverage, based on the idea that limited competition for information may indicate investment opportunities in which public information is not fully reflected in the market price of the equity. Bottom-up managers build their portfolios one stock at a time, focusing on characteristics of single stocks rather than a broad economic theme or portfolio-level targets.

22.3.3   Fundamental Bottom-Up Equity Valuation Models

Two popular approaches among bottom-up investors are discounted cash models and the enterprise valuation model.

It is reasonable to view the value of an asset as the present value of the expected stream of future cash flows discounted for time and risk. For example, if V_0 is the value of an asset and div_t is the cash flow expected at the end of time period t, and if the appropriate discount rate is k for the cash flow distributed at the end each of period, then the value of the asset is as follows in Equation 22.3:

$$V_0 = \sum_{t=1}^{\infty} \frac{E[div_t]}{(1+k)^t} \tag{22.3}$$

To make Equation 22.3 equation easier to solve, assumptions are often made about uncertain future dividend payments and discount rates. For example, for the most extreme case of simplification, if it is assumed that the first cash flow of div_1 is known and that once it is paid, the cash flows grow at the rate of g in each consecutive period, then the perpetuity with growth formula can be employed as follows in Equation 22.4:

$$V_0 = \frac{div_1}{k-g} \tag{22.4}$$

The constant growth model is known to fail to value all assets well, as the model gives a firm a zero value if it is assumed that there will be no cash distributions in the first year.

The enterprise valuation model attempts to calculate the total value of a firm and then extracts the value of the firm's equity by noting that the value of the firm should equal the sum of equity and debt values. In particular, the **enterprise value** of a firm is defined as the market value of its operating assets as shown in Equation 22.5:

Total Value of Assets = Enterprise Value + Cash

Total Value of Assets = Debt + Equity

Therefore,

Equity = Enterprise Value + Cash − Debt $\qquad$ (22.5)

The market value of a firm's operating assets is calculated using the free cash flow generated by the firm. **Free cash flow to the firm (FCFF)** is the total cash flow that is available for distribution to shareholders and bondholders of the firm. The FCFF is considered to be available for distribution to all suppliers of capital, because the cash needed to support the firm's operations as well as investments is already accounted for.

In particular, FCFF is defined in Equation 22.6.

FCFF = Net Income + Noncash Charges

$\qquad$ + [Interest Expense × (1 − Tax Rate)]

$\qquad$ − Investments in Fixed Assets and Working Capital $\qquad$ (22.6)

Noncash charges refer to expenses that do not represent any cash payment. Depreciation is an important example of a noncash charge. The after-tax cost of interest is added back to net income to calculate the cash that is available for distribution to both shareholders and bondholders. However, to account for the tax benefits that interest expense provides, the after-tax value of interest expense is added back.

Finally, the model accounts for the cash that is used to make fixed investments or working capital investments. For example, cash may be used to acquire equipment and machinery (fixed-asset investment), to purchase raw material (working capital), or to provide credit to customers (working capital).

Example: The net income available to shareholders of Digital Corporation is $400 million. Annual depreciation and interest expense are $40 million and $30 million, respectively. The firm invests $10 million in new equipment during the year and increases its inventory by $5 million. The marginal tax rate for Digital Corporation is 30%. What is the FCFF of Digital Corporation?

$$FCFF = \$400 + \$40 + \$30 \times (1 - 0.3) - \$10 - \$5 = \$446 \text{ million}$$

To obtain the current enterprise value (EV_0) of a firm using all projected values of free cash flow to the firm, $FCFF_t$, a risk-adjusted discount rate, k, should be used as indicated in Equation 22.7.

$$EV_0 = \sum_{t=1}^{\infty} \frac{FCFF_t}{(1 + k)^t} \tag{22.7}$$

22.3.4 Four Procedures within the Fundamental Investment Process

This section reviews four procedures within a fundamental equity manager's investment process. The four procedures are: (1) understand the business of the company; (2) study the company's management; (3) read and digest the financials; and (4) create and defend the valuation of the company.

THE BUSINESS OF THE COMPANY: An analysis of the business side of a company takes into consideration two important things: the company's ability to generate stable above-average returns and whether the company has a defensible competitive position. Additional factors that need to be examined include the company's relative cost position, its market share and product quality, and the talent of its employees.

THE COMPANY'S MANAGEMENT: Management's compensation and checks and balances that exist between key members of management are important. While the company's culture may be difficult to ascertain, studying the officers of the firm may give a good sense of the company's culture.

FINANCIALS: Examination of the financial statements is a major part of fundamental analysis. Systematic methods exist such as the DuPont model. The **DuPont model** evaluates a firm based on a company's gross value rather than its net value, and breaks a firm's ROE into three major components: profit margin, asset turnover, and leverage. The relation is as follows:

ROE = Profit Margin × Asset Turnover × Leverage, or

ROE = (Net Income/Revenues) × (Revenues/Assets) × (Assets/Book Equity)

$$\tag{22.8}$$

The DuPont model provides an organized and uniform way to analyze changes over time in the ROE as well as to attribute performance to the components of ROE.

The following characteristics on the balance sheet warrant special concern because they are critical in showing strengths or weaknesses in a company: capital structure, fixed charges, coverage ratio, changes in working capital, any off-balance sheet financing, and pension fund issues.

VALUATION: Arriving at a value for a company begins with how the valuation of a company stacks up relative to its peers and the broad market including comparing its earnings with those of similar companies.

22.3.5 Four Mechanics of Fundamental Strategies

This section discusses four mechanics of the traditional fundamental investment process.

IDEA GENERATION: The first, and by far the most critical, step is to generate good investment ideas. Some managers screen the universe of stocks based on fundamental ratios or technical indicators so as to reduce the total number of stocks to a manageable size. Others read industry newsletters, research reports, market commentary, academic research, or other written sources of information to gain investment insights. Additionally, some managers attend investment conferences, trade conferences, and idea luncheons or dinners to develop new ideas. The value of a solid network of colleagues cannot be overestimated in uncovering and refining new ideas.

OPTIMAL IDEA EXPRESSION: The next step is how to best express an idea by determining the best investment decisions that can be made based on the investment idea. During this process, the manager considers what trade should be executed to extract the highest return from the idea and what price level will either confirm or negate the idea's validity.

SIZING THE POSITION: Sizing the position works in conjunction with the previous step. Positions are generally sized according to the level of the manager's conviction regarding the idea.

EXECUTING THE TRADE: When executing their trades, managers need to consider whether they should buy aggressively (lift offers), sell aggressively (hit bids), or trade passively (join or improve bids or offers). Other important considerations when executing trades include the liquidity of the underlying security, whether a major announcement is due out, and the availability of the stock to be borrowed in the case of a short sale. Fundamental managers—or, more particularly, head traders—often examine the average daily volume of each stock in an attempt to assess the underlying liquidity of each position.

22.3.6 The Top-Down Approach of Fundamental Analysis

Top-down fundamental analysis is the use of economy-wide or industry-wide information to obtain enhanced abilities to predict levels and changes of key economic characteristics. The goal of a top-down fundamental analyst is to forecast how market values will be driven by a few broad investment and macroeconomic themes. Managers seek to forecast macroeconomic forces that would drive a sector's return, and implement their views through diversified portfolios such as a portfolio of exchange-traded funds (ETFs). They tend to focus on the current stage of the business cycle, inflationary expectations, and monetary and fiscal policies. The following are some examples of the types of inquiries these managers may make:

- What impact might global protectionism have on economic growth?
- To what extent will emerging economies fuel global economic growth?

- If oil prices rise or fall substantially, what are the implications for equity markets and various industries?

Top-down long/short managers seek enhanced risk-adjusted returns through a strong understanding of macroeconomic forces and their impact on financial markets, and they strive to understand various interactions among different segments of capital markets such as lead-lag relations between the fixed-income, currency, commodity, real estate, and stock market sectors.

22.3.7 Top-Down Managers and Schools of Thought

Global macro managers primarily employ top-down management. According to Ahl (2001), there are essentially three possible schools of thought to be considered by macro managers.

Feedback-based global macro managers assume that markets are rational most of the time but that there can exist periods of severe irrationality. Such periods can arise either because people have made money too easily and become complacent or because they have lost money too quickly and become stressed or distressed. As a result, feedback-based global macro managers attempt to read the financial market's psychology, sell into bursting bubbles, and buy into post-crash recoveries.

Information-based global macro managers rely primarily on collecting micro-level information to better understand the global macro picture. Their hypothesis is that an information gap is created by the delay in the release of official macroeconomic statistics. This gap then opens the door for pricing inefficiencies, which will persist until the macro information has been disseminated into the public domain.

Model-based global macro managers rely primarily on financial models and economic theories to analyze market movements, detect policy mistakes of central banks and governments, or extract implied market expectations and compare them to sensible estimates.

22.3.8 Two Risks of Directional Fundamental Strategies

The two primary risks of fundamental investment strategies are fundamental risk and the risk from uncertainty generated by noise traders.

FUNDAMENTAL RISK: **Fundamental risk** emanates from an unexpected change in the fundamental value of a security, causing an apparent arbitrage opportunity to generate losses on the part of the investor. For example, suppose the same commodity is produced and traded in two countries. A trader observes the gap between the two prices of the commodity and determines that it is much wider than its historical range. Given that there is free trade in the commodity, the trader believes the gap will approach its historical value and therefore takes a long position where the commodity is selling at a low price and a short position where the price is high. However, the country where the commodity is trading at a high price unexpectedly decides to impose tariffs on importation of the commodity. In this case, there has been a fundamental change in the economic relation between the two commodities, and the trader is likely to face some losses.

NOISE TRADERS: The textbook description of the efficient market hypothesis assumes that investors are rational and act only on information that can affect the fundamental value of securities. The term **noise traders** refers to those investors who trade securities for reasons not related to the fundamental value of securities. For instance, some investors may sell securities in order to meet liquidity needs, while others may decide to buy securities simply because their prices have been increasing in recent days. That is, they follow a momentum strategy. Recent developments in the field of behavioral finance have identified a number of biases that impact investors' behavior and lead them to act as noise traders. The risk of price changes due to noise traders is also a source of risk (and alpha) to traders using technical analysis. For example, a trader implementing a signal-to-noise ratio views noise trading as a source of opportunities but also a driver of the strategy's risk.

22.4 DIRECTIONAL STRATEGIES AND BEHAVIORAL FINANCE

Substantial debate exists regarding the assumptions and predictions of the efficient markets hypothesis. The premise that investors are rational and value securities without any biases has been questioned by behavioral financial economists. Behavioral finance is commonly justified on two main building blocks: (1) limits to arbitrage, which states that rationally-behaving traders may have difficulty undoing dislocations that are caused by less rational traders; and (2) cognitive psychology.

Cognitive psychology is a broad category that attempts to capture the many types of deviations from full rationality to reflect how people think, including analysis of the emotional components that may affect investors' decision-making abilities. For example, market panics are events in which fear selling and herding behaviors are believed to occur.

The following list includes popular behavioral biases and other effects that often are described in attempts to better understand investor behavior that departs from ultra-rationality. It should be noted that hedge funds see such periods of irrationally behaving markets and trades by less rational market participants as ideal periods and situations in which to generate alpha.

22.4.1 Sentiment Sensitivity

Sentiment, in the context of investment analysis, is broadly defined as beliefs about future cash flows and risks that are not justified by an objective analysis of the facts. Due to limits of arbitrage, ultra-rational investors may not be aggressive enough to force prices back to their fundamental values.

Baker and Wurgler (2006, 2007) contend that, for a variety of reasons, investors may become too optimistic or pessimistic about certain sectors of the market or the overall market and cause prices to deviate substantially from their fundamentals. Some proposed examples include the Internet bubble and burst of 2000 and the real estate bubble and burst of 2007–9. The authors construct a sentiment index incorporating six underlying proxies or indicators of sentiment. The **six sentiment indicators** are: (1) the discounts on closed-end funds; (2) the turnover of New York

Stock Exchange (NYSE) shares; (3) the number of initial public offerings (IPOs); (4) the average first-day returns on IPOs; (5) the equity share in new issues; and (6) the dividend premium. The **dividend premium** is defined as the difference between the average market-to-book-value ratios of dividend payers and nonpayers. They show that the behavior of the index has a significant relationship with the behavior of certain stocks, such as those that have small capitalizations and are younger, unprofitable, and highly volatile, or nondividend-paying, or stocks in financial distress.

There have been other approaches to the construction of sentiment indices, and studies have shown that these indices may explain the behavior of certain stocks through business cycles.

Digital and social media have been used to create measures of investor sentiment. For example, Liew and Wang (2016) created a sentiment index based on the number of tweets that were made about impending IPOs, showing that Twitter sentiment predicts the cross-section of IPO returns. By breaking down the first-day performance of IPOs using the opening price and open-to-close return of first-day trading, they identify both a positive predictive relationship and a negative predictive relationship, respectively. They conclude: "We document that Tweet sentiment matters for IPO first-day performances but the nature of this relationship appears very complex."

22.4.2   Overconfidence

Studies in psychology have demonstrated that traders systematically exhibit overconfidence in their ability to value firms and make price and earnings predictions. They become overly bullish about stocks they are optimistic about, or overly bearish with respect to stocks they regard with pessimism. Overconfidence has been proxied through responses to the following question: "How good are you at investing?" When asked such a question about investment skill and knowledge, many investors are inclined to attribute to themselves superior skills. Unfortunately, it has been shown that many people are poor at calibrating probabilities and confidence intervals. Alpert and Raiffa (1982) show that 98% confidence intervals constructed by study participants include the true quantities only about 60% of the time. Fischhoff, Slovic, and Lichtenstein (1977) document miscalibration of probabilities. They find that events that people think are certain to occur only occur only 80% of the time. Finally, many argue that overconfidence leads investors to overtrade their portfolios, incurring high levels of transaction costs and drags on performance. Barber and Odean (2001) examine the trading activities in discount brokerage accounts and find that the more someone trades, the worse the person performs on average. They find that men trade more and thus do worse than women.

22.4.3   Behavioral Biases From Over-Reliance on the Past

ANCHORING EFFECTS. **Anchoring** occurs when a person is biased due to prior views and cannot properly integrate new information. In other words, during decision-making under uncertain circumstances, anchoring occurs when individuals over-rely on an initial piece of information to make subsequent judgments. In the stock market, anchoring may lead investors to believe that a stock that was trading for $100 a few weeks earlier and is now trading for $20 must be cheap, and therefore the investor may decide to buy the stock even though the fundamental value of the stock may now be $20 or lower.

Studies have shown that the cognitive bias of anchoring is present in sell-side analysts' forecasts of earnings. For example, there is evidence that analysts make optimistic forecasts when the forecasted earnings per share (EPS) are lower than the industry median. In other words, industry-median EPS estimates serve as an anchor, and therefore earnings estimates of poorly performing companies tend to be too high and close to the industry's median. On the other hand, earnings of firms that have been performing well tend to be underestimated. As a result, there is evidence that future stock returns are significantly higher than forecasted for firms with above-median EPS forecasts.

CONFIRMATION BIAS. **Confirmation bias** occurs when one selectively employs evidence that supports a given claim or belief and minimizes contradictory evidence (aka "selective hearing"). Duong, Pescetto, and Santamaria (2010) directly test for confirmation bias in the context of value versus glamour investing and fundamental analysis in the UK. Value stocks are defined as those with a high fundamentals-to-price ratio (high book-to-market ratio, earnings-to-price ratio, and cash-flow-to-price ratios); alternatively, glamour stocks are those that have a low fundamentals-to-price ratio. Using sample data consisting of UK stocks from 1991 to 2007, the researchers document investors' asymmetric reactions to both good and bad news. Value investors underreact to good news and process bad news overconfidently, whereas glamour investors underreact to bad news and process good news overconfidently. In other words, each type of investor reacts more strongly to the news that confirms the group's prior beliefs.

LOSS AVERSION/DISPOSITION EFFECT. The **loss aversion/disposition effect** captures the notion that investors typically prefer to avoid losses more than to acquire gains. Empirical and laboratory evidence demonstrates that people have stronger reactions to losses than to gains. Kahneman and Tversky (1979) critiqued the expected utility theory and developed their alternative prospect theory. In **prospect theory,** agents underweight those outcomes that are probable vis-à-vis those outcomes that are certain. Such tendencies contribute to the risk aversion in choices involving sure gains and the risk-seeking preference in choices involving sure losses. One example is that many investors lock in small profits and fail to cut off losses quickly, in opposition to the adage (and often tax-preferable strategy) "Let your winners run and cut your losses."

REPRESENTATIVENESS: The representativeness bias is a decision-making shortcut that uses past experiences to guide the decision-making process. The term *representativeness* indicates that when investors are confronted with a new experience and need to make a judgment or decision about that situation, their brains automatically rely on past experiences and mental representations that seem similar to this new situation in an effort to guide their judgments and decisions. For example, investors who have seen Internet companies perform well in the past may consider any dot-com company to be a fast-growing firm. In other words, the person over-relies on categories to decide if a firm will be growing quickly going forward.

22.4.4 Other Potential Sources of Pricing Anomalies

MARKET FRICTION EFFECTS: **Market frictions** are impediments to costless trading—such as transaction costs, taxes, and regulations—that can create market imperfections and make it too costly or too risky to implement certain arbitrage strategies. The textbook definition of arbitrage assumes that markets are perfect. For example, it is generally suggested that there are no barriers to shorting overvalued securities. However, in the real world, it may be costly or even impossible to short certain securities.

AGENCY RELATIONSHIP EFFECTS: An agency relationship (i.e., a principal–agent relationship) arises whenever an owner of an asset hires an agent to manage that asset on the owner's behalf. This relationship gives rise to certain problems and costs. For example, how would the owner know that the agent is managing the asset for the sole benefit of the owner, or that the agent is not taking too much risk? The owner may have to hire auditors and install monitoring systems to ensure that the assets are properly managed. This will be costly. One implication of an agency relationship is that in order to reduce the chance of underperformance relative to their peers, agents may decide to follow the crowd rather than invest in unique strategies. Also, there is a risk that the owner may not be patient enough to stay with certain strategies. Suppose an agent identifies a highly undervalued security. For the price of this security to reach its potential fundamental value, other market participants must be convinced that the security is indeed undervalued. This could take many months, and in the meantime the security may decline even further. The owners of the asset may look at the temporary losses, conclude that the trader lacks the necessary skills, and decide to withdraw their funds.

22.5 DIRECTIONAL TRADING AND FACTORS

This section discusses directional strategies based on return factors, which represent a new and growing area of research and applications. Factor returns are detailed in Chapter 8.

Recall that there are three primary types of return factors: statistical, fundamental, and dynamic (Ang 2014). In recent decades, much of the trading of equities, and to a lesser extent, bonds, has been driven by strategies related to dynamic or time-varying factors. Ang (2014) lists five major factors: value stocks versus growth stocks, winning stocks versus losing stocks (momentum), illiquid securities versus liquid securities, risky bonds versus safe bonds, and option strategies based on volatility.

Strategies based on dynamic factors can be relative value trades in which a portfolio contains long positions in some securities and short positions in other securities differentiated by their factors. For example, an investor may be long growth stocks and short value stocks (or vice versa) based on their forecasts of relative performance. Alternatively, strategies based on dynamic factors can be directional trades. For example, a long-only equity manager may allocate entirely towards value stocks based on a forecast that value stocks will perform well.

22.5.1 Emphasis on Value versus Growth Investing

Long/short managers vary concerning investment style classifications analogously to how mutual funds differ in terms of styles, such as value, growth, and blend.

Value long/short managers employ traditional valuation metrics, such as the book-to-market ratio, earnings-to-price (E/P) ratio, dividend yield, and the ratio of P/E to earnings growth rate (i.e., the PEG ratio), to look for undervalued companies. Value stocks tend to have low betas relative to growth stocks. When anticipating down markets, managers may take a value investment approach, but in anticipation of rising markets, they increase their allocations to growth companies, thereby blending the two approaches.

The **growth approach** to fundamental long/short equity investing is to over-weight companies perceived as having higher potential to deliver large increases in revenues, earnings, and/or cash flows. Long/short growth managers are attracted by top-line growth numbers and are willing to look past weak current earnings in the presence of aggressive sales growth. Often they invest in small high-tech companies because large companies in mature industries generally lack the same growth opportunities.

22.5.2 Directional Trading Based on Momentum

Momentum in equities is commonly defined as the tendency of stocks that have performed well in the last 6 to 12 months to continue to perform well (and for stocks that have performed poorly in the last 6 to 12 months to continue to perform poorly). Empirical analysis indicates that momentum has been a powerful factor in explaining equity returns for decades.

There is evidence that, even prior to the discovery of the momentum effect, the market has experienced momentum crashes. A momentum crash is said to have occurred when the momentum factor exhibits reversed correlation to short term returns and stocks that have been performing well (poorly) in the past 6 months experience a dramatic collapse (recovery) in the next month. For example, dramatic momentum crashes caused returns of the highest decile momentum stocks to under-perform those in the lowest decile by 200% in part of 1932 and over 100% in the ensuing months in 2009 (Daniel and Moskowitz 2016).

22.5.3 Emphasis on Illiquidity Premiums

Asset allocators within alternative investments are often motivated to invest in private investments in order to receive higher average returns based on a potential illiquidity premium. An illiquidity premium is a higher return on illiquid investment, such as private partnerships, than liquid securities, such as listed equities. Scholars have examined listed securities to ascertain whether the more illiquid of the listed securities offer higher average returns than the more liquid securities. The empirical results are unclear.

Chapter 30 discusses the illiquidity premium in the context of listed and private real estate and, to a lesser extent based on data availability, in equities (i.e., listed equities versus private equity). Empirical examination of the issue is made more difficult by problems with measuring point-to-point returns on private securities and by other issues that arise when examining fund returns. For example, fund returns are driven not only by the performance of the fund's underlying assets but also by other issues such as fees, interest expenses, leverage differentials, and risk differentials.

The potential importance and success or failure of various factor-based directional strategies is difficult to predict. However, it seems highly likely that factor-based investment strategies and analysis will continue to evolve and will continue to grow in popularity among sophisticated asset allocators and investors.

REFERENCES

Ahl, P. 2001. "Global Macro Funds: What Lies Ahead?" *AIMA Newsletter*, April.

Alpert, M. and H. Raiffa. 1982. "A Progress Report on the Training of Probability Assessors." In *Judgment under Uncertainty: Heuristics and Biases*, eds. D. Kahneman, P. Slovic, and A. Tversky. Cambridge: Cambridge University Press, pp. 294–305.

Ang, A. 2014. *Asset Management: A Systematic Approach to Factor Investing*. New York, NY: Oxford University Press.

Baker, M. and J. Wurgler. 2006. "Investor Sentiment and the Cross-Section of Stock Returns." *Journal of Finance* 61 (4): 1645–80.

Baker, M. and J. Wurgler. 2007. "Investor Sentiment in the Stock Market." Working Paper, National Bureau of Economic Research. www.nber.org/papers/w13189.

Barber, B. and T. Odean. 2001. "Boys Will Be Boys: Gender, Overconfidence, and Common Stock Investing." *Quarterly Journal of Economics* 116 (1): 261–92.

Burnside, C., M. Eichenbaum, and S. Rebelo. 2011. "Carry Trade and Momentum in Currency Markets." *Annual Review of Financial Economics* (3): 511–35.

Daniel, K. and T. J. Moskowitz. 2016. "Momentum crashes." *Journal of Financial Economics* http://dx.doi.org/10.1016/j.jfineco.2015.12.002.

Duong, C., G. Pescetto, and D. Santamaria. 2010. "Fundamental Analysis in Value-Glamour Contexts." Working Paper, Canterbury Christ Church University, UK.

Fischhoff, B., P. Slovic, and S. Lichtenstein. 1977. "Knowing with Certainty: The Appropriateness of Extreme Confidence." *Journal of Experimental Psychology: Human Perception and Performance* 3 (4): 552–64.

Kahneman, D. and A. Tversky. 1979. "Prospect Theory: An Analysis of Decision under Risk." *Econometrica* 47 (2): 263–91.

Liew, J. and G. Wang. 2016. "Twitter Sentiment and IPO Performance: A Cross-Sectional Examination." *Journal of Portfolio Management* 42 (4): 129–35.

Moskowitz, T., T. Ooi, and L. Pedersen. 2012. "Time Series Momentum." *Journal of Financial Economics* 104.

CHAPTER 23

Multivariate Empirical Methods and Performance Persistence

M ost methods in Level I of the CAIA curriculum focused on single-factor linear models. This chapter builds on those chapters with an emphasis on multi-factor and nonlinear methods that are essential to the analysis and management of alternative investments. This material is fundamental to the challenges faced by an asset allocator in determining the mix between traditional assets and alternative assets in a portfolio, as well as in determining the relative weights within the alternative asset portion of the portfolio.

23.1 STATISTICAL FACTORS AND PRINCIPAL COMPONENT ANALYSIS

Chapter 8 discusses factor models in which asset returns are described as being determined by the product of asset-specific sensitivities (typically betas) and market-wide variables (factors). This section details principal component analysis, a popular method of identifying statistical factors.

23.1.1 Principal Component Analysis and Types of Factors

Recall from Chapter 8 that there are three major categories of asset factors: macro, dynamic, and statistical. Macro and dynamic factors are verified by selecting an economic series and testing empirically to ascertain the factor's ability to explain past return premiums. For instance, potential economic factors that might be tested include inflation, productivity, and economic growth. Potential dynamic factors in a study of stock returns might include value, momentum, and size.

The key to macro and dynamic factor identification is that it starts with selecting existing and known variables and then testing them with return data. The key to statistical factors is that the data themselves (asset returns) are used to identify potential factors. **Principal component analysis (PCA)** is a linear statistical method that identifies the set of orthogonal factors from a data set that maximize the percentage of explained variation.

For example, the returns of a large sample of stocks might be examined using PCA in which the data set of returns is a matrix through time and across assets. A PCA analysis identifies subsets of stocks that tend to behave similarly with respect to one or more of the factors that it creates. The researcher can then examine the attributes of those firms to see which attributes seem to be driving the relations. Perhaps the researcher identifies that that the associations are linked to geographic regions, industries, sustainability, or governance. The key is that first the return data are used to identify empirical associations. Then the researcher analyzes the empirical associations to ascertain any links to characteristics that identify the factors. An example below illustrates the process.

23.1.2   The Basics of Principal Component Analysis

PCA is easily performed using statistical software such as SAS, SPSS, MiniTab, R, Python, and even as add-ins to EXCEL. An investment researcher simply identifies a set of assets and forms a matrix or table of their returns through time. The statistical programs then estimate variance-covariance matrices and generate two primary results for our purposes: loadings for each of the principal components and eigenvalues. These outputs are explained in more detail later. First, this section describes the process of obtaining the results.

The process of PCA reduces the dimensionality of the matrix. Recall that one example of a PCA in investments is to gather a large set of assets and returns. For example, a researcher might assemble a data set of perhaps 60 monthly returns for perhaps 200 firms forming a 60×200 matrix of returns. PCA reduces the data set along the dimension of firms to perhaps 3–10 from 200. In other words, rather than viewing the data set as having 200 separate firms, the result of the process is to identify perhaps 3–10 factors (principal components) that explain perhaps 90% or more of the return variation.

Here is how the software identifies the factors. First, the software searches for a vector of loadings (i.e., a set of loadings with one value for each asset) that maximizes the portion of the total return variance that can be explained by a single factor. The first vector of loadings that provides the maximum explanation of variance is the loadings of the first principal component. Next, the software searches for a second vector of loadings that maximizes the explanation of the remaining variance (which identifies the loadings of the second principal component). The process continues until the point where an additional principal component fails to explain enough variance to satisfy a user-specified (or default) criterion. The process utilizes vectors of factor loadings that are orthogonal (uncorrelated) with each other so that the marginal percentage of the variance explained by each additional principal component declines and does not alter the loadings of the previously-identified factors.

23.1.3   The Two Primary Outputs of Principal Component Analysis

A primary output of PCA is eigenvalues. An **eigenvalue** is a number that, in the case of a principal components analysis of investment returns, can be used to indicate the proportion of the return variance that is explained by each factor. For example, consider the eigenvalues in Exhibit 23.1.

The cumulative percentage of the variance explained by the first principal component is 80% which is found as its eigenvalue (4.0) divided by the sum of the eigenvalues (5.0). Some software programs automatically calculate the cumulative percentages explained and may even refer to the cumulative percentages as the eigenvalues because they are scaled representations.

EXHIBIT 23.1 Hypothetical Eigenvalues and Cumulative Percentages Explained

	Factor #1	Factor #2	Factor #3	Factor #4	...	Total
Eigenvalues	4.0	0.6	0.2	0.1	...	5.0
Cum. Pct. Explained	80%	92%	96 %	98%	...	100%

APPLICATION 23.1.3

An analyst performs a PCA with a very small criterion for limiting the number of principal components. The software generates the following eigenvalues:

	Factor #1	Factor #2	Factor #3	Factor #4	Factor #5	...	Total
Eigenvalues	22.0	14.0	11.0	1.9	0.9	...	50.0

What cumulative percent of the variance is explained by each factor? If the analyst had set a criterion of 5% additional variance explained, how many principal components would the software have shown?

The marginal percent of the variance explained by each factor is: 44.0%, 28.0%, 22.0%, 3.8%, and 1.8%, found by dividing each eigenvalue by the sum of the eigenvalues. The cumulative explanation is 44.0%, 72.0%, 94.0%, 97.8%, and 99.6%.

The **factor loadings** of each principal component are a vector of values (scores) with one loading for each asset (e.g., stock or bond) that inform the researcher of the responsiveness of each asset to each principal component. This is demonstrated in the example of the next section.

23.1.4 An Example of Applying and Interpreting a Principal Component Analysis

Consider the hypothetical weekly returns on US Treasury bills over a 2-year period for maturities of 1 week to 26 weeks depicted in Exhibit 23.2. An investment analyst simply inserts the return matrix into software that performs a PCA.

The analyst set a criterion that resulted in the process stopping at three factors because factors beyond three contributed minimal increased explanation of the variance. The analysis indicates that three factors explained a great deal of the variation in Treasury returns (which is consistent with actual studies). Next, the analyst examines principal components loadings or scores that are generated for each security for each factor as indicated in Exhibit 23.3.

The analyst graphs the loadings or scores and notes against the bond maturities (not shown). The graphs of the loadings of the first principal component tends to form a straight line, the graph of the loadings for the second principal component forms a gentle curve, while the results for the third principal component form a curve with a degree of curvature that changes over the maturity range.

EXHIBIT 23.2 Hypothetical Input Data Set of Bond Returns

		Tbill Returns			
		Weeks to Maturity			
		1	2	3 ...	26
	1	0.06%	0.07%	0.11% ...	0.19%
	2	−0.05%	0.01%	−0.01% ...	0.27%
Time	3	0.10%	0.01%	0.13% ...	0.18%
Period	4	0.06%	0.07%	0.03% ...	0.28%
	5	−0.05%	−0.04%	−0.05% ...	0.25%
	6	0.09%	0.01%	0.05% ...	0.14%
	7	0.04%	0.07%	0.09% ...	0.10%
	8	0.00%	0.11%	−0.02% ...	0.14%
	9	−0.07%	−0.02%	0.13% ...	0.10%
	10	0.06%	0.02%	0.00% ...	0.09%
	11	0.05%	−0.01%	0.07% ...	0.28%
	12	0.01%	−0.04%	0.05% ...	0.20%
	:	:	:	:	:
	104	0.09%	0.09%	0.06% ...	0.09%

EXHIBIT 23.3 Sample Output of Principal Component Loadings

	Factor #1	Factor #2	Factor #3
1-Week Tbill	0.02	.08	−.02
2-Week Tbill	0.04	.06	−.06
3-Week Tbill	0.07	.04	−.08
:	:	:	:
26-Week Tbill	0.42	.08	1.65

Actual analyses of the loadings of principal components of short-term Treasury returns indicate that there are three components that are often interpreted as relating to shifts in the height, slope, and curvature of the term structure of interest rates. An analysis of corporate bonds would likely note a default-risk-related factor by noting that the loadings or scores were related to bond ratings.

Had a PCA been applied to the returns of a number of hedge funds, the analyst might have noted the characteristics of the funds in relation to their loadings and perhaps concluded that the results were related to degrees of leverage, strategies, and home currencies.

Of course, if the characteristics that drive returns are already known, then PCA may not be as useful. A key strength of PCA occurs when the dimensions of the original data are vast: hundreds of securities with hundreds or thousands of returns through time for each security. The PCA may be able to reduce a dimension of the problem from hundreds or thousands to a small number of factors. In doing so, the analyst may develop a more clear understanding of the number of sources of return variation and, perhaps, the nature of the underlying sources of risk.

23.1.5 Three Key Differences Between Principal Component Analysis and Factor Analysis

A method similar to PCA is factor analysis. **Factor analysis (FA)** is a statistical method that seeks to identify factors and their coefficients through optimization of a specified model with explicit statistical assumptions. Three important differences between PCA and FA as typically applied are summarized below in the context of analyzing security returns:

1. FA typically makes specific statistical and modeling assumptions about the return process, while PCA does not require a definite model because it simply maximizes explained variance.
2. FA generates different factor scores when different numbers of factors are allowed in the model, while PCA's loadings do not change as the number of components considered is increased.
3. PCA can identify a factor driven almost entirely by one security (e.g., one stock or bond with a very volatile and unusual risk profile), while FA seeks factors that drive at least two securities.

While some descriptions within software packages and elsewhere may describe PCA as a special case of factor analysis, the methods are quite distinct.

23.2 MULTI-FACTOR MODELS AND REGRESSION

Whereas the single-factor market model (detailed in Level I of the CAIA curriculum) assumes that an asset's market exposure is the only risk that is priced (i.e., affects expected return), more than one risk factor is included in multi-factor models, as introduced in Part 2 of the Level II CAIA curriculum. Empirical analysis of multiple factors often utilizes multiple regression. A **multiple regression model** is a regression model with more than one independent variable.

23.2.1 Selecting Factors for Multi-factor Regression

In alternative investments, it is clear that a wide variety of variables explain *realized* returns. However, it is not clear the extent to which return factors determine *expected* returns (i.e., have expected risk premiums). In other words, just because realized returns are correlated with a particular factor does not necessarily imply that the factor has a nonzero risk premium. An alternative investment analyst must be especially careful when selecting variables, such as risk factors, to be independent variables in a multiple regression. The interpretation of a return regression's intercept as an estimate of the investment's alpha requires that the regression model be well specified. Any omitted risk factors will be captured in the regression's intercept and will be falsely attributed to alpha.

For example, if an equity manager makes an investment in a fund that includes commodities, and if an index representing the commodity market factor is not included in the regression, then any returns attributable to the commodity return factor may be counted as alpha. The Fama–French model, discussed in Chapter 8, is a very popular multi-factor model in the analysis of equity returns. Equation 23.1 is the empirical model of the Fama–French approach, in which realized returns of an investment are explained not only by estimated exposure to the stock market index (R_m), but also by estimated exposure to the anomaly factors of value and size:

$$R_{it} - R_f = a_i + b_{mi}(R_{mt} - R_f) + b_{1i}(R_{st} - R_{bt}) + b_{2i}(R_{ht} - R_{lt}) + e_{it} \qquad (23.1)$$

Equation 23.1 specifies a multiple regression model with R_f as the riskless return. By including the returns corresponding to the size factor, $R_s - R_b$, and the value factor, $R_h - R_l$, an analyst can expect that the returns of asset i in time period t, R_{it}, will be more fully explained and that the parameters that estimate the exposure of the asset to each of the factors (the value of each b) will be more accurately estimated. A typical result of adding more true factors to a model is that the r-squared increases and the estimated intercept (a_i) declines. The r-squared increases as the additional factors are explaining a greater portion of the variance in the dependent variable. The estimated alpha typically declines as returns that were previously attributed to the intercept are now explained by systematic risk exposure (and a risk premium) to the anomaly factors of size and value (betas). A major challenge in multiple regression is deciding which independent variables (factors) to include.

23.2.2 Multicollinearity

Level I of the CAIA curriculum detailed three major challenges with simple regression (outliers, autocorrelation, and heteroskedasticity), each of which is also a challenge in multiple regression. In addition, multiple regression adds the challenge of potential multicollinearity. **Multicollinearity** is when two or more independent variables in a regression model have high correlation to each other. A primary method of detecting multicollinearity is to examine the correlations between the independent variables.

When two independent variables are highly correlated, there are two primary adverse effects to regression results. The **two primary adverse effects of multicollinearity** are: (1) the estimates of the slope coefficients for each of the correlated independent variables may be highly inaccurate; and (2) the standard errors for the correlated independent variables may be inflated (large). With multicollinearity, even though the r-squared of a regression may be high, it can be difficult to find independent variables with coefficients that have significant t-statistics.

There are several corrections for multicollinearity. In the case of returns as independent variables, one potential method for correction is to form return spreads between the correlated independent variables. For example, consider a multiple regression equation with a US stock index and a non-US stock index both serving as independent variables. Because the contemporaneous returns of US and non-US stocks tend to have high correlation with each other, this multiple regression model probably has multicollinearity. The estimated slope coefficients for each of the highly correlated factors would be unreliable and are likely to be statistically insignificant. To avoid this issue, the analyst might start with a US equity index return series as one independent variable and then add the difference (spread) between the returns of the US stock index and the non-US stocks as a second independent variable.

This transformation serves to reduce the correlation between the independent variables, now making it possible to better separate the effects of each market segment independently.

23.2.3 Selecting the Number of Factors and Overfitting

Once the list of potential return factors is determined, the next challenge is to determine which of the independent variables should be included and retained in the regression equation. Especially when multicollinearity is a potential issue, rather than running a "kitchen sink" regression that includes all potential variables, a stepwise regression technique is more appropriate. **Stepwise regression** is an iterative technique in which variables are added or deleted from the regression equation based on their statistical significance. At each step, the variables with the greatest *t*-statistics are added to or retained in the model, and variables with insignificant *t*-statistics are deleted from the model.

Although stepwise regression can be an extremely fast way to consider many independent variables and reduce the number of variables ultimately included, the analyst should be cognizant of the temptation for data dredging. Searching across large data sets with numerous potential independent variables can locate statistically significant relations over the time period of the regression, but these results may fail to predict or explain the dependent variable using data from outside the sample. Analysts must also be careful to not include too many variables in the regression to avoid overfitting the model. **Overfitted models** explain the past well (i.e., the model explains the data used to fit the model), but they do not predict future relations well. Ideally, the analyst's knowledge should be used to limit the variables under consideration to those that make economic sense.

23.3 PARTIAL AUTOCORRELATIONS AND REGRESSION

Level I of the CAIA curriculum discussed partial autocorrelations and reported estimated autocorrelations for many asset indices. This section details their intuition and estimation.

23.3.1 Intuition of Partial Autocorrelations

A return autocorrelation is commonly estimated as a simple Pearson correlation coefficient between the returns of a series separated by one or more time periods. For example, in the case of a daily return series of 100 days, the first order autocorrelation would be estimated as the correlation between two arrays: days 1 to 99, and days 2 to 100. The second order autocorrelation would be estimated as the correlation between two arrays separated by two days: days 1 to 98, and days 3 to 100, and so forth.

The problem with Pearson correlations as return autocorrelations is that the nth order estimated autocorrelation coefficient is driven at least in part by the 1st through n^{th} autocorrelations and so it is not clear what the *marginal* contribution of the nth order autocorrelation is. The **n^{th} order partial autocorrelation coefficient** is designed to denote the marginal or incremental autocorrelation contribution of only the return that is lagged n periods.

EXHIBIT 23.4 Regression Goodness-of-Fit Results

Regression Statistics	
Multiple R	0.5951
R Square	0.3542
Adjusted R Square	0.3045
Standard Error	0.0213
Observations	71.0000

23.3.2 Estimation of Partial Autocorrelations

Formulas exist for estimating partial autocorrelations of a few orders. However, the formulas become very complex beyond second-order partial autocorrelations. An easy method to estimate the first n partial autocorrelations is simply to perform a multivariate regression of the return of each time period on the n previous observations:

$$R_t = a + b_1 R_{t-1} + b_2 R_{t-2} + \ldots + b_n R_{t-n} + e_t \tag{23.2}$$

where R_t is the return of an asset in time t, a is the estimated intercept of the regression and e_t is the residual (estimated error) for time t. In Equation 23.2, b_i is the estimated i^{th} order partial autocorrelation coefficient, for $i = 1, \ldots, n$.

23.3.3 Partial Autocorrelations of a Return Series Based on Appraisals

This section demonstrates the estimation of partial autocorrelation using multiple regression in the case of timberland returns. Timberland returns are selected for this demonstration because the returns are based on appraisals—which are well known to reflect value changes on a delayed basis and therefore exhibit strong positive auto-correlations of first order and higher orders.

Exhibit 23.4 reports summary statistics of the regression (a fifth-order version of Equation 23.2). The 19 years of data contained 76 quarterly observations. The estimation of up to a fifth-order autocorrelation means that the first observation in the regression comes from the sixth time period because time periods 1 to 5 are used to form the five independent variables. The R square of 0.3542 indicates that 35% of the variability in the dependent variable is explained by the independent variables (five previous periods of returns).

Exhibit 23.5 reports the estimated intercept and slope coefficients along with their standard errors.

Finally, Exhibit 23.6 reports the estimated autocorrelation coefficients using simple Pearson correlation coefficients.

Note that the second-order autocorrelation coefficient in the multiple regression (Exhibit 23.5) (estimated as a partial autocorrelation coefficient) is only 0.10 while the estimate based on Pearson correlations (in Exhibit 23.6) is 0.26. The difference confirms the concern that simple correlations between the returns in periods t and t-2 may be biased indicators of the causality of R_{t-2} on R_t. In other

EXHIBIT 23.5 Regression Coefficient Results

	Coefficients	Standard Error
Intercept	0.0055	0.0035
X Variable 1	0.2394	0.1212
X Variable 2	0.1008	0.1059
X Variable 3	−0.0010	0.1065
X Variable 4	0.5226	0.1057
X Variable 5	−0.2069	0.1205

EXHIBIT 23.6 Pearson Autocorrelation Coefficients

Order	1	2	3	4	5
Pearson Autocorrelation Coefficients	0.2273	0.2632	0.1455	0.5407	0.0518

words, the value of 0.26 for the second-order autocorrelation in Exhibit 23.6 is driven by both the first- and second-order partial autocorrelation coefficients.

23.4 THREE DYNAMIC RISK EXPOSURE MODELS

The multiple regression models considered so far make the key assumption that the return to a fund or security (i.e., the dependent variable) is linearly related to the factors or independent variables in the model. However, hedge funds and other alternative investments often have nonlinear exposures to market factors due to the positions held or the trading strategy implemented. A **nonlinear exposure** of a position to a market factor is when the sensitivity of the position's value varies based on the magnitude of the change in the market factor's value.

23.4.1 The Nonlinear Exposure of Perfect Market-Timing Foresight

Positions with nonlinear exposures include long or short positions in call or put options. Also, event-driven strategies, such as merger arbitrage or distressed investments, can create nonlinear payoff diagrams similar to those of short positions in put options. Strategies that generate nonlinear exposures also include market-timing strategies, such as managed futures funds, which may expand long positions after a rise in a market and expand short positions after a fall in markets and therefore vary their exposures to factors based on market price levels.

For example, consider a perfect market timer that profits from a market move in either direction by taking the appropriate market-directional bet based on perfect forecasting ability. The single-period profits or losses of this hypothetical trader would be the same as having free long positions in option straddles, meaning long a call and long a put with the same strike price. The diagram of potential profit or loss against the single-period market return would be a perfect V shape, with the bottom of the V on the origin (the intersection of the vertical and horizontal axes).

A simple linear regression performed using returns from several periods may indicate no explanatory power, since the relation is a mix of positive and negative slopes (exposures to factors). In other words, a perfect market-timing strategy would generate high returns both for when the market rose substantially and when it fell substantially and would not experience negative returns. One solution to this nonlinear payoff structure would be to use a nonlinear model that permitted the regression coefficients to change, producing different exposures for different markets (i.e., different ranges of the independent variable).

This section describes **three dynamic risk exposure models** that can be used to estimate the effectiveness of market-timing strategies and other nonlinear exposures: a dummy variable approach, a separate regression approach, and a quadratic approach.

23.4.2   The Dummy Variable Approach to Dynamic Risk Exposures

The effectiveness of market-timing strategies can be analyzed by a comparison of their average risk exposures to up markets and their average risk exposures to down markets. Equation 23.3 models different responses of the returns of a fund to up markets and down markets:

$$R_{it} - R_f = a_i + \{[b_{i,d} + (D_1 \times b_{i,diff})] \times (R_{mt} - R_f)\} + e_{it} \qquad (23.3)$$

The dummy variable, D_1 , is set equal to 1 when excess returns on the market index, $R_{mt} - R_f$, are positive and set equal to zero when the excess returns are zero or negative. The down market beta, $b_{i,d}$, is the responsiveness of the fund's return to the market return when the market return is less than the riskless rate (i.e., when the market's excess return is negative, or down). The coefficient $b_{i,diff}$ is the difference between the sensitivities or betas of the fund's return to up and down markets. The up market beta, $b_{i,u}$, (not directly included in Equation 23.3) is the responsiveness of the fund's return to the market return when the excess market return is positive, and is estimated as the sum of $b_{i,d}$ and $b_{i,diff}$.

Inspection of Equation 23.3 indicates that in down markets, the coefficient of the market's excess returns is simply $b_{i,d}$ (the down beta), whereas in up markets, the coefficient is $b_{i,d} + b_{i,diff}$, which is the model's estimate of the up market beta.

Suppose, for example, that $b_{i,d} = 0.5$ and $b_{i,diff} = 0.7$. When the market index is earning a positive excess return, $D_1 = 1$, and the total beta exposure of the fund is 1.2, which is the sum of the down beta coefficient, 0.5, and the dummy beta coefficient during up markets, 0.7. When the market index is generating a negative excess return, $D_1 = 0$, and the total beta exposure of the fund is 0.5. When $b_{i,diff}$ is greater than zero, the manager is demonstrating a valuable market-timing skill by increasing exposure to market risk during times of positive excess returns and reducing market exposure during times of negative excess returns. Conversely, a negative value of $b_{i,diff}$ indicates a negative alpha with regard to market timing.

Mathematically equivalent models to Equation 23.3 can be formed through algebra. For example, a model can be derived with explicit up and down betas. An advantage to the model in Equation 23.3 is that it can automatically be used to test for a difference between the up and down betas by testing whether $b_{i,diff}$ statistically differs from zero. Note that $b_{i,diff}$ is the key measure of market-timing skill in this model.

23.4.3 The Separate Regression Approach to Dynamic Risk Exposures

A similar approach to the dummy variable approach is to perform separate regressions based on subsamples. If the regression is being performed on a time series, then the analyst simply breaks the data set into two or more subsamples based on a specified condition, especially an independent variable such as a market factor. For example, one subsample could include markets with positive market price changes, and the other subsample could include markets with a negative market change.

For example, Black (2006) finds that hedge funds of funds' behavior changed dramatically from the 1990–97 period to the 1999–2004 period, using 1998's experience with Long-Term Capital Management as a dividing line in hedge fund risk exposures. Using the entire time frame of 1990 to 2004 would have not only obscured the change in behavior over this time period but also would have obscured the degree to which behavior could be well described within each subperiod.

23.4.4 The Quadratic Approach to Dynamic Risk Exposures

Another approach to assessing market-timing skill uses a quadratic curve (i.e., a squared term) rather than a dummy variable or separate regressions. Consider another skilled but imperfect market timer, such as a skilled trend follower. That market timer might tend to perform exceedingly well with large underlying up or down (i.e., large directional) moves in the market, have modest profits in markets with smaller directional moves, and perform with likely losses during directionless markets. Henriksson and Merton (1981), as well as Treynor and Mazuy (1966), discuss models to explain market-timing performance. One such model is:

$$R_{it} - R_f = \alpha_i + b_{im}(R_{mt} - R_f)^2 + e_{it} \tag{23.4}$$

Equation 23.4 provides an accurate fit for a U-shaped profit-loss diagram. In the nonlinear model of Equation 23.4, the squared value of the excess return on the market is used to explain the performance of the fund's excess return. A statistically significant and positive beta coefficient on the squared term in Equation 23.4 is an indication that the manager has been able to successfully time the market, earning positive returns in both strong market rises and strong market declines. A significant negative value of b_{im} indicates that the manager has perverse market-timing skill, in which the average market-timing decision is detracting value from the fund. However, a positive estimated beta in Equation 23.4 can also be obtained by purchasing option straddles. The costs of the option straddles, which would be captured by the intercept, may outweigh the benefits. Further insight into the potential for skill would therefore include examination of the estimated intercept as well as considering how many managers were tested in the process, since the indication of skill may have been generated by luck.

23.5 TWO APPROACHES TO MODELING CHANGING CORRELATION

The assumption that volatilities and correlations are constant over time and over market conditions facilitates simpler modeling, but the dynamics of the data often conflict with this assumption. The return distributions of hedge funds and hedge fund indices are nonstationary, meaning that return volatilities and correlations vary through time. This section discusses two approaches for modeling changing correlation: conditional correlation and rolling window.

23.5.1　Conditional Correlation Modeling Approach

A **conditional correlation** is a correlation between two variables under specified circumstances. For example, an analyst may estimate the correlation coefficient between a hedge fund's returns and the returns of an equity index during only those months in which the stock market rose by 1% or more. The correlation coefficient being estimated would be a conditional correlation coefficient rather than an unconditional correlation coefficient because the behavior being measured is based on or applicable to a limited set of circumstances. Conditional correlation is constant across conditions when the relation between two variables is completely linear.

Conditional correlation estimation and analysis of differences between estimates can be used to understand nonlinear relationships and is similar to the separate regression approach discussed in Section 23.4.3. The differences are that: (1) the regression-based approach can include multiple factors; and (2) regression coefficients differ from correlation coefficients by a scale factor related to volatility ratios.

23.5.2　Interpreting an Example of Conditional Correlations

Consider the statistics in Exhibit 23.7. Underlying Exhibit 23.7 are the correlations, standard deviations, and mean returns during two subsamples based on whether each month experienced a rise or decline for the S&P 500 Index as proxied by an S&P 500 exchange-traded fund. The "up" subsample includes the months when the S&P 500 Index experienced a nonnegative total return. In that subsample, the S&P 500 rose with a monthly average return of 3.1%. The "down" subsample is the remaining months in which the index fell. During the second subsample, the S&P 500 Index experienced an average monthly return of −3.8%.

EXHIBIT 23.7　Change in Hedge Fund Risk, Return, and Correlation on Up versus Down Returns in the S&P 500 Index. Monthly Returns, March 1994 to December 2018.

	Correlation (Up)	Correlation (Down)	Change in Correlation Up - Down	Standard Deviation (Up)	Standard Deviation (Down)	Average Return (Up)	Average Return (Down)
Hedge Fund Index	0.25	0.49	−0.24	5.7%	6.1%	1.3%	−0.7%
Convertible Arbitrage	0.26	0.35	−0.09	4.4%	8.3%	0.8%	−0.1%
Emerging Markets	0.23	0.55	−0.32	11.3%	12.8%	1.7%	−1.6%
Equity Market Neutral	0.33	0.19	0.14	3.9%	14.6%	0.7%	−0.4%
Event Driven	0.34	0.52	−0.19	3.9%	6.9%	1.3%	−0.6%
Distressed	0.28	0.55	−0.28	4.1%	7.0%	1.3%	−0.4%
Risk Arbitrage	0.31	0.43	−0.12	3.1%	4.4%	0.8%	−0.1%
Fixed Income Arbitrage	0.06	0.42	−0.36	3.5%	6.8%	0.6%	0.0%
Macro	0.09	0.16	−0.07	8.7%	7.4%	1.2%	0.1%
Long/Short Equity	0.42	0.49	−0.07	6.8%	8.4%	1.7%	−1.3%
Managed Futures	−0.01	−0.36	0.35	10.8%	12.4%	0.5%	0.1%
Multistrategy	0.15	0.31	−0.16	4.0%	5.6%	0.9%	−0.1%
S&P 500 Index				8.1%	10.8%	3.1%	−3.7%

Exhibit 23.7 displays the changes to the estimated correlation coefficients, standard deviations, and mean returns between the two subsamples. For example, the last line indicates that the mean monthly return of the S&P 500 was 6.8% lower in the down sample (−3.7% for falling equity markets) than in the up sample (3.1%). The other rows indicate the correlation, standard deviation, and mean return changes for indices corresponding to 12 hedge fund strategies. In each case, the subsample differs based on whether the S&P 500 Index was up or down for the associated months. All of the hedge fund strategies had lower average monthly returns in the down sample months for the S&P 500 than in the up months.

Importantly, 10 of the 12 hedge fund indices had a higher correlation to equity market returns in down markets than they had in up markets. When the correlation in the down sample is higher than the correlation in the up sample, it is termed negative conditional correlation. The negative conditional correlation in Exhibit 23.7 is undesirable for hedge fund investors, as investors desire lower correlations during times when stock prices are declining to mitigate losses, and higher correlations when stock prices are rising to extend profits. Positive conditional correlation of investment returns to market returns is when the correlation in the up sample is higher than the correlation in the down sample. Investors prefer investment strategies with positive conditional correlation, since the strategies offer higher participation in profits during markets that rose and lower participation in losses during markets that declined. The only indices exhibiting positive conditional correlation during this period were managed futures and equity market-neutral funds.

It should be noted that the results of Exhibit 23.7, like most similar empirical analyses of correlation, are subject to being dominated by the most extreme outcomes. The two particularly bad months for the S&P 500 (August 1998 and October 2008) exert a strong effect on estimated correlations. The managed futures index was up in both of those months, and the equity market neutral index was near zero in both months, which likely explains why those indices alone had estimated positive conditional correlation. Careful analysis should be used to judge whether predictions of future behavior should be so heavily influenced by the two largest outliers in terms of S&P 500 returns.

23.5.3 Variations on Conditional Empirical Analyses

Conditional correlation analysis is not limited to separating a sample into only two subsamples or to separating a sample based only on the behavior of the variable with which the correlations are being estimated. For example, an analyst might examine the correlation between hedge fund strategies and equity returns in three market conditions: increased interest rates, decreased interest rates, and stable interest rates.

Further, parameters other than correlation, such as volatilities and means, can be analyzed on a conditional basis. Conditional correlation and other conditional analyses can be viewed as general methods of examining the behavior of estimated parameters relative to one or more identifiable variables. The development and application of advanced methods to model the dynamic behavior of return distributions is an important frontier of alternative investments.

23.5.4 Rolling Window Modeling Approach

Another method to model changing correlation caused by the dynamic exposures of an investment strategy is to use a rolling window analysis. **Rolling window analysis** is a relatively advanced technique for analyzing statistical behavior over time, using overlapping subsamples that move evenly through time. When analysts use multiple time periods in a regression or correlation analysis, the data set is typically divided into two, three, or four subperiods of time, with every observation included in only one subsample. A rolling window analysis chooses a time width for the window, such as 36 months, and performs the regression or correlation analysis for each contiguous 36-month period in the data. The subperiods use overlapping data as the window moves from the first 36 months of data to the last 36 months of data.

For example, using 10 years of data, a rolling window analysis with a window of 36 months would produce 85 outputs of 36 observations each. The first analysis and output would use the data from months 1 to 36, the second from months 2 to 37, and the final from months 85 to 120. These 85 subsamples can be used to conduct a rolling window regression analysis of the returns of a fund against the returns of several market indices. The output of the first regression would show the estimated relation between the dependent and independent variables over the first 3-year (36-month) period (months 1 to 36). The second regression would be the same as the first regression except it would delete the first monthly observation and add the observation of the 37th month.

As the regression walks forward in time, the sensitivity of fund returns to each market variable can change to reflect the dynamic allocations of the fund manager. Put together, the estimated parameters, perhaps with their confidence intervals, can be graphed through time to illustrate the dynamic nature of the estimates. It should be noted that even though this rolling window approach would generate 85 sets of regression results, the regressions use overlapping data and are therefore not independent statistical tests. With 10 years of data, there are only three statistically independent 3-year regressions that can be performed.

APPLICATION 23.5.4A

A 50-week rolling window analysis is performed with exactly 4 years of data (208 weeks). How many windows (observation intervals) would there be and how many statistically independent windows would there be?

The 208 weeks of data would generate 159 windows of analysis, but there would be only four independent analyses, such as 1–50, 51–100, 101–150, and 151–200.

Rolling window analysis and other forms of multi-period analysis using longer-term returns, such as monthly returns, are often appropriate for determining long-term style drifts. Some fund strategies, such as equity market-neutral, managed futures, and global macro, are more likely to alternate signs of exposures too quickly to be well measured with a long-term analysis. Shorter-term changes in exposures are better analyzed with shorter-term return intervals, such as daily return data.

23.6 FOUR MULTI-FACTOR APPROACHES TO UNDERSTANDING RETURNS

A large set of returns can often be better understood by organizing the data into groups or analyzing the returns relative to common factors. This section discusses four approaches to multi-factor empirical methods based on four principles: asset classes, strategies, market-wide factors, and specialized market factors. Each approach organizes or analyzes individual investment data using a different principle. Empirical analyses based on each approach have generated important conclusions, which are summarized at the end of each section. The discussion focuses on hedge fund returns but applies to other classes of assets as well.

23.6.1 Understanding Style Analysis and Fund Groupings Based on Asset Classes

Multi-factor return models can use the returns of underlying asset classes to explain the returns of investment pools. For example, the returns of convertible arbitrage hedge funds are often explained based on the returns of asset classes such as equities, bonds, and options.

Style analysis is the process of understanding an investment strategy, especially using a statistical approach, based on grouping funds by their investment strategies or styles. The key question in a style analysis is this: do investment funds of the same stated investment style have returns that can be explained by the same underlying return factors?

The modern approach to performing style analysis on traditional mutual funds was pioneered by Sharpe (1992), who: (1) groups mutual funds by their stated investment styles; and (2) analyzes the performance of each group (i.e., style) relative to the performance of various potential underlying asset classes. Sharpe attributes the returns of mutual funds to the returns of indices corresponding to traditional financial security classes related to the most common holdings of the mutual funds. In other words, Sharpe's style analysis regresses mutual fund returns (as the dependent variable) on the returns of various asset classes (as the independent variables). Sharpe selects several distinct bond indices and numerous indices of stocks based on size, country, and other attributes as the independent variables. His results indicate that up to 90% of each mutual fund's returns is explained by the returns of a few underlying asset classes. The balance of returns may be attributable to manager skill, including security selection and market timing, or luck.

Fung and Hsieh (1997) use data on hedge funds to apply a style analysis approach analogous to that conducted by Sharpe but to alternative investments. They focus on using indices of traditional asset returns to explain the returns of hedge funds. Contrary to Sharpe's results for mutual funds, Fung and Hsieh find that the amount of variation of hedge fund returns that is explained by financial asset class returns is low: R-squared measures are less than 25% for almost half of the hedge funds studied.

In summary, traditional mutual fund returns are well explained by the returns of the asset classes that the funds hold, but the same is not true for hedge funds. Empirical evidence indicates that the returns on most hedge funds are not well explained by passive return indices of their underlying assets. For example, managed futures funds hold positions in commodity futures, but an analyst should not expect that a particular managed futures fund will have returns that are highly correlated to commodity price indices. Managed futures funds have actively traded long and short positions, and their returns depend more on the extent to which managers can time changes in commodity prices. Managed futures funds also trade a wide variety of markets, where positions in currencies, equity indices, and interest rate markets will dilute the exposure of managed futures funds to the commodity markets.

23.6.2 Understanding Funds Based on Strategies

Another interesting question is whether funds with the same stated investment strategy or style have similar returns or have returns that respond to similar risk factors. For example, in traditional investments, the returns of an equity fund are compared with the returns of other equity funds to detect the extent to which the equity funds respond to the same underlying risk factors, such as Fama–French factors. The analysis is often taken to a finer level of detail so that a US large-cap growth fund is compared with other such funds. Grouping funds by strategies or styles and analyzing the returns of funds with the returns of other funds of similar style is commonly performed in both traditional and alternative investments.

The stated strategy or style of a traditional mutual fund is usually quite clear from examining its publicly available listings of assets and from the fact that most traditional mutual funds maintain relatively stable portfolios. However, hedge fund portfolios are often opaque, can be very diverse, and can have changing portfolios and risk exposures. Further, a hedge fund may not identify itself as following a particular style that can be used to associate that hedge fund with other hedge funds. Even if a group of hedge funds can be identified with the same style (e.g., equity market timing), the funds within that style group may have very different trading strategies and very different returns. Finally, a hedge fund's strategy or style may change or drift through time.

Fung and Hsieh use data on hedge funds and PCA (principal component analysis, discussed in the first section of this chapter) to find return commonalities among hedge fund returns. Fung and Hsieh find that the returns of many hedge funds can be moderately explained by viewing most of the funds as behaving as if they belong in one of five groups or trading styles, which they labeled as: (1) systems/opportunistic; (2) global macro; (3) value; (4) systems/trend following; and (5) distressed. They estimate that these five hedge fund styles explain about 45% of the cross-sectional variation in hedge fund returns. Their work suggests that cross-sectional hedge fund returns are better explained by their trading styles than by their correlations with traditional asset classes. For example, the returns of a global macro fund tend to be explained better by the fund's tendency to behave like other global macro funds than by its mixture of underlying traditional asset classes.

In summary, a hedge fund's return is explained better by its trading style than by the returns of hedge funds with the same stated style or the returns of the asset classes that it trades. For example, an equity market-neutral fund is unlikely to have returns highly correlated with all other equity market-neutral funds, because the returns of these funds are driven by distinct idiosyncratic risks. Also, an equity market-neutral fund is unlikely to have returns highly correlated with underlying equity market indices, because the fund strives to hedge its returns against equity market fluctuations. Rather, an equity market-neutral fund with trades based on a trading style, such as trend following, is more likely to have returns correlated with other funds that use trend following, whether they are equity market-neutral funds or not.

23.6.3 Understanding Funds Based on Market-wide Factors

The pioneering work of Fama and French, discussed in Chapter 8, indicates that individual equity returns can be explained by identifiable market-wide factors, such as size. The key to this type of analysis is the reliance on an arbitrage-free model of returns that applies to all assets and all funds in the market. Researchers develop relevant factors by: (1) developing a concept of how the returns experienced by underlying securities in the market might vary based on a particular variable (e.g., size); (2) dividing the sample into two subgroups based on that variable (e.g., a large-cap group and a small-cap group); (3) estimating the return spread from being long one of the groups and short the other group; and (4) empirically examining whether returns from the entire sample of securities are consistently explained by the return spread.

The factors in a Fama–French style of analysis are referred to as tradable because an investor could receive the returns of each factor by holding long positions in one set of stocks (e.g., small-cap stocks) and short positions in another set of stocks (e.g., large-cap stocks). When the factors are tradable, there are two important economic implications: (1) the intercept of the model in an efficient market must be equal to the riskless rate; and (2) the model itself can be described as an arbitrage-free relationship, because if the model did not have a mean-zero error term or intercept equal to the riskless rate, there would be an arbitrage opportunity. In other words, if some error terms were consistently positive or negative, a market participant could earn superior risk-adjusted returns with long positions in the assets with generally positive error terms, and short positions in the assets with consistently negative error terms. Fama and French identified a market factor, a size factor, and a value factor. Other researchers report evidence of many other factors.

How can this market-wide factor approach of Fama and French be extended to alternative investments? To what extent can hedge fund returns be well explained by market-wide factors?

Fung and Hsieh (2004) propose seven observable and tradable factors:

1. The return of the S&P 500 minus the risk-free return.
2. Small-cap stock returns minus large-cap stock returns.
3. The return of the 10-year Treasury bond minus the risk-free return.
4. The return of Baa-rated bonds minus the return of the 10-year Treasury bond.
5. The return of a portfolio of call and put options on bonds.
6. The return of a portfolio of call and put options on currencies.
7. The return of a portfolio of call and put options on commodities.

The options portfolios (factors 5, 6, and 7) refer to portfolios of calls and puts that are constructed to mimic the behavior of a series of look-back options. A **look-back option** has a payoff that is based on the value of the underlying asset over a reference period rather than simply the value of the underlying asset at the option's expiration date. Fung and Hsieh estimate that 90% of the return variation in *diversified* portfolios of hedge funds can be explained by the seven factors. However, individual hedge fund returns are not so well explained.

23.6.4   Understanding Funds Based on Specialized Market Factors

A final and emerging approach to analyzing hedge fund returns with multiple factors is related to hedge fund replication. As detailed in Chapter 26, hedge fund replication is the process of mimicking the performance of a particular hedge fund investment strategy using different assets or a different investment process. For example, a convertible bond arbitrage fund may hold long positions in convertible bonds, hedged with short positions in equities that are selected using a proprietary model and the skilled discretion of the fund's manager. One hedge fund replication strategy might be to try to replicate the convertible bond strategy's returns using different underlying assets, such as a portfolio of equity indices, bond indices, and call options. This strategy is often used to create liquid products that attempt to replicate a strategy that uses illiquid securities by designing a strategy that uses liquid securities as underlying assets. Another fund replication strategy might be to try to replicate the returns of a skill-based proprietary strategy using a naïve and mechanical trading model applied to positions similar to the positions being held by the fund being replicated.

In the context of multi-factor return models, hedge fund replication involves identifying specialized market factors and estimating fund exposures to those factors such that a portfolio of other securities can be constructed that generates beta similar to a selected fund.

The difference between this approach and the market-wide factor approach is that here, the factors are selected to be tailored to the specifics of a particular fund rather than gathered as market-wide factors. Factors in a market-wide approach are selected based on how they explain returns of all of the assets in a market. The **specialized market factors** in a specialized market factor approach are specifically identified and selected to represent the returns to a specific fund rather than the overall market. The factors may be identified empirically by searching for historical correlations between a fund's returns and potential factors, or they may be identified through an understanding of the fund's strategy.

In summary, the specialized market factor approach to hedge fund replication uses the returns of specially chosen factors to explain the return of each particular fund. This approach assumes that the manager's beta exposure and pursuit of alpha may be predictable enough that the returns of the fund can be closely linked to these specialized market-based factors. For example, the returns to a US merger arbitrage hedge fund may be highly correlated with a factor that contains hedged positions in all announced US mergers.

23.7   EVIDENCE ON FUND PERFORMANCE PERSISTENCE

Perhaps the most important question with respect to all alternative investment managers, not just hedge fund managers, is this: can the manager systematically repeat good performance? Asset returns driven by multiple factors raise substantive challenges in performance attribution relative to single-factor approaches. An obvious approach is to use a multiple factor model in a full performance attribution analysis. This section briefly discusses empirical methods used to examine performance persistence that do not explicitly adjust for multiple factors.

23.7.1   Performance Persistence Based on Return Correlations

One simple approach to estimating performance persistence is to examine the correlation between samples of earlier returns and subsequent returns. For example, Brown, Goetzmann, and Ibbotson (1999) simply regress past hedge fund returns on more recent hedge fund returns. Over the 6 years studied, they find that three of the years had persistent positive performance, with positive coefficients between the returns of subsequent and earlier periods. However, they also find that three of the years had negative coefficients. They conclude that there is no evidence of performance persistence in their hedge fund sample.

A problem with examinations of return persistence based on correlations or regressions is that the results could be driven by short-term serial correlation of returns, which does not reflect true long-term performance correlations. Serial correlation is the same as autocorrelation: it is the correlation of a variable, such as return, in one time period (e.g., year) to the same variable in another time period. Further, although serial correlation of returns may be an indication of true skill persistence, it may also be due to the inaccuracy of smoothed or managed pricing. For example, if farmland is valued using appraisal methods that are slow to react to true price changes, the return series based on the appraised values will contain positive serial correlation. However, the observed return persistence does not indicate a trading opportunity because the values are not tradable market values.

23.7.2   Performance Persistence Based on Risk-Adjusted Returns

Another problem with the examination of serially correlated asset returns occurs when the returns are not risk adjusted. Since high-risk assets should consistently generate higher returns than low-risk assets, return persistence in a sample may simply reflect heterogeneous risks. Returns need to be risk-adjusted either when the risks differ between funds or when the risks of individual funds shift through time.

This type of empirical test contains a joint hypothesis. A **joint hypothesis** is a test with results that depend on two hypotheses: (1) the hypothesis that the test method is valid; and (2) the hypothesis being tested, such as a null hypothesis that return persistence does not exist. A finding that the null hypothesis cannot be rejected indicates either: (1) that that the test was not valid (perhaps because the risk-adjustment method did not properly adjust for risk); or (2) that performance does not persist. For example, perhaps a factor-based model was used to adjust for risk and the factors were not well specified. The problem of a test based on risk-adjusted performance analysis is that, especially within alternative investment analysis, there is much uncertainty about how to adjust for risk.

Returns driven by multiple factors raise special concerns that the method used to adjust for factors is not valid. One approach to adjusting for risk is to measure risk as the volatility of total returns. For example, Park and Staum (1999) measure skill by the ratio of excess return as measured by the CAPM divided by the standard deviation of the hedge fund manager's returns. They use this skill statistic to rank hedge fund managers on a year-by-year basis and then compare this ranking to the following year's skill ranking. Using this risk-adjusted approach, they find strong evidence that hedge fund manager skill persists from year to year.

23.7.3 Performance Persistence Based on Portfolio Returns

Empirical analyses of return persistence vary by time periods analyzed, time intervals used, and investments examined. To reduce the confounding effects of multiple factors and high idiosyncratic risk on statistical analysis, researchers often group individual securities into portfolios. Aggarwal, Georgiev, and Pinato (2007) group funds into portfolios and find that a portfolio of equity-based hedge funds during a 31-month period has estimated alphas that are significantly more predictive than predictions based on short in-sample periods of 6 to 9 months.

Overall, the evidence is mixed on whether alternative investment managers can generate consistently superior risk-adjusted returns. The mixed conclusions could be due to different samples of funds, different time periods tested, or different methods implemented. The difficulty of empirically identifying and predicting alpha emphasizes the need to understand markets, understand individual fund strategies, and conduct rigorous qualitative due diligence on each hedge fund manager. There is one firm conclusion: improved models of risk and return will help investigators better understand the extent to which true risk-adjusted performance does or does not persist.

REFERENCES

Aggarwal, R., G. Georgiev, and J. Pinato. 2007. "Detecting Performance Persistence in Fund Managers." *Journal of Portfolio Management* 33 (2): 110–19.

Black, K. H. 2006. "The Changing Performance and Factor Risks of Funds of Funds in the Modern Period," in *Funds of Hedge Funds: Performance, Assessment, Diversification and Statistical Properties*, ed. Greg N. Gregoriou, Oxford, UK: Elsevier, pp. 99–106.

Brown, S., W. Goetzmann, and R. Ibbotson. 1999. "Offshore Hedge Funds: Survival and Performance, 1989–95." *Journal of Business* 72 (1): 91–118.

Fung, W. and D. Hsieh. 2004. "Hedge Fund Benchmarks: A Risk-Based Approach." *Financial Analysts Journal* 60 (5): 65–80.

Fung, W. and D. Hsieh. 1997. "Empirical Characteristics of Dynamic Trading Strategies: The Case of Hedge Funds." *Review of Financial Studies* 10 (2): 275–302.

Henriksson, R. and R. Merton. 1981. "On Market Timing and Investment Performance II: Statistical Procedures for Evaluating Forecasting Skills." *Journal of Business* 54 (4): 513–33.

Park, J. and J. Staum. 1999. "Performance Persistence in the Alternative Investment Industry." Paradigm Capital Management Working Paper.

Sharpe, W. 1992. "Asset Allocation: Management Style and Performance Measurement." *Journal of Portfolio Management* 18 (2): 7–19.

Treynor, J. and K. Mazuy. 1966. "Can Mutual Funds Outguess the Market?" *Harvard Business Review* 44: 131–36.

CHAPTER 24

Relative Value Methods

A relative value strategy attempts to identify two or more positions that have diverged from their predicted price relation and to seek superior risk-adjusted performance by establishing positions (typically long and short) that will gain if the assets move closer to the predicted relation (i.e., converge). In other words, relative value strategies take a combination of long and short positions in instruments that are perceived as having values or returns that are linked together and are predicted to have an attractive probability of converging values. This linkage could be based on an economic relation between the two securities or on empirical observations.

A relative value strategy may be viewed as having a thesis that two or more assets are relatively mispriced and that their valuations are likely to converge. The distinction between directional strategies (which also seek to identify mispriced assets) and relative value strategies is that relative value strategies seek to hedge out directional risk.

24.1 OVERVIEW OF RELATIVE VALUE METHODS

Relative value strategies vary in three primary ways: (1) the method or theory by which assets are viewed as being linked; (2) the method or theory through which potential opportunities are determined; and (3) the markets or securities in which the trades take place. Relative value strategies can be implemented in the context of equity, fixed income, commodity, currency, and the related derivatives markets.

For example, consider a hedge fund with a thesis that the stock prices of two oil companies (neither of which hedge their commodity exposures) are likely to be highly linked and, in the absence of major firm-specific events, will tend to follow similar paths (i.e., exhibit high return correlation). This is an example of the first way in which relative value strategies are formed. The second thesis is how a trading opportunity might be identified. For example, the hedge fund might hypothesize that when their daily returns diverge by a prespecified percentage—for no apparent reasons based on underlying economic fundamentals—the divergence is temporary and a trade should be placed. Perhaps the divergence was a consequence of some large idiosyncratic purchase or sale orders by institutions altering their portfolio weights. The relative value strategy speculates that the return pattern will reverse.

Other potential relations between securities include the stock prices of a manufacturer and a key supplier, or a negative relation between equity returns and estimates of their volatility. If the relation between two securities or economic variables is strong and stable, then they could be attractive bases of an arbitrage or a relative value strategy.

24.1.1   Arbitrage and Risks in Relative Value Strategies

Relative value strategies rely on market inefficiencies. Almost the entire modern finance literature is concerned with the relation between risk and return and how investors seek improved combinations of risk and return. The efficient market hypothesis (EMH), which was discussed in CAIA Level I, is founded on the idea that competitive markets almost never offer investors free lunches, meaning that investors should not expect to earn large positive average returns without taking higher levels of risk. Modern portfolio theory informs investors on how to diversify the unnecessary risks of their investments so that they bear only those risks that are rewarded by the marketplace. Therefore, the idea that substantial arbitrage opportunities may arise and may last for relatively long periods of time appears to contradict much of what is discussed in finance books.

The textbook definition of **arbitrage** refers to a situation in which an investor is able to earn virtually riskless positive profits while making little or no investment. The simplest example is when the same asset is trading at different prices in two separate markets, and the cost of trading in these markets is rather negligible. In this case, a trader would short the asset in the market where the price is relatively high and use the proceeds to buy the same asset in the market where the price is lower. Assuming that the prices would eventually converge, the trader is expected to earn a riskless positive profit with little or no investment. Such easily exploitable arbitrage opportunities are not likely to arise often and, if they do, they are not likely to last for an extended period of time.

24.1.2   Pure Arbitrage and Risk Arbitrage

Almost all potentially available arbitrage opportunities involve some degree of risk, at least in the interim. The term **pure arbitrage** is often used to denote an arbitrage opportunity that involves a level of risk so near zero (or some might argue is "zero risk") that any risk can be ignored as inconsequential. The term **risk arbitrage** is often used by the investment industry to describe profit opportunities that involve enough risk that it is appropriate to explicitly indicate that the supposed arbitrage comes with nontrivial risk. Some argue that the term arbitrage implies zero risk; yet taken to the extreme all activity involves some level of risk. On the other hand, the concept of generating superior returns with arbitrage strategies is so appealing that it leads some to label highly risky strategies as being "arbitrage." In this chapter the term arbitrage is used to identify strategies with very little risk, but too much to be considered pure arbitrage.

24.1.3   Limits to Arbitrage

Limits to arbitrage refers to the idea that investment strategies that seek to earn superior risk-adjusted returns are limited in size by a constraint on investors with regard to the degree of leverage that they can cost-effectively arrange and the level of risk that they can tolerate.

A number of factors limit arbitrage and/or risk arbitrage activities. These factors are typically ignored when "no-arbitrage" conditions are imposed for the sake of constructing asset valuation models. In real-world cases, the limits to arbitrage constrain the amount of capital traders are willing or able to commit to relative value strategies. As a result, risk arbitrage relative value opportunities may persist through time.

24.1.4   Two Examples of Nearly Pure Arbitrage

This section provides two examples of nearly pure arbitrage with one based on rates and the other based on prices.

UNEQUAL RISKLESS BORROWING AND LENDING RATES: Suppose a local community bank offers a promotion to its customers with a 4% annual lending rate good for loans of up to 1 year while a neighboring local bank offers a promotion promising to pay 5% per year for up to 1 year for deposits into new accounts.

The arbitrage opportunity is this: an arbitrageur can borrow a sum of money for 1 year from the bank charging a 4% lending rate and deposit that amount in a Federally insured bank offering a 5% return on deposits for the same term. At the end of the year, arbitrage profit amounts to (Borrowed Sum) × (5% – 4%). Although scenarios of bank defaults or governmental actions could in theory cause a loss, this would traditionally be termed pure arbitrage.

LONG A STOCK ON MARGIN, SHORT A CALL, AND LONG A PUT: Consider a long position in a stock, a long position in a put, and a short position in a call (with both options on the same stock with the same strike price and tenor) with a net value financed with a term loan requiring a payment including interest (when the options expire) that is less than the strike price of the two options.

Put-call parity describes a no-arbitrage relation between European calls and puts on the same nondividend paying asset with the same strike price and tenor (time-to-expiration). Assuming that both the call and put are European options with maturity date T and strike price K on the same stock, the combined payoffs from the stock and two options should equal K at time T. If the amount due on the margin loan is less than K, there is an arbitrage opportunity. Note that there is risk that the counterparties to the long put position will default. In most cases, such as exchange-traded options, the risk would be so minimal that this would traditionally be termed pure arbitrage.

24.1.5   Two Examples of Risk Arbitrage

Consider the following two examples illustrating risk arbitrage opportunities:

LONG STOCK ABC IN TORONTO AND SHORT ABC IN NY: Assume that a dually listed mining company stock currently trades at USD 50 on the New York Stock Exchange and CAD 55 on the Toronto Stock Exchange. The current market exchange rate is 0.90 USD per CAD.

Note that, with the exchange rate at 0.90, the equilibrium value in the foreign exchange market of CAD 55 expressed in USD would be 49.50 (i.e., 55 x 0.90). The stock values indicate an arbitrage opportunity worth 0.50 USD. An arbitrage trade would be to go long the stock in Toronto (−49.50 USD) and short the stock in New York (+50.00), generating a cash inflow of 0.50 USD ignoring trade frictions. Note that in a well-functioning market, the currency adjusted prices should return to an equilibrium in which the trade can be closed with no cash required or generated. For example, if the USD and CAD traded at parity, both stock prices would be the same and no cash would be generated or need to close the trades. If the CAD strengthened to be worth double the USD (i.e., 1.00 CAD = 2.00 USD) then the price of the stock in NY expressed in USD would tend towards being twice the value of the price expressed in CAD and the positions could be closed with no cash required or generated.

However, the relation between the two prices of the stock (currency adjusted) in the two locations could stray even further out of equilibrium (given that the current prices are already out of equilibrium). For example, international trade disputes may arise that effect their relative prices. So it might be inappropriate to view this as pure arbitrage. Note that the hedge underlying this arbitrage opportunity did not require currency forward contracts or similar derivatives. This important issue is discussed in detail in Chapter 40.

LONG STOCK X AT $90 AND SHORT STOCK Y AT $120 WHEN STOCK X OWNS 80% OF STOCK Y:

> Assume X Corporation owns 80% of Y Corporation's equity. Both have 100 million shares outstanding. Shares of X Corporation are trading at $90 a share, while shares of Y Corporation are trading at $120 a share. Is this a pure arbitrage opportunity?

> Consider a trader long 100 shares of Stock X and short 80 shares of Stock Y. The arbitrage-like characteristic of this trade is that the $9,000 purchase of X has 80 underlying shares of Stock Y long worth $120 each for a total long holding of Y of $9,600. The trader invests $9,000 in Stock X, receives $9,600 from shorting Stock Y, has a net exposure to Stock Y of zero, and has ownership of other assets inside Stock X.

> In theory, the shares of X and Y should adjust to reflect the potential arbitrage. But what if the owners of the shares in Stock Y that were borrowed by the trader demand to have them back before share prices have converged? What if the prices drift even further apart, and thus the trader is forced to cover his short positions? Further, suppose that Stock X becomes entangled in a massive lawsuit and liquidates the holdings in Y to cover losses? It might be more appropriate to term this strategy as risk arbitrage.

24.2   TYPES OF PAIRS TRADING AND THE FOUR TYPICAL STEPS

Relative value strategies often focus on trades involving two securities. For example, the convertible arbitrage strategy as detailed in the CAIA Level I curriculum involves the relative values of a convertible bond and stock in the same corporation (although in practice convertible arbitrage often involves more than two positions). Capital structure arbitrage was also detailed in the CAIA Level I program as involving two securities of the same firm. This section focuses on pairs trading. **Pairs trading** generally refers to a simultaneous long and short position in two securities that share many similarities, such as bonds with similar ratings, equities in similar industries, and futures contracts with the same underlying but different delivery dates.

Relative value strategies can involve portfolios of three or more securities, but trading of similar pairs of securities (i.e., pairs trading) is a more common short-term relative value strategy that is the focus of much of this chapter.

The implementation of a pairs-trading strategy consists of the following four typical steps:

1. IDENTIFY THE CANDIDATE PAIRS: In this step, technical or fundamental analysis can be used to identify security pairs that are closely related, such that a large spread between the two returns can be forecasted to revert towards some normal level.
2. IDENTIFY PAIRS WITH A DIVERGENT SPREAD: Once candidate pairs are identified, their price paths are monitored to determine if their returns have diverged to a predetermined threshold.
3. CONSTRUCT AND SIZE THE PORTFOLIO: Given the information collected in the previous two steps, the portfolio manager will have the estimates needed to create a long/short portfolio. The trader establishes a long position in the asset with recent underperformance and a short position in the asset with recent overperformance.
4. EXIT STRATEGY: The criteria for exiting such strategies should typically be at least partially predetermined. The timing of the exit is perhaps the most difficult part of the strategy. Suppose that the portfolio manager observes that, after placing the trade, the spread between the two prices is actually increasing. There are two possible decisions. First, the portfolio manager may consider this to be an even better opportunity and therefore adds to the positions. Alternatively, the portfolio manager may conclude that the underlying thesis of the trade has proven to be incorrect and therefore closes the positions. Similar decisions need to be made in other scenarios. For example, if the spread persists without increasing or decreasing, how long should the positions be maintained? If the spread diminishes or even reverses, at what point should the trader close the positions? Should the trade be closed in one step or in stages?

The next three sections provide detail regarding three major applications of pairs trading: (1) pairs trading of equities based on statistics; (2) pairs trading of commodities based on spreads; and (3) pairs trading of fixed income securities based on rates.

24.3   STATISTICAL PAIRS TRADING OF EQUITIES

Pairs trading of equities is commonly performed using statistical analysis rather than fundamental analysis. The development of statistical pairs trading is attributed to Nunzio Tartaglia, who, along with a team of statisticians and mathematicians, worked at Morgan Stanley in the 1980s. Their objective was to use quantitative models to identify and implement arbitrage opportunities in a systematic and algorithmic manner. One of the strategies successfully developed by this team was statistical pairs trading. **Statistical pairs trading** is a relative value strategy trade with one long and one short position in securities with an observed long-term close statistical relation of returns and a recent observation of a marked but presumably short-term departure from that statistical relation.

If the underlying assumption of the strategy, which is that the two prices should converge and that the spread should be zero, is valid, then the resulting portfolio return will typically have low correlation with changes in the overall market; that is, it may not be beta neutral, but the beta will typically be low. Also, since the two stocks are likely to come from the same industry, the portfolio is likely to have low exposure to the sector. In most instances, equal amounts are invested in long and short positions; therefore, the strategy tends to be monetary neutral as well.

24.3.1 Statistical Pairing using the Co-Integration Approach

The first step is to identify candidate pairs. In other words, how can appropriate pairs of securities be identified for which it is believed that their returns are linked through time? One popular approach to finding these candidate pairs is co-integration. The **co-integration approach** is a statistical technique that detects whether a linear combination of two nonstationary time-series variables is itself stationary. Co-integration is used by traders to specify how the prices of securities may be related through time.

It is important to note that cointegration is different from correlation. Stocks that are highly correlated may not necessarily be good candidates for pairs trading. The following discussion clarifies the difference between correlation and co-integration. Dispersion trades and correlation trades, mostly implemented in the options markets, are discussed in Chapter 37.

Consider two stocks with prices given as p_t and s_t. **Co-integrated stock prices** exist when a linear combination of the two is a stationary process. Loosely speaking, a process is said to be **stationary** if its statistical properties do not change through time; for example, its means and standard deviations remain the same. Specifically, two stock prices are said to be co-integrated if the random variable u_t as specified by the following linear combination of two security prices, is stationary for a given value of a:

$$\ln(p_t) - a \times \ln(s_t) = u_t \tag{24.1}$$

Note that the natural logs of prices rather than the prices themselves are used. The reason is to focus on returns rather than prices and the rate of return from the investment strategy is related to changes in the log of prices. Equation 24.1 requires that a linear combination of p_t and s_t (in which one of the values is scaled by some value of the parameter a) forms a stationary process (u_t).

For example, suppose the logs of the two price processes are given by the processes in Equations 24.2 and 24.3:

$$\ln(p_t) = \eta_{1t} + \varepsilon_t \tag{24.2}$$

$$\ln(s_t) = \eta_{2t} + \upsilon_t \tag{24.3}$$

Here, η_{1t} and η_{2t} are the common trends present in the two price processes, and ε_t and υ_t are stationary random noises. If the common trends are related according to $\eta_{1t} = a \times \eta_{2t}$, then the linear combination given in Equation 24.1 will be stationary (with a as a constant). Intuitively, the relative size of the positions in p and s can be scaled by a to hedge the trends in a pairs trade. If the noise terms (ε_t and υ_t) are stationary, then the paired assets form a stationary process that facilitates identification of diverging prices. There are well-known tests that allow one to determine whether two price series are co-integrated.

Depending on the extent to which the two random noises of Equations 24.2 and 24.3 (ε_t and υ_t) are correlated, the two price series could have different levels of correlations. However, regardless of the level of correlation, the logs of the two prices will be co-integrated if the nonstationary parts of the price series are represented by two related common trends.

There are statistical methods other than co-integration for identifying potential candidates. Further, most traders supplement their statistical analysis with at least some fundamental analysis. For example, pairs of securities found to be appropriate for pairing based on statistical analysis of past returns can be further studied using fundamental analysis (e.g., are they in the same industry?) to ensure that the statistical results are not obtained only by chance—that there are underlying economic reasons for the two stock prices to move together.

24.3.2 Identification and Timing of Trade Entry Opportunities

Once the potential pairing candidates have been identified, the portfolio manager will monitor their price movements through time to select a trade entry point. The portfolio manager sets predetermined thresholds which will signal if the spread between two candidate stocks is wide enough to be exploited. The most common approach is to set the threshold proportional to the historical standard deviation of the spread. This means that if the spread has been historically very volatile, then the two prices have to diverge by a relatively large amount before a trade is triggered.

For example, a threshold for a trade for a pair of moderately volatile securities may be a 1% deviation in recent returns. Using computers, the prices of every pair of securities identified as candidates for trading will be scanned and compared to their thresholds to generate potential points to enter trades.

Finally, the portfolio manager must develop precise exit strategies. For instance, the strategy might require the manager to exit the positions if the prices converge as anticipated, do not converge within a specified period, or if the spread increases beyond a set level. Alternatively, the strategy could require the manager to exit the positions after a prespecified period of time no matter what has happened to prices.

24.3.3 The Nature and Performance of Pairs-Trading Strategies

One of the most cited research papers in this area is by Gatev et al. (2006), who find that annualized returns of up to 11% above Treasury rates were potentially generated by systematic pairs-trading strategies. The abnormal returns reported by this study remain significant even after adjusting for transaction costs. The average holding period for the pairs in the strategy was 4 months. The authors highlight the importance of diversification and recommend that in order to have relatively stable returns, a portfolio consisting of at least 20 pairs should be constructed.

Another important study examines the sources of returns behind potential profits in pairs trading and how idiosyncratic news, common news, and liquidity affect the strategy's performance. Engelberg, Gao, and Jagannathan (2009) contend that idiosyncratic news, which temporarily decreases the liquidity in one of the stocks in a pair, increases the probability of finding profitable opportunities. The conclusion is that news affecting both stocks in a pair may lead to a larger reaction in one of the stocks due to differences in their liquidity levels, leading to a divergence of prices and a pairs-trading opportunity. Accordingly, liquidity differentials could be one of the main drivers of profitability within pairs trading.

Pairs trading tends to be a contrarian strategy. It tends to buy shares in the security within a pair that has fallen the most, and simultaneously sells shares in the more sluggish security that has fallen less in price (or not at all). Conversely, the pairs strategy tends to sell shares in the security within a pair that has risen the most, and simultaneously buys shares in the more sluggish security that has risen less in price (or not at all). Therefore, pairs traders are suppliers of liquidity to the market, and may represent an important source of return to the strategy. Supplying liquidity, especially in times of greater volatility, serves the marketplace by offering anxious buyers and sellers the opportunity to execute their trades at better prices than are being offered by other traders in the market.

24.4 PAIRS TRADING IN COMMODITY MARKETS BASED ON SPREADS

This section details pairs trading based on spreads using the commodity markets as an example. Relative value strategies in commodities can be executed across three risk dimensions. The **three dimensions of commodity relative value strategies** are: (1) location; (2) correlation; and (3) time. The location dimension refers to the same commodity having potentially different prices at different locations in the world. The correlation dimension refers to relative prices of two similar commodities possibly diverging from historical norms. The time dimension refers to prices of the same commodity possibly being different based on when the commodity is scheduled for delivery. For example, consider a spread trade that is long crude oil for delivery in October in the United Kingdom and short heating oil for delivery in December in the United States. This trade has all three risk dimensions: location, correlation, and time. Some traders may also discuss quality spreads, which trade on the price differences between different qualities of commodities, such as wheat or coffee.

In contrast, relative value arbitrage strategies in equity and fixed-income markets are generally limited to two dimensions: correlation and time. A share of stock, irrespective of currency, tends to trade at the same price (adjusted at currency market exchange rates) everywhere in the world (or else allows for very quick and very low cost arbitrage trading), so there is typically little or no location dimension.

24.4.1 Commodity Derivatives Calendar Spreads

Commodity spreads are strategies that seek to take advantage of trading opportunities based on relative commodity prices that can be executed entirely in derivatives markets. These can involve futures contracts, forward contracts, OTC swaps, options, and swaptions. Perhaps the simplest strategy is a calendar spread. A **calendar spread** involves taking opposing long/short positions in the futures market for delivery at different times in the future. These trades can be designed to provide liquidity or insurance against an unforeseen event, or to express a view.

Depending on their market views, traders can enter two types of calendar spreads: bull spreads and bear spreads. A **bull calendar spread** is long the nearby (near-term) contract and short the distant (long-term) contract. In markets that are in backwardation, the investor is hoping for the spread to widen; in contango markets, the bull spread investor is hoping for the price difference to narrow. The losses of a bull spread investor tend to be limited because, in an efficient market, price differences cannot exceed carrying costs (adjusted for convenience yields). If at some point the differences do exceed carrying costs, arbitrageurs would drive prices toward a level reflecting fair carrying costs.

A **bear calendar spread** is long the distant (long-term) contract and short the nearby (near-term) contract. In markets in backwardation, the bear spread speculator wants the spread to narrow, whereas in contango markets the bear spread speculator wants the price difference to widen. In theory, it is possible to see a rise in the price of the near-term contract without a similar rise in the price of the long-term contract (e.g., due to a workers' strike or weather). Therefore, in principle, the potential risk in a bear spread could be unlimited or at least very large.

For example, a typical calendar spread trade involves a trade such as shorting March natural gas futures (i.e., establishing short positions, selling futures, or agreeing to make delivery) and establishing long positions (agreeing to take delivery) of natural gas in April. This is a bear calendar spread that could be profitable in an unexpectedly mild winter (when natural gas prices decline) but could lose money in an unexpectedly cold winter (when natural gas prices rise).

The other side of these spreads may be utilities that purchase more natural gas for delivery in March than they expect to need to ensure adequate supplies. If the winter is mild, they will sell the surplus gas inventories toward the end of the season, which will push down the price for delivery in March. Traders may also take the other side of this trade by buying natural gas for March delivery and selling it for delivery in April. If a natural gas shortage develops due to an exceptionally cold winter or supply disruptions, this trade will be profitable.

Traders who establish the previous calendar spread of natural gas contacts may be viewed as writing a synthetic weather derivative. A **synthetic weather derivative** is a set of derivative positions with returns that are substantially driven by weather conditions. Speculators may implement synthetic weather derivative strategies as a potential source of returns by providing protection from the economic consequences of adverse weather occurrences to major commodity users or producers.

24.4.2 Estimating the Profitability of Calendar Spread Trading

The profit and loss (P&L) from a spread position can be calculated after the spread is closed. Assume the following scenario (see Exhibit 24.1). In March, a calendar spread trader observes a contango in the crude oil forward curve. Anticipating a flattening of the curve and a narrowing of the spread, the trader goes long three July light sweet crude oil futures contracts (traded on NYMEX) at $44.37, simultaneously shorting three December light sweet crude oil futures at $50.78. In April and May, an oversupply of crude in the world markets causes prices to slump across the board. At the beginning of June, the spreader closes out the July contract at $35.18 and the December contract at $38.16.

The profit for the combined position can now be determined. The first step, shown in Exhibit 24.1, is to compute the profit or loss per unit (e.g., barrel) of

EXHIBIT 24.1 Profit and Loss Calculation

	July (1st Leg)	December (2nd Leg)	Total
March, open	Long: −$44.37	Short: +$50.78	
June, close	Short: +$35.18	Long: −$38.16	
Net per barrel	−$9.19	$12.62	$3.43

the underlying commodity. The second step is to estimate the position's total profit or loss by multiplying the profit or loss per underlying commodity unit times the number of commodity units per contract and the number of contracts, as shown in Equation 24.4.

$$\text{Position P\&L} = \text{P\&L}_{\text{barrel}} \times \text{Contract} \times \text{Position Size} = \$3.43 \times 1{,}000 \times 3 = \$10{,}290$$
$$(24.4)$$

Since the size of the NYMEX light sweet crude oil contract is 1,000 barrels, and the size of the trader's spread position is three contracts, the total gain of the trader's position (ignoring trading and financing costs and collateral yield) is $10,290.

APPLICATION 24.4.2

Wheat contracts typically trade in contracts for delivery of 5,000 bushels. Assume that May wheat contracts currently sell for $5.50 per bushel, which is $0.20 more than the futures price of wheat contracts with delivery in July, due to anticipated harvesting. A commodity trader with a sophisticated weather forecasting model anticipates highly abnormal weather that will drive the two futures prices to being equal. If the trader is correct, what will the profit be on a calendar spread position that is long 30 July contracts and short 30 May contracts?

It is not necessary to know absolute prices in calculating the profit or loss of a spread trade. In this example, the spread between the two dates is assumed to decline from $0.20 per bushel to $0.00 per bushel. The $0.20 per bushel profit is multiplied by 5,000 bushels times 30 contracts to calculate the total profit on the position of $30,000 (i.e., using Equation 24.4).

24.4.3 Processing Spreads

Spreads between contracts are based on different economic reasons for their association.

Processing spreads seek to take advantage of the relative price difference between a commodity and products the commodity can be used to produce. Two popular processing spreads are crush spreads and crack spreads. A **crack spread** is a processing spread that involves buying crude oil (in the spot or futures markets) while selling a combination of products derived from crude oil (heating oil and gasoline). A crush spread involves buying soybeans and selling a combination of soybean meal and soybean oil.

Crack spreads are typically used by oil refineries and their counterparties reflecting the cracking or breaking apart of large oil molecules in the process of refining crude oil into gasoline and heating oil. The typical producer hedge position would involve going long crude oil futures (to hedge future input purchases) and short gasoline and heating oil (to hedge against potential decreases in the price of the outputs, or distillates). The crack spread locks in the refiner's margin, which is the revenue earned for refining each barrel of crude oil.

It is a common practice to express the crack spread in terms of a ratio as $X:Y:Z$, where X represents the number of barrels of crude oil, Y represents the number of barrels of gasoline, and Z represents the number of barrels of heating oil, subject to the constraint that $X = Y + Z$. Typical crack spreads are 3:2:1, 5:3:2, and 2:1:1. Commonly traded benchmark crack spreads include Gulf Coast 3:2:1 and Chicago 3:2:1.

Crush spreads are a processing spread typically used as hedges by soybean processors, with its name derived from the physical crushing of soybeans into oil and meal. A typical crush spread would involve going long soybean futures (to ensure the processor against potential input price increases) and short soybean oil futures and soybean meal futures (to ensure against potential output price decreases). The analysis of crush spreads is very similar to the prior example presented for crack spreads.

Processing spreads, such as crush spreads, are frequently used by producers to lock in favorable margins. For example, a soybean processor may wish to buy the spread in the futures market (buy soybean futures and sell soybean meal and soybean oil futures) because these contracts can be used to lock in the purchase and sales prices of the processor's business. However, there are no natural sellers of this spread (i.e., no business makes soybeans from soybean oil and meal). Instead, there are three separate natural participants on the other side of the three components of the spread:

1. Farmers who sell soybean futures (to lock in revenues).
2. Livestock feed producers who buy soybean meal (to lock in feeding costs).
3. Vegetable oil manufacturers who buy soybean oil (to lock in purchasing costs).

24.4.4 The Economics of Processing Spreads to Producers and Speculators

There are two conditions that hold for producers that are hedging:

1. Producers take long futures positions to hedge against rising input prices.
2. Producers take short futures positions to hedge against falling output prices.

In other words, producers who choose to hedge are generally long the commodity they use as input to their production process in a nearer-term expiration month. Producers tend to short the commodities that they output in a later period.

Speculators seek a source of return from providing liquidity to commodity users and producers. Speculators typically provide liquidity by selling the spread to permit the processor to lock in a favorable margin and then either: (1) immediately attempt to find buyers or sellers to unwind the individual components of their spread trade; or (2) hold the spread position as a speculation based on an expectation that they can unwind the entire transaction at a more favorable price.

It should be noted that futures exchanges set lower margins for bona fide hedging spreads in which a producer goes long futures on the input and goes short futures on the output. On the flip side, a spread trader who goes long the output and short the input is subject to higher margin requirements despite providing hedgers with needed liquidity.

24.4.5 Substitution Commodity Spreads

Substitution spreads are positions across commodities that can serve as alternatives for one another in terms of either production or consumption. There are **two types of commodity substitutes:** production substitutes and consumption substitutes.

1. For example, a producer may be able to use the same capital equipment to produce different products, such as a farmer's ability to use land to grow corn or soybeans, because land suitable for growing soybeans is usually also suitable for growing corn. Oil refineries can also vary the mix of refined products that they produce because a refinery can be adjusted, within limits, to favor production of heating oil, jet fuel, or gasoline, depending on seasonal demand.
2. A consumer may be able to substitute one commodity for another driven by their relative prices. For example, a utility may have the flexibility to utilize different fuels for electricity generation (e.g., natural gas can be substituted for oil-based fuels in the long run).

PRICE RATIOS AS MEASURES OF SUBSTITUTION: The general premise of substitution spreads is that the relative pricing relation between easily substitutable commodities should be stable. If the price of one becomes too expensive, consumers will switch to the substitute. This results in a price drop for the original and a price rise for the substitute, forcing the ratio back to normal.

RATIOS OF THE NATURAL LOGARITHMS OF SUBSTITUTABLE COMMODITIES: To normalize ratios of contracts with different pricing specifications and contract sizes, one can study natural logs of the ratios of prices. The reason for this type of normalization is that price distributions can be approximated by a lognormal distribution, and therefore the distribution of the resulting ratio can be approximated by a normal distribution. This facilitates the testing of the difference to see if it is statistically significant. For example, one might look at the natural log of a series of ratios of heating oil to natural gas prices, such as depicted in Equation 24.5:

$$\text{Substitute Test Statistic}_t = \ln\left[\frac{\text{Close Price (Heating Oil)}_t}{\text{Close Price (Natural Gas)}_t}\right] \quad (24.5)$$

For the purposes of illustration, let's assume that the nearest-maturity NYMEX heating oil futures contract (HO) traded at $2.5620 per gallon yesterday, while the same maturity NYMEX Henry Hub natural gas futures contract (NG) traded at $8.112 per 10,000 million British thermal units (MMBtu). The HO/NG test statistic would be estimated as follows:

$$\text{Substitute Test Statistic}_{\text{yesterday}} = \ln\left[\frac{\text{HO}_{\text{yesterday}}}{\text{NG}_{\text{yesterday}}}\right] = \ln\left(\frac{2.5620}{8.112}\right) = -1.15$$

RATIOS OF LOG PRICES AS TEST STATISTICS: To determine whether the spread has experienced a change substantial enough to warrant a spread trade, measures of the spread's normal level and what constitutes a substantial deviation from that normal level are required. A test statistic at traders' disposal is the difference from a 100-day moving average, calculated as follows in Equation 24.6:

100-Day Statistic

$$= \frac{\text{Substitution Statistics}_t - (100 \text{ Day MA of Substitution Statistics})}{(100 \text{ Day Standard Deviation of Substitution Statistic})}$$

$$(24.6)$$

The term in parentheses in the numerator of Equation 24.6 serves as a measure of a ratio's normal test statistic level. The entire numerator indicates the amount that the current test statistic appears to deviate from its normal level. Finally, the denominator scales the measure into the number of standard deviations.

DETERMINING ENTRY AND EXIT POINTS WITH A SUBSTITUTION TEST STATISTIC: Entering a spread long means going long the product in the numerator of the price ratio and shorting the product in the denominator. The assumption of the long spread position is that the product in the denominator has become too expensive relative to the product in the numerator. Shorting the spread means the opposite: shorting the product in the numerator and going long the product in the denominator. The assumption of the short spread position is that the product in the numerator has become too expensive relative to the product in the denominator.

   The critical values of the statistic that would trigger entering or exiting a spread position are determined statistically (optimizing over historical series of logs of price ratios of related securities). In other words, strategies based on different entry and exit points are tested with historic data to identify the parameters that would have worked best in the past.

EXAMPLE OF A SUBSTITUTION SPREAD TRADE: For example, assume that the critical value of a substitute trade statistic for entry is 2.75, and the critical value for exit is 0. A long entry into the spread would be triggered if the 100-day statistic fell below –2.75 (i.e., execute pair trade: long heating oil, short natural gas), whereas a short position in the spread would be established if the 100-day statistic rose above 2.75 (i.e., execute pair trade: short heating oil, long natural gas). Traders following this strategy typically exit long spreads when the 100-day statistic rises above zero and exit short spreads when the 100-day statistic falls below zero.

In practice, though, the speed of price reversion of a substitution spread will primarily be driven by somewhat long-term changes in the technologies and assets underlying the production and consumptions processes. Substitution spread trades are generally riskier than processing spreads or calendar spreads.

24.4.6   Quality and Location Spreads

Quality spreads are similar to substitution spreads, except that the spread is across different grades of the same commodity. A common quality spread executable in futures markets involves spring wheat and hard red winter wheat. Most other quality spreads involve OTC transactions.

   For example, there is a liquid OTC market in jet fuel, which is very similar to diesel fuel/heating oil. Similarly, there are many grades of coffee that are traded OTC but only a few grades that are listed on futures exchanges.

   Location spreads are trades that involve the same commodity but different delivery and storage locations. A common location spread involves Brent crude oil, delivered in the United Kingdom, and West Texas Intermediate (WTI) crude oil, delivered in the United States. Location spreads are primarily traded using OTC derivatives, though some location spreads can be executed using listed futures contracts.

Some location spreads have an arbitrage component if the sides of the spread differ by sufficient time to allow delivery between locations. For example, if a long crude oil futures position in one location settles 1 month prior to the settlement of a short crude oil futures position, then it may be possible to take delivery in one location, incur transportation and storage costs, and then make delivery in the other location in time to satisfy the short position.

However, if the location spread is made without sufficient time to make settlement through delivery, then the trade is a **correlation trade.** In other words, the trade will have an outcome that is driven by the statistical correlation between two values.

24.4.7   Intramarket Relative Value Strategies

Many of the strategies used by active commodity managers and hedge funds combine the trading of commodity derivatives with the trading of the underlying commodities in the physical or spot markets. These strategies are designed to either implement a potential arbitrage opportunity or to use commodity futures markets the same way that commercial users do: as hedging vehicles to manage the exposure of a particular transaction to various risks.

Storage strategies seek to profit from changes in the benefits and costs of commodity storage and often use leased storage facilities to hold physical commodities for delivery at a later date, when the return on storing a commodity exceeds its costs. These strategies are more complex than futures-based strategies and are both labor and capital intensive. Storage strategies are typically hedged transactions, involving a simultaneous purchase of the physical asset in the spot market and the sale of the commodity in the futures or OTC forward market for future delivery. A storage strategy is equivalent to a calendar spread in that the transaction involves holding the same commodity over time.

Transportation strategies use spot commodity markets to execute location trades by moving commodities when the benefits of price differentials exceed transportation costs. The strategy involves leased transportation services, such as tankers, bulk shipping, or pipelines, to physically move a commodity from a location where the commodity's price is relatively low (presumably due to a local surplus) to a location where the price is higher (presumably due to a local shortage).

Some transportation and storage strategies carry risks that futures-based strategies do not. For example, market participants using OTC contracts must be willing to assume the attendant credit risk of counterparties used in these transactions. The participants must also be prepared to bear the risks associated with storing and transporting potentially hazardous commodities, including the potential headline and reputational risks.

24.5   PAIRS TRADING IN RATES FROM FIXED INCOME AND CURRENCY MARKETS

Relatively long-term trades based on rate differentials are often carry trades. In its simplest form, a **carry trade** consists of being short one rate (e.g., borrowing in a low-interest-rate currency) and being long another rate (e.g., lending in a high-interest-rate currency) in an attempt to earn the spread without hedging the risk that the spread will change. The goal of such a trade is to capture the rate differential, such as an interest rate differential.

For example, consider a carry trade in the currency markets in which the potential funding currency (i.e., the currency to be borrowed) carries an annual interest rate of 0.5% versus 5.25% in the target currency (i.e., the currency to be lent or invested in). To initiate the trade, the trader would borrow in the funding currency, convert the proceeds into the target currency at the current exchange rate, and buy bonds using the target currency. This would earn the trader a positive carry (or profit) of 4.75% as long as the exchange rate does not change. Carry trading across currencies remains profitable as long as the target currency does not depreciate by more than the interest rate differential.

The currency carry trade has three risks: (1) the funding currency interest rate rises, thereby increasing borrowing costs; (2) the funding currency appreciates against the target currency; and (3) the target currency investment does not yield as much as initially expected.

A potential problem is that in informationally efficient capital markets the expected return on a carry trade should be proportional to its systematic risks, which would generally be zero. Therefore, the likelihood that the funding currency will appreciate against the target currency and/or the funding costs will rise relative to the returns in the target currency is high.

Covered interest rate parity explains the parity of carry trades in an informationally efficient market. **Covered interest rate parity** relates the spot and forward exchange rates to differences in short-term interest rates in the two currencies. Let S_0 denote the spot number of units of a trader's foreign currency unit (FCU) equivalent to one unit of a home (domestic) currency unit, DCU, and F_t as the corresponding forward value (units of FCU per DCU) with settlement in t years. Also, let r_{DCU} and r_{FCU} denote annualized short-term riskless interest rates on instruments denominated in DCUs and FCUs, respectively.

According to covered interest rate parity, the covered (hedged) return from investing in the DCU-denominated instrument should be related to the rate of return on the FCU-denominated instrument as indicated in Equation 24.7:

$$(1 + r_{DCU})^t \times \frac{F_t}{S_0} = (1 + r_{FCU})^t \qquad (24.7)$$

For example, assume the euro (the home currency) is currently in parity with the USD, the euro-based 1-year riskless interest rate is 10.00%, the 1-year forward rate is 1.03 USD per euro (indicating strengthening of the euro to the dollar), and that covered interest rate parity holds. Find the dollar-based riskless 1-year interest rate (FCU).

$$(1 + .1000)(1.03/1.00) = 1.1330$$

$$r_{DCU} = 13.3\%$$

In order for the interest rate differential to persist with higher US dollar interest rates, it must be that the dollar is expected to depreciate against the euro.

APPLICATION 24.5

Suppose annual short-term interest rates in the United States and Japan are 4% and 1%, respectively (i.e., $r_{DCU} = 4\%$ and $r_{FCU} = 1\%$). In addition, the current spot rate and the 1-year forward rate for the yen (JPY) versus USD are 120 and 116.54, respectively (i.e., 120 JPY = 1 USD in the spot market, and the forward market is quoting 116.54 JPY = 1 USD). Does covered interest rate parity hold, assuming zero transaction costs? If the riskless interest rate in United States were 5%, what would the forward rate be for interest rate parity to hold with the other values remaining constant?

In response to the first question: $(1 + 0.04)(116.54/120) = (1 + 0.01)$. It can be verified that this equality holds, and covered interest parity is satisfied.

In response to the second question with F the forward rate: $(1.05)(F/120) = (1.01)$. So: $F = 120*1.01/1.05 = 115.43$. Note that the larger interest rate spread is offset by a larger basis in the forward curve (in terms of absolute values).

An important implication of the above application is that the value of the currency of the country with the higher interest rate—USD in this case—should on average decline versus the value of the currency of the country with the lower interest rate. If the strategy is hedged against exchange rate changes (e.g., using a forward contract on the two exchange rates) then, to the extent that the relevant markets are informationally efficient, the strategy is riskless and should return the riskless rate.

24.6 RELATIVE VALUE MARKET-NEUTRAL STRATEGIES AND PORTFOLIO RISKS

Understanding the *sources* of risk and return is a crucial part of analyzing any trading strategy. Even if a strategy has offered attractive returns in the past, managers and asset allocators must be aware of the sensitivities of the strategy to both systematic and idiosyncratic uncertainty as well as the sources of return (i.e., why an asset might offer competitive or superior risk-adjusted returns).

The previous sections of this chapter have focused on trades involving two assets. The total exposure of an investor implementing one or more of these trading strategies on large sets of opportunities will be determined by the combination of many such trades. This final section discusses management of related risks.

24.6.1 Risks of Pairs-Trading Strategies

A pairs-trading strategy is almost never a riskless strategy. As discussed in the following paragraphs, the strategy could experience losses. Therefore, it is important to understand the extent to which a pairs-trading strategy has exposures to systematic and idiosyncratic risk. If there are substantial exposures to systematic sources of risk, then the strategy cannot be considered an arbitrage strategy and its return represents compensation for bearing systematic risks. More importantly, if exposures to systematic sources of risk are dominant, then the benefits of having a diversified portfolio of pairs-trading strategies will be limited. On the other hand, if the idiosyncratic sources of risk are most important, then it will be essential for the manager to have a fully diversified portfolio of such strategies, as the rate of return from such a portfolio could come close to representing an arbitrage opportunity as the size of the portfolio increases and the diversifiable risk is diversified away.

A key issue in each risk is the extent to which the risks are systematic (requiring a risk premium to be borne) or idiosyncratic (diversifiable). The following sources of risk have been identified for pairs strategies:

NOISE TRADERS' RISK: **Noise traders' risk** is performance dispersion caused by idiosyncratic trading. In the same way that noise traders could create a spread between two co-integrated prices, they could cause the spread to widen even further. This would lead to losses, possibly forcing the manager to close the positions before the two prices had even begun to converge. This risk is mostly idiosyncratic and thus could be diversified away.

FUNDAMENTAL RISK: In this case, the spread between the two stocks could become permanent due to a fundamental change in the two firms. For example, one of the two firms could develop a new product that would change the fundamental relation between the firms (e.g., Apple developing the iPhone and therefore becoming less connected to the computer industry). This risk is mostly idiosyncratic and thus could be diversified away.

CORPORATE EVENT RISK: Corporate events, such as mergers and spin-offs, are most likely to change the relation between the two stocks. This risk is a combination of idiosyncratic and systematic risks. Since industry mergers and acquisitions tend to be somewhat correlated, there is a common risk factor present in a pairs-trading strategy that involves the same industry. To diversify this risk, it is important to use numerous pairs of stocks, with many pairs coming from different industries.

SYNCHRONIZATION RISK: **Synchronization risk** arises when market participants are slow to react to increased divergence between two stocks, leading the portfolio manager to consider closing the positions because the convergence has not taken place during a specific period. For example, empirical evidence has shown that speed of convergence for related stocks changes through time. This indicates that this risk likely affects a large set of pairs of stocks and therefore may not be fully diversifiable. However, it is not clear if this represents a systematic source of risk in which the investor is compensated for bearing this risk.

LIQUIDITY RISK: Stocks that are candidates for pairs trading must be scanned for sufficient liquidity. Since each strategy involves at least four transactions, bid-ask spreads and market impact could severely hamper the performance of the strategy. Liquidity is not constant, and it tends to disappear during periods of financial stress. Therefore, this risk tends to be systematic and thus is not fully diversifiable. In fact, since pairs trading is a contrarian strategy, one could argue that the strategy compensates investors for providing liquidity to the rest of the market.

SHORT-SALE RISK: **Short-sale risk** could arise if the investor is forced to cover the short positions at unattractive prices because the shares have been called in by the lenders perhaps due to a short squeeze. The investor could face a short squeeze if a large number of investors are forced to cover their short positions. A short squeeze tends to be firm specific and therefore its risk can be diversified away.

MODEL RISK: Since pairs trading is essentially a statistical arbitrage strategy, it relies on the assumption that the underlying models of stock returns and their estimated parameters are accurate and stable through time. To the degree that there are shared flaws in the statistical models employed for different pairs (or markets change to make the model obsolete), this risk could affect all the strategies being implemented by investors and therefore cannot be diversified away.

FINANCING RISK: Relative value trades, especially in the fixed income and currency markets, are implemented using leverage. Leveraged trades can experience increased risks when: (1) the term of the borrowing does not equal the term of the lending (an asset-liability mismatch); (2) the prime broker has an ability to reduce the amount or increase the cost of available leverage during times of stressed market conditions; and (3) financing agreements may cause a trader to stay with a position longer than they would otherwise choose.

Clearly, pairs-trading strategies have exposures to some sources of systematic risk (e.g., liquidity), and therefore a portion of the return they generate can be considered compensation for bearing those risks. Systematic risk may explain only part of the excess return. The unexplained part of the return is attributed to idiosyncratic risks (e.g., the presence of noise traders, complexity of the strategy, and leverage risk) or managerial skill.

24.6.2 Equity Market-Neutral Strategy

Broadly speaking, an equity market-neutral strategy refers to one or more strategies whose returns have limited exposure to equity market fluctuations. The correlation coefficient and beta of a portfolio with an overall market index are the most common measures of market neutrality. It is important to note that when two return streams are uncorrelated (i.e., have a negligible correlation coefficient), it does not mean that they are statistically independent. Correlation coefficients and market betas are useful in determining whether two return streams are *linearly* related to each other but may fail in signaling nonlinear relations.

For example, consider X, a normally-distributed random variable with a mean of zero, and Y, a variable equal to X^2. It can be verified that the correlation coefficient between X and Y is zero. However, these two random variables are clearly not independent—they are closely related—but their relation is nonlinear (i.e., between X and X^2). Therefore, correlation coefficients and betas from linear regressions can be deceptive indicators of risk and the relation between assets when the relation is nonlinear.

The issue of nonlinear relations between assets may appear to be a technical point that is irrelevant to the practical study of an equity market-neutral strategy. However, returns on many derivative securities, such as options, are nonlinear functions of returns on their underlying assets. Similar nonlinearity can be generated through dynamic trading strategies. For example, consider a fund with a portfolio that consists of two long positions: deep out-of-the-money calls and deep out-of-the-money puts, both on an equity index. For small changes in the equity index, the market beta between the fund's returns and the market could be near zero, driven mostly by changes in volatility; but for large changes, the performance of the fund will be closely linked to the performance of the market. This means that one has to examine the market neutrality of a fund's return under a variety of market conditions and with a broader view of risk than is found through risk measures that report linear relations among relatively minor market movements.

Further, even if a portfolio is uncorrelated with or independent from the overall market, it might have significant exposure to specific industries, sectors, or other sources of risk in the economy. For example, it might be exposed to credit, currency, or volatility factors. Therefore, an equity market-neutral portfolio does not mean a riskless portfolio, and the appropriate rate on such a portfolio will not be a risk-free benchmark. This issue is explored in the next section.

24.6.3   Risks Related to Equity Market Neutrality

The risks of Section 24.6.1 apply broadly to strategies involving hedge funds and other potentially complex strategies. The hedge fund industry has developed several specific terms describing risks that are especially relevant to equity market-neutral strategies. The risks in Section 24.6.1 are not limited to pairs-trading strategies and may not exist in some pairs-trading strategies. Similarly, the risks in this section are not limited to equity market-neutral trading strategies and may not exist in some equity market-neutral strategies.

> MONETARY NEUTRALITY: A portfolio that is **monetary neutral** has equal long and short exposures to a specified currency. For example, consider a portfolio that has equal euro exposure in long and short positions. This euro-neutral strategy is approximately self-financing, as the proceeds from the short positions can, in principle, be used to fund the long positions.

> BETA NEUTRALITY: A **beta neutral** portfolio generates returns that are not linearly correlated with the market risk associated with the specified beta. In this strategy, the equity market betas of long and short positions are equal to each other. Note that this does not mean that equal amounts are invested in long and short positions. For instance, if a long position consists of low-beta (e.g., value) stocks, and a short position consists of high-beta (e.g., growth) stocks, then the size of the long position needs to be levered up in order to match the high beta of the short position.

> SECTOR NEUTRALITY: A **sector neutral** portfolio generates returns that are uncorrelated with economic sectors, including industries or industry groups. For example, a fund manager may take long positions in the stocks of energy firms and short positions in the stocks of technology firms. Even if the two

positions are of the same size and have the same beta with respect to the changes in the overall market, the portfolio likely has significant exposures to the energy and technology sectors. On the other hand, a manager may choose to create long and short positions using energy stocks. This portfolio will have little exposure to changes in the overall energy sector but may not be beta neutral.

An important question that arises is whether an equity market-neutral strategy will generate any excess return (i.e., any return in excess of the riskless rate). After all, if markets are efficient, then a truly market-neutral strategy should generate a riskless expected return. If an equity market-neutral portfolio generates consistent positive excess returns in an efficient market, one would argue that those returns are compensations for exposures to systematic risk factors other than equity risk (e.g., credit, currency, volatility, or liquidity factors). Alternatively, one can argue that markets are not always efficient, and pockets of inefficiency arise in financial markets. The goal of equity market-neutral strategies is to exploit these inefficiencies while not exposing the portfolios to substantial amounts of other systematic risks.

REFERENCES

Gatev, E. W., N. Goetzmann, and K. Geert Rouwenhorst. 2006. *The Review of Financial Studies* 19 (3): 797–827.

Engelberg, J., P. Gao, and R. Jagannathan. 2009 "An anatomy of pairs trading: the role of idiosyncratic news, common information and liquidity." Third Singapore International Conference on Finance.

CHAPTER 25

Valuation Methods for Private Assets: The Case of Real Estate

This chapter discusses important methods for managing portfolios of private assets. The chapter uses a portfolio of private real estate as an example. The methods include evaluating implications of depreciation and other income tax issues, formulating private asset returns from transactions data, and interpreting appraisals.

25.1 DEPRECIATION TAX SHIELDS

Markets in which the income from assets is subject to different effective tax rates and in which investors are exposed to different marginal tax rates raise important issues. While the direct effects of income taxation are obviously important to taxable investors (e.g., family offices), taxation is also important to tax-exempt institutions, such as most foundations, endowments, and pension funds. An institution that is exempt from income taxation should typically consider the taxation of various assets because the pre-tax expected returns of assets traded in competitive markets should vary inversely with the extent to which the assets offer tax advantages. For example, in the US most municipal bonds offer returns free of Federal income taxes. Municipal bonds therefore offer lower pre-tax expected risk-adjusted returns than their taxable counterparts (e.g., corporate bonds). Institutions exempt from such taxation should generally prefer corporate bonds to municipal bonds, while the most highly taxed investors should favor municipal bonds.

There are numerous aspects of an investment that affect its taxation, such as depreciation (in real estate), depletion allowances (in energy enterprises), long-term capital gains, and others. This section details depreciation in general and real estate in particular as having very important and widespread effects regarding taxation.

The primary potential tax advantage of real estate around the world is the deductibility of depreciation on buildings for income tax purposes. Thus, a property generating net cash revenues from rent and leases of €5,000,000 per year will generate taxable income of only €3,500,000 per year if the taxpayer is able to claim €1,500,000 per year in depreciation expense.

The tax advantages relating to the deductibility of depreciation for income tax purposes are important and widely misunderstood. Simply put, effective income tax rates depend on the extent to which the depreciation allowed for tax purposes exceeds, equals, or is lower than the actual decline in the value of the asset being depreciated. If the depreciation allowed for tax purposes exceeds the actual economic decline in the value of the asset (which it usually does), then effective income tax rates can be substantially lower than stated income tax rates.

25.1.1 Valuation of the Depreciation Tax Shield

The **depreciation tax shield** is the prospective stream of reduced income taxation that a particular investor will experience as a result of being able to deduct depreciation. Equation 25.1 depicts the tax shield in year t.

$$\text{Depreciation Tax Shield}_t = \text{Depreciation}_t \times \text{Tax}_t \tag{25.1}$$

where Depreciation_t is the amount of depreciation for tax accounting purposes that the investor can deduct in year t, and Tax_t is the investor's marginal income tax rate in year t. Thus, $\text{Depreciation Tax Shield}_t$ is the amount by which the investor's income taxes in year t are reduced as a result of being able to deduct depreciation at the tax rate, Tax_t.

Financial decision-making should adjust future expected cash flows for time and risk. This analysis of the tax advantages of depreciation focuses on the present value of the depreciation tax shield. The present value (PV) of the depreciation tax shield is computed by discounting the incremental stream of cash flows at an appropriate interest rate as indicated in Equation 25.2.

$$\text{PV Depreciation Tax Shield} = \sum_{t=1}^{T} \frac{\text{Depreciation}_t \times \text{Tax}_t}{(1 + R_d)^t} \tag{25.2}$$

Assuming that tax rates are constant and that the investor will be able to enjoy the tax shield with certainty, the cash flows can be discounted at the riskless rate, R_f. But, to be precise, the tax advantages depend on the firm having sufficient profits to utilize the depreciation deduction effectively. Therefore, Equation 25.2 uses R_d as the discount rate on the depreciation tax shield. Note that $R_d > R_f$ for firms with a positive probability of default. To summarize, the **discount rate for the depreciation tax shield** should take into account the uncertainty of the investor having adequate future profits or other mechanisms of utilizing the taxation benefits of the depreciation and should exceed the riskless rate to the extent that the uncertainty exists.

25.1.2 Computation of the Depreciation Tax Shield

For example, a building with a €10,000,000 depreciable base that can be evenly depreciated over 20 years (using straight-line depreciation) will permit deduction of an annual depreciation of €500,000 per year. At a marginal tax rate of 40%, the annual depreciation tax shield (i.e., reduction in taxes) is €200,000 per year. At a discount rate of 5%, the present value of the 20-year tax shield is €2.49 million.

However, the depreciation taken against the building lowers the book value of the building over time. When the real estate is ultimately sold, the taxpayer will typically owe taxes on the profit. The taxable profit is composed of the gain between the purchase and sales prices as well as recaptured depreciation. **Recaptured depreciation** is the amount of the accumulated depreciation taken on an asset between the purchase and sales date that is recovered by the sales price exceeding the purchase price. Thus, in many cases, the taxable profit on the date of the asset's sale will include €1 for each €1 of accumulated depreciation. Although depreciation does not typically change the total nominal amount of taxes paid (if tax rates are constant), it does *defer* those taxes.

A potential long-term and very substantial tax advantage to a real estate investment program is when the accounting value for tax purposes of an asset steps-up to the current market value when the owner dies, as is permitted in the US. This seemingly simple provision may allow real estate investors to enjoy tax-shelter-generated cash flow for decades before passing the assets on free of income taxes on gains to their heirs (if the basis is stepped-up).

Depreciation, even if recaptured, reduces the present value of taxes. For example, assuming that the building in the previous example is sold after 20 years for a value above its original cost, the taxpayer will owe taxes on the recaptured depreciation of €10,000,000. Continuing with a marginal tax rate of 40% and a discount rate of 5%, this tax liability of €4,000,000 in 20 years has a present value of €10,000,000 $\times 0.40/(1.05)^{20}$, or €1.51 million. Thus, the net gain to the taxpayer from being able to deduct depreciation is €2.49 million – €1.51 million = €0.98 million.

25.1.3 Viewing Depreciation as Generating an Interest-Free Loan

If the asset being depreciated for tax purposes is holding steady or appreciating in market value, then the ability to depreciate the asset may be viewed as an interest-free loan from the government to the taxpayer (i.e., the reduced taxes may be viewed as a loan against future taxes). In other words, relative to not having the asset and paying full income taxes on all revenues at the stated tax rates, the investor may be viewed as using depreciation as a shield to postpone taxes and increase the discounted value of all future cash flows.

APPLICATION 25.1.3

Consider a real estate investment held by a taxpayer with substantial income, who is in a 25% tax bracket on all income. A property offers $1 million per year in depreciation over the next 8 years. However, the depreciation will be recaptured for tax purposes when the property is sold at the end of 8 years. What is the present value of the combined tax effects of depreciating the property and recapturing the depreciation based on an interest rate of 8.75%?

The benefit is an 8-year $250,000 annuity found by multiplying the annual depreciation amount by the tax rate. The cost is the need to pay taxes at the end of 8 years on $8 million of recaptured depreciation (i.e., $2 million). Assuming for computational simplicity that the 8th and final year of depreciation is both deducted and recaptured in the 8th year, the benefits and costs can be computed in a single step with a payment of $250,000, a future value of –$2 million, $N = 8$, and interest rate = 8.75, for a net benefit of $374,314, which may be viewed as the value of an interest-free loan generated by the tax shield.

Note in Application 25.1.3 that the real estate investor enjoyed a $250,000 higher cash flow each year for 8 years as a result of the depreciation tax shield and a negative $2,000,000 cash flow at the end of the 8 years. This is, in effect, a sequence of interest-free loans from the government to the taxpayer relative to not having the tax shield.

Depreciation tax shields are offered not only in the US, but also in many other countries around the world. For example, based on a study by Pricewaterhouse-Coopers International, Lee and Swenson (2012) analyze the countries belonging to the European Union and find that all of them offer some type of depreciation tax shield (via either expensing or rapid depreciation).

25.2   DEFERRAL OF TAXATION OF GAINS

In many countries, real estate can offer taxable investors the advantage of deferred taxation of investment gains until the assets are liquidated. As in the case of common stocks, gains are typically taxed on the sale of the investment rather than being marked to market. Some investments, such as a series of short-term commodity investments that are rolled over annually (or more often) cause annual taxation of gains.

25.2.1   Return with Annual Taxation of Gains

Annual taxation of gains causes after-tax growth to be equal to the product of the pre-tax rate of gain (r) and 1 minus the marginal tax rate (1 – tax):

$$\text{After-Tax Return without Tax Deferral} = r \times (1 - \text{Tax Rate}) \qquad (25.3)$$

For example, an investment growing at 10% per year experiences an after-tax growth rate of 6% when applying a tax rate of 40%. Thus, a euro placed in a 20-year investment using the same rates would grow to €1 × $(1.06)^{20}$ = €3.2071.

25.2.2   Return with Deferred Taxation of Gains

Deferral of taxation of gains is included by compounding an investment forward at its pre-tax rate and subtracting taxes upon liquidation. For example, €1 growing for 20 years at 10%, with gains taxed at 40% at the end of 20 years, would grow as shown:

$$\text{After-Tax Future Value of } €1 = €1 \times (1.10^{20} - 1)(1 - 0.40) + €1$$

$$= €3.4365 + €1$$

$$= €4.4365$$

Using these numbers, tax deferral allows accumulation of 55.7% more profit: (€3.4365 – €2.2071)/€2.2071. The general formula for the after-tax rate using an annual taxation of gains that is equivalent to earning r for T years with tax deferral is shown in Equation 25.4:

$$\text{After-Tax Return with Tax Deferral} = [1 + [(1 + r)^T - 1] \times (1 - \text{Tax Rate})]^{\frac{1}{T}} - 1$$

$$(25.4)$$

Note that the annual after-tax return for the preceding example can be found as the rate that equates the after-tax future value (€4.4365) to the initial investment of €1, as indicated in the following equation:

$$\text{After-Tax Rate} = \left(\frac{€4.4365}{1}\right)^{\frac{1}{20}} - 1 = 7.73\%$$

Tax deferral of gains has the effect of increasing the after-tax gains from 6% to 7.73%. Alternatively, note that the pre-tax rate equivalent to 7.73% after tax is found by dividing by $(1 - \text{tax})$, which generates 12.88%. Thus, tax deferral of gains relative to annual taxation of gains is equivalent to being able to earn 12.88% pre-tax rather than 10%.

APPLICATION 25.2.2

An investor is comparing the after-tax rates of return on an investment offering a pre-tax return of 5.2% per year. Inside one investment wrapper, the return is fully taxed each year. Another wrapper defers taxation until the funds are withdrawn. Assuming an investor with a 35% tax rate and a 10-year investment horizon, compute the after-tax returns of the investment using both wrappers.

The wrapper with annual taxation is computed using Equation 25.3 as $5.2\% \times (1 - 0.35) = 3.38\%$. The wrapper with deferred taxation is computed using Equation 25.4 (and a future value of 1.66019) as $[1 + (1.66019 - 1) \times (1 - 0.35)]^{1/10} - 1 = 3.635\%$.

25.2.3 Depreciation, Deferral, and Leverage Combined

As previously indicated, the ability to deduct depreciation as an expense for income tax purposes is, in most cases, tantamount to deferral of income taxes (rather than a reduction in total taxable income). Deferral of income taxes is also available to real estate because capital gains are generally not taxed until realized through a transaction, and, as discussed in the previous section, may not be taxed at all. Finally, leveraged real estate can offer taxable investors the advantage of deducting interest payments on the debt financing of real estate for income tax purposes in the periods when an interest payment is made.

Taken together, the income tax benefits of leveraged real estate can be especially valuable to investors in very high tax brackets. Returning to the example on depreciation at the end of Section 25.1.2, the potential value of the depreciation tax deduction to a taxable investor, almost €1 million in the example, is especially substantial when leverage is applied. If the building in the example (perhaps worth €12,000,000, including land) is financed with 6:1 leverage, the entire €0.98 million depreciation tax shield can be generated with only €2 million of equity investment.

25.3 COMPARING AFTER-TAX RETURNS FOR VARIOUS TAXATION SCENARIOS

This section works through five numerical examples of real estate corresponding to five taxation scenarios. The scenarios progress from the scenario in which depreciation generates the smallest tax advantage, to the scenario in which depreciation generates the largest tax advantage.

25.3.1 Real Estate Example without Taxation

Consider a real estate property that cost $100 million and will be sold after 3 years. For simplicity, ignore inflation and assume that the true value of the property will decline by 10% each year due to wear and aging. Assume that the cash flows generated by the property each year are equal to the sum of 10% of the property's value at the end of the previous year plus the amount by which the property declined in value.

For example, operating cash flow at the end of year 1 is equal to $20 million, found as 10% of $100 million plus the difference between $100 million and $90 million. These numbers are illustrated in Exhibit 25.1 and are constructed to generate a 10% IRR on a pre-tax basis. The 10% IRR should be expected because the assets earn 10% above and beyond depreciation each year. The IRR is computed using the initial investment ($100 million), the operating cash flows for each year, and the assumption that the property can be sold at the end of the third year at its year 3 value ($72.90 million). The IRR is 10%.

25.3.2 After-Tax Returns When Depreciation Is Not Allowed

This section continues with the previous real estate example and modifies the example to include taxation at a stated rate of 40% of income. A **stated rate of income tax** is the statutory income tax rate applied to reported income each period.

EXHIBIT 25.1   A Stylized Depreciable Real Estate Property: No Taxes ($ in millions)

	End of Year 0	End of Year 1	End of Year 2	End of Year 3
True property value	$100.00	$90.00	$81.00	$72.90
Operating cash flow	$0	$20.00	$18.00	$16.20
– Depreciation	$0	–$10.00	–$9.00	–$8.10
– Taxes	$0	$0	$0	$0
Net income	$0	$10.00	$9.00	$8.10
Sales proceeds				$72.90
Total cash flow	–$100.00	$20.00	$18.00	$89.10
IRR = 10.0%				

The stated tax rate can differ from the effective tax rate. The **effective tax rate** is the actual reduction in value that occurs in practice when other aspects of taxation are included in the analysis, such as exemptions, penalties, and timing of cash flows. For example, a corporation with $100 million of taxable income that is taxed at a 10% statutory rate would experience a lower effective tax rate if the tax law granted the corporation the opportunity to pay the taxes several years later and without penalty.

To include taxation without depreciation, assume that the operating cash flows from each year are fully taxed, even though the cash flows overstate the income because the value of the property is declining through time. In other words, depreciation expense is not allowed for tax purposes in this example. Depreciation may be viewed as a way of marking an asset to market. If the property were marked-to-market in the first year, the $20 million of operating cash flow would not be fully taxed, since the process of marking the property's value to market would generate a $10 million offsetting loss through depreciation.

Exhibit 25.2 illustrates the incomes and cash flows. The property is sold at a loss to its initial purchase price. Because depreciation is not allowed, assume that this loss is allowed to offset the investor's taxable income in that year, thereby generating reduced taxes in the third year. Assume through this section that the investor has sufficient income from other investments to utilize any tax losses generated by this investment. Depreciation, which is not included in Exhibit 25.2, can have a substantial effect on measured performance. Depreciation as a measure of the decline in the value of an asset can be either an estimation of the true economic decline that the asset experiences, or an accounting value based on accounting conventions.

As indicated in Exhibit 25.2, the after-tax IRR of the property is 5.8%. Note that the after-tax IRR is less than 6%, which would be 60% of the 10% pre-tax IRR.

This result illustrates the **first principle of depreciation and returns:** when accounting depreciation either is not allowed for tax purposes or is allowed at a rate that is slower than the true economic depreciation, the after-tax IRR will be less than the pre-tax IRR reduced by the tax rate. In this example, the pre-tax IRR of 10% reduced by the tax rate of 40% is 6%. The actual after-tax IRR of 5.8% is lower by more than 40% compared to the pre-tax IRR, demonstrating that the present value of the taxes exceeds 40% of the present value of the profits. Thus, when depreciation for tax accounting purposes either is not allowed or is allowed

EXHIBIT 25.2 A Stylized Depreciable Real Estate Property: No Depreciation ($ in millions)

	End of Year 0	End of Year 1	End of Year 2	End of Year 3
True property value	$100.00	$90.00	$81.00	$72.90
Operating cash flow	$0	$20.00	$18.00	$16.20
Pre-tax profit	$0	$20.00	$18.00	$16.20
−Taxes	$0	−$8.00	−$7.20	−$6.48
Net income	$0	$12.00	$10.80	$9.72
Sales proceeds				$72.90
Capital loss tax shield (40% of loss)				$10.84
Total cash flow	−$100.00	$12.00	$10.80	$93.46
IRR = 5.8%				

on a deferred basis relative to true economic depreciation, the after-tax return will generally be less than the pre-tax return reduced by the stated income tax rate.

The intuition of the first principle is that by disallowing a deduction for depreciation on a timely basis, the investor is, in an economic sense, paying taxes before they are due. The investor may be viewed as providing an interest-free loan to the government by paying taxes in advance of when the taxes would be paid if the investor were being taxed on true economic income as it occurred. Thus, the effective tax rate exceeds the stated tax rate.

25.3.3 Return When Accounting Depreciation Equals Economic Depreciation

This section continues with the real estate example of the previous two sections and modifies the example to include depreciation for tax accounting purposes that is allowed at a rate that matches the true economic depreciation of decline in the value of the property. Exhibit 25.3 illustrates the incomes and cash flows. Since the property is sold at its depreciated value, there is no income tax due on its sale.

As indicated in Exhibit 25.3, the after-tax IRR of the property is 6%. Note that this after-tax IRR is exactly 60% of the pre-tax IRR (10%). This stated income tax rate of 40% causes a 40% reduction in the IRR earned by the investor, so the effective tax rate equals the stated tax rate. This illustrates the **second principle of depreciation and returns:** when depreciation for tax accounting purposes matches true economic depreciation in timing, the after-tax return generally equals the pre-tax return reduced by the stated income tax rate.

It should be noted that the speed of the depreciation method does not affect the aggregated taxable income (summed through all of the years). Rather, the rate of the depreciation changes the timing of the taxes. When the time value of money is included, the rate of the depreciation changes the after-tax IRR and the effective tax rate.

25.3.4 Return When Accounting Depreciation Is Accelerated

This section demonstrates the most common situation in practice: accelerated depreciation. **Accelerated depreciation** is when accounting depreciation for tax purposes

EXHIBIT 25.3   A Stylized Depreciable Real Estate Property: Economic Depreciation ($ in millions)

	End of Year 0	End of Year 1	End of Year 2	End of Year 3
True property value	$100.00	$90.00	$81.00	$72.90
Operating cash flow	$0	$20.00	$18.00	$16.20
– Depreciation	$0	–$10.00	–$9.00	–$8.10
Pre-tax profit	$0	$10.00	$9.00	$8.10
– Taxes	$0	–$4.00	–$3.60	–$3.24
Net income	$0	$6.00	$5.40	$4.86
Sales proceeds				$72.90
Total cash flow	–$100.00	$16.00	$14.40	$85.86
IRR = 6.0%				

EXHIBIT 25.4   A Stylized Depreciable Real Estate Property: Accelerated Depreciation ($ in millions)

	End of Year 0	End of Year 1	End of Year 2	End of Year 3
True property value	$100.00	$90.00	$81.00	$72.90
Operating cash flow	$0	$20.00	$18.00	$16.20
Profit before depreciation	$0	$20.00	$18.00	$16.20
– Depreciation	$0	–$20.00	–$20.00	–$20.00
Pre-tax profit	$0	$0	–$2.00	–$3.80
– Taxes	$0	$0	$0.80	$1.52
Net income	$0	$0	–$1.20	–$2.28
Book value end of period	$100.00	$80.00	$60.00	$40.00
Sales proceeds				$72.90
– Capital gain taxes (40% of profit)				–$13.16
Total cash flow	–$100.00	$20.00	$18.80	$77.46
IRR = 6.3%				

writes off the value of an asset more quickly than it is actually declining in market value. In fact, in practice, it is typically the case that accounting depreciation for tax purposes writes off the value of real estate assets that are actually increasing in value through time. For simplicity, accelerated depreciation is modeled as $20 million in each of the first 3 years. Exhibit 25.4 illustrates the incomes and cash flows. Since the property is sold above its depreciated value, there is income tax due on its sale.

As indicated in Exhibit 25.4, the after-tax IRR of the property is 6.3%. Accelerated depreciation, shown in Exhibit 25.4, generates an after-tax IRR that exceeds the after-tax IRR that was found in Exhibit 25.3 when accounting depreciation matched the true economic depreciation. The reason is that accelerated depreciation defers income taxes, effectively serving as an interest-free loan from the government to the investor, enhancing the value of the property. The resulting effective tax rate is less than the stated tax rate. This illustrates the **third principle of depreciation and returns:** when depreciation for tax accounting purposes is accelerated in time relative to true economic depreciation, the after-tax return generally exceeds the pre-tax return reduced by the stated income tax rate.

25.3.5   Return When Capital Expenditures Can Be Expensed

This section analyzes an extreme situation in which capital expenditures are allowed to be immediately and fully deducted, or expensed, for income tax purposes. Such treatment is generally allowed for smaller and shorter-term assets, such as minor equipment, but not for real estate. The point here is to illustrate the most extreme possible form of accelerated depreciation. Exhibit 25.5 illustrates the incomes and cash flows. The initial purchase price of $100 million can be expensed, generating $40 million of tax savings (i.e., offsets to the investors' other taxable income). Since the property is sold above its depreciated value ($0), there is income tax due on the full proceeds of its sale.

As indicated in Exhibit 25.5, the after-tax IRR of the property is 10%. Amazingly, being able to expense outlays immediately on an investment causes the after-tax

EXHIBIT 25.5   A Stylized Depreciable Real Estate Property: Expensed ($ in millions)

	End of Year 0	End of Year 1	End of Year 2	End of Year 3
True property value	$100.00	$90.00	$81.00	$72.90
Operating cash flow	–$100.00	$20.00	$18.00	$16.20
Pre-tax profit	–$100.00	$20.00	$18.00	$16.20
– Taxes	$40.00	–$8.00	–$7.20	–$6.48
Net income	$0	$12.00	$10.80	$9.72
Sales proceeds				$72.90
– Capital gain taxes (40% of profit)				–$29.16
Total cash flow	–$60.00	$12.00	$10.80	$53.46
IRR = 10%				

IRR to equal the pre-tax IRR (10%). The intuition is that all cash inflows and outflows are reduced by 40%. The scale of the cash flows is reduced and any NPV for the project is similarly reduced (by 40%). However, the relative values and timing do not change. Thus, the IRRs of the pre-tax and after-tax cash flows are the same. In practice, major capital expenditures cannot typically be expensed in the year of purchase. However, the case parallels the benefits of fully tax-deductible retirement investing. This illustrates the **fourth principle of depreciation and returns:** when all investment outlays can be fully and instantly expensed for tax accounting purposes, the after-tax return generally equals the pre-tax return.

The reduced taxation afforded by depreciation is due to the depreciation tax shield. A depreciation tax shield is a taxable entity's ability to reduce taxes by deducting depreciation in the computation of taxable income. The present value of the depreciation tax shield is the present value of the tax savings generated by the stream of depreciation. Real estate equity investment tends to offer substantial depreciation tax shields to taxable investors.

The above discussions regarding depreciation and taxes have shown that when depreciation for tax accounting purposes occurs at the same rate as true economic decline in the value of the asset, the value of the depreciation tax shield drives the effective tax rate to equal the stated tax rate. In other words, the after-tax IRR will equal the pre-tax IRR reduced by the stated tax rate. However, as is often the case, when real estate depreciation for tax purposes is allowed to substantially exceed the true economic depreciation, the value of the depreciation tax shield can cause the effective income tax rate on the property to be substantially lower than the stated tax rate.

APPLICATION 25.3.5

Consider four investments with otherwise equivalent characteristics. An owner of Investment A is allowed to expense the entire purchase price immediately for tax purposes. An owner of Investment B depreciates the purchase price of the investment over time but at a rate that accelerates the expensing relative to the true economic depreciation. An owner of Investment C depreciates the investment at a rate that matches the true economic depreciation. An owner of Investment D depreciates the investment at a rate that is slower than the true economic depreciation. The pre-tax rate of return on the cash flows is 12%. What can be said about the after-tax rates of return of each investment for a taxpayer in an income tax bracket of 25%?

The answer is that the after-tax rate of return

- for Investment A is 12%;
- for Investment B is between 9% and 12%;
- for Investment C, when economic depreciation equals depreciation for tax purposes, the after-tax rate of return is 9%, which equals the pre-tax rate of return (12%) times 1 minus the 25% tax rate; and
- for Investment D the after-tax rate of return is less than 9%.

25.3.6 Depreciation and Heterogenous Marginal Tax Rates Among Investors

As an asset offering a depreciation tax shield, real estate requires specialized analysis. Depreciation is a noncash expense that can have important effects on taxes and after-tax rates of return. Generally, real estate buildings offer taxable investors in the equity of the real estate the opportunity to receive a depreciation tax shield that can be very valuable and needs to be considered in decision-making.

Most equity positions in real estate possess average to above-average income tax benefits.

Competition should drive the prices and expected returns of investments to reflect the taxability of the investment's income. Entities in zero or low-income tax brackets should generally prefer investments that are highly taxed; whereas investors in high-income tax brackets should prefer investments that offer income tax advantages, such as the opportunity to claim accelerated depreciation. Tax-exempt investors and investors in very low-income tax brackets may find the rates of return on equity real estate to be insufficient to support equally high asset allocations to real estate. Nevertheless, substantial real estate is held by and typically should be held by tax-exempt investors due to the other advantages offered by real estate

25.4 TRANSACTION-BASED INDICES: REPEAT-SALES

The two main methods used to estimate transaction-based price indices are the repeat-sales method (RSM) and the hedonic-pricing method (HPM). While this discussion focuses on real estate, the principles are applicable to various privately-traded heterogenous assets, such as intellectual property (e.g., artwork) and infrastructure.

Transaction-based real estate indices are estimated based on actual contemporaneous property sales of sample properties that trade in each period. The **main problems of transaction-based indices** are that each individual property is unique and each individual property is sold infrequently and at erratic time intervals. Nevertheless, transaction-based real estate indices can serve as a good basis for real estate valuation under the following three conditions:

1. They are based on enough data and rigorous econometric methods.
2. Any differences in properties trading in different periods are controlled for.
3. Statistical noise is minimized.

This section details the repeat-sales approach while Section 25.5 details the hedonic-pricing approach.

25.4.1 Overview and Example of the Repeat-Sales Method

A repeat sale occurs when a specific property is traded at least two times during the sample period used. Differences in properties through time (e.g., additions) are controlled for by using price-change information only from properties that have not changed substantially. The periodic returns on all properties are then estimated from the percentage changes in the observations with repeat sales. The **repeat-sales method (RSM)** regresses the percentage price changes observed in properties on a sequence of time-dummy variables.

The following example illustrates how a repeat-sales method can be used to construct an index based on prices estimated according to the RSM. The example is adapted from Geltner et al. (2014). Assume two properties and two periods of time. Suppose that the first investor purchased his property for $100,000 at the beginning of the first period and sold it for $115,500 at the end of the second period; that is, the property was held for two full periods. Suppose the second investor purchased her property at the beginning of the second period for $200,000 and sold it at the end of that period for $210,000.

Given this information, the time-dummy variable for the first time period would be 1 for the first investor and zero for the second investor. The time-dummy variable for the second time period would be 1 for both investors, since they both held their investments during that period. Exhibit 25.6 presents the corresponding regression model data. Note that with two observations and two unknown variables the solution does not require statistical regression but it is used for simplicity.

The time-dummy coefficients for the two periods are then estimated. The estimated coefficients correspond to the annual return on the investments represented

EXHIBIT 25.6 Setup of the "Regression" Model Data

Dependent Variable	Time-Dummy Variables	
	Time Period 1	Time Period 2
$115,500/$100,000 = 1.155	1	1
$210,000/$200,000 = 1.05	0	1

by the two properties. In this simple example, the regression yields a 10% return as the coefficient of the dummy variable representing the first period, and a 5% return as the coefficient of the dummy variable representing the second period. The dependent variables may be transformed using the log function before the regression is estimated; that is, logs of total returns, 1.155 and 1.050, may be used as dependent variables in which case the coefficients can be viewed as continuously compounded returns.

In this example:

For the first investor: $\$100,000 \times 1.10 \times 1.05 = \$115,500$

For the second investor: $\$200,000 \times 1.05 = \$210,000$

As long as the data contain at least one sale per period, the repeat-sales model can find returns for each period. Statistical techniques, such as ordinary least squares (OLS), weighted least squares (WLS), and time-weighted dummies, can be selected in the optimization.

In the US, the CoStar Commercial Repeat-Sale Index (CCRSI) publishes a repeat-sales index that measures returns for commercial real estate. The index is based on 1,154 repeat sales in March 2018 and 190,000 repeat sales since 1996. The CCRSI family of indices report monthly and quarterly returns on 30 sub-indices in the CoStar index family. The sub-indices include breakdowns by region of the country (Northeast, South, Midwest, and West); by property sector (office, industrial, retail, multi-family, hospitality, and land); by transaction size and quality (general commercial and investment grade); and by market size (composite index of the prime market areas in the country).

25.4.2 Two Advantages of the Repeat-Sales Method

There are two primary advantages of the repeat-sales method:

1. The RSM calculates changes in home prices based on sales of the same property. Therefore, this method avoids the problem of trying to explain price differences in properties with varying characteristics. Thus, the repeat-sales method does not require detailed information on property characteristics.
2. The RSM is relatively robust to specification error in the application of the model. Typically, this type of error arises when the wrong regression model is selected to explain variations in the dependent variables.

25.4.3 Three Disadvantages of the Repeat-Sales Method

There are three primary disadvantages of the repeat-sales method:

1. The main disadvantage of the RSM is that the sample of properties (with two or more transactions) from which the price changes and the resulting index are calculated typically represents a small portion of all the properties that are transacted during a given period of time (i.e., transacted only once). This data scarcity problem can be severe when trying to apply this method during a short period

of time. This disadvantage can be important because properties that were sold only once during a certain time period (and are therefore not considered when using the RSM) are also important signs of real estate market movements. As a result, the RSM may suffer from a sample selection bias.

2. The RSM assumes that the property being traded does not experience changes, when in reality all properties depreciate and age, and some are renovated.

3. When the RSM is updated, it generates backward adjustments in the historical series of returns, and thus previously estimated returns for certain years in the past may change. This problem occurs because a property recording a new "second sale" links back to the earlier "first sale" in estimation history.

25.5   TRANSACTION-BASED INDICES: HEDONIC

Having reviewed the other major form of transaction-based valuation methods (the repeat-sales method) in the previous section, this section details the hedonic-pricing method (HPM).

25.5.1   Overview of the Hedonic-Pricing Method

The price of every real estate asset is determined by the overall supply and demand conditions in the local real estate market, as well as by the different set of attributes of each asset. The **hedonic-pricing method (HPM)** assumes that each of these attributes has its own market price. Examples of these attributes include the number of rooms, the size of the lot, the number of bathrooms, and so on. In other words, properties can be viewed as bundles of attributes and characteristics. We can observe the market price and the attributes or characteristics of the properties. It is thus required to unbundle and determine the implicit price or contribution of each of these attributes (i.e., the hedonic price) within the observed market price, including precise location, that renders them virtually unrepeatable and unique.

Of course, each property also has property-specific attributes including its precise location that makes the property unique. Regression can be used because, through its error term, regression allows for prices to deviate from the values that are fitted based on the limited number of shared characteristics available to serve as independent variables in the regression.

The attributes of a property may be internal (location, size, number of rooms, age) or external (accessibility to schools, crime rate in the neighborhood, level of air pollution). Some attributes may be difficult to measure or quantify, such as charm and layout. However, the HPM is market-priced-based and is relatively inexpensive to apply when data are readily available.

The concept of a hedonic price index (applied to real estate transactions) involves using observed real estate transactions of some properties to estimate the prices of all properties, including those that did not transact.

25.5.2   Three Steps to Calculating a Hedonic Price Index

The three steps of calculating a hedonic price index using transaction prices are:

1. Model the value of real estate properties as being a function of specified characteristics of the properties that can be observed and for which data are available.

2. Use a sample of prices observed from recent transactions to fit the parameters of the real estate valuation model; that is, determine the implicit price of each attribute.
3. Use the estimated valuation parameters for the various characteristics to estimate the values of the properties that are within the index but did not transact.

25.5.3 A Simplified Example of the Hedonic-Pricing Approach

As a very simplified example, a model of office properties may be valued using a model with two variables: size (square feet of space) and quality (Class 1, 2, or 3). Data on recent office property transactions are recorded with a transaction price, size, and quality class for each. The parameters (i.e., regression coefficients) for the size and quality attributes (i.e., independent variables) are estimated based on an econometric model, with price per square foot as the dependent variable. In this example, size and quality are the independent variables. The estimated parameters from the model are then used to infer the prices of all properties. These prices are then used to calculate values of other properties and the index representing the overall market.

Exhibit 25.7 illustrates hypothetical data. Suppose that six offices (A through F) of different sizes (in square feet) and quality types (from 1 to 3, where 1 is the highest) have recently transacted at the prices shown. How can this information be used to predict or fit the price of a seventh office?

First, a regression equation is estimated using an econometric method—in this case the OLS (ordinary least squares) method—and tested with a 10% level of statistical significance. The natural logarithm of price is the dependent variable, while size and quality serve as the independent variables. The natural logarithm (ln) of price is used as the dependent variable because it provides a better estimation when estimating hedonic regressions. The estimated regression equation is therefore as follows (note that t-statistics are in parentheses under the respective coefficients:

$$\ln(\text{Price}) = 11.13151 + (0.000918 \times \text{Size}) - (0.1159316 \times \text{Quality})$$

$$(3.06)\,(-1.86)$$

The R^2 of the regression is 0.95 indicating that 95% of the variation is explained. The coefficients on the variables size and quality have the expected sign and are statistically significant at 10%.

EXHIBIT 25.7 Hypothetical Prices, Sizes, and Qualities of Six Office Properties

	Sale Price	Size (Sq. Ft.)	Quality
Office A	$110,000	840	3
Office B	$145,000	1,155	2
Office C	$152,000	1,035	1
Office D	$133,000	970	2
Office E	$205,000	1,250	1
Office F	$ 95,000	760	3

Let us now suppose that we need to estimate the price of a new office, G, which is of quality type 2 and has 1,020 square feet. Using the estimated equation, we get:

$$\ln(\text{Price}) = 11.13151 + (0.000918 \times 1{,}020) - (0.1159316 \times 2)$$

$$\ln(\text{Price}) = 11.8360068$$

Calculating $e^{\ln(\text{price})}$, we get the estimated price of office G: $e^{11.8360068}$ = $138,136.

APPLICATION 25.5.3

A hedonic pricing model is estimated using linear regression with ln(Price) as the dependent variable. The intercept of the regression, a, is 10, and the slope coefficients are 0.001200 and -0.1000 for the independent variables Size and Quality, respectively. A property not included in the sample has a size of 1,000 square feet and a quality value of 3. What is the property's estimated value based on the regression results?

Inserting the estimated parameters into the regression equation generates $54,176:

$$\ln(\text{Price}) = 10 + (0.001200 \times 1{,}000) - (0.1000 \times 3)$$

$$\ln(\text{Price}) = 10 + 1.200 - 0.3 = 10.9$$

$$e^{\ln(\text{Price})} = e^{\ln(10.9)} = \$54{,}176$$

25.5.4 Three Primary Advantages of the Hedonic-Pricing Model

There are three primary advantages of the HPM:

1. The HPM uses all observations (transactions) and is not limited to repeat sales. This advantage is particularly useful when the length of the sample period is short.
2. The HPM is versatile, as hedonic indices can be adapted to take into consideration the characteristics deemed relevant to the market being analyzed. For example, the HPM has been used to estimate the effect of the following on housing prices: the presence of air pollution, scenic views versus industrial views, the perceived risk of only partially compensated expropriations, and the existence of open space and protected areas.
3. The HPM avoids backward adjustments of historical returns when an index is re-estimated with "second sale" transactions data.

25.5.5 Three Primary Disadvantages of the Hedonic-Pricing Model

There are three primary disadvantages of the HPM:

1. The HPM requires a large amount of data on several hedonic (both internal and external) variables. The collection of this data can be costly and time-consuming.
2. As in the case of the repeat-sales model, the HPM may also suffer from sample selection bias. This arises when the properties that are sold are not representative of the universe of properties. For example, a sample selection bias will arise if, in a normal market, the owners of properties with rising values tend to sell their properties, while the owners of properties with falling values tend not to sell their properties.
3. The HPM is exposed to specification error. That is, not all attributes of properties may have been included. For example, the model may not include the noise level of various localities situated near factories.

25.6 SAMPLE BIAS AND THE REPEAT-SALES AND HEDONIC-PRICE METHODS

The primary difference between hedonic-price indices and repeat-sales indices is that hedonic-price indices include all properties that transacted at least once, whereas repeat-sales indices include data from only those properties that transacted multiple times. Both indices are transaction-based indices.

Transaction-based real estate indices suffer from sample selection bias to the extent that the properties that are represented in the index differ from the aggregated mix of all such assets. For example, in transaction-based indices, a bias arises to the extent that properties transacted during a particular period are used to calculate an index which may not be representative of the entire universe of properties. A bias toward a particular type of property, location of property, size of property, and so forth, would interfere with the representativeness of the sample. Although the effects of sample selection bias also influence residential property indices, they are likely to be especially severe for commercial properties because the universe of commercial properties is typically small and the number of transactions in any particular time period is even smaller. The effects of randomness on the attributes of a sample tend to be larger when the sample is small.

There is another reason to be concerned about sample selection bias other than the idea that the sample of properties with transactions will deviate from the universe of all properties due to randomness. As Haurin (2005) points out:

> In a normal market, the real values (i.e., deflated values) of some properties will rise while others may decline. If the owners of properties with falling values tend to choose not to sell their properties, while owners of properties with rising values tend to choose to sell (or vice versa), then the sample of transacted properties is clearly not random and is biased towards a particular price outcome. It is also plausible that the choices of whether to sell properties with rising and falling values change over the real estate cycle and thus

the nature of the sample selection bias will change over time. This changing bias results in an estimated transaction-based price index that differs from a theoretical price index that would track market values of the stock of all properties.

Thus, there may be systematic reasons to believe that the sample of properties that have transacted will have substantially different characteristics from the universe of properties and that, more importantly, the differences in characteristics will be related to recent price changes. The result is that the sample will reflect price changes unrepresentative of the universe.

25.7   APPRAISAL-BASED INDICES

This section discusses appraisals and, implicitly, indices based on appraisals. **Appraisal-based indices** are derived from the asset values estimated by appraisers, which may track a particular subpopulation. In theory, all assets included in this type of index can be appraised every period, although this is not always the case. This section focuses on real estate; however, the principles can apply to other assets that are frequently valued through appraisals.

25.7.1   Approaches to Appraisals

There are three primary means of appraising real estate: the sales comparison approach, the cost approach, and the income capitalization approach. Each method has its own advantages depending on the situation and type of real estate involved. These methods are most common for commercial real estate.

1. The **sales comparison approach,** in which a real estate asset is evaluated against those of comparable (substitute) properties that have recently been sold. Value adjustments may be made for characteristics such as square footage, date of sale, location, and amenities.
2. The **cost approach,** which assumes that a buyer will not pay more for a property than it would cost to build an equivalent one. A property's value can be estimated by adding the depreciated value of any improvements to the land value of the property. This approach is often suggested when valuing newer structures.
3. The **income approach,** which is similar to the discounted cash flow method used for valuing stocks and bonds. Several years of net operating income are projected for a specific property or portfolio of properties and then discounted using an appropriate discount rate. This approach is particularly useful when valuing income-producing real estate assets, such as commercial real estate.

25.7.2   Two Advantages of Appraisal-Based Models

There are two primary advantages of appraisal-based models:

1. In general, they do not suffer from a small sample size problem (as does the repeat-sales method and, to a lesser extent the hedonic approach, both of which are discussed in previous sections of this chapter).
2. All properties can be appraised frequently.

25.7.3 Three Disadvantages of Appraisal-Based Models

There are three primary disadvantages of appraisal-based models:

1. Appraisals are inherently subjective and backward-looking, thus introducing errors in prices. Typically, properties are fully reappraised only periodically. This causes a "stale appraisal" effect (i.e., dated appraisals), which adds to the lag.
2. Appraisal-based indices are smoothed compared with actual changes in real estate market values. Thus, measures of volatility of the value of commercial real estate assets are underestimated using appraisal-based indices. Fortunately, unsmoothing techniques, presented in Chapter 18, help mitigate this problem.
3. Appraisal methods tend to rely on data from comparable properties. Therefore, the quality of the appraisal will depend critically on the quality of available data. As a result, appraisals may not be accurate in situations in which comparable properties cannot be identified (e.g., the current property is rather unique) or there is a significant time lag between the time the data has become available and the time the appraisal takes place.

Chapter 18 provides extensive analysis and detail on the issues that arise when allocating to private assets that are valued based on appraisals, and listed assets that are valued based on observable market values.

25.8 NOISY PRICING

Estimated values for privately-traded heterogenous assets can be obtained either by evaluating transaction prices of those assets that actually sell or by using appraised values produced by professional appraisers. Both types of values are noisy because they are inexact estimates of true market value (i.e., they contain error relative to the true value of the assets). As illustrated in Geltner et al. (2014), this error falls primarily into two major types: purely random error or noise and temporal lag bias. This section discusses noisy pricing in the context of real estate properties.

25.8.1 Random Pricing Errors and Reservation Prices

The **purely random error or noise** arises because of the structure of the real estate market, where transactions involve negotiations between two parties and the resulting transaction price is one value from a range of prices that could have resulted from those negotiations. **Temporal lag bias** arises when transaction prices are related to past prices because of the structure of the market. For example, the reported transaction price may have been negotiated a few months before and therefore does not reflect the current market conditions.

In addition, a tradeoff between these two types of errors arises when one attempts to construct an optimal value estimation method. This occurs because it is difficult to reduce the lag bias without increasing the random error, and hard to reduce the random error without increasing the lag bias.

To understand this problem of noisy pricing, consider the concept of reservation price. The **reservation price** is the lowest price at which a potential seller is willing to sell a property, or the highest price a potential buyer is willing to pay for a property.

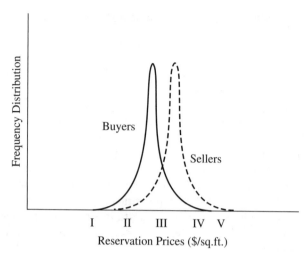

EXHIBIT 25.8   Buyer's and Seller's Reservation Price
Frequency Distributions at a Given Point in Time

Exhibit 25.8 shows that the cross-sectional reservation price distribution of potential buyers and sellers overlaps for a particular population of properties and at a certain instant in time. It is in this overlapping region (i.e., the price region where prices range between values II and IV) where real estate transactions may take place, as some sellers will have reservation prices at least as low as the reservation prices of some buyers.

One can argue that these reservation prices will tend to be distributed around III on the horizontal axis of Exhibit 25.8, which is the hypothetical true market value of the population of properties at a given point in time and once they are adjusted for quality. Unfortunately, III is empirically unobservable, and all one can examine are valuations drawn from the probability distribution in III. The **transaction price noise** or **transaction price error** is the difference between any given price observation and the unobservable true market value. Assuming, among other things, that all transaction price observations occur at the same point in time, this error will be unbiased.

25.8.2   Appraisals and Appraisal Error

Real estate appraisals are also noisy because they are based on opinions (however rational and professional the appraisers may be); thus, five different appraisers may arrive at five different appraisals. The **appraisal error** is difference between a particular empirical appraised value and the unobservable true market value.

Unlike transaction prices, the appraised-value cross-sectional dispersion may or may not be centered on the true value. This implies that appraised values may be biased. To reduce the random estimation error, more transaction data are necessary. And to obtain more transaction data, transactions must be recorded reaching further back in time. One can thus reduce the random noise, but at the expense of increasing the temporal lag, or decrease lag but increase noise. This noise versus lag tradeoff has a concave form, which implies that there are diminishing returns in the process (e.g., the more transaction data that one has, the more accurate will be the inferences about real estate market values, but at a decreasing rate).

25.8.3   The Square Root of *N* Rule

More specifically, the accuracy of an estimated market value based on n observations will tend to be inversely proportional to the square root of the number of observations (e.g., transaction price data) that one can examine. This is the law of statistical inference known as the square root of n rule.

For example, consider an appraiser that uses two comparables to generate an estimate of a property's value. If the appraiser can use four comparables instead of just two, the estimated value will have about 71% (i.e., $1/\sqrt{2}$) as much error ($4/2 = 2$). But if the same appraiser can use eight comparables instead of just two, the estimated value will have only about 50% (i.e., $1/\sqrt{4}$) as much error. Thus, one can reduce the error of the estimated value from 71% to 50% by increasing the number of comparables from four to eight. However, comparable data become available only when transactions take place, and transactions occur through time. In our case, in order to use, for example, eight comparables rather than two, and reduce the error by 50%, the appraiser would have to reach, on average, four times as far back in time.

REFERENCES

Geltner, D., N. G. Miller, J. Clayton, and P. Eichholtz. (2014). *Commercial Real Estate Analysis and Investment*. Mason: OneCourse Learning.

Haurin, D. R. 2005. "US Commercial Real Estate Indices: Transaction-Based and Constant-Liquidity Indices ." *BIS White Papers* 21, April.

Lee, N. and C. Swenson. 2012. "Are Multinational Corporate Tax Rules as Important as Tax Rates?" *International Journal of Accounting* 47 (2): 155–67.

Accessing Alternative Investments

The relative merits of various forms of access to asset classes are key factors in the asset allocation process. Chapter 26 discusses hedge fund replication approaches – which attempt to generate hedge-fund-like returns outside of direct investments in traditional hedge funds. Chapters 27 and 28 discuss asset-class specific access approaches with Chapter 27 focused on hedge funds and Chapter 28 focused on real estate and commodities. Chapters 29 and 30 center on private equity. Chapter 29 delves deeply into private partnership details and, especially, concerns with their principal-agent conflicts of interest. Chapter 30 discusses performance computation details.

CHAPTER 26

Hedge Fund Replication

This chapter discusses hedge fund replication methods and potential applications of products developed using these methods. The subject of hedge fund replication was first examined by academics in the early 2000s while attempting to develop performance benchmarks for hedge funds. Later, in 2007, following initiatives by major investment banks (such as Merrill Lynch, Goldman Sachs, Credit Suisse, and Morgan Stanley) and other firms to introduce investable hedge fund replication products, there was renewed interest in the subject among academics and practitioners.

This chapter examines, from both a theoretical and an empirical standpoint, the respective benefits and limits of two main approaches to hedge fund replication: factor-based replication and bottom-up replication (also called algorithmic replication). The chapter also briefly discusses the payoff-distribution replication approach, examines the potential benefits that replication products could offer investors, and provides a brief summary of some of the empirical evidence regarding the performance of these products.

26.1 AN OVERVIEW OF REPLICATION PRODUCTS

Fundamentally, **hedge fund replication products** (also called clones or trackers) are created to capture the traditional and alternative betas underlying the expected return and risk of a hedge fund benchmark. **Alternative betas** refer to exposures to risk, risk premiums, and sources of return that are not normally available through investments in traditional assets—or, if they are available, are commonly bundled with other risks. For instance, publicly traded equities have exposures to a number of factors, including volatility and commodity price risks. These two risks are generally considered alternative sources of risk, but in the case of common stocks, they are bundled with pure equity risk, which dominates the behavior of common stocks. Other examples of alternative betas are risks associated with currency investments, momentum or trend-following strategies, and structured products, such as convertible bonds and certain tranches of asset-backed securities.

Available replication products are based on statistical techniques (e.g., a factor-based) or bottom-up (algorithmic) trading models. The **algorithmic factor replication approach** (i.e., the bottom-up approach) attempts to trade the underlying securities in a manner consistent with the trading approach taken by most active managers within a particular strategy. To the degree that tracker products are designed to track benchmarks based on active managers, factor-based and algorithmic approaches are meant to capture a substantial portion of the common strategy return and to reflect fund managers' common exposures to various traditional and alternative betas. Additionally, these tracker products are designed to capture the common strategy alpha earned by managers, as represented by the excess return of the fund strategy relative to a passive benchmark consisting of traditional sources of risk (e.g., MSCI World Index). In other words, if the overall strategy, rather than just the top managers, generates alpha, then replication products are created to capture all or some of that alpha.

26.2   POTENTIAL BENEFITS OF REPLICATION PRODUCTS

Before discussing the various approaches to hedge fund replication, the potential benefits that one may receive from using a replication product are examined. The term *using* is employed, rather than *investing,* because investors may benefit from these products even if they do not make any allocations to them, as replication products can lead to a better understanding of the underlying risks of hedge funds and allow investors to build better benchmarks against which to measure their hedge fund investments. The reason that investors may allocate to hedge funds in the first place needs to be understood. In other words, why is it of some potential value to replicate hedge funds?

The potential benefits of investing in hedge funds depend on the various strategies. Some strategies have significant systematic risks and therefore allow investors to earn relatively high risk-adjusted returns through exposures to directional market risks. Equity long/short funds and some global macro funds fall into this category. The primary benefit that investors seek in investing in these return enhancers is to improve the risk-adjusted returns of their portfolios. This benefit can come from earning alpha or by investing in alternative beta exposures that are underweighted in an investor's traditional portfolio. The alpha is typically measured relative to the performance of all underlying beta exposures, whether they are traditional betas or alternative betas.

Alternative beta exposures may include those taken by a global macro fund that invests in global equity and foreign currency markets while managing the risks of those investments. Liquidity risk is another important alternative source of return not available through investments in traditional assets. Liquidity risk is one of the primary sources of return to a distressed securities strategy. Finally, a time-varying traditional source of beta could be considered an alternative source of beta. For instance, a passive equity index has a constant and positive equity beta, while an equity long/short manager is likely to have a time-varying beta, which could even become negative during bear markets. Equity beta is considered a traditional source of return, while a dynamic beta that results from an actively managed portfolio is considered an alternative beta and, assuming that the manager has some market-timing skill, serves as a source of alpha.

Some strategies, however, have less systematic exposure to equity, fixed-income, or commodity markets, and are classified as risk diversifiers. Some commodity trading advisers (CTAs) and global macro funds, as well as most relative value funds, such as convertible and merger arbitrage, fall into this category. These funds provide returns that are not highly correlated with returns on traditional assets and can therefore help reduce the overall risk of a portfolio. Similar to return enhancers, a secondary benefit provided by risk diversifiers is exposure to alternative sources of risk and return. For instance, convertible bond arbitrage funds provide exposures to risks associated with implied volatility, credit, and illiquidity, earning a relatively low rate of return while reducing the overall risk of a traditional portfolio.

26.3 THE CASE FOR HEDGE FUND REPLICATION

Prior to the bursting of the Internet bubble and the resulting bear market that began in 2000, there was a widely held market belief that the returns to actively managed alternative investment funds were composed primarily of alpha (excess return above that available in an equally risky passive investment product) and small amounts of beta (return due to a strategy's exposure to investable market factors). Since then, the return streams associated with passive investable indices, active managers, and other alternative or structured products have severely challenged this belief system.

In the traditional mutual fund arena, research continues to question the existence of manager alpha (e.g., see Bodie, Kane, and Marcus 2010). Even in the alternative investment area, where greater amounts of informational inefficiencies may be expected, studies have shown that the alpha of many hedge fund strategies is consistently positive but that there has been a general decline in overall alpha in the past decade.[1]

26.3.1 Estimating the Risk and Return of Funds of Funds

Exhibit 26.1 displays a one-factor estimate of the rolling beta and rolling alpha of the Center for International Securities and Derivatives Markets (CISDM) Fund of Funds Index, for which the S&P 500 Index is used as the benchmark. Both the beta and the alpha are estimated using a 24-month rolling window. The alpha is estimated based on the following model:

$$R_{t,CISDM} - r_f = \alpha_t + \beta_t(R_{t,SP} - r_f) \tag{26.1}$$

Here, $R_{t,CISDM}$ is the estimated 24-month mean return of the CISDM Fund of Funds Index, $R_{t,SP}$ is the estimated 24-month mean return on the S&P 500 Index, β_t is the beta of the CISDM Index to the S&P 500, α_t is the alpha of the CISDM index, and r_f is the monthly rate for 30-day London Interbank Offered Rate (LIBOR). All variables are estimated using a linear regression and a 24-month rolling window.

From Exhibit 26.1, it can be seen that since 1995, there has been significant variation in the estimated beta of the hedge fund index. A rise is observed from about 2004 to 2007, and then a general decline since then. However, a general decline in the value of alpha is observed since 2001, with the most recent estimates hovering around zero.

26.3.2 Three Theories for Increased Beta and Decreased Alpha in Hedge Fund Returns

There have been various explanations for increases in beta and declines in alpha: changes in trading strategies, increased liquidity, technological advances that have

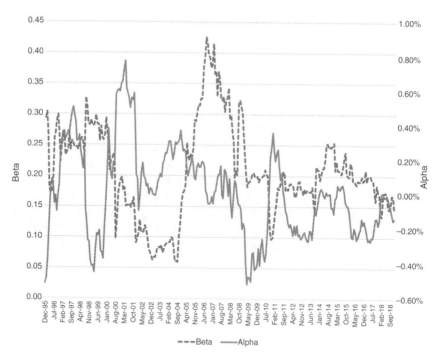

EXHIBIT 26.1   Twenty-Four Month Rolling Estimates of Betas and Alphas of the CISDM Fund of Funds Index Relative to the S&P 500 Index, 1994–2018
Source: CISDM, Bloomberg, and authors' calculations.

all but eliminated information premiums, or regulatory intervention. These explanations have given rise to three alternative hypotheses:

1. The fund bubble hypothesis.
2. The capacity constraint hypothesis.
3. The increased allocation to active funds hypothesis.

The **fund bubble hypothesis** assumes that successful hedge fund managers can earn substantially greater returns than successful fund managers in the traditional space, but that bubbles cause inferior managers to dilute overall industry performance. Investment bubbles provide an opportunity for less skilled traditional fund managers to become hedge fund managers. The fund bubble hypothesis simply states that as the supply of investment capital to the hedge fund space increases, so does the number of less qualified managers who enter the industry and provide inferior returns that dilute the overall performance of the hedge fund industry.

The **capacity constraint hypothesis** argues that most alpha is a zero-sum game and that increased supply of managers pursuing alpha dilutes superior performance. In this hypothesis, only a few managers can offer alpha on a consistent basis. In short, the growth in assets under management sharply reduces the per capita amount of alpha available in the marketplace. In addition, unless new strategies or sources of alpha are discovered, further declines in alpha can be expected.

The **increased allocation to active funds hypothesis** argues that as hedge fund investment becomes more popular, the risk-adjusted performance of hedge funds will be adversely affected by the trading decisions of investors who have allocations to both these funds and traditional assets. This causes the systematic risks or betas of hedge funds to increase as more capital flows into them and, during periods of financial stress, investors may be forced to liquidate both their traditional and their alternative investments. The liquidation in stressed markets increases the overall correlation between traditional and alternative asset classes since common correlation measures are heavily weighted towards extreme outcomes.

The common theme flowing through these three hypotheses is that, although star managers exist whose ability to provide meaningful returns is not questioned, the investment management universe also includes managers who either are mandated to invest in accordance with a given benchmark or do not have the skill to surpass that benchmark. Note that the lack of manager outperformance is not necessarily manager induced. For example, some managers may be constrained by the mandates of their contracts; in this case, often the clients have made an asset allocation decision that requires the manager to remain within certain limits. Client intervention, however, plays a very limited role within absolute return vehicles, whereas the decline of alpha is pronounced and without many mitigating factors. The real questions in the replication or tracking literature remain the degree to which the representative benchmark is investable, and the degree to which the investable replication or tracker fund adequately reflects the risks and returns of the representative benchmark.

26.3.3 The Aggregate Alpha of the Hedge Fund Industry

Since hedge fund replication products attempt to capture the overall performance of hedge funds or hedge fund strategies, it is important to examine whether the hedge fund industry can generate alpha on an aggregate level. While there is ample evidence that some hedge fund managers are able to provide alpha, it is not clear whether the entire strategy can and should be able to generate positive alpha on a consistent basis. The main argument against the ability of the entire industry to generate alpha is rooted in the concept of informational market efficiency, discussed in the CAIA Level I curriculum. However, if security markets are perfectly efficient, then paying positive fees to active managers implies inefficient markets for asset management.

In other words, there is potential inconsistency to simultaneously assuming that financial markets are dominated by rational investors who arbitrage away pricing inefficiencies and that there are irrational people who invest with professional money managers who, according to the efficient market hypothesis, do not add any value. Why should professional money managers exist at all, and why should some investors be willing to pay them substantial fees to manage their assets?

The presence of active money managers seems to imply that markets are not efficient, as thousands of hedge funds, private equity funds, and active mutual funds earn substantial fees when, according to the efficient market hypothesis, they should underperform active strategies on an after-fee basis. However, if markets were highly inefficient, many more traders would enter the active money management business to earn a portion of those fees and, in the process, help make markets more efficient. Therefore, it seems that there must be a fine balance between efficiency and inefficiency. This leads to markets being efficiently inefficient, as discussed in Chapter 22.

Finding the right manager takes time and resources, and therefore investors have to decide whether to spend search costs to find an active asset manager or allocate their capital to a passive strategy. Of course, there are investors who lack the resources, the patience, or the skills to identify good active managers, and as a result, they allocate randomly to both good and bad managers. In fact, one can argue that these asset allocators are more likely to invest with bad managers, as the skilled managers tend to have capacity constraints.

The performance of these allocators will depend on their relative allocations to good and bad managers, but their overall performance after fees is likely to be worse than that of passive investors due to the fees. In addition, if these allocators represent a relatively large portion of investors, then the overall performance of active managers is likely to be worse than that of passive managers. Therefore, whether replication products add value or not depends on the relative number of active allocators who are able to spend resources to eliminate unskilled managers from the pool of available hedge fund managers. However, if due diligence is too costly and finding skilled managers too uncertain, then unskilled managers will not be eliminated from the available pool, and the overall performance of the industry will suffer.

26.3.4 Replication Products as a Source of Alpha

It is commonly argued that replication products cannot possess alpha, because they are not managed by skilled managers. However, replication products that track a benchmark consisting of one or more actively managed funds may be able to capture the alpha provided by the benchmark. In the extreme case, if a replication product can perfectly replicate the return properties of the benchmark, then by definition it will capture the alpha provided by the benchmark as well. If the benchmark consists of a group of top managers, then the replication product may even be able to capture the alpha provided by top-tier managers. Whether in practice one can create such a perfect replication product is discussed later.

Since hedge fund replication products carry lower fees than actively managed portfolios, the possibility of providing alpha to investors who allocate to these products increases. On the other hand, if the replication product cannot gain access to attractive sources of returns used by managers in the underlying benchmark, then replication products will not be able to generate the level of alpha provided by managers. In short, whether replication products can generate alpha is an empirical question.

26.3.5 Replication Products as a Source of Alternative Beta

Replication products have the potential to give investors access to some of the alternative sources of beta. Whether this potential can be realized in practice depends greatly on the set of securities used to create the replication product. For example, if liquid publicly traded securities are used to create the replicating portfolio, then clearly the product cannot provide exposure to illiquidity risk. This in turn means that any return that can be attributed to illiquidity risk will not be present in the replicating product's performance.

As new passive investable products are created, replication products are given a greater chance to offer investors access to many sources of alternative betas. For example, exchange-traded funds (ETFs) based on convertible bonds and volatility have become available. These ETFs make it possible to create investable products that attempt to track convertible bond arbitrage and volatility trading strategies.

For instance, a strategy consisting of a long position in the convertible bond ETF and a short position in an equity index ETF could generate returns that are similar to a simple convertible arbitrage strategy. An interesting question that arises is whether these can still be considered sources of alternative beta now that they are available to all investors through traditional investment vehicles? To the degree that these new investment products bundle an alternative source of beta with other traditional sources of risk, they may still be considered alternative assets. For example, a convertible bond ETF provides exposure to the options embedded in convertible bonds while exposing investors to credit, equity, and interest rate risks. Some of these risks are commonly hedged away by active managers, and thus a convertible bond arbitrage fund may have little exposure to equity or interest rate risks. Therefore, the embedded option of a convertible bond and its implied volatility can still be considered potential sources of alternative beta. Also, to the degree that a replicating product can capture the dynamic beta of a hedge fund, the product could be a source of alternative beta.

26.4 UNIQUE BENEFITS OF REPLICATION PRODUCTS

In the previous sections, it was argued that replication products have the potential to provide many of the benefits that motivate investors to allocate to hedge funds. Namely, they could act as both return enhancers and risk diversifiers. This section examines the benefits that are somewhat unique to replication products and are generally not offered by most hedge funds. These represent the strongest rationales for the development of various replication products and the reasons why some investors consider allocating to them.

26.4.1 Two Reasons to Use Replication Products

Whether the unique benefits provided by hedge fund replication products make a strong case for increased allocations to these products depends primarily on the investor's initial reason for investing in hedge funds. One reason is seeking manager skill. If access to some unique sources of risk premium (e.g., illiquidity) and skills displayed by top-tier managers are the main reasons, then replication products will not be considered viable alternatives to hedge funds. Another reason is to seek exposure to a benchmark deemed by the investor to be attractive. If the goal is to capture the alpha and the beta that are represented by the *benchmark* that underlies the replication product, then these products may be attractive to some investors.

26.4.2 Two Key Issues Regarding Fund Replication Benefits

The two key questions in this discussion are:

1. Can an investor identify top-tier managers a priori, and do these managers display significant persistence in their performance?

2. Can hedge fund replication products track performance of various strategies even during different market cycles?

Regarding the first question, academic and industry research provides mixed results. Some studies show that top-tier funds do display return persistence, but their outperformance is partially eroded through time. This is because capital flows to top-performing funds, leading to some erosion of their superior performance.[2] Other studies show no performance persistence among hedge fund managers—or, if there is any, it tends to disappear after a few months.[3] The second question is discussed later in the chapter.

26.4.3 Eight Potential Unique Benefits from Hedge Fund Replication

This section examines eight unique benefits that hedge fund replication products can potentially provide.

1. LIQUIDITY AS A REPLICATION BENEFIT: Tracker products invest primarily in liquid instruments (e.g., ETFs or futures) and are therefore able to offer liquidity terms (both purchase and redemption) to investors that most fund managers cannot match. Most replication products do not have lockup periods or the ability to erect gates to slow investor withdrawals. Though it is difficult to quantify the redemption premium required by fund investors, evidence from the secondary market for hedge fund investments shows that during periods of market distress (e.g., 2007–8), investors were willing to accept a discount of 20% on the net asset value (NAV) of their hedge fund investments in order to exit a fund.[4] Even though this reflects the cost of a liquidity premium during a market crisis, the potential always exists for market distress and so redemption liquidity is likely to be valuable.

   Hedge fund investors are bound by the redemption policies of the hedge funds. An investor in a hedge fund often has to manage liquidity by attempting to anticipate the behavior of other investors, who may decide to redeem quickly, leaving the long-term investor with the least liquid (and least attractive) remnants of a fund's portfolio. An investor who executes a replication strategy does not face these problems. The investor will enjoy whatever liquidity is on offer from the actual market and is not hurt if other investors decide to exit early.[5]

   Hedge fund investors can achieve some degree of liquidity and reduce exposure to the behavior of fellow investors by using a managed account platform (i.e., a separately managed account). The key advantage to a managed account is complete control by the investor. By pulling trading privileges, the investor has the ability to manage the cash and liquidate the account at any time. In theory, this gives the investor better than daily liquidity, as the account can be liquidated whenever the market is open. Of course, these advantages come at a cost. For example, one cost is the reduced size of the pool from which managers are selected. Many large managers do not accept managed accounts, and those that do require rather large minimum account sizes and have other additional administrative requirements.

2. Transparency as a Replication Benefit: Replication products can afford to be highly transparent in terms of their trading strategies, including security holdings. Moreover, since replication products operate primarily in the most liquid segments of the markets (e.g., exchange-traded securities), trades implemented tend to have negligible price impact when trading is focused on the most liquid ETFs. Further, since trades are often primarily algorithmic, suppliers of tracker products can disclose a substantial amount of information about the trading process. As discussed previously, hedge fund investors could receive a high degree of transparency by using a managed account platform. However, while such an approach increases transparency in terms of portfolio positions, it may not provide complete transparency in terms of the trading process of the portfolio manager.

3. Flexibility as a Replication Benefit: Most replication products can be very flexible in terms of the risk profile they offer investors. An investor may be able to specify a particular hedge fund strategy benchmark that the product is designed to track, as well as its volatility and other desired statistical properties. These products can be especially suited for use in separate accounts designed to meet individual investors' unique requirements. Funds of funds (FoFs) may be able to put investors' assets to work rather quickly by investing in a replication product.

4. Lower Fees as a Replication Benefit: Replication products charge lower total fees than do hedge funds. The lower fees for replication products may offset the higher gross returns that individual hedge fund managers may generate, reducing the differential net-of-fee returns generated by both products. Further, once other costs such as market impact, due diligence, monitoring, and liquidity are taken into account, replication products may be able to offer net returns that are comparable to those offered by individual funds and FoFs.

Exhibit 26.2 indicates that for a given hypothetical level of return, the higher expenses in both direct hedge fund and FoF investments require a hedge fund-based product to produce a substantially higher gross return compared to that of a replication product, if investors are to receive the same net return. In Exhibit 26.2, only 62.78% and 50.47% of the gross returns earned by hedge funds and FoFs, respectively, flow to the investors. In contrast, 83.33% of the gross returns of replication products are earned by investors. Further, if these products were used in structured products, the structuring fees applied to tracker investments would be significantly lower due to their transparency and liquidity.

5. Hedging as a Replication Benefit: If replication products are created using liquid financial instruments, then it should be possible to short the replication product. This creates a number of potential opportunities for investors. For example, if an investor cannot reduce her allocation to a hedge fund, she might be able to hedge some of its risks by shorting a replication product that is designed to mimic its strategy.

6. Lower Due Diligence and Monitoring Risks as a Replication Benefit: Recent experience has shown that hedge funds and FoFs have significant due diligence and operational risk exposure. Replication products entail lower operational risk, imposing substantially lower due diligence and monitoring costs on their investors. In addition, hedge funds and FoFs may deviate from their expected

EXHIBIT 26.2 Net Fee Comparisons of Three Methods of Access

	Hedge Funds	Funds of Funds	Replication Products
Net return assumed to be earned by investors	7.00%	7.00%	7.00%
Management fee—fund level	2.00%	2.00%	1.00%
Performance fee—fund level	20.00%	20.00%	
Estimated operating expenses-fund level	0.40%	0.40%	0.40%
Management fee—FoF level		1.00%	
Performance fee—FoF level		10.00%	
Estimated operating expenses—FoF level		0.40%	
Gross return required to achieve comparable net return	11.15%	13.87%	8.40%
% of gross return earned by investors	62.78%	50.47%	83.33%

investment styles, exposing investors to style drift risk. Since replication products are calibrated to a defined hedge fund strategy benchmark, investors have minimal exposure to style drift.

7. DIVERSIFICATION AS A REPLICATION BENEFIT: In some replication approaches, diversified factors, such as the returns on ETFs or futures contracts, are used to create portfolios that mimic the performance of hedge funds. This creates replication products that are highly diversified. Even when the product's positions are concentrated in a few economic sectors or countries, diversified instruments such as ETFs and futures are normally employed to gain these exposures.

8. BENCHMARKING AS A REPLICATION BENEFIT: The preceding benefits would accrue only to investors who allocate to replication products. However, the benchmarking benefit does not require any allocation to the replication product. If a replication product were able to capture the properties of the returns to a given hedge fund strategy, then it would represent an investable benchmark which can be used by investors to estimate the value added by their managers. In addition, the investor may be able to negotiate incentive structures that are tied to the manager's performance relative to a replication product.

26.5 FACTOR-BASED APPROACH TO REPLICATION

There are two major approaches to hedge fund replication: factor-based and algorithmic approaches. This section provides details regarding the factor-based approach. Recall from Part 2 that factor-based models look through securities (which are viewed as bundles of factor exposures) to the underlying associations that drive returns. By focusing on the underlying factors, factor-based approaches seek to form portfolio exposures that mimic the factor exposures of a specified benchmark.

The **underlying assumption of the factor-based replication approach** is that a substantial portion of a fund's returns can be explained by a set of asset-based factors such that construction of a portfolio composed of long and/or short positions in a set of suitably selected risk factors can minimize the tracking error with respect to a predefined benchmark. The benchmark may consist of a single manager or, more commonly, an equally weighted benchmark of multiple managers, such as a hedge fund index.

26.5.1 Four Primary Issues in Constructing a Factor-Based Replication Product

The following four issues are addressed in constructing a replication product using the factor-based approach:

1. CHOICE OF BENCHMARK: The benchmark to be replicated must be selected carefully. The most common practice is to use a publicly available index, such as one of the strategy indices from Hedge Fund Research (HFR) or CISDM. It is also possible to create a custom benchmark that meets certain criteria. For example, a custom benchmark for a strategy (e.g., equity long/short) may be created by ensuring that only those managers who clearly follow such a strategy are added to the benchmark, rather than relying on each manager's self-declared strategy.

   When deciding on a suitable benchmark, a decision should also be made on whether to use an investable hedge fund index or a noninvestable hedge fund index for replication. Choosing between investable and noninvestable versions of a hedge fund index involves a tradeoff between better replication and targeting a higher return. While tracking products have a much better fit with investable hedge fund indices, as the underlying hedge funds may invest in more liquid securities, noninvestable hedge fund indices often have higher returns than those of investable hedge fund indices, perhaps due to investments in less liquid securities or to the closure of highly successful funds to new investors.

2. CHOICE OF FACTORS: The factors should be readily investable. Otherwise, the replication product will fail to serve its main purpose. In addition, investors should decide whether a fixed set of factors will be used or the most suitable set of factors will be selected using some statistical method (e.g., stepwise regression).

3. LENGTH OF ESTIMATION PERIOD: The parameters of the model generally have to be estimated using historical performance data. In general, a longer data series has more data which by itself means smaller errors in the estimated values of the parameters. However, when there are changes in the characteristics of the benchmark and/or the factors through time, longer estimation periods may lead to a mimicking portfolio that reflects average market conditions over several months rather than current market conditions.

4. NUMBER OF FACTORS: Using a large set of factors will generally lead to better in-sample fit but may lead to poor out-of-sample performance. Using a small set of factors, on the other hand, may increase tracking error, resulting in both poor in-sample fit and poor out-of-sample performance.

   Aside from these four primary issues, there are many other technical issues to consider, such as adjusting the benchmark's return series for stale prices, adjusting net returns for fees, selecting the appropriate econometric technique to be employed, and using overlays such as volatility control or stop-loss control.

26.5.2 Three Steps to Factor-Based Replication

The following steps are involved in setting up a factor-based replication program once the issues described in the previous section have been resolved.

STEP 1: ESTIMATE WEIGHTS OF RISKY ASSETS

Weights of risky assets can be estimated using Equation 26.2:

$$R_{t,HF} - r_f = \beta_1 \times (F_{1t} - r_f) + \beta_2 \times (F_{2t} - r_f) + \cdots + \beta_K \times (F_{Kt} - r_f) + \varepsilon_t$$
(26.2)

where $R_{t,HF}$ is the total rate of return for month t on the benchmark that is being replicated, r_f is the short-term riskless rate (e.g., 30-day T-bill) for month t, F_{it} is the random total rate of return on factor i for month t, β_i is the exposure of the benchmark to factor i, and ε_t is the return on the benchmark that cannot be explained by the combination of factors being used in Equation 26.2. Note that the betas represent the weight of each risky asset in the replicating portfolio. The weight of cash is determined later (see Step 2).

The in-sample fit of the model from Equation 26.2 is estimated using the R-squared of the regression. If the variance of the error term from Equation 26.2 is small, then the in-sample R-squared would be high, indicating a good fit for the model. However, even if the in-sample R-squared is close to 1.0, it does not mean that the out-of-sample tracking error will be small, since most hedge funds actively trade during the month, resulting in changes to allocations for various securities and asset classes (which tend to cause changes in factor exposures). In these cases, the estimated portfolio weights for the tracking product are likely to generate significant tracking error in out-of-sample periods.

Two important points should be kept in mind while running the regression following Equation 26.2. First, all factors should represent investable assets, as the resulting portfolio needs to be investable. Excess returns on different equity, fixed-income, and commodity ETFs or futures contracts can be used to represent the factors. ETFs and futures trade in liquid markets, provide immediate access to various sources of return, and typically represent diversified portfolios.

Second, returns in excess of a riskless rate must be used on both sides of the equation to relax the requirement that the betas estimated from the equation should add up to 1.0. In this setting, the weight of cash is the free (or slack) variable and is determined given the weights (i.e., betas) of the risky assets.

STEP 2: ESTIMATE THE WEIGHT OF CASH

Once the betas (i.e., the weights) for the risky assets are estimated, the weight for cash in the replicating portfolio is given by Equation 26.3:

$$\beta_{Cash} = 1 - \sum_{i=1}^{K} \beta_i$$
(26.3)

Following this procedure ensures that the weights of all assets, including cash, sum to 1.0. If the weight of cash is negative, then the product will use leverage to create the mimicking portfolio.

STEP 3: INVEST IN DIFFERENT ASSETS

The parameters of the preceding equations are estimated using T observations, with T being the observation for the most recent month; that is, $t = 1, \ldots, T$. The out-of-sample return on the replicating portfolio—the realized return at time $T + 1$—is given by Equation 26.4:

$$R_{Re,T+1} = \hat{\beta}_{t,T} F_{1,T+1} + \ldots + \hat{\beta}_{K,T} F_{T+1} \tag{26.4}$$

Note that the process can be repeated every month or so as new observations on the performance of the benchmark and the factors become available.

26.5.3 Two Key Concepts Regarding Factor-Based Replication

Two common questions arise in the context of factor-based replication that relate to two key concepts regarding factor-based annuities.[6]

VIEW COMMONALITY: How can hedge fund returns be replicated using a relatively small set of factors? After all, each hedge fund may invest in hundreds of securities, and thus several hundred securities will underlie a hedge fund index.

View commonality refers to the fact that when the views of individual hedge fund managers (measured by their exposures) are aggregated in a hedge fund index, they tend to cluster into common themes that drive the overall performance of the index. For instance, if most equity long/short hedge fund managers have positive views on energy stocks, they may attempt to exploit this view by allocating assets to various companies that have exposure to the energy sector. In the index, these views are aggregated and are represented by increased exposure of the index to the energy sector, which could be captured by the replication product through increased allocations to an energy ETF.

EXPOSURE INERTIA: How can the appropriate weights of the mimicking portfolio be estimated if the weights of the actively managed product change over time? If managers are dynamically changing the weights of their portfolios, then the true values of the betas are constantly changing and thus can only be estimated with substantial errors. In addition, the estimated betas would reflect what the managers were holding on average over several months, not necessarily what they are holding now.

Exposure inertia asserts that the overall weights of an index consisting of actively managed portfolios can be empirically estimated because the overall exposures change relatively slowly through time. The idea here is that a large number of hedge fund managers underlying a hedge fund index can reduce the speed at which the common views or exposures change over time. If the core themes that drive hedge fund returns change rapidly, then the factor-based replication models would not be able to immediately identify the appropriate weights for the mimicking portfolio. This is particularly true when monthly (or more frequent) data are used to estimate the parameters of the model. However, even though one hedge fund may actively change its exposures rapidly, the index is likely to display a more stable behavior because of its exposure to many managers.

26.5.4 Research on Factor-Based Replication

There are two primary research results of efforts to test hypothetical factor-based replication products:

MOST HYPOTHETICAL FACTOR-BASED HEDGE FUND REPLICATION PRODUCTS PERFORMED POORLY: There are many academic and industry research papers on factor-based benchmarking and replication of hedge funds. For example, Schneeweis et al. (2003) examined European-based hedge funds for five strategies: fixed-income arbitrage, convertible arbitrage, funds of funds, long/short equity, and event-driven. Hasanhodzic and Lo (2007) attempted to replicate the return distributions of several hedge fund strategies.

The results confirm that perfect replication is not possible, and some of the benefits of hedge funds may not carry completely over to replication products. They generally conclude that none of the methods generate fully satisfactory results, and that the factor-based approach to hedge fund replication faces a series of formidable challenges. These challenges notably include the difficulty of identifying the right factors, as well as the difficulty of replicating, in a robust manner, the time-varying exposures of hedge fund managers with these factors.

SOME FACTOR-BASED REPLICATION PRODUCTS GENERATE PROMISING RESULTS: Lee and Lo (2014) analyze the performance of ASG Global Alternatives Fund, a hedge fund replication product that uses a factor-based replication technique. The authors conclude that hedge fund beta replication did achieve its objective of providing investors with the liquid portion of the expected returns and the diversification benefits of hedge funds without the complexities and fees of hedge fund investments. Agarwal and Naik (2004) used a multi-factor model in which the risk factors were buy-and-hold and option based. The authors obtained in-sample adjusted R-squareds ranging from 40.5% to 91.6%, while the 1-year out-of-sample results were too short to draw any meaningful conclusion from them.

Overall, a review of the studies that attempt to replicate hedge fund returns through a factor replication approach leads to the conclusion that replication accuracy is not satisfactory. In-sample R-squared is not sufficiently high to indicate satisfactory in-sample fit, while out-of-sample results suggest that hedge fund return replication is approximate at best. However, in isolated cases (i.e., particular strategies) some moderate replication success has been observed.

26.5.5 Comparison of Factor-Based Approaches to Payoff-Distribution Approaches

The **payoff-distribution approach** to replication aims to produce a return distribution that matches a desired distribution (e.g., that of the benchmark). While this approach was first developed to match the distribution of a hedge fund benchmark, later developments employed this technique to create return distributions that possessed some desirable properties rather than matching a particular hedge fund strategy. The payoff-distribution approach was developed by Amin and Kat (2003), based on initial theoretical work done by Dybvig (1988) and later applied by Robinson (1998). The objective of this method (matching the return distributions) is far less ambitious than the one pursued in the factor-based approach to hedge fund replication (matching returns).

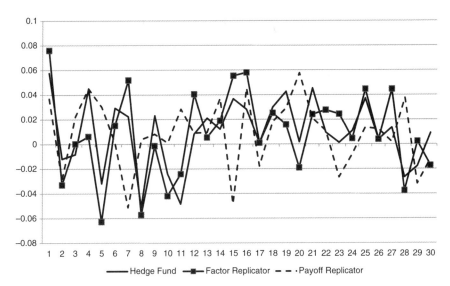

EXHIBIT 26.3 Hypothetical Returns on a Hedge Fund and Two Replicators
Source: Authors' calculations.

For instance, the following simple numerical example can highlight the difference between the factor-based replication approach and the payoff-distribution replication approach. Exhibit 26.3 displays the monthly returns on a hypothetical hedge fund and the returns on two replicators: a factor-based replicator and a payoff-distribution replicator.

The hypothetical factor-based replicator in Exhibit 26.3 illustrates successful tracking of the performance of the hedge fund on a monthly basis. The correlation between the two in the illustration is nearly 0.80. However, the factor-based replicator does not produce the same mean return, standard deviation, skewness, and kurtosis as those of the hedge fund. On the other hand, the payoff-distribution replicator almost exactly matches the higher moments of the distribution of the hedge fund's return, but does a poor job of tracking the monthly returns on the hedge fund. It can be seen that monthly return from the payoff replicator has very low correlation to the monthly return on the hedge fund.

An important point is that the payoff distribution cannot, and does not try to, match the mean return on the hedge fund. First, the average returns on the clones were, in most cases, very different from that of the index being replicated.

Research efforts to match second and higher payoff-distributions have also been disappointing but have differed depending on the strategy. Although the volatility values obtained for the clones were relatively close to those obtained for the hedge fund indices, authors have reported mixed results regarding the equalities of estimated skewness and kurtosis values for the clones and those of the observed returns on the hedge fund indices. The best replication process was obtained with the short-selling index, and the worst was obtained with the equity market-neutral index. The payoff-distribution approach was able to match the distribution in less than half the cases. These results imply that even if one is willing to ignore the differences in mean returns, not all hedge fund distributions can be matched with relative satisfaction.

Finally, an important point is that the good results obtained for at least some hedge fund strategies have been achieved only when a long out-of-sample period was used. In some cases, it took close to 8 years to obtain payoff distributions that matched the return distribution of the hedge fund indices. Further, the authors show that the replicating portfolio performs poorly in terms of matching the correlation of hedge fund indices with other assets. For an investor with limited patience, the payoff-distribution approach to hedge fund replication can lead to disappointment.

26.6 THE ALGORITHMIC (BOTTOM-UP) APPROACH

The algorithmic (or bottom-up) approach is substantially different from the factor-based approach (or the payoff-distribution approach). The **algorithmic approach** does not rely on a predefined benchmark; it involves implementing a simplified version of the actual trading strategy employed by funds that follow the particular strategy. For instance, the most basic type of merger arbitrage strategy involves taking long positions in target firms and short positions in acquiring firms. Similarly, basic convertible arbitrage involves taking a long position in convertible bonds of a firm and a specific short position in the equity of the same firm such that the equity risk of the convertible bond is hedged away. In both cases the algorithmic approach mimics the strategies using the same types of positions but with a rules-based approach for selecting events, position sizes and timing rather than case-by-case discretionary judgment.

Accordingly, the algorithmic approach is suitable only for well-defined strategies that involve systematic trading and exclude manager discretion as a primary source of return. Other examples of relatively well-defined strategies include trend-following (e.g., CTAs) and some equity long/short (e.g., momentum and value/growth).

To the degree that a systematic trading process representing the fund strategy can be developed and monitored, systematic algorithmic trading strategies can be implemented using an algorithmic or bottom-up approach. The funds implementing the bottom-up approach essentially hold some of the same securities as those of the hedge funds being replicated. In times of market distress, such as during the global financial crisis of 2007–8, bottom-up replication managers faced difficulty meeting redemption requests, which, in turn, adversely affected the value of their funds. However, if liquidity risk and event risk are significant contributors to the alpha of hedge fund strategies, investing in hedge funds or bottom-up replication products may be the only way to access this portion of returns.

26.7 THREE ILLUSTRATIONS OF THE ALGORITHMIC (BOTTOM-UP) APPROACH

This section provides three examples of how to implement algorithmic investment strategies.

26.7.1 An Illustration of the Algorithmic Approach: Merger Arbitrage

Merger arbitrage is a strategy that can be implemented by buying a portion of all announced mergers and shorting the acquiring firms. Profitability of this strategy depends on the percentage of mergers that are successfully completed and on the manager's ability to buy shares of the target company at a price below the deal price. Returns are also comprised from selling short stock of the acquiring company, which may decline over the course of merger negotiation, and from rebates received on cash generated from selling short the acquirer's stock.

The following hypothetical example illustrates how merger arbitrage works. Men's Clothing, a men's dress clothes retailer, initiates a hostile takeover bid for Women's Store, another retailer, on November 26, 2019. In this stock-for-stock transaction, Men's Clothing initially offers 1.15 shares for every 1 share of Women's Store shares. The day the deal is announced, shares of Women's Store close at $56.29 and shares of Men's Clothing close at $50.60, representing a $58.19 bid. Subsequently, Men's Clothing increases the bid price initially to a 1.2 share ratio, representing a $60.72 bid. Finally, the ratio is increased to 1.25 shares, representing a $63.25 bid. before completing the acquisition on June 19, 2020. The acquisition process has taken a total of 205 days to complete from the day of initiation of the first bid. On the day the deal is completed, the price of Men's Clothing is $55.67.

If a fund manager is implementing a merger arbitrage using this deal, she would buy shares of Women's Store and sell short shares of Men's Clothing after the bid is announced, using the original stock to stock transaction ratio of 1.15. Exhibit 26.4 describes the profit from merger arbitrage involving acquisition of Women's Store by Men's Clothing assuming the fund manager buys 1,000 shares of Women's Store and sells short 1,150 shares of Men's Clothing. In this example, we are assuming Men's Clothing pays a dividend of $0.54 per share during the holding period, and the annual short rebate is 1%.

EXHIBIT 26.4 Profit-and-Loss Statement for the Example Merger Arbitrage Trade

Description		Amount
Gain on Women's Store long position	$1,000 \times [(55.67 \times 1.25) - 56.29]$	13,297.50
Loss on Men's Clothing short position	$-1,000 \times 1.15 \times (55.67 - 50.60)$	−5,830.50
Dividend paid on short position	$-1,000 \times 1.15 \times 0.54$	−621.00
Short rebate at 1% rate	$1,000 \times 1.15 \times 50.60 \times 1\% \times 205/365$	326.82
Total profit (loss) from strategy		7,172.82
Initial investment	$1,000 \times 56.29$	56,290.00
Return on investment over 205 days	7,172.82 / 56,290.00	12.74%
Annualized return	$(1 + 12.74\%)^{\left(\frac{365}{205}\right)} - 1$	23.81%

The main risk of a merger arbitrage strategy stems from mergers not being completed for numerous reasons, such as failure to arrange adequate financing, another bidder emerging in the process and offering a higher price for the same company, and willingness of the target company to stay independent by deploying various anti-takeover measures. If mergers are not completed, an investor stands to lose on both the long and the short side of the trade.

26.7.2 An Illustration of the Algorithmic Approach: Convertible Arbitrage

Convertible arbitrage is another hedge fund strategy that can be implemented in an algorithmic setting. The simple version of the convertible arbitrage strategy involves purchasing a portfolio of convertible bonds and then hedging out the equity risk of the convertible bond portfolio by using short equity positions in the underlying companies. Essentially, the strategy is equivalent to a combination of a long position in a bond, a long position in a call option, and a short position in shares of stock. The arbitrager's goal is to purchase a convertible bond with an implicit option that is underpriced (i.e., the implied volatility of the option's underlying stock is lower than the volatility that the arbitrager expects). The arbitrager attempts to profit from the underpriced option while avoiding directional risk by using a delta-neutral hedging strategy. Generally, if the underlying equity experiences volatility that substantially exceeds the implied volatility, the strategy earns a profit.

For example, assume that a convertible bond is trading at 106% of par; that is, a bond with a $1,000 face value is currently trading at $1,060. Assume that the bond pays semiannual coupons at an annual rate of 5%. This bond converts to 16.5 shares of stock and currently has a delta of 0.602. For demonstration purposes, we will make the delta of our portfolio zero by selling short the appropriate number of shares. Assuming that the current stock price is $28.12, the number of shares that need to be sold short to make the convertible bond delta neutral is 22.69 (1,060 × 0.602/28.12). Therefore, the dollar value of stock held short to create a delta-neutral position is $638.04 (22.69 × 28.12). Now, suppose the stock price moves up by 1%. This will cause the value of the convertible bond to increase by more than 0.602% (the delta of the convertible bond) because the positive gamma of the option means that the bond's delta will increase as the stock price increases. Exhibit 26.5 shows the value of the portfolio before and after a 1% increase in the stock price.

After a 1% increase in the price of the stock, the value of the short position in stock (which has a gamma of zero) becomes –$644.42 (–638.04 × 1.01). At the same time, the value of the convertible bond becomes greater than $1,066.38 (greater than 1,060 × 1.00602) because the delta of the convertible increased as the stock price increased. Note that the gain in the value of the convertible bond more than offsets the loss in the short position in the stock. This is what is supposed to happen when

EXHIBIT 26.5 Hedging of Convertible Bonds

	Before	After	Change
Long convertible bond	1,060.00	>1,066.38	>6.38
Short stock	−638.04	−644.42	−6.38
Portfolio value	421.96	>421.96	>0

EXHIBIT 26.6   Sources of Returns to Convertible Arbitrage

Source	Contribution
Interest earned	2.50%
Short stock rebate	0.10%
Dividend payment	−0.20%
Cost of leverage	−0.80%
Return from hedging activities in excess of time decay	0.40%
Unlevered return in 6 months	2.00%
Unlevered return in 1 year	4.00%
Levered (4x) return in 1 year	16.00%

the convertible bond is delta-hedged and the convertible has positive gamma. If the stock price had fallen in value, there would be a profit to the convertible arbitrage because the delta of the convertible would decrease, thereby reducing the loss from the convertible's price decline to being smaller than the gain from the short stock position.

After any stock price increase, the delta of the convertible bond has increased, so additional shares are sold short to return the position to being delta-neutral. Conversely, when the stock price declines, the convertible bond's delta declines and the short position needs to be reduced through the purchase of shares. This hedging activity keeps the strategy delta-neutral. The strategy generates return from volatility that exceeds market expectations (as imbedded in the bond's original price) and positive gamma. The trading of the underlying stock merely hedges out directional risk by restoring the position to delta-neutrality.

Convertible bond arbitrage returns are driven by several additional sources. Interest received from the convertible bond and the short stock rebate provide return, while dividend payments and the interest cost of leverage diminish return. Usually, significant leverage is employed in convertible arbitrage strategies to generate returns that are comparable to those earned by other hedge fund strategies. The sources of return for this strategy over a 6-month period are illustrated in Exhibit 26.6.

26.7.3   An Illustration of the Algorithmic Approach: Momentum Strategies

There is substantial academic and industry research on the profitability of momentum (trend-following) strategies. A simple version of a momentum strategy involves long positions in a portfolio of stocks, commodities, or currencies that have outperformed over previous periods, and short positions in a portfolio of stocks, commodities, or currencies that have underperformed over previous periods; 6 months and 12 months are common periods on which to identify momentum in equities. This strategy has produced impressive rates of return in back-testing. A momentum strategy can be illustrated using a CTA.

CTAs are prime examples of hedge-fund-like strategies that predominantly employ trend-following strategies. CTAs primarily invest in futures contracts across currencies, commodities, interest rates, and stock indices. They may also use options on futures and, in some cases, currency forwards to implement their strategies.

Roughly two-thirds of CTA funds follow systematic trend-following strategies, but the systematic managers have the bulk of the money managed by CTAs. CTAs extensively use computer algorithms to find patterns in prices and can go long and short in any market. They also employ significant leverage to enhance returns.

Consider a very simple CTA trading strategy. Suppose a fund manager follows a 20-day and 50-day look-back strategy to trade crude oil futures contracts. This implies that the manager looks at what the prices of crude oil futures contracts were 20 and 50 days ago, and compares those prices to the current price. If the current price is higher than prices from both 20 days ago and 50 days ago, then the manager opens a long position in a certain number of crude oil futures contracts. The number of contracts is dependent on the risk capital allocated to crude oil. If a large amount of risk capital is allocated to crude oil, a large number of futures contracts are purchased.

On the other hand, if the current price is between the price from 20 days ago and the price from 50 days ago, the manager does not do anything, since the trend-following strategy is indicating a mixed signal. If, however, the current price is lower than prices from both 20 days ago and 50 days ago, then the manager sells short a certain number of crude oil contracts. Thus, the manager can have a long position, a short position, or no position in crude oil futures at any point in time depending on where current price is relative to prices from previous days.

CTAs often trade a number of types of futures contracts simultaneously so that when the futures price of oil signals no trade, the CTA may put the risk capital to work in other contracts (e.g., other commodities). Volatility of commodities or currencies plays a predominant role in deciding how much risk capital to allocate to each market. If a commodity has higher volatility, a smaller amount of risk capital is allocated to that particular commodity so that the contribution of volatility from that commodity is similar to the volatility from other commodities in the portfolio. This is similar to the approach employed in products based on the risk parity approach to asset allocation.

NOTES

1. See Fung and Hsieh (2007); Fung et al. (2008); Naik et al. (2007).
2. Billio et al. (2014); Getmansky et al. (2015).
3. See Jagannathan et al. (2012).
4. See Brown et al. (1999); Bares et al. (2003).
5. See www.hedgebay.com.
6. See Kamel (2007).
7. See Drachman and Little (2010).

REFERENCES

Agarwal, V. and N. Y. Naik. 2004. "Risks and Portfolio Decisions Involving Hedge Funds." *Review of Financial Studies* 17 (1): 63–98.

Amin, G. S. and H. M. Kat. 2003. "Hedge Fund Performance 1990–2000: Do the 'Money Machines' Really Add Value?" *Journal of Financial and Quantitative Analysis* 38 (2): 252–74.

Bares, P., R. Gibson, and S. Gyger. 2003. "Performance in the Hedge Fund Industry: An Analysis of Short and Long-Term Persistence." *Journal of Alternative Investments* 6 (3): 25–41.

Billio, M., L. Frattarolo, and L. Pelizzon. 2014. "A Time-Varying Performance Evaluation of Hedge Fund Strategies through Aggregation." *Bankers, Markets & Investors* 129 (March–April): 40–58.

Bodie, Z., A. Kane, and A. Marcus. 2010. *Investments*. 9th edn. Maidenhead, UK: McGraw-Hill/Irwin.

Brown, S. J., W. N. Goetzmann, and R. G. Ibbotson. 1999. "Offshore Hedge Funds: Survival and Performance, 1989–1995." *Journal of Business* 72 (1): 91–118.

Drachman, J. and P. Little. 2010. "Enhancing Liquidity in Alternative Portfolios." Credit Suisse Asset Management. https://www.credit-suisse.com/pwp/am/downloads/marketing/tl_201006_lab_us_apac_jp__ie_lux_sp_scand_uk_.pdf.

Dybvig, P. H. 1988. "Inefficient Dynamic Portfolio Strategies or How to Throw Away a Million Dollars in the Stock Market." *Review of Financial Studies* 1 (1): 67–88.

Fung, W. and D. A. Hsieh. 2007. "Will Hedge Funds Regress towards Index-like Products?" *Journal of Investment Management* 5 (2): 46–65.

Fung, W., D. A. Hsieh, N.Y. Naik, and T. Ramadorai. 2008. "Hedge Funds: Performance, Risk, and Capital Formation." *Journal of Finance* 63 (4): 1777–1803.

Getmansky, M., P. A. Lee, and A. W. Lo. 2015. "Hedge Funds: A Dynamic Industry in Transition." *Annual Review of Financial Economics* 7: 483–577.

Hasanhodzic, J. and A. W. Lo. 2007. "Can Hedge-Fund Returns Be Replicated? The Linear Case." *Journal of Investment Management* 5 (2): 5–45.

Jagannathan, R., A. Malakhov, and D. Novikov. 2012. "Do Hot Hands Exist among Hedge Fund Managers? An Empirical Evaluation." *Journal of Finance* 65 (1): 217–55.

Kamel, T. 2007. "Hedge Fund Replication." Iluka Hedge Fund Consulting. www.ilukacg.com.

Lee, P. A. and A. W. Lo. 2014. "Hedge Fund Beta Replication: A Five-Year Retrospective." *Journal of Investment Management* 12 (3): 5–18.

Naik, N. Y., T. Ramadorai, and M. Stromqvist. 2007. "Capacity Constraint and Hedge Fund Strategy Returns." *European Financial Management* 13 (2): 239–56.

Robinson, B. 1998. "Efficiency Cost of Guaranteed Investment Products." *Journal of Derivatives* 6 (1): 25–37.

Schneeweis, T., H. Kazemi, and V. Karavas. 2003. "EUREX Derivative Products in Alternative Investments: The Case for Hedge Funds." CISDM – Center for International Securities and Derivatives Markets Working Paper Series. https://www.etfexpress.com/sites/default/files/import_attachments/Eurex%20Derivative%20Products%20in%20Alternative%20Investments%20-%20The%20Case%20for%20Managed%20Futures.pdf.

CHAPTER 27

Diversified Access to Hedge Funds

O ne of the key considerations in alternative investing is the relative merit of different ways of accessing assets. This chapter reviews and discusses methods of accessing a diversified exposure to the performance of hedge funds.

27.1 EVIDENCE REGARDING HEDGE FUND RISK AND RETURNS

Level I of the CAIA curriculum focuses on the standalone risks and returns of hedge funds and other assets. This section discusses the correlations, systematic risks, portfolio effects, and portfolio risks of exposures to hedge funds.

27.1.1 Evidence Regarding Performance of Hedge Funds by Strategies

Inferring future performance based on analysis of historic returns of assets is fraught with peril. Asset returns do not generally adhere to a random walk with a constant mean. Over periods of multiple months, assets such as equities have been observed to trend (i.e., exhibit momentum). Over periods of multiple years, equities have generally been observed to exhibit mean-reversion. To the extent that returns exhibit mean-reversion, especially over long time horizons, the past level of total long-term return performance is a perverse indicator of future total return performance.

Exhibit 27.1 examines 21 years of historical total return data for 12 hedge fund strategies (although the returns for four of the strategies are not available over the entire period because their inception dates are subsequent to January of 1998). For comparison purposes, the returns of the MSCI World and S&P 500 equity indices are included.

The returns in Exhibit 27.1 are annualized geometric total returns. The 21 years of return data are divided into three 7-year periods. Note that the first 7-year period (1998–2004) is a period of generally increasing equity market prices with a moderate bear market in the middle. The second 7-year period (2005–11) covers a generally slightly increasing equity market with a substantial global financial crisis in the middle. The third 7-year period (2012–18) covers a strongly increasing equity market with no major, long-lasting decline.

EXHIBIT 27.1 Annualized Mean Returns of Various Strategies

Strategy	1998–2004	2005–2011	2012–2018	Mean	Sharpe Ratio
Credit Suisse Global Macro	10.20%	9.40%	2.50%	7.40%	1.02
HFRI Macro: Systematic Diversified	11.80%	8.90%	−0.30%	6.80%	0.58
HFRI ED: Merger Arb	7.40%	5.50%	3.40%	5.40%	1.06
HFRI ED: Distressed/ Restructuring	11.30%	4.80%	4.60%	6.90%	0.76
Credit Suisse ED: Multi Strat	8.80%	5.70%	2.90%	5.80%	0.54
HFRI RV: Convert Arb	9.90%	4.10%	4.40%	6.10%	0.49
HFRI RV: Corporate	5.70%	3.70%	4.60%	4.70%	0.44
HFRI RV: Multi-Strat	n.a.	4.30%	4.50%	4.40%	0.49
HFRI EH: Equity Mkt Neutral	6.20%	2.10%	3.20%	3.80%	0.61
HFRX Activist	n.a.	5.90%	6.20%	6.00%	0.29
HFRX RV: Vol	n.a.	2.50%	3.80%	3.20%	0.19
HFRI EH: Short Bias	n.a.	−2.90%	−6.40%	−4.70%	−0.61
Mean of Funds	8.90%	4.50%	2.80%	5.40%	0.89
MSCI World	4.60%	2.20%	16.50%	7.80%	0.38
S&P 500	4.80%	2.60%	21.20%	9.60%	0.54
1-Year Treasury Bill Rate	3.60%	2.30%	1.50%	2.20%	

There are three key observations regarding Exhibit 27.1:

1. HEDGE FUND RETURNS HAVE BEEN GENERALLY DECLINING: The mean return of the combined hedge funds has declined over the three periods from 8.9% to 4.5% to 2.8%. Some of the decline between the first two periods may be attributable to the inclusion of four new strategies in the later two periods, while some of the decline may be from declining short-term interest rates earned on cash holdings. The four strategies had modest returns—especially short bias. However, the new strategies only explain part of the decline.

HEDGE FUND MEAN RETURNS ARE NOT FULLY EXPLAINED BY EQUITY RETURNS: The overall hedge fund average returns declined through time across all three time periods, even though the equity market's worst performance was in the middle period (2005–11). Further, equity market turmoil was greatest in the middle periods and generally did not coincide with unusually high or low general hedge fund returns. Thus, aggregated hedge fund performance did not appear to be driven by positive correlations to equity market returns or volatility.

THE 21-YEAR TOTAL RETURNS OF HEDGE FUNDS HAVE BEEN LOWER THAN EQUITIES: The 21-year mean annualized returns of the combined hedge funds was 5.4% unadjusted for risk. The MSCI World Index and S&P 500 Index had averaged returns of 7.8% and 9.6%, respectively (as indicated by the average geometric returns of the three time periods). Risk adjustment is discussed later. To the extent that hedge fund returns will exhibit very long-term mean-reversion (based perhaps on the long-term ebb and flow of cash into and out of hedge funds), it is possible that hedge funds will return to more attractive profitability than that experienced in 2012–18. In other words, "efficiently inefficient" market theory might imply that hedge funds will find greater profit opportunities in the future after a long period of consolidation during which more and more dollars were "chasing" fewer and fewer profitable opportunities. This time period of low hedge fund returns was also characterized by falling interest rates, low stock market volatility, and low dispersion across stocks and sectors. Hedge funds may find greater profit opportunities when the volatility and dispersion of stock and stock index returns increase.

27.1.2 Evidence Regarding the Systematic and Total Risk of Hedge Funds

Exhibit 27.1 and the discussion of the previous section did not risk-adjust the returns. Exhibit 27.2 provides the annualized volatilities of the monthly returns for the hedge funds and the two equity indices for January 2005 through December 2018. The time period was based on the maximum observation period for which data were available on all strategies. All hedge fund strategy indices indicated lower risk than the two equity indices, with most fund strategies experiencing substantially lower return volatility. Note that the volatility of the mean return of all the hedge fund strategies enjoyed a very low annual volatility of 3.6%.

Exhibit 27.3 summarizes the betas of each strategy with respect to the S&P 500 index. Taken together, Exhibits 27.2 and 27.3 indicate a profoundly lower total risk and systematic risk to *indices* of hedge fund returns compared to the risks of equity market indices. Together, Exhibits 27.2 and 27.3 indicate a mean return from an equally weighted average of the returns of the 12 strategies (or less than 12 in the case of unavailable data for up to four of the strategies in the early years) of 5.4% per year with a volatility of only 3.60%.

There are three key observations regarding Exhibits 27.2 and 27.3:

INDIVIDUAL FUND STRATEGY INDICES TENDED TO EXHIBIT ABOUT HALF THE TOTAL RISK AND ABOUT ONE-THIRD THE SYSTEMATIC RISK AS THE EQUITY INDICES:

EXHIBIT 27.2   Annualized Volatilities of Various Strategies

Credit Suisse Global Macro	5.08%
HFRI Macro: Systematic Diversified	7.99%
HFRI ED: Merger Arb	3.02%
HFRI ED: Distressed/ Restructuring	6.21%
Credit Suisse ED: Multi Strat	6.70%
HFRI RV: Convert Arb	7.96%
HFRI RV: Corporate	5.64%
HFRI RV: Multi-Strat	4.48%
HFRI EH: Equity Mkt Neutral	2.61%
HFRX Activist	12.93%
HFRX RV: Vol	5.33%
HFRI EH: Short Bias	11.24%
Volatility of Monthly Mean Return of All 12 Fund Strategies	3.60%
MSCI World	14.78%
S&P 500	13.82%

EXHIBIT 27.3 36-Month Betas of Various Strategies

Strategy	1998–2000	2001–2003	2004–2006	2007–2009	2010–2012	2013–2015	2016–2018	Mean
Credit Suisse Global Macro	0.09	−0.02	0.17	0.12	0.06	0.22	0.13	0.11
HFRI Macro: Systematic Diversified	0.30	0.28	0.83	−0.06	0.06	0.13	0.15	0.24
HFRI ED: Merger Arb	0.13	0.10	0.31	0.16	0.11	0.11	0.11	0.15
HFRI ED: Distressed/ Restructuring	0.24	0.11	0.30	0.34	0.29	0.33	0.27	0.27
Credit Suisse ED: Multi-Strat	0.29	0.11	0.46	0.26	0.45	0.38	0.37	0.33
HFRI RV: Convert Arb	0.10	0.01	0.12	0.54	0.30	0.16	0.21	0.21
HFRI RV: Corporate	0.15	0.11	0.12	0.39	0.21	0.21	0.19	0.20
HFRI RV: Multi Strat	0.08	0.07	0.10	0.28	0.17	0.15	0.15	0.14
HFRI EH: Equity Mkt Neutral	0.07	−0.06	0.14	0.04	0.17	0.10	0.09	0.08
HFRX Activist	n.a.	n.a.	0.84	0.75	0.89	0.60	0.62	0.74
HFRX RV: Vol	n.a.	n.a.	−0.06	0.04	0.05	0.08	0.41	0.10
HFRI EH: Short Bias	n.a.	n.a.	−1.33	−0.61	−0.72	−0.39	−0.87	−0.78
Mean of Fund Returns	0.16	0.08	0.21	0.19	0.17	0.17	0.15	0.16

Holding a broad portfolio of funds within a strategy generated returns that are half that of the equity markets, roughly bringing approximate parity between fund index Sharpe ratios and equity market Sharpe ratios given the low riskless interest rates over much of the period. Further, the systematic risks of the hedge funds indicate substantially lower systematic risk (and more attractive risk-adjusted returns) from investing in a portfolio of fund of funds compared to the equity market indices. Volatility of some types of individual hedge funds and individual strategies may be low due to their low net market exposure as well as the tendency of some fund types to hold illiquid and infrequently valued securities. Note that standard deviation is not a complete measure of risk, as the returns to some hedge fund strategies are not normally distributed, but exhibit extreme levels of skewness and kurtosis.

AVERAGE HEDGE FUND RETURNS TENDED TO EXHIBIT APPROXIMATELY ONE-THIRD THE TOTAL RISK OF THE EQUITY INDICES: Diversification (even naïve diversification based on equal weights of all strategies) across all strategies further lowers the total risk of hedge funds to the point of generating historically attractive Sharpe ratios relative to equity indices.

AVERAGE HEDGE FUND RETURNS TENDED TO EXHIBIT APPROXIMATELY ONE-SIXTH THE SYSTEMATIC RISK OF THE EQUITY INDICES: The systematic risk of the twelve strategies viewed as a whole were so low as to make the averaged returns of the strategies as a whole quite attractive relative to equity market indices over the same time period.

27.1.3 Evidence Regarding Correlations and Diversification of Hedge Funds

Exhibit 27.4 displays the monthly return correlations between all 12 hedge fund strategies over their available histories (up to 21 years). As expected, the short bias index exhibited negative correlation with the other strategies. The frequency of relatively low return correlation coefficients is consistent with the argument that large portfolios of hedge funds offer much lower risks than broad equity market indices and that therefore their required returns should be much lower.

27.2 APPROACHES TO ACCESSING HEDGE FUNDS

There are three basic approaches for institutional investors to gain hedge fund exposure in their portfolios: direct, delegated, and indexed.

27.2.1 The Direct Approach and Its Three Advantages

The direct approach consists of investing directly in a number of single-manager hedge funds to create a portfolio. With more than 8,200 single-manager hedge funds globally from which to choose, this approach requires extensive resources to identify and research managers, as well as the relevant experience and expertise to determine the appropriate blend of strategies, styles (how each manager executes the same strategy), and funds.

In spite of these obstacles, institutional investors are increasingly choosing to invest directly in hedge funds for a variety of reasons. The three major reasons are:

1. The cost savings from avoiding the extra layer of fees charged by a fund of hedge funds.
2. Access to cost-effective, experienced consultants to assist implementing the approach.
3. The ability to have improved control and transparency in the asset allocation and due diligence process.

The direct approach may, however, be challenging for those investors who are constrained by the minimum net worth levels and sophistication standards required by regulators in many countries, as well as the fact that the median hedge fund requires a minimum investment of \$500,000. As a result, small or medium-sized investors may not be able to create a fully diversified portfolio of hedge funds while keeping their total allocations at a reasonable level.

27.2.2 The Delegated Approach and Its Five Services

In a fund of hedge funds approach to investment, portfolio selection and management are delegated to another party. This delegated approach provides the following five services:

EXHIBIT 27.4 Return Correlations Between 12 Hedge Fund Strategies

Correlation Matrix	Credit Suisse Global Macro	HFRI Macro: Systematic Diversified	HFRI ED: Merger Arb	HFRI ED: Distressed / Restructuring	Credit Suisse ED: Multi Strat	HFRI RV Convert Arb	HFRI: Corporate	HFRI RV: Multi-Strat	HFRI EH: Equity Mkt Neutral	HFRX Activist	HFRX RV Vol	HFRI EH: Short Bias
Credit Suisse Global Macro	1.000	0.323	0.676	0.406	0.458	0.329	0.360	0.517	0.379	0.383	0.069	−0.199
HFRI Macro: Systematic Diversified	0.323	1.000	0.290	0.151	0.306	0.021	0.041	0.117	0.250	0.099	0.002	−0.069
HFRI ED: Merger Arb	0.676	0.290	1.000	0.571	0.691	0.539	0.540	0.524	0.431	0.676	0.288	−0.551
HFRI ED: Distressed / Restructuring	0.406	0.151	0.571	1.000	0.850	0.713	0.864	0.805	0.422	0.705	0.248	−0.626
Credit Suisse ED: Multi Strat	0.458	0.306	0.691	0.850	1.000	0.640	0.723	0.729	0.515	0.729	0.307	−0.661
HFRI RV Convert Arb	0.329	0.021	0.539	0.713	0.640	1.000	0.776	0.845	0.356	0.716	0.176	−0.524
HFRI: Corporate	0.360	0.041	0.540	0.864	0.723	0.776	1.000	0.866	0.336	0.684	0.218	−0.595
HFRI RV: Multi-Strat	0.517	0.117	0.524	0.805	0.729	0.845	0.866	1.000	0.384	0.707	0.216	−0.561
HFRI EH: Equity Mkt Neutral	0.379	0.250	0.431	0.422	0.515	0.356	0.336	0.384	1.000	0.575	0.262	−0.360
HFRX Activist	0.383	0.099	0.676	0.705	0.729	0.716	0.684	0.707	0.575	1.000	0.265	−0.705
HFRX RV Vol	0.069	0.002	0.288	0.248	0.307	0.176	0.218	0.216	0.262	0.265	1.000	−0.213
HFRI EH: Short Bias	−0.199	−0.069	−0.551	−0.626	−0.661	−0.524	−0.595	−0.561	−0.360	−0.705	−0.213	1.000
Average Correlation	0.336	0.139	0.425	0.464	0.481	0.417	0.438	0.468	0.323	0.439	0.167	−0.460

1. SOURCING MANAGERS: As significant allocators of capital, funds of hedge funds are actively sought out by hedge funds as clients. Access to higher-quality hedge funds is typically based on the size and quality of the fund of hedge funds, established relationships with the hedge funds, and the quality of the fund of hedge fund's client base.

2. DUE DILIGENCE: Due diligence is the process of understanding, reviewing, and analyzing the strategy, management, and operations of a hedge fund manager. This is perhaps one of the most important value propositions that differentiate a fund of hedge funds manager for investors who are deciding between a direct and a delegated hedge fund investment program. Unfortunately, several large funds of hedge funds have been marred by underlying manager blowups and frauds that have caused some institutional investors to reassess the value of a fund of hedge funds' due diligence process.

   There is, however, some academic evidence justifying the payment of an additional layer of fees in return for more robust operational due diligence. Operational due diligence is the process of evaluating the policies, procedures, and internal controls of the operations of an asset management organization. Brown, Fraser, and Liang (2008) estimate that, net of fees, the largest funds of hedge funds outperformed the smallest funds of hedge funds by a statistically significant +2.69% per year from 1995 to 2006, and that Sharpe ratios for large funds of hedge funds were twice those of smaller funds of hedge funds. Larger funds of hedge funds may outperform because their scale allows them to invest more in due diligence and risk management processes as well as potentially accessing managers with higher returns that require higher minimum investments. Small funds of hedge funds are at a competitive disadvantage because, due to their small size, they are not able to generate sufficient fees to cover the fixed and necessary costs of substantial initial due diligence. More information on operational due diligence can be found in Chapters 33 and 34.

3. STRATEGY AND FUND SELECTION: The fund of hedge funds is responsible for selecting appropriate strategies and a proper mix of funds for each strategy. While funds of hedge funds may have access to preferred hedge funds as well as experienced insight regarding which strategies are likely to outperform going forward, institutional investors are catching up. Historically, institutional investors have also used funds of hedge funds to reduce the risk of negative headlines should one of the underlying hedge fund investments blow up. The dissemination of hedge fund knowledge and expertise across the industry has minimized this value proposition of funds of hedge funds.

4. PORTFOLIO CONSTRUCTION: Once the strategies and funds have been selected, the fund of hedge funds has to decide on position sizing: that is, how much to allocate to each strategy and each fund to build the portfolio. The allocation will depend on the specific objectives of the fund of hedge funds in combination with the terms of the fund of hedge funds offering, including the strategies permitted and liquidity provisions for investors. The portfolio construction process includes evaluating the expected correlations among the underlying hedge funds, ensuring that the fund of hedge funds is adequately diversified by strategy and style, and making sure that the combined liquidity provisions of the underlying hedge funds conform to the terms offered by the fund of hedge funds.

5. RISK MANAGEMENT AND MONITORING: The fund of hedge funds manager monitors each underlying hedge fund to ensure that its performance profile is consistent with the fund's investment objectives and the fund of hedge funds' overall objectives. Some funds of hedge funds employ sophisticated risk-management processes to monitor the underlying hedge funds' positions, while others may employ multi-factor sensitivity analysis to gauge risk exposure to various market factors and to analyze a fund's potential risk.

27.2.3 The Indexed Approach

The third approach, the indexed approach, involves investing in index-type products. This approach allows an investor to select a representative hedge fund index and invest through a financial product that aims to replicate the performance of that index. Indexed financial products are typically sold as certificates or principal-guaranteed notes issued by a creditworthy financial institution whose returns are typically linked to the performance of a referenced fund of hedge funds or specific hedge fund index.

Recently, other products (e.g., liquid alternative mutual funds and exchange-traded funds [ETFs]) have proliferated that claim to provide hedge fund exposure without some of the major drawbacks of direct investing in hedge funds. Advantages may include lower fees, better liquidity, and improved transparency. Liquid alternative funds employ constrained hedge fund strategies that are offered in a mutual fund structure with daily liquidity. These funds are constrained in terms of the liquidity of

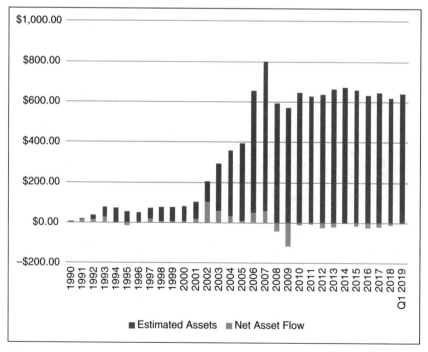

EXHIBIT 27.5   Estimated Growth of Fund of Funds 1990–Q1 2019
Source: Hedge Fund Research (HFR) 2019a.

the underlying securities in which they can invest, the amount of leverage they can employ, and their use of short positions. Replication strategies, discussed in detail in Chapter 26, come in many variations. They typically identify market factors to which hedge funds are exposed and may replicate the return pattern through the use of derivatives or through algorithmic approaches.

Exhibit 27.5 shows the tremendous long-term growth of the fund of hedge funds industry, increasing assets under management (AUM) from $1.9 million in 1990 to over $640 billion in 2019. Fund of hedge funds assets peaked in 2007 at $798.6 million as institutions made their initial hedge fund allocations via funds of hedge funds. During the financial crisis of 2008–9, fund of hedge funds assets dropped to a low of $571.3 billion due to a combination of negative performance, withdrawals on the heels of the Madoff fraud, and institutional investors investing directly in hedge funds.

27.3   CHARACTERISTICS OF FUNDS OF HEDGE FUNDS

Fund of hedge funds can be analyzed with respect to three key characteristics.

27.3.1   Approach to Manager Selection

There are many ways to populate each strategy allocation with hedge funds. Exactly how a fund of hedge funds manager selects managers is a key issue. Typically, the portfolio manager or strategy expert searches for the combination of hedge funds that can best meet the objectives of the fund of hedge funds. Also, the returns to some strategies can be closely tracked with just a few funds, while other strategies may require a larger number of funds. This process, however, involves many factors, including whether the identified hedge fund is open to new investment. Unlike mutual funds, which are easy to access for investors, hedge funds are not always open to new investors. Some of the best hedge funds are closed to new investors after reaching the manager's capacity constraint. The capacity constraint is the AUM level beyond which the manager believes that additional capital will increase market impact and reduce potential returns.

Portfolio managers at funds of hedge funds are constantly looking to improve their current hedge fund rosters by building a short list of hedge funds approved for investment. Occasionally, an underlying fund needs to be replaced, which entails coordinating redemption cash flow timing as well as reallocating the capital. Managers of funds of hedge funds are constantly attending conferences, capital introduction events, networking events, and endless meetings with managers, all in an effort to keep their short lists updated with quality managers.

Funds of hedge funds may subscribe with data vendors and may set up quantitative screens to help make their searches more efficient. An example of such a method is the Bifurcated Fund Analysis Model (BFAM) by Liew, Mainolfi, and Rubino (2002). The **Bifurcated Fund Analysis Model** helps determine whether a potential hedge fund manager's return characteristics are a good fit from two vantage points: (1) the attractiveness from a mean-variance perspective; and (2) the rankings from a flexible peer group scoring method.

27.3.2   Four Types of Funds of Hedge Funds Based on Diversification

Broadly speaking, funds of hedge funds can be grouped based on the number of underlying strategies, the number of underlying hedge funds, or a stated objective:

Diversified funds of hedge funds attempt to diversify a portfolio by allocating assets to a larger number of hedge funds (typically 30 to 50) that follow different strategies and are generally expected to have returns that have low correlations with one another.

Concentrated funds of hedge funds typically allocate assets to a relatively small number of hedge funds compared to diversified fund of hedge funds (typically 5 to 10).

Single-strategy funds of hedge funds allocate assets across several hedge funds (typically 5 to 15) following the same strategy, theme, or group of strategies. Their goal is to provide exposure to a particular subset of the hedge fund universe. Examples of single-strategy funds of hedge funds include funds that allocate exclusively to equity hedge funds, managed futures funds, emerging markets, or emerging managers.

Tactical funds of hedge funds invest in a group of hedge funds (typically 5 to 10) to opportunistically gain exposure to a specific market factor. A recent example of this was the proliferation of credit-based strategic funds of hedge funds in 2009 to profit from the credit dislocation of 2008.

27.3.3   Exposure of Funds of Hedge Funds Returns to Four Potential Biases

As with most aggregations of fund returns, potential performance biases are key to interpreting historical performance.

Funds of hedge funds voluntarily report assets, performance, and other fund information to commercial databases that track them. These service providers greatly facilitate information gathering and performance comparisons among the many funds. Moreover, many experts feel that the data on returns measured by fund of hedge funds databases are usually of a much better quality than the data on individual hedge funds. In particular, some of the usual hedge fund biases are significantly reduced or even eliminated when applied to funds of hedge funds (see Fung and Hsieh 2002), as indicated by the following four levels of potential bias:

1. LITTLE OR NO HEDGE FUND SURVIVORSHIP BIAS: Funds of hedge funds provide audited track records, which include full historical allocations to all winners and losers, regardless of whether the underlying funds voluntarily reported to a database. As a result, the historical track record of a hedge fund that stops reporting to databases will be included in the track record of all funds of hedge funds that have invested in that fund and reported their performance.

2. NO HEDGE FUND SELECTION BIAS: While hedge funds may choose not to report to databases, their track record will be embedded in the performance of any fund of hedge funds that was invested in it. As a result, looking at fund of hedge funds databases increases the potential universe of funds captured to include those that do not report to databases.

3. NO INSTANT HISTORY BIAS: When a fund of hedge funds adds a new hedge fund to its portfolio, the historical track record of that hedge fund is not included in the historical track record of the fund of hedge funds. As a result, returns from funds of hedge funds are less susceptible to instant history bias.
4. LESS SURVIVORSHIP BIAS: The mortality rate of funds of hedge funds is much lower than that of individual hedge funds. The performance differential between surviving and liquidated funds of hedge funds is also smaller than that of individual hedge funds. According to Liang (2003), the annual survivorship bias for hedge funds is +2.32% per year, while the bias for funds of hedge funds is +1.18%.

As a result, fund of hedge funds returns are likely to deliver a more accurate estimate of the actual investment experience of hedge fund investors than are single hedge fund returns or hedge fund indices.

27.3.4 Four Key Issues Comparing Funds of Hedge Funds and Multi-strategy Funds

Level I of the CAIA curriculum detailed the similarities and differences between funds of hedge funds and multi-strategy funds. This section discusses four key issues in selecting between funds of hedge funds and multi-strategy funds.

1. FEES: Funds of hedge funds charge an additional layer of fees on top of the fees charged by the underlying hedge funds. In many cases, they are able to negotiate fee breaks with underlying managers as a way to offset the additional layer of fees at the funds of hedge funds level. Many multi-strategy funds, which do not have the additional layer of management and incentive fees, may pass on the cost of their infrastructure to the fund, and in many cases, these costs are substantial. However, multi-strategy fund fees may be lower than those of funds of hedge funds and the underlying managers, if for no other reason than the reduction of netting risk.
2. LEVERAGE: While both funds of hedge funds and multi-strategy funds may use leverage, it's important to understand how that leverage is used, its tenor (how long it is locked in), and its impact on the overall fund. Leverage in a funds of hedge funds can cause losses when an individual fund blows up, but those losses are usually limited to specific underlying funds and do not contaminate the rest of the portfolio. Leverage in a multi-strategy fund, in contrast, can put the entire fund at risk, as the strategies are not isolated unless housed in a series of bankruptcy-remote special purpose vehicles.
3. TACTICAL MOVES: Funds of hedge funds typically take longer to make tactical moves, as they must provide notice to redeem, wait for the funds to disburse the money, and then reallocate to new funds. Since the capital in a multi-strategy fund is internal, multi-strategy funds can make tactical moves more quickly to take advantage of market conditions if a team is already in place to execute the strategy.
4. COMPENSATION: While multi-strategy funds' compensation arrangements with their trading teams vary widely across firms, they generally fall into one of two categories. In the first category, multi-strategy funds pay their internal teams based on their aggregate performance. This was the original compensation model for multi-strategy funds, but it created a talent-retention issue when the best traders decided to strike out on their own.

In the second category, multi-strategy funds pay each internal team based on the profits each generates. This approach is the most widely used compensation structure today because it helps retain top talent and is aligned with investors' interest in paying for performance. Unfortunately, it also creates netting risk for investors when profitable teams in a multi-strategy fund get paid even though the aggregate fund reports negative returns. These compensation charges are frequently included in expenses that are passed on to investors.

OTHER CONTRASTS BETWEEN MULTI-STRATEGY FUNDS AND FUNDS OF HEDGE FUNDS: Exhibit 27.6 highlights major differences between funds of hedge funds

EXHIBIT 27.6   Funds of Hedge Funds Compared with Multi-strategy Funds

	Funds of Hedge Funds	**Multistrategy Funds**
Asset allocation	Open architecture; can select from hedge fund universe	Captive managers
Portfolio diversification	More diverse in strategies, styles, and funds (for diversified FoF)	Narrower in strategies and styles
Investor sophistication level	Low	High
Minimum capital investment	Low	High
Headline risk	Lower, but market generally aware of underlying manager allocations	Higher; each captive manager puts fund at risk
Transparency	Typically, fund names, strategies, and allocation percentages disclosed	Varies, but typically strategy allocations and weights disclosed
Performance	Lower	Higher
Returns volatility	Lower	Higher
Operational risk	Low	High
Cross-collateralization (at what level leverage is applied)	Underlying fund level	At the strategy and/or overall fund level
Basis of risk analysis	Generally at the underlying hedge fund level	Security level
Ability to make tactical changes	Takes longer to redeem and reallocate	Capital can be moved quickly to take advantage of market conditions
Risk management	Important	Critical
Fund liquidity	Moderate	Moderate
Standard fees:		
Management fee (plus underlying HF fees)	1.0%	2.0%
Incentive fee	Up to 10%	20%
Pass-through expenses	No	Varies, but yes in many cases
Are incentive fees paid on net returns?	No	Yes, mostly
Knowledge transfer to investors	Yes	No

Source: CISDM.

and multi-strategy funds. Note that, compared to multi-strategy funds, funds of hedge funds tend to have lower minimum capital requirements, return volatility, operational risk, and headline risk. Also, compared to multi-strategy funds, funds of hedge funds tend to have more diverse strategies, better knowledge transfer to investors, a large universe of managers and no pass-through expenses. On the other hand, compared to funds of hedge funds, multi-strategy funds tend to have better performance.

27.4   FUND OF HEDGE FUNDS PORTFOLIO CONSTRUCTION

The construction of a portfolio of hedge funds by a fund of hedge funds manager may initially appear to be a very daunting task. Questions arise, such as: what are the different strategies to which to allocate? Are the strategies' definitions exhaustive? How much should be allocated to each strategy? How much should be allocated to each fund? Such questions are forever being debated within thoughtful funds of hedge funds.

This section highlights some practical issues that may be encountered when portfolios are weighted or sized, first discussing some overly simple allocation methods and then some relatively advanced methods.

27.4.1   Assets-Under-Management Weighted Approach and its Three Challenges

The most standard allocation process is to use an asset-weighted approach that allocates to strategies based on the AUM reported by each strategy. However, the AUM-weighted approach has three key challenges:

DECLINING ALPHA: Unlike many standard allocation processes, employing AUM weights may lead to highly suboptimal allocations. Hedge fund strategies that have generated attractive alpha (excessive risk-adjusted returns) may attract capital inflows. The theory of efficient markets implies that the additional inflows may cause the alpha to lessen and eventually disappear. Following this reasoning, an allocation process in which the largest allocation goes to the most popular strategies, or the strategies with the most AUM, may not be optimal. In fact, some funds of hedge funds even argue that a better approach would be allocating to hedge fund strategies in which flows are shrinking or receding.

BIASED AUMs: The dynamic nature of assets flowing across hedge fund strategies makes following AUM weights challenging over time. The cost of accessing these data and the fact that one vendor may monitor a hedge fund universe that vastly differs from that of another vendor or uses different strategy classifications further complicates the analysis. Therefore, even the AUM numbers are a bit suspect and may be biased to include only those hedge fund managers who may be looking to raise more assets.

FLAWED STRATEGY CLASSIFICATIONS: Consider also that, given the vast differences in strategy definitions for hedge funds, even classifications become a bit fuzzy across time. For example, a multi-strategy hedge fund with a large convertible arbitrage allocation may be initially classified as convertible arbitrage. Over time, if convertible arbitrage opportunities wane, the fund may increase allocations to equity hedge and event-driven strategies. It may not always be clear that the classification system will account for such changes.

Also, if a new hedge fund strategy attracts a large amount of assets and the vendor does not have that particular strategy classified, there may be a significant amount of time before the new classification is defined. These are just some of the issues that have to be thought through carefully before pursuing an allocation process based on predefined-strategy AUM. Once strategies are defined and weights are determined, investors need to size the allocation to each of the underlying hedge funds. Typically, fund of hedge funds are organized across strategy experts, such as a portfolio manager who covers equity hedge funds and a portfolio manager who covers global macro/commodity trading adviser (CTA) funds. Portfolio managers are generally supported by analysts who are responsible for creating a shortlist of funds to satisfy the targeted allocations for each strategy.

In an example in which a hedge fund manager has initial success from his original strategy, asset inflows will follow, and the fund may branch out and add even more strategies as AUMs increase. Since hedge fund strategies are not perfectly correlated, this diversification process adds benefits on two important fronts for the manager: by lowering overall fund volatility and by increasing overall fund capacity. The largest hedge funds, therefore, often look more like multi-strategy hedge funds than single-strategy funds. This typical style drift may not be properly accounted for by data vendors or may be reported on a lagged basis.

27.4.2 Equally Weighted Approach

Equally weighted approaches are also known as 1/N diversification (where N is the number of funds in the portfolio) because the target allocation to each of the portfolio's assets is equal to 1/N. The equally weighted approach to strategies does not require a view on any particular strategy—it simply invests equally in each strategy. This approach is the most objective and, in theory, the most simple to initially implement. Note, however, that from a rebalancing standpoint, this strategy will reallocate away from the successful strategies and towards the unsuccessful strategies. Therefore, rebalancing to 1/N will perform relatively poorly if fund performance persists and will perform relatively well if fund performance mean-reverts.

The equal-weighting approach does not take into account that some strategies are more volatile than others or that some strategies have lower correlations with other strategies, thereby affecting diversification. The equal-weighting strategy may be difficult to implement precisely in practice due to the potential inability to liquidate or trade any strategy each month without prohibitive transaction costs. Many hedge funds have lockup periods and redemption schedules and may occasionally impose gates against redemptions.

At a minimum, a naïve (i.e., equally weighted allocation) across strategies provides a good baseline on which to further improve by using one of the strategies in the next sections.

27.4.3 Equal Risk-Weighted Approach

Equal weighting across strategies does not account for the differing volatility (or annualized standard deviation) of individual strategies, and constrains a high-volatility strategy to have the same weighting as a low-volatility strategy. One way to normalize for the different volatilities is to size the allocations inversely proportional to each strategy's volatility. For example, highly volatile strategies would get a smaller allocation, while less volatile strategies would get a larger allocation. Equation 27.1 depicts the weight for each asset, i, for a portfolio of N funds. The sum of the inverse standard deviations is the denominator, and the strategy's inverse standard deviation is the numerator. Thus, the weights sum to 1.0.

$$\text{Equally Risk Weighted}_i = \frac{(\text{Standard Deviation of Fund i})^{-1}}{\sum_{K=1}^{N} (\text{Standard Deviation of Fund } k)^{-1}} \quad (27.1)$$

In practice, some analysts employ rolling standard deviations, but then the choices of window length and frequency of data come into question: should one use the data at daily, monthly, or annual intervals, and how many observations should be used? With the many different ways used to compute volatility, this process has many options.

When hedge funds have experienced a few months of extreme performance, including or excluding one monthly data point will have a profound influence on the rolling standard deviations used. As with most weighting strategies there is the practical issue that periodic reallocation across strategies raises challenges when the underlying fund has constraints on liquidity.

Standard deviation is an imperfect measure of volatility because it penalizes upside deviations as much as downside deviations. One of several alternatives to standard deviation when estimating and sizing allocations is to use semivolatility or semideviations, which measure only downside volatility.

This inverse-weighting approach is a simplified version of the risk-parity approach. In a risk-parity approach, each asset class makes the same contribution to the total volatility of the portfolio. Assuming that all asset classes, or in this case all hedge funds, have the same correlation with each other, then the weights obtained in Equation 27.1 will be the same as risk parity. That is, the weights are selected so that each fund will make the same contribution to the total volatility of the portfolio.

Once the inputs to the model have been determined and a rebalancing discipline has been created, this allocation process provides some comfort to adherents. Its biggest drawbacks are that it uses historical information to allocate capital without considering whether markets have changed, doesn't take into account any cross-correlations with other strategies, is very dependent on the time frame selected, and, in times of particular stress in the markets, produces results that may not be representative of long-term volatility levels.

27.4.4 Mean-Variance (Unconstrained and Constrained) Approach

Probably the best-known allocation method is based on mean-variance optimization (MVO). This method involves finding optimal allocations across strategies that increase the ex post Sharpe ratio. Some have argued that MVO, which uses historical data for inputs, is error maximizing, as it overly favors historically strong-performing investments and overly emphasizes prior diversification benefits. In addition, MVO assumes that returns are normally distributed, which is not the case for hedge funds. These are legitimate reasons to be wary of the MVO allocation approach, which can create ex post optimal, but not practical or feasible, portfolios.

Constraints are often used to improve diversification by reducing the dominant weights that unconstrained optimization may suggest for some strategies. While the results of the MVO unconstrained approach may appear to be attractive on the surface, the lack of diversification among strategies subjects the portfolio to tail risk events.

27.4.5 Mean-Variance Approach with Constraints on Higher-Moments

Mean-variance optimization may not be appropriate, as the returns for hedge fund strategies are not normally distributed, as is evidenced by negative skewness and excess kurtosis. Some evidence indicates that the underlying strategies have distributional characteristics that allow portfolio skewness and kurtosis to be substantially improved relative to the portfolios designed by the equally weighted or MVO approaches. For example, Black (2006, 2012) documents skew-reduction techniques by including the Cboe Volatility Index (VIX) in a hedge fund portfolio. If a hedge fund portfolio has higher moments and short volatility exposures, a long position in VIX futures or call options can offset those risks and return the portfolio of VIX and hedge funds to a return profile that is closer to normally distributed.

There are many objectives that can be satisfied using portfolio optimization, including minimizing standard deviation, minimizing drawdown, or minimizing the correlation or beta to specific market indices. Optimization methods assume the stability of the return distribution over time, which tends to break down during fat tail events, especially across hedge fund strategies. As a result, much caution should be taken when using these methods. Some analysts will use volatility and correlation estimates from times of market crisis to understand the sensitivity of optimization results to inputs that can vary substantially over time.

27.4.6 Personal Allocation Biases Approach

When a fund of hedge funds manager has had a very bad experience with a given strategy, typically due to performance or operational issues, the manager's personal biases will have a direct influence on future asset allocation decisions. Some funds of hedge funds avoid mortgage-backed and fixed-income arbitrage funds altogether, while others may exclude all quantitative or black-box models. Institutional investors may have written mandates to avoid certain strategies that may have blown up in the past. Such biases are conspicuously present across asset allocation methods in practice, as legacy experiences weigh in on current decisions.

27.5 WAYS THAT FUNDS OF HEDGE FUNDS CAN ADD VALUE

One of the most important debates with respect to funds of hedge funds concerns whether they deserve their "fees on top of fees" and whether they add any value with respect to a randomly selected portfolio of, say, 20 to 40 hedge funds. Fund manager selection is a key part of the value proposition of hedge funds. As can be seen in Exhibit 27.7, there is a wide dispersion in returns across managers in each

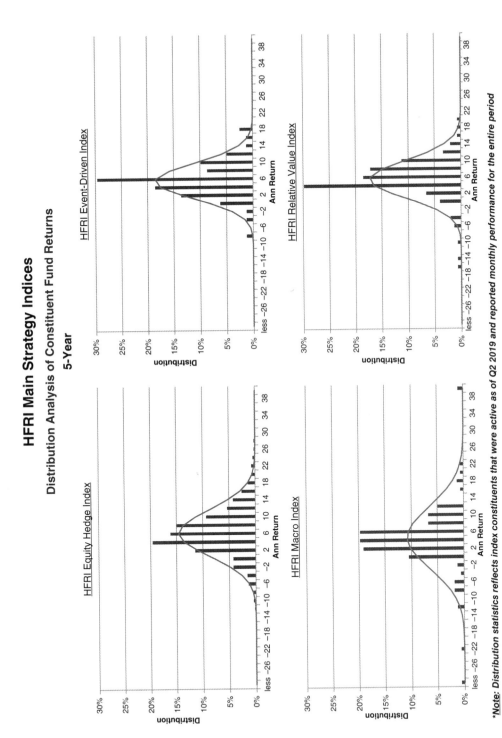

EXHIBIT 27.7 Distribution Analysis of Constituent Fund Returns over 5 Years
Source: Hedge Fund Research (HFR), 2019b.

Note: Distribution statistics reflects index constituents that were active as of Q2 2019 and reported monthly performance for the entire period

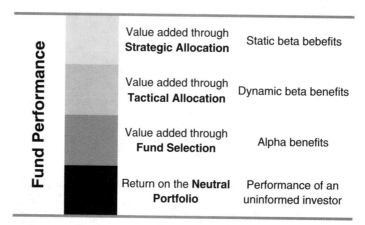

EXHIBIT 27.8   Approaches to Add Value by Fund-of-Funds Managers
Source: Darolles and Vassie (2010).

of the hedge fund styles tracked by HFR. Funds of funds that can select hedge funds with median and above median returns can reduce the risk of large losses in the fund of funds portfolio.

A study by the EDHEC-Risk Institute (Darolles and Vassie 2010) sought to quantify the impact of various factors over time. The research analyzed three ways for a fund of hedge funds manager to add value as indicated in Exhibit 27.8: Strategic allocation, tactical allocation, and fund selection.

27.5.1   Evidence on the Three Levels at Which Funds of Hedge Funds Can Add Value

From a universe of more than 1,000 funds of hedge funds, Darolles and Vassie (2010) studied the performance attribution of 184 funds of hedge funds that had a continuous track record from January 2000 to July 2009. They compared the results of these funds of hedge funds against the returns of a predefined neutral portfolio of an uninformed investor (as defined in the study). The research concluded that of the three approaches, strategic allocation accounts for a large part (68%) of funds of hedge funds return variability, with the balance explained by the other two factors.

The second part of the study sought to assess the extent to which the sources of value added over the neutral portfolio by funds of hedge funds managers are regime dependent. The study divided the same observation period into two market regimes: normal market conditions (January 2000 to June 2007) and stressed market conditions (June 2007 to July 2009). These are displayed in Exhibit 27.9 and Exhibit 27.10.

In addition, the study classified the performance of funds of hedge funds into one of two groups depending on their performance versus the neutral portfolio: positive value added and negative value added. In other words, which of these three approaches added the most value during normal market conditions and during stressed market conditions?

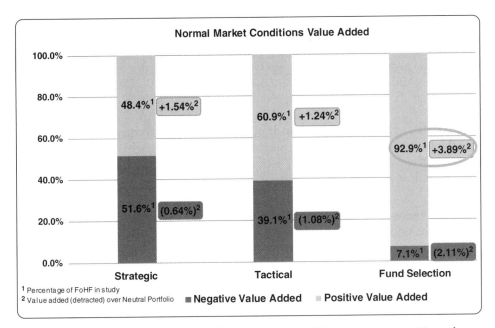

EXHIBIT 27.9   Three Approaches to Add Value by Fund of Funds Managers in Normal
Market Conditions
Source: Darolles and Vassie (2010).

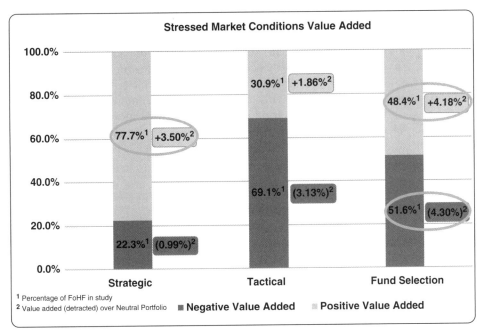

EXHIBIT 27.10   Three Approaches to Add Value by Fund of Funds Managers in Stressed
Market Conditions
Source: Darolles and Vassie (2010).

The researchers made the following conclusions:

1. The value added of strategic allocation is positively skewed in both market regimes, especially in stressed market conditions when this approach was most valuable (as 77.7% of funds of hedge funds were able to add 3.50% annually).
2. Tactical allocation appears to produce limited value added.
3. Fund selection is a double-edged sword. In normal market conditions, 92.9% of funds of hedge funds had an annual positive outperformance of 3.89% over the neutral portfolio by using the fund selection approach. In stressed market conditions, however, only 48.4% of funds of hedge funds added value of 4.18% annually.

27.5.2 General Evidence on the Performance of Funds of Hedge Funds

This section briefly summarizes evidence on the performance of funds of hedge funds relative to direct access to hedge funds or indices.

Funds of hedge funds provide significant diversification potential because they have relatively low volatility and drawdowns. This is particularly true of funds of hedge funds as compared to individual hedge funds. This suggests that a fiduciary who is primarily concerned about the downside risk associated with hedge fund investments should consider a funds of hedge fund vehicle.

This risk reduction, however, generally comes at the cost of lower annualized returns, because average returns of funds of hedge fund indices have typically been only a little more than half of those of hedge fund indices over the same period. This is in line with the empirical literature and can be explained by the so-called double layer of fees of funds of hedge funds and the survivorship impact that creates a meaningful upward bias in the reported performance of individual hedge fund indices.

On a risk-adjusted basis, research also indicates that funds of hedge funds offer a slightly lower information ratio. This suggests either that funds of hedge fund managers have not done a particularly good job at selecting superior hedge funds or that the fees they charge wipe out the benefits they deliver. Several studies have confirmed these results and tend to confirm that, on average, funds of hedge funds underperform hedge funds after fees.

27.6 INVESTABLE HEDGE FUND INDICES

The first investable hedge fund indices were launched in January 2001 by Zurich Financial Services and Schneeweis Partners and were soon followed by several others. All investable hedge fund indices share the goal of offering investors the opportunity to access the overall returns of the entire hedge fund market at a relatively low cost. But as their construction rules, weighting, and rebalancing policies differ widely, significant variations in their performance result.

Index providers face a tradeoff between including more funds to be more representative and using fewer funds to facilitate management. To be investable requires that the hedge fund indices select only a limited number of liquid and open hedge funds. Most index providers impose strict selection criteria (e.g., minimum track record, minimum AUM, sufficient liquidity, absence of a lockup period, daily or weekly valuation, minimum transparency, willingness to accept additional investors, and commitment to provide sufficient capacity) in order to select the funds that are eligible to enter their index.

The process of selecting hedge funds based on certain criteria leads to adverse selection. That is, it is likely that the hedge fund managers who are willing to belong to an investable index would have characteristics different from those of the universe of all managers. As illustrated by Lhabitant (2007), the set of all investable indices included only 4 of the largest 25 hedge funds worldwide, despite the fact that those funds managed a total of more than $300 billion.

Adverse selection is likely to lead to lower returns for the index, because it is often assumed that top-performing managers are less likely to agree to belong to an index.

Beyond the question of representation, several criticisms of the selection process used by investable index providers have been raised. Since investable hedge fund indices are created with the implicit goal of launching a tracking vehicle, it is essential that their historical pro forma performance looks attractive to potential investors. Therefore, index providers have a tendency to select index members among funds with good track records. This does not, however, guarantee good performance in the future. For most strategies and providers, a simple comparison between noninvestable and investable indices indicates underperformance of the investable indexes.

27.7   ALTERNATIVE MUTUAL FUNDS

Level I of the CAIA curriculum discussed alternative mutual funds (AMFs) in detail. AMFs are also known as liquid alternative funds. The next three sections summarize three potential benefits of AMFs to managers, three potential benefits to investors, and three potential risks. The final section discusses alternative exchange-traded funds.

27.7.1   Three Potential Benefits of Offering Alternative Mutual Funds

First, a hedge fund manager might be able to raise significantly more capital through an AMF. Even if a hedge fund is able to attract a tiny portion of total mutual fund assets, the fund could easily multiply its asset base several-fold. This reason alone can untangle the puzzle of why a lower-fee mutual fund might be offered by a hedge fund manager. With a larger asset base, the fund manager might end up earning more than what he could earn with the performance fee on a smaller hedge fund.

Second, AMFs allow a hedge fund manager to diversify the fund's investor base beyond those who are investing in the hedge fund. Traditional mutual fund investors are retail investors who usually do not qualify for investing in hedge funds based on regulatory standards such as a minimum level of income or net worth. A mutual fund also offers a hedge fund manager the ability to sell the fund through multiple retail channels, enabling it to raise assets from a diverse set of investors.

Third, increased regulations have closed the gap between hedge funds and mutual funds. In the case of the United States, with the implementation of the

Dodd–Frank Act (2010), many hedge fund managers, albeit reluctantly, had to register as investment advisers. Since a US mutual fund manager must also be registered as an investment adviser, a hedge fund manager can easily launch a US mutual fund once registered. In addition, having a mutual fund removes certain restrictions that are placed on a hedge fund. For example, a mutual fund can attract as many investors as are willing to invest in the fund, whereas a hedge fund may face restrictions on the number of investors that it can accommodate.

27.7.2   Three Benefits of Alternative Mutual Funds to Investors

Besides offering hedge fund strategies in a mutual fund structure, the main benefits of AMFs for investors are transparency, daily liquidity, and low fees, while operating in a regulated framework that offers various safeguards to both retail and institutional investors. Operational risks of the alternative mutual fund may be lower than those of a similar hedge fund that operates in an unregulated environment, reducing possibilities of losses due to fraud and the level of due diligence that might be necessary.

Second, the lack of minimum eligibility requirement for investing in them. There are many investors who would not be able to access hedge fund-like strategies if alternative mutual funds were not available. Having a hedge fund-like strategy in a portfolio offers the benefit of diversification for most retail investors who hold stock and bond funds. At times of market stress, diversification can protect a portfolio from having large drawdowns and can improve risk-adjusted return.

Finally, a key advantage of alternative mutual funds is their lower fees compared to hedge funds. Whereas hedge funds usually charge an incentive fee in addition to a hefty management fee of around 2% of AUM, mutual funds in the US cannot charge an asymmetric incentive fee, and their management fees are usually lower than 2%. Funds organized under the Undertakings for the Collective Investment in Transferable Securities (UCITS) structure or in Canada are allowed to charge the asymmetric incentive fee commonly found in unlisted hedge funds.

27.7.3   Three Risks of Alternative Mutual Funds

AMFs have some risks that one needs to study carefully before investing. This section discusses three of the risks.

Perhaps the biggest risk for an AMF is liquidity. Even with the provision of not investing more than 15% of assets in illiquid assets, funds may at times find themselves facing unforeseen redemption requests, which might require them to sell assets that have low liquidity. A surge in redemption requests usually depletes the most liquid assets first and subsequently requires the selling of assets that are less liquid. This results in two unfavorable conditions for the fund. First, as the fund starts selling less liquid assets at depressed prices, the net asset value (NAV) of the fund suffers. This leads to an exodus of investors who want to leave the fund before others, exacerbating an already dire situation.

Another risk for AMFs originates in the excessive leverage inherent in different securities they may invest in. Even though AMFs in the US are not permitted to have more than 33% leverage, they may invest in securities that are themselves leveraged. For example, AMFs may invest in levered ETFs or futures contracts, which have high leverage that is not accounted for if one is looking at only the amount borrowed by a fund. Leverage has both advantages and disadvantages. It offers high returns when markets move in a fund's favor, but brings disastrous effects when markets move against a fund. Significant attention needs to be paid in analyzing portfolio holdings and investment policies of an AMF before investing.

Finally, a risk that is more operational in nature is related to trade allocation when the same investment manager operates a hedge fund and an AMF side by side. As hedge funds earn incentive fees in addition to higher management fees, the temptation is great for a fund manager to allocate favorable trades to the hedge fund to maximize his personal benefit at the expense of AMF investors.

27.7.4 Three Advantages of Exchange-Traded Alternative Funds

Some hedge fund strategies have also been offered through ETFs since 2009. ETFs combine many of the features of mutual funds with the trading features of common stocks. ETFs offer three distinct advantages over mutual funds.

First, ETFs can be bought or sold throughout the trading day, making it easy to get into or out of any position. Second, ETFs disclose their holdings at the start of every trading day, unlike mutual funds, which disclose holdings once a quarter. Third, ETFs offer tax advantages over mutual funds because they have lower turnover and they allow for in-kind redemptions. In-kind redemption allows an ETF to deliver a group of securities that have appreciated in value in exchange for shares of the ETF, thereby avoiding the taxable event that would have occurred if those appreciated securities had been sold in the open market.

The largest ETF in terms of market value that follows a hedge fund strategy is IQ Hedge Multi-Strategy Tracker ETF (QAI), which has averaged about $1 billion in assets. The underlying strategy of this ETF is hedge fund replication (discussed in Chapter 26) through investment in other ETFs. The IQ Hedge Multi-Strategy Tracker ETF uses empirical correlations to try to match the returns of the HFRI (Hedge Fund Research) Fund of Funds Composite Index as closely as possible.

REFERENCES

Black, K. 2006. "Improving Hedge Fund Risk Exposures by Hedging Equity Market Volatility, or How the VIX Ate My Kurtosis." *Journal of Trading* 1 (2): 6–15.

Black, K. 2012. "An Empirical Exploration of the CBOE Volatility Index (VIX) Futures Market as a Hedge for Equity Market and Hedge Fund Investors." *Research in Finance* 28: 1–18.

Brown, S. J., T. L. Fraser, and B. Liang. 2008. "Hedge Fund Due Diligence: A Source of Alpha in a Hedge Fund Portfolio Strategy." *Journal of Investment Management* 6 (4): 23–33.

Darolles, S. and M. Vassie. 2010. "Do Funds of Hedge Funds Really Add Value: A Post Crisis Analysis." EDHEC-Risk Institute. http://faculty-research.edhec.com.

Fung, W. and D. Hsieh. 2002. "Hedge-Fund Benchmarks: Information Content and Biases." *Financial Analysts Journal* 58 (1): 22–34.

Hedge Fund Research (HFR). 2019a. Global Hedge Fund Industry Report, First Quarter 2019. www.hedgefundresearch.com.

Hedge Fund Research (HFR). 2019b. Global Hedge Fund Industry Report, Second Quarter 2019. www.hedgefundresearch.com.

Lhabitant, F. 2007. "Delegated Portfolio Management: Are Hedge Fund Fees Too High?" *Journal of Derivatives & Hedge Funds* 13: 220–32.

Liang, B. 2003. "Hedge Funds, Funds-of-Funds, and Commodity Trading Advisors." Working Paper, Case Western Reserve University, Cleveland, OH.

Liew, J., F. Mainolfi, and D. Rubino. 2002. "Bifurcated Fund Analysis Model." *MFA Reporter*, November 12–15.

CHAPTER 28

Access to Real Estate and Commodities

This chapter examines access to two important real assets: real estate and commodities. The chapter discusses the main unlisted real estate funds available (open-end funds and closed-end funds), as well as the most important listed real estate funds (REITs and exchange-traded funds [ETFs] based on real estate indices). The chapter also discusses how investors can obtain access to the risk and returns of commodity-related investments. Until the introduction of futures-based investment products and other derivatives, indirect investments (e.g., equity ownership of firms specializing in direct commodity market production) was the principal means by which many investors obtained exposure to this asset class. Derivatives provide cost-effective means of accessing commodity returns, but require especially careful and effective management.

28.1 UNLISTED REAL ESTATE FUNDS

This section discusses unlisted real estate funds. These include open-end and closed-end real estate funds, as well as funds of funds. The section also discusses the most important advantages and disadvantages of privately-held real estate funds.

28.1.1 Open-End Funds

Open-end real estate funds allow investments and redemptions (usually after an initial lockup period) at any time, have an indefinite life, and can cause performance problems due to using stale redemption prices. The redemption price is calculated based on the quarterly appraisal value of the portfolio of properties, making the redemption price a stale price since appraisals are performed with a lag and a tendency towards smoothing. This stale pricing can create serious performance problems for long-term investors of open-end real estate funds. For example, when real estate prices are increasing, a rush of buyers will invest in the fund at the last quarterly price, which does not yet entirely reflect the upturn in the real estate market. The resulting new cash will dilute the subsequent fund return and hurt fund performance of long-term investors. In a declining real estate market, a rush of sellers trying to benefit from the relatively high appraisal value of the previous quarter will hurt the other investors in the fund and may lower the manager's future performance due to exiting investors taking advantage of stale pricing.

US open-end real estate funds are typically required to fund redemptions out of the income received from the underlying portfolio of properties. If there is not enough earned income to fund redemption requests, investors wanting to redeem their shares must wait until other investors in the fund (who were first in asking to redeem their shares) are paid. These restrictions are not usually present in European open-end real estate funds.

Property unit trusts (PUTs) are the main open-end investment product used by pension funds and insurance funds in the UK to obtain a diversified exposure to the UK real estate market. The values of these unlisted investment vehicles are calculated using the appraisal method. **Unauthorized PUTs** are unregulated unit trusts that may be offered only to institutional investors in the UK. All issued units are purchased by these investors, who are completely exempt from capital gains tax or corporation tax (e.g., pension funds and charities). **Authorized PUTs (APUTs)** are issued in the UK and are intended mainly for retail investors and offer exemption from capital gains tax on disposals of investments in the fund. Furthermore, there is no extra tax liability for exempt or corporate investors on distributions from the fund, but credit for any tax paid into the fund is not available.

According to Baum (2012), APUTs are not particularly attractive to tax-exempt investors because the structure has an absolute tax cost that they can circumvent by investing in an unauthorized PUT. Finally, offshore PUTs are tax-effective for many UK and international institutional investors who are either tax-exempt or nonexempt. **Property authorized investment funds (PAIFs)** are investment vehicles authorized by the UK's Financial Conduct Authority that can invest in real estate directly or indirectly (mainly though shares in UK REITs). The Financial Conduct Authority requires PAIFs to value their positions on a daily basis. APUTs can be converted to PAIFs if certain conditions are met.

28.1.2 Closed-End Real Estate Funds

Closed-end real estate funds issue an initial number of shares to investors before any real estate investments are made and are unlisted, and have a specific investment period (e.g., 3 years) and fund-termination period (e.g., 4 to 6 years before the termination period concludes), at which time the fund must distribute all cash flows to investors. Investors cannot redeem their positions through the fund structure but instead must liquidate their shares or units by trading them in the secondary market, which tends to be quite illiquid (and hence the decision in this chapter to categorize this investment vehicle as an unlisted real estate product). In the United States, shares or units are tradable only on a matched-bargain basis. A **matched-bargain system** for trading securities functions by matching buy offers directly with sell offers rather than involving a market-maker who can provide liquidity.

In the United States and internationally, the majority of closed-end real estate funds follow the format of the limited partnership. One of the main advantages of limited partnerships is that they are tax-neutral (i.e., tax-transparent) investment vehicles. A **tax-transparent investment vehicle** is nontaxable and simply flows through all accounting information to its investors. The closed-end real estate funds just described should not be confused with **closed-end real estate *mutual* funds (CEMFs)**, which are exchange-traded mutual funds that have a fixed number of shares outstanding and that represent only a small portion of the listed real estate industry. Shares in closed-end real estate mutual funds are traded on stock exchanges; therefore, they should be classified as a listed real estate investment. CEMFs invest in REITs and real estate operating companies and offer the possibility of gaining a diversified exposure to the real estate asset class with just a small amount of capital. Real estate closed-end mutual funds usually liquidate their real estate portfolios and return capital to shareholders after an investment term (typically 15 years), the length of which is stated at the fund's inception.

28.1.3   Real Estate Funds of Funds

Real estate funds of funds invest in other real estate funds rather than investing directly in real estate assets. While funds of funds in the UK (and the United States) are open-ended, in most of the rest of Europe they are closed-ended. Real estate funds of funds provide higher diversification than investing in only a few real estate funds, and are run by managers who are specialists in the real estate arena. The downside to investors in real estate funds of funds is that they are charged two fees: the first by the fund of funds manager, and the second by the managers of the underlying real estate funds. Exhibit 28.1 summarizes the main characteristics of unlisted real estate funds.

28.1.4   Nontraded REITs

Nontraded REITs are not listed on any exchange and should therefore not be considered listed REITs, although they have some features in common with listed REITs. For instance, in the United States, they are registered and available to retail investors. **Nontraded REITs** were created in the United States in 1990, and even though they are registered with the Securities and Exchange Commission as public companies, their shares are not available on an exchange and are thus essentially illiquid (and therefore difficult to value). Investors can usually sell their shares after a year under a limited repurchase program.

The estimated life span of a nontraded REIT is usually 7 to 10 years, at which time it ends in a liquidity event. Nontraded REITs must pay out at least 90% of their taxable income to shareholders in order to preserve their status as being exempt from federal corporate income taxes. Nontraded REITs are available only to investors who meet suitability standards, and they represent about 20% of the total market capitalization for all publicly-registered REITs (in the United States).

Upfront fees associated with investing in a nontraded REIT are usually between 12% and 15%. The contrast of nontraded REITs with these high initial fees and a structure with a finite life with a listed REIT (without a term limit) is discussed in Chapter 29 in the context of a performance comparison between listed and nonlisted performance.

One of the major challenges for nontraded REITs occurs during the ramp-up phase, when investors have the expectation of receiving future dividend payments at a time when the REIT needs to cover relatively high initial fees and there are only a few assets ready to generate cash flow.

The **life cycle of a nontraded REIT** has four distinct phases, although in practice some of the phases may overlap to some extent. The first phase is the capital-raising stage. Usually no additional new capital is available after this initial stage ends. In the

EXHIBIT 28.1   Main Characteristics of Unlisted Real Estate Funds

	Open-End Real Estate Funds	Closed-End Real Estate Funds
Percentage of total unlisted real estate funds	Around 30%	Around 70%
Types of real estate assets held	Tend to be lower-risk or core real estate	Higher-risk private equity (PE) real estate funds
Life of fund	Indefinite life	Termination date, at which time the fund distributes all cash flows to investors
Liquidity (to investors)	Redemptions (monthly, quarterly, or annually); in the UK, PUTs also have a small amount of trading in the secondary marker	Do not offer redemptions; investors can trade their positions in the secondary market (if it exists), although it is not liquid
Redemption price	Based on appraisals of properties owned by the fund	Based on proceeds from properties at the termination date
Fund structure	In the UK, PUTs are the most common open-end structure used by pension funds	Closed-end funds are very prevalent in the PE industry. In the U.S., most PE consists of limited partnerships or limited liability corporations; globally, limited partnerships are the most common structure
Tax status	Tax-free for qualifying pension funds	Limited partnerships are tax-neutral
Fees	50 to 200 bps (U.S.), and 20 to 150 bps (UK); yearly performance fees may also be charged	50 to 200 bps (U.S.), and 20 to 150 bps (UK); yearly performance fees may also be charged

second phase, the REIT acquires its portfolio of properties with the capital raised in the initial phase. In the third phase, the REIT manages the assets it owns, attempting to generate positive cash flows and to increase value (this is the asset management phase). The final stage is known as the disposition phase. During this stage, an exit strategy is executed to return the investors' original investment and any capital gains or losses that may result from the liquidity event.

Similar to the case of listed REITs, nontraded REITs can be classified into three main categories: equity, mortgage, and hybrid. Furthermore, there are seven broad property categories in which a traded or nontraded REIT may invest: (1) apartments or multi-family properties; (2) office space; (3) industrial facilities; (4) retail space; (5) hospitality properties; (6) healthcare properties; and (7) self-storage properties.

Nontraded REITs can explicitly select two types of strategies or a combination of the two. The first is a current income strategy (also known as distributions), which is associated with higher current yields but at the expense of lower overall total returns. The second is a long-term price appreciation strategy. In the case of a nontraded REIT, this strategy is realized at the sale of the assets.

Nontraded REITs have received the following three main criticisms (Husson, McCann, and Taveras 2012). The **three main criticisms of nonlisted REITs** are: (1) their illiquid nature may give investors a misleading sense of low return volatility; (2) they command high fees, and often involve significant conflicts of interests; and (3) they often use leverage to fund current dividend payments, a practice that may divert attention from their potential inability to generate future dividends.

28.1.5 Four Potential Advantages of Unlisted Real Estate Funds

Four potential advantages of unlisted real estate funds are:

1. UNLISTED REAL ESTATE FUNDS HELP DIVERSIFY REAL ESTATE SPECIFIC RISK: Large sums of money are required to build a diversified portfolio of real estate physical assets. Baum and Struempell (2006) report that more than £1 billion is required to form a diversified portfolio of offices in London. Assuming a structure of 50% debt and 50% equity financing, 20 investors committing £25 million each would be required to raise the needed capital to form an unlisted real estate fund. However, £25 million can afford the purchase of only one or two offices of average lot size in London. Further, unlisted funds may offer better knowledge of the specific real estate investments that will be made.
2. ACCESS TO SKILLED MANAGERS: Skilled managers (specialized in either a market sector or a specific geography) may be attracted to these structures because they can generate better investment opportunities with higher returns and/or lower risk.
3. TARGETED EXPOSURES: Some unlisted real estate funds target real estate investments in specific subsectors or regions.
4. TAX-ADVANTAGED INCOME: In general, unlisted real estate funds offer tax-advantaged income to taxable investors.

28.1.6 Three Potential Disadvantages of Unlisted Real Estate Funds

Three potential disadvantages of unlisted real estate funds are:

1. CASH DRAG: Cash invested in unlisted real estate funds will not necessarily be drawn by the fund manager immediately. This occurs because cash will be drawn from investors as it is needed by the fund to purchase the respective real estate assets. Therefore, the investor will not be able to attain immediate full exposure to real estate assets when allocating funds to unlisted real estate funds.
2. LARGER FEES: Fees charged by unlisted real estate funds can be substantial and larger than those offered by listed real estate funds. Fees are charged yearly and amount to between 50 and 200 basis points in the United States and between 20 and 150 basis points in the UK. Performance fees may also be charged (relative either to an index or to absolute returns). Performance fees can add up when the manager uses substantial leverage and the appraisal values of the properties are increasing. Finally, initial offering fees can be substantial.
3. LEVERAGE AND THE J-CURVE EFFECT: The short-term performance of unlisted funds is usually affected by the costs involved in the initial placement and in buying the initial portfolio of properties. Once these costs are amortized, unlisted funds need

to outperform the direct market to compensate for the short-term underperformance. Leverage is one mechanism used to attain higher returns. While use of leverage can be an advantage of real estate investment, it increases the risk of such assets, which could be exacerbated because the underlying asset is illiquid.

28.2   LISTED REAL ESTATE FUNDS

This section discusses real estate funds listed on exchanges and also presents the main advantages and disadvantages of publicly traded real estate funds.

28.2.1   REITs and REOCs

A REIT is a professionally managed investment vehicle that invests in a portfolio of real estate assets, typically with the goal of generating income (mainly rental income) for its shareholders. Listed REIT shares are listed on stock exchanges (which is the focus of this section), although unlisted REITs are also common. In general, REITs do not have to pay corporate taxes on profits as long as a large proportion of income (90% in the United States) is distributed to shareholders as dividends. This feature, which is also present in the case of mutual funds, represents a major tax advantage when compared to the typical investment in corporate stocks that pay income taxes. Other important features of REITs were discussed in Level I.

Traditionally, REITs have been the most important listed real estate investment vehicle. REITs and analogous entities are common in the United States, the UK, Canada, Germany, Singapore, and Australia. These and many other countries have adopted the US REIT approach. Also, in recent years, a number of alternative listed real estate investment vehicles have been launched. These new investment vehicles include options and futures on real estate indices, exchange-traded funds based on real estate indices, and closed-end real estate mutual funds.

Large REITs are actively managed and are vertically integrated firms, as they can be involved in the following activities: land acquisition and holding, development, ownership (supply of financial capital and portfolio management), operation (asset and property management), and tenant services.

A **real estate operating company (REOC)** is similar to a REIT, except that a REOC reinvests its earnings into the business rather than passing them along to shareholders (and hence they do not get the same tax advantage enjoyed by investors in REITs). REOCs reinvest their earnings because their goal is to search for capital gains rather than passive cash flows. Furthermore, REOCs are more flexible than REITs in terms of the kinds of real estate investments they can make.

28.2.2   Exchange-Traded Funds Based on Real Estate Indices

Most ETFs trade on exchanges at approximately the same price as the net asset value of their underlying assets due to provisions that allow for the creation and redemption of shares at NAV. ETFs have the advantage of being a relatively low-cost investment vehicle, are tax-efficient, and offer stock-like features (liquidity, dividends, the possibility to go short or to use with margin, and in some cases the availability of calls and puts on the ETF).

While the first ETFs were based on only stock and bond indices, ETFs are now also based on assets such as real estate, currencies, and commodities. Exchange-traded funds based on real estate indices or portfolios of REITs and listed in US exchanges track the following:

- Global real estate values (such as the SPDR DJ Global Real Estate ETF).
- Global regions (such as the iShares FTSE EPRA/NAREIT Developed Europe Index Fund, the iShares FTSE EPRA/NAREIT Americas Index Fund, and the Invesco China Real Estate ETF).
- Broad US exposures (such as through the First Trust S&P REIT Index Fund).
- US sectors (such as through the iShares FTSE NAREIT Residential Index, the iShares FTSE NAREIT Industrial/Office Index, the iShares FTSE NAREIT Retail Index, and the iShares FTSE NAREIT Mortgage REITs Index).
- US mortgages (such as through the iShares Mortgage Real Estate ETF and the Vanguard Mortgage-Backed Securities ETF).

There are even real estate ETFs with leverage up to 3× (e.g., ProShares Ultra Real Estate with 2×) and ETFs with short exposures up to 3× (e.g., ProShares UltraShort Real Estate with −2×).

Subject to the possible disconnect between private real estate values and public market prices, ETFs facilitate access to real estate assets for both small and large investors; and similar to options and futures on real estate indices, ETFs based on real estate indices can be used either to hedge risks or to speculate.

28.2.3 Four Potential Advantages of Listed Real Estate Funds

Four potential advantages of listed real estate funds are:

1. DIVERSIFICATION: Similar to unlisted real estate funds, listed real estate funds help diversify real estate specific risk. Very large sums of money are needed to build a diversified portfolio of real estate physical assets. Listed real estate funds such as REITs facilitate exposure to investments in real estate assets requiring even lower sums of money than the typical open-end real estate fund.
2. LIQUIDITY AND DIVISIBILITY: Listed real estate funds have liquidity and divisibility. In general, REITs are fairly liquid investments. This is one of the main advantages of REITs compared to unlisted real estate funds. Also, their divisibility implies that investors can have indirect access to real estate assets in the precise amount that they wish to invest.
3. CONSTANT EXPOSURE: Listed real estate funds provide constant and instant exposure to a real estate portfolio. Cash invested in unlisted real estate funds will not necessarily be drawn by the fund manager immediately. This is because cash will be drawn from investors as it is needed by the unlisted fund to purchase the respective real estate assets. Therefore, the investor will not be able to attain immediate full exposure to real estate when allocating capital to unlisted real estate funds.
4. HIGH INFORMATION FLOW: Listed real estate funds are regulated and provide substantial and timely information. Similar to the case of other securities listed on exchanges, such as stocks and bonds, listed real estate funds are required

to disclose financial and other related information about the fund. This allows investors to make relatively informed decisions.

28.2.4   Two Potential Disadvantages of Listed Real Estate Funds

Two potential disadvantages of listed real estate funds are:

1. VOLATILITY RELATIVE TO THEIR NET ASSET VALUE (NAV): REITs often trade at a substantial discount or premium to their NAV. In the case of US REITs, there were fluctuations between a discount to NAV of 40% and a premium of 20% between 1990 and 2010. Several explanations have been offered to explain this phenomenon. For example, some attribute the problem to the practice of smoothing appraisals of direct investments made by REITs, which, they argue, render these valuations as less informative reflections of REIT values than REIT share prices. However, other market participants disregard the information content of REIT share prices because they contend that the prices are an unreliable indication of short-term market sentiment and exhibit contagion with the overall equity market.

2. HIGH CORRELATION WITH EQUITY MARKET RETURNS: Listed real estate funds such as REITs may have a high correlation with the stock market (and not with the underlying real estate index). It has been observed that often the shares of REITs follow more closely the behavior of stock market indices (especially mid-sized and small stocks) than the trends of the real estate index underlying the REIT.

Exhibit 28.2 summarizes the main characteristics of REITs and ETFs regarding types of real estate assets that they hold, liquidity, redemption price, tax status, and fees.

28.2.5   Global REITs

Similar to the case of allocating funds to stocks on a worldwide basis, global real estate investing makes sense as long as financial markets across countries are not perfectly correlated. By investing internationally, an investor in real estate may well gain access to a higher efficient frontier (i.e., benefit from a higher expected return for a given level of risk) than if investing only in a domestic real estate market.

Global REITs are real estate investment trusts that invest in global real estate products. They are the premier listed investment vehicle for gaining access to international real estate markets. In general, and similar to the case with US REITs, trusts on non-US REITs do not have to pay corporate taxes on profits as long as a large proportion of income (90% in the United States, the UK, and Japan, and 85% in France, for example) is distributed to shareholders as dividends.

Global REITs also differ on the rules related to their management and their use of leverage. Many non-US REITs are externally managed by outside companies. However, in the United States, REITs are normally managed by their executives or trustees. Regarding leverage, whereas US REITs have no limits on the amount of

EXHIBIT 28.2 Main Characteristics of Listed Real Estate Funds

	REITs	ETFs
Types of real estate assets held	Can be equity REITs, mortgage REITs, or mixed	ETFs track a real estate index; there are also short and ultra-short ETFs
Liquidity (to investors)	Traded on the secondary market	Traded on the secondary market
Redemption price	Secondary market traded price	Secondary market traded price
Tax status	REITs do not pay taxes at the company level if they comply with a number of restrictions; this means that no capital gains taxes are charged on the disposal of assets	ETFs are tax-neutral
Fees	Most REITs have annual managers' fees, property management fees, trustees' fees, and other expenses; brokerage fees must also be added when buying or selling REIT shares in the marker	As most real estate ETFs invest in REITs, there are two layers of fees: the fees from the REIT and the fees from the ETF; brokerage fees must also be added

debt financing they can employ, REITs in other countries do have debt ceilings. For example, Australian REITs have a debt-to-equity ratio limit of 3 to 1 under certain circumstances.

The global REIT market has experienced rapid growth during the past decade, particularly in the case of REITs from emerging markets such as China and India. Approximately three-quarters of the companies in the global real estate securities market consist of REITs or REIT-like structures, with the remaining portion accounted for by non-REIT owner-operators and real estate development companies.

There are over 30 nations (including the US, Netherlands, Australia, Canada, Belgium, Japan, South Korea, France, Hong Kong, and Taiwan) that have listed REITs with many other countries for which REIT legislation is either in progress or under consideration. The first country that adopted the REIT structure was the United States (1960), followed by the Netherlands (1969) and Australia (1971), meaning that REITs have been in existence for more than five decades.

Finally, Exhibit 28.3 briefly compares traded and nontraded REITs as they pertain to investment objective, liquidity, volatility, investors, and fees.

EXHIBIT 28.3 Comparison between Traded and Nontraded REITs

	Traded REITs	Non-Traded REITs
Investment objective	Current income and share price appreciation	Current income and eventual capital appreciation
Liquidity	May be bought and sold at any time; either listed on an exchange or traded over-the-counter (OTC)	Investors should plan to hold through planned exit event
Volatility	Daily share price volatility based on supply and demand	No daily share price volatility until repricing 18 months after close of offering period, when underlying value of real estate holdings may fluctuate up or down
Investors	Available to any person or entity with a brokerage account	Available only to qualified investors through a professional financial adviser
Fees	Initial offering fees and/or commissions for secondary market transactions; annual asset-based management fees	Front-end fees of 12% to 15% of investment; acquisition, asset management, disposition, and incentive fees during term.

Source: Taken from Investment Program Association (2013).

28.3 COMMODITIES

The **return to commodity beta** may be defined as the return from direct exposure to changes in commodity prices, which result from holding a passive long position in a commodity. For example, to deliver oil-based commodity beta, an investor can use a number of investment vehicles that capture the price change in a particular oil-based commodity investment.

Within the past two decades, the number of investable commodity indices and commodity-linked investments has increased dramatically. Subsequent sections provide an outline of the wide range of investment products that are currently available to acquire commodity beta exposure. Since most commodity investments are in some way linked to commodity indices, the characteristics of commodity indices and enhanced commodity indices, as well as the calculation of their returns, are discussed.

28.3.1 Direct Physical Ownership of Commodities

Most investors avoid holding physical commodities because storage can be cumbersome and expensive, and they prefer to avoid committing large amounts of capital.

For example, barrels of oil require a storage tank as well as transportation from the purchase site. In fact, some commodities are perishable (e.g., many agricultural and livestock commodities), making them virtually impossible to store for an extended period based on speculation. Precious metals are an exception. Investors often hold precious metals in the form of bullion or coinage. Gold is especially easy to store, and gold investors have historically preferred to hold physical gold rather than gold derivatives.

In short, real assets such as physical commodities require a degree of active management simply to maintain their value. Research suggests that over the long term, the prices of physical (i.e., spot) commodities have not kept up with inflation, which is in stark contrast to the returns generated by other forms of commodity investment, such as commodity futures and indices.[1] As a result, most commodity investments are made through derivatives contracts, such as futures contracts, forward contracts, swaps, options, and swaptions. These derivatives allow the long side to benefit from price increases in the commodity without the need to physically store the commodity.

28.3.2 Indirect Ownership of Commodities

The most common method of obtaining commodity exposure is through synthetic or **indirect commodity investments** involving equity, fixed income, and derivative instruments. Most investors actually have this type of exposure embedded in their traditional investment portfolios. These exposures can be as simple as owning traditional stock or bond investments in companies that are involved in the production, transportation, and marketing of commodities, or they can be one of a number of more specialized commodity-based investments discussed in the following sections.

A great deal of institutional investment in commodities takes the form of index-based investments. The primary vehicle used by institutional investors for exposure to commodity indices is a commodity index swap.

28.3.3 Commodity Index Swaps

A **commodity index swap** is an exchange of two cash flows in which one of the cash flows is based on the price of a specific commodity or a commodity index, whereas the other cash flow is fixed. Similar to other types of swaps, the contract specifies a term for the swap, the frequency of the payments, and leverage (both direction and magnitude). The buyer (i.e., receiver) of the swap will agree to make fixed payments on specific dates in exchange for payments that are tied to the value of a specific commodity or commodity index. The seller or payer of the swap pays the variable price and receives the fixed price. The net cash flow is determined by the difference between the actual subsequent market price and the fixed price.

Similar to a futures contract that has a market value of zero when the contract initiated, the initial market value of a commodity swap is near zero. Specifically, the size of the fixed payments is negotiated between the two parties such that each side perceives the initial market value of the swap is near zero or positive.

For many major commodities, a commodity swap can be replicated using a portfolio of futures contracts. Therefore, it is natural to ask why investors use swaps when they can use futures contracts. The primary reason is that the swap provides flexibility. The underlying commodity index and other terms can be chosen to meet the specific needs of the investor when there may not be exchange-traded futures contracts that would meet those needs. Also, if the swap is long-term, futures contracts of long maturity may not be available or may lack liquidity. Further, investors sometimes prefer this structure because it allows them to maintain control of their cash. While most commodity indices include a hypothetical collateral return equal to that of Treasury bills, a majority of investors can achieve higher actual collateral returns by managing the cash themselves. The cash can also be used in portable alpha strategies or, if desired, held in Treasury bills.

Commodity index swaps are preferred by institutional commodity investors because swaps are competitively priced, with multiple dealers making markets in swaps on several major commodity indices. Swaps also experience greater counterparty risk than do the commodity futures markets. Competition among dealers provides multiple counterparties to spread the default risk that stems from over-the-counter (OTC) swap transactions. The principal drawback of OTC swaps is that relatively few investors have direct access to this market, as it is limited to institutional investors. Also, the *secondary* market for commodity swaps is illiquid, so early termination or modification of swap agreements typically requires negotiating with the original counterparty. It is important to note that in recent years, certain OTC products have been moved to exchanges, and this trend is likely to continue.

28.3.4   Public Commodity-Based Equities

Owning the equity of a firm that derives a substantial part of its revenue from the sale of physical commodities appears to be a reasonable way of gaining exposure to commodities. However, not all of these investments have returns that are highly correlated with specific commodities. For example, the returns of integrated oil companies (like Exxon Mobil) and gold-mining companies (like Goldcorp) tend to be at least moderately correlated with the prices of crude oil and gold, respectively, but the returns of food companies typically have only minor correlation with the prices of grains and livestock. There is evidence that commodity producers engage in selective hedging, in which they actively alter their hedge ratios based on their views of future commodity prices.[2] Hedging activity, to the extent that it is not disclosed in public filings, can result in unpredictable commodity exposures for indirect commodity investors. Therefore, indirect commodity investments derive at least some of their returns from the active management of commodities.

Using equities for commodity exposure subjects the investor to substantial stock market exposure, a risk that can result in a decoupling of realized returns from those sought by exposure to a particular commodity. In addition to the underlying commodity and stock market risks, an investor that established a position in the equity securities of companies engaged in the sale of physical commodities is also subject to each company's underlying business risk.

In various studies, an index of commodity-producing equities had similar long-run returns as an index of commodity futures contracts, and the long-run volatility of the commodity futures index was lower than that of the commodity equity portfolio.[3] However, the long-term returns and volatility tell only part of the story. The same studies have shown that the portfolio of commodity-based equities had a higher correlation with the S&P 500 than with the portfolio of commodity futures.

Exhibit 28.4 displays a scatter plot of monthly returns on the S&P GSCI against the monthly returns on the S&P North American Natural Resources Index, which measures performance of equities of North American companies belonging to this

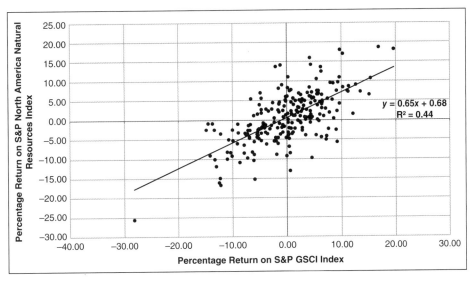

EXHIBIT 28.4 S&P GSCI versus S&P North American Natural Resources Index monthly returns from 1996 to 2016
Source: Bloomberg and authors' calculations.

sector. We can see that there is indeed a positive relationship between the two indices. The slope of the regression is 0.65, which indicates that for one percentage increase in the S&P GSCI, the equities of commodity-producing firms increase by 0.65% on average. The R-squared of the regression is about 44%, which is statistically significant but also indicates that only 44% of the monthly return volatility on these equities can be explained by changes in the commodity futures index.

28.3.5 Bonds Issued by Commodity Firms

Somewhat similar to owning equities of commodity producing firms is attempting to gain exposure to commodities through owning bonds issued by firms that derive a substantial portion of their revenue from the sale of commodities. However, if a company is rated as investment grade, the yield on these bonds generally has low sensitivity to the commodity market in which the company is involved. Specifically, the bond price will fluctuate less with the value of the commodities that provide the basis of the firm's revenue than with economy-wide changes in interest rates and general credit spreads.

28.3.6 Commodity-Based Mutual Funds and Exchange-Traded Products

Other ways to gain exposure to commodities are through commodity-based mutual funds or exchange-traded products. These vehicles typically use one of four methods to acquire commodity exposure:

1. commodity index funds or swaps;
2. equities of commodity-based companies;

3. physical commodities;
4. commodity futures.

Commodity-based mutual funds are available in different active and passive structures, including commodity-based equity funds and passive commodity index-tracking funds, which benchmark to commodity price indices as well as stocks of commodity producers. While index mutual funds, which track commodity indices, are generally considered passive funds, they have opportunities to attempt to outperform their benchmarks by actively managing the collateral portion of the investments.

Commodity-based mutual funds generally have fees and cost structures similar to other types of mutual funds.[4] Commodity-based exchange-traded funds (ETFs) generally offer exposures similar to those of commodity mutual funds. Long-only commodity index-based ETFs may track broad-based commodity indices (such as the iShares S&P GSCI Commodity-Indexed Trust) or commodity sub-indices (such as the PowerShares DB Energy Fund). These ETFs generate their returns directly—by holding commodity futures contracts—or indirectly (such as through swaps). ETFs are also available that track the spot price of individual commodities, such as the SPDR Gold Shares (GLD), which tracks the price of physical gold. Rather than tracking commodity futures, the GLD ETF holds gold bullion (which is more a function of gold investment; many other specific commodity ETFs hold their exposures in the form of derivative contracts).

While most commodity ETFs track commodity prices (based on commodity futures or spot commodities), some ETFs track the equity prices of firms engaged in commodity production. For example, the VanEck Vectors Agribusiness ETF tracks the stocks of agribusiness firms.[5] As previously discussed, equities provide a less pure exposure to commodity prices than derivatives-based commodity ETFs, since their performance is influenced by factors that drive the equity markets as well as factors that drive commodity prices.[6] Some commodity-related ETFs offer leveraged or leveraged inverse commodity exposures.

ETFs may trade at a premium or a discount relative to the net asset value of the fund. For ETFs with liquid underlying securities, large premiums or discounts are rare because they can be arbitraged away. If the ETF is trading at a premium, authorized participants will purchase the securities in the ETF basket, exchange them for ETF units, and then sell the units on the exchange to earn a profit. If the ETF is trading at a discount, authorized participants will buy the ETF, exchange the ETF for units of the securities that are in the ETF basket, and sell the securities in the market to earn a profit. However, some commodity ETFs do not invest in physical commodities or securities that directly track spot prices, so there could be large tracking errors between the actual performance of the ETF and the benchmark that it is supposed to track. Some ETFs that use futures and swaps to replicate the benchmarks may have large tracking errors. Generally, commodity ETFs that use full replication, such as the iShares Silver Trust (SLV) and GLD, have the lowest tracking errors, followed by ETFs that use futures, followed by swap-based ETFs.[7]

28.3.7　Public and Private Commodity Partnerships

Some commodity investment vehicles have structures similar to private real estate partnerships or REITs. Private commodity partnerships offer long-term ownership of real assets used in mining and energy markets. Whereas equity real estate vehicles own and operate income-producing properties, commodity partnerships might own the extraction rights to a natural gas field, a pipeline, railcars, storage facilities, or refining operations related to natural resource extraction. Partnerships are organized as pass-through entities. The income from ownership of the assets is distributed to the partners, typically without taxation at the partnership level. Income can be in the form of lease income—for example, if the partnership owns a pipeline—or from the sale of such commodities as crude oil or natural gas. In either case, the income paid by the partnership is usually correlated with the price of some commodity, so investors see many partnerships as a highly correlated substitute for direct commodity investments.

In the United States, master limited partnerships are a popular structure for obtaining exposure to energy commodities and enterprises. A master limited partnership (MLP) is a tax-efficient structure that can be used to gain access to sources of returns that are correlated to certain parts of the commodity sector and has its shares (called "units") traded on a public exchange, such as the NYSE or NASDAQ. As partnerships, MLPs are pass-through entities for tax purposes, meaning they do not pay taxes at the corporate level. As currently defined by the US Tax Code, MLPs are required to generate at least 90% of their income from activities with "qualified sources," such as depletable natural resources.[8]

As discussed in CAIA Level I, many MLPs operate in the midstream energy sector, owning pipelines and distribution assets that earn revenues for transporting energy that are relatively uncorrelated to the price of the energy products transported. MLPs typically operate in asset-intensive businesses with high barriers to entry, which can also help ensure their cash flow stability but with which there are unique risks. Some of these risks are due to the legal structure of MLPs, and some are from the market in which they operate. MLPs, particularly in times of market stress, can demonstrate equity-like volatility and drawdowns. The majority of MLPs continue to be held by retail investors who may react to negative news by selling their positions. Historically, MLPs have increased their distributions in aggregate. However, individual MLPs can change and, in some cases, decrease their distributions for strategic, competitive, or other business reasons. The MLP marketplace remains small compared to domestic equities and bonds. Investors with larger portfolios may experience difficulty in efficiently building or reducing their positions due to limited trading volumes. Much of the market's investable value is represented by a limited number of MLPs. A key attraction of MLPs has been their comparatively high yields. An overall rise in interest rates could diminish MLPs' appeal if they are not able to generate a commensurate growth in distributions. MLPs typically distribute a very high percentage of their free cash flow and, as such, need to regularly access the capital markets for debt and equity to finance their growth.

28.3.8 Commodity-Linked Investments

A **commodity index-linked note** is a debt instrument that pays a return linked to the performance of a commodity (e.g., natural gas or aluminum) or a basket of commodities over a defined period. The note may not pay any interim coupons, with the only payoff distributed on the maturity date, when the note pays the initial principal amount plus return, if any, based on the percentage change in the underlying commodity.

Index-linked notes appeal primarily to investors who prefer to hold bonds, often for regulatory purposes. Many investors are obligated to own securities and have difficulty entering futures contracts. Furthermore, futures contracts and swaps require frequent margin and/or collateral postings. Index-linked note structures do not require collateral, since the structure is already fully collateralized. Finally, there is a secondary market for index-linked notes. A swap contract cannot generally be transferred, but ownership of notes is easily transferred.

A **commodity exchange-traded note** (ETN) is a debt instrument that is traded on an exchange but is different from an ETF; instead of being a share in an actual portfolio of assets, the ETN is a note issued by a financial institution that promises to pay ETN holders the return on some index over a certain period of time, and then return the principal of the investment at maturity. This means that if the company issuing the ETN defaults, ETN holders could lose a portion or all of their investment.

The credit risk exposure associated with ETNs is generally higher than the counterparty risk inherent in a commodity index-linked swap. In the case of the latter, swap counterparties post collateral at regular intervals, so counterparty risk is usually no more than a few percentage points of the total notional size of the swap.

The primary advantage of an ETN is that the issuer promises to pay exactly the return on some index, minus fees and expenses; therefore, there is little tracking error. Further, some ETNs are able to deliver the returns of a particular index that may not be available in an ETF framework. For example, the underlying securities could consist of derivative products, which in some instances may not be held in an ETF structure. Finally, in some jurisdictions, investors may face different tax treatment depending on whether they choose to invest in ETFs or ETNs.[9]

ETNs are frequently referred to as prepaid forward contracts. **Prepaid forward contracts** are fully collateralized forward contracts for delivery. Thus, a commodity exchange traded note is economically equivalent to a prepaid forward contract on the index value. Commodity indices have a high turnover rate, so profits and losses are usually treated as short-term capital gains and are therefore taxed as ordinary income, at a relatively high rate. However, since an ETN is based on the index value (rather than futures contracts), an ETN may qualify for long-term capital gains tax treatment (at a lower rate) if it is held for a minimum period of time, which is often defined as more than 1 year.

Long-maturity index-linked futures contracts on several commodity indices are also available. These are economically equivalent to ETNs, except that they are listed on futures exchanges rather than stock exchanges. The key difference between these contracts and typical commodity futures contracts is that long-maturity index-linked futures contracts are fully margined, meaning the trader must post 100% collateral at the time of investment (although market-makers and other commercial users of these contracts are allowed to post much smaller margin amounts). Long-maturity index-linked futures contracts offer one of the least expensive and least leveraged solutions for retail investors. Furthermore, there is less counterparty credit risk associated with futures exchange trades than with ETNs.

28.3.9 Commodity-Based Hedge Funds

Hedge funds are active players in the commodity markets. Before 2000, commodity hedge funds were primarily focused on absolute return and relative value strategies. However, in response to institutional investment in commodities, a number of firms have launched long-biased commodity hedge funds. There are two categories of long-biased funds.

The first group is similar to long-only equity funds, in which managers typically hold long positions in futures contracts rather than physical commodities. Funds in this group look to identify undervalued commodities to purchase and hold in unhedged portfolios. These funds have been successful in attracting assets that would otherwise be placed in commodity index funds. Active managers may be able to avoid unfavorable rolls and to overweight or underweight commodities based on fundamental, quantitative/statistical, or technical models. The fund managers are typically benchmarked to a particular index, with compensation schemes tied to their performance relative to the fund's benchmark. Lockups are short, and both liquidity of the investments the fund makes and transparency are higher compared to other hedge funds.

The second group of long-biased funds is involved in the physical markets. These funds are engaged in the purchase, storage, and transportation of commodities. Because they also limit their use of hedging, their returns are influenced by the direction of commodity prices. These managers tend to specialize in particular commodities or commodity sectors. Investors in these funds are seeking returns generated through a combination of active management (alpha) and commodity beta. Investments with these managers are fairly illiquid, often requiring long notice periods prior to redemptions. Competitors include trading companies, shipping firms, and the commodity trading desks of major financial firms.

Hedge funds that focus exclusively on commodity investments are by no means restricted to long-only funds. Hedge fund strategies include a number of methods, including cash management, long/short positions, and instrument choice.[10] In these hedge funds, there is no guarantee that a manager will maintain a long position in commodities, as the manager may choose to take short positions or to hedge some or most of the fund's commodity exposure.[11] Commodity hedge funds also use market-timing strategies.

Historically, the correlation between commodity hedge fund returns and the returns of the underlying commodities has been low. Exhibit 28.5 displays the empirical relation between HFR's index of hedge funds that specialize in energy and basic commodities and the S&P GSCI. The relation is positive, but weak, a point that is underscored by both the regression's weak slope and low R-square. While there is a positive relation between the commodity hedge fund index and the commodity index, the relation between average commodity hedge fund returns and the commodity index is not positive: a study of individual hedge funds shows that since 2006, the average correlation between commodity hedge funds and the S&P GSCI is not significantly different from zero.

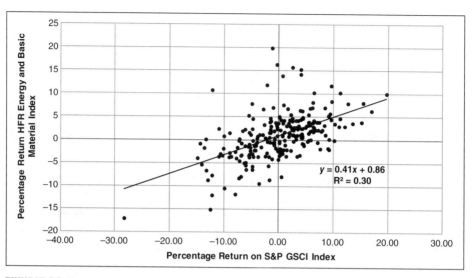

EXHIBIT 28.5   Correlation between Commodity Hedge Funds and S&P GSCI monthly returns from 1996 to 2016

28.4   COMMODITY TRADE FINANCING AND PRODUCTION FINANCING

Financing for the production, storage, and transportation of commodities has historically been provided by merchant banks, vertically integrated commodity firms, and investment banks. A number of private investment funds have also been organized to compete in the high-margin segments of this business.

The strategies related to financing physical commodities can be executed in a number of ways. Most commonly, investment funds will provide financing for the extraction or shipping of bulk commodities, with the commodities pledged as collateral for the loans. Other strategies involve purchasing commodities for future delivery directly from the producers. In effect, the producers are borrowing money that will be repaid with commodities. This provides working capital to the producers and an effective hedge for producers against a decline in the price of the commodity.

For investment funds, these transactions typically offer higher margins as they are custom transactions that frequently involve operational, credit, and political risk. Many commodity producers operate primarily in parts of the world with elevated political risks. Purchasing commodities for future delivery from producers operating in precarious environments carries considerable risks (e.g., expropriation). These risks, and the resulting profits, have traditionally gone to multi-national banks and other financial intermediaries. As recent regulations have forced financial institutions to dramatically reduce risk-weighted assets, profit opportunities—and their related risks—have grown for investment funds as they have stepped up to fill the gap.

28.5   LEVERAGED AND OPTION-BASED STRUCTURED COMMODITY EXPOSURES

While most externally managed commodity investments are delivered through standard index-based structures such as swaps, ETFs, and structured notes, an array of complex structures, such as principal-protected notes, levered notes, options, and swaptions are available to investors.

28.5.1   Leveraged and Inverse Commodity Index-Based Products

Most commodity index-based products have traditionally been designed to provide an unleveraged long exposure to a commodity index; however, there is a variety of ETFs and ETNs providing unleveraged inverse (short), leveraged long, or leveraged inverse exposure to a variety of investable indices, including commodities. Managers of leveraged exchange-traded products primarily use swaps or futures contracts to provide holders with either 2× or even 3× long or short exposure to the daily returns of an underlying index (the majority of products reset their exposure on a daily basis). Return expectations for these structured products are mired in confusion. Earlier chapters use binomial trees to debunk similar common myths such as being able to create wealth through diversification return in efficient markets. The following points clarify two areas of confusion.

WHEN STRUCTURED COMMODITY RETURNS ARE $NPV = 0$: In the absence of fees, trading costs, excessive financing costs, and inefficiently priced underlying commodities, structured commodity exposures through ETFs and ETNs offer $NPV = 0$ returns. It is sometimes falsely argued that structured leverage products are inherently wealth-destroying due to the mathematics of return variation. For example, it is claimed that the return of a leveraged commodity exchange-traded product (ETP) will be $NPV < 0$ if the returns of the underlying commodity have a variance greater than zero. For example, it can be shown that the multi-period returns of a leveraged long-exposure ETP can be negative even over a period in which the underlying commodity has risen in price. However, the argument can be made about the effect of return variability of the underlying commodity itself. When the underlying commodity experiences variable returns with an arithmetic mean of zero (e.g., equal numbers of periods of returns of +10% and −10%), the commodity will decline in value (e.g., earning 10% in one year and −10% in another year will compound to a loss of 1%). Leverage simply magnifies this effect. Note that expected excess total returns of a L-1 leveraged ETP with daily adjustment should be L times the returns of the underlier $(1 + 2L)$, not $(1 + r)^L$. The illusion can also be caused by misuse of expected geometric mean returns.

POOR HISTORIC RETURNS OF STRUCTURED COMMODITY PRODUCTS AND MEAN-REVERSION: Observation of past structured commodity returns often indicate poor performance for leveraged exposures and short exposures through structured ETPs. But it is inefficiently priced underlying assets (primarily mean-reverting returns) that cause poor historic returns of leveraged long commodity ETPs. Also, long-term positive risk premiums in underlying commodity returns cause negative excess returns in short ETP exposures. But assets with negative betas must offer negative expected returns in equilibrium. Structuring itself cannot consistently destroy or create wealth in the absence of market inefficiencies, trading costs, excessive financing costs, and fees.

28.5.2   Leveraged Notes

Index-linked notes may offer leveraged exposure to commodity indices as well. These are referred to as leveraged notes. A **leveraged note** is an indexed note that offers leveraged exposure (e.g., 3×) to a specified commodity index. Because these notes can lose 100% of their value when a daily decline of more than 33% in the index is experienced, the issuer and investor can be viewed as having or needing options.

The investor benefits from the implicit limited liability of the note and an asymmetric exposure, since any loss on the note cannot exceed the amount invested while profits are unlimited. The main benefit, which also serves as the primary risk, of leveraged notes is the high daily commodity exposure. In a 3× leveraged note, each $1,000 invested controls $3,000 of commodity exposure, so speculators can add significant leverage to their exposure to daily returns on a targeted commodity index.

28.5.3   Principal-Guaranteed Notes

Many investors prefer a form of index-linked notes referred to as principal-guaranteed notes as discussed in Level I of the CAIA curriculum. **Principal-guaranteed commodity notes** are structured products that offer investors the upside opportunity to profit if commodity prices rise, combined with a downside guarantee that some, potentially all (depending on the note's terms), of the principal amount will be returned at the maturity of the structure. Notes containing so-called contingent protection clauses will not return the investor's principal unless the stated contingencies are met. Also, in the event the issuer, or counterparty, of a particular note files for bankruptcy, the note's purchasers essentially become unsecured creditors and risk losing up to all of their investment.[12]

There are two common structures for principal-guaranteed notes. The first structure, and the most common, is the **cash-and-call strategy or participation note**, in which the principal guarantee comes from the issuer purchasing maturity- and principal-matched zero-coupon bonds, while the commodity-linked upside exposure comes through the issuer purchasing call options.

For instance, assume that an investor wants exposure to commodities but wants to avoid a loss of principal. The capital committed by the investor is $1,000. The issuer can create a principal-protected product with exposure to commodities by following these steps. First, to protect the principal, a 5-year, $1,000 zero-coupon bond yielding 5% is purchased for $783.53, which leaves $216.47 for the purchase of call options on the benchmarked commodity index. Next, upon the maturity of the bond, the $1,000 principal is returned to the investor. If the note is invested in Treasuries, then there is essentially no risk of default on the part of the issuer. If the zero-coupon bond is a liability of the issuer, then there is a chance that the principal will not be fully realized. In this case, the risk of the principal and the performance of the product will reflect the credit quality of the issuer. Finally, if the commodity price has increased sufficiently and the call option expires in-the-money, the investor will receive all or only a portion of the gains. Otherwise, the investor will receive the principal.

The second, less common, structure for principal-guaranteed notes is a dynamic strategy, or **constant proportion portfolio insurance (CPPI)**, which varies the size of the commodity investment based on the cost of insuring the principal guarantee. Using the previous example, the initial price of the zero-coupon bond is $783.53, which is set as the floor value. This floor value changes over time, as rising yields reduce the cost of the zero-coupon bond, while the passage of time increases the cost of the zero-coupon bond, as there is less time remaining to earn interest.

In the dynamic strategy, commodity investments are held as long as their value exceeds the cost of purchasing the zero-coupon bond to insure the portfolio.

28.6   KEY CONCEPTS IN MANAGING COMMODITY EXPOSURE

This final section on commodity exposures discusses roll return, price cycles, and key determinants of commodity returns.

28.6.1   Roll Return

Roll return, or roll yield, is the profit or loss from holding a futures contract due to the change in the basis (where basis equals spot price minus futures price). A popular view of roll return is that it is obtained from rolling up or down a commodity's forward curve from the future toward the present with the passage of time.

Obviously, if a downward sloping commodity forward curve (i.e., in backwardation) remains downward sloping (and does not shift down), roll return will be positive for a long futures or forward position. Conversely, roll return will be negative when the forward curve persistently slopes up (contango) and does not shift up.

On the one hand, the efficiency of commodity derivative markets should prevent any roll-return-based strategies from consistently generating a risk-adjusted profit. In other words, forward curves will tend to evolve through time such that there are no risk-adjusted expected profits from efforts to implement market-timing strategies based on roll return. However, in practice, popular strategies have emerged. For example, difficult-to-store commodities and those that are subject to supply or demand shocks tend to have larger convenience yields and are more likely to be in backwardation and numerous strategies exist that attempt to generate superior returns through positive roll returns.[13] Investors using commodity indexes should note that the weighting scheme of each index can have a substantial impact on its returns due to roll return and that:

1. Roll return for a particular commodity changes over time with changes in interest rates, storage costs, and convenience yields. A commodity's forward curve may flip from backwardation to contango with changes in the cost of carry.
2. Commodities in backwardation typically exhibit high volatility due to their low inventory levels.
3. Focusing strictly on roll return may negatively impact the degree of diversification of the commodity index, as commodities that tend to all be in backwardation or all in contango may share significant correlation with one another.

28.6.2   Commodity Prices and Cycles

This section discusses three potential cycles in the context of commodities and commodity returns.

> COMMODITY PRICES AND THE BUSINESS CYCLE: Commodity prices are strongly influenced by the level of business activity and therefore any cycles in business activities may be useful in managing commodity exposures. The impacts of business cycles tend to vary across commodity sectors and often within sectors.

For example, while most energy commodities tend to respond similarly to the business cycle, agricultural commodities exhibit greater heterogeneity in their responses to business cycle effects. These differences are related to storability and demand sensitivity to economic activity as well as exogenous factors affecting supply of some commodities. However, it is difficult to generalize the impacts of the business cycle on commodity prices. The relations are confounded by the impact of other macroeconomic factors such as currency exchange rates and changes in technology. The clearest relations between business cycles and commodity prices tends to be found in energy and industrial metals.

COMMODITY PRICES AND SUPERCYCLES: Examination of commodity prices suggests four supercycles during 1865–2009, with each cycle lasting around 30 to 40 years.[14] The 2007–9 global economic crisis was preceded by a commodity price boom that was unprecedented in its magnitude and short duration. The real prices of energy and metals more than doubled in the 5 years from 2003 to 2008, while the real prices of food commodities increased 75%. The remarkable strength of this upswing in commodity prices reflected the extraordinary resilience of growth performance of major emerging countries that demanded commodities.

COMMODITY SUPERCYCLES VERSUS SHORT-TERM FLUCTUATIONS: Supercycles differ from short-term fluctuations restricted to financial factors in two ways. First, they tend to span a much longer period, with upswings of 10 to 35 years, generating 20- to 70-year complete cycles. Second, they are observed over a broad range of commodities, mostly inputs for industrial production and urban development of an emerging economy. For example, the economic growth in the United States from the late nineteenth through the early twentieth century led to a supercycle expansion in commodity prices that was rather well sustained and prolonged. Another upswing took place during the postwar reconstruction in Europe and was further enhanced by Japanese postwar economic emergence. These two earlier supercycles in commodity prices were driven by the resurgence of demand for raw materials during the industrialization of a major economy or a group of economies. Likewise, the current phase of supercycle expansion can be attributed to rapid and sustained Chinese industrialization and urbanization. Similar to previous supercycles, the current cycles will end when the growth rates in China, India, and other emerging economies moderate.

28.6.3 Commodity Prices and Key Economic Variables

This section discusses three potentially key economic variables that influence commodity returns.

COMMODITIES AND INTEREST RATES: High real interest rates increase the opportunity costs of investors who hold commodities in storage, which leads to a temporary reduction in the potential demand for storable commodities.[15] First, high interest rates reduce the potential demand for storable commodities (or increase the potential supply) through three channels: (1) by increasing the incentive for extraction today rather than tomorrow; (2) by decreasing firms' desire to carry inventories; and (3) by encouraging investors to shift out of commodity contracts into fixed-income instruments.

COMMODITIES AND CENTRAL BANK POLICIES: When studying tactical asset allocation and commodity futures, Jensen, Johnson, and Mercer (2002) show that the main benefits of holding long commodity positions are during the times when the US Federal Reserve Bank is tightening monetary policy. Given that commodity prices are a significant part of the inflation calculation in most countries, commodity prices are likely to be strong during times of high and rising inflation. Central banks seek to tighten monetary policy and raise interest rates to reduce inflation and slow a rapidly growing economy.

The mechanism through which changes in a central bank's policies can affect commodity prices is as follows. (1) A central bank is attempting to reduce inflationary pressures in the economy begins a contractionary monetary policy. (2) The policy change raises the real interest rate in the short run as the nominal rate increases without a corresponding increase in the inflation rate. (3) The increase in interest rates and potential decline in economic growth rates lead to a decline in real commodity prices. That is, commodity prices will rise at a rate that is lower than the rate of inflation. Once the central bank is satisfied that inflation is under control, expansionary monetary policies are implemented, reversing the previous price declines.

Commodity prices generally have an inverse correlation to the value of the US dollar, as a strong dollar is often experienced during times of weak commodity prices. If tighter monetary policy in the US increases interest rates as well as the value of the US dollar, commodity prices are likely to weaken. As the US dollar strengthens, commodity prices tend to fall, as consumers of commodities in countries with relatively weak currencies experience import price inflation which can reduce demand for commodities.

COMMODITIES, INFLATION, AND COMMODITY PRICE PATTERNS: The above two sections indicate that commodity prices follow a rather predictable pattern as a central bank's monetary policies are adjusted in response to business cycles, rising and falling as the inflation rate increases and declines. While demand and inflation impacts tend to dominate the pricing relations for various forms of energy—and, to a lesser extent, industrial metals—interest rate effects tend to dominate the pricing relationship for many agricultural and livestock commodities, which may provide a business cycle hedge rather than an inflation hedge.

NOTES

1. Gorton and Rouwenhorst (2006); Bhardwaj et al. (2015).
2. Stulz (1996).
3. Gorton and Rouwenhorst (2006); Bhardwaj et al. (2015).
4. Burkart (2006).
5. For a description of agribusiness and categories tracked, please refer to MOO exchange-traded fund.
6. Jensen and Mercer (2011).

7. See Guo and Leung (2014); Murphy and Wright (2010).
8. Benham et al. (2015).
9. Jensen and Mercer (2011).
10. Burkart (2006).
11. Till and Eagleeye (2005).
12. SEC (2011).
13. Till and Eagleeye (2005).
14. Erten and Ocampo (2013).
15. Frankel (2006).

REFERENCES

Baum, A. and P. Struempell. 2006. "Managing Specific Risk in Property Portfolios." University of Reading.

Baum, A. E. and D. Hartzell. 2012. *Global Property Investment: Strategies, Structures, Decisions*. Oxford: Wiley-Blackwell.

Benham, F., E. Walsh, and R. J. Obregon. 2015. *Evaluating Commodity Exposure Opportunities*. Available at SSRN.

Bhardwaj, G., G. Gorton, and G. Rouwenhorst. 2015. *Facts and Fantasies about Commodity Futures Ten Years Later*. No. w21243. National Bureau of Economic Research.

Burkart, D. W. 2006. "Commodities and Real-Return Strategies in the Investment Mix." CFA Institute.

Erten, B. and J. A. Ocampo. 2013. "Super Cycles of Commodity Prices Since the Mid-Nineteenth Century." *World Development* 44 (C): 14–30.

Frankel, J. 2006. "Commodity Prices, Monetary Policy, and Currency Regimes." NBER Working Paper C0011.

Gorton, G. and K.G. Rouwenhorst. 2006. "Facts and Fantasies about Commodity Futures." *Financial Analysts Journal*, CFA Institute.

Guo, K. and T. Leung. "Understanding the Tracking Errors of Commodity Leveraged ETFs." Columbia University.

Husson, T., C. McCann, and C. Taveras. 2012. "A Primer on Non-Traded REITs and Other Alternative Real Estate Investments." Securities Litigation and Consulting Group, Fairfax, VA.

Jensen, G. R. and J. M. Mercer. 2011. "Commodities as an Investment." *Research Foundation Literature Reviews* 6 (2): 1–33.

Jensen, Gerald R., Robert R. Johnson, and Jeffrey M. Mercer. 2002. "Tactical Asset Allocation and Commodity Futures." *Journal of Portfolio Management* 28 (4 Summer): 100–11.

Murphy, R. and C. Wright. 2010. "An Empirical Investigation of the Performance of Commodity-Based Leveraged ETFs". Symmetry Partners and Central Michigan University.

European Commission. 2011. "Impact Assessment of the Common Agricultural Policy towards 2020." Annex 4, SEC (2011) 1153 final/2.

Stulz, R. M. 1996. "Rethinking Risk Management." *Journal of Applied Corporate Finance* 9 (3): 8–25.

Till, H. and J. Eagleeye. 2005. "Commodities: Active Strategies for Enhanced Return." *Journal of Wealth Management* 8 (2): 42–61. Also in *The Handbook of Inflation Hedging Investments*, ed. R. Greer, New York: McGraw-Hill, pp. 127–57.

CHAPTER 29

Access Through Private Structures

This chapter explores the issues of accessing assets through unlisted (private) structures relative to listed structures. The focus is on the institutional and conceptual differences between private and listed structures. Chapter 30 focuses on evidence regarding the historical performance differences. This chapter begins with a general discussion of private versus listed access and then reviews various private structures for accessing investment exposures and concludes with a discussion of the secondary market for private equity partnership interests.

29.1 OVERVIEW OF ISSUES IN PRIVATE VERSUS LISTED INVESTMENT ACCESS

It should be noted that the word "public" does not necessarily mean that the structure is listed for trading on an exchange—it sometimes simply means that it is approved for sale to the general public by regulators. Most institutions investing in private equity seek intermediation, typically through private equity funds, as few have the experience and management expertise that would allow them to directly invest in unquoted companies. Note that private fund structures sometimes use limited liability companies rather than limited partnerships. However, this chapter generally refers to limited partnerships, general partners (GPs, the sponsor of the fund), and limited partners (LPs, the investors with limited control over the fund's major investment decisions).

29.1.1 Financial Market Segmentation

In financial markets, market segmentation refers to differences in market characteristics (especially valuation) emanating from differences in the clienteles (i.e., participants) using the markets. In finance, a **market clientele** is a general type of market participant that dominates a particular market. Financial market segmentation can lead to price differences (and especially differences in risk premiums) for similar assets trading in different markets. The different prices (and risk premiums) are typically attributed to the differences in the clienteles that participate in the markets, such as having different risk preferences. Equity markets are segmented between private and listed access.

29.1.2   Major Potential Advantages of Listed Assets

Although advantages and disadvantages to investors depend on the investor and the circumstances, the seven following potential advantages tend to be more available to investors using listed assets rather than privately organized assets (the list is not ranked):

1. GREATER LIQUIDITY: Can be traded on one or more exchanges.
2. LOWER MANAGERIAL FEES: The total fees usually are less than the sum of management and incentive fees of private partnerships.
3. EASIER DIVERSIFICATION: Can be purchased in small quantities to facilitate diversification.
4. VISIBLE INDICATIONS OF MARKET VALUE: The market prices continuously signal the market's consensus of the asset's value based on available information, allowing simplified and better performance and risk estimation.
5. REGULATORY OVERSIGHT: The initial and ongoing regulatory disclosure requirements may provide some protections against adverse managerial behaviors including fraud.
6. GREATER ACCESS TO FINANCING: The listed structures may facilitate better debt and secondary equity funding.
7. TAX SIMPLIFICATION: Income tax information may be available more quickly and reported using easier forms.

29.1.3   Major Potential Advantages of Privately Organized Assets

Although advantages and disadvantages to investors depend on the investor and the circumstances, the seven following potential advantages tend to be more available to investors using privately organized assets rather than listed assets (the list is not ranked):

1. ILLIQUIDITY PREMIUM: The investor's expected return may include a premium for bearing the risk of poor liquidity.
2. MORE INCENTIVIZED MANAGERS: Heavy performance-based fees may attract managers with better connections and provide greater incentives for them to generate profits.
3. GREATER ASSET TARGETING BY INVESTORS: Investors may be able to select partnerships that invest in assets more closely related to their preferences or needs.
4. APPEARANCE OF STABLE VALUES: The use of appraisals, quarterly sent asset values, and managerial judgment may smooth reported prices and returns.
5. GREATER INVESTOR OVERSIGHT: The rights of limited partners to terminate or otherwise control managers (and the low number of partners relative to the number of shareholders in a public company) may reduce agency conflicts.
6. GREATER MANAGERIAL FLEXIBILITY: The private structure may provide more freedom for managers to operate with flexibility and maximize value creation.
7. TAX BENEFITS: For taxable investors, private structures may better flow through tax advantages such as depreciation and depletion. For the general partners, carried interest may be taxed at highly preferred long-term capital gains rates in some jurisdictions.

29.1.4 Rational Investing with High Fees

As discussed in various locations throughout the CAIA Level I and II curricula, the total fees collected by private equity fund managers are often high on an absolute basis and relative to managers of other investment structures. If sophisticated institutional investors have been rational in selecting private structures for numerous decades, it must be that these structures are at least perceived to offer attractive returns before fees that are able to offset the fees.

In examining the various potential advantages to private assets in the previous section, which of the advantages to privately held assets (relative to listed assets) would justify the decisions of major institutional investors to repeatedly select access through private structures with high fees? In other words, what advantage or advantages available through private structures can offset the high fees?

The empirical evidence on the size of illiquidity premiums (see Chapter 30) indicates that return enhancement for bearing illiquidity is relatively minor (compared to the size of private equity fees). Many institutional investors do not pay income taxes yet they invest heavily in private equity, so income tax advantages do not appear to justify the fees. Other potential advantages listed in Section 29.1.3 also appear unable to justify rational investing in such high fee structures except for those involving better management (Numbers 2 and 6). If private structures are better able to attract the greatest talent, provide powerful incentives to those managers, and allow managers flexibility to best apply their talents and energy, then perhaps the private structures can be attractive even on an after-fee basis.

29.1.5 Private Structures as a Superior Governance Paradigm

In a nutshell, it can be argued that private structures such as those found in private equity are the most efficient structures to create wealth in fields such as buyouts and venture capital. This view proposes that private partnerships represent a superior governance paradigm for private equity that attracts superior managers and incentivizes them to unlock tremendous wealth. The gains through this superior paradigm are claimed to be sufficiently high to: (1) compensate skilled general partners; and (2) reward the limited partners who are skilled enough to select superior managers and work effectively with them.

Within this paradigm, private equity GPs create wealth through: (1) assembling a top management team; (2) selecting portfolio companies with high return potential; (3) working with or replacing the management teams of those portfolio companies; (4) tapping the GP's networks to bring in personnel and contacts to optimize the potential success of each portfolio company; and (5) assisting the successful portfolio companies to perform exits that maximize the creation of wealth. To the extent that private equity GPs have exceptional skill in these key tasks, the partnerships should offer LPs attractive returns net of fees.

As a corollary, unskilled investors may consistently select partnerships with GPs who possess insufficient skills to overcome fees. Investments in private structures by unskilled LPs may offer high potential loss exposures, limited protections, and the potential to be adversely affected by the flexibility of the structures with regard to fees and other sources of conflicts of interest.

29.2   UNLISTED MANAGER–INVESTOR RELATIONSHIPS

At the heart of unlisted structures are concerns regarding conflicts of interest in the manager–investor relationship. In 2019, ILPA (The Institutional Limited Partners Association) released the third edition of the *ILPA Private Equity Principles* with the goal of "improving the private equity industry … to further partnership between LPs and GPs."

These principles provide a suitable foundation to understand the issues involved. There are **three ILPA guiding principles:** (1) alignment of interest; (2) governance; and (3) transparency. The following sections summarize some of the key elements considered to be especially important by limited partners. The *Principles* have received quite limited endorsement by GPs.

29.2.1   GP and Fund Economics

WATERFALL STRUCTURE: (1) Best practice is for full return of investor contributions and preferred returns *first;* (2) enhance investor protections under the deal-by-deal method.

CALCULATION OF CARRIED INTEREST: (1) Calculate carried interest on a *net after-tax profit basis;* (2) calculate preferred return from the capital contribution date to the distribution date; (3) carried interest should ideally utilize a "hard hurdle."

RECYCLING DISTRIBUTIONS: (1) The amount of total distributions that are subject to recycling provisions should have either a mutually agreed cap, or a monitoring threshold.

CLAWBACK: (1) Actual and potential clawback liabilities should be determined and clearly disclosed to the LPs as of the end of every reporting period. (2) All clawback amounts should be gross of taxes paid and paid back no later than 2 years following recognition of the liability. (3) The clawback period must extend beyond the term of the fund, including liquidation and any provision for LP giveback of distributions. (4) LPs should have robust enforcement powers, including the ability to directly enforce the clawback against individual GPs.

MANAGEMENT FEES: (1) Management fees should not exceed reasonable operating expenses and salaries; and (2) full disclosure of the economic arrangement between the GP and its placement agents.

FEE INCOME BEYOND THE MANAGEMENT FEE: (1) No fees should be charged to portfolio companies.

REASONABLE ORGANIZATION AND PARTNERSHIP EXPENSES: (1) Costs related to the formation of the fund should be reasonable and capped at an amount appropriate to the size of the fund. (2) GPs should seek whenever possible to include provisions common across the majority of a fund's side letters into the LPA itself. (3) Expenses shared between the GP and the Partnership include: broken-deal expenses, technology, cyber security and software upgrades, and specific LP expenses. (4) Expenses allocable to the Partnership include: LPAC meetings/annual investor meeting, third-party administration, travel, interest expenses and fees, audits, legal expenses, indemnification, insurance, and litigation expenses, and regulatory expenses. (5) Expenses covered under the management fee include: consultants' fees, ESG-related expenses, placement agent fees, operating partners/consultants, and unforeseen expenses.

29.2.2   Fund Term and Structure

GENERAL PARTNER COMMITMENT AND OWNERSHIP: (1) The GP's equity commitment to the fund should be substantial; (2) the GP's equity should not be transferable; and (3) the GP should not co-invest only in selected deals.

FUND TERM EXTENSIONS: (1) Extensions should be in 1-year increments and require majority approval of the LP Advisory Committee or the LPs; and (2) the GP should be required to liquidate the fund within one year of the expiration of the term of the fund.

VEHICLES INVESTING ALONGSIDE THE FUND: (1) Investments by such additional vehicles should be made at the same time as the fund and should be sold at the same time; and (2) investment results of any alternative vehicles should be aggregated with the investment results from the fund for the purpose of determining distributions.

29.2.3   Key Person

IDENTIFICATION AND CHANGES TO KEY PERSON(S): (1) Any significant change in that team should allow LPs to reconsider their decision to commit through the operation of the key person provisions; and (2) LPs should be notified in a timely manner of any personnel changes, not solely key persons, with the potential to impact fund performance, and immediately notified when key person provisions are tripped.

TIME AND ATTENTION: (1) Key persons should devote substantially all their business time to the fund, its predecessors and successors within a defined strategy, and its parallel vehicles; and (2) key persons for the fund, as identified in the LPA, must not act as a GP for a separate fund managed by the same firm with substantially equivalent investment objectives until after the investment period ends.

KEY PERSON TRIGGERS AND PROCESS TO REMOVE: (1) A "key person" or "for cause" event should result in a suspension of the investment period; (2) in the event of an investment period suspension triggered by the key person provision, the GP should not otherwise use fund assets; and (3) any such vote to reinstate the investment period or to remove the GP should exclude the LP interests held by the GP or its affiliates.

GP REMOVAL AND REPLACEMENT: (1) Provisions that exculpate or indemnify GPs in advance for material breaches of the agreement or fiduciary duties should be precluded, and (2) termination of GPs for cause should require only a majority of LPs.

29.2.4   Fund Governance

FIDUCIARY DUTY: (1) GPs should clear all potential conflicts of interest with the LP Advisory Committee (LPAC); and (2) as a general rule, GPs shouldn't undertake action that constitutes or could potentially constitute a conflict of interest between the fund, a portfolio investment, and/or a portfolio manager on one hand and the GP, key persons, affiliates, etc. on the other, without prior written approval from the LPAC.

INVESTMENT MANAGEMENT CONSIDERATIONS: (1) The GP should diversify across industry and time periods; (2) the GP should accommodate LP exclusion policies; and (3) the GP should commit to directing all appropriate investment opportunities to the fund during the investment period.

CHANGES TO THE FUND: (1) For any changes to the fund requiring an LP vote, "no responses" should be treated as abstentions and excluded from both the numerator and denominator; (2) super majority interests are recommended for LPA amendments, dissolving the fund without cause, and GP removal; and (3) simple majority interests are recommended for investment period suspensions and reinstatement of the investment period.

GP-LED SECONDARY TRANSACTIONS: (1) GPs should engage the LPAC at the earliest opportunity around the objectives and logic for the transaction, process of the transaction, and terms and framing of the deal; (2) GPs should ensure processes are fair and transparent; and (3) GPs should engage an experienced adviser to solicit bids at the cost of the GP and not the fund.

CROSS-FUND INVESTMENTS: (1) GPs should seek to limit the number of overlapping investments between funds.

CO-INVESTMENT ALLOCATIONS: (1) GPs should disclose to all LPs in advance a framework for how co-investment opportunities, interests, and expenses will be allocated among the fund and any participating co-investors; and (2) any parallel vehicles or any affiliates of the GP should be permitted to participate in co-investment opportunities, but only in the same securities and on the same terms as the LPs in the fund.

LPAC BEST PRACTICES: (1) The mandate of the LPAC should be clearly disclosed and should generally include matters specific to evaluating conflicts of interest as presented by the GP; (2) GPs should be able to articulate the rationale for how LPAC members are selected; (3) LPACs should meet regularly on a pre-agreed cadence, with the option to attend remotely via telephone or video; (4) the cost of LPAC participation in LPAC meetings should be borne by the fund; (5) simultaneously with each closing, the list of LPAC members should be disclosed to all LPs in the fund, and (6) the GP or the LPAC should appoint a rotating chair to chair LPAC meetings

AUDITOR INDEPENDENCE AND SCOPE 3 OF FUND AUDIT: (1) The auditor of a private equity fund should be independent and focused on the best interests of the partnership as a whole, rather than the interests of the GP.

29.2.5 Financial Disclosures

FEES AND EXPENSES: (1) All fees charged to portfolio companies should be 100% offset against the management fee and accrue to the benefit of the fund; and (2) the presentation of allocable and charged fees and expenses should be consistent with provisions in the limited partnership agreement and side letters and should be presented such that it can be referenced within that pre-agreed language.

OTHER FINANCIAL INFORMATION, QUARTERLY: (1) LPs should receive quarterly: unaudited profit and loss statements, information on material changes in investments and expenses, a summary of all capital calls and distribution notices, management comments about changes during the quarter, and an explanation of quarter-to-quarter valuation changes.

FINANCIAL DISCLOSURES, ANNUAL: (1) GP annual reporting should include: concentration risk, foreign exchange risk, leverage, realization, and ESG risk at the fund level, and leverage, realization, strategy, reputational, ESG risk at the portfolio company level; and (2) annual reports and audited financial statements should be provided within 90 days of year-end.

CAPITAL CALLS AND DISTRIBUTIONS: (1) Capital calls and distributions should be consistent with the ILPA Standardized Reporting format.

SUBSCRIPTION LINES OF CREDIT: (1) Quarterly and annual reporting should include a schedule of fund-level leverage; and (2) subscription facility terms should be disclosed or available to LPs on request.

PORTFOLIO COMPANY INFORMATION: (1) Sensitive portfolio company information should be provided separately from fund-level reporting; and (2) valuation information should be disclosed on a quarterly basis.

FINANCIAL AND PERFORMANCE REPORTING: (1) Performance figures should be displayed both gross and net of accrued carried interest, as well as the methodology used; and (2) at the end of a fund's life, LPs should be provided with a detailed breakdown of each historical cash flow.

FUND MARKETING MATERIALS: (1) Marketing materials for a fund should include: values for each unrealized portfolio company in prior funds, explanations for valuations that deviate from audited statements, performance of prior funds on a gross and net basis, and description of any pending or threatened litigation, political contributions made by the manager or any associated individuals.

INFORMATION ACCESS AND FUND AUDITS: (1) The fund auditor has ultimate responsibility to ensure that financial reports are free from fraud.

29.2.6 Notification and Policy Disclosures

ESG POLICIES AND REPORTING: GPs should consider an ESG policy.

OTHER POLICY DISCLOSURES AND NOTIFICATIONS: Any policy or event with a significant effect on the fund or its investors should be disclosed to all LPs upon their issuance or modification.

29.3 SIDE LETTERS TO LIMITED PARTNERSHIP AGREEMENTS

An increasingly important practice in partnership agreements is the use of side letters. In the context of private partnerships, side letters are agreements between the GP and one or more LPs that specify special arrangements governing their relationship, often the granting of concessions or other favorable treatments to one or more of the LPs. One of the most important such arrangements can be with regard to co-investing, which is detailed in Section 29.4. This section discusses side letters negotiated between GPs and LPs involving issues other than co-investing.

The following issues involving side letters are detailed by Anderson (2016).[1]

MOST FAVORED NATION (MFN) CLAUSES: LPs may negotiate side letters that grant the LP most favored nation status. **Most favored nation status** is a term from international trade that is used in private partnership negotiations to refer to the negotiated right of an LP to be treated with any and all benefits being offered to any other LP. The purpose of the clause from a particular LP's perspective is to ensure that the interests of other LPs are not placed ahead of the LP with a most favored nation clause.

ECONOMIC TERMS: Side letters may be used to negotiate specific and potentially special economic terms governing the relationship between the sponsor (GP) and the LP that differ from the economic terms of the limited partnership agreement of the main fund.

REPORTING: Side letters may be negotiated by an LP that require the GP to provide financial reports, tax reports, and potentially other reports that the LP requires or prefers for their management and reporting. An example is a requirement for the GP to provide greater detail in periodic reporting regarding portfolio companies.

CONFIDENTIALITY: Side letters may contain clauses with regard to issues regarding confidentiality. LPs may be in positions in which it is necessary for them to report certain information to their investors, jurisdictional authorities, or other parties of interest. The terms of these side letters may be used to negotiate exceptions to otherwise potentially stringent restrictions on dissemination of information regarding the main fund and its investments. A somewhat similar issue regards use of name rights. **Use of name clauses** in a side letter provide limits to the disclosure of the identity of LPs by the sponsor to provide LPs with anonymity (subject to limits imposed on the sponsor such as requirements to disclose LP identities in reporting to regulators or other government authorities).

EXCUSE RIGHTS: Side letters may delineate particular excuse rights. Anderson[2] describes excuse rights. **Excuse rights** potentially allow LPs to opt out of particular investments in the main fund with three main areas for negotiation of excuse rights: (1) legal requirements (based on jurisdictions); (2) LP internal policy requirements (e.g., ESG); and (3) religious (e.g., *Shari'ah*).

CO-INVESTMENTS: Side letters may create co-investing relationships and specify the terms of those relationships as discussed in Section 29.4.

ESG: Side letters may detail agreement of the GP to invest and otherwise function in harmony with the ESG-related objectives and constraints of one or more investors. The heterogeneity of the LPs with respect to the scope and nature of ESG concerns in this increasingly prevalent area of investor concern can raise complexities for the GP.

TRANSFER OF INTERESTS: Side letters may specify the terms under which one or more LPs will be able to transfer their rights of ownership to other investors (e.g., accessing the secondary market for such interests as detailed in Section 29.6).

CREDIT FACILITIES: Side letters may be used by the GP to solidify the LP's obligation to meet commitments to cash investments. The ability of the GP to enforce capital calls can be an important aspect of the GP's ability to use these commitments to obtain financing, such as a credit facility. The use of collateralized credit facilities to support short-term financing is discussed in Chapter 30 as a source of potential conflicts of interest between GPs potentially manipulating reported IRRs (internal rates of return) and LPs seeking reliable cash flow projections and maximization of NPVs (net present values).

29.4   CO-INVESTMENTS

Much of the focus on private equity funds in the CAIA curriculum is on so-called blind pool equity funds. A **blind pool equity fund** aggregates capital obtained from its partners into a single fund (i.e., the main fund) that has a stated investment mandate but that generally does not involve limited partners in deal sourcing. This section focuses on ways of investing in private equity outside of blind pool structures, namely, co-investing.

29.4.1   Overview of Co-Investing

Co-investment refers to the practice of investors being invited by the sponsors of private equity funds (typically GPs) to make investments into one or more pre-specified portfolio companies using structures other than a main private equity fund. Institutions increasingly invest in companies directly or alongside main PE funds in the form of co-investments. Some LPs generally look for such opportunities and even ask for co-investment rights. But co-investing differs from being an LP in a blind pool fund and therefore requires additional knowledge and skills.

As noted by Greene and Rigdon (2016),[3] co-investment typically involves one or more LPs of the main fund being invited by the GP to invest in one or more of the portfolio companies through a "sponsor-controlled investment vehicle typically a limited partnership or limited liability company." However, in addition to co-investing in a partnership controlled by the GP of the main fund, co-investing also occurs through three other vehicles. **Three alternative co-investing structures** involve:[4] (1) the LP invests directly into one or more of the portfolio companies of the main fund; (2) one or more LPs use a GP-controlled fund created apart from the main fund for the purposes of investing in one or more of the same portfolio companies selected for the main fund; and (3) making investments in co-investment programs in which the specific investments are identified and decisions on whether to co-invest are made on an ongoing and deal-by-deal basis.

The second investing structure discussed above is a top-up fund. A **top-up fund** is used to co-invest in one or more future investments of the main fund. An **annex fund** is used to co-invest in one or more pre-existing investments.[5]

Terms for co-investing are often described in detail in side letters between the GP and the investors participating in the co-investing.[6] These issues may include lock-step provisions. A **lock-step provision** in a co-investment agreement specifies that the terms and conditions of the co-investor–GP relationship is the same as the terms and conditions of the LP–GP relationship. The co-investing may be performed in the context of bridge financing. In the context of private equity financing, **bridging** is when the GP makes an investment in the main fund while agreeing to sell that investment at a subsequent time to co-investors such that co-investors receive bridge-financing from the main fund between the time the investment is made and the time that the co-investor(s) takes ownership. Side letters are detailed in Section 29.3.

From the LP perspective, an LP's primary view of co-investments is often as a way of enhancing their overall returns primarily from accessing a private company while paying lower management fees or carried interest charges than found in the main PE fund or potentially paying no management or carried interest fees. While GPs may charge low or no management fees for providing this access to co-investment opportunities, they may charge other fees such as transaction fees. To be able to go this low or no-fee, no-carried-interest route, the LP generally needs to be an existing investor in the GP's main fund. Further, co-investing opportunities may be linked to whether or not the LP has a good relationship with the GP or is able to offer expertise in a particular field.

From the GP perspective,[7] co-investment can increase the size of the fund and, potentially, the level of diversification. Co-investing can allow a manager to make larger investments without dedicating too much of the main fund's capital to a single transaction, which is why co-investments can increase the level diversification within the main fund. Further, co-investing can provide financing that facilitates the transition from one partnership to a successor partnership when the GP has not been able to arrange sufficient financing yet to launch a main fund.

Finally, not all co-investment deals come without fees and carried interest. Some LPs co-invest by paying promote rather than carried interest. In the context of private equity, **promote** is a fee based on profits that is similar to carried interest but is typically associated with more specific duties such as the creation and marketing of a specific investment opportunity.

29.4.2 Investment Processes for Co-Investing

There is no set universal model for co-investments. The main differences between co-investing and direct investing include how the investments in the portfolio companies are sourced and selected (in the main fund the sponsor makes the decisions and in co-investing the LPs tend to be able to pick which investments they help fund). However, generally, opportunities are deals that the fund manager has prescreened, selected, structured, and priced. The following points summarize the co-investment processes:

- Portfolio strategies of LPs typically include a reserve of between 10% and 20% to be allocated to co-investments. Many investors do not appear to have a specific allocation and tend to do co-investments on an opportunistic basis, but a PE investment program requires a critical mass for being able to pursue co-investments.
- The sponsor of the main fund generally organizes the co-investment for the LPs. The GP usually needs a significant number of primary fund commitments to generate a meaningful co-investment deal flow. LPs need to express their interest in co-investments at the time of the fund commitment and reinforce this through regular follow-up calls and meetings.

- Importantly, the efficient execution of the process, be it turning a deal down quickly or working in parallel with and at the same pace as the GP, is critical to successful co-investing.
- Co-investing requires a different skill set than does main fund investing, as LPs need to have much greater insight into individual deals. Even if they are unable to form a view on the attractiveness of individual investments, they may still be attracted by potential savings on management fees and carried interest.

For smaller LPs, the fact that an occasionally too-high minimum amount is required for co-investments can cause problems. In such situations, the opportunity for co-investing may have to be passed up, especially if the amount required for co-investing is close to the amount the small institution originally committed to a fund. One way of overcoming this is to approach other investors and do the co-investment alongside them.

Co-investing can be viewed as a way to overcome some of the restrictions of the investing in the main limited partnership structure. However, co-investing is not a panacea and clearly is not for the risk-averse or inexperienced PE investor.

29.4.3 Evidence on the Performance of Co-Investments

Co-investing is often pitched to LPs as a way to obtain access to private equity with a known GP and to reduce costs when the LPs are waiting for other opportunities in which to deploy funds. However, when the GP offers lower cost access to one or more of their portfolio companies, it may create concerns on the part of the LP regarding the quality of the opportunity they are being offered. In fact, a study by Fang, Ivashina, and Lerner (2015) addresses this important issue in the private equity industry. These researchers find that direct investments have significantly outperformed co-investments and industry-standard benchmarks. Specifically, the study finds:

- The evidence of underperformance of co-investments may be associated with the higher risk of such deals.[8]
- Importantly, the evidence found a sharp contrast between the performance of "solo" deals, in which institutional investors source direct investments independently from GPs, and that of co-investment deals. This points to a potential conflict of interest and a potential principal–agent problem because GPs may selectively offer deals to their LPs.
- Crucially, however, the results of the study are based on deals in which LPs took no active role in sourcing opportunities and only co-invested in deals offered to them, apparently based on deal size. (The deals were nearly five times larger than the funds' average deals.)

That co-investments are viewed as being offered only by GPs to their LPs reflects a specific modus operandi that is not necessarily representative.[9] Practitioners point out that it is important that LPs generate their co-investment deal flows like any other direct investor would.[10] The PE market environment has a strong influence on the types of industries from which these co-investment opportunities come and on the timing of the flows. Co-investment opportunities emerge particularly in periods when deal flow for larger investments is good but fundraising is difficult. In this situation, and also when funds do not wish to be overexposed to one particularly large deal, GPs are likely to turn to their LPs and propose a co-investment.

29.4.4   Potential Advantages of Co-Investing

In addition to avoiding the double layer of management fees, co-investing potentially offers the LP a number of potential advantages:

- SUPERIOR RETURNS: Theoretically, co-investing offers enhanced returns by reducing fees and increasing exposure to portfolio companies selected by the LP for their potential upside.
- Targeted investment tool: Commitments to PE funds are a relatively blunt allocation tool. Co-investments are a tool for building a targeted allocation to specific investments. If an LP follows the policy of co-investment only in portfolio companies that are already profitable or that would reach profitability soon, this could, for example, mitigate the exposure to cash-burning start-ups. Also, it may be difficult to find funds that specifically target, say, eco-innovation, but it is very likely that a number of funds have one or another company active in this sector in their portfolios. Co-investing allows the LP to tilt the portfolio balance in a desired direction or fill specific target allocations in the LP's portfolio.
- Better management of portfolio diversification: Co-investments can mitigate an institutional portfolio of funds' overdiversification or overexposure. Co-investments provide flexibility to capitalize on industry-specific and country-specific opportunities as they arise. They may also be an answer to funds with liquidity management problems and can be a meaningful strategy with a first-time team, serving as a tool to assist fund managers in the execution of transactions. In the context of an overcommitment strategy, prospective co-investment opportunities allow an LP not to execute the option if the liquidity is insufficient to honor the resulting increase in capital calls. Moreover, it could be used for managing foreign exchange risks, as usual hedging products would be too uneconomical for PE funds, with their long lifetimes and volatile cash flows.
- Mitigating dilution: For investments in small funds, co-investments also improve downside protection, as they mitigate the dilution of a fund's shareholding when available resources are insufficient for follow-on investing. This can be attractive when funds lack sufficient capital for follow-on investment (particularly in a venture context), allowing them to boost their firepower on certain deals without resorting to collaboration with other GPs, which can potentially lead to conflicts and rivalry. However, if disputes on an investment arise, relationships with LPs and future fundraisings can be negatively affected.
- Dual level of review for investments: The institutional investor can leave the difficult work of deal sourcing and assessment to experienced industry experts. Even though LPs need to do some due diligence, they can save significant time, as much of the screening is done by fund managers, as is a large degree of the time-consuming task of monitoring.
- Improved monitoring: As an indirect benefit, a co-investment allows for improved monitoring of the funds and a further reduction of the information

asymmetry between fund managers and their investors. It can help LPs better understand the investment process and environment, allowing for better fund selections and reinvestment decisions. The information co-investors receive is quite important because it gives an idea about how the fund managers operate and often goes beyond the standard reporting LPs usually receive.

- Establishing relationships to invitation-only funds: For LPs who face problems getting access to top funds, co-investments form an important part of a strategy that helps to land slots in a handful of sought-after funds. Moreover, an LP can benefit from the investment skills of such funds even if not yet invested and get access to transactions of top-tier PE firms.
- Reduction of the J-curve effect: Co-investments, like secondaries, are viewed as leading to a reduction of the J-curve effect and improved capital deployment and returns. Smoothing the cash-flow J-curve (that is, the concentrations in outflows due to capital calls during the early years of an investment program) may make sense in some situations but will be difficult to achieve, as there is usually too little and too inconsistent quality deal flow to have a meaningful impact on sizable portfolios.

Importantly, co-investing conforms to the important characteristics of real options and can maximize a fund investment's upside by increasing the exposure to the best-performing portfolio companies. However, it is definitely not a guarantee for higher returns in the asset class and, in fact, is often seen as quite difficult to execute.

29.4.5 Potential Expected Disadvantages of Co-Investing

Indeed, there are also disadvantages to take into consideration when engaging in co-investments:

- Unbalanced portfolios: Because an LP's participation in co-investing may build up additional exposure to certain companies, industries, or geographies, risks can increase very specifically with regard to individual portfolio companies. If few and too large co-investments are undertaken, there is also the danger of holding an overly concentrated portfolio of directly held investments.
- Increased fiduciary risk: For investment decisions taken outside a formal partnership structure, there is exposure to fiduciary risk. If things go wrong at the investment level, LPs may be exposed to legal liabilities and reputational risks.
- Conflicts of interest: There is a wide consensus that investors should focus on committing to the very best funds irrespective of co-investing rights or opportunities. Moreover, co-investing can become a source of conflicts of interest between LP investors in the same main fund. Co-investing LPs are likely to give preference to their specific investments even if this is detrimental to the main fund's performance.
- Disagreements among LPs: Problems associated with failing co-investments can become complicated when one company with several co-investing LPs goes bankrupt, leading to disagreements between the parties involved. Also, fund managers may be inclined to spend more time on particular portfolio companies if they receive additional management fees or carried interest, or if the co-investing LP is of strategic importance for them.

- Allocation of Fees: Co-investing can increase the potentially serious issue of the allocation of expenses between the GP, the LPs of the main fund, and the co-investors. Fee allocation is receiving increasing attention as an issue tied to inherent conflicts of interest between the parties to private equity investments.

29.5 CASH COMMITMENTS AND ILLIQUIDITY

An important issue in private equity (and some other private investments such as private real estate) is the efficient management of cash. One reason for the importance of cash management is the uncertainty regarding the size and timing of cash outflows from the investor (e.g., capital calls) and cash flows to the investor (e.g., distributions). The second reason is the potentially large costs or difficulties in liquidating private investments to raise cash or quickly locating attractive private investments to deploy excess cash.

29.5.1 The Costs of Excess Liquidity

Private equity fund limited partners do not pay in all of their capital on the first day of an investment; rather, the money is drawn by the fund over time. Therefore, cash must be available to meet undrawn capital commitments that occur with uncertain size and timing.

The total return on private equity is typically based on all resources dedicated to private equity including cash. If a large part of the capital remains uninvested or parked in low-returning assets such as Treasury bills, the resulting drag on total return can be substantial. Therefore, liquidity management is one of the key performance drivers in private equity. It can be a difficult task to put money to work efficiently (i.e., carry minimal cash balances) while maintaining target allocations in the portfolio.

In theory, Treasury bills and other short-term low-risk investments in a competitive market have zero NPVs. Therefore, cash invested in money market opportunities theoretically should not generate opportunity costs to serve as a drag on total *risk-adjusted* return. However, in practice, private funds and institutional investors in private assets have substantial ongoing expenses (and limited leverage) that necessitates that funds allocated to private investments generate positive NPVs.

29.5.2 The Costs of Illiquidity

Effective liquidity risk management helps ensure the ability of a pension fund, endowment fund, or other institutional investor to meet its cash flow obligations, which may not be completely predictable, as they are affected by external market conditions. Low levels of liquidity increase the probability that a fund may be unable to meet a cash commitment.

As in the case of an ordinary loan, when an LP is unable to meet a capital call by the GP (i.e., the LP defaults on its commitments), the GP can restructure the relationship. In this situation, the LP may lose the paid-in capital or suffer other penalties, with the GP holding the paid-in capital as collateral. Default can also involve a reputational penalty as a defaulting investor might not be allowed by GPs to invest in other PE funds.

During the global financial crisis, insufficient liquidity caused some institutional investors to sell a portion of their illiquid assets at deep discounts in secondary markets, to delay the funding of important projects, and, in some cases, to borrow funds in the debt market during a period of extreme market stress.

29.5.3 Overcommitment Strategies

To keep a program permanently and fully invested in portfolio companies, an overcommitment strategy may need to be employed. An **overcommitment** is a pledge to invest more in funds than the investor has currently available as resources. The purpose is to increase private investments and avoid idle cash. In an **overcommitment strategy**, future anticipated distributions (or other anticipated cash inflows) are forecast as being available to honor the capital calls to new funds.

In cases in which distributions are insufficient, the LP is taking on commitment risk. **Commitment risk** describes the situation in which an LP may become a defaulting investor if the proceeds from exiting funds are not sufficient to pay the capital calls of newly committed funds. This can occur due to shortfalls in distributions from funds or to other factors such as exchange rate changes that have an adverse impact on the resources available to respond to capital calls.

29.5.4 The Challenge of Identifying Illiquidity and Managing Cash Flows

Funding risk, also referred to as default risk within the private equity industry, is the risk that an investor will not be able to meet capital commitments to a private equity fund in accordance with the terms of its obligation to do so. If this risk materializes, an investor can lose the full investment, including all paid-in capital, which is why it is of paramount importance for investors to manage their cash flows to meet their funding obligations effectively. The financial crisis in 2008 highlighted the importance of managing funding risk.

Funding risk can be measured through a funding test or through cash flow models that take extreme cases into account. The funding test analyzes the undrawn commitments in relation to the resources available for commitments. Alternatively, a cash flow model provides the investor with a simulation of the expected capital calls and distributions in the future. Investors can reduce the funding risk by assessing their future commitment plan with cash flow simulations and cautious planning.

29.5.5 Four Benefits of Private Equity Cash Flow Models

Modeling the cash flows of private equity investments (or other private investments) is an important part of the liquidity management process and potentially allows one to do the following:

1. Improve investment returns for the undrawn capital.
2. Increase the profit generated by the private equity allocation through overcommitment.
3. Calculate an economic value when a discount rate is available.

4. Monitor the cash flows and risk–return profiles of a portfolio of private equity funds.

Achieving a high total return for the overall investment program is a complex task that requires not only technical skills, particularly in quantitative modeling and financial engineering, but also a high degree of judgment and management discipline. There is no quick fix for this, and only a disciplined approach can deliver small improvements that eventually add up to a significant impact. As a result, it is likely to take many years before an investment program is able to reach sustainable levels of high total return and a stable long-term allocation.

29.5.6   The Overcommitment Ratio

An overcommitment ratio is the ratio of total commitments to resources available for commitment for a private equity investor as indicated in Equation 29.1.

Overcommitment Ratio =

Total Commitments/Resources Available for Commitments   (29.1)

APPLICATION 29.5.6

Consider an investor with a new $200 million allocation to private equity that decides to commit to $280 million of new private equity investments over the next 4 years in order to be fully invested, given the potential for time lags and undrawn capital. The overcommitment ratio would be 1.40, or 140%, found as $280 million/$200 million. Note that the ratio is not annualized.

A key cause of liquidity problems occurs when an investor follows an overly aggressive overcommitment strategy. Overcommitment ratios of less than 100% suggest an inefficient use of resources; 125% to 140% ratios have been documented. Investors seek to deploy an overcommitment strategy that strikes a balance between being substantially underexposed to their strategic allocation to the asset class and being unable to fund capital calls, as discussed in the next section.

29.5.7   The Optimal Overcommitment Ratio

The **optimal overcommitment ratio** is the level of the overcommitment ratio that minimizes the sum of two discounted expected costs: (1) the opportunity cost of idle capital from excess liquidity; and (2) the costs of adverse events from inadequate liquidity including lost investment opportunities and forced liquidations. The opportunity costs of idle capital reflect the lower risk-adjusted return available to excess liquidity relative to the risk-adjusted returns expected from long-term private investments. The potential direct costs of adverse events include both the potential inability to take on attractive projects due to lack of liquidity and the potential losses from being forced to liquidate an existing investment at unattractive prices (due to an inability to fund capital calls or to generate cash for other purposes such as a spending rate).

29.5.8 Commitments, the Global Financial Crisis, and Liquidity

During the 2008 crisis, it became very difficult for managers to exit investments, as private equity funds could not float initial public offerings and real estate funds could not sell properties. As a result, distributions were much slower than expected. When distributions slowed and capital calls continued, some endowments and foundations found it challenging to meet their commitments, as they had previously assumed that the pace of distributions would be sufficient to fund future capital calls.

In the aftermath of the 2008 financial crisis, many pension funds and endowments have begun to reevaluate their asset allocation policies and, in the process, are paying increased attention to their risk and liquidity management practices. The strategy depends on estimating cash flows within the investor's organization (e.g., estimating the annual spending rate) as well as cash flows to and from investments, especially the size and timing of capital calls and exits.

29.6   THE SECONDARY MARKET FOR PE PARTNERSHIPS

An important issue in private equity fund investing is the extent to which the secondary market in PE partnerships offers opportunities to manage private equity exposures either through buying existing interests in desirable funds or liquidating positions in existing funds that are no longer attractive to the investor. This section details the secondary market for PE partnerships.

Secondary private equity market transactions refer to the buying and selling of pre-existing limited partnership interests in private equity and other alternative investment funds. Kießlich (2004) suggests that the first secondary PE transaction took place in 1979, with David Carr buying Thomas J. Watson's stake in a venture capital fund when Watson had to exit after being appointed the new ambassador to the Soviet Union.

The genesis of the secondary *market* is said to date back to the infamous Black Monday in October 1987 and to the world economic crisis of the early 1990s. These two events produced a large need for liquidity among many financial institutions, especially those with illiquid assets such as private equity, which in turn created a new market for secondary interests in PE funds or companies. Since then, a sizable secondary market has emerged, which allows investors to sell their interests in limited partnerships in order to generate liquidity or pursue strategic objectives or to buy interests in order to manage exposures.

29.6.1 Secondary PE Market Development

The development of a secondary market has usually been portrayed as a market response to the illiquidity of fund investments that constrains the universe of investors to those with appropriate profiles. Often intermediated by specialized investment banks, secondary stakes are bought by investors who are primarily attracted by one or more of three advantages. The potential **advantages of secondary market PE purchases** are: (1) the potential discount at which a transaction may take place; (2) the shorter period during which the invested capital is locked in and management fees are paid; and (3) the portfolio diversification properties of secondaries.

Historically, the secondary market has been largely driven by the sale of interests in PE funds, with LPs being forced to exit prematurely. Initially, the secondary market was viewed by many as a market of last resort for those desperate to liquidate PE positions. A number of recent developments have led to changes in this perception:

- Large institutions regularly exit from private equity as part of an overall portfolio management and reallocation strategy.
- Some LPs entering the PE market are interested in secondary transactions as a means of getting *exposure to PE assets quickly* without having to commit capital over a period of 10 to 12 years, as is typical for primary fund investors. Given that it normally takes several years for a fund to reach the cash flow breakeven point, a secondary acquisition of a 4-year-old fund reduces this period significantly and potentially even eliminates it.
- Such LPs also seek a *reduction of risks* by using secondary transactions in order to achieve a wider and more balanced vintage-year spread.
- While the secondaries' total value to paid-in (TVPI) ratios are generally lower due to their shorter life, the *strong IRR performance* has significantly contributed to the rising amount of commitments to secondary funds.
- The different dynamic (i.e., less early loss recognition) in the secondary market can be employed as a means to *counteract the J-curve effect* of primary fund investments.
- There is increasing experience in conducting secondary transactions that are considered successful by buyers as well as sellers.
- Respected players, such as US university endowments and pension funds, are routinely investing in secondary funds-of-funds specialists.

Today, investing in secondary transactions has become an accepted investment strategy and an active portfolio management tool in its own right, and the market has grown substantially in size and maturity. Additionally, in recent years an active market for the sale of directly held portfolio companies has emerged. Here, it is the GPs who want or are under pressure to sell, mainly as their fund is approaching the end of its contractual lifetime. In such **synthetic secondaries,** portfolio companies are packaged up and sold to another manager, usually with the backing of a secondary fund specialist. In fact, dedicated secondary direct strategies have only recently become recognized as independent strategies requiring highly specialized fund managers. This market is attractive due to its inefficiencies, but such opportunities are hard to value, and the due diligence is complex.

29.6.2 PE Secondary Market Size

The secondary market began to take off following the burst of the dot-com bubble. At that time, institutions and particularly individual investors who had previously enthusiastically committed to VC funds felt the liquidity squeeze acutely and often could not afford to meet further capital calls.

It is estimated that the global volume of secondary transactions increased tenfold in the first decade of the twenty-first century. This market has grown significantly, mirroring the substantial expansion in the primary fundraising market in private equity. Secondaries were probably about 10% of the total PE market in 2005. It is important to emphasize that the total supply was significantly larger, however.

Data by Greenhill (2019) show a steady increase in the volume of transactions in the secondary market from $25 billion in 2011 to $74 billion in 2018. Also, as shown in Exhibit 29.1, which displays secondary market pricing history expressed as average high bids as a percentage of NAV, the secondary transactions have been taking place at increasingly smaller discounts to NAV in recent years. These transactions took place at discounts of about 40% in 2009, about 15% in 2010–12, and often less than 10% since 2014. This points out that the secondary market is no longer driven entirely by the desire of LPs to sell their positions because of liquidity needs.

Despite its increasing importance and growth in the volume of transactions, the secondary market has remained highly opaque. Although various data vendors tried to build specific Internet platforms for secondary transactions, information about market conditions is often spurious, and little is known about prices at which transactions finally settle. Historically, around 3% to 5% of outstanding LP exposure comes to market, which represents the pool from which potential buyers can fish. In the end, less than 2% of the outstanding exposure, calculated as the sum of NAV and unfunded commitments, is actually traded each year.[11]

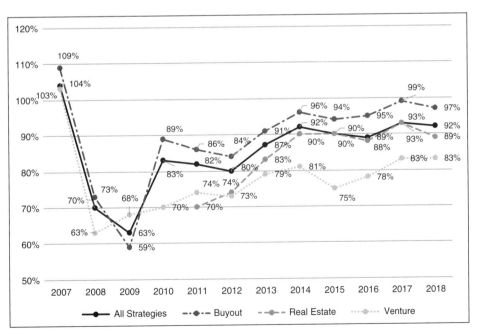

EXHIBIT 29.1 Evolution of Average Secondary Marketing Pricing
Source: Greenhill (2019).

29.6.3   PE Buyer Motivations

On the buy side, the secondary market has historically been dominated by dedicated secondary funds and other funds of funds. Apart from the portfolio management considerations mentioned previously, the obvious reasons why investors want to buy relate mainly to the potential attractiveness of secondary stakes.

- To begin with, secondaries can still be distressed sales that take place at a significant discount to the most recent NAV. Under certain market conditions, stakes in funds are offered by LPs who are generally in need of liquidity or, specifically related to their PE activities, face a nontrivial risk of default on future capital calls from fund managers. Such assets can be a bargain for those who have at their disposal a sufficient degree of liquidity to meet the unfunded commitments of the fund investments.
- An important advantage of secondary investments is that they are subject to less uncertainty when compared with commitments to primary funds, which represent blind pools of capital. At the time of making a commitment, primary investors do not know how their capital will eventually be deployed by the fund—apart from the broad investment guidelines specified in the limited partnership agreement. By the time a secondary transaction takes place, a significant share of the fund's capital has already been invested in portfolio companies. Prospective buyers can analyze them in detail and have indicators that help distinguish between companies that developed according to plan and those that did not.[12]

In recent years, a growing number of nontraditional buyers have entered the market, including pension funds, insurance companies, endowments, foundations, family offices, sovereign wealth funds, and hedge funds.

29.6.4   PE Seller Motivations

The reasons why LPs decide to dispose of their holdings on the secondary market are diverse. Broadly speaking, one may differentiate between sales that are motivated primarily by liquidity constraints and those that are related to the strategic repositioning of an investor's portfolio. As far as liquidity-motivated sales are concerned, the desire to transfer stakes in a limited partnership is usually cyclical, in line with macroeconomic developments. Understanding these different reasons is important for assessing the informational content of transaction prices in the secondary market.

- Sellers may be motivated by active portfolio management considerations. As the secondary market has matured, it has been increasingly used strategically. Sell-side LPs may decide to divest their entire stake in a particular fund or even offer their entire portfolio of fund investments. Others, however, may decide to sell only a certain share of their stake in a partnership, signaling their continued confidence in the fund manager.
- Sometimes LPs are dissatisfied with the performance of a fund or a portfolio of funds and lose confidence in a management team. Selling their stakes in such funds can generate capital that can be redeployed into new opportunities.

- Conversely, an LP may want to lock in returns in situations in which the fund manager is not likely to materially increase the performance of the underlying portfolio companies during the remainder of the lifetime of the fund.
- Another strategic reason to sell may lie in an unintended overexposure to private equity. This so-called **denominator effect** usually arises in periods of financial stress, when prices of marketable instruments decline much faster than valuations of illiquid investments, resulting in a higher-than-targeted share of the latter.

Despite such good reasons for an LP to sell, this raises the question of whether an early exit is against the main purpose of private equity, namely to be patient until the "pearls" emerge. Generally, institutions are justifiably reluctant to sell.[13] Although the existing investor may occasionally be under pressure to exit a fund, from an economic point of view the case for selling is far from clear under normal circumstances and raises the question of sourcing and proper pricing of secondary transactions.

29.6.5 The Secondary Market PE Investment Process

Secondary transactions can be difficult to access and tend to be open only to well-connected investors who are trusted to efficiently assess PE assets, safeguard confidential information, and execute the transaction with minimal fuss. The secondary sales process can be highly complex and time-consuming.

29.6.6 Sourcing PE Secondary Opportunities

While transactions involving individual funds or small portfolios are usually negotiated bilaterally, intermediated auctions have become increasingly common for larger and more complex transactions. This process is facilitated by financial intermediaries, who are involved in the majority of deals in the secondary market and ensure that the sales process is competitive. Used mainly by sellers, intermediaries help identify buyers and structure offerings of fund interests. Financial intermediaries are either specialized secondary advisers or placement agents, generally charging a transaction fee between 1% and 2% of the value of the transaction.

Typically, a number of LPs are contacted to sound out their potential interest. In cases in which a large portfolio is being sold, intermediaries may divide it into subsets to improve the chances of finding interested buyers. LPs make bids in a managed auction for the particular stakes they want to purchase; these decisions are based on confidential information the intermediary provides about the funds' holdings and their valuation. Many secondary auctions involve two rounds.

After a first round of bidding, the seller and the intermediary invite a subgroup of potential buyers to participate in the second round. During this round, interested buyers have the opportunity to revise their bids in light of new information they might have acquired in the process. While the set of information the intermediary provides is the same for all interested buyers, large LPs with diversified portfolios often have an important competitive advantage in that they have superior proprietary information about the fund manager, the manager's previous track record, and the quality of the current investments.

29.6.7   Valuing Secondary PE Stakes

Prices in the secondary market are generally expressed in terms of discounts or premiums relative to a fund's NAV. However, differences in discounts to NAV across funds may be a misleading indicator of valuation. In other words, the NAV reported by the GP may be of limited relevance to the determination of a fair value for the fund. Valuations of funds can be considered to be fair only if they are equal to the risk-adjusted present value of the fund's overall expected cash flows, which include not only those that are related to the investments a fund has already made but also future cash flows that are associated with the undrawn commitments the buyer needs to fund.

The secondary value is estimated by projecting future cash flows and discounting the expected future cash flows on a rate based on the buyer's expectations about the asset's performance:

$$P_0 = \sum_{t=0}^{T} \frac{CF_t}{(1 + IRR_{Buyer})^t} \qquad (29.2)$$

with P_0 denoting the secondary value as estimated by prospective buyer, CF_t the fund's expected cash flow at time t, T the fund's anticipated maturity, and IRR_{Buyer} the buyer's required or expected IRR. This value reflects the expected cash flows from both funded and unfunded commitments and thus will generally be different from the NAV reported by the GP; this is because the accounting impact is usually the reference point for the seller. The discount can be expressed as follows:

$$Discount_t = \frac{NAV_t - P_t}{NAV_t} \qquad (29.3)$$

APPLICATION 29.6.7

A prospective secondary-market private equity investor forecasts a total of five equal cash flows from a fund of $1 million per year over the next 5 years (i.e., years 1–5). The buyer's required internal rate of return (IRR) is 18%. The fund's current net asset value (NAV) is $3.5 million. What is the fund's estimated discount?

The present value of the cash flow stream at 18% is $3.127 million using Equation 29.2. The discount using Equation 29.3 is [(3.500 − 3.127)/3.500)], which equals 10.7%.

The cash flow projection needs to take a number of factors into account: in particular, projected future capital calls, the expected exit values, exit timing for current portfolio investments, and the return on future investments made using such drawdowns. **Exit value** refers to the price that the fund can receive when portfolio companies are sold through initial public offerings (IPOs) or strategic sales. Exit timing refers to the period during which portfolio companies are expected to be sold and exit values are realized. This analysis is generally based on a combination of GP guidance, investor insight, and market analysis. All public investments inside the fund are valued using a mark-to-market analysis, taking potential lockups into consideration that may suggest that the market prices be discounted.

The resulting projected gross cash flows are then run through the partnership's legal structure, taking future management fees and the distribution waterfall into account to arrive at a net cash flow stream for the fund. Once the projected net cash flows are determined, the present value is calculated by discounting the net cash flows at an appropriate discount rate. This target rate varies across market segments, with mezzanine funds usually having a lower target rate than buyout funds, which in turn have a lower target rate than VC funds, reflecting their specific risk characteristics.

Secondary market prices are only of limited use as benchmarks for fair market value, as they are not observable. Transactions are confidential, and the final settlement price is generally known to only the buyer and the seller (and the intermediary, to the extent that a transaction has been facilitated by a specialist agent). The secondary market price reflects current market conditions for those who participate in the market as either sellers or buyers but reveals little about the underlying value of the portfolio, which is held until maturity.

Exhibit 29.1 displays pricing levels based on secondary-market pricing historical data. First, note that the secondary prices are almost always discounted relative to NAV. Second, the discounts reached their highest values during the global financial crisis. Third, the average discounts for buyout funds are typically smaller than those of venture capital funds. This can be explained by the fact that portfolio companies of venture capital funds are more difficult to value, and therefore there is greater uncertainty regarding their NAVs.

29.6.8 Limitations of the PE Secondary Market

Undoubtedly, the secondary market would not have reached its current level of significance if it had not brought about important advantages for both sellers and buyers of interests in limited partnerships. However, as the secondary market has not materially altered the fundamental characteristics of fund investments, the challenges investors face in measuring and managing the particular risks that come with commitments to limited partnerships remain essentially unchanged. As significant as the development of the secondary market may be for constructing efficient portfolios, it should not be perceived as a game changer in terms of risk management in illiquid investments.

Although the secondary market has expanded rapidly in recent years, it has remained small relative to the primary market, with only a few percent of primary commitments being transacted in the secondary market. Importantly, the secondary market, just like other financial markets, may dry up precisely at the time when it is needed most. The year 2009 provides a warning. Although a maximum amount of supply came to market, the actual transaction volume collapsed, as sellers were not prepared to accept discounts that were at times 60% or higher unless they were under exceptional pressure to create liquidity.

NOTES

1. See Anderson (2016).
2. Ibid.
3. See Greene and Rigdon (2016).
4. Ibid.
5. Ibid.
6. Ibid.

7. Ibid.

8. See Fang et al. (2015).

9. Ibid.

10. Ibid.

11. See Cornelius et al. (2013).

12. Note, however, that this advantage can be significantly reduced, and even eliminated, in early secondary transactions. Sometimes called purchased primaries, such transactions take place at a very early stage of the fund. In extreme cases, the buyer agrees to buy the seller's commitment at a time when the fund has not yet made any acquisitions.

13. For example, according to Private Equity International (2006), for CalPERS, conducting a sale is not an option.

REFERENCES

Anderson, G. 2016. "Investor Side Letters," in Tom Alabaster, *Global Investment Funds: A Practical Guide to Structuring, Raising and Managing Funds*. Woking: Globe Law & Business.

Cornelius, P., C. Diller, D. Guennoc, and T. Meyer. 2013. *Mastering Illiquidity: Risk Management for Portfolios of Limited Partnership Funds*. Chichester: John Wiley & Sons.

Fang, L., V. Ivashina, and J. Lerner. 2015. "The Disintermediation of Financial Markets: Direct Investing in Private Equity." *Journal of Financial Economics* 116 (1): 160–78, April 2015.

Greene, D. and A. Rigdon, 2016. "Private Equity Co-Investment," in Tom Alabaster, *Global Investment Funds: A Practical Guide to Structuring, Raising and Managing Funds*, Globe Law & Business Ltd.

Greenhill. 2019. Global Secondary Market Trends & Outlook for 2018. White Paper. https://www.greenhill.com/en/content/greenhill%E2%80%99s-secondary-market-analysis-another-record-transaction-volume.

Private Equity International. 2006. "Orphans in the Portfolio." *Private Equity International*, May.

CHAPTER 30

The Risk and Performance of Private and Listed Assets

This chapter focuses on one of the most crucial issues of asset allocation in general and access in particular: the extent, if any, to which illiquid private investments tend to provide higher expected returns (adjusted for market risks) than listed investments. Presumably, the justification for higher long-term returns in private structures is that investors are compensated for the risk of illiquidity in the form of an expected premium return. If so, investors such as those endowments to whom exposure to at least some illiquidity is not a large problem should invest in private structures to receive liquidity premiums (assuming that there are not enough investors willing to hold illiquid assets if there is no premium).

Any higher returns to private equity investors would require some advantage to private structures, such as enabling higher risk-adjusted returns on assets. Perhaps private structures could generate higher risk-adjusted returns because of advantages discussed in Chapter 29, including potentially lower organizational costs, greater managerial flexibility, lower financing costs, better management, and/or less need to maintain liquidity at the fund level. However, managers may demand some or all enhanced returns through private structures by levying higher fees.

This chapter examines evidence on the relative risks and performance of private and listed assets, including private real estate and private equity.

30.1 EVIDENCE ON AN ILLIQUIDITY PREMIUM FROM LISTED ASSETS

In the context of a position in an asset or a portfolio of assets, **asset illiquidity** refers to the difficulty of closing a position on a timely basis at a price that is minimally affected by the urgency with which the position is closed. A highly illiquid position can usually be closed quickly, but typically at an unfavorable price from the perspective of an urgent trader.

The **illiquidity of assets** can be viewed in two primary ways: the amount of *time* required to close a position at a price that is not affected by matters of urgency; or the amount of lost *value* from closing a position with urgency rather than with patience.

30.1.1 A Factor-Pricing-Based Explanation for an Illiquidity Premium

The key issue is whether illiquid assets offer higher returns for investors willing to bear the risks of illiquidity. The importance of illiquidity is clear in the context of return factors. If illiquid securities have bid-asked spreads that rise and/or prices that drop during periods of market turmoil (especially during bear markets) then illiquid securities generate relatively low returns in "bad times" and relatively high returns in "good times." This is exactly the condition (detailed in Chapter 8) under which investors should demand a risk premium (in the form of higher expected returns) for holding less liquid securities.

30.1.2 Empirical Evidence of an Illiquidity Premium in US Treasuries

Discussion of an illiquidity premium (enhanced expected return) for holding illiquid positions is not limited to the comparison of private and listed positions. Various securities markets often list securities with a spectrum of liquidity. For example, the US Treasury market contains recently issued bills, notes, and bonds that are termed "on-the-run" issues. An **on-the-run issue** is the most recently issued Treasury security or other asset that is regularly issued with a given maturity. For example, the US Treasury offers bills, notes, and bonds on a weekly or quarterly or other basis, such as a 13-week bill or a 10-year note. Starting with the time that a security (e.g., a 10-year Treasury note) is issued, that security is "on-the-run" until another security with the same original maturity is issued (e.g., a new 10-year Treasury note). In other words, each on-the-run issue becomes off-the-run when a newer security is issued, with the newer security becoming the new on-the-run issue.

When a security is recently issued, many of the purchasers of the on-the-run security (especially those who participated in the initial auction of the security) are quite willing to trade the security and a relatively high level of trading takes place that generally diminishes through time as more and more of the issue becomes held by long-term investors. When the security becomes off-the-run, its trading level typically drops substantially.

The higher level of trading of on-the-run issues has been generally associated with smaller bid-asked spreads and higher prices (i.e., lower yields) compared to off-the-run issues. The reason is quite simple: everything else being equal, investors should prefer the higher trading volumes and lower spreads of the on-the-run issues.

Pasquariello and Vega (2009)[1] review evidence that "most recently issued (i.e., on-the-run, new, or benchmark) government bonds of a certain maturity are generally more expensive and liquid than previously issued (i.e., off-the-run or old) bonds maturing on similar dates." They find evidence that liquidity differentials among Treasuries are economically significant and increase when "the dispersion of beliefs across informed traders is high." So, even in one of the world's most liquid and homogeneous markets (in terms of credit risk), higher returns can be earned by bearing slightly increased illiquidity risk.

30.1.3 Empirical Evidence of an Illiquidity Premium in US Equities

Pastor and Stambaugh (2003)[2] provide empirical evidence that liquidity risk is related to higher expected stock returns using merely the differences in liquidity among publicly-traded equities. More recently, Ben-Rephael, Kadan and Wohl[3] analyze historical returns in US equities and conclude that "Stock liquidity has improved over the recent four decades... accompanied by a dramatic increase in trading activity," that "the characteristic liquidity premium of U.S. stocks has significantly declined over the past four decades," and that illiquidity in recent years "is significantly priced only for the smallest common stocks."

Ahimud, Hameeb, Kang, and Zhang[4] examined illiquidity premiums in equities in 45 global markets and concluded that: "the average illiquidity return premium across countries is positive and significant, after controlling for other pricing factors" and that "a commonality exists across countries in the illiquidity return premium."

Given the relatively small differences in liquidity between the listed securities analyzed in the above discussions and viewing the conclusions of these studies, a reasonable inference would be that classes of alternative investments with high levels of illiquidity (e.g., private equity partnerships) may need to be priced to offer substantially higher long-term returns (see Khandani and Lo's 2009 analysis[5] of illiquidity premia).

30.2 PRIVATE VERSUS LISTED REAL PERFORMANCE: THE CASE OF REAL ESTATE

Due especially to the availability of excellent long-term data, real estate markets in the US serve as a good place to examine the relative performance of similar real estate assets accessed through private versus listed structures. The evidence on the general performance of public listed REITs relative to that of private real estate stands in stark contrast to the proposition that private investments generate higher average returns than their public counterparts due to a premium for bearing the illiquidity of private assets.

30.2.1 The Case Against Unlisted Real Estate Pools based on Historical Performance

Empirical analysis of private real estate fund performance is somewhat easy relative to analysis of private equity because underlying real estate assets exhibit generally lower cross-sectional dispersion (compared to venture capital portfolio companies) especially when divided into core properties, value-added properties, and opportunistic properties. However, comparison of public and private real estate returns is somewhat complicated by two issues: (1) REITs and private real estate may have various levels of leverage; and (2) performance of unlisted real estate returns is not generally based on market prices.

Cambridge Associates compares the returns on the FTSE® NAREIT All Equity Index and NCREIF Property Index in the "Real Estate Index and Selected Benchmark Statistics December 31, 2017"[6] report. That analysis indicates that the annualized 25-year returns of public real estate (10.89%) exceeded that of private properties (8.39%) by 2.5%. The 2.5% difference is roughly equal to the amount by which the annualized total fees of private real estate structures are generally believed to exceed the fees of REITs (i.e., listed real estate structures). However, return differentials may be partly or fully attributable to leverage differences or differences in risk of the underlying real estate portfolios.

30.2.2 Listing: Increased Risk or the Appearance of Increased Risk?

The NCREIF Property Index (NPI) of private properties and the NAREIT Index of listed REITs indicated tremendous divergence in reported performance in 2008 and 2009 as discussed in Chapter 18. There are two primary competing explanations for this divergence in performance:

1. The REIT Index's substantial price decline followed by a near 100% price increase accurately represents the true changes in the values of real estate properties adjusted for the effects of leverage. The NPI's delayed and muted response was due to the use of appraisals, which mute the true fluctuations.
2. The REIT Index's returns and their high volatility emanate from a contagion effect of public equity markets (i.e., from the volatility in the US stock market driven by stress) which is a source of risk uncorrelated with the underlying economic fundamentals of real estate. The low volatility of the NPI's returns could then be viewed as being a response that more accurately reflects the realities of the real estate market and the actual values at which property transactions were occurring.

In the first explanation, listed REIT prices are informationally efficient. In the second explanation, listed REIT prices can diverge enormously from reflecting true real estate values due to stress in the public equity markets. There is substantial disagreement on which of these explanations is more accurate. The problem with resolving whether publicly-traded real estate values are highly correlated with private real estate values is that, unlike with publicly-traded securities, values of private property cannot be observed unless they are traded frequently.

Empirical efforts to resolve the issue have not generated a definitive conclusion. However, Fisher et al. (2003) empirically analyzed publicly-traded real estate versus appraised private properties and concluded that "the general pattern of price discovery seems to involve the NAREIT Index typically moving first . . . followed last by the appraisal-based NCREIF Index. The total time lag between NAREIT and NCREIF can be several years, as measured by the timing of the major cycle turning points."

The evidence that REIT valuation and private real estate valuation diverge substantially may indicate that the real estate investment market is segmented. Many institutions, such as endowments, may have limited need for liquidity throughout their entire portfolios and may view their investments with longer-term horizons. These investors may be drawn to private real estate investments in the belief that these investments have relatively low risk (given their steady cash flows and relatively low dispersion in values at the longer-term horizon point at which the investment might be liquidated). Such institutions may view listed REITs as riskier due to their volatile market prices.

Investors with shorter-term horizons and a higher need for liquidity may perceive listed REITs as providing the liquidity they desire with low transaction costs. These shorter-term investors may perceive private real estate as having just as much risk or higher risk than REITs because of the steep price discounts and higher transaction costs that they may be forced to bear in liquidating private real estate during periods of stress. Within this market segmentation view, both public and private real estate are accurately priced for their respective clienteles. Barriers to arbitrage activity, such as transaction costs and short-selling limitations, allow the valuations to diverge on a short-term basis.

30.2.3 The Case Against Unlisted Real Estate Pools Based on Risk-Adjusted Performance

Numerous studies explicitly adjust for the leverage differentials between listed REITs and private real estate funds (including unlisted but publicly-registered REITs). Further, many of those studies control for or adjust for differences in the risks of the underlying assets. For example, private real estate funds often include more aggressive types of properties such as core-plus, value-added, or even opportunistic.

Case[7] provides extensive analysis of the relative performance of real estate accessed through private funds and through listed funds (listed REITs). In addition to reporting the dismal performance of private real estate relative to listed REITs from his own analysis of the data, Case asserts that "Every academic study ever conducted has found that public real estate outperformed private real estate." Case summarizes numerical evidence from nine such published studies to support his characterization of the evidence.

In summary, evidence from the US real estate market indicates that returns from private structures on a risk-adjusted basis do not offer an illiquidity premium. In fact, historical risk-adjusted real estate returns using private real estate funds are likely to be lower than returns on listed real estate funds (i.e., listed REITs) due, presumably, to the relatively higher fees of private real estate structures, especially fees associated with initial offerings. Both annual fees and initial offering fees of nonlisted real estate pools are discussed in Chapter 28. Note that private structures generally have limited lives during which to earn back large initial expenses, while listed REITs tend to have lower initial offering expenses and do not have term limits. The fee differential would require private real estate funds to generate large gross returns over relatively short terms, which may explain the lower use of core real estate properties in private funds than in most listed REITs.

30.3 CHALLENGES WITH THE PME METHOD TO EVALUATING PRIVATE ASSET PERFORMANCE

The previous section analyzed the relative performance of listed and private real estate pools. Real estate fund performance is somewhat simplified by the homogeneity of the cash flow patterns generated by the underlying assets. Private equity, such as venture capital and leveraged buyouts, tends to offer cash flows that vary markedly across investments in terms of timing, size, and even sign. The substantially varied cash flow patterns and the potential for fund managers to manipulate the size and timing of cash flows raise serious issues with respect to evaluation of performance. The challenges emanate from the use of cash-flow-weighted methods such as IRR (internal rate of return) and the PME (public market equivalent) method, which in turn emanate from the lack of competitive market prices for the private securities. The PME method was introduced in Level I of the CAIA curriculum as a premier method of evaluating private equity fund performance. The PME method is further explained in Chapter 17 of this book. This section discusses many of the challenges with the PME method. Throughout the sections that follow the PME method is discussed based on IRR as the metric (i.e., based on the LN PME method as detailed in Chapter 17).

30.3.1 The Interim Internal Rate of Return (IIRR) and Multiple Solutions

Interim IRRs and final IRRs are commonly used in analysis of returns from private structures. The Interim Internal Rate of Return (IIRR) uses the NAV prior to the completion of an investment in place of final distributions and is the discount rate that makes the present value of the distributions, the contributions, and the NAV equal to zero. More formally, the IIRR is found by solving the following equation:

$$\sum_{t=0}^{T} \frac{D_t}{(1 + IIRR_T)^t} - \sum_{t=0}^{T} \frac{C_t}{(1 + IIRR_T)^t} + \frac{NAV_T}{(1 + IIRR_T)^T} = 0 \qquad (30.1)$$

As with other IRR computations, the IIRR for a PE fund (and especially IRRs based on the PME method) can have multiple solutions, although this is rare in practice. As detailed in Level I of the CAIA curriculum, the number of solutions to an IRR problem can be up to and including the number of sign changes in the cash flows through time. Ordinarily, a PE fund would have capital calls (negative flows to the investor) followed only by distributions (positive flows to the investors) and therefore would have no more than one IRR. However, the cash flows of the PME method will tend to have two sign changes in its cash flow stream in any scenario in which the PE fund outperformed the public market on a cash-weighted basis (see Chapter 17). The issue of multiple IRRs is very problematic since there is no simple way of concluding that one of the IRRs is useful and one of them should be ignored.

Exhibit 30.1 illustrates the use of the concepts just presented with two simplified hypothetical cash flow streams. Suppose that Exhibit 30.1 represents the listed values for distributions, contributions, and NAVs for two PE funds (named PE Fund 1 and PE Fund 2) that belong to the vintage-year 2020 buyout funds.

Positive numbers correspond to years in which investors received net distributions, negative numbers correspond to years in which investors made net contributions, and the figures for 2026 correspond to the NAVs of each of the two funds at the end of that year.

Note that because the final cash flow (in Year 2026) is a NAV, any IRR computations become IIRRs. Note also that one would need to compare these IIRRs to the discount rates or the required rates of return applicable to each PE fund in order to determine whether these IIRRs, in retrospect, were attractive (i.e., were greater than the required minimum returns).

EXHIBIT 30.1 Simulated Distribution of Two Funds (€ million), 2026 values are NAVs

	2020	2021	2022	2023	2024	2025	2026
PE Fund 1	−200	−800	200	−2,000	−600	2,000	3,500
PE Fund 2	−1,500	−1,500	−800	−200	500	1,500	5,000

Solving Equation 30.1 using a financial calculator or Excel (function IRR or XIRR) generates an IIRR of 12.53% for PE Fund 2 in Exhibit 30.1. Using a standard financial calculator, the cash flows are entered for each time period, and the calculator performs the trial-and-error search when the IRR key is selected and the compute key is pressed.

APPLICATION 30.3.1

What is the IIRR of PE Fund 1 in Exhibit 30.1?

As just noted, a solution may be found using a financial calculator by entering the cash flows (and NAV if applicable) and computing IRR following the same procedure as for PE Fund 2. Computation for PE Fund 1 indicates an IIRR of 16.53%, which is more profitable than PE Fund 2 by 4%. However, it can be essential to take into account that the cash flows of PE Fund 1 from left to right have three sign changes. Therefore, there can be up to three different IIRRs that solve for Equation 30.1 in the case of PE Fund 1. In cases of IIRR computations with multiple sign changes, none of the solutions can be trusted.

30.3.2 The IRRs under the PME Method Cannot be Calculated in Some Cases

Like the IRR (discussed in detail in Level I of the CAIA curriculum) and the IIRR, the PME method does not always have an IRR solution. As in the case of IRR, numerous methods have been developed to address this unlikely shortcoming.

To see the problem, consider the cash flows of a private investment and the hypothetical market accumulation cash flows in Exhibit 30.2. Note that the market index's return is zero in most periods in order to simplify the arithmetic.

The IRR of the "PE Fund Flows" in Exhibit 30.2 is equal to zero since the sum of the contributions (capital calls) equals the sum of the distributions. Note that the PME method has cash flows ("Hypothetical Cash Flows") that have two sign changes indicating that there could be up to two IRRs. However, in this case, the hypothetical cash flows in the last line of Exhibit 30.2 have no solution for IRR since the NPV is negative over all discount rates. The hypothetical investment in the market lost money when the market plummeted by 50%. Viewing the last line of Exhibit 30.2 as an NPV problem can be used to show that there is no discount rate which sets NPV

EXHIBIT 30.2 PME Analysis for a PE Fund with Problematic Cash Flows

Period	0	1	2	3	4	5	6
PE Fund Flows	−100	−50	0	50	50	0	50
Market Index	100	100	50	50	50	50	50
Market Return	n.a.	0	−0.50	0	0	0	0
Hyp Mkt Acc	100	150	75	25	−25	−25	−75
Hyp Cash Flows	−100	−50	0	50	50	0	−25

equal to zero and therefore there is no IRR for the PME-based cash flows. Other metrics of performance may be used to analyze the PME-based cash flows such as profitability index, given a discount rate.

30.3.3 IRR Does not Adjust for Scale and Timing

The well-known problems with IRR include the fact that the IRR does not indicate the effect of the size of an investment nor the longevity of the project on wealth (e.g., net present value). Since the PME method for generating cash flows (and interpreting the cash flows with IRRs) is based on two IRRs (the IRR of the actual cash flows of the private investment and the cash flows of the hypothetical investment in a public market index), the problems with IRR are magnified. The problems with IRR can be addressed by using other methods such as NPV which require a discount rate.

For example, consider the IRRs of the three sets of cash flows in Exhibit 30.3.

If an endowment could only pick one of these assets in which to invest, which asset would be best (assuming that the investments cannot be repeated or purchased in larger scale)? While the third asset has the lowest IRR, it has the highest NPV (for a discount rate such as 10%). The problem with Asset #1 is that most of the cash earned the attractive IRR for only 1 year—even though the asset does not end until Year 5. The problem with Asset #2 is that it is of inconsequential scale relative to Asset #3. Hence, IRR incorrectly ranks the attractiveness of the investment opportunities.

In traditional corporate investment decisions, such unusual and heterogeneous cash flow patterns may be unrealistic. But the cash flows in Exhibit 30.3 illustrate very real problems that arise in the analysis of PE funds with pooled performance and problems through comparing IRRs under the PME method. Performing an NPV analysis solves these problems; however, NPV requires the input of an appropriate discount rate. Further, the NPV may need to be adjusted for the scale (size) of the cash flows in order to provide useful ranking.

30.3.4 The PME Method Can be Effective in Evaluating Performance

Recall from Chapter 17 that the PME method compares the traditional IRR of an investment in a hypothetical PE fund (using the cash flows from the fund) with the IRR of a hypothetical cash flow stream based on a simulation of investing the same cash flows in a public equity market using a public equity market index. Case #1 at the top of Exhibit 30.4 repeats an analysis from Chapter 17 for a private

EXHIBIT 30.3 Assets with Scale and Timing Differences

Period	0	1	2	3	4	5	IRR
			(millions of dollars)				
Asset 1	−100	115	0	0	0	10	19.8%
Asset 2	−1	0	0	0	0	2.5	20.1%
Asset 3	−100	0	0	0	0	225	17.6%

EXHIBIT 30.4 PMEs for Three Scenarios

Case #1: Example from Chapter 17 (Exhibit 17.4)

Period	0	1	2	3	4	5	6	7	8
PE Fund Flows	−100	−50	−40	0	0	0	70	80	280
Market Index	100	60	75	90	99	110	132	165	198
Market Return	n.a.	−.40	.25	.20	.10	.1111	.20	.25	.20
Hyp Mkt Acc	100	110	177.5	213.0	234.3	260.3	242.4	223	−12.40
Hyp Cash Flows	−100	−50	−40	0	0	0	70	80	267.60

Case #2: Slightly Lower PE Fund Distribution in Year 8

Period	0	1	2	3	4	5	6	7	8
PE Fund Flows	−100	−50	−40	0	0	0	70	80	200
Market Index	100	60	75	90	99	110	132	165	198
Market Return	n.a.	−.40	.25	.20	.10	.1111	.20	.25	.20
Hyp Mkt Acc	100	110	177.5	213.0	234.3	260.3	242.4	223	67.40
Hyp Cash Flows	−100	−50	−40	0	0	0	70	80	267.60

Case #3: Slightly Higher Public Equity Market Return in Period 1

Period	0	1	2	3	4	5	6	7	8
PE Fund Flows	−100	−50	−40	0	0	0	70	80	280
Market Index	100	60	75	90	99	110	132	165	198
Market Return	n.a.	−.30	.25	.20	.10	.1111	.20	.25	.20
Hyp Mkt Acc	100	120	190.0	228.0	260.8	278.7	264.4	250.5	20.60
Hyp Cash Flows	−100	−50	−40	0	0	0	70	80	300.60

Case #1: PE Fund IRR = 12.75%; PME IRR = 12.30%

Case #2: PE Fund IRR = 9.57%; PME IRR = 12.30%

Case #3: PE Fund IRR = 12.75%; PME IRR = 13.48%

investment that outperformed the public market on a cash-flow-weighted basis. The outperformance of the private investment can be seen from the negative value (−12.40) in the last year of the hypothetical accumulation using public market returns (the second to last line). The outperformance of the private investment in Case #1 can also be seen from a comparison of IRRs and as indicated as the bottom of Exhibit 30.4.

Cases #2 and #3 indicate different scenarios that illustrate the usefulness of the PME approach. In Case #2, the PE fund is assumed to have only been able to generate a €200 distribution in the final period rather than the €280 distribution in Case #1. As can be seen at the bottom of Exhibit 30.4 the IRR of the PE fund drops to 9.57%, which is below the IRR of the PME method (12.30%) indicating that the PE fund underperformed the market index. In Case #3, the public market index is assumed to have performed better by only having dropped by 30% in the first year rather than 40%. The resulting IRRs at the bottom of the exhibit indicate that the PME approach rises to 13.48%, indicating that the PE fund underperformed the index.

30.3.5 The PME Method Can be Manipulated

A substantial issue in PE fund performance reporting is the potential for IRRs in general, and especially IRRs of pooled time periods, to be manipulated by managers or investors in an attempt to portray more favorable results. One particularly troublesome issue within IRR computation involves the use of lines of credit. In the case of a private equity fund, a **subscription-secured line of credit (SLOC)** is a borrowing facility that is collateralized with the capital commitments to the fund from its investors.

For example, consider a fund with total commitments of €800 million that commences in Year 2020. Rather than calling the capital from its investors in 2020, the fund uses a SLOC to borrow €800 million at 5% simple interest to invest in portfolio companies. Three years later (in 2023), the fund exits one or more of its portfolio companies to receive €120 million in cash, calls the €800 million of commitments from its investors, and uses those proceeds to repay the SLOC (including €120 million in interest). Two years later (in 2025) the fund liquidates its portfolio and distributes a final payout to its investors of €1,500 million. Note that the timing and size of the cash flows are stylized and simplified to keep the arithmetic simple.

Exhibit 30.5 summarizes the cash flows of the fund under two scenarios. The first scenario uses the SLOC to make the investments in year 2020 while waiting until 2023 to call investor capital. In the second scenario, the fund calls the investors' capital in 2020 to make the investment.

From the investor viewpoint in Scenario #1, the LPs respond to capital calls in 2023 by paying €800 and receiving €1,500 million 2 years later for an IRR of 36.93%. In Scenario #2, the LPs respond to capital calls in 2020 by paying €800 million, and end up receiving €120 million 3 years later and €1,500 million a total of 5 years later for an IRR of 15.73%. Note that the latter IRR requires use of the financial functions of a calculator to avoid having to perform a trial and error search.

EXHIBIT 30.5   Hypothetical Fund Investment with and without a SLOC

Scenario 1: With a SLOC (€ million)

Year:	2020	2021	2022	2023	2024	2025
SLOC Cash flows	+800			−920		
Portfolio Cashflows	−800			+120		+1,500
Investor Cash Flows				−800		+1,500
IRR = 36.93%						

Scenario 2: Without a SLOC (€ million)

Year:	2020	2021	2022	2023	2024	2025
Portfolio Cash flows	−800			+120		+1,500
Investor Cont.	−800			+120		+1,500
IRR = 15.73%						

APPLICATION 30.3.5

Consider a PE Fund that called €500 from its investors and invested the €500 in portfolio companies in Year 0. In Year 4, the Fund receives €100 and distributed the €100 to investors from the sale of several portfolio companies. Finally, in Year 6 the Fund is terminated with €1,000 distribution to its investors. The resulting cash flows from the perspective of the investors are:

Year 0	Year 1	Year 2	Year 3	Year 4	Year 5	Year 6
−500	0	0	0	+100	0	+1,000

What is the IRR of this cash flow schedule?

Using the IRR function on a financial calculator produces IRR= 14.58%.

Now consider a second scenario in which the only difference is the use of a SLOC. The PE Fund borrows €500 in Year 0 using a SLOC to make the €500 portfolio company investments. The Fund calls the €500 capital commitments from its investors in Year 4. The SLOC's principal (€500) and interest (5% simple annual interest is €100 for the 4 years) is paid in Year 4 using the investor contributions and the €100 from the sale of some portfolio companies. What is the investors' IRR under the second scenario (using the SLOC)?

The cash flows of the second scenario from the perspective of the Fund's investors are:

Year 0	Year 1	Year 2	Year 3	Year 4	Year 5	Year 6
0	0	0	0	−500	0	+1,000

IRR = 41.42%

The 2018 annual report for KKR[8] acknowledges the potentially IRR-increasing effect of credit facilities and their potential use of such credit:

> *KKR's Private Markets funds may utilize third-party financing facilities to provide liquidity to such funds. The above net and gross IRRs are calculated from the time capital contributions are due from fund investors to the time fund investors receive a related distribution from the fund, and the use of such financing facilities generally decreases the amount of invested capital that would otherwise be used to calculate IRRs, which tends to increase IRRs when fair value grows over time and decrease IRRs when fair value decreases over time.[9]*

30.4 MULTIPLE EVALUATION TOOLS

This section discusses the use of multiple metrics to evaluate private asset performance. The motivation to using multiple evaluation tools is twofold: (1) each tool by itself can produce erroneous signals; and (2) a single PE fund performance measure can be gamed by PE fund managers more easily than a set of measures. Therefore, the use of multiple measures may provide more accurate and complete performance analysis.

Recall from CAIA Level I that there are three popular ratios of cash inflows to initial costs: the TVPI, the DPI, and the RVPI. The **distribution to paid-in (DPI) ratio,** or realized return, is the ratio of the cumulative distribution to investors to the total capital drawn from investors. The **residual value to paid-in (RVPI) ratio,** or unrealized return, is the ratio of the total value of the unrealized investments (as measured by NAV) to the total capital drawn from investors during the previous time periods. Finally, the **total value to paid-in (TVPI) ratio** is a measure of the cumulative distribution to investors plus the total value of the unrealized investments relative to the total capital drawn from investors.

30.4.1 Simple Cash Flow Multiples

Due to the difficulties with the IRR and IIRR—including multiple solutions, no solutions, and failure to adjust for scale and timing—the IRR and IIRR are not the only performance measures used by the industry. The TVPI, the DPI, and the RVPI ratios (simple ratios that use cash flows and NAVs not adjusted for time and risk) can be formed based on cash flows unadjusted for time and risk. This section uses the cash flows from Exhibit 30.1 (repeated here for convenience) to illustrate the computation of simple cash flow multiples (and later the computation of a more advanced ratio).

Simulated Distribution of Two Funds (€ million), 2026 values are NAVs

	2020	2021	2022	2023	2024	2025	2026
PE Fund 1	−200	−800	200	−2,000	−600	2,000	3,500
PE Fund 2	−1,500	−1,500	−800	−200	500	1,500	5,000

In the case of PE Fund 1, the TVPI is found by inserting the cash flows into Equation 30.2:

$$TVPI_T = \frac{\sum_{t=0}^{T} D_t + NAV_T}{\sum_{t=0}^{T} C_t} \tag{30.2}$$

$$TVPI_T = \frac{200 + 2{,}000 + 3{,}500}{200 + 800 + 2000 + 600} = 1.58$$

The ratio indicates that 58% more cash is received (or indicated by a NAV) than is paid out.

APPLICATION 30.4.1A

What is the TVPI for PE Fund 2?

Inserting the cash flows and NAV from the previous exhibit into Equation 30.2 indicates that in the case of PE Fund 2, the TVPI is 1.75.

Thus, PE Fund 2 has a higher ratio of total distributions and NAV to total contributions between 2020 and 2026 than does PE Fund 1. As mentioned previously, this measure does not take into account the time value of money. Also, note that even though the drawdowns or paid-in capital are negative in the exhibit (given that they represent a use of cash to PE funds), their values are expressed in positive numbers in the denominator of the equation. This convention is followed because it generates a more meaningful sign (i.e., a positive value) for the TVPI index, which is more easily interpreted than benefit-to-cost ratios are usually expressed and interpreted.

The same procedure is followed when calculating the total value of drawdowns in the case of the next two indices (DPI and RVPI). For DPI, the distributions are inserted into Equation 30.3. In the case of PE Fund 1, the DPI is determined as follows:

$$DPI_T = \frac{\sum_{t=0}^{T} D_t}{\sum_{t=0}^{T} C_t} \tag{30.3}$$

$$DPI_T = \frac{200 + 2{,}000}{200 + 800 + 2{,}000 + 600} = 0.61$$

APPLICATION 30.4.1B

What is the DPI for PE Fund 2?

Inserting the distributions and contributions from the previous exhibit into Equation 30.3 indicates that in the case of PE Fund 2, the DPI is 0.50.

DPI analysis indicates that PE Fund 1 has a higher ratio of total distributions to total commitments between 2020 and 2026 than does PE Fund 2. As mentioned previously, these measures do not take into account the time value of money (except partially through the use of a NAV in the RVPI and TVPI).

Finally, use Equation 30.4 when calculating the residual value to paid-in (RVPI) ratio:

$$RVPI_T = \frac{NAV_T}{\sum_{t=0}^{T} C_t} \tag{30.4}$$

For PE Fund 1, the RVPI is:

$$RVPI_T = \frac{3,500}{(200 + 800 + 2,000 + 600)} = 0.97$$

APPLICATION 30.4.1C

What is the RVPI for PE Fund 2?

Inserting the NAV and contributions from the previous exhibit into Equation 30.4 in the case of PE Fund 2, the formula gives us an RVPI of 1.25.

It can be seen that PE Fund 2 has a higher ratio of NAV to total contributions than does PE Fund 1. Again, note that this measure does not consider the time value of money. However, these three ratios can be useful general indicators of the performance of each of the PE funds.

30.4.2 Multiples based on the PME Method

The cash flows and NAVs used in forming multiples in the previous section can be adjusted for time at various rates, such as public market equivalent rates, assumed reinvestment rates, or risk-adjusted discount rates. Equations 30.5 and 30.6 illustrate the PME approach by compounding the distributions (D_t) and contributions (C_t) forward using index values. Specifically, each value is multiplied by the ratio of the value of an index at time T (I_T) to the value of the index at time t (I_t).

$$FV(D) = FV(Distributions) = \sum_{t=0}^{T} \frac{D_t \times I_T}{I_t} \tag{30.5}$$

$$FV(D) = FV(Contributions) = \sum_{t=0}^{T} \frac{C_t \times I_T}{I_t} \tag{30.6}$$

Note that multiplying each cash flow at time t by I_T/I_t is tantamount to compounding each cash flow forward by all the returns on the market index from time t to time T.

An important ratio based on the PME approach is the **PME ratio,** which uses future values calculated by compounding cash flows forward through time using the annual returns of a public market index and then adding in the NAV at time T to form a ratio of value received to value paid out. The following equation provides the PME ratio, which is the future value of distributions (including NAV as an estimate of future distributions) to the future value of contributions.

$$PME\ Ratio = \frac{FV(D) + NAV}{FV(C)} \tag{30.7}$$

We can use the information from the two example funds, PE Funds 1 and 2, to calculate the PME ratios using Equation 30.7. PE Funds 1 and 2 of have an $FV(D)$

of €5,131 and €4,959, respectively, and an $FV(C)$ of €7,438 and €6,568, respectively. Given their interim NAVs, the PME ratios of the two funds are 1.16 and 1.52. This indicates that the two funds outperformed the public index and that PE Fund 2 performed better than PE Fund 1 according to the PME ratio.

APPLICATION 30.4.2A

Suppose that the 3-year cash flows of a PE investment are $-100, +50,$ and $+150,$ respectively. The NAV of the fund is 50 in Year 3. Given that a public equity index had the values 120, 135, and 125 over the same 3-year period, what are the $FV(D)$, $FV(C)$, and PME ratios over the 3 years?

The relevant future values of distributions $FV(D)$ and contribution $FV(C)$ are:

$$FV(D) = [50 \times (125/135)] + [150 \times (125/125)] = 196.3$$

$$FV(C) = 100(125/120) = 104.17$$

The PME ratio is therefore $\dfrac{(196.3 + 50)}{104.17} = 2.36.$

Since the ratio is higher than 1.0, it is concluded that this private equity investment has outperformed the public market index by a substantial amount.

30.4.3 Private Equity Fund Benchmark Analysis

A benchmark analysis can be performed based on the previous computations for PE Funds 1 and 2 in Exhibit 30.1 and the following five observations collected for 31 PE funds categorized as vintage-year 2020 buyout funds, from inception to December 31, 2026:

1. The maximum return (measured using the IIRR) registered by a PE fund was 34.80%.
2. The highest quartile of PE funds had a return of 13.20% or more.
3. The median return was 6.50%.
4. The lowest-quartile funds had returns of 0% or less.
5. The minimum return was −9.50%.

Based on the information provided, a table can be constructed, shown in Exhibit 30.6, to help visualize the performance of PE Funds 1 and 2 as a classic benchmark analysis.

It can be seen in Exhibit 30.6 that PE Fund 1 (introduced in Exhibit 30.1) had an excellent IIRR when compared to its peers, as its IIRR was located in the top quartile of returns corresponding to the 31 PE funds used in the sample. In the case of PE Fund 2, the observed return was less impressive, although its IIRR was still above the median PE fund return of the sample.

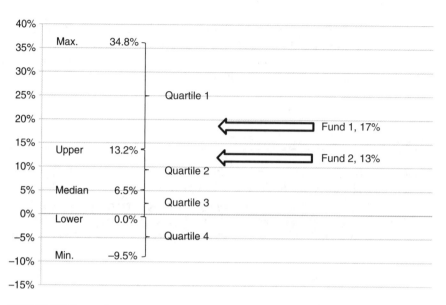

EXHIBIT 30.6   Performance Benchmarking

30.4.4   Applying a PME Analysis to the Example PE Funds

To compare the returns offered by the two PE funds introduced in Exhibit 30.1 to those of the public index, start by calculating the gap between the IIRR of each PE fund and the public market equivalent. The value of the public index during the 2020–26 period is shown in Exhibit 30.7.

Based on the public equity market index values in Exhibit 30.7, the PME method can be applied to PE Funds 1 and 2 in Exhibit 30.1. The PME IIRR for PE Fund 1 is 9.1% and for PE Fund 2 is 2.5%. Therefore, the gap, or excess IIRR, for the IIRR of PE Fund 1 (16.5%) relative to the PME IIRR of PE Fund 1 (9.1%) is 7.4%. For PE Fund 2, its IIRR under the PME method is 2.5%, underperforming the fund's IIRR of 12.5% by 10%. The annual return for the public index was −1.1%, found as $\{[(5542/5926)]^{\wedge}(1/6)\} - 1$. Both PE funds outperformed the returns that could have been earned by an investor through the public market.

30.4.5   Summary of Results Using Multiple Evaluation Tools

Exhibit 30.8 summarizes the various metrics for PE Funds 1 and 2 derived in the previous sections. The comparison of the two funds is substantially simplified because the IIRRs were based on the same time length (6 years) and the amount invested was similar (3,600 for Fund 1 and 4,000 for Fund 2). However, the timing of the contributions (capital calls) was quite different. Fund 1 had much of its capital called

EXHIBIT 30.7   Public Index Value, 2020 to 2026

	2020	2021	2022	2023	2024	2025	2026
Public index	5,926	4,625	3,064	3,558	3,821	4,715	5,542

EXHIBIT 30.8 Summary of Example PE Funds

		Metrics Not Based on PME Method			
	DPI	RVPI	TVPI	IIRR	Length
1	0.61	0.97	1.58	16.5%	6 Yrs.
2	0.50	1.25	1.75	12.5%	6 Yrs.

		Metrics Based on PME Method			
Fund	FV(D)	FV(C)	PME Ratio	PME IIRR	Spread to PME
1	5,131	7,438	1.16	9.1%	7.4%
2	4,959	6,568	1.52	2.5%	10.0%

in 2023 and 2024, while Fund 2 had most of its capital called in 2020 and 2021. The differences in the timing of the contributions had a major impact on the PME IIRRs because the public market index fell substantially from 2020 to 2022 and rose substantially from 2022 to 2026.

The similar size and longevity eliminated many of the problems with evaluating the relative performance of the two funds with a single metric. Nevertheless, multiple metrics should be used, especially when it is possible that managers are gaming the metrics through lines of credit or other mechanisms.

30.5 IRR AGGREGATION PROBLEMS FOR PORTFOLIOS

In addition to all of the problems with IRR as a measure of the performance of an individual asset, there are problems with aggregating performance measures of a portfolio of assets across similar time periods or across only partially overlapping time periods. The challenges are exacerbated when, as is usually the case with private equity and other private assets, there is no reliable indication of each asset's value. A PE portfolio is an aggregation of funds, so the performance of a portfolio is either an aggregation of the performance measures used for the individual funds (IRR, IIRR, TVPI, DPI, or RVPI) or the performance measure of pooled cash flows. This section explores the application of several approaches.

30.5.1 Equally Weighting IRRs or IIRRs

This section discusses several approaches. In the absence of market values with which to weight assets within a portfolio in estimating the portfolio's attributes, equal weighting of IRRs, IIRRs, and other performance and risk measures may be suitable in the case of a portfolio of assets held in similar sizes. The simple arithmetic mean of the PE funds' performance measures is depicted in Equation 30.8:

$$IIRR_{P,T} = \frac{1}{N} \sum_{t=1}^{N} IIRR_{i,T} \qquad (30.8)$$

In Equation 30.8, $IIRR_{P,T}$ is the IIRR of portfolio P at the end of period T, $IIRR_{i,T}$ is the IIRR of fund i at the end of time period T, and N is the number of funds in the portfolio. Note that this calculation works for either IIRR or IRR. Note also that this average IIRR may give misleading signals about the performance of the portfolio. For example, the simple average would be different from the IIRR calculated using other methods. Therefore, the simple average IIRR has to be used with caution.

APPLICATION 30.5.1

Consider Fund A with an investment of €100 in Year 0 and a NAV of €110 in Year 1, and Fund B with an investment of €200 in Year 0 and a NAV of €288 in Year 2. What is the simple average of the IIRRs for a PE portfolio composed of these two funds?

The IIRR of Fund A is 10%, and the IIRR of Fund B is 20%, so the simple average of the IIRR is 15%.

A simple alternative to the average is to use the median. In small samples or samples with a pronounced skew, the median can differ markedly from the mean.

30.5.2   Commitment-Weighting IRRs or IIRRs

The commitment-weighted average of the funds' performance measures (in this case IIRRs) is given in Equation 30.9:

$$IIRR_{P,T} = \left(\frac{1}{\sum\limits_{i=1}^{N} CC_i} \right) \sum_{i=1}^{N} CC_i \times IIRR_{i,T} \tag{30.9}$$

Here, CC_i is the commitment made to fund i. In this case, the IIRR of each investment is weighted by the relative size of the commitment of each investment. The **commitment-weighted IRR** is an average calculated by weighting the rates of return by commitment. The commitment-weighted IRR does not capture the true weight of each fund's actual value. However, it might be useful for measuring the LP's skill in selecting and allocating the right amount to funds.

APPLICATION 30.5.2

Consider Fund A with an investment (and commitment) of €100 in Year 0 and a NAV in Year 1 of €110, and Fund B with an investment (and commitment) of €200 in Year 0 and a NAV of €288 in Year 2. What is the commitment-weighted average of the IIRRs for a PE portfolio composed of these two funds?

The IIRR of Fund A is 10%, and the IIRR of Fund B is 20%. The commitment-weighted average of the IIRRs is 16.67%, found as [(100/300) ×10%] + [(200/300) × 20%].

30.5.3 Pooled Cash Flows for Weighting IRRs or IIRRs

In the previous weighting approaches, the IRR or IIRR for each fund is estimated using the projected (in the case of IIRR) cash flows and estimated net asset values or (in the case of IRR) using the realized cash flows. Given these data, a portfolio IRR or IIRR can be obtained by pooling (i.e., combining) all of the data from the individual funds (e.g., realized cash flows, projected cash flows, and/or estimated residual values) and calculating the pooled IIRR or IRR as if they were from one single fund by solving the equation for $IIRR_{P,T}$:

$$\sum_{t=0}^{T} \sum_{i=0}^{N} \frac{CF_{i,t}}{(1 + IIRR_{P,T})^t} + \sum_{i=0}^{N} \frac{NAV_{i,T}}{(1 + IIRR_{P,T})^T} = 0 \tag{30.10}$$

Here, $CF_{i,t}$ is the net cash flow during period t between the fund i and the investor, T is the number of periods, $NAV_{i,T}$ is the latest NAV of the fund i, $IIRR_{P,T}$ is the IIRR of the portfolio P at the end of time period T, and N is the number of funds in the portfolio. In the case of IRRs, the NAV in Equation 30.10 would be replaced by the realized terminal distribution.

The **pooled IRR or IIRR** is a measure that attempts to capture investment timing and scale, and is calculated by estimating all actual and projected cash flows, aggregating them, and treating all funds as if they were one composite fund. This composite fund's cash-flow series is then used to calculate the pooled IRR or IIRR. The advantage of this measure is that it takes the scale and timing of cash flows from various funds into account and may be indicative of LP's skills. A potential disadvantage is that larger cash flows will be given more weight, so in a composite portfolio of small early-stage funds and large later-stage or buyout funds, the larger funds will tend to dominate the results.

To illustrate the pooled IRR approach, return to the two PE Funds in Exhibit 30.1 that were analyzed in the discussion of multiple metrics. The pooled cash flows from the two funds are, from 2020 to 2026: −1700, −2300, −600, −2200, −100, 3500 and 8500. The IRR of the pooled cash flow stream is 13.85%, which is slightly closer to the 12.53% IRR of PE Fund 2 than it is to the 16.53% IRR of PE Fund 1. Presumably this is because the total of contributions to PE Fund 2 is 4,000, while the total of contributions to PE Fund 1 is 3,600. The commitment-weighted IRR is 14.43% and the equally-weighted IRR is 15.53%.

APPLICATION 30.5.3

Consider Fund A with an investment of €100 in Year 0 and a NAV of €110 in Year 1, and Fund B with an investment of €200 in Year 0 and a NAV of €288 in Year 2. What is the pooled IIRR for a PE portfolio composed of these two funds?

The cash flows are −300 in Year 0, +110 in Year 1, and +288 in Year 2. Using a calculator to perform the search, the pooled IIRR is 18.01%.

30.5.4 Time-Zero-Based Pooling

Each weighting method generates results of questionable meaning when applied across vintage years when the different time periods reflect substantially different economic conditions. The problem of pooling cash flows with substantially different starting dates is especially severe in the case of cash-flow pooling since the aggregated cash flows across vintage years can create multiple sign changes in the pooled cash flow stream which can lead to multiple IRRs or IIRRs.

For example, returning to PE Fund 1 and PE Fund 2 in Exhibit 30.1, suppose that rather than both funds starting in Year 2020, PE Fund 1 began in Year 2023 and generated the same cash flow stream as in Exhibit 30.1 but in Years 2023–29. While the IRRs of the two funds separately are, of course, unchanged, the time-zero-based pooled cash flows over Years 2020–29 have a pooled IR of 13.54%, which is 31 basis points lower than the pooled IRR when both funds had the same starting date (13.85%).

APPLICATION 30.5.4

Return to PE Fund 1 and PE Fund 2 in Exhibit 30.1. Supposing that rather than both funds starting in Year 2020, PE Fund 2 began in Year 2023 and generated the same cash flow stream as in Exhibit 30.1 but in Years 2023–29. Find the time-zero-based pooled cash flows and calculate the time-zero-based IRR.

The time-zero-based cash flow stream is:

−200	−800	200	−3,500	−2,100	1,200	3,300	500	1,500	5,000

The time-zero-based pooled cash flows have a pooled IRR of 14.22%.

In analyses of portfolios with multiple funds that have different starting dates, some analysts use time-zero-based pooling. **Time-zero-based pooling** (or **time-zero pooling**) is the process of pooling or summing cash flows across funds of different vintages by treating the funds as if they all started on the same date. In other words, the nth annual cash flow of each fund would be summed to form the nth annual cash flow of the pooled data. The PE Funds in Exhibit 30.1 had the same starting date and therefore did not need to be altered. The next section provides an example.

30.5.5 Contrasting the Weighting Approaches for IRR and IIRR

Arguably, cash-flow pooled measures give the most meaningful IRR or IIRR of the portfolio. However, it may also make sense to use the others, depending on what one wishes to measure. For example, the simple average can be a good indicator of the selection skills, while the commitment-weighted average can be useful in assessing the added value resulting from the decision of what size commitment to make to each specific fund.

EXHIBIT 30.9 Three Weighting Measures for a Three-Fund Portfolio

| Fund | Annual Cash Flows | | | | | | | Total | |
	2020	2021	2022	2023	2024	2025	2026	IRR	Commitment
1	−50	−150	50	150	250			35.8%	200
2		−200	−100	100	200	250		23.2%	300
3			−300	−200	100	100	250	−3.5%	500
Sum	−50	−350	−350	50	550	350	250		1,000

Time-Zero-Based Analysis:

Years:	0	1	2	3	4
Cash Flows:	−550	−450	250	450	750

Summary of IRRs

Simple Average	18.5%
Median	23.2%
Commitment-Weighted	12.4%
Pooled	15.6%
Time-Zero Pooled	13.8%

Consider the three funds in Exhibit 30.9 that have three different vintages. This exhibit depicts the various measures of their combined performance in terms of IRR.

The time-zero-based pooling approach forms the cash flows −550, −450, 250, 450, and 750 by summing the first through fifth cash flows of each fund. Once the cash flows have been pooled, the analysis proceeds like any single fund analysis. Note, however, that the PME method could not be applied directly to the summed cash flows, because each total cash flow sums individual cash flows from different points in time.

The homogeneity of the three funds in Exhibit 30.9, especially with respect to the length of each project in years, mutes the dispersion between the IRRs resulting from the various weighting schemes. The point is less that some measures are more flawed than others, and rather that no single measure is perfect and that analysis of IRRs and IIRRs should include a variety of metrics and examination of their relationships to the individual funds. Similarly, analysis should extend beyond IRR and IIRR analysis to include PME methods as well as the various ratios discussed in this chapter. NPV analysis can be very helpful.

30.6 THE CASE AGAINST PRIVATE EQUITY

Ludovic Phalippou in *Private Equity Laid Bare*[10] presents a formidable case against private equity investing through limited partnership agreements that are fraught with conflicts of interest and potentially high fees. Phalippou argues that historical returns to private equity LPs are overstated.

Numerous studies have been performed on both buyout fund and venture capital fund performance. The results are sensitive to the type of fund, the time interval examined, and the method of estimating the returns of unlisted funds. Generally, performance measures in these studies indicate substantially worse performance by private equity funds than are often claimed by managers and investors. For example, Phalippou and Gottschalg (2009) cite valuation problems and selection bias as distorting examination of private equity fund performance. They found "average net-of-fees fund performance" that, after adjusting for risk, indicates annual underperformance of 6%. Interestingly, they estimate annual fees to be 6%.[11] The finding that the high fees collected by GPs offset the alpha generated by the underlying assets is shared by others.

Overall, the studies tend to indicate three key findings. The **three key empirical findings regarding PE fund performance** are: (1) venture capital fund performance tended to exceed that of buyout funds; (2) private equity outperformance and performance persistence have generally been lower in more recent years (e.g., since 2000) than in early years (e.g., prior to 2000); and (3) risk-adjustment of returns and netting of fees tended to lower private equity performance to unattractive levels except for venture capital returns in earlier years and especially for those investors who enjoyed an "early mover advantage" and access to the best managers.

30.7 TWO PROPOSITIONS REGARDING ACCESS THROUGH PRIVATE VERSUS LISTED STRUCTURES

Previous sections in this chapter, in Chapter 29, and in Level I of the CAIA curriculum discussed concerns with private structures including performance manipulation, high fees, and conflicts of interest. Substantial differences of opinion remain. Many large institutional investors have reported enormous success from investments in private funds, especially prior to 2000.

Institutional investors should consider the following two propositions in deciding the extent, if any, with which to allocate to assets accessed through private versus listed structures.

PRIVATE STRUCTURES SHOULD BE USED ONLY TO ACCESS ASSET CLASSES THAT CONTAIN SUPERIOR INVESTMENT OPPORTUNITIES AND ONLY IF HIGHLY SKILLED GPS CAN BE IDENTIFIED AND ACCESSED: Private structures allow flexibility that enables LP investors to offer superior GPs the levels of compensation and flexibility that can attract the world's best private equity managers. In effect, private equity can be a superior governance paradigm that can generate tremendous increases in wealth through superior portfolio company selection and management.

MANAGERS WITH UNREMARKABLE SKILL OR MANAGERS IN MARKETS WITH MODEST INVESTMENT OPPORTUNITIES SHOULD BE ACCESSED WITH LISTED STRUCTURES: Listed structures tend to offer investor protections and lower fees that are appropriate for investment opportunities and managers that offer modest pre-fee returns.

NOTES

1. See Pasquariello and Vega (2009).
2. See Pástor and Stambaugh (2003).
3. See Ben-Rephael et al. (2015).

4. See Amihud et al. (2015).
5. See Khandani and Lo (2009).
6. https://www.cambridgeassociates.com/wp-content/uploads/2018/05/WEB-2017-Q4-Real-Estate-Benchmark-Book.pdf accessed June 1, 2019.
7. Brad Case, "Equity Investing in Real Estate Through Public and Private Markets." National Association of Real Estate Investment Trusts, Inc. (NAREIT), November 7, 2017.
8. KKR & Co. LP. Form 10-K filed 02/23/18 for the period ending 12/31/17, page 12.
9. Ibid.
10. See Phalippou (2017)
11. See Phalippou and Gottschalg (2009).

REFERENCES

Amihud, Y., A. Hameed, W. Kang, and H. Zhang. 2015 "The Illiquidity Premium: International Evidence." *Journal of Financial Economics* 117 (2): 350–68.

Ben-Rephael, A., O. Kadan, and A. Wohl. 2015. "The Diminishing Liquidity Premium." *Journal of Financial and Quantitative Analysis* 50 (1–2): 197–229.

Fisher, J., D. Gatzlaff, D. Geltner, and D. Haurin. 2003. "Controlling for the Impact of Variable Liquidity in Commercial Real Estate Price Indices." *Real Estate Economics* 31 (2): 269–303.

Khandani, A. E. and A. W. Lo. 2009. "Illiquidity Premia in Asset Returns: An Empirical Analysis of Hedge Funds, Mutual Funds, and U.S. Equity Portfolios." MIT Working Paper.

Pasquariello, P. and C. Vega. 2009. "The on-the-run liquidity phenomenon." *Journal of Financial Economics* 92 (1): 1–24.

Pástor, L. and R. F. Stambaugh. 2003. "Liquidity Risk and Expected Stock Returns," *Journal of Political Economy* 111 (3): 642–85.

Phalippou, L. 2017. *Private Equity Laid Bare*. Self-published: CreateSpace.

Phalippou, L. and O. Gottschalg. 2009. "The Performance of Private Equity Funds, Review of Financial Studies." 22 (4): 1747–76.

Due Diligence & Selecting Managers

Alternative investments are noted for the wide dispersion of returns between bottom and top quartile managers. Given this large dispersion, due diligence and manager selection is of utmost importance. Chapter 31 discusses liquidity risk and tactical asset allocation models. In chapter 32, fund manager selection and the screening of investment opportunities is the focus. Due diligence should be separated into two unique components, investment due diligence as discussed in chapter 33 and operational due diligence as discussed in chapter 34. While investment due diligence is vital, many investors today use an operational veto, refusing to invest in a strategy if something is wrong with the structure or practice of the fund's operations. Once deciding that a manager is attractive after performing both investment and operational due diligence, the techniques in chapter 35 focus on the due diligence of the structure, fees, and risks of the specific fund vehicle.

CHAPTER 31

Active Management and New Investments

The decision to add an investment often involves two aspects that are discussed in this chapter: (1) tactical asset allocation; and (2) the pursuit of an enhanced combination of risk and return through active management. This chapter begins with a discussion of tactical asset allocation (TAA), followed by a discussion of the Fundamental Law of Active Management. The chapter also discusses funds as financial intermediaries and the role of secondary markets in private partnership units. Due diligence is detailed in Chapters 32–35.

31.1 TACTICAL ASSET ALLOCATION

Earlier chapters introduced the asset allocation process, with a focus on the strategic asset allocation process, asset allocation models such as the mean-variance approach, and the investment policy statement. The strategic asset allocation is the process of setting the long-term target weights for major asset classes. Tactical asset allocation (TAA) has a long history and has been used by large and small asset owners. Generally, tactical asset allocation is an active and dynamic strategy that shifts capital to those asset classes that an asset allocator believes offers the most attractive risk–return combination over a short- to medium-term time horizon. However, there is no well-established and uniform definition of TAA; different authors and investment firms use the term to mean different things.

One thing that all uses of TAA seem to have in common is that it represents a form of active management of a portfolio. TAA will add value if it can systematically take advantage of temporary market inefficiencies and departures of asset prices from their fundamental values. Over time, strategic asset allocation is the most important driver of a portfolio's risk–return characteristics. TAA can add value if: (1) there are short- to medium-term inefficiencies in some markets; and (2) a systematic approach can be designed to exploit these inefficiencies while overcoming the risks and costs that are associated with active portfolio management.

TAA is driven by the balance between its potential benefits and costs. The potential benefit of TAA is to reach a more preferred allocation (in terms of risk and expected net return) over a short to medium time horizon. The costs of TAA include transactions costs (commissions and bid–asked spreads), managerial costs, and, in some cases, potential adverse taxation consequences. The Fundamental Law of Active Management, discussed in the next section, models the tradeoff between risk and return.

31.2   THE FUNDAMENTAL LAW OF ACTIVE MANAGEMENT

The **Fundamental Law of Active Management (FLOAM)**, explained by Grinold (1989), expresses the risk-adjusted value added by an active portfolio manager as a function of the manager's skill to forecast asset returns and the number of markets to which the manager's skill can be applied (breadth).

31.2.1   The Central Relation of the FLOAM

Equation 31.1 represents the central relation of the FLOAM.

$$IR = IC \times \sqrt{BR} \tag{31.1}$$

where IR is the information ratio, IC is the information coefficient, and BR is the strategy's breadth. The **information ratio** (IR) is equal to the ratio of the manager's estimated alpha (i.e., risk-adjusted expected outperformance) divided by the estimated volatility of that alpha. The **information coefficient** (IC) is a measure of the manager's skill, and represents the correlation between the manager's forecast of asset returns and the actual returns to those assets. The **breadth** (BR) is the number of independent forecasts (or "bets") that the manager can skillfully make during a given period of time (e.g., 1 year).

   The left side of the FLOAM (i.e., Equation 31.1) is analogous to a Sharpe ratio of the manager's return-to-risk ratio in that it measures the estimated added expected return to an active strategy relative to the volatility of that potential added return. The right side of Equation 31.1 asserts that the benefit-to-cost ratio of active management is a product of the manager's skill (IC) and the number of opportunities that the manager has to deploy that skill. Therefore, the FLOAM indicates that the value added by active management increases with the ability of the manager to forecast returns and the number of independent assets, sectors, or markets to which the forecasting skill can be applied.

   The FLOAM can be applied to allocate within security selection, sectors, or even asset classes. Clearly, when FLOAM is applied to the process of selecting securities from a universe of 5,000 or more, there should be greater potential for adding value, as the breadth could be large. This insight has been used as an argument against TAA. In other words, the amount of value that can be added through active asset allocation by a portfolio manager needs to be much higher if that skill is to be applied to only a handful of independent asset classes (i.e., if BR is small).

APPLICATION 31.2.1

Suppose active manager A has the skill to select stocks from a universe of 2,000 securities and generate an information ratio (IR) of 1.2. This means that the expected alpha of this manager's portfolio is 20% higher than the volatility of that alpha. Active manager B can generate the same information ratio (1.2) using 15 asset classes. What are the managers' information coefficients?

Using Equation 31.1:

Active manager A has an information coefficient of 0.027:

$$1.2 = IC \times \sqrt{2000}$$

$$IC = 0.027$$

Active manager B has an information coefficient of 0.310:

$$1.2 = IC \times \sqrt{15}$$

$$IC = 0.310$$

In this example, active manager B has to be about 11.5 times more skillful using active management among asset classes than active manager A, who is using security selection to achieve the same IR with a much larger number of independent forecasts. Note that in Equation 31.1, any of the variables can be solved given the value of the other two.

The FLOAM, as previously described, assumes that the asset allocator has an unfettered ability to utilize the potential information ratio for each of the independent forecasts (the breadth) that the manager can skillfully identify. The next section expands the model to include constraints on the manager's ability to exploit all potential opportunities.

31.2.2 The FLOAM and the Transfer Coefficient

The FLOAM, as expressed in Equation 31.1, assumes that the manager faces no constraints in the asset allocation decision with regard to an ability to invest in all assets that appear to offer an attractive alpha. In practice, portfolio managers face a number of constraints, both internal and external. For instance, the manager is constrained by the limits imposed by strategic asset allocation. In addition, there could be regulatory constraints on allocations to some asset classes. Finally, there are implementation costs associated with active management. This is particularly important when considering alternative investments. The costs associated with changing allocations from, say, private equity to a real asset could exceed the perceived alpha of the switch. Even altering allocations to more liquid segments of alternative investments, such as commodity trading advisers (CTAs) and some hedge fund strategies, could be costly.

A modified version of the FLOAM takes into account that some allocations may have to be substantially different from the ideal allocation recommended by the manager's forecasting skill. This extended or modified FLOAM adds a transfer coefficient and can be written as:

$$IR = IC \times \sqrt{BR} \times TC \qquad (31.2)$$

where *TC* is the transfer coefficient. The **transfer coefficient** (TC): (1) measures the ability of the manager to implement her recommendations; (2) has an upper limit of one and a lower limit of zero; and (3) indicates the correlation between the forecasted active returns and the active weights. When TC is equal to one, it means the manager is able to implement all her recommendations—meaning that she is able to assign high weights to those assets appearing to offer high alpha. A TC of zero indicates no correlation between the portfolio weights and the perceived alpha associated with each weight.

Clearly, TC will be less than one when a portfolio of alternative asset classes is considered. Both hard constraints, such as no short selling of funds, and soft constraints, such as high transaction costs associated with the rebalancing of alternative assets, will reduce the value of TC well below one. The information ratio in this modified version of the FLOAM therefore depends on three determinants: the information coefficient, the breadth, and the transfer coefficient.

APPLICATION 31.2.2

Consider two similarly skilled active managers, each with an IC of 0.50. Active manager C can apply his skills to only 16 asset classes, whereas active manager D can apply her skills to 100 securities. What level of transfer coefficient does each manager need to have in order to generate an information ratio of 1.2?

Using Equation 31.2:

$$IR = IC \times \sqrt{BR} \times TC$$

Active Manager C:

$$1.2 = 0.5 \times \sqrt{16} \times TC$$

$$= 0.60$$

Active Manager D:

$$1.2 = 0.5 \times \sqrt{100} \times TC$$

$$= 0.24$$

By having greater breadth, active manager D can achieve an IR of 1.2 with a TC of only 0.24.

31.2.3 The Tradeoff Between the Information Coefficient and Breadth and Its Key Driver

Setting aside temporarily the transfer coefficient, the FLOAM indicates that the information ratio can be increased through increases in the information coefficient, the breadth, or both. While FLOAM presents IC and BR as somewhat independent parameters, they tend to be dependent in practice. For example, it is highly unlikely for a manager to have the skill to forecast returns (i.e., generate an IC on a large number of independent securities (when breadth is large)).

Notice that the key word in breadth is independent. This occurs when a manager applies one or more models to a set of securities that are not highly correlated, and therefore the forecast errors are independent from each other. This is a very strong requirement that is unlikely to be fully satisfied. In other words, in practice there is a tradeoff between IC and BR. The key driver of the tradeoff is that the more markets to which the manager tries to apply her skills, the less accurate the forecasts are likely to become (and the lower the IC). By focusing on a few asset classes, the manager might be able to develop separate forecasting models for each and therefore generate forecasts with independent errors.

Note that the information coefficient tends to be much higher when applied to asset classes than when applied to individual securities. The random returns on individual security prices contain a significant amount of noise, which makes forecasting models less accurate. Available empirical evidence suggests that expected returns on various asset classes or portfolios behave in a more predictable way through various market cycles. But the breadth is limited when dealing with asset classes because there are far more underlying securities than there are asset classes.

31.3 COSTS OF ACTIVELY REALLOCATING ACROSS ALTERNATIVE INVESTMENTS

The FLOAM model seeks the benefits of alpha through active management, but the model does not address the potential costs of moving between assets that occurs with active management. There are costs associated with actively managing portfolios, especially those that consist of alternative assets. This section reviews the key costs and begins with a potential cost of liquidating a position in a fund that has incentive fees.

31.3.1 Incentive Fees and Forgone Loss Carryforward

A common reason to wish to exit a fund is that it has performed poorly, potentially having generated losses in recent years. The **forgone loss carryforward** of a fund with incentive fees is an opportunity cost potentially borne by every investor in a fund with an asymmetric incentive fee structure that arises from the inability to recapture incentive fees.

Forgone loss carryforward arises when an existing investor loses the fee benefits of owning a fund below its high-water mark. The cost to the investor results from a managerial decision to liquidate a fund with a net asset value (NAV) below its high-water mark. Because a manager collects performance fees only when NAV is above the most recent high-water mark at the end of the relevant accounting period, a manager who is underwater (i.e., whose net asset value is below the most recent high-water mark) does not accrue performance fees until a new high-water mark is achieved.

The cost of loss carryforward should be taken into account when the decision is being made to replace a poorly performing manager with another manager. Going forward with the existing manager means that any positive returns realized from the poorly performing manager will be gross of performance fees until the fund returns to its high-water mark. While any return earned on an investment with a new manager will be subject to (i.e., net of) performance fees. This means the new manager will need to outperform the old manager by the amount of the performance fee just to break even on the decision to switch managers. If the drawdown is large from the previous high-water mark on which incentive fees were collected, the savings on remaining with the manager can be large relative to switching to an equally successful alternative manager.

For example, if an existing manager experiences a drawdown of 25%, then the next 33.33% return $(0.75 \times 1.3333 = 1.0)$ generated by the manager is free from incentive fees. Consider a $10 million investment in a fund trading 25% below its high-water mark and having an incentive or performance fee of 20%. Assume that in the ensuing period the old fund returned to its high-water mark by gaining 33.33%. Also assume that over the ensuing periods (and ignoring the time value of money for simplicity), the new fund earned a return that exceed 33.33% by α. What is the value of α that would equation the after-fee returns of the two funds?

To calculate α assume that the old fund earns $r = 33.33\%$ and that the new fund earns $33.33\% + \alpha$ before fees. The after-fee gains of the two funds equal:

After fee Return on Old Fund: $r = 33.33\%$

After fee Return on New Fund: $(33.33\% + \alpha)(1 - 20\%)$

$$33.33\% = (33.33\% + \alpha)(1 - 20\%)$$

$$\alpha = (.3333/.8) - .3333 = 41.67\% - 33.33\% = 8.34\%$$

So the new fund's total return would have to be 41.67%, an alpha of 8.34% relative to the old fund, to break even with the return on the old fund after fees.

APPLICATION 31.3.1

OLDE Fund with 15% incentive fees is 10% below its high-water mark (NAV). Assume that an investor leaves the fund to invest in a new fund with 15% incentive fees. If the OLDE fund returns to its previous high-water mark in the next period, how much would the new fund have to earn that period to generate an identical after-fee return as the OLDE fund? Ignore taxes.

The OLDE fund must earn 11.11% to return to the high-water mark from being 10% down. The new fund would have to earn r before fees to generate

11.11% after fees:

$$11.11\% = r(100\% - 20\%)$$

$$r = 11.11\%/80\% = 13.89\%$$

31.3.2 Two Potential Costs of Staying with a Manager Below its High-Water Mark

While the loss carryforward represents a potential cost for replacing a manager that has recently experienced some losses, there are three primary reasons that an investor may still wish to replace a manager with a carryforward loss (assuming that the strategy of the fund is equally as attractive as the strategies of other funds).

First, the investor may be concerned that the old manager does not have an adequate incentive to generate performance until the high-water mark is reached. That is, because of the lack of incentive on the part of the manager, the recent poor performance may continue for some time while the manager puts greater effort into other professional opportunities or clients, or does not offer sufficient compensation to retain and attract quality traders and other employees.

Second, other investors may withdraw their funds, making the investor's relative position in the fund too large or jeopardizing the viability of the fund. Most investors want to avoid this situation, because if they decide to redeem their shares in the future, the fund's NAV and operations could be adversely affected when a relatively large part of the assets under management (AUM) is redeemed.

31.3.3 Two Types of Potential Costs of Replacing Managers Unrelated to Incentive Fees

There are two primary types of other costs associated with replacing managers other than forgone loss carryforwards or concerns with the management of funds that are in decline. These include: forgone earnings on dormant cash, and administrative costs of closing out one position and opening another.

A liquidation at a particular net asset value typically generates two rounds of cash being distributed to the investor. There is a lag between the striking of the net asset value for liquidation and the receipt of both rounds of cash. Both lags cause forgone interest on dormant cash. This cost is borne by the investor, and depends on a fund's practices with regard to interest payments on cash balances. Industry practices vary, but it is common to find that funds do not pay a market interest rate on the value of undistributed cash balances. In these cases, the cost of forgone interest depends on how quickly cash is returned to the investor. Opportunity losses also occur during the time after the cash is distributed to the investor but before the investor is able to place the cash into new investments that offer returns equal to or in excess of market rates.

The other type of cost is related to transaction and administrative fees. Closing out old positions and opening new positions entails administrative fees and due diligence costs. These costs will vary by investor. Large, experienced investors may have long lists of managers to choose from, and therefore due diligence costs may be relatively small. However, additional due diligence could be a significant cost for investors who have a relatively small allocation to the relevant asset class and must search for an attractive replacement fund.

31.4 KEYS TO A SUCCESSFUL TACTICAL ASSET ALLOCATION PROCESS

TAA has to overcome significant costs and barriers if it is to be applied to portfolios of alternative asset classes. This section discusses the keys to a successful TAA process.

31.4.1 The TAA Process and Return Predictability

A key component of a successful TAA process is the development of sound models that can consistently forecast returns across asset classes. This point may appear to contradict the basic tenet of the efficient market hypothesis that asset returns are essentially unpredictable. There is strong evidence that returns to asset classes are indeed predictable (Pesaran 2010). It is beyond the scope of this chapter to discuss the academic and industry findings regarding the sources of predictability in asset returns.

What is less clear is whether this predictability is the result of foreseeable changes in risk premiums or market inefficiency. In other words, is return predictability explained by risk premiums that change through time? Or is return predictability the result of informational market inefficiency? Studies have not been able to conclusively rule out that some asset return predictabilities using low-frequency data (e.g., annual frequency) represent temporary inefficiencies in markets (Asness, Moskowitz, and Pedersen 2013; Hull and Qiao 2017).

31.4.2 The TAA Process and Model-based Return Prediction

The effectiveness of a TAA strategy is largely dependent on constructing a good model of return prediction. Absent an ability to forecast expected returns and/or risks, there would seem to be few reasons to embark on TAA given the costs discussed in previous sections.

The first step in developing a TAA strategy is to forecast excess returns by constructing fundamental and technical models that can predict asset class returns, using a set of explanatory variables for fundamental models and signals for technical models.

Evidence indicates that return models may have varying predictive strengths during different economic regimes or points in economic cycles. Note from the FLOAM that the potential value added through a TAA process is higher when the models' errors are not correlated with each other (so that the aggregated risk from errors is reduced). Therefore, multiple forecasting models should be used to maximize the value added by the TAA strategy.

A good forecasting model must include economically meaningful signals and have a research process that correctly identifies those signals. In addition, the model must have performed well in the past using out-of-sample data.

31.4.3 Three Important Characteristics of Sound TAA Model Development

The following are three important characteristics of sound model development:

1. USE OF ECONOMICALLY MEANINGFUL SIGNALS. Economically meaningful signals are those signals with rational, intuitive explanations for their expected predictive power. For example, evidence indicates that the slope of the term structure of interest rates has been an effective indicator of the business cycle. This finding not just an empirical observation: it is intuitive and rational. Theoretically, a flat or downward-sloping yield curve is associated with a decreasing expected and realized inflation rate which, in turn is theoretically consistent with slower economic activity. A model that uses inputs with a strong basis in economic theory is likely to provide signals that identify fundamental shifts in the economy.

2. ABSENCE OF DATA MINING. The manager should be able to confirm that the predictive results are not due to data mining. Data mining in this context occurs if an analyst or investment manager tries a large variety of models, explanatory variables, and return models to see which models and variables best explain historic data. The one that performs best is chosen as the most accurate one to implement the TAA strategy on live data. Ex post, with enough models, variables, and data it is always possible to find models and explanatory variables that can explain past random processes. The question is whether there are *economic* reasons to think that ex ante the model would have worked. More importantly, out-of-sample validations (i.e., validations based on data not used to identify potentially successful models or explanatory variables) must be done to guard against data mining. Out-of-sample tests of the strategy, such as in other time periods or countries, can help confirm that the strategy's success is not simply the result of finding a model and identifying explanatory variables that explain one historical period.

3. AVOIDANCE OF OVERFITTING. Models that have a large number of explanatory variables can produce impressive explanatory power (e.g., R-squareds), especially when there is limited data. While models with smaller numbers of explanatory variables are likely to produce less impressive R-squareds using the same sample data, they are generally more likely to reproduce their in-sample predictive power out of sample. In addition, models that use fewer variables are more likely to be stable through time; that is, the estimated relations do not change radically because of small changes in the data.

31.4.4 SAA Models and Unconditional Analyses

Linear regression of investment returns on various fundamental variables is the most common approach for testing and developing fundamental models. A key point in understanding the application of these models is to differentiate between an *unconditional approach* to generate strategic asset allocation (SAA) weights or a *conditional* approach to generate TAA weights.

For an extremely simplified example, consider the regression of historic equity returns on a single variable (i.e., simple linear regression). If the single variable selected is a constant (i.e., a column of 1s) then the intercept will be the historic mean and the dispersion of the residuals will indicate volatility. Note that it is the historic mean returns and estimated volatilities that serve as major inputs into many approaches to SAA, especially mean-variance asset allocation models. As the process is updated through time with the arrival of new data, the regression results (means and volatilities) will remain mostly unchanged, especially if a very long series is used.

The point of the previous paragraph is to emphasize that *strategic* asset allocation can be viewed as relying on *unconditional* empirical analyses. In other words, an **unconditional empirical analysis approach to asset allocation** uses the historic means and volatilities (and correlations) within an SAA approach to form asset weights without regard to the current condition of the economy and markets. Note that the results of long-term historical analyses change slowly, so SAA weights also tend to change very slowly through time.

31.4.5 TAA Models Based on Conditional Analyses

This section examines TAA approaches and the use of conditional expectations. As in the SAA approach, linear regressions are used. But the regression results are used to create *conditional* expectations of asset returns. Unlike unconditional expected returns, which use the average historical returns on the asset to form expectations, conditional expectation models obtain estimates of expected returns that are functions of the *current values* of a set of predictive variables.

As in the previous section, a regression is performed. However, the same asset returns (emerging markets equity returns) are now regressed against the constant (one) and the lagged values of the term spread from the term structure of interest rates in the local bond market. An asset allocator can use the regression results to generate an expected return on this emerging market *conditioned* on the term spread. Specifically, the best estimate of the future expected return of the emerging equity market (i.e., the dependent variable) is now equal to the estimated intercept plus the estimated slope coefficient *times the current value of the term spread*. In other words, the current term spread is used to inform the asset allocator of an expected emerging equity market return under the current economic conditions (i.e., in the case of the current term spread).

The forecast of the emerging market's equity returns will change as its term spread changes. In other words, conditional expected returns are used to generate tactical weights (e.g., in a mean-variance model). These weights may change drastically if there is a fundamental change in economic conditions leading to substantial changes in the conditioning variables. This result is that the approach is conducive to *tactical* asset weights.

A **conditional empirical analysis approach to asset allocation** uses the current condition of the economy and markets (along with empirical measures such as means, volatilities, and correlations) within a TAA approach to form asset weights (tactical weights) that change with current conditions. Current conditions can change somewhat rapidly, but SAA weights also tend to change very slowly through time.

Therefore, TAA can be viewed as SAA when conditional expected returns (and other measures) are used as inputs in the asset allocation process rather than unconditional expected returns and measures.

For example, annual returns on an equity index were regressed against lagged dividend yields using almost 100 years of data. The regression results are presented in Exhibit 31.1.

EXHIBIT 31.1   Equity Returns Versus Lagged Dividend Yield

Intercept	3.30%
Coefficient of Dividend Yield	1.04
R-squared	0.04
Historical Means	
Equity Returns	7.70%
Annual Dividend Yield	4.20%

As expected, this simple model lacks significant predictive power, as the slope coefficient, 1.04, is not statistically significant (the *t*-stat is 0.97). Still, it can be used to demonstrate how to employ such models. The unconditional mean return on the equities is 7.7% per year. To calculate the conditional mean, we need the current value of the dividend yield, say 2.11%. Therefore, the conditional mean return on the equity index is:

$$E[\text{Equity Return} \mid \text{CurrentDivYld}] = 3.3\% + (1.04 \times 2.11\%) = 5.5\%$$

The conditional mean return of 5.5% differs from the historic mean of 7.7%. Further, this estimate of equity returns may change substantially through time as the recent dividend yield changes. This 100-year historic mean return (and therefore the unconditional mean) will change very little.

31.4.6   Technical Analysis Underlying TAA Models

While regression models based on fundamental economic relationships can be useful in implementing TAA strategies, models based on technical analysis can be used to supplement these models; in some cases, research has shown that they may even perform better than fundamental models. Faber (2013) has produced one of the most cited studies in this area. The approach employed in Faber's study is very simple but has produced results that seem to indicate that technical analysis has been a viable basis for a successful TAA approach.

The model uses six asset classes: US large cap (S&P 500), non-US developed markets (MSCI EAFE), US 10-year government bonds, commodities (S&P GSCI), real estate investment trusts (NAREIT Index), and 90-day US Treasury bills.

The objective is to build a simple model that can be used to highlight the use of technical signals in performing TAA for traditional asset classes. The strategy examines a very simple quantitative TAA model, which is based on a trend-following model. The model uses the following buy and sell rules: increase exposure to 20% of the portfolio if the current price is above the 10-month simple moving average, and reduce exposure to 0% of the portfolio if the current price is below the 10-month simple moving average.

The model is mostly a risk-reduction technique that signals when a portfolio manager should reduce exposure to a risky asset class in favor of a less risky investment. The hypothetical allocations are updated monthly, and the cash not allocated to risky strategies is invested in Treasury bills. Exhibit 31.2 presents the results reported using data covering 1973–2012.

EXHIBIT 31.2   Global Tactical Asset Allocation

	Buy and Hold	TAA
Annual Realized Returns	9.92%	10.48%
Annual Realized Volatility	10.28%	6.99%
Sharpe Ratio	0.44	0.73
Maximum Drawdown	−46.12%	−9.54%

Source: Based on 1973–2012 results from Faber (2013).

The buy-and-hold strategy is an equally weighted portfolio. The model clearly performed well in the past although it is important to note that transaction costs and fees were not taken into account. Therefore, it is reasonable to assume that the mean return would have been closer to being the same as the mean return of the buy-and-hold strategy (9.92%) if trading costs had been taken into account. However, the risk reduction of the TAA strategy would not be impacted by these costs and it indicates a substantial advantage relative to the buy-and-hold strategy.

31.5   ADJUSTING EXPOSURES TO ILLIQUID PARTNERSHIPS

This section discusses illiquid limited partnerships in the context of implementing portfolio management decisions such as TAA; namely acquisition and disposal of partnership interests in secondary markets. Specifically, this section examines the illiquidity of a limited partnership (LP) in private equity (PE). Active management of PE is constrained because LP investments are designed to be long term and illiquid. The opportunities to increase a particular investment in an existing partnership or to sell one are limited.

This section begins with a review of the terms and financial economics of PE limited partnerships as a foundation for an ensuing discussion of the issues involved with actively managing PE limited partnerships in the context of TAA.

31.5.1   The Primary Markets for PE Funds

The organized primary PE market is dominated by funds, generally structured as limited partnerships, which serve as the primary financial intermediaries. Fund management companies, also referred to as PE firms, set up these funds. PE funds are unregistered investment vehicles in which investors, or limited partners (LPs), pool money to invest in privately held companies. Investment professionals, including venture capitalists and buyout managers, manage these funds and are known as general partners (GPs) or fund managers. Tax, legal, and regulatory requirements drive the structuring of these investment vehicles with the goal of increasing transparency (investors are treated as investing directly in the underlying portfolio companies), reducing taxation, and limiting liability (investors' liabilities are limited to the capital committed to the fund). From a strictly legal standpoint, limited partnership shares are illiquid; in practice, however, secondary transactions in private equity occasionally take place, in which investors sell their interests to other investors before the termination of the fund.

31.5.2   PE Funds as Intermediaries

PE funds serve as financial intermediaries by facilitating investment in private equity. There are several motivations to using PE funds as intermediaries. Private equity funds step into the funding process when traditional lenders are not willing or able to provide funding. For example, banks may be unwilling to lend to an entrepreneur or be involved in leveraged buyouts because of the significant risk that is involved. In the case of lending to an entrepreneur, the product or the intellectual property is not well understood, and of course the firm has no track record that the bank could use to evaluate its riskiness. Also, some of these lenders (e.g., banks) are not willing or allowed to take equity positions in these firms. This means they cannot fully participate in the significant upsides that PE investments could provide. The result is that this complex sphere of investing is dominated by sophisticated managers and investors using partnership structures generally not often accessed by noninstitutional investors.

31.5.3   PE Fund Incentives and Terms

Another important reason for the existence of PE firms is the presence of certain economic inefficiencies in the traditional corporate structure. In some cases, management may not be given proper incentives to maximize the value to the shareholders of a corporation. Private equity seeks to address this problem by tightly aligning the interests of managers and investors to achieve increased efficiency and higher returns to the providers of capital. PE funds principally serve the following functions.

PE funds pool investors' capital for investing in private companies. The management screens, evaluates, and selects potential companies. Then the management helps foster the growth and development of their portfolio companies. Finally, the management assists in exit opportunities for portfolio companies.

The essence of the limited partner's involvement with a PE fund is to provide capital to general partners that they trust to manage the partnership with expertise and diligence. The limited partner–general partner relationship is primarily a principal–agent relationship. Because information in PE markets is incomplete and highly asymmetric, the relationship requires some specific agreements to cover the resulting problems of moral hazard and conflict of interest.

The fund usually has a contractually limited life of approximately 10 years, often with a provision for an extension of 2 to 3 years. The fund manager's objective is to realize, or exit, all investments before or at the liquidation of the fund.

The initial years require limited partners (LPs) to meet their contractual obligations to invest when required up to their capital commitment. A significant portion, though not typically all, of committed capital is drawn down during the investment period, typically the first 3 to 5 years, during which new opportunities are identified. After that, during the divestment period, only the existing portfolio companies with the highest potential are further supported, with some follow-on funding provided to extract the maximum value through exits. The manager's efforts during this time are concentrated on realizing or selling investments.

In later years of the partnership, the LPs should receive distributions when realizations (sales of portfolio companies) are made, or when interest payments, dividends, or recapitalizations are received. Funds may have a reinvestment provision, wherein the proceeds of realizations within the investment period or a similar time frame may be reinvested in new opportunities and not distributed to investors. Under this scenario, the fund is self-liquidating as the underlying investments are realized. However, these returns come mostly in the second half of the fund's lifetime.

These distributions to investors can also take the form of securities of a portfolio company, known as in-kind distributions, provided that these securities are publicly tradable or distributed when the fund gets liquidated. Legal documentation may also allow for some reinvestment of realizations, normally subject to a cap amount.

In summary, most PE funds require several years of cash contributions (the commitment) and eventually generate cash flows or distributions-in-kind in the years prior to the termination. These cash flow patterns need to be taken into account by investors attempting to liquidate an existing position or obtain a new position in an existing fund. For example, during the worst times of the global financial crisis (e.g., 2008), PE investors with liquidity problems faced the prospect of receiving almost no value in their attempts to liquidate their existing PE LP positions due to the reluctance of potential buyers to take on the burden of completing the commitments in an environment in which prospects for success were dim.

31.6   THE SECONDARY MARKET FOR PE LP INTERESTS

Secondary transactions refer to the buying and selling of preexisting limited partnership interests in private equity and other alternative investment funds.

31.6.1   Secondary PE Market Emergence and Development

The development of the secondary market in PE has usually been portrayed as a market response to the illiquidity of fund investments that constrained the universe of investors to those who could tolerate the lack of liquidity. The genesis of the secondary market is said to date back to the massive stock market declines of Black Monday on October 19, 1987 and to the world economic crisis of the early 1990s. The secondary market also gained in size following the burst of the dot-com bubble. At that time, institutions and particularly individual investors who had previously enthusiastically committed to venture capital funds felt the liquidity squeeze acutely and often could not afford to meet further capital calls.[1]

These events produced a large need for liquidity among many financial institutions, especially those with illiquid assets such as private equity, which in turn created a new market for secondary interests in PE funds or companies. Since then, a sizable secondary market has emerged, which allows investors to sell their interests in limited partnerships in order to generate liquidity or pursue strategic objectives.

Initially, the secondary market was largely driven by the sale of interests in PE funds, with LPs being forced to exit prematurely. Thus, the PE secondary market was viewed by many as a market of last resort for those desperate to liquidate PE positions. The secondary market not only suffered from a limited track record but also largely lacked transparency and was characterized by an unhealthy predominance of sellers over buyers.

A number of recent developments have led to changes in the perception of the PE secondary market from being only a refuge for desperate sellers and a bargain bin for buyers searching for huge discounts. The motivations of buyers and sellers in the PE secondary market are detailed in later sections (31.6.3 and 31.6.4).

31.6.2 PE Secondary Market Size and Overview

It is estimated that the global volume of secondary transactions increased tenfold in the first two decades of the twenty-first century. The PE secondary market has grown significantly, mirroring the substantial expansion in the primary fundraising market in private equity. Secondaries were probably about 10% of the total PE market in 2005. It is important to emphasize that the total supply was significantly larger, however. Recent data by Cogent Partners (Greenhill 2019) show a steady increase in the volume of transactions in the secondary market: from $25 billion in 2011 to $74 billion in 2018. Also, as shown in Exhibit 31.3, the secondary transactions have been taking place close to the net asset value in recent years. These transactions took place at discounts of about 40% in 2009, about 15% in 2010–12, and moderating to 10% or less in 2017–18. This points out that the secondary market is no longer driven entirely by the desire of LPs to sell their positions because of liquidity needs.

Despite its increasing importance and growth in the volume of transactions, the secondary market has remained opaque. Although various data vendors tried to build specific Internet-based platforms for secondary transactions, information about market conditions is often spurious, and little is known about prices at which transactions finally settle. Historically, around 3% to 5% of outstanding LP exposure comes to market. In the end, less than 2% of the outstanding exposure, calculated as the sum of NAV and unfunded commitments, is actually traded each year.[2]

In recent years, an active market for the sale by PE funds of directly held portfolio companies has emerged. Here, it is the GPs who want or are under pressure to sell, mainly as their fund is approaching the end of its contractual lifetime. In such

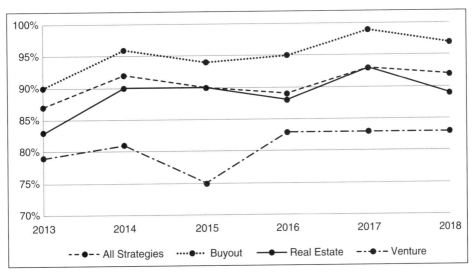

EXHIBIT 31.3 Evolution of Average Secondary Market Pricing
Source: Greenhill (2019).

synthetic secondaries, *portfolio companies* are packaged up and sold to another PE fund manager.

Today, investing in secondary transactions has become an accepted investment strategy and an active portfolio management tool in its own right, and the market has grown substantially in size and maturity. This market is attractive due to its inefficiencies, but such opportunities are hard to value, and the due diligence is complex.

31.6.3 PE LP Seller Motivations

The reasons why LPs decide to dispose of their holdings on the secondary market are as diverse as those for buyers. Broadly speaking, one may differentiate between sales that are motivated primarily by liquidity constraints and those that are related to the strategic repositioning of an investor's portfolio. Understanding these different reasons is important for assessing the informational content of transaction prices in the secondary market.

Sellers may be motivated by active portfolio management and reallocation considerations. As the secondary market has matured, it has been increasingly used for tactical asset allocation. Sell side LPs may decide to divest their entire stake in a particular fund or even offer their entire portfolio of fund investments. Others, however, may decide to sell only a certain share of their stake in a partnership, signaling their continued confidence in the fund manager.

Sometimes LPs are dissatisfied with the performance of a fund or a portfolio of funds and lose confidence in a management team. Selling their stakes in such funds can generate capital that can be redeployed into new opportunities.

Conversely, an LP may want to lock in returns in situations in which the fund manager is not likely to materially increase the performance of the underlying portfolio companies during the remainder of the lifetime of the fund.

Another strategic reason to sell may lie in an unintended overexposure to private equity. This so-called denominator effect usually arises in periods of financial stress, when prices of marketable instruments adjust much faster than valuations of illiquid investments, resulting in a higher-than-targeted share of the latter. As far as liquidity-motivated sales are concerned, the desire to transfer stakes in a limited partnership is usually cyclical, in line with macroeconomic developments.

Despite such good reasons for an LP to sell, this raises the question of whether an early exit is against the main idea of private equity, namely to be patient until the "pearls" emerge, and, by and large, institutions are justifiably reluctant to sell.[3] Although the existing investor may occasionally be under pressure to exit a fund, from an economic point of view the case for selling is far from clear under normal circumstances and raises the question of sourcing and proper pricing of secondary transactions.

31.6.4 PE LP Buyer Motivations

On the buy side, the secondary market has historically been dominated by dedicated secondary funds and other funds of funds. Apart from the portfolio management considerations mentioned previously, the obvious reasons why investors want to buy relate mainly to the potential attractiveness of secondary stakes.

To begin with, secondaries are often distressed sales that take place at a significant discount to the most recent NAV. Under distressed market conditions, stakes in funds are offered by LPs who are generally in need of liquidity or, specifically related to their PE activities, face a nontrivial risk of default on future capital calls from fund managers. Such assets can be a bargain for those who have at their disposal a sufficient degree of liquidity to meet the unfunded commitments of the fund investments.

An important advantage of secondary investments is that they are subject to less uncertainty when compared with commitments to primary funds, which represent blind pools of capital. At the time of making a commitment, a primary investor does not know how the fund's capital will eventually be deployed—apart from the broad investment guidelines specified in the limited partnership agreement. By the time a secondary transaction takes place, a significant share of the fund's capital has already been invested in portfolio companies. Prospective buyers can analyze them in detail and have indicators that help distinguish between companies that developed according to plan and those that did not.[4] In recent years, therefore, a growing number of nontraditional buyers have entered the market, including pension funds, insurance companies, endowments, foundations, family offices, sovereign wealth funds, and hedge funds.

Some institutional investors enter the secondary PE market as a means of getting rapid exposure to PE assets with a diverse range of vintage years. Other LPs use secondary transactions to avoid committing capital to the 10 to 12-year investment horizon of newly PE funds. The different dynamic in the secondary market can be employed as a means to counteract the J-curve effect of primary fund investments. Given that it normally takes several years for a fund to reach the cash flow breakeven point from its inception, a secondary acquisition of a 4-year-old fund reduces this period significantly, generating expected cash flows quickly and shortening the duration of the investment relative to new offerings.

31.6.5 Sourcing Secondary PE Fund Opportunities

While transactions involving individual funds or small portfolios are usually negotiated bilaterally, intermediated auctions have become increasingly common for larger and more complex transactions. This process is facilitated by financial intermediaries, who are today involved in the majority of deals in the secondary market and ensure that the sales process is competitive. Used mainly by sellers, intermediaries help identify buyers and structure offerings of fund interests. Financial intermediaries are either specialized secondary advisers or placement agents, generally charging a transaction fee between 1% and 2% of the value of the transaction.[5]

Typically, a number of LPs are contacted to sound out their potential interest. In cases in which a large portfolio is being sold, intermediaries may divide it into subsets to improve the chances of finding interested buyers. LPs make bids in a managed auction for the particular stakes they want to purchase; these decisions are based on confidential information the intermediary provides about the funds' holdings and their valuation. Many secondary auctions involve two rounds. After a first round of bidding, the seller and the intermediary invite a subgroup of potential buyers to participate in the second round. During this round, interested buyers have the opportunity to revise their bids in light of new information they might have acquired in the process. While the set of information the intermediary provides is the same for all interested buyers, large LPs with diversified portfolios often have an important competitive advantage in that they have superior proprietary information about the fund manager, the manager's previous track record, and the quality of the current investments.

31.6.6 Valuing Secondary Stakes

While prices in the secondary market are generally expressed in terms of discounts or premiums relative to a fund's NAV, this can be misleading. To determine a fund's fair value, the NAV reported by the GP is of limited relevance. Valuations of funds can be considered to be fair only if they are equal to the present value of the fund's overall expected cash flows, which include not only those that are related to the investments a fund has already made but also future cash flows that are associated with the undrawn commitments the buyer needs to fund.

The secondary price is estimated by discounting the expected future cash flows, based on the buyer's expectations about the asset's performance:

$$P_0 = \sum_{t=0}^{T} \frac{CF_t}{(1 + IRR_{\text{Buyer}})^t} \tag{31.3}$$

with P_0 denoting the secondary price offered by the buyer, CF_t the fund's expected cash flow at time t, n the fund's maturity, and IRR_{Buyer} the buyer's required or expected IRR. This value reflects the present value of the expected cash flows from both funded and unfunded commitments and thus will generally be different from the NAV reported by the GP; this is because the accounting impact is usually the reference point for the seller.

The discount can be expressed as follows:

$$\text{Discount}_t = (\text{NAV}_t - P_t)/\text{NAV}_t \tag{31.4}$$

APPLICATION 31.6.6

A prospective secondary-market private equity investor forecasts a total of five equal cash flows from a fund of $1 million per year over the next 5 years (i.e., years 1–5). The buyer's required internal rate of return (IRR) is 18%. The fund's current NAV is $3.5 million. What is the fund's estimated value to the buyer and the estimated discount?

The value of the expected cash flow stream to the buyer using a discount rate of 18% is $3.127 million using Equation 31.3. The discount using Equation 31.4 is [(3.500 − 3.127)/3.500], which equals 10.7%. The buyer is offering a price 10.7% below the fund's reported NAV.

In practice, the cash flow projections need to take a number of factors into account: in particular, the expected exit value and exit timing for current portfolio investments, any projected future capital calls, and the expected cash flows on any future investments made using such drawdowns. Exit value refers to the price that the fund can receive when portfolio companies are sold through initial public offerings (IPOs), strategic sales, or other methods of exit.

Exit timing refers to the period during which portfolio companies are expected to be sold and exit values are realized. This analysis is generally based on a combination of GP guidance, co-investor insight, and market analysis. All public investments are valued using a mark-to-market analysis, taking potential lockups into consideration. The resulting projected gross cash flows are then run through the partnership's legal structure, taking future management fees and the distribution waterfall into account to arrive at a net cash flow stream for the fund. Once the projected net cash flows are determined, the present value is calculated by discounting the net cash flows at an appropriate discount rate. This target rate varies across market segments, with mezzanine funds usually having a lower target rate than buyout funds, which in turn have a lower target rate than VC funds, reflecting their specific risk characteristics. Furthermore, target rates mirror market conditions, which vary over time.[6]

Secondary market prices are only of limited use as benchmarks for fair market value, as they are not observable. Transactions are confidential, and the final settlement price is generally known to only the buyer and the seller (and the intermediary to the extent that a transaction has been facilitated by a specialist agent). The secondary market price reflects current market conditions for those who participate in the market as either sellers or buyers but reveals little about the underlying value of the portfolio, which is held until maturity.

Exhibit 31.3 displays secondary market pricing history, which is expressed as average high bids as a percentage of NAV. First, we can see that the secondary prices are almost always discounted relative to NAV. Second, the discounts reached their highest values during the most recent financial crisis. Third, the average discounts for buyout funds are typically smaller than those of venture capital funds. This can be explained by the fact that portfolio companies of venture capital funds are more difficult to value, and therefore there is greater uncertainty regarding their NAVs.

31.6.7 Limitations of the Secondary Market for PE Interests

Undoubtedly, the secondary market would not have reached its current level of significance if it had not brought about important advantages for both sellers and buyers of interests in limited partnerships. However, as the secondary market has not materially altered the fundamental characteristics of fund investments, the challenges investors face in measuring and managing the particular risks that come with commitments to limited partnerships remain essentially unchanged. As significant as the development of the secondary market may be for constructing efficient portfolios, it should not be perceived as a game changer in terms of tactical asset allocation, active management, or risk management in illiquid investments.

Although the secondary market has expanded rapidly in recent years, it has remained small relative to the primary market, with only a few percent of primary commitments being transacted in the secondary market. Importantly, the secondary market, just like other financial markets, may dry up precisely at the time when it is needed most. The year 2009 provided a warning. Although a maximum amount of supply came to market, the actual transaction volume collapsed, as sellers were not prepared to accept discounts that were at times 60% or higher unless they were under exceptional pressure to create liquidity.

NOTES

1. Brown and Berman (2003) reported that in the United States at the time, 400 individuals were looking for bailouts and were willing to sell at a discount rather than become defaulting investors. Secondary specialists like Coller Capital or Landmark Partners were even able to close a number of so-called walk-away deals in which they paid the original investors nothing for the position and in exchange agreed to cover future capital calls.
2. See Cornelius et al. (2013).
3. For example, according to Private Equity International (2006), for CalPERS, conducting a sale is not an option.
4. Note, however, that this advantage can be significantly reduced, and even eliminated, in early secondary transactions. Sometimes called purchased primaries, such transactions take place at a very early stage of the fund. In extreme cases, the buyer agrees to buy the seller's commitment at a time when the fund has not yet made any acquisitions.
5. See Talmor and Vasvari (2011).
6. See Cornelius et al. (2013).

REFERENCES

Asness, Clifford S., Tobias J. Moskowitz, and Lasse Heje Pedersen. 2013. "Value and momentum everywhere." *The Journal of Finance* 68 (3): 929–85.

Brown, E. and P. Berman. 2003. "Take My Venture Fund—Please!" *Forbes*, June 23.

Cogent Partners. 2015. "Secondary Market Trends and Outlook." White Paper, January.

Cornelius, P., C. Diller, D. Guennoc, and T. Meyer. 2013. *Mastering Illiquidity: Risk Management for Portfolios of Limited Partnership Funds.* Chichester, UK: John Wiley & Sons.

Cornelius, P., K. Juttmann, and R. de Veer. 2009. "Industry Cycles and the Performance of Buyout Funds." *Journal of Private Equity* 12 (4): 14–21.

Faber, M. 2013. "A Quantitative Approach to Tactical Asset Allocation." Mabane Faber Research White Paper.

Greenhill, 2019, Global Secondary Market Trends & Outlook for 2018. https://www.greenhill.com/en/content/greenhill%E2%80%99s-secondary-market-analysis-another-record-transaction-volume.

Grinold, R. 1989. "The Fundamental Law of Active Management," *Journal of Portfolio Management* 15 (3): 30–37.

Hull, Blair and Xiao Qiao. 2017. "A practitioner's defense of return predictability." *The Journal of Portfolio Management* 43 (3): 60–76.

Pesaran, M. Hashem. 2010. "Predictability of asset returns and the efficient market hypothesis." In: D. Giles and A. Ullah, ed. *Handbook of Empirical Economics and Finance.* Taylor & Francis, 281–312.

Private Equity International. 2006. "Orphans in the Portfolio." May.

Talmor, E. and F. Vasvari. 2011. *International Private Equity.* Chichester, UK: John Wiley & Sons, Chapter 7.

CHAPTER 32

Selection of a Fund Manager

This chapter discusses selection of private equity funds. Private equity funds are selected as the focus of the chapter; however, most of the material applies generally to a variety of private fund structures. The chapter discusses the process of screening the universe of potential funds to identify those on which due diligence is performed, and the priorities in selecting the funds that will be included in the portfolio. The process of due diligence is detailed in Chapters 33–35.

32.1 THE IMPORTANCE OF FUND SELECTION ACROSS MANAGERS THROUGH TIME

Gaining access to the top performers is critical to the success of the fund selection process. Exhibit 32.1 displays relative performances of upper and lower quartiles of private equity funds by vintage year. As can be seen, for some vintage years, the differences between the internal rates of return (IRRs) of top-quartile and bottom-quartile managers exceed 15%. Therefore, the skill to select top-quartile funds is considered the core competence of fund selection and is the key performance driver for private fund allocations.

The private equity (PE) industry is evolving. Decades ago there were only a few players in a largely underexplored (i.e., inefficient) PE market that offered rich pickings. Access and due diligence were seen as everything. In more recent years, the PE market has become highly competitive.

As the market matures, investors may find that selection of high-quality managers is not sufficient to ensure high performance and should increasingly focus on managing all aspects of the investment process well, including the evaluation of overall conditions of the industry. In other words, PE fund selection may increasingly involve knowing the market conditions under which managers should be selected at all.

32.2 THE RELATIONSHIP LIFE CYCLE BETWEEN LPS AND GPS

A key to selecting managers is to understand the life cycle of the relationship between fund GPs and their LP investors.

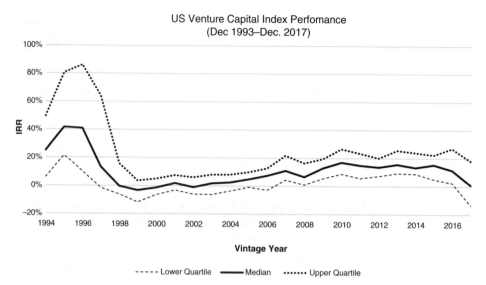

EXHIBIT 32.1   US Private Equity and Venture Capital Index Performance as of December 2017
Source: Cambridge Associates, 2018.

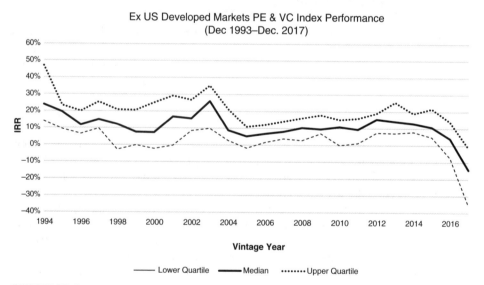

EXHIBIT 32.2   Ex-US Developed Markets Private Equity and Venture Capital Index Performance as of December 2017
Source: Cambridge Associates, 2018.

32.2.1   The Relationship Between PE GPs and LPs

PE funds generally have finite lives, such as 12 years. The initial years of the fund involve selecting and funding portfolio companies. To maintain continuous investment in new portfolio companies, GPs need to raise new funds as soon as the capital from their latest active fund is fully invested (or reserved for follow-on investments), that is, about every 3 to 5 years. GPs with good relationships with LPs in prior funds seek to continue those relationships as they launch new funds. PE GPs, for their part, want financially strong, dependable, knowledgeable, and long-term LPs. LPs should have industry expertise and familiarity with the nuts and bolts (particularly valuations and benchmarking) of the PE business.

An LP investing in a successful PE fund will likely have a favorable view of the GP as a manager and will seek further investments with that manager (who will likely be happy to continue to work with the LP through new funds rather than go through the process of attracting a new limited partner). Thus, relationships between LPs and GPs follow a life cycle and are forged through various rounds of investment, eventually resulting in a virtuous circle of growing experience and fund size.

Anecdotal evidence suggests that experienced market players profit from forging long-term relationships. Fund managers usually cannot get rich through their first few funds. However, a favorable track record is an asset in itself. For more reputable managers, fundraising is less costly. Fund managers can minimize their expenses by turning first to those who invested in their previous partnership, provided that the fund's performance was satisfactory.

While it is easy to see how fund managers benefit from a loyal and reliable investor community, these long-term relationships can also be advantageous for LPs. It is especially desirable for a PE investor to hold on to good fund managers, as the best teams will have an established investor base (i.e., a set of established and loyal clients). In the opaque PE market, the search for and due diligence of funds is a costly exercise, and LPs have reason to prefer familiar fund managers to investment proposals from unfamiliar managers. Long-term relationships may provide LPs with access to a quality deal flow of co-investment opportunities in portfolio companies within an established framework. There is likely to be improved investment planning as LPs make clear their intentions to participate in follow-on funds. Predictable closings put money to work more efficiently.

Thus, there is a symbiotic relationship between LPs and GPs. From the perspective of the LP, the success of an LP's investment strategy can depend on its relationships with GPs. LPs with established relationships with historically successful GPs often have preferred access to subsequent funds. GPs often focus on specific segments (such as stages or sectors) of the market. This specialized focus, for example in the case of venture capital, can often limit the access of LPs without established GP relationships to identify and access high-quality fund managers.

32.2.2 Adverse Selection and GP–LP Relationships

Adverse selection exists in the PE market. GPs of unproven quality or GPs with relatively unattractive track records cannot be highly selective in their search for investors in new funds. They may be forced to accept investments from inexperienced LP investors who may require substantial time with the GP to learn about PE and may need extensive communication with the GP during the fund's early years.

Inexperienced LP investors usually lack access to top managers because follow-on funds of successful managers are often fully subscribed by the GP's previous investors or well-known and established LPs in the PE market. The inexperienced LPs will tend to be forced to select managers from a pool of GPs with limited track records in terms of either success, number of funds, or both.

The **consequence of adverse selection in PE funds** is the higher probability that both unproven GPs and inexperienced LPs will form relationships with each other, both will underperform and both may eventually exit the market. However, it is an oversimplification to assume that investors invest only in top performers and that below-average funds are unable to continue. As in most relationships, there is a certain degree of tolerance for mistakes and failures, at least over a period of time. It is clear that there are limits to disappointing results, but all things being equal, investors will tend to go with fund managers they already know or who have been referred to them through their network, even if the fund's performance has been subpar at times.

32.2.3 Overview of the Life Cycle Aspect of the GP–LP Relationship

The life cycle of the GP–LP relationship (see Exhibit 32.3) focuses on the long-term pattern of GPs as they create multiple funds through time. The **GP–LP life cycle** can be divided into three phases: (1) entry and establish (the phase involving the GP's initial funds); (2) build and harvest (or grow and compete, the phase in which the GP's funds thrive and grow); and (3) decline (lost competition), exit (gave up or made it), or transition to new managers (spinouts). These three potential outcomes lead toward the termination of the original relationship.

32.2.4 The Entry and Establish Phase

During the **entry and establish phase,** substantial entry barriers into the PE market exist for both GPs and LPs and, lacking a verifiable track record, new teams find it difficult to raise their first fund. Furthermore, analysis of historical benchmark data supports the hypothesis that new teams suffer from higher mortality than do established or institutional-quality fund managers. First-time funds note the

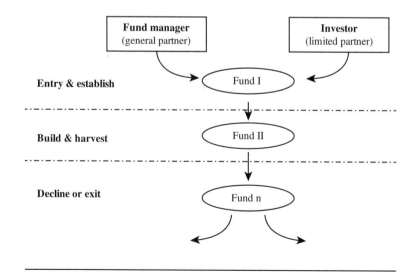

EXHIBIT 32.3   Fund Manager–Investor Relationship Life Cycle

EXHIBIT 32.4 Characteristics of the GP–LP Life Cycle Phases

Fund Characteristic	Entry and Establish	Build and Harvest	Decline or Exit
Investment strategy	Differentiation	Star brand	Unexciting
Fundraising	Difficult fundraising	Loyal LP base	LPs leave and are replaced by other typical investors (secondary plays, new entrants in market)
Performance	Unknown: either top or out	Likely top performer	Not top but consistent performer
Size	Fund is too small	Fund size is right	Fund size too large/too many funds
Economies of scale	Fund is too small to get rich	Best alignment of interests	Senior managers made it
Management team	Management team forming	Management team performing	Succession issues, spinouts

importance of differentiation or innovation as applied to fundraising and thus often pursue specialized investment strategies. The main differences between this phase as well as the other phases are summarized in Exhibit 32.4.

New LPs also face entry barriers, suffering the initial informational disadvantages that make it extremely difficult to identify or gain access to the best managers, particularly when their funds are oversubscribed. For LPs, it takes the disciplined execution of a long-term investment strategy to build up a portfolio of funds that gives attractive and sustainable returns.

32.2.5 The Build and Harvest Phase

The **build and harvest phase** of PE funds is when the size of the investments tends to grow, the profitability of the investments is strong, and both the GPs and LPs receive the greatest rewards. Since investors are mainly interested in the cash returned, the fund manager–investor relationship tends to be relatively stable throughout the build and harvest phase. Lerner and Schoar (2004) present evidence on the high degree of continuity in the investors of successive funds, and the ability of sophisticated investors to anticipate funds that will have poor subsequent performance.

32.2.6 The Decline or Exit Phase

Eventually, the relationship ends in decline or exit. The exit may occur as a spinout. Not surprisingly, the terms marriage and divorce are often used in the context of relationships between fund managers and their investors. A gradual decline may occur either as a result of past successes, which potentially decrease the financial motivation of senior fund managers, or due to an improperly planned succession, which leads to the departure of middle management. In addition, the LPs may eventually end the relationship if they lose confidence or trust in the team (for example, if the team becomes arrogant or fails to deliver). Some LPs do not invest in follow-on funds and may be replaced by less deep-pocketed or experienced investors, or by secondary investors who choose to invest as a one-off financial play.

32.3   FUND RETURN PERSISTENCE

Fund performance persistence refers to the tendency of a fund's under- or over-performance in one time period to be likely to be followed be similar under- or overperformance. This section discusses fund return persistence starting with the fund return persistence hypothesis.

32.3.1   The Fund Performance Persistence Hypothesis

The **fund performance persistence hypothesis** is the proposition that fund managers generate returns that contradict the weak-form efficient markets hypothesis by offering excess returns in two or more non-overlapping time periods that exhibit statistically significant correlation.

When considering private equity's modus operandi and the observation that GPs have differential and proprietary skills, the performance persistence hypothesis appears to be highly plausible because distinct organizational capabilities could credibly explain the top-performing GPs' superior value creation.[1] The lack of a public auction of initial offerings of the funds offered by top managers could inhibit informationally-efficient pricing.

Supporting fund performance persistence is the proposition that top-performing GPs build extensive industry networks which give them an advantaged deal flow and allow them to identify the most promising deals. Associated with such a network is domain expertise (that is, specialized knowledge of the industry sector in which the GP is operating). Finally, and largely independent from industries, top-performing GPs are said to have the ability to create value through operational improvement in portfolio companies.

Gatekeepers market their benchmarking services for checking and comparing GPs' performance as well as their ability to sell access to these "top team" fund managers. **Gatekeepers** are professional advisers operating in the PE market on behalf of their clients:[2] in particular, consultants and account managers, funds of funds, and placement agents. However, the fact that the performance persistence argument is neat, simple, and intuitively sensible means that there is a risk that any evidence that conflicts with this conventional wisdom meets with skepticism.

On a theoretical level, significant performance persistence poses a problem, especially given the anecdotal evidence that some top-performing funds do not accept all the money that investors are willing to provide. Why don't these fund managers increase their income by increasing fund size or fees? Kaplan and Schoar (2005) mutual fund argue that, given the diseconomies of scale displayed by private equity funds, top-performing funds limit their size so that they can deliver higher returns to their investors. Higher performance will enable these fund managers to raise additional funds going forward, potentially maximizing long-term profitability. Further, private equity funds may want to limit their offerings to those investors who are known to have the resources to respond to capital calls and to invest in follow-on funds.

32.3.2   Evidence Regarding Fund Performance Persistence

There has been a wide consensus among investors that some alternative investments exhibit performance persistence. Private equity funds are an often-cited example of links between prior fund returns and those in the future. GPs' performance persistence in private equity has long attracted the interest of practitioners as well as academics.[3] What evidence there is seems to support the performance persistence hypothesis.

Available empirical evidence strongly supports the presence of persistence for all private equity strategies until the late 1990s. For example, for venture capital (VC), Conner (2005) found that follow-on funds raised by fund managers whose prior fund's performance was in the top quartile had a 44% chance of achieving a top-quartile internal rate of return (IRR). If the distribution of returns across GPs was perfectly random and previous returns were irrelevant, this figure would be 25%.

Although past private equity GP performance persistence is widely accepted as a fact, recent research has called more recent performance persistence into question. These studies have shown that while persistence exists for certain strategies, the degree of persistence has weakened considerably since 2000. For example, the performance persistence of follow-on funds relative to the performance persistence of the previous funds has weakened since 2000.[4] Going forward, LPs may not be able to rely on simple screening criteria based on prior performance and may need to reflect on how they can create value under these circumstances. This also implies greater focus on aspects of manager selection and monitoring that form distinct parts of the investment process, that can be efficiently structured, and that are among the keys to sustainable outperformance in private equity.

32.3.3 Transition Matrices and Return Persistence in PE Funds

A **transition matrix** is a square matrix that denotes the frequency (or probability) of subsequent outcomes based on prior outcomes. Each prior outcome (i.e., in this case performance of an original private equity fund in a prior time period) is matched with each subsequent outcome (i.e., in this case performance of a follow-on private equity fund in a subsequent time period). The goal is to indicate the historic rates at which particular levels of performance in a prior period are associated with subsequent performance.

For example, consider the transition matrix in Exhibit 32.5. An initial sample of "prior" or "current" funds is divided into tertiles ranked by return performance. The "prior fund" is then linked to a successive fund ("the next fund") with the same GP. The successive funds are also divided into tertiles based on their return performance. These linked pairs of sequential funds form nine possible performance paths: (1) from lower tertile performance to lower tertile performance (the upper left corner) of Exhibit 32.5 (2) from lower tertile performance to middle tertile performance (the

EXHIBIT 32.5 Transition Matrix of Private Equity Funds (Phalippou and Gottschalg 2009)

		Next Fund		
		Lower 3rd	Middle 3rd	Upper 3rd
Current Fund	Lower 3rd	43%	29%	28%
	Middle 3rd	30%	41%	29%
	Upper 3rd	26%	32%	42%

EXHIBIT 32.6 Transition Matrix of Venture Capital Fund Performance (Harris, Jenkinson, and Stucke 2014)

VC Funds		Current Funds (whole sample)			
		1	2	3	4
Previous Fund Quartile	1	48.5%	16.7%	24.2%	10.6%
	2	28.9%	34.2%	20.2%	16.7%
	3	22.0%	29.4%	29.4%	19.3%
	4	14.8%	17.3%	29.6%	38.3%

upper center); ... (9) from higher tertile performance to higher tertile performance (the lower right corner).

Performance persistence is supported to the extent that the frequency rates observed on the diagonal from upper left to lower right (i.e., 43%, 41%, and 42%) exceed the frequency expected in the absence of performance persistence (33%). Casual analysis of Exhibit 32.5 indicates historical tendencies of the returns of one fund in one time period to persist into similar performance in a successive fund in a subsequent time period. For example, bad performance is repeated 43% of the time (compared to 33% if returns are not correlated through time) and good performance is repeated 42% of the time. Funds reversed their performance from lower to higher only 28% of the time and from higher to lower only 26% of the time.

A more recent study summarized in Exhibit 32.6 indicates that venture capital funds grouped into quartiles based on historic performance also experienced persistence. The diagonal of persistence indicates outcomes (48.5%, 34.2%, 29.4%, and 38.3%) that substantially exceed the 25% average of outcomes generated without persistence.

32.3.4 Persistence of Return Persistence in PE Funds

Exhibits 32.5 and 32.6 indicated likely return persistence over a long time period (1984–2011) based on casual observation. Exhibits 32.7 and 32.8, which are adapted from Harris, Jenkinson, and Stucke (2014), display the transition matrix of buyout funds divided into two time periods: pre-2001 and post-2000. The purpose of the exhibits is to indicate whether the evidence regarding persistence is changing through time.

EXHIBIT 32.7 Transition Matrix of Pre-2001 Buyout Fund Performance (Harris, Jenkinson, and Stucke 2014)

Buyout Funds		Current Funds (pre-2001)			
		1	2	3	4
Previous Fund Quartile	1	37.5%	25.0%	18.8%	18.8%
	2	30.4%	21.7%	30.4%	17.4%
	3	21.4%	25.0%	32.1%	21.4%
	4	17.4%	26.1%	30.4%	26.1%

EXHIBIT 32.8 Transition Matrix of Post-2000 Buyout Fund Performance (Harris, Jenkinson, and Stucke 2014)

Buyout Funds		Current Funds (post-2000)			
		1	2	3	4
Previous Fund Quartile	1	22.0%	28.8%	30.5%	18.6%
	2	24.5%	22.6%	32.1%	20.8%
	3	15.4%	28.2%	38.5%	17.9%
	4	21.4%	14.3%	32.1%	32.1%

Focusing again on the diagonal frequency rates, in the earlier time period (pre-2001) three of the four rates exceeded 25%, with a high of 38.5%, but one was only 22%. In the later time period (post-2000), two of the rates exceeded 25% and two did not (although the rates exceeding 25% were much higher than the rates falling short of 25%). Note also that the maximum rate along the diagonal in the later sample (38.5%) exceeded the maximum diagonal rate from the earlier time period (37.5%).

It is important to note that these results are not universally supported, as other studies report different figures for the transition matrix. The differences are primarily driven by the variety of databases that are employed and the adjustments that researchers make in order to improve the integrity of the data. For example, some researchers assume that the book values of mature funds that have been partially liquidated and that have remained inactive for several years is zero, while others accept the values reported by the fund manager.

Exhibit 32.9 reproduces a chart provided by Preqin, a well-known source of data in the alternative investments industry. The chart covers the overall private equity fund universe for 1982–2017. Casual analysis of Exhibit 32.9 indicates that over the period covered by the study, 36% of top-quartile funds produced follow-on funds that ranked in the top quartile in terms of performance. On the other hand, only 15% of top-quartile funds produced follow-on funds that ranked in the bottom quartile.

These and other results point to the follow broad conclusions: performance persistence is present for poor-performing buyout and VC funds. The persistence may have weakened in recent years but still indicates that performance persistence could be an economically significant factor in manager selection.

32.3.5 Six Challenges to the Performance Persistence Hypothesis

There has been increasing skepticism in recent years regarding the performance persistence hypothesis. There are six primary challenges to the performance persistence hypothesis:

1. AMBIGUITIES REGARDING DEFINITION OF "TOP PERFORMANCE": Conscious of the widespread belief in performance persistence, LPs' preoccupation with track record, and LPs' tendency to meet only with "top-quartile" managers, GPs may frame the measurement of their past performance in whatever way will support the proposition

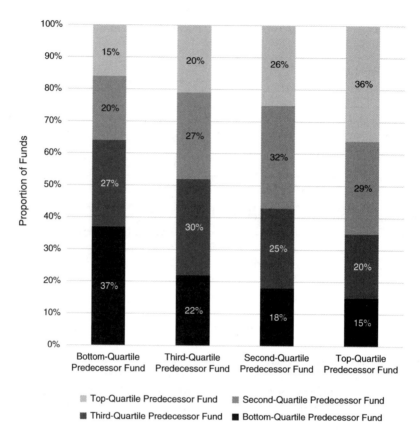

EXHIBIT 32.9   Overall Private Equity Relationship between Predecessor and Successor Fund Quartiles

that they have persisted as being "top." Although the quartiles' mathematical definition is clear, what the numbers refer to is vague. Results can be manipulated by selecting between: (1) potential performance measures such as the funds' internal rates of return or multiples; (2) computation intervals such as the funds' interim or final returns; (3) fee treatment such as the funds' gross returns or returns to LPs net of fees and carried interest; (4) criteria for selection of the peer group (e.g., do they include private equity as a whole or do they differentiate between, say, buyouts and venture capital?).

2. COMPARING HETEROGENOUS FUNDS: If the definition of success is based on the quartile position in the benchmark, comparison should be made against funds that are subject to the same market conditions in order to assure that "apples" are being compared to "apples" (e.g., the vintage-year cohort of the peer group). However, from vintage year to vintage year, the composition of the peer group will change; rarely can two funds managed by the same management team be measured against the same peers because GPs raise funds in irregular intervals. Therefore, the firms that raised the funds that made up the previous vintage year's peer group may not be out looking for investors at the same time for their next round of fundraising. Drawing the conclusion

that success as measured by quartiles is primarily a result of the GPs' skills assumes that all funds had equal starting positions and faced an identical group of competitors.

3. IS THE PERFORMANCE LUCK OR SKILL? Performance may depend on talented individuals and on the processes and culture of the GP as an organization. While it seems an accomplishment to be in the top quartile, a GP has only a handful of opportunities to manage successive funds through time. Assuming that a manager can start a new fund every 6 years, the manager may have only four funds that have been completely liquidated and that therefore offer unambiguous performance figures. This is hardly enough data on which to estimate the impact of the manager's skills with high statistical confidence.[5]

4. THE EFFECT OF CHANGES IN FUND SIZE THROUGH TIME: First-time managers tend to improve their performance in successive funds; however, research suggests a positive relation between fund size and performance up to a point where for very large funds their performance tends to decline again. As first-time funds are usually smaller than the average, the performance improvement may be linked to the change in fund size.[6]

5. SECULAR MARKET TRENDS: In situations with sectors in which all managers generate extreme performance at the same time (for example, in the high performance of the VC market at the end of the 1990s relative to other PE funds), performance is likely to be driven by a secular trend in that sector rather than by individual talent. In other words, the performance persistence among a group of managers in a particular sector may be due to the existence of a long-term trend of high or low performance in that sector rather than an indication of managerial talent.

6. PERFORMANCE DISPERSION IS HETEROGENEOUS IN THE PE MARKET: The dispersion in the performance of one manager may differ from the dispersion of another. A high dispersion manager may have a 50%/50% chance of being in the highest and lowest quartiles, while a low dispersion manager has a 50%/50% chance of being in the second and third quartiles. If half of the managers are high dispersion and half are low dispersion the key diagonals in a transition matrix (i.e., the four frequency rates of remaining in the same quartile) will all be 50%!

32.3.6 Performance Persistence Implementation Issues

Even if investors believe in the performance persistence hypothesis, in practice they may find it difficult to make meaningful use of it: by the time there is sufficient evidence that a firm is really successful, the effect may be gone. The main problem is that empirical analyses of performance persistence in private equity are based on data for funds close to the end of their lifetime. Only funds aged between at least 6 and 8 years are sufficiently mature for drawing conclusions regarding performance. However, GPs raise subsequent funds in intervals of 2 or 3 years. Accordingly,[7] the performance of the most recent fund cannot be reliably estimated in time for investors to decide on commitments for the next fund.

Section 32.3.5 discussed "Ambiguities regarding definition of top performance." The challenges raised in the immediately previous paragraph as well as the ambiguities raised in Section 32.3.5 can make it difficult for investors to use top-quartile performance as an effective screening criterion.[8]

32.4   MORAL HAZARD, ADVERSE SELECTION, AND THE HOLDUP PROBLEM IN FUND MANAGEMENT

For the PE fund investors, the limited partnership agreement (LPA) is an important document that defines the fund's legal framework, terms and conditions. The LPA has two main categories of clauses: (1) investor protection clauses; and (2) economic terms clauses.

1. Investor protection clauses cover investment strategy, including possible investment restrictions, key person provisions, termination and divorce, the investment committee, the LP advisory committee, exclusivity, and conflicts.
2. Economic terms clauses include management fees and expenses, the GP's contribution, and the distribution waterfall. The distribution waterfall defines how returns are split between the LP and GP and how fees are calculated. LPAs are continuously evolving, given the increasing sophistication of fund managers and investors, new regulations, and changing economic environments.

In essence, the LPA lays out conditions aimed at both aligning the interests of fund managers with their investors and discouraging the GP from cheating (moral hazard), lying (adverse selection), or engaging in opportunism (holdup problem) in whatever form.

Moral hazard and adverse selection take place when there is asymmetric information between two parties (e.g., LPs and GPs). **Adverse selection within funds** takes place before a transaction is completed, when the decisions made by one party (e.g., a GP or LP) cause less desirable parties to be attracted to the transaction. For example, if an LP decides to seek GPs that charge very low fees and offer funds with very favorable terms, the LP is likely to attract unskilled GPs that claim to be skilled.

Moral hazard, in contrast, takes place after a transaction is completed and can be defined as the changes in behavior of one or more parties as a result of incentives that come into play once a contract is in effect. For example, with asymmetric fee structures and without proper monitoring, a GP may take excessive risk in order to increase the potential performance fee. If management fees dominate the compensation, an unskilled manager may decide to take minimal levels of risk and just collect the management fee.

In economics, the **holdup problem** is a situation in which two parties (in the case of private equity, a GP and an LP) refrain from cooperating due to concerns that they might give the other party increased bargaining power and thereby reduce their own profits. Incentives are designed so that the fund manager's focus is on maximizing terminal wealth and performance, and ensuring that contractual loopholes are not exploited (e.g., by claiming to have produced overly optimistic interim results).

32.5   SCREENING WITH FUNDAMENTAL QUESTIONS

Chapters 33–35 discuss detailed due diligence for prospective funds under serious consideration. Proper due diligence of funds such as hedge funds and private equity funds can require extensive and expensive analysis. The **fund screening process** involves reducing the universe of potential investments into a much smaller subset on which full due diligence can be performed. This section provides fundamental questions that may be appropriate as part of a screening process for funds ranging from private equity funds to highly liquid hedge funds. They are a prelude to, not a substitute for, a thorough due diligence review.

32.5.1 Three Fundamental Questions Regarding the Nature of a Fund's Investment Program

This section contains three fundamental questions regarding the nature of the fund's investment program. The answers to these three questions are critical:

1. What is the investment objective of the fund?
2. What is the investment process of the fund manager?
3. What is the nature and source of any value added by the fund manager?

A fund manager should have a clear and concise statement of the fund's investment objective, be able to describe the investment process, and explain how and why the fund manager is able to generate attractive returns. The next three sections explore these questions in greater detail.

32.5.2 Three Detailed Questions Regarding the Investment Objective

The investment objective of a fund specifies the goals, nature, and strategies of the fund's investment program. The first question regarding a fund manager's investment objective can in turn be broken down into three more specific questions:

1. In which markets and assets does the fund manager invest?
2. What is the fund manager's general investment strategy?
3. What is the fund manager's benchmark, if any?

Although these questions may seem straightforward, they are often surprisingly difficult to answer, and documentation may not provide the information needed. Consider the following language from a fund disclosure document, in which the manager desires to maintain a flexible investment mandate:

> *The principal objective of the Fund is capital appreciation, primarily through the purchase and sale of securities, commodities, and other financial instruments, including without limitation, stocks, bonds, notes, debentures, and bills issued by corporations, municipalities, sovereign nations, or other entities; options, rights, warrants, convertible securities, exchangeable securities, synthetic and/or structured convertible or exchangeable products, participation interests, investment contracts, mortgages, mortgage- and asset-backed securities, real estate, and interests therein; currencies, other futures, commodity options, forward contracts, money market instruments, bank notes, bank guarantees, letters of credit, and other forms of bank obligations; other swaps and other derivative instruments; limited partnership interests and other limited partnership securities or instruments; and contracts relating to the foregoing; in each case whether now existing or created in the future.*

Let's analyze this statement in light of our three investment objective questions. The first question is not answered appropriately, as the manager has not disclosed a narrow set of markets for investment consideration. The manager's investment strategy, capital appreciation, is a goal for nearly all investment funds, so this manager needs to be more specific. Finally, the manager does not provide a benchmark in the documentation.

By contrast, consider the following language from a second fund disclosure document:

> *The Fund's investment objective is to make investments in U.S. public equity securities. The Fund applies a long/short equity strategy designed to have a positive (i.e., net long) but varying exposure to the equity market. The goal of the strategy is to generate a long-term return in excess of that generated by the value-weighted overall U.S. public equity market.*

This very brief paragraph helps answer all three investment objective questions. First, the manager identifies that the fund invests in public equity securities. Second, the manager discloses that the fund uses a long/short investment strategy. Last, since the manager states that the fund's objective is to outperform an overall value-weighted US public equity market, the investor can conclude that a suitable benchmark might be based on an index such as the S&P 500. An initial meeting with a manager is an opportunity to obtain sufficiently detailed responses to these questions regarding the investment objective, such that the investor may make an informed decision as to the appropriateness of the strategy in relation to the investor's own objectives.

32.5.3   Four Detailed Questions Regarding the Investment Process

Most investors prefer a well-defined investment process, as it can offer insights into the repeatability of a strategy's investment results. The investment process of a fund comprises the methods the fund uses to formulate, execute, and monitor investment decisions. The articulation and documentation of the process can be vital to an understanding of the likely range of investment results generated by the process. Consider the following language from another fund disclosure document:

> *The manager makes extensive use of computerized technology in both the formulation and execution of many investment decisions. Transaction decisions will generally be made and executed algorithmically according to trading strategies embodied in software running in computers used to support the Fund's trading activities.*

The above paragraph describes a so-called black-box trading system, based on computer algorithms developed to quantify the manager's investment insight, and is itself the core of the investment process. Many participants in the fund industry consider themselves to be skill-based, so many fund investment processes are less computerized than this example and reflect the procedures by which the manager's skill and discretion are translated into implementable trading decisions.

The description of the investment process should provide answers to the following four questions:

1. Who makes the investment decisions, such as which decisions are made by investment committees and which are made by individuals?
2. Who are the key people in those committees and individual decisions?
3. How are the decisions actually made (e.g., majority, consensus, sole decision-maker)?
4. How are the portfolios and positions monitored?

Investment process risk is the potential loss from failure to properly execute the stated investment strategy. Although investment process risk cannot be quantified, it may be related to measurable events, such as the loss of key personnel in key functions or breakdowns in communication and trading systems when algorithmic strategies are followed. In many cases, this can be reduced through the use of a key personnel clause. A key personnel clause is a provision that allows investors to withdraw their assets from the fund, immediately and without penalty, when the identified key personnel are no longer making investment decisions for the fund. Other sources of investment process risk can be addressed by having robust communication and algorithmic systems that have been stress tested.

32.5.4 Two Detailed Questions Regarding the Value Added by the Fund Manager

The final set of fundamental questions relates to the nature and source of any value added by the fund manager. These questions help develop an initial understanding of the potential value of the investment program. It requires prospective managers to provide an explanation of how and why the manager is able to generate attractive returns.

There are several ways that fund managers can add value, such as offering attractive risk premiums for bearing risks like illiquidity and exploiting tax advantages to offer attractive after-tax returns. This section focuses on the most common argument for the source of superior returns: using available information to identify mispriced assets.

Investors seek consistently superior risk-adjusted returns. In this endeavor, a prospective investor must ask two questions:

1. What enables a manager to identify alpha?
2. What reasons are there to believe that the alpha will persist (i.e., what makes the manager smarter than other managers)?

There are two primary information-based explanations for superior investment performance in competitive markets based on information: information gathering and information filtering.

1. Information gatherer or searcher: **Information gathering** indicates the ability of the manager to create access to information or to have access to better information than do other managers. Thus, the manager's competitive advantage may

not be in analyzing information but in developing a superior information set. The manager may have a wider or deeper information set that allows a competitive edge, or the manager may have a differentiated strategy or unique position that enables a focus on a specific segment of the market and the ability to gather better information. The advantage is a proprietary information set accumulated over time.

2. Information filterer or analyzer: Another way to generate attractive returns is to have superior skill in filtering and analyzing information. **Information filtering** is the fund manager's ability to use data available to others but to be better able to glean tradable insights from it. Generally speaking, quantitative, computer-driven equity managers access the same information set as everyone else, but the successful managers have better algorithms to extract more value. These successful managers are able to process generally available information more quickly or more effectively.

Fundamental managers use a mosaic approach to data gathering, piecing together many sources of publicly available information and developing insights that others who did not do the legwork would be unlikely to discover. This could include site visits to retail stores to talk to customers and employees, scrubbing industry data such as capacity utilization, or analyzing individual business units in companies with multiple product lines.

To have and maintain a competitive investment edge based on information, a fund manager must demonstrate at least one of these competitive advantages. Some managers may claim success as both information gatherers and information filterers, and in other cases, the distinction may be blurred. Consider the following language from a fund disclosure document indicating information gathering:

> "The General Partner will utilize its industry expertise, contacts, and proprietary databases to identify superior investment ideas." Another manager claims to be an information filterer: "The General Partner will analyze available investment opportunities using its proven methods of determining value." Some managers may not fall neatly into one category or the other: "The General Partner will use its extensive experience, knowledge, databases, and contacts to locate and analyze investment opportunities."

32.6 HISTORICAL PERFORMANCE REVIEW

Clearly, investment performance is the purpose of investing. To what extent, if any, do past results indicate future results? Weisman and Abernathy suggest that relying on a *hedge fund* manager's past performance history can lead to disappointing investment results. Section 32.3.5 discussed six challenges with relying on private equity performance persistence. Consequently, historical performance history, though potentially useful for validation purposes, cannot be relied on solely in selecting a fund manager.

32.6.1 Two Critical Decisions Regarding A Performance Review

The performance review is an analysis of past investment results that forms the heart of many due diligence reports. Even though past performance cannot guarantee future results, it provides insight into the fund manager's performance (risk, return, and correlation) in difficult market cycles, as well as some guidance as to the likelihood of the fund manager's success. Two critical decisions that should be carefully decided before performance reviews are commenced:

1. When should the performance review be executed?
2. How much weight should past performance be given?

Analysis of performance should generally *follow* rather than lead the other aspects of due diligence. Behavioral theory warns of a confirmation bias, whereby an analyst tends to falsely interpret information as supporting previous beliefs or preferences. Since a performance review is more quantitative and objective in nature than other aspects of due diligence, there is a strong reason to believe that a performance review should be performed subsequent to the more subjective aspects of due diligence. The goal is to prevent confirmation bias, in which an investor first identifies historically successful funds and then subconsciously favors those funds throughout the due diligence process. This confirmation bias is especially dangerous to the extent that past performance is not indicative of future performance. There is also a danger of herd behavior, also known as the bandwagon effect in psychology. **Herd behavior** is the extent to which people are overly eager to adopt beliefs that conform to those of their peers.

A number of biases, including those just discussed, can distort the due diligence process by causing the performance review to disproportionately influence the entire due diligence process, or may cause the performance review itself to be flawed. Leading these biases is the **bias blind spot,** which is people's tendency to underestimate the extent to which they possess biases. The bottom line is that if material flaws are uncovered in the analysis of the manager's strategy, structure, or administration, then the due diligence process should cease before evaluating performance.

The importance of past performance should be thoughtfully weighted in due diligence. Funds with extraordinary reports of past performance may have simply been lucky, may have benefited from market conditions that will not persist, may be more likely to experience future capacity problems, may have taken excess risks, or may be more likely to have reported fraudulent or deceptive results. Funds with mixed performance may in some cases have better prospects for superior future returns. A strategic investigator considers these dynamics and performs due diligence that is not dominated by reported past performance.

32.6.2 Reliance on Past Performance

The underlying issue in investigating the source of attractive returns is to determine which fund managers can sustain superior performance. An investor cannot rely on historical fund performance data as the sole means of selecting good managers over bad managers, because all fund performance contains random noise. For example, even in a perfectly efficient market in which no manager can generate alpha, sheer luck causes some managers to have higher returns and some to have lower returns. Analysis of past data may provide useful information regarding risk, but analysis of historical returns cannot reliably predict alpha. The more reliable method for ascertaining the potential for alpha is rigorous and thoughtful analysis.

It should be noted that competition tends to erode informational advantages over time, as other managers discover the sources of returns from successful funds. Thus, an analysis of the sources of returns should include an analysis of whether an informational advantage should be expected to persist via either proprietary data or investment in continuously sought-after new sources.

To summarize, in a competitive market (and excluding transaction costs), every cent by which one investor outperforms the market index on a risk-adjusted basis must be offset with a cent by which another investor underperforms. Successful fund managers should know the exact nature of their competitive advantage and how to continue to exploit it. Many investors chase past performance by selecting funds with attractive performance records without paying much attention to the sources and causes of the outperformance. But successful alternative investment professionals tend to focus on identifying managers through superior analysis of their strategies and the sources of their returns.

32.6.3 Comprehensive Listing of Current and Past Assets under Management

A historical analysis of performance should begin with the generation of a comprehensive listing of *all* assets under management directed by the fund manager. The investor should verify how many unique strategies, funds, and separate accounts the fund manager advises as well as the assets under management for each fund. This is important not only for the collection of performance data but also to give the investor some sense of the fund manager's investment capacity and how thin the investment manager may be spread across multiple products, all relying on continually refreshed investment insights. It is essential to learn about any funds or accounts that have been terminated to avoid selection bias in analyzing performance.

Verifying the assets of the fund manager may not be as easy as it sounds. First, the fund manager may have onshore and offshore accounts or funds. Second, the fund manager may use multiple prime brokers and custodians to keep and trade its assets. The investor should find out how many custodians and prime brokers the fund manager uses and get all monthly statements from each. Only then can the investor piece together the total size of the fund manager's assets.

There are three important questions to ask:

1. How long has the fund manager been actively managing each current *and previous fund*?
2. Have the manager's performance results been consistent over time and across funds?
3. How do the investment strategies of the funds compare and contrast?

For funds, 5 years is generally sufficient to qualify as a long-term track record. The consistency of performance through time and across all funds provides insight regarding risk. Performance should be linked to the investment strategies and styles. If multiple funds pursue similar investment opportunities, then the issue of trade allocation must be resolved. Trade allocation, in this context, refers to the process by which—and priorities with which—an attractive investment opportunity is distributed among the manager's various funds and accounts.

32.6.4 Drawdowns

Past drawdowns provide indications of past risk that should be carefully considered in the due diligence process. Drawdowns should be analyzed in the context of the fund's strategy, the fund's leverage, and the performance of market indices. The analysis should indicate the fund's response to periods of market stress, as well as the fund's relative sensitivities to both market and idiosyncratic risk. For example, large drawdowns in a market-neutral fund may indicate a lapse of fund manager skill. Drawdowns in directional fund strategies may simply indicate market risk.

In addition to examining the size of drawdowns, the investor should examine how long it took for the fund manager to recoup the losses. The fund manager should explain the causes of past drawdowns and, ideally, how those losses might be mitigated in the future.

32.6.5 Statistical Return Data and Five Classic Issues

The statistical data section of a performance review covers the basic summary information that is expected of all active managers, including returns over a variety of time periods, volatilities of returns, and performance measures such as the Sharpe ratio and the information ratio (IR). There are numerous issues to be considered once the data are assembled. Five classic issues are related to virtually any use of past data to predict the future.

1. ACCURACY: Are the measures accurate? Performance may be intentionally misrepresented, as in the case of fraud, or inadvertently wrong due to data errors or computation errors. **Expectation bias** is synonymous with confirmation bias and is a tendency to overweight those findings that most agree with one's prior beliefs. Thus, a confident manager is more likely to unknowingly accept and report erroneous data if those data portray the fund's performance favorably.
2. REPRESENTATIVENESS: Are the measures representative of the fund's total experience, or is there cherry-picking or other selection bias? Marketing pressures may lead managers to report or emphasize more favorable time periods, higher-performing accounts or funds, and those performance measures that are most favorable.
3. STATIONARITY: Are past results likely to predict future results? In liquid markets, competition should be expected to eliminate substantial market inefficiencies. Thus, high past performance should be expected to attract competition and eventually dilute profit opportunities rather than persist through a stationary return-generating process.
4. GAMING: Are the performance numbers gamed? In the context of investment management, **gaming** is investment activity driven by a desire to generate favorable statistical measures of performance rather than to benefit investors. A survey in the spring 2010 issue of the *Journal of Alternative Investments* found that 27% of respondents believed that hedge funds engage in deliberate cheating by subjectively valuing securities to smooth returns and reduce volatility.[9]

   Even without such misconduct, performance measures such as the Sharpe ratio are imperfect and should be interpreted with caution due to the ability of managers to boost the measures using market tactics and valuation techniques.

For example, if an investment manager can shift profits from highly profitable time periods to time periods with heavy losses, the estimated volatility can be substantially reduced. A reduction in reported volatility increases the Sharpe ratio even though true performance has not changed.

5. APPROPRIATENESS: Are the performance measures used appropriate for the underlying investments and strategies? Sharpe ratios and other performance measures can be misleading statistics because of nonnormal returns, nonlinear strategies, smoothed prices, and other phenomena common to alternative investments. Analysts should also be concerned with past correlation and/or autocorrelation being unrepresentative of future correlation or autocorrelation. Most correlations increase in stressed markets. Correlation-based and volatility-based risk measures that do not include periods of high market stress will underrepresent future risk.

32.6.6 Statistical Return Analysis, Computation Horizons, and Intervals

Risk management analysis and systems based on short-term annualized volatilities (e.g., daily data) may substantially understate risk over longer time periods. For example, in the late 1990s, a well-known publisher of financial information on mutual funds assigned low-risk ratings to growth funds, especially high-tech growth funds, even though common sense indicated that these equity funds were riskier than most funds. The volatilities and drawdowns of these funds were very low when based on daily, weekly, or monthly returns because performance was so consistently positive during the tremendous bull market in that sector; however, a longer-term and more thoughtful analysis of returns, such as returns over 10 years or longer, would have indicated the tremendous risk inherent in these funds, which had exploded in price to unprecedented valuation levels. In March 2000, the prices of these growth funds began a precipitous decline, and investors relying on these supposedly safe funds, rather than on common sense, experienced massive losses.

The possibility of large directional movements over months or even years may have been underweighted because of a focus on volatility computations based on short time intervals. Risk management may fail when numbers are not interpreted in context and with substantial investment experience. For example, even if daily price volatility does not change, monthly price volatility can explode or collapse, based on whether returns experience positive or negative autocorrelation. Note that a string of alternating daily returns (+1%, –1%, +1%, –1% . . .) has substantial daily volatility but generates little monthly volatility. However, a string of correlated daily returns (–0.5%, –0.6%, –0.6% . . .) has less daily volatility but generates huge directional moves. The relation between short-term and long-term volatility is driven by autocorrelation.

Level I of the CAIA curriculum indicates that the volatility of returns over T periods (σ_T) is equal to the single-period volatility (σ_1) times the square root of the number of time periods when returns have no autocorrelation. Thus, annual volatility is only about 16 times larger than daily volatility based on 256 trading days per year and zero autocorrelation. If daily price volatility is 1%, annual volatility is about 16%. However, when returns are perfectly autocorrelated, the same daily volatility generates much higher annualized volatility: $\sigma_T = T\sigma_1$. Thus, annual volatility is about 256 times higher than daily volatility based on 256 trading days per year and perfect positive autocorrelation. A performance report, risk analysis, or risk management system that relies on annualized volatilities of short-term returns is underreporting long-term volatility to the extent that short-term returns exhibit positive autocorrelation that is ignored. Large directional moves, often during periods of market stress, can be caused by high autocorrelation.

32.7 MANAGER SELECTION AND DEAL SOURCING

Manager selection is not mechanical; it requires industry experience and resources to conduct both research and due diligence. Unfortunately, this is easier said than done, and the advice to focus on top funds is probably as helpful as the observation that to become rich, one needs to acquire a lot of money. Further, it is more difficult to identify superior managers than it is to eliminate obviously inferior managers.

32.7.1 Determination of the Wish List of Fund Characteristics

The development of an investment strategy is important to efficiently manage the process of selecting fund managers, and it forms the starting point of the selection process. Based on the investment strategy of the investor and the resulting portfolio design, a wish list of fund characteristics needs to be established. This wish list defines the types of proposals that are consistent with the investment strategy of the investor. Next, an active deal sourcer identifies wish-list funds to be specifically targeted for investment. Investors can make a market mapping, in which all management teams are ranked by their perceived attractiveness (see Exhibit 32.10).

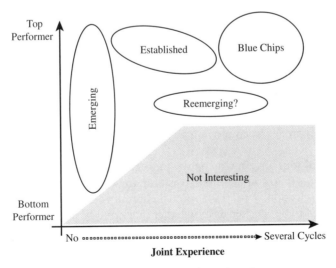

EXHIBIT 32.10   Market Mapping of Fund Performance through Several Business Cycles

32.7.2 Classifying Management Teams

Despite the reservations regarding the performance persistence hypothesis, track record remains an important factor to take into consideration when assessing a management team's competence for an alternative asset fund. Attractive teams are normally those that have been able to generate top performance during several market cycles, as they are the most likely to continue to do so in the future. One way to classify manager teams is to rank them according to two dimensions: (1) the quality of their track record (i.e., their financial performance in previous ventures) from bottom to top performer; and (2) the duration of their joint experience (i.e., their previous involvement as a management team) from none to several market cycles. From this, the following classification is suggested:

- A **blue chip management team** is a team that has been able to generate a top-quartile performance for all of its funds through at least two business cycles (i.e., a sequence of more than three funds).
- An **established management team** is a team that has been able to generate a top-quartile performance for most of its funds (more than three funds) through at least two business cycles.
- An **emerging management team** is a team with limited joint history but with all the characteristics to become an established team.
- A **reemerging management team** is a previously blue chip or established team that has been through a restructuring following recent poor performance or some significant operational issues and has regained the potential to reemerge as an established or a blue chip team.

Teams not included in the preceding categories are not usually considered by most investors. Although in specific situations (for example, in emerging markets) the overall market opportunity may be very interesting, it will not be possible to find teams with track records comparable to those of teams in more established PE markets.

32.7.3 Deal Sourcing

Investors in PE funds need to use their network of industry contacts to identify and establish communication with high-quality fund managers. It is critical to get as many opinions and leads as possible; this can be achieved by having discussions with other investors or entrepreneurs, employing advisers and consultants, and researching the press.

Reactive deal sourcing, in which investors evaluate a portion of the large number of general partners who contact them to ask for an investment, is not an efficient way of approaching selection. With this approach, literally hundreds of private-placement memoranda need to be checked as to whether they comply with the set wish-list characteristics or investment criteria. First-time teams often have to approach as many investors as possible, but top teams typically get referred to limited partners by word of mouth and therefore need to be actively sourced. Developing long-term relationships and exploring opportunities that fit the set criteria are critical. For this purpose, teams have to be identified and approached even before they start their fundraising.

This process requires establishing a calendar of when teams are expected to go to the market to raise capital for their next fund offering.

Databases and conferences may provide opportunities for investors to find information regarding GPs and their upcoming fund offerings. Firms like Preqin and PitchBook, as well as a variety of print publications, make it their business to provide information about funds coming to market as well as the historical performance of funds. Investors attending conferences may have an opportunity to hear from managers or schedule one-on-one meetings efficiently at or near the conference venue. Banks, consultants, and brokerage firms may offer capital introduction or manager research services that can make investors aware of newly formed and experienced funds.

Under the performance persistence hypothesis (that past performance and future performance of a team are correlated), funds raised by teams that have performed well in the past tend to be oversubscribed. If returns have been high, LPs from prior funds are highly motivated to commit to follow-on funds, and GPs will reward their loyalty with virtually guaranteed access to future funds.

In fact, the PE industry is a close community where past relationships provide access to funds in high demand, while newcomers may find it difficult to access all of the funds that they hope to invest in. GPs are interested in maintaining their relationships with the existing LP base. Searching for new LPs is an expensive exercise, and it creates uncertainty regarding the timing of closing and future relationships.[10] Consequently, fund managers tend to avoid this exercise whenever possible. In the extreme, it will not even be known to outside parties that the team may be raising a new fund.

While top teams give priority allocations to their previous investors, they may also allocate a share of the new fund to investors who could add value, such as deal flow, exit opportunities, and industry expertise. Access is far less a problem for LPs who are financially strong and have demonstrated that they are long-term players in the market. For newcomers, however, this is a significant barrier to entry. This means that an investor building a new allocation to private equity may not be able to invest with the top teams, even when the investor has knowledge of their fundraising schedules.

32.8 FUND CULTURE

A dimension of selecting investment managers that is often overlooked is the subjective analysis of a fund's culture. **Fund culture** refers to the principles, professionalism, ethics, character, and governance exhibited by and integrated within fund management. Charles Ellis, founder of Greenwich Associates and renowned author, has written much on the topic. Ellis views the fund's culture as an important factor in identifying managers who will provide superior active management. Analysis of the professionalism, governance, and ethical standards of a fund's management may be a valuable part of selecting an investment manager.

The previous sections discussed potential conflicts of interest and incentives that could lead a manager to manipulate reported performance and/or alter risks in an attempt to game investors. Of course, most fund managers are professionals who serve the interests of their clients and perform their responsibilities with integrity.

How can a prospective investor gauge the integrity of a fund manager? Each fund manager may be viewed as possessing a fund culture.

A fund culture can also be viewed as a generally shared set of priorities and values within the fund's organization. At the most positive end are investment teams with a fund culture of rigid adherence to the highest professional standards of conduct. However, some investment teams may develop fund cultures that sacrifice such standards in pursuit of pragmatism or even with disregard for investor interests. One of the strongest protections against operational risk is a fund culture that fosters competence, honesty, and diligence. Evidence of the true culture of a fund can be found by examining its systems of risk management and methods of performance valuation, performance reporting, and employee compensation. The attitude of fund employees, especially key employees, can reveal the seriousness with which the fund acts with regard to conforming to regulations and adhering to high standards of conduct. Investors should consider the likelihood that negative attitudes towards adherence to regulations may be accompanied by negative attitudes towards adherence to fiduciary responsibilities.

32.9 DECISION-MAKING AND COMMITMENT AND MANAGER SELECTION

Exhibit 32.11 depicts a model of the PE fund selection process. Due diligence, detailed in Chapters 33–35, can be seen primarily as information gathering and evaluation and not as a decision-making tool. In practice, the distinction is seldom made; due diligence is used to eliminate inferior funds and to accept the remaining proposals. The results of the due diligence process should be used only as input for a decision-making process that takes into consideration not only the quality of the investment proposal but also the program's portfolio composition.

Finally, this is not a one-sided decision. Teams may have their own due diligence criteria for selecting potential investors. They should examine whether the investor's commitment is long-term, whether the investor understands the business, whether the investor has a reputation for being difficult, and whether the investor has been a defaulting investor (one who has previously reneged on capital commitments) or is at risk of defaulting due to financial distress. In a case in which public institutional investors seek to become LPs, their investment restrictions (particularly those related to industry sectors and geography) and their transparency requirements need to be acceptable to the fund managers. In order to protect the GP's private information,

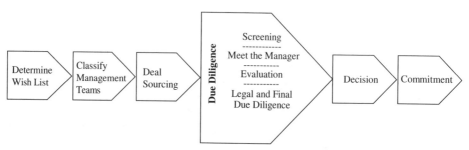

EXHIBIT 32.11 PE Fund Manager Selection Process

some PE fund managers may not allow commitments from investors who are required to publicly disclose information regarding their investment programs, such as US pension plans subject to the Freedom of Information Act.

NOTES

1. Meerkatt et al. (2008).
2. Talmor and Vasvari (2011).
3. See, for instance, Von Braun (2000); Tierney and Folkerts-Landau (2001); Scardino (2004); Kaplan and Schoar (2005); Rouvinez (2006); Hendershott (2007); Sorensen (2007); and Phalippou and Gottschalg (2009).
4. See Chung (2012); Braun et al. (2013); and Harris et al. (2014).
5. Korteweg and Sorensen (2014) concluded that "top-quartile performance does not necessarily imply top-quartile skills," making it difficult for investors to differentiate between luck and skill. Some LPs try to do the analysis on the underlying portfolio company data, where the statistical significance will be reached more quickly. This may give information on many aspects of the GP's investment approach but not on the GP's portfolio management.
6. This is consistent with Manninena, Jääskeläinena, and Maula (2010), who found no significant institutional learning among GPs.
7. See Burgel (2000) or Conner (2005).
8. In the set of data used by Conner (2005), firms that raised a subsequent fund did so 2.9 years on average after raising the predecessor fund.
9. See Goltz and Schroeder (2010).
10. See also Lerner and Schoar (2004). The authors presented the theory that by choosing the degree of illiquidity of the security, private equity fund managers can influence the type of investor the firm will end up attracting. This allows managers to screen for deep-pocketed investors (i.e., those who have a low likelihood of facing a liquidity shock), as they can reduce the GP's cost of capital in future fundraising efforts. The authors' analysis is based on the assumption of an information asymmetry about the quality of the manager between the existing investors and the market. The GP faces a problem when having to raise funds for a subsequent fund from outside investors, because the outsiders cannot determine whether the manager is of poor quality or the existing investors were hit by a liquidity shock. Transferability constraints are less prevalent when private equity funds have LPs that are known to be subject to few liquidity shocks (e.g., endowments, foundations, and other investors with long-term commitments to private equity).

REFERENCES

Braun, R., T. Jenkinson, and I. Stoff. 2013. "How Persistent Is Private Equity Performance? Evidence from Deal-Level Data." Working Paper, August 13. Available at http://ssrn.com/abstract=2314400 or http://dx.doi.org/10.2139/ssrn.231.

Burgel, O. 2000. *UK Venture Capital and Venture Capital as an Asset Class for Institutional Investors.* London: BVCA.

Chung, J.-W. 2012. "Performance Persistence in Private Equity Funds." Working Paper, Chinese University of Hong Kong, November 24.

Conner, A. 2005. "Persistence in Venture Capital Returns." *Private Equity International,* March 2.

Goltz, F. and D. Schroeder. 2010 "Hedge Fund Transparency: Where Do We Stand?" *Journal of Alternative Investments* 12 (4): 20–35.

Harris, R. S., T. Jenkinson, S. N. Kaplan, and R. Stucke. 2014. "Has Persistence Persisted in Private Equity? Evidence from Buyout and Venture Capital Funds." February 28. Available at http://papers.ssrn.com/sol3/papers.cfm?abstract_id=2304808.

Hendershott, R. 2007. "Using Past Performance to Infer Investment Manager Ability." Preliminary Paper, November. Available at www.scu.edu/business/mindwork/winter08/upload/hendershott-past_performance_nov07.pdf.

Kaplan, S. N. and A. Schoar. 2005. "Private Equity Performance: Returns, Persistence, and Capital Flows." *Journal of Finance* 60 (4): 1791–1823.

Korteweg, A. G. and M. Sorensen. 2014. "Skill and Luck in Private Equity Performance." Working Paper 179, Rock Center for Corporate Governance at Stanford University, October 29. Available at http://papers.ssrn.com/sol3/papers.cfm?abstract_id=2419299.

Lerner, J. and A. Schoar. 2004. "The Illiquidity Puzzle: Theory and Evidence from Private Equity." *Journal of Financial Economics* 72 (1): 3–40.

Manninena, O., M. Jääskeläinena, and M. Maula. 2010. "Access versus Selection: What Drives Limited Partners' Private Equity Returns?" Working Paper, Aalto University, Finland, November 1.

Meerkatt, H., J. Rose, M. Brigl, H. Liechtenstein, M. J. Prats, and A. Herrera. 2008. *The Advantage of Persistence: How the Best Private-Equity Firms "Beat the Fade."* Boston: Boston Consulting Group and IESE Business School of the University of Navarra. www.bcg.com/documents/file15196.pdf.

Phalippou, L. and O. Gottschalg. 2009. "The Performance of Private Equity Funds." *Review of Financial Studies* 22 (4): 1747–76.

Rouvinez, C. 2006. "Top Quartile Persistence in Private Equity." Private Equity International, June.

Scardino, J. 2004. "Past Performance a Guide to Likely Future Performance in Private Equity." *Private Equity Monitor.*

Sorensen, M. 2007. "How Smart Is Smart Money? A Two-Sided Matching Model of Venture Capital." *Journal of Finance* 62: 2725–62

Talmor, E. and F. s. 2011. "Gatekeepers." In *International Private Equity.* Chichester, UK: John Wiley & Sons.

Tierney, J.F. and D. Folkerts-Landau. 2001. *Structured Private Equity: An Old Market Becomes an Emerging Asset Class.* Frankfurt: Deutsche Bank Global Markets Research.

Von Braun, E. 2000. "Selektion und Strukturierung von Private Equity Fonds-Portfolios." Paper presented at the IIR Private Equity & Venture Capital Conference, Munich.

CHAPTER 33

Investment Process Due Diligence

In law, due diligence is defined as the care that a reasonable person exercises to avoid harm to other people or their property and has been a long-term issue in securities law and securities regulation. In the context of investing, **fund due diligence** is the process of performing a review of an investment fund with an appropriate level of competence, care, and thoroughness. Top-level oversight of traditional public investments requires little or no knowledge of day-to-day issues involving investment processes and operations underlying the assets of a portfolio. For example, an institution establishing a position in a huge, well-known fund, such as the Vanguard 500 Index Fund, might do so without investigating Vanguard's investment process or operations and with little analysis of the investment other than its stated objective, expense ratio, and long-term performance relative to the S&P 500 Index.

Issues regarding investment processes and operations, however, are essential to institutional investors in private investments, especially those with sophisticated or rapid trading technologies. This chapter details the challenges involved with overseeing alternative investments and investigating and monitoring their investment process. The focus of this chapter is on private fund structures, such as those used in private equity funds and hedge funds. The principles involved, however, are applicable to other investments as well, including investments in private infrastructure funds, managed futures funds, and separately managed accounts.

33.1 OVERVIEW OF INVESTMENT DUE DILIGENCE

In many discussions of fund organization, the fund's investment process is viewed as a subset of its operations. This chapter deals exclusively with the investment process while Chapter 34 discusses noninvestment operations.

33.1.1 Due Diligence Approaches

Due diligence procedures generally have been conducted by internal staff using questionnaires and other materials to provide structure, organization, and a comprehensive view of risks. Best practices include carefully compiling and utilizing lists of requested documents (e.g., offering, organizational, and governance) with reviews by attorneys to ensure that they are appropriate. In many cases, the investor's internal staff conducts most or all of the due diligence and staff may be dedicated entirely to performing the due diligence function.

Alternative due diligence approaches include: (1) the use of employees in which due diligence is all or part of their job description; (2) the use of external consultants and firms to perform due diligence tasks; or (3) a combination of internal employees and external consultant. Thorough background checks on the fund's principals should be carefully conducted—a task that increasingly is outsourced. The fund's service providers should be interviewed, including prime brokers, administrators, custodians, and providers of pricing and other data. Procedures to monitor personal trading and communications should be reviewed as well as fund governance procedures. An onsite visit is considered to be part of best practice, although due diligence without an onsite visit, called a **desk review,** is sometimes used. Institutional investors in alternative assets increasingly rely on experienced external consultants to assist with these due diligence processes.

Institutional investors may find it useful to use the resources of two not-for-profit organizations: the Standards Board for Alternative Investments (SBAI) and the Alternative Investment Management Association (AIMA). The SBAI publishes Standards for Alternative Investments, which addresses key issues relating to alternative investment practices, including disclosure, valuation, risk management, fund governance, and shareholder conduct. Due diligence questionnaires can be used to organize an internal due diligence process or to evaluate and monitor due diligence activities performed by external consultants. AIMA publishes information on due diligence questionnaires that can be especially helpful.

33.1.2 Importance of Investment Due Diligence

In 2014, in the US the Office of Compliance Inspections and Examinations in coordination with the SEC issued a Risk Alert entitled "Investment Adviser Due Diligence Processes for Selecting Alternative Investments and Their Respective Managers." (SEC 2014) The stated purpose of the alert is to:

> *highlight . . . risks and issues that the staff has identified in the course of examinations regarding investment adviser due diligence processes for selecting alternative investments and alternative investment managers.*

The Risk Alert "describes factors that firms may consider to (i) assess their supervisory, compliance, and/or other risk management systems related to these risks, and (ii) make any changes, as may be appropriate, to address or strengthen such systems." The document provides an excellent overview of those areas of increasing concern regarding investor due diligence for alternative investments.

The Risk Alert notes that "the due diligence process can be more challenging for alternative investments due to the characteristics of private offerings, including the complexity of certain alternative investment strategies." The document concludes that the staff "hopes that this [document] concerning the due diligence practices of advisers will help to support the compliance programs of registrants." The document calls on advisers that exercise discretion to purchase alternative investments on behalf of clients to determine whether such investments:

> *(i) meet the clients' investment objectives; and (ii) are consistent with the investment principles and strategies that were disclosed by the manager to the adviser (as set forth in various documents, such as advisory disclosure documents, private offering memoranda, prospectuses, or other offering materials provided by the manager).*

The first point highlights the requirement to ensure that the stated investment strategy of an investment is suitable for the client. The second point is designed to ensure that the fund manager follows the stated or anticipated investment and operational processes.

33.1.3 Three Internal Fund Functions

A fund's activities or functions are often classified into three categories: investment, operational, and business. However, all three functions are sometimes described as being part of the fund's operations and, in particular, part of operational due diligence.

This chapter focuses on the investment process. Investment activities span the investment process, involving all aspects of determining and implementing investment decisions. These activities are often described as front office activities.

Operational activities (the focus of Chapter 34) include the direct support of investment activities, often described as middle office and back office operations. Operational activities include data entry, data processing, data management, record keeping, and trade reconciliation and documentation.

Business activities include the indirect support of the investment activities of the fund, including all of the normal activities of running any similarly sized organization, such as human resources management, technology, infrastructure, and facility maintenance. Due diligence of business activities is discussed in Chapter 35.

33.1.4 Differentiating Between Investment Process and Operational Due Diligence

The best way to differentiate between the investment, operational, and business activities or functions of a fund is by the people involved in the activities and whether they are identified as investment personnel, operations personnel, or business personnel. For example, an employee entering trade decisions for execution is performing a task that may be viewed as operational in nature. But typically that employee is considered to be a member of the investment team, and the function is therefore an investment function.

33.1.5 Costs and Importance of Due Diligence

Fund due diligence is expensive, in terms of both money and time spent. Anson (2006) mentions that effective due diligence requires 75 to 100 hours of work reviewing a fund manager. According to Brown, Fraser, and Liang (2008), the cost of due diligence depends on a series of factors, including: time spent; level of thoroughness; and whether accounting firms, law firms, third-party service providers, and consulting firms are used. These authors assume "a conservative cost of due diligence of $50,000 to $100,000 per fund." However, they contend that effective due diligence of funds in the selection of fund managers can generate alpha for the investor's portfolio.

There is no substitute for taking the time and effort to perform detailed due diligence on a private investment fund. Although the concept of due diligence covers a wide variety of professional responsibilities, this chapter focuses on performing due diligence in selecting a fund manager. Due diligence may be viewed as the initial phase of building a relationship with a fund manager.

33.1.6 Due Diligence Checklists and Questionnaires

Checklists and questionnaires can be a good starting point for organizing and facilitating a due diligence process. Several examples of checklists and questionnaires are available online. Investors may compile checklists based on these samples, while adjusting the components to suit their needs. However, the keys to a successful due diligence program extend far beyond questionnaires and checklists. This chapter focuses on best practices with respect to investment process due diligence.

33.2 THE INVESTMENT STRATEGY OR MANDATE

A critical initial part of due diligence is a review of the fund manager's investment strategy. The **investment strategy or mandate of a fund** refers to the sets of objectives, principles, techniques, and procedures the fund uses to construct and modify its portfolio.

33.2.1 Details on Components of the Investment Strategy

At the core of each fund is the investment strategy or mandate. An investment mandate is an explicit or implicit statement of the allowable and intended strategy, goals, and/or risks of an investment program. The investment mandate and its stated investment strategy are typically disclosed in the various documents provided to investors prior to their decision to invest in the investment vehicle. Descriptions of investment mandates vary tremendously in length and specificity. The investment strategy should be clearly and carefully described in various documents, including the fund's offering documents and marketing material.

A description of the investment strategy should include a list of the markets and securities in which the fund invests, the extent of anticipated and permitted use of leverage and financial derivatives, limits to risk exposures, limits to position sizes, the identities and roles of the investment team, the fund's risk management procedures, what benchmark (if any) is appropriate for the fund, what competitive advantage the fund manager brings to the table, the current portfolio position, the source of investment ideas, and the strategy's capacity. Some of these issues were briefly discussed in Chapter 32 on selection of managers. Of special concern is the risk that the actual investment strategy will differ from the stated investment strategy or the permitted investment strategies.

33.2.2 The Investment Mandate and Strategy Drift

A critical aspect of a fund's risk is the potential divergence between the stated investment strategy or mandate of the fund and the actual investment strategy. Offering documents often include extremely broad language allowing the fund to operate in virtually any market with effectively no constraints to protect the manager from allegations of implementing disallowable trades. The **stated investment strategy of a fund** is the investment strategy that a diligent investor would expect the fund to pursue, based on a reasonable analysis of information made available by the fund.

The actual investment strategy of a fund may deviate from its previously stated strategy but should never stray outside the strategies permitted in its offering documents. The actual investment strategy may differ from the stated investment strategy for three primary reasons: strategy (style) drift; operational errors; and fraud. All three reasons are causes for concern.

Strategy drift (or style drift) is the change through time of a fund's investment strategy based on purposeful decisions by the fund manager in an attempt to improve risk-adjusted performance in light of changing market conditions. Investment strategy drift includes moving into new markets, new investments, new position sizes and direction, and risk exposures that previously have not been experienced. For example, a manager may find that a strategy is not working as anticipated and may make changes in an attempt to better control risk and/or generate better returns.

33.2.3 Strategy Drift and Leverage

Investment strategy drift is often a signal that the initial investment strategy is failing to generate the returns previously experienced or envisioned. A prominent example is increased leverage, which can be a warning signal that the original investment strategy is offering lower returns than originally expected. The fund's investment team may be using leverage to prop up the performance of an investment strategy with deteriorating performance.

Reduced returns to a strategy, before adding leverage, can be a signal of increased competition in the markets from other investors crowding into the strategy. At other times, increased leverage can represent potential overconfidence of the investment team. In both cases, the higher leverage increases the likelihood of large losses and fund failure.

Operational errors can cause unintentional changes to an investment strategy through human error, including poor risk management systems and controls. Operational errors are discussed in Chapter 34. Intentional deviations of the actual investment strategy from the strategies permitted within the offering documents in disregard of investor interests, however, are examples of fraud. Legal and documentation issues are discussed in Chapter 35.

33.2.4 Investment Markets and Securities

Investors should document the markets and securities in which the fund manager invests. For some fund managers, the answer is not so obvious. For instance, global macro managers typically have the broadest investment mandate possible, meaning they can invest in equity, bond, commodity, and currency markets across the world using a variety of investment vehicles. When looking at global macro managers, the investor may have to accept that they can and will invest in whatever market they deem fit.

Closely related to the investment markets are the types of securities in which the fund manager invests. For some strategies, this is straightforward. For instance, the fund's documentation may indicate that the fund manager invests only in the stocks of a particular country. However, other strategies are not so clear. Often, fund disclosure documents are drafted in very broad and expansive terms to allow maximum flexibility to the portfolio manager. Although they may prefer not to put it in writing, managers may be more forthcoming verbally as to historical norms and future expectations about likely investment vehicles.

The purpose of due diligence is not to legally bind the fund manager, but to document the types of securities necessary to implement the investment strategy.

The ability to take derivatives positions should be clear. Derivatives are a two-edged sword, not inherently good or bad. Used one way, they can hedge an investment portfolio and reduce risk. Used in other ways, they can increase the leverage of the fund and magnify the risks taken by the fund manager. It is very important that the investor determine the fund manager's strategy for using derivatives, the types of derivatives used, and in which markets positions in derivatives are traded.

The global financial crisis of 2007 to 2009 underscores the dangers of entering derivative transactions with counterparties that can default, so the investor should ensure that the fund manager has a process in place to evaluate counterparties and ensure proper diversification with these entities. Further, the crisis revealed the challenges of placing even a conservative value on complex derivative deals, for which identifying and valuing underlying assets can be difficult. The investor, then, needs to understand the manager's process for valuing fund holdings (discussed in a subsequent section of this chapter).

A subsequent section of this chapter discusses due diligence regarding the risk of the portfolio from securities including options, short-selling, and volatility derivatives.

33.2.5   Competitive Advantage and Source of Investment Ideas

A key question during the due diligence process is the nature of the fund manager's competitive advantage. What is the competitive advantage of the prospective fund manager that makes the fund an attractive investment?

For instance, there are many merger arbitrage managers; those who invest in announced deals, potential deals, cross-border deals, particular market capitalization ranges, and so forth. But specialization alone does not represent a competitive advantage. An example of a potential competitive advantage may be a merger arbitrage fund with special expertise such as a large in-house legal staff to review the regulatory or antitrust implications of the announced deals.

Chapter 32 discussed potential competitive investment management in the context of private equity. That discussion included the concepts of information advantages, such as being a better gatherer of information or a better analyzer or filterer of information. Thus, a fund manager's competitive advantage could be a research department obtaining information better than others or processing that information into profitable trades better or faster than other fund managers.

The due diligence process should discover, evaluate, and document the perceived competitive advantage, under which market conditions the fund manager's ideas work best, and when opportunities for the manager's strategy are most available. The process should also evaluate the potential for the perceived competitive advantage to persist.

33.2.6   Fund Assets Under Management Capacity for Effective Management

Linked to the competitive advantage and source of investment ideas is the fund's capacity. **Fund capacity** refers to the maximum amount of assets under management that allows the fund manager to implement the investment strategy effectively. Fund managers might dilute their skill by allowing a greater amount of capital into the fund than is optimal from the perspective of the existing investors. Too much money chasing a limited-capacity investment idea moves the price of the security away from the investor, cutting into the alpha that might have otherwise come from the idea. Initial evidence that a fund is nearing capacity is rising trading costs from increasing market impact as the fund attempts to execute larger transactions. Ultimately, the evidence that capacity has been exceeded is when returns decline because the manager cannot deploy all of the assets effectively. The due diligence process should investigate potential capacity constraints and query the fund managers with respect to the potential capacity of the fund and potential policies regarding closing the fund to new investors.

33.2.7 Key Persons and Investment Strategy

Investment fund management is to a large degree a people business. Consequently, part of the due diligence process involves ascertaining who the key people are in the investment process and the vulnerability of the fund to losses of those personnel. The fund's chief investment officer (CIO) typically oversees the investments and the investment process. If one or several of the named key investment experts depart the team or stop committing sufficient time to the investment management of the fund, what would happen to the fund's competitive advantage and prospective returns?

33.3 THE INVESTMENT IMPLEMENTATION PROCESS AND ITS RISKS

The **investment process** includes the methods a manager uses to formulate, execute, and monitor investment decisions, and spans the range of investment activities including: the design and revision of the investment strategy; sourcing of ideas; determination of transactions; setting of leverage; and the placing, execution, and allocation of trades.

33.3.1 Implementing the Investment Strategy

The procedures and personnel directly involved in investment activities are often referred to as the front office. Understanding and documenting a fund manager's investment process are not always straightforward tasks. Some fund managers rely on a largely quantitative, systematic investment process, such as a black-box process. Other managers pursue a more discretionary process that relies on the subjective and qualitative investment decisions made by just one person or a small team of investment professionals.

Analysis of quantitative investment processes focuses on the software that captures the fund's investment strategy. Analysis of discretionary investment processes focuses directly on the judgment and skill of individuals. The investment process in discretionary cases centers on the investment management governance process, which is the explicit or implicit set of procedures through which investment decisions are made. For example, one fund may assemble talented managers who function independently in an entrepreneurial culture and compete to persuade a centralized leader or committee that their decisions have merit. In other cases, major investment decisions are tightly controlled by committee processes, with portfolio managers exercising reduced latitude.

33.3.2 Investment Process Risk

Investment process risk is economic dispersion caused by imperfect application of the decisions, activities, policies, and procedures within the front office and ensuing errors or purposeful decisions that result in exposures that are inconsistent with the investment mandate, such as inappropriate levels of leverage and inappropriate levels or types of asset risk.

Investment process risk is especially prevalent in the hedge fund industry because of the industry's skill-based nature and potentially high level of transactions. A starting point for investment process risk analysis is precisely identifying the nature of the fund's investment strategy. For example, does the fund have an active and highly hedged strategy, such as a quantitative equity market-neutral hedge fund, or does the fund have a more passive and unhedged strategy, such as a fund of funds?

Investment process errors are an idiosyncratic risk caused by problems with the fund manager's structure and operations unrelated to market conditions. However, investment process risk can be caused by and exacerbated by market turmoil. The stress and potentially increased level of trading activity during market turmoil can cause higher probabilities of errors. Further, improperly implemented investment processes, such as style drift, inappropriate application of leverage, and inappropriate systematic and idiosyncratic risk exposures, tend to lead to losses during periods of extremely high market volatility because those periods usually occur with generally declining security prices.

33.3.3 Detecting Investment Process Risk

The detection of investment process risk can include quantitative historical performance analysis. Historical and current investment returns of a fund should be analyzed against the returns of market indices and similar funds to infer the extent to which the fund's returns are consistent with the market environment. Investment process risk can also be detected qualitatively. The key to optimal control of investment process risk is a sound, well-defined, well-designed investment process. A well-defined investment process clearly specifies the functions of the investment team; a well-designed investment process maximizes the potential benefits of the stated investment strategy while minimizing the costs of investment process risk.

Assessing the stability and reliability of a fund manager's investment process is essential to assessing risk. In the case of quantitative, systematic investment processes, much of the investment process resides in a fund's software or computer algorithms. A fund's computer algorithms are procedures within the software that determine trading decisions or other outputs. The fund manager may be unwilling to reveal the details of the computer algorithms because they represent part or all of the fund manager's competitive advantage. Prospective investors may decide not to invest in any investment process they do not understand. This is a blunt risk management policy, but an investor who cannot understand the investment process may not be able to comprehend the risks associated with the process. This lack of transparency in the investment process contributes to the investment process risk borne by the investor. Investors may mitigate this risk through diversification into other funds but must ultimately decide whether the potential returns merit the risks of a process that lacks transparency.

Given transparency, the way to manage the risk is to carefully examine and understand the details of the investment process. It is not necessary to read the underlying computer code behind every computer algorithm of a quantitative manager. Instead, the investor must understand the structure of the algorithms. The investor should determine which computer algorithms are used to evaluate different financial instruments and whether each computer algorithm includes all relevant variables. For instance, with respect to convertible bond arbitrage, appropriate economic inputs might be the underlying stock price, the historical volatility, the implied volatility, the current term structure of interest rates, the credit rating of the instrument, the duration of the bond, the convertible strike price, and any call provisions in the bond indenture. The investor should understand the purpose of the computer algorithms with respect to pursuit of alpha and control of risk.

All investment processes involve interaction of both people and computers. For example, even with a black-box investment process, there are people and a governance process involved with the design and adjustment of the mechanical process. Whether quantitatively or qualitatively focused, the investment process needs to be qualitatively analyzed for soundness through analysis of its framework of governance. This framework includes the organizational chart, along with the existence, nature, composition, and documentation of the responsibilities of all investment personnel and investment committees. The committee framework includes the processes for selecting members, selecting officers, scheduling meetings, forming agendas, and voting, as well as the process for recording, approving, distributing, and preserving the minutes. The framework also includes the detail, accuracy, and importance of procedure manuals. The analysis seeks to ascertain the susceptibility of the investment process to conflicts of interest, fraud, and incompetence.

According to the Risk Alert, investors are reviewing regulatory documents to research the firms and personnel related to an investment decision. Web-based sources of regulatory documents include information on investment professionals and firms in the Financial Industry Regulatory Authority's BrokerCheck and information on registered firms and their personnel in the SEC's Investment Adviser Public Disclosure website. The information gathered can inform investors of potential regulatory issues or control weaknesses with regard to the fund's manager.

33.4 ASSET CUSTODY AND VALUATION

This section discusses two important and related issues: reviewing the procedures for custody of the fund's assets and the procedures for valuing (i.e., pricing) those assets.

33.4.1 Custody of Fund Assets

Fund investors must be concerned about the custody of assets. A major tool in preventing fraud and detecting fraud in the case of an investment fund is the careful review of custodians and the policies and procedures for safeguarding the assets.

Custody refers to the holding of assets by a financial institution for the benefit of a customer. The investor in a fund has a direct ownership interest in a fund. The fund, in turn, places the fund's assets with a custodian. Thus, the fund is the direct owner of the assets being held by the custodian.

Managed accounts, or separate accounts, provide safe and transparent custody of assets because in a managed account, the assets are managed by an external manager but remain in the investor's account at a brokerage firm. Thus, the investor retains custody of the assets, so it is virtually impossible for the fund manager to withdraw the funds. Given that the account belongs to the investor, the investor can access account positions, balances, and performance in real time. This allows the investor to see returns on a much more frequent and independent basis, if desired, and to evaluate them. There is likely to be no question about the valuation of the securities in the account, as the prices of the positions should be determined by the custody bank or broker, not by the fund manager.

An investor in a fund typically has no direct control over the assets under custody and typically there is no direct transparency for the fund investor to view the positions and their values in real time directly from the custodian.

This lack of transparency and control raises numerous questions for the due diligence process. Are assets segregated for the fund investors as a group or for individual investors in the fund? Are controls in place to prevent the movement of funds into the fund manager's personal accounts or other inappropriate accounts? Are legal agreements with prime brokers effective in preventing commingling of assets with the assets of the brokers, or will fund manager assets become commingled with brokerage assets, making it difficult to disentangle assets, such as during the bankruptcy of the European prime brokerage operations of Lehman Brothers?

The Risk Alert noted that advisers are seeking greater information, including position-level transparency and separately managed accounts. **Position-level transparency** in the context of funds refers to regular, prompt, and detailed disclosure by the fund manager of the fund's securities holdings and the ability of the fund advisers or investors to see the exact positions underlying their funds and the values as reported by the custodian. Although some managers are reluctant to provide position-level transparency (which may reveal their proprietary trading strategies), investors can benefit from position-level transparency by being better able to understand and manage their aggregate risks.

33.4.2 Current Portfolio Position

Due diligence includes obtaining a current snapshot of the current positions of the fund. The investor should ascertain the fund's current long and short exposures, determine the amount of cash held by the fund, and evaluate its appropriateness. Too much cash indicates an investment strategy that may be stuck in neutral or waiting for attractive investment opportunities; too little cash may indicate potential liquidity issues. The investor should analyze the number of positions the fund manager holds and the nature of those holdings to indicate the extent to which the fund is exposed to systematic and idiosyncratic risks as well as the extent to which the portfolio is consistent with the investment mandate.

There can be substantial information value for investors in the analysis of both current and historical portfolio positions. Rather than estimating risk from a time series of returns, investors with access to positions can calculate the risk directly from the portfolio holdings. Investors should also be concerned with return attribution, which evaluates the contribution to risk and return based on long vs. short positions or the specific sectors in which the manager is invested.

Fund managers may be reluctant to reveal current positions in order to prevent other traders from transacting based on the information. Further, some managers may even be reluctant to reveal older positions to prevent others from ascertaining and potentially copying their strategy.

When position-level data are provided, it should be reported directly from the fund's custodian or administrator, as this third-party verification makes it difficult for the manager to understate the risk of the fund. The direct position link from the custodian verifies the true positions of the fund.

Because it is often vital that investors understand the size, leverage, and concentration of positions, if managers will not provide transparency down to specific holdings, investors should request that the holdings be confidentially reported to a third-party risk system that can report measures of risk to the investors. The risk monitoring system used to analyze the positions should aggregate the positions and provide statistics on leverage, concentration, and security types. The system may even enable scenario analysis and value at risk calculations without disclosing the manager's individual positions or the details of trading positions to the prospective investor.

A final question the investor should ask the fund manager is how the current portfolio has been positioned in light of current market conditions. This should not only provide insight into how the fund manager views the current financial markets but also shed some light on the anticipated investment strategy going forward.

33.4.3 Principles of Fund Asset Valuation

Valuation can be the object of powerful conflicts of interest. Investors select funds on the basis of risk-adjusted returns, and incentive fees are paid on reported returns. Accordingly, some managers may manipulate reported returns to enhance their income or maximize the probability of retaining or growing investor assets. Therefore, it is imperative that traders and portfolio managers do not value (i.e., price) their own positions for risk management and reporting purposes. Valuation of positions for reporting and risk control purposes should be determined through and reported directly from an independent source with an independently derived process.

To reduce the opportunities to manipulate prices, external pricing services are often used to value the positions held by a fund, especially funds holding illiquid assets. Portfolio pricing is particularly important for fund managers that invest in esoteric and illiquid securities, such as collateralized debt obligations (CDOs), distressed debt, private investments in public equity (PIPEs), or convertible bonds. Fund managers are believed to be able to earn consistent abnormal returns for securities with greater complexity and less liquidity. However, these sources of return premiums generate ambiguity and uncertainty in the pricing of positions.

33.4.4   Four Implications of Conflicts of Interest in Fund Asset Valuation

Conflicts of interest between fund owners (principals) and fund managers (agents) may provide incentives for the fund manager to manage, manipulate, or misrepresent asset values and fund returns.

Four implications from potential conflicts of interest are manager attempt to: (1) obscure or delay losses; (2) smooth returns by shifting performance between reporting periods; (3) vary risks to recoup losses or lock in profits; and (4) inflate valuations to increase fees. Each of these implications is detailed next.

1. Fund managers may have an incentive to obscure losses to avoid reporting inferior performance and provide time to recoup losses. The valuation procedure should prevent managers from being able to influence reported valuations.
2. Fund managers may have an incentive to smooth returns. If performance is smoothed over a long period of time, the fund appears to have lower volatility and higher risk-adjusted returns, which can assist in attracting and retaining assets. Managers smooth returns by moving profits from periods of high performance to periods of low performance and by moving losses from periods of low performance to periods of high performance. For example, at the end of a very successful period, a manager can smooth returns by placing a reduced value on the end-of-period positions. The reduced valuations lower the prior period's financial performance and provide an immediate gain for the next period. At the end of an unsuccessful period, a manager can smooth returns by placing an increased value on the end-of-period positions.
3. Fund managers have an incentive to vary risks to game performance evaluation. A fund manager with a benchmark has an incentive to lock in profits by lowering risk when profits have already exceeded the benchmark. In so doing, the manager is increasing the probability of outperforming the benchmark over the reporting period. Conversely, a manager underperforming a benchmark has an incentive to take high risks in an effort to reach the benchmark by the end of the reporting period. Analysis of frequent and accurate fund valuation can assist in revealing managerial attempts to game performance evaluation. As discussed in CAIA Level I, this conflict of interest can be reduced when the degree of managerial coinvesting in the fund exceeds 30% of the manager's net worth.
4. Fund managers have an incentive to inflate net asset valuations (overstating the values of long positions and understating the values of short positions) in order to increase the size of fees or to accelerate the timing of their distribution. Many investment managers have implied long positions in call options to the extent that they can reap generous incentive fees and other compensation from staying in business and accumulating profits, while enjoying limited downside in the case of losses.

Separately managed accounts (rather than investment funds and other pools) may provide investors with greater transparency, better monitoring, greater control, and reduced likelihood of incurring unauthorized fees or having assets be misappropriated. However, managed accounts may also increase the fund manager's concerns regarding loss of control over the release of position and trading details that could be used by other traders. Use of separately managed accounts is a matter of negotiation between investors and fund managers.

33.4.5 Challenges in Listed Asset Valuation

For publicly traded markets such as equities and futures, valuation challenges are less acute but still offer the possibility of unscrupulous behavior. Publicly-traded stocks have both a bid price and an offer price. For a large, frequently traded stock like IBM, for which the price is high and the spread is small (e.g., a bid price of $101.86 and an offer price of $101.87), the issue of whether to use the bid price or the offer price is trivial, as the spread is 1 cent on a large per-share price. Smaller and less liquid stocks may have a substantially wider bid-ask spread, especially when expressed as a percentage of the price.

A conservative approach to valuing positions is to consistently use whichever price generates a lower portfolio value. For example, the fund manager with a long position should mark to the bid price, whereas a fund manager that is short could mark the position to the offer. In addition to being conservative, using the less favorable price tends to more accurately describe the liquidation value of the portfolio, since orders to liquidate involve selling at bids and buying at offers. However, a common practice in the fund industry is to take the midmarket price, exactly between the bid and the offer prices, and use this for both short and long positions.

Even the prices of publicly traded securities can be manipulated. For smaller stocks with lighter trading, the price manipulation can be greater. For example, a buy or sell order placed at the close of trading can "paint the tape" with a price that substantially increases portfolio values. A buy order can be placed to try to support the valuation of long positions, and a sell order can be placed to support the value of short positions. Last-minute orders can cause the closing bid, offer, and last trade prices to be different at the end of the day than they would have been if the trades were placed earlier in the day, giving other market participants time to react before the market closed.

Any such transactions in securities for the purpose of artificially altering reported closing prices is a form of market manipulation. Anecdotally, trading volume at the end of months and quarters does typically spike, perhaps indicating that investors are attempting to make their portfolios look better at those arbitrary measurement points or to exit positions or risks that the manager would rather not disclose.

33.4.6 Valuation of Illiquid Assets and Level 1, 2, and 3 Assets

For stocks and bonds that are not publicly traded, the solution to valuing or marking the portfolio becomes especially problematic. Many fund managers mark to model. **Mark to model** means the use of valuation models to estimate the likely prices at which illiquid securities would transact. This valuation may be subjective, biased, and unreliable. Even third-party models designed to be objective and unbiased can generate highly erroneous indications of prices at which transactions would take place during periods of extreme illiquidity and turmoil. Mark-to-model accounting has been the source of numerous investment disasters.

The Financial Accounting Standards Board in the US defines three types, or levels, of assets in the context of determining fair asset values using Generally

Accepted Accounting Principles (GAAP). The levels reflect the degree of uncertainty in estimating fair asset values, with Level 1 assets being priced with the most certainty.

Level 1 assets are those assets that can be valued based on an unadjusted market price quote from an actively traded market of identical assets. **Level 2 assets** are best valued based on nonactive market price quotes, active market price quotes for similar assets, or nonquoted values based on observable inputs that can be corroborated. **Level 3 assets** are valued based on the estimated fair values for assets that are subject to the greatest uncertainty and may be valued based on models with ambiguous inputs such as volatility.

For example, a traditional equity traded in a large public market would generally be considered a Level 1 asset. A distressed debt security traded infrequently and/or valued based on market prices of similar securities would generally be considered a Level 2 asset. Finally, an untraded structured product tailored to the tax rates and tax needs of a specific investor would generally be a Level 3 asset.

The valuation of highly illiquid investments such as private equity can pose substantial problems, given the often limited operating history of the investment which may include that the company has yet to generate a profit. Private equity and other private real assets are appraised assets, valued not by the consensus reflected in market prices nor in accurate models. Private equity valuations are often performed according to industry standards, such as the International Private Equity and Venture Capital Valuation Guidelines (IPEV Valuation Guidelines).

Regardless of the nature of the firm's valuation practices, such practices must always be documented ex ante. Firms must document their policy and procedure for valuing illiquid or hard-to-value assets, disclose any material information relative to how such values are determined (particularly in the case of subjective, unobservable inputs), and document, through the use of valuation memos or similar material, that the process was applied.

33.4.7   Internal Valuation of Assets

Internally gathered or determined valuations should always be supported by the following:

- The use of a knowledgeable but disinterested party in performing the valuation.
- Documentation and justification for the valuation method used.
- Documentation of all inputs and assumptions.
- Review, if not approval, of the final value by yet another knowledgeable, independent party.

The bottom line is that the due diligence process must document how the fund manager prices positions and, in particular, how the manager uses models to price positions. The analysis of the pricing procedures for illiquid securities must be especially detailed. If the fund manager uses a mark-to-model methodology for less liquid securities, then the investor should analyze how the fund manager's model works under periods of market stress.

33.5 RISK ALERT'S ONE ADVANTAGE AND SIX OBSERVATIONS ON THIRD-PARTY INFORMATION

The Risk Alert discusses the trend among investment advisers to use third parties as sources of additional information, such as portfolio information aggregators (risk aggregators). **Portfolio information aggregators (risk aggregators)** are third-party service providers who collect and process information from various private investments to report and assess the combined risks to investment advisers. The alert identified six categories and provided observations.

33.5.1 Advantages of Portfolio Information Aggregators

A potential advantage of using portfolio information aggregators is that fund managers may be more willing to provide portfolio details to these aggregators rather than directly to investment advisers. A risk aggregator can download the positions held in each fund in an investor's portfolio directly from the prime brokers, verifying actual positions and reducing the risk of fraud or understated risk. Without disclosing actual positions to investors, the risk aggregation system can give fund-level and portfolio-level disclosures of betas, leverage, and risk, including options and futures positions. Top risk aggregation systems also can perform scenario analysis, stressing how an investor's portfolio across all fund investments would fare if the market conditions of previous events, such as the 2007–9 global financial crisis, were to repeat in the future.

33.5.2 The Risk Alert Made Two Observations on Third Party Information Regarding Asset Values

The first two involve information on the fund's assets.

1. INCREASING INDEPENDENT VERIFICATION: Advisers are increasingly contacting a fund's third-party service providers to independently verify information regarding the fund's assets and the existence of its alternative investment relationships. Advisers also are conducting some due diligence on key service providers to ensure that the service providers adequately meet the needs of the investment.

    Some advisers will invest only in funds with independent third-party administrators. Their goal is to mitigate investment and operational risks related to key fund administration services, such as "performing net asset value calculations, fund accounting, trade reconciliation, and processing and recording shareholder activity."

2. INCREASING RELIANCE ON TRANSPARENT INVESTMENT REPORTS: Another trend is increasing reliance on the transparency reports (of investment positions) directly from and independently produced by third-party administrators. The information sought includes the fund's (1) net asset value and the percentage of its investments that are confirmed by the administrator with independent custodians; (2) custodians holding its investments; (3) percentage of investments that are priced by a third-party administrator; and (4) assets and liabilities which are

measured at "fair value" and are categorized using the fair value hierarchy (Level 1, 2, or 3) established under FASB ASC 820, Fair Value Measurements.

33.5.3   The Risk Alert Made Four Observations on Four Trends in Due Diligence

The last four observations noted due diligence trends with increasing and widespread usage that presumably indicate a professional consensus regarding their importance.

1. ADDITIONAL QUANTITATIVE ANALYSES AND RISK MEASUREMENT: The Risk Alert discussed quantitative analyses and risk measurement and identified key areas for which increased effort is needed to detect performance manipulation and to supplement decision making. An area of increased concern involves the "detection of manipulation of performance returns" by fund managers. SEC staff had observed advisers using quantitative analysis to detect aberrations in returns that might identify "falsified or otherwise manipulated" returns and their managers.

   The following three measures of returns were noted: (1) the **bias ratio,** which attempts to indicate when returns have been manipulated and thus do not exhibit a distribution consistent with competitive markets; (2) indications of serial correlation (i.e., correlation of returns between different time periods); and (3) measures of skew (i.e., the tendency of a return distribution to have higher tail risk.

2. INCREASED QUANTITATIVE ANALYSIS OF INVESTMENT DECISIONS: Another area of increased quantitative analysis and risk measurement noted was the "supplementation of investment-level decision making." SEC staff also observed increased use of quantitative risk measures to make investment-level decisions. The goals included using statistical techniques, such as factor analysis, to indicate whether returns are consistent with the stated investment strategy and sophisticated quantitative analysis of returns to detect potential problems before they become severe.

3. VALUATION SHOULD BE BASED MORE ON EXTERNAL DEALER QUOTES: For exchange-traded securities, the fund's own back office team can easily value the fund using pricing feeds from market data systems, combined with position reports from the custodian, prime broker, and administrator. Less liquid positions traded in the over-the-counter (OTC) market, such as mortgage-backed or convertible securities, should be valued through the use of external dealer quotes rather than by the models or prices supplied by a trading desk. Objectivity and independence in the valuation process are essential.

4. AVOID AMBIGUITY IN VALUATION, PERFORMANCE REPORTING, AND RISK MEASUREMENT: Systems of valuation, performance reporting, and risk measurement that permit ambiguity or subjectivity are fertile ground for operational risk. Relatively minor incidents of bending rules to one's advantage, if unchecked, can evolve into more reckless behavior and create incentives for additional rule breaking to cover up past indiscretions. Note that fund collapses have begun with minor losses that were obscured and became a gateway to increasingly desperate risk taking in an attempt to restore profitability.

33.6 PORTFOLIO RISK REVIEW

Section 33.3 discussed the risk involved with errors in the investment process. This section focuses on the risk of the investment strategy in the absence of processing errors.

33.6.1 Risk Review Overview

Understanding the risks embedded in a fund manager's investment strategy, investment process, and current portfolio is an especially critical task of due diligence. Investors need to consider the manager's compliance and risk management systems, as well as the degree to which leverage is employed and controlled.

Market risk has both a general meaning and a narrower interpretation. In discussions of investment process, the market risk in the investment process describes any systematic *or* idiosyncratic dispersion in economic outcomes attributable to changes in market prices and rates. Thus, the market risk of a fund might be used to describe any potential for portfolio losses that are caused by changes in market prices, market rates, or market conditions. However, market risk also has a narrower interpretation in the context of asset pricing models. In this narrower interpretation, market risk is used synonymously with systematic risk to refer to the portion of an asset's total risk that is attributable to changes in the value of the market portfolio or to a return factor that drives general market returns. For the purposes of this chapter, market risk refers to the more general definition.

Market risk directly affects the total risk of a fund through its presence in the firm's stated investment strategy. However, market risk also has an important role in determining the total risk of a fund through its synergistic risk effects with other types of risk. A **synergistic risk effect** is the potential for the combination of two or more risks to have a greater total risk than the sum of the individual risks. Fluctuations in market prices are a source of risk. However, when the level of operational errors is positively related to the volatility of market prices, there is a synergistic effect that deserves careful consideration.

Quantitative risk analysis is usually focused on historical analysis of past risk and return. However, very few fund collapses can be predicted based on analysis of past returns alone. The following subsections discuss aspects of a quality risk review other than historical performance analysis.

33.6.2 Chief Risk Officer

The **chief risk officer (CRO)** oversees the fund manager's program for identifying, measuring, monitoring, and managing risk. Larger funds often establish a senior executive who oversees risk across all funds and separate accounts. Often, especially with smaller funds, the CFO serves as the risk officer. This is a good solution, as long as the CFO is not also the chief investment officer (CIO).

The CIO and the CRO should not be the same person. If so, there is a conflict in risk control because risk management should function separately from investment management. Without this independence, there can be no assurance that risk will be properly identified, promptly reported, and appropriately managed.

If the amount of leverage is not contractually specified in the limited partnership agreement, then the CRO should set a limit. The CRO must monitor the leverage in each fund and account to ensure that it is consistent with that fund's investment strategy. Finally, the CRO should establish the position limits for any one investment within a fund portfolio. Due diligence requires documentation of the CRO's responsibilities and evaluation of the quality of the programs that the CRO oversees.

33.6.3   Three General Questions of a Risk Review

There are three important questions that must be answered to understand the risk profile and risk management of the fund:

1. What are the types and levels of risk involved in the fund manager's strategy?

    Investors need to understand the fund's investment strategy and the risks associated with that strategy. For example, the fund manager may pursue an equity long/short strategy, in which case the due diligence process should involve an analysis of the management of the risks of short selling.

2. What risks are measured, monitored, and managed?

    Next, it is important to determine what risks the fund manager measures, monitors, and/or manages. Are there risks that are not measured and monitored?

3. How and with what measures are risks monitored and managed?

    Finally, the due diligence process should determine which risk measures are reported (e.g., standard deviation of returns, semivariance, Sortino measure, value at risk). Which methods are used to estimate the risk measures (e.g., historical data, scenario analysis)? How does the fund manager monitor risk and use the measures to manage the risk of the portfolio?

    For example, one way to control risk is by setting limits on the size of any investment position and adjusting those position limits with a system based on risk measurement. Another way to manage risk is to monitor position or portfolio volatility or tracking error relative to an upper boundary.

33.6.4   Key Risks of Special Concern in a Risk Review

This section discusses three key risks: short volatility risk; counterparty risk; and short-selling risk.

SHORT VOLATILITY RISK reflects the extent to which the fund manager may short volatility. Shorting volatility is a strategy whereby a fund manager: (1) sells (i.e., writes) call or put options, especially out-of-the-money options, without an offsetting (hedging) position; or (2) establishes positions in volatility derivatives (discussed in detail in Chapters 36 and 37) that move inversely to volatility levels, in particular, equity volatility levels.

Being short volatility exposes the fund to the potential for enormous losses, especially during periods of stress. These exposures can be attractive to managers but difficult to detect. The reason that short volatility risk can be attractive to fund managers is that bearing short volatility risk can generate high probabilities of small, regular profits. Short volatility risk can be detrimental to investors, however, as it can generate very large losses during market turmoil, even if the probabilities are small. The reason these exposures can be difficult to detect is due to the complexity of financial derivatives that provide that exposure.

COUNTERPARTY RISK can be difficult to detect and dangerous to investors. Fund managers frequently establish positions in over-the-counter derivative instruments. The counterparty to such trades is often a large investment house or a large money center bank. When a fund manager establishes these derivatives, the fund takes on the credit risk that the counterparty might fail to fulfill its obligations under the derivative contract by declaring bankruptcy. A counterparty is most likely to fail during periods of enormous market stress and when its derivative positions have large unrealized losses. These are also the conditions under which a fund may be in distress and find that its derivatives with large unrealized profits have become worthless due to counterparty risk.

SHORT-SELLING RISK brings the potential for massive losses along with the complexities involved with implementing a short-selling strategy. The potential losses are theoretically unlimited because the asset being shorted typically has no upper bound on its price. The complexities of short-selling include the potential for the security lender to demand the return of the securities and the potential of a short-squeeze.

33.6.5 Risk Reviews and Leverage

Leverage is a key factor in risk, and therefore leverage management is a key factor in understanding and controlling investment process risk. Investment process risk stems from the leverage inherent in the investment mandate as well as the risk that the actual leverage will stray from the levels of risk anticipated in the investment mandate. A fund's history of leverage use should be part of an institution's due diligence, and monitoring leverage after investing in a fund should be ongoing.

Another major concern of a leveraged fund is that the risk inherent in the fund's investment strategy is similar to the risk borne by other leveraged and active traders because many funds are crowding a particular trade. For example, if numerous highly leveraged funds are pursuing very similar strategies, the funds may begin to act like a herd by having similar positions. If one fund liquidates or deleverages its positions quickly, the market impact of such trading may trigger liquidations and deleveraging by the other funds, which can spiral into rapid, large losses. Analysis of the risk from herd trading requires knowledge of the fund's positions, knowledge of the likely or actual positions of similar funds, and an understanding of the degree of liquidity in the relevant markets, so that the potential price impacts of herd trading can be evaluated.

Some fund managers specifically limit the leverage they employ. This limit is typically set in the private placement memorandum, so that the fund manager is legally bound to stay within a leverage limit. Many fund managers, however, do not document a limit on the amount of leverage that they may apply. If a fund intends to use leverage, the due diligence process should document the highest amount of leverage applied by the fund manager, as well as the average leverage of the fund since inception. One of the reasons for the demise of Long-Term Capital Management was the massive amount of leverage employed in its strategy.

33.6.6 How Leverage Magnifies Losses and Probabilities of Various Loss Levels

A fund with a leverage factor or ratio of L (L = Assets/Equity) has short-run returns that have L times the volatility of its assets. However, the probability of large losses increases by a factor greater than L. To illustrate, consider two funds with assets of identical risk, one without leverage and one with leverage. There may be a tendency to view a particular percentage equity loss (e.g., −20%) as being L times more likely to be reached with the leveraged fund than with the unleveraged fund. But the probability for large equity losses in the leveraged fund is far more than L times the probability that the unleveraged fund will experience such a loss.

Unusual events are often described as N-sigma events. An N-sigma event is an event that is N standard deviations from the mean. An unleveraged fund with an asset volatility of 10% experiences a two-sigma event when its value falls more than 20% or rises more than 20% (ignoring the mean return).

For normally distributed variables, a two-sigma loss should occur with a probability of about 2.3%. Thus, the unleveraged fund with assets that have a volatility of 10% should have about a 2.3% probability of experiencing a loss equal to or greater than 20%. Note that a fund leveraged 2:1 with the same asset volatility (10%) experiences a 20% loss in equity when the fund's assets drop by only 10%, a one-sigma event. The probability of the assets experiencing a 10% loss is almost 16%, more than seven times higher than the probability of a 20% loss!

APPLICATION 33.6.6A

Assume an unleveraged fund and an otherwise identical fund that is leveraged 3:1 (L = 3). To simplify the math, assume that the expected return of each fund is 0% and that the returns of the assets have a daily standard deviation of 2%. When markets decline, the equity of the unleveraged fund experiences the same percentage loss as the assets of the fund, because in the case of an unleveraged fund, assets = equity. For example, a three-sigma loss causes the assets of each fund to decline by 6% in one day ($3 \times 2\% = 6\%$). The three-sigma event causes the unleveraged fund to lose 6% in assets and 6% in equity. What is the probability that a fund leveraged 3:1 will experience a 6% drop in equity assuming that the returns are normally distributed?

For the leveraged fund to suffer the same loss in equity (6%), it needs to experience only a 2% loss in assets, which is only a one-sigma event. Assuming the normal distribution for simplicity, the probability of a one-sigma loss (15.9%) is more than 100 times the probability of a three-sigma loss (0.135%). Thus, with only 3:1 leverage, the leveraged fund in this example is more than 100 times more likely to lose 6% than an unleveraged fund with the same assets.

This discussion has illustrated the potential role of leverage in magnifying the risk of the equity for relatively modest events (two or three sigmas) and relatively modest leverage (2:1 or 3:1). However, extremely stressed markets have been measured as having experienced double-digit sigma events and highly leveraged traders sometimes hold positions with double-digit leverage (i.e., $L>10$). For extreme events or larger leverage, an analysis would demonstrate much more dramatic relative probabilities.

33.6.7 Subscription and Redemption Risks

Rising subscriptions to a fund can also be a source of drag on fund performance. First, as it may take time to get invested in the less liquid ideas, cash may be a drag on the portfolio return. Second, unless new investors are charged for trading costs, subscriptions result in transaction costs that are typically borne by all investors as the new money is invested. As more capital flows into a fund, the trades get larger, and inferior ideas are implemented as the manager's best ideas reach their investment capacity.

Large redemptions from investment pools can have an impact on fund performance. If a fund manager is fully invested at the time of these large asset flows, fund performance typically suffers. For redemptions, the fund manager must sell securities to fund the withdrawals. This means that transaction costs are incurred and typically borne by all investors unless specifically charged to the investor requiring the redemption. In anticipation of potential withdrawal requests, portfolios may be tilted away from less liquid positions toward securities with greater liquidity but less alpha potential. Obviously, funds have varying levels of portfolio liquidity depending on the investment mandate.

33.7   FOUR WARNING INDICATORS AND AWARENESS SIGNALS REGARDING INVESTMENTS

The Risk Alert noted four "warning indicators or awareness signals" regarding investments that "led advisers to conduct additional due diligence analysis, to request that the manager make appropriate changes, or to reject (or veto) the manager or the alternative investment."

Investment Warning Indicators or Awareness Signals:

1. Manager unwillingness to provide transparency.
2. Investment returns inconsistent with the investment strategy.
3. Lack of clarity in the investment process.
4. Lack of controls and segregation of duties.

33.8   FOUR WARNING INDICATORS AND AWARENESS SIGNALS REGARDING RISK MANAGEMENT

The Risk Alert noted four "warning indicators or awareness signals" regarding risk management that "led advisers to conduct additional due diligence analysis, to request that the manager make appropriate changes, or to reject (or veto) the manager or the alternative investment."

Risk Management Warning Indicators or Awareness Signals:

1. Concentrated positions.
2. Insufficiently knowledgeable investment personnel.
3. Investment strategy drift.
4. Overly complex or opaque investment descriptions.

REFERENCES

Anson, M. 2006. *The Handbook of Alternative Assets*, 2nd ed. Hoboken, NJ: John Wiley & Sons.

Brown, Stephen, Thomas Fraser, and Bing Liang 2008. "Hedge Fund Due Diligence: A Source of Alpha in Hedge Fund Portfolio Strategy," New York University Working Paper, January 21.

Securities and Exchange Commission (SEC). 2014. "Investment Adviser Due Diligence Processes for Selecting Alternative Investments and Their Respective Managers," National Exam Program, Risk Alert 4, no. 1 (28 January 2014): www.sec.gov/ocie/announcement/risk-alert---selecting-alternative-investments-and-managers.html.

CHAPTER 34

Operational Due Diligence

For the purposes of this Chapter, operations is defined as including all operations except investment operations (discussed in Chapter 33) and business activities and governance of the fund (discussed in Chapter 35).

Feffer and Kundro (2003) studied more than 100 fund liquidations over a 20-year period and attributed half of all fund failures to operational risk. They contend that structural problems with funds contributed to substantial investor losses and that investors could have avoided these problems by following a comprehensive due diligence process. **Operational due diligence (ODD)** refers to the process of evaluating operational risk to ensure that investors will not be subject to the financial or reputational risks of investing in funds (or the applicable fund advisers) that may experience losses and/or suspend redemptions for noninvestment reasons. A broad interpretation of operational risk is that it is any economic dispersion caused by operations within the investment, operational, or business activities. This chapter uses a narrower definition of operational risk that focuses on the view of a fund's operations and excludes the investment process and business activities.

34.1 OPERATIONS: OVERVIEW, RISKS, AND REMEDIES

The primary purpose of ODD is to detect unacceptable levels of potential operational risk before investing in a fund. The **operational risk of a fund** may be viewed as having three sources: operational errors; agency conflicts; and operational fraud.

34.1.1 Operational Errors, Agency Conflicts, and Operational Fraud

Operational errors are inadvertent mistakes made in the process of executing a fund's investment strategy. For example, in some circumstances, errors in executing trades may occur, such as the execution of a trade in the wrong size or direction. Trading errors become more possible and the likely impact of those trading errors may increase during chaotic markets, when errors may not be detected quickly and prices may move substantially before corrective action is taken. Errors can also be of greater consequence when the fund's investment universe or strategy is complex/high volume and the systems in place to capture these have an element of manual input. Operational errors may also be defined as a breach of a fund's regulatory guidelines, for example in relation to UCITS vehicles where counterparty and position limits are tightly defined. In these cases, the breach is further defined as either "passive" (inadvertent, due to market movement), or "active," where guidelines are breached as a result of incorrect investment or trading decisions.

Analysis of agency conflicts is an essential part of ODD. Operational risk includes the intentional actions of fund employees that are contrary to the interests of investors, but can increasingly include unintentional actions made in good faith, but on the basis of fraudulent or misleading information, such as emails or calls from agents purporting to be genuine counterparties with whom the firm should interact. Agency costs can be reduced when incentive-based compensation schemes are used to bring the interests of the fund manager (the agent) into closer alignment with the interests of the investors (the principals). However, optimal compensation schemes allow the interests of investors and the interests of the fund manager's employees to remain in conflict because the expense of resolving some conflicts may be too costly, and all interests can never be perfectly aligned. An extreme example of a conflict of interest is a **rogue trader** who intentionally departs from the investment mandate due to incentives to generate performance or to recoup losses that jeopardize a trader's career.

Gaming refers to strategic behavior to gain benefits from circumventing the intention of the rules of a particular system.

Operational fraud from the perspective of an investor is any intentional, self-serving, deceptive behavior in the operational activities of a fund that is generally harmful to the investor. Operational fraud can be reduced through separation of duties, checks and balances, third-party audit, etc.

34.1.2 Operational Due Diligence is Driven by Operational Risk

Operational risk is a general term that refers to a series of risks that are not purely investment related in nature. But what exactly are these risks? Exhibit 34.1 provides a summary of key operational risk areas typically covered by investors during ODD reviews to ensure that risks are appropriately addressed by the manager.

EXHIBIT 34.1 Key Operational Risk Areas Typically Reviewed during Operational Due Diligence

Post-investment operational processes	Cash management
Valuation	Collateral and custody management
Legal function	Compliance function
Fund and firm service providers	Fund reporting
Legal documentation	Financial documentation
Regulatory interactions	Information technology
Information security	Business continuity and disaster recovery
Board of directors	Tax practices
Insurance	Counterparty management
Human capital and training	Assets under management and fund flows
Client concentration	Conflicts of interest
Investment allocations	

34.1.3 Prevention, Detection, and Mitigation of Operational Risk by Asset Managers

Three major components to controlling operational risk are prevention, detection, and mitigation. Prevention of operational risk lies in the development of sound systems and policies and procedures, and the proper hiring, training, retention, and compensation of personnel. Systems should be designed to optimally reduce operational risk and to detect risk. Personnel should be selected and managed in light of their potential degree of conflicts of interest; they should possess commensurate integrity, willingness to admit errors, and ability to mitigate operational risks.

34.1.4 Mitigation of Operational Risk by Investors

Christory, Daul, and Giraud (2006) analyzed operational default for funds and reached the following three conclusions regarding operational risk mitigation:

1. A diversified portfolio of at least 40 funds provides reasonable diversification against operational risk.
2. Investors should conduct an informed operational due diligence examination that takes into consideration the relative importance of the main risk factors affecting funds in general.
3. When investors assess the operational risk of funds properly, the information can be valuable in developing a more accurate return and risk profile for the fund.

Going beyond the third conclusion, Brown et al. (2009) conclude:

Operational risk is of course not the only factor explaining fund failure. We find that there is a significant positive interaction with [investment] risk, which suggests that funds with high degrees of operational risk are more subject to failure from excessive [investment] risk. This is consistent with rogue trading anecdotes that suggest that fund failure associated with excessive risk taking occurs when operational controls and oversight are weak.

34.1.5 Perverse Incentives and Internal Control Procedures

The desire of portfolio managers, traders, and, indeed, all fund employees is to retain existing assets, attract new assets, and increase revenues. Therefore, it is in their best interest to report high and consistent performance. However, the incentives that motivate fund managers to report high and consistent performance can cause unintended consequences from perverse incentives.

For example, there is an incentive for a fund manager to reduce investment risks when substantial profits have accrued to lock in an acceptable level of performance and the continued opportunity to manage assets. Conversely, there is an incentive for a fund manager to increase risks when substantial losses have accrued to increase the chance of recouping the losses and reaching an acceptable level of performance to sustain retention of assets.

The call-option-like nature of performance-based fees also provides fund managers with the incentive to take high risks. The risk-taking incentive varies based on the moneyness of the option. The net result is that portfolio managers and traders have incentives to take higher risks (and, in some cases, lower risks) than are appropriate given the investment mandate and market conditions. This principal–agent conflict can be largely resolved by requiring the fund manager to invest a significant portion of their personal net worth in the fund.

Internal control procedures can mitigate operational risk and reduce the consequences of perverse incentives. Risk managers must have the skills, dedication, authority, and support to design, implement, and monitor risk management systems that provide reasonable protections from investment process risks. The ongoing monitoring of the financial performance, risks, and current market values of portfolios and positions allows early detection of investment process problems and other operational problems. Proper valuation is the core of the monitoring process, since valuation is central to performance measurement and risk measurement.

34.1.6   Oversight of the Trade Life Cycle

During the ODD process, investors take measures to analyze the operational risks in each of the steps in the trade life cycle. One area this analysis focuses on is the independent oversight in place among different internal departments. For example, some funds may employ fund accounting and operations departments with the designated task of supporting the post-trade life cycle process. In other cases, this process may be shared by individuals with multiple responsibilities, including those of managing the investment portfolio or for risk management. In other cases, these processes may be outsourced, in whole or in part.

Due to the potential for manipulation and conflicts, it is considered best practice not only to segregate the investment and operational functions but also to balance separations among the various systems used in different functions of the trading process while still promoting process efficiency. Trading and risk management are **tasks of portfolio management** that should be performed by different people to have the optimal reduction in operational risk.

Another area of consideration is the level of oversight of clearing and valuation, especially when performed by third parties such as the fund administrator or third-party valuation agent. For example, if a reconciliation is performed between the fund and the administrator, and the lists of trades and settlement prices do not completely match, what happens next? It is considered best practice for fund administrators to maintain internal procedures by which such situations are researched independently of the fund.

34.1.7   Potential Veto Power of Due Diligence Teams

The importance of operational due diligence is highlighted by a Risk Alert from the SEC that notes an increase in the establishment of dedicated operational due diligence groups that have veto-level authority over the selection of fund managers recommended by the investment due diligence team, as well as a veto right after selection, in the event of any material operational change. This trend reflects the importance of ODD as rising to the point to override positive views on the fund's investment process potential. The Risk Alert noted that the scope of the groups may include "evaluation of the manager's policies and procedures regarding valuation"—indicating the importance of best practices in asset valuation.

34.2 FOUR KEY OPERATIONAL ACTIVITIES

Noninvestment operational activities are often termed middle-office and back-office activities and are performed by middle-office and back-office personnel. Note that virtually any activity in a fund involves some aspects of investments. The terms front office, middle office, and back office often are delineated by the expertise and job description of the personnel involved in the activities rather than by the extent to which the activities are generally related to investments.

Foremost concerns with regard to operational risk are errors, fraud, and perverse incentives. Cash management procedures should be given extra scrutiny. Noninvestment activities include providing support to the investment personnel with respect to data, recordkeeping, and documentation.

Noninvestment operational activities generally include the following four primary functions:

1. ALLOCATION: The predetermined process of dividing a trade into the various accounts and funds for which the trade was intended.
2. EXECUTION: The process of completing a trade. After the investment team decides to implement a trade, it may be placed by the investment team or in operations by a trading desk. In either case, the process of completing a trade involves policies and procedures for directing, communicating, and working the trade. Risk management should be built into the process to ensure that trades are consistent with the investment policy and risk limits of the fund.
3. POSTING AND SETTLEMENT: The process of logging the trade (posting) and the process of reconciling the trade with confirmations from third parties.
4. RECONCILIATION: The process of reviewing internal records of trades against external records of those trades, such as those provided by the prime broker, the administrator, or counterparty.

34.2.1 Overview of Due Diligence Regarding Execution

Trade execution refers to the process by which a fund completes a securities trade. In practice, after the decision has been made to trade, an execution process commonly begins. The trades are typically communicated by investment personnel to a centralized trading desk. Some smaller funds may not maintain dedicated trading desks; in these cases, trades are typically executed by investment personnel. In the context of an ODD review, the separation of investment and trading activities is considered best practice in order to lessen the potential for conflicts of interest.

Another consideration is the method by which these trades are transmitted. Trading instructions are typically transmitted electronically through electronic messaging or an order management system (OMS). These software systems assist funds in managing the trade life cycle process. The running list of all trades desired and completed during each trading day is commonly referred to as a **trade blotter**. After trading instructions are received by the centralized trading function, trades can then be executed with brokers or counterparties via either electronic interface or telephone. Funds may record these telephone conversations in case there is a discrepancy regarding the actual executed trade and the instructions provided by the fund. For electronic trading, different technology protocols, such as the Financial Information eXchange (FIX) protocol, may be used.

34.2.2 Overview of Due Diligence Regarding Posting

Posting is a term commonly used to refer to the process by which trades are logged internally at a fund, whether through order management or through fund accounting systems. **Internal settlement** refers to the firm's or fund's process of reconciling third-party trade confirmations for executed trades with its internal systems and trade blotters, and transferring the cash and securities to complete the trade. Depending on the types of securities processed, settlement procedures may occur practically in real time through automated reconciliations or may take several days to settle. The actual process of trade execution posting and settlement has multiple steps.

34.2.3 Overview of Due Diligence Regarding Trade Allocation

Trade allocation refers to the process by which trades are divided among the firm's various funds and/or accounts with best practice for a fund to maintain a predetermined trade allocation policy that does not favor one of the firm's funds or accounts at the expense of another. **Pro rata allocation** is a common allocation method by which a firm allots shares in the securities purchased to different funds and accounts based on predetermined proportionate amounts, such as assets under management, or a fund's predetermined target allocation size.

Fund managers need to be careful when they manage accounts with differing fee structures. They may be tempted to place more profitable trades, such as IPOs, into the accounts that pay more lucrative performance fees to the fund manager. To avoid this conflict, the fund should have written policies on trade allocation which are regularly reviewed for compliance testing.

34.2.4 Overview of Due Diligence Regarding Reconciliation

After trades have been executed, posted, internally settled, and allocated among the firm's funds, the final step is reconciliation. **Reconciliation** refers to the process by which a fund conducts another internal review to ensure that the internal details of the trade (buy/sell, security description, trade size, and price) are accurately matched with the details provided by the fund's counterparties.

This reconciliation is typically performed as a **two-way reconciliation**, which is a reconciliation between the fund's trading records and the prime broker. Some funds will use a third-party administrator. In those cases, a **three-way reconciliation (or triangular reconciliation)**, is performed between the trading counterparties, the fund itself, and the administrator.

Due to the enhanced oversight provided by the addition of the fund administrator, it is considered best practice for a triangular reconciliation to be performed as opposed to a two-way reconciliation. The timing of the completion of the reconciliation process depends on a number of factors, including whether a trade anticipated by the fund failed to execute, which is commonly known as a **trade break**. The type of securities being traded may also influence the timing of the completion of the reconciliation process.

For liquid securities, most reconciliations are typically completed on what is known as a **T+1 basis,** which means that one business day after the trade date—referred to as T—the trade would be reconciled. Other securities, such as bank debt, do not generally settle as quickly and may not be reconciled for several days. An additional consideration relates to the frequency of reconciliations. Although it is considered best practice to conduct frequent (i.e., daily) reconciliations, some funds may opt to conduct less frequent reconciliations. Reasons for this include the increased operational work related to performing these reconciliations, as well as the potential additional expenses charged by fund administrators to conduct this work. However, longer times to reconciliation can increase the cost of trade errors, as errors will tend to be detected more slowly and the financial markets will have more time to move further away from the originally intended price.

34.3 ANALYZING FUND CASH MANAGEMENT AND MOVEMENT

The operational steps regarding trades just described relate to the movement of securities held by funds. Related, and also a key ODD consideration, is a fund's management and movement of cash.

34.3.1 Four Primary Purposes of Fund Cash

The ways in which funds deal with cash can be grouped into four primary categories:

1. Cash for fund expenses.
2. Cash to facilitate trading.
3. Cash flows to and from investors.
4. Unencumbered cash.

34.3.2 Analyzing Cash for Fund Expenses

The operation of a fund requires frequent recurring cash expenses, such as office rent and salaries, as well as less frequent expenses, such as audit and legal bills. In order to manage cash for fund expenses, there are a number of best practices funds typically employ. Investors should understand and scrutinize which expenses are charged to the manager and which are charged to the fund. Best practices are for the manager to pay office rent and salaries out of the management and incentive fees, while investors typically pay the audit and legal costs of the fund.

Vendor Invoices and Segregation of Duties: When an invoice for a fund expense is submitted to a fund by a third party, it is considered best practice to have an individual who is not associated with approving payment of the invoice log the invoice into the firm's accounting systems and review it (to avoid having payments approved and processing by one person for personal gain). Another safeguard is to have a preapproved list of vendors that are eligible to receive payments with new vendors added to the list only with approvals from multiple individuals within the firm. Another common practice is to require multiple approvals from different departments throughout the firm and/or require one approval by a senior individual (i.e., from an A list) and one or more junior individuals (i.e., from a B list). Some funds require higher levels of approval based on the amount of the expense. Analyzing the approval process to ensure appropriate oversight and controls of approval channels is a key goal of ODD analysis.

ROLES OF THE ADMINISTRATOR AND BANKS: The administrator may oversee the transfer of cash to process expenses as part of a fund's cash controls. After an internal approval of the expenditure, the next step typically involves review and approval by the fund administrator with a focus on questions related to the amount of the expenditure and whether it is a common vendor that is frequently used. The fund administrator will ensure that the approvals were granted according to the fund's policies. It is best practice for the fund administrator to be sent copies of the actual invoices received, so that the administrator may directly contact the vendor to determine the validity of the invoice or conduct additional inquiry regarding the expense if any further questions arise. After approvals are granted by the fund administrator, the bank can process payment to the vendor.

34.3.3 Analyzing Cash to Facilitate Trading

The second primary category of cash is that used by funds to facilitate trading. A previous section on trading briefly addressed cash for trade execution. Depending on the type of transaction, funds may also have positive cash balances on account with trading counterparties. A common example of a situation such as this arising would be with a swap counterparty. In these cases, a key consideration during the ODD process is to analyze what happens to this cash. One option would be for positive balances of cash to sit at the counterparty, waiting for the next trade to be executed. In other cases, funds recall this cash, which is sometimes referred to as sweeping cash, an option that has two primary advantages for funds:

RREDUCTION OF COUNTERPARTY EXPOSURE: By taking unnecessary cash balances back from the counterparty, the fund is minimizing its counterparty exposure.

OPTION TO REINVEST OR EARN INTEREST: By sweeping back the cash from the counterparty to its own accounts, the fund now has the ability to use the cash for trading or other purposes, such as to earn interest.

The frequency by which cash is swept varies among funds. Some prefer the ease of leaving cash with a commonly used counterparty rather than sweeping back the cash and later depositing it again with the same counterparty for future trading. Others may sweep cash daily, weekly, or monthly. It is generally considered best practice to sweep cash more frequently or when cash reaches a certain threshold amount.

34.3.4 Four Reasons for Analyzing Cash to And From Investors

The third primary category of fund cash relates to cash used to process capital inflows and outflows, which are also called **subscriptions and redemptions,** respectively. Typically, the fund administrator is involved in processing the subscriptions and redemptions of investor funds subject to fund oversight. Similar to the movement of cash for fund expenses, a number of internal fund review processes and administrator checks are typically in place regarding this capital. It is imperative that instructions for wiring funds are verified and correct and that controls are in place for changing these instructions. Such oversight is crucial for several reasons, including these four:

1. Ensuring that capital subscriptions are placed into the appropriate funds.
2. Monitoring the process so that redemptions are not paid out to the wrong individuals or in incorrect amounts.
3. Evaluating subscription and redemption timing to ensure that it complies with fund terms and timing guidelines.
4. Reviewing subscription and redemption documentation to ensure that all appropriate procedures are in place for complying with regulations, such as anti-money-laundering and accredited investor provisions.

34.3.5 Analyzing Unencumbered Cash

The fourth primary category of fund cash relates to cash that is not currently being used for trading but may be used in the future for either trading or another purpose; this type of cash is referred to **unencumbered cash.** Funds typically earn interest on unencumbered cash by depositing the cash in liquid vehicles, such as checking accounts or interest-bearing money market accounts. Best practices for ODD involve examining the procedures for managing these cash balances.

34.4 ANALYZING EXTERNAL PARTIES AND CHECKING PRINCIPALS

Operational due diligence includes contact with and analysis of external service providers. This section focuses on analysis of prime brokers, fund administrators, and external sources of information. Prime brokers and fund administrators are key service providers for hedge funds but are less frequently employed by managers of private equity and real assets funds.

34.4.1 Analyzing Fund Prime Brokers

Fund prime brokers are institutions that facilitate fund trading by aggregating a portion, or all, of a fund's cash and securities as well as providing services for leverage and short selling. As part of the ODD process, fund investors focus on solvency of prime brokers, noting prime broker failures in the past in which funds were unable to reclaim cash balances held at the institution in a timely manner. In part to diversify the risk of prime broker insolvency, it is now common for funds to use two or more prime brokers.

The ODD goals include understanding the solvency of the prime broker(s). Also ODD seeks general background information including the specific ways in which the prime brokers may interact with the fund in areas such as trade processing, ongoing counterparty management, and oversight, as well as with other service providers, such as fund administrators.

34.4.2   Analyzing Fund Administrators

Fund administrators commonly perform fund accounting, shareholder services, and are responsible for reviewing the valuations of securities held by funds (although not responsible for independently valuing securities for which valuations are not readily available). After 2008, most hedge funds moved from internal administration to external administration or at least an external verification of internal valuations. For private equity and real assets fund managers that don't have an external administrator, it is important to have an appropriate segregation of duties between the investment team and the administration and valuation team.

FOR ILLIQUID POSITIONS: It is considered best practice for the fund to provide the administrator with copies of the minutes of any internal valuation committee meetings as well as the pricing supports used by the fund in valuing illiquid positions. In cases in which the manager directly prices a large portion of a fund's holdings, it is considered best practice for the fund to engage a third party, known as a **valuation agent,** to conduct an independent valuation of these positions.

FOR MODERATELY ILLIQUID POSITIONS: In the case of positions with modest liquidity, such as certain over-the-counter (OTC) positions that are priced through broker quotes, it is typically considered best practice to obtain multiple broker quotes. One way that administrators typically attempt to independently verify the prices submitted to funds by brokers is through the creation of shared email in-boxes for pricing feeds to independently verify the pricing data eventually submitted by the fund. Not all administrators, however, may universally follow rigorous processes in this regard; therefore, it is up to investors to evaluate the robustness of the level of administrator oversight through ODD.

FOR LIQUID POSITIONS: Another potential task of administrators is obtaining security prices from additional sources other than those used by the fund manager to enhance the accuracy of prices. By using multiple sources, less reliance is placed on the prices provided by one vendor or broker. As can be expected, in many cases the prices from these multiple sources may not exactly match. In these situations, different rules may be followed, including discarding large outlier prices and taking averages.

COMPUTING THE FUND'S NAV: Fund administrators help produce the fund's **net asset value (NAV)**, which is the value of the fund after liabilities have been subtracted and is used in the production of investor statements to report the value of investors' holdings in the fund at different points in time and to calculate fees, redemptions, and subscriptions.

After the administrator and the fund are both satisfied with the valuations obtained for a fund during a particular period (e.g., monthly), a final NAV is agreed on, which is known as **cutting the NAV.** The administrator prepares and distributes individual investor account statements.

From an operational risk perspective, *continued delays* in the production of NAVs can be representative of larger underlying problems between the fund and the administrator. Continued NAV production delays can signal that there are undiagnosed operational problems present. This effect can guide investors to focus more heavily on certain parts of their ODD.

34.4.3 Overview of Investigative Due Diligence

Investigative due diligence, sometimes known as background investigation, is an essential part of the larger ODD process. The Risk Alert noted a professional consensus regarding the importance of background checks of fund principals. Third parties increasingly are performing independent background checks of principals as well as checks on the corporate entity/firm to supplement the fund's own reviews regarding "employment history, legal and regulatory matters, news sources, and independent reference checks."

34.4.4 Three Models of Selecting Personnel for Investigation

Investors traditionally perform background investigations on key fund personnel as well as on the management company entity for the fund. It should be noted that there are no universal rules with regard to which individuals should be investigated. During the course of an ODD review, an investor may learn that an individual with a seemingly unimportant title may turn out be a key individual in the organization's operations. In these cases, flexibility in the approach employed to select individuals for investigation is often merited. There are three common approaches investors use to assist them in determining which individuals to investigate:

1. EQUITY OWNERSHIP MODEL: Under the **equity ownership model** approach, an investigation would be performed on all personnel who have equity ownership in the management company of the fund organization. This is generally feasible from a cost and investigation-duration perspective for a small fund organization with two or three owners. In larger fund organizations, which typically have a large number of owners, such searches can become prohibitively expensive and lengthy.
2. INVESTMENT DECISION-MAKING AUTHORITY MODEL: The **investment decision-making authority model** approach focuses on performing background investigations on those individuals who have authority to make investment decisions and act (i.e., trade) on such decisions. This generally includes portfolio managers, traders, and those involved with the investment process on a daily basis.
3. RISK CONTROL MODEL: Under the **risk control model** approach, background investigations are performed on all individuals, both investment and noninvestment focused, who control risk within an organization. These include portfolio managers and traders, as well as senior operational personnel, such as the chief financial officer and chief compliance officer, and those with authority to move cash.

34.4.5 Five Areas of Background Investigation

The fund manager should authorize investors to perform an independent background check that fully discloses all civil, criminal, and regulatory actions against the fund manager or any of its principals over their entire careers.

FIVE AREAS COMMONLY INCLUDED IN BACKGROUND INVESTIGATIONS: (1) criminal searches; (2) civil searches; (3) regulatory searches; (4) media searches; and (5) factual information searches

Criminal searches include reviews of all records related to criminal activities. Areas typically range from arrest and conviction records to traffic violations.

Civil searches include reviews of civil litigation records, bankruptcy records, foreclosures, tax cases, and other judgments and liens.

Regulatory searches include reviews of regulatory filings, records of financial regulators, office of foreign asset control, and global sanctions.

Media searches include the Internet-based searches of web content, broad media searches of industry periodicals, and social media screens.

Factual information searches include confirmation and review of previous employment and educational endeavors, asset records such as property and vehicles, fictitious-name databases, other business interests outside the fund, and reference checks.

34.4.6 Organizing and Interpreting Information from Background and Other Investigations

Depending on where these investigations are performed jurisdictionally, different levels of detail may be available. This is in part due to differing privacy laws across countries, as well as to the different structures of the previously noted areas of investigation, such as court system structures. In most cases, fund personnel are required to sign releases in order to provide permission for institutions to release certain information about a person's previous affiliation with the institution. Additionally, data protection rules in some jurisdictions (e.g., the General Data Protection Regulation in the EU), require controllers of personal data to ensure appropriate technical and organizational measures are in place to implement data protection principles.

Traditionally, most investors simply outsourced the background investigation process to third-party investigative firms. This approach suffered from a separation between the investigative firms and the fund's direct ODD process. As a result, it is increasingly common for investors to combine the background investigation and ODD processes under a single entity, such as a third-party ODD consulting firm. Under these integrated reviews, investors benefit from more comprehensive deep-dive due diligence reviews and can subsequently make more informed investment decisions.

Evaluating the results of the investigative process can be a very subjective matter, on which reasonable minds may disagree. For example, if a fund manager had been previously convicted of financial crimes, most investors would agree that this would be a deal breaker, and they would not invest with this manager. However, in matters unrelated to financial services, consider the situation of a fund manager who is charged with driving while intoxicated but pleads guilty to a lesser charge, such as reckless driving. Individual investors might evaluate such circumstance differently when coming to an overall investigative due diligence assessment of a fund.

It is becoming increasingly popular for investors to conduct *ongoing* investigative due diligence on fund management companies and key personnel. These ongoing investigations typically focus on items that may change over time, such as arrest records and civil litigation. In these cases, investors follow different approaches with regard to the scope and timing of such searches; however, the goal is to ensure that some degree of ongoing investigative due diligence is performed, rather than having the initial review be the final source of information.

34.4.7   Independent Service Provider Verification of Fund Operational Data

Two primary areas of fund data verification are asset and position verification. **Asset verification** refers to the process by which an investor independently confirms a fund's level of asset holdings with third parties, such as fund administrators, prime brokers, and banks. Position verification refers to the process of confirming the holdings of actual fund positions with third parties, such as prime brokers and custodians.

The goal of such confirmations is to provide an independent comparison with regard to the asset level the fund manager is reporting and that which third parties are reporting. All verifications should be performed before an investment is made, as well as on a regular basis for as long as the investor retains an allocation to the fund.

34.4.8   Checks with Other Investors

Ownership information of funds is generally private. Fund managers often provide a list of selected existing investors who have agreed to serve as references. Talking to these existing clients is a necessary step to check the veracity of the fund manager's statements and to receive an indication of existing client satisfaction. The best questions for these existing investors include the following:

- Have the financial reports been timely?
- Have the reports been easy to understand?
- Has the fund manager responded effectively to questions about such topics as financial performance?
- Has the fund manager done what was promised, such as maintaining the investment strategy?
- What concerns does the current investor have regarding the fund manager or the fund's performance?
- Would the current client invest more money with the fund manager?

However, a sample of reference checks derived from a list of current investors the manager provides is a biased sample of investors. An unbiased sample of investors would be derived from a list of all current investors and former investors. The problem with obtaining a representative sample of all investors past and present is identifying former investors and current investors not provided by the fund manager as references. Further, if these other investors can be identified, it may be difficult to obtain their open and honest opinions with regard to any problems with the fund manager. The best way to receive good information from these investors is by establishing an extensive network of industry professionals committed to openness and honesty. Informal reference checks with these contacts, as well as with the listed references and the outside service providers, should include an open-ended summary question, such as: is there anything else about this fund and its manager that I should know that would help me make a better decision with regard to this potential investment?

34.5   ANALYZING FUND COMPLIANCE

The management of compliance risks within a fund is typically overseen by a designated compliance department. Some smaller funds may not maintain dedicated compliance departments but instead outsource the function. The **four areas commonly overseen by the compliance department** are: (1) initial and ongoing personnel training on compliance-related matters; (2) testing of the implementation of compliance policies; (3) monitoring and managing conflicts of interest; and (4) ensuring adherence with regulatory requirements in the jurisdictions in which the firm operates.

The compliance department should maintain and distribute a manual containing compliance policies and procedures as well as the firm's Code of Ethics and Conduct. Compliance is responsible for ensuring that all employees are aware of the policy and maintain procedures to ensure that employees are in continuous compliance with the policies. Common areas include regulations on outside business activities, gifts and entertainment, material nonpublic information, and personal trading.

34.5.1   Personal Trading Compliance of Fund Employees

A key fund compliance policy, which is known as **personal account dealing,** relates to the trading of securities by employees of the firm for their own accounts. The policies implemented in this regard typically apply not only to employees but also to their significant others as well as other immediate family members. One of the key concerns is **front running,** or trading ahead, in which employees or others attempt to trade for their own accounts in advance of the firm's trading for client accounts. Front running places the interests of the firm's employees ahead of its investors.

The majority of personal trading procedures specify a list of securities, known as **covered securities,** which are securities commonly held in client accounts and to which the policies apply. In practice, most funds typically exclude from the list of covered securities investments such as mutual funds and exchange-traded funds, and securities only traded in passively managed client accounts. The reason for these exclusions is the reduced likelihood that an employee would benefit from front running anticipated fund trades.

34.5.2   Common Compliance Risks Regarding Personal Trading

Pre-clearance of personal account trades is a process by which employees must seek approval from compliance before executing a trade. Pre-clearance requests may be submitted in a number of formats, including via email or through a designated personal account dealing management system.

Post-clearance refers to the process by which the compliance department collects employee brokerage statements and then attempts to reconcile them to pre-clearance requests. It is considered best practice for the compliance department of a fund to collect employee brokerage statements directly from brokers and independent of the employee. It is becoming more common for firms to engage a third-party software solution to automate the pre-clearance and post-clearance/reconciliation process.

A **restricted list** is a list of securities that the firm has prohibited employees from trading because the firm has received material nonpublic information regarding a particular security, which is commonly referred to as being *conflicted out of a security*. Restricted lists can also include names that are restricted based on an investment restriction due to environmental, social, or governance factors. During the ODD process, investors seek to gauge who is responsible for maintaining this list and what controls are in place to prevent employees from trading in restricted names.

Blackout periods are common practice in situations where employees are able to trade names within firm portfolios, whereby employees cannot trade these securities within a specified number of days before or after a portfolio trades that security.

Minimum holding periods are requirements that prohibit an employee from purchasing a security and then selling it within a predefined period of time and have the goal of preventing employees from actively trading in their personal accounts.

Maximum number of trades in a given time frame may also be imposed to avoid individuals from trading excessively.

In certain cases, funds may employ a **hardship exemption procedure,** wherein an employee is allowed, with permission, to sell a security, especially at a loss, even if it is within the minimum holding period. A hardship exemption is commonly permitted to allow employees to limit personal losses.

34.5.3   Compliance Risks Regarding Nonpublic and Inside Information

Another common compliance risk consideration is insider trading, a scheme in which employees of a fund use what is known as material nonpublic information (MNPI), sometimes referred to as insider information, in their investment process. In many countries, front running and insider trading are illegal and subject to criminal prosecution. In countries where there are no regulations regarding these activities, CFA Charterholders and CAIA Charterholders are required to abide by the Standards of Practice Handbook, which prohibit these activities globally, even in countries where they aren't illegal.

Many firms are regularly in possession of MNPI, such as law firms and investment banks that negotiate merger deals before they are publicly announced. Corporate insiders, such as CEOs and CFOs are also regularly in possession of MNPI, especially regarding corporate revenues and earnings before they are publicly announced. Firms should develop policies that define material nonpublic information and place controls on who has access to this information. Fund managers may come into contact with MNPI through conversations with these attorneys, bankers, and corporate executives, as well as through expert networks. Procedures should be put into place preventing those in possession of MNPI from disseminating or trading on this information.

The technical legal definitions of what constitutes MNPI can vary across jurisdictions. Many of the high-profile fund cases that have been reported involving insider trading relate to the use of expert networks, which are organized by third-party for-profit firms. **Expert networks** are comprised of professionals and academics from various disciplines and industries that provide advice and consultations to funds conducting research, but in some cases have been found to use currently employed or recently retired employees from publicly traded companies to obtain MNPI. These types of networks typically impose prohibitions on their experts with regard to communication of MNPI.

The use of such networks by funds does not intrinsically represent a high degree of operational risk. Compliance departments can take a number of steps to institute better controls over such networks, including these eight practices:

1. Reviewing expert network policies regarding MNPI and ensuring that the policies comply with both applicable laws and the fund's policies.

2. Supplementing or tailoring the expert's policies to ensure they are suitable for the funds/firm.
3. Requiring preapproval for investment personnel before allowing conversations with experts.
4. Requiring analysts to read a predetermined script at the start of each call, making clear the purpose of the call and the information they do/do not wish to receive.
5. Having compliance personnel listen in on either all or a sample of expert calls.
6. Imposing a suitable cooling off/hiatus time frame post-employment at either a publicly listed company/or in a government position before engaging with such consultants.
7. Setting an appropriate limit on the number of times the same expert can be consulted each quarter.
8. Monitoring fund trading activity after expert conversations for unusual patterns, as well as employee personal trading.

It should be noted that these same practices can be employed when third-party research sources that are not part of formal expert networks are used, such as freelancers. In addition to preventing intentional use of MNPI, compliance training can ensure that employees recognize and report when they believe they are in the possession of MNPI.

34.5.4 Electronic Communication Monitoring

Most funds use electronic communications (e.g., email, instant messaging, and remote device communications) to facilitate their daily investment and operational procedures. Some jurisdictions require funds to archive electronic communications often to prevent the transmission of MNPI. Two common methods of oversight are:

1. Lexicon-based searches that locate messages containing keywords or phrases that may signal MNPI and warrant further investigation; and
2. Perusing a randomly selected fixed percentage of firm-wide and department-wide emails

34.5.5 Analyzing the Work of Third-Party Compliance Consultants

To ease the burden on internal fund compliance departments, funds may sometimes work with third-party compliance consultants. These consultants may perform a number of tasks, including these four actions:

1. Performing mock regulatory audits.
2. Updating compliance policies and procedures to comply with new regulations.
3. Assisting with, or completely running, compliance testing programs.
4. Assisting with regional compliance expertise in satellite offices where the firm may have little to no internal compliance personnel.

It is generally considered best practice for a fund to use a third-party compliance consultant to augment the work of the internal compliance function.

34.6   ONSITE MANAGER VISITS

Onsite manager visits form a crucial step in the operational due diligence process.

34.6.1   Selection of Visit Location

After the documentation review process (further detailed in Chapter 35) is complete, the next stage in the process is for investors to go onsite with a manager at the fund's office to conduct an in-person meeting. One consideration that may arise in setting the location for the office review is the question of what to do should the GP maintain multiple offices. In the context of setting a meeting location focused on operational risk, it is commonly considered best practice to focus the onsite meeting where the majority of fund operational procedures are performed. Of course, it is not unheard of to visit multiple locations should it be deemed necessary to meet face-to-face with individuals in multiple offices.

34.6.2   Desk Reviews Are Not Best Practice

Some investors may omit the onsite visit during ODD due to budget constraints or a policy that only requires onsite visits for managers or strategies deemed as higher risk. This type of ODD review is a desk review, which is limited to a review based solely on documents collected and perhaps conference or video calls. The desk review approach is not considered to be best practice. Three reasons LPs may argue in favor of desk reviews are the following:

1. Lower cost of desk reviews compared to onsite visits.
2. Shortened overall review time for desk reviews.
3. Belief in equal information collection by both review processes.

Although desk reviews may result in lower costs and shorter ODD review processes, not including an onsite visit with the GP during the ODD process typically results in a less comprehensive review. This can subsequently expose investors to increased levels of operational risk.

Four reasons LPs may argue that desk reviews are inadequate include:

1. An onsite visit allows the LP to verify that the employees of the GP have knowledge of the written procedures and how closely they are followed in regular practice.
2. That a visit to the GP's office allows the due diligence team to interview a broad group of key personnel, which allows the LP to evaluate the competency of the GP's team.
3. A desk review may not provide an overview of the IT architecture of the GP's operations. An onsite visit allows the LP to view demonstrations of IT systems, especially those used to place and settle trades.
4. While GPs may provide electronic copies of a variety of documents to facilitate desk reviews, some documents will only be available for review of physical copies at the GP's office. Such documents may include valuation procedures, SEC exam letters, and the firm's complete compliance manual.

34.6.3 Risk Alert's Three Tasks on Desk versus Onsite Reviews

The Risk Alert asserts that onsite visit requirements are part of adviser reviews. Onsite visits address three important tasks: "(i) understand the culture of the manager; (ii) detect instances where dominant individuals and inadequate control environments may exist; (iii) and provide increased access to review documents and to speak with the manager's personnel."

34.7 ELEMENTS AND KEY CONCERNS OF THE ODD PROCESS

This section returns to a "big picture" view of ODD to summarize the myriad ODD issues discussed above.

34.7.1 Eight Core Elements of The ODD Process

The alternative investment ODD process employed by investors typically has seven primary steps and an eighth step (ongoing monitoring) in the event that an investment is made: (1) document collection; (2) document analysis; (3) onsite visit; (4) service provider reviews and confirmations; (5) investigative due diligence; (6) process documentation; (7) operational decision; (8) ongoing monitoring (if the investment is made).

An investor performing ODD will often go back to the manager several times requesting additional documents. However, prospective LPs must be conscious of the time needed by GPs to respond to requests. Thus, LPs must engage in a balancing act so as not to overly burden the fund manager with too many separate requests. Instead, it is often considered prudent to bundle requests for follow-up items, such as additional documents. Increasingly, many of the documents that ODD professionals require are available online via secure portals administered by the GP, and access to these can be beneficial and less burdensome on all parties.

34.7.2 Five Explanations for the Expanding Scope of Operational Due Diligence

The scope of ODD has grown in recent years. There are a number of explanations for the expanding scope of items covered during operational due diligence. These include the following:

1. Expanded regulatory requirements.
2. Increased availability of overall due diligence resources.
3. Continued presence of fund fraud or operational failures.
4. Increasing operational sophistication and automation of investment processes.
5. Greater reliance on trading models and related risk management systems.

34.7.3 External Sources of Review and Confirmation

External third-party service providers should be viewed as more than simply sources of documents. The Risk Alert suggested that advisers who do not apply a consistent program of oversight of third-party service providers (e.g., periodic reviews of whether the terms of agreements were being followed) are more likely to have deficiencies. Similarly, the ODD procedures followed by investors should engage fully with external service providers, such as prime brokers, administrators, banks, IT consultants, legal counsels, compliance consultants, valuation agents, and auditors. Other common service providers may include custodians, personnel recruiting firms, preemployment screening firms, risk analysis services, marketers, and fund distributors.

As part of the service provider review process, LPs may reach out to other more investment-related service providers, such as trading counterparties. One example would be a swap counterparty that may be used by GPs. From an ODD perspective, the reviews of these counterparties will typically focus not on the investment merits of any interaction with such counterparties but on the operational interaction between the GP and the counterparties, as well as the terms of such arrangements.

NINE KEY OPERATIONAL WARNING INDICATORS OR AWARENESS SIGNALS are: (1) lack of a qualified third-party administrator; (2) unknown or unqualified auditor; (3) multiple changes in third-party service providers; (4) concerns noted in the audited financial statements, including related-party transactions; (5) unfavorable indications from background checks of key personnel; (6) findings of undisclosed conflicts of interest; (7) inadequate operational infrastructure and compliance programs; (8) questionable fair valuation process; and (9) lack of transparency.

34.8 INFORMATION TECHNOLOGY AND META RISKS

Information technology has been and will continue to be an increasing aspect of most ODD processes.

34.8.1 Information Technology

Private fund managers, as with most traditional public fund managers, are heavily reliant on information technology (IT). There are several documents associated with IT that can be analyzed. Information technology documentation typically includes a review of various aspects of a fund's IT function, including policies related to hardware, software, and ongoing support. Private funds typically maintain documentation of IT policies and procedures that address the ways in which firms manage these issues.

IT raises concerns regarding scalability that are especially critical. **Operational scalability** refers to the firm's ability to build on existing systems in order to continue to support growth in an organized manner, including via the addition of new resources, without material disruption. The concept extends beyond IT. For example, operational scalability would be a concern if sufficient fund account personnel were not added to support new fund launches.

34.8.2 Five Key Questions Regarding Information Technology

When reviewing documents regarding IT, common considerations for LPs include these five questions:

1. What is the organization of the firm's IT function?

2. What process is in place with regard to the rolling out of new revisions of IT software and hardware?
3. How does the firm approach information security issues, including protecting data, managing firewalls, and updating credentials for employees and consultants?
4. What escalation procedures are in place to manage IT issues that may arise during the course of the firm's operations?
5. What is the firm's IT hardware and software support management plan? If the fund maintains multiple offices, how is this process managed for the different locations?

Business continuity planning, disaster recovery, and cybersecurity, all of which are heavily based on IT, are discussed in Chapter 35.

34.8.3 Evaluating Meta Risk

In 2008, a report of the Investors' Committee of the President's Working Group on Financial Markets titled "Principles and Best Practices for Fund Investors" references the concept of **meta risks,** which are defined as "the qualitative risks beyond explicit measurable financial risks. They include human and organizational behavior, moral hazard, excessive reliance on and misuse of quantitative tools, complexity and lack of understanding of market interactions, and the very nature of capital markets in which extreme events happen with far greater regularity than standard models suggest."

In an operational risk context, meta risks is the catch-all category used to account for all noninvestment-related risks that are not covered by a particular category, with examples ranging from a fund manager's expenditures on expensive office decorations, or a fund manager who is confrontational or defensive during an onsite meeting. The process of assessing the importance of meta risks is inherently subjective but may be an area in which a highly skilled operational risk professional can add value.

34.9 FUNDING, APPLYING, AND CONCLUDING ODD

This chapter concludes with a discussion of how ODD is funded and applied.

34.9.1 Four Approaches to Resource Allocation for Operational Due Diligence

There are four popular approaches to allocating resources for ODD: dedicated, shared, modular, and hybrid:

1. Dedicated: A **dedicated operational due diligence approach** is an ODD framework in which an investment organization has at least one employee whose full-time responsibility is vetting the operational risks of fund managers.
2. Shared: A **shared operational due diligence approach** is a framework in which the responsibility for ODD is shared by multiple individuals who have responsibility for investment due diligence but in which no full-time, dedicated ODD staff are employed.

3. Modular: A **modular operational due diligence approach** is one whereby the ODD process is classified into functional components and divided among specialists with relevant domain-specific knowledge. Domain experts typically have responsibilities in addition to their ODD duties and collaborate on their ODD work through the leadership of an operational generalist who serves as an information aggregator.

4. Hybrid: A **hybrid operational due diligence approach** refers to some combination of the dedicated, shared, and modular approaches. An example is employing a full-time ODD analyst (dedicated framework) while leveraging off in-house domain experts as needed (modular framework).

34.9.2 Documenting the Operational Due Diligence Process

The Risk Alert noted that advisers with detailed documentation on policies and procedures were more likely to consistently apply due diligence processes.

Individual organizations approach the ODD documentation process in different ways. Some organizations may produce a brief summary memo that outlines only the key concerns from the ODD process. While such summary memorandums are efficient for review, it is often considered best practice to produce a more detailed document or detail/substantiation of the review process. The length of ODD process documentation reports has grown to keep up with the broadened scope of ODD reviews.

These detailed documents typically begin with an executive summary section, which summarizes the key findings from the ODD review. It is also considered best practice not only to document concerns in the executive summary section, but also to detail fund and firm strengths uncovered during the ODD process. The other sections of the report typically provide detailed analysis of each of the operational risk review areas covered during the ODD process. One of the key benefits of producing a detailed report summarizing ODD analysis is that in the event that an investment is made with a fund, the document facilitates the ongoing monitoring process. Should an investment not be made initially, the detailed ODD report can be used to facilitate a revised review of the same manager if the fund is still of interest to investors in the future.

In documenting ODD reports, some investors attempt to assign quantitative operational risk scores to the different operational risk areas covered. These scores can then be weighted based on predetermined factor weightings in order to produce a weighted average operational risk score, which could drive the frequency and level of ongoing or further due diligence. While such approaches may be useful for high-level operational risk analysis or comparing scores among different fund managers, it is generally considered best practice to use more of an information-based approach to operational risk analysis and to focus on the actual operational practices employed rather than just scores.

34.9.3 Operational Decision-Making and Allocation Considerations

The end result of the ODD process is to facilitate the development of an operational risk determination, sometimes referred to as an operational decision. An **operational**

EXHIBIT 34.2 Common Allocation Conclusions and Resulting Actions from the Operational Due Diligence Process

Conclusion	Common Possible Resulting Actions
High level of operational risk that is unacceptable to investors	Decision is made to make no investment with the fund initially. The decision may be reevaluated to make an allocation in the future if the fund makes operational improvements
Intermediate level of operational risk that is acceptable, but still concerning to investors	A reduced allocation is made to the fund
Low level of operational risk where operational risks may still be present but classified as relatively low risk by an investor	An allocation of the original amount anticipated is made

decision by an investor, or investment organization, can typically result in a number of common allocation conclusions (no investment, reduced allocation, or originally anticipated investment) as summarized in Exhibit 34.2.

In reference to Exhibit 34.2, it should be noted that in each case, an investor can share with the fund under review feedback relating to the operational risk concerns discovered. This feedback can then be used by the fund to repair operational deficiencies, with the goal of securing an initial or increased allocation from an investor in the future.

It should also be noted that the guidelines in Exhibit 34.2 are simply general guidelines. Individual investors may make different determinations relating to the severity of certain operational deficiencies. This relates to a key operational risk concept known as factor weighting. **Factor weighting in the context of ODD** refers to the importance (i.e., weight) that individual investors give to different operational risk considerations when coming to an overall operational decision. For example, some investors may choose to equally weight the various operational risk factors analyzed. Other investors may view certain items, such as fund accounting and valuations, as holding more operational risk, and therefore give those areas more weight when making operational decisions. Note that factor weights vary across strategy, where trading systems may be more important in managed futures and liquidity risk and leverage structure more important in fixed income arbitrage. The ODD analyst should build separate risk models for each fund strategy.

While there is flexibility in assigning factor weights, there is a series of market norms regarding what is considered operational best practice in certain areas that guide investors in the factor weighting process. **Operational benchmarking** is the process of comparing operational best practices to the actual procedures in place at a fund. Operational best practices may vary by strategy, as hedge funds have different procedures and regulations than private equity or real estate funds. It should also be noted that the factor weighting process is not necessarily quantitative in nature; qualitative weights, such as designating a particular operational risk area as "very important," may also take place.

There is a general consensus that certain practices are no longer acceptable to the majority of investors. One example of this would be a hedge fund that self-administers its own funds. In some cases the issue of self-administration would be referred to as an **operational threshold issue,** meaning that it is an issue that must be satisfied in order to have a particular investor continue to consider allocating to a particular fund. Another example of an operational threshold issue for all types of funds, including private equity and real asset funds, would be to use an unknown or inexperienced auditor. To be clear, investors typically do not view each operational risk area to be a threshold issue. For example, most investors would apply a degree of flexibility to the number of approvers required to sign off on cash transfers.

REFERENCES

Brown, S., W. Goetzmann, B. Liang, and C. Schwarz. 2009. "Estimating Operational Risk for Hedge Funds: The ω-Score." *Financial Analysts Journal* 65 (1): 43–53.

Christory, C., S. Daul, and J. R. Giraud. 2006. "Quantification of Hedge Fund Default Risk." *Journal of Alternative Investments* 9 (2): 71–86.

Feffer, S. and C. Kundro. 2003 "Understanding and Mitigating Operational Risk in Hedge Funds: A Capco White Paper." The Capital Markets Company Ltd.

Investors' Committee of the President's Working Group on Financial Markets. 2008. "Principles and Best Practices for Fund Investors." Report.

Securities and Exchange Commission (SEC). 2014. "Investment Adviser Due Diligence Processes for Selecting Alternative Investments and Their Respective Managers." *National Exam Program, Risk Alert* 4, no. 1 (January 28, 2014): www.sec.gov/ocie/announcement/risk-alert---selecting-alternative-investments-and-managers.html.

CHAPTER 35

Due Diligence of Terms and Business Activities

The focus of this chapter on due diligence is the terms of the fund–investor relationship especially as indicated through analysis of a fund's structure and legal documents from the investor's perspective. Primarily, this chapter discusses the implications of legal documents and other findings from the due diligence procedure on the appropriateness of the fund for the investor conducting the due diligence. The chapter also includes a discussion of the business activities, continuity planning, and disaster recovery.

35.1 DUE DILIGENCE DOCUMENT COLLECTION PROCESS

One of the primary purposes of document collection is to allow investors to begin to develop an initial assessment of a fund manager's operational risk profile before the onsite visit. An **operational risk profile** is an outline or summary of potential losses or other exposures of a fund due to errors or failures within the fund's functions other than those purely attributable to the fund's investment strategy.

This chapter focuses on the three most common document types that are typically collected and reviewed during the operational due diligence (ODD) process: (1) legal documentation; (2) financial documentation; and (3) information technology documentation. There are three primary sources of documentation for investors during an ODD review: (1) fund managers themselves; (2) fund service providers; and (3) regulatory filings.

What documents should investors collect? Exhibit 35.1 outlines a list of key documents commonly collected during an ODD review. There is no universal set of terms that private equity fund managers use when naming documents. One example is the compliance manual. Some managers may maintain a document similar to a compliance manual but refer to it as a code of ethics. If an investor does not refer to the exact name used by the fund when requesting a certain document, the GP (general partner) might simply reply that the fund does not maintain the document requested. Oftentimes, this problem can be overcome by LPs (limited partners) in two ways. The first is by engaging in discussions with GPs when submitting document requests to provide perspective on the goals of the LP document request. A second way is to develop documentation requests in such a way as to not be overly self-limiting.

Another common issue that typically arises during the LP document collection stage is that a fund manager may choose not to distribute certain documentation

EXHIBIT 35.1 Common Documents Collected During an Initial Operational Due Diligence Review

Document Type	Example Documents	Notes
Fund-specific legal documentation	Fund offering memorandum	
	Subscription documents	
	Articles of association (if applicable)	
	Limited partnership agreement (if applicable)	
	Fund formation documents	
Firm legal and compliance documentation	Firm formation documents	Another document commonly asked for associated with formation is a certificate of good standing, or equivalent, which in part shows that no outstanding taxes or liens are in place
	Compliance manual	If not included in compliance manual: • Employee personal trading procedures • Electronic communication policy • Anti-money-laundering policies and procedures
	Code of ethics	
Financial documents	Audited financial statements	If no audits are available, previous fund audits are typically collected
Marketing communications	LP investor Letters	
	Samples of recent marketing materials	Examples include presentations (commonly called pitch books) and GP letters to LPs
Other documentation	Firm organizational chart	
	Business continuity and disaster recovery plan	
	Valuation policy and procedures	
	Details of insurance coverage	LPs may also ask for actual copies of insurance certificates in addition to a summary of coverage
	Operations policy manual	
	Information technology policies and procedures	

outside the fund's office (e.g., the compliance manual which some GPs view as proprietary). There are a myriad of reasons GPs typically cite for this, including confidentiality concerns. In this case, there are two common approaches LPs typically employ.

The first is to collect what is known as compromise documentation, which allows investors to collect part of a document or a sample of a document for their files while still allowing the fund to appropriately manage any document distribution concerns. LPs can negotiate compromise documentation through requesting the table of contents of the manual. This table of contents not only serves as a placeholder in an LP's due diligence files with regard to compliance-related documentation, but also provides the LP with an understanding of what items are covered within the compliance manual itself, therefore facilitating further analysis in this area.

The second approach for dealing with a GP who will not release documents outside the fund's office is for the LP to review the documents at the manager's office during the onsite visit stage of the ODD process.

Increasingly, investor responses are in the form of a specific list of questions and answers on a form known as a due diligence questionnaire (DDQ). Many GPs will typically have some sort of DDQ already prepared. These GP-prepared DDQs will typically provide answers to commonly asked questions about the firm, such as historical asset figures.

35.2   FUND GOVERNANCE

Fund governance is the interconnected system of controls and procedures that determine oversight, independence, and transparency throughout the fund.

35.2.1   Fund Governance through Internal Committees

One common governance structure in place at funds is based on internal committees which are responsible for providing oversight and transparency across a number of investment and operational areas. There are **five common operational fund committees**: (1) operations committee; (2) valuation committee; (3) business continuity and disaster recovery committee; (4) best execution committee; and (5) compliance committee.

35.2.2   Fund Governance through Boards of Directors

Another common fund governance mechanism is a fund's board of directors. The **fund's board of directors** is a group of individuals who are responsible for fulfilling regulatory obligations, exercising legal rights, and providing limited independent oversight of funds. These individuals may be standalone professionals or may work for third-party professional directorship companies that specialize in providing directors for hire.

Common duties of fund board members include these six: (1) overseeing the enforcement of any redemption gates; (2) reviewing and approving the audited financial statements of a fund; (3) approving amendments to legal documentation; (4) approving the fund manager's use of certain mechanisms or altering the original terms of the mechanisms; (5) reviewing fund manager valuations and overseeing the enforcement of valuation practices and procedures; and (6) reviewing the ongoing performance of fund service providers and approving new fund service provider appointments. An example of a mechanism in the fourth duty indicated above is an audit holdback. An **audit holdback** is a mechanism by which a fund manager retains a portion of an investor's redeemed capital until the finalization of a fund's audit to provide a capital buffer to the fund manager should the final financial figures be different from expectations.

35.2.3   Limited Partner Control and Communication

The law and the **limited partnership agreement (LPA)** define and restrict the degree of control LPs have over the activities of GPs, relating, for example, to waiving or accepting investment restrictions, extending the investment period or fund duration, handling key-person-related issues, or participating in an LP advisory committee. An **LP advisory committee (LPAC)** has responsibilities that are defined in the LPA and normally relate to dealing with conflicts of interest, reviewing valuation methodologies, and any other consents predefined in the LPA. LPs can make decisions with either a simple majority (e.g., the decision to extend the investment period or the fund's duration) or a qualified majority (e.g., the decision to remove the GP without cause). A **qualified majority** is generally more than 75% of LPs rather than the 50% required for a simple majority.

Occasionally, LPs may be offered positions on the investment committee. However, it is not clear whether LPs should actually take on this role. Generally, professionals recognize that fund managers should make investment and divestment decisions without the direct involvement of investors, so as not to dilute the responsibility of the manager, create potential conflicts of interest with nonparticipating investors, or expose LPs to the risk of losing their limited liability (in limited partnership structures, an overactive LP could become reclassified as a GP, thereby losing his or her limited liability). Also, investors do not normally have the legal rights or the required skills and experience to make such decisions.

Another important element of corporate governance is reporting to LPs. Various associations or industry boards, such as the Institutional Limited Partners Association (ILPA), have released guidelines for reporting. The obligation to disclose in compliance with these guidelines is increasingly being made part of contractual agreements. While some GPs reduce the level of detail provided to the bare minimum and share it with all LPs, others share different levels of detail depending on the specific type of investor.

35.3   STRUCTURAL REVIEW OF THE FUND AND FUND MANAGER

The **structural review** is a key part of the due diligence process and involves analysis of the organization of the fund, the organization of the fund manager, registrations, and outside service providers.

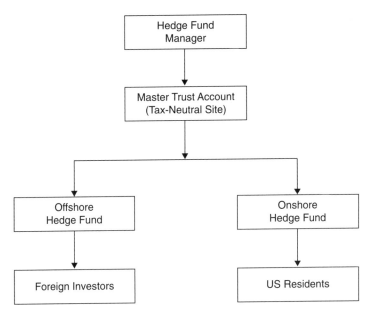

EXHIBIT 35.2 Master Trust Account for US-Based Fund
Source: Anson (2006).

35.3.1 Fund Organization

The **primary equity investor motivations of designing fund legal structures** are: (1) to facilitate the implementation of tax efficiency; and (2) to limit liability among the entities involved. For tax efficiency, the fund manager may invest the fund's assets through an offshore master trust account or fund, discussed later. For limited liability, the funds are organized through partnerships with outside investors as limited partners.

35.3.2 Master–Feeder Trusts

The fund manager may manage the assets of both funds in a master trust account, as illustrated in Exhibit 35.2. The **master trust** is the legal structure used to invest the assets of both onshore investors and offshore investors in a consistent if not identical manner, so that both funds share the benefit of the fund manager's insights and avoid tax inefficiency. Investors access the master trust through feeder funds. A **feeder fund** is a legal structure through which investors have access to the investment performance of the master trust. Onshore and offshore investors use separate feeder funds to access the master trust. Investors in both of these feeder funds benefit from the separation of funds because tax consequences flow appropriately to each investor. Together, the master trust and feeder funds are referred to as a master–feeder structure.

Consider a fund manager who has two investors: one based in the United States with $10 million to invest, and one in another country with $15 million to invest. The manager knows that some US investors may be required or prefer to have their funds remain in the United States, whereas many non-US investors prefer to have their money outside the United States. Where should the fund be located? If the fund is located in the United States, the non-US investor may have to pay income taxes both to the United States and to a home country. The best way to resolve this problem is to set up two funds, one onshore (for US investors) and one in an offshore domicile that avoids double taxation (for non-US investors).

The **purpose of the master trust** is tax neutrality, not evasion. In Bermuda, for example, master trust funds pay only a corporate licensing fee, not corporate income tax. This ensures that there are no tax consequences to the fund investors at the master trust level. Instead, the tax consequences for the investors occur at their country of domicile through the feeder funds. Investors in the onshore, or US-based, feeder fund are subject to the US Internal Revenue Code, whereas investors in the offshore feeder fund are subject to the tax codes of their respective domiciles—including the United States, if a US investor has chosen to invest through the offshore vehicle.

Fund structures are not always as complicated as that presented in Exhibit 35.2. For example, many fund managers in the United States operate only within the United States, have only an onshore fund, and accept only US investors. Nonetheless, the popularity of fund investing has resulted in operating structures that are sometimes nearly as creative as the fund strategies themselves.

35.3.3 Side Pocket Arrangements

In a **side pocket arrangement,** illiquid investments held by a fund (e.g., commonly a hedge fund) are segregated from the rest of the portfolio commonly because they are difficult to value, can interfere with equitable treatment of investors entering and leaving the fund, and prevent future investors from participating in the returns to assets in the side pocket. Valuation of side pocket investments is typically performed on a less frequent and less accurate basis than is computation of the net asset value (NAV) of the liquid portion of the hedge fund.

The use of side pockets can be controversial. Although side pockets are typically used to separate liquid and illiquid assets within the fund, the best practice is for the performance of all side pockets (including those initiated by the investor) to be included in the performance of the fund for all periods. Investors must inquire as to the existence and nature of the fund's side pockets, how and when they are used, and whether the performance of side pockets is included in the fund returns.

35.3.4 Registrations

The investor should document any regulatory registrations and obtain and retain copies of documents required by and for regulatory authorities. If the fund manager is registered with the local regulatory authority, such as the US Securities and Exchange Commission (SEC) or the UK Financial Conduct Authority (FCA), the investor should ascertain the date of the original registration and whether there are any civil, criminal, or administrative actions outstanding against the fund manager. Investors need to determine the regulatory requirements in each manager's local jurisdiction and ensure that the manager is current with the appropriate authorities.

35.3.5 Fund Manager Organization and Ownership

In addition to analyzing the organization of the fund itself (as discussed above), the investor should analyze the organization of the fund's manager. The ownership structure of the fund manager must be documented. It is imperative to know who owns the company that advises the fund, whether it is an external party, active employees, or some combination of the two. The extent to which ownership is shared among the fund manager's employees is important, as sharing the ownership of the fund management company with employees can encourage proper alignment of interests and retention of key personnel.

An organizational chart of personnel is mandatory, with particular attention paid to separation of duties. Of special importance is the chief financial officer (CFO). The **chief financial officer (CFO)** is typically the investor's most important link of investors to the fund manager because the CFO is ultimately responsible for reporting the fund's performance numbers. Consequently, the investor should make sure that the CFO has a strong background in accounting for investments, preferably including a major professional accounting designation.

The investor must determine which senior managers are in charge of the key functions: trading, information systems, marketing, risk management, and research. Managerial talent should be assessed in the context of the fund's investment activities. For example, short selling of equities is very different from long-only investing; thus, before investing money with a long/short fund manager, an investor should determine the extent of the relevant manager's background and expertise in shorting equities.

Finally, it is important to understand the compensation structure and incentives of each key employee. Which employees have the potential to earn equity ownership or stock options in the firm? Are incentives awarded on individual performance, or is there also a team component to compensation? Are the people making investment decisions able to earn bonuses based on the performance of the fund? It is clearly a benefit to have employees properly motivated by performance-based compensation, but conflicts of interest must be identified.

35.4   TERMS FOR LIQUID PRIVATE FUNDS

The issues faced by funds with highly illiquid assets (e.g., most private equity funds) differ from those faced by funds with liquid assets such as most hedge funds and managed futures funds. Funds with liquid assets tend to trade more frequently and offer its LPs rights to redeem their shares. This section discusses issues more commonly related to hedge funds than private equity funds.

35.4.1   Redemptions

Terms regarding **redemptions** and withdrawals are specified in the subscription agreement. Some funds provide monthly liquidity (i.e., transfers are made at or immediately after the end of each month), but the norm is quarterly or semiannual redemption rights. This allows for controlled cash flows to and from the fund, especially for the purpose of matching redemptions and subscriptions to minimize the impact of investor flows on the fund. Also, limited partners must usually give notice to the fund manager that they intend to redeem. The **notice period** is a fund requirement, typically ranging from 30 to 90 days, for LPs to inform the GP in advance of a redemption to give the fund manager the ability to position the fund's portfolio and liquidity to meet the redemption request.

A risk to consider is whether the redemption provisions provided by the fund manager match the liquidity of the underlying securities in which the fund manager invests. For example, the distressed debt market is one of the least liquid securities markets. Liquidity can be virtually nonexistent and is typically available only by private negotiation between two parties. Even in this scenario, it can take several months to find a willing seller and buyer. If a distressed debt fund manager has liberal redemption provisions, a liquidity mismatch could cause a run on the fund's assets when there is no ready market into which the assets of the fund can be liquidated.

35.4.2 Lockups and Their Two Potential Benefits

The Risk Alert noted that redemption terms and liquidity of a fund's portfolio are essential when assessing liquidity issues.[1] Some investors experienced unanticipated and problematic redemption restrictions during the financial crisis of 2008–9. All investors should closely examine potential redemption restrictions to evaluate their appropriateness for an investor's liquidity needs given the liquidity of the investor's other holdings. Although the Risk Alert did not emphasize the issue, lenient redemption restrictions for funds are not always good. In fact, they may be problematic if the fund's net asset value could be adversely affected by redemptions from other investors.

More and more hedge funds are requiring lockup periods for their investors. A **lockup period** is a provision preventing, or providing financial disincentives for, redemption or withdrawal of an investor's funds for a designated period, typically 1 to 3 years for hedge funds, and up to 10 years or more for real estate and private equity funds. During this period, the investor cannot redeem the investment. Lockup periods can refer to the time period immediately following an investor's initial investment, which means that every investor in the fund may be operating under a different timeline or can be triggered subsequently by events. Due diligence requires careful assessment of the provisions regarding redemptions as well as the potential risks and conflicts of interest that they can create.

Lockup periods provide two benefits. First, they give the fund manager time to implement the investment strategy. Imagine how difficult it might be to implement a sophisticated investment strategy, especially in less liquid securities, while worrying about funding redemption requests. Second, withdrawals of capital by one limited partner can disadvantage the remaining partners through transaction costs borne by the fund.

Funds may require either a hard lockup period or a soft lockup period. A **hard lockup period** disallows withdrawals for the entire duration of the lockup period. A **soft lockup period** allows investors to withdraw capital from the fund before the expiration of the lockup period but only after the payment of a redemption fee, which is frequently 1% to 5% of the withdrawal amount, discouraging investors from causing liquidity disruptions by leaving the fund and allowing the fund manager to recoup some of the costs associated with liquidating a portion of the fund portfolio to redeem shares or to make up for the drag on performance from a cash balance that the fund manager maintains to fund investor redemptions.

35.4.3 Gates

Investors also need to evaluate the fund documents to understand whether gates are allowed. A **gate** is a provision describing the terms under which the fund may limit investor withdrawals even when the investor has satisfied the lockup period. Although investors may desire to exit the fund, the hedge fund manager may lock the gates, preventing investor capital from leaving. Gating typically occurs during times of market turbulence and constrained liquidity, as the hedge fund manager may perceive that liquidating enough assets to fund investor withdrawals will have a substantially negative impact on the value of the fund and the fund's other investors.

35.5 TERMS FOR ILLIQUID PRIVATE FUNDS

The LPA (limited partnership agreement) is a key document with details regarding important issues in the GP–LP relationship.

35.5.1 The LPA, Fund Term, and Distributions

In some cases, the length of the fund's life is specified as in the case of a private equity fund with a typical life of roughly 10 years (with possible extensions of up to perhaps 3 more years). Normally, the extension of a fund's life is approved annually by a simple majority of LPs or members of the LPAC, 1 year at a time versus 2 or more at once, during which time management fees are either reduced or eliminated altogether to stimulate quick exits.

Normally, in the case of limited life funds such as private equity funds the proceeds are distributed to investors as soon as is feasible after the fund's assets are sold. However, in some cases, LPs grant fund managers the discretion to reinvest some of the proceeds that are realized during the investment period.

35.5.2 Advisory Committee

Fund advisory committees serve as a source of objective input for fund managers. An advisory committee is composed of representatives from the fund and investors in the fund. The advisory committee may provide advice on the valuation of particular investments, especially illiquid investments. The advisory committee may also advise the fund manager as to whether the fund should be opened up to new investors and how much more capacity the fund manager should take. Although advisory committees serve as useful devices for control by limited partners, they are more common in the private equity world than in hedge funds. Also, the exercise of control by limited partners increases the risk that they will be deemed to be participating in the management of the fund and therefore will no longer be afforded the protection of limited liability.

35.5.3 Termination and Divorce

In the case of illiquid private partnerships such as private equity funds, LPAs may foresee a for-cause removal of the GP and include a **bad-leaver clause,** which, if exercised (normally following a simple majority vote of the LPs), causes investments to be suspended until a new fund manager is elected or, in the extreme, the fund is liquidated. In practical terms, conditions leading to a for-cause removal are difficult to both define and determine. Issues are highly subjective, and taking matters to court carries high legal risk for an investor, as it is very difficult and lengthy to prove wrongdoing.

The good-leaver clause enables investors to cease additional funding of the partnership with a vote requiring a qualified majority, generally more than 75% of LPs. This "without-cause" clause provides a clear framework for shutting down a partnership that is not working, or when confidence is lost. The good-leaver clause sometimes provides for compensation amounting to 6 months to 1 year of management fees; the bad-leaver clause provides no such compensation and foresees no entitlement to carried interest. This contrasts with the good-leaver clause but includes a vesting schedule, so that part of the carry remains available to incentivize the new team being hired.

In deciding whether to exercise one of these clauses, reputation considerations play a key role, as the market consists of a small number of players who repeatedly interact with one another. GPs who are removed with or without cause may subsequently be unable to raise funds or participate in investment syndicates with other partnerships. To avoid such disastrous outcomes, GPs tend to agree on a fund restructuring to prevent a forced removal.

35.6 GENERAL TERMS FOR PRIVATE FUNDS

The legal documentation supporting an investment in a fund (the private placement memorandum, subscription agreement, and side letter agreement) sometimes contains terms negotiated between the fund's attorneys and the attorneys of prospective investors rather than standardized across all investors. Therefore, due diligence includes careful analysis of the legal documents that need to be signed to invest in a fund.

35.6.1 Type of Investment and Liability Limits

The due diligence process should reveal the precise degree of liability shielding. Most private fund investments are structured as limited partnerships, although some managers offer separate accounts for their investors. A limited partnership can provide a liability shield for the investor. A **limited liability shield** or financial firewall is a legal construct that prevents creditors from pursuing restitution from investors or other participants involved in an economic activity beyond the amount of capital that they have contributed. For example, the limited liability structure limits investor losses to the amount contributed, even when a highly leveraged hedge fund experiences losses greater than the value of the assets contributed by investors.

Any excess risk is borne by the fund manager as the general partner. However, if limited partners act in some capacity beyond their role as passive investors, the limited liability shield may be pierced. Due diligence requires analysis of the integrity of the liability shield and the activities that could render the shield ineffective, such as becoming actively involved in the day-to-day management of the organization.

Separate accounts do not typically offer limited liability to the investor; therefore, there can be more risk associated with this type of investment. Investors in separate accounts may be responsible for losses beyond their investment to cover losses from the use of margin or the use of derivatives. There are potential advantages to separate accounts, however, that may offset potential liability exposure. These potential advantages relative to a limited partnership include facilitated risk reporting, reduced risk of fraud, increased transparency, increased liquidity, and elimination of adverse effects from redemptions or subscriptions by fellow limited partners.

35.6.2 Subscription Amount

Virtually all funds have a minimum subscription amount, specifying the smallest initial investment that the fund manager will allow. Generally, this amount is quite high for two reasons. First, the fund may be using a safe harbor provision that limits the number of investors. The manager will not want to expend these limited slots on investors with small subscriptions but with the same level of reporting requirements as the largest investors. Second, higher capital commitments help ensure that only sophisticated investors with a large net worth subscribe in the fund. Hedge funds are designed for sophisticated investors who not only understand the risks, but are also in a financial position to bear those risks.

Some funds also have a maximum subscription amount. This is done so that no single investor becomes too large relative to other investors in the fund. Redemptions from one very large investor can intensify or create acute liquidity problems. Also, the fund manager may have capacity issues that limit the size of the fund or the effective and prompt deployment of a very large initial capital contribution.

35.6.3 Investor Relations

Ideally, the fund manager should designate a primary contact person for investors. This representative handles investor issues regarding performance reporting, subscriptions and redemptions, increased investment, and meetings. These duties should be delegated to the investor relations team, which frees the CEO to keep the fund manager on course rather than having to take client phone calls.

35.7 PRIVATE PLACEMENT MEMORANDUM (PPM)

Across the spectrum of legal documentation, one of the key documents that is collected and reviewed is the offering memorandum. **The offering memorandum (OM) or private placement memorandum (PPM)** is the central controlling legal document for the fund. This section refers to this document as the OM/PPM.

35.7.1 Four Key Functions of the OM/PPM

The OM/PPM is the central legal authoritative source of the private fund under review. An offering memorandum seeks to accomplish four key functions:

1. limited partner education;
2. risk disclosure;
3. risk assignment;
4. assignment of decision-making authority.

LIMITED PARTNER EDUCATION: When analyzing an OM/PPM, an investor may notice that the actual document itself is quite long, often exceeding 100 pages. One of the reasons for the length of these documents is that they provide a great amount of education to limited partners about a variety of issues. The OM/PPM includes factual information about not only the specific investment strategy of fund but also a number of related items, including key fund and GP personnel, and the GP organization. For private equity funds in particular, this factual background information may also cover information about funds from prior vintage years managed using the same investment strategy.

RISK DISCLOSURE: The second primary function of the OM/PPM is to serve as a vehicle for risk disclosure including any illiquidity concerns. The OM/PPM serves not only to highlight these risks but also to provide a number of detailed disclosures related to such risks.

RISK ASSIGNMENT: **Risk assignment** in the context of fund documentation refers to anticipated ways for placing responsibility for different risks with different parties. Two common related legal terms contained in OM/PPMs that assign risk are exculpation and indemnification.

Exculpation is a contractual term that relates to freeing someone from blame. **Indemnification** relates to a duty to make good on a loss. Exculpation and indemnification clauses are used in OM/PPMs to outline a limited set of legal standards at which predefined parties would be liable for certain actions or losses. Common legal standards employed include gross negligence, fraud, willful malfeasance, bad faith, and dishonesty. Following is an example of a typical indemnification clause—this one for the GP—that would be contained in a private equity fund OM:

> *The General Partner is liable to creditors for the debts of the Partnership. However, none of the affiliated parties, nor any person designated to wind up the affairs of the Partnership pursuant to the partnership agreement, will be liable for any loss or cost arising out of, or in connection with, any activity undertaken (or omitted to be undertaken) in connection with the Partnership, including any such loss sustained by reason of any investment or the sale or retention of any security or other asset of the Partnership, except for any liability caused by his, her, or its fraud, gross negligence, or willful misconduct.*

This indemnification clause outlines that the GP and affiliated parties would be liable for the debts of the partnership under a specific set of legal standards (i.e., fraud, gross negligence, or willful misconduct). In other circumstances, such as an honest error, the GP would not be liable to LPs indicating exculpation.

ASSIGNMENT OF DECISION-MAKING AUTHORITY: Decision-making authority is perhaps best understood by way of example. Let's say a private equity fund makes an inadvertent fund accounting error, which causes the fund to be late in paying the legal bill of fund counsel. Let us further assume that as per its arrangement with fund counsel, all legal bills not paid in a timely manner accrue interest at a rate of 1.5% per month. The error in our example went unnoticed for 3 months, and therefore the fund had an obligation to the law firm that was 4.5% greater than it would have been had the error not occurred. Who should be responsible for paying the additional 4.5%?

On the one hand, the argument could be made that GP accounting personnel did not make the error intentionally and that it came up in the legitimate course of business. Such errors, it could be argued, should not be considered the GP's fault and so the fund should be responsible for this additional 4.5%. On the other hand, it could be argued that it was the GP's fault that this error occurred and that as the GP has a responsibility to prevent such errors, the additional expense should be absorbed by the GP at the management company level.

This example is representative of a number of conflicts that may arise in practice. Carefully drafted OM/PPMs can help by providing guidelines and mechanisms for resolving such issues in advance. For example, perhaps the OM/PPM makes clear that such decisions are the exclusive realm of the GP. The OM/PPM outlines these rules prior to an investor committing capital to the fund. If an investor doesn't like the rules, the time to seek to negotiate certain risk assignment terms is generally prior to investing.

35.7.2 Side Letters

Investors can often request to enter into what is known as a **side letter** to negotiate such terms, which is an agreement between an investor and the fund that amends the OM/PPM to afford a specific investor with certain negotiated provisions. Examples of common items negotiated in side letters could be additional fund transparency or beneficial redemption rights. It should be noted that side letters do not apply to all LPs in a pooled fund structure—just those designated in the side letter. Performing due diligence on these types of issues and negotiating any side letter terms prior to investing is critical, because there is often little room for negotiation after the capital has been committed.

35.7.3 Different Purposes of Legal Counsel Reviews and ODD Document Reviews

Analysis of the actual terms of an OM/PPM is a detailed process that requires knowledge of common document terms of private funds in general, as well as understanding the specifics associated with the particular fund under review. It should be noted that in the context of an ODD review, although the OM/PPM deals with matters related to law, a review of the document by an LP may differ from a review by legal counsel. The goals of such reviews may be different.

A review by an LP's law firm, for example, may be focused on detecting terms in the document that may violate certain investor guidelines or laws, such as the Employee Retirement Income Security Act (ERISA). Thus, the focus of legal counsel reviews is on legal issues.

An LP ODD review, however, may focus on risk analysis and term negotiation. An example of a negotiation might involve the omission of a key person provision that provides LPs with options to redeem capital should key individual(s) associated with the fund cease to be associated with the fund and GP. Because it is not illegal in and of itself for a GP's OM/PPM to omit a key person provision, the absence of such a clause might not be cause for concern during review of the document by LP legal counsel. However, in the context of an LP ODD review, the omission of such a clause may raise concerns. Thus, the focus of ODD reviews is on economic and risk implications. Integrating the economic and risk implications of key fund legal terms, such as key person provisions, into the broader operational risk assessment process is where ODD can add value over a pure legal analysis of the legal terms of documents such as OM/PPMs.

35.7.4 Analyzing Other Common Private Placement Memorandum Terms

OM/PPMs are lengthy documents covering a wide variety of fund terms. Other key areas that are commonly focused on by LPs during a review of the OM, and associated considerations, are outlined in Exhibit 35.3.

EXHIBIT 35.3   Key Areas of Offering Memorandum Considered During the Operational Due Diligence Review

Area Reviewed	Comments
Fund and associated entity domicile	Common domiciles are Delaware for US-based funds and the Cayman Islands for non-US (i.e., offshore) funds
Distributions	Distribution terms outline the ways, amounts, and timing of capital that is returned to investors. Commonly, 100% of distributions are paid directly to LPs until certain criteria are met, including recouping their original investment and a predefined rate of return. Distributions then typically proceed under a predefined schedule, with the GP sharing in a portion of the profits
Capital commitments and unfunded commitments	These terms describe the process by which LPs commit capital to a fund, including minimum commitment amounts. OMs also typically contain terms that if capital is called from other LPs and they cannot meet the commitments, other LPs may be responsible for meeting these unfunded commitments.
Tax considerations	While tax considerations vary across jurisdictions, OMs will typically detail key tax considerations for the fund and LPs. Although the goal of this LP analysis is not to produce a formal tax opinion, gaining an understanding of the tax structure and anticipated consequences of a fund's investments should be considered during an ODD review
Conflicts of interest	**Conflicts of interest** refer to the ability of the GP, funds, or key personnel to participate in other activities that may present a potential conflict with the fund under review. Three examples of common conflicts of interest that may be in place: 1. Allocation of investment opportunities among multiple funds 2. Conflicts relating to asset dispositions 3. Participation in outside business activities

35.8 FUND FEES AND EXPENSES

Fund fees are also commonly analyzed as part of the OM/PPM review process. Management fees provide a base compensation so that the fund manager can support the ongoing activities of funds. In addition to a standard management fee, compensation to fund managers is typically highly performance driven through incentive fees (performance fees). Also, funds such as private equity funds may charge a number of other fees, including sales and distribution charges, fund start-up expenses, deal fees, advisory fees, and monitoring fees paid by portfolio companies.

35.8.1 Timing of Fee Collection

With regard to fees in general, from an ODD perspective, LPs should be conscious of the timing of the collection of fees. Fees may be collected in one of two ways:

1. Fee collection in advance: This refers to fees being collected at the beginning of the period in which they are due (e.g., the beginning of the month).
2. Fee collection in arrears: This refers to fees being collected at the end of the period in which they are due (e.g., the end of the month).

Due in part to considerations related to the time value of money, it is generally considered advantageous to the LP for a fund to collect fees in arrears as opposed to in advance.

In the case of private equity, fees are on a commitment basis, rather than being levied only against capital that has been invested. If fees were based only on invested capital, management might have an incentive during the investment period to pursue volume instead of quality. Also, the fees on committed but uninvested funds can be viewed as paying for the staffing required for due diligence during the investment period. At the end of the investment period or with the raising of subsequent funds, fees ramp down and are levied only against capital still under management. Fees are adjusted according to the proportion of the portfolio that has been divested.

35.8.2 Fee Offsets

Investors need to determine if fees that are earned by the GP offset the stated management fees. When management fees are low, the fund manager may be looking for other compensation, such as that earned by sitting on the boards of directors of portfolio companies, providing advisory or management services, or advising on or structuring transactions. To counter these incentives for distraction from investment management or the double payment of fund management services, a fee-offset arrangement may be implemented, in which fees are fully or partially netted against management fees. Fee-offset clauses have become standard in LPAs.

35.8.3 Details Regarding Incentive Fees

Managers of private funds typically earn performance-based fees known as carried interest, performance fees, or incentive fees. The amount and timing of these payments can provide valuable insights into other operational risk areas, such as employee compensation and retention approaches. When evaluating the language in the OM/PPM with regard to performance-based fees in the context of an ODD, review questions to consider include these four:

1. Is there a hurdle rate or preferred rate?
2. Is a deal-by-deal or fund-as-a-whole approach applied?
3. Who determines which individuals or groups participate in performance-based fee distributions?
4. What are the vesting periods for the payout of performance-based fees to team members?

Level I of the CAIA curriculum introduced the issues of hurdle rates (i.e., preferred rates) and accounting on a deal-by-deal versus fund-as-a-whole approach, as well as the distinction between soft-hurdle rates versus hard-hurdle rates, catch-up periods, and clawbacks.

Careful study of these terms in the OM/PPM review process should include analysis of the incentives, unintended consequences, and conflicts of interest inherent in virtually any compensation scheme.

For example, a preferred return or hurdle rate tends to incentivize the managers (as, effectively, holders of out-of-the-money calls) to make riskier investments to generate higher potential returns that exceed the hurdle rates and increase the expected payouts. Though high hurdle rates aim to provide an incentive for fund managers to outperform, they can also have the opposite effect. Managers of funds with overly high hurdle rates (or of struggling funds) can be demotivated if it becomes unlikely that they will receive carried interest.

There are also some perverse incentives regarding harvesting of profits with preferred returns. GPs are faced with the dilemma of whether to realize an investment over a short period of time to optimize the IRR or to hold on to it and try to optimize the multiple. For example, is it better to generate a 50% IRR for a period of 3 months, which yields only a 1.11× multiple on capital invested, or only a 10% IRR for a period of 3 years, leading to a 1.33× multiple? The standard preferred return, being based on the IRR, gives incentive to the former. The kind of fee structure and its details can be an important determinant of managerial decisions.

35.8.4 GP's Contribution

Excessive risk-taking can be reduced or eliminated if managers have a significant portion of their personal wealth in the fund. In this case the manager, being directly exposed to fund losses, has reduced incentive to take excessive risks, to work on nonfund-related activities, or to abandon ship once the prospects for generating carry and launching a follow-on fund become highly unlikely.

Typically, LPs in private funds contribute perhaps up to 99% of the fund's capital. The GP often contributes perhaps 1% of the fund's capital as a standard and acceptable contribution. This capital contribution by GPs, also known as **hurt money,** should be contributed in cash rather than through waiving of management fees (or through surplus from the management company's budget). Typically, the GP's contribution to the fund is a significant share of his or her personal wealth, whereas the LPs' investment, although in absolute terms far higher, represents an immaterial share of the institution's overall assets.

An objective of requiring the GP to contribute capital is to better align the interests of the LPs and GPs by placing them in the same position in the fund's capital structure. Too large a contribution by the GP relative to the GP's wealth can cause excessive risk aversion in decision-making relative to the preferences of the LPs, while too little a contribution may not provide alignment of preferences. In the case of wealthy managers and depending on the size of the fund, even 1% may at times be too low.

It is a challenge to determine the appropriate contribution level for a GP: one that provides a reasonable incentive, but is not excessively onerous. An analysis of profits earned from past investments, salaries, budget surpluses, and so forth may provide useful information for determining a contribution level that is appropriate for a particular GP.

35.9 PRIVATE FUND AUDITED FINANCIAL STATEMENT REVIEW

The primary *financial* documentations reviewed by LPs during the due diligence process are the audited financial statements of a fund, sometimes referred to simply as audits. These audits are prepared by a third party known as an auditor. In some cases, an existing fund is being analyzed for which audited financial statements are available.

Depending on the jurisdiction in which the fund is based, the accounting standards used by the auditors may differ. Common accounting standards include Generally Accepted Accounting Principles (GAAP) and International Financial Reporting Standards (IFRS). Different countries that use GAAP may have their own specific versions, such US GAAP or UK GAAP. The choice of accounting and audit standards not only influences the presentation of the audited financial statements, but also governs the underlying assumptions used in preparing these statements.

Depending on the format used, the rules for the presentation of items—such as fund expenses—may differ. Additionally, the sections included in the financial statements may vary based on format. The common sections of audited financial statements that should be reviewed by LPs during the ODD process are outlined in Exhibit 35.4.

Note that the financial statements typically contain a notes section at the end that provides a number of important disclosures and additional information related to fund operations. The seven main areas typically covered by financial statement notes are:

1. organization and business;
2. summary of significant accounting policies;
3. investments;
4. commitments and contingencies;
5. related-party transactions;
6. financial highlights;
7. subsequent events.

EXHIBIT 35.4 Common Sections of Audited Financial Statements

Audited Financial Statement Section	Comments
Opinion Letter	This section provides a summary of the auditor opinion of the financial statements. An auditor opinion that is qualified means that the auditor is certifying the statements subject to a qualification. In limited circumstances, qualified audit opinions may be used to designate acceptable deviations from accounting standards. In other cases, qualified opinions may be used to raise red flags to investors, which should be thoroughly vetted during the operational due diligence process
Statement of Assets and Liabilities	Commonly known as the **balance sheet**, this section provides a summary of assets, liabilities, and partners' capital
Statement of Operations	Commonly known as the **income statement**, this section provides a summary of income and expenses
Statement of Cash Flows	This section outlines the movements of cash throughout the fund as well as financing-related cash flow activities
Statement of Changes	This section, sometimes known as the statement of changes in partners' capital, outlines items related to partner capital allocations, contributions, and withdrawals
Schedule of Investments	This section typically details portfolio holdings and may classify them in summary form according to predefined categories, such as by sector or region

A common consideration for LPs when investing in private equity is that an investor may be committing capital to a brand-new fund with no history or one that is the next series in a vintage-fund framework. This new fund typically has no operating history and therefore no audited financial statements. LPs can often overcome these concerns by reviewing the audits for funds of the previous vintage. Although not an exact indication of the financial state of the fund under review to which the LP is considering allocating capital, this review of similar funds can often provide useful insights into the overall management of finances of previous funds. Additionally, investors can gain familiarity with the format and style of the statements, which will typically use the same auditor across vintages unless a firm-wide or strategy-wide switch of the auditor takes place.

35.9.1 Valuation Policies

Investment managers need to have a documented valuation policy for their portfolio holdings. Internal control processes need to be in place that ensure a consistent process that is free of conflicts. When hedge funds charge incentive fees based on unrealized profits, it is imperative that the valuation of positions is as accurate and as conflict-free as possible.[2] Funds of funds managers that invest in external investment firms or resellers of investment products need to verify investment performance of those external investments.[3] Even if the fraud or misrepresented performance was external to your firm, the disclosure or reliance on false information can make your firm liable if steps were not taken to verify this information.

35.10 BUSINESS ACTIVITIES, CONTINUITY PLANNING, DISASTER RECOVERY, AND INSURANCE

Like any other organization, an investment fund requires personnel that support information technology, infrastructure, human resource management functions, and other activities that reinforce operations. Although business activities are not typically described as operational activities, due diligence and ongoing monitoring of the fund's business activities should be addressed as part of operational due diligence.

Business continuity and disaster recovery plans should be carefully reviewed. How would the fund respond to an emergency in which the facilities normally used for their investment processes and other operations become unavailable? How is the organization equipped to deal with losses of key personnel? Along a related line, what insurance coverage does the fund have, such as errors and omissions insurance? The information needs to be collected, verified, and analyzed.

35.10.1 Business Continuity Planning and Disaster Recovery

Business continuity planning and disaster recovery (BCP/DR) encompasses the umbrella term business continuity planning and the key subset of disaster recovery plans. BCP/DR addresses concerns that the fund manager's operations are vulnerable to a disruptive event (e.g., a natural disaster or terrorism) or a more localized business disruption (e.g., the firm's office becomes temporarily inaccessible or inoperable due to a fire or infrastructure failure).

Business continuity planning includes the development and management of an organization's overall strategies, practices, and procedures for maintaining the critical functions of the organization in the event of an unexpected business interruption. The letter "P" may refer to the words "plans" or "planning." The acronym BCP is sometimes shortened to BC.

Disaster recovery (DR) represents the specific plans and processes to re-establish critical business functions in a crisis. Disaster recovery is sometimes referred to as DRP, indicating a focus on the actual disaster recovery *plans*.

BCP/DR has become commonplace and its analysis is a key part of due diligence. Many fund managers employ sophisticated trading models that require considerable computing power. The loss of trading and computing functionality can severely hurt a fund manager's performance if investment insights cannot be implemented. Further, inability to manage existing positions exposes a fund to increased risk, especially substantial during the market turbulence that may coincide with a disaster.

The fund manager should have a disaster recovery plan if a natural or other disaster shuts down trading and investment operations. The plan could involve leased space at a disaster recovery site owned by a computer service provider, a backup trading desk in a remote location, or shared facilities with other trading desks. It is important to be able to access trading and client records from laptops or remote servers if the regular office space becomes unavailable. A firm needs to be able to have continuous communication with its staff and clients. Fund managers need to be able to strike the NAV of each fund on a regular schedule. Plans to overcome interruption of critical tasks performed by third-party service providers also need to be covered.[4]

Questions that must be answered regarding a disaster plan are these: in the event of a disaster, how would the fund manager monitor and manage its investment positions and its risk exposures? How would the fund trade without its current data sources, hardware, and software? How would the fund manager maintain connectivity with its employees if they cannot get to the recovery site? Due diligence can ascertain whether an adequate disaster plan is in place at the fund management company, as well as with the external service providers.

35.10.1.1 Focus on Information Technology

A large part of BCP/DR is related to the management of information technology and cybersecurity issues. Although BCP/DR is not exclusively the purview of information technology, reviewing BCP/DR documentation with an IT focus in mind can certainly add value during the ODD process.

When reviewing BCP/DR documentation, a key consideration relates to gauging an understanding of the implementation and testing of technology policies and procedures. Testing refers to a firm conducting dry runs of simulated business disruptions or disaster events. PE firms' BCP/DR will typically describe policies for testing of the plans. The following are five examples of key considerations during a review of BCP/DR documentation:

1. Is testing described from a personnel perspective, technology perspective, or both?
2. How is employee contact information shared and updated throughout the firm so that employees may remain in touch in the event of a disaster?
3. How frequently is it anticipated that testing will be performed?
4. If any issues arise during the testing process, which GP groups will review the testing results?
5. How frequently will the firm revise its BCP/DR?

For private funds such as private equity funds, some investors question the benefit of analyzing BCP/DR documentation. This questioning is based on the fact that private equity funds do not typically trade as frequently as do most hedge funds. The thinking goes that any business disruptions would not be as detrimental to PE funds due to this more limited trading activity.

However, even funds with illiquid assets, such as private equity funds, do engage in a number of time-sensitive projects, which a business disruption could materially affect. For example, from an operational perspective, if a business disruption occurred during the quarter-end close of the accounting books of the fund, a delay could significantly influence the fund's ability to distribute investor statements. For these reasons, it is therefore considered best practice to incorporate a review of BCP/DR documentation into an ODD assessment even for a private equity fund.

Cybersecurity is becoming an increasingly important part of the ODD process as investors seek to ensure that their fund managers remain compliant with regulatory requirements.[5] Investors should confirm that fund managers have processes in place to install firewalls, backup and encrypt data, and to prevent cyberattacks and other frauds such as malware, ransomware, data security, and identify theft using client information. Investors should also investigate that managers regularly follow and update those processes and include processes that address similar risks at critical external vendors.

35.10.1.2 Fund Insurance

A key area that is sometimes overlooked as part of the ODD process is the level of insurance coverage in place at the fund. Some types of insurance held by funds are general in nature and not necessarily specific to the fund or financial industry. Other types are more appropriately customized to the work of the fund. The **common types of fund insurance coverage** include errors and omissions (E&O), directors' and officers' liability coverage (D&O), general partner liability coverage, and employment practices liability coverage.

E&O insurance (i.e., errors and omissions or professional liability insurance) covers the insured against financial damages from mistakes, negligence, inaccuracies, and other professional failures (subject to exclusions and limits). E&O insurance, unlike the other insurances listed in the previous paragraph, is important to the prospective LP because E&O insurance often covers the risk that investment process and operational errors by the fund managers will directly imperil the value of the LP's investment. Note that most types of professional liability insurance specifically exclude the very coverage and risks most related to investment process and operational risks (e.g., negligence, errors, and omissions).

NOTES

1. "Investment Adviser Due Diligence Processes for Selecting Alternative Investments and Their Respective Managers." *National Exam Program, Risk Alert* 4, no. 1 (28 January 2014): www. sec.gov/ocie/announcement/risk-alert—selecting-alternative-investments-and -managers.html.
2. "SEC Charges London-Based Hedge Fund Adviser and U.S.-Based Holding Company for Internal Control Failures." (December 12, 2013) https://www.sec.gov/news/press-release/ 2013-259.
3. "Investment Advisers Paying Penalties for Advertising False Performance Claims." SEC Press Release (August 25, 2016) https://www.sec.gov/news/pressrelease/2016-167.html.
4. Compliance Alert (June 2007) "Advisers' Disaster Recovery Plans: Provisions to Include in a Firm's DRP." https://www.sec.gov/about/offices/ocie/complialert.htm#P62_10474. SEC IM Guidance Update (June 2016): https://www.sec.gov/investment/im-guidance-2016-04 .pdf.
5. http://www.marcumllp.com/insights-news/cybersecurity-101-for-fund-managers.

REFERENCE

Anson, Mark. 2006. *Handbook of Alternative Assets* 2nd ed. Hoboken, NJ: John Wiley & Sons.

Volatility and Complex Strategies

Complex securities (e.g., structured products) and complex strategies (e.g., hedge funds and managed futures) are important aspects of alternative investing. Part 8 begins with two chapters (Chapters 36 and 37) that discuss volatility and volatility-related strategies with an emphasis on equity markets. Chapter 38 begins with a discussion of complexity risk premiums and related issues and concludes with a discussion of asset based investing with and without structuring. Chapter 39 discusses innovative structured products. Finally, Chapter 40 concludes the book with a study of some complex issues using international real estate investing, and especially currency differences, as a case in point.

CHAPTER 36

Volatility as a Factor Exposure

Investors are familiar with common positions with returns that are tied to the directional returns of underlying real or financial assets. This chapter discusses products and strategies with returns that are tied to changes in levels of asset volatilities, correlations, or dispersions. These increasingly popular products and strategies can enable investors to better manage the risks of their portfolios and to better position their portfolios to benefit from superior market predictions. Further, volatility itself is increasingly being considered as an important factor in investment and risk management.

36.1 MEASURES OF VOLATILITY

Obviously, understanding volatility products and strategies relies on understanding the properties and behavior of volatility. However, the nuances of volatility and volatility-related strategies can be challenging to understand deeply. This section details the concepts of implied volatility and realized volatility.

36.1.1 Implied Volatility and Realized Volatility

Implied return volatility is the volatility over the remaining life of an option that is inferred from an option price under assumptions including risk-neutrality, the validity of the specified option pricing model, and the accuracy of the model's inputs other than volatility. Although the implied volatility is usually estimated using market prices, it is estimated with a specific option pricing model that contains assumptions about the underlying asset's return process. For example, in the derivation of the Black–Scholes option pricing model, the option's underlying asset is assumed to follow a Geometric Brownian Motion (GBM) in which the instantaneous returns of the asset: (1) have a constant variance through time; (2) are normally distributed; and (3) are uncorrelated through time.

Further, the implied volatility does not generally represent an accurate and unbiased consensus of the realized volatility expected by market participants due to risk premiums. An option position has exposure to changes in volatility; therefore, implied volatilities should be expected to differ from expected realized volatilities in order to reflect risk premiums related to volatility.

As detailed in CAIA Level I, the **realized return volatility** of an asset is the actual variation (typically measured as the standard deviation of returns) that occurs over a specified time period using a specified return measurement interval (e.g., daily or weekly return granularity). In practice, observed returns are discrete, not continuous, and all three of the properties of a GBM process (homoscedastic, normally distributed, and uncorrelated returns) are violated in practice. The next section discusses limitations of realized volatility as a measure of dispersion that emerge when the previous assumptions do not hold.

36.1.2 Three Limitations of Realized Volatility as a Measure of Dispersion

As standard deviations, realized return volatilities are simply single estimated measures describing the dispersion of a frequency distribution of a sample of outcomes. Assets with similar realized return volatilities may have experienced tremendously different returns. Note these three limitations on realized volatility: (1) realized volatility does not describe the shape of the return distributions; (2) assets with identical realized volatilities may differ with respect to whether their underlying returns exhibited trending, mean-reversion, or minimal autocorrelation; and (3) realized volatility does not describe whether the dispersion primarily occurred near a particular price of the underlying asset or during a particular time period within the sample.

To illustrate these three shortcomings of realized volatility as a complete description of dispersion, consider six assets on which various fund managers execute volatility strategies: Assets A, B, C...F. Assume that all six assets experience the same realized volatility of returns, but with the following unexpected differences:

1. Asset A experienced a single extremely large return and many very small returns, while Asset B experienced mostly moderately sized returns.
2. Asset C experienced returns that tended to trend in a single direction, while asset D experienced returns that alternated signs and therefore tended to mean-revert.
3. Asset E experienced low volatility for most of the time period followed by enormous shocks near the end of the time period (when the underlying asset's price was relatively high), while Asset F experienced the opposite pattern.

Most volatility strategies will perform very differently across these six assets even though all of the assets experienced the same realized volatility. To complicate matters further, note that the granularity with which the returns are measured (e.g., daily returns or weekly returns) can substantially alter the characteristics of its returns.

36.1.3 Six Properties of Realized Volatility

Sinclair (2013) presents six stylized observations regarding realized volatility, many of which are key assumptions behind some volatility arbitrage portfolio strategies and risk management techniques. The following summarizes the key observations.

1. Realized volatility is not constant. Realized volatility slowly mean-reverts and clusters. As such, many traders model volatility using a variety of generalized

autoregressive conditional heteroscedasticity (GARCH) and regime switching approaches.

2. Realized volatility tends to stay low for some extended period of time until a market shock occurs and volatility transitions to a higher level for some period of time.

3. The volatility of short-term changes in realized volatility can be high, but in the long run, volatility tends to revert toward some long-term average level.

4. Empirical and laboratory evidence suggests that higher volatility increases investors' risk aversion. This indicates that higher realized volatility tends to be negatively correlated with returns on most risky assets.

5. Equity market realized volatility tends to increase in bear markets and decrease in bull markets. In addition, a decline in the stock price of a firm increases its leverage and riskiness, resulting in higher volatility.

6. The rate at which realized equity volatility rises in bear markets exceeds the rate at which realized volatility falls in bull markets.

36.2 VOLATILITY AND THE VEGAS, GAMMAS, AND THETAS OF OPTIONS

The sensitivity of an asset to changes in its underlying factors such as volatility are key to risk management. The risk exposures of various option strategies and option portfolios are often expressed using the Greeks—risk measures introduced in CAIA Level I.

36.2.1 Option Vegas

Vega indicates the sensitivity of an option value to a change in the volatility of the option's underlying asset. Strictly speaking, the vega of a portfolio describes the response of the portfolio's *model value* to a change in the volatility of the underlying asset assumed within the model while holding all other variables constant. In practice, vega may be somewhat loosely viewed as measuring the response of the current *price* of a portfolio to a change in the market's *anticipated* volatility of the returns of the portfolio's underlying asset.

Many investors in volatility strategies seek to create positions with predetermined levels of sensitivity to changes in implied volatility (i.e., reach target exposures to vega) while minimizing exposure to small and large changes in the value of the underlying asset (i.e., minimizing delta). Some traders may seek to earn a volatility risk premium by implementing positions that short vega.

The formulas (using the Black–Scholes option pricing model) for the vega (v) of both call options and put options on an asset, S, are identical and are depicted in Equation 36.1:

$$v = \frac{\partial p}{\partial \sigma} = SN'(d)\sqrt{T} \tag{36.1}$$

where p is the option value (call or put), σ is the volatility of the underlying asset, $N'(d)$ is the (noncumulative) probability density function of the normal distribution at d, which means that $N'(d)$ is the density function (where d is the same as d as discussed in Level 1) and T is the option's time to expiration or tenor.

36.2.2   Scaling of the Vega of an Option

As a derivative of an option value with respect to its implied volatility, the vega of an option is easy to interpret. However, there is an important scaling issue involved in actual vega usage. While Equation 36.1 expresses the "textbook" vega (i.e., the actual partial derivative of an option value with respect to its volatility), practitioners adjust the formula in Equation 36.1 to scale vega to indicate the risk of a one basis point change in volatility. In other words, practitioners and financial data providers implicitly report vega as $SN'(d)\sqrt{T}/100$; a measure that might better be described as *vega per basis point*.

Vega, as shown in Equation 36.1, measures the instantaneous rate of response of an option value to a change of one full unit in volatility, such as a change from 0.20 (i.e., 20%) to 1.20 (i.e., 120%). Vega per basis point divides the vega in Equation 36.1 by 100 so that it measures the instantaneous rate of response of an option value to a change of one basis point in volatility, such as a change from 0.20 (i.e., 20%) to 0.21 (i.e., 21%).

Note in any case that as a first-order derivative, vega indicates the rate of change in an option value with respect to an infinitesimal shift in volatility as shown in Equation 36.1. If the vega per basis point of an option is $0.20 it means that for an infinitesimal increase in its implied volatility, the option's value will rise at the rate of $0.20 for every basis point of implied volatility.

For example, consider a nondividend-paying stock with a value of $50 that has a call option and a put option trading with 0.25 years to expiration with the same strike price and tenor. Assuming that N'(d) is 0.20 for both options, the "textbook" vega of both options (based on Equation 36.1) would be $50 * 0.20 * $\sqrt{25}$ or $5.00. The much more common measure of vega would be $0.05, which is the vega per basis point found by dividing the "textbook" vega by 100. Each option would rise towards a value increase of $0.05 (i.e., $5.00 × 0.01) as the option's implied volatility rose towards an increase of 0.01 from, say, 0.25 to 0.26 (i.e., by 1% from 25% towards 26%).

36.2.3   Vega as an Approximation for Finite Shifts

The previous paragraph described that a value movement "would rise towards a value increase of $0.05" rather than simply saying that the value would move by $0.05. The reason is that the relation between value and volatility is nonlinear, so vega (as a partial derivative) is only a precise measure when dealing with infinitesimal shifts. For a large (discrete) shift, higher-order derivatives would be necessary in order to generate an accurate approximation. For the purposes of this section, higher-order effects are ignored. Equation 36.2 depicts a linear (first-order) approximation that illustrates the use of vega to estimate option value changes.

$$\Delta p \approx v \Delta \sigma \qquad\qquad (36.2)$$

Viewing v in Equation 36.2 as "vega per basis point", for a vega of $0.30, a change in volatility of 0.02 (e.g., two basis points from 0.20 to 0.22) would cause a call or put to rise in value by approximately $0.60 ($0.30 × 2).

APPLICATION 36.2.3

Consider a nondividend-paying stock that has a call option and a put option trading with 0.25 years to expiration and with the same strike price and tenor. The vega per basis point of the call option is $0.40. Use a first-order approximation to estimate the change in a call option value and a put option value for a decline in volatility from 0.30 to 0.28.

First, note that the vega of the put must equal the vega of the call ($0.40). Inserting $0.40 into Equation 36.2 for v and -2 for $\Delta\sigma$ generates Δp as approximately $-\$0.80$ for both the put and the call (correctly reflecting that a decline in volatility lowers both the call and put values).

36.2.4 Four Observations on Option Vegas

Note the following four observations based on Equation 36.1:

1. Vega is always positive for a long position in a call or put option because all three terms on the right side of Equation 36.1 are positive.
2. The vega of a call and a put with the same underlying asset, strike price, time to expiration, and implied volatility must be equal because they share the same formula for vega. Note from put–call parity arranged as follows, Call – Put = Stock – Bond, that implied volatility does not appear on the right side so its effects must cancel out of left side. In other words, "Stock-Bond" (the right side of the equation) may be viewed as a financed long position in a stock which has a vega of zero. Therefore, "Call – Put" with the same underlying asset, strike price, and tenor (the left side of the equation) has a net vega of zero (meaning that the vega of the call and put must equal each other).
3. The vega of an option approaches zero as the time to expiration approaches zero, as seen in Equation 36.1 with T approaching zero.
4. The vega of an option approaches zero as the value of the underlying asset approaches zero or infinity. Therefore, vega approaches zero for deep in-the-money and out-of-the-money options because the normal probability density function, $N'(d)$ in Equation 36.1, approaches zero going out either tail of the normal distribution.

The last two observations are consistent with the relation between the time value of call options and their moneyness depicted in Exhibit 36.1. The differences in the time value of the three call options (i.e., the excess of the call option values above the lower bound) are primarily driven by volatility and time to expiration through the quantity $\sigma\sqrt{T}$. In other words, the three curves may be viewed as indicating differing tenor, differing implied volatility, or a combination.

Exhibit 36.1 helps illustrates changes in option values with respect to vega. A shift upward or downward in volatility can be viewed as moving the option value to a higher or lower curve in Exhibit 36.1. As time passes, everything else equal, option values will move downward to lower curves.

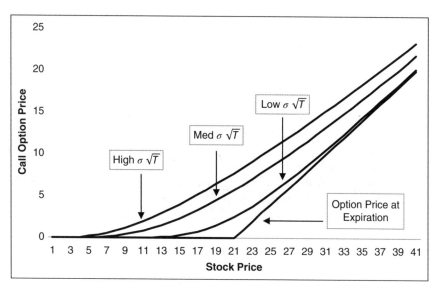

EXHIBIT 36.1   Call Option Values at Three Levels of Implied Volatility and/or Tenor

36.2.5   Option Gammas

An option's gamma is the second-order partial derivative of its value with respect to the value of the underlying asset (i.e., it is also the first-order partial derivative of an option's delta with respect to the value of the underlying asset since delta is the first-order partial derivative of the option's value with respect to the value of its underlying asset).

Equation 36.3 provides two formulas to describe the gamma of an option. The gamma, γ, is expressed as a function of its vega on the right side of Equation 36.3. Note that gamma is the same for a call or put option with the same strike price, tenor, and underlier.

$$\gamma = \frac{N'(d)}{S\sigma\sqrt{T}} = \frac{v}{(\sigma S^2 T)} \tag{36.3}$$

Note that in Equation 36.3 the terms are all nonnegative. Therefore, gamma and vega must share the same positive sign for simple calls or puts. The long volatility exposure of a long option position is represented by its positive gamma; short option positions are short volatility and have negative gamma.

Graphically, the gamma of an option indicates the degree of *curvature* in the relation between option price and the price of the underlying asset. Note in Exhibit 36.1 that the lowest curve has sharp curvature near the money—indicating a high value of gamma. The highest curve is less sharp and indicates low (but positive) gamma. All three curves have greater gamma near the money and little or no gamma far into or out of the money.

36.2.6   Putting Option Vegas, Gammas, and Thetas Together

Gamma is the degree of nonlinearity of long positions in options with respect to the price of their underlying asset (i.e., is a measure of the degree of curvature) that provides call option owners (who are long gamma) with the highly desirable combination of experiencing increasing rates of gain as the underlying asset moves up and decreasing rates of loss as the underlying asset moves down. Put option owners experience the highly desirable combination of experiencing increasing rates of gain as the underlying asset moves down and decreasing rates of loss as the underlying asset moves up.

Vega captures the sensitivity of options to volatility that is driven by gamma. If an option has near-zero gamma (e.g., is deeply into the money), its vega will be small. It is an option's positive gamma that makes anticipation of higher volatility cause higher option values.

A portfolio with large positive gamma will benefit greatly from large directional movements in the underlying asset in one direction but will suffer relatively smaller losses from directional movements in the other direction. Of course, there is no "free lunch" if options are competitively priced. Positive gamma portfolios tend to be long options and therefore have a negative theta. A negative theta means that as an underlying asset experiences minimal price movement (and minimal volatility is expected to continue) the options on that asset will decline in value as time passes.

In summary, gamma (which comes from asymmetric payoffs) is the primary reason that options sell for a premium above their intrinsic value (i.e., their value at expiration). This positive time value to a call option emanates from the virtually unlimited gains to a call option with relatively limited loss. That time value will decay through time, as measured by the option's theta, if the anticipated volatility fails to occur.

36.3   EXPOSURES TO VOLATILITY AS A FACTOR

A key issue exists in the distinction between the sign of an option's vega and whether or not the option is long volatility or short volatility. This section explores this important and problematic issue.

36.3.1   Long and Short Volatility

Consider a very broad equity-market index and options on that index. When an option or any other investment has returns that are negatively correlated with the volatility level of the market index, the position is said to be **short volatility** or "short vol" (i.e., short the volatility of the market or other specified asset). When an investment's value tends to rise with increases in the volatility level of market returns, the position is said to be **long volatility** (i.e., long vol). A key aspect of long and short volatility is that it is a description of an *empirically observed correlation* or tendency.

Long positions in at-the-money equity options are generally viewed as being long volatility with respect to the volatility of their underlying assets (and short positions in at-the-money options are viewed as being short volatility with respect to the volatility of their underlying assets).

However, note that a short-dated call option (on an equity index) that is deeply into-the-money behaves very much like its underlying index. Note from the fifth observation on realized volatility discussed in a previous section, that an equity index has negative correlation with equity market volatility. Therefore, according to this definition of being long or short volatility, a long position in the index itself is therefore short volatility. It follows that a deep in-the-money call option on an equity index, like the index itself, is short volatility. In other words, a long position in a deep in-the-money call option is short volatility. This is because the effect of declining equity market prices on the value of a deep-in-the-money call option on equities through its positive delta will tend to dominate the value-increasing effect of the increased volatility on the value of the deep in-the-money option through its positive vega.

Thus, long positions in options are not always long volatility. The assertion that all long option positions on equities are long equity-market volatility (and all short option positions are short volatility) is usually made in the context of delta-neutral portfolios in which the effects of directional movements in the underlying equity market have been hedged away.

There are numerous securities or financial derivatives that have been developed in recent years (detailed in later sections) that have been engineered to be either long or short volatility. Interest in these products as well as investment funds and other pools that focus on volatility has soared in recent years. Portfolios can be long or short volatility based not only on their direct option exposures, but also through exposures to myriad other products engineered to have strong exposures to volatility.

36.3.2 Distinctions between Positive Vega and Long Volatility Exposures

The concepts of positive vega and long volatility are related. There is no clear consensus on the exact distinctions between the concepts. This section compares and contrasts vega and vol.

Recall that vega is the partial derivative of an asset (e.g., an option) with respect to the implied volatility of a specified asset (e.g., the implied volatility of the option's underling asset). As a partial derivative, vega is the response of the value of an asset (usually an option) to changes in volatility (in the underlying asset) *holding all other variables constant* (especially holding constant the value of the option's underlying asset).

A long position in any simple option has a positive vega. Simple long or short positions in a traditional asset, such as an equity index, have a vega of zero.

Discussions of long and short volatility exposures tend to focus on *empirically observed correlations* between an asset's returns and volatility levels. An asset (such as a long position in a put or an at-the-money call) that's price *tends* to rise when realized equity-market volatility increases is generally viewed as being long volatility. Assets that tend to decline in volatile equity markets (including most short positions in options) are generally viewed as being short volatility.

Observed correlations differ from partial derivatives because in the case of observed correlations the other variables (e.g., the price level of a related asset) are not held constant.

Practical distinctions between long vega and long volatility are complex. For example, long positions in equities have a vega of zero but are often described as being short equity-market volatility (i.e., short vol) because their returns are negatively correlated with equity market volatility. The idea that equities are short volatility when they have no vega may initially seem counterintuitive. Note that all of the returns of an equity index are generated by its delta of one because its vega is zero. However, the claim that being long equities is being short volatility makes sense when "being short volatility" is defined as an empirical observation that equity indexes tend to fall during periods of high equity market volatility.

Deep in-the-money equity call options have a positive vega but tend to be negatively correlated with equity market volatility and so are short vol.

In summary:

- Vega: Positive vega exists for an asset when the partial derivative of its price with respect to implied volatility is positive (holding underlying asset price levels constant). All long option positions have positive vegas (assuming the options are simple options) and all short option positions have negative vegas.
- Vol: An asset is long volatility when its price is empirically observed as being positively correlated with volatility levels and is short volatility when its price is observed as being negatively correlated with volatility levels. Options may be long or short volatility depending on whether they are puts or calls and their moneyness.

The above discussion focuses on static positions in assets. The effects of dynamic portfolio weighting strategies on the volatility of a portfolio adds another layer of complexity.

36.3.3 Using Volatility Derivatives to Hedge Market Risk

A key proposition regarding volatility derivatives is that they can be used to hedge long positions in traditional assets such as an equity portfolio. The justification for this proposition is the empirical observation that long positions in equities are *short* volatility as discussed in the previous sections. The proposition that volatility derivatives can be used to hedge long positions in traditional assets has very important implications for evaluating the systematic risks of volatility products and their expected returns.

Most investors have substantial investments in traditional asset classes, and therefore are long market risk (and, presumably, short volatility). Some investors take long positions in volatility derivatives to hedge their traditional portfolios. That is, the gains from long volatility investments tend to offset the losses from their risky traditional asset portfolio during times of financial market crisis and rising market volatility.

36.3.4 Volatility as an Unobservable but Unique Risk Factor

Factor exposures are the underlying drivers of the returns to assets as discussed in Chapter 8. Volatility is one of the most important factor exposures. Volatility is generally viewed as an economy-wide factor. Specifically, volatility is an important macro factor in multi-factor asset pricing models.

Volatility as a risk factor is not immediately observable; therefore, we need to estimate it or find proxies for it. A number of methods have been developed for measuring the volatility factor and estimating its statistical properties. The two most commonly used measures are implied volatility and realized volatility. Implied volatility is derived from the price of liquid options, whereas realized volatility is estimated by observing a time series of returns.

Volatility is not directly traded through traditional assets. Investment products must be created in order to trade volatility directly. We will later discuss that long volatility positions, at least in equity markets, typically have high carrying costs. Implied volatility can be isolated and traded using options, and products exist where the implied volatility of an asset can be observed and traded. Since the global financial crisis of 2008–9, as investor attention to understanding and trading volatility has increased substantially, the number of these products has increased, along with their trading volume.

As discussed in Chapter 8, legitimate risk factors must carry risk premiums that are unique; that cannot be explained by other risk factors. In other words, true risk factors should not be highly correlated with each other. For example, the value and momentum factors are unique since they are not highly correlated with each other or other factors (e.g., size factor).

In this context, supporting the claim that volatility is a unique factor, Rennison and Pedersen (2012) show that there is a low correlation (i.e., less than 30%) between the return to selling straddles and the returns to the underlying markets. They also find that the correlations between commodity volatility versus commodity futures, currency volatility versus carry strategies, and interest rate swaptions versus long credit investments are also less than 30%. Equity volatility and long stock investments have a 50% correlation of returns. Volatility strategies across the four markets (commodities versus equities versus rates versus currencies) also have low correlations of between 17% and 32% for all pairs.

This evidence not only supports the idea that volatility is a risk factor, but also that assets directly related to volatility are a unique asset class. Investment products that allow investors to access the risk premium attached to the volatility factor are considered a separate asset class.

Volatility plays an important role as a factor in a wide variety of asset classes. For example, options prices are linked to the anticipated volatility of the assets underlying the options as seen by the direct relationship between option prices and volatility in option pricing models, such as the Black–Scholes option pricing model. Thus, volatility is clearly a factor exposure to option returns. Of course, option returns also contain large factor exposures to the returns of the underlying assets.

In recent years, a large and growing set of volatility derivatives has emerged. **Volatility derivatives** are engineered to provide pure plays on volatility with returns that are driven substantially, explicitly, and directly by exposure to the volatility factor.

36.3.5 The Volatility Factor Has a Negative Risk Premium

Chapter 8 discusses how the risk premium on an asset class is comprised of a basket of risk premiums reflecting the various factor exposures of that asset class. In other words, each risky asset class offers an increased return for any increased exposure to systematic risk. For example, investors may seek to earn the equity risk premium, perhaps 4% or more per year over a riskless rate, by holding long positions in stocks or stock market indices. Investors also can own investment-grade and high-yield corporate bonds, both of which are expected to earn a credit risk premium. This section on volatility discusses the risk premiums on products with values that are tied directly to the levels of return volatilities (i.e., to volatility as a risk factor).

If a factor exposure provided consistent positive returns in all market conditions, it would lead to arbitrage. Thus, long factor exposures should tend to generate gains in some markets (e.g., bull markets) and especially losses in bear markets. Over several economic cycles, we should expect positive average returns to factor exposures that contain positive market beta (or other sources of systematic risk) and negative average returns (relative to the riskless rate) to factor exposures that contain negative betas. Thus, risk premiums earned through traditional factor exposures tend to be positive during normal time periods, negative during periods of financial and economic distress, and positive over the long run.

The level of return volatility exhibits a *negative* correlation to the returns of the market index. This negative correlation has been characterized by the tendency of equity markets to "take the escalator up and the elevator down." That negative correlation may be due to investor utility functions and behavioral factors such as loss aversion. In equity markets, there is increased demand for put options by investors (institutional investors in particular) when equity markets experience turmoil such as declines in price levels. This negative correlation between demand for long positions in puts and equity market price levels is an often-cited reason for the negative correlations between implied volatility and equity market returns.

As discussed in Chapter 8, risk factors that perform poorly during poor economic conditions must offer a positive risk premium. The positive risk premium is the incentive that investors need to hold a positive market beta asset that is expected to perform poorly when other risky assets are also expected to perform poorly.

While we typically think of positive risk premiums as being attached to positive exposures to factors, long volatility products are expected to perform well when other risky assets are performing poorly. Therefore, long volatility products have a negative market beta and carry a *negative* risk premium. The greater the extent to which an asset has a negative exposure to the volatility factor (i.e., is short volatility), the higher the positive risk premium. The positive expected return to being short volatility (which provides the counterparty with protection against the downside risk of equity markets) is similar to the positive expected premiums that insurance companies seek from providing protection to the buyers of insurance policies.

For example, the Cboe Volatility Index (VIX) futures contract is positively correlated to equity market volatility and these contracts tend to decline in value due to a negative risk premium. An investor establishing a long position in the VIX contract enjoys the hedging benefit of a negative equity beta but pays for that protection through the negative risk premium. In other words, products that generate hedging benefits by having returns that are positively correlated to volatility offer a **negative volatility risk premium,** which means they tend to have expected returns less than the riskless rate.

While correlation determines the sign of the volatility risk premium, supply and demand explain the size of the premium. There are many potential natural buyers of tail risk protection who seek to hedge their risky investments by entering volatility derivatives with positions that are long volatility. Given aversion to large losses, there is a limited number of traders willing to short volatility (and they will demand a premium for doing so). This is similar to the arguments made regarding normal backwardation of commodity futures by Keynes.

The volatility risk premium must be large enough to balance the supply and demand. It should be noted that shorting volatility exposes a trader to losses (i.e., tail risk) at the worst times: times of market distress. Therefore, there is reason to expect that the volatility risk premium will be substantially negative in equity markets as long as volatility itself is negatively correlated with equity returns.

36.3.6 Evidence That Short Volatility Earns a Positive Risk Premium

If being short volatility earns a positive risk premium, then being long volatility should tend to pay a risk premium, thereby generating low or negative average returns (i.e., lower than the riskless rate). The VIX futures contract (to be detailed in the next chapter) and several VIX-related exchange-traded products (ETPs, also detailed later) offer a pure play on exposure to the US equity market volatility factor. The VXX was an ETP that demonstrated the long-term effect of positive volatility exposure (from long positions in VIX futures contracts). Being long, the VXX was a pure play on being long volatility. VXX's performance was a profound demonstration of the negative volatility risk premium. VXX declined 99.99% over its 10-year lifetime! The VXX matured in January 2019 and was replaced with series B of the VXX ETN (also issued by Barclays). The maturity of VXX was pre-scheduled to occur 10 years after being created in 2009.

Investors with short volatility positions should earn a consistent profit from bearing exposure to the volatility factor. In terms of option prices, this consistent profit to short option positions would emanate from implied volatility consistently exceeding realized volatility. If so, options are frequently "overpriced" (relative to a risk-neutral world). If so, option writers consistently earn returns in excess of the riskless rate because the implied volatility priced into the options they are selling consistently exceeds the realized volatility. Rennison and Pedersen (2012) estimate the volatility risk premium to be about 10% of the level of implied volatility, which can be earned through options and volatility trading strategies in the equity, interest rate, currency, and commodity markets. In an efficient market, the excess return earned by option writers is compensation for bearing the risk of the volatility factor.

Exhibit 36.2 summarizes the estimated historic risk premiums to short straddle positions across 14 different options markets. The evidence in Exhibit 36.2 indicates that the risk–return tradeoff for strategies exposed to the volatility factor can compare favorably to the risk premiums that can be earned through exposure to equity and credit factors.

Over an even longer sample period, Cboe data reported in Exhibit 36.3 show that the *implied* volatility of S&P 500 options exceeded *realized* volatility in over 88% of all calendar quarters studied. Both exhibits indicate the consistently low or negative historical returns from being long products that are long S&P 500 volatility.

EXHIBIT 36.2 Quantifying the Volatility Risk Premium, June 1994–June 2012

Option Market	Average One-Month Implied Volatility	Average One-Month Realized Volatility	Implied Volatility–Realized Volatility Difference	Average Annual Excess Return to Selling Straddles	Standard deviation of Short Straddle Returns
Equity indices	20.3%	18.1%	2.2%	3.9%	3.9%
Commodity	37.4%	33.0%	4.4%	6.1%	5.2%
Currencies	10.3%	9.4%	0.9%	1.2%	1.7%
10-Year Interest Rate Swaptions	23.4%	20.4%	3.0%	1.3%	1.0%

Source: Rennison and Pedersen (2012).

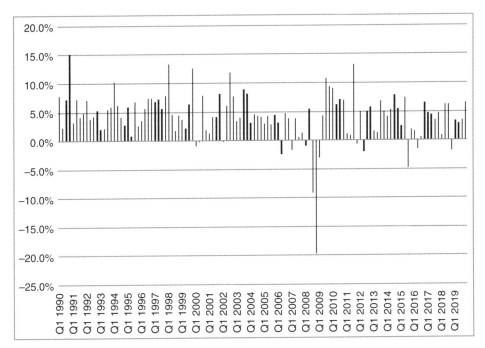

EXHIBIT 36.3 Quarterly Average 30-Day Richness of S&P 500 Options Implied Volatility Minus Realized Volatility, January 1990–December 2019
Source: Cboe.

36.4 MODELING VOLATILITY PROCESSES

The starting point for theory-based modeling of volatility derivatives is the specification of the underlying processes. Most valuation models for cash securities are based on continuous processes in which security prices (ignoring dividends) experience price changes in infinitesimal amounts that occur with a constant volatility. Many volatility derivative models and some option models are based on changing volatility. **Volatility risk** is the economic dispersion caused by changes in volatility.

36.4.1   Volatility Processes with Jump Risk

According to Nossman and Wilhelmsson (2009), there is a positive expected return to short positions in products that are tied to the implied volatility of options to compensate sellers for two volatility risk premiums: one for volatility diffusion and a second for volatility jump. **Volatility diffusion risk** is the risk of volatility changes that represent the continuous accrual of small changes in the volatility of an asset through time. **Volatility jump risk** is the risk of potentially large periodic and sudden upward changes in the level of volatility.

To understand these two types of volatility risk, consider the following representation of returns on an equity index:

$$\frac{S_{t+\Delta} - S_t}{S_t} = \mu_t \Delta + \sigma_t \Delta \tilde{W} \tag{36.4}$$

Here, S_t is the equity price at time t, μ_t is the expected rate of return, σ_t is the standard deviation of the rate of return, $\Delta \tilde{W}$ is a Wiener process, and Δ is the length of time (e.g., one day). Equation 36.4 is a continuous-time diffusion process that does not allow for discontinuities or jumps in its values. In some applications, such as the Black–Scholes option pricing model, the volatility parameter is assumed to be continuous and constant.

Robust valuation of volatility products must allow for volatility to change. The following is a general representation of a process with changes in volatility:

$$\sigma_{t+\Delta} - \sigma_t = \gamma \Delta + \delta \Delta \tilde{Y} + \phi \Delta \tilde{J} \tag{36.5}$$

In Equation 36.4, $\Delta \tilde{J}$ represents a source of uncertainty generating jumps in volatility. Also in Equation 36.5, $\tilde{\phi}$ is a random variable that determines the volatility of changes in volatility and permits both negative and positive jumps in volatility. Level II of the CAIA program discusses specific models that allow volatility to change, including the Heston model and the Bates model.

36.4.2   Volatility Processes and Regime Changes

In financial markets, a **regime change** occurs when an observed behavior of a financial series experiences a dramatic shift. For example, a major macroeconomic shift, such as a new central bank policy target combined with severe tightening of monetary policy, could cause changes in the behavior of interest rates through time that might be described as a regime change.

In modeling traditional assets, it may often be reasonable to assume that the regime does not change. For example, the return-generating process of a large listed equity in a developed market might be little changed through time. However, volatilities and correlations in financial markets appear at times to experience substantial regime changes.

Exhibit 36.4 displays an example of a volatility process driven by Equation 36.5.

Some investors model stock market volatility as a **mixture model or a regime switching model,** which models equity market volatility as some mixture of two return distributions. That is, the model has no jump component in Equation 36.5.

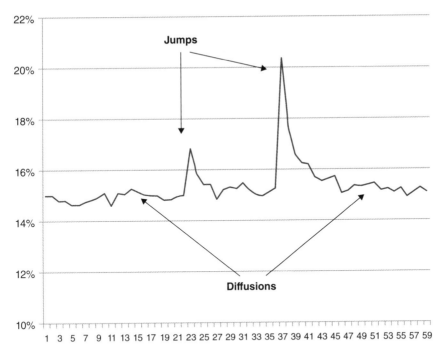

EXHIBIT 36.4 Example of a Volatility Process

However, the model has two different versions of Equation 36.5, with one having a much higher value for δ and one having a much lower value of δ. It is assumed that volatility switches between these two processes in a random fashion.

For example, a low-volatility market with a positive mean return may prevail for perhaps 80% of the time, and a high-volatility market with a negative mean return may prevail much less frequently, the remaining 20% of the time. Because volatility clusters, the probability of staying within a current regime (either high or low volatility) is higher than the probability of switching to a new regime in the next time period. **Volatility clustering** occurs in a price series when large changes are likely to be followed by more large changes and periods of small changes are likely to be followed by more small changes.

36.4.3 Two Reasons Why Volatility Strategies Tend to Recover Quickly

The return to volatility strategies can be highly volatile. However, while long-only investments in stocks, credit, or commodities may take 1 to 2 years to recover from a drawdown, volatility strategies historically have recovered from a drawdown in less than a year. Two reasons are behind this shorter period to recover from drawdowns in volatility strategies.

First, there is a high degree of *mean-reversion in realized volatility,* which means periods of high volatility do not last very long, and, as realized volatility declines, suppliers of long volatility products recover their losses. Realized volatility tends to experience spikes when a major event occurs (e.g., a major political/military crisis or the announcement of a huge corporate loss). Then the realized volatility eventually tends to decline towards a more normal level. The reason for volatility spikes is because major events tend to cluster (e.g., one military action can beget others, just as one major corporate announcement of an unexpected loss is often followed by other firms reacting to similar underlying economic headwinds). After a volatility spike, if no additional events soon ensue, then the market returns towards more normal volatility levels.

Second, there is *increased demand after a crisis* for long volatility products by investors in traditional asset classes. The increased demand for long volatility is met through an increase in the anticipated volatility risk premium demanded by traders willing to take short volatility positions.

36.4.4   Reasons Why Volatility Mean-Reversion Cannot Arbitraged

It is important to point out that while realized volatility may display a strong degree of mean-reversion, this does not prove that mean-reversion can be used as the basis of highly profitable volatility trading strategies. It is true that competition tends to prevent levels of asset prices from displaying strong degrees of mean-reversion in efficient markets since a tradable asset with a price that clearly exhibits mean-reversion could be exploited to generate substantial and almost risk-free returns. Realized volatility is not directly traded. Other nontradable market values such as interest rates and inflation rates can exhibit mean-reversion since there is no ability for traders to directly exploit all patterns in rates. Similarly, commodity prices can show patterns of price changes and volatility relative to harvesting seasons in the case of foods and heating seasons in the case of energy products such as natural gas. However, these patterns are not necessarily able to be arbitraged.

36.5   IMPLIED VOLATILITY STRUCTURES

An implied volatility can be derived for each option differentiated by the underlying asset, the tenor of the option, the moneyness of the option, and the type of option (e.g., call versus put). This section discusses the construction and analysis of implied volatility structures. An **implied volatility structure** is a representation of the various implied volatilities of a set of options relative to their tenor, moneyness, or type.

36.5.1   Methods of Computing Implied Volatility

In the case of the Black–Scholes option pricing model, implied volatility computations rely on values such as the price of the underlying asset and the riskless rate, which can be readily observed. The problem with the Black–Scholes option pricing model is that its assumptions are highly restrictive, including the assumption that the underlying asset has a constant volatility. Other option pricing models relax the assumption of a constant volatility but, in turn, can involve parameters requiring a great deal of subjective judgment. Each estimate of implied volatility is therefore specific to a particular option pricing model.

36.5.2   Implied Volatility Structures and Moneyness

Exhibit 36.5 illustrates a popular implied volatility structure that focuses on the relationship between implied volatilities and moneyness. The exhibit illustrates a volatility skew. A **volatility skew** indicates that options that differ by moneyness have different implied volatilities.

Exhibit 36.5 shows out-of-the-money (OTM) put options, at-the-money (ATM) put options, and in-the-money (ITM) put options. Put options are ATM when the price/strike is near 100%, OTM below 100%, and ITM above 100%. Exhibit 36.5 indicates ITM options as having lower implied volatility than ATM options, which in turn have lower implied volatility than OTM options. In equity index options, the graph for a single expiration date seems to look like a smile or a smirk. A volatility structure with a **smile or a smirk** is where out-of-the-money put options have higher levels of implied volatility than other options. OTM call options tend to have a lower implied volatility than put options a similar distance from the current market price. These smiles or smirks may be generated by negatively skewed return distributions, institutional demand for the downside risk-protection offered by long positions in equity put options, or perhaps the negative correlation between returns and changes in volatility.

36.5.3   Implied Volatility Surfaces

An **options volatility surface** is a volatility structure that plots implied volatility for a wide variety of options in a given instrument across both expiration dates and strike prices. For example, an options volatility surface, as shown in Exhibit 36.6, would essentially combine the information from Exhibit 36.5 across all expiration dates for a given asset.

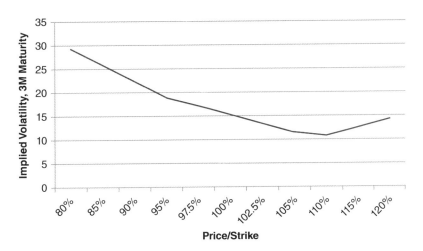

EXHIBIT 36.5   Example of Volatility Smile or Smirk from 30-Day S&P 500 Put Options on April 26, 2016
Source: Bloomberg.

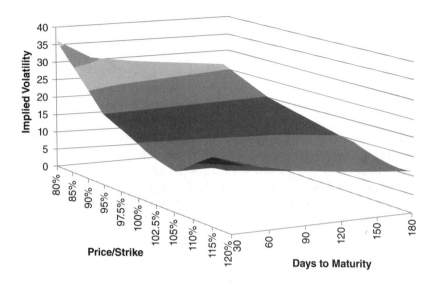

EXHIBIT 36.6   Example of a Volatility Surface
Source: Bloomberg.

36.5.4   Four Key Reasons for Implied Volatility Structures and Surfaces

Nontrivial implied volatility structures and surfaces are driven by expectations of future realized volatility in the underlying asset and other factors. There are four primary reasons that implied volatilities differ on options with the same underlying asset but with different strike prices or tenors.

First, even under the assumption that the expected realized volatilities of the asset over different time horizons are equal, differences in implied volatility would be observed because of the insufficiency of sigma as a description of the return distribution when return distributions are skewed or have nonzero excess kurtosis. If the returns of the underlying asset are not normally distributed, then the skewness and the kurtosis of the asset over different time horizons could drive differences between expected realized and implied volatilities due to the effects of skewness and kurtosis on expected option payoffs.

Second, volatility structures can be driven by expectations of time-varying volatility in the underlying asset's returns such as expectations of seasonal effects. Seasonal effects on anticipated volatility could include earnings announcements, revelation of actual revenues near major holiday periods, or potential seasonal trading patterns such as year-end tax-related transactions.

Third, the volatility of the underlying asset measured over different lengths of time (corresponding to different option tenors) or with different return granularity (e.g., measuring returns on a daily or weekly basis) can differ due to any autocorrelation in the returns of the underlying asset. Note that assets such as the overall market index are observed as having degrees of positive autocorrelation (i.e., trending returns or momentum) and negative autocorrelation (mean-reversion) that differ depending on the time lengths of the observation interval as well as the granularity of the returns.

Finally, risk aversion drives differences between implied and expected realized volatilities. If the implied volatilities of options tended to equal the expected realized volatilities of the option's underlying asset, then there would tend to be no expected compensation for bearing any systematic risk of holding the option. Therefore, implied option volatilities will tend to be lower than the expected realized volatility to the extent that a long position in the option contains positive beta exposure to the market. Time varying risk premiums could therefore drive differences between implied volatilities of options on the same asset leading to nontrivial implied volatility structures and surfaces.

36.5.5 Two Explanations for High Implied Volatilities of Out-of-The-Money Puts

An issue of particular importance in option trading and portfolio risk management is the implied volatility of deeply out-of-the money (DOOM) put options on a broad equity index (such as the S&P 500). Deeply out-of-the-money puts on equity indices provide highly desirable protection to investors seeking limits on their portfolio's downside exposure. However, the implied volatilities of deeply out-of-the-money puts tend to be substantially higher than the implied volatilities of puts with different moneyness. Consider two potential explanations for the relatively high implied volatilities of deeply out-of-the-money put options.

First, the high implied volatilities of deeply out-of-the money put options on broad market indices could reflect the skewness of the returns of the underlying equity index. The negative skewness could be due to the relatively high probability of market "crashes" and any tendencies of the underlying asset to follow an asymmetrical jump process.

Second, the high implied volatilities of deeply out-of-the money put options on broad market indices could be caused by option writers requiring a large risk premium for writing such puts. The demand for long positions in deep out-of-the-money puts emanates from portfolio managers or direct investors wishing to purchase protection from the tail risk of the equity market. It should be noted that, in theory, option payouts can be replicated using dynamic portfolio strategies in the option's underlying asset. However, such strategies may be difficult to implement given, for instance, market closures and discontinuous jumps. To the extent that these puts provide protection from large losses that cannot be obtained elsewhere and that is highly prized by investors, the put prices would have to contain a premium to induce speculators to write the options. Evidence indicates that the above relation of high implied volatilities on out-of-the-money puts is not as strong in the case of individual securities. Perhaps the reason being that the need for portfolio insurance is not strong for individual securities.

Note that the explanations are not mutually exclusive: both could be true. Broad equity markets are well known to have higher probabilities of massive declines than massive gains (i.e., taking the escalator up and the elevator down). Thus, the higher implied volatilities of out-of-the-money puts appear to be driven at least in part by skewness in the returns of the underlying asset. Evidence is mixed and inconclusive regarding the role of risk premiums in driving the high implied volatilities of deeply out-of-the- money puts.

REFERENCES

Black, K. and E. Szado. 2016. "Performance Analysis of CBOE S&P 500 Options-Selling Indices." INGARM Working Paper.

Nossman, M. and A. Wilhelmsson. 2009. "Is the VIX Futures Market Able to Predict the VIX Index? A Test of the Expectation Hypothesis." *Journal of Alternative Investments* 12 (2): 54–67.

Rennison, G. and N. Pedersen. 2012. "The Volatility Risk Premium." PIMCO Viewpoint White Paper.

Sinclair, E. 2013. *Volatility Trading*. Hoboken, NJ: John Wiley & Sons.

CHAPTER 37

Volatility, Correlation, and Dispersion Products and Strategies

This chapter explores volatility-related financial derivative securities and strategies related to volatility, correlation, and dispersion among returns of securities such as equity indices.

37.1 COMMON OPTION STRATEGIES AND THEIR VOLATILITY EXPOSURES

In the previous chapter, the relation between volatility and options was shown to be less definitive than the relation between vega and options. Vega, as a partial derivative, is positive for simple long option positions and negative for short option positions. Volatility exposure, as an empirical tendency, is not always positive for long option positions even for options on equity indices. For example, deeply in-the-money call options on the market index, like the index itself, can exhibit negative volatility. This section discusses common option strategies and their exposures to volatility.

Theory predicts that each asset's expected return depends on its factor exposures. Investors can expect a positive volatility risk premium through equity-market option strategies that are short volatility. Short option positions are short vega and tend to be short volatility (with deep-in-the-money call options on the equity market being a potential exception). However, individual option exposures (e.g., being long or short a call or a put) have exposures to factors other than volatility that determine their expected return. For example, a long position in a call option on a market index has a positive market beta while a put option has a negative market beta.

37.1.1 Option Writing, Theta, and Time Decay

The theta of an option is the partial derivative of the option's price with respect to time. Theta depends on the tenor of the option. The formula for the theta of a call or put option assuming, for simplicity, that the riskless interest rate is zero, $\theta_{r=0}$, is given in Equation 37.1:

$$\theta_{r=0} = -SN'(d)\sigma/2\sqrt{T} \tag{37.1}$$

where S is the price of the underlying asset, σ is the volatility of the returns of the underlying asset, $N'(d)$ is the (noncumulative) probability density function of the normal distribution at d (where d is explained in Level I), and T is the option's tenor or time to expiration.

Note that $\theta_{r=0}$ is negative since $N'(d)$, σ and T are all positive. Also, note that $\theta_{r=0}$ is high when $N'(d)$ is high—which tends to occur when the option is near-the-money. Finally, note that $\theta_{r=0}$ increases as T approaches zero (i.e., as the option nears expiration).

Theta is a measure of time decay—the decline in the value of an option caused by the passage of time while other values such as the price of the underlying asset and its anticipated volatility are stable. However, theta describes only one component of an option's return, so it is inappropriate to view theta (time decay) as causing long positions in options to have a negative or low expected return. The expected returns of assets depend on factor exposures in an informationally efficient market.

The formula for the value of an option exactly at-the-money (and with the riskless rate equal to zero) illustrates time decay nicely because d (in the Black–Scholes option pricing model) is simply $\sigma/2\sqrt{T}$. Continuing to assume that the riskless rate is zero, if the anticipated volatility is constant, the value of the at-the-money option is proportional to $\sqrt{T}$ as illustrated in Exhibit 37.1.

Continuing the previous assumptions, consider a 12-month at-the-money option that, by definition, has 100% of the premium of a 1-year option. A 6-month option, everything else equal, has 71% (the square root of 0.5) of the premium of a 1-year option, while a 3-month option has 50% (the square root of 0.25) of the premium of a 1-year option. Thus a long position of a 1-year option held for 9 months and a short position of a 3-month option held until expiration have offsetting time decay (holding all other variables constant).

Of course, in practice an option's underlying asset value and volatility change through time. The long gamma of long option positions offer an asymmetrical combination of large profit potential and modest loss potential to holders of long positions in options that (in an efficient market) offset the negative theta such that the expected return of an option depends on its factor exposures, not its theta.

EXHIBIT 37.1 Time Decay (Theta) of an At-the-Money Option Accelerates toward the Expiration Date of an Option Holding Volatility Constant

37.1.2   Writing Option Straddles and Strangles as a Short Volatility Strategy

A single position in an equity call or put is not a pure play on volatility because it contains substantial directional risk to the underlying equity. Note that a portfolio consisting entirely of short positions in equity call options contains a substantial negative market beta whereas a portfolio consisting entirely of long positions in equity call options contains a substantial positive market beta. This section discusses option straddles that can be used to lower this directional risk.

A long option straddle contains a long position in a call option and a long position in a put option on the same asset with the same expiration date and strike price. A strangle is analogous to a straddle except that the strike prices of the call and the put differ. A **short straddle** position contains a short call option and short put option on the same asset and with the same strike price. A **short strangle** position contains a short call option and short put option on the same asset but with different strike prices. Straddles and strangles were detailed and diagrammed in CAIA Level I.

Exhibit 37.2 depicts a long position in an option straddle with the top curve depicting values prior to expiration and the "V" on the bottom depicting values at expiration. The slope of the relations at each point is equal to the delta of the straddle. As illustrated in Exhibit 37.2, to varying degrees the directional risks of the call and put in a straddle offset each other, therefore reducing the straddle's market beta. Note that, prior to expiration, there is a value at which the straddle's delta is zero. This occurs where the long call's positive delta exactly offsets the long put's negative delta and depicts delta-neutrality (such as when the call option's delta is 0.5 and the put option has the same strike price, tenor, and underlying asset).

Straddles can offer a more pure play on volatility than a position in a single call option or a single put option because the straddle is less directional. A long

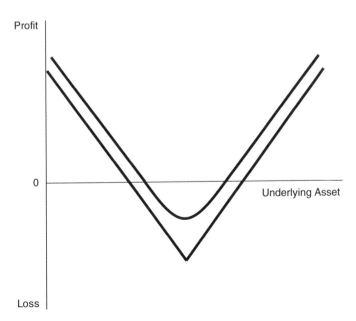

EXHIBIT 37.2   Long Straddle Before and at Expiration

straddle, like a long call or put, is long volatility whereas a short straddle (the mirror image of Exhibit 37.2) is short volatility. Strangles offer similar exposures to straddles in this regard. An at-the-money (ATM) straddle has a near zero market beta and therefore offers exposure to the volatility factor with minimal short-term exposure to directional risk in the assets underlying the options.

37.1.3   Writing Option Butterflies and Condors as Volatility Strategies

While selling (writing) straddles or strangles offers a moderately pure way to earn the volatility risk premium, it exposes sellers to potentially unlimited losses should the underlying asset make a large move. Some investors prefer positions with more limited risk, such as iron butterflies or iron condors, which are illustrated in Exhibit 37.3. In a short position in an **iron butterfly,** the trader sells a bull spread and a bear spread such that the two spreads share the same middle strike price. In a short position in an **iron condor,** a trader sells an out-of-the-money bull spread and an out-of-the-money bear spread. Note that bull spreads and bear spreads are detailed in the CAIA Level I curriculum.

The shape of payoff (or profit loss) diagrams such as those in Exhibit 37.3 indicate whether the positions are long or short volatility. Specifically, a payoff that forms a convex function to the value of the underlying asset (i.e., curves upward) is long volatility because it tends to generate larger profits or smaller losses when the underlying asset makes large directional moves. Convexity indicates a positive second derivative (positive gamma). A payoff that forms a concave function to the value of the underlying asset (i.e., curves downward) in Exhibit 37.3 is short volatility because it generates larger losses or smaller gains when the underlying asset makes large directional moves. Both diagrams in Exhibit 37.3 are concave near the middle of the horizontal axis (near an inner strike price).

In a short straddle or strangle (not illustrated in Exhibit 37.3) the potential losses from large directional movements are potentially very large—the consequence of being consistently short volatility (concave). Conversely, a long straddle or strangle is long volatility (convex).

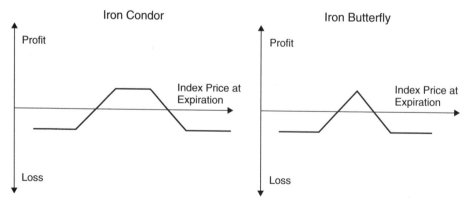

EXHIBIT 37.3   Payoff Diagrams for Short Iron Condor and Iron Butterfly Strategies

Returning to Exhibit 37.3, in both a short condor and a short butterfly, the tails of the risk exposures have limited downside exposures to large directional moves (due to long options positions on each tail). The limited losses to short iron condors and short iron butterflies are in contrast to the potentially unlimited losses of short straddles and strangles.

Both diagrams in Exhibit 37.3 are concave near the middle strike prices; they generate losses when the price of the underlying asset moves substantially to the right or left, and therefore represent short volatility strategies. Note, however, that after the underlying asset in a short condor or butterfly position makes a large directional move, the position can be viewed as switching from being short volatility to being long volatility as can be seen from observing in Exhibit 37.3 that the functions are convex on each tail (i.e., near the outside strike prices).

37.2 VOLATILITY AND DELTA-NEUTRAL PORTFOLIOS WITH OPTIONS

Chapter 21 in Part 5 (Methods and Strategies) details the method of hedging the delta risk of an option with a position in the option's underlying asset. Delta-neutral portfolios that include net long or short positions in options can be used to manage exposures to volatility or to speculate on realized volatility. This section discusses: (1) the relation between the performance of delta-neutral portfolios with options to changes in volatility; and (2) volatility-related strategies using delta-neutral portfolios.

37.2.1 General Performance Drivers of Delta-Neutral Portfolios with Options

The performance of a discretely hedged delta-neutral portfolio held to the option's expiration date is primarily driven by: (1) the level and nature of the variation that occurs in the price of the options' underlying asset; and (2) the strategy (frequency) for rehedging. These two drivers interact.

Equation 36.3 demonstrated that an option's (or portfolio's) gamma, γ, and vega, v, are linked ($\gamma = v/\sigma S^2 T$) such that they always share the same sign. Thus, a portfolio that is long vega will be long gamma. The goal of being long vega in a portfolio using a delta-neutral hedging strategy is to benefit from the long gamma through realized volatility in the underlying asset that exceeds market expectations.

The nature of the variation is previously detailed to include the timing of the variation relative to the option's tenor and relative to the option's moneyness, as well as the shape of the frequency distribution formed by the underlying asset's returns. The strategy for rehedging denotes the frequency of rehedging which can be based on the length of time between rebalancing or the distance that the underlying asset must move before triggering rebalancing. Rehedging or rebalancing often includes an intentional bias towards a net bullish position or a net bearish position based on market views. However, a delta-neutral strategy would involve best efforts to return the portfolio to having no directional risk.

37.2.2 Four Key Points Regarding Delta-Neutral Option Portfolios

Four key points regarding delta-neutral option portfolios hedged with the underlying asset of the option(s) are as follows:

(i) Delta-neutral portfolios that are long options are long vega and gamma and generate performance that is driven by the relation between the realized volatility of the underlying asset and the implied volatility of the options when the positions are established. However, the effect of realized variation of the underlying asset on the portfolio's profitability is complex. The portfolio's performance is driven not just by the realized volatility of the returns of the underlying asset but also by the *nature* of that variation including the timing of that variation relative to the option's expiration date, the location of the underlying asset's variation relative to the option's strike price, and the higher moments of the frequency distribution of the price changes in the underlying asset (i.e., skewness and kurtosis).

(ii) The time interval selected for rebalancing a hedge back to delta neutrality will not affect the expected profitability of the position (in the absence of trading costs) if the underlying asset's price changes form a random walk. Note that no sequence of trades can generate an expected risk-adjusted profit for any asset with returns that form a random walk.

(iii) Rebalancing the portfolio more frequently to maintain delta neutrality will tend to enhance expected returns (prior to transactions costs) if the returns of the option's underlying asset are mean reverting and will detract from the portfolio's expected returns if the returns of the option's underlying asset tend to trend.

(iv) Hedging activities (rebalancing) will tend to lower directional risk and accelerate the *recognition* of profits. However, hedging activities themselves do not generate expected profits unless the returns of the option's underlying asset have a predictable pattern such as mean-reversion. Rapid rehedging (rebalancing) will tend to increase transactions costs.

37.2.3 Delta Normalization and Exposure to Volatility

A problem with using vega as usually defined is that the volatilities underlying different options are often substantially different as detailed in the previous chapter on volatility structures (e.g., smiles and smirks) and volatility surfaces.

Use of vega to control the risk of a portfolio of options implicitly assumes that all option implied volatilities change by the same absolute amount. Thus, if one option's implied volatility shifts from 10% to 11%, another option's implied volatility is implicitly assumed to shift by the same absolute amount, say from 20% to 21%. However, volatilities can change by different magnitudes in some ways that are at least partially predictable. For instance, an option with an initial implied volatility of 40% may be more likely to experience a larger absolute shift in volatility than an option with an initial implied volatility of 20%.

A common approach to improve hedging across options with different tenors and/or moneyness is to normalize the vega for differences in the absolute size of volatility shifts. **Vega normalization** across options is the process of adjusting the vegas of each option to represent identical relative changes. For example, the effects of the change in the implied volatility of one option from 10% to 10.1% might be modeled based on proportions such that this 0.1% shift would be viewed as being comparable to the change in the implied volatility of another option from 20% to 20.2% (since the changes are equal on a relative basis).

Other normalization approaches can be used depending on the assumed relations between changes in volatilities of options that differ by factors such as tenor or price.

37.3 ADVANCED OPTION-BASED VOLATILITY STRATEGIES

This section provides details on three major types of option-based strategies related to volatility trading.

37.3.1 Vertical Intra-Asset (Skew) Option Spreads

A **vertical spread** is a combination of long calls and short calls (or short puts and long puts) having the long options with one strike price (the long leg) and the short options with a different strike price but with the same expiration dates. The spread is intra-asset when it involves options from the same asset. The vertical spread is a type of skew spread.

While a vertical spread that is created using the same number of long and short options is a pure vertical spread, a **ratio spread** is a vertical spread with unequal numbers of long and short option positions. For example, a pure vertical spread would be long 10 March 100 strike calls and short 10 March 120 strike calls, while a ratio vertical spread may be long 10 March 100 strike calls and short 20 March 120 strike calls.

At expiration, a vertical spread will have a minimum value of zero, when both options expire out-of-the-money. The maximum value will be equal to the difference between strike prices when both options are in-the-money.

37.3.2 Vertical Spreads with Delta-Hedging

A common strategy is to use vertical spreads in equity securities while hedging delta risk. The strategy commonly sells (writes) ATM puts and buys OTM puts. The two puts generate: (1) a profit equal to the difference between the initial put prices if the underlying asset is above both strike prices at expiration (since they both expire worthless); (2) a somewhat limited loss if the underlying asset falls well below the lowest strike price at expiration; and (3) a bullish exposure to the value of the underlying asset near expiration when the value of the underlying asset is between the two strike prices.

To create a pure volatility play, the entire position can be delta-hedged to remove the trader's exposure to changes in the underlying asset. The bullish exposure to the underlying asset can be hedged with a short position in the underlying asset.

Consider the exposure of the portfolio prior to the option expirations. A major driver of the returns of the puts is changes in their implied volatilities. Note that the larger price and vega of the short ATM put relative to the OTM put means that the portfolio is net short volatility. Therefore, the combination of the two puts will tend to fall in value (rise in value) when implied volatility increases (decreases) as long as the implied volatilities of the two puts move by similar amounts.

Note that prior to expiration, the ATM option (held short) must have a higher value than the OTM option (held long) and therefore the combination of puts always has a negative value prior to expiration. Therefore, the strategy tends to benefit from the net time decay in the value of the options (holding all other values constant).

The delta-hedge involves holding a short position in the stock (or index) underlying the puts in order to hedge the strategy against price changes in the stock (or index). The process of expanding and contracting the size of the stock position (i.e., delta-hedging as the net delta of the puts changes) is not generally intended to create profits—it is intended to remove directional risk. The delta-hedged portfolio will tend to make money (lose money) when the realized volatility of the underlier (i.e., stock or index) is less than (greater than) the implied volatility of the puts.

37.3.3   Horizontal Intra-Asset (Skew) Spreads

The second type of intra-asset spread, a horizontal spread, differs in terms of the expiration dates or tenors of its options. A **horizontal spread** is a combination of long calls and short calls (or short puts and long puts) having the long options with one expiration date (the long leg) and the short options with a different expiration date but with the same strike prices. The spread is intra-asset when it involves options from the same asset. The horizontal spread is a type of skew spread.

While vertical spreads tend to have relatively significant exposures to directional moves in the underlying assets, horizontal spreads have much lower directional exposures. Horizontal spread returns are driven by changes in relative implied volatilities between options of different tenors, which in turn are often driven by the timing of new information such as an event.

An example of a trade using a horizontal spread occurs when a stock is set to release earnings in the next week, and the implied volatility of 1-month options has risen substantially more than the implied volatility of 3-month options. A trader may sell the 1-month options and buy the 3-month options in anticipation that the spread between the two implied volatilities will narrow after the earnings announcement due to a decline in the volatility of the short-term option. The trader will profit if the spread between the implied volatilities of two options narrows following the announcement and if the price movement of the stock does not cause larger losses due to the position's negative gamma.

37.3.4   Inter-Asset Option Spreads

Traders often analyze the volatility spread between options on two different assets. An **inter-asset option spread** involves a long option position in one asset and a short option position in another asset. For example, the spread can be between two equities in the same sector, two currency pairs, or two commodities. The spread can be entered due to a catalyst in one leg of the trade—an earnings announcement, a central bank meeting, or an important geopolitical event—or the spread may be entered on the basis of analyzing past return relations between the two.

Trades are based on anticipated changes in the relation between the implied volatilities of options on the two assets. Traders will establish long option positions on the asset with implied volatility that the trader expects will rise (relative to the implied volatility of the other asset) and will establish short positions in options on the other asset.

Consider the case of this inter-asset spread in which the risk of changes in the value of each index has been hedged out to being delta-neutral using positions in the underlying assets. By being delta-neutral to each index, the strategy focuses on the relative implied volatilities between the two indices rather than the differences in their returns.

The implied volatility spread between the two indices essentially has two components to it. The first is the levels of implied volatilities of the stocks within each index. The second is the correlation between the stocks within each index. During periods of turmoil, the correlation among many assets typically rises. Lows in the spread between the implied volatilities of the two indices will tend to occur when the overall level of volatility is low, whereas highs will tend to occur when overall volatility is high. Accordingly, the side of the trade that is long the NASDAQ index option and short the S&P 500 index option is long volatility and will tend to gain in a period of market turmoil if the options are delta hedged (and will underperform in a period of low market volatility).

37.4 VARIANCE-BASED AND VOLATILITY-BASED DERIVATIVE PRODUCTS

Markets, including financial markets, are the institutions through which modern economies gain the enormous benefits of trade. The ability to transfer and manage *risk* through financial markets is just as vital to the health of a modern society as the ability to trade intellectual property, commodities, and finished goods. Modern economies need efficient and effective products to transfer risks such as volatility.

Financial derivative products such as variance swaps and volatility swaps exist and are introduced in the CAIA Level I curriculum. Variance swaps offer returns tied explicitly to a measure of realized volatility. While sophisticated strategies also exist that can serve similar purposes, they tend to require investors to perform daily rehedging or to struggle with issues such as the path dependencies of options. Volatility derivatives allow investors to manage exposure to realized volatility more easily.

This chapter discusses a variety of volatility products available to investors in the following order: variance swaps, futures contracts on volatility, and other products.

37.4.1 Variance Swaps and Variance Futures on Realized Variance

This section focuses on derivatives that are direct plays on *realized* variance (i.e., the observed variance of the returns on a specified asset over a specified time period). The next section discusses contracts that are direct plays on *implied* volatility.

Over-the-counter (OTC) variance swaps can be used to take a position with payoffs driven by the realized variance of returns observed for its underlying asset. As discussed in Level I of the CAIA curriculum, in a variance swap one party (the variance swap buyer) receives the annualized variance realized by a specified asset and pays a predetermined variance (the variance strike rate). The other party to the swap (the variance swap seller) pays the annualized variance realized by the same asset and receives the (predetermined) variance strike rate.

The predetermined variance strike rate in the variance swap is negotiated by the parties to the swap. The parties may determine the strike rates that they find to be acceptable through examination of the level of implied volatilities from options. In other words, option implied volatilities may provide a basis for determining an appropriate strike rate for a variance swap. Note that this makes sense since the payoffs to a delta-neutral option portfolio with an exposure to volatility is a similar play on the relation between realized volatility and implied volatility.

The variance swap rate is usually set at a value for which both sides enter the contract without requiring an initial fee.

For example, assume that in a variance swap (with a notional value of $100,000) the predetermined variance strike rate of the variance swap is 6.00 at the initiation of the agreement. Further assume that the realized variance that occurs in the underlying asset is observed to be 5.50. The buyer of the variance swap loses 0.5 times the notional amount of the swap of $100,000 for a loss of $50,000. The 0.5 loss is found by subtracting the variance strike rate (6.00) from the realized variance (5.50). Of course, the counterparty receives the $50,000. If the realized variance turned out to be 6.50, the variance swap seller would owe the buyer 0.5 times the notional amount of the swap.

While variance swaps are commonly OTC traded, variance futures are listed but are relatively lightly traded. Variance futures are available on the EURO STOXX 50 Index, the Eurex, and the Chicago Mercantile Exchange (CME). Variance futures contracts are like other futures contracts except that the underlying value over which settlement amounts are determined are realized (observed) variances in the returns of the specified assets (or observed variance swap rates).

The key point is that variance futures contracts and OTC variance swaps offer market participants the opportunity to contract directly on the realized volatility of various assets such as market indexes. The next section introduces very actively traded and important contracts based on *implied* volatilities.

37.4.2 Implied Volatility Indices

A key innovation underlying the explosion in trading of volatility-based products has been the establishment of a standardized method of reporting implied volatility. Recall that the implied volatility of an asset usually refers to the inferred standard deviation of returns of the asset based on the observed prices of options on that asset and the specification of a particular option pricing model. However, the VIX computations discussed in this section are based on implied volatilities from the formula for variance swaps rather than from option pricing models.

The **CBOE Volatility Index (VIX)** (less formally, the VIX Index or simply the VIX) is a trademarked market-based approximation of the 30-day implied volatility of the S&P 500 that is calculated and disseminated in real time by the CBOE. The VIX Index serves as a direct underlier to futures contracts and to options. While much attention has been focused on the VIX for the S&P 500 equity index, VIX indices are now available on a host of popular indices throughout the world. The VIX approach can be applied to virtually any index on which there are actively traded options.

These VIX indices, and the derivatives based on those indices, have facilitated a breakthrough in the ability of market participants to manage their risk exposures to the key uncertainty facing investors: market volatility. VIX-related products have achieved enormous levels of popularity in the wake of the global financial crisis of 2008 and now represent a large portion of volatility trading.

37.4.3 Computation of the CBOE Volatility Index (VIX)

The VIX index is designed to approximate the implied volatility of an option on the S&P 500 that has exactly 30 days to expiration. Since options on the S&P 500 have a variety of strike prices and have exactly 30 days to expiration only once per month, it is necessary for the CBOE to use a weighted average of actual S&P 500 options. The exact formula is complex and relies on the formula for the valuation of a variance swap rate rather than an option pricing model.

First, consider the problem that the most popular option contracts have exactly 30 days to expiration only once per month (i.e., 30-days prior to their expiration date). In order to arrive at a value for the VIX index, the variance swap rate is calculated for two expiration dates: the dates immediately prior to and after 30 days.

The VIX index is then calculated using a complex formula that generates volatility-like values from the interpolated values of variance rates. Data based on option prices of all available strike prices are used in the calculation for VIX, with the exception of any options with no bid price and any options with smaller deltas than those options with no bid price. The key point is that VIX index computations are based on the volatility levels inferred from a large set of available option prices on the respective index.

37.4.4 Futures Contracts on the CBOE Volatility Index (VIX)

Futures contracts and options on those contracts are actively traded on the value of various VIX indices just like futures contracts and options are actively traded on other values such as the price of corn, the level of a stock index, and various interest rates. For example, a wide range of futures contracts on the CBOE S&P 500 30-day VIX are traded with monthly settlement dates. Weekly settlement dates on that contract are available over the nearest four weeks.

The **VIX term structure** is the relation between the prices of VIX futures contracts and their settlement dates, usually expressed as a graph. Using the available spectrum of settlement dates, a term structure of futures contract rates can be observed as shown in Exhibit 37.4. Exhibit 37.4 depicts a typical example of the relation between the futures contract rates on the 30-Day S&P 500 VIX futures contract and their settlement dates. The ten settlement dates are connected with a line that passes through each actual rate as a visual aid. The straight and dashed line with a value of 17.68 represents the current spot rate of the CBOE 30-Day VIX Index (for the S&P 500).

At the settlement date, each futures contract is settled based on the value of the VIX on that settlement day. The holder of a long (short) position in a single futures contract will receive (pay) $1,000 for every point by which the VIX at the settlement date exceeds the price at which the contract was entered, or will pay (receive) $1,000 for every point by which the VIX falls short of the original contract price.

For example, an investor wishing to speculate that market volatility will decline or remain steady might establish a short position in the October contract in Exhibit 37.4 at a value of 18.09. The size of the contract is $1,000 per point

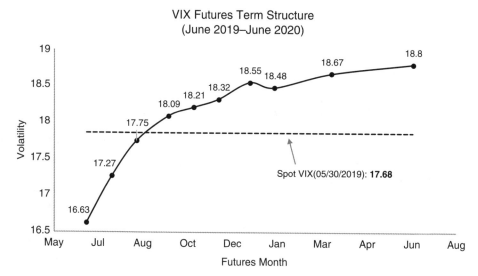

EXHIBIT 37.4 Term Structure of Implied S&P 500 Volatilities from VIX Futures Contracts

(although a separately traded mini-contract is available for $100 per point). If the VIX index remains steady at 17.68 until the contract settles, the speculator will gain 0.41 points ($410 per contract) at settlement.

A portfolio manager wishing to hedge against a potential market correction that would accompany a spike in market volatility may establish a long position on the same VIX futures contract. This portfolio manager would lose $410 under the same scenario. The portfolio manager may view this as the cost of having purchased "insurance" (i.e., hedged against the possibility of market turmoil) for the portfolio for a few months.

APPLICATION 37.4.4

A trader wishes to speculate that a market crisis with unexpectedly large equity price volatility will occur in the next few weeks. The trader enters a position in ten VIX futures contracts at a price of 15.60. Modest market turmoil ensues and the trader receives a total profit (ignoring trading costs) of $15,000 when the contract settles. What direction was the trader's position (long versus short) and what was the price of the futures contract at settlement?

A trader anticipating an unexpected rise in equity market volatility would establish long positions in the VIX futures contracts. The trader's $15,000 profit is $1,500 for each of the ten contracts. Each contract point is worth $1,000, meaning that the contract rose by 1.50 points. Therefore, the contract must have settled at 17.10.

Note that the time period of the volatility on which each of the monthly set-tlement dates depicted in Exhibit 37.4 depends exceeds the settlement date by a 30-day horizon. For example, consider a VIX futures contract with a settlement date of June 20. On June 20 the contract will settle based on option prices that have an expiration date 30 days later (July 20). Thus the settlement will ultimately occur based on the market's June 20 anticipation of the volatility that will occur dur-ing the next 30 days (i.e., June 20 to July 20). For example, a futures contract on May 1 with a settlement date of June 20 is based on options that expire in 80 days (i.e., on July 20). Thus, the relevant volatility for the June contract is the implied volatility between June 20 and July 20 even though the futures contract is trading on May 1.

In addition to futures contracts, a spectrum of liquid options exists on the VIX. The options contracts settle based on the value of the actual VIX index on the option expiration date. Like the futures contracts on the VIX, the settlement (expiration) dates are weekly for up to 6 weeks and monthly up to roughly 1 year.

Like the term structure of interest rates, the VIX term structure is often upward sloping and can be humped or downward sloping when the current VIX level is much higher than usual. However, compared to the term structure of interest rates, the VIX futures term structure can be very volatile when anticipated volatility in the equity markets shifts. For example the level of the short end of the VIX term structure roughly doubled in a single day in February 2018. Speculators who were short the VIX futures contract (i.e., short volatility) as a way of "selling insurance" and "collecting insurance premiums" lost enormous sums of money to the holders of long positions in VIX futures contract and similar derivatives that were long volatility. Many such speculators were using the ETPs (Exchange-traded products) detailed in the next sections rather than establishing positions directly in the futures contracts.

37.4.5   The S&P 500 VIX Short-Term Futures Index

Many market participants face challenges when considering the use of futures posi-tions to establish long-term exposures, especially exposures to volatility. First, note that short positions in futures contracts expose traders to unlimited potential losses. Futures trading can be highly leveraged and some institutions are not allowed to establish direct positions in futures contracts. Further, note that in order to main-tain a long-term exposure using futures positions a trader with contracts nearing settlement must regularly roll the position over into more distant months. As with all futures contracts, hypothetical returns to a long-term futures strategy depend on when the contracts are rolled. Finally, note that the risk of VIX futures contracts can vary markedly between the nearby contract and the deferred contracts because the VIX futures term structure (e.g., Exhibit 37.4), much like the term structure of interest rates, often experiences much larger shifts on its short end than on its long end.

In order to address the challenges of using VIX futures contracts to gain con-tinuous, long-term exposure to volatility, a suite of products, mostly ETPs, has been created. At the core of many of these products are indices designed to indicate the returns of futures strategies that are rebalanced daily to maintain a fixed hypothetical settlement date. A key such index is the S&P Short-Term VIX Futures Index. The **S&P 500 Short-Term VIX Futures Index** is a benchmark index that mimics the performance of a hypothetical portfolio of VIX futures contracts with a fixed weighted time-to-settlement of 30 days, formed using a time-weighted combination of the prices of the front and second month VIX futures contracts.

The weights of the two contracts (one with less than 30 days and one with more than 30 days) are adjusted each day to linearly approximate the hypothetical price of a 30-day futures contract. The weighting moves away from the shorter-term contract toward the longer-term contract as the times to settlement of both contracts diminish. The result roughly simulates a rollover strategy that rolls 1/30th of the portfolio into the more distant contract each day (ignoring holidays and weekends for simplicity) in order to keep the weighted average settlement date at a 30-day horizon. The linear interpolation of the two contract prices is depicted in Equation 37.2:

$$\text{30-Day Hypothetical Contract Price} = P_s(T_l - 30)/(T_1 - T_s)$$

$$+ P_1(30 - T_s)/(T_1 - T_s) \qquad (37.2)$$

where P_s is the price of the shorter-term contract, T_s is the number of days to settlement of the shorter-term contract, P_1 is the price of the longer-term contract, and T_1 is the number of days to settlement of the longer-term contract. For example, suppose that the nearby VIX futures contract has 10 days to settlement and a price of 20.10, while the first deferred contract has 40 days to settlement and a price of 20.40. A hypothetical contract with 30 days to settlement can be estimated using Equation 37.3 as the following linear combination of the contracts with 10 and 40 days to settlement, noting that there are 30 days between the settlements of the two contracts:

$$\text{30-Day Hypothetical Contract Price} = 20.10(40 - 30)/(40 - 10)$$

$$+ 20.40(30 - 10)/(40 - 10) = 20.30$$

$$= 20.10(10/30) + 20.40(20/30)$$

The intuition of the formula is especially clear in the last equation. The 30-day hypothetical price is a weighted average of the 10-day and 40-day price. The weights (10/30 and 20/30) add together to $30/30 = 1$. They weight the two times-to-settlement (10 and 40) to 30: $10 * 10/30 + 40 * 20/30 = 30$. In five more days, the weights would be 5/30 and 25/30 with times to settlement of 5 and 35. Five more days later, the weights would shift to 0/30 and 30/30 so all the weight would be on the 30-day contract. One day after that the formula would be a weighted average of the 29-day contract and the 59-day contract.

The previous exercise shows how every trading day the hypothetical price of a 30-day VIX futures contract is estimated (by interpolation). The S&P 500 VIX Short-Term Futures Index calculates returns every trading day from the change in the hypothetical 30-day VIX futures prices.

APPLICATION 37.4.5

Consider the information on two futures contracts over a 2-day period in Exhibit 37.5.

EXHIBIT 37.5 Future Contracts over a 2-day Period

	Nearby Contract	Deferred Contract
Days to Settlement on Monday	15	45
Contract Price on Monday	15.00	16.20
Days to Settlement on Tuesday	14	44
Contract Price on Tuesday	14.10	15.00

Calculate the price of a hypothetical 30-day contract on Monday and Tuesday and use the prices to calculate the price change between the 30-day hypothetical contracts on the two dates.

Using Equation 37.2, the hypothetical contract is priced at 15.60 on Monday (note that it is an equally weighted average since it lies equally between the two in time), whereas at 14.58 on Tuesday it lies closer to the deferred contract as the times to settlement of the contracts diminish and the weight on the longer contract increases. The price change of the hypothetical 30-day contract is −1.02.

There is also a Mid-Term VIX Futures Index that holds a combination of the fourth, fifth, sixth, and seventh month VIX futures contracts. Notice the large risk premium paid by investors taking long positions in the Short-Term VIX Futures Index contract, which can exceed 3% for each month, as shown in Exhibit 37.4. Long positions would earn a large return during a stock market crash, such as occurred in 2008, but have a very high cost of carry. Positions in inverse, or short volatility, exchange-traded products have earned a positive return over some extended periods of time. Investors can access each futures contract separately in the futures markets, or trade exchange-traded products linked to the short-term or mid-term indices.

37.4.6 Options, Exchange-Traded Notes, and Other VIX-Related Products

The previous sections discussed how observed option prices are used to infer the implied volatility of the underlying index (e.g., the S&P 500). Next, the implied option volatilities are summarized in a single measure and reported as the VIX Index. The two left-most boxes in Exhibit 37.6 illustrate the process.

The VIX Index serves as the underlier to VIX futures contracts with a wide range of settlement dates. These actual futures contract prices are linearly interpolated to construct the price of a futures contract on the VIX index with a time-to-settlement

EXHIBIT 37.6   Diagram of Information Flow from Option prices to ETPs

of 30 days. The daily changes in the series of hypothetical 30-day futures prices are used to construct a return index for VIX futures. The third and fourth boxes in Exhibit 37.6 illustrate the process.

Finally, the return index based on the hypothetical 30-Day VIX futures prices is used to structure a spectrum of financial derivatives, especially exchange-traded products. These products are engineered to overcome challenges with the direct use of VIX futures contracts by market participants. The derivatives offer continuous exposure to a constant settlement date, they do not require the investor to roll contracts, the derivatives offer limited liability, and they can avoid restrictions on the direct use of futures contracts.

A spectrum of exchange-traded products (ETPs) is available (especially exchange-traded notes (ETNs)) to provide exposures similar to long and short positions in VIX futures contracts. The ETPs differ by long versus short exposures, leveraged versus unleveraged exposures, and short-term or mid-term exposures. The VXX is a massive unlevered ETN that provides long exposure with returns similar to those of the S&P 500 Short-Term VIX Futures Index. SVXY is a large unlevered ETN that provides short exposure to the same index. There is also an S&P 500 VIX Mid-Term Index that indicates returns on a rollover strategy of long positions in the four-month through seven-month time horizon of the VIX term structure.

While the S&P 500 VIX asset complex offers the most diverse and liquid product universe, the methods used to calculate the S&P 500 VIX index have been applied to a number of other assets globally. Moran (2014) explains that dozens of volatility-based indices are now available, with more than 40 exchange-traded products tracking several of these indices. The CBOE currently publishes volatility indices on equity markets (NASDAQ, S&P 500, Dow Jones Industrial Average, Emerging Markets, China and Brazil ETFs, single stocks); commodities (oil, gold); and currencies (yen, pound, and euro). There even is a "VIX of the VIX," the VVIX, which measures the volatility of VIX options.

37.4.7   The VIX Term Structure and Its Slope as a Proxy for Portfolio Insurance

VIX futures contracts with different settlement dates have prices that reflect different time horizons or windows of volatility. Usually, the VIX futures curve is upward sloping, or in contango: the price or rate of the front month VIX futures contract is higher than the underlying VIX index, and the values of the deferred VIX futures contracts are higher still. Since each futures contract must converge to the value of the VIX index at settlement, a consistent upward slope in the VIX term structure causes long positions in the futures contracts to generate consistent losses. These consistent losses to long positions in VIX futures contracts are consistent with the consistent negative returns on the VXX (an ETP with long exposure to VIX futures). It is also consistent with the consistent positive returns until February 2018 on the inverse ETP (XIV) which had a short exposure to VIX futures similar to SVXY.

The losses to long volatility exposures (whether through long VIX futures contracts or VXX) are similar to insurance premiums that car owners or homeowners pay to insure against losses. In this case, long positions in VIX futures (or similar positions through ETPs) act as insurance for those investors who are using the futures contracts to hedge long positions in equities and other similarly risky assets. The insurance will pay off if there is a spike in the VIX, which is normally associated with a drop in risky asset prices. Other exposures with similarity to buying protection through insurance contracts include long positions in VIX futures and long positions in call options on VIX futures.

The slope of the VIX term structure tends to indicate the level of expected profit from being short volatility (as the contracts ride the VIX term structure down its curve towards settlement). Therefore, the slope of the VIX futures contracts is an indicator of the market price of insurance against spikes in the VIX and declines in prices of risky assets.

Being long the VIX should be expected to be very profitable as a financial crisis or liquidity event unfolds. As discussed in Chapter 8, a key aspect of asset factors and their risk premiums is the extent to which the asset performs well or poorly during "bad economic times." Long volatility exposure such as VIX futures contracts and the ETP VXX tend to pay very well when market turmoil erupts and equity prices decline. That highly desirable factor exposure drives its negative risk premium. Otherwise, there would not be a balance between the supply and demand for the exposure.

37.5 CORRELATION SWAPS

A **correlation swap** is a derivative that transfers the risk from the swap's seller to its buyer such that the actual average correlation among a specified set of individual stocks is higher than the swap's strike correlation. The net payment between the seller and the buyer is based on the difference between the average correlation rate and the strike correlation rate multiplied by the notional value of the swap.

37.5.1 Mechanics of a Correlation Swap

A correlation swap has a realized correlation received by the swap buyer (from the seller) and a fixed strike correlation received by the swap seller (from the buyer). Thus, a correlation swap buyer is "long" realized volatility. The payment made by the swap seller is based on the actual average realized correlation. The realized correlation is a market-weighted average of the return correlations between each pair of individual assets specified in the portfolio or index over the prespecified reference period.

The buyer of a correlation swap agrees to pay a specific correlation (the strike correlation) and receive the market-weighted average correlation realized among the constituents of an index for a specific dollar amount per correlation point. The strike correlation rate is fixed and is negotiated by the parties prior to the swap's inception. Kelly (1994) defines the average correlation measure and how the average correlation relates to the implied volatility smile.

For example, if the strike correlation rate of a correlation swap agreed to by both parties is 0.35, while the realized average correlation turns out to be 0.40, then the swap would require the swap buyer to pay 0.35 and receive the 0.40 actual average realized correlation for a net flow to the swap buyer of 0.05 times the notional principal amount.

APPLICATION 37.5.1

A correlation swap based on four assets has a strike correlation rate of 0.40 and a notional value of $100,000. Three of the assets experience actual realized return correlations between each other of 0.50. One of the assets experiences returns that have zero correlation with the other three assets. The market weights of the assets are all equal. Calculate the net payment to be made and identify whether the net payment is received by the buyer or the seller.

The four assets have six realized correlations. Three of the correlations are 0.50 and three are 0.00. Given that the asset weights are equal, the average realized correlation is 0.25. The payment amount is $(0.25 - 0.40) \times \$100,000 = -\$15,000$. The payment is made by the buyer to the seller.

37.5.2 Modeling the Relation between Correlations, Security Volatility, and Portfolio Volatility

The value of a correlation swap is driven by the market-weighted average correlation between each pair of components. The average correlation between each pair of components also drives the relation between the variance of the returns of a portfolio and the average variance of the components. This section describes a highly simplified approximation to the average correlation coefficient.

The variance of the rate of return on a portfolio is given by the weighted average of variances as well as the weighted average of correlations:

$$\sigma_p^2 = \sum_{i=1}^{N} w_i^2 \sigma_i^2 \sum_{i}^{N-1} \sum_{j>i}^{N} w_i w_j \sigma_i \sigma_j \rho_{ij} \qquad (37.3)$$

Here σ_p^2 is the variance of the rate of return of a portfolio (or index), w_i is the weight of security i in the portfolio or index, and ρ_{ij} is the correlation between security i and j. In order to simplify the analysis, consider four very strong assumptions: (1) the portfolio is equally weighted; (2) the variance of the returns of each individual asset is the same; (3) the return correlations between each pair of assets, $\rho_{average}$, is the same and positive; and (4) the number of assets in the portfolio, N, is very large so that we can approximate $((N-1)/N)$ as equaling one. Under these assumptions the pairwise correlation coefficient, ρ_{Average}, will be (recognizing that it is an approximation to the true correlation):

$$\rho_{\text{average}} \approx \sigma_p^2 / \sigma_i^2 \tag{37.4}$$

where σ_i^2 is equal to the variance of each asset in the portfolio. Note that Equation 37.3 has two desirable properties. For a very large portfolio of uncorrelated assets, the variance of the portfolio will approach zero; confirming that the correlations among the assets is zero. For a portfolio of perfectly positively correlated assets, the variance of the portfolio will equal the variance of each asset; confirming that the correlations are one. If the variance of the portfolio is half the variance of the individual assets (e.g., 0.01 versus 0.02) then the correlation coefficient is approximately 0.25.

APPLICATION 37.5.2

A very large portfolio is comprised of equally weighted and equally correlated assets. The individual assets each have a volatility of 0.50, while the portfolio has a volatility of 0.20. Using the approximation formula for an average correlation coefficient within the portfolio, find the approximated correlation coefficient between the asset pairs.

Converting the volatilities to variances and inserting the values into the approximation in Equation 37.4:

$$\rho_{\text{average}} \approx .04/.25 = 0.16$$

The assets in the portfolio have an assumed (or average) correlation coefficient of approximately 0.16. Note that any one of the three values in the approximation could serve as the missing value.

37.5.3 Motivations to Correlation Trading

Correlations between the returns of individual equities typically rise during equity market turmoil and, especially, during large equity market declines (i.e., in extreme bear markets most correlations go to one). Equity correlations tend to drift downward during periods of relative market calm. Therefore, strategies positively exposed to realized correlations (e.g., the buyer of a correlation swap) are long volatility.

Correlation among equities and equity returns tend to be negatively correlated. Therefore, strategies positively exposed to realized correlations tend to have negative betas.

Being a buyer of a correlation swap is profitable when realized correlations are high (relative to the swap's strike correlation) and therefore being a correlation swap buyer can be expected to be profitable during spikes in equity volatility (and equity market downturns). An equity correlation swap buyer therefore tends to be long volatility and short beta. In order to be consistent with a negative volatility risk premium in the market, the price of a correlation swap must be higher than the anticipated correlations such that selling correlation (i.e., being a correlation swap seller and therefore being short volatility) has often been—on average—a profitable strategy (similar to writing portfolio insurance to the swap buyer).

37.6   DISPERSION TRADES

The term dispersion is used here to denote the degree to which the returns of assets within a portfolio (or index) deviate from each other. Dispersion is therefore synonymous with the degree to which the returns are uncorrelated. Dispersion matters because the dispersion among the returns of the portfolio's assets drives the total risk of a portfolio relative to the total risks of the underlying assets. The implied volatilities of options on the portfolio depend on the total risks of their underlying assets. Therefore, the relation between the implied volatility of an option on a portfolio and the implied volatilities of options on each of the portfolio's individual assets is driven by the anticipated return correlations (i.e., anticipated dispersion of returns) between the individual assets.

A dispersion trade combines a long (short) position in an index option with short (long) positions in the options of the index's constituent assets. Note that the value of a portfolio of options on individual assets is higher than the value of an option on a portfolio (index) of those same assets (assuming that the options all have the same expiration dates and that the strike price of the index option is equal to the sum of the strike prices of the individual asset weighted by the index's weights). Therefore, if there are no changes in volatilities or correlations over the lives of the options, then the trader who is long the option on the index (portfolio) and short a portfolio of options will make money.

Dispersion trades are generally hedged to be delta-neutral. The profitability of the trade will be based on the degree of dispersion between the returns of the index's components (which can be viewed as the lack of correlation between the realized returns of the index's components). A dispersion trade that is short index options and long options on the components of the index (and delta-hedged) will benefit from high dispersion (i.e., low correlation among the returns of the index's components). The dispersion trade can be comprised of call options or put options.

To better understand the exposure of a dispersion trade, consider the case of a dispersion trade based on call options that is short an index call option and long call options on the components. This dispersion trade benefits when dispersion is high among the returns of the index components because the profits from call options on the individual stocks that rise will more than offset the losses from the call options on the individual stocks that fell (due to positive gamma).

However, gains from individual stocks that rise will tend to offset the losses on the individual stocks that fall, leaving the value of the index and its call options unaffected by the dispersion. This means the index option experiences little change while the long calls on the individual stocks produce net gains. The result is the same for a dispersion trade with put options. However, in the case of a dispersion trade based on put options, the profits from put options on the individual stocks occur when stocks fall and those profits more than offset the losses from put options on the individual stocks that rise.

A dispersion trade has similar factor exposures to a correlation swap. A dispersion trade that is short the index option will benefit from high dispersion—which is when the realized correlations among the components of the index are less than the implied correlations imbedded in the relative option prices. Correlation swaps allow investors to gain this exposure more directly.

Historical evidence is that the correlation implied by the relation between index option prices and individual option prices is typically higher than the average correlation actually realized by the underlying components. Accordingly, exposures that are short realized correlation have tended to make money over the long term. Exposures that are long realized correlation (i.e., strategies that have large positive payoffs in "bad times," such as rising correlation in bear markets) have tended to lose money over the long term.

In summary, when market participants take the risk of losing money when realized correlations will be relatively high (which tends to occur in bear markets), they will tend to consistently earn a profit. This is a risk premium for accepting exposure that generates losses "in bad times" (as detailed in Chapter 8). Two strategies that take the risk of losing money when realized correlations are relatively high are: (1) dispersion trades that are short the index option; and (2) being the seller of a correlation swap.

37.7 SUMMARY AND COMMON THEMES OF VOLATILITY, CORRELATION, AND DISPERSION TRADING

In terms of the pricing of volatility and volatility products, one common theme abounds. Consistent with asset pricing theory, investors are willing to pay (i.e., accept a negative risk premium) for long exposure to volatility, variance, and correlation. In other words, volatility, variance, and correlation are all high in "bad times" and therefore long exposures to them makes money. Since volatility, variance, and correlation all have a negative correlation to the broader equity market, being long these exposures has a negative beta, a negative risk premium, and can be used as a hedge against systematic risk. Passive long exposures to volatility, variance, and correlation should produce a negative return on average (relative to the riskless rate) over very long periods of time. Passive short exposures to volatility, variance, and correlation have positive betas and positive risk premiums and should therefore produce positive average return (relative to the riskless rate) over very long periods of time.

Exhibit 37.7 summarizes the response of volatility, correlation, and dispersion to the health of the economy as well as summarizing the typical returns of various exposures.

Exhibit 37.8 summarizes the correlation to the market and the sign of the risk premiums of four exposures. Note that being long vol, being a correlation swap buyer, and being long the index in a dispersion swap all tend to pay off well in a bear market. This highly desirable payoff means that, to the extent that markets are informationally efficient, the expected return of the strategies should include a negative risk premium.

EXHIBIT 37.7   Summary of Relations between "Bad Times" and Trading Characteristics

	In "Bad Times"	In "Other Times"
Equity Volatility	High	Low
Correlations among stocks	High	Low
Dispersion among stocks	Low	High
Return to Equity	Low	High
Return to Long Volatility	High	Low
Return to Correlation Swap Buyer	High	Low
Return to Dispersion Trade with Long the Index Option	High	Low

* Throughout the exhibit high volatility is assumed strongly negatively correlated with the returns of the equity market index (bad times).

EXHIBIT 37.8   Summary of Characteristics of Volatility, Correlation, and Dispersion*

	Correlation to Market	Sign of Risk Premium
Long Equities	Positive	Positive
Long Equity Volatility	Negative	Negative
Correlation Swap Buyer	Negative	Negative
Dispersion Trade with Long the Index Option	Negative	Negative

* Each "Positive" and "Negative"' is reversed if the position is changed from "Long" to "Short" (or "Buyer" to "Seller" in the case of the correlation swap.

37.8   VOLATILITY HEDGE FUNDS AND THEIR STRATEGIES

With increased investor attention to volatility products and the trading of volatility products, more focus has been placed on funds that primarily trade volatility.

37.8.1   Four Subcategories of Volatility Hedge Funds

Eurekahedge maintains four volatility fund indices based on their portfolio composition and investment goals: Short Volatility, Long Volatility, Relative Value Volatility, and Tail Risk indices. **Tail risk funds** are designed specifically to provide their investors with protection against large, broad market declines. Long volatility strategies are a less aggressive variant of the tail risk strategy. While, as the name suggests, they should profit from increases in volatility, they may at times hold small or neutral volatility positions. Short volatility strategies chiefly are designed to extract the volatility or correlation risk premium inherent in stock indices and other assets. Relative value volatility strategies are designed to capitalize on volatility mispricings, and will buy volatility deemed undervalued and sell volatility deemed overvalued. While relative value volatility funds will hold long and short volatility positions, their overall position is often neutral.

37.8.2 Relative Value Volatility Funds

As evidenced by the name, relative value volatility funds try to profit from mispricings and will take volatility positions in a variety of assets, often globally, with the goal of buying underpriced implied volatility and selling overpriced implied volatility. While the fund holds a number of positions, the net vega exposure is small, as the fund will hold long and short positions. These funds may engage in a variety of strategies. They may buy or sell implied or realized volatility they perceive to be cheap or rich based on quantitative or fundamental measures, using options, variance swaps, and VIX products. They may trade intra- and inter-asset spread positions. They may also trade correlation, either through a dispersion trade or through a correlation swap. Many of the funds may also seek to capture the bid–ask spread in the options markets by making markets in a number of assets simultaneously and then managing the risks of the resulting positions.

37.8.3 Short Volatility Funds

Short volatility funds typically take positions designed to earn the volatility risk premium in stock indices, currencies, interest rates, or commodities. This premium is compensation for the risk that volatility increases, an occurrence that, again, occurs during equity market downturns or other events specific to the commodity or the currency markets. As an analogy, investors implementing a carry trade with long positions in high-yielding currencies will typically suffer losses during times of increasing systemic risk. Long volatility and tail risk funds will take long volatility or, less commonly, long correlation positions. These funds often research macroeconomic and microeconomic events to find stocks, sectors, indices, or other asset classes where future realized volatility may exceed the volatility implied by the option prices.

Short volatility funds will exhibit a bias toward carrying a net short implied or realized volatility position. While they may deploy both intra- and inter-asset spreads, these funds seek to profit chiefly from harvesting the volatility and cor-relation risk premium. As a result, positions held would include short variance swaps, short volatility products, dispersion trades, and correlation swaps. While the funds will tend to be short volatility, they can vary the exposure based on market conditions.

37.8.4 Long Volatility and Tail Risk Funds

Tail risk funds can be viewed as insurance products that protect their investors against broad market declines. While these funds gain during times of turmoil, investors should expect small declines in calm conditions as their long options or other protective positions decay. The profile of long volatility funds will be similar to that of tail risk funds in the sense that they should profit during market declines. However, they may not always require such a position, and they may hold short volatility positions that partially offset their long positions, so the gains during turmoil and the losses during calm markets may be smaller in magnitude. Long volatility funds will take positions similar to tail risk funds, but can vary their volatility exposure and hold more inter- and intra-asset spread positions, as these funds, unlike tail risk funds, do not have a mandate to provide protection at all times.

The first year of the Eurekahedge Tail Risk Index, 2008, is disappointing, possibly due to the relative immaturity of these funds. Second, tail risk funds purportedly provide constant protection against black swans, while long volatility funds may not always be providing this protection. Nassim Taleb defines a **black swan** as an event or occurrence that deviates beyond what is normally expected of a situation and that would be extremely difficult to predict. Market events with large impact, such as the failure of Long-Term Capital Management or Lehman Brothers, tend to fit this definition of a black swan.

37.8.5 Returns of the Four Volatility Fund Indices

Exhibit 37.9 lists the cumulative returns for the four volatility indices. The return history starts in 2005 for three of the four fund types, and begins in 2008 for the Tail Risk Index. Accordingly, Exhibit 37.9 only displays the time period during which all four types of funds have data available. The indices were created in 2015, and consist of the same group of funds for the entire period, which makes these returns subject to survivorship and instant history biases.

The annualized returns and volatilities over the 11-year period are as shown in Exhibit 37.9. Note that the tail risk funds, which provide protection (e.g., portfolio insurance) against tail risk exhibit a negative average long-term return consistent with its negative beta and negative risk premium. Also, note that the averaged tail risk fund returns exhibited substantially greater variability than the other strategies.

Exhibit 37.10 contains the cumulative returns for each volatility fund index. Caution should be used in interpreting the historical evidence in Exhibits 37.9 and 37.10 as being reliable forecasts of future performance, especially because the historical returns are observed over a relatively short period of time. The primary takeaway of the exhibits is that tail risk funds have exhibited a negative risk premium consistent with their negative beta and potential attractiveness as a provider of portfolio protection against tail risk.

EXHIBIT 37.9 Annualized Average Returns on Volatility Funds

	Long	Relative Value	Short	Tail
Annualized return	5.69%	8.81%	5.51%	−7.89%
Volatility	4.37%	2.07%	4.24%	7.16%

Source: Eurekahedge and author calculations.

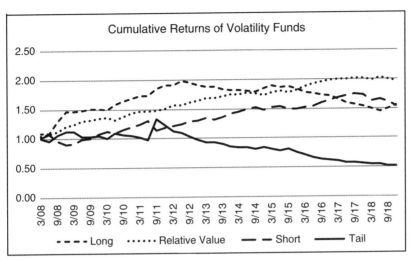

EXHIBIT 37.10 Cumulative Returns on Volatility Funds
Source: Eurekahedge and author calculations (http://www.eurekahedge.com/
Indices).

NOTES

1. When using options to trade volatility, the path that the underlying asset takes can influence the risks to the investor. For example, an investor's exposure to volatility of the asset will decrease as the delta of an option tends to the extremes: when an option is very deep in or out-of-the-money, any changes in volatility will have a very small impact on the option price.
2. Since 2014, the VIX calculation has included the use of SPX weekly options; prior to that, only the standard monthly expiries were used. The exact details can be found on the CBOE website at www.cboe.com.
3. In foreign exchange, this dynamic may exist in currency pairs commonly targeted due to the positive carry in the pair.

REFERENCES

Black, K. and E. Szado. 2016. "*Performance Analysis of CBOE S&P 500 Options-Selling Indices.*" INGARM Working Paper.
Kelly, Michael A. 1994. "Correlation: Stock Answer." *Risk* 7 (8): 40–43.
Moran, M. 2014. "Thirty Volatility Indexes: Worldwide Tools to Gauge Sentiment and Diversify Portfolios." *Journal of Index Investing* (Spring): 69–87.

CHAPTER 38

Complexity and Structured Products

This chapter begins with a discussion of complexity and related topics as part of a foundation on which to understand financial economics. The chapter then covers asset-based lending and asset-backed securities.

38.1 UNCERTAINTY, AMBIGUITY, AND OPACITY

Before discussing complexity in Section 38.2, this section discusses two related concepts: ambiguity and opacity. These topics raise key issues in the context of the investor–fund manager relationship as a principal–agent relationship.

38.1.1 Knightian Uncertainty

Knight (1921) made the distinction between two sources of unpredictability: risk and uncertainty. One source of unpredictability he termed risk—which occurs when an investor understands the probabilities of various outcomes but is unsure as to which outcome will occur. For example, consider an individual randomly drawing a ball from a bag of 50 red balls and 50 black balls in which the red balls are worth more than the black balls. The individual understands the probability of selecting each color (50%/50%) and the economic risk of the alternatives.

The other source of variability is Knightian uncertainty. **Knightian uncertainty** occurs when an investor cannot form reasonable quantified estimates of either the possible outcomes or their associated probabilities. Returning to the bag of balls, consider that the individual is now randomly drawing a ball from a bag with unknown quantities of various colors. The individual in this instance does not know the probabilities of selecting various colors.

Let's look at two unique examples. First, consider an investor in a binary or digital option on an equity index that offers two outcomes (both of which are well known in advance). In the case of a publicly-traded equity index as the option's underlying asset, the investor would have a solid basis for developing reasonable estimates of the probabilities of each of the two outcomes. The investor would face risk as identified by Knight.

Secondly, now consider an investor in a black-box investment strategy offered as a private deal in the form of a managed account overseen by a friend (who has simply indicated that the prospects are attractive). The investor faces Knightian uncertainty by not having a reasonable basis on which to form quantifiable estimates of the possible payoffs or their associated probabilities.

38.1.2 Ambiguity

Ambiguity in the context of investment risk, like Knightian uncertainty, is lack of knowledge with regard to the potential future returns of an asset and their associated probabilities. Aversion to ambiguity implies that assets with ambiguity should offer risk premiums relative to otherwise equivalent assets without ambiguity.

Olsen and Troughton (2000) surveyed 314 professional money managers. Their results contradict the perception that risk is primarily viewed as being synonymous with return dispersion. Their survey responses indicated that "risk is more a function of the possibility of incurring a loss than of variability of return." Their work indicates that Knightian uncertainty (ambiguity) is a key issue in investment management and may be a key driver of investment risk premiums. Note that traditional investment analysis associates risk premiums only with the narrow definition of risk—the lack of foresight with regard to which outcomes will occur from investments that have known return probability distributions.

38.1.3 Opacity and the Theoretical Incentive to Create Complexity

Opacity, in the context of investments, is the extent to which an asset lacks clarity with regard to various characteristics, especially potential financial outcomes and their associated probabilities. Opacity is the opposite of transparency. In the context of investments, transparency exists when investors are able to understand the characteristics, risks, and details with regard to an investment or a strategy.

Opacity can be motivated or driven by a variety of factors. Sato (2014) discusses what might be described as investor-hostile sources of opacity. In the context of delegated portfolio management, opacity can emanate from principal–agent problems and the incentive for managers to obscure the sources of return variability in order to reduce the likelihood of being perceived as an unskilled manager. Sato notes that, in theory, markets will evolve such that investment managers overseeing opaque investments can command higher fees than investment managers overseeing transparent investments.

The key implication is that financial engineering can be used to create opaque investments from transparent investments (e.g., mortgage derivatives from mortgages) thereby enabling investment managers to charge higher fees by managing the opaque investments. Thus, complexity can be engineered to generate opacity (i.e., increased supply of opaque securities, such as some financial derivatives) that, in turn, can lead to increased demand for the services of investment managers and fund managers that oversee opaque investments. Complexity is discussed further in the next section.

Sato recognizes that other motives may exist for complexity and opacity that are investor-friendly; potentially delivering value to the investor. For example, complexity and opacity can be unintended consequences of creating investment opportunities that facilitate better risk management. This is referred to here and in the CAIA Level I curriculum as "completing the market." Completing the market is the process of providing new investment opportunities that allow investors to select payoffs in various states that better maximize their expected utility.

38.2   ASSET AND STRATEGY COMPLEXITY

This section discusses the role of complexity within modern portfolio theory.

38.2.1   Complexity, Passive Indexation, and Active Management

In the context of securities, **complexity** is the degree of complication that may make precise estimation of probabilities and outcomes more difficult. Without any complexity, the benefits of analysis would be insignificant. Therefore, the existence of complexity and active management are complementary to one another.

Let's examine the increased and large amount of assets in passively indexed investment strategies. Broad diversification and passive indexation are increasingly popular strategies. However, if investors singularly followed market-weighted diversification and passive indexation, then markets would not incorporate information into asset prices. Prices would be impacted only by asset flows and not security analysis.

As discussed in the Level I CAIA curriculum, efficiently inefficient markets is the theory that there is a reward available to superior investors for processing information and pursuing active investment strategies that enable market prices to approach informational efficiency. The return for superior active investing must be sufficient to induce analysts to gather and process information, otherwise there would be no incentive for analysis and the market could not sustain informational market efficiency of any level.

38.2.2   Complexity Crashes

Section 38.3 discusses several past financial crises that might well be described as "complexity crashes" in which highly complex securities, such as structured products, experienced severe declines in market values due to a combination of adverse economic events and the opacity of the complex securities. Simply put, in a severe crisis it is difficult to be confident as to the value of a complex security and, under stressful market conditions, investors liquidating complex positions might need to offer steep discounts to attract buyers. The term "complexity crash" here is used analogously to the use of "momentum crashes." A momentum crash is a well-known term in financial markets to indicate a general and severe decline in assets with high exposure to momentum factors.

38.2.3   The Complexity Risk Premium

The **complexity risk premium,** if it exists, would be the enhanced return offered to opaque investments to compensate the investors for the risk of increased losses and/or the added costs of financial analysis in evaluating complex products.

The existence of a particular risk premium can be based on empirical evidence, economic reasoning, or a combination of both. The question regarding whether or not returns on complex securities include a complexity risk premium is unlikely to be completely resolved.

Economic reasoning generates mixed evidence regarding the existence of a general complexity risk premium across asset classes. For example, the decision to invest in products that have high complexity could be based on the investor's belief that the product offers a positive risk premium as a reward for performing the necessary due diligence and bearing complexity risk.

Alternatively, the decision to invest in products that have high complexity could be based on the investor's belief that complex products "complete the market" (thereby enhancing the investor's ability to manage risk) and therefore are worth holding even if the risk premium is negative. For example, a commodity-linked bond may allow a fixed-income mutual fund to speculate on the price of commodities indirectly in a case where the fund is not allowed by regulators to gain direct exposure to commodities.

The two preceding hypotheses are based on quite rational behavior by the investor. It is possible that investors err substantially in analyzing complex investments and invest in some complex investments based on misestimation of future returns. When investors lack the skill to detect discernable attributes of a strategy, then complex securities may have a negative risk premium, have no unique benefits to risk management, and be brought to investors as a result of aggressive marketing tactics. These types of offerings often have high fees available to their originators and managers but are marketed to investors that may not sufficiently appreciate the cost and benefits of the investment.

The complexity risk premium is difficult to measure. Empirically, the evidence is insufficient due to the limited number of financial crises as well as the tendency of complex securities to have other factor exposures such as illiquidity.

38.2.4 Complexity as a Return Characteristic or Factor

Clearly, the returns of highly complex products such as CDOs exhibit correlation with overall market returns. In fact, it is reasonable to assert that CDOs have even been the *cause* of huge market declines and even economic declines. But whether complexity is an *economy-wide return factor* is not clear.

Ang (2014) cites four criteria of economy-wide factors—two of which seem to be met by complexity risk: a return history for "bad times" and being "implementable." However, two of the criteria may not be fully met: being justified by academic research (i.e., compelling logic as to why the risk premium should exist) and having exhibited premiums in the past that are expected to persist.

Without doubt, complexity (and opacity) are important characteristics. An analogy is the idea that the credit risk premium is widely viewed as a factor, but characteristics that generate credit risk, such as default probabilities and losses given default, are not, per se, viewed as risk factors. So, perhaps complexity risk and opacity risk are simply important characteristics.

38.3 CASES IN COMPLEXITY AND PERVERSE INCENTIVES

This section reviews three instances in which financial innovations helped investors "complete markets," but in which perverse incentives and complexity also generated conflicts of interest between investor interests and investment manager interests. Each case is based in fixed income markets and the increasing complexity of financially engineered securities.

38.3.1 Treasury Strips in the 1980s

The 1980s were generally a time period of very high, but declining, interest rate levels in the US. Investors in long-term US Treasury bonds had suffered egregious losses during the generally-increasing levels of US interest rates in the 1970s. In the 1980s, a new investment product gained popularity: US Treasury Strips.

US Treasury Strips are financially engineered zero-coupon securities formed by parsing a non-callable US Treasury note or bond into a set of securities with maturities corresponding to each of the promised coupon and principal payments. Thus, a 10-year Treasury note with 20 coupon payments and one principal payment could be divided into US Treasury strips serving as zero-coupon bonds with maturities ranging from 6 months to 10 years. The prices of strips were quoted on the basis of the price per $100 of face value. Given high interest rates in the US in the early 1980s, it was not unusual to see long-term strips trading at $20–30 per $100 of face value.

Treasury strips offered investors US government-guaranteed zero-coupon investments with a spectrum of maturities that allowed the investors to cash-flow-match their liabilities. For example, an investor wishing to lock-in the nominal cash flows to fund a child's anticipated need for 4 years of tuition payment could simply purchase these strips (with face values that matched expected tuition payments) to form a cash-flow-matched hedge (setting aside inflation concerns regarding the eventual tuition bills). This ability to accomplish better cash-flow-matching through new securities is an excellent example of "completing the market," although this is not intended to imply that a single innovation can perfectly complete the market.

However, the introduction of Treasury strips brought complexities to retail investors accustomed only to coupon bonds. First, the bonds did not offer the traditional relation between yields, coupons, and prices such that bond prices could be easily judged to depend on small differences between yields and coupons. Many investors did not understand the importance of purchasing a strip at $26 rather than $25. Second, brokers found that they could receive enormous bid-asked spreads and circumvent a guideline that fees should be less than 5% because fees were measured relative to face value rather than transaction prices.

Some investors were encouraged to "roll" the strips as interest rates declined. Thus, an investor might be encouraged to buy a 20-year strip at a high asked price of $25 only to be encouraged to sell the strip a year later at a low-bid price of $26 (which generates only a 4% total return in a market of high and declining interest rates). The complexity of zero-coupon bond returns masked the large reduction in return being caused by the enormous but opaque bid-asked spreads (when viewed as a percentage of price rather than face value). The inherent broker–customer conflicts of interest from commission-based compensation schemes in some cases worked against the tremendous potential advantages that the zero-coupon opportunities provided to investors seeking cash-flow-matching at targeted maturity dates.

38.3.2 Collateralized Mortgage Obligations in the 1990s

In the late 1980s and early 1990s, Collateralized Mortgage Obligations (CMOs) became popular serving much the same role as US Treasury strips discussed in the previous section: they took a security offering a long string of cash flows through the future (pools of residential mortgages) and parsed them into sets of products (CMOs) that offered targeted maturity date exposures.

The CMO investors experienced a crisis in 1994 when the US economy experienced a massive but mercifully short-lived increase in interest rates that is recounted by Ehrbar (2013). Chapter 24 of the CAIA Level I curriculum details the CMO products and the financial crisis of 1994. Very briefly, rising interest rates caused those CMOs subject to the most extension risk to experience massive market value losses of up to 80% on products that were US government-backed against default risk and were sure to provide a full return of capital, in some cases with a time period as short as 6 months.

The CMO crisis vividly illustrates the points regarding complexity and conflicts of interest discussed earlier in this chapter. Portfolio managers schooled in the simple and moderately transparent sequential-pay CMOs of the late 1980s often did not realize the huge complexities built into highly engineered CMO products in the early 1990s (e.g., TACs as discussed in CAIA Level I).

Why did such a mismatch occur between the complexity of the new CMO products and the sophistication of the portfolio managers? The work by Sato discussed earlier provides a potential explanation below.

Sell-side financial institutions developed innovative securities that passed popular interest rate risk stress tests while purporting to have attractive expected returns. Extrapolating from Sato's theses, the institutions created these opaque financial derivatives because there were unattractive fees on CMOs that offered transparency. By creating complexity and opacity, the institutions could compete for market share. It is quite difficult to contend that the enormous complexity of the most highly engineered CMOs "completed the market" in a valuable way when, in fact, they had dangerous features that escaped detection when analyzed using the conventional stress tests of the era.

38.3.3 Residential Mortgage-Backed Securities in the 2000s

The role of losses from residential mortgage-backed securities (RMBS) in the global financial crisis is generally well-known and is discussed in Level I of the CAIA curriculum. Unlike the previous two sections on US Treasury Strips and CMOs, the RMBS in this section often contained substantial credit risk (i.e., default risk). This section discusses RMBS and the global financial crisis in the context of complexity, opacity, and conflicts of interest.

As indicated in Chapter 26 and exemplified in the case of Carlisle Capital Corporation, at the core of the global financial crisis was the assignment of AAA-ratings to RMBS that experienced massive declines in prices. The exact holdings and risks of many RMBS (e.g., the quantity and credit quality of subprime mortgages) were often not well known to their investors. Investors often relied on rating agencies to perform the task of evaluating the risks. Obviously, the rating agencies were not able to fully understand the risks of these highly complex structures.

RMBS brought substantial improvements to financing of home ownership that doubtlessly saved homeowners many billions of dollars of interest and provided investors with cost-effective access to diversification and superior risk management through the years prior to the crisis. However, the complexity of the structures that enabled advanced financial engineering of their tranches also camouflaged the inherent inadequacies of the methods being used to analyze the risks of the structures.

38.3.4 Five Key Takeaways from the Three Fixed Income Cases

Five key takeaways from this section on three cases involving complexity and fixed income instruments are:

1. The effects of the innovations discussed in the previous sections (US Treasury strips, CMOs, and RMBSs) are not all negative: these innovations have generated tremendous financing advantages for decades to investors facing the challenges of managing risk efficiently and cost-effectively in the face of incomplete markets.
2. Complexity can be a necessary consequence of the financial engineering that has been deployed to help serve investors by completing the market.
3. Complexity often causes opacity and, in some cases, may be an intentional tool for creating opacity.
4. Opacity and complexity can cause or exacerbate adverse outcomes to individual investors or even to the entire world economy.
5. Complexity for the sake of opacity can be a perverse consequence of principal–agent conflicts, namely conflicts of interest between investment managers and clients, as well as conflicts of interest between sell-side institutions and investors. However, the ability of knowledgeable investors to seek less complex products with which to meet their investment goals should act to undo efforts by others to create opacity.

38.4 ASSET-BASED LENDING

An **asset-based loan** (ABL) is a secured loan backed by various types of collateral pledged by the borrower. The value, type, and quality of the collateral determine the amount of the loan that can be extended, the advance rate, and the interest rate of the loan. Hedge funds and private equity funds making these loans are said to be part of the shadow banking system. The **shadow banking system** consists of various nontraditional lenders who fill a void in lending created when traditional lenders reduce credit availability due to increased capital requirements or other governmental policies.

38.4.1 A Typical Borrower in Asset-Based Lending

The typical borrower using an asset-based loan is a small or midsize company, and the typical size of the ABL ranges from $10 million to $50 million, although there are loans that are significantly larger. Borrowers can be in various industries and sectors, including retail, distribution, manufacturing, wholesale, and service companies. A typical ABL candidate has an asset-rich balance sheet, with a significant amount (half or more) of its total assets in working capital. These assets are often in the form of inventory or accounts receivable.

Similar to other types of lending, an asset-based lender looks for a borrower with a strong management team that has a proven track record of managing the operational complexities of its business, strength (if not market leadership) within its industry, and a strong ability to service its debt. Furthermore, given the nature of the ABL, it is important that borrowers have strong financial accounting and information technology (IT) systems that enable reliable data on asset performance as well as on operational results.

Unlike in the cash flow-based lending market, the ABL market relies far less on external credit ratings (i.e., those provided by credit rating agencies such as Moody's, Standard & Poor's, and Fitch). Given the collateralized, secured nature of asset-based lending, this type of lending is typically done with borrowers whose credit risk is similar to noninvestment-grade borrowers.

Geographically, the ABL market is well developed in the United States, with established markets in Europe and Canada as well. Lenders have extended credit to multi-national companies with assets residing in geographies outside the areas just mentioned, with certain caveats. Lenders need to be able to get a security interest in the underlying collateral, as well as gain comfort that, in the event of restructuring, there is precedent on how creditors can get recovery on their loan. Practically speaking, structures such as a special purpose vehicle are formed to own the collateral. Lenders may also utilize a lockbox. A **lockbox** is a bank account set up to protect the lender by receiving collections of accounts receivable so that the proceeds can be used to support the debt.

38.4.2   Why Borrowers Select Asset-Based Lending

In the corporate credit arena, a lender can lend to a corporation based on two different frameworks: asset-based lending or cash flow-based lending. In the cash flow-based lending model, a cash flow-based lender provides unsecured loans and typically looks at prospective cash flows to support the loan. Prospective cash flows are estimated through analysis of earnings before interest, taxes, depreciation, and amortization (EBITDA) adjusted for cash as a proxy. EBITDA or a similar measure is then combined with a multiplier to determine how much leverage is prudent to extend to the prospective borrower.

During business and economic downturns, many businesses will see their earnings (and cash flows) contract. This often translates into difficulty accessing financing. To make matters worse, during difficult economic conditions, lenders typically also become more bearish and adjust their leverage multiple downward, further shrinking the amount of credit available to a particular borrower.

For an asset-based lender, the loan is secured by specified assets, and many asset-based lenders feel that asset valuation tends to be less volatile than earnings multiples when it comes to determining available credit to a borrower. This also benefits some types of borrowers because the availability of credit tends to remain more stable over different business and economic environments.

38.4.3   Features of Asset-Based Lending

ABL begins with an examination of the collateral assets available to support additional loans. The **collateral amount** is the sum of available assets to support debt. However, lenders do not typically extend credit equal to the collateral amount considering the likely reductions that would occur in the event of a forced liquidation. The collateral amount is reduced in a process called margining to estimate a borrowing base. The **borrowing base** is therefore the maximum potential quantity of credit the lender is willing to extend after reducing collateral values considering the level of outstanding debt that would be senior to the loan.

Collateral amounts are reduced to a borrowing base either through reduction by a discount factor or by application of an advance rate. An **advance rate** is the ratio of credit extended for every dollar of collateral (i.e., the borrowing base). The two terms, discount factor and advance rate, describe the same concept. For example, for an asset with an advance rate of 80%, if the asset is valued at $100, $80 of credit (borrowing base) can be extended. Alternatively, the exercise could describe a discount factor of 20% as lowering the $100 collateral amount to the $80 borrowing base.

The reduction of collateral amounts to borrowing bases depends on the type of collateral and the mix of assets within the collateral package. Assets that are easier to value and have better liquidity are generally deemed to be more attractive as collateral by the lenders, who tend to apply a higher advance rate in calculating the borrowing base. The specific terms involving valuation of the underlying collateral as well as the advance rate are highly negotiable and vary dramatically across borrowers. For example, the advance rate against a particular borrowing base can fluctuate over time.

Seasonal overadvance is a temporary allowance by which the lender allows for a higher advance rate to account for seasonal effects in which the working capital need of the borrower is higher. For example, retailers' busiest season is typically in November and December, and in preparation for that season, they usually need to build inventory. The need to purchase more goods will lead to higher working capital needs, and a seasonal overadvance provides some flexibility to allow higher borrowing.

Traditional overadvance is typically used for a corporate transaction, such as an acquisition or a leveraged buyout (LBO). In a **traditional overadvance,** lenders allow for a greater advance rate, and the additional borrowing is then amortized over several years and can be added to an existing term loan or as a separate facility.

In connection to the amount of borrowing in excess of the regular advance rate, there may be an excess cash flow sweep (i.e., additional cash flow is redirected to repay the additional borrowing) to bring the loan back to the regular advance rate. The metrics used to analyze an overadvance are closer to traditional cash flow lending inasmuch as the lender looks at expected ability to service the debt, historical performance of the company, and the total leverage of the borrower.

38.4.4 Discount Rates for Various Assets in Asset-Based Lending

There are four major categories of assets often pledged for ABL: accounts receivable, inventory, equipment, and real estate.

Accounts receivable collateral is measured by various factors, such as the diversification of client base (the more diversified, the better), length of term, typical collection period, and dilution in determining the advance rate. In most cases, advance rates on typical portfolios of accounts receivable range from 70% to 85%. In some cases, it makes sense for the borrower to provide credit insurance and boost the advance rate of the accounts receivable to 90%.

The advance rates seen for inventory range widely depending on the type of inventory and the expected ease of liquidation. Common industry practice is to set the value of the inventory as a percentage (80–90%) of liquidation value, net of the cost of liquidation. In evaluating the value of inventories, the lender typically hires a third party who is a professional appraiser. The appraiser will usually have experience in handling the liquidation of the particular type of inventory. Measures such as how quickly the inventory can be converted into sellable merchandise, profit margin, whether the inventory is a commodity, and the mix of the inventory all factor into the appraisal value and ultimately into the borrowing base.

For commodity-oriented inventory, the advance rate can go as high as 80%. Equipment and real estate are similarly discounted based on the perceived liquidity of each asset and the availability of ready buyers.

38.4.5   Use of Asset-Based Lending Proceeds

The use of the proceeds of an ABL typically varies depending on the type of borrower. Larger, higher-quality borrowers typically use asset-based loans to finance working capital. Because of their size and credit quality, these are typically the borrowers that can finance most of their liabilities through public or private credit markets. These borrowers may use ABLs either to fund seasonal changes in their working capital (i.e., borrow to finance higher inventory during restocking, and the inventory collateralizes the borrowing) or to finance certain corporate actions, such as opportunistic asset purchases, share repurchases, or special dividends.

Smaller and midsize borrowers tend to use ABLs more extensively in their overall capital structure. For these borrowers, the asset-based borrowing may include longer-term loans that are backed by hard assets, such as real estate or equipment. Additionally, companies that are in active acquisition mode may also use ABLs as part of their acquisition financing in addition to other, more junior debt. In addition, borrowers that are in stress or distress may also rely on ABLs, since their credit profiles render them unsuitable for cash flow-based lending. These types of borrowers typically need capital that they can rely on as management restructures the business or weathers the current situation. In this scenario, the ABL may act as a bridge loan that provides some temporary liquidity as well as operational and financial flexibility as the owners execute a turnaround. As the turnaround is completed, the company may repay the ABL and go back to financing its liabilities in the cash flow market.

38.4.6   Asset-Based Loan Structures and Collateral

A typical ABL credit facility is composed of a revolver and a term loan. A **revolver,** or a **revolving line of credit,** is a credit line with a preapproved limit that's available for a prespecified period. As the borrower takes out some capital, the amount of available credit is reduced by that amount. Unlike a term loan, the borrower can repay the amount of borrowing at any time before the end of the period, and the same amount will again become available for future borrowings. The borrower typically uses the revolver to finance working capital needs. As the need for working capital fluctuates over time, the revolver structure allows the borrower to access more credit as the business needs grow and to repay the loan (and free up future capacity) as cash comes in or business slows down. A **term loan** typically has either an amortizing or a bullet structure to reduce and terminate the loan, and is secured against longer-term assets (real estate, or machinery).

Often, term loans are provided against capital expenditures such as new machinery. A term loan typically makes up a third or less of the total ABL facility. Typical tenors for ABLs range from 3 to 5 years; however, the terms of these deals tend to be highly customizable and can involve significant negotiation between the borrower and the lender.

The most common assets to back an ABL facility are inventory and accounts receivable. In other words, these assets are fairly liquid with easy-to-determine values. As discussed, longer-term assets (real estate or equipment) tend to be used to back term loans. An important part of the negotiation is determining what types of assets are not eligible for inclusion in the collateral package of the ABL. For example, past-due account receivables and incomplete work-in-process inventory are commonly excluded from the collateral package.

As the ABL market matures, lenders have grown to acknowledge that borrowers may be able to offer valuable collateral in the form of intangible assets, such as brand name and intellectual property (e.g., patents and trademarks). As expected, valuation of intangible assets tends to be more complex than that for tangible assets such as inventories. Third parties with particular expertise in evaluating the value of specific intangible assets are likely to be involved, as well as legal counsel (also likely with specific expertise, such as expertise in intellectual property law), to make sure that the relevant asset comes with a perfected security interest. Market practice has shown that borrowers that are able to borrow against intangible assets tend to be more creditworthy borrowers whose brand name is well established in the market and/or that have intellectual property that can be sold or monetized separately from the physical products of the company.

38.4.7 Asset-Based Lender Protection and Covenants

For a cash flow-based loan, one of the key covenants is the **net leverage covenant**, which is a restriction on maximum leverage calculated as the amount of senior or total debt, net of cash, as a multiple of EBITDA. However, for an asset-based loan, there is typically no leverage covenant. This means that the ABL borrower has more flexibility in the amount of borrowing that it can incur, especially if the business has a volatile earnings stream. ABL lenders are more focused on ensuring that the borrower has enough liquidity in order to meet its cash needs. Liquidity can be measured as either available cash or unused capacity under the existing facility given the borrowing base.

Therefore, an ABL lender is focused on analyzing the cash flow from the underlying operations of the business relative to cash needs, such as interest payments on the loan (and other debts, if they exist), taxes, any dividends or distributions to shareholders, and capital expenditures. The one credit metric that ABL lenders tend to be most focused on is the fixed charge coverage covenant.

The **fixed charge coverage ratio** is a ratio equal to (EBIT + fixed charge)/(fixed charge + interest) where fixed charges include rent/lease payments, utilities, insurance, and salaries. The key to this calculation is determining what constitutes a fixed charge. Fixed charges are inserted into the formula as a positive number which in the case of the numerator means adding back in the fixed charges to EBIT that were subtracted out of revenue to calculate EBIT. The fixed charge coverage covenant is a restriction on the minimum amount by which the measure of cash flow in the numerator covers the fixed charges (plus interest) in the denominator. A ratio of less than one means that the firm is not generating enough cash to pay the fixed costs, while a ratio of greater than one indicates more than enough cash to pay the fixed costs.

APPLICATION 38.4.7

An unlevered firm with EBIT of $10 million and fixed charges of $5 million needs to report its fixed charge coverage ratio. Calculate the ratio and interpret the result.

The fixed charge coverage ratio is:

$$(\text{EBIT} + \text{fixed charge})/(\text{fixed charge} + \text{interest})$$

$$= (\$10,000,000 + \$5,000,000)/\$10,000,000 = 1.5$$

The ratio indicates that the firm's operations have been generating enough cash to more than cover its fixed charges such as rent, leasing payments, utilities, insurance, and salaries.

In practice, some asset-based facilities are structured such that the fixed charge coverage covenant does not come into play until the borrower's unused loan capacity falls below a certain limit. This gives the borrower additional flexibility, as the liquidity limit does not kick in until the point at which the lender indicates that the borrower's access to liquidity has fallen below a specified level (typically 10% to 20% of the asset-based facility). Naturally, larger and more creditworthy corporate borrowers tend to have better terms regarding this type of feature, also known as a springing covenant.

Another feature for some asset-based facilities is limiting the lender's recourse ability if the borrower fails to meet the liquidity test by blocking the borrower from accessing a portion of the loan. Although this seems to make asset-based loans less attractive to borrowers, the borrower benefits from not having to accept financial covenant tests that could lead to default on the loan if the borrower breaches a specified covenant.

For cash flow-based loans, there are often negative covenants. These nonfinancial covenants effectively prohibit the borrowers from undertaking certain actions that are seen as detrimental to the lenders. An example of a negative covenant is the prohibition on borrowers paying a special dividend to the shareholders of the company. Without this type of negative covenant, a borrower such as a family-owned business is able to distribute cash to the owners as long as the liquidity test is met.

38.5 RISKS OF ASSET-BASED LOANS

This section discusses five specialized or unique risks regarding asset-based lending.

38.5.1 Collateral Valuation Risk of Asset-Based Loans and Lender Remedies

The nature of the underlying assets backing the loan tends to change on a day-to-day basis. For example, accounts receivables change daily as new accounts are added to the mix and existing accounts are converted into cash. Inventories change as finished goods are sold and new materials are purchased. Similarly, the mix of inventory changes as raw materials enter production and work-in-process converts parts into finished products, sometimes within the span of a day. These changes in the assets and, consequently, the value at which these assets can be liquidated, is not always reflected in periodic financial statements.

Thus, asset-based lenders bear the risk that the value of the collateral backing the loan may be different from what they expected. Lenders mitigate this risk by closely monitoring the collateral. Periodic reports on inventory composition, third-party valuation, and accounts receivable aging are examples of how lenders manage valuation risk. These periodic reports are provided by the borrower in frequencies ranging from monthly to weekly or even daily. The most creditworthy borrowers tend to be able to report inventory composition or accounts receivable aging on a monthly basis, but in extreme scenarios lenders may require daily reporting. Third-party valuation reports tend to be costly, and, in terms of balancing risk mitigation and cost, these reports may be done on a semiannual or quarterly basis rather than more frequently.

38.5.2 Risks Regarding Process and People in Asset-Based Loans

Given the data and labor-intensive monitoring required regarding the underlying assets, lenders need to have a fairly sophisticated system that enables easy reporting by the borrowers as well as easy information retrieval for the lending team. But systems alone are not sufficient.

The lender needs a dedicated team with the right skill set to collect and analyze the data from the borrower. This is particularly true for borrowers that submit data daily. Monitoring of information and the ability to detect signals of deteriorating liquidity, such as an increasing number of days to collect accounts receivable, is key in mitigating losses. Therefore, if the lender does not have the right processes and people, data collection alone is not entirely useful. In fact, having more data can backfire, as the systems are overwhelmed and the lender is not able to get useful information from the borrower data.

38.5.3 Risks Regarding Hedging of Asset-Based Loans

Asset-based lending is generally a long-only strategy. Given the smaller nature of a typical borrower, the highly idiosyncratic nature of small businesses, and the unique features of the specific ABL facilities, hedging is difficult. Hedging a long portfolio filled with small issuers with a short portfolio composed of larger bond issuers (because it is difficult to find borrowers for shorting middle-market bonds) introduces basis risk, in which the lender is betting on the health of small businesses versus larger businesses. Historical data tend to indicate that smaller businesses tend to be more negatively affected by business cycle downturns, whereas larger businesses have more levers to pull, including more diversified business lines and more ways to access capital, such as existing relationships with banks or the ability to tap capital markets globally.

38.5.4 Legal Risks of Asset-Based Loans

One of the risks, in the event that the lender needs to collect the collateral, is that it finds itself in a position where it is unable to exercise ownership of the collateral. In a secured transaction, attachment of security interest is vital. **Attachment of security interest** under US law consists of the very important steps needed to make sure that the lender has the necessary legal rights to take possession of collateral in the event of default. In addition, lenders need to perfect the security interest. **Perfecting the security interest** occurs when the party seeking to establish ownership of an asset takes the necessary actions in order to assure that no other party, such as another creditor or a bankruptcy trustee, will be able to claim the same asset as collateral in the event that the debtor becomes insolvent.

There are various methods for perfecting a security interest. For example, legal documents can be prepared to perfect a security interest, or the party can take possession of the collateral. The process will be different for different jurisdictions. There are risks to the lender if the paperwork required to attach and perfect the security interest is not complete or is not done properly. Lenders need to have access to the right legal expertise and representation to make sure that they do not find themselves stripped of the collateral that was expected to be theirs in the event of default.

38.5.5   Risks Regarding Timing of Exits from Asset-Based Loans

In the event that the borrower gets into financial distress and the lender needs to seize the collateral backing the loan, there is the risk that the collateral value has fallen below what the lender is owed. For example, a loan backed by inventory that is largely composed of seasonal merchandise, such as toys, may lose its value after the holiday season. Furthermore, if the merchandise does not get sold quickly and consumer tastes and preferences change, that would further harm the cash value of the collateral. Not all risk is removed just because the lender is able to take control of the collateral, as the time taken to liquidate the collateral and changing market conditions can translate into significant exit risk for the lender.

38.6   ASSET-BACKED SECURITIES

Structured products were introduced in CAIA Level I, where it was asserted that the concept of structuring is essential to modern finance and investments. Financial structuring is the practice of engineering unique financial opportunities from existing asset positions. This process enables diverse investors to hold claims with different risk exposures (or other characteristics) from the same assets.

38.6.1   The Creation of Asset-Backed Securities

To create asset-backed securities (ABS), an entity creates a special purpose vehicle (SPV) to which it sells the respective assets. The SPV is funded by issuing financial securities to investors. Most asset-backed securities are issued in three separate classes of tranches (classes A, B, and C). The highest tranche (class A, or senior tranche) is typically the largest tranche, has the highest credit rating, and is supported by the junior tranches. The B and C tranches have lower credit ratings (or no credit ratings) and thus offer higher prospective yields to compensate investors for added risk. The lower tranches suffer most or all of the initial losses when a credit event occurs. However, if the losses are large enough, the A tranche will also experience losses.

Principal payments are distributed to each tranche according to a predetermined priority scheme. In a sequential-pay tranche structure of fixed income securities, the senior tranche receives all initial principal payments (both scheduled and pre-paid) until all tranche holders have been completely paid off. After that, the next most senior tranche is entitled to receive all the principal payments, and so on. Each tranche will collect interest (coupon) payments as long as the tranche's principal has not been paid off. Each tranche has a different average maturity to adapt to different investor clienteles.

38.6.2   Growth of Various Types of Asset-Backed Securities

Exhibit 38.1 depicts the growth in three major types of asset-backed securities: those backed by automobile loans, housing-related loans, and student loans. Asset-backed securities collateralized by credit card loans shrank markedly due to the global financial crisis. The post-crisis regulatory environment accentuated the market decline, as ABS products were blamed for creating and amplifying the crisis. In the post-crisis period, new and stricter capital requirements became mandatory for the issuance of new ABS.

The next sections discuss two types of ABS: auto loans and credit card receivables. Credit cards and auto loans are **recourse loans,** which means that the borrower is personally liable for repaying any outstanding balance on the loan. This implies that lenders are allowed to garnish wages or levy accounts to collect what is owed, even after they have taken collateral. On the other hand, in a **nonrecourse loan,** the lender can collect only the collateral at hand.

From an investor's perspective, the shorter duration and amortizing plans of asset-backed securities facilitate a reduction in the portfolio's interest rate and possibly credit risk.

38.6.3   Auto Loan-Backed Securities

Auto loan-backed securities (ALBS) receive cash flows from customer payments assembled from a specific pool of automobile loans or leases. The loans can be issued by commercial banks, financial subsidiaries of auto companies, independent finance companies, or small financial companies dedicated to auto loans. Auto loan (and auto lease) asset-backed securities have historically represented between a fifth and a quarter of the asset-backed securities market in the United States.

Auto loan-backed securities do not have government backing and are therefore subject to credit risk. Auto loans are typically classified as prime, near-prime, or subprime. The credit risk and performance of ALBS depend on the structure of the ABS and the performance of the underlying auto loan collateral. Auto loan-backed securities based on subprime loans usually include a provision that protects either investors in the senior ABS tranches or the entire structure. In the case of subprime auto loan-backed securities, one common credit enhancement is overcollateralization.

Moreover, most subprime ALBS contain a credit enhancement provision that redirects any interest received on the underlying auto loan portfolio in excess of interest payments on junior ABS tranches to a reserve account, which offers an additional credit safeguard planned to benefit senior tranches (Culp and Forrester

EXHIBIT 38.1 US Asset-Backed Securities Outstanding ($ Billions)

Year	Automobile	Credit Card	Student Loans	Other	Total
1985	0.9	0.0	0.0	0.4	1.3
1986	10.5	0.0	0.0	1.3	11.8
1987	14.2	2.4	0.0	2.0	18.6
1988	13.5	9.1	0.0	3.5	26.2
1989	14.1	20.0	0.0	3.2	37.3
1990	19.9	42.1	0.0	3.9	65.9
1991	27.8	59.0	0.2	4.3	91.3
1992	37.4	70.8	0.4	7.2	115.8
1993	43.0	75.1	0.8	12.4	131.3
1994	40.5	98.6	3.4	18.3	160.9
1995	53.4	131.0	6.5	22.4	213.2
1996	67.3	168.2	14.3	39.4	289.2
1997	81.2	191.6	25.9	56.4	355.1
1998	90.1	201.3	31.5	69.0	391.9
1999	109.9	216.8	36.4	86.8	449.9
2000	140.8	240.1	44.8	102.0	527.6
2001	167.0	268.2	48.2	109.6	593.0
2002	187.3	294.5	59.3	105.2	646.3
2003	190.9	304.7	88.4	113.3	697.4
2004	175.3	298.6	123.1	116.1	713.2
2005	194.6	287.3	160.1	132.6	774.7
2006	195.4	291.6	201.1	151.3	839.4
2007	181.0	324.8	230.2	170.6	906.6
2008	140.4	316.0	238.5	156.5	851.4
2009	127.0	300.7	241.0	151.3	820.0
2010	115.1	217.3	242.2	143.9	718.4
2011	115.4	164.3	235.8	143.2	658.7
2012	140.9	128.2	235.1	152.8	657.0
2013	160.0	124.5	230.1	172.5	687.0
2014	178.4	136.5	218.1	184.8	717.7
2015	189.1	128.6	201.8	196.8	716.4
2016	193.6	130.5	188.6	208.9	721.6
2017	203.0	128.9	177.1	235.3	744.3
2018	222.8	123.8	170.9	289.8	807.3
2019	264.3	122.2	170.1	293.8	850.4

Note: This table does not include CDOs, *2019 data is as of Q2.*
Source: Securities Industry and Financial Markets Assosiation (SIFMA).

2015). Finally, the quality of the originator's underwriting standards also influences an investor's decision to invest in a specific ALBS.

The interest rates on the underlying auto loans are affected by the borrowers' income, employment history, credit scores (categorized as prime, nonprime, or subprime), and other variables. The cash flows of auto loan-backed securities are managed by servicers, which are paid a fixed fee (usually 0.5% to 2.0% of the pool's remaining collateral balance). Servicers collect and process borrowers' payments to the loan pool and then pay investors in this asset-backed security. They also endeavor to collect payments due from delinquent borrowers. The credit rating of auto loan-backed securities is affected in part by the creditworthiness of the servicer and also by its experience.

38.6.4 Auto Loan-Backed Securities and Prepayments

Throughout fixed income structured products, unscheduled principal payments (prepayments) can be extremely important. Elsewhere in the CAIA curriculum, prepayments are discussed using mortgages as an example. In this section, they are discussed in the context of auto loans.

Auto loan-backed securities receive cash flows not only from monthly loan payments (interest and scheduled principal repayments) but also from prepayments made by borrowers. Predicting prepayment speeds can be a vital process in valuing auto loan-backed securities, and in understanding and managing the associated risks. A fully prepaid loan provides an investor in a corresponding asset-backed security with early return of principal but takes away the investor's ability to earn the original interest rate on the old loan. Similarly, if a borrower does not fully prepay a loan but merely makes additional (unscheduled) partial principal repayments, investors in auto loan-backed securities experience effects similar to those of the full prepayment scenario but at a smaller magnitude. As a result, prepayments affect not only the cash flows relating to the principal but also reduce the expected subsequent interest payments.

In general, the rate of prepayments on these auto loan asset-backed securities will be affected by a number of factors. A key factor is the current level of interest rates relative to the rates being charged on the loans in the pool. Borrowers will have a greater incentive to refinance when current loan rates are low relative to the rates on existing loans. Refinancing, however, is not an important factor explaining prepayments in the case of auto loans. This is both because auto loans are generally small and because the value of a vehicle may depreciate at a faster pace than the outstanding balance of the loan in the first few years. Prepayments nonetheless can also originate due to the following factors: sales and trade-ins involving full loan payment, loss or destruction of an automobile, repossession and subsequent resale of a vehicle, and payoff of the loan by the borrower with cash.

Analysts build fundamental models of prepayment speeds and analyze past prepayment rates and macroeconomic factors in their effort to predict future prepayment rates. It is thus important that investors consider the speed of prepayments, which can be measured by the conditional prepayment rate (CPR).

38.6.5 Credit Card Receivables

When a customer makes a purchase on a credit card, the issuer of the credit card (i.e., the lender) provides credit to the cardholder (i.e., the borrower). The sum that the cardholder owes the lender is a receivable to the credit card issuer.

A **credit card receivable (CCR)** is an asset-backed security in which a pool of credit card receivables is used as collateral, as in the case of auto loans discussed above. The cash flows received by CCRs consist of annual fees, interest, and principal payments. CCRs are structured differently than other asset-backed securities (such as those based on auto loans and mortgages). This is because credit card receivables, which have a short-term life span and tend to be paid off within a year (i.e., much faster than an auto loan or a mortgage), support the outstanding certificates issued by the trust, which usually have maturities of 3, 5, or 10 years.

Credit card debt does not have an actual maturity date, because principal repayment is not scheduled (i.e., it is regarded as a nonamortizing loan). This characteristic led to the development of a structure, the master trust, which is better adapted to the short-term nature of CCRs because it allows issuers to sell more than one series from the same pool of credit card receivables. This is accomplished by including more receivables every time a new series is sold.

Because of the ongoing series of credit card receivables being added to the trust, CCRs are structured so as to pay periodic interest to their holders, but no principal is paid during a prespecified lockout period (which may last anywhere from 1.5 years to 10 years). If credit card users make principal payments during the lockout period, these cash flows are used to pay for new credit card receivables, with the aim of maintaining a relatively constant overall value of the receivables. Once the lockout period is over, principal payments are channeled to CCR holders in what is termed the principal amortization period.

The credit risk of the underlying collateral in the master trust can change over time because credit card issuers can add receivables to the trust and also change the terms on existing receivables. This requires rating agencies to constantly examine the performance of the receivables in the trust.

38.6.6 Credit Card Receivables Credit Enhancements

Credit enhancements of credit card receivables can be internal, external, or a combination of both, and are required if the structure is to receive higher credit ratings. The three most typical external credit enhancements from credit card receivables are: (1) cash collateral accounts; (2) third-party letters of credit; and (3) collateral invested amounts. Each is detailed next.

1. Cash collateral accounts: These are accounts funded when a series is issued and created by the securitization trust, which can be used to fund principal and/or interest on the certificates and other trust expenses when the excess spread turns negative.
2. Third-party letters of credit: These are backed by external institutions that provide protection against losses from defaults.
3. Collateral invested amounts (also known as CIAs): These consist of privately-placed ownership interests in the securitization trust, and are subordinate in payment rights to all investor certificate holders.

The four most common internal credit enhancements from credit card receivables are: (1) senior/subordinated certificates; (2) spread accounts; (3) excess finance charges; and (4) overcollateralization. Each is detailed next.

1. Senior/subordinated certificates: These refer to the internal credit enhancement to more senior tranches from the existence of less senior tranches that incur losses first.

2. Spread accounts: If certain performance indicators fall below specific thresholds, any "excess spread" earned on the collateral will be deposited into an account for the benefit of the CCR holders.
3. Excess finance charges: These are defined as the difference between the gross yield on the pool of securitized receivables and the cost of financing those receivables and serve to strengthen credit.
4. Overcollateralization: This occurs when the total quantity of receivables (assets) is greater than the sum of the nonequity tranches which strengthens the credit of the nonequity tranches.

REFERENCES

Ang, A. 2014. *Asset Management: A Systematic Approach to Factor Investing*. New York, NY: Oxford University Press.

Culp, C. L. and J. P. Forrester. 2015. "Have Pre-Crisis Levels of Risk Returned in U.S. Structured Products? Evidence from U.S. Subprime Auto ABS, CLOs, and Insurance-Linked Securities Markets." *Journal of Structured Finance* 21 (1): 10–44.

Ehrbar, A. 2013. "The Great Bond Massacre." *Fortune*, February 3. http://fortune.com/2013/02/03/the-great-bond-massacre-fortune-1994/.

Knight, F. H. 1921. *Risk, Uncertainty and Profit*. New York, NY: Harper.

Olsen, R. A. and G. H. Troughton. 2000. "Are Risk Premium Anomalies Caused by Ambiguity?" *Financial Analysts Journal* 56 (2): 24–31. 10.2469/faj.v56.n2.2341.

Sato, Y. 2014 "Opacity in Financial Markets." *The Review of Financial Studies* 27 (12): 3502–46. 10.1093/rfs/hhu047.

CHAPTER 39

Insurance-Linked Products and Hybrid Securities

The first part of this chapter explores insurance-linked securities (ILS), a relatively new asset class. The second part of the chapter discusses mezzanine finance products and the use of hybrid securities in project finance.

39.1 NONLIFE ILS: CATASTROPHE BONDS

Catastrophe bonds are a type of insurance-linked security. **Insurance-linked securities (ILS)** are tradable financial instruments with payoffs and values affected by an insured loss event, such as a natural disaster, longevity risk, or life insurance mortality. ILS represent a convergence between capital and insurance markets. Institutional investors have increasingly regarded reinsurance as a new asset class, having invested around $50 billion in an array of insurance-linked securities over the past decade. ILS offer exposure to nonfinancial risks and thus are generally regarded as being uncorrelated with the general financial markets. In subsequent sections another important ILS group of products, longevity-risk-related products, is detailed.

39.1.1 Overview of Catastrophe Bonds

Catastrophe bonds (cat bonds) are risk-linked debt securities that represent the largest portion of the ILS market, are typically structured as private placements, and are designed to transfer specific risks from issuers—typically insurance or reinsurance companies—to investors. These specific risks are usually those having to do with natural disasters, such as hurricanes and earthquakes in the United States, Europe, or Japan.

The occurrence of major catastrophic events in the early 1990s led to the development of the cat bond market in the second half of the decade. Those events were Hurricane Andrew in 1992 (Florida, United States, $17 billion of insured losses), the Northridge earthquake in 1994 (California, United States, $15 billion), and the Kobe earthquake in 1995 (Kobe, Japan, $3 billion). The large losses that these events imposed on insurance companies highlighted the need for supplementary risk capital throughout the industry, encouraging insurers and reinsurers to search for new sources of additional risk capital and new ways to spread the risk among a larger group of investors with the capacity to bear those risks. It was believed that this would allow insurance companies to continue offering protection against these types of events without the need to increase the insurance rates to such high levels that coverage would no longer be affordable. Furthermore, the low interest rate environment following the global financial crisis of 2008–9 encouraged institutional investors to search for investment opportunities in new high-yielding assets.

The cat bond industry grew exponentially from a few hundred million dollars in bonds outstanding at the end of the 1990s to around $13 billion by 2007. The growth in cat bond issuance came to a stop after the 2008–9 global financial crisis and the bankruptcy of Lehman Brothers. Lehman Brothers had sponsored four cat bonds, for which the market value of the investments in their special purpose vehicles (SPVs) was smaller than the fully redeemable value of the bonds used to finance the SPVs. Eventually, the market resumed its growth, and by 2019, the total amount of bonds outstanding reached a record $39 billion.

39.1.2   Mechanics of Catastrophe Bonds

Exhibit 39.1 diagrams how a cat bond works. First, a sponsor (insurer or reinsurer) enters a contract to transfer specific risks with an SPV or a securitization fund created specifically for that transaction. This securitization fund issues cat bonds to investors, and the money received from investors is invested in risk-free assets held in a collateral trust account, thus virtually eliminating credit risk. If no covered event takes place, investors receive variable interest (from the risk-free assets) plus a risk premium. However, if a catastrophic event takes place, the fund covers the losses of the protection buyer. When the bond matures, investors receive their principal minus any funds that would have been used to cover catastrophe losses during the life of the bond.

The capital supplied by investors when they buy cat bonds is used to compensate any covered losses from a catastrophic event as specified in the bond. Thus, the investors are protection sellers. If no catastrophic event occurs, investors receive all the coupon payments from the bond and the bond's principal. However, if a catastrophic loss does take place, investors will usually forgo some of the coupon payments and suffer a partial or complete loss of principal. Furthermore, investors in cat bonds should be aware of the potential relative illiquidity of these securities.

39.1.3   Risks and Returns of Catastrophe Bonds

Investors in cat bonds have received relatively high returns when no catastrophic event has occurred. Historically, such risks have had occurrence frequencies of 1 in 50

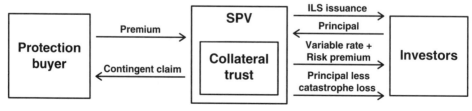

EXHIBIT 39.1   Diagram of a Cat Bond
Source: Based on a diagram presented in Weistroffer (2010).

to 1 in 100 years, and investors have been paid a spread over a short-term benchmark that has fluctuated between 4% and 10% (Sterge and Van der Stichele 2015). The occurrence of a prespecified event triggers the loss of part of or the entire bond's principal, which is used to cover the issuer's indemnities.

Catastrophe bonds are attractive to investors because the occurrence of a trigger event is virtually uncorrelated with financial risks (e.g., market risk, credit risk, and interest rate risk). Maturities of cat bonds typically range between 1 and 5 years, with most bonds having a 3-year maturity. Cat bonds are floating-rate bonds, and coupons are usually paid quarterly. Annual expected losses are modeled by three specialized firms and have historically ranged between 50 and 500 basis points (at issuance), with a size-weighted average of 160 basis points (Sterge and Van der Stichele 2015).

39.1.4 Role of Catastrophe Bonds in Managing Risks to Insurers

Cat bonds are generally used by insurers as a substitute for traditional catastrophe reinsurance. **Reinsurance** is insurance that is purchased by an insurance company from one or more other insurance companies, known as the reinsurer. The insurance company and the reinsurer enter into a reinsurance agreement, which details the conditions upon which the reinsurer would pay a share of the claims incurred by the insurance company.

The goal of a reinsurance program is to diversify the risk, which enables the insurance company to offer insurance at competitive rates to its customers, and to maintain its financial viability in the face of substantial insurance claims resulting from major and widespread natural disasters. A healthy reinsurance marketplace helps ensure that insurance companies can remain solvent because the risks and costs are spread out. By sponsoring cat bonds, both insurance and reinsurance companies can hedge their exposure to catastrophe risk.

39.2 FOUR TRIGGER TYPES OF CAT BONDS

In a cat bond transaction, payment depends on the occurrence of a triggering event (Edesess 2014; NAIC 2012). There are four basic types of triggers: (1) indemnity triggers, which are based on the actual claims incurred by the sponsoring insurance company or companies; (2) industry loss triggers, which are based on an industry-wide index of claims; (3) parametric triggers, which are based on assumed claims from an actual physical event (such as the magnitude of an earthquake or the wind speed of a hurricane); and (4) modeled triggers, which are based on estimated claims generated by a computer model.

39.2.1 Indemnity Triggers

An **indemnity trigger** is a type of trigger that initiates principal reductions based on the level of actual excess claims paid by the issuer. The **cat bond attachment point of the trigger** is a numerical value indicating the point at which at least a fraction of principal must be "attached" to cover claims. The **exhaustion point** is the level of claims loss at which the principal is "exhausted" and investors are not legally responsible for any additional claims. Related to attachment point is the **attachment probability,** which, typically based on historical information about natural disasters, indicates the estimated probability that the cat bond's attachment point will be reached.

The indemnity trigger is advantageous for the issuer because it will have to pay claimants essentially the same amount the cat bond pays the issuer (i.e., there is no "basis risk"). On the other hand, the indemnity trigger is disadvantageous to the investor because it must wait until all claims are settled. More specifically, if there has been a triggering event (e.g., an earthquake), the investor may have to wait a long time after the bond matures to reclaim a portion or the entire principal.

Furthermore, the indemnity trigger creates moral hazard because the issuer has the incentive to underwrite excessive risks—for example, homes built in areas where the risk of being struck by an earthquake is high—because actual losses are hedged. Because of this increased risk or moral hazard, investors usually require an extra return for investing in indemnity trigger transactions.

39.2.2 Industry Loss Triggers

An **industry loss trigger** is a trigger in which principal reductions in the cat bond are based on index estimates made by an independent third party of the total industry losses due to the occurrence of an insured event. For example, consider the case of a triggering event that takes place when total industry losses exceed $8 billion. In this case, investors are accountable for the percentage of the industry that corresponds to the cat bond's issuer's share.

In an industry loss trigger type, the issuer bears basis risk because the claims that it must pay may not correspond exactly to its share of the industry loss. Furthermore, the estimated total industry losses assessed by the independent third party and the actual total industry losses may not be exactly the same. The industry loss trigger type is more advantageous to the investor because claims are settled faster. This occurs once industry losses are estimated by the independent third party, which surveys the participants in the industry for their estimates. Furthermore, moral hazard is diminished given that the issuer bears some basis risk.

39.2.3 Parametric Triggers

A **parametric trigger** offers coverage when a certain threshold is surpassed based on previously specified natural parameters. According to Edesess (2014), a parametric trigger is based on the occurrence of a specific natural event, such as wind speed exceeding 120 km/hr (in a specified location), a category 5 hurricane, or an earthquake exceeding 7.0 on the Richter scale. While this poses basis risk to the issuer, it is advantageous to the investor because little or no waiting time is required before settlement of the bond following a triggering event, resolution of losses is rapid and transparent, and the danger of moral hazard is low. However, investors in parametric trigger type cat bonds bear basis risk because there may be a mismatch between the actual loss incurred by the sponsor and the transaction recovery (Kusche 2013).

39.2.4 Modeled Triggers

In a **modeled trigger,** the coverage is based on claims generated by a computer model, developed by an independent modeling company. Catastrophe modeling software is used to estimate an exposure portfolio, which provides estimates of losses given various severities of a natural disaster. If a catastrophic event takes place, the event parameters are compared with the exposure portfolio, and the bond will be triggered if the modeled losses surpass a previously specified threshold. Therefore, given that involved parties do not have to deal with a company's actual claims, loss resolution after a triggering event can be faster, although the issuer preserves some basis risk.

39.3 CAT BOND VALUATION, PERFORMANCE, AND DRAWBACKS

This section begins with a model that attempts to explain the market-clearing price of cat bonds.[1] The section then discusses index returns and potential drawbacks to cat bonds.

39.3.1 Establishing The Coupon Rate To Investors In Cat Bonds

To model cat bond valuation, the total coupon rate received by investors is disaggregated into two components: one that accounts for the time value of money (typically based on the LIBOR rate) and a second (the spread) that relates to the extra return demanded by investors for taking on the risk of suffering a potential cat loss:

$$\text{Total Coupon Rate to Investors} = \text{LIBOR} + \text{Spread} \qquad (39.1)$$

The following equation is then used to estimate the spread for each exposure:

$$\text{Spread} = \text{Constant} + [\text{Loss Multiplier} \times \text{Expected Loss (\%)}] \qquad (39.2)$$

where the loss multiplier parameter is a function of the uncertainty in the estimated expected loss. Since it is not possible to actually know the true value of the expected loss, one is forced to rely on cat modeling firms, which use computer software to produce estimates of the true expected loss. In its simplest form, expected loss is given by:

$$\text{Expected Loss (\%)} = \frac{\text{Probability of Event} \times \text{Annual Monetary Loss}}{\text{Principal}} \qquad (39.3)$$

Note that Equation 39.3 allows for a constant as a component of the spread which can adjust for a premium for bearing risk or as a complexity premium.

As an example of the use of this model, Bodoff and Gan (2009) use all years of data between 1998 and 2008 and fit the parameters of their model by inspecting results for US wind cat bonds (related to losses arising from very high winds in Florida, the Southeast United States, and/or the Northeast United States), and obtain the following equation, which approximates the spread, when issued, of any cat bond that covers US wind:

$$\text{Spread} = 3.33\% + [2.40 \times \text{Expected Loss (\%)}]$$

The intercept, 3.33%, and the slope, 2.40, are statistically significant variables. One can use expert judgment to improve the modeled spread by including some of the additional factors that affect the actual issuance spread (trigger type, market conditions, etc.).

APPLICATION 39.3.1

Suppose a 3-year cat bond covering US wind has just been issued. Based on the equation estimated by Bodoff and Gan (2009), with an intercept of 3.33% and a slope coefficient of 2.40, find the estimated spread assuming an expected loss of 1.40% per annum. Then, assuming 3-year LIBOR is 1.7% per annum, calculate the total coupon rate (%) to investors for this bond.

First, recall that the spread is given by Equation 39.2. Using the numbers provided in this application, the spread should be equal to:

$$\text{Spread (\%)} = 3.33\% + (2.40 \times 1.4\%) = 6.69\%$$

Using Equation 39.1, the total coupon rate to investors should be equal to:

$$\text{Total Coupon Rate} = 1.7\% + 6.69\% = 8.39\%$$

Note that with both equations, any variable in the middle expression could be computed if values of all the other variables were provided.

39.3.2 Cat Bond Index Returns

The Swiss Re Cat Bond Total Return Index is one of the most widely used cat bond indices. This index tracks the total rate of return for all outstanding cat bonds denominated in US dollars and is updated on a weekly basis each Friday. Swiss Re also calculates, among other indices, the following cat bond indices: global, US wind, and California earthquake. Exhibit 39.2 shows the cumulative wealth starting with $100 invested in catastrophe bonds between 2002 and continuing to 2018 based on the Swiss Re Cat Bond Total Return Index. Exhibit 39.2 also indicates the timing of several major catastrophic events that occurred during this period.

39.3.3 Potential Drawbacks and Alpha of Investing in Cat Bonds

Investing in cat bonds has some drawbacks.

Low Liquidity: First, investors should bear in mind that these types of bonds are less liquid than most equities and corporate bonds issued by the largest firms.

Returns Skewed to Left: In addition, their payoff distribution is highly skewed and has significant tail risk to the downside.

Credit Risk: Catastrophe bonds may be subject to credit risk. However, even though this risk is supposed to be relatively small for these securities,

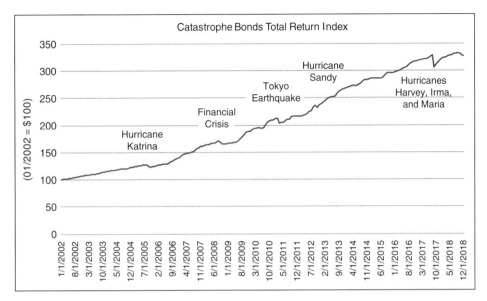

EXHIBIT 39.2 Catastrophe Bonds Total Return Index
Note: The graph shows a cumulative wealth index based on the Swiss Re Cat Bond Total Return Index.
Source: Bloomberg.

alternatives have been devised to mitigate and manage this risk, including an extra collateral account, a guarantee provided by a parent company, a letter of credit by a bank or another financial institution, the use of credit default swaps, and credit insurance through bond insurance firms.

With drawbacks usually come risk premiums:

ALTERNATIVE BETA RISK PREMIUM: Jaeger, Müller, and Scherling (2010) argue that ILS returns are essentially driven by alternative beta. This means that they offer a positive expected return that should be considered compensation for the event risk assumed by investors.

ALPHA OPPORTUNITIES: Jaeger, Müller, and Scherling (2010) also contend that alpha-generating strategies based on security selection, market timing, and complexity arbitrage may exist. The first two sources are similar to what one finds in traditional equity and bond investments. However, complexity arbitrage arises because these securities are difficult to price and may trade in markets that are not entirely efficient. **Complexity arbitrage** is the process of attempting to earn short-term, very low-risk profits from pricing discrepancies attributable to highly complicated investment features. The authors caution that alpha strategies will be difficult to implement because many of them are costly to execute and constrained by their small size.

Kusche (2013) notes that many institutional investors that invest in cat bonds are not concerned about diversification within the catastrophe bond asset class because their allocation to cat bonds is often relatively small compared to their overall portfolio. Instead, these investors focus on the most attractive risk–return profiles among cat bonds and thus invest in, for example, US wind-driven cat bonds, as these bonds have exhibited the highest risk-adjusted margins.

39.3.4 Catastrophe-related Derivative Securities

Finally, there are also other catastrophe-related securities than cat bonds. For example, cat derivatives are financial instruments indexed to catastrophic events. When one of these types of rare events occurs, these products pay a specified cash flow to their holders. Catastrophe derivatives are generally based on an index reflecting the severity of the catastrophic event. The size of the payment is usually proportional to the characteristics of the event or to the losses suffered by the holder as a consequence of the catastrophic event. These types of financial securities may trade in organized exchanges or over the counter (OTC).

39.4 LONGEVITY AND MORTALITY RISK-RELATED PRODUCTS

This section examines another class of insurance-linked securities, life ILS. Life ILS introduce longevity risk and mortality risk. The section also considers the investment attributes of life insurance settlements, a life insurance-linked security that has gained increasing interest in the past two decades, in spite of being controversial to some participants.

39.4.1 Longevity Risk

Longevity risk is any potential risk that arises from a higher realized average life expectancy of pensioners and policyholders than initially projected. Longevity improvements around the world are attributable to declining infant mortality rates, improved living conditions, and better medical care. Life insurance companies and pension funds are, among other institutions, affected by longevity risk. Governments' fiscal balance sheets can also be severely affected by longevity risk.

Longevity risk has arisen mainly because people are living longer than expected (particularly since the 1990s), and as a result, payments associated with annuities purchased by retirees or pension funds have been extending longer than originally forecasted. For example, life expectancy at age 60 in advanced economies in Europe rose from 15 years in 1910 to 24 years 100 years later, and it is generally expected to improve further. This means that while in 1910 an annuity purchased by a 60-year-old retiree was expected to make 15 years of payments, the same annuity today is expected to make 24 or more years of payments. The most relevant measure of longevity risk is life expectancy at pensionable age.

Longevity risk represents a threat to systemic financial stability for two reasons. One factor is the threats to the fiscal solvency of countries given that governments are exposed to longevity risk through pension liabilities. A second factor is threats to the solvency of private corporations and financial institutions that are vulnerable to longevity risk, mostly through their defined benefit pension plans or issuance of nonpension annuities.

Governments are exposed to longevity risk in three ways: (1) through their liabilities in defined benefit public pension plans; (2) through social security programs; and (3) through being regarded as the "holders of last resort" of the longevity risk borne by financial institutions and individuals. The exposure of governments to longevity risk is large, and thus it increases the already large costs of aging populations.

39.4.2 Hedging Longevity Risk

Longevity risk can be hedged using index-based and indemnity-based longevity swap contracts (OSFI 2014). A **longevity swap contract** takes place when a pension plan administrator agrees to make fixed payments to a counterparty based on specified mortality assumptions, while the counterparty agrees to make floating payments based on either the pension plan's actual mortalities (indemnity-based contract) or an agreed-upon mortality index (index-based contract). Thus, these contracts allow the counterparty to assume the longevity risk for a price.

Exhibits 39.3 and 39.4 illustrate the functioning of each contract. Note that the margin included in the fixed cash flows stands for the risk premium demanded by the counterparty to assume longevity risk and expenses.

In the case of indemnity-based longevity contracts, if a pension plan's beneficiaries live longer than was originally assumed, the pension plan will receive higher payments from the counterparty, thus helping to offset the plan's ex post higher pension costs. In the case of index-based contracts, if there is an increase in general longevity (as measured by the respective index), this will cause higher payments from the counterparty to the plan.

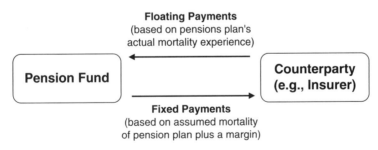

EXHIBIT 39.3   Indemnity-Based Longevity Contract
Source: Based on OSFI (2014).

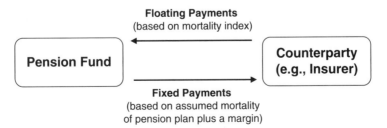

EXHIBIT 39.4   Index-Based Longevity Contract
Source: Based on OSFI (2014).

Index-based longevity swaps have the advantage that they are readily available and much more marketable than indemnity longevity swaps. Index-based longevity swaps can also bring in counterparties that do not want to hold specific longevity risk.[2]

39.4.3 Four Longevity Hedging Risks

Pension plans and other financial institutions that use indemnity-based longevity contracts to hedge longevity risk are exposed to four key risks:[3]

1. COUNTERPARTY RISK: This is the risk that the counterparty to the contract will not fulfill its obligations.
2. ROLLOVER RISK: This risk arises when pension plans agree to enter into hedging contracts for a shorter period of time than the liabilities they are aiming to cover.
3. BASIS RISK: This risk arises when index-based longevity risk hedging contracts are used, as there is a chance that the mortality experience of the pension plan could diverge from that of the index associated to the respective contract.
4. LEGAL RISK: This risk arises because longevity risk hedging contracts are private (not exchange traded) and require more careful scrutiny of their terms.

39.4.4 Mortality Risk

Mortality risk is the risk of a person (or group of individuals) passing away sooner than expected. Such an event could create financial distress at the individual level if the deceased is the family wage earner and passes away without life insurance.[4] This risk is also borne by companies writing life insurance if a large number of sooner-than-expected mortalities occur. Mortality risk is the opposite of longevity risk.

A related concept is that of extreme mortality risk. **Extreme mortality risk** arises because of the threat of very high mortality rates due to natural disasters, pandemics, and terrorist attacks rather than idiosyncratic causes of death.

39.4.5 Mortality Risk and Structured Products

Here is how a transaction can be structured with regard to mortality risk. An SPV is used for the securitization to hold assets in a collateral account. The SPV enters into an agreement with an insurance company to offer a call option to the insurance company on the SPV's assets, in exchange for a premium paid by an insurance company. At the same time, the SPV issues bonds to investors. Returns generated by the collateral account are swapped with a highly rated counterparty in exchange for a LIBOR-based interest rate.

Relatively high mortality (as measured by an index) causes reduction in the principal amounts owed by the SPV to the bondholders of the SPV. The insurance company receives payments generated by these reductions of principal repayment to bondholders. The principal reductions and corresponding gains to the insurance company occur if the index measuring mortality rates goes above a threshold of, say, 130% of the base value (known as the attachment point), and may increase proportionally until it reaches a threshold of, say, 150% (known as the exhaustion point), at which point the insurance company receives the full amount and investors receive no principal repayment. The extreme (catastrophic) mortality bonds issued by the SPV can be tranched. For example, the structure may include two tranches with different attachment and exhaustion points.

An innovation is the use of a credit wrap to improve the credit rating of a specific tranche. A **credit wrap** is a credit enhancement in which an insurance company guarantees the payment of interest and principal of a specific debt in exchange for an insurance premium. Wrapped bonds yield lower spreads because of the risk reduction that they achieve.

39.4.6 Main Risks of Catastrophic Mortality Bonds

The main risk in mortality bonds (a massive increase in mortality) is assumed to come from a pandemic or a similar disease that severely affects death rates. These types of extreme and rare events are very difficult for insurance companies to model.

According to Krutov (2010), five factors affect mortality rates. The **five mortality rate factors** are: (1) catastrophic events; (2) random fluctuations; (3) misestimation of mortality trends; (4) miscalculation of claim levels; and (5) data issues.

Furthermore, extreme mortality securitization entails independent modeling of three main elements of mortality rates. The **three main elements of mortality rates** are: (1) baseline mortality; (2) the terrorism element (effect of terrorist acts on mortality rates); and (3) the pandemic component (effect of major epidemics of severe infectious diseases on mortality rates). Pandemics are the main cause of potential jumps in mortality rates. Most life insurance policies do not include war as a covered cause of death.

The risks of catastrophic mortality bonds may be partly systematic and thereby offer lower diversification benefits than those provided by nonlife cat bonds. The reason is that an event such as a pandemic could lead to disruptions in many markets that negatively affect most financial securities, increasing their correlations.

39.5 LIFE INSURANCE SETTLEMENTS

Life insurance settlements, or life settlements, consist of the transfer of the ownership of an existing life insurance policy (including the sale, bequest, or assignment of an existing life insurance policy or the benefits of such policies) by its owner to a third party. The buyer of the policy becomes its beneficiary and becomes responsible for payments of any remaining premiums.

39.5.1 Mechanics and Details of Life Insurance Settlements

Life insurance policies in life settlements (not the case of viatical settlements discussed in Section 39.6) have to be from policyholders who are not terminally ill (although they may be sick or elderly). There is a dispute in some US states and in other countries about the legality of life insurance settlements.

The **cash surrender value of a life insurance policy** is the price at which the insurance company will buy back its commitments under the contract. If the price offered to the owner of a life insurance policy by a third party is greater than the cash surrender value of the policy, it is financially beneficial to the policyholder to sell the policy to a third party rather than surrender it to the insurance company. There are rational economic reasons for a policyholder to sell a life insurance policy (rather than surrender it) if the policyholder is unable to make required premium payments or if the policyholder otherwise perceives great benefits from immediate cash and has no other preferable options to obtain that cash.

From the point of view of an investor (i.e., purchaser of the insurance settlement), the transaction could be valuable if the discounted value of the expected future benefits of the life insurance policy exceed the total present value of the expected premium payments to be made and the cost to acquire the policy. The investor who purchases the insurance policy expects to benefit on average from the purchased policy if the price paid is less than the net present value of all the cash flows (premiums and life insurance benefits) associated with the contract. In other words, both parties benefit (relative to a policy surrender) if:

$$\text{Surrender Value} < \text{Purchase Price} < \text{NPV of Nonsurrender Cash Flows} \qquad (39.4)$$

The beneficiaries of the insurance policy are giving up potential benefits equal to the difference between the NPV of the nonsurrender cash flows and the price of the transaction. However, the beneficiaries gain immediate access to cash and do not run the risk of being unable to pay the premiums.

39.5.2   Path of Life Insurance Policy Values Through Time

Many life insurance policies are structured in a way whereby the premium payments remain level even though the rate of mortality increases over time as the policyholder ages. Effectively, in the beginning, the premiums paid on such a policy are higher than necessary for the expected level of claims in the short run. After a certain period, however, the situation reverses and the premiums no longer cover the increasing present value of the expected claims as the policyholder's mortality rate rises with age.

Thus the financial value of a life insurance policy becomes positive at some point if the policyholder survives long enough for the cost of the premiums to match the gains in the contract's value (although the premiums are sunk costs). The policy has likely been profitable to the life insurance company because the overpayments in the early years of the policy more than offset the underpayment toward the end of the policyholder's life. From the insurance company's perspective, their reserves from the policy have been built up from the beginning and can be used to pay claims, most of which come later.

This simplified example explains how an existing insurance policy could have monetary value to the policyholder who has been paying premiums for several years. On an expected basis, the present value of the future premiums could be lower than the present value of the death benefit, often by a significant amount. The difference is even greater for a policyholder whose health condition has significantly deteriorated since the initial underwriting and those whose mortality rate has thus increased beyond the initial expected value.

39.5.3 Modeling Life Insurance Settlements

The typical life insurance settlement can be represented as a bond having negative, fixed-coupon payments (the annual premiums), a known principal (the face value of the policy), and an unknown duration (the policyholder's life expectancy). For example, consider the case of a policyholder with a life expectancy of 10 years and a life insurance policy with a face value of $1,000,000. The annual premium on the policy is 3%. Assuming a discount rate of 10% and ignoring commissions, fees, and taxes, the net present value of the policy to the policyholder can be calculated. The policyholder has to make annual payments of $30,000 on the policy (i.e., $1,000,000 \times 3\%$) during each of the 10 years. The net present value of the policy to the policyholder is then:

$$\text{NPV} = \sum_{t=0}^{10} \frac{-30,000}{(1+0.1)^t} + \frac{1,000,000}{(1+0.1)^{10}} = 201,206$$

If the surrender value of the insurance policy is less than NPV ($201,206), then there will be a price at which both the policyholder and the investor could benefit from the transaction. Note that the calculation is similar to that of a bond with a negative coupon payment of $30,000 and a positive face value of $1,000,000.

APPLICATION 39.5.3

A life insurance owner has a life expectancy of 5 years and a life insurance policy with a face value and death benefit of $500,000. Her annual premium on the policy is 4%, and its cash surrender value is $200,000. Find the excess of the NPV of the policy to its cash surrender value if the market discount rate is 8%.

The present value of 5 years of $20,000 premium payments represents a liability to the policy owner of $-79,854$. The present value of the death benefit in 5 years is $+$340,292. The net present value to the policy owner is $260,437, which exceeds the cash surrender value by $60,437.

39.6 OVERVIEW OF VIATICAL SETTLEMENTS

A **viatical settlement** is a transaction in which a sick policyholder sells his or her life insurance policy at a discount to its face value. The buyer obtains the face value of the policy when the original policyholder passes away.

39.6.1 Viatical Settlements, Life Settlements, and Secondary Markets

It is sometimes difficult to distinguish viatical settlements from life settlements. However, the transaction is a viatical settlement if the life expectancy of an insurance policyholder is less than 2 years.

Viatical settlements are tightly regulated in many US states. Some regard investors in viatical settlements as providers of an important public service, because they allow a person with a terminal disease to obtain funds when they are most needed (e.g., to pay for better medical care).

The United States, Germany, the UK, and other countries have developed secondary markets for life insurance policies. The contracts are termed traded endowment policies (TEPs) or simply traded policies. The life settlement market is essentially institutional. The market for life insurance policies is expected to continue to grow as investors and policyholders gain knowledge about this transaction, and also as baby boomers age. Unfortunately, many policyholders do not know that they have the option to sell unaffordable or unnecessary life insurance policies, and let their policies lapse.

39.6.2   Investment Benefits, Risks, and Drawbacks of Viatical Settlements

From an investor point of view, life settlements offer the potential advantage of having low correlations with traditional investments. Therefore, life insurance policies and other longevity-based financial securities tend to be good candidates for enhancing portfolio diversification. However, and similar to the case of other fixed-income assets, the value of life settlements can be affected by interest rate changes. Other risks that affect an investment in life insurance settlements include longevity risk, policy availability risk, credit risk, operational risk, and changes in tax legislation and regulation.

Unfortunately, and similar to the case of catastrophic mortality bonds, data on the investment performance of life settlements is sparse. Furthermore, life settlements can be illiquid investments. These two factors complicate the estimation of the value of investments in life settlements and the calculation of net asset values to be reported to investors (e.g., in the case of hedge funds investing in life settlements). Finally, another potential drawback of investing in life settlements is that they often involve substantial legal risks. Legal due diligence is thus an essential component of the life settlement investment process.

39.6.3   Returns on Life Insurance Settlements

Braun, Gatzert, and Schmeiser (2011) obtain an indirect estimate of the investment attributes of life insurance settlements by analyzing the net asset value (NAV) performance of 17 open-end funds that were exclusively dedicated to investing in US life insurance settlements between December 2003 and June 2010. During this 6.5-year period, life settlement funds recorded a cumulative return of 37.3%. However, results from this study should be taken with caution. The calculation of the NAVs of these funds is subject to potentially severe valuation and liquidity risks.

In a more recent study, Januário and Naik (2014) examine settlement transactions by original policy owners using a data set containing all information in relation to 9,000 policies with aggregate net death benefits of $24 billion. These policies had been purchased in the secondary market by Coventry First from original policy owners between January 2001 and December 2011. The authors find that:

"... by selling their policies in the secondary market, policy owners received more than four times the ... cash surrender value they would have received had they surrendered their policies to their respective life insurance companies ... The [annualized] internal rate of return on the life settlements in our sample is 12.5%. (3)"

39.7   HYBRID PRODUCTS: MEZZANINE DEBT

Mezzanine finance, also known as mezzanine debt (MD) is described in the CAIA Level I curriculum. Here, we introduce advanced mezzanine debt features and their potential complexity.[5]

The next five subsections present an overview of: (1) step-up rates; (2) subordinated debt with PIK interest; (3) subordinated debt with profit participation; (4) subordinated debt with warrants; and (5) project finance.

39.7.1   Subordinated Debt with Step-Up Rates

Subordinated debt with step-up rates is a mezzanine debt product that is used in cases in which a firm cannot take on more debt with a fixed-rate scheme, because the current levels of senior and subordinated debt are exhausting the current cash flows. Interest rates in subordinated debt with step-up rates increase as the debt ages. The step-up schedule can be adapted to the firm's projected cash flows following a time-based or a criteria-based schedule. More often, a hybrid model that combines time-based or a criteria-based schedule.

Consider firm XYZ, which cannot take on more debt with a fixed-compensation mechanism due to the high levels of senior debt it already has on its balance sheet and short-term forecasts of insufficient cash flow to support fixed rate debt. The firm is offered subordinated debt with the time-based step-up rate mechanism depicted in Exhibit 39.5, in which interest payments increase toward the end of the life of the

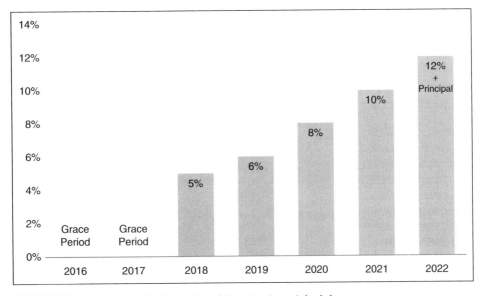

EXHIBIT 39.5   Example of a Time-Based Step-Up Rate Schedule

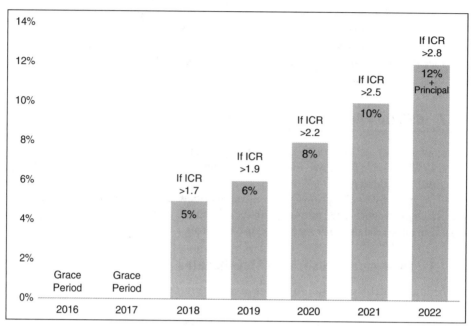

EXHIBIT 39.6 Example of a Criteria-Based Step-Up Rate Schedule

loan (a time at which, presumably, the company will have both created additional cash flows to service the debt and paid down outstanding senior debt).

A problem with the time-based step-up rate is that there is no guarantee that the company will have experienced sales and margins high enough to honor its debt in the years in which interest rates increase. An alternative consists of designing a mechanism in which interest rates increase only if certain financial parameters have been met, such as in the next example.

Suppose that firm XYZ will pay higher interest rates in future years only if the interest coverage ratio (ICR) is greater than a certain value, as shown in Exhibit 39.6. For example, the firm will pay an interest rate of 8% in 2020 if the ICR exceeds 2.2 that year. Use of the ICR is just one example of a criterion; any agreed-upon criterion could be used.

The time-based and criteria-based step-up rate mechanisms are often too rigid. In practice, market participants use a hybrid mezzanine rate step-up model. A hybrid mezzanine rate step-up model has a step-up schedule in which a certain level of fixed interest rates are paid each year, independent of firm performance (this would be the time-based step-up rate part), and additional interest is paid depending on firm performance and based on an agreed criterion (this would be the criteria-based step-up rate part).

39.7.2 Subordinated Debt with PIK Interest

Subordinated debt with **payment-in-kind (PIK) interest** is a type of obligation that does not provide any cash flows (interest or principal repayment) from the borrower to the lender prior to the maturity of the loan (or the refinance date), but rather accrues an increasing debt balance. This means that both interest and principal payments become due in one balloon (bullet) payment when the debt matures.

EXHIBIT 39.7 PIK Interest Example

Year	Beginning Debt Balance	PIK interest	Ending Debt Balance
1	£1,000,000	£120,000	£1,120,000
2	£1,120,000	£134,400	£1,254,400
3	£1,254,400	£150,528	£1,404,928
4	£1,404,928	£168,591	£1,573,519
5	£1,573,519	£188,822	£1,762,341
Total PIK Interest		£762,341	

Consider a 5-year, £1,000,000 non-amortizing loan at 12% PIK annual compounding interest rate. The total PIK interest to be paid by the borrower can be calculated as follows. The PIK interest owed for the first year would be £120,000 (i.e., $£1,000,000 \times 0.12$), which is paid in a security issued by the borrower and is added to the principal amount of the debt, increasing the total amount owed to £1,120,000 at the end of the first year. During the second year, the 12% annual rate is applied against the new principal balance, resulting in a total amount of £134,400 (i.e., $£1,120,000$ million $\times 0.12$). The same process continues until the fifth year (see Exhibit 39.7). The total PIK interest, which will be paid in the fifth year, amounts to £762,342 (rounded), which when combined with the principal determines a balloon payment of £1,762,342.

APPLICATION 39.7.2

A 5-year bond with an initial principal amount of $2,000,000 is a nonamortizing loan with a 10% PIK annual compounding interest rate. Calculate all the cash payments that investors will receive, assuming that there is no default.

Without amortization and with the PIK feature, there will be no cash interest payments prior to maturity. The principal of the bond will increase at the 10% PIK annual compounding interest rate through the entire maturity of the bond. Growing $2,000,000 for 5 years at 10% results in a value of $3,221,020, which is the total cash due when the bond matures in 5 years. The value may be found using the same math as is used to compute future values.

Interest on PIK loans provides the lender with three sources of cash flow: (1) an arrangement and/or a commitment fee; (2) the (accrued or compounded) interest; and (3) sometimes, a ticking fee. A **ticking fee** is a payment paid by the borrower to the lender to account for the time lag between the commitment on a loan and the actual disbursement.

PIK toggle notes or bonds are a variant of a PIK bond that allows the borrower to pay interest (partly or in full) in each period, or to accrue a part or the whole interest payment due. Usually, if the borrower pays only part or nothing at all, the overall interest rate is increased following certain rules (often between 25 and

100 basis points). PIK toggle notes usually stipulate specific cash flow triggers that would effectively trigger interest payments during a certain period. PIK toggle notes often come with light covenants.

39.7.3 Subordinated Debt with Profit Participation

A **subordinated debt with profit participation scheme** provides a risk balance between debt and equity to mezzanine lenders, offering a level of downside protection and also a way to participate in the upside potential. The following example illustrates a profit participation scheme.

Suppose a £10 million loan is arranged as part of a profit participation model. The loan will be repaid at maturity. The profit participation scheme (PPS) is 4% of earnings before interest and taxes (EBIT), with annual floors and caps of £160,000 and £250,000, respectively. The forecasted EBIT for the next 4 years are £3,200,000, £3,500,000, £3,800,000, and £5,200,000.

In the first year, the PPS provides a payment of £128,000 (i.e., 4% of £3,200,000). This is lower than the floor payment of £160,000; therefore, the floor would be binding in 2016 and would require a payment of £160,000. The same phenomenon happens in the next 2 years. However, in the fourth year the continuing rise in EBIT causes the PPS is equal to £208,000, which is greater than the floor of £160,000 but lower than the cap of £250,000. Therefore, this is the payment for that year.

39.7.4 Subordinated Debt with Warrants

None of the mezzanine debt products presented so far are likely to be attractive to a mezzanine lender when a firm has exhausted its capacity to assume further senior and subordinated debt and has unpredictable future cash flows. In such cases, to justify assuming the risk that comes with the investment, the lender may seek an equity exposure to the firm. A warrant is a security that fits perfectly in this situation, as it allows the investor to benefit from the potential upside in the equity value of the firm. Long positions in equity warrants included with a subordinated debt issue can be call and put warrants or a combination of both.

Warrants are similar to equity options, but they differ in that they: (1) are generally issued by unlisted firms and are thus regarded as OTC securities; (2) are dilutive when issued by the firm itself since their exercise is satisfied by additional shares of common stock; (3) tend to have much longer maturities (often years) than traditional equity options (which usually have maturities measured in months); and (4) are not standardized securities.

Warrants are often attached to bonds or preferred stocks as a sweetener, as they allow investors to potentially receive an extra return (coming from the warrant) above the coupons received from the bond (or the fixed dividend received in the case of a preferred stock). In turn, warrants allow borrowers to make considerably lower interest payments compared to subordinated loans of similar risk with no warrants attached. Subordinated debt with warrants is different from other mezzanine securities because it eventually grants investors actual equity in the firm.

Consider the following example: firm ABC issues bonds with a $100 face value. The bonds also have warrants attached, providing each bondholder the right to purchase 10 shares of firm ABC stock at $15 per share over the next five years.

Subordinated debt with warrants differs from a convertible bond because in the case of convertibles, the option is exercised by handing over the underlying bond rather than being exercised independently of the debt security. Subordinated debt with warrants offers two distinct advantages to issuers: lower interest costs and less restrictive covenants compared to most other bonds. Investors in convertibles are willing to accept lower yields and less restrictive covenants in exchange for receiving both a more senior security that provides comparative income stability (the debt) and the possibility of enjoying a high return if the underlying value of the shares rises (the warrant).

39.7.5   Project Finance and Public–Private Partnerships

This final section on complex or advanced mezzanine financing briefly discusses the uses of mezzanine debt and financing in project finance. **Project finance** is capital intended to support a specific purpose, such as real estate projects and infrastructure projects, either on a private basis or in a public–private partnership. Public–private partnerships (PPPs) are discussed later in the section. The majority of the funding in project finance (around 75%) comes from debt products. The high long-term cost of using standard fixed-coupon, long-term bonds (10 to 15 years) would render many of these projects financially unfeasible. In these cases, lenders will be willing to fund projects only if they can provide senior, nonrecourse loans that are secured by all the assets of the project.

Public–private partnerships (PPPs)[6] represent cooperation between government and business jointly working toward a specific mutual target, assuming investment risks and sharing revenues and costs based on a predefined distribution. Projects are financed through a mixture of equity and debt financing, with debt financing in the neighborhood of 70% or more, and may often use mezzanine finance products. The public authority (public party) specifies its requirements in terms of outputs, which set out the public services that the facility (public infrastructure) is intended to provide but does not specify how these services or assets are to be provided. The private sector designs, finances, builds, and operates the facility to meet these long-term output specifications.

PPP project financing is usually arranged by creating a special purpose vehicle and designing a risk-sharing, cash flow-based lending structure in which limits are set to liabilities and off-balance-sheet financing. The project company (private party) receives payments (from the public-sector party or from the general public as users of the facility) over the life of the PPP contract on a pre-agreed-upon basis, which are intended to repay the financing costs and give a return to investors. The facility remains in public-sector ownership, or it is reverted to public-sector ownership at the end of the PPP contract.

NOTES

1. See Bodoff and Gan (2009).
2. See Gaches (2012). Luciano and Regis (2014) report that the largest-ever longevity swap transaction has been for a notional amount of £5 billion (the buyer of the contract was Aviva and the seller was Swiss Re and SCOR).

3. See OSFI (2014).
4. This section and the following are based mainly on Krutov (2010).
5. This section is based mainly on Nijs (2012).
6. See Bult-Spiering and Dewulf (2006) and Svedik and Tetrevova (2012).

REFERENCES

Bodoff, N. and Y. Gan. 2009. "An Analysis of the Market Price of Cat Bonds." Casualty Actuarial Society E-Forum, Spring.

Braun, A., N. Gatzert, and H. Schmeiser. 2011. "Performance and Risks of Open-End Life Settlement Funds." Working Papers on Risk Management and Insurance 73, March.

Bult-Spiering, M. and G. Dewulf. 2006. *Strategic Issues in Public–Private–Partnerships*. Oxford, UK: Blackwell Publishing.

Edesess, M. 2014. "Catastrophe Bonds: An Important New Financial Instrument." EDHEC–Risk Institute, July.

Gaches, A. 2012. "Index-Based Longevity Swaps: The Next Big Thing?" In "Longevity Risk Management for Institutional Investors." Special issue, *Institutional Investors Journal* (Fall): 64–68.

Jaeger, L., S. Müller, and S. Scherling. 2010. "Insurance-Linked Securities: What Drives Their Returns?" *Journal of Alternative Investments* 13 (2): 9–34.

Januario, A. and N. Naik. 2014. "Testing for Adverse Selection in Life Settlements: The Secondary Market for Life Insurance Policies." http://bvlzl.de/Newsletter/2014_12/Markets_USA_01.pdf.

Krutov, A. 2010. *Investing in Insurance Risk*. London: Risk Books.

Kusche, P. 2013. "The New Alternative Asset: Insurance-Linked Securities." *Journal of Structured Finance* 19 (2): 52–58.

Luciano, E. and L. Regis. 2014. "Risk–Return Appraisal of Longevity Swaps." In "Pension and Longevity Risk Transfer for Institutional Investors." Special issue, *Institutional Investors Journal* (Fall): 99–108.

NAIC. 2012. "A Comprehensive Overview of the Insurance-Linked Securities Market." National Association of Insurance Commissioners, Capital Markets Special Reports.

Nijs, L. 2012. *Mezzanine Financing*. Croydon, UK: Wiley Finance.

OSFI. 2014. "Longevity Insurance and Longevity Swaps." Office of the Superintendent of Financial Institutions Canada. www.osfi-bsif.gc.ca.

Sterge, A. and B. Van der Stichele. 2015. "Understanding Cat Bonds." AQR Capital Management.

Svedik, J. and L. Tetrevova. 2012. "Financing and Mezzanine Capital in the Context of PPP Projects in the Czech Republic." In *Recent Researches in Business and Economics: Proceedings of the 4th WSEAS World Multiconference on Applied Economics, Business and Development (AEBD '12)*, edited by Zeljko Panian, 113–17. Athens: WSEAS Press.

Weistroffer, D. 2010. "Insurance-Linked Securities: A Niche Market Expanding." Deutsche Bank Research.

CHAPTER 40

Complexity and the Case of Cross-Border Real Estate Investing

This chapter discusses real estate investing with multiple currencies. It is a case study of the complexity of alternative investing.

40.1 TRADITIONAL VIEW OF CURRENCY-HEDGING FOR CROSS-BORDER REAL ESTATE INVESTING

Real estate investors are traditionally viewed as being exposed to foreign exchange risk when investing abroad. Currency exposure is particularly relevant in the case of international real estate investments. This is because a property's revenues have relatively low volatility, especially when compared to other asset classes, particularly exchange-traded assets such as stocks. This fact renders exchange rate movements a main factor affecting cross-border real estate risks and returns in the short run (from the point of view of an unhedged foreign investor).

40.1.1 Cross-Border Return as a Function of Rates

A US investor receiving an expected cash flow of €10 million faces two risks in terms of the cash flow measured in US dollars: the volatility of the cash flow, and the volatility of the exchange rate. Similarly, the investor can be viewed as facing two risks regarding the value of the real estate holdings: the volatility of the asset in the local currency, and the volatility of the exchange rate.

For example, to the US investor, a property with a current worth, V_0, of €100 million can be viewed as having a return, R, based on the next period value, V_1, as shown in Equation 40.1:

$$(V_1 - V_0)/V_0 = \{[V_0 \times [1 + r] \times [1 + fx]] - V_0\}/V_0 \approx r + fx \qquad (40.1)$$

where r is the percentage change in the property as valued in euros and fx is the percentage change in the value of euros expressed in terms of US dollars. The formula in Equation 40.1 is an approximation because it ignores the cross-product: $r \times fx$. The scale of the investment (i.e., €100) is irrelevant to the return, R.

Note that Equation 40.1 depicts the US investor's return, measured in US dollars, as being directly related to the change in the value of a euro relative to US dollars. Thus if the euro appreciates 5% relative to the US dollar, a US real estate investor would earn an additional 5% return in terms of US dollars from investing in European real estate (on top of whatever return the real estate generated in its home currency—in this case euros). If the property also rose in value (expressed in euros) by 3%, the US investor evaluating performance in US dollars would receive an approximated return of 8%. The added 5% return occurs from the currency-driven profit of turning euros back into dollars after the euros have appreciated by 5% relative to the dollars.

APPLICATION 40.1.1

A European investor purchases a US property, values that property at the beginning of the year as being worth 75 million euros, and is certain that its value in US dollars will grow by 4% per year. The investor wishes to know the total return (expressed in euros based on market exchange rates) under two scenarios: (1) if euros appreciate 2% relative to the US dollar; and (2) if euros depreciate 2% relative to the US dollar. Find the total return and next-period value of the property for each scenario.

The first scenario's total return from Equation 40.1 is 6% approximated as (4% + 2%) with a next-period approximated value of €106 million. The second scenario's total return from Equation 40.1 is 2%, generating a next-period value of €102 million.

The above examples illustrate a view in which changes in exchange rates cause risk to a cross-border investor who does not currency-hedge. Within this view, the unhedged investor in foreign real estate will have higher performance (measured in the home currency) when the foreign currency strengthens (relative to the investor's domestic currency) and lower performance when the currency weakens. As indicated in subsequent sections, this "risk" may be illusory. Also, to the extent that an investor is exposed to currency risk, the decision *not* to currency-hedge can be viewed as diversifying the investor's total risk from being fully exposed to one currency (the investor's home currency) to being spread across two or more currencies.

Finally, note that Equation 40.1 depicts the value of the real estate at Time t directly as V_t. However, V_t could easily be expanded into a valuation based on one or more variables such as expected cash flow. For example, if V_t is as expressed as a product of the expected value of the first annual cash flow and a price-to-cash-flow multiple, then the equation could link return performance to expected cash flows, explicitly indicating that real estate returns were driven by expected cash flows.

40.1.2 The Key Traditional Currency Risk Assumption of Cross-Border Investing

The **key traditional currency risk assumption** is that the return of a foreign investment to an investor expressed in the investor's home currency is subject to currency risk based on the belief that the nominal price of the foreign asset is non-negatively correlated with changes in the value of its currency. In the context of the example in Application 40.1.1, the asset was assumed to rise in value by 4% in terms of US dollars irrespective of the strength or weakness of the US dollar in currency markets. This implied covariance of zero is consistent with the traditional assumption that foreign asset ownership adds currency risk.

Obviously, the above assumption is violated in the long run for major currency devaluations. If a country experienced massive inflation (and therefore its currency depreciated substantially relative to other currencies), one would expect that the return of a real asset expressed in its home currency (r in Equation 10.1) would reflect the high inflation rate. In other words, high rates of inflation ultimately cause nominal prices (and nominal returns) of real estate and other real assets to rise to keep their inflation-adjusted prices (i.e., real prices) in equilibrium with other investment opportunities.

The importance of the relation between currency values and real asset values can be seen in Equation 40.1. If fx is highly negative (e.g., −25%) then it would be expected, or would at least be possible, that r would have a tendency to be highly positive as nominal prices adjusted to keep real prices stable. Traditional currency risk models, such as the model in the previous section, ignore this potentially important issue. This issue is revisited in later sections.

40.1.3 Currency Risks and Return Variances

Equation 40.1 can be viewed as expressing the percentage total return in the value of the property in the investor's domestic currency as the sum of the total return of the property (including cash flows) in the investor's foreign currency plus (or minus) any appreciation (or depreciation) in the foreign currency relative to the investor's home currency.

Under the scenario in Application 40.1.1 of a European investor, recall that a 2% depreciation in the value of the US dollar relative to the euro would add 2% to the return measured in euros. Therefore, the total return in euros would be 6%, found as the sum of the US dollar return (4%) and the −2% effect from the strengthening in the euro relative to the dollar.

The risk of an investor in foreign assets under this model can be effectively viewed as a two-asset portfolio if the returns of r and fx (property and currency, respectively), are both thought of as assets. Analogous to the case of a two-stock portfolio, this international investment's variance can be decomposed as follows:

$$\sigma_d^2 = \sigma_{fx}^2 + \sigma_r^2 + 2\text{cov}(fx, r) \tag{40.2}$$

where σ_d^2 is the variance of the international real estate investment return, expressed in domestic currency terms; σ_{fx}^2 is the variance of the foreign exchange rate; σ_r^2 is the variance of the foreign real estate asset's return measured in its currency; and $\text{cov}(fx, r)$ is the covariance between the foreign exchange rate and the foreign real estate asset's nominal return.

Equation 40.2 nicely illustrates the idea that there are three components to the risk of foreign investment viewed from the perspective of the returns to the investor as measured in the investor's home currency: (1) the volatility of the asset's return in its own currency, σ_r^2; (2) the volatility of the exchange rate (i.e., the exchange

rate between the investor's home currency and the currency in which the investment is domiciled), σ^2_{fx}; and (3) the covariance between the return on the investment
expressed in the currency in which the real estate domiciled and the exchange rate
between the two currencies (i.e., the investor's home currency and the asset's home
currency). Equation 40.2 depicts the traditional assumption that currency fluctuations (i.e., $\sigma^2_{fx} > 0$) add risk and that cov(fx, r) > 0 adds even more risk.

APPLICATION 40.1.3

Return to the European investor in Application 40.1.1 who purchased a US
property and is concerned about the total return of the property when viewed
in euros. Assume that the investor views the US dollar total return as having a
standard deviation of 20% and views the standard deviation of the exchange
rate between euros and the US dollar as being 15%. Find the total variance of
the euro-based return of the property under two scenarios regarding the covariance between the foreign exchange rate and the foreign real estate's return: (1)
covariance = 0%; and (2) covariance = 1%.

Equation 40.2 expresses the variance of the investor's total return viewed in
the investor's home currency as the sum of two variances and twice the covariance. First, note that the variances are 0.0400 and 0.0225. For Scenario 1, the
total variance is the sum of the variances: 0.0400 + 0.0225 = 0.0625. Under
Scenario 2, the total variance adds in twice the covariance for a total of 0.0825.
Exchange rate volatility is assumed to add total risk, and a positive covariance
increases the risk further.

Equation 40.2 nicely summarizes the relation of cross-border risk to its components and provides insight into the "key traditional currency risk assumption"
discussed in Section 40.1.2. Specifically, the "key traditional currency risk assumption" is that the covariance between fx and r is zero, meaning that the term cov(fx,
r) drops out of the equation. Under the assumption that cov(fx, r) = 0 and taking the
square root of both sides of Equation 40.2 generates Equation 40.3:

$$\sigma_d = \sqrt{(\sigma^2_{fx} + \sigma^2_r)} \quad \text{for} \quad \rho(fx, r) = 0 \tag{40.3}$$

where $\rho(fx$, $r)$ is the correlation coefficient between fx and r. By ignoring correlation (i.e., assuming that it is zero), the currency risk of investing cross-border, σ^2_{fx},
is viewed as adding to the investment risk (which includes σ^2_r).

40.1.4 Risk when Domestic Investment Returns Fully Adjust for Currency Devaluation

This subsection discusses cases in which the correlation coefficient between fx and r
is negative one or positive one. It discusses the correlation coefficient between fx and

r rather than the covariance in order to simplify the equations for the extreme cases of perfect positive and perfect negative correlation.

As shown in Equation 40.4, if the correlation coefficient between *fx* and *r* is one then:

$$\sigma_d = \sigma_r + \sigma_{fx} \qquad \text{for} \qquad \rho(fx, r) = 1 \qquad (40.4)$$

Equation 40.4 indicates that the total volatility of foreign investments is the sum of the two volatilities (the return *volatility* of the foreign investment and the volatility of *fx*).

In summary, a nonnegative correlation coefficient (i.e., a nonnegative covariance) between *r* and *fx*) generates a risk that lies on or between the values for σ_d in Equations 40.3 and 40.4. In all such cases, exchange rate volatility is viewed as adding to the total risk of an investor in foreign assets.

A correlation coefficient of negative one indicates that all of the return risk of the foreign asset is driven by currency risks so that the asset's price (measured in the currency of its domicile) moves inversely to the value of the currency in which it is domiciled. Although unrealistic, this case is instructive.

To be precise, the condition that the correlation coefficient between *fx* and *r* have a negative sign (i.e., that nominal asset prices are inversely correlated to the exchange rate) requires specification of the exchange rate (e.g., dollars per euro, or euros per dollar). Specifically, in this discussion the exchange rate is the number of units of the currency in which the investor is located per unit of the currency in which the asset is domiciled. Equation 40.4 depicts the case of $\rho(fx, r) = -1$.

$$\sigma_d = |\sigma_r - \sigma_{fx}| \qquad \text{for} \qquad \rho(fx, r) = -1 \qquad (40.5)$$

With the correlation coefficient between *fx* and *r* equal to negative one, the return *volatility* of the foreign investment is the absolute value of the difference between the *volatilities* of *fx* and *r*. In other words, if the only uncertainty in a foreign asset's return volatility is inversely and perfectly correlated to exchange rates then they would hedge each other strongly.

APPLICATION 40.1.4

Consider a US investor who purchased a French property and is concerned about the total return of the property when viewed in US dollars. Assume that the investor views the euro-based total return as having a standard deviation of 30% and also views the standard deviation of the exchange rate between the US dollar and euros as being 30%. Find the total volatility of the dollar-based return of the property under three scenarios regarding the correlation coefficient between the foreign exchange rate and the foreign real estate's return: $\rho = -1$, $\rho = 0$, and $\rho = +1$.

Equations 40.3, 40.4, and 40.5 can be used to solve for the volatility of the investor's total return viewed in dollars. For $\rho = 0$ Equation 40.3 generates $\sigma_d = 42.4\%$. For $\rho = 1$ Equation 40.4 generates $\sigma_d = 60.0\%$. For $\rho =$

(continued)

−1 Equation 40.5 generates $\sigma_d = 0\%$. Depending on the assumed correlation between domestic asset returns and foreign exchange rates, the currency risk of cross-currency investments can add to the investor's risk or reduce it (even to zero).

The key issue regarding the currency risk of cross-border investing is whether the returns of the foreign asset measured in the currency of its domicile is positively correlated, uncorrelated, or negatively correlated with the exchange rate between the investor's home currency and the asset's home currency. This important issue is explored further in Section 40.2.

40.1.5   Risk and a Focus on Single Currency Risk Measures

This analysis of foreign investment views currency risk as having added to the investment's total risk due to the operation of the assets such as real estate in a jurisdiction with a different currency, especially when domestic return versus exchange rate correlations are positive. This view of additional risk is based on measuring risk in the currency of the investor's home country. However, it is not clear that investor wealth and risk should be measured with respect to a single currency. Some institutional investors may have a global investor base. In addition, investors who minimize currency risk measured in terms of a single currency are likely maximizing their risk exposure to the risk of unanticipated inflation in that same currency. A strong argument can be made that investors should consider having their wealth exposed to a diversified basket of currencies to avoid concentration of inflation risk in a single currency.

40.2   FUNDAMENTALS OF CURRENCY RISK AND HEDGING IN PERFECT MARKETS

This section continues the analysis of the proposition that a cross-border investment has added risk (currency risk) due to the domicile of the assets (such as real estate) being in a jurisdiction with a different currency than the domestic currency of the investor. The previous section demonstrated that the key issue is the magnitude and direction of the correlation coefficient between the returns of an asset in its own currency and changes in the exchange rate between the two jurisdictions. This section provides important insights regarding the correlation between asset returns and exchange rates by beginning with an examination of the case of assets trading in perfect markets.

40.2.1   Currency Risk and the Law of One Price

Consider arbitragable real assets such as precious metals trading in perfect markets (i.e., without impediments to exchange such as transaction costs, transportation costs, or taxes). The prices of assets that can be arbitraged must, in theory, adhere to the law of one price in the absence of trading frictions. The law of one price states, for example, that the price of gold expressed in any currency must be equal throughout the world when adjusted for market foreign exchange rates. Any inequality in gold prices, adjusted for current market FX rates (foreign exchange rates), can be quickly arbitraged and, if necessary, the gold can be transported geographically to equilibrate price discrepancies between local markets.

A subsequent section demonstrates that in a perfect market an investor will receive the same returns on identical assets measured in the investor's home currency regardless of which currency and domicile is used to obtain the exposure. Note that it is somewhat analogous (and more easily understood) that *returns* would be the same for a speculator trading gold whether the trades were measured and denominated in ounces or grams.

To the extent that markets are well-functioning, it is not necessary to hedge currency risk. Note that while the law of one price holds perfectly only in perfect markets for identical goods, it should hold approximately in markets with modest trading frictions. In imperfect markets, purchasing power parity should tend to drive returns of highly similar assets towards having equal long-term returns. The next sections demonstrate and discuss the implications of the law of one price for managing currency risk.

40.2.2 Example of No Currency-Hedging Needed

Consider a German-based trader concerned about managing returns in his or her domestic currency (euros). The trader is considering the purchase and sale—1 year later—of gold using either: (1) German custody and transacting in euros; or (2) Swiss custody and transacting in Swiss francs. Presumably, the second alternative involves two currency transactions: converting euros into Swiss francs to purchase gold in Switzerland at Time 0, and then converting Swiss francs back to euros when the gold is sold at Time 1.

Exhibit 40.1 depicts a scenario in which the Swiss franc trades on par with the euro at Time 0 and then experiences a massive devaluation between Times 0 and 1. Exhibit 40.1 uses large and unrealistic values to keep the arithmetic simple and avoid rounding.

In Alternative #1, the German trader buys gold at 1,000 euros and sells it at 1,000 euros one period later for a 0% return. In Alternative #2 the German: (1) converts 1,000 euros to 1,000 francs; (2) buys the gold in Switzerland for 1,000 francs at Time 0; (3) sells the gold in Switzerland for 1,250 francs at Time 1; and (4) at Time 1 converts the francs back to euros at 0.80 euros per franc for a final position of 1,000 euros and a return of 0%. Both strategies generate the same return even though there is no attempt to hedge currency risk.

EXHIBIT 40.1 Simplified Hypothetical Currency and Gold Prices

Time	Gold Price Francs	Francs per euro	German Gold Price	Euros per Franc
0	1,000	1:1	1,000	1:1
1	1,250	1.25:1.00	1,000	0.80:1.00

The reason that the two alternatives generate equal returns is that the prices in Exhibit 40.1 conform to the law of one price: the currency-adjusted *market* value of gold is the same in both countries both at Time 0 and Time 1. Arbitrage is assumed to force the market value of the gold at the same time to be the same in both countries (Germany and Switzerland), adjusted at current market exchange rates.

APPLICATION 40.2.2

A UK trader invests in gold by: (1) converting her British pounds to US dollars; (2) purchasing gold in the US using US dollars; and (3) 1 year later selling the gold for US dollars and converting the dollars back to British pounds. The market price of gold (measured in British pounds) over the same 1-year time period in the UK declined by 3%. Assuming: (1) there are no taxes, transaction costs, or other frictions; (2) that the US dollar strengthened by 4% relative to the British pound; and (3) gold is arbitragable, what would be the UK trader's return if she did not hedge against currency fluctuations using forward contracts or any other hedging tools?

The answer is 3%. The law of one price dictates that the return to the UK trader would be the same (3% given as the gold price change in the UK) by investing through US dollars or British pounds. The 4% figure is irrelevant to the answer.

40.2.3   Currency Risk and the Law of One Price
with Currency-Hedging

This section repeats the exercise of the previous section except that the traders hedge their perceived exposure to currency risk by locking in the exchange rate of anticipated currency conversions using FX forward contracts. The example uses the same data (Exhibit 40.1) and builds on the same example of two strategies (domestic and foreign).

The German-based trader continues to consider German custody and euros, but now considers a supposedly currency-hedged approach to speculate using Swiss francs and Swiss custody of the gold by: (1) converting euros into Swiss francs to purchase gold in Switzerland at Time 0; (2) entering a forward contract to sell Swiss francs for euros at Time 1; (3) selling the gold for francs at Time 1; and (4) converting the francs back to euros using the forward contract.

Continuing with the data in Exhibit 40.1, in Alternative #1, as before, the German trader buys gold at 1,000 and sells it at 1,000 for a 0% return. In Alternative #2 the German: (1) converts 1,000 euros to 1,000 francs; (2) buys the gold in Switzerland for 1,000 francs at Time 0; (3) sells the gold in Switzerland for 1,250 francs at Time 1; and (4) converts the francs back to euros using the exchange rate locked in by the forward contract (rather than the market exchange rate as assumed in the previous example).

Here is the key issue: the only way that the two alternatives (domestic and foreign investment in gold) generate the same outcome (a 0% return) is if the forward price of the FX contract *happens* to equal 0.80 francs per euro (the subsequently observed market exchange rate). Any other forward price (and there is no reason to believe that the devaluation could be precisely predicted) causes the German trader to experience a return based not solely on changes in the price of gold, but, rather, based on the subsequent value of the Swiss franc relative to the euro. In an attempt to hedge against currency risk, the trader has inadvertently exposed the trade to currency risk.

This is the key implication: for arbitragable assets obeying the law of one price, currency exchange rate risk can be an illusion. An attempt to hedge against it can actually cause the trader to incur FX risk. The primary implication of this result is that for arbitragable assets and, to a lesser extent, any assets trading in reasonably well-functioning markets, the "key traditional currency risk assumption" discussed in Section 40.1 is violated because currency-hedging is not necessary. Traders implementing currency-hedging strategies for arbitragable assets outside their domicile would introduce currency risk into their portfolio and the financial derivatives used in a misguided attempt to hedge risk would actually be a risk-increasing speculation in the FX market.

40.2.4 Currency Risk and Currency-Hedging of Fixed Income Securities

If the German-based trader purchases fixed income securities rather than gold, the implications for currency risk and hedging completely change. For example, consider that the alternatives are establishing a long position in a one-period (short-term) high-quality German bond or a one-period high-quality Swiss bond (accomplished with conversion of euros to francs at Time 0 and from francs back to euros at Time 1).

Since both bonds would mature at par, the major risk *is* the currency risk faced by the trader. That risk is generated by changes in the euro/franc exchange rate. Thus, investment in high-quality, short-term fixed income assets is a case in which currency risk hedging using a forward contract is fully appropriate if the objective is to minimize risk measured in terms of the investor's home currency.

The key takeaway is that whether or not multiple currencies cause currency risk and whether currency-hedging is appropriate is driven by the types of assets being utilized and their ability to be arbitraged. The following sections move away from the pristine cases of perfect markets, arbitragable assets, and fixed income assets to address the issue of when currency-hedging is and is not appropriate for alternative investments.

40.3 CURRENCY RISK AND HEDGING OF ALTERNATIVE INVESTMENTS

Building on the previous sections, this section discusses the potential currency risks of investing in an asset (such as an alternative asset) that resides in a foreign country and is primarily traded in that country's currency but is not able to be arbitraged. For example, private equities in one country cannot be well arbitraged against private equity in another country. Nevertheless, the implication from Section 40.2 that currency-hedging is not beneficial may still be relevant. A key starting point for this discussion is price stickiness.

40.3.1 Price Stickiness, Asset Values, and Expected Future Cash Flows

The perfect market and law of one price discussions in the previous sections do not reflect price stickiness. **Price stickiness** is the extent to which some prices are slow to respond to changes in economic circumstances. For example, the price changes of gasoline at local gas stations, gold jewelry at department stores, and beef at the local butcher shop may lag the price changes in global commodity market prices by several days or much longer. The prices and expected cash flows of corporate assets (and many other domestic assets) may also respond to changes in the value of its home currency on a delayed basis.

Consider the impact of sticky product prices on corporate asset values. The prices that a manufacturer expects to receive from sales of its product may persist unchanged for months after its home currency experiences a large change in value (e.g., a surge of inflation). In fact, few firms (other than perhaps commodity producers) would be expected to continuously change the nominal price of its product with each change in the value of its currency as reflected by worldwide currency exchange rates.

Note that the value of an enterprise depends on the net of revenues and expenses. While the above discussion has focused on product prices and revenues, it is important to also take into account the response of the enterprise's expenses to changes in the value of the domestic currency. It is likely that wages, rents, and locally produced goods will also experience little or no price changes in the short run (i.e., exhibit price stickiness). Thus, the net effect of changes in the value of the local currency on profits and asset values may be negligible in the short-run.

The key point is that market values and expected cash flows from investments may exhibit behavior much more consistent with price stickiness than with the law of one price. In other words, when the currency of the country in which an asset is domiciled changes in value relative to other currencies, there may be little or no shift in the asset's value or expected cash flows (as measured in the home currency) in the short-term.

40.3.2 Price Stickiness, Currency Risk, and Unlevered Corporate Assets

The extent to which expected cash flows, market values, and market returns of investments do or do not respond quickly to changes in the global value of its currency has a direct and clear impact on whether investments in such assets should be currency-hedged by foreign investors. Consider oil refineries with a primary major cost of crude oil and outputs of refined petroleum products, most of which trade in world commodity markets. The domicile of the refinery and its local currency should not be a huge determinant of asset returns (i.e., unlevered equity returns).

For example, consider a German trader comparing returns of US-based equities owning refineries in the US and European-based equities owning refineries in Europe. Absent major disruptions within each jurisdiction, in the theory of perfect markets the returns should be approximately equal (assuming equal operating efficiencies, labor costs, etc.). The key point here is if the German trader converts euros to US dollars, invests in a US refinery, and then liquidates the position back to euros (at market exchange rates) the expected total return should be the roughly same as investing directly in an otherwise identical German refinery using euros. While it may be unreasonable to assume that both companies operate identically, the point is that the conversion to a foreign currency and back, of and by itself, should have no impact on relative performance if refineries of various jurisdictions were being arbitraged by traders (which was discussed using gold as an example in a previous section).

Returning to the refinery values, note, however, that the transaction would not *appear* to have been free from currency fluctuations to the trader. The German trader would likely have experienced that the exchange rate from euros to US dollars at the inception of the investment differed from the exchange rate at the end of the investment when the US dollars were converted to euros. But to the extent that speculators arbitrage refinery asset values towards a single valuation standard, the local currencies should be irrelevant. Thus, the relative values of the refineries adjusted by market exchange rates should lead to equal currency-adjusted returns in a well-functioning market.

Unlevered investments in unlevered assets, such as alternative assets, may or may not require currency-hedging depending on the nature of the assets, revenues, and expenses in terms of price stickiness. Exhibit 40.2 summarizes the contrasts.

The key question is whether the values or operating revenues of investable assets are sticky. On the one hand, high volume goods that trade in global markets, such as commodities, may have little or no price stickiness and require little currency-hedging. But to the extent that assets have barriers to international trade, substantial transportation costs, high trading costs, and substantial taxation, the prices of those assets may deviate from those predicted by the law of one price for substantial periods of time.

40.3.3 Currency Risk and Levered Assets

The use of leverage inside a corporation can affect the conclusions of the previous sections in the context of an investor holding the equity of a levered foreign corporation. Since leverage magnifies equity volatility it might seem as though investing in levered foreign corporations magnifies the currency risk. However, leverage typically involves promised cash flows fixed in the local currency of the borrower. To the extent that the debt of the foreign corporation is nominally fixed in its country of domicile, large nominally fixed interest expenses act to lower the currency risk exposure to a foreign investor. For example, cross-border real estate investment would typically be almost entirely financed by fixed-rate debt in the local currency. The locally denominated revenues and locally denominated expenses tend to hedge the currency risk.

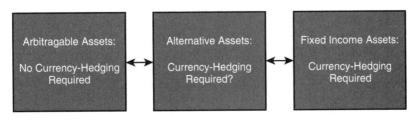

EXHIBIT 40.2 Relative Importance of Currency-Hedging by Asset Type

If being *long assets* domiciled in a foreign currency causes the investor to be *exposed to declines* in the value of the foreign currency, then being *short debt* (i.e., owning leveraged assets) causes the investor to be *exposed to increases* in the value of the foreign currency.

Consider a European investor holding a long position in US real estate with a substantial mortgage denominated in US dollars when an extreme devaluation occurs causing the value of the US dollar to fall quickly by 25% relative to the euro and other major currencies. Clearly, the market value of the US mortgage (expressed in a European investor's home currency of euros) falls proportionately (25%). The European investor enjoys a gain from the decline in the value of debt owed when measured in the investor's home currency. However, the European investor will experience a decline in the value of the real estate to the extent that property values in the US are sticky and do not rise when the US dollar devalues.

On the one hand, it may be reasonable to assume that the US dollar value of properties would rise substantially (due to each US dollar being worth less in global markets and, presumably, the high rate of US inflation that caused the devaluation). On the other hand, if the US economy is in disarray (associated with the inflation that caused the decline in the value of the US dollar) it might be reasonable to assume that, at least in the short run, US property values would decline even when measured in US dollars.

As in the case of other foreign investments (except fixed income assets and arbitragable assets in a well-functioning market), the net effect of changes in relative currency values on investor returns can be complex. One conclusion is especially clear: the traditional currency risk assumption that the return of a foreign investment, expressed in an investor's home currency, is subject to well-defined and predictable levels of currency risk is erroneous.

40.4 ACCESSING FOREIGN ASSETS WITH FUTURES AND QUANTO FUTURES

Chapter 19 discusses access to various assets through derivatives. This section discusses access to foreign assets such as equities using futures contracts.

40.4.1 Quanto Financial Derivatives

A regular equity futures contract or option contract (e.g., on an equity index) is traded in the home country where the underlying equities are primarily domiciled and the contracts are settled in the home currency. For example, a regular futures contract on the US S&P 500 Index traded in the US is settled in US dollars such that payoffs will be based on a fixed basis of US dollars per point of the index. For example, a contract trading with a scale of $250 per point would cause the long side to gain $500 if the index rose by 2.00 points.

A **quanto derivative** is generically viewed as a quantity-adjusted financial derivative in which payoffs are found as a quantity-adjusted product (i.e., the product of the change in the underlying asset price and another value such as an exchanged rate). As an example, a **quanto option** (quantity-adjusting option) contract might adjust the payoff of the option into a different currency using a prespecified (fixed) exchange rate. Thus, while a regular option may terminate with a payoff of $4, an otherwise identical quanto option might convert the payoff to euros at a prespecified exchange rate of $1.25 per euro for a payout of $5.

40.4.2 Quanto Futures Contracts

A quanto futures contract has a payoff that is adjusted by a factor such as an exchange rate that alters the nature (not just the size) of the contract's risk exposure. For example, consider two futures contracts on one unit of the Nikkei 225 equity index during a time period in which the Nikkei 225 index rose by 1% from 20,000¥ to 20,200¥. The payoff of a "regular" (i.e., nonquanto) futures contract (perhaps trading in Japan) is 200¥ from the short side to the long side. The other futures contract (perhaps trading in the US) is a quanto futures contract in which the 200¥ index change is quantity-adjusted at settlement into another currency—in this case USD—on a prespecified basis. The payoff is, in effect, multiplied by a hypothetical USD/¥ exchange rate such as being equal to one. Thus, this example of a quanto futures contract would have a payoff of $200 from the short side to the long side even though the underlying price change of the index was denominated in yen. Available quanto futures contracts include contracts on equity indices and commodities that settle in one currency even though the price of the underlier is based on another currency.

Note that most futures contracts are "quantity-adjusted" in the sense that settlement of a commodity contract or equity index contract often has a multiplier (such as 5,000 bushels of wheat or 250 times the S&P 500 Index). These multipliers merely serve to scale the size of a single contract to a convenient level. A quanto futures contract includes a quantity adjustment such as a currency exchange rate that changes the nature of the contract's risk exposure—not just the size. In the example of the previous paragraph, the quanto futures contract on the Nikkei 225 replaces exposure to fluctuations in the value of the yen to exposure to fluctuations in the value of the dollar since the settlement is denominated in dollars.

40.4.3 Futures-based Strategies versus Direct Cash Investment in Foreign Assets

The difference between the returns and risks of a regular (i.e., nonquanto) futures contract and a quanto futures contract are usually driven by currency exchange rate risk. However, discussion of currency exchange rate risk and investor preferences can become quite complicated. This section simplifies the discussion by focusing on comparing the returns of two straightforward strategies to invest in foreign assets: (1) a direct cash investment in a foreign stock index fund; and (2) a synthetic strategy using a regular futures contract (fully collateralized in the currency of the foreign stock index).

Specifically, the cash strategy is a 1-year investment by a US investor in a Japanese equity index via a Japanese-domiciled equity index fund. The cash strategy is initiated by converting domestic currency (USD) to the foreign currency (yen), immediately buying the Japanese equity index fund with the yen, and then, after 1 year, liquidating the Japanese fund (in yen) and converting the yen back to USD at the exchange rate prevailing at the end the year.

The synthetic strategy attempts to mimic the above cash strategy by establishing a long position in a regular (nonquanto) futures contract on the Japanese equity index with settlement in 1 year occurring in yen. The futures position is assumed to be fully collateralized by money market deposits in yen.

Both the Japanese stock index fund and the futures contract are assumed to have identical underlying assets. For simplicity, it is assumed that the yen-based and dollar-based interest rates are both 0%. Trading frictions, expense ratios, taxes, and marking-to-market are ignored in this example. For this example, it is further assumed that the Japanese equity index rises 10% (in yen) over the year and the yen is assumed to strengthen 5% against the USD over the year.

The cash and synthetic strategies detailed above will have identical 1-year returns even though the futures contract is nonquanto:

1. THE DIRECT INVESTMENT APPROACH (I.E., A CASH INVESTMENT STRATEGY): A US investor in the index fund of Japanese equities (as detailed above) will generate a return of 15.50% in terms of USD; found as the product of one plus the yen-based gain in the Japanese index (1.10) and one plus the appreciation of the yen over the dollar (1.05) minus one.

2. A LONG POSITION IN FOREIGN CASH (YEN) AND A REGULAR FUTURES CONTRACT: The regular (nonquanto) futures contract would generate a 10% gain in the form of settlement in yen made to the investor. The 10% gain in the notional value of the futures in yen combined with the fully (i.e., 100%) collateralized principal invested in the money market assets (in yen) means that the strategy delivers 110% of the original investment in the form of yen. The yen are then converted back to USD at the end of the year. Note that the 5% strengthening of the yen relative to the USD (along with the 10% futures profits) would generate a total gain of 15.5%, which is equivalent to the direct investing approach.

   The point is that there is no difference between this synthetic futures-based approach and a direct investment approach assuming that the futures contract is nonquanto and that the full collateral is held in the foreign currency. Note, that using a quanto futures strategy or holding the collateral in USD will generate a different return than the cash strategy.

   Next, the example is extended to using a quanto futures contract (and foreign-denominated collateral):

3. A LONG POSITION IN FOREIGN CASH (YEN) AND A LONG QUANTO FUTURES CONTRACT: The quanto futures contract generates a 10% gain in US dollars because the index points are treated as USD values. The US investor gains 5% (measured in dollars) on the collateral (held in yen) due to the yen strengthening by 5%. Although the US investor gains 10% on the quanto futures contract, it is in dollars, so the US investor loses the benefit of the 5% gain from the strengthening in the yen on the 10% profit. The total return is 15%. In this example, the difference is small (15.5% in the cash strategy versus 15% in the regular futures strategy); but for a long term investment or during market turbulence the difference could be large.

   In summary, the synthetic strategy that replicates a direct investment in foreign equities (the cash strategy) is to use a regular futures contract rather than a quanto contract and to place full collateral in the foreign currency. Note that an investor wishing to avoid direct exposure to foreign currencies can use a quanto futures contract with collateral posted in the investor's home currency.

40.5 OVERVIEW OF INTERNATIONAL REAL ESTATE INVESTING

As institutional investors gain experience investing in a variety of domestic real estate projects, they often look to other countries for new real estate opportunities. Institutional investors pursuing direct access to real estate assets often begin investing abroad by becoming a limited partner in an international project somewhat similar to the domestic opportunities with which they are already familiar and experienced.

40.5.1 Characteristics of International Real Estate Markets

Historically, institutions have dominated investments in commercial real estate throughout most markets and most countries, with the vast majority of properties held domestically. Challenges facing new investors include lack of knowledge with regard to local institutions, agency costs, regulatory restrictions on foreign ownership, transaction costs, taxation, political risks, economic risks, exchange rate risk, and access to local services.

London-based real estate advisor Savills[1] estimated the world's wealth in general and real estate in particular. Their 2017 estimates (measured in trillions of US dollars) are:

Equities	$70.1
Outstanding securitized debt	$100.20
Gold	$6.50
Agricultural land and forestry	$27.20
Commercial real estate	$32.30
Residential real estate	$168.50
Total	$404.80

Over half of the estimated wealth was in real estate with total global real estate estimated at $228 trillion. These estimates include the holdings of institutional investors, corporations, as well as individuals.

40.5.2 Global Real Estate Taxes and Transaction Costs

Return characteristics, taxes, and transaction costs associated with direct foreign real estate investing can vary extensively from one country to another (see Exhibit 40.3 for developed markets and Exhibit 40.4 for emerging markets). For example, Exhibit 40.3 shows that rental income taxes for foreigners across a group of developed countries can be as low as 0.00% (Sweden) and as high as 48.56% (Switzerland). Similarly, capital gains taxes can be as low as 1.62% (Netherlands) and as high as 34% (Finland).

Similarly, high variability in income tax and capital gains tax rates applicable to foreign investors can be observed across major emerging markets (Exhibit 40.4). **Roundtrip costs,** which are the total costs of buying and selling a residential property, including legal fees, sales and transfer taxes, registration fees, and real estate

EXHIBIT 40.3 Return Characteristics, Taxes, and Transaction Costs Associated with Direct Foreign Real Estate Investing: Developed Market

Country	Gross Rental Yield	Rental Income Tax	Roundtrip Cost	Capital Gains Tax
Austria	1.96%	24.92%	11.20%	27.50%
Belgium	4.56%	8.11%	19.22%	16.50%
Canada	3.95%	25.00%	8.05%	33.00%
Denmark	4.84%	1.63%	2.23%	24.00%
Finland	4.11%	22.50%	6.99%	34.00%
France	2.79%	10.00%	18.45%	33.00%
Germany	2.95%	2.71%	12.71%	n.a.
Hong Kong	2.35%	11.40%	34.11%	n.a.
Ireland	7.09%	10.05%	9.07%	33.00%
Japan	2.66%	3.40%	13.36%	15.00%
Netherlands	3.72%	13.42%	8.25%	1.62%
New Zealand	5.48%	0.94%	4.52%	n.a.
Norway	3.09%	20.80%	4.69%	24.00%
Spain	4.00%	19.00%	11.09%	19.00%
Sweden	n.a	0.00%	8.25%	30.00%
Switzerland	3.33%	48.56%	6.21%	n.a.
United Kingdom	2.71%	n.a.	10.03%	28.00%
United States	2.91%	30.00%	9.82%	15.00%

Source: www.globalpropertyguide.com (accessed on June 6, 2019).

EXHIBIT 40.4 Return Characteristics, Taxes, and Transaction Costs Associated with Direct Foreign Real Estate Investing: Emerging Markets

Country	Gross Rental Yield	Rental Income Tax	Roundtrip Cost	Capital Gains Tax
Argentina	2.45%	14.70%	10.79%	15.00%
Brazil	n.a	15.00%	11.50%	15.00%
China	2.10%	5.00%	7.35%	20.00%
India	2.32%	7.87%	11.88%	30.00%
Mexico	n.a	25.00%	8.13%	25.00%
Poland	5.50%	13.50%	6.73%	n.a.
Russia	3.22%	20.00%	23.11%	20.00%
South Africa	3.88%	12.80%	14.65%	13.65%
Turkey	1.93%	14.60%	9.50%	n.a.

Source: www.globalpropertyguide.com (accessed on June 6, 2019).

agents' costs and fees, also show a very high dispersion across countries. Overall, the exhibits make it clear that it is of the utmost importance for investors to understand the specific characteristics of each real estate market in which they might consider allocating funds.

The assumptions made to obtain these numbers are explained on the web page.

40.5.3 Benefits Of International Real Estate Investing

Investing in international real estate offers two primary potential opportunities.

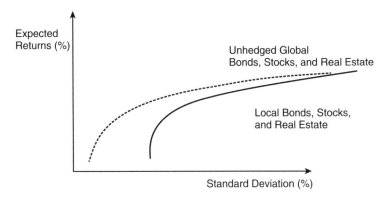

EXHIBIT 40.5   Global (Unhedged) versus Local Efficient Frontiers

Expanded Opportunities to Pursue Alpha: One of the reasons for expanding into international real estate investing is the expectation of achieving higher risk-adjusted returns abroad than in a single country approach (i.e., the home country). The economies of emerging markets grew at nearly twice the rate of those of developed markets during the past decades, albeit with greater volatility. Economic and population growth in emerging markets has been accompanied by fast urbanization, with a resulting impetus in the demand for new and improved office space, retail space, and housing.

Diversification Benefits: Investors are likely to benefit from the diversification benefits offered by global real estate investments rather than a single (home country) approach. Domestic real estate markets are influenced by national and international economic variables. To the extent that these national economic variables and business cycles are nonsynchronous with the economic factors and business cycles in other countries, one would expect relatively low correlations across international real estate returns. Therefore, a diversified investment in international real estate markets should have a relatively large potential for benefiting investors by offering access to different cash flow streams and risk exposures.

In theory, an efficient frontier that includes global bonds, stocks, and real estate dominates a frontier that includes only local or domestic bonds, stocks, and real estate because it offers a larger investment set of assets to choose from, which are not perfectly correlated. Graphically, this set corresponds to the efficient frontiers depicted in Exhibit 40.5, where for each possible level of expected return the investor can anticipate a lower level of total risk when combining local and international investments rather than investing only domestically.

40.6 HETEROGENOUS INVESTMENT TAXATION ACROSS JURISDICTIONS

An essential element of real estate portfolio allocation, even for tax-free institutions, is income taxation. The key idea is this: investors in high income tax brackets should concentrate on (i.e., overweight) real estate investments that offer substantial income tax advantages, and investors in low or zero income tax brackets should generally avoid (i.e., underweight) investments that offer substantial income tax advantages. This is similar to the idea that tax-exempt investors should focus on high-tax investments and not invest in tax-exempt bonds (e.g., municipal bonds). In both cases *pre-tax* equilibrium expected returns on tax-advantaged securities should be lower than for highly taxed securities (adjusted for risk).

Pension funds are usually tax exempt in their own domicile but may suffer withholding taxes when investing abroad. There may also be other types of taxes for foreign investors in real estate. For example, there are a few cases of countries that charge an annual flat tax (in percentage) on the value of properties owned by foreigners. There may also be other taxes, such as property taxes and sales taxes. Exhibits 40.3 and 40.4 in Section 40.5 indicate the range of tax rates on rental income. Chapter 25 discusses the important roles of depreciation expensing and capital gains tax rates in financial analysis and asset allocation. The complexity of the problem makes the use of expert tax advice of the utmost importance.

40.7   CHALLENGES TO INTERNATIONAL REAL ESTATE INVESTING

The growth in international real estate investing, while widening the potential pool of investments and enhancing diversification, comes with challenges. The previous sections of this chapter discuss challenges of multiple currencies. Here, the following potential challenges are discussed: agency relationships, information asymmetries, liquidity and transaction costs, and political, economic, and legal risks.

40.7.1   Three Reasons Why Agency Relationships Are Important

Institutional real estate ownership typically involves agency relationships, which are important drivers of performance. Agents can fulfill two important functions: serving as managers of the operations of each property; and serving as decision-makers in purchasing and selling properties.

The size and nature of a portfolio manager's allocations should be based on the investor's abilities to select, monitor, and manage agency relationships, because the success of the real estate investment is substantially driven by the performance of the managers.

There are three reasons that agency relationships are especially important in the selection and management of real estate relative to the management of other investments, such as passive public equity funds:

1. INEFFICIENT MARKETS FOR MANAGERS: The market for agents such as real estate managers is not highly efficient. In an efficient market, buyers get what they pay for. For example, in a truly efficient market for athletes, a team owner who hires the most expensive athletes will tend to have the greatest athletes. However, in an inefficient market, buyers cannot be confident that they will earn returns that are on par with the cost and risk of the investment. To the extent that the market for real estate managers is inefficient, an investor's ability to select superior managers with appropriate compensation levels and schemes should be taken into consideration when determining allocations to real estate.

2. PRIVATE ACCESS REQUIRES GREATER DILIGENCE: In the case of direct property ownership through partnerships with a small number of investors, the investor's relationship with real estate managers may be important, as the real estate investor cannot rely on other investors to monitor and control the managers. In the case of public equity investing, an investor can remain passive, becoming involved in issues only in limited cases of shareholder activism. Most real estate ownership requires greater contact with real estate managers over the life of the project. Therefore, an investor's ability to have effective ongoing relationships with managers can justify higher allocations to real estate.

3. ALPHA IS A KEY PERFORMANCE DRIVER: In a perfectly efficient market, managers cannot consistently generate abnormal profits. Real estate properties often trade in relatively inefficient markets wherein superior managers can consistently generate superior performance. Therefore, investors who can select and monitor managers who are successful in assembling portfolios of real estate properties can justify higher allocations to real estate.

These aspects of private (i.e., unlisted) real estate emphasize the importance of superior real estate management. Investors must be able to identify capable managers and maintain successful relationships with those managers. The conclusion is simple: investors with the contacts, access, and capabilities necessary for successful property acquisition and management should consider overweighting private real estate. However, investors unable or unwilling to acquire and maintain superior management capabilities should consider underweighting private real estate.

40.7.2 Relative Inefficiency of Global Real Estate Markets

In general, real estate markets around the world are less efficient than major markets for stocks and bonds. This feature creates challenges for investors who want to assess real estate prices and investment prospects. Furthermore, in the case of international real estate investments, the inherent geographical distance between investors and managers will most likely hinder the investor's abilities to select, monitor, and manage agency relationships. One should expect foreign investors to be poorly informed relative to most domestic investors, and this is likely to be reflected in inferior performance.

According to Geltner et al. (2014, 626):

> *The information costs (to foreign investors) can come in two varieties, both leading to underperformance. The first is that investors do not have the necessary information and therefore make mistakes. They buy lemons; they pay too much when they buy and get too little when they sell. Alternatively, they could try to solve the problem by buying information, for example from local brokers, or by establishing local offices and employing local people.*
>
> *However, that would simply translate the cost of the information disadvantage into the payment of fees and salaries, likewise eroding the return. In any event, these information costs imply that diversification, dubbed as the only free lunch in financial markets, is no longer free.*

There exists evidence that domestic investors earn higher returns than foreign investors when both invest in the same real estate market. This "home effect" might be explained by the fact that domestic investors are closer to information, and they know more about the local real estate market and the legal and tax situation. For example, Eichholtz, Schweitzer, and Koedijk (2001) and Eichholtz, Gugler, and Kok (2011) report evidence that the property market is not efficient, and domestic real estate investors tend to outperform international real estate investors, everything else being the same, when they invest in the same market and product. According to Baum and Hartzell (2012), this is one of the reasons why foreign investors often decide to invest through a joint venture with a local partner.

Note that investments in large publicly traded real estate markets or other large publicly traded markets do not typically require the ability to select superior managers and to monitor them. In an informationally efficient market, an investor with poor ability to select and monitor managers can earn average market returns by holding a well-diversified portfolio of publicly traded securities. Thus, investors with little or no expertise in real estate or in optimizing agency relationships, such as most foreign real estate investors, may do best by holding well-diversified portfolios of REITs or other market-traded real estate securities. With high levels of diversification and in relatively efficient markets, investor performance should closely track the performance of the overall market without requiring superior management capabilities.

However, investors should bear in mind that management fees charged by international real estate funds tend to be higher than those charged by domestic real estate funds, reflecting the higher costs of running a fund that invests abroad.

40.7.3 Information Asymmetries

Due to the uniqueness of most real estate investments, prices of real estate properties offered for sale are more likely to vary widely from their true economic values compared to homogeneous assets trading in relatively efficient markets. The information asymmetries between buyers and sellers can be quite high and cause information costs. In a more efficient market, such as large markets for public equities, there are numerous well-informed buyers and sellers seeking to buy securities that they identify as being underpriced and to sell securities that they perceive to be overpriced. The large number of such informed investors tends to force market prices toward levels that reflect available information. Therefore, a poorly informed investor can be somewhat confident that transactions in efficient markets will generate normal returns.

Investors with poor information (and analysis) should be concerned that transactions in relatively inefficient markets may systematically generate inferior returns. The net result is that investors with access to superior information and analysis of private real estate should consider overweighting international private real estate, while those with more limited information and analysis should consider underweighting international private real estate.

40.7.4 Liquidity and Transaction Costs

Private real estate is typically highly illiquid. The illiquidity of real estate is driven by uniqueness and transaction costs, among other factors. Real estate transaction costs are relatively high. The costs of acquiring and eventually liquidating properties can include sales commissions (agent fees) and legal fees that range between 2%

and 7%, depending on the country and the amount of the sale, and other costs, including transfer taxes, search costs, and financing costs, approaching a total of 10%. Property transfer taxes, which are rare in the United States, can be relatively high in some countries. They can range from 1% or 2% in Turkey, China, and Mexico to 5% or even 7% in Australia, France, the Netherlands, and Spain.

The substantial length of the real estate sales process is due to the complexities involved. For instance, sellers typically have to prepare the relevant documentation and hire a brokerage firm to market a property, and potential buyers often have to spend a considerable amount of time searching, performing due diligence, and dealing with financing. Furthermore, negotiations between the two parties can take substantial time.

Large interests in private real estate are often restricted to a fixed size that may be inconvenient to traders, thus limiting the liquidity of the interest (i.e., lumpiness). For example, many direct private equity real estate investments take place with a single institutional investor or a small number of institutional investors serving as limited partners. An investor cannot typically adjust the size of the existing limited partnership to increase or decrease his allocation to the interest. Furthermore, in attempting to liquidate the interest, a seller may have difficulty finding a buyer who is both interested in the underlying property and satisfied with the size of the interest being offered.

Illiquidity is a problem that worsens in the case of international real estate investments. This occurs because the foreign investor will be at a disadvantage in dealing with local brokers, especially if the investor is following an active trading strategy. For example, selling offices in London when the market is thought to have reached a plateau to move to New York City, where it is considered to be at the bottom, cannot be accomplished immediately (as can be done with stocks and bonds), especially if other market participants share the same expectations about the London office market. Illiquidity is higher during periods of weak real estate demand, when the selling of a property can take up to a year or more. Owners usually set minimum reservation prices below which they are unwilling to sell, thus exacerbating the illiquidity problem.

Finally, the obstacles and risks discussed in these sections are less important today than they were in the past, particularly in the case of countries belonging to trading blocs. However, other risks are inevitably intrinsic to international investment in real estate.

40.7.5 Political, Economic, and Legal Risks

This chapter, and indeed this book, concludes with three risks that, among others, should be considered when considering the challenging and potentially attractive opportunities to invest in diverse assets throughout the world.

POLITICAL RISKS: Political risk can be defined very broadly as the risk that returns from investments could be adversely affected as a result of instability or political changes in a country. Political risk is particularly relevant for real estate investments and even more for foreign investors. This is because real estate is part of the heritage of a country, and local governments are key actors in such areas as zoning, taxes, and tenant protection. Some examples of political risk faced by foreign real estate investors are the establishment of new limits on nondomestic property ownership, land and property expropriations, and excessive taxes on foreign investors

(Contreras et al. 2014). The illiquidity of directly held real estate investments makes it difficult to escape a rise in political risk.

ECONOMIC RISKS: **Economic risk** in this context is the likelihood that macroeconomic conditions (e.g., changes in monetary and tax policies) and government regulation in a country will affect an investment. In the case of government regulation, there may be restrictions in place on foreigners owning real estate assets. There may also be barriers to the repatriation of profits, an obstacle that may be particularly harmful for foreign direct real estate investments. Some of these issues are gradually becoming less important, especially within trading blocs.

LEGAL RISKS: Investors in real estate need to verify that, when they purchase a property, they are obtaining a good title, free of encumbrances and liens. In theory, title insurance in the US can often provide protection against the legal risks of property acquisition. However, legal risks vary from country to country. For example, Girgis (2007) documents that real estate fraud became a very real menace in specific jurisdictions. Specifically, as a result of identity theft, homeowners' titles have been illegally transferred and mortgages have been registered against those titles, all without the homeowners' knowledge or consent. The management of real estate legal risks is closely related to many aspects of the real estate due diligence process.

NOTE

1. Article dated April 10, 2017 and accessed at https://www.savills.com/blog/article/216300/residential-property/how-much-is-the-world-worth.aspx (March 26, 2019).

REFERENCES

Baum, A. E. and D. Hartzell. 2012. *Global Property Investment: Strategies, Structures, Decisions*. Chichester, UK: Wiley-Blackwell.

Contreras, V., U. Garay, M. A. Santos, and C. Betancourt. 2014. "Expropriation Risk and Housing Prices: Evidence from an Emerging Market." *Journal of Business Research* 67 (5): 935–42.

Eichholtz, P., N. Gugler, and N. Kok. 2011. "Transparency, Integration, and the Costs of International Real Estate Investments." *Journal of Real Estate Finance and Economics* 43 (1): 152–73.

Eichholtz, P., M. Schweitzer, and K. Koedijk. 2001. "Testing International Real Estate Investment Strategies." *Journal of International Money and Finance* 20 (3): 349–66.

Geltner, D., N. Miller, J. Clayton, and P. Eichholtz. 2014. *Commercial Real Estate Analysis and Investments*. Mason, OH: OnCourse Learning.

Girgis, J. 2007. "Mortgage Fraud, the Land Titles Act and Due Diligence: The *Rabi v. Rosu* Decision." *Banking and Finance Law Review* 22: 419–34.

Index

Bold page numbers indicate keyword definitions or explanations.